Dear Student,

John Wiley & Sons and SCIENCE NEWS magazine are writing to alert you to a special Web site, containing up-to-date news of psychology, offered free to students who have bought this textbook.

We are delighted to provide you with the most recent research in psychology as it emerges. In psychology, important findings are being revealed continually. Together, SCIENCE NEWS and *Psychology: Mind, Brain, & Culture* can show you how researchers do their work and what impact the results may have on your life.

Through a special arrangement, John Wiley & Sons, the publisher of this text, has been able to include recent psychology articles from SCIENCE NEWS and to post new ones, as they are published, on the Web site dedicated to *Psychology: Mind, Brain, & Culture*. Professor Paul Wellman from Texas A & M University is selecting the Science News psychology articles to be posted on the site. Dr. Wellman has added questions connecting the articles to the text, to help you see the value of current, ongoing research in psychology as it relates to the topics covered in the text.

As a student who has purchased a new copy of *Psychology: Mind, Brain, & Culture*, you can use the password to access our Web site and review these psychology articles. Be sure to tear out the card containing your personal password and keep it in a safe place.

SCIENCE NEWS, the premier magazine providing news of science to nonscientists, is also an important source of information for students, teachers, and researchers. Its reporters talk to scientists, attend meetings, and read the latest publications in all scientific fields, then present the findings and their implications in appealing, informative stories.

As another special service, SCIENCE NEWS magazine offers you a discounted subscription. You can get 52 issues of SCIENCE NEWS for only $29.00. To subscribe at this special student rate, call 800-552-4412 and press 0 to speak to a representative. Visit www.sciencenews.org to sample the magazine's excellent coverage of news in science and to explore the site's special features.

We hope you enjoy sampling the most exciting new research in psychology on the *Psychology: Mind, Brain, & Culture* Web site—a free service from John Wiley & Sons and SCIENCE NEWS.

Sincerely yours,

The Editors

WESTEN WEB SITE

Valuable student resources are available on this web site that will enhance your understanding of concepts learned in class. Links to several psychology web sites are provided as well as online quizzes and SCIENCE NEWS articles.

THREE EASY STEPS TO ACCESS THE WEB SITE

1) Go to

www.wiley.com/college/wave/westen

2) Enter identification

6012655-50204-4677-6

3) Create User name _____

Password _____

$\mathcal{W}$HAT STUDENTS ARE SAYING ABOUT WESTEN . . .

In the first edition of Westen's *Psychology: Mind, Brain, and Culture*, we invited students to e-mail their comments about the book to the author. Here is what they were moved to write after reading it.

❝Your book TRULY held my interest. For the first time, I felt that the author wanted me to understand the material. So often I feel that the authors of my textbooks assume that I'm already familiar with the subject, or that they just want to flaunt their intelligence by using complicated words and the like. The examples you used were helpful and interesting, they really made the different concepts clearer. I just had to let you know that you've made me happy—at least I know that there's ONE textbook out there in the American educational system that is informative and, at the same time, engaging. If only all books could be like that!❞
—Rachel Healy, *Fordham University*

❝I just wanted to compliment you on how well you wrote your textbook. I feel it is the most easy to read text that I have come across yet. Everything in your book flows and is so easy to understand. A job well done.❞
—Gregg McAuliffe, *JRI Health*

❝This was one of the rare books that kept to its format throughout the entire text. The main issues were presented in easy to read columns before each chapter, readdressed in exact order within the text, and highlighted in summary at the end of the chapter. Finally, a text that is clear and true to its aim!❞
—John J. Lagos, *Framingham State College*

❝I have been meaning to write to you to express my appreciation ever since I started starring and tallying up the funny yet subtle 'ha-has' and witty remarks you sprinkled your book with . . . This book was direct and understandable, despite the 'complex' and highly interpretive nature of this subject matter. I often found myself reading random chapters and picture captions for the simple sake of enjoyment and enrichment, even when I should have been doing something else, like reading the assigned pages . . . I felt compelled to inform you of how useful, applicable, and entertaining (the funnies 'rocked my psyche') I found your book. I'm not even going to sell it back to the bookstore after our exam, I like it so much.❞
—Marlena Marie Wojcik, *Northwestern University*

❝I want to compliment you on your book, *Psychology: Mind, Brain, & Culture*. I have always had a difficult time comprehending information through reading but I have found that your method of summarizing the chapters has been extremely helpful in allowing me to recall and understand what I have read.❞
—Roberta Myer, *University of California-Davis*

❝I wanted to let you know that I am thoroughly enjoying reading your book. It is very organized, so I can easily follow the format and you have used language that is easy to understand (which is refreshing). I like that you begin each chapter with a real life story or example. It immediately draws the reader in. Also, all of the examples and anecdotes you provide add a lot to the book and make it easier to understand. I have frequently come up with examples in my own life that support the ideas that you have presented. I appreciate your subtle humor.❞
—Elizabeth Chiarello, *Trinity College*

PSYCHOLOGY

MIND, BRAIN, & CULTURE

SECOND EDITION

DREW WESTEN
HARVARD UNIVERSITY

JOHN WILEY & SONS, INC.

New York   Chichester   Weinheim   Brisbane   Singapore   Toronto

DEDICATION

To Laura

EXECUTIVE EDITOR — Christopher Rogers
SENIOR MARKETING MANAGER — Charity Robey
SENIOR PRODUCTION EDITOR — Elizabeth Swain
DESIGN SUPERVISORS — Ann Marie Renzi/Kevin Murphy
TEXT DESIGN — Nancy Field
SENIOR PHOTO EDITOR — Hilary Newman
PHOTO RESEARCHER — Jennifer Atkins
FINE ART CONSULTANT — Steven Diamond
ILLUSTRATION COORDINATOR — Anna Melhorn

COVER ART © Therese May, "Therese," 1969, 72" x 90", fabric, machine, applique. Photo by Sharon Risedorph.

This book was set in 10/12 Palatino by Ruttle, Shaw & Wetherill, Inc. and printed and bound by Von Hoffmann, Inc. The cover was printed by Phoenix.

This book is printed on acid-free paper.

Recognizing the importance of preserving what has been written, it is a policy of John Wiley & Sons, Inc. to have books of enduring value published in the United States printed on acid-free paper, and we exert our best efforts to that end.

The paper on this book was manufactured by a mill whose forest management programs include sustained yield harvesting of its timberlands. Sustained yield harvesting principles ensure that the number of trees cut each year does not exceed the amount of new growth.

Library of Congress Cataloging in Publication Data:
Westen, Drew, 1959–
    Psychology : mind, brain & culture / Drew Westen. — 2nd ed.
      p.   cm.
    Includes bibliographical references and index.
    ISBN 0-471-24049-4
    1. Psychology.
  BF121.W44 1998
  150—dc21   97-51291
                                          CIP

Printed in the United States of America

10 9 8 7 6 5 4 3 2 1

Preface

Psychology: Mind, Brain, & Culture emerged from my several years of teaching introductory psychology at the University of Michigan. My goal was to try to translate a style of teaching into the written word, a style that is at once personal and informal—engaging students by presenting material relevant to their own concerns and interests—yet highly conceptual and scientifically rigorous. Translating a lecture style into a book is no easy task because so much of effective teaching happens through interaction, eye contact, and humor, which all too often elude capture on the written page. So this has been quite a challenge.

WRITING FOR A BROAD RANGE OF STUDENTS

In moving to a second edition, another challenge emerged. Over the last three years, I have received dozens of e-mails from around the world—many from professors who are using the book, but even more from their students. (These e-mails have been truly a pleasure to read and have reminded me of the importance of intermittent reinforcement, especially while in the midst of expending the thousand or so hours necessary to update the book for the second edition!) Aside from an occasional e-mail from some perceptive reader informing me that I had confusingly labeled the axes of some figure (thanks, by the way), perhaps the most striking thing about these e-mail messages has been the range of colleges and universities from which they have come.

I had hoped to write a book with the scientific rigor and conceptual complexity to be used at some of the top universities in the world; judging from the list of professors and universities who have adopted the book, that seems to have happened. But I also wanted to write a book that students would actually enjoy reading, and I hoped the book might find its way into the hands of students from a broad spectrum of colleges and universities, whose professors had faith in their ability to do what most cognitive-developmentalists suggest is optimal for learning: to tackle material at the top of their capacity instead of a level or two down. Some of the most rewarding e-mails have, in fact, come from some of the most unlikely places, including some junior colleges where professors who were willing to take a gamble thought the writing style might compensate for the high conceptual level of the book. But some professors who wanted to use the book have worried about the bottom third of their classes, who may need more guidance as they are reading to be sure they get the gist.

So the question was how to revise the book so that it could reach the widest audience without "dumbing it down" or killing perhaps the most distinctive feature of the book, the writing. So in careful consultation with both my editors at Wiley and a number of professors who are currently using the book, I decided to add two features, which have turned out, I think, to be helpful to students at every level: Interim Summaries, which periodically provide students with the gist of what they have just read; and an advanced discussion that appears in many chapters, called "One Step Further," which professors can choose either to assign or instruct students to ignore, depending on their interests. In addition, I have added more subheads to the text to help the students organize the concepts as they read.

KEEPING PACE WITH EMERGING KNOWLEDGE

The other major change in the second edition is content. The first edition was written and rewritten from 1986 through 1995, with round after round of reviews and constant updating to keep up with the field. It was thus a very up-to-date book, with an organization that fit the 1990s. Nevertheless, some subfields—particularly those in which neuroscience is prominent—are moving so quickly that even a book crafted in the mid-1990s is behind the times. So I have substantially rewritten and reorganized several chapters, most of them in the first third of the text, to be sure that this book brings students forward into the 21st century instead of backward into the late 19th. Professors who have used the book will find this most apparent in Chapter 3 on the biological bases of psychology; in Chapter 4, on sensation and perception; in Chapter 5, on learning; in chapters 6 and 7, on memory and cognition; and in Chapter 17, on attitudes and social cognition.

In all of these cases, new data simply made parts of the old organization problematic. For example, the study of stereotypes (Chapter 17) has become one of the hottest, most fascinating areas of social psychology, with work by Claude Steele and his colleagues showing that an intervention as seemingly harmless as asking participants to report their race along with other demographic data will decrease the performance of individuals from groups stereotypically viewed as less competent.

Although I cannot highlight all of the changes, I will mention a few of the most important ones. *Chapter 2* on research methods now has a state-of-the art discussion of neuroimaging techniques, which reflects, in part, my own attendance at a weeklong functional MRI "bootcamp" designed to help researchers in the behavioral sciences move into research involving functional neuroimaging. *Chapter 3* on the biological basis of mental life and behavior is substantially rewritten, moving away from the old "the temporal lobes do X" approach to a more current understanding of neural pathways that do not always so neatly place themselves in one region of the brain or another. *Chapter 4* on sensation and perception includes new sections on object identification and geon theory, motion perception, and "what" and "where" pathways in visual processing. *Chapter 6* is completely rewritten, beginning with a discussion of the "second cognitive revolution" that is currently taking place as researchers begin to shift from a computer metaphor to the metaphor of mind-as-brain and increasingly rely on parallel processing models of cognition. It also covers several important areas not covered in the first edition, such as the components of working memory, the neuropsychology of working memory, everyday memory, misremembering, and evolutionary approaches to memory. *Chapter 7*, on thought and language, is also completely rewritten, addressing issues of bounded rationality, everyday cognition, analogical reasoning, implicit thought, and the neuropsychology of thinking. It also provides a clear, more detailed discussion of connectionism and gives some perspective on the Chomskyian revolution. *Chapter 17* is also completely rewritten, beginning with a state-of-the-art discussion of recent thinking about dimensions on which attitudes vary (such as accessibility, strength, and ambivalence) and routes to attitude change, covering some of the most exciting new research on subtle forms of racism, applying developments in cognitive science (such as the increased focus on implicit processes and connectionist models) to social psychology, and concluding with a discussion of evolutionary approaches to social psychology.

The other major difference in the two editions is my better understanding of the history of the discipline and the recurrence and revision of ideas over time.

Between this edition and the last, I added more on the history of psychology, and I now offer a broader view of where we have come from and where we are going.

AIMS AND CORRESPONDING FEATURES

I set out in the first edition to write a textbook with five objectives: to focus on both the biological basis of psychology and the role of culture in shaping basic psychological processes; to provide a conceptual orientation that would capture the excitement and tensions in the field; to help students understand the logic of scientific discovery and hypothesis-testing as applied to psychological questions; to suggest ways of integrating psychological theories and knowledge across subfields; and to employ a language that would be sophisticated but engaging. A sixth aim, more clearly articulated in the second edition, is to find ways to help students who need more structure in learning the material without placing barriers in the way of students who like to read a good story and do not want the narrative disrupted with pedagogical devices. The features of the book follow from these six aims.

BIOLOGY AND CULTURE: A MICRO TO MACRO APPROACH

A consistent theme of the book, introduced in the first chapter, is that biology and culture form the boundaries of psychology: Understanding people means attending simultaneously to biological processes, psychological experience, and the cultural and historical context. The focus on biological and neural underpinnings echoes one of the major trends in contemporary psychological science, as technological developments allow progressively more sophisticated understanding of the neural substrates of psychological experience. The focus on culture has been a central feature of this book since I began work on it in 1986. *Cross-cultural material is not tacked onto this book; it is integral to it.* My first book, *Self and Society* (1985), was on culture and personality, and a background in anthropology and sociology informs my understanding of the way people think, feel, learn, behave, and develop.

Each chapter of this book contains two extended discussions that show the way psychological experience is situated between the nervous system and cultural experience.

FROM MIND TO BRAIN

- "From Mind to Brain" integrates concepts and findings from biopsychology and the neurosciences, discussing such issues as the way damage to the brain can alter personality. The latest research in neuroscience is also integrated throughout the text.

GLOBAL VISTA

- "A Global Vista" uses ethnographic examples and cross-cultural studies to explore psychological phenomena in other cultures, with an eye to addressing the universality or culture-specificity of psychological theories and observations. For example, menopause has a very different meaning, and hence different symptoms, in a Mayan village than it does in North America, and parenting styles fostering autonomy

> that are adaptive in Western, technologically developed societies are not necessarily optimal everywhere. In addition, cross-cultural research is integrated into the structure of each chapter, so that students do not balkanize cross-cultural issues as distinct from the "psychology of white people" but instead ask cross-cultural questions from the start.

These special features flow integrally from the text and are not presented as isolated "boxes." In this way, students will not get the message that the biological and cultural material is somehow superfluous or added on. In this edition, we have screened these features with color to highlight their importance and to help break up what can otherwise seem like a sea of words, without compromising their content or flow with the rest of the narrative.

CONCEPTUAL ORIENTATION

The book is conceptually oriented. It attempts, within the limits of my objectivity and expertise, to give a fair and compelling account of the different perspectives psychologists take in understanding psychological phenomena. I have a healthy respect for each approach and assume that if thousands of my colleagues find an approach compelling, it probably contains something that students should know. Feedback from professors who have used the book over the past three years has been extremely helpful in alerting me to places in which my biases did creep in. The coverage in this edition is more balanced.

- From the start, students are challenged to think about psychological phenomena from multiple perspectives. Chapter 1 is not perfunctory; it introduces four perspectives—*psychodynamic, behavioral, cognitive,* and *evolutionary*—in enough depth to allow students to begin conceptualizing psychological data rather than simply memorizing a list of facts, names, or studies. Based on feedback from professors, I have expanded the evolutionary coverage in the first chapter of this edition, so that students can get a firmer grasp of how evolutionary thinking can be applied across the range of psychological phenomena and how it can be tested empirically.

- At the same time, I have avoided slavishly introducing paragraphs on each perspective in every chapter, since some perspectives obviously apply better to certain phenomena than to others. For example, Chapter 6 on memory is organized primarily around cognitive information-processing models. It does, however, conclude with an evolutionary perspective which, like many contemporary cognitive models, challenges the view of an all-purpose, general processing brain, suggesting that the brain may have modules that process very specific information relevant to survival and reproduction.

- Although I have made every effort to present controversies in a balanced and dispassionate way, the danger in doing so is that one loses one's voice, and the last thing I wanted to write was a book with intellectual laryngitis. Thus, in "Commentary" sections, I periodically comment on issues of method that bear on the conclusions being reached; or after presenting both sides of a debate, I let the reader know where I stand on controversial issues, such as the existence of repressed memories of sexual abuse. I have presented versions of some of these commentaries on National Public Radio's "All Things Considered."

RESEARCH FOCUS

This book takes psychological science seriously. A student should come out of an introductory psychology class not only with a sense of the basic questions and frameworks for answering them but also with an appreciation for how to obtain psychological knowledge. Thus, Chapter 2 is devoted to research methods; the style reflects an effort to engage, not intimidate, so students may see how methods actually make a difference. The statistical supplement that immediately follows it, which even the most seriously math-phobic can understand, is included in the body of the text rather than cast off at the end as an impenetrable appendix. In addition, throughout each chapter, students read about specific studies so that they can learn about the logic of scientific investigation. In this edition I have done this earlier in the text, beginning in the first chapter, and continuing with the detective stories that constitute good research in Chapter 3 (on the biological basis of mental processes and behavior) and Chapter 4 (on sensation and perception). By providing the details of experimental design (e.g., how does imaging research really work?), the more biological chapters in particular can read more like a story about living, evolving subdisciplines.

The research presented in this book is also up to date. Like Sisyphus, I have been pushing the boulder of citations up the hill every year, updating and re-thinking as it acquires new weight. At the same time, I have included many classic citations and have tried to convey the way theories and hypotheses have evolved, not just their latest renditions for the sake of appearing current.

INTEGRATIVE APPROACH

Solo-authoring an introductory text is probably presumptive evidence of mental instability (and is clearly a cause of it as well), but I could not have produced this book any other way because my aim was to engage students in the enterprise of thinking about the whole person, not just the parts. As one psychologist put it (Holt, 1976), the human psyche is not the handiwork of an obsessive-compulsive god who created cognition on one day, affect on another, motivation on another, and so forth, and made sure they all stayed neatly in their own territories. Too often our efforts to classify and label lead us to try to separate the inseparable. The integrative bent of the book stems primarily from my own work as a researcher, which has focused on integrating clinical and experimental perspectives as well as concepts and methods from different psychological traditions.

Wherever possible, this book tries to delineate some of the links that our best intellectual efforts often obscure. For example, Chapter 7 presents connectionist models in some detail, linking them to concepts of association described in Chapter 1, Chapter 5 on associative learning, and Chapter 6 on associative memory. Chapter 11 on emotion, stress, and coping ties together evolutionary thinking about the adaptive functions of emotion, research on the neural substrates of positive and negative affect, research on operant conditioning, and approaches to affect regulation in thinking about how emotion regulates thought and behavior.

LANGUAGE

Above all, I wanted to avoid writing in "textese," a language that presents dry summaries of data for students to memorize instead of engaging them in *thinking* about psychology. *Psychology: Mind, Brain, & Culture* offers a solid and comprehensive account of the principles of psychology in what I hope is an accessible, lively, and thought-provoking style.

- Throughout the book, I aim at clarity and introduce terminology only when it enlightens, not obscures. I am not shy about using metaphor or weaving a narrative, but not a single term in this book is defined by context alone. If students need to understand a concept, they will see the definition in the same sentence in which the word is boldfaced. I have also tried to keep the language at a level appropriate to college students, but if they have to look up an occasional word, I will not lose sleep over it. (I had to look up a few in writing it!)

- As a teacher and writer, I try to make use of one of the most robust findings in psychology: that memory and understanding are enhanced when target information is associated with vivid and personally relevant material. Each chapter begins, then, with an experiment, a case, or an event that lets students know why the topic is important and why anyone might be excited about it. None of the cases is invented; this is real material, and the questions raised in the opening study or vignette reemerge throughout each chapter. Chapter 2, for example, begins with the case of a young woman who lost her entire family in a car accident and found herself suddenly contracting one minor ailment after another until finally starting to talk about the event with a psychologist. I then present an experiment by James Pennebaker on the influence of emotional expression on physical health to show how a researcher can take a striking phenomenon or philosophical question (the relation between mind and body) and turn it into a researchable question. A major change in this edition can be seen in the way I raise fundamental issues in each subfield at the beginning of the chapter, gradually address them as the chapter proceeds, and generally return to them in a more systematic way in the conclusion.

PEDAGOGICAL FEATURES

I have tried to avoid pedagogy that is condescending or unnecessary. One student complained to me in an e-mail message that her biggest problem with the book was that her roommate kept stealing it from the bookshelf and reading it! In my experience students never follow up on annotated recommendations for future reading, so I have not cluttered the ends of chapters with them. Similarly, because all terms are defined in the text, there is no need to list key terms at the end of the chapter; students can use the index and the glossary if they have trouble locating them. On the other hand, students do need some guidance in studying the material. Three features address this issue: interim summaries, chapter summaries, and a new feature called "One Step Further."

INTERIM SUMMARIES   In this edition I have added interim summaries at the end of major sections. Their aim is to recap the "gist" of what has been presented, not only to help students consolidate their knowledge of what they have read but also to alert them if they didn't get something important. The inclusion of these summaries reflects both feedback from professors and the results of research which suggests that distributing conceptual summaries throughout a chapter and presenting them shortly after students have read the material is likely to optimize learning.

CHAPTER SUMMARIES

As in the first edition, each chapter concludes with a summary of the major points, organized under the headings in which they were presented. These summaries are essentially an outline of the chapter. Student feedback on their organization and level of detail has been very positive.

▶ ONE STEP FURTHER

In this edition I have added a new feature, called "One Step Further." Like the other recurring features in the book, these discussions flow naturally from the text but are highlighted in color. Generally, these are advanced discussions of some aspect of the topic, usually with a strong methodological, conceptual, or neuroscientific focus. These sections are intended to be assigned by professors who prefer a high-level text, or to be read by students who find the topic intriguing and want to learn even more about it even if it isn't assigned. Highlighting these sections gives professors—and students—some choice about what to read or not to read. For example, in Chapter 3, this feature describes some of the latest research on non-motor functions of the cerebellum. In Chapter 4, it addresses signal detection theory, which some professors consider central to introductory coverage of sensation and perception, whereas others consider this material too advanced. In Chapter 5, this feature addresses the theoretical question, "What makes reinforcers reinforcing?" and integrates Gray's work on affect-mediated systems of approach and avoidance, Davidson's work on cortical pathways involved in approach and avoidance, and integrative theories of emotion and reinforcement stemming back to Dollard and Miller. In each case, the material can be skipped without any break in the narrative if the professor chooses not to assign it.

ORGANIZATION

I tried to organize **Psychology:** *Mind, Brain, & Culture* in a way that would be convenient for most instructors yet follow a coherent design. Of course, different instructors organize things differently, but I do not think many will find the organization idiosyncratic.

Teaching the material in the order presented is probably optimal, for chapters do build on each other. For example, the consciousness chapter presupposes knowledge of the distinction posed in Chapter 6 between implicit and explicit memory. However, if instructors want to rearrange the order of chapters, they can certainly do so, as material mentioned from a previous chapter is cross-referenced so that students can easily find any information they need.

ILLUSTRATION AND DESIGN

When I began this enterprise, I had no idea what it meant to put together a whole textbook. As a person with minimal use of his right hemisphere, I assumed that some editorial type would come up with figures and tables. This assumption was obviously an example of a well-known psychological phenomenon, wishful thinking. After ten years of working on this project, I think I finally figured out how to educate the right hemisphere, even if mine does not work so well. I took tremendous care to select and design only figures and tables that actually add something and that do not just make the pages look less ominous. Additionally, in this edition, the illustrations were designed with a more vibrant, bolder color palette and larger, bolder labels for better clarity and legibility. The same is true of photo selection, which involved collaboration of the author, editors, and a very talented photo research department committed to finding images that would provoke thought and not simply provide momentary respite from the prose. We also worked with the best designers in the business to create a design that is sophisticated and readable, adding the color background screens to the three categories of embedded essays (From Mind to Brain, A Global Vista, and One Step Further) and a bolder, more dynamic palette to their design elements.

SUPPLEMENTARY MATERIALS

Accompanying the text is an integrated supplements package that includes the following components.

For Instructors

Test Bank and Instructor's Manual: The new edition of the test bank has been written by *The Princeton Review,* the leading publisher of course-preparation materials, and reviewed by Professor Runi Mukerji of the State University of New York at Old Westbury and Professor Brenda Byers of Texas A & M University. Known for getting excellent results through their test-preparation publications and courses, *The Princeton Review* and John Wiley & Sons provide instructors with carefully edited materials and techniques that will help them most effectively test students who use this text and in turn achieve positive results with their own students. The *Instructor's Manual* has been written by The Princeton Review and Professor Paul Wellman of Texas A&M University, and reviewed by Professor Dean McKay at Fordham University, and contains cross-references to the text, the *Test Bank,* and *Study Guide* as well as links found in the *On-Line Guide* with tips for instructors on how to incorporate Web material (see below) into the classroom.

Computerized Test Bank: All of the paper *Princeton Review Test Bank* questions are incorporated into this easy-to-use software program that enables instructors to create, save, customize, and print exams.

Instructor's Resource CD-ROM: Created and developed by Professor Paul Wellman of Texas A&M University, this CD includes digital slide shows of 450 original lecture slides and 215 art slides that can be sequenced and customized by instructors to fit any lecture. It also includes the complete *Instructor's Manual* and entire *Test Bank,* and a *Science News* archive containing the most important and current articles on psychology research from 1997 to the present. These *Science News* research pieces will be updated bi-weekly on the new Web site.

Transparencies: Full-color traditional acetates of illustrations from the text will be provided in special cases for those who cannot use the slides or our CD.

The Psychology Web Site for Instructors: The new Web site includes a Listserve that instructors can join to receive updates every two weeks about new Web links, new technology and how to integrate it into the classroom, new search engine information, and continually updated information on new images available for lecture presentations. An exciting new Web feature will be *In the News,* a unique feature organized and updated bimonthly by Paul Wellman, which will contain news stories from *Science News* magazine and discussion questions that tie each article directly to related material in the text. The site also contains useful tips on creatively using the *Instructor's Resource CD* and the digital slide presentations, and describes the changes made to the new edition of the text. Instructors will also have access to

WebCT, a more powerful web site program that allows professors to set up an on-line course with chat rooms, bulletin boards, quizzing, and student tracking. The WebCT version will be fully loaded with our content for immediate use.

For Students:

Art Notebook: Packaged with every text, this notebook contains all of the art illustrations in *Psychology: Mind, Brain, & Culture* that students will see in lecture from the art slides and transparencies. Students can easily take notes in class on the illustrations contained in the slide shows on the *Instructor's Resource CD-ROM* without having to bring their text to class, and then use this notebook to study for exams.

The Psychology Web Site for Students: Packaged with every text will be a password that will be the students' key to the new Web site. Here students will have access to the latest research through *Science News* articles, updated biweekly and specifically tied into each of the chapters they study. Over 100 Web sites with descriptions researched and written by Paul Wellman will be included on the site, separated by text chapter, that will guide students through the most useful and accurate information available on the Web. Students can take practice quizzes here, written by Professor Runi Mukerji, that are scored and also can be sent directly to their instructors.

Study Guide: Written by Alastair Younger at the University of Ottawa, and edited and reviewed by *The Princeton Review* so it ties in well with the *Test Bank* and *Instructor's Manual,* the study guide offers students a great way to review the material in the text and test their knowledge. Each chapter in the text has a corresponding chapter in the study guide. Six tools help students master the material: chapter outlines, learning objectives, key terms, fill-in exercises, critical thinking exercises, and sample test questions with answers.

On-Line Guide: This paperback Web guide will be included with every copy of the text and covers the basics of student use of the Internet and how to use search engines most efficiently to find the exact information you're looking for. A special chapter covering *Mental Health Net* is included as well as a complete section of URLs relating Web links to topics in each chapter of the text.

Videos: There are a number of videotapes available to adopters of the text that are new to this edition. Please contact your local Wiley representative for details of this exciting new program.

Acknowledgments

This project began many years ago—in 1987—and several people have played important roles in getting it off the ground. The initial plan for the book was to co-write it with a very talented writer, Jean Stein, who helped write the first draft of the first half of the first edition. Her involvement ended a year after the project began, and the writing and content are now very different because of the many rounds of revisions the book has undergone since then. Nevertheless, many flashes of sparkle, felicitous turns of phrase, and clear passages remain from her efforts, for which I am extremely grateful. Several other people also contributed in the early stages, notably Judy Block, Barbara Misle, Carol Holden, and Karen Schenkenfeldter. Like Jean, they helped lay the foundations, and their efforts, too, are greatly appreciated. Since then, I have gained from the work of multiple research assistants (some of whom are now colleagues), including (but not limited to) Lauren Korfine, Patricia Harney, Colleen Coffey, and Michelle Levine. To all of them I am very grateful.

REVIEWERS

Over the past ten years, this book has been shaped by the insightful comments of dozens of colleagues and would look nothing like it does now without their tireless efforts. In particular, I would like to thank Walt Lonner of Western Washington University, who advised me on cross-cultural coverage for many chapters and gave feedback on several, and Paul Watson of the University of Tennessee for his uncanny ability throughout the years to notice where my prose was getting sloppy, my thoughts confused, or my coverage idiosyncratic. Several others provided invaluable feedback on multiple chapters of the new edition:

General Reviewers, Second Edition

Eugene Aidman, University of Ballarat
Paul Bloom, University of Arizona
Toni L. Blum, Stetson University
Joanna Boehnert, University of Guelph
John Bonvillian, University of Virginia
Douglas A. Bors, University of Toronto at Scarborough
Bruce Bridgeman, University of California at Santa Cruz
James Butler, James Madison University
Simone Buzwell, Swinburne University of Technology
James Dalziel, University of Sidney
Hank Davis, University of Guelph
Mark Dombeck, Idaho State University
Richard Eglsaer, Sam Houston State University
Nellie Georgiou, Monash University
Leonard Green, Washington University

Linda Hort, Griffith University
Robert F. Mosher, Northern Arizona University
Andrew Neher, Cabrillo College
Dorothy C. Pointkowski, San Francisco State University
Laura Reichel, Metropolitan State College of Denver
Paul Roberts, Murdoch University
Hillary Rodman, Emory University
Alexander Rothman, University of Minnesota
David A. Schroder, University of Arkansas
Norm Simonson, Univeristy of Massachusetts
Paul Stager, York University
Margo A. Storm, Temple University
David Uttal, Northwestern University

Paul J. Watson, University of
Tennessee at Chattanooga

Paul Waxer, York University
Cara Wellman, Indiana University

In addition, a special team of reviewers with expertise related to specific chapters took time to provide especially thorough reviews and critiques of chapters in their area of expertise for this edition:

Expert Reviewers, Second Edition

Gary Allen, University of South Carolina, *Chapter 6*

Elaine Baker, Marshall University, *Chapter 9*

Richard Belter, University of West Florida, *Chapters 15 and 16*

Kathleen Bey, Palm Beach Community College, *Chapter 12*

John D. Bonvillian, University of Virginia, *Chapters 3, 7, 8, and 13*

Bruce Bridgeman, University of California, Santa Cruz, *Chapter 3*

Nathan Brody, Wesleyan, *Chapter 8*

Susan Calkins, University of North Carolina at Greensboro, *Chapters 11, 12, and 13*

Toon Cillessen, University of Connecticut, *Chapter 14*

Patricia Colby, Skidmore College, *Chapter 11*

William Domhoff, University of California, Santa Cruz, *Chapter 9*

Wendi Gardner, Northwestern University, *Chapter 11*

Leonard Green, Washington University, *Chapter 5*

Joseph Guido, Providence College, *Chapters 9, 11, 12, 17, and 18*

Robert Guttentag, University of North Carolina at Greensboro, *Chapters 9 and 13*

Richard Halgin, University of Massachusetts at Amherst, *Chapters 15 and 16*

Douglas Herrmann, Indiana State University, *Chapter 6*

Julia Jacks, University of North Carolina at Greensboro, *Chapters 1, 17, and 18*

Robert Johnston, College of William and Mary, *Chapter 10*

Kevin Kennelly, University of North Texas, *Chapter 6*

Randy J. Larsen, The University of Michigan, *Chapter 11*

Len Lecci, University of North Carolina at Wilmington, *Chapters 8 and 12*

Matthew Margres, *Chapters 3–8.*

Ann Meriwether, University of Michigan, *Chapters 13 and 14*

John B. Nezlek, College of William and Mary, *Chapters 17 and 18*

Constance Pilkington, College of William and Mary, *Chapter 18*

Felicia Pratto, University of Connecticut, *Chapters 17 and 18*

David Rabiner, University of North Carolina at Greensboro, *Chapters 2, 15, and 16*

Hillary Rodman, Emory University, *Chapters 3 and 4*

David Schroeder, University of Arkansas, *Chapter 17*

Alan Searlman, St. Lawrence University, *Chapter 6*

Richard Schiffman, Rutgers University, *Chapter 4*

Steven Sloman, Brown University, *Chapter 7*

Chehalis Strapp, Western Oregon University, *Chapter 7*

Malcolm Watson, Brandeis University, *Chapters 13 and 14*

Billy Wooten, Brown University, *Chapter 4*

David M. Wulff, Wheaton College, *Chapters 9 and 12*

Prior to publication of this edition and the last, a large number of introductory psychology professors from around the world with a wide range of areas of expertise provided detailed reviews of every chapter of the book. Their comments have shaped every aspect of it. Special thanks go to the following:

GENERAL REVIEWS FOR PRIOR DRAFTS

Gordon Allen, Miami University
Harvard L. Armus, University of Toledo

Robert Batsell, Southern Methodist University
Carol M. Batt, Sacred Heart University

Col. Johnson Beach, United States Military Academy-West Point

John B. Best, Eastern Illinois University

John Bonvillian, University of Virginia

Robert Brown, Georgia State University

Mark Byrd, University of Canterbury (New Zealand)

Barbara K. Canaday, Southwestern College

George A. Cicala, University of Delaware

John M. Clark, Macomb Community College

Margaret Cleek, University of Wisconsin-Madison

Peter Ditto, Kent State University

Allen Dobbs, University of Alberta

Eugene B. Doughtie, University of Houston

J. Gregor Fetterman, Arizona State University

Nelson Freedman, Queens University

Herbert Friedman, The College of William and Mary

Mauricio Gaborit, S. J., St. Louis University

Adrienne Ganz, New York University

Mark Garrison, Kentucky State University

Marian Gibney, Phoenix College

William E. Gibson, Northern Arizona University

Marvin Goldfried, State University of New York-Stony Brook

Mary Alice Gordon, Southern Methodist University

Charles R. Grah, Austin Peay State University

Mary Banks Gregerson, George Washington University

Timothy Jay, North Adams State College

James Johnson, Illinois State University

Lance K. Johnson, Pasadena City College

Lynne Kiorpes, New York University

Stephen B. Klein, Mississippi State University

Keith Kluender, University of Wisconsin-Madison

James M. Knight, Humboldt State University

James Kopp, University of Texas-Arlington

Emma Kraidman, Franciscan Children's Hospital, Boston

Philip Langer, University of Colorado-Boulder

Peter Leppmann, University of Guelph

Alice Locicero, Lesley College

Richard M. Martin, Gustavus Adolphus College

Donald McBurney, University of Pittsburgh

Eleanor Midkiff, Eastern Illinois University

David Mitchell, Southern Methodist University

David I. Mostofsky, Boston University

John Mullennix, Wayne State University

John Nezlek, The College of William and Mary

J. Faye Pritchard, La Salle University

Freda Rebelsky, Boston University

Bradley C. Redburn, Johnson County Community College

Daniel Roenkert, Western Kentucky University

Lawrence Rosenblum, University of California-Riverside

Kenneth W. Rusiniak, Eastern Michigan University

Ina Samuels, University of Massachusetts-Boston

Karl E. Scheibe, Wesleyan University

Richard Schiffman, Rutgers University

Robert Sekuler, Brandeis University

Norman Simonson, University of Massachusetts-Amherst

Steven Sloman, Brown University

J. Diedrick Snoek, Smith College

Sheldon Solomon, Skidmore College

Perry Timmermans, San Diego City College

D. Rene Verry, Millikin University

Paul Watson, University of Tennessee-Chatanooga

Russell H. Weigel, Amherst College

Joel Weinberger, Adelphi University

Cheryl Weinstein, Harvard Medical School

Paul Wellman, Texas A & M University

Macon Williams, Illinois State University

Jeremy M. Wolfe, Massachusetts Institute of Technology

Todd Zakrajsek, Southern Oregon State College

Thomas Zentall, University of Kentucky

STUDENT FOCUS GROUPS

We also benefitted considerably from student response in focus groups. Many thanks to the faculty members and graduate students who coordinated them, as well as to the students who provided their feedback.

- **Canisius College**   *Coordinator:* Harvey Pines
- **Johnson County Community College**   *Coordinator:* Tody Klinger
- **Ohio State University**   *Faculty Coordinator:* Alexis Collier
- **Southern Illinois University-Carbondale**   *Coordinator:* Gordon Pitz
- **University of Minnesota-Minneapolis**   *Coordinator:* Gail Peterson
- **University of New Mexico-Albuquerque**   *Coordinator:* Robert J. Sutherland
- **University of Oklahoma-Norman**   *Coordinator:* Richard Reardon
- **University of Tennessee-Knoxville**   *Coordinator:* William H. Calhoun

Finally, I'd like to offer my deep appreciation to the extraordinary team at Wiley. Foremost, Chris Rogers has shepherded this project for several years and helped elaborate its vision. He has been a wonderful friend and editor, a rare combination of scholar, businessman, and empathic soul who understands the torment of textbook authorship (when he isn't, by virtue of his role, contributing to it). In this edition, Rachel Nelson assumed much of the editorial responsibility for the project and did a superb job. In this edition and the last, Harriett Prentiss went through every word of every paragraph and probably taught me more about writing than anyone since my twelfth-grade English teacher. Anna Melhorn and Hilary Newman have done a superb job developing the art work and photography programs, respectively. They performed an impressive balancing act in giving me autonomy while sharing their expertise whenever my defective right hemisphere led me astray. My thanks also go to Art Ciccone, who helped render accurate technical illustrations in the first edition; the artists at J. A. K. Graphics, who did an extraordinary job of turning my sketches into illustrations that are both aesthetically appealing and edifying; Ann Marie Renzi, who supervised the design; Elizabeth Swain, who carefully oversaw production; Kristen Karyczak and Caroline Ryan, who helped pull the final project together; and Charity Robey, Senior Marketing Manager. More generally, I couldn't ask for a better publisher, from the extraordinary efforts of a gifted editorial and production staff, to the marketing and sales force who put this book in your hands, and to a CEO, Will Pesce, and a Chairman of the Board, Brad Wiley, II, who are committed to publishing textbooks that edify and excite rather than just sell.

About the Author

Drew Westen

Drew Westen is Associate Professor of Psychology at the Harvard Medical School and Chief Psychologist at the Cambridge Hospital, in Cambridge, Massachusetts. He received his undergraduate degree from Harvard, an M.A. in Social and Political Thought from the University of Sussex (England), and a Ph.D. in Clinical Psychology from the University of Michigan, where he taught introductory psychology for several years. While at the University of Michigan, he was honored two years in a row by the *Michigan Daily* as the best teaching professor at the university, and was the recipient of the first Golden Apple Award for outstanding undergraduate teaching. His major areas of research are personality disorders, emotion regulation, implicit processes, and adolescent psychopathology. Much of his theoretical work has attempted to bridge cognitive, behavioral, psychodynamic, and evolutionary perspectives. His series of videotaped lectures on abnormal psychology, called *Is Anyone Really Normal?*, was published by the Teaching Company, in collaboration with the Smithsonian Institution. He also provides psychological commentaries on political issues for "All Things Considered" on National Public Radio. His main love outside of psychology is music. He writes comedy music and has performed as a stand-up comic in Boston.

Contents in Brief

Contents

Glenys Barton, "Three Faced Head 1990, Small Madonna 1990." Courtesy Angela Flowers Gallery, London.

CHAPTER *1*

Psychology: The Study of Mental Processes and Behavior

A 15-year-old girl we will call Susan was hospitalized in a psychiatric unit because of severe adjustment problems. The most notable characteristic of her case was a dramatic change in her IQ score, which had dropped 50 points in less than five years, from 120 to 70. IQ is a measure of intelligence, and 120 is quite high, whereas 70 is on the border of mental retardation. As IQ scores in adolescence and adulthood typically remain fairly stable, a change of even 10 or 15 points in such a short time span is remarkable.

Susan had a poorly controlled case of epilepsy, a disorder characterized by abnormal patterns of electrical activity in the brain. In epilepsy, nerve cells in the brain discharge, or "fire," without appropriate stimulation. This leads to alterations in consciousness and behavior called *seizures,* characterized by brief periods of psychological "absence" from reality or violent muscle movements. Epilepsy can usually be controlled with medication (Smith & Darlington, 1996), but Susan was one of the unfortunate minority for whom nothing seemed to work.

Susan was peculiar in a number of ways. She was extremely egocentric, focusing only on her own perspective and interrupting conversations with her own concerns. She had difficulty sticking to the subject and would often blurt out inappropriate thoughts. When asked questions, she would often delay for up to a minute before answering. Finally, she was overly preoccupied with religion, a phenomenon observed in a small percentage of people with epilepsy (Daiguji, 1990; Tucker et al., 1987).

According to Susan, her only problem was that her mother no longer lived with her; Susan's mother had abandoned the family five years earlier, and Susan had never recovered emotionally. As soon as her mother returned, she insisted, she would be fine again. However, the medical team treating Susan—I was part of that team—had a different prognosis. We suspected Susan had a degenerative brain disease—a deteriorating brain—that was responsible for both the epilepsy and her plummeting IQ score.

Several months after her release from the hospital, something strange happened: Susan's IQ rose almost 30 points, her social and academic difficulties diminished somewhat, and her seizures decreased in frequency. She would never return to normal, but the change was extraordinary. When I heard of this dramatic improvement, I presumed that her doctors had probably hit upon a new medication, but like many psychological hypotheses, this one turned out to be wrong. In fact, what had prompted Susan's dramatic improvement was just what she had predicted: Her mother had returned.

Susan's case is unusual because rarely does an environmental change lead to such a remarkable improvement in brain functioning. Yet it illustrates a central issue that has vexed philosophers for over two millennia and psychologists for over a century—namely, the relation between mental and physical events, between meaning and mechanism.

Humans are complex creatures whose psychological experience lies at the intersection of biology and culture. To paraphrase one theorist, Erik Erikson (1963), psychologists must practice "triple bookkeeping" to understand an individual at any given time, simultaneously tracking biological events, psychological experience, and the cultural and historical context. Susan had **lesions,** or damaged areas, throughout her brain, but she also had emotional "lesions"—a broken heart as well as a broken brain. Together these misfortunes created a syndrome that probably neither alone would have produced. Yet even this interaction of mind and brain does not fully account for Susan's syndrome, for in most cultures throughout human history, people have lived in small communities with their extended families, and mothers have not had the option of moving far away from their children. Had she lived in another place or another time, Susan may not have experienced either a rapid decline or a remarkable recovery.

At this intersection of biology and culture lies **psychology,** *the scientific investigation of mental processes and behavior*. All psychological processes occur through the interaction of cells in the nervous system, and all human action occurs in the context of cultural beliefs and values that render it meaningful. Psychological understanding thus requires a constant movement between the micro-level of biology and the macro-level of culture. But psychology is not simply about cells or societies. It is simultaneously about mind, brain, and culture.

This chapter begins by exploring the biological and cultural boundaries and borders that frame human psychology. We then examine the theoretical perspectives that have focused, and often divided, the attention of the scientific community for a century.

INTERIM SUMMARY   **Psychology** is the scientific investigation of mental processes and behavior. Understanding a person requires attention to the individual's biology, psychological experience, and cultural context.

THE BOUNDARIES AND BORDERS OF PSYCHOLOGY

Biology and culture establish both the possibilities and the constraints within which people think, feel, and act. On the one hand, the structure of the brain sets the parameters, or limits, of human potential. Most ten-year-olds cannot solve algebra problems because the neural circuitry essential for abstract thought has not yet matured. Similarly, the capacity for love has its roots in the innate tendency of infants to develop an emotional attachment to their caretakers. These are biological givens.

On the other hand, most adults throughout human history would find algebra problems as mystifying as would a preschooler because their culture never provided the groundwork for this kind of reasoning. And though love may be a basic potential, the way people love depends on the values, beliefs, and practices of their society. In some cultures, people seek and expect romance in their marriages, whereas in others, they do not select a spouse based on affection or attraction at all.

FROM MIND TO BRAIN

THE BOUNDARY WITH BIOLOGY

The biological boundary of psychology is the province of **biopsychology** (or **behavioral neuroscience**), which investigates the physical basis of psychological phenomena such as memory, emotion, or stress. Instead of studying thoughts, feelings, or fears, behavioral neuroscientists (some of whom are physicians or biologists rather than psychologists) investigate the electrical and chemical processes in the nervous system that underlie these mental events. Their aim is to link mind and body, psyche and brain.

The connection between mind and brain became increasingly clear during the nineteenth century, when doctors began observing patients with severe head injuries. Language and memory were often greatly curtailed in these patients, who might also show dramatic alterations in their personalities. A socially appropriate, genteel businessman and devoted father could suddenly become lewd and cantankerous and lack affection for loved ones following a severe blow to the head. These observations led researchers to experiment by *producing* lesions surgically in animals in different neural regions to observe the effects on behavior. This method is still used today, as in research on emotion, which has begun to identify the neural pathways involved in fear reactions (LeDoux, 1995). In this research, psychologists lesion one brain structure at a time along pathways hypothesized to be involved when rats learn to fear an object associated with pain. When a lesion disrupts learning, the researcher knows that the lesioned area, or other areas connected to it, is involved in fear.

Since its origins in the nineteenth century, one of the major issues in behavioral neuroscience has been **localization of function,** or the extent to which different parts of the brain control different aspects of functioning. In 1836, a physician named Marc Dax presented a paper in which he noted that lesions on the left side of the brain were associated with *aphasia,* or language disorders. The notion that language was localized to the left side of the brain (the left hemisphere) developed momentum with new discoveries linking

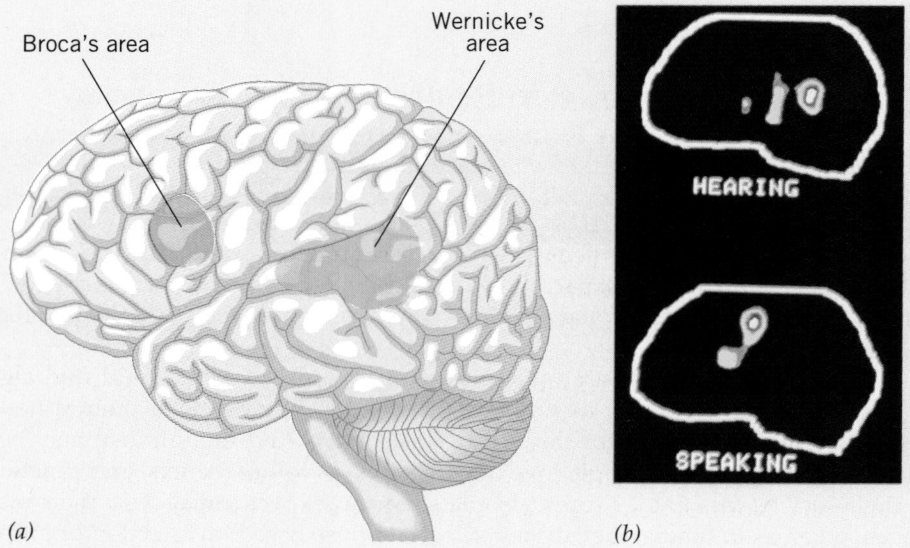

FIGURE 1.1
Broca's and Wernicke's areas. (*a*) Discovery of different effects of lesions to Broca's and Wernicke's areas led to increased sophistication about localization of function. Broca's aphasia involves difficulty producing speech, whereas Wernicke's aphasia typically involves difficulty comprehending language. (*b*) A positron emission tomography (PET) scan is a computerized imaging technique that allows researchers to study the functioning of the brain as the person responds to stimuli. The PET scans here show activity in Wernicke's and Broca's areas.

specific language functions to specific regions of the left hemisphere. Paul Broca (1824–1880) discovered that brain-injured people with lesions in the front section of the left hemisphere were often unable to speak fluently but could comprehend language. Carl Wernicke (1848–1904) showed that damage to an area a few centimeters behind the section Broca had discovered could lead to another kind of aphasia, in which the person can neither understand language nor speak comprehensibly (Figure 1.1). Individuals with this form of aphasia may speak fluently, apparently following rules of grammar, but the words they utter make little sense ("I saw the bats and cuticles as the dog lifted the hoof, the pauser").

One of the metaphors that underlies neuropsychological thinking compares the brain to an electronic machine with a complex series of circuits. Particular experiences or behaviors reflect patterns or sequences in the activation of cells that are "wired" together. To offer an analogy, no single point on a television screen means anything on its own because each pixel or dot can be used in millions of different configurations. The *pattern* in which that dot is activated gives it meaning, just as the pattern of firing cells determines the meaning of a neural event.

Contemporary neuroscientists no longer believe that complex psychological functions "happen" exclusively in a single localized part of the brain. Rather, the circuits for psychological events, such as emotions or thoughts, are distributed throughout the brain, with each part contributing to the total experience. A man who sustains lesions to one area may be unable consciously to distinguish his wife's face from the face of any other woman—a disabling condition indeed—but may react physiologically to her face with a higher heart rate or pulse (Bruyer, 1991; Young, 1994). Technological advances over the last two decades have allowed researchers to pinpoint lesions precisely, and even to watch computerized portraits of the brain light up with activity (or fail to light up, in cases of neural damage) as people perform psychological tasks (Alivisatos & Petrides, 1997; Nadeau & Crosson, 1995).

A GLOBAL VISTA

THE BOUNDARY WITH CULTURE

Humans are not only collections of cells; they are also themselves the "cells" of larger groups, such as tribes or nations, which similarly impose their stamp on psychological functioning. The emergence of agriculture and cities, generally known as *civilization,* occurred less than ten thousand years ago. Before that time, and until well into the twentieth century in much of this planet's southern hemisphere, humans lived in small bands composed largely of their kin. Several bands often joined together into larger tribes in order to trade mates, protect territory, wage war on other groups, or participate in communal rituals.

The anthropologists who first studied these "exotic" cultures in Africa, Australia, North America, and elsewhere were struck by their differentness from their own cultures. Their observations raised a central issue that psychology has been slow to address: To what extent do cultural differences create psychological differences? What can we make of someone who becomes terrified because he believes that a quarrel with kin has offended the forest and may bring disaster upon his family? Does he share our psychological nature, or does each society produce its own psychology?

The first theorists to address this issue were psychologically sophisticated anthropologists like Margaret Mead and Ruth Benedict, who were interested in the relation between culture and personality (LeVine, 1982). Impressed with the wide variation of cultural beliefs and practices across the globe, they argued that individual psychology is fundamentally shaped by cultural values, ideals, and ways of thinking. As Benedict put it, "The life history of the individual is first and foremost an accommodation to the patterns and standards traditionally handed down in the community" (1934, p. 2). As children develop, they learn to behave in ways that conform to cultural standards. The openly competitive, confident, self-interested style generally rewarded in North American society would be unthinkable in Japan, where communal sentiments are much stronger. Japanese manufacturing companies do not lay off workers during economic downturns as do their North American and European counterparts because they believe corporations are like families and should treat their employees accordingly. Even ways of thinking—using witchcraft to explain disease or manipulating things that do not exist in reality, such as negative numbers—are shaped through interactions with others and become woven into the individual's own psychological fabric (Vygotsky, 1978; Wertsch & Kanner, 1992).

In the middle of the twentieth century, **psychological anthropologists,** who study psychological phenomena in other cultures by observing people in their natural settings (see Bock, 1988; Mathews & Moore, 1998; Suarez-Orozco et al., 1994), turned their interest to the way economic realities shape childrearing practices, which in turn mold personality (Kardiner, 1945; Whiting & Child, 1953). Then, as now, people in much of the Third World were leaving their ancestral homelands seeking work in large cities. Working as a laborer in a factory requires different attitudes toward time, mobility, and individuality than farming or foraging. A laborer must be able and willing to punch a time clock, move where the work is, work for wages, and spend all day away from kin (see Inkeles & Smith, 1974). Notions we take

Margaret Mead was a leading figure among anthropologists and psychologists trying to understand the relation between personality and culture. Here she is pictured among the Manus of Micronesia in the late 1920s.

Working in a factory requires attitudes, behaviors, and personality traits such as punctuality that require years, if not generations, to form.

for granted—such as arriving to work within a prescribed span of minutes—are not "natural" to human beings. Punctuality is necessary for shiftwork in a factory or for changing from class to class in a modern school, and we consider it an aspect of character or personality. Yet punctuality was probably not even recognized as a dimension of personality in most cultures before the contemporary era and was certainly not a prime concern of parents in rearing their children.

After the 1950s, interest in the relation between culture and psychological attributes waned for decades. Within psychology, however, a small group of researchers developed the field of **cross-cultural psychology,** which attempts to test psychological hypotheses in different cultures (Berry et al., 1992, 1997; Lonner & Malpass, 1994; Triandis, 1980, 1994). Interest in cross-cultural psychology has blossomed recently as issues of diversity have come to the fore in the political arena. Psychologists have now been reflecting more carefully on the extent to which decades of research on topics such as memory, motivation, psychological disorders, or obedience have yielded results about *people* or about a particular *group* of people. Do individuals in all cultures experience depression? Do toddlers learn to walk and talk at the same rate cross-culturally? Do people dream in all cultures, and if so, what is the function of dreaming? Only cross-cultural comparisons can distinguish between universal and culturally specific psychological processes.

INTERIM SUMMARY Biopsychology (or **behavioral neuroscience**) examines the physical basis of psychological phenomena such as motivation, emotion, and stress. Although different neural regions perform different functions, the neural circuits that underlie psychological events are distributed throughout the brain and cannot be "found" in one location. At one other boundary of psychology, cross-cultural investigation is essential to try to distinguish psychological processes that are universal from those that are more specific to particular cultures.

FROM PHILOSOPHY TO PSYCHOLOGY

Questions about human nature, such as whether psychological attributes are the same everywhere, were once the province of philosophy. Early in this century, however, philosophers entered a period of intense self-doubt, wrestling with the limitations of what they could know about topics like morality, justice, and the nature of knowledge. At the same time, psychologists began to apply the methods and technologies of natural science to psychological questions. They reasoned that if physicists can discover the atom and industrialists can mass-produce automobiles, then psychological scientists can uncover basic laws of human and animal behavior.

Philosophical Roots of Psychological Questions

The fact that psychology was born from the womb of philosophy is of no small consequence. Many of the issues at the heart of contemporary psychological research and controversy are classic philosophical questions. One of these is whether human action is the product of **free will** or **determinism**—that is, whether we freely choose our actions or whether our behavior is really caused, or determined, by things outside our control. Those who champion free will follow in the footsteps of seventeenth-century French philosopher Rene Descartes (1596–1650), who contended that human action follows from human intention—that people choose a course of action and act on it. In contrast, proponents of determinism, from the Greek philosopher Democritus onward, assert that behavior follows lawful patterns like everything else in the universe, from falling rocks to planets revolving around the sun. Psychological determinists believe that the actions of humans and other animals are determined by physical forces, internally by genetic processes and externally by environmental events.

This issue has no easy solution. Subjectively, we have the experience of free will. I could choose to stop writing—or you to stop reading—at this very moment. Yet here we are, continuing into the next sentence. Why? What determined our choice to forge ahead? And how can mental processes exercise control over physical processes such as moving a pen or turning a page? Humans are material beings, part of nature, like birds, plants, and water. When we choose to move, our limbs exert a force that counters gravity and disturbs molecules of air. How can a nonmaterial force—will—displace material forces? No one has ever proposed a satisfactory solution to the **mind–body problem,** the question of how mental and physical events interact. However, psychological phenomena such as the decline and subsequent rise of Susan's IQ put the mind–body problem in a new light by drawing specific attention to the way psychological meaning (despair at her mother's absence) can become transformed into mechanism (physiological events such as seizure activity).

Psychologists do not tackle philosophical issues such as free will directly, but these classic philosophical questions reverberate through many contemporary psychological discussions. Research into the genetics of personality and personality disturbances provides an intriguing, if disquieting, example. People with antisocial personality disorder have minimal conscience and a tendency toward aggressive or criminal behavior. In an initial psychiatric evaluation one man boasted about the way he had terrorized his former girlfriend for an hour by brandishing a knife and telling her in exquisite detail the ways he intended to slice her flesh. This man could undoubtedly have exercised his free will to continue or discontinue his behavior at any moment and hence was morally (and legally) responsible for his acts. He knew what he was doing, he was not hearing voices commanding him to behave aggressively, and he thoroughly enjoyed his victim's terror. A determinist, however, could offer an equally compelling case. Like many violent men, he was the son of violent alcoholic parents, who had beaten him severely as a child. Both physical abuse in childhood and parental alcoholism (which can exert both genetic and environmental influences) render an individual more likely to develop antisocial personality disorder (see Cadoret et al., 1995;

People who deliberately inflict injury on others for political purposes that seem bizarre but were fully aware of what they were doing press the limits of what we mean by free will or personal responsibility. The Unabomber, who embarked on a 20-year killing spree to protest modern technology, was surely emotionally unstable, although his disorder did not meet the legal criteria for insanity.

TABLE 1.1 PHILOSOPHICAL ISSUES AND PSYCHOLOGICAL QUESTIONS	
PHILOSOPHICAL ISSUE	EXAMPLES OF CONTEMPORARY PSYCHOLOGICAL QUESTIONS
Free will versus determinism: Do people make free choices or are their actions determined by forces outside their control?	What causes patients with antisocial personality disorder to produce criminal behavior?
Nature versus nurture: To what extent do psychological processes reflect biological or environmental influence?	To what extent is intelligence inherited, and how do genes and environment interact to influence intellectual functioning?
Rationalism versus empiricism: To what extent does knowledge about the world come from observation and experience or from logic and reasoning?	How do children come to understand that other people have thoughts and feelings?
Reason versus emotion: To what extent are people guided by their knowledge or by their feelings (and to what extent should they be)?	Should people choose their mates based on "gut" feelings, or should they carefully weigh a potential partner's costs and benefits if they want to have a happy, long-lasting marriage?
Continuity versus discontinuity with other animals: To what extent are humans similar to other animals (that is, to what extent is human psychology continuous with the psychology of other animals)?	To what degree can studying fear responses in rats inform psychologists about the nature of human emotions?
Individualism versus relationality: To what extent are humans fundamentally self-interested or oriented toward relating to and helping other people?	Do people ever really help others without any benefit to themselves or are they motivated by other considerations, such as desires to feel good about themselves or avoid guilt?
Conscious versus unconscious: To what extent are people conscious of the contents of their minds and the causes of their behavior?	Can people describe themselves accurately, or are they unaware of many aspects of their personality?

Zanarini et al., 1990). In the immediate moment, perhaps, he had free will, but over the long run, he may have had no choice but to be the person he was.

Other philosophical questions set the stage for psychology and remain central to contemporary psychological theory and research. Many of these questions, like free will versus determinism, take the apparent form of choices between polar opposites, neither of which can be entirely true. Does human behavior reflect nature (biology) or nurture (environmental influence)? Does knowledge come from observing the world or from thinking about it? Several of these fundamental questions are summarized in Table 1.1.

From Philosophical Speculation to Scientific Investigation

Philosophical arguments have thus set the agenda for many of the issues confronting psychologists, and in our lifetimes, psychological research may shed light on questions that have seemed unanswerable for 2500 years. The fact that psychology was born from the womb of philosophy, however, has had another monumental influence on the discipline. Philosophers searched for answers to questions about the nature of thought, feeling, and behavior in their minds, using

Wilhelm Wundt is often called the "father of psychology" for his pioneering laboratory research. This portrait was painted in Leipzig, where he founded the first psychological laboratory.

logic and argumentation. By the late nineteenth century an alternative viewpoint emerged: If we want to understand the mind and behavior, we should investigate it scientifically, just as physicists study the nature of light or gravity through systematic observation and experimentation. Thus, in 1879, Wilhelm Wundt (1832–1920), often described as the "father of psychology," founded the first psychological laboratory in Leipzig, Germany.

Wundt hoped to use scientific methods to uncover the elementary units of human consciousness that combine to form more complex ideas, much as atoms combine into molecules in chemistry. One of the major methods he and his students used was **introspection,** the process of looking inward and reporting on one's conscious experience. The kind of introspection Wundt had in mind, however, was nothing like the introspection of philosophers, who tended to speculate freely on their experiences and observations. Instead, Wundt trained observers to report verbally everything that went through their minds when presented with a stimulus or task. By varying the objects presented to his observers and recording their responses, he concluded that the basic elements of consciousness are sensations (such as colors) and feelings. These elements combine into more meaningful perceptions (such as of a face or a cat), which can be combined into still *more* complex ideas by focusing attention on them and mentally manipulating them.

Wundt never believed that experimentation was the only route to psychological knowledge. Experimentation is essential for studying the basic elements of mind, he argued, but other methods—such as the study of myths, religion, and language in various cultures—are essential for understanding higher mental processes. The next generation of experimental psychologists, however, took a different view, motivated by their wish to divorce themselves from philosophical speculation and to establish a fully scientific psychology. Wundt's student, Edward Titchener (1867–1927), advocated the use of introspection in experiments in hopes of devising a periodic table of the elements of human consciousness, much like the periodic table discovered by chemists. Because of his interest in studying the structure of consciousness, the school of thought he initiated was known as **structuralism.** Unlike Wundt, Titchener believed that experimentation was the only appropriate method for a science of psychology and that concepts such as "attention" implied too much free will to be scientifically useful. As we will see, the generation of experimental psychologists who followed Titchener went even further, viewing the study of consciousness itself as unscientific because the data—sensations and feelings—could not be observed by anyone except the person reporting them.

Structuralism was one of two competing schools of thought that dominated psychology in its earliest years. The other was functionalism. Instead of focusing on the *contents* of the mind, **functionalism** emphasized the role—or *function*—of psychological processes in helping individuals adapt to their environment. A functionalist would not be content to state that the idea of running tends to come into consciousness in the presence of a bear showing its teeth. From a functionalist perspective, it is no accident that this particular idea enters consciousness when a person sees a bear but not when he sees a flower.

One of the leaders of functionalism, Harvard psychologist William James (1842–1910), penned the first textbook in psychology in 1890. (If you think *this* one is long, try reading James's 1400-page, two-volume set.) James was more comfortable with philosophical arguments than Titchener, and he believed that experimentation was only one path to psychological knowledge. Knowledge about human psychology, he argued, could come from many sources, including not only introspection but also the study of children, other animals (whose introspective reports may not be very useful), and people whose minds do *not* function adequately (such as the mentally ill). James viewed the structuralists' attempt to catalog the elements of consciousness as not only misguided but profoundly boring.

Consciousness exists because it serves a function, and the task of the psychologist is to understand that function. James was interested in explaining, not simply describing, the contents of the mind. As we will see, functionalism bore the clear imprint of the evolutionary theory of Charles Darwin, whose work has once again begun to play a central role in psychological theory a century later.

Structuralism and functionalism were two early "camps" in psychology that attracted passionate advocates and opponents. As we will see, they were not the last.

INTERIM SUMMARY   Although many contemporary psychological questions derive from age-old philosophical questions, by the end of the nineteenth century psychology emerged as a discipline, which aimed to answer questions about human nature through scientific investigation. Among the earliest schools of thought were **structuralism** and **functionalism.** Structuralism attempted to use **introspection** to uncover the basic elements of consciousness and the way they combine. Functionalism attempted to explain psychological processes in terms of the role, or function, they serve.

PERSPECTIVES IN PSYCHOLOGY

A tale is told of several blind men in India who came upon an elephant. They had no knowledge of what an elephant was, and eager to understand the beast, they reached out to explore it. One man grabbed its trunk and concluded, "An elephant is like a snake." Another touched its ear and proclaimed, "An elephant is like a leaf." A third, examining its leg, disagreed: "An elephant," he asserted, "is like the trunk of a tree."

Psychologists are in some ways like those blind men, struggling with imperfect instruments to try to understand the beast we call human nature and typically touching only part of the animal while trying to grasp the whole. Structuralism and functionalism provided the earliest perspectives in psychology. In this

FIGURE 1.2
An ambiguous figure. The indentation in the middle could be either an indentation in a vase or a nose. In science, as in everyday perception, knowledge involves understanding "facts" in the context of a broader interpretive framework.

chapter and throughout the book, we examine four perspectives that guide current psychological thinking, offering sometimes competing and sometimes complementary points of view on phenomena ranging from antisocial personality disorder to the way people make decisions when choosing a mate.

These perspectives are similar in many respects to the intuitive perspectives people take in daily life. The importance of perspective can be illustrated by a simple perceptual phenomenon. Consider Figure 1.2. Does it depict a vase? The profiles of two faces? The answer depends on one's perspective on the whole picture.

This picture was used by a German school of psychology in the early twentieth century, known as **Gestalt psychology.** The Gestalt psychologists argued that perception is not a passive experience through which people take photographic snapshots of details of the world around them. Rather, they argued, perception is an active experience of imposing order on an overwhelming panorama of details by seeing them as parts of larger wholes (or *gestalts*).

On simple perceptual tasks, then, the way people understand specific details depends on their interpretation of the object as a whole. This is equally true of complex scientific observations, which always occur within the context of a broader view, a theoretical perspective. To take a clinical example (an example from the therapeutic practice of psychology), a patient with an irrational fear, or *phobia,* of elevators may be told by one psychologist that her problem stems from the way thoughts and feelings were connected in her mind as a child. A second psychologist informs her that her problem results from an unfortunate connection between something in her environment, an elevator, and her learned response—avoidance of elevators. A third—examining the same data, no less—concludes that she has faulty wiring in her brain that leads to irrational anxiety.

What can we make of this state of affairs, in which experts disagree on the meaning and implications of a simple symptom? And what confidence could anyone have in seeking psychological help? The alternative is even less attractive: A psychologist with no perspective at all would be totally baffled and could only recommend to this patient that she take the stairs. Perspectives are like imperfect lenses through which we view some aspect of reality. They are frequently too convex or too concave, and they often leave their wearers blind to data on the periphery of their understanding. Without them, however, we are totally blind.

PARADIGMS AND PSYCHOLOGICAL PERSPECTIVES

Thomas Kuhn, a philosopher of science, studied the history of science to learn about the relationship between scientific "facts" and scientists' interpretations. Kuhn (1970) observed that science does not progress through the accumulation of facts, as many had believed. Rather, scientific progress depends on the development of better and better paradigms. A **paradigm** is a broad system of theoretical assumptions that a scientific community uses to make sense of a domain of experience. For example, the scientific community of physicists develops paradigms to make sense of the domain of the physical world; economists develop paradigms to explain market forces.

A paradigm has several key components. First, it includes a set of theoretical assertions that provide a **model,** or abstract picture, of the object of study. In economics, this model includes laws of supply and demand. Second, a paradigm includes a set of shared metaphors that compare the object under investigation to another that is readily apprehended (such as "the mind is like a computer"). Metaphors provide mental models for thinking about something that may be unfamiliar in a way that seems more familiar and understandable. Third, a paradigm includes a set of methods that members of the scientific community agree will, if properly executed, produce valid and useful data. Astronomers, for example, agree that telescopic investigation provides a window to events in space.

According to Kuhn, the social sciences and psychology differ from the older natural sciences (like physics and biology) in that they lack an accepted paradigm upon which most members of the scientific community agree. Instead, he proposes, these young sciences are still splintered into several schools of thought, or what we will call **perspectives.** The four psychological perspectives we examine offer the same kind of broad orienting approach as a scientific paradigm, and they share its three essential features. Focusing on these particular perspectives does not mean that other, less comprehensive approaches have not contributed to psychological knowledge or that nothing can be studied without them. A researcher interested in a specific question, such as whether preschool programs for economically disadvantaged children will improve their functioning later in life (Reynolds et al., 1995), does not need to endorse a broader outlook. But perspectives generally guide psychological investigations.

In the following sections we examine the **psychodynamic, behaviorist, cognitive,** and **evolutionary perspectives.** In many respects, these perspectives have evolved independently, and each places at its center phenomena that others tend to ignore.

INTERIM SUMMARY   A **paradigm** is a broad system of theoretical assumptions employed by a scientific community that includes shared models, metaphors, and methods. Psychology lacks a unified paradigm but has a number of schools of thought, or **perspectives,** that can be used to understand psychological events.

THE PSYCHODYNAMIC PERSPECTIVE

A friend has been dating a man for five months and has even jokingly tossed around the idea of marriage. Suddenly, her boyfriend tells her he has found someone else. She is shocked and angry and cries uncontrollably but a day later asserts that "he didn't mean that much to me anyway." When you try to console her about the rejection she must be feeling, she says, "Rejection? Hey, I don't know why I put up with him as long as I did," and jokes that "bad character is a genetic abnormality carried on the Y chromosome" (more on that later). You know she really cared about him, and you conclude that she is being defensive—that she really feels rejected. You draw these conclusions because you have grown up in a culture influenced by the psychoanalytic theory of Sigmund Freud.

In the late nineteenth century, Sigmund Freud (1856–1939), a Viennese physician, developed a theory of mental life and behavior and an approach to treating psychological disorders known as **psychoanalysis.** Since then, many psychologists have maintained Freud's emphasis on **psychodynamics,** or the dynamic interplay of mental forces. Psychodynamic psychologists make several basic assumptions. First, people's actions are determined by the way thoughts, feelings, and wishes are connected in their minds. Second, many of these mental events occur outside of conscious awareness. And third, these mental processes may conflict with one another, leading to compromises among competing motives. Thus, people are unlikely to know precisely the chain of psychological events that leads to their conscious thoughts, intentions, feelings, or behaviors.

Origins of the Psychodynamic Approach

Freud originated his theory in response to patients whose symptoms, although real, were not based on physiological malfunctioning. At the time, scientific think-

Sigmund Freud poring over a manuscript in his home office in Vienna around 1930.

ing had no way to explain patients who were preoccupied with irrational guilt after the death of a parent or were so paralyzed with fear that they could not leave their homes. Freud made a deceptively simple deduction, but one that changed the face of intellectual history: If the symptoms were not consciously created and maintained, and if they had no physical basis, only one possibility remained: Their basis must be unconscious.

Just as people have conscious motives or wishes, Freud argued, they also have powerful unconscious motives that underlie their conscious intentions. The reader has undoubtedly had the infuriating experience of waiting for half an hour as traffic crawls on the highway, only to find that nothing was blocking the road at all—just an accident in the opposite lane. Why do people slow down and gawk at accidents on the highway? Is it because they are concerned? Perhaps. But Freud would suggest that people derive an unconscious titillation or excitement, or at least satisfy a morbid curiosity, from viewing a gruesome scene, even though they may deny such socially unacceptable feelings.

Metaphors of the Psychodynamic Approach

Freud likened the relation between conscious awareness and unconscious mental forces to the visible tip of an iceberg and the vast, submerged hulk that lies out of sight beneath the water. Before Freud's time, most people believed that their own and others' actions were directed by their conscious wishes and beliefs. In contrast, Freud argued that these conscious desires themselves may reflect *unconscious* conflicts and compromises.

One patient, for example, came to a psychotherapist because she was always choosing men who were unobtainable. She explained that she was only attracted to men who were exciting, charismatic, and ultra-successful. As she explored her dating history in therapy, a pattern emerged: If she could actually win these "special" men, she became disinterested. Exploring her childhood history revealed that her father was a flashy, charismatic, and highly successful businessman whose love and respect she felt she never could obtain. As an adult, she was attracted to men much like her father, but she was also afraid that they would reject her as her father had in many ways. As a result, she was caught in an impasse, looking for men like her father but rejecting them as soon as they showed interest. Recent research in fact supports the view that the relationship between children and their parents is crucial in shaping later social relationships, and that these patterns of relating may be transmitted from generation to generation through parent–child interactions beginning in infancy (Bretherton, 1990; Main, 1995; Main, Kaplan, & Cassidy, 1985; van IZjendoorn, 1995).

Another psychodynamic metaphor compares the mind to a battleground in which warring factions struggle for expression. Imagine a young man growing up in a culture such as our own, which views homosexuality with considerable hostility. The young man has sexual feelings only toward other males, but these feelings conflict with societal norms and with his conscience, which has been shaped by social and parental attitudes. The high suicide rate among homosexual teenagers attests to the intensity of the pain this conflict can produce (Hartstein, 1996).

One option for this man is to acknowledge his homosexual feelings and ultimately accept them, a path that increasing numbers of gay men and lesbian women are now choosing. Alternatively, he may resolve the conflict unconsciously. For instance, he might **repress** his wishes, that is, keep himself unaware of them to avoid emotional distress. Freud maintained, however, that things are rarely that simple. Unconscious motives may be out of sight, but they are not out of mind. They will continue to press for satisfaction, and the stronger their force, the more intense the efforts to deny them may be. Thus, the man might convince himself that he is not really homosexual and join a crusade against homosexuality. In doing so, he exerts considerable effort trying to eradicate the homosexuality outside of him, when his real aim is to stifle the homosexual feelings and impulses within. Interestingly, recent experimental research finds that homophobic men—men who report particularly negative attitudes toward homosexuality—show heightened sexual arousal when viewing photos of homosexual intercourse in comparison to their less homophobic peers (Adams et al., 1996).

Methods and Data of the Psychodynamic Perspective

The methods used by psychodynamic psychologists flow from their aims. Psychodynamic understanding seeks to *interpret meanings*—to infer underlying wishes, fears, and patterns of thought from an individual's conscious, verbalized thought and behavior. Accordingly, a psychodynamic clinician observes a patient's dreams, fantasies, posture, and subtle behavior toward the therapist. The psychodynamic perspective thus relies substantially on the *case study* method, which entails in-depth observation of a small number of people (Chapter 2).

The data of psychoanalysis can be thoughts, feelings, and actions that occur anywhere, from a vice president jockeying for power in a corporate boardroom to a young child biting his brother for refusing to vacate a hobbyhorse. The use of any and all forms of information about a person reflects the psychodynamic assumption that people reveal themselves in everything they do (which is why psychoanalysts may not always be the most welcome guests at dinner parties).

Psychodynamic psychologists have typically relied primarily on clinical data to support their theories. Because clinical observations are open to many alternative interpretations, this has led to skepticism about psychodynamic ideas among many research psychologists. However, a growing number of researchers who are both committed to scientific method and interested in psychodynamic concepts have subjected these concepts to experimental tests (see Fisher & Greenberg, 1985, 1996; Shedler et al., 1993; Westen, 1990, in press). For example, several studies have now documented that people who avoid conscious awareness of their negative feelings are at increased risk for a range of health problems such as asthma, heart disease, and cancer (Weinberger, 1990). One recent study found that individuals who chronically remain unaware of unpleasant feelings tend to have high levels of a hormone that suppresses the body's capacity to fight disease (Brown et al., 1996).

INTERIM SUMMARY   The **psychodynamic perspective** proposes that people's actions reflect the way thoughts, feelings, and wishes are associated in their minds; that many of these processes are unconscious; and that mental processes can conflict with one another, leading to compromises among competing motives. Although psychodynamic psychologists are making increasing use of experimental methods, their primary method is the analysis of case studies, since their primary goal is to interpret complex meanings hypothesized to underlie people's actions.

THE BEHAVIORIST PERSPECTIVE

You are enjoying an intimate dinner at a little Italian place on Main Street when your partner springs on you an unexpected piece of news: The relationship is over. Your stomach turns and you leave in tears. One evening a year or two later, your new flame suggests dining at that same restaurant. Just as before, your stomach turns and your appetite disappears.

The second broad perspective that developed in psychology early in this century, **behaviorism,** argues that the aversion to that quaint Italian cafe, like many

THE FAR SIDE   By GARY LARSON

Unbeknownst to most students of psychology, Pavlov's first experiment was to ring a bell and cause his dog to attack Freud's cat.

Animals of many species can learn to strike some "unnatural" poses.

reactions, is the result of *learning*—in this case, instant, one-trial learning. Whereas the psychodynamic perspective emphasizes internal mental events, behaviorism focuses on the relation between objects or events in the environment (**stimuli**) and an organism's response to those events. Indeed, John Watson (1878–1958), a pioneer of American behaviorism, considered mental events outside the province of a scientific psychology altogether, and B. F. Skinner (1904–1990), who developed behaviorism into a full-fledged perspective years later, stated, "There is no place in a scientific analysis of behavior for a mind or self" (1990, p. 1209).

Origins of the Behaviorist Approach

At the same time Freud was developing psychoanalytic theory, Ivan Pavlov (1849–1936), a Russian physiologist, was conducting experiments on the digestive system of dogs. During the course of his experiments, Pavlov made an important and quite accidental discovery: Once his dogs became accustomed to hearing a particular sound at mealtime, they began to salivate automatically whenever they heard it, just as they would salivate if food were presented. The process that had shaped this new response was learning. Behaviorists argue that human and animal behaviors—from salivation in Pavlov's laboratory to losing one's appetite upon hearing the name of a restaurant associated with rejection—are largely acquired by learning. Psychologists today have even begun to identify the biochemical changes in brain cells and the neural circuits involved as humans and other animals learn (Lavond, Kim, & Fitzgerald, 1993; Martinez & Derrick, 1996).

The behaviorist perspective, particularly as it developed in the United States, sought to do away with two ideas propounded by the philosopher Descartes. Descartes stressed the role of reason in human affairs; he believed that thought can generate knowledge that is not derived from experience. To be human is to reflect upon one's experience, and to reflect is to create new insights about oneself and the world. Descartes also proposed a dualism of mind and body, in which mental events and physical events can have different causes. The mind, or soul, is free to think and choose, while the body is constrained by the laws of nature.

Behaviorists asserted that the behavior of humans, like other animals, can be understood entirely without reference to internal states such as thoughts and feelings. And they attempted to counter **Cartesian dualism** (the doctrine of dual spheres of mind and body) by demonstrating that human conduct follows laws of behavior, just as the law of gravity explains why things fall down instead of up.

The task for behaviorists was to discover the ways in which environmental events, or stimuli, control behavior. John Locke (1632–1704), a seventeenth-century British philosopher, had contended that at birth the mind is a *tabula rasa,* or blank slate, upon which experience writes itself. In a similar vein, John Watson later claimed that if he were given 12 healthy infants at birth, he could turn them into whatever he wanted, doctors or thieves, regardless of any innate dispositions or talents, simply by controlling their environments (Watson, 1925).

The Environment and Behavior

The dramatic progress of the natural sciences in the nineteenth century led many psychologists to believe that the time had come to wrest the study of human nature away from philosophers and put it into the hands of scientists. For behaviorists, psychology is the *science of behavior,* and the proper procedure for conducting psychological research should be the same as that for other sciences—rigorous application of the scientific method, particularly experimentation.

Scientists can directly observe a rat running a maze, a baby sucking on a plastic nipple to make a mobile turn, or even the rise of a rat's heart rate at the sound of a bell that has previously preceded a painful electric shock. But no one can directly observe unconscious motives. Science, behaviorists argued, entails making observations on a reliable and calibrated instrument that others can use to make precisely the same observations. If two observers can view the same data very differently, as often occurs with psychodynamic inferences, then prediction and hypothesis testing are impossible.

According to behaviorists, psychologists cannot even study *conscious* thoughts in a scientific way because no one has access to them except the person reporting them. Structuralists like Titchener had attempted to understand the way conscious sensations, feelings, and images fit together, using introspection as their primary method. Behaviorists like Watson questioned the scientific value of this research, since the observations on which it relied could not be independently verified. They proposed an alternative to psychodynamic and introspective methods: Study observable behaviors and environmental events and build a science around the way people and animals *behave*. Hence the term *behaviorism*. In recent years, some behaviorists have been more comfortable acknowledging the existence of mental events but do not believe such events play a *causal* role in human affairs; they tend to see mental processes as byproducts of environmental stimulation, not as independent causes of behavior.

Perhaps the most systematic behaviorist approach was developed by B. F. Skinner. Building on the work of earlier behaviorists, Skinner observed that the behavior of organisms can be controlled by environmental consequences that either increase *(reinforce)* or decrease *(punish)* their likelihood of occurring. Subtle alterations in these conditions, such as the timing of an aversive consequence, can have dramatic effects on behavior. Most dog owners can attest that swatting a dog with a rolled-up newspaper after it grabs a piece of steak from the dinner table can be very useful in suppressing the dog's unwanted behavior, but not if the punishment comes an hour later. Researchers from a behaviorist perspective have discovered that this kind of learning-by-consequences can be used to control some very unlikely behaviors in humans. For example, by presenting people with feedback on their biological or physiological processes *(biofeedback)*, psychologists can help them learn to control "behaviors" such as headaches, chronic pain, and blood pressure (Arena & Blanchard, 1996; Lisspers & Ost, 1990; Paran, Amir, & Yaniv, 1996).

B. F. Skinner offered a comprehensive behaviorist analysis of topics ranging from animal behavior to language development in children. In Walden Two, *he even proposed a utopian vision of a society based on behaviorist principles.*

Metaphors, Methods, and Data of Behaviorism

A primary metaphor of behaviorism is that humans and other animals are like machines. Just as pushing a button starts the coffee maker brewing, presenting food triggered an automatic or reflexive response in Pavlov's dogs. Similarly, opening this book probably triggered the learned behavior of underlining and note taking. Some behaviorists also view the mind as a "black box" whose mechanisms can never be observed. A stimulus enters the box, and a response comes out; what happens inside is not the behaviorist's business. Other behaviorists are interested in what might occur in that box but are not convinced that current technologies render this information accessible to scientific investigation. They prefer to study what *can* be observed—the relation between what goes into it and what comes out.

The primary method of behaviorism is experimental. The experimental method entails framing a hypothesis, or prediction, about the way certain environmental events will affect behavior and then creating a laboratory situation to test that hypothesis. Consider two rats placed in simple mazes shaped like the letter T, as shown in Figure 1.3. The two mazes are identical in all respects but one: Pellets of food lie at the end of the left arm of the first rat's maze but not of the second. After a few trials (efforts at running through the maze), the rat that obtains the reward will be more likely to turn to the left and run the maze faster. The ex-

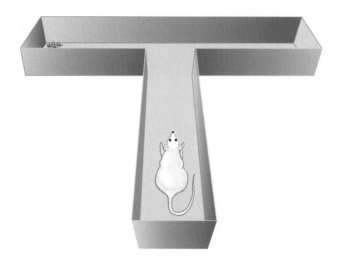

FIGURE 1.3
A standard T-maze from a behaviorist experiment. The experimenter controls the rat's behavior by giving or eliminating rewards in one arm or the other of the T.

perimenter can now systematically modify the situation, again observing the results over several trials. What happens if the rat is rewarded only every third time? Every fourth time? Will it run faster or slower? Because these data can be measured quantitatively, experimenters can test the accuracy of their predictions with great precision, and they can apply them to practical questions, such as how an employer can maximize the rate at which employees produce a product.

Behaviorism was the dominant perspective in psychology, particularly in North America, from the 1920s to the 1960s. In its purest forms it has lost some favor in the last two decades as psychology has once again become concerned with the study of mental processes. Many psychologists have come to believe that thoughts *about* the environment are just as important in controlling behavior as the environment itself (Bandura, 1977, 1991; Mischel, 1990; Mischel & Shoda, 1995; Rotter, 1966, 1990), and some contemporary behaviorists define behavior broadly to include thoughts as private behaviors. Nevertheless, traditional behaviorist theory continues to have widespread applications, from helping people quit smoking or drinking to enhancing children's learning in school.

INTERIM SUMMARY   The **behaviorist perspective** focuses on learning and studies the way environmental events control behavior. Behaviorists reject the concept of "mind" or view mental events as the contents of a black box that cannot be known or studied scientifically. Scientific knowledge comes from studying the relation between environmental events and behavior using experimental methods.

THE COGNITIVE PERSPECTIVE

In the past 30 years psychology has undergone a "cognitive revolution." Today the study of **cognition,** or thought, dominates psychology in the same way that the study of behavior did in the middle of the twentieth century. Indeed, when chairpersons of psychology departments were asked to rank the ten most important contemporary psychologists, eight were cognitive psychologists (Korn, Davis, & Davis, 1991). One could argue that the history of psychology has seen a shift from the "philosophy of mind" of the Western philosophers, to the "science of the mind" in the work of the structuralists, to the "science of behavior" in the research of the behaviorists, to the "science of behavior and mental processes" in contemporary, cognitively informed psychology.

Cognitive psychology has roots in experiments conducted by Wundt and others in the late nineteenth century, which examined phenomena such as the influence of attention on perception and the ability to remember lists of words. Gestalt psychology, too, was arguably a cognitive psychology, in its focus on the way people organize sensory information into meaningful units. In large measure, though, the cognitive perspective owes its contemporary form to a technological development—the computer. Many cognitive psychologists use the metaphor of the computer to understand and model the way the mind works. From this perspective, thinking is **information processing:** The environment provides inputs, which are transformed, stored, and retrieved using various mental "programs," leading to specific response outputs. Just as the computer database of a book store may code its inventory according to topic, title, author, and so forth, human memory systems encode information in order to store and retrieve it. The coding systems we use affect how easily we can later access information. Thus, most people would find it hard to name the forty-second president of the United States (but easy to tell which recent president came from Arkansas) because they do not typically code presidents numerically.

To test hypotheses about memory, researchers need ways of measuring it. One way is simple: Ask a question like, "Do you remember seeing this object?" A second method is more indirect: See how quickly people can name an object they saw some time ago. Our memory system evolved to place frequently used and more recent information in the front of our memory "files" so that we can get to it faster. This makes sense, since dusty old information is less likely to tell us about our immediate environment. Thus, *response time* is a useful measure of memory.

For example, one investigator used both direct questions and response time to test memory for objects seen weeks or months before (Cave, 1997). In an initial session, she exposed undergraduate participants in the study to over 100 drawings presented rapidly on a computer screen and asked them to name them as quickly as they could. That was their only exposure to the pictures. In a second session, which occured weeks or months later, she mixed some of these drawings in with other drawings the students had not previously seen and asked them either to tell her whether they recognized them from the earlier session or to name them. When asked directly, participants were able to distinguish the old pictures from new ones with better-than-chance accuracy as many as 48 weeks later; that is, they correctly identified which drawings they had seen previously more than half the time. Perhaps more striking, as Figure 1.4 shows, they were also faster at naming the pictures they had seen previously than those they had not seen almost an entire year later! Thus, exposure to a visual image appears to keep it toward the front of our mental "files" for a very long time.

The cognitive perspective is useful not only in examining memory but also in understanding processes such as decision making. When people enter a car showroom, they have a set of attributes in their minds: smooth ride, sleek look, good gas mileage, affordable price, and so forth. At the same time, they must process a great deal of new information (the salesman's description of one car as a "real steal," for instance) and match it with stored linguistic knowledge. This allows them to comprehend the meaning of the dealer's speech, such as the connotation of "real steal" (from both his viewpoint and theirs). In making a decision, they must process the information they are receiving, taking into account both the importance of particular attributes and the quality of each car on those dimensions.

Origins of the Cognitive Approach

The philosophical roots of the cognitive perspective lie in a series of questions about where knowledge comes from that were first raised by the ancient Greek philosophers and later pondered by British and European philosophers over the last four centuries (see Gardner, 1985). Descartes, like Plato, reflected on the remarkable truths of arithmetic and geometry and noted that the purest and most

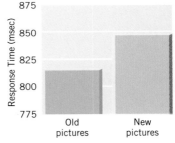

FIGURE 1.4
Response time in naming drawings 48 weeks after initial exposure. This graph shows the length of time participants took to name drawings they saw 48 weeks earlier ("old" drawings) versus similar drawings they were seeing for the first time. Response time was measured in milliseconds (thousandths of a second). As can be seen, at 48 weeks—nearly a year—participants were faster at naming previously seen pictures.

People categorize an object that resembles a dog by comparing it to examples of dogs, generalized views of dogs, or characteristic features of dogs stored in memory.

useful abstractions—such as a circle, a hypotenuse, pi, or a square root—could never be observed by the senses. Rather, this kind of knowledge appeared to be generated by the mind itself. Other philosophers, however, emphasized the role of experience in generating knowledge. Locke proposed that complex ideas emerge from the mental manipulation of simple ideas; these simple ideas are products of the senses, of observation.

The behaviorists roundly rejected Descartes's view of an active, reasoning mind with knowledge that can be independent of experience. Cognitive psychologists, in contrast, have shown more interest in questions raised by Descartes and other **rationalist** philosophers, who emphasized the role of reason in creating knowledge. For example, cognitive psychologists have studied the way people form abstract concepts or categories. These concepts are derived in part from experience, but they often differ from any particular instance the person has ever perceived, which means that they must be mentally constructed (Medin et al., 1997; Smith, 1995). Children can recognize that a bulldog is a dog even if they have never seen one before because they have an abstract concept of "dog" stored in memory that goes beyond the details of any specific dogs they have seen.

Metaphors, Methods, and Data of Cognitive Psychology

Both the cognitive and behaviorist perspectives view organisms as machines that respond to environmental input with predictable output. Some cognitive theories even propose that a stimulus evokes a series of mini-responses inside the head, much like the responses the behaviorist studies outside the head (Anderson, 1983). But the metaphors used by cognitive psychologists differ from those of behaviorists. As noted earlier, some behaviorists view the mind as a black box whose contents are unobservable and therefore problematic for a scientific psychology; most actually object entirely to the concept of mind. The cognitive perspective, in contrast, has filled the box with software—mental programs that produce output. In fact, the cognitive perspective is often more interested in how mental programs operate than in either the particular stimulus or the end result.

Recently, cognitive psychologists have begun to use the brain itself as a metaphor for the mind (McClelland, 1995; Rumelhart, McClelland & PDP Research Group, 1986). According to this view, an idea can be conceived as a network of brain cells that are activated together. Thus, whenever a person thinks of the concept "bird," a set of nerve cells becomes active. When confronted with a stimulus that resembles a bird, part of the network is activated, and if enough of the network becomes active, the person concludes that the animal is a bird. From this point of view, a person is likely to recognize a robin as a bird quickly because it resembles most other birds and hence activates most of the "bird" network immediately. Correctly classifying a penguin takes longer because it is less typically "birdlike" and activates less of the network.

Like behaviorism, the primary method of the cognitive perspective is experimental, but with one important difference: Cognitive psychologists use experimental procedures to infer mental processes at work. For example, when people try to retrieve information from a list (such as the names of states), do they scan all the relevant information in memory until they hit the right item? One way psychologists have explored this question is by presenting subjects with a series of word lists of varying lengths to memorize, such as those in Figure 1.5. Then they ask the participants in the study if particular words were on the lists. If participants take longer to recognize that a word was *not* on a longer list—which they do—they must be scanning the lists sequentially (that is, item by item), because additional words on the list take additional time to scan (Sternberg, 1975).

Cognitive psychologists originally tended to study processes such as memory and decision making that had little to do with emotion or motivation. In more recent years, however, some have attempted to use cognitive concepts and metaphors to explain a much wider range of phenomena (Cantor & Kihlstrom, 1987; Sorrentino & Higgins, 1996). Cognitive research on emotion, for example, documents that the way people think about events plays a substantial role in generating emotions (Lazarus, 1993; Roseman et al., 1995). For example, people are more likely to become angry when they perceive a situation as negatively affecting their goals, perceive someone else as the cause, and have difficulty imagining a way out of it (Smith et al., 1993).

LIST A	LIST B
Nevada	Texas
Arkansas	Colorado
Tennessee	Missouri
Texas	South Carolina
North Dakota	Alabama
Nebraska	California
Michigan	Washington
Rhode Island	Idaho
Massachusetts	
Idaho	
New York	
Pennsylvania	

FIGURE 1.5
Two lists of words used in a study of memory scanning. Presenting participants in a study with two lists of state names provides a test of the memory-scanning hypothesis. Iowa is not on either list. If an experimenter asks whether Iowa was on the list, participants take longer to respond to list A than to list B because they have to scan more items in memory.

INTERIM SUMMARY The **cognitive perspective** focuses on the way people process, store, and retrieve information. Cognitive pyschologists are interested in questions such as how memory works and how people solve problems and make decisions. The primary metaphor underlying the cognitive perspective is the mind as computer. In recent years, many cognitive psychologists have begun to turn to the brain itself as a source of metaphors. The primary method of the cognitive perspective is experimental.

THE EVOLUTIONARY PERSPECTIVE

- The impulse to eat in humans has a biological basis.
- The sexual impulse in humans has a biological basis.
- Caring for one's offspring has a biological basis.
- The fact that most males are interested in sex with females, and vice versa, has a biological basis.
- The higher incidence of aggressive behavior in males than in females has a biological basis.
- The tendency to care more for one's own offspring than for the offspring of other people has a biological basis.

Most people fully agree with the first of these statements, but many have growing doubts as the list proceeds. The degree to which inborn processes determine human behavior is a classic issue in psychology, called the **nature–nurture controversy.** Advocates of the "nurture" position maintain that behavior is primarily learned and not biologically ordained. Other psychologists, however, point to the similarities in behavior between humans and other animals, from chimpanzees to birds, and argue that some behavioral similarities are so striking that they must reflect shared tendencies rooted in biology. Indeed, anyone who believes the sight of two male teenagers "duking it out" behind the local high

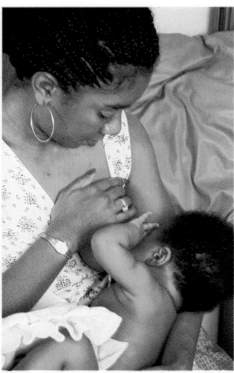

The notion that birds instinctively care for their children (a) is widely accepted, but the corresponding claim that humans have innate mechanisms that elicit caretaking behavior (b) is more controversial.

(a)   (b)

school for the attention of a popular girl is distinctively human should observe the behavior of rams and baboons. As we will see, many, if not most, psychological processes reflect an *interaction* of nature and nurture, as in the case of Susan's epileptic seizures, which waxed and waned with her mother's presence. Human life is like a gray fabric, with strands of genetics (white) and environmental influence (black) so tightly interwoven that one can rarely discern the separate threads (Kagan & Snidman, 1991).

The evolutionary perspective argues that many behavioral proclivities, from the need to eat to concern for our children, became prevalent in human populations because they helped our ancestors survive and rear healthy offspring. Why, for example, was Susan, whose case opened this chapter, so devastated by her mother's absence? From an evolutionary perspective, a deep emotional bond between parents and children prevents them from straying too far from each other while children are immature and vulnerable. Breaking this bond leads to tremendous distress.

Like the functionalists at the turn of the century, evolutionary psychologists believe that most enduring human attributes at some time served a function for humans as biological organisms (Buss, 1991). They argue that this is as true for physical traits—such as the presence of two eyes (rather than one), which allows us to perceive depth and distance—as for cognitive or emotional tendencies such as the child's distress at the absence of her caregivers. The implication for psychological theory is that understanding human mental processes and behaviors requires insight into their evolution.

Origins of the Evolutionary Perspective

The evolutionary perspective is rooted in the writings of Charles Darwin (1859). Darwin did not invent the concept of evolution, but he was the first to propose a mechanism that could account for it—**natural selection.** Darwin argued that nat-

Similar behavior in humans and other animals may suggest common evolutionary roots.

ural forces select traits in organisms that are **adaptive,** that is, that help them adjust to and survive in their environment. This occurs naturally because organisms endowed with fewer features that help them adapt to their particular environmental circumstances, or *niche,* are less likely to survive and reproduce; in turn, they have fewer offspring who survive and reproduce.

A classic example of natural selection occurred in Birmingham, Liverpool, Manchester, and other industrial cities in England (Bishop & Cook, 1975). A light-colored variety of peppered moth common in rural areas of Britain also populated most cities, but as England industrialized in the nineteenth century, light-colored moths became scarce in industrial regions and dark-colored moths predominated.

How did this happen? With industrialization, the air became sooty, darkening the bark of the trees on which these moths spent much of their time. Light-colored moths were thus easily noticed and eaten by predators. Prior to industrialization, moths that had darker coloration were selected *against* by nature because they were conspicuous against light-colored bark. Now, however, they were *better* able to blend into the background of the dark tree trunks (Figure 1.6). As a result, they

Charles Darwin revolutionized human self-understanding in 1859 by rewriting the family tree.

(a)   *(b)*

FIGURE 1.6

The natural selection of moth color. As environmental conditions changed in industrial England, so, too, did the moth population. In (*a*), where two pepper moths rest on the dark bark of an oak tree in Manchester, the darker moth is better camouflaged. With industrialization, darker moths were better adapted to their environments. In contrast, (*b*) shows a light-colored oak bark typical of rural Wales, where the light moth is extremely difficult to see and hence better able to evade its predators.

survived to pass on their coloration to the next generation. Over decades, the moth population changed to reflect the differential selection of light and dark varieties. Since England has been cleaning up its air through more stringent pollution controls in the past 30 years, the trend has begun to reverse.

The peppered moth story highlights a crucial point about evolution: Because adaptation is always relative to a specific niche, evolution is not synonymous with progress. A trait or behavior that is highly adaptive can suddenly become maladaptive in the face of even a seemingly small change in the environment. A new insect that enters a geographical region can eliminate a flourishing crop, just as the arrival of a warlike tribe (or nation) into a previously peaceful region can render prior attitudes toward war and peace maladaptive. People have used Darwinian ideas to justify racial and class prejudices ("people on welfare must be naturally unfit"), but sophisticated evolutionary arguments contradict the view that adaptation or fitness can ever be absolute. Adaptation is always relative to a niche.

Ethology, Sociobiology, and Evolutionary Psychology

If Darwin's theory of natural selection can be applied to characteristics such as the color of a moth, can it also apply to behaviors? It stands to reason that certain behaviors, such as the tendency of moths to rest on trees in the first place, evolved because they helped members of the species to survive. In the middle of the twentieth century the field of **ethology,** which studies animal behavior from a biological and evolutionary perspective (Hinde, 1982), began to apply this sort of evolutionary approach to understanding animal behavior. For example, several species of birds emit warning cries to alert their flock about approaching predators; some even band together to attack. Konrad Lorenz, an ethologist who befriended a flock of black jackdaws, was once attacked by the flock while carrying a wet black bathing suit. Convinced that the birds were not simply offended by the style, Lorenz hypothesized that jackdaws have an inborn, or *innate,* tendency to become distressed whenever they see a creature dangling a black object resembling a jackdaw, and they respond by attacking (Lorenz, 1979).

▶ *It is seldom that I laugh at an animal, and when I do, I usually find out afterwards that it was at myself, at the human being whom the animal has portrayed in a more or less pitiless caricature, that I have laughed. We stand before the monkey house and laugh, but we do not laugh at the sight of a caterpillar or a snail, and when the courtship antics of a lusty greylag gander are so incredibly funny, it is only [because] our human youth behaves in a very similar fashion.*

(LORENZ, 1979, P. 39)

If animal behaviors can be explained by their adaptive advantage, can the same logic be applied to human behavior? Just over two decades ago, Harvard biologist E. O. Wilson (1975) christened a new, and controversial, field called **sociobiology,** which explores possible evolutionary and biological bases of human social behavior. Sociobiologists and **evolutionary psychologists,** who apply evolutionary thinking to a wide range of psychological phenomena, note that genetic transmission is not limited to physical traits such as height, body type, or vulnerability to heart disease. Parents also pass onto their children behavioral and mental tendencies. Some of these are universal, such as the need to eat and sleep or the capacity to perceive certain wavelengths of light to which the eye is attuned. Others differ across individuals. As we will see in later chapters, recent research in **behavioral genetics**—a field that examines the genetic and environmental bases of differences among individuals on psychological traits—suggests that heredity is a surprisingly strong determinant of many personality traits and intellectual skills. The tendencies to be outgoing, aggressive, or musically talented, for example, are all under partial genetic control (Loehlin, 1992; Loehlin et al., 1988; Plomin et al., 1997).

Perhaps the fundamental concept in all contemporary evolutionary theories is that evolution selects organisms that maximize their reproductive success. **Reproductive success** refers to the capacity to survive and produce offspring. Over many generations, organisms with greater reproductive success will have many more descendants because they will survive and reproduce more than other organisms, including other members of their own species. Central to evolutionary psychology is the notion that the human brain, like the eye or the heart, has evolved through natural selection to solve certain problems associated with survival and reproduction, such as selecting mates, using language, competing for scarce resources, and cooperating with kin and neighbors who might be helpful in the future (Tooby & Cosmides, 1992).

For example, we take for granted that people usually tend to care more about, and do more for, their children, parents, and siblings than for their second cousins or nonrelatives. Most readers have probably received more financial support from their parents in the last five years than from their aunts and uncles. This seems natural—and we rarely wonder about it—but *why* does it seem so natural? And what are the causes of this behavioral tendency? From an evolutionary perspective, individuals who care for others who share their genes will simply have more of their genes in the gene pool generations later. Thus, evolutionary theorists have expanded the concept of reproductive success to encompass **inclusive fitness,** which refers not only to an individual's own reproductive success but also to her influence on the reproductive success of genetically related individuals (Daly & Wilson, 1983; Hamilton, 1964).

According to the theory of inclusive fitness, natural selection should favor animals whose concern for kin is proportional to their degree of biological relatedness. In other words, animals should devote more resources, and offer more protection, to close relatives than to more distant kin. The reasons for this are strictly mathematical. Imagine you are sailing with your brother or sister and with your cousin, and the ship capsizes. Neither your sibling nor your cousin can swim, and you can save only one of them. Whom will you save?

Most readers, after perhaps a brief, gleeful flicker of sibling rivalry, will opt for the sibling—because first-degree relatives such as siblings share much more genetic material than more distant relatives such as cousins. Siblings share half of their genes, whereas cousins share only one-eighth. In crass evolutionary terms, two siblings are worth eight cousins. Evolution selects the neural mechanisms that make this preference feel natural—so natural that psychologists have rarely even thought to explain it.

At this point the reader might object that the real reason for saving the sibling over the cousin is that you know the sibling better; you grew up together, and you have more bonds of affection. This poses no problem for the evolutionary theorist, since familiarity and bonds of affection are probably the psychological mechanisms selected by nature to help you in your choice. When human genes were evolving, close relatives typically lived together. People who were familiar and loved were more often than not relatives. Humans who protected others based on familiarity and affection would be more prevalent in the gene pool thousands of years later because more of their genes would be available.

Metaphors, Methods, and Data of the Evolutionary Perspective

Darwin's theory of natural selection is part of a tradition of Western thought since the Renaissance that emphasizes individual self-interest and competition for scarce resources. Its major metaphor is borrowed from another member of that tradition, the sixteenth-century philosopher Thomas Hobbes (1538–1679): Wittingly or unwittingly, we are all runners in a race, competing for survival, sexual access to partners, and resources for ourselves and our kin.

Evolutionary methods are frequently deductive; that is, they begin with an observation of something that already exists in nature and try to explain it with logical arguments. For instance, evolutionary psychologists might begin with the fact that people care for their kin and try to deduce an explanation. This method is very different from experimentation, in which investigators create circumstances in the laboratory and test the impact of changing these conditions on behavior.

Many psychologists have challenged the deductive methods of evolutionary psychologists, just as they have criticized psychodynamic explanations of individual cases. They argue that predicting behavior in the laboratory is much more difficult and convincing than explaining what has already happened.

Evolutionary psychologists are increasingly making use of experimental and other procedures that involve prediction of responses in the laboratory (Buss et al., 1992). For example, two recent studies, one from the United States and one from Germany, have used evolutionary theory to predict the extent to which grandparents will invest in their grandchildren (DeKay, 1998; Euler & Weitzel, 1996). According to evolutionary theory, one of the major problems facing males in many animal species, including our own, is paternity uncertainty—the lack of certainty that their presumed offspring are really theirs. Female primates (monkeys, apes, and humans) are always certain that their children are their own because they bear them. Males, on the other hand, can never be certain of paternity because their mate could have copulated with another male. (Psychological language is typically precise but not very romantic.)

If a male is going to invest time, energy, and resources in a child, he wants to be certain that the child is his own. Not surprisingly, males of many species develop elaborate ways to try to minimize the possibility of accidentally investing in another male's offspring, such as guarding their mates during fertile periods and killing off infants born too close to the time at which they began copulating with the infants' mother. In humans, infidelity (and suspicion of infidelity) is one of the major causes of spouse battering and homicide committed by men cross-culturally (Daly & Wilson, 1988).

Evolutionary psychologists have used the concept of paternity uncertainty to make some very specific, and novel, predictions about patterns of *grandparental* investment in children. As can be seen in Figure 1.7*a*, the father's father is the least certain of all grandparents that his grandchildren are really his own, since he did not bear his son, who did not bear *his* child. The mother's mother is the most certain of all grandparents because she is sure that her daughter is hers, and her daughter is equally certain that she is the mother of *her* children. The other two grandparents (father's mother and mother's father) are intermediate in certainty. This analysis leads to a hypothesis about the extent to which grandparents will invest in their grandchildren: The greatest investment should be seen in maternal grandmothers, the least in paternal grandfathers, and intermediate levels in paternal grandmothers and maternal grandfathers.

To test this hypothesis, in one study U.S. college students ranked their grandparents on a number of dimensions, most notably level of emotional closeness and amount of time and resources their grandparents invested in them (DeKay, 1998). On each of these dimensions, the pattern was as predicted: Maternal grandmothers, on the average, were ranked as the most invested of all four grandparents and paternal grandfathers as the least invested. Figure 1.7*b* shows the percent of college students who ranked each grandparent a 1—that is, most invested or most emotionally close. A similar pattern emerged in a German study (Euler & Weitzel, 1996). Although a critic could generate alternative explanations, these studies are powerful because the investigators tested hypotheses that were not intuitively obvious or readily predictable from other perspectives.

INTERIM SUMMARY   The **evolutionary perspective** argues that many human behavioral tendencies evolved because they helped our ancestors survive and reproduce. Psychological processes have evolved through the natural selection of traits that help organisms adapt to their environment. Evolution selects organisms that maximize their reproductive success, defined as the capacity to survive and reproduce as well as to maximize the reproductive success of genetically related individuals. Although the primary methods of evolutionary theorists have traditionally been deductive and comparative, evolutionary psychologists are making increasing use of experimental methods.

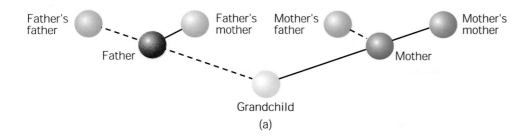

(a)

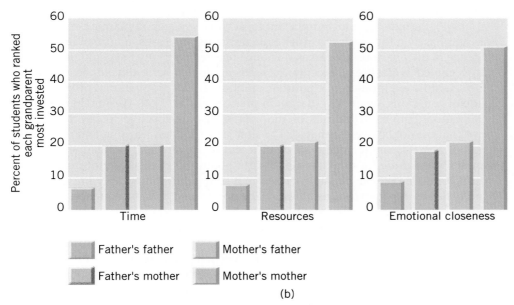

(b)

FIGURE 1.7

(a) Certainty of genetic relatedness. Dashed lines indicate uncertainty of genetic relatedness, whereas solid lines indicate certainty. As can be seen, the father's father is least certain that his presumed grandchild is his own (dashed lines between both himself and his son and his son and the son's child), whereas the mother's mother is most certain. Each of the other two grandparents are sure of one link but unsure of the other. (b) Rankings of grandparental investment. This graph shows the percent of participants in the study who ranked each grandparent the highest of all four grandparents on two kinds of investment and on emotional closeness to them. Students ranked their maternal grandmothers most invested and close and their paternal grandfathers least invested and close on all three dimensions. Similar findings emerged when participants were asked to rate each grandparent on the same dimensions using a 1–7 scale. (Based on DeKay, 1998.)

PUTTING PSYCHOLOGICAL PERSPECTIVES IN PERSPECTIVE

We have seen that what psychologists study, how they study it, and what they observe reflect not only the reality "out there" but also the conceptual lenses they wear. In many cases adherents of one perspective know very little—and may even have stereotypic views or misconceptions—about other perspectives. The reader will no doubt be tempted at times to conclude that a particular perspective is the right one. This condition unfortunately afflicts most of us who make our careers donning a set of theoretical lenses and then forgetting that we are bespectacled. Before succumbing to this fate, be forewarned that the different perspectives often contribute in unique ways depending on the object under investigation. Deciding that one perspective is valid in all situations is like choosing to use a telescope in-

Behavior that seems "natural" to us, like the bond between grandparent and grandchild, may well be the handiwork of natural selection.

stead of a microscope without knowing whether the objects of study are amoebas or asteroids.

Contributions of Each Perspective

Psychologists disagree on the relative merits of the different perspectives, but each has made distinctive contributions. Philosophers have long speculated about the relative value of "reason" and "passion" in human life; the psychodynamic perspective focuses above all on the passionate—on motivation and emotion. From a psychodynamic standpoint, people rarely associate anyone or anything of any importance with just one feeling, which means that we are likely to find ourselves at times in conflict, and recent research supports this view (Caccioppo et al., 1997). Perhaps the most important legacy of the psychodynamic perspective is its emphasis on the pervasive role of unconscious processes in human life. The existence of unconscious processes was once rejected by many psychologists but has now gained widespread acceptance as technologies have developed that allow the scientific exploration of cognitive, emotional, and motivational processes outside of conscious awareness (Bargh, in press; Schacter, 1992; Westen, in press).

Among the contributions of the behaviorist perspective to psychology are two that cannot be overestimated. The first is its focus on learning and its postulation of a *mechanism* for many kinds of learning: reward and punishment. Behaviorists have offered a fundamental insight about the psychology of humans and other animals that can be summarized in a simple but remarkably important formula: *Behavior follows its consequences.* The notion that the consequences of our actions shape the way we behave has a long philosophical history, but the behaviorists were the first to develop a sophisticated, scientifically based set of principles about the way environmental events shape behavior. This leads to the second major contribution of the behaviorist approach, its emphasis on **empiricism**—the belief that the path to scientific knowledge is systematic observation and, ideally, experimental observation.

The cognitive perspective focuses on the *reason* pole of the reason–passion dichotomy. Most of what is distinctive about *Homo sapiens*—and what lent our species its name (*sapiens* means "knowledge" or "wisdom")—is our extraordinary capacity for thought and memory. This capacity allows actors to perform a two-hour play without notes, three-year-old children to create grammatical sentences they have never heard before, and scientists to develop vaccines for viruses that cannot be seen with the naked eye. In only three decades since the introduction of the first textbook on cognition (Neisser, 1967), the cognitive perspective has transformed our understanding of thought and memory in a way that 2500 years of philosophical speculation could not approach. Like the behaviorist perspective, the contributions of the cognitive perspective reflect its commitment to empiricism and experimental methods.

Finally, the evolutionary perspective asks a basic question about psychological processes that directs our attention to phenomena we might easily have taken for granted: *Why* do we think, feel, or behave the way we do as opposed to some other? Although many psychological attributes are likely to have developed as accidental byproducts of evolution with little adaptive significance, the evolutionary perspective forces us to examine *why* we feel jealous when our lovers are unfaithful, *why* we are so skillful at recognizing the emotions people are feeling just by looking at their faces, and *why* children are able to learn new words so rapidly in their first six years that if they were to continue at that pace for the rest of their lives they would scoff at *Webster's Unabridged*. In each case, the evolutionary perspective suggests a single and deceptively simple principle: We think, feel, and behave these ways because doing so helped our ancestors adapt to their environments and hence to survive and reproduce.

TABLE 1.2 MAJOR SUBDISCIPLINES IN PSYCHOLOGY

SUBDISCIPLINE	EXAMPLES OF QUESTIONS ASKED
Biopsychology: investigates the physical basis of psychological phenomena such as thought, emotion, and stress	How are memories stored in the brain? Do hormones influence whether an individual is heterosexual or homosexual?
Developmental psychology: studies the way thought, feeling, and behavior develop through the lifespan, from infancy to death	Can children remember experiences from their first year of life? Do children in daycare tend to be more or less well adjusted than children reared at home?
Social psychology: examines interactions of individual psychology and group phenomena; examines the influence of real or imagined others on the way people behave	When and why do people behave aggressively? Can people behave in ways indicating racial prejudice without knowing it?
Clinical psychology: focuses on the nature and treatment of psychological processes that lead to emotional distress	What causes depression? What impact does childhood sexual abuse have on later functioning?
Cognitive psychology: examines the nature of thought, memory, and language	What causes amnesia, or memory loss? How are people able to drive a car while engrossed in thought about something else?
Industrial/organizational (I/O) psychology: examines the behavior of people in organizations and attempts to help solve organizational problems	Are some forms of leadership more effective than others? What motivates workers to do their jobs efficiently?
Educational psychology: examines psychological processes in learning and applies psychological knowledge in educational settings	Why do some children have trouble learning to read? What causes some teenagers to drop out of school?
Experimental psychology: examines processes such as learning, sensation, and perception in humans and other animals	How often should a rat, pigeon, or human be rewarded to produce optimal learning? Do braille readers have heightened abilities to perceive with their fingers than people who read with their eyes?
Health psychology: examines psychological factors involved in health and disease	Are certain personality types more vulnerable to disease? What factors influence people to take risks with their health, such as smoking or not using condoms?

Applying and Integrating the Perspectives

Psychology has a number of subfields (Table 1.2), and the perspectives psychologists take tend to differ among (and even within) these areas of investigation. For example, *developmental psychology* studies the way thought, feeling, and behavior develop through the lifespan, from infancy to death. Developmental psychologists researching the influence of television on children's aggressive behavior tend to take a cognitive or an integrated cognitive-behavioral approach, guided by the hypothesis that what children observe influences the way they behave (Hughes & Hasbrouck, 1996; Singer, 1986). Research on the close ties that form between infants and their parents, on the other hand, has drawn heavily on the work of John Bowlby (1969, 1988), who was both a psychoanalyst and an ethologist. *Social psychology* examines interactions of individual psychology and social

How might a psychologist from each of the four perspectives explain why a soldier would go off for war, leaving behind loved ones and risking his life for his country?

phenomena. Social psychologists study phenomena such as prejudice, mob violence, peer pressure, and the way people process information about themselves and others. Social psychology has been increasingly influenced in recent years by the cognitive perspective (Markus & Zajonc, 1985), as researchers have tried to understand how the way people process information can lead them to discriminate against members of minority groups, behave aggressively, or respond to people who behave in ways that seem unjust (Berkowitz, 1993; Darley, 1990; Devine, 1989).

Although the different perspectives have often developed in isolation from one another, some attempts at integration have occurred, particularly in clinical work, where the goal of helping patients has at times been strong enough to induce psychologists to cross territorial lines. For example, many psychologists who treat patients are **cognitive-behavioral,** accepting the behaviorist principle that learning is the basis of behavior but also emphasizing the role of mental processes in determining the way individuals respond to their environment (Bandura, 1977, 1986; Goldfried & Davison, 1994; Meichenbaum, 1977). Thus, a person who is terrified of speaking in a group may not only have an automatic fear reaction every time he considers saying something but may also be inhibited from speaking by beliefs that he will look stupid or that people will not like him. A small group of psychologists have taken an even more integrative stance, bringing together aspects of cognitive-behavioral and psychodynamic theory (Arkowitz, 1997; Wachtel, 1997). These therapists might attend not only to the person's conscious thoughts and fears in groups but also to less conscious beliefs, fears, or conflicting motives that might be triggered outside of conscious awareness. For example, alongside one patient's fear of saying something "dumb" was an equally strong fear that what he had to say might actually be *too smart,* so that speaking would make him feel guilty that he was outdoing or humiliating other people in the room.

INTERIM SUMMARY   Although the different perspectives tend to offer radically different ways of approaching psychology, each has made distinctive contributions. These perspectives have often developed in mutual isolation, but efforts to integrate aspects of them are likely to continue to be fruitful, particularly in clinical psychology.

COMMENTARY

How to Grasp an Elephant from Trunk to Tail Without Getting Skewered on the Tusks

Many readers may have wondered, in reading about the perspectives described in this chapter, where the author stands on them. Does he see vases, profiles, or simply random collections of white and black dots? Forewarned is forearmed: The best way to inoculate oneself against the subtle intrusions of an author's biases in any field is to know what they are.

My own point of view reflects, and is shaped by, the fact that I am both a researcher and a clinician. Much of my research has been at the intersection of cognitive science and psychodynamic psychology, since I believe the former offers insight into the dynamics of thought and memory, whereas the latter delves into the dynamics of motivation and emotion. My understanding of motivation and emotion has also been heavily influenced by evolutionary and behaviorist principles, particularly the idea that human emotions have evolved to regulate our behavior in adaptive ways, by rewarding or punishing different courses of action. As a freshman in college I took a year-long course on the evolutionary bases of human social behavior taught by one of the leaders of that emerging approach, which forever sensitized me to questions about the adaptive functions and evolution of psychological processes. Thus, I am a hybrid—in the vernacular, a mutt—and the words "psychodynamic," "behavioral," "cognitive," and "evolutionary" have all appeared in the titles of articles I have written for professional journals.

An advantage of being a mutt is recognizing some of the limitations of the pure-bred positions and the impact that inbreeding can have on the health of a perspective. I sometimes find my fingers tapping impatiently when psychoanalysts or evolutionary psychologists spin elaborate theoretical yarns without subjecting their hypotheses to rigorous scientific scrutiny. I am sometimes struck, as well, by the problems that can occur when studies of cognitive processes neglect or minimize the role of emotion and motivation. When people think about issues that matter to them, which is most of the time, their thinking is frequently biased toward the conclusions they want to reach, as when fans on opposite sides of a college football stadium see a pass-interference call entirely differently or lovers fail to see each others' foibles and failings—until they are ready to break up, at which point they may see *nothing but* foibles and failings. I have trouble with the underlying assumptions of the behaviorist perspective, or at least of its most radical proponents, because experimental studies on thought and memory and my patients' life stories have impressed me with the richness and importance of the thoughts, feelings, and personal meanings that guide human action. At the same time, I believe the principles of learning elucidated by behaviorists must be at the heart of any theory of mind and behavior, and as a clinician, I consider the therapeutic contributions of the behaviorist perspective among the most important of any theoretical perspective. I once even attended the annual conventions of both the Association for the Advancement of Behavior Therapy and the American Psychoanalytic Association in the same year!

Being a mutt requires a high tolerance for ambiguity and conflict. However, the obvious contributions of each of the perspectives, despite their often contradictory assumptions, will likely motivate me for the rest of my career to search for ways to integrate aspects of them, as I believe a whole elephant is more valuable than part of one. ■

SUMMARY

THE BOUNDARIES AND BORDERS OF PSYCHOLOGY

1. **Psychology** is the scientific investigation of mental processes and behavior. Understanding a person means practicing "triple bookkeeping": simultaneously examining the person's biological makeup, psychological experience and functioning, and the cultural and historical moment.

2. **Biopsychology** (or **behavioral neuroscience**) examines the physical basis of psychological phenomena such as motivation, emotion, and stress. **Cross-cultural psychology** attempts to test psychological hypotheses in different cultures. Biology and culture form the boundaries, or constraints, within which psychological processes operate.

3. A classic question inherited from philosophy is whether human action is characterized by **free will** or **determinism,** that is, whether people freely

choose their actions or whether behavior follows lawful patterns. A related issue is the **mind–body problem**—the question of how mental and physical events interact—a contemporary version of which addresses the genetics of personality.

4. The field of psychology began in the late nineteenth century as experimental psychologists attempted to wrest questions about the mind from philosophers. Most shared a strong belief in the scientific method as a way of avoiding philosophical debates about the way the mind works. Among the earliest schools of thought were structuralism and functionalism. **Structuralism,** developed by Edward Titchener, attempted to use introspection as a method for uncovering the basic elements of consciousness and the way they combine with one another into ideas (that is, the *structure* of consciousness). **Functionalism** looked for explanations of psychological processes in their role, or *function,* in helping the individual adapt to the environment.

PERSPECTIVES IN PSYCHOLOGY

5. A **paradigm** is a broad system of theoretical assumptions employed by a scientific community to try to make sense of a domain of experience. Psychology lacks a unified paradigm but has a number of schools of thought, or **perspectives,** which are broad ways of understanding psychological phenomena. A psychological perspective, like a paradigm, includes theoretical propositions, shared metaphors, and accepted methods of observation.

6. The **psychodynamic perspective** originated with Sigmund Freud. From a psychodynamic perspective, conflict is central to mental life, as are unconscious processes. Thus, the mind is like a battleground, and consciousness is like the tip of an iceberg. Because a primary aim is to interpret the underlying meanings or motives behind human behavior, psychodynamic psychologists tend to rely on case studies as a method for investigating the mind.

7. The **behaviorist perspective** focuses on the relation between environmental events (or **stimuli**) and the responses of the organism. Skinner proposed that all behavior can ultimately be understood as learned responses and that behaviors are selected on the basis of their consequences. A primary metaphor underlying behaviorism is the machine; many behaviorists have also considered the "mind" to be an unknowable black box, whose contents cannot be studied scientifically. The primary method of behaviorists is laboratory experimentation.

8. The **cognitive perspective** focuses on the way people process, store, and retrieve information. **Information processing** refers to taking input from the environment and transforming it into meaningful output. The metaphor underlying the cognitive perspective is the mind as computer, complete with software. In recent years, however many cognitive psychologists have used the brain itself as a metaphor for the way mental processes operate. The primary method of the cognitive perspective is experimental.

9. The **evolutionary perspective** argues that many human behavioral proclivities exist because they helped our ancestors survive and produce offspring that would likely survive. It proposes the mechanism of **natural selection,** through which natural forces select traits in organisms that are adaptive in their environmental niche. The basic notion of evolutionary theory is that evolution selects organisms that maximize their **reproductive success,** defined as the capacity to survive and reproduce. The primary methods are de-

ductive and comparative, although evolutionary psychologists are increasingly relying on experimental methods.

10. Although the four major perspectives largely developed independently, each has made distinctive contributions, and some areas of integration have occurred, particularly in clinical psychology. The **cognitive-behavioral** approach accepts many behaviorist principles but emphasizes as well the role of thought processes, such as expectations, in learning.

Jacob Lawrence, "The Library," 1960. National Museum of American Art, Smithsonian Institution/Art Resource, NY."

CHAPTER *2*

Research Methods in Psychology

*S*andra was 19 years old when she received a call that would change her life forever. Her parents and only brother had been killed in an automobile accident. Like most people, Sandra initially reacted with shock and tremendous grief, but over the course of the next year, she gradually regained her emotional equilibrium. Sometimes when she would think of her family her eyes would well up, but as the months passed, she knew she had little choice but to go on.

About a year after the accident, though, Sandra noticed that something was different. She was constantly ill with one cold, sore throat, or flu after another. After a few trips to the health service, an astute doctor asked her if anything out of the ordinary had happened in the last year. When she mentioned the death of her family, the doctor recommended she see a psychologist. She did—and was free from physical illness for over a year from the day she entered the psychologist's office.

Was it an accident that Sandra's health improved just as she began expressing her feelings about the loss of her family with a psychologist? Research by James Pennebaker and his colleagues (1990) suggests that the timing may not have been coincidental. In one study, they demonstrated this relationship using a stressful experience much less calamitous than Sandra's: the transition to college. For most people, entering college is an exciting event, but it can also be stressful, since it often means leaving home, breaking predictable routines, finding a new group of friends, and having to make many more decisions independently.

To assess the impact of emotional expression on health, Pennebaker and his colleagues assigned college freshmen to one of two groups. Students in the first group were instructed to write for 20 minutes on three consecutive days about "your very deepest thoughts and feelings about coming to college," including "your emotions and thoughts about leaving your friends or your parents—or even about your feelings of who you are or what you want to become." Students in the other group were asked "to describe in detail what you have done since you woke up this morning"; they were explicitly instructed *not* to mention their emotions, feelings, or opinions.

The results were dramatic (Figure 2.1). Students in the emotional expression group made significantly fewer visits to the health service in the following two to three months than those who simply described what they had done that day. The effect largely wore off by the fourth month, but it was remarkable given how seemingly minor the intervention had been.

Philosophers have speculated for centuries about the relation between mind and body. Yet here, psychologists were able to demonstrate **empirically**—that is, through observation—how a psychological event (in this case, simply expressing

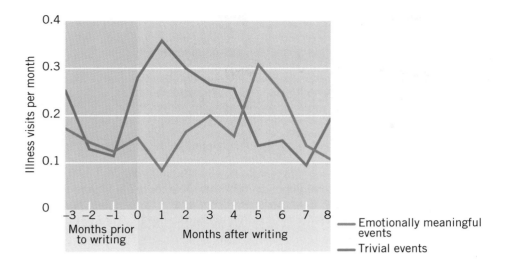

FIGURE 2.1
Emotional expression and health. The figure shows the number of visits to the health service per month for students writing about emotionally meaningful or trivial events. In the three months prior to writing, students in the two groups showed no clear differences in number of visits to the health center. Directly following writing (month 0), however, students who wrote about trivial events were much more likely to seek medical attention. Thus, expressing feelings has an impact on health, although without continued attention to emotion, the impact disappears. *Source:* Adapted from Pennebaker et al., 1990, p. 533.

feelings about a stressful experience) can affect the body's ability to protect itself from infection. The methods psychologists use to address issues ranging from the relation between mind and body to the impact of daycare on children are the topic of this chapter. We begin by describing the features of good psychological research. How do researchers take a situation like the sudden improvement in Sandra's health upon entering therapy and turn it into a researchable question? How do they know when the findings apply to the real world? Then we describe three major types of research: experimental, descriptive, and correlational. Next, we discuss how to distinguish a good research study from a bad one. We conclude by returning to some central questions worth bearing in mind throughout the chapter: How do the theoretical perspectives psychologists adopt affect the methods they choose? What methods—or combination of methods—provide the most conclusive results? What do we gain and what do we lose when we "domesticate" a psychological phenomenon and bring it into the laboratory? And how do we know when we have asked the right questions in the first place?

CHARACTERISTICS OF GOOD PSYCHOLOGICAL RESEARCH

The tasks of a psychological researcher trying to understand human nature are in some respects similar to the tasks we all face in our daily lives as we try to predict other people's behavior. For example, a student named Elizabeth is running behind on a term paper. She wants to ask her professor for an extension but does not want to risk his forming a negative impression of her. Her task, then, is one of prediction: How will he behave?

To make her decision, she can rely on her observations of the way her professor normally behaves, or she can "experiment," by saying something and seeing how he responds. Elizabeth has observed her professor on many occasions, and her impression—or theory—about him is that he tends to be rigid. She has noticed that when students arrive late to class he looks angry and that when they ask to meet with him outside of class he often seems inflexible in scheduling appointments. She thus expects—hypothesizes—that he will not give her an extension. Not sure, however, that her observations are accurate, she tests her hypothesis by speaking with him casually after class one day. She mentions a "friend" who is

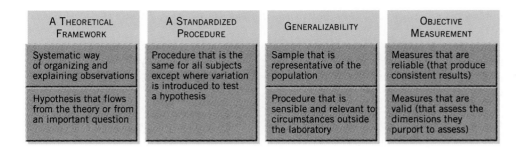

Figure 2.2
Characteristics of good psychological research. Studies vary tremendously in design, but most good research shares certain attributes.

having trouble finishing the term paper on time, and she carefully observes his reaction—his facial expressions, his words, and the length of time he takes to respond. The professor surprises her by smiling and advising her that her "friend" can have an extra week.

In this scenario, Elizabeth is doing exactly what psychologists do: observing a psychological phenomenon (her professor's behavior), constructing a theory, using the theory to develop a hypothesis, measuring psychological responses, and testing the hypothesis. Psychologists are much more systematic in applying scientific methods, and they have more sophisticated tools, but the logic of investigation is basically the same.

Like an architect or carpenter, researchers have a number of tools at their disposal. Just as a carpenter would not use a hammer to turn a screw or loosen a bolt, a researcher would not rely exclusively on any single method to lay a solid empirical foundation for a theory. Nevertheless, most of the methods psychologists use—the tools of their trade—share certain features: a theoretical framework, standardized procedures, generalizability, and objective measurement (Figure 2.2). We examine each of these in turn.

THEORETICAL FRAMEWORK

Psychologists study some phenomena because of their practical importance. They may, for example, conduct studies on the impact of divorce on children (Kalter, 1987, 1990; Wallerstein, 1988, 1991) or the effect of the human immunodeficiency virus (HIV), which causes acquired immunodeficiency syndrome (AIDS), on the nervous system (Kelly et al., 1996). In most cases, however, research is grounded firmly in theory.

A **theory** is a systematic way of organizing and explaining observations; it includes a set of propositions, or statements, about the relations among various phenomena. For example, a theory might propose that having a pessimistic attitude promotes poor physical health, for two reasons: Pessimists do not take good care of themselves, and pessimism taxes the body's defenses against disease by keeping the body in a constant state of alert. People frequently assume that a theory is simply a fact that has not yet been proven. As suggested in Chapter 1, however, a theory is always a mental construction, an imperfect rendering of reality by a scientist or community of scientists, which can have more or less evidence to support it. The scientist's thinking is the mortar that holds the bricks of reality in place.

In most research, theory provides the framework for the researcher's specific hypothesis. A **hypothesis** is a tentative belief or educated guess about the relationship between two or more variables. A **variable** is any phenomenon that can differ, or vary, from one situation to another or from one person to another; in other words, it is a characteristic that can take on different values (such as IQ scores of 115 or 125). Researchers measure variables they believe have important connections with each other. For example, a research team interested in the links between optimism and health decided to test the hypothesis that optimism (variable 1) is related to speed of recovery from heart surgery (variable 2). The researchers found that patients undergoing coronary artery bypass operations who are optimistic are quicker to recover than people who are pessimistic (Scheier & Carver, 1993).

In this case, optimism and health are variables because different people are more or less optimistic (they vary on degree of optimism) and recover more or less quickly (they vary on recovery rate). A variable that can be placed on a continuum—such as degree of optimism, intelligence, shyness, or rate of recovery—is called a **continuous variable.** In contrast, some variables are comprised of groupings or categories, such as gender, species, or whether a person has *had* a heart attack. A **categorical variable** of this sort cannot easily be placed on a continuum; people are either male or female and cannot usually be located on a continuum between the two.

STANDARDIZED PROCEDURES

In addition to being grounded in theory, good psychological research uses **standardized procedures;** that is, it exposes the participants in a study to as similar procedures as possible. For example, in the study of emotional expression and health that opened this chapter, the experimenters instructed students to write for 20 minutes a day for three days. If instead they had let the students write as long as they wanted, students in one group might have written more, and the experimenters would not have been able to tell whether differences in visits to the health service reflected the *content* of their writing or simply the *quantity.*

GENERALIZABILITY FROM A SAMPLE

Psychological research typically studies the behavior of a subset of people in order to learn about a larger **population.** The population might be as broad as all humans or as narrow as preschool children with working mothers. A **sample** is a subgroup of the population that is likely to be **representative** of the population as a whole—that is, similar enough to other members of the population that conclusions drawn from the sample are likely to be true of the rest of the population. The individuals who participate in a study are called **participants** (or **subjects**).

A representative sample contributes to the generalizability of a study's conclusions. **Generalizability** refers to the applicability of the findings to the entire population of interest to the researcher. Participants in the study of emotional expression and health were U.S. college students. Would the study have had the same results in a sample of soldiers who might consider writing about feelings weak or sentimental? Would the results have been different in a culture that discourages expression of unpleasant feelings?

For a study to be generalizable, its procedures must also be sound, or **valid.** To be valid, a study must meet two criteria. First, it must employ methods that convincingly test the hypothesis. This is often called **internal validity**—validity of the design itself. If a study has fatal flaws—such as an unrepresentative sample, or a failure to standardize aspects of the design that could affect the way participants respond—its internal validity is jeopardized. Second, the study must establish **external validity,** which means that the findings can be generalized to situations outside, or external to, the laboratory. Does expressing feelings on paper for three days in a laboratory simulate what happens when people express feelings in their diary or to a close friend? Often researchers must strike a balance between internal and external validity, because the more tightly a researcher controls what participants experience, the less the situation may resemble life outside the laboratory.

INTERIM SUMMARY   Psychological research is generally guided by a **theory**—a systematic way of organizing and explaining observations. The theory helps generate a **hypothesis,** or tentative belief about the relationship between two or more variables. **Variables** are phenomena that differ or change across circumstances or individuals; they can be either **continuous** or **categorical,** depending on whether they form a continuum or are comprised of categories. **Standardized procedures** expose participants in a study to as similar procedures as possible. Although psychologists are typically interested in knowing something about a **population,** to do so they usually study a **sample,** or subgroup, that is likely to be representative of the population. To be **generalizable,** a study must have both **internal validity** (a valid design) and **external validity** (applicability to situations outside the laboratory).

OBJECTIVE MEASUREMENT

As in all scientific endeavors, objectivity is an important ideal in psychological research. The reader of a study wants to be confident that the results are not simply the experimenter's subjective impression. Variables must therefore be defined in a way that enables researchers to quantify or categorize them. For example, one research team wanted to learn about the friendship patterns of children who had been physically abused by their parents (Parker & Herrera, 1996). Does abuse at home tend to disrupt the ability to form close friendships? Based on the theory that abuse makes children more aggressive and less trusting, the researchers hypothesized that abused children would show more conflict and less intimacy than nonabused children when interacting with a friend.

To test this hypothesis, the researchers had to overcome two major hurdles: how to distinguish abused from nonabused children and how to measure variables such as degree of conflict. To identify abused children, the investigators received permission from the state agency charged with the protection of children to locate children whose parents had beaten or kicked (or in one case, burned) them in the past 2.5 years to such a degree that the state had had to intervene. Nonabused children were recruited from flyers posted in similar neighborhoods, and their records were checked with the protective services agency to make sure they had no reported histories of abuse.

To assess friendship patterns, the researchers asked the children to nominate their closest friend and obtained parental permission to bring the children and their best friend into the laboratory for a two-hour session. In the laboratory, the children interacted with their friend in a standardized series of tasks, ranging from chatting with each other while the experimenter allegedly worked on some paperwork to playing particular games that allowed the opportunity for cooperation, conflict, competition, negotiation, and generosity between the partners. The researchers wanted to see how the children interacted on several different types of tasks to increase the likelihood that they would observe the way the children actually behave in many situations.

The interactions between the pairs of children were videotaped and later rated on several dimensions such as conflict and intimacy. For example, each segment of the laboratory session was rated on a conflict scale based on the presence of disagreements, insults, and fights, ranging from 0 *(no conflicts)* to 3 *(five or more conflicts)*. Each segment was also rated for intimacy, defined as disclosure of personal or private information involving sharing of thoughts and feelings, on a scale from 1 *(little or no disclosure)* to 4 *(extensive discussion of feelings or discussion of things that could lead to considerable vulnerability)*. In terms of variables, the researchers were interested in the relation between a categorical variable (whether

TABLE 2.1   INTIMACY AND CONFLICT IN THE FRIENDSHIPS OF ABUSED AND NONABUSED CHILDREN

VARIABLE	ABUSED	NONABUSED
Intimacy	2.39	2.87
Conflict	.72	.25

Source: Adapted from Parker and Herrera, 1996.

Note: For intimacy, the table shows the average intimacy rating across all tasks on which the children interacted. For conflict, the two groups differed only in the amount of conflict shown during the game-playing task. The table shows the average amount of conflict during that task. Other differences between abused and nonabused children's friendships were specific to one gender or the other. For example, abused girls showed less positive emotion in their interactions with their friends than nonabused girls, whereas boys showed more negative emotion in interactions with their friends than nonabused boys. Thus, abuse seems to take some of the pleasure out of girls' friendships but to increase the hostility in boys'.

or not the pair included an abused child) and two continuous variables (degree of conflict and degree of intimacy). As can be seen in Table 2.1, the friendships of abused children showed more conflict and less intimacy than those of nonabused children.

To study a variable, then, the researcher must first devise a technique to measure it. A **measure** is a concrete way of assessing a variable, a way of bringing an often abstract concept down to earth, such as coding intimacy between children on a 1–4 scale. In the research linking optimism to health, the investigators used a questionnaire to measure optimism. The questionnaire included items such as "I hardly ever expect things to go my way" and "In uncertain times, I usually expect the best." The investigators measured recovery from heart attack by assessing concrete behaviors, such as how quickly the patients began to sit up in bed, walk around the hospital room after surgery, or return to work. In the study of emotional expression and health, the investigators obtained actual records of visits from the campus health service as a rough measure of illness. This was a better measure than simply asking people how often they got sick, since people may not be able to remember or report illness objectively. (One person's threshold for being "sick" might be much lower than another's.)

For some variables, measurement is not a problem. Researchers typically have little difficulty distinguishing males from females. However, for some characteristics, such as conflict in friendships, optimism, and health, measurement is much more complex. In these cases, researchers need to know two characteristics of a measure: whether it is reliable and whether it is valid.

Reliability

Reliability refers to a measure's ability to produce consistent results. Using a measure is like stepping on a scale: The same person should not register 145 pounds one moment and 152 a few minutes later. Similarly, a reliable psychological measure does not fluctuate substantially despite the presence of random factors that may influence results, such as whether the participant had a good night's sleep or who coded the data. Reliability in this technical sense is not altogether different from reliability in its everyday meaning: A test is unreliable if we cannot count on it to behave consistently, just as a plumber is unreliable if we cannot count on him consistently to show up when he says he will. An unreliable measure may sometimes work, just as an unreliable plumber may sometimes work, but we can never predict when either will perform adequately.

Three kinds of reliability are especially important. **Test–retest reliability** refers to the tendency of a test to yield relatively similar scores for the same individual over time. If a measure is reliable, people who are retested should receive scores close to their initial scores, unless they have changed dramatically. Another kind of reliability is **internal consistency.** A measure is internally consistent if several ways of asking the same question yield similar results. For example, suppose a researcher asks two questions designed to assess self-esteem: "Do you like yourself?" and "Do you think you are a good person?" If people who answer "yes" to the first question are very likely to answer "yes" to the second, then the test is internally consistent; that is, the two items are assessing the same underlying dimension. A third kind of reliability is **inter-rater reliability.** If two different interviewers rate an individual on some dimension, both should give the person similar scores. To make sure that a test has inter-rater reliability, raters must be trained to use precise definitions of the phenomena they are measuring. When the researchers studying abused children's friendships rated conflict and intimacy, they thus used very specific definitions of each (defining intimacy, for example, in terms of disclosure of personal information and putting a premium on discussion of feelings and information that would make the children vulnerable to their friends.) Obtaining inter-rater reliability on data of this sort often requires developing detailed coding procedures to guarantee that different raters are similarly "calibrated," like two thermometers recording temperature in the same room.

The distinctions among these kinds of reliability can be clarified by returning to the plumbing analogy. A plumber establishes his *test–retest* reliability by showing up when he says he will on different occasions and by performing competently on each occasion. He establishes *internal consistency* by fixing an overflowing commode with as much dispatch as he would a stopped-up sink. He can boast *inter-rater reliability* if his customers agree in their assessment of his work. If he fails any of these reliability tests, he is unlikely to be called again, just as an unreliable measure will not be used in another study.

Validity

When the term **validity** is applied to a psychological measure, it refers to the measure's ability to assess the variable it is supposed to measure. For example, readers are all familiar with IQ tests, which are supposed to measure intelligence. One way psychologists have tried to demonstrate the validity of IQ test scores is to show that they consistently predict other phenomena that require intellectual ability, such as school performance. As we will see in Chapter 8, IQ tests and similar tests such as the Scholastic Aptitude Test (the SAT) are, in general, highly predictive of school success (Anastasi & Urbina, 1997), although they are not without their critics (Elliott, 1988). Some of the measures people intuitively use in their daily lives have much less certain validity, as when Elizabeth initially presumed that her professor's inflexibility in arranging meetings with students was a good index of his general flexibility (rather than, say, a tight schedule).

To ensure the validity of a psychological measure, researchers conduct validation research. **Validation** means demonstrating that a measure consistently relates to some objective criterion or to other measures that have themselves already demonstrated their validity. For example, the Affect Intensity Measure (AIM) is a self-report measure of emotional intensity on which people report how strongly they typically experience their emotions (Larsen & Diener, 1987). To assess the validity of the instrument, the psychologists who developed the AIM measured the extent to which study participants responded physiologically to emotion-arousing events in the laboratory, by examining variables such as heart rate. They also measured the extent to which participants' moods actually fluctuated in daily life by having them carry beepers and record the intensity of their feelings when beeped periodically. Participants who described themselves as emotionally intense on the AIM tended to be the most physiologically reactive in the laboratory and reported more intense emotions when their emotional experiences were monitored at various times throughout a normal day. These findings supported the validity of the AIM.

Multiple Measures

One of the best ways to obtain an accurate assessment of a variable is to employ multiple measures of it. **Multiple measures** are important because no psychological measure is perfect. A measure that assesses a variable accurately 80 percent of the time is excellent—but it is also inaccurate 20 percent of the time. In fact, built into every measure is a certain amount of **error,** or discrepancy between the phenomenon as measured and the phenomenon as it really is. For example, IQ is a good predictor of school success *most* of the time, but for some people it overpredicts or underpredicts their performance. Multiple measures therefore provide a safety net for catching errors. The study of abused children's friendships, for example, used several measures of intimacy: global intimacy, peak intimacy (highest recorded level of intimacy across all tasks), amount of "relationship talk," and physical closeness and positive touching. Global intimacy proved the best measure, although taking the average of multiple measures often produces the most reliable results.

Virtually all good psychological studies share the ingredients of psychological research outlined here: a theoretical framework, standardized procedures, generalizability, and objective measurement. Nevertheless, studies vary considerably in design and goals. The following sections examine three broad types of research (Table 2.2): experimental research, which tries to demonstrate cause-and-effect relationships; descriptive research, which attempts to describe psychological phenomena; and correlational research, which attempts to assess the relations among variables such as IQ and school achievement. As we will see, the lines among these types are not hard and fast. Many studies categorized as descriptive, such as studies of small numbers of patients with brain lesions that affect their ability to recognize people's faces, actually include experimental components, and correlational questions are often built into experiments. The aim in designing research is scientific rigor and practicality, not purity; the best strategy is to use whatever systematic empirical methods are available to explore the hypothesis.

INTERIM SUMMARY Just as researchers take a sample of a population, they similarly take a "sample" of a variable—that is, they use a **measure** of the variable, which provides a concrete way of operationalizing it. A measure is **reliable** if it produces consistent results—that is, if it does not show too much random fluctuation. A measure is **valid** if it accurately assesses or "samples" the construct it is intended to measure. Because every measure includes some component of error, researchers often use **multiple measures** of the same construct (in order to assess more than one sample of the relevant behavior).

EXPERIMENTAL RESEARCH

In **experimental research,** investigators manipulate some aspect of a situation and examine the impact on the way participants respond. Experimental methods are particularly important because they can establish cause and effect—*causation*—directly. An experiment can demonstrate causation by proving that manipulating one variable leads to predicted changes in another. The researchers studying the impact of emotional expression on health could be confident that

TABLE 2.2   COMPARISON OF RESEARCH METHODS

METHOD	DESCRIPTION	USES AND ADVANTAGES	POTENTIAL LIMITATIONS
Experimental	Manipulation of variables to assess cause and effect	• Demonstrates causal relationships • Replicability: study can be repeated to see if the same findings emerge • Maximizes control over relevant variables	• Generalizability outside the laboratory • Many complex phenomena cannot be tested • Does not offer insight into personal meanings
Descriptive			
Case study	In-depth observation of a small number of cases	• Reveals individual psychological dynamics • Allows study of complex phenomena not easily reproduced experimentally • Provides data that can be useful in framing hypotheses	• Generalizability to the population • Replicability: study may not be repeatable • Researcher bias • Cannot establish causation
Naturalistic observation	In-depth observation of a phenomenon as it occurs in nature	• Reveals phenomena as they exist outside the laboratory • Allows study of complex phenomena not easily reproduced experimentally • Provides data that can be useful in framing hypotheses	• Generalizability to the population • Replicability • Observer effects: the presence of an observer may alter the behavior of the participants • Researcher bias • Cannot establish causation
Survey research	Asking people questions about their attitudes, behavior, etc.	• Reveals attitudes or self-reported behaviors of a large sample of individuals • Allows quantification of attitudes or behaviors	• Self-report bias: people may not be able to report honestly or accurately • Cannot establish causation
Correlational	Examines the extent to which two or more variables are related and can be used to predict one another	• Reveals relations among variables as they exist outside the laboratory • Allows quantification of relations among variables	• Cannot establish causation

writing emotionally about a stressful experience *caused* better health because participants who did so were subsequently healthier than those who did not.

The emphasis on experimentation as a way of understanding nature derives in part from Sir Francis Bacon (1561–1626), a British philosopher who was writing as England took its first steps into the modern age in the sixteenth century. According to Bacon, the best way to test our understanding of nature is to bend it to do something it normally does not do (Smith, 1992). Scientists who understand the laws of physics—or behavior—ought to be able to "bend nature" in a laboratory to do something scientifically interesting or practically useful. College students do not typically write for 20 minutes a day for three consecutive days about the experience of beginning college, but when researchers bent nature this way, they found some very practical, and theoretically interesting, impacts on physical health.

The logic of experimentation is much more straightforward and intuitive than many people think. Elizabeth used it implicitly when she tested her professor's flexibility, as we all do multiple times a day in one situation after another. An experimenter manipulates variables that are outside the participants' control, independent of their actions; these are known as **independent variables.** The aim is to assess the impact of these manipulations on the way participants subsequently respond. Because participants' responses depend on both the participant and the independent variable, they are known as **dependent variables.** The independent variable, then, is the variable the experimenter manipulates; the dependent variable is the one the experimenter measures to see if the manipulation has had an effect.

To assess cause and effect, experimenters present participants with different possible variations, or **conditions,** of the independent variable and study the way participants react. In the study of emotional expression and health, the experimenters used an independent variable (emotional expression) with two conditions (express or do not express). They then tested the impact on health (dependent variable).

Consider a series of classic studies conducted in the 1950s by Harry Harlow and his colleagues (Harlow & Zimmerman, 1959). They were interested in determining which of two theories better explained why infant monkeys become emotionally attached to their mothers. One theory hypothesized that the basis for this attachment was the mother's role as the source of food. An alternative theory suggested that infant monkeys are drawn by the security and comfort mothers provide their young. To test these two hypotheses, the researchers conducted an experiment in which infant monkeys were separated from their mothers and raised in social isolation. Each monkey shared its cage with two surrogate or replacement "mothers," one made of wire and the other also made of wire but covered with terrycloth (and hence softer).

The independent variable—the variable manipulated by the researchers—was the placement of the milk bottle. In one experimental condition, a bottle was attached to the wire mother, whereas in the other condition it was attached to the cloth mother (Figure 2.3). The dependent variable was the infant monkeys' response, notably the amount of time they spent holding onto each of the two mothers and which mother they turned to when frightened. The researchers found that whether the wire or the cloth surrogate was the source of milk did not matter: The infants showed a clear preference for the cloth surrogate. Harlow and his colleagues concluded that security and comfort were more important than simple nourishment in the development of attachment to the mother.

Experiments vary widely in both their designs and their goals, but the steps in conceiving and executing them are roughly the same, from the starting point of framing a hypothesis to the ultimate evaluation of findings (Figure 2.4). Although these steps relate specifically to the experimental method, many apply to descriptive and correlational methods as well.

FIGURE 2.3
Surrogate mother in Harlow's monkey studies. Monkeys were separated from birth from their mothers and given the choice of spending time with a wire mother or a terrycloth mother. Regardless of which "mother" fed the baby monkey, it preferred the soft terrycloth mother, suggesting that security, not nourishment, is the basis of attachment in monkeys.

INTERIM SUMMARY   In **experimental research,** psychologists manipulate some aspect of a situation (the **independent variables**) and examine the impact on the way participants respond (the **dependent variables**). This allows researchers to assess cause and effect.

STEP 1: FRAMING A HYPOTHESIS

The first step in constructing an experiment is to develop a hypothesis that predicts the relationship between two or more variables. For example, Gordon Bower and his associates have investigated the impact of mood on memory (Bower, 1981, 1989; Gilligan & Bower, 1984). Based on a cognitive theory of the way people store

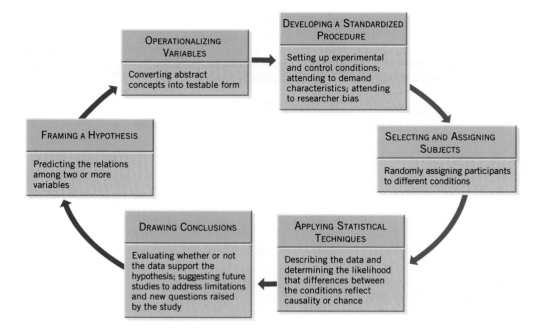

FIGURE 2.4
Conducting an experiment requires systematically going through a series of steps, from the initial framing of a hypothesis to drawing conclusions about the data obtained. The process is circular, as the conclusion of one study is generally the origin of another.

and retrieve memories, they hypothesized that people who are in a positive mood while learning information will be more likely to remember pleasant aspects of that information. Conversely, people in a negative mood while learning will be more likely to remember negative information. This hypothesis states a relationship between two variables: *mood state* when learning material (the independent variable) and later ability to *recall* that material (the dependent variable).

STEP 2: OPERATIONALIZING VARIABLES

The second step in experimental research is to operationalize the variables. **Operationalizing** means turning an abstract concept into a concrete variable defined by some set of actions, or operations. Bower operationalized the independent variable, mood state, by hypnotizing participants to feel either happy or sad (the two conditions of the independent variable). He then had participants read a psychiatric patient's descriptions of various happy and sad memories. Bower operationalized the dependent variable—the ability to recall either positive or negative information—as the number of positive and negative memories the participant could recall 20 minutes later.

STEP 3: DEVELOPING A STANDARDIZED PROCEDURE

The next step in constructing an experiment is to develop a standardized procedure, so that the only things that vary from participant to participant are the independent variables and participants' performance on the dependent variables. Standardized procedures maximize the likelihood that any differences observed in participants' behavior can be attributed to the experimental manipulation, allowing the investigator to draw inferences about cause and effect.

In Bower's study, the experiment would have been *contaminated*, or ruined, if different participants had heard different stories or varying numbers of positive and negative memories. These differences might have influenced the number of positive and negative memories participants would later recall. Bower's method of inducing happy or sad mood states also had to be standardized. If the experimenter induced a negative mood in one participant by hypnotizing him and in another by asking him to try to imagine his mother dying, differences in recall could stem from the different ways mood was induced.

Control Groups

Experimental research typically involves dividing participants into groups who experience different conditions of the independent variable and then comparing the responses of the different groups. In Bower's experiment, the two groups consisted of participants who were hypnotized to be in a happy mood in one group and those who were hypnotized to be in a sad mood in the other. Experiments often include another kind of group or condition, called a control group. Instead of being exposed to the experimental manipulation, participants in the **control group** experience a neutral condition. Although Bower's experiment did not have a control group, a control condition for this experiment could have been a group of participants who were brought under hypnosis but were not given any mood induction. By comparing participants who were induced to feel sad while reading the story with those who were not induced to feel anything, Bower could have seen whether sad participants recall more sad memories (or fewer happy ones) than neutral participants. Examining the performance of participants who have not been exposed to the experimental condition gives researchers a clearer view of the impact of the experimental manipulation.

Protecting Against Bias

Researchers try to anticipate and control the many sources of bias that can affect the results of a study. Investigators must sometimes ensure that participants do not know too much about the study because this knowledge could influence their performance. Some participants try to respond in the way they think the experimenter wants them to respond. (They are nice people but lousy participants.) The ways participants' perceptions of the researcher's goals influence their responses are known as the **demand characteristics** of a study. To prevent demand characteristics from biasing the results, psychologists sometimes conduct **blind studies,** in which participants are kept unaware of, or blind to, important aspects of the research. If participants in the study of emotional expression and health had known why their subsequent health records were important, they might have tried to avoid the doctor as long as possible if they were in the experimental group. If they believed the hypothesis, they might even have been less likely to *notice* when they were sick.

Blind studies are especially valuable in researching the effect of interventions such as medications on psychological symptoms. Researchers in these studies have to contend with **placebo effects,** in which giving a participant a pill, for example, produces an effect because participants *believe* it will produce an effect. Participants who think they are taking a medication often find that their symptoms disappear after they have taken what is really an inert, or inactive, substance such as a sugar pill (a placebo). Simply believing that a treatment is effective can sometimes prove as effective as the drug itself. In a **single-blind study,** participants are kept blind to crucial information, such as the condition to which they are being exposed (in this case, placebo versus medication). In this case, the participant is blind, but the experimenter is not.

The design of an experiment should also guard against researcher bias. Experimenters are usually committed to the hypotheses they set out to test, and, being human, they might be predisposed to interpret their results in a positive

An Italian faith healer works miracles—a likely example of the powerful effect of a placebo.

light. An experimenter who expects an anti-anxiety medication to be more effective than a placebo may inadvertently overrate improvement in participants who receive the medication. Experimenters may also inadvertently communicate their expectations to participants—by probing for improvement more in the medication group than in the control group, for example. The best way to avoid the biases of both participants and investigators is to perform a **double-blind study.** In this case, both participants *and* researchers who interact with them are blind to the experimental condition to which each participant has been exposed until the research is completed.

STEP 4: SELECTING AND ASSIGNING PARTICIPANTS

Having developed standardized procedures, the researcher is now ready to find participants who are representative of the population of interest. Experimenters typically place participants randomly in each of the experimental conditions (such as sad mood, happy mood, or neutral mood). Random assignment is essential for internal validity; it minimizes differences between participants in different groups that cannot be attributed to the independent variable. If all participants in the sad condition were male and all those in the happy condition were female, Bower could not tell whether his participants' responses were determined by mood or by sex. In this case the sex of the participants would be a **confounding variable,** a variable that could produce effects that are confused, or confounded, with the effects of the independent variable. The presence of confounding variables compromises the internal validity of a study by making inferences about causality impossible.

Ideally, the samples psychologists use to test general hypotheses about mental and behavioral processes should be representative of the human population as a whole. From a practical point of view, however, collecting data on participants from multiple cultures, or even from a true cross section of a single society, is very difficult. Because so many researchers are based on college campuses, the most frequently studied population is largely white, middle-class, 18- to 20-year-old Americans—a fact that led one somewhat cynical observer to call psychology the "science of the behavior of the college sophomore" (Rubenstein, 1982). Although this constraint is too seldom acknowledged in research studies, it undoubtedly limits the generalizability of many research findings.

Should one therefore discount all North American or European psychological research because it depends on student participants? To do so, a critic would need a good reason to believe that people in other cultures or other age groups would respond differently on the particular task at hand. In the case of Bower's research, for example, there is little reason to suspect that the relation between mood state and recall would differ from a Canadian college student to an Australian aborigine, although the only way to know is to test the hypothesis cross-culturally.

In contrast, consider the findings of a remarkable study that examined genetic influences on the tendency to become divorced (Jockin, McGue, & Lykken, 1996). Using methods that will be described in Chapter 3, the researchers were able to determine that more than one-third of the tendency to become divorced can be explained by genetic influences on personality, and that this was especially true for women. Of particular importance in accounting for the finding is that the tendency to become upset, which is heavily influenced by genes, is also associated with increased risk for divorce. As we will see, the link between genes and emotional distress is probably universal across cultures, but the link to divorce is not. Many cultures do not permit divorce, and women in many cultures have not been allowed to initiate divorce. Even where divorce is permitted, divorce rates vary substantially. If only 10 percent of couples divorce, findings from a U.S. sample, where 50 percent of marriages end in divorce, may not be applicable, because divorce would presumably occur in only the most extremely distressed couples. This could either increase or decrease the role of genetically influenced traits such as negative emotionality; the only way to know is to *replicate,* or repeat, the study cross-culturally.

STEP 5: APPLYING STATISTICAL TECHNIQUES TO THE DATA

Once an investigator has selected participants and conducted an experiment, the next step is to analyze the data. When psychologists present and analyze data, they are typically confronted with two tasks. First, they must describe the findings in a way that summarizes their essential features **(descriptive statistics)**; second, they must draw inferences from the sample to the population as a whole **(inferential statistics)**. Descriptive statistics are a way of taking what may be a staggeringly large set of observations, sometimes made over months or years, and putting them into a summary form that others can comprehend in a table or graph.

Almost *any* time two groups are compared, differences will appear between them simply because no two groups of people are exactly alike. The task for the researcher is to try to infer whether the differences that do emerge are meaningful or simply random. This is the job of inferential statistics. In experimental research, the goal is to test for differences between groups or conditions to see if the independent variable really had an impact on the way participants responded. Figure 2.5 shows the results of Bower's study in which participants heard about the psychiatric patient while they were either happy or sad. As this figure reveals, the average number of positive and negative memories recalled by participants varied according to mood. Happy participants recalled almost eight happy story incidents but fewer than 6.5 sad ones, whereas sad participants recalled over eight sad but fewer than six happy incidents. The supplement that immediately follows this chapter addresses descriptive and inferential statistics in enough detail to allow the reader to make sense of most articles in psychological journals. (Fight the urge to skip it—it is comprehensible even to the seriously math phobic and is even occasionally interesting.)

STEP 6: DRAWING CONCLUSIONS

The final step in experimental research, drawing conclusions, involves evaluating whether or not the hypothesis was supported, that is, whether the independent and dependent variables were related as predicted. It also entails interpreting the findings in light of the broader theoretical framework of the study and assessing their generalizability to phenomena outside the laboratory. Most studies conclude by acknowledging their limitations and pointing toward future research that might address unanswered questions. The findings of the study of emotional expression and health, for example, raised an intriguing question: What if people think about a stressful event but do not focus on their feelings about it? In fact, subsequent studies showed that focusing on the feelings is essential to reaping the health rewards of thinking about stressful or distressing experiences (Pennebaker, 1990).

INTERIM SUMMARY   Conducting a study, particularly an experiment, entails a series of steps. The first is framing a hypothesis that predicts the relations among two or more variables. The second is to **operationalize** variables—to turn abstract constructions into concrete form defined by a set of actions or operations. The third step is to develop a standard-

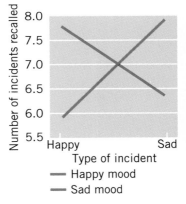

FIGURE 2.5
The influence of mood on memory. Happy participants stored and later retrieved more happy incidents, whereas sad participants were more likely to recall sad incidents. *Source:* Bower, 1981.

ized procedure, so that only the variables of interest vary. In experimental research, researchers often divide participants into different groups, who experience different conditions of the independent variable; some participants are often assigned to a **control group**—a neutral condition against which participants in various experimental conditions can be compared. The fourth step is to select samples that are as representative as possible of the population of interest. The fifth step is to analyze the data using statistical techniques. The final step is to draw conclusions from the data to help assess whether the hypothesis was supported and whether the results are likely to generalize.

LIMITATIONS OF EXPERIMENTAL RESEARCH

Because experimenters can manipulate variables one at a time and observe the effects of each manipulation, experiments provide the "cleanest" findings of any method in psychology. No other method in psychological research can determine cause and effect so unambiguously. Furthermore, experiments can be replicated, or repeated, to see if the same findings emerge with a different sample; the results can thus be corroborated or refined.

Experimental methods do, however, have their limitations. First, for both practical and ethical reasons, many complex phenomena cannot be tested in the laboratory. A psychologist who wants to know whether divorce has a negative impact on children's intellectual development cannot manipulate people into divorcing in order to test the hypothesis. Researchers frequently have to examine phenomena as they exist in nature.

When experiments are impractical, psychologists sometimes employ **quasi-experimental designs,** which share the logic and many features of the experimental method but do not afford the experimenter as much control over all relevant variables, such as random assignment of participants to different conditions (Campbell & Stanley, 1963). An experimenter interested in the impact of divorce on memory, for example, might compare the ability of children from divorced and nondivorced families to retrieve positive and negative memories. The researcher would also test to be sure the two groups did not differ on variables that could potentially influence the results, such as age, gender, and socioeconomic status (social class). Although quasi-experimental designs cannot provide the degree of certainty about cause-and-effect relationships that experiments offer, they are probably the most common designs used in psychology. Reality, unfortunately, is both the object of scientific inquiry and its major impediment.

A second limitation of the experimental method centers on the problem of external validity. Researchers can never be certain how closely the phenomena observed in a laboratory parallel their real-life counterparts. In some instances, such as the study with which this chapter opened, the implications seem clear: If briefly writing about stressful events can improve health, imagine what talking about them with a professional over time might do. And in fact, research shows that people who get help for *psychological* problems through psychotherapy tend to make fewer trips to the doctor for *medical* problems (Gabbard et al., 1996). In other cases, external validity is more problematic. Do the principles that operate in a laboratory study of memory apply when a person reflects on past events to decide whether or not to stay in a relationship (Ceci & Bronfenbrenner, 1991; Neisser, 1976; Rogoff & Lave, 1984)?

A third limitation is emphasized by psychologists who take an **interpretive** (also called *hermeneutic*) stance on methodology (Messer et al., 1988). They argue that the aim of a science of human mental life and behavior is not *predicting* behavior but *understanding* the highly idiosyncratic personal meanings that lead to an individual's actions. One person may commit suicide because he feels he is a failure; another may kill himself to get back at a relative or spouse; another may do so to escape intense or chronic psychic pain; still another individual might take his life because cultural norms demand it in the face of a wrongdoing or humiliation. From an interpretive point of view, explaining a behavior such as suicide means understanding the subjective meanings behind it, not predicting it from some combination of variables. Interpreting meanings of this sort typically requires in-depth interviewing that is beyond what can be accomplished in an experiment.

Despite its limitations, the experimental method is the bread and butter of psychology. No method in psychology is more definitive than a well-executed experiment. Nevertheless, few would desire a steady diet of bread and butter, and scientific investigation is nourished by multiple methods and many sources of data.

INTERIM SUMMARY   Experiments are the only methods in psychology that allow researchers to draw unambiguous conclusions about cause and effect. The limits of experimental methods are the difficulties of bringing some complex phenomena into the laboratory, the question of whether the results apply to phenomena outside the laboratory, and the problem of exploring idiosyncratic personal meanings that may lead to an individual's actions.

DESCRIPTIVE RESEARCH

The second major type of research, **descriptive research,** attempts to describe phenomena as they exist rather than to manipulate variables. Do people in different cultures use similar terms to describe people's personalities, such as "outgoing" or "responsible" (Paunonen et al., 1992)? Do members of other primate species compete for status and form coalitions against powerful members of the group whose behavior is becoming oppressive? Do young women with anorexia have personality characteristics that distinguish them from their peers (Bruch, 1973; Vitousek & Manke, 1994)? To answer such questions, psychologists use a variety of descriptive methods, including case studies, naturalistic observation, and survey research. Table 2.2 summarizes the major uses and limitations of these descriptive methods as well as the other methods psychologists use.

CASE STUDY METHODS

A **case study** is an in-depth observation of one person or a small group of individuals. Case study methods are useful when trying to learn about complex psychological phenomena that are not yet well understood and require exploration or that are difficult to produce experimentally. Some of the most famous case studies in psychology are Sigmund Freud's studies of his early patients. Freud sought to discover the origin of his patients' symptoms (such as a little boy's fear of horses or a physically healthy woman's inability to breastfeed her baby) in their past experiences. Researchers tend to describe cases they believe are representative of a population, much as Freud used the case of the little boy who was afraid of horses to set forth some hypotheses about the origins of phobias. Single-case designs can also be used in combination with quantitative or experimental procedures (Kazdin & Tuma, 1982). For example, some researchers assess change in patients over time by coding videotaped psychotherapy sessions for qualities such as emotion, self-esteem, or defensiveness (Hilliard, 1993).

Case studies are often useful when large numbers of subjects are not available, either because they do not exist or because obtaining them would be extremely difficult. For example, extensive case studies of patients who have undergone surgery to sever the tissue connecting the right and left hemispheres of the brain (in order to control severe epileptic seizures) have yielded important information about the specific functions of the two hemispheres (Chapter 3).

A major limitation of case study methods is their small sample size. Because case studies examine only a small group of participants, generalization to a larger population is always uncertain. An investigator who conducts intensive research on one young woman with anorexia and finds that her self-starvation behavior is strongly tied to her wishes for control might be tempted to conclude that control issues are central in cases of this disorder. They may well be, but they may also be idiosyncratic to this particular person. One way to minimize this limitation is to use a multiple-case-study method (Rosenwald, 1988), extensively examining a small sample of people individually and drawing generalizations across them.

A second limitation of case studies is their susceptibility to researcher bias. Investigators tend to see what they expect to see. A psychotherapist who believes that anorexic patients have conflicts about sexuality will undoubtedly see such conflicts in her anorexic patients because they are operative in everyone. In writing up the case, she may select examples that demonstrate these conflicts and miss other issues that might be just as salient to another observer. Because no one else is privy to the data of a case, no other investigator can examine the data directly and draw any different conclusions unless the therapy sessions are videotaped; the data are always filtered through the psychologist's theoretical lens.

Case studies are probably most useful at either the beginning or end of a series of studies that employ quantitative methods with larger samples. Exploring individual cases can be crucial in deciding what questions to ask or what hypotheses to test because they allow the researcher to immerse herself in the phenomenon as it appears in real life. A case study can also flesh out the meaning of quantitative findings by providing a detailed analysis of representative examples.

NATURALISTIC OBSERVATION

A second descriptive method, **naturalistic observation,** is the in-depth observation of a phenomenon in its natural setting. For example, Frans de Waal, a primatologist (researcher who studies primates, such as humans and chimpanzees), has spent years both in the wild and at zoos observing the way groups of apes or monkeys behave. de Waal (1989) describes an incident in which a dominant male chimpanzee in captivity made an aggressive charge at a female. The troop, clearly distressed by the male's behavior, came to the aid of the female and then settled into an unusual silence. Suddenly, the room echoed with hoots and howls, during which two of the chimps kissed and embraced. To de Waal's surprise, the two chimps were the same ones who had been involved in the fight that had set off the episode! After several hours of pondering the incident, de Waal suddenly realized that he had observed something he had naively assumed was unique to humans: reconciliation. This led him to study the way primates maintain social relationships despite conflicts and acts of aggression. His research led him to conclude that for humans, as for our nearest neighbors, "making peace is as natural as making war" (p. 7).

Psychologists also observe humans "in the wild" using naturalistic methods, as in the classic studies of Genevan school children by the Swiss psychologist Jean Piaget (1926). Piaget and his colleagues conducted their research in playgrounds and classrooms, taking detailed notes on who spoke to whom, for how long, and on what topics. Piaget found that young children often speak in "collective monologues," talking all at once; they may neither notice whether they are being listened to nor address their comments to a particular listener. An advantage of nat-

Naturalistic observation can lead to novel insights, such as the importance of peacemaking in primates.

uralistic observation over experimental methods is that its findings are clearly applicable outside the laboratory.

Most people behave somewhat differently when they are aware that someone is watching them; thus, a limitation of observational methods is that the very fact of being watched may influence behavior, if only subtly. Researchers often try to minimize this bias in one of two ways. One is simply to be as inconspicuous as possible—to blend into the woodwork. The other is to become a participant-observer, interacting naturally with subjects in their environment. Naturalistic observation shares other limitations with the case study method, such as the problem of generalizability. When can a psychologist conclude that after she has seen one baboon troop, she has seen them all? Researcher bias can also pose limitations since observers' theoretical biases can influence what they look for and therefore what they see. As with case studies, this limitation can be minimized by observing several groups of participants or by videotaping interactions, so that more than one judge can independently rate the data.

Finally, like other descriptive studies, naturalistic observation primarily *describes* behaviors; it cannot demonstrate *why* they take place. Based on extensive observation, a psychologist can make a convincing *argument* about the way one variable influences another, but this method does not afford the luxury of doing something to participants and seeing what they do in response, as in experimental designs.

Jean Piaget observes children on a playground.

SURVEY RESEARCH

A third type of descriptive research, **survey research,** involves asking a large sample of people questions, usually about their attitudes or behaviors. For instance, in 1976, a team of researchers embarked on a massive study of over 2200 Americans to see whether conceptions of mental health and attitudes about treatment for emotional problems had changed since the administration of a similar survey 20 years earlier (Veroff et al., 1981). Survey research can yield rigorous quantitative findings by attaching numbers to participants' responses. The researcher might ask people how many times they saw a mental health professional in the last year or to rate the extent to which they believe that seeing a therapist is a sign of weakness on a seven-point scale (where 1 = strongly disagree and 7 = strongly agree). The two most frequently used tools of survey researchers are **questionnaires,** which participants fill out by themselves, and **interviews,** in which researchers ask questions using a standard format.

Selection of the sample is extremely important in survey research. For example, pollsters want to be sure that their predictions of election results accurately reflect a large and heterogeneous population. Researchers typically want a **random sample,** a sample selected from the general population in a relatively arbitrary way that does not introduce any systematic bias. A researcher seeking a random sample of residents of Montreal, for instance, might choose names out of the phone book.

Random selection, however, does not always guarantee that a sample will accurately reflect the **demographic characteristics** (such as gender, race, and socioeconomic status) of the population in which the researcher is interested. A telephone survey based on a random sample of Montreal residents listed in the phone book may overrepresent people who happen to be home answering the phone during the day, such as older people (and underrepresent poor people who do not have a phone). Where proportional representation of different subpopulations is important, researchers select a stratified random sample. A **stratified random sample** specifies the percentage of people to be drawn from each population

THE FAR SIDE   By GARY LARSON

"So, you're a *real* gorilla, are you? Well, guess you wouldn't mind munchin' down a few beetle grubs, would you? ... In fact, we wanna see you chug 'em!"

category (age, race, etc.) and then randomly selects participants from *within* each category. Researchers often use census data to provide demographic information on the population of interest and then match this information as closely as possible in their sample. The 1976 mental health study was stratified along a number of lines, including age, sex, race, marital status, geographical region, and education.

The major problem with survey methods is that they rely on participants to report on themselves truthfully and accurately. Unfortunately, most people tend to describe their behaviors and attitudes in more flattering terms than others would use to describe them (Greenwald, 1984; John & Robins, 1994). How many people are likely to admit their addiction to *General Hospital* or *Leave It to Beaver* reruns? In part, people's answers may be biased by their conscious efforts to present themselves in the best possible light. They may also unconsciously shade the truth because they want to feel intelligent or psychologically healthy (Shedler, Mayman, & Manis, 1993). In addition, participants may honestly misjudge themselves. Measuring people's attitudes toward the disabled by questionnaire typically indicates much more positive attitudes than does measuring how far they *sit* from a disabled person when entering a room (see Wilson, 1996).

INTERIM SUMMARY   **Descriptive methods** describe phenomena as they already exist rather than manipulate variables. A **case study** is an in-depth observation of one person or a group of people. Case studies are useful in generating hypotheses, exploring complex phenomena that are not yet well understood or difficult to examine experimentally, or fleshing out the meaning of quantitative findings. **Naturalistic observation** is the in-depth observation of a phenomenon in its natural setting. It is useful for describing complex phenomena as they exist outside the laboratory. **Survey research** involves asking a large sample of people questions, usually about their attitudes or behavior, through **questionnaires** or **interviews.** By obtaining **random** or **stratified random samples,** psychologists can gain substantial information about a representative sample of the population. Unlike experiments, descriptive methods cannot unambiguously establish cause and effect.

CORRELATIONAL RESEARCH

The aim of **correlational research** is to determine the degree to which two or more variables are related, so that knowing the value (or score) on one allows prediction of the other. Correlational analyses can be applied to data from experiments, case studies, or naturalistic observation, but most often, correlational designs rely on survey data such as self-reports. Do children who are shy, fearful, and inhibited in the second year of life remain similarly timid and socially uncomfortable when they are older (Schwartz, Snidman, & Kagan, 1996)? Are people who are highly prejudiced more likely to think simply than less prejudiced people, or are prejudice and intellectual sophistication unrelated to each other? These are the kinds of questions that can be addressed using correlational designs.

For example, one study examined the extent to which people who frequently experience one emotion, such as guilt, experience others, such as shame (Izard et al., 1993). Participants completed questionnaires asking them to rate how frequently in their lives they experience various emotions, on a scale from 1 *(never)* to 5 *(very often).* Do people who frequently feel guilty also often feel ashamed, fearful, or angry? To answer this question, the researchers correlated guilt with other emotions. To **correlate** two variables means to assess the extent to which being high or low on one measure predicts being high or low on another. The statistic that allows a researcher to do this is called a correlation coefficient. A **correlation coefficient** measures the extent to which two variables are related (literally,

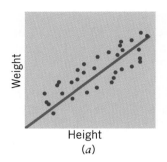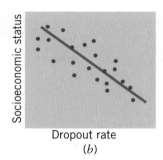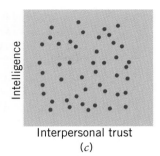

FIGURE 2.6

(*a*) Positive, (*b*) negative, and (*c*) zero correlations. A correlation expresses the relation between two variables. The panels depict three kinds of correlations on hypothetical scatterplot graphs, which show the way data points fall (are scattered) on two dimensions. Panel (*a*) shows a positive correlation, between height and weight. A comparison of the dots (which represent individual participants) on the right with those on the left shows that those on the left are lower on both variables. The dots scatter around the line that summarizes them, which is the correlation coefficient. Panel (*b*) shows a negative correlation, between socioeconomic status and dropout rate from high school. The higher the socioeconomic status, the lower the dropout rate. Panel (*c*) shows a zero correlation, between intelligence and the extent to which an individual believes people can be trusted. The dots are randomly distributed across the diagram, indicating that being high on one dimension predicts nothing about whether the participant is high or low on the other.

co-related, or related to each other). A correlation can be either positive or negative. A **positive correlation** means that the higher individuals measure on one variable, the higher they are likely to measure on the other. This also means, of course, that the lower they score on one variable, the lower they will score on the other. A **negative correlation** means that the higher participants measure on one variable, the *lower* they will measure on the other. Correlations can be depicted on **scatterplot graphs,** which show the scores of every participant along two dimensions (Figure 2.6).

Correlation coefficients vary between +1.0 and −1.0. A strong correlation—one with a value close to either positive or negative 1.0—means that a psychologist who knows a person's score on one variable can confidently predict that person's score on the other. For instance, one would expect a strong negative correlation between level of alcohol in a person's blood and his ability to recite the alphabet backward; the higher the alcohol level, the fewer letters accurately recited backward. A weak correlation hovers close to zero, either on the positive or the negative side. Variables with a correlation close to zero are unrelated and thus cannot be used to predict one another, such as adult weight and IQ score.

To return to the study of emotions, one might hypothesize that people who tend to feel one unpleasant emotion also tend to feel others. That is, guilt, fear, and shame should all be positively correlated with one another. Table 2.3 presents the correlations among various emotions as a **correlation matrix**—a table presenting the correlations among a number of variables. The strongest positive correlation (.61) is between shame and guilt: People who tend to feel guilty also tend to feel ashamed. The negative correlations between joy and the unpleasant emotions are all relatively weak (−.14 to −.30). This suggests, somewhat counterintuitively, that people who frequently experience unpleasant feelings do not necessarily tend to lack positive feelings.

The virtue of correlational research is that it allows investigators to study a whole range of phenomena that vary in nature—from personality characteristics to attitudes—but cannot be produced in the laboratory. Like other nonexperimental methods, however, correlational research can only *describe* relationships among variables (which is why it is actually sometimes categorized as a descriptive method, rather than placed in its own category). When two variables corre-

TABLE 2.3   CORRELATIONS AMONG VARIOUS EMOTIONS

	GUILT	SHAME	FEAR	JOY
Guilt	—	.61	.54	−.23
Shame		—	.51	−.30
Fear			—	−.14
Joy				—

Source: Adapted from Izard et al., 1993.

Note: The dashes represent correlations between a variable and itself (e.g., fear with fear), which by definition are 1.0 (a perfect correlation). Note that only half a table is needed to present a correlation matrix because any correlations below the dashes would be redundant, having already been presented elsewhere in the table.

late with each other, the researcher must infer the relation between them: Does one cause the other, or does some third variable explain the correlation?

Media reports on scientific research often disregard or misunderstand the fact that *correlation does not imply causation.* If a study shows a correlation between drug use and poor grades, the media often report that "scientists have found that drug use leads to bad grades." That *may* be true, but an equally likely hypothesis is that some underlying aspect of personality (such as alienation) or home environment (such as poor parenting, abuse, or neglect) produces both drug use *and* bad grades (Shedler & Block, 1990). Similarly, in 1986 the Meese Commission, established by President Ronald Reagan, reviewed the evidence (most of it correlational) linking pornography to violence, particularly crimes against women, and concluded that pornography leads to rape. Just because rapists read pornography, however, does not prove that pornography *leads to* rape. Many people who do not commit rapes also read pornography. In rapists, both pornographic viewing and violent sexual behavior may reflect a third variable, disturbed sexuality (see Mould, 1990).

INTERIM SUMMARY   **Correlational research** assesses the degree to which two variables are related; a **correlation coefficient** quantifies the association between two variables. Correlational research can shed important light on the relations among variables, but correlation does not demonstrate causation.

FROM MIND TO BRAIN

RESEARCHING THE BRAIN

The methods psychologists use are only as powerful as the technologies and statistical tools that support them. For example, the invention of a seemingly simple mathematical device—the correlation coefficient—set the stage for psychologists to begin answering questions about the influence of heredity on traits such as intelligence, anxiety, and shyness that were previously mere topics of speculation. In the last two decades, a new set of technologies has emerged in one area of psychology that has revolutionized our understanding of human thought and memory: the study of the brain (Barinag, 1997; Posner & Raichle, 1996). Advances in these technologies are proceeding at such a bewildering rate that the next decade may well yield as much new knowledge about the basic mechanisms of human thought, feeling, and behavior as humans have accumulated since the dawn of civilization.

Scientists began studying the functioning of the brain by examining patients who had sustained damage or disease (lesions) to particular neural regions. As noted in Chapter 1, physicians discovered the promise of *lesion studies* in the mid-nineteenth century when they observed patients with left-hemisphere damage who had speech or language impairments. They reasoned that one way to infer what a neural structure normally does is to see what happens when it is *not* working. Experimental psychologists subsequently discovered that they could learn about the function of a particular region by *creating* a lesion in an animal and examining the effects.

In the middle of the present century, neurosurgeons began to learn about the functions of different parts of the brain in humans by stimulating them during surgery using a mild electrical current. This procedure was necessary to "map" the brain of a given patient to avoid damaging essential regions, such as those involved in language. Observing that stimulation of certain regions seemed to yield similar effects *across* patients, researchers began to use this method to learn about the functions of particular neural structures.

Another major advance in understanding the brain came in the 1930s, with the development of the **electroencephalogram,** or **EEG.** The EEG capitalizes on the fact that every time a nerve cell fires it produces a measurable quantity of electrical activity. Researchers can measure this activity in a region of the brain's outer layers by placing electrodes on the scalp. The EEG is frequently used to diagnose disorders such as epilepsy as well as to study neural activity during sleep. It has also been used to examine questions such as whether the two hemispheres of the brain respond differently to stimuli that evoke positive versus negative emotions, which they do (Davidson, 1996).

A major step forward occurred when scientists discovered ways to use X-ray technology and other methods to produce pictures of soft tissue (rather than the familiar bone X-rays), such as the living brain. These **imaging techniques** use computer programs to convert the data taken from brain-scanning devices into visual images of the brain. One of the first such

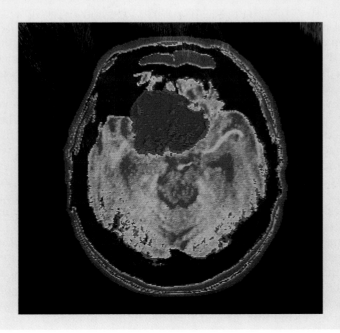

A CT scan of a patient with a tumor (shown in purple).

techniques to be developed was **computerized axial tomography,** commonly known as a **CT scan** or **CAT scan.** A CT scanner rotates an X-ray tube around a person's head, producing a series of X-ray pictures. A computer then combines these pictures into a composite visual image. CT scans can pinpoint the location of abnormalities such as neuronal degeneration and abnormal tissue growths (tumors). A related technology, **magnetic resonance imaging (MRI),** can accomplish similar tasks without using X-rays.

A quantum leap forward has occurred with the development of two imaging techniques that actually allow researchers to observe the brain in action rather than simply to detect neural damage. These techniques rely on properties of cells in the brain, such as the amount of blood that flows to cells that have just been activated, that can be measured using sophisticated instruments designed by physicists and engineers. By having participants perform tasks such as solving mathematical problems, watching images, or retrieving memories, researchers are able directly to observe the links between mind and brain. One technique, **positron emission tomography (PET),** requires injection of a small quantity of radioactive glucose (too small a dose to be dangerous) into the bloodstream. Nerve cells use glucose for energy, and they replenish their supply of glucose from the bloodstream. As these cells make use of glucose that has been radioactively "tagged," a computer produces a color portrait of the active parts of the brain. Researchers and clinicians can thus examine ongoing activity in various regions in patients suffering from disorders such as schizophrenia, yielding clues to the structures and pathways in the brain that underlie the symptoms of these diseases (Buchsbaum et al., 1996; Holcomb et al., 1996).

Another technique, called **functional magnetic resonance imaging (fMRI),** uses MRI to watch the brain as the individual carries out tasks such as recognizing an object visually or looking at emotionally evocative pictures (Breiter et al., 1996; Puce et al., 1996). Functional MRI works by exposing the brain to pulses of a phenomenally strong magnet (strong enough to lift a truck) and measuring the response of chemicals in blood cells going to and from various regions, which become momentarily "lined up" in the direction of the magnet. For example, one research team used fMRI to study the parts of the brain that are active when people generate mental images, such as of a horse, an apple, or a house (D'Esposito et al., 1997). When we conjure up a picture of a horse in our minds, do we activate different parts of the brain than when we simply hear about an object but do not picture it? In other words, how are memories *represented* in our brains? Do we actually form visual images, or do we really think in words?

The investigators set out to answer this question by asking seven participants to carry out two tasks with their eyes closed, while their heads were surrounded by the powerful magnet of the MRI scanner. In the first experimental condition, participants listened to 40 concrete words and were asked to try to picture them in their minds. In the second condition, they listened to 40 words that are difficult to picture (such as "treaty" and "guilt") and were asked simply to listen to them. (This is called a *within-subjects* experimental design, because instead of placing each subject in one condition or the other, each subject is exposed to *both* conditions. Differences in the way subjects respond to the two conditions are then compared within, rather than across, subjects.) The experimenters then used fMRI to measure whether the same or different parts of the brain were activated under the two conditions. They hypothesized that when people actually picture objects, their brains would show activity in regions involved in forming and remembering visual images and their meanings, regions that are also acti-

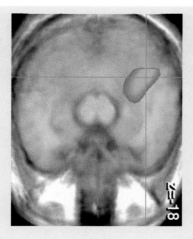

FIGURE 2.7
The figure shows an averaged view of the brains of participants in the study using fMRI. The red area indicates the region of the brain that, on average, showed the highest activation in the visual imagery condition after subtracting out activation that occurred in the non-imagery condition; in other words, this region showed significantly more activation while participants were forming mental images than when performing a control task.

vated when people actually see an object, such as a horse. When people just hear words, in contrast, these vision centers should not be active. That is precisely what the investigators found, as can be seen in Figure 2.7.

Researchers are still a long way from mapping the micro-details of the brain. The *resolution*, or sharpness, of the images produced by most scanning techniques is still too fuzzy to allow psychologists to pinpoint, for example, the different neural networks activated when a person feels guilty versus sad or angry. Further, people's brains differ, so that a single map will not work precisely for every person; averaging the responses of several participants can thus sometimes lead to imprecise results. Nevertheless, if progress made in the last decade is any indication, imaging techniques will continue to increase in precision at a dazzling pace, and so will our knowledge of mind and brain.

A GLOBAL VISTA

CROSS-CULTURAL RESEARCH

To some degree, human nature is the same everywhere because the brain and its genetic blueprints are so similar. But the *expression* of those blueprints can be as varied as an adobe hut and a high-rise apartment. Determining the extent to which psychological findings in one culture apply to people around the globe presents challenges as important and difficult as brain mapping.

Like anthropological fieldwork, in which an investigator lives in another culture and observes daily events, many cross-cultural investigations involve naturalistic observation, usually supplemented with quantitative methods. For example, when Western researchers wanted to explore the origins of social behavior in infants reared in a culture very different from their own, they studied Efe pygmies in the tropical rain forests of Zaire, who survive by hunting, gathering food, and trading with neighboring agricultural peoples (Tronick et al., 1992). The Efe establish camps composed of huts arranged in a semicircle, usually consisting of about 20 people. Researchers armed with laptop computers recorded minute-by-minute observations of the social life of Efe infants and toddlers in the camps. They found that, unlike Western children, who are groomed for independence, Efe children are

Among the Efe, as in many cultures, children are rarely alone.

surrounded by other people virtually every hour of their lives, preparing them well for a communal lifestyle as adults.

Other researchers rely on correlational and experimental methods to investigate psychological phenomena across cultures. In the 1940s anthropologists created the Human Relations Area Files, a database on hundreds of cultures taken from detailed observations by anthropologists. The information is indexed under categories such as supernatural beliefs, treatment of outsiders, rituals, infant care, and childrearing practices. This allows researchers to test hypotheses by correlating variables with each other across cultures, asking questions such as, "Do cultures that treat children harshly tend to have physically violent adults?" (Ember, 1997; Naroll et al., 1976). Studies since the 1950s have examined the correlations between various childrearing variables and cultural practices (Whiting & Child, 1953). For example, harsh childhood discipline correlates with beliefs in evil deities (Rohner, 1986). Apparently, cultural views of the gods are not independent of children's views of the godlike figures in their lives—their parents. Cross-cultural psychologists have also applied experimental procedures in other countries to test whether the findings of Western studies on phenomena replicate cross-culturally (see Berry et al., 1992, 1997; Triandis, 1994).

Psychologists interested in the cross-cultural validity of their theories face many difficulties, however, in transporting research from one culture to another. The same stimulus may mean very different things to people in different cultures. How might people from Bali, whose culture emphasizes *control* of emotions in the face of events such as grief, respond to instructions to describe a stressful event in full emotional detail in a study of emotional expression and health? Would they comply, or would this experimental situation itself be stressful because it forced them to violate a cultural norm? Or how might people from a culture like the Efe, who have had minimal exposure to photographs, respond to a study asking them to judge what emotion people are feeling from pictures of faces? Creating an equivalent experimental design often requires using a *different* design, but then is it really the same experiment?

Similarly, when employing a questionnaire cross-culturally, researchers must be very careful about translation because even minor changes or ambiguities could make cross-cultural comparisons invalid. To minimize distortions in translation, researchers use a procedure called back-translation, in which a bilingual speaker translates the items into the target language, and another bilingual speaker translates it back into the original language (usually English). The speakers then repeat the process until the translation back into English matches the original. Even this procedure is not always adequate; sometimes concepts simply differ too much across cultures to make the items equivalent. Asking a participant to rate the item "I have a good relationship with my brother" would be inappropriate in Japan, where speakers distinguish between older and younger brothers and lack a general term to denote both (Brislin, 1986). Once again reality poses obstacles to research, but we have to try to hurdle them if we want to learn about the psychology of *people* rather than of particular *peoples*.

INTERIM SUMMARY   Researchers study the relation between mental and neural processes using a number of methods, including case studies of patients with brain damage, experimental lesion studies with animals, **electroencephalograms (EEGs),** and computerized **imaging techniques** that allow researchers to study the brain in action, such as **CT, PET, and fMRI.** The aim of cross-cultural research is to assess the extent to which psychological processes vary across cultures. Researchers studying psychological phenomena cross-culturally use a variety of methods, including naturalistic observation, correlational studies linking one cultural trait to another, and experiments.

HOW TO EVALUATE A STUDY CRITICALLY

Having explored the major research designs, we now turn to the question of how to be an informed consumer of research. In deciding whether to "buy" the results of a study, the same maxim applies as in buying a car: *caveat emptor,* let the buyer beware. The popular media often report that "researchers at Harvard have found . . ." followed by conclusions that are tempting to take at face value. In reality, most studies have their limitations. To evaluate a study critically, the reader should examine the research carefully and attempt to answer seven broad questions (Figure 2.8).

DOES THE THEORETICAL FRAMEWORK MAKE SENSE?

The first step in evaluating a study is to consider whether the theory and the specific hypothesis to be tested make sense. Do the authors specify precisely what they mean by the concepts they use? Do all definitions of a key concepts refer to the same thing? For example, if the study explores the relation between social class and intelligence, does the article explain why social class and intelligence should have some relationship to each other? Do the authors clearly and consistently define both social class and intelligence?

IS THE SAMPLE ADEQUATE AND APPROPRIATE?

The next step is to examine the sample and determine if it adequately represents the population from which it is drawn. If researchers want to know about emotional expression and health in undergraduates, then a sample of undergraduates is perfectly appropriate. If they want to generalize to other populations, however, they need to use other samples, such as adults drawn from the local community, or people from Bali, to see if the effects hold. Another important issue is whether

1. Assess the study's theoretical framework.

Does the theory make sense?
Does the hypothesis make sense?
Are terms defined logically and consistently?

2. Assess the adequacy and appropriateness of the sample.

Is it representative of the population of interest?
Is it of sufficient size to test the hypothesis?

3. Assess the adequacy of the measures and procedures.

Are the measures reliable and valid?
Did the investigators properly control confounding
   variables?

4. Examine the data.

Do the data demonstrate what the authors claim?
Could the data be explained some other way?

5. Examine the conclusions drawn by the investigators.

Do the conclusions follow from the data?
Does the study have limitations that affect the
   interpretation or generalizability of the findings?
Can the findings be understood in the context of
   previous research?

6. Consider the meaningfulness of the study.

Does the study pass the "so what" test?
Do the theory and data shed any new light on the
   phenomenon under investigation?

7. Evaluate the ethics of the study.

Did the costs outweigh the benefits?
Did the investigators carefully consider the welfare
   of human and animal subjects?

FIGURE 2.8
Steps in evaluating a study critically. Examining a study critically means considering every aspect of the investigation, from the theory underlying it to its ethics.

the sample is large enough to allow for adequate statistical tests of the findings' significance (Chapter 2 Supplement).

WERE THE MEASURES AND PROCEDURES ADEQUATE?

The third broad question is whether the measures and procedures were well suited to the hypothesis being tested. Do the measures assess what they were designed to assess? Were proper control groups chosen to rule out alternative explanations and to assure the validity of the study? Did the investigators fail to notice any confounding variables that might have influenced the results? For example, if the study involved interviewing participants, were some of the interviewers male and some female? If so, did the gender of the interviewer affect how participants responded?

ARE THE DATA CONCLUSIVE?

Another step in evaluating a study is to examine the data presented. Do they demonstrate what the author claims? Typically, data in research articles are presented in a section entitled "Results," usually in the form of graphs, charts, or tables. In evaluating a study critically, the reader should carefully examine the data presented in these figures and ask whether any alternative interpretations could explain the results as well as or better than the researcher's explanation. Often, data permit many interpretations, and the findings may fit a pattern that the researcher rejected or did not consider.

ARE THE BROADER CONCLUSIONS WARRANTED?

Still another question is whether the researcher's broad conclusions fit both the theory presented and the data of the study. Does the study have limitations that render the conclusions invalid or applicable only under certain circumstances? An experiment may nicely test a phenomenon in a very specific domain, but then the investigator may try to generalize the findings to other areas with different properties. A reader should be wary of a research article that describes the effects of overcrowding on rats and then tries to draw broad conclusions about the need for human population control.

DOES THE STUDY SAY ANYTHING MEANINGFUL?

The sixth question in evaluating a study is the "so what?" test: Are the results meaningful? Does the study tell us anything we did not already know? Does it lead to questions for future research? The meaningfulness of a study depends in part on the importance, usefulness, and adequacy of the theoretical perspective from which it derives. Important studies also tend to produce findings that are in some way surprising or help choose between theories that offer opposing predictions.

IS THE STUDY ETHICAL?

A final question concerns ethics. If the study uses human or animal subjects, does it treat them humanely, and do the ends of the study—the incremental knowledge it produces—justify the means? The study of emotional expression and health required that the investigators have access to participants' medical records. Given the unreliability of self-reports of doctor visits, this seems justified, but the researchers no doubt took extra measures to assure confidentiality, such as requesting permission from participants to find out the *number* of visits but not specific details.

Individual psychologists were once free to make ethical determinations on their own, and the vast majority have always carefully considered the welfare of participants in designing studies. Today, however, the American Psychological Association (APA) publishes guidelines that govern psychological research practices (APA, 1973, 1997), and universities and other institutions have boards that review proposals for psychological studies, with the power to reject them on ethical grounds.

▶ ONE STEP FURTHER

Ethical Questions Come in Shades of Gray

The ethical issues involved in research are not always black and white. For example, in 1991, Jacob, Krahn, and Leonard published a study of problem solving in alcoholic fathers and their adolescent children. Participants were offered a sizable honorarium, or payment, to participate in the study ($400). During one procedure, alcoholic beverages were made available to participants in order to explore the impact of alcohol consumption on the parent–child interaction. Not surprisingly, the alcoholics availed themselves of this opportunity, with a mean consumption of 3.4 ounces.

The study itself was very strong methodologically and overcame numerous problems of previous research. For instance, many studies have used college students as participants. Yet even college students who display symptoms of alcohol abuse may not be a representative sample. Some students abuse alcohol during college because of its novelty, peer pressure, and cultural norms of college behavior but later have normal drinking patterns. Studies that *have* used actual alcoholics as participants have often relied on self-reports. Unfortunately, self-reports of alcohol consumption are notoriously unreliable among alcoholics, who may be unwilling or unable (because of denial or memory lapses) to provide accurate information. Thus, Jacob and colleagues could argue that their study was of particular value in offering new insights into an important topic.

Other psychologists, however, expressed concerns about the ethics of the research. The study essentially paid alcoholics to drink, thereby colluding in a disorder that has substantial negative consequences for families (Koocher, 1991; Stricker, 1991). As one commentator noted, $400 is a substantial payment for participation in a study, especially since roughly one-quarter of the participants were unemployed (Koocher, 1991). Jacob and colleagues responded that they had safeguarded the welfare of the participants in a number of ways, such as sending them home in taxis to prevent them from driving under the influence (Jacob & Leonard, 1991). Furthermore, most participants drank less than two drinks during the procedure, hardly an amount likely to influence the lives of men who had been drinking heavily for 10 to 20 years. Nevertheless, this example demonstrates the ambiguity that sometimes arises when researchers are confronted with ethical decisions.

Deception in Psychological Research

Many studies keep participants blind to the aims of the investigation until the end; some even deceive participants, giving them a "cover story" so that demand characteristics will not bias their responses. For example, in one experiment researchers wanted to study the conditions under which people can be induced to make false confessions (Kassin & Kiechel, 1996). They led college student participants to believe that they would be taking a typing test with another participant, who was really an accomplice, or *confederate*, of the experimenters. The experimenters explicitly instructed the participants not to touch the ALT key on the computer, since that would allegedly make the computer crash, and all data would be lost. Sixty seconds into the task, the computer seemed to stop functioning, and the experimenter rushed into the room accusing the participant of having hit the forbidden key. To assess whether false incriminating evidence could convince people that they had actually done something wrong, in one condition the confederate (allegedly simply waiting to take the test herself) "admitted" having seen the participant hit the ALT key; in a control condition, the accomplice denied having seen anything. The striking finding was that in the experimental condition about half of the participants came to believe that they *had* hit the key and destroyed the experiment. Obviously, if they had known what the experiment was really about, the experiment would not have worked.

From an ethical standpoint, the use of deception raises questions about **informed consent**—the participant's ability to agree (or refuse) to participate in an informed manner. Can individuals really give informed consent to participate in a study whose aims they do not know? Some psychologists argue that "the use of intentional deception in the research setting is unethical, imprudent, and unwarranted scientifically" (Baumrind, 1985). Others, however, point to evidence demonstrating that participants in deception experiments actually tend to enjoy the experience more, learn more from their participation, and rarely object to the deception when they are "debriefed" at the end (Christensen, 1988).

Only a small proportion of experiments actually involve deception, and APA guidelines permit deception only if a study meets four conditions: (1) The research is of great importance and cannot be conducted without the use of deception; (2) participants can be expected to find the procedures reasonable once they are informed of them after the experiment is completed; (3) participants can withdraw from the experiment at any time; and (4) experimenters debrief the participants afterward, explaining the purposes of the study and removing any stressful aftereffects. Many universities address the issue of deception by asking potential participants if they would object to being deceived temporarily in a study. That way, any participant who is deceived by an experimenter has given prior consent to be deceived.

Ethics and Animal Research

A larger ethical controversy concerns the use of nonhuman animals for psychological research (Bowd & Shapiro, 1993; Ulrich, 1991). By lesioning a region of a rat's brain, for example, researchers can sometimes learn a tremendous amount about the function of similar regions in the human brain. Such experiments, however, have an obvious cost to the animal, raising questions about the moral status of animals, that is, whether they have rights (Plous, 1996; Rollin, 1985). Again the issue is how to balance costs and benefits: To what extent do the costs to animals justify the benefits to humans? The problem, of course, is that, unlike humans, animals cannot give informed consent.

To what extent can humans use, and even breed, other sentient creatures (that is, animals who feel) to satisfy intellectual or other human interests? Groups such as Mobilization for Animals (1984) argue that animal research in psychology has produced little of value to humans, especially considering the enormous suffering animals have undergone. Most psychologists dispute this claim (Miller, 1985). They note that animal research has led to important advances in behavioral therapy, biofeedback, and potential treatments for serious disorders such as Alzheimer's disease (a degenerative brain illness that ultimately leads to death). Animal research has also contributed to the understanding of such phenomena as stress, weight gain, and the effects of aging on learning and memory. The difficulty lies in balancing the interests of humans with those of other animals and advancing science while staying within sensible ethical boundaries (Bowd, 1990). Accordingly, institutional review boards examine proposals for experiments with nonhuman animals as they do with human participants and may similarly veto proposals they deem unethical. ◀

INTERIM SUMMARY To evaluate a study, a critical reader should ask a number of broad questions, including whether the study's theoretical framework makes sense and the hypotheses flow sensibly from it, the sample is appropriate, the measures and procedures are valid and reliable, the data fit the theory, and the results are meaningful. An additional concern is whether the study is ethical. Whether a study entails deception or poses potential harm to humans or other animals, the ethical question is one of weighing potential costs against benefits.

SOME CONCLUDING THOUGHTS

As we have seen, psychological research has the power to tackle questions that have seemed unanswerable for centuries. Can talking about unpleasant experiences reduce the risk of illness? Yes. Is the brain equipped to produce mental images that people can generate from memory and scan as they try to find their way around a new city? Yes. Is psychology essentially the same cross-culturally, or do humans think, feel, and behave in entirely different ways depending on their culture? Neither. These are solid answers that only solid empirical procedures could have provided.

At the outset we posed a series of questions. How do the theoretical perspectives psychologists adopt affect the methods they choose? What methods—or combination of methods—provide the most conclusive results? What do we gain and what do we lose when we "domesticate" a psychological phenomenon and bring it into the laboratory? And how do we know when we have asked the right questions in the first place?

Psychologists with a behavioral or cognitive orientation are almost uniformly committed to experimental investigation. The philosopher of science Karl Popper (1963), among others, has argued that the criterion that distinguishes science from other practices (and from mere speculation) is the formulation and evaluation of testable hypotheses that can be refuted if they are untrue. Preferably, these hypotheses should not be intuitively obvious, so they can put a theory to the test. From this standpoint, the behaviorist and cognitive perspectives have the greatest scientific support, although psychodynamic and evolutionary psychologists are increasingly relying on experimental methods.

The phenomena that most readily lend themselves to experimental investigation, however, are not necessarily the most important to study. For instance, as we saw in Chapter 1, researchers have offered competing theories for over a century about the extent to which specific parts of the brain perform specific functions. We now know that many functions are, in fact, localized to specific structures and pathways, although most functions are distributed across circuits in many parts of the brain, not just a single region. The question of how the brain is organized was no less important before the advent of brain imaging techniques than after, and researchers did the best they could with the technologies available, such as lesion and EEG studies. Similarly, based on case studies, psychodynamic theorists have asserted for a century that much of human mental life is unconscious. We did not have the technologies to test that proposition adequately, either, until the last 15 years, but it turned out to be correct.

Should a hypothesis be discarded simply because it is difficult to assess? To do so would confuse the truth-value of a hypothesis with its testability. A sophisticated theory of human nature may include many accurate propositions that are difficult to test empirically precisely because humans are complex creatures, and psychology is only a century old. Science, like all human cognition, involves constructing a story, or a map, of a phenomenon we want to understand, using all the information at our disposal. That means tentatively accepting hypotheses supported by our strongest methods, even more tentatively holding other theoretical beliefs that have *some* basis in more limited methods, and gradually weeding out those beliefs that do not withstand closer scientific scrutiny when the technologies are available to test them.

In its broadest sense, a scientific, empiricist attitude in psychology means keeping one's eyes wide open in as many settings as possible and constantly testing what one believes. Philosophers of science sometimes distinguish between the **context of discovery** (in which phenomena are observed, hypotheses are framed, and theories are built) and the **context of justification** (in which hypotheses are tested empirically). Case studies, naturalistic observation, and surveys are often most useful in the context of discovery precisely because the investigator is *not* structuring the situation. The more experimenters exert control, the less they see unconstrained behavior—behavior as it occurs in nature. Descriptive methods often foster the kind of exploration that leads researchers to ask the right questions. In the context of justification, where hypotheses are put to the test, the best designs are experimental, quasi-experimental, and sometimes correlational. By using inferential statistics, researchers can assess the likelihood that their theories and hypotheses have merit.

The road to psychological knowledge is paved in many directions. Just as an optimal study uses multiple measures, so an optimal science of mental life and behavior uses multiple methods of observation. The remainder of this text examines the discoveries to which the various methods have led, beginning with the biological bases of mental processes and behavior.

INTERIM SUMMARY   Descriptive methods tend to be most useful in the **context of scientific discovery,** whereas experimental methods tend to be most useful in the **context of justification.** A scientific, empiricist attitude means using whatever methods one can to study a phenomenon, continually testing one's hypotheses, and applying experimental and quasi-experimental methods wherever possible to assess cause and effect.

SUMMARY

CHARACTERISTICS OF GOOD PSYCHOLOGICAL RESEARCH

1. Good psychological research typically has a number of features: a theoretical framework, standardized procedures, generalizability, and objective measurement.

2. A **theory** is a systematic way of organizing and explaining observations that includes a set of propositions about the relations among various phenomena. A **hypothesis** is a tentative belief or educated guess that purports to predict or explain the relationship between two or more **variables;** variables are phenomena that differ or change across circumstances or individuals. A variable that can be placed on a continuum is a **continuous variable.** A variable comprised of groupings or categories is a **categorical variable.**

3. A **sample** is a subgroup of a **population** that is likely to be **representative** of the population as a whole. **Generalizability** refers to the applicability of findings based on a sample to the entire population of interest. For a study's findings to be generalizable, its methods must be sound, or **valid.**

4. A **measure** is a concrete way of assessing a variable. A good measure is both reliable and valid. **Reliability** refers to a measure's ability to produce consistent results. The **validity** of a measure refers to its ability to assess the construct it is intended to measure.

EXPERIMENTAL RESEARCH

5. In **experimental research,** investigators manipulate some aspect of a situation and examine the impact on the way participants respond in order to assess cause and effect. **Independent variables** are the variables the experimenter manipulates; **dependent variables** are the participants' responses, which indicate if the manipulation had an effect.

6. Conducting a study entails a series of steps: framing a hypothesis, operationalizing variables, developing a standardized procedure, selecting participants, testing the results for statistical significance, and drawing conclusions. **Operationalizing** means turning an abstract concept into a concrete variable defined by some set of actions, or operations.

7. A **control group** is a neutral condition of an experiment in which participants are not exposed to the experimental manipulation. Researchers frequently perform **blind studies,** in which participants are kept unaware of, or "blind" to, important aspects of the research. In a **single-blind study,** only participants are kept blind; in **double-blind studies,** participants and researchers alike are blind.

8. A **confounding variable** is a variable that could produce effects that might be confused with the effects of the independent variable.

9. Limitations of experimental studies include the difficulty of bringing com-

plex phenomena into the laboratory, the question of external validity (applicability of the results to phenomena in the real world), and limited possibility of exploring personal meanings. An **interpretive** stance on methodology argues that the aim of a science of human action is not the *prediction* of behavior but the *understanding* of the highly idiosyncratic personal meanings that lead to an individual's actions.

DESCRIPTIVE RESEARCH

10. Unlike experimental studies, **descriptive** methods cannot unambiguously demonstrate cause and effect. They describe phenomena as they already exist rather than manipulate variables to test the effects. Descriptive methods include case studies, naturalistic observation, and survey research.

11. A **case study** is an in-depth observation of one person or a small group of people. **Naturalistic observation** is the in-depth observation of a phenomenon in its natural setting. Both case studies and naturalistic observation are vulnerable to researcher bias—the tendency of investigators to see what they expect to see. **Survey research** involves asking a large sample of people questions, often about attitudes or behaviors, using **questionnaires** or **interviews.**

CORRELATIONAL RESEARCH

12. **Correlational research** assesses the degree to which two variables are related, in an effort to see whether knowing the value of one can lead to prediction of the other. A **correlation coefficient** measures the extent to which two variables are related; it may be positive or negative. A **positive correlation** between two variables means that the higher individuals measure on one variable, the higher they are likely to measure on the other. A **negative correlation** means that the higher individuals measure on one variable, the lower they will measure on the other, and vice versa. *Correlation does not demonstrate causation.*

13. Researchers studying the relation between mental and neural processes use a number of methods, including case studies of patients with brain damage, experimental lesion studies with animals, **electroencephalograms (EEGs),** and computerized **imaging techniques,** such as **CT, PET,** and **fMRI.**

14. Researchers studying psychological phenomena cross-culturally use a variety of methods, including naturalistic observation, correlational studies linking one cultural trait to another, and experiments.

HOW TO EVALUATE A STUDY CRITICALLY

15. To evaluate a study, a critical reader should answer several broad questions: (1) Is the study's theoretical framework sensible, and do the hypotheses flow sensibly from it? (2) Is the sample adequate and appropriate? (3) Were the measures and procedures valid and reliable? (4) Are the data conclusive? (5) Are the broader conclusions warranted? (6) Does the study say anything meaningful? (7) Is the study ethical?

SOME CONCLUDING THOUGHTS

16. Where they can be used, experimental methods are the strongest, but the optimal path to psychological knowledge is through the use of multiple methods.

Statistical Principles In Psychological Research

Statistics are far more intuitive than most people believe, even to people who do not consider mathematics their strong suit. As described in Chapter 2, psychologists use descriptive statistics to summarize quantitative data in an understandable form. They employ inferential statistics to tell whether the results reflect anything other than chance. We discuss each in turn.

SUMMARIZING THE DATA: DESCRIPTIVE STATISTICS

The first step in describing participants' responses on a variable is usually to chart a frequency distribution. A **frequency distribution** is exactly what it sounds like—a method of organizing the data to show how frequently participants received each of the many possible scores. In other words, a frequency distribution represents the way scores were distributed across the sample. The kind of frequency distribution that a professor might observe on a midterm examination (in a very small class, for illustration) is shown in Table 2S.1 and again graphically in Figure 2S.1. The graph, called a **histogram**, plots ranges of scores along the x axis and the frequency of scores in each range on the y axis. The rounded-out version of the histogram drawn with a line is the familiar "curve."

MEASURES OF CENTRAL TENDENCY

Perhaps the most important descriptive statistics are **measures of central tendency,** which provide an index of the way a typical participant responded on a

TABLE 2S.1   DISTRIBUTION OF TEST SCORES ON A MIDTERM EXAMINATION

98
92
87
87
84
78
74
70
60
730

$$\text{Mean} = \frac{730\,(\text{total of scores})}{9\,(\text{number of students})} = 81.1$$

Note: The mean is the average of all scores (in this case, 81.1). The mode is the most common score (87). The median is the score in the middle of the distribution, with half of all scores above it and half below it (84).

measure. The three most common measures of central tendency are the mean, the mode, and the median. The **mean** is simply the statistical average of the scores of all participants, computed by adding up all the participants' scores and dividing by the number of participants. The mean is the most commonly reported measure of central tendency and is the most intuitively descriptive of the average participant.

Sometimes, however, the mean may be misleading. For example, suppose as part of a larger study a team of researchers wanted to know how much money the typical rural family in Peru earns per year. Now suppose they found, in a sample of ten families, that eight earned $2000 per year, one earned $100,000 per year, and one earned $300,000 (Table 2S.2). Relying strictly on mean income as the measure of central tendency, the researcher would conclude that rural Peruvians are, on the average, a wealthy bunch, with a mean annual income of $41,600. However, this would obviously misrepresent the majority, whose meager incomes were averaged in with their wealthy landowning neighbors.

"How do you expect me to average 55 miles an hour if I don't speed?"

FIGURE 2S.1
Histogram showing a frequency distribution of test scores. A frequency distribution shows graphically the frequency of each score (how many times it occurs) distributed across the sample.

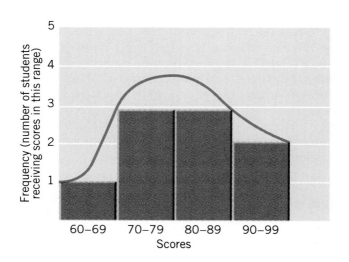

TABLE 2S.2	WHEN A MEAN IS MISLEADING		
FAMILY NUMBER	ANNUAL INCOME (IN DOLLARS)		
1	2,000		
2	2,000		
3	2,000		
4	100,000		
5	2,000		
6	2,000		
7	2,000		
8	300,000	$\text{Mean} = \dfrac{\text{sum of all incomes}}{\text{number of families}} = \dfrac{\$416,000}{10} = \$41,600$	
9	2,000		
10	2,000	Mode = $2000	

In this case, both the mode and the median would be more useful measures of central tendency, because a mean can be strongly influenced by extreme and unusual scores in a sample. The **mode** (or *modal score*) refers to the most *common* score observed in the sample. In this case, $2000 is the modal income because eight of ten families had an income of $2000. In Table 2S.1, the modal test score is 87, whereas the mean is 81.1. One or two students with particularly low scores pulled down the class mean. The mode, however, can be a misleading measure of central tendency if the sample has more than one frequent score and these frequent scores are far apart from one another. In the Peruvian example what if five families had an income of $2000 and four had an income of $40,000. The mode would be $2000 but would not really be representative of the whole sample.

The **median** refers to the score that falls in the middle of the distribution of scores, with half scoring below and half above it. Reporting the median essentially allows one to ignore extreme scores on each end of the distribution that

In Peru as in much of Latin America, mean income is a misleading measure of central tendency.

TABLE 2S.3   THE STANDARD DEVIATION

SCORE	DEVIATION FROM THE MEAN	D²
98	98 – 91 = 7	49
94	94 – 91 = 3	9
91	91 – 91 = 0	0
87	87 – 91 = –4	16
85	85 – 91 = –6	36
455	0	110

$$\text{Mean} = 455/5 = 91$$

$$\text{Standard deviation} = \frac{\sqrt{\Sigma D^2}}{N} = \frac{\sqrt{110}}{5} = \frac{\sqrt{22}}{5} = 4.7$$

Note: The table presents the scores of five students on an examination (column 1). Computing a standard deviation is actually quite intuitive. The first step is to calculate the mean score, which in this case is 91. The next step is to calculate the difference, or deviation, between each participant's score and the mean score, as shown in column 2. The standard deviation is the average deviation of participants from the mean. The only complication is that taking the average of the deviations always produces a mean deviation of zero because the sum of deviations is by definition zero (see the total in column 2). Thus, the next step is to square the deviations (column 3). The standard deviation is then computed by taking the square root of the sum of all the squared differences, divided by the number of participants.

would bias a portrait of the typical participant. In the Peruvian example in which eight of ten families lived on $2000 per year, median income, like modal income, is $2000 because $2000 falls in the middle of the distribution. Half of the families sampled earn $2000 or less, and half earn $2000 or more, even though those who are wealthier earn *substantially* more. The median test score on the midterm examination in Table 2S.1 is 84; half the scores fall above and half below.

VARIABILITY

As the above examples demonstrate, another important descriptive statistic is a measure of the **variability** of scores, that is, how much participants' scores differ from one another. Variability influences the choice of measure of central tendency. The simplest measure of variability is the **range** of scores, which refers to the difference between the highest and the lowest value observed on the variable. In the Peruvian case, values of the income variable run from $2000 to $300,000, for a range of $298,000.

The range can be a biased estimate of variability, however, in much the same way as the mean can be a biased estimate of central tendency. Income does range considerably in this sample, but for the majority of Peruvians studied, variability is minimal (ranging from $2000 to $2000—no variability at all). Hence, a more useful measure is the **standard deviation (SD),** which again is just what it sounds like: the amount that the average participant deviates from the mean of the sample. Table 2S.3 shows how to compute a standard deviation.

THE NORMAL DISTRIBUTION

When researchers collect data on continuous variables (such as weight or IQ) and plot them on a histogram, the data usually approximate a normal distribution, like the distribution of IQ scores shown in Figure 2S.2. In a **normal distribution,**

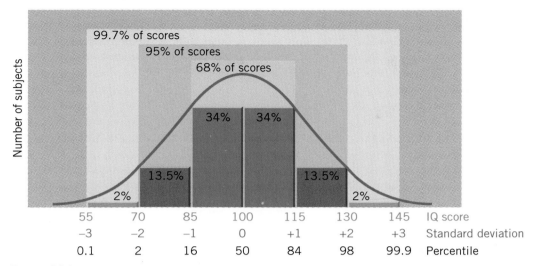

FIGURE 2S.2
A normal distribution. IQ scores approximate a normal distribution, which looks like a bell-shaped curve; 68 percent of scores fall within one standard deviation of the mean (represented by the area under the curve in blue). The curve is a smoothed-out version of a histogram. An individual's score can be represented alternatively by the number of standard deviations it diverges from the mean in either direction or by a percentile score, which shows the percentage of scores that fall below it (to the left on the graph).

the scores of most participants fall in the middle of the bell-shaped distribution, and progressively fewer participants have scores at either extreme. In other words, most individuals are about average on most dimensions, and very few are extremely above or below average. Thus, most people have an IQ around average (100), whereas very few have an IQ of 70 or 130. In a distribution of scores that is completely normal, the mean, mode, and median are all the same.

Participants' scores on a variable that is normally distributed can be described in terms of how far they are from average, that is, their deviation from the mean. Thus, a person's IQ could be described either as 85 or as one standard deviation below the mean, for the standard deviation in IQ is about 15. A participant two standard deviations below the mean would have an IQ of 70, which is bordering on mental retardation. For normal data, 68 percent of participants fall within one standard deviation of the mean (34 percent on either side of it), 95 percent fall within two standard deviations, and over 99.7 percent fall within three standard deviations. Thus, an IQ above 145 is a very rare occurrence.

Knowing the relation between standard deviations and percentages of participants whose scores lie within different parts of a distribution allows researchers to report **percentile scores,** which indicate the percentage of scores that fall below a score. Thus, a participant whose score is three standard deviations above the mean is in the 99.7th percentile, whereas an average participant (whose score does not deviate from the mean) is in the 50th percentile.

INTERIM SUMMARY Descriptive statistics allows researchers to summarize data in a readily understandable form. The first step in describing the data is often to provide a **frequency distribution,** which shows how frequently participants received each of the many possible scores. The most important descriptive statistics are **measures of central tendency,** which provide an index of the way a typical participant responded on a measure. The **mean** is the statistical average of the scores of all participants; the **mode** is the most common score; the **median** is the score that falls in the middle of the distribution. Another important descriptive statistic is **variability,** which refers to the extent to which participants tend to differ from one another. The **standard deviation** describes how much the average participant deviates from the mean. When psychologists collect data on continuous variables, they often find that the data approximate a **normal distribution,** with most scores toward the middle. Participants' scores on a normally distributed variable can be described in terms of the number of standard deviations from the mean or as **percentile scores,** which indicate the percentage of scores that fall below them.

TESTING THE HYPOTHESIS: INFERENTIAL STATISTICS

When researchers find a difference between the responses of participants in one condition and another, they must infer whether these differences likely occurred by chance or reflect a true causal relationship. Similarly, if they discover a correlation between two variables, they need to know the likelihood that the two variables simply correlated by chance. As the philosopher David Hume (1711–1776) demonstrated two centuries ago, we can never be entirely sure about the answer to questions like these. If someone believes that all swans are white and observes 99 swans that are white and none that are not, can the person conclude with certainty that the hundredth swan will also be white? The issue is one of probability: If the person has observed a representative sample of swans, what is the likelihood that, given 99 white swans, a black one will emerge next?

STATISTICAL SIGNIFICANCE

Psychologists typically deal with this issue in their research by using tests of **statistical significance.** These procedures determine whether the results of a study are likely to have occurred simply by chance (and thus cannot be meaningfully generalized to a population) or whether they reflect true properties of the population. Statistical significance should not be confused with practical or theoretical significance. A researcher may demonstrate with a high degree of certainty that, on the average, females spend less time watching football than males, but who cares? Statistical significance means only that a finding is unlikely to be an accident of chance.

Beyond describing the data, then, the researcher's second task in presenting and analyzing data is to draw inferences from the sample to the population as a whole. Inferential statistics help sort out whether or not the findings of a study really show anything. Researchers usually report the likelihood that their results mean something in terms of a **probability value** (or **p-value**). A *p*-value represents the probability that any positive findings obtained with the sample (such as differences between two experimental conditions) were just a matter of chance. In other words, a *p*-value is an index of the probability that positive findings obtained would not apply to the population and instead reflect only the peculiar characteristics of the particular sample.

How many swans must one observe before concluding that all swans are white?

TABLE 2S.4 CHILDREN'S PROSOCIAL RESPONSE TO ANOTHER PERSON'S DISTRESS DURING THE SECOND YEAR OF LIFE			
	PERCENTAGE OF EPISODES IN WHICH THE CHILD BEHAVED PROSOCIALLY		
TYPE OF INCIDENT	TIME 1	TIME 2	TIME 3
Witnessed distress	9	21	49
Caused distress	7	10	52

Source: Adapted from Zahn-Waxler et al., 1992.

To illustrate, one study tested the hypothesis that children increasingly show signs of morality and empathy during their second year of life (Zahn-Waxler et al., 1992). The investigators trained 27 mothers to dictate into a tape recorder reports of any episode in which their one-year-olds either witnessed distress (e.g., seeing the mother burning herself on the stove) or caused distress (e.g., pulling the cat's tail, teasing a sibling, or biting the mother's breast while nursing). The mothers dictated descriptions of these events over the course of the next year; each report included an account of the way the child responded to the other person's distress. Coders then rated the child's behavior using categories such as prosocial behavior, defined as efforts to help the person in distress.

Table 2S.4 shows the percentage of times the child behaved prosocially during these episodes at each of three periods: time 1 (13–15 months of age), time 2 (18–20 months), and time 3 (23–25 months). As the table shows, the percentage of times the child behaved prosocially increased dramatically over the course of the second year of life, regardless of whether the child witnessed or caused the distress. When the investigators analyzed the changes in percentages over time for both types of distress (witnessed and caused), they found the differences statistically significant. A jump from nine to 49 prosocial behaviors in 12 months was not likely to be accidental.

By convention, psychologists accept the results of a study whenever the probability of positive findings attributable to chance is less than 5 percent. This is typically expressed as $p < .05$. Thus, the smaller the p-value, the more certain one can feel about the results. A researcher would rather be able to say that the chances that her findings are spurious (that is, just accidental) are 1 in 1000 ($p < .001$) than 1 in 100 ($p < .01$). Nevertheless, researchers can never be *certain* that their results are true of the population as a whole; a black swan could always be swimming in the next lake. Nor can they be sure that if they performed the study with 100 different participants they would not obtain different findings. This is why replication—repeating a study to see if the same results occur again—is extremely important in science. For example, in his studies of mood and memory described in Chapter 2, Bower hit an unexpected black swan: His initial series of studies yielded compelling results, but some of these findings failed to replicate in later experiments. He ultimately had to alter parts of his theory that the initial data had supported (Bower, 1989).

The best way to ensure that a study's results are not accidental is to use a large sample. The larger the sample, the more likely it reflects the actual properties of the population. Suppose 30 people in the world are over 115 years old and researchers want to know about hearing ability in this population. If the researchers test 25 of them, they can be much more certain that their findings are generalizable to this population than if they study a sample of only two of them.

These two could have been born with hearing deficits that have no connection to their age or could be unusual in their hearing ability.

Most people intuitively understand the importance of large numbers in sampling, even if they do not realize it. For example, tennis fans recognize the logic behind matches comprised of multiple sets and would object if decisions as to who moves on to the next round were made on the basis of a single game. Intuitively, they know that a variety of factors could influence the outcome of any single game other than the ability of the players, such as fluctuations in concentration, momentary physical condition (such as a dull pain in the foot), lighting, wind, or which player served first. Because a single game is not a large enough set of observations to make a reliable assessment of who is the better player, many sports rely on a best-of-three, best-of-five, or best-of-seven series.

INTERIM SUMMARY   To assess whether the results of a study likely reflect anything other than chance, psychologists use inferential statistics, notably tests of **statistical significance.** They usually report a **probability value,** or *p*-**value,** which represents the probability that any positive findings obtained (such as a difference between groups, or a correlation coefficient that differs from zero) were accidental or just a matter of chance. By convention, psychologists accept *p*-values that fall below .05 (that have a probability of being accidental of less than 5 percent). The best ways to protect against spurious findings are to use large samples and to try to replicate findings in other samples.

COMMON TESTS OF STATISTICAL SIGNIFICANCE

Choosing which inferential statistics to use depends on the design of the study and particularly on whether the variables assessed are continuous or categorical. If both sets of variables are continuous, the researcher simply correlates them to see whether they are related and tests the probability that a correlation of that magnitude could occur by chance. For many kinds of research, however, the investigator wants to compare two or more groups, such as males and females, or participants exposed to several different experimental conditions. In this case, the independent variables are categorical (male/female, condition 1/condition 2). If the dependent variables are also categorical, the appropriate statistic is a **chi-square** test (or χ^2). A chi-square compares the observed data with the results that would be expected by chance and tests the likelihood that the differences between observed and expected are accidental. For example, suppose a researcher wants to know whether patients with antisocial personality disorder are more likely than the general population to have had academic difficulties in elementary school. In other words, she wants to know whether one categorical variable (a diagnosis of antisocial versus normal personality) predicts another (presence or absence of academic difficulties, defined as having failed a grade in elementary school). The researcher collects a sample of 50 male patients with the disorder (since the incidence is much higher in males and gender could be a confounding variable) and compares them with 50 males of similar socioeconomic status (since difficulties in school are correlated with social class). She finds that, of her antisocial sample, 20 individuals failed a grade in elementary school, whereas only two of the normals did (Table 2S.5). The likelihood is extremely small that this difference could have emerged by chance, and the chi-square test would therefore show that the differences are statistically significant.

In many cases, the independent variables are categorical, but the dependent variables are continuous. This was the case in the study of emotional expression described in Chapter 2, which placed participants in one of two conditions (writing about emotional events or about neutral events) and compared the number of visits they subsequently made to the health service (a continuous variable). The question to be answered statistically regards the likelihood that the mean number

TABLE 2S.5 TYPICAL DATA APPROPRIATE FOR A CHI-SQUARE ANALYSIS

		School Failure	
		Present	Absent
Diagnostic Group	Antisocial	20	30
	Normal	2	48

Note: A chi-square is the appropriate statistic when testing the relation between two categorical variables. In this case, the variables are diagnosis (presence or absence of antisocial personality disorder) and school failure (presence or absence of a failed grade). The chi-square statistic tests the likelihood that the relative abundance of school failure in the antisocial group occurred by chance.

of visits to the doctor made by participants in the two conditions differed by chance. If participants who wrote about the transition to college made .73 visits to the health service on the average whereas those who wrote about a neutral event made 1.56, is this discrepancy likely to be accidental or does it truly depend on the condition to which they were exposed?

When comparing the mean scores of two groups, researchers use a *t*-test. A **t-test** is actually a special case of a statistical procedure called an **analysis of variance (ANOVA),** which can be used to compare the means of two or more groups. ANOVA assesses the likelihood that mean differences among groups occurred by chance. To put it another way, ANOVA assesses the extent to which variation in scores is attributable to the independent variable. Once again, a larger sample is helpful in determining whether mean differences between groups are real or random. If Pennebaker and his colleagues tested only two participants in each condition and found mean differences, they could not be confident of the findings because the results could simply reflect the idiosyncrasies of these four participants. If they tested 30, however, and the differences between the two conditions were large and relatively consistent across participants, the ANOVA would be statistically significant.

Chi-square, *t*-tests, and analysis of variance are not the only statistics psychologists employ. They also use correlation coefficients and many others. In all cases, however, their aim is the same: to try to draw generalizations about a population without having to study every one of its members.

INTERIM SUMMARY   Whether one uses inferential statistics such as **chi-square** or **analysis of variance (ANOVA)** depends on the design of the study, particularly on whether the variables assessed are continuous or categorical.

SOME CONCLUDING THOUGHTS

Inferential statistics are extremely important in trying to draw inferences from psychological research, but they are not fool-proof. In fact, some psychologists are now debating whether significance testing is really useful (see Abelson, 1997; Hunter, 1997; Shrout, 1997). One problem with significance testing is that *p*-values are heavily dependent on sample size. With a large enough sample, a tiny correlation will become significant, even though the relation between the two variables may be miniscule. Conversely, researchers often mistakenly infer from nonsignificant findings that no real difference exists between groups, when they simply have not used a large enough sample to know. If group differences *do* emerge, a *p*-value is meaningful because it specifies the likelihood that the findings could have occurred by chance. If group differences do *not* emerge, however, a *p*-value can be misleading because true differences between groups or experimental conditions may not show up simply because the sample is too small or the study is not conducted well enough.

For these reasons, some psychologists have called for other methods of reporting data that allow consumers of research to draw their own conclusions. For example, instead of reporting the size of the *p*-value, one approach is to report the size of the *effect* of being in one group or another, such as how much difference an experimental manipulation made on the dependent variable. *Effect size* can be reported as the number of standard deviations the average participant in one condition differs from the average participant in another on the dependent variable. For example, if participants who write about an emotional event for four days in a row go to the health service .73 times and those who write about a neutral event go 1.56 times, the meaning of that discrepancy is unclear unless we know the standard deviations of the means. If the SD is around .75, then students who write about emotional events are a full standard deviation better off than control subjects—which is definitely a finding worth writing home about. If the SD is .25, the effect size is *three* standard deviations, which means that writing about emotional events would put the average participant in the experimental condition in the 99th percentile of health in comparison with participants in the control condition, which would be an extraordinary effect. This example illustrates why researchers always report SDs along with means: .73 vs 1.56 is a meaningless difference if we do not know how much the average person normally fluctuates from these means.

In the final analysis, perhaps what statistics really do is to help a researcher tell a compelling story (Abelson, 1995). A good series of studies aims to solve a mystery, leading the reader step by step through all the possible scenarios, ruling out one suspect after another. Statistics can lend confidence to the conclusion, but they can never entirely rule out the possibility of a surprise ending.

SUMMARY

SUMMARIZING THE DATA: DESCRIPTIVE STATISTICS

1. The most important descriptive statistics are **measures of central tendency,** which provide an index of the way a typical participant responded on a measure. The **mean** is the statistical average of the scores of all participants. The **mode** is the most common or frequent score or value of the variable observed in the sample. The **median** is the score that falls right in the middle of the distribution of scores; half the participants score below it and half above it.

2. **Variability** refers to the extent to which participants tend to differ from one another in their scores. The **standard deviation** refers to the amount that the average participant deviates from the mean of the sample.

TESTING THE HYPOTHESIS: INFERENTIAL STATISTICS

3. To assess the results of a study, psychologists use tests of **statistical significance** to determine whether positive results are likely to have occurred sim-

ply by chance. A **probability value,** or *p*-**value,** represents the probability that positive findings (such as group differences) were accidental or just a matter of chance. By convention, psychologists accept *p*-values that fall below .05 (that have a probability of being accidental of less than 5 percent). The best way to ensure that a study's results are not accidental is to use a large enough sample that random fluctuations will cancel each other out.

4. The choice of which inferential statistics to use depends on the design of the study, particularly on whether the variables assessed are continuous or categorical. Common statistical tests are **chi-square** and **analysis of variance (ANOVA).**

5. Tests of statistical significance are not without their limitations. With a large enough sample size, significant differences are likely to emerge whether or not they are meaningful, and *p*-values do not adequately reflect the possibility that *negative* findings occurred by chance. Thus, some psychologists have begun to advocate the use of other methods for making inferences from psychological data, such as effect size. Statistical techniques are useful ways of making an argument, not fool-proof methods for establishing psychological truths.

Biological Bases of Mental Life and Behavior

*I*n 1917, an epidemic broke out in Vienna that quickly spread throughout the world. The disease was a mysterious sleeping sickness called encephalitis lethargica. *Encephalitis* refers to an inflammation of the central nervous system that results from infection. (*Lethargica* simply referred to the fact that extreme lethargy, or lack of energy, was a defining feature of the disease.) The infection that led to the disease was thought to be viral, although the viral agent was never discovered. The epidemic disappeared as unexpectedly as it emerged, though not until 10 years had passed and 5 million people had fallen ill to it (Cheyette & Cummings, 1995; Sacks, 1993).

The acute phase of the illness, during which symptoms were most intense, was characterized by extreme states of arousal. Some patients were so under-aroused that they seemed to sleep for weeks; others became so hyperaroused they could not sleep at all (Sacks, 1973). Roughly one-third of those who con-tracted the disease died during its acute phase, but those who seemingly recov-ered did not know what would later hit them. Delayed-onset symptoms usually

arose five to ten years later and were re-markably diverse, including severe de-pression, mania (a state that often in-cludes extreme grandiosity, extraordinarily high energy, and little need for sleep), sexual perversions, ab-normal twitching movements, sudden episodes in which the person would shout obscenities, and severe conduct problems in children afflicted with the disorder (Cheyette & Cummings, 1995).

For most of the survivors of the epi-demic, the most striking and tragic symptom was brain deterioration within the years following the acute phase of the illness, leaving many in a virtual state of sleep for almost 40 years. These sur-vivors were aware of their surroundings, but they did not seem to be fully awake. They were motionless and speechless, without energy, motivation, emo-tion, or appetite. And they remained in that stuporous state until the develop-ment of a new drug in the 1960s. The drug, L-dopa, suddenly awakened many from their slumbers by restoring a chemical in the brain that the virus had de-stroyed.

Ms. B contracted a severe form of encephalitis lethargica when she was 18 (Sacks, 1973). Although she recovered in a few months, she began to show signs of the post-encephalitic disorder four years later. For almost half a century she was unable to perform any voluntary movements, to speak, or even to blink for long periods of time. Ms. B was not in a coma. She was aware of the events around her, but she could not react to them physically or emotionally.

Ms. B began to come alive within days of receiving L-dopa. After one week, she started to speak. Within two weeks she was able to write, stand up, and walk between parallel bars. Eventually her emotions returned, and she reestablished contact with her family—or what was left of it. She had fallen asleep a vibrant young woman of 22. She awakened a woman of 67.

To comprehend Ms. B's experience requires an understanding of the **nervous system**—the interacting network of nerve cells that underlies all psychological activity. At the time of the outbreak physicians had difficulty finding a link between many symptoms that seemed unrelated, such as the inability to move and the tendency to develop compulsions or scream obscenities. Only recently have researchers begun to understand how the damaged parts of the brain could produce such a seemingly incomprehensible picture.

We begin by examining the neuron, or nerve cell, and the way neurons communicate with one another to produce thought, feeling, and behavior. After briefly exploring the hormones that work with neurons to create psychological experience, we then consider the extraordinary organization of billions of neurons in the central nervous system (the brain and spinal cord) and in the peripheral nervous system (neurons in the rest of the body). We conclude with a brief discussion of the role of biology and genetics in understanding human mental life and behavior. Throughout, we wrestle with some thorny questions about how physical mechanisms are translated into psychological meanings and consider whether our subjective experience is little more than a shadow cast by our neurons, hormones, and genes.

NEURONS: BASIC UNITS OF THE NERVOUS SYSTEM

Nerve cells, or **neurons,** are the basic units of the nervous system. Appreciating a sunset, swaying to music, pining for a lover 500 miles away, or praying for forgiveness—all of these acts reflect the coordinated action of thousands or millions of neurons. We do not, of course, *experience* ourselves as systems of interacting nerve cells, any more than we experience hunger as the depletion of sugar in the bloodstream. We think, we feel, we hurt, we want. But we do all these things through the silent, behind-the-scenes activity of neurons, which carry information from cell to cell within the nervous system as well as to and from muscles and organs.

No one knows how many neurons are in the nervous system; the best estimates range from 10 to 100 billion in the brain alone (Stevens, 1979). Some neurons connect with as many as 30,000 neurons, although the average neuron transmits information to about 1000 (Damasio, 1994).

The nervous system is composed of three kinds of neurons: sensory neurons, motor neurons, and interneurons. **Sensory neurons** (also called *afferent neurons*) transmit information from sensory cells called receptors (that is, cells that *receive* sensory information) to the brain, either directly or by way of the spinal cord. Thus, sensory neurons might send information to the brain about the sensations perceived as a sunset or a sore throat. **Motor neurons** (or *efferent neurons*) transmit commands from the brain to the glands and muscles of the body, most often through the spinal cord. Motor neurons carry out both voluntary actions, such as grabbing a glass of water, and vital bodily functions, such as digestion and heartbeat. **Interneurons** connect other neurons with one another and comprise the vast majority of neurons in the brain and spinal cord.

ANATOMY OF A NEURON

No two neurons are exactly alike in form, size, and shape, but their cellular structure is basically the same. The main part of the neuron is the **cell body,** or *soma* (Figure 3.1). The cell body includes a nucleus that contains the genetic material of the cell (the chromosomes) as well as other structures vital to cell functioning. Like other cells, the neuron is surrounded by a membrane made of lipids (fats) and proteins that transport chemicals across the membrane and receive signals from other cells. Neurons are held in place in much of the nervous system by *glial cells* ("glial" means glue), which also insulate the neurons from messages not "intended" for them.

Branchlike extensions of the cell body, called **dendrites,** receive information from other cells. If a neuron receives enough stimulation through its dendrites and cell body, it passes information to other neurons through its axon. The **axon** is a long extension—occasionally as long as several feet—that frequently has two or more offshoots, or **collateral branches.**

The axons of all but the shortest neurons in the nervous system are covered with a **myelin sheath,** a tight coat of cells composed primarily of lipids. Myelinated axons give some portions of the brain a white appearance (hence the term *"white matter"*). The "gray matter" of the brain gets its color from cell bodies, dendrites, and unmyelinated axons.

The myelin sheath insulates the axon from chemical or physical stimuli that might interfere with the transmission of nerve impulses, much as the coating of a wire prevents electrical currents from getting crossed. The myelin sheath can also dramatically increase the speed of transmission of messages. It does this by capitalizing on the fact that between the cells that form the sheath are small spaces of "bare wire" called **nodes of Ranvier.** When a neuron **fires** (is activated enough to send information to other neurons), the electrical impulse is rapidly conducted from node to node, like an express train that does not have to stop at every station.

Not all axons are myelinated at birth. The transmission of impulses along these axons is slow and arduous, which helps explain why babies have such poor motor control. As myelination occurs in areas of the nervous system involved in motor action, an infant becomes capable of reaching and pointing. Such developmental achievements can be reversed in *demyelinating* diseases such as multiple sclerosis. In these disorders, degeneration of the myelin sheath on large clusters of axons can cause jerky, uncoordinated movement, although for reasons not well understood, the disease often goes into remission and the symptoms temporarily disappear. Multiple sclerosis and other diseases that progressively strip axons of their myelin may be fatal, particularly if they strike the neurons that control basic life-support processes such as the beating of the heart.

At the end of an axon are **terminal buttons,** which send signals from a neuron to adjacent cells and are triggered by the electrical impulse that has traveled down the axon. These signals are then typically received by the dendrites or cell bodies of other neurons, although they may also be received by muscle or gland cells. Connections between neurons occur at **synapses.** Two neurons do not actually touch at a synapse; instead, a space exists between the two, called the **synaptic cleft.** Not all synapses actually occur at terminal buttons at the end of an axon; in the brain, many synapses are located directly on it.

INTERIM SUMMARY   The nervous system is the interacting network of nerve cells that underlies all psychological activity. **Neurons** are the basic units of the nervous system. **Sensory neurons** carry sensory information from sensory receptors to the central nervous system. **Motor neurons** transmit commands from the brain to the glands and muscles of the body. **Interneurons** connect neurons with one another. Neurons generally have a **cell body, dendrites** (branchlike extensions of the cell body), and an **axon** that carries information to other neurons. Neurons connect at **synapses.**

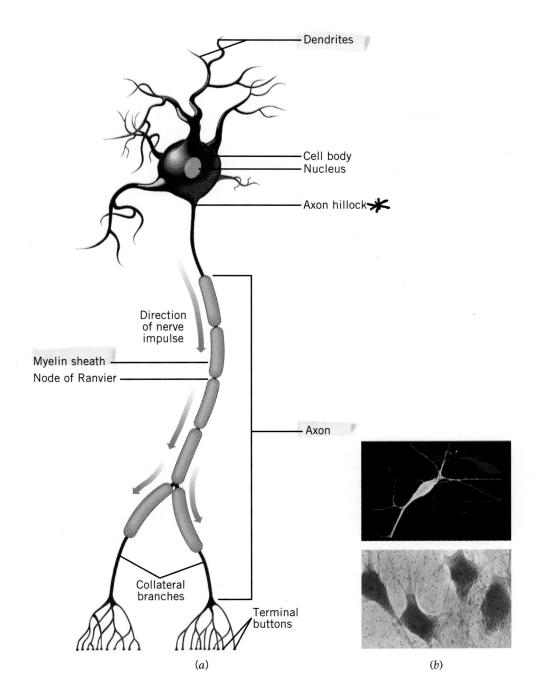

Dendrites

Cell body
Nucleus

Axon hillock

Direction
of nerve
impulse

Myelin sheath
Node of Ranvier

Axon

Collateral
branches

Terminal
buttons

(a)

(b)

FIGURE 3.1
The anatomy of a neuron. (*a*) The branched fibers called dendrites receive neural information from other neurons and pass it down the axon. The terminal buttons then release neurotransmitters, chemicals that transmit information to other cells. (*b*) As can be seen, actual neurons differ in their shape throughout the nervous system. The top photo shows a neuron in the most evolutionary recent part of the brain, the cerebral cortex, which is involved in the most complex psychological processes. The bottom photo shows neurons in the spinal cord, which is a much older structure. These images were magnified using an electron microscope.

FIRING OF A NEURON

Most neurons communicate at the synapse through a process that involves electrical and chemical changes. To understand this process, we examine how neurons function in their normal resting state and the events that lead them to fire.

Resting Potentials

When a neuron is "at rest," its membrane is *polarized*, like two sides of a battery: Inside the membrane is a negative electrical charge, whereas the fluid outside the cell has a positive charge. This polarized state reflects the fact that the cell membrane naturally lets some chemicals in, keeps others out, and actively pumps some in and out. (In a sense, neurons are never really at rest, since they use vast amounts of energy to pump chemicals across their membranes.)

A combination of chemicals normally exists inside and outside the membrane, the most important of which are sodium (Na^+), potassium (K^+), and chloride (Cl^-) ions. (An *ion* is an atom or small molecule that carries an electrical charge.) Outside the cell is a fluid much like the seawater within which the most primitive cells appear to have evolved millions of years ago. Thus, sodium and chloride ions tend to concentrate on the outside of the cell. (Sodium chloride, or NaCl, is salt.) The cell membrane of a neuron is typically not permeable to positively charged sodium ions; that is, these ions cannot easily get through the membrane, so they tend to accumulate outside the neuron. The membrane is also completely impermeable to a variety of negatively charged protein ions inside the cell that are involved in carrying out its basic functions. As a result, the electrical charge is normally more negative on the inside than on the outside of the cell.

This "resting" condition, in which the neuron is not firing, is called the **resting potential.** (It is called a *potential* because the cell has a stored-up source of energy, which has the potential to be used.) At its resting potential, the difference between the electrical charge inside and outside the neuron is about –70 millivolts (mV). (A volt is a standard unit of electricity, and a millivolt is one-thousandth of a volt.) Researchers discovered this by inserting tiny electrodes (materials that conduct electricity) on the inside and outside of the cell membrane of animals with the largest neurons they could find and measuring the electrical potential across the membrane.

Graded Potentials

When a neuron is stimulated by another, one of two things can happen. The stimulation can reduce the membrane's polarization, decreasing the voltage discrepancy between the inside and the outside. For instance, the resting potential might move from –70 to –60 mV. Alternatively, stimulation from another neuron can *increase* polarization. Typically, a decrease in polarization **(depolarization)** stems from an influx of positive sodium ions. As a result, the charge inside the cell membrane becomes less negative. The opposite state of affairs—increasing the electrical difference between the inside and outside of the cell—is called **hyperpolarization.** This condition usually results from an outflow of potassium ions, which are also positively charged, or an influx of negatively charged chloride ions; as a result, the potential across the membrane becomes even more negative.

Most of these brief voltage changes occur at synapses along the neuron's dendrites and cell body; they then spread down the cell membrane like ripples on a pond. These spreading voltage changes, which occur when the neural membrane receives a signal from another cell, are called **graded potentials,** and they have two notable characteristics. First, their strength diminishes as they travel along the cell membrane away from the source of the stimulation, just as the ripples on a pond grow smaller with distance from a tossed stone's point of impact. Second, graded potentials are cumulative, or additive. If a neuron is simultaneously depolarized by +2 mV at one point on a dendrite and hyperpolarized by –2 mV at an adjacent point, the two graded potentials add up to zero and essentially cancel each other out. In contrast, if the membrane of a neuron is depolarized at multiple points, a progressively greater influx of positive ions occurs, producing a "ripple" all the way down the cell body to the axon.

Action Potentials

If this cumulative electrical "ripple" crosses a certain threshold, depolarizing the membrane at the axon from its resting state of –70 mV to about –50 mV, a sudden

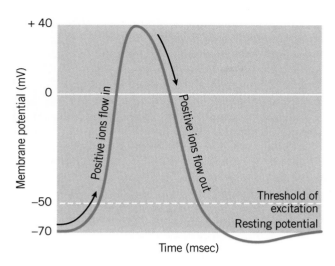

FIGURE 3.2
An action potential. This figure depicts the firing of a neuron as recorded by two electrodes, one inside the membrane of the axon and the other just outside the membrane. When a neuron is depolarized to about –50 mV (the threshold of excitation), an influx of positively charged ions briefly creates an action potential. An outpouring of positive ions then contributes to restoring the neuron to its resting potential. (This outpouring actually overshoots the mark briefly, so that for a brief instant after firing the potential across the membrane is slightly more negative than –70mV.)

change occurs. For a flicker of an instant, the membrane is totally permeable to positive sodium ions, which have accumulated outside the membrane. These ions pour in, changing the potential across the membrane to about +40 mV (Figure 3.2). Thus, the charge on the inside of the cell becomes momentarily positive. An outpouring of positive potassium ions then rapidly restores the neuron to its resting potential, rendering the charge inside the cell negative once again. This entire electrochemical process typically takes less than 2 milliseconds (msec, or thousandths of a second).

The shift in polarity across the membrane and subsequent restoration of the resting potential is called an **action potential,** or the "firing" of the neuron. The action potential rapidly spreads down the length of the axon to the terminal buttons. Unlike a graded potential, an action potential (or *nerve impulse*) is not cumulative. Instead, it has an **all-or-none** quality: It either occurs or does not. In this sense, the firing of a neuron is like the firing of a gun. Unless the trigger is pulled hard enough, the amount of pressure placed on the trigger below that threshold does not matter. Once the threshold is crossed, however, the trigger gives way, the gun fires, and the trigger springs back, ready to be pulled once more.

Although action potentials seem more dramatic, in many ways the prime movers behind psychological processes are graded potentials. Graded potentials create *new* information at the cellular level by integrating signals from multiple sources (multiple synapses). Action potentials, in contrast, can only pass along information already collected without changing it.

INTERIM SUMMARY   When a neuron is at rest (its **resting potential**), it is polarized, with a negative charge inside the cell membrane and a positive charge outside. When a neuron is stimulated by another, its cell membrane is either **depolarized** or **hyperpolarized.** The spreading voltage changes along the cell membrane that occur as one neuron is excited by other neurons are called **graded potentials.** If the cell membrane is depolarized by enough graded potentials, the neuron will fire. This is called an **action potential,** or nerve impulse.

TRANSMISSION OF INFORMATION BETWEEN CELLS

When a nerve impulse travels down an axon, it sets in motion a series of events that can lead to transmission of information to other cells. Figure 3.3 presents a simplified diagram of a synaptic connection between two neurons. The neuron that is sending an impulse is called the **presynaptic neuron** (that is, *before* the synapse); the cell receiving the impulse is the **postsynaptic neuron.**

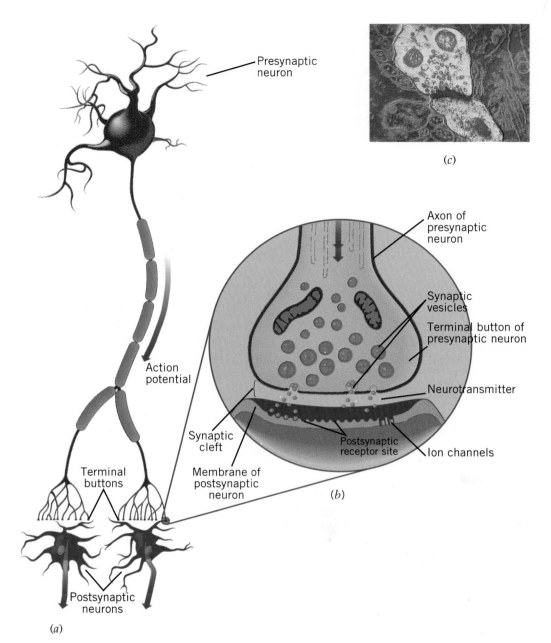

(c)

Presynaptic neuron

Axon of presynaptic neuron

Synaptic vesicles

Terminal button of presynaptic neuron

Neurotransmitter

Action potential

Synaptic cleft

Postsynaptic receptor site

Ion channels

Membrane of postsynaptic neuron

(b)

Terminal buttons

Postsynaptic neurons

(a)

FIGURE 3.3

(a) Transmission of a nerve impulse. When an action potential occurs, the nerve impulse travels along the axon until it reaches the synaptic vesicles. The synaptic vesicles release neurotransmitters into the synaptic cleft. (b) The neurotransmitters then bind with postsynaptic receptors and produce a graded potential on the membrane of the postsynaptic neuron. Receptors are strings of amino acids (the building blocks of proteins) suspended in the fatty membrane of the postsynaptic neuron. Typically, several strands of these proteins extend outside the cell into the synapse, where they detect the presence of neurotransmitters and may transport them through the membrane. Other strands remain on the inside of the cell and send information to the nucleus of the cell, alerting it, for example, to open or close channels in the membrane (called ion channels) in order to let various ions in or out. (c) An electron micrograph of a synapse.

Neurotransmitters and Receptors

Within the terminal buttons of a neuron are small sacs called **synaptic vesicles.** These sacs contain **neurotransmitters** (also called *transmitter substances*), chemicals that transmit information from one cell to another. When the presynaptic neuron fires, the synaptic vesicles in its terminal buttons move toward the cell's membrane (the presynaptic membrane). Some of them adhere to the membrane and break open, releasing neurotransmitters into the synaptic cleft.

Once in the synaptic cleft, some of these chemical molecules then bind with protein molecules in the *post*synaptic membrane called **receptors.** Receptors act like locks that can be opened only by particular keys. In this case, the keys are neurotransmitters in the synaptic cleft. When a receptor binds with the neurotransmitter that fits it—in both molecular structure and electrical charge—the chemical and electrical balance of the postsynaptic cell membrane changes, producing a graded potential—a ripple in the neuronal pond.

The Effects of Neurotransmitters

Neurotransmitters can either *increase* or *decrease* neural firing. **Excitatory neurotransmitters** depolarize the postsynaptic cell membrane, making an action potential more likely. (That is, they *excite* the neuron.) In contrast, **inhibitory neurotransmitters** hyperpolarize the membrane (increase its polarization); this reduces the likelihood that the postsynaptic neuron will fire (or *inhibits* firing). Excitatory neurotransmitters thus grease the wheels of neural communication, whereas inhibitory neurotransmitters put on the brakes. A neuron can also release more than one neurotransmitter, affecting the cells to which it is connected in various ways.

Aside from being excitatory or inhibitory, neurotransmitters differ in another important respect. Some, like the ones we have been describing, are released into a specific synapse and only affect the neuron at the other end of the synaptic cleft (the postsynaptic neuron). Others have a much wider radius of impact and remain active considerably longer. Once released, they find their way into multiple synapses, where they can affect any neuron within reach that has the appropriate chemicals in its membrane. The primary impact of these transmitter substances, called *neuromodulators*, is to increase or decrease (that is, *modulate*) the impact of other neurotransmitters released into the synapse.

Types of Neurotransmitters

A decade ago, researchers only knew of a handful of neurotransmitters. Progress in the understanding of neural transmission has proceeded so rapidly, however, that we now know of at least 75 substances that can transmit messages between neurons. For example, **epinephrine** and **norepinephrine** are involved in emotional arousal, particularly fear and anxiety. **Endorphins** are chemicals that elevate mood and reduce pain (Watkins & Mayer, 1982). Endorphins have a range of effects, from the numbness people often feel immediately after tearing a muscle (which wears off once these natural pain killers stop flowing), to the "runner's high" athletes sometimes report after a prolonged period of exercise (see Hoffman, 1997). The word "endorphin" comes from *endogenous* (meaning "produced within the body") and *morphine* (a chemical substance derived from opium that elevates mood and reduces pain). Opium and similar narcotic drugs kill pain and elevate mood because they stimulate receptors in the brain specialized for endorphins. Essentially, narcotics "pick the locks" normally opened by endorphins.

Table 3.1 describes some of the best-understood neurotransmitters, although our knowledge remains incomplete. We will briefly examine five of them: glutamate, GABA, dopamine, serotonin, and acetylcholine.

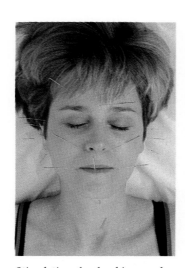

Stimulation of endorphins may be responsible in part for the pain-killing effects of acupuncture.

TABLE 3.1   PARTIAL LIST OF NEUROTRANSMITTERS

TRANSMITTER SUBSTANCE	SOME OF ITS KNOWN EFFECTS
Glutamate	Excitation of neurons throughout the nervous system
GABA (gamma-aminobutyric acid)	Inhibition of neurons in the brain
Glycene	Inhibition of neurons in the spinal cord and lower brain
Dopamine	Emotional arousal, pleasure, and reward; voluntary movement; attention
Serotonin	Sleep and emotional arousal; aggression; pain regulation
Acetylcholine (ACh)	Learning and memory
Epinephrine and norepinephrine	Emotional arousal, anxiety, and fear
Endorphins and enkephalins	Pain relief and elevation of mood

Note: The effect of a neurotransmitter depends on the type of receptor it fits. Each neurotransmitter can activate different receptors, depending on where in the nervous system the receptor is located. Thus, the impact of any neurotransmitter depends less on the neurotransmitter itself than on the receptor it unlocks; in fact, some neurotransmitters can have an excitatory effect at one synapse and an inhibitory effect at another.

Glutamate and GABA   **Glutamate** (glutamic acid) and **GABA** (gamma-aminobutyric acid) are two of the most widespread neurotransmitters in the nervous system. Glutamate can excite nearly every neuron in the nervous system, whereas GABA has the opposite effect in the brain, playing an inhibitory role. One of the reasons glutamate and GABA are so important is that they not only bind with specific receptors like other neurotransmitters but they also act directly on the axons of neurons, lowering or raising their threshold for firing.

Glutamate is involved in many psychological processes, but recent research suggests that it may play an important role in learning (Blokland, 1997; Izquierdo & Medina, 1997). Some people respond to the MSG (monosodium glutamate) in Chinese food with neurological symptoms such as tingling and numbing because this ingredient activates glutamate receptors.

Roughly one-third of all the neurons in the brain use GABA for synaptic communication (Petty, 1995). GABA is particularly important in the regulation of anxiety; drugs like valium and alcohol that bind with its receptors tend to reduce anxiety. Low levels of GABA may also be related to both severe depression and mania.

Dopamine   **Dopamine** has wide-ranging effects in the nervous system (Baldessarini & Tarazi, 1996). Some neural pathways that rely on dopamine are involved in the experience of pleasure and in the learning of behaviors associated with reward. Drugs ranging from marijuana to heroin increase the release of dopamine in these pathways; the addictive quality of many drugs is related in part to this effect (Wicklegren, 1996). Other dopamine pathways are involved in movement, attention, decision making, and other cognitive processes. Abnormally high levels of dopamine in some parts of the brain have been linked to schizophrenia (Chapter 15).

Degeneration of the dopamine-releasing neurons in a part of the brain called the *substantia nigra* (literally, "dark substance") causes **Parkinson's disease,** a disorder characterized by uncontrollable tremors, a general slowing down, and difficulty both initiating behavior (such as standing up) or stopping movements that are already in progress (such as walking forward). Physicians discovered the role of the substantia nigra in this disorder when they noticed the lack of this region's

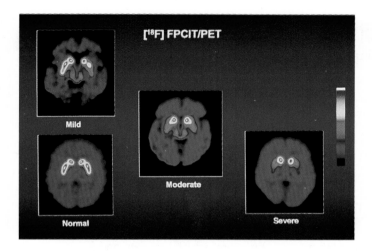

These PET scans contrast the brain of a normal volunteer (left) with that of a patient with Parkinson's disease (center and right). Areas of the brain that normally use dopamine and control movement are less active in the Parkinsonian brain. Brighter areas indicate more activity.

typical coloration in an autopsied Parkinson's patient; the dark color is normally a byproduct of chemical reactions involving dopamine. Although disordered movement is the most visible sign of Parkinson's disease, other symptoms can include depression and a general slowing of thought that parallels the slowing of behavior (Rao et al., 1992; Tandberg et al., 1996).

Because the victims of encephalitis lethargica described at the beginning of this chapter showed Parkinsonian symptoms, researchers believed the dopamine-rich neurons in the substantia nigra and areas of the brain connected to it had been destroyed; autopsies of patients with the disease corroborated this hypothesis. Physicians therefore tried treating these patients, who had virtually been asleep for decades, with L-dopa, a chemical that readily converts to dopamine and had recently proven effective in treating Parkinson's disease. Dopamine itself cannot be administered because it cannot cross the *blood–brain barrier*, which normally protects the brain from foreign substances in the blood. (The blood–brain barrier results from the fact that the cells in the blood vessels of the brain tend to be so tightly packed that large molecules have difficulty entering).

Unfortunately, only a small percentage of even L-dopa gets past the blood–brain barrier. The rest affects neurons in the rest of the body and can cause side effects such as nausea, vomiting, and shortness of breath. The L-dopa that *does* make its way into the brain can also have unwanted consequences because the brain uses dopamine for neural transmission in many regions and for different purposes. L-dopa can thus reduce Parkinsonian symptoms, but it can also produce disordered thinking (such as hallucinations) or movement disorders other than Parkinson's. For example, Ms. B, the victim of the 1917 encephalitis epidemic, developed a "touching tic," whereby she had to touch everything she passed. For many patients, however, symptoms such as tics were a minor price to pay for reawakening.

Serotonin   Like other neurotransmitters, **serotonin** serves a variety of functions. It appears to be involved in the regulation of mood, sleep, eating, arousal, and pain. Decreased serotonin in the brain is common in severe depression, which often responds to medications that increase serotonin activity. People who are depressed often have trouble sleeping and eating, in part because the disruption of serotonin activity that may accompany depression can also affect these other functions.

Serotonin plays an inhibitory role in most sites in the nervous system. For example, serotonin appears to inhibit neural circuits involved in aggression. Low serotonin levels have been found in aggressive rhesus monkeys (Higley et al., 1992) as well as in antisocial adult humans and delinquent children (Kruesi et al., 1992). Studies that have manipulated serotonin levels experimentally, using

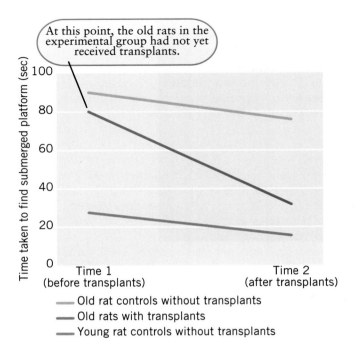

FIGURE 3.4
Neural transplants and learning in aged rats. The investigators compared three groups: old rats without transplants, old rats with transplants, and unimpaired young rat controls. The investigators tested the rats' learning ability by seeing how long they would take to learn to swim to a platform submerged under water. Old rats given transplants showed remarkable improvements in their ability to learn this task compared to untreated old rats, as measured by their response time. *Source*: Adapted from Bjorklund & Gage, 1985.

chemicals that affect the availability of serotonin in the brain, have similarly found an association between low serotonin and aggression, at least in males (Cleare and Bond, 1997).

Acetylcholine   Another neurotransmitter of considerable importance is **acetylcholine (ACh),** which is involved in learning and memory. For example, experiments have shown increased ACh activity in rats learning to discriminate one stimulus from another, in comparison to rats in control conditions that do not require learning (Butt et al., 1997).

A key piece of evidence linking ACh to learning and memory is the fact that patients with Alzheimer's disease, which destroys memory, show depletions in ACh. Transplanting tissue rich in ACh has led to markedly improved functioning in learning-impaired rats. The results of one such study are reproduced in Figure 3.4. In this study, old rats with neural transplants performed substantially better on a learning task than same-aged peers without the transplants (Bjorklund & Gage, 1985). Brain-grafting techniques of this sort hold the promise of helping patients with a variety of degenerative neurological disorders (such as Parkinson's disease), although their use in humans remains years away (Iwashita et al., 1994).

INTERIM SUMMARY   Within the terminal buttons of the **presynaptic neuron** are **neurotransmitters,** such as glutamate, GABA, dopamine, serotonin, and acetycholine. Neurotransmitters transmit information from one neuron to another as they are released into the synapse from the synaptic vesicles. They bind with **receptors** in the membrane of the postsynaptic neuron, which produces graded potentials that can either excite or inhibit the postsynaptic neuron from firing.

THE ENDOCRINE SYSTEM

Neurotransmitters are not the only chemicals that transmit psychologically significant messages. The **endocrine system** is a collection of glands that secrete chemicals directly into the bloodstream; these chemicals are called **hormones**

(Figure 3.5). Like neurotransmitters, hormones bind with receptors in cell membranes, but because they travel through the bloodstream, they can simultaneously activate many cells in the body as long as these cells are equipped with the right receptors. The chemical structure of some hormones is similar or even identical to that of some neurotransmitters. The hormone **adrenalin,** for example, is the same compound as the neurotransmitter epinephrine; similarly, the chemical structure of the hormone **noradrenalin** is the same as norepinephrine.

The endocrine system is thus a second system for intercellular communication, but it does not rely on the kind of intricate "wiring" between cells used by the nervous system. The difference between the methods of communication used by the two systems is like the difference between word of mouth—which requires transmission from one person to the next—and mass media—which can communicate information to millions of people at once. The endocrine system "broadcasts" its signals by releasing hormones into the bloodstream. Its messages are less specific but readily "heard" throughout the body.

In many instances the endocrine and nervous systems send simultaneous messages. When a person faces an emergency, the adrenal glands release adrenalin into the bloodstream. At the same time, neurons send "word-of-mouth" impulses by releasing epinephrine and its close cousin, norepinephrine, into synapses at strategic locations in the nervous system. These parallel actions ready the body for emergency in a variety of ways, such as increasing heart rate and diverting blood to the muscles and away from internal organs such as the stomach. People typically remain in a slightly aroused state and continue to feel jittery after a crisis (or a horror movie) is over because the bloodstream continues to contain elevated levels of adrenalin for minutes or even hours after the neurons have stopped firing.

Endocrine glands perform many functions other than readying the body for

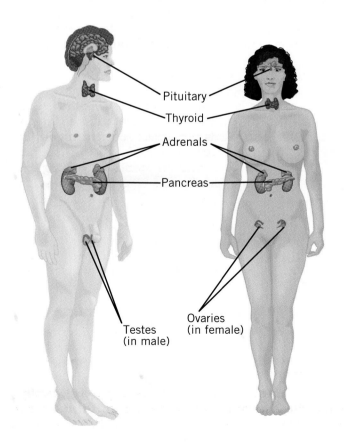

Pituitary

Thyroid

Adrenals

Pancreas

Testes
(in male)

Ovaries
(in female)

FIGURE 3.5
The major endocrine glands. The endocrine system is a series of glands that rely on hormonal communication to activate cells throughout the body.

emergency. The **pituitary gland** is an oval structure about the size of a pea that is located in the brain. It is often described as the "master gland" because some of the hormones it releases stimulate and regulate the other glands. The pituitary is connected more directly to the central nervous system than any of the other endocrine glands.

The **thyroid gland**, located in the neck, releases a hormone that controls metabolism (transformation of food into energy). The thyroid gland also affects energy levels and mood (Haggerty et al., 1993). People with **hypothyroidism**, or an underactive thyroid (*hypo* means "under"), sometimes require artificial replacement of thyroid hormones to relieve sluggishness and depression. One study found a 10 percent incidence of undiagnosed hypothyroidism in patients complaining of depression (Gold & Pearsall, 1983).

The **adrenal glands** are located above the kidneys. (The Latin *ad renal* means "toward the kidney.") These glands secrete adrenalin and other hormones during emergencies. Another endocrine gland, the **pancreas,** is located near the stomach and produces hormones that control blood-sugar level.

The **gonads** influence sexual development and behavior. The male gonads, or **testes,** are located in the testicles; the most important hormone they produce is **testosterone.** The female gonads, the **ovaries,** produce **estrogens.** In both sexes, these hormones control not only sex drive but also the development of secondary sex characteristics such as growth of breasts in females, deepened voice in males, and pubic hair in both sexes.

INTERIM SUMMARY   The **endocrine system** is a collection of glands that control various bodily functions through the secretion of **hormones.** The endocrine system complements the cell-to-cell communication of the nervous system by sending global messages through the bloodstream. Hormones are like neurotransmitters, except that they travel through the bloodstream and can thus activate many cells simultaneously.

THE PERIPHERAL NERVOUS SYSTEM

Although the endocrine system plays an important role in psychological functioning, the center of our psychological experience is the nervous system. The nervous system has two major divisions, the central nervous system and the peripheral nervous system (Figures 3.6 and 3.7). The **central nervous system (CNS)** consists of the brain and spinal cord; the **peripheral nervous system (PNS)** consists of neurons that convey messages to and from the central nervous system. We begin with the peripheral nervous system, which has two subdivisions: the somatic and the autonomic nervous systems.

THE SOMATIC NERVOUS SYSTEM

The **somatic nervous system** transmits sensory information to the central nervous system and carries out its motor commands. Sensory neurons receive information through receptors in the eyes, ears, skin, muscles, and other parts of the body such as the tongue. Motor neurons direct the action of skeletal muscles. Because the somatic nervous system is involved in intentional actions, such as standing up or shaking someone's hand, it is sometimes called the *voluntary nervous system.* However, the somatic nervous system also directs some involuntary or automatic actions, such as adjustments in posture or balance.

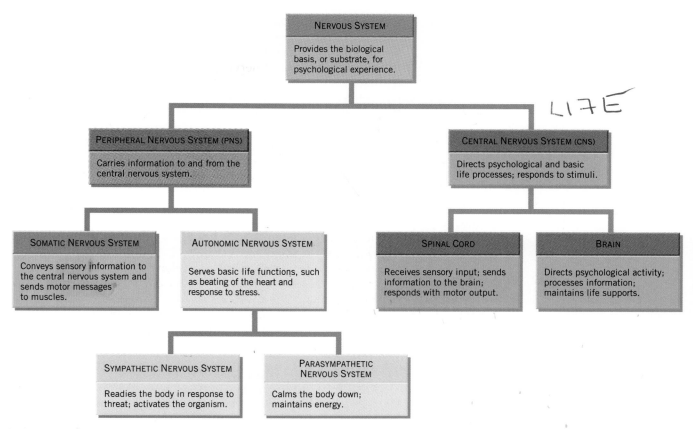

FIGURE 3.6
Divisions of the nervous system.

THE AUTONOMIC NERVOUS SYSTEM

The **autonomic nervous system** conveys information to and from internal bodily structures that carry out basic life processes such as digestion and respiration. It consists of two parts: the sympathetic and the parasympathetic nervous systems. Although these systems work together, their functions are often opposed or complementary. In broadest strokes, one can think of the sympathetic nervous system as an emergency system and the parasympathetic nervous system as a "business-as-usual" system (Figure 3.8).

The **sympathetic nervous system** is typically activated in response to threats. Its job is to ready the body for fight or flight, which it does in several ways. It stops digestion, since diverting blood away from the stomach re-directs the blood to the muscles, which may need extra oxygen for an emergency response. It increases heart rate, dilates the pupils, and causes hairs on the body and head to stand erect. It is also involved in other states of intense activation, such as ejaculation in males.

By preparing the organism to respond to emergencies, the sympathetic nervous system serves an important adaptive function. Sometimes, however, the sympathetic cavalry comes to the rescue when least wanted. A surge of anxiety, tremors, sweating, dry mouth, and a palpitating heart may have helped prepare our ancestors to flee from a hungry lion, but they are less welcome when trying to deliver a speech. Similar physiological reactions occur in panic attacks, which include symptoms such as intense anxiety, tremors, and palpitating heart (Chapter 15).

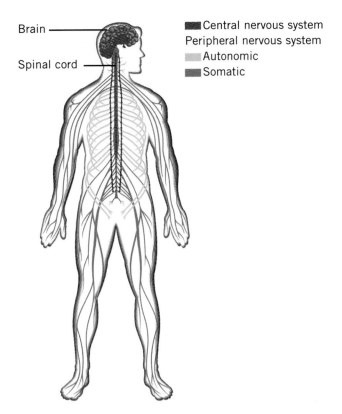

Brain

Spinal cord

■ Central nervous system
Peripheral nervous system
▨ Autonomic
■ Somatic

FIGURE 3.7
The nervous system. The nervous system consists of the brain, the spinal cord, and the neurons of the peripheral nervous system that carry information to and from these central nervous system structures.

The **parasympathetic nervous system** supports more mundane, or routine, activities that maintain the body's store of energy, such as regulating blood-sugar levels, secreting saliva, and eliminating wastes. It also participates in functions such as regulating heart rate and pupil size. The relationship between the sympathetic and parasympathetic nervous systems is in many ways a balancing act: When an emergency has passed, the parasympathetic nervous system resumes control, reversing sympathetic responses and returning to the normal business of storing and maintaining resources.

A good illustration of the way these two systems interact—and how their interaction can be derailed—is sexual activity. In males, the parasympathetic nervous system controls the flow of blood to the penis; it is thus responsible for engorging the blood vessels that produce an erection. In females, parasympathetic processes are similarly involved in vaginal lubrication. Ejaculation, however, is controlled by the sympathetic nervous system, which is likely involved in female orgasms as well.

The capacity to become excited and experience orgasm thus depends on the synchronized activation of the parasympathetic and sympathetic nervous systems. If a man experiences sympathetic activation too early, he loses his capacity to sustain an erection and may ejaculate prematurely. Conversely, if he does not experience sympathetic activation, ejaculation will not take place (Kimble, 1992). In women, poor coordination of sympathetic and parasympathetic activity may inhibit vaginal lubrication and thus hinder sexual pleasure.

In a society that places a premium on sexual performance, a few disappointing sexual experiences can disrupt the delicate balance between sympathetic and parasympathetic activation. For example, a man who experiences a brief period of difficulty maintaining sexual excitement may begin to see himself as a failure sexually and become more anxious with each new encounter. The anxiety, in turn,

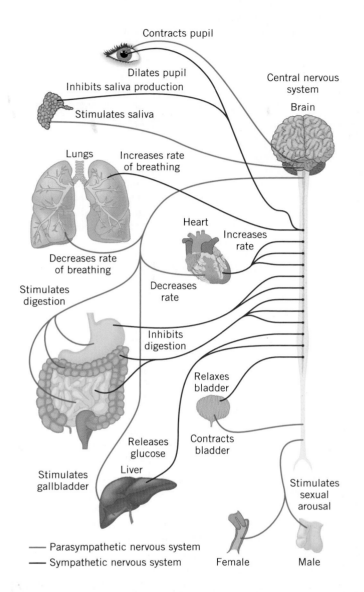

Contracts pupil

Dilates pupil

Inhibits saliva production

Stimulates saliva

Central nervous system

Brain

Lungs

Increases rate of breathing

Decreases rate of breathing

Heart

Increases rate

Decreases rate

Stimulates digestion

Inhibits digestion

Relaxes bladder

Contracts bladder

Releases glucose

Stimulates gallbladder

Liver

Stimulates sexual arousal

— Parasympathetic nervous system
— Sympathetic nervous system

Female   Male

FIGURE 3.8
The sympathetic and parasympathetic divisions of the autonomic nervous system.

The sympathetic nervous system is involved in fight-or-flight responses in the face of threat.

can inhibit the parasympathetic activation that normally leads to erection, setting in motion a cycle in which sympathetic activation and feelings of anxiety fuel each other and create a full-fledged problem in sexual functioning. This example illustrates the interaction of psychological experience, physiological processes, and culture. Based on cultural standards of sexual performance, a transitory dysfunction (failure to sustain an erection) leads the person to feel anxious and inadequate, which then exacerbates the initial psychobiological condition.

Interim Summary   The nervous system consists of the **central nervous system (CNS)** and the **peripheral nervous system (PNS).** Neurons of the PNS carry messages to and from the central nervous system. The PNS has two subdivisions: the somantic nervous system and the autonomic nervous system. The **somantic nervous** system consists of sensory neurons that carry sensory information to the brain and motor neurons that direct the action of skeletal muscles. The **autonomic nervous system** controls basic life processes such as beating of the heart, workings of the digestive system, and breathing. It consists of two parts, the **sympathetic nervous system,** which is activated primarily in response to threats (but is also involved in general emotional arousal), and the **parasympathetic nervous system,** which is involved in more "mundane" activities such as maintaining the body's energy resources and restoring the system to an even keel following sympathetic activation.

The Central Nervous System

The peripheral nervous system reflects a complex job of neural wiring, but the human central nervous system is probably the most remarkable feat of electrical engineering ever accomplished. Understanding the way it functions requires some knowledge of its evolution.

Evolution of the Central Nervous System

If an engineer were to design the command center for an organism like ours from scratch, it would probably not look much like the human central nervous system. The reason is that, at every evolutionary juncture, nature has had to work with the *structures* (collections of cells that perform particular functions) already in place. The modifications made by natural selection have thus been sequential, one building on the next. For example, initially no organisms had color vision; the world of the ancestors of all contemporary sighted organisms was like a black-and-white movie. Gradually the capacity to perceive certain colors emerged in some species, conferring an adaptive advantage on organisms that could now, for instance, more easily distinguish one type of vegetation from another. The human central nervous system, like that of all animals, is like a living fossil record: The further down one goes (almost literally, from the upper layers of the brain down to the spinal cord), the more one sees ancient structures that evolved hundreds of millions of years ago and were shared—and continue to be shared—by most other vertebrates (animals with spinal cords).

It is tempting to think of nature's creatures as arranged on a scale from simple to complex, beginning with organisms like amoebas, then moving up the ladder perhaps to pets and farm animals, and on to the highest form of life, ourselves (see Butler & Hodos, 1996). And in a sense, there is something to this; after all, *we* can dissect the brain of a frog, but a frog cannot return the favor.

One must always remember, however, that natural selection is a process that favors *adaptation to a niche,* and different niches require different adaptations. I would not trade my brain for that of my dog, no matter how endearing he might be, because I would rather be the one throwing than fetching. But my dog has abilities I lack, either because we humans never acquired them or because over time we lost them as our brains evolved in a different direction. My dog can hear things I cannot hear, and he does not need to call out in the dark, "Who's there?" because his nose tells him. And anyone who thinks humans and insects are easy to place on a single, evolutionary scale has never stared a scorpion in the face and asked, "Who is better adapted, you or I?" (Do not try this experiment at home.)

The Evolution of Vertebrates

Our understanding of the evolution of the human nervous system still contains heavy doses of guesswork, but a general outline looks something like the following (Butler & Hodos, 1996; Healy, 1996; Killacky, 1995; Kolb & Whishaw, 1996; MacLean, 1982, 1990). The earliest precursors to vertebrate animals were probably fishlike creatures whose actions were less controlled by a central "executive" like the human brain than by specific, or "local," reactions at particular points along the body. These organisims were likely little more than stimulus–response machines whose actions were controlled by a simple fluid-filled tube of neurons that evolved into the spinal cord. Sensory information from the environment entered the upper side of the cord, and neurons exiting the underside produced automatic responses (reflexes). Vision and smell were likely the first senses to develop and were shared by our most immediate prevertebrate ancestors.

Through evolution, the front end of the spinal cord became specialized to allow more sophisticated processing of information and more flexible motor responses (Figure 3.9). Presumably this end developed because our early ancestors moved forward, head first—which is why our brains are in our heads instead of our feet. The primitive vertebrate brain, or *brainstem*, appears to have had three parts. The foremost section, called the *forebrain*, was specialized for sensation at a very immediate level—smell, and eventually taste. The middle region, or *midbrain*, controlled sensation for distant stimuli—vision and hearing. The back of the brainstem, or *hindbrain*, was specialized for movement, particularly for balance

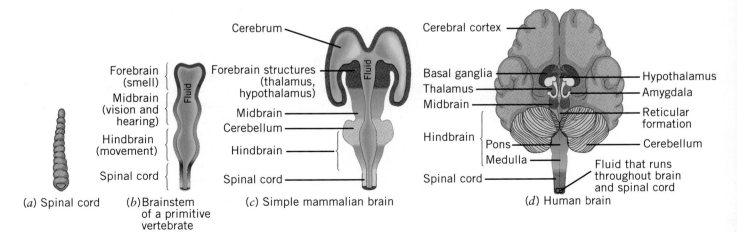

FIGURE 3.9
Evolution of the human brain. (*a*) The earliest central nervous system in the ancestors to contemporary vertebrates was likely a structure similar to the contemporary spinal cord. (*b*) The primitive brain, or brainstem, allowed more complex sensation and movement in vertebrates. (*c*) Among the most important evolutionary developments of mammals was the cerebrum. (*d*) The human brain is a storehouse of knowledge packed in a remarkably small container, the human skull. *Source:* Adapted from Kolb & Whishaw, 1990.

(Sarnat & Netsky, 1974). The hindbrain was also the connecting point between the brain and spinal cord, allowing messages to travel between the two. This rough division of labor in the primitive central nervous system still applies in the spinal cord and brainstem of humans. Many human reflexes, for example, occur precisely as they did, and do, in the simplest vertebrates: Sensory information enters one side of the spinal cord (toward the back of the body in humans, who stand erect), and motor impulses exit the other.

As animals, and particularly mammals, evolved, the most dramatic changes occurred in the hindbrain and forebrain. The hindbrain sprouted an expanded *cerebellum,* which increased the animal's capacity to put together complex movements and make sensory discriminations. The forebrain of contemporary mammals is also probably very different from that of its ancestors. It evolved many new structures, most notably those that comprise the **cerebrum,** the part of the brain most involved in complex thought, which greatly expanded the capacity for processing information and initiating movement (see Finlay & Darlington, 1995). Thus, even relatively simple mammals such as hedgehogs and opossums are able to discriminate and respond to more subtle features of the environment than most fish, whose less developed cerebrum renders them less "cerebral" (Diamond & Hall, 1969). In "brainier" mammals, and especially in humans, considerable evolution has occurred in the many-layered surface of the cerebrum known as the **cortex** (from the Latin word for "bark"). In fact, 80 percent of the human brain's mass is cortex (Kolb & Whishaw, 1996).

The Human Nervous System

Although the human brain and the brains of its early vertebrate and mammalian ancestors differ dramatically, most of the differences are the result of additions to, rather than replacement of, the original brain structures. Two very important consequences flow from this. The first, as we have seen, is that many neural mechanisms are the same in humans and other animals; others differ across species that have evolved in different directions from common ancestors. Generalizations between humans and animals as seemingly different as cats or rats are likely to be more appropriate at lower levels of the nervous system, such as the spinal cord and brainstem, because these lower neural structures were already in place before these species diverged millions of years ago. The human brainstem (which includes most of the structures below the cerebrum) is almost identical to the brainstem of sheep (Kolb & Whishaw, 1996), but the two species differ tremendously in the size, structure, and function of their cortex. Much of the sheep's cortex is devoted to processing sensory information, whereas a greater part of the human cortex is involved in forming complex thoughts, perceptions, and plans for action.

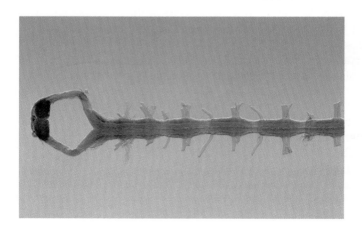

The nervous system of the earthworm includes a spinal cord and a small, simple brain.

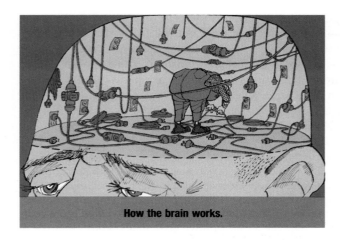

How the brain works.

The second implication is that human psychology bears the distinct imprint of the same relatively primitive structures that guide motivation, learning, and behavior in other animals. This is a sobering thought, which led Darwin to place species on our family tree that we might consider poor relations; led Freud to view our extraordinary capacities to love, create, and understand ourselves and the universe as a thin veneer (only a few millimeters thick, in fact) over primitive structures that motivate our greatest achievements and our most "inhuman" atrocities; and led Skinner to argue that the same laws of learning apply to humans as to other animals.

The human nervous system is thus a set of hierarchically organized structures built layer upon layer over millions of years of evolution. The most primitive centers send information to, and receive information from, higher centers; these higher centers are in turn integrated with, and regulated by, still more advanced areas of the brain. Behavioral and cognitive precision progressively increases from the lower to the higher and more recently evolved structures (Luria, 1973). Thus, the spinal cord can respond to a prick of the skin with a reflex without even consulting the brain, but more complex cognitive activity simultaneously occurs as the person makes sense of what has happened. We reflexively withdraw from a pinprick, but if the source is a vaccine injection, we inhibit our response—though often milliseconds later, since information traveling to and from the brain takes neural time. Responding appropriately requires the integrated functioning of structures from the spinal cord up through the cortex.

Before discussing the major structures of the central nervous system, an important caveat, or caution, is in order. A central debate since the origins of modern neuroscience in the nineteenth century has centered on the extent to which certain functions are localized to specific parts of the brain. One of the most enlightening things about watching a brain scan in action as a person performs even a simple task is just how much of the brain actually "lights up" much of the time. Different regions are indeed specialized for different functions; a severe blow to the head that damages the back of the cortex is more likely to disrupt vision than speech. Knowing that a lesion at the back of the cortex can produce blindness thus suggests that this region is *involved in visual processing* and that it must be relatively intact for normal visual functioning to occur. But this does not mean that this region is the brain's "center" for vision. Every thought, feeling, or psychological attribute is always the result of a *network* of neurons acting in combination.

In the pages that follow, we describe a series of structures as if they were discrete entities. In reality, evolution did not produce a nervous system with neat boundaries. Distinctions among structures, of course, are not simply the whims of neuroanatomists; they are based on qualities such as the appearance, function, and cellular structure of adjacent regions. Nevertheless, where one structure ends and another begins is to some extent arbitrary. Axons from the spinal cord synapse with neurons far into the brain, so that parts of the brain could actually be called spinal. Similarly, progress in the understanding of the brain has led to increased recognition of different functions served by particular clumps of neurons or axons *within* a given structure. Where researchers once asked questions such as "What does the cerebellum do?" today they are more likely to ask about the functions of specific parts of the cerebellum.

INTERIM SUMMARY   The design of the human nervous system, like that of other animals, reflects its evolution. Early precursors to the first vertebrates (animals with spinal cords) probably had minimal centralized control over behavior and instead tended to react with reflexive responses to environmental stimulation at specific points of their bodies. As vertebrates evolved, the front end of the spinal cord became specialized to allow more complex sensory processing and movement. The most primitive vertebrate brain, or brainstem, included a **forebrain** (specialized for sensing nearby stimuli, notably smells and tastes), a **midbrain** (specialized for sensation at a distance, namely vision and hearing), and a **hindbrain** (specialized for control of movement). This rough division of labor persists in contemporary vertebrates, including humans. The forebrain of humans and other contemporary vertebrates includes an expanded **cerebrum,** with a rich network of cells comprising its outer layers or **cortex,** which allows much more sophisticated sensory, cognitive, and motor processes. The human nervous system is a hierarchically organized system with an overall structure that follows its evolution. Evolutionarily more recent centers control, rechannel, and receive feedback from many of the processes that begin at lower levels.

THE SPINAL CORD

As in all vertebrates, neurons in the human spinal cord produce reflexes, as sensory stimulation activates rapid, automatic motor responses. In humans, however, the main function of the **spinal cord** is to transmit information between the brain and the rest of the body. The spinal cord sends information from sensory neurons in various parts of the body to the brain, and it relays motor commands back to muscles and organs (such as the heart and stomach) via motor neurons. In some animals, notably certain species of fish, the spinal cord is more autonomous from the brain. Swishing back and forth in water requires less subtle coordination of movements than walking or climbing, so the spinal cord in these animals can control movement without much involvement of the brain except under special circumstances, such as attack by a predator (Butler & Hudos, 1996).

The spinal cord in humans is segmented, with each segment controlling a different part of the body. By and large, the upper segments control the upper parts of the body and the lower segments the lower body (Figure 3.10). As in the earliest vertebrates, sensory information enters one side of the spinal cord (toward the back of the body), and motor impulses exit the other (toward the front). Outside the cord, bundles of axons from these sensory and motor neurons join together to form 31 pairs (from the two sides of the body) of **spinal nerves;** these nerves carry information to and from the spinal cord to the periphery. Inside the spinal cord, other bundles of axons (*spinal tracts,* which comprise much of the white matter of the cord) send impulses to and from the brain, relaying sensory messages and motor commands. (Outside the central nervous system, bundles of axons are usually called **nerves;** within the brain and spinal cord, they are called **tracts.**)

When the spinal cord is severed, the result is loss of feeling and paralysis at all levels below the injury, which can no longer communicate with the brain. Even with less severe lesions, physicians can often pinpoint the location of spinal damage from patients' descriptions of their symptoms alone. If a patient complains of a lack of feeling in the upper part of the foot and nerve damage to the foot or brain

Actor Christopher Reeves, now an activist for research on spinal cord injuries, become a quadriplegic after breaking his neck, which severed the connection between the brain and all his muscles below the point of the injury.

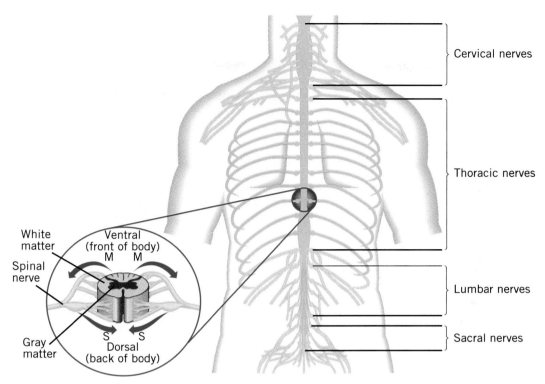

Cervical nerves

Thoracic nerves

Lumbar nerves

Sacral nerves

White matter

Spinal nerve

Gray matter

Ventral (front of body)
M   M

S   S
Dorsal (back of body)

FIGURE 3.10

The spinal cord. Segments of the spinal cord relay information to and from different parts of the body. Sensory fibers relay information to the back of the spine (dorsal), and motor neurons transmit information from the front of the spinal cord (ventral) to the periphery.

has been ruled out, the lowest segment of the spinal cord (the sacral segment) has probably been damaged (Figure 3.10).

<u>INTERIM SUMMARY</u>   The central nervous system (CNS) consists of the brain and spinal cord. The **spinal cord** carries out reflexes, transmits sensory information to the brain, and transmits messages from the brain to the muscles and organs. Each of its segments controls sensation and movement in a different part of the body.

THE HINDBRAIN

Directly above the spinal cord in humans are several structures that comprise the **hindbrain:** the medulla oblongata, cerebellum, and parts of the reticular formation. Another small hindbrain region, the *pons,* is not yet well understood, although it may play some role in learning (Figure 3.11). As in other animals, hindbrain structures link the brain to the spinal cord, sustain life by controlling the supply of air and blood to cells in the body, and regulate arousal level. With the exception of the cerebellum, which sits at the back of the brain and has a distinct appearance, the structures of the hindbrain merge into one another and perform multiple functions as information passes from one structure to the next on its way to higher brain regions.

Medulla Oblongata

Anatomically, the lowest brainstem structure, the **medulla oblongata** (or simply **medulla**), is actually an extension of the spinal cord. Although quite small—about an inch and a half long and three-fourths of an inch wide at its broadest part—the

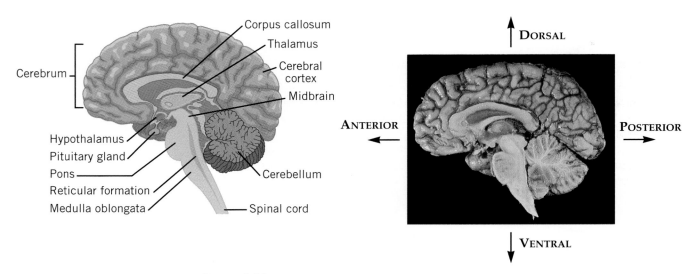

FIGURE 3.11
Cross-section of the human brain. The drawing and accompanying photo show a view of the cerebral cortex and the more primitive structures below the cerebrum. Not shown here are the limbic system and basal ganglia, which are structures within the cerebrum. Also marked on the photo are common terms used to describe location in the brain. For example, a structure toward the front of the brain is described as *anterior* (*ante* means "before"). Not shown are two other directions: *lateral* (toward the left or right side) and *medial* (toward the middle). Thus, a neural pathway through the upper sides of the brain might be described as *dorsolateral* (*dorsal* meaning toward the top of the head, and *lateral* meaning toward the side).

medulla is essential to life, controlling such vital physiological functions as heartbeat, circulation, and respiration. Neither humans nor other animals can survive destruction of the medulla.

The medulla is the link between the spinal cord and the rest of the brain. Here, bundles of axons cross over from each side of the body to the opposite side of the brain. As a result, most of the sensations experienced on the right side of the body, as well as the capacity to move the right side, are controlled by the left side of the brain, and vice versa. Thus, if a person has weakness in the left side of the body following a stroke, the damage to the brain was likely on the right side of the brain.

Cerebellum

The **cerebellum** (Latin for "little cerebrum") is a large structure at the back of the brain. For decades researchers have believed that the cerebellum is exclusively involved in coordinating smooth, well-sequenced movements (such as riding a bike) and in maintaining balance and posture. Staggering and slurred speech after a few too many drinks stem in large part from the effects of alcohol on cerebellar functioning. The cerebellum also takes a pounding when the head is repeatedly snapped back in boxing. Over the span of a boxer's career the damage may be permanent, leading to a movement disorder or slurred speech, particularly if the boxer refuses to retire as his reflexes slow and he takes more punches on the chin. More recently, however, researchers using positron emission tomography (PET) and functional magnetic resonance imaging (fMRI) scans have found the cerebellum to be involved in sensory and cognitive processes as well, such as learning to associate one stimulus (such as a sound) with another (such as a puff of air on the eye, which leads to an eyeblink reflex)(Blaxton et al., 1996; Cabeza et al., 1997).

Repeated battering of the brain in boxing can lead to damage to the cerebellum.

► ONE STEP FURTHER

Tracking Down the Functions of the Cerebellum

Some researchers have begun to wonder whether the role of the cerebellum in movement reflects in part its involvement in processing *sensory* information. When people move, they receive constant feedback about the position of their bodies and the objects they are touching. If they did not, they would constantly fall. The question for researchers is how to tell whether the cerebellum is actually involved in movement, in sensory processes that make smooth movement possible, or both.

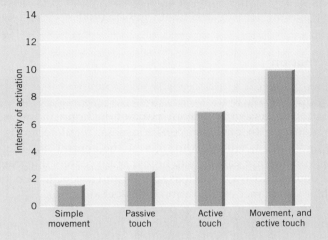

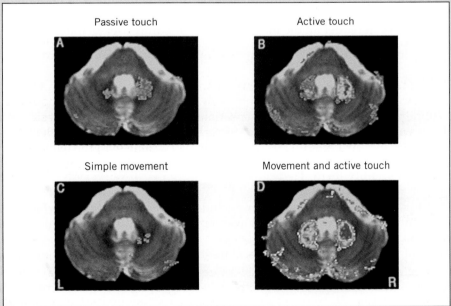

FIGURE 3.12
The relation between sensory and motor tasks and activation of the lateral cerebellum. The graph and accompanying photos show the amount of increased activation of the lateral cerebellum for each of four tasks involving sensory and motor processes. The cerebellum was most active when participants had to combine sensory and motor responses. (Data in the chart are for the right hand; the left hand produced similar findings.) In the brain images, the bright green indicates some activation; the yellow, more activation; and the red, high activation.

To try to tease apart these two possibilities, researchers in one study observed the activity of the brain using fMRI while participants performed each of four tasks (Gao et al., 1996). In a passive touch condition, participants did nothing other than observe the feeling of sand paper lightly rubbed against their fingers. In an active touch condition, they were asked to judge whether the sand paper rubbed on each of their hands was equally coarse—a test of sensory discrimination between two stimuli. In a simple movement condition, they were instructed to reach for, grab, and drop an object repeatedly. Finally, in a condition that combined movement and sensory discrimination, they were asked to pick up an object in each hand and judge whether the two objects were the same. The study was intended to assess whether sensory processing, movement, or both lead to activation of the side portions of the cerebellum (the *lateral* cerebellum).

The results are shown in Figure 3.12. As can be seen, simple movement led to slight activation, as did simple sensation (passive touch). However, sensory discrimination—and especially the combination of sensory discrimination plus movement—led to the strongest activation of the cerebellum, suggesting that the cerebellum (or at least its lateral regions) may be involved in combining sensory and motor information.   ◄

Reticular Formation

The **reticular formation** is a diffuse network of neurons that extends from the lowest parts of the medulla in the hindbrain to the upper end of the midbrain. The reticular formation sends axons to many parts of the brain and to the spinal cord. Its major functions are to maintain consciousness, regulate arousal levels, and modulate the activity of neurons throughout the central nervous system. The reticular formation also appears to help higher brain centers integrate information from different neural pathways (such as sounds and associated images) by calling attention to their simultaneous activation (Munk et al., 1996).

Reticular damage can affect sleep patterns as well as the ability to be alert or attentive. Damage to the reticular formation is a major cause of coma. In fact, humans can lose an entire side (or hemisphere) of the cerebrum—about 50 billion cells—without losing the capacity for consciousness, whereas lesions to the reticular formation can render all the information in the cortex useless (Baars, 1995).

THE MIDBRAIN

The **midbrain** consists of the tectum and tegmentum. The **tectum** includes structures involved in vision and hearing. These structures largely help humans orient to visual and auditory stimuli with eye and body movements. When higher brain structures are lesioned, people can often still sense the presence of stimuli, but they cannot identify them. The **tegmentum**, which includes parts of the reticular formation and other neural structures, serves a variety of functions. Many are related to movement; the tegmentum includes the substantia nigra, which deteriorates in Parkinson's disease and was apparently destroyed by encephalitis lethargica.

Recent research suggests that these midbrain structures also play an important role in learning to produce behaviors that minimize unpleasant (aversive) consequences and maximize rewards—a kind of learning studied for years by behaviorists (Chapter 5). Neurons deep inside the tectum are part of a system of neurons involved in generating unpleasant feelings and linking them, through learning, to actions that can help the animal escape or avoid them (Brandao et al., 1994). Chemical or electrical activation of these pathways in rats produces "freezing" (a characteristic fear response) and efforts to escape. Other *nuclei* (collections of neurons in a region of the brain that serve a shared function) in the tegmentum are involved in the experience of pleasure or reward, which is crucial to learning to produce actions that lead to positive consequences (Johnson et al., 1996; Nader & van der Kooy, 1997). For example, rats will learn to perform behaviors that lead to morphine injections in regions of their tegmentum (Jaeger & van der Kooy, 1996).

INTERIM SUMMARY   The hindbrain includes the **medulla oblongata,** the **cerebellum,** and parts of the **recticular formation.** The medulla regulates vital physiological functions, such as heartbeat, circulation, and respiration, and forms a link between the spinal cord and the rest of the brain. The cerebellum has long been seen as the lowest brain structure involved in movement, but parts of it also appear to be involved in learning and sensory discrimination. The reticular formation is most centrally involved in consciousness and arousal. The midbrain consists of the **tectum** and **tegmentum.** The tectum is involved in orienting to visual and auditory stimuli. The tegmentum is involved, among other things, in movement and arousal. Hindbrain structures are also part of neural circuits that help humans learn to approach or avoid stimuli associated with reward and punishment.

THE FOREBRAIN

The **forebrain,** which is involved in complex sensory, emotional, cognitive, and behavioral processes, consists of the hypothalamus, thalamus, and cerebrum. Within the cerebrum are the basal ganglia and limbic system, which are called **subcortical** structures (*sub,* or *below,* the cortex). The outer layers of the cerebrum, or cortex, are so complex that we will devote a separate section to them.

Hypothalamus

Situated in front of the midbrain and adjacent to the pituitary gland is the **hypothalamus.** Although the hypothalamus accounts for only 0.3 percent of the brain's total weight, this tiny structure helps regulate behaviors ranging from eating and sleeping to sexual activity and emotional experience. In nonhuman animals, the hypothalamus is involved in species-specific behaviors, such as responses to predators. For example, electrical stimulation of the hypothalamus in cats can produce rage attacks—filled with hissing, growling, and biting (Bandler, 1982; Lu et al., 1992). The hypothalamus works closely with the pituitary gland and provides a key link between the nervous system and the endocrine system, largely by activating pituitary hormones. When people undergo stressful experiences (such as taking a psychology exam or getting into a heated argument), the hypothalamus activates the pituitary, which in turn puts the body on alert by sending out hormonal messages.

One of the most important functions of the hypothalamus is *homeostasis*—keeping vital processes such as body temperature, blood-sugar (glucose) level, and metabolism (use and storage of energy) within a fairly narrow range. For example, as people ingest food, the hypothalamus detects a rise in glucose level and responds by shutting off hunger sensations. Chemically blocking glucose receptors (cells that detect glucose levels) in cats can produce ravenous eating, as the hypothalamus attempts to maintain homeostasis in the face of misleading information (Batuev & Gafurov, 1993; Berridge & Zajonc, 1991; Katafuchi et al., 1985).

Thalamus

The **thalamus** is a set of nuclei located above the hypothalamus. Its various nuclei perform a number of functions; one of the most important is to provide initial processing of sensory information and to transmit this information to higher brain centers. In some respects the thalamus is like a switchboard for routing information from neurons connected to visual, auditory, taste, and touch receptors to appropriate regions of the brain. However, the thalamus plays a much more active role than a simple switchboard. Its function is not only to *route* messages to the appropriate structures but also to *filter* them, highlighting some and de-emphasizing others.

The thalamus is ideally situated for performing this function, since it receives *projections* (that is, axons leading to it) from several sensory systems, as well as feedback from higher cortical centers in the brain. Thus, the thalamus can collect information from multiple senses and determine the extent to which information is converging on something important that may require more detailed processing. The thalamus also receives input from the reticular formation, which "highlights" some neural messages. Recent studies using PET and other techniques suggest that the reticular formation and thalamus may be the anatomically "lower" sections of a neural circuit that directs attention and consciousness toward potentially significant events (Kinomura et al., 1996; Newman, 1995).

The Limbic System

The **limbic system** is a set of structures with diverse functions, including emotion, motivation, learning, and memory. The limbic system includes the septal area, the amygdala, and the hippocampus (Figure 3.13).

The role of the **septal area** is only gradually becoming clear. Early research linked it to the experience of pleasure: Stimulating a section of the septal area proved to be a powerful reinforcer for rats, which would walk across an electrified grid to receive the stimulation (Milner, 1991; Olds & Milner, 1954). More recent research suggests that, like most brain structures, different sections of the septal area likely have distinct, though related, functions. For example, one part of the septal area appears to be involved in relief from pain and other unpleasant emotional states (Yadin & Thomas, 1996). Another part seems to help animals learn to avoid situations that *lead* to aversive experiences, since injection of chemicals that temporarily block its functioning makes rats less able to learn to avoid stimuli associated with pain (Rashidy-Pour et al., 1995). These regions receive projections from midbrain and thalamic nuclei involved in learning.

The **amygdala** is an almond-shaped structure (amygdala is Latin for "almond") involved in many emotional processes, especially learning and remembering emotionally significant events (Aggleton, 1992; LeDoux, 1995; Sarter &

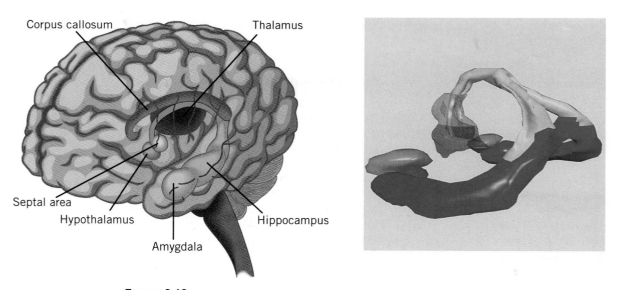

FIGURE 3.13

The limbic system. The limbic system, located within the cerebrum, consists of the septal area, amygdala, and hippocampus. The drawing shows the parts of the limbic system, and the photo shows the way it looks using computer imaging.

Markowitsch, 1985). One of its primary roles is to attach emotional significance to events. The amygdala appears to be particularly important in fear responses. Lesioning the amygdala in rats, for example, inhibits learned fear responses; that is, the rats no longer avoid a stimulus they had previously connected with pain (LaBar & LeDoux, 1996).

The amygdala is also involved in recognizing emotion, particularly fearful emotion, in other people. One study using PET technology found that presenting pictures of fearful rather than neutral or happy faces activated the left amygdala and that the amount of activation was strongly correlated with the amount of fear displayed in the pictures (Morris et al., 1996). From an evolutionary perspective, this suggests that humans have evolved particular mechanisms for detecting fear in others and that these "fear detectors" are anatomically connected to neural circuits that *produce* fear. This makes sense, since fear in others is likely a signal of danger to oneself. In fact, infants as young as 9 to 12 months show distress when they see distress on their parents' faces (Campos et al., 1993).

The **hippocampus** is particularly important in memory (see, e.g., Schachter, 1992, 1996; Squire, 1991). This was demonstrated dramatically in a famous case study by Brenda Milner and her colleagues (Milner et al., 1968; Scoville & Milner, 1957). A man identified as H. M. underwent surgery to control life-threatening epileptic seizures. The surgeon removed sections of his cortex and some underlying structures. Unfortunately, one of those structures was the hippocampus, and although H. M. was now free of seizures, he was also "free" of the capacity to remember new information.

Actually, that is only half the story, and the other half has, in the last 15 years, changed our understanding of memory. H. M. *did* lose his memory in the sense that psychologists and laypeople alike have traditionally understood memory. For example, every time he met Dr. Milner, who studied him over 20 years, he had to be reintroduced; invariably, he would smile politely and tell her it was a pleasure to make her acquaintance. But as we will see in Chapter 6, we now know that certain kinds of memory do not involve the hippocampus, and H. M. retained those capacities. For example, on one occasion H. M.'s father took him to visit his mother in the hospital. Afterward, H. M. did not remember anything of the visit, but he "expressed a vague idea that something might have happened to his mother" (Milner et al., 1968, p. 216). His capacity to form associations (such as the connection between his mother and a sense of unease) was intact, even though he could not recall the events that led to those associations.

The Basal Ganglia

The **basal ganglia** are a set of structures located near the thalamus and hypothalamus that are involved in movement. Damage to the basal ganglia can cause changes in posture and muscle tone or various kinds of abnormal movements. The basal ganglia have been implicated in Parkinson's disease and in the epidemic of encephalitis lethargica that struck millions early in the twentieth century. The dopamine-rich neurons of the substantia nigra (in the midbrain) normally project to the basal ganglia. When these neurons die, as in Parkinson's, they stop sending signals to the basal ganglia, which in turn cease functioning properly to regulate movement. Some neural circuits involving the basal ganglia appear to inhibit movement, whereas others initiate it, since lesions in different sections of the basal ganglia can either release movements (leading to twitches or jerky movements) or block them.

Damage to the basal ganglia can also lead to mood and memory disorders, as higher regions of the brain fail to receive necessary activation (see Federoff et al., 1992; Krishnan, 1993; Lopez-Villegas et al., 1996). In addition, at least one neural pathway in the basal ganglia is part of a circuit involved in memory that leads from the cerebellum to the cerebral cortex (Cabeza et al., 1997).

INTERIM SUMMARY   The forebrain consists of the **hypothalamus, thalamus,** the **subcortical** structures of the **cerebrum** (the limbic system and basal ganglia), and the **cerebral cortex.** The hypothalamus is involved in regulating a wide range of behaviors, including eating, sleeping, sexual activity, and emotional experience. Among its other functions, the thalamus provides initial processing of sensory information and transmits this information to higher brain centers. The **limbic system** includes the **septal area, amygdala,** and **hippocampus.** The precise functions of the septal area are unclear, although it appears to be involved in learning to act in ways that avoid pain and produce pleasure. The amygdala is crucial to the experience of emotion. **Basal ganglia** structures are involved in the control of movement and also play a part in mood and memory.

THE CEREBRAL CORTEX

Although many components of normal behaviors are produced below the cortex—in the spinal cord and medulla up through the limbic system and basal ganglia—the cerebral cortex coordinates and integrates these components. The cortex consists of a three-millimeter-thick layer of densely packed interneurons; it is grayish in color and highly convoluted (that is, filled with twists and turns). The convolutions appear to serve a purpose: Just as crumpling a piece of paper into a tight wad reduces its size, the folds and wrinkles of the cortex allow a relatively large area of cortical cells to fit into a compact region within the skull. The hills of these convolutions are known as **gyri** (plural of **gyrus**) and the valleys as **sulci** (plural of **sulcus**).

In humans, the cortex performs three functions. First, it allows the flexible construction of sequences of voluntary movements involved in activities such as changing a tire or playing a piano concerto. Second, it permits subtle discriminations among complex sensory patterns; without a cerebral cortex, the words *gene* and *gem* would be indistinguishable. Third, the cortex makes possible symbolic thinking—the ability to use symbols such as words or pictorial signs (like a flag) to represent an object or concept with a complex meaning. The capacity to think symbolically enables people to have conversations about things that do not exist or are not presently in view; it is the foundation of human thought and language.

Primary and Association Areas

The cortex consists of regions specialized for different functions, such as vision, hearing, and body sensation. Each of these areas can be divided roughly into two zones, called primary and association cortex. The **primary areas** process raw sensory information or (in one section of the brain, the frontal lobes) initiate movement. The **association areas** are involved in complex mental processes such as forming perceptions, ideas, and plans. They were given this name in the nineteenth century because of the belief that higher mental functioning revolves around the association of one idea with another.

The primary areas are responsible for the initial cortical processing of sensory information. Neurons in these zones receive sensory information, usually via the thalamus, from sensory receptors in the ears, eyes, skin, and muscles. When a person sees a safety pin lying on her dresser, the primary or sensory areas receive the simple visual sensations that make up the contours of the safety pin. Activation of circuits in the visual association cortex enables the person to recognize the object as a safety pin rather than a needle or a formless shiny object.

Neurons in the primary areas tend to have more specific functions than neurons in association cortex. Many of these neurons are genetically wired to register very basic, and very specific, attributes of a stimulus. For example, some neurons in the primary visual cortex respond to horizontal lines but not to vertical lines;

other neurons respond only to vertical lines (Hubel & Wiesel, 1963). Some neurons in the association cortex are equally specific in their functions, but many develop their functions through experience. The brain may be wired from birth to detect the contours of objects like safety pins, but a person must learn what a safety pin is and does. From an evolutionary perspective, this combination of "hard-wired" and "flexible" neurons guarantees that we have the capacity to detect features of *any* environment that are likely to be relevant to adaptation but can also learn the features of the *specific* environment in which we find ourselves.

Lobes of the Cerebral Cortex

The cerebrum is divided into two roughly symmetrical halves, or **cerebral hemispheres,** which are separated by the **longitudinal fissure.** (A fissure is a deep sulcus, or valley.) A band of neural fibers called the **corpus callosum** connects the **right** and **left hemispheres.** Each hemisphere consists of four regions, or **lobes:** occipital, parietal, frontal, and temporal. Thus, a person has a right and left occipital lobe, a right and left parietal lobe, and so forth (Figure 3.14). Once again, it is important to bear in mind that nature did not create clearly bounded cortical regions and rope them off from one another; the functions of adjacent cortical regions tend to be related, even if some cells are called "occipital" and others "temporal."

The Occipital Lobes   The **occipital lobes,** located in the rear portion of the cortex, are specialized for vision. Primary areas of the occipital lobes receive visual input from the thalamus. The thalamus, in turn, receives information from the receptors in the retina via the optic nerve. The primary areas respond to relatively simple features of a visual stimulus, and the association areas organize these simple characteristics into more complex maps of features of objects and their position in space. Damage to the primary areas leads to partial or complete blindness.

The visual association cortex, which actually extends into neighboring lobes, projects (that is, sends axons carrying messages) to several regions throughout the cortex that receive other types of sensory information, such as auditory or tactile (touch). Areas that receive information from more than one sensory system are called **polysensory areas.** The existence of polysensory areas at various levels of

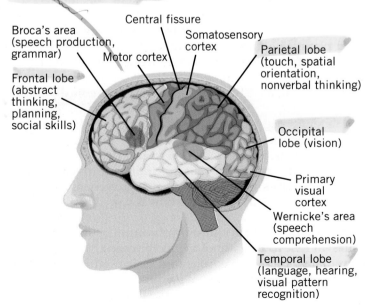

Broca's area
(speech production,
grammar)

Central fissure

Somatosensory
cortex

Motor cortex

Parietal lobe
(touch, spatial
orientation,
nonverbal thinking)

Frontal lobe
(abstract
thinking,
planning,
social skills)

Occipital
lobe (vision)

Primary
visual
cortex

Wernicke's area
(speech
comprehension)

Temporal lobe
(language, hearing,
visual pattern
recognition)

FIGURE 3.14
The lobes of the cerebral cortex. The cortex has four lobes, each specialized for different functions and each containing primary and association areas.

the brain (including subcortical levels) helps us, for example, to associate the sight of a car stopping suddenly with the sound of squealing tires.

The Parietal Lobes   The **parietal lobes** are located in front of the occipital lobes. They are involved in several functions, including the sense of touch, detection of movement in the environment, locating objects in space, and the experience of one's own body as it moves through space. A person with damage to the primary area of the parietal lobes may be unable to feel a thimble on her finger, whereas damage to the association area could render her unable to recognize the object she was feeling as a thimble or to understand what the object does.

The primary area of the parietal lobe, called the **somatosensory cortex,** lies directly behind the **central fissure,** which divides the parietal lobe from the frontal lobe. Different sections of the somatosensory cortex receive information from different parts of the body (Figure 3.15). Thus, one section registers sensations from the hand, another from the foot, and so forth. The parietal lobes are also involved in complex visual processing, particularly the posterior (back) regions nearest to the occipital lobes.

The Frontal Lobes   The **frontal lobes** are involved in a number of functions, including movement, attention, planning, social skills, abstract thinking, memory, and some aspects of personality (see Goldman-Rakic, 1995; Russell & Roxanas, 1990; Stuss & Benson, 1984). Figure 3.15 shows the **motor cortex,** the primary zone of the frontal lobe. Through its projections to the basal ganglia, cerebellum, and spinal cord, the motor cortex initiates voluntary movement. The motor cortex and the adjacent somatosensory cortex send and receive information from the same parts of the body.

As the figure indicates, the amount of space devoted to different parts of the body in the motor and somatosensory cortexes is not directly proportional to their size. Parts of the body that produce fine motor movements or have particularly dense and sensitive receptors take up more space in the motor and somatosensory cortexes. These body parts tend to serve important or complex functions and thus require more processing capacity. In humans, the hands, which are crucial to exploring objects and using tools, occupy considerable territory, whereas a section of the back of similar size occupies only a fraction of that space. Other species have different cortical "priorities"; in cats, for example, input from the whiskers receives considerably more space than input from "whiskers" on the face of human males.

In the frontal lobes, the primary area is motor rather than sensory. The association cortex is involved in planning and putting together sequences of behavior. Neurons in the primary areas then issue specific commands to motor neurons throughout the body.

Damage to the frontal lobes can lead to a wide array of problems, from paralysis to difficulty thinking abstractly, focusing attention efficiently, coordinating complex sequences of behavior, and adjusting socially (Damasio, 1994; Grattan & Eslinger, 1991). Lesions in other parts of the brain that project to the frontal lobes can produce similar symptoms if the frontal lobes fail to receive normal activation. For example, the victims of encephalitis lethargica could not initiate movements even though their frontal lobes were intact because projections from the basal ganglia that normally activate the frontal lobes were impaired by dopamine depletion.

In most individuals, the left frontal lobe is also involved in language. **Broca's area,** located in the left frontal lobe at the base of the motor cortex, is specialized for movements of the mouth and tongue necessary for speech production. It also plays a pivotal role in the use and understanding of grammar. Damage to Broca's area causes **Broca's aphasia,** in which a person may have difficulty speaking, putting together grammatical sentences, and articulating words, even though he

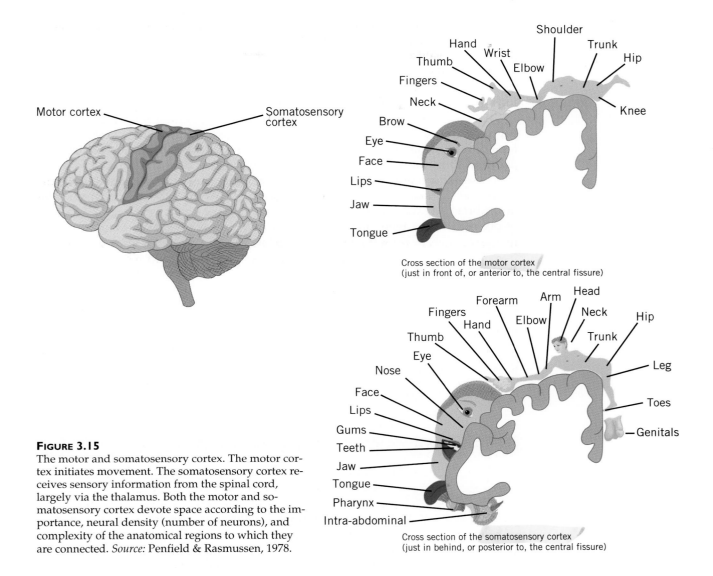

FIGURE 3.15
The motor and somatosensory cortex. The motor cortex initiates movement. The somatosensory cortex receives sensory information from the spinal cord, largely via the thalamus. Both the motor and somatosensory cortex devote space according to the importance, neural density (number of neurons), and complexity of the anatomical regions to which they are connected. *Source:* Penfield & Rasmussen, 1978.

may remain able to comprehend language. Individuals with lesions to this area occasionally have difficulty comprehending *complex* sentences if subjects and objects cannot be easily recognized from context. For example, they might have difficulty decoding the sentence, "The cat, which was under the hammock, chased the bird, which was flying over the dog."

The Temporal Lobes The **temporal lobes,** located in the lower side portions of the cortex, are particularly important in audition (hearing) and language. The connection between hearing and language makes evolutionary sense because language, until relatively recently, was always spoken (rather than written). The primary cortex receives sensory information from the ears, and the association cortex breaks the flow of sound into meaningful units (such as words). Cells in the primary cortex respond to particular frequencies of sound (that is, to different tones) and are arranged anatomically from low (toward the front of the brain) to high frequencies (toward the back).

For most people the left hemisphere of the temporal lobe is specialized for language, although some linguistic functions are shared by the right hemisphere. **Wernicke's area,** located in the left temporal lobe, is important in language comprehension. Damage to Wernicke's area may produce **Wernicke's aphasia,** characterized by difficulty understanding what words and sentences mean. Patients with Wernicke's aphasia often produce "word salad": They may speak fluently and expressively, as if their speech were meaningful, but the words are tossed together so that they make little sense. In contrast, right temporal damage typically results in nonverbal deficits, such as difficulty recognizing songs, faces, or paintings.

Although psychologists once believed that hearing and language were the primary functions of the temporal lobes, more recent research suggests that the temporal lobes have more than one region and that these different regions serve different functions (Rodman, 1997). For example, one region is comprised of visual association cortex involved in identifying objects. As demonstrated in lesion studies with monkeys and humans, neurons toward the back (posterior regions) of the brain adjacent to the occipital lobes are involved in discriminating qualities of objects such as their shape and size. Toward the front of the brain (anterior), temporal neurons are more involved in memory for objects seen previously.

INTERIM SUMMARY   The **cerebral cortex** includes **primary areas,** which usually process raw sensory data (except in the frontal lobes), and **association areas,** which are involved in complex mental processes such as perception and thinking. The cortex consists of two hemispheres, each of which has four lobes. The **occipital lobes** are involved in vision. The **parietal lobes** are involved in the sense of touch and in perception of movement and space. The **frontal lobes** serve a variety of functions, such as coordinating and initiating movement, attention, planning, social skills, abstract thinking, memory, and aspects of personality. Sections of the **temporal lobes** are important in hearing, language, and visual object recognition.

FROM MIND TO BRAIN

THE IMPACT OF FRONTAL AND TEMPORAL LOBE DAMAGE ON PERSONALITY

If damage to the brain can affect such specific functions as language, what can it do to the complex patterns of emotion, thought, and behavior that constitute an individual's personality? Psychologists define personality much as laypeople do, as both a person's reputation (the way people tend to perceive him) and the enduring psychological attributes (mental processes) that create this reputation. Personality thus includes an individual's characteristic ways of feeling, of thinking about himself and the world, and of behaving. We hold people responsible for their personalities and tend to associate personality more with the "mind" or the "soul" than with the brain. We condemn people for aspects of their personality or character in a way that we do not for mental retardation or physical handicaps.

But is personality really so independent of the brain that serves as its biological substrate? Can a damaged brain create a damaged soul for which a person bears no more responsibility than for paralysis caused by an automobile accident? In fact, damage to parts of the brain can alter personality so that someone literally becomes a different person. Lesions to the frontal and temporal lobes provide striking examples.

Patients with frontal damage often make tactless comments and are described as callous, grandiose, boastful, and unable to understand other people's perspectives. They are also prone to lewd, bawdy, or childish joking (Ron, 1989; Russell & Roxanas, 1990; Stuss et al., 1992). A famous early report of such symptoms was the case of a construction worker named Phineas Gage. In 1848 an explosion sent a metal bar of more than an inch in diameter through Gage's skull, damaging association areas of his frontal lobes. Previously known as a decent, conscientious man, Gage was described following the accident as childish and irreverent. He was also unable to control his impulses and was constantly devising plans that he would abandon within moments (Blumer & Benson, 1984; Damasio, 1994). According to his doctor, the accident disrupted the balance between Gage's intellect and his "animal propensities."

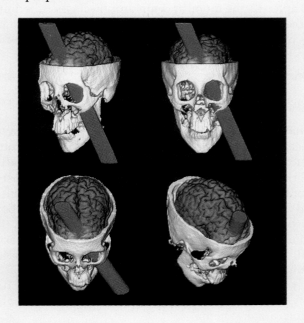

Computerized images from four angles reconstruct the likely path of the rod through Phineas Gage's frontal lobes.

Another broad class of personality alterations associated with frontal lobe lesions includes indifference, apathy, and loss of motivation. A 46-year-old man suffered a skull fracture in a car accident and consequently had a portion of his left frontal lobe removed. Although his physical and cognitive abilities returned to normal, his personality changed dramatically. Prior to the accident, his friends described him as friendly, active in the community, talkative, animated, and happy. He was a warm, loving father and husband and a successful salesperson. After his injury, he became quiet, spent most of his time alone smoking, and spoke only in response to questions. His altered behavior makes sense neuropsychologically, since the frontal lobes are involved in initiating activity. The patient spoke in an intelligent but very "matter of fact" manner, and he was completely indifferent to his wife and children, who eventually stopped seeing him (Blumer & Benson, 1984).

Another type of brain pathology associated with specific types of personality change is temporal lobe epilepsy, a seizure disorder characterized by abnormal electrical activity in the brain that begins in the temporal lobe. A 43-year-old businessman began to experience seizures and personality changes after he suffered a head injury in a car accident. After his injury he became excessively verbose and preoccupied with irrelevant details; he could literally spend hours discussing small, tangential details before returning to the point he was trying to make. (No, he did not become a professor or textbook author.) His inability to maintain a fluent conversation, as well as his short temper, eventually led to a breakdown in communication with his wife and periods of marital separation (Blumer & Benson, 1984).

These cases challenge the way most of us intuitively understand ourselves and other people, particularly in the West, where cultural beliefs emphasize personal responsibility and the separation of mind and body. How does a person respond to a once loving spouse or father who no longer seems to care? Is he the same husband or father, or does the same body now house a different person? Is he accountable for the way he behaves?

The courts were faced with just such a dilemma in sentencing children who survived encephalitis lethargica, some of whom developed sexual perversions and became sex offenders (Cheyette & Cummings, 1995). As we will see in Chapter 12, the moral and philosophical issues become even more complex in the face of evidence that personality is partly innate and that some people are born with a tendency to behave antisocially or indifferently to other people.

Cerebral Lateralization

We have seen that the left frontal and temporal lobes tend to play a more important role in speech and language than their right-hemisphere counterparts. This raises the question of whether other cortical functions are **lateralized,** that is, localized on one or the other side of the brain, and if so, how extensively.

Global generalizations require caution because most functions that are popularly considered to be lateralized are actually represented on both sides of the brain in most people. However, some division of labor between the hemispheres does exist, with each side **dominant** for (that is, in more control of) certain functions. In general, at least for right-handed people, the left hemisphere tends to be dominant for language, logic, complex motor behavior, and aspects of consciousness (particularly verbal aspects). Many of these left-hemisphere functions are analytical, breaking down thoughts and perceptions into component parts and analyzing the relations among them.

Drawing by Sidney Harris.

The right hemisphere tends to be dominant for nonlinguistic functions such as forming visual maps of the environment. Studies indicate that it is involved in the recognition of faces, places, and nonlinguistic sounds such as music. The right hemisphere's specialization for nonlinguistic sounds also seems to hold in nonhuman animals: Japanese macaque monkeys, for example, process vocalizations from other macaques on the left but other sounds in their environment on the right (Petersen et al., 1984). Recent research indicates that the region of the brain that constitutes Wernicke's area of the left temporal lobe in humans may have special significance in chimpanzees as well, since this region is larger in the left than right hemisphere in chimps as in humans (Gannon et al., 1998).

Split-Brain Studies   A particularly important source of information about cerebral lateralization has been case studies of **split-brain** patients—individuals whose corpus callosum has been surgically cut, blocking communication between the two hemispheres. Severing this connective tissue is a radical treatment for severe epileptic seizures that spread from one hemisphere to another and cannot be controlled by other means.

In their everyday behavior, split-brain patients generally appear normal (Sperry, 1984). However, their two hemispheres can actually operate independently, and each may be oblivious to what the other is doing. Under certain experimental circumstances, the disconnection between the two minds housed in one brain becomes apparent. To understand the results of these experiments, bear in mind that the left hemisphere, which is dominant for most speech functions, receives information from the right visual field and that the right hemisphere receives information from the left. Normally, whether the right or left hemisphere receives the information makes little difference because once the message reaches the brain, the two hemispheres freely pass information between them. Severing the corpus callosum, however, blocks this sharing of information (Gazzaniga, 1967).

Figure 3.16a depicts a typical split-brain experiment. A split-brain patient is seated at a table, and the surface of the table is blocked from view by a screen so the individual cannot see objects on it. The experimenter asks the person to focus on a point in the center of the screen. A word (here, *key*) is quickly flashed on the left side of the screen. When information is flashed for only about 150 milliseconds, the eyes do not have time to move, ensuring that the information is sent to only one hemisphere. The patient is unable to identify the word verbally because the information never reached his left hemisphere, which is dominant for speech. He can, however, select a key with his left hand from an array of objects hidden behind the screen because the left hand receives information from the right hemisphere, which "saw" the key. Thus, the right hand literally does not know what

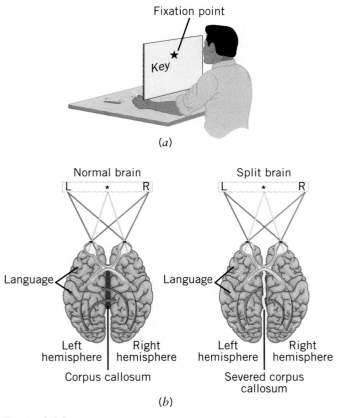

FIGURE 3.16
A split-brain study. In a typical split-brain study (a), a patient with a severed corpus callosum sees the word *key* flashed on the left portion of the screen. Although he cannot name what he has seen, as speech is lateralized to the left hemisphere, he is able to use his left hand to select the key from a number of objects because the right hemisphere, which has "seen" the key, controls the left hand and has *some* language skills. Part (b) illustrates the way information from the left and right visual fields is transmitted to the brain in normal and split brains. When participants focus their vision on a point in the middle of the visual field (such as the star in the diagram), anything on the left of this fixation point (for instance, point L) will be sensed by receptors on the right half of each eye. These receptors are located in the retina, at the back of the eye. This information is subsequently processed by the right hemisphere. Conversely, receptors in the left part of each eye's retina register information from the right visual field and pass this information along to the left hemisphere. In the normal brain, information is readily transmitted via the corpus callosum between the two hemispheres. In the split-brain patient, the severed neural route means the right and left hemispheres "see" different things. *Source:* Part (a) adapted from Gazzaniga, 1967.

the left hand is doing, and neither does the left hemisphere. Figure 3.16*b* illustrates the way visual information from the left and right visual fields is transmitted to the brain in normal and split-brain patients.

This research raises an intriguing question: Can a person with two independent hemispheres be literally of two minds, with two centers of conscious awareness, like Siamese twins joined at the cortex? Consider the case of a 10-year-old boy with a split brain (LeDoux et al., 1977). In one set of tests, the boy was asked about his sense of himself, his future, and his likes and dislikes. The examiner asked the boy questions in which a word or words were replaced by the word *blank.* The missing words were then presented to one hemisphere or the other. For example, when the boy was asked, "Who _____?" the missing words *are you* were projected to the left or the right hemisphere. Not surprisingly, the boy could only answer verbally when inquiries were made to the left hemisphere. The right hemisphere could, however, answer by spelling out words with letter tiles with the left hand (because the right hemisphere is usually not entirely devoid of language) when the question was flashed to the right hemisphere. Thus, the boy could describe his feelings or moods with both hemispheres.

Many times the views expressed by the right and left hemispheres overlapped, but not always. One day, when the boy was in a pleasant mood, his hemispheres tended to agree (both, for example, reporting high self-esteem). Another day, when the boy seemed anxious and behaved aggressively, the hemispheres were in disagreement. In general, his right-hemisphere responses were consistently more negative than those of the left, as if the right hemisphere tended to be in a worse mood. Researchers using other methods have also reported that the two hemispheres differ in their processing of positive and negative emotions and that these differences may exist at birth (Davidson, 1995; Fox, 1991). Left frontal regions are generally more involved in processing positive feelings that motivate approach toward objects in the environment, whereas right frontal regions are more related to negative emotions that motivate avoidance or withdrawal. One of my own patients received frontal damage in a horseback-riding accident and has unsuccessfully undergone every form of treatment for a severe and deadening depression possible, thus far to no avail. The damage was actually in the right hemisphere and appears to have destroyed inhibitory mechanisms that normally *control* right frontal emotional activation.

Sex Differences in Lateralization   Psychologists have long known that females typically score higher on tests of verbal fluency, perceptual speed, and manual dexterity than males, whereas males tend to score higher on tests of mathematical ability and spatial processing, particularly geometric thinking (Bradbury, 1989; Casey et al., 1997; Maccoby & Jacklin, 1974). In a study of students under age 13 with exceptional mathematical ability (measured by scores of 700 or above on the SAT), boys outnumbered girls 13 to 1 (Benbow & Stanley, 1983). On the other hand, males are much more likely than females to develop learning disabilities with reading and language comprehension. Although these sex differences are not particularly large (Caplan et al., 1997; Hyde, 1990), they have been documented in several countries and have not consistently decreased over the last two decades despite social changes encouraging equality of the sexes (see Bradbury, 1989; Randhawa, 1991). Psychologists have thus debated whether such discrepancies in performance might be based in part on innate differences between the brains of men and women.

Some data suggest that women's and men's brains may indeed differ in ways that affect cognitive functioning. At a hormonal level, research with human and nonhuman primates indicates that the presence of testosterone and estrogen in the bloodstream early in development influences aspects of brain development (Clark & Goldman-Rakic, 1989; Gorski & Barraclough, 1963). One study found that level of exposure to testosterone during the second trimester of pregnancy predicted the speed with which children could rotate mental images in their minds at age 7 (Grimshaw et al., 1995). Some evidence even suggests that women's spatial abilities on certain tasks are lower during high-estrogen periods of the menstrual cycle, whereas motor skills, on which females typically have an advantage, are superior during high-estrogen periods (Kimura, 1987).

Perhaps the most definitive data on gender differences in the brain come from recent research using fMRI technology (Shaywitz et al., 1995). In males, a rhyming task led to activation of Broca's area in the left frontal lobe. The same task in females produced frontal activation in *both* hemispheres (Figure 3.17). Thus, in females, language appears less lateralized.

Cultural factors appear to play a significant role in shaping the skills and interests of males and females as well. Parents tend to talk to little girls more, and they encourage boys to play with mechanical objects and discourage them from many verbal activities such as writing poetry. Furthermore, despite efforts to remove gender biases from textbooks, a study comparing high school chemistry textbooks from the early 1970s with their current editions found that males are still shown three times more often in illustrations and examples than females, subtly perpetuating the view of chemistry as a male discipline (although the ratio had dropped from 5 to 1) (Bazler & Simonis, 1991). Some of the most interesting evidence of the impact of culture comes from a study that followed girls from ages 11 to 18 (Newcombe & Dubas, 1992). The best predictors of spatial ability at age 16 were two psychological attributes at age 11: wishing to be a boy and having a more stereotypically masculine view of what they would like to be. To what extent these psychological attributes themselves could be influenced by biology, however, is unknown.

INTERIM SUMMARY   Some psychological functions are **lateralized,** or processed primarily by one hemisphere. In general, the left hemisphere is more verbal and analytic, and the right is specialized for nonlinguistic functions. Although the differences tend to be relatively small, males and females tend to differ in cognitive strengths, which appears to be related in part to differences between their brains, including in the extent of lateralization of functions such as language.

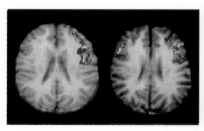

FIGURE 3.17
Gender differences in cortical activation during a rhyming task. The photo on the left shows that for males, rhyming activated only Broca's area in the left frontal lobe. For females (right photo), this task activated the same region in both hemispheres. (From the angle at which these images were taken, left activation appears on the right.) *Source:* B. A. Shaywitz, et al., 1995. NMR/Yale Medical School.

A GLOBAL VISTA

ENVIRONMENT, CULTURE, AND THE BRAIN

The issue of how, and in what ways, cultural practices and beliefs influence cognitive abilities raises an intriguing question: Since all abilities reflect the actions of neural circuits, can environmental and cultural factors actually affect the circuitry of the brain?

We have little trouble imagining that *biological* factors can alter the brain. **Tumors,** or abnormal tissue growths, can damage regions of the brain by putting pressure on them, leading to symptoms as varied as blurred vision, searing headaches, or explosive emotional outbursts. High blood pressure or diseases of the blood vessels can lead to **strokes,** in which blood flow to regions of the brain is interrupted. If the interruption occurs for more than about 10 minutes, the cells in that area die, leading to changes in psychological functioning such as paralysis, loss of speech, or even death if the stroke destroys neural regions vital for life support such as the medulla or hypothalamus. Trauma to the nervous system caused by automobile accidents, blows to the head, or falls that break the neck can have similar effects, as can infections caused by viruses, bacteria, or parasites.

But what about psychological blows to the head, or, conversely, experiences that enrich the brain or steer it in one direction or another? As we saw in Chapter 2, monkeys separated from their mothers for long periods of time develop abnormal electroencephalograms (EEGs), suggesting that social and environmental processes can indeed alter the structure of the brain. A fascinating line of research indicates that early sensory enrichment or deprivation can affect the brain in fundamental ways that may be relevant to the experience of children in different social and cultural environments (Heritch et al., 1990; Rosenzweig et al., 1972). In one series of studies, young male rats were raised in one of two conditions: an enriched environment, with 6 to 12 rats sharing an open-mesh cage filled with a variety of toys; or an impoverished one, in which rats lived alone without toys or companions (Cummins et al., 1977). Days or months later, the experimenters sacrificed the rats and weighed their forebrains. The brains of enriched rats tended to be heavier than those of the deprived rats, indicating that different environments can alter the course of neural development.

Is the same true of humans? And can cultural differences become translated into neurological differences? The human brain triples in weight in the first two years and quadruples to its adult weight by age 14 (Winson, 1985). This means that social, cultural, and other environmental influences can become *built into* the brain (Shore, 1995), particularly into the more evolutionarily recent cortical regions involved in complex thought and learning (Damasio, 1994). For instance, many native Asian language speakers have difficulty distinguishing *la* from *ra* because Asian languages do not distinguish these units of sound. One study found that Japanese people who heard sound frequencies between *la* and *ra* did not hear them as *either la or ra*, as do Americans (Goto, 1971). If children do not hear certain linguistic patterns in the first few years of life (such as the *la–ra* distinction, the French *r*, or the Hebrew *ch*), they may lose the capacity to do so. Thus, these patterns may have to be laid down with different and much less efficient neural machinery later on (Lenneburg, 1967).

This schoolboy from Shanghai may be using somewhat different neural circuits than a schoolchild across the globe who writes in a language that is not pictographic.

Many Asian languages also differ from languages derived from Latin (such as French, English, and Spanish) in that they are *tone languages*, which means that intonation—the rising and falling of the voice—is used to distinguish otherwise identical words. In Mandarin Chinese, for example, saying the word *mao* with a rising tone means "cat" and with a falling tone, "hat." The processing of tone, like music, is typically more lateralized to the right hemisphere in the West. A study of Chinese subjects suffering from Broca's aphasia, however, suggests that being a native Chinese speaker may shift this function to the left hemisphere. These patients, with documented left-hemisphere damage, had considerable difficulty producing tone (Packard, 1986). Another study found similar evidence for left-hemisphere processing of tone in Norwegian, a non-Asian language that uses tone as well (Moen, 1993). In this study, which focused on normal individuals without brain damage, participants were better able to discriminate tone with their right ear than their left, suggesting a left-hemisphere superiority for tone processing. As we will see in later chapters, cultures shape not only language but also fundamental ways of thinking and feeling, which themselves rely on, and shape the connections among, billions of neurons. Thus, mind, brain, and culture may not be so easily divisible.

MIND, BRAIN, AND GENE

Having described the structure and function of the nervous system, we conclude with a brief discussion of the influence of genetics on psychological functioning. Few people would argue with the view that hair and eye color are heavily influenced by genetics or that genetic vulnerabilities contribute to heart disease, cancer, and diabetes. Yet, as we saw in Chapter 1, as soon as one suggests genetic roots to human behaviors or to differences between individuals, clouds of controversy begin to collect. In part, the controversy reflects realistic concerns about branding certain people or races as genetically inferior. In part, though, a resistance to genetic explanations is based in strongly held cultural beliefs that "all men are created equal" and that anyone can do almost anything with hard work and perseverance.

GENETICS

Psychologists interested in genetics study the influence of genetic blueprints—**genotypes**—on observable psychological attributes or qualities—**phenotypes.** The phenotypes that interest psychologists are characteristics such as quickness of thought, extroverted behavior, and the tendency to become anxious or depressed. The **gene** is the unit of hereditary transmission. Although a single gene may control eye color, genetic contributions to most complex phenomena, such as intelligence or personality, reflect the action of many genes.

Genes are encoded in the DNA (deoxyribonucleic acid) contained within the nucleus of every cell in the body. Genes are arranged along **chromosomes**—strands of paired DNA that spiral around each other (Figure 3.18). Human cells have 46 chromosomes, except sperm cells in males and egg cells in females, each of which has 23. The union of a sperm and an egg creates a cell with 46 chromo-

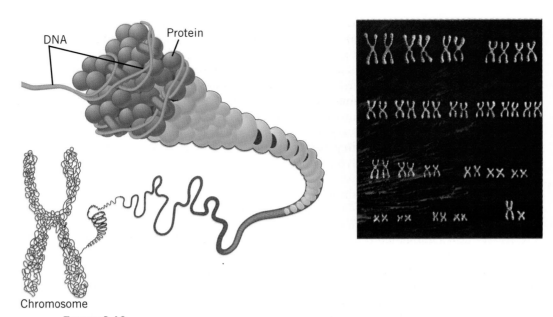

FIGURE 3.18

Human chromosomes. A drawing and magnified photograph of human chromosomes.

somes, half from the mother and half from the father. Children receive a somewhat random selection of half the genetic material of each parent, which means that the probability of sharing any particular gene with a parent is 1 out of 2, or .50. This number represents the **degree of relatedness** between parent and offspring.

Because children and their parents are related by .50 and parents and *their* parents are related by .50, the degree of relatedness between grandchildren and grandparents is .25, or .5 × .5. In other words, a grandmother passes on half of her genes to her daughter, who passes on half of those genes to her child; the likelihood that the grandchild receives any particular gene from her maternal grandmother through her mother is thus .25. Siblings are also related by .50 because they have a .25 chance of sharing a gene from their mother and a .25 chance from their father; added together, this means that they are related by .50 on the average. Table 3.2 shows the degree of relatedness for various relatives.

The fact that relatives differ in degree of relatedness enables researchers to tease apart the relative contributions of heredity and environment to phenotypic differences between individuals. If the similarity between relatives on attributes

TABLE 3.2 DEGREE OF RELATEDNESS AMONG SELECTED RELATIVES	
RELATION	**DEGREE OF RELATEDNESS**
Identical (MZ) twin	1.0
Fraternal (DZ) twin	.50
Parent/child	.50
Sibling	.50
Grandparent/grandchild	.25
Half-sibling	.25
First cousin	.125
Nonbiological parent/adopted child	0

such as intelligence or conscientiousness varies with their degree of relatedness, this suggests genetic influence, especially if the relatives did not share a common upbringing (such as siblings adopted into different families). Particularly important for research on the genetic basis of behavioral differences are identical and fraternal twins. **Monozygotic (MZ, or identical) twins** develop from the union of the same sperm and egg. They share the same genetic makeup, so their degree of genetic relatedness is 1.0. In contrast, **dizygotic (DZ, or fraternal) twins** develop from the union of two sperm with two separate eggs. Like other siblings, their degree of relatedness is .50, since they have a 50 percent chance of sharing the same gene for any characteristic.

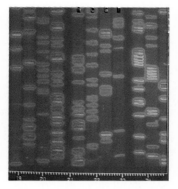

Data from the Human Genome Project, an international collaborative effort to map the genetic structure of all 46 human chromosomes.

BEHAVIORAL GENETICS

A relatively new field called behavioral genetics has produced rapid advances in our understanding of the relative roles of genetics and environment in shaping mental processes and behavior. Recent evidence suggests that genetic influences are far greater than once believed in a number of domains, including personality, intelligence, and mental illness (Fuller & Thompson, 1978; Gottesman, 1991; Kendler & Diehl, 1993; McGue et al., 1993; Plomin et al., 1997). Studies of twins provide psychologists a golden opportunity to examine the role of genetics because MZ and DZ twins typically share similar environments but differ in their degree of genetic relatedness. If a psychological attribute is genetically influenced, MZ twins should be more likely than DZ twins and other siblings to share it. This method is not free of bias; identical twins may receive more similar treatment than fraternal twins, since they look the same. Thus, behavioral geneticists also compare twins reared together in the same family with twins who were adopted separately and reared apart (Bouchard et al., 1991; Loehlin, 1989, 1992; Lykken et al., 1992; Tellegen et al., 1988).

The findings from these studies have allowed psychologists to estimate the extent to which differences among individuals on psychological dimensions such as intelligence and personality are **heritable,** or determined by genetic factors. A **heritability coefficient** quantifies the extent to which variation in the trait across individuals (such as high or low levels of conscientiousness) can be accounted for by genetic variation. A coefficient of 0 indicates no heritability at all, while a coefficient of 1.0 indicates that a trait is completely heritable.

An important point, but one that is often misunderstood, is that heritability refers to genetic influences on *variability among individuals*; it says nothing about the extent to which a trait is genetically determined. An example should make this clear. The fact that humans have two eyes is genetically determined. For all practical purposes, however, humans show no variability in the expression of the trait of two-eyedness because virtually all humans are born with two eyes. Thus, the heritability of two-eyedness is 0; genetic variability is not correlated with phenotypic or observed variability because virtually no variability exists. In contrast, the trait of eye *color* has a very high degree of heritability (approaching 1.0) in a heterogeneous population. Thus, heritability refers to the proportion of variability among individuals on an observed trait (phenotypic variance) that can be accounted for by variability in their genes (genotypic variance).

Several studies of the personality characteristics of twins have produced heritability estimates from .15 to .50 (that is, up to 50 percent heritability) on a broad spectrum of traits, including conservatism, neuroticism, nurturance, assertiveness, and aggressiveness (Plomin et al., 1997). Some findings have been very surprising and counterintuitive. For example, identical twins reared apart, who may never have even met each other, tend to have very similar vocational interests and levels of job satisfaction (Arvey et al., 1989; Moloney et al., 1991). Researchers have even found a genetic influence on religious attitudes, beliefs, and values

Jerry Levey and Mark Newman, separated at birth, met when a colleague did a double-take at a firefighters' convention.

(Waller et al., 1990). Remarkably, the likelihood of *divorce* is influenced by genetics, since personality traits such as the tendency to be unhappy are partly under genetic control and influence life events such as divorce (Jockin et al., 1996). Heritability estimates for IQ are over .50.

In interpreting findings such as these, however, some caveats are in order. First, as emphasized by leading behavioral geneticists but too readily forgotten, heritability in the range of 50 percent means that environmental factors are equally important—they account for the other 50 percent (Plomin & Rende, 1991). Second, estimates of heritability depend in part on who one includes in the sample. Children who are severely malnourished may show less heritability of IQ than others because malnutrition can place constraints on intellectual potential that can suppress the impact of hereditary differences. In contrast, excluding diverse populations from a sample can lead to the mistaken conclusion that cultural or environmental factors make little difference. Including Bosnian and North American participants in a study of the relative roles of heredity and environment in shaping feelings of mistrust would likely yield much stronger estimates of environmental impact than studying only North Americans because of the recent turmoil, civil war, and genocide in Bosnia. As we will see throughout the book, in most domains, psychologists have become less interested in parceling out the relative roles of genes and environment than in understanding the way genetic and environmental variables *interact*.

INTERIM SUMMARY   Psychologists interested in genetics study the influence of genetic blueprints **(genotypes)** on observable qualities **(phenotypes).** Research in behavioral genetics suggests that a surprisingly large percent of the variation among individuals on psychological attributes such as intelligence and personality reflects genetic influences, which interact with environmental variables in very complex ways. **Heritability** refers to the proportion of variability among individuals on an observed characteristic (phenotypic variance) that can be accounted for by genetic variability (genotypic variance).

SOME CONCLUDING THOUGHTS

When I entered the field as a graduate student less than 20 years ago, a person could be a competent psychologist in many areas of research without being terribly well informed about the brain or genetics. To be sure, knowing more was better than knowing less. Understanding the brain's hierarchical organization was useful in understanding motivation, just as knowing about medications that impact the brain was important in working with patients with severe psychiatric disorders.

But 20 years ago a cognitive psychologist with minimal knowledge about the brain could develop hypotheses and design important experiments—because we knew so little about the function of the hippocampus in memory or the role of the frontal lobes in attention and problem solving. When researchers debated whether people use mental images of verbal propositions to solve spatial problems, they had to design very clever experiments that might test the advantages of one explanation over the other. (Now, we ask participants to rotate mental images in their minds and scan their brains to see where they show the most activation relative to control tasks such as simply looking at pictures.)

Today, things are very different. As we will see throughout this book, scarcely an area of research in psychology has been left untouched by the explosion of new information about the brain, biology, and behavioral genetics. We now know that different memory systems reflect different neural pathways, and we can no longer study "memory" as if it were one system. We know that pleasant and unpleasant feelings occur through the activation of separate neural pathways that rely on different neurotransmitters, so we can no longer view happiness and sadness as opposite ends of a continuum. And we know that genetic factors contribute substantially to success in school, work, and marriage. Thus, if we discover, for example, that children of divorce are more likely themselves to have problems sustaining long-term relationships, we must at least consider the possibility that *genetic* vulnerabilities—to sadness or anxiety, for example—might render them, like their parents, less able to sustain a relationship.

Does this mean that psychological experiences are nothing but biological events dressed up in cognitive or emotional clothing? No. The grief of losing a parent or lover is not adequately explained as the activation of neural circuits in the hypothalamus, amygdala, and cortex. And the most sophisticated brain-scanning techniques yield little of value if psychologists cannot associate what is happening in the brain with psychologically meaningful processes. For example, if we do not understand how people think and feel as they make moral decisions, we will have no idea what tasks to have them perform while scanning their brains to learn about the neural underpinnings of morality.

Thus, psychologists are increasingly focusing on *brain–behavior relationships*. To study the biological side of human nature is not to commit oneself to an image of a disembodied brain divorced from its psychological, social, and cultural context. An understanding of the biological underpinnings of human mental life and behavior should not *reduce* its richness; it should *add to* it. We will never comprehend the complexities of motivation, personality, development, or social interaction simply by "looking under the hood" of our skulls or of our genes. But as the explosion of research that has come at the end of the millenium has shown, we will never again understand these phenomena *without* looking under the hood. We have reached a new level of self-understanding, and we can never turn back.

SUMMARY

NEURONS: BASIC UNITS OF THE NERVOUS SYSTEM

1. The firing of billions of nerve cells provides the physiological basis for psychological processes.
2. **Neurons,** or nerve cells, are the basic units of the nervous system. **Sensory neurons** carry sensory information from sensory receptors to the central nervous system. **Motor neurons** transmit commands from the brain to the glands and muscles of the body. **Interneurons** connect neurons with one another.

3. A neuron typically has a **cell body, dendrites** (branchlike extensions of the cell body), and an **axon** that carries information to other neurons. Axons are often covered with **myelin** for more efficient electrical transmission. Located on the axons are **terminal buttons,** which contain **neurotransmitters,** chemicals that transmit information across the **synapse** (the space between neurons through which they communicate).

4. The "resting" voltage at which a neuron is not firing is called the **resting potential.** When a neuron stimulates another neuron, it either **depolarizes** the membrane (reducing its polarization) or **hyperpolarizes** it (increasing its polarization). The spreading voltage changes that occur when the neural membrane receives signals from other cells are called **graded potentials.** If enough depolarizing graded potentials accumulate to cross a threshold, the neuron will **fire.** This **action potential,** or nerve impulse, leads to the release of **neurotransmitters** (such as glutamate, GABA, dopamine, serotonin, and acetylcholine). These chemical messages are received by **receptors** in the cell membrane of other neurons, which in turn can excite or inhibit those neurons. *Neuromodulators* can increase or reduce the impact of other neurotransmitters released into the synapse.

The Endocrine System

5. The **endocrine system** is a collection of glands that control various bodily functions through the secretion of **hormones.** The endocrine system complements the cell-to-cell communication of the nervous system by sending global messages through the bloodstream.

The Peripheral Nervous System

6. The **peripheral nervous system (PNS)** consists of neurons that carry messages to and from the central nervous system. The peripheral nervous system has two subdivisions: the somatic nervous system and the autonomic nervous system. The **somatic nervous system** consists of the sensory neurons that receive information through sensory receptors in the skin, muscles, and other parts of the body, such as the eyes, and the motor neurons that direct the action of skeletal muscles. The **autonomic nervous system** controls basic life processes such as the beating of the heart, workings of the digestive system, and breathing. It consists of two parts, the **sympathetic nervous system** (which is activated in response to threats) and the **parasympathetic nervous system** (which returns the body to normal and works to maintain the body's energy resources).

The Central Nervous System

7. The **central nervous system (CNS)** consists of the brain and spinal cord. It is hierarchically organized, with an overall structure that follows its evolution. Evolutionarily more recent centers regulate many of the processes that occur at lower levels.

8. Aside from carrying out reflexes, the **spinal cord** transmits sensory information to the brain and transmits messages from the brain to the muscles and organs.

9. Several structures comprise the **hindbrain.** The **medulla oblongata** controls vital physiological functions, such as heartbeat, circulation, and respiration,

and forms a link between the spinal cord and the rest of the brain. The **cerebellum** appears to be involved in a variety of tasks, including learning, discriminating stimuli from one another, and coordination of smooth movements. The **reticular formation** maintains consciousness and helps regulate activity and arousal states throughout the central nervous system, including sleep cycles.

10. The **midbrain** consists of the tectum and tegmentum. The **tectum** includes structures involved in orienting to visual and auditory stimuli as well as others involved in linking unpleasant feelings to behaviors that can help the animal escape or avoid them. The **tegmentum** includes parts of the reticular formation and other nuclei with a variety of functions, of which two are particularly important: movement and the linking of pleasure to behaviors that help the animal obtain reward.

11. The **forebrain** consists of the hypothalamus, thalamus, and cerebrum. The **hypothalamus** is involved in regulating a wide range of behaviors, including eating, sleeping, sexual activity, and emotional experience. The **thalamus** is a complex of nuclei that perform a number of functions; one of the most important is to provide initial processing of sensory information and transmit this information to higher brain centers.

12. The **cerebrum** includes a number of **subcortical** structures as well as an outer layer, or **cortex**. The subcortical structures are the limbic system and the basal ganglia. Structures of the **limbic system** (the **septal area, amygdala,** and **hippocampus**) are involved in emotion, motivation, learning, and memory. **Basal ganglia** structures are involved in the control of movement; they also appear to play a part in mood and memory.

13. In humans, the **cerebral cortex** allows the flexible construction of sequences of voluntary movements, enables people to discriminate complex sensory patterns, and provides the capacity to think symbolically. The **primary areas** of the cortex receive sensory information and initiate motor movements. The **association areas** are involved in putting together perceptions, ideas, and plans.

14. The **right** and **left hemispheres** of the cerebral cortex are connected by the **corpus callosum.** Each hemisphere consists of four sections or lobes. The **occipital lobes** are specialized for vision. The **parietal lobes** are involved in a number of functions, including the sense of touch, movement, and the experience of one's own body and other objects in space. The functions of the **frontal lobes** include coordination of movement, attention, planning, social skills, conscience, abstract thinking, memory, and aspects of personality. Sections of the **temporal lobes** are important in hearing, language, and visual object recognition. Some psychological functions are **lateralized,** or primarily processed by one hemisphere.

15. Cultural and environmental factors can modify not only behavior but also the structure of the brain.

MIND, BRAIN, AND GENE

16. Environment and genes interact in staggeringly complex ways that psychologists are just beginning to understand. Psychologists interested in genetics study the influence of genetic blueprints **(genotypes)** on observable psychological attributes or qualities **(phenotypes).** Studies in **behavioral genetics** suggest that a substantial portion of the variation among individuals on many psychological attributes such as intelligence and personality are **heritable.** Heritability refers to the proportion of variability among individuals on an observed trait (phenotypic variance) that can be accounted for by variability in their genes (genotypic variance).

Saul le Boff, Untitled.

CHAPTER *4*

Sensation and Perception

A woman in her early twenties damaged her knee in a fall. Following surgery, she experienced sharp, burning pain so excruciating that she could not eat or sleep. The pain ran from her ankle to the middle of her thigh, and the slightest touch—even a light brush with a piece of cotton—provoked a feeling of intense burning. Surgical attempts to relieve her pain gave her no relief or only temporary relief followed by even more severe pain (Gracely et al., 1992). Tragically, her pain persisted indefinitely.

Another case had a happier ending. A 50-year-old man suffering from chronic lower back pain underwent surgery after unsuccessful attempts to treat it with exercise and medication. Like roughly 1 percent of patients who undergo this procedure (Sachs et al., 1990), he, too, developed severe burning pain and extraordinary sensitivity to any kind of stimulation of the skin. Fortunately, however, the pain disappeared after three months of treatment.

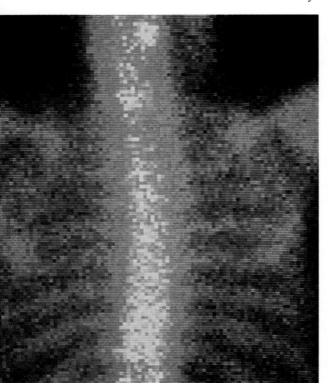

These patients suffered from a disorder called *painful neuropathy*, which literally means a painful illness of the neurons. Painful neuropathy can result from either an accident or from surgery. What essentially happens is that the brain interprets signals from receptors in the skin or joints that normally indicate light touch, pressure, or movement as excruciating pain. Researchers are unclear whether the problem lies in the peripheral or the central nervous system. Physical trauma might rewire peripheral nerves, so that they connect with the wrong sensory receptors and transmit an erroneous message to the brain; alternatively, the brain may adapt to nerve damage by becoming hypersensitive to any stimulation of the affected region (Gracely et al., 1992).

Whether the damage is peripheral or central, this syndrome raises some intriguing questions about the way the nervous system translates information about the world into psychological experience. Does the intensity of sensory experience normally mirror the intensity of physical stimulation? In other words, when pain increases or the light in a theater seems extremely bright following a movie, how much does this reflect changes in reality versus changes in our *perception* of reality? And if neurons can become accidentally rewired so that touch is misinterpreted as burning pain, could attaching neurons from the ear to the primary cortex of the occipital lobes produce visual images of sound?

These are some of the central questions underlying the study of sensation and perception. **Sensation** refers to the process by which the sense organs gather information about the environment and transmit this information to the brain for initial processing. **Perception** is the process by which the brain organizes and interprets these sensations. Sensations are immediate experiences of qualities—red, hot, bright, and so forth—whereas perceptions are experiences of objects or events that appear to have form, order, or meaning (Figure 4.1). The distinction between sensation and perception is useful though somewhat artificial, since sensory and perceptual processes form an integrated whole, translating physical reality into psychological reality.

FIGURE 4.1
From sensation to perception. Take a careful look at this picture before reading further, and try to figure out what it depicts. The photograph makes little sense until you recognize a Dalmatian, nose to the ground, walking toward a tree in the upper left corner. When people first look at this photo, their eyes transmit information to the brain about which parts of the picture are white and which are black; this is sensation. Sorting out the pockets of white and black into a meaningful picture is perception.

Why do sensation and perception matter? When students first approach this topic, they often think, "Oh, that rods-and-cones stuff I learned when I was ten," and wonder what it has to do with psychology. I was one of those students. What drew me to psychology were questions such as how memory works and why people fall in love. It was only years later that a simple and obvious fact penetrated my thick skull (and my apparently thin cortex): *Sensation and perception are the gateway from the world to the mind.* Memory involves the mental reconstruction of past experience—but what would we remember if we could not sense, perceive, and store images or sounds to re-create in our minds? Or consider love. What would love be if we could not feel another person's skin against ours? Could lovers experience the sense of comfort and security they feel when they mold into each other's arms if the skin were not laden with pressure detectors? (Okay, it isn't Shakespeare, but you get the point.) Without our senses, we are literally senseless—without the capacity to know or feel. And without knowledge or feeling, there is little left to being human.

We begin the chapter with sensation, exploring basic processes that apply to all the senses (or *sensory modalities*—the different senses that provide ways of knowing about stimuli). We then discuss each sense individually, focusing on the two that allow sensation at a distance, vision and hearing (or *audition*), and more briefly exploring smell *(olfaction),* taste *(gustation),* touch, and *proprioception* (the sense of the body's position and motion). Next we turn to perception, beginning with the way the brain organizes and interprets sensations and concluding with the influence of experience, expectations, and needs on the way people make sense of sensations. Does a hamburger taste the same to someone who is starving as to someone who has just eaten? Does an X-ray of a finger look different to a radiologist than to a layperson? And do people *learn* to organize visual sensations into meaningful three-dimensional shapes or are we born with certain processes that organize our experience?

INTERIM SUMMARY   **Sensation** is the process by which sense organs gather information about the environment and transmit it to the brain for initial processing; **perception** is the

Sensation is an active process in which humans, like other animals, focus their senses on potentially important information.

related process by which the brain selects, organizes, and interprets sensations. Sensation and perception are the gateway from the external world to the mind.

BASIC PRINCIPLES

Throughout this discussion, three general principles repeatedly emerge. First, *there is no one-to-one correspondence between physical and psychological reality.* What is "out there" is not directly reproduced "in here." Of course, the relation between physical stimuli and our psychological experience of them is not random; as we will see, it is actually so orderly that it can be expressed as an equation. Yet the inner world is not simply a photograph of the outer. The degree of pressure or pain experienced when a pin presses against the skin—even in those of us *without* painful neuropathy—does not precisely match the actual pressure exerted. Up to a certain point, light pressure is not experienced at all, and pressure only feels like pain when it crosses a certain threshold. The inexact correspondence between physical and psychological reality is one of the fundamental findings of **psychophysics,** the branch of psychology that studies the relation between attributes of the physical world and our psychological experience of them.

Second, *sensation and perception are active.* Sensation may seem passive—images are cast on the retina at the back of the eye; pressure is imposed on the skin. Yet sensation is first and foremost an act of translation, converting external energy into an internal version, or *representation,* of it. People also orient themselves to stimuli to capture sights, sounds, and smells that are relevant to them. We turn our ears toward potentially threatening sounds to magnify their impact on our senses, just as we turn our noses toward the smell of baking bread. We also selectively focus our consciousness on parts of the environment that are particularly relevant to our needs and goals (Chapter 9).

Like sensation, perception is an active process, which organizes and interprets sensations. The world as subjectively experienced by an individual—the *phenomenological world*—is a joint product of external reality and the person's creative efforts to understand and depict it mentally. People often assume that perception is like photographing a scene or tape recording a sound and that they need only open their eyes and ears to capture what is "really" there. In fact, perception is probably more like stitching a quilt than taking a photograph. The phenomenological world must be constructed from sensory experience, just as the quilt maker creates something whole from threads and patches.

The world as perceived represents an interaction between the perceiver and the perceived. (George Braque, Landscape with Houses, 1908-9, oil on canvas, 65.5x54cm. Collection: Art Gallery of New South Wales. ©1998 Artists Rights Society (ARS), New York, ADAGP, Paris. Reproduced with permission.)

If perception is a creative, constructive process, to what extent do people perceive the world in the same way? Does red appear to one person as it does to another? If one person loves garlic and another hates it, are the two loving and hating the same taste or does garlic have a different taste to each? To what extent do people see the world the way it really is?

Plato argued that what we perceive is little more than shadows on the wall of a cave, cast by the movement of an unseen reality in the dim light. What does it mean to say that a cup of coffee is hot? Relative to what? Do fish perceive the depths of the ocean as cold? And is grass *really* green? A person who is color blind for green, whose visual system is unable to discriminate certain wavelengths of light, will not see the grass as green. Is greenness, then, an attribute of the object (grass), the perceiver, or some interaction between them? These are philosophical questions at the heart of sensation and perception.

The third general principle is that *sensation and perception are adaptive.* From an evolutionary perspective, the ability to see, hear, or touch is the product of millions of adaptations that left our senses exquisitely crafted to serve functions that facilitate survival and reproduction (Tooby & Cosmides, 1992). Frogs have "bug detectors" in their visual systems that automatically fire in the presence of a potential meal. Similarly, humans have neural regions specialized for the perception of faces and facial expressions (Adolphs et al., 1996; Phillips et al, 1997). Human infants have an innate tendency to pay attention to forms that resemble the human face, and over the course of their first year they become remarkably expert at reading emotions from other people's faces (Chapter 13). Attending to their parents' facial cues (such as concern or fear) can mean the difference between approaching or escaping a predator, and reading faces is as important for later adjustment and adaptation as reading words is in a literate culture.

The specific ways sensory systems are constructed reflects evolutionary pressures. Consider something we take for granted, like the placement of the eyes (Figure 4.2). Among vertebrates, the eyes can be placed frontally, as in humans, or laterally (on the sides), as in rabbits. Frontal placement is common in predators, who rely on sensory input from two eyes to pinpoint distance. Lateral placement is more common among animals who are frequently prey, for it provides them with an expanded field of vision; if they cannot have eyes in the back of their head, at least they have something close.

INTERIM SUMMARY   Three basic principles apply across all the senses: There is no one-to-one correspondence between physical and psychological reality; sensation and perception are active, not passive; and sensory and perceptual processes reflect the impact of adaptive pressures over the cource of evolution.

SENSING THE ENVIRONMENT

Although each sensory system is attuned to particular forms of energy, all the senses share certain common features. First, they must translate physical stimulation into sensory signals. Second, they all have thresholds below which a person does not sense anything despite external stimulation. Children know this intuitively when they tiptoe through a room to "sneak up" on someone—who may suddenly hear them and turn around. The tiptoeing sounds increase gradually in intensity as the child approaches, but the person senses nothing until the sound crosses a threshold. Third, sensation requires constant decision making, as the individual tries to distinguish meaningful from irrelevant stimulation. We are unaware of most of these sensory "decisions" because they occur so rapidly and unconsciously. Alone at night, people often wonder, "Did I hear something?" Their

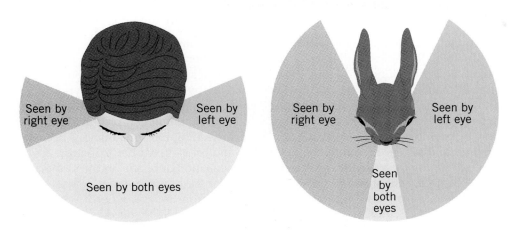

FIGURE 4.2
Eye placement and field of vision. Frontal placement of the eyes allows depth perception but reduces the field of vision. Lateral eye placement has the opposite result. Regardless of eye placement, animals expand their range of vision by moving their eyes and heads. *Source:* Adapted from Sekuler & Blake, 1994, pp. 28–29.

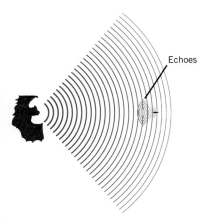

Echoes

FIGURE 4.3
Echolocation in the bat. Bats use echolocation to detect stimuli in the dark, such as insects. They send out pulses of sound waves and home in by sensing the echoes that bounce off their prey. As they prepare to intercept, they send out pulses at a more rapid rate to get the precise coordinates. *Source:* Griffin, 1959, p. 86.

answers depend not only on the intensity of the sound but also on their tendency to attach meaning to small variations in sound. Fourth, sensing the world requires the ability to detect *changes* in stimulation, to notice when a bag of groceries has gotten heavier or a light has dimmed. Finally, efficient sensory processing means "turning down the volume" on information that is redundant; the nervous system tunes out messages that continue without change. We examine each of these processes in turn.

TRANSDUCTION

Sensation requires converting energy in the world into internal signals that are psychologically meaningful. The more the brain processes these signals—from sensation to perception to cognition—the more meaningful they become.

Sensation typically begins with an environmental stimulus, a form of energy capable of exciting the nervous system. We actually register only a tiny fraction of the energy surrounding us, and different species have evolved the capacity to process different types of information. Honeybees can sense the Earth's magnetic field and essentially relocate important landmarks, such as places they have found food, by their compass coordinates (Collett & Baron, 1994). Bats are nocturnal creatures, but instead of relying on vision in darkness (like cats), they "see with their ears," using a process called echolocation. **Echolocation** enables animals such as bats, whales, and porpoises to obtain information about the size, location, and movement of objects by emitting waves of sound (mechanical energy that causes particles of air or water to vibrate) and sensing the resulting echoes as these waves bounce off objects (Griffin, 1959). The ears and brains of bats evolved to detect very tiny air movements caused by echoes from small flying insects. As the bat approaches its prey, it emits faster pulses of sound to help it locate the insect in space (Figure 4.3). SONAR (the acronym for "sound navigation and ranging") uses similar principles to navigate the ocean. Instruments such as SONAR or Geiger counters for detecting X-ray radiation expand the range of our senses to detect energy for which they lack the sensitivity.

Creating a Neural Code   Specialized cells in the nervous system, called **receptors,** transform energy in the environment into neural impulses that can be interpreted by the brain (Loewenstein, 1960; Miller et al., 1961). Receptors respond to different forms of energy and generate action potentials in sensory neurons adjacent to them. In the eye, receptors respond to particles of light; in the ear, to the movement of molecules of air. The process of converting physical energy or stimulus information into neural impulses is called **transduction.** The brain then interprets the impulses generated by sensory receptors as light, sound, smell, taste, touch, or motion. It essentially reads a neural code—a pattern of neural firing—and translates it into a psychologically meaningful "language."

In 1826, Johannes Müller proposed that whether a neural message is experienced as light, sound, or some other sensation results less from differences in stimuli than from the particular neurons excited by them. Müller's hypothesis, known as the **doctrine of specific nerve energies,** is bolstered by reports of syndromes such as painful neuropathy, in which a cotton ball can produce a sensation of burning instead of a light touch because receptors presumably become rewired to different neural fibers. Extending and revising Müller's doctrine, psychologists now recognize that the nature of a sensation depends on the pathways in the brain it activates. Electrical stimulation of the primary visual cortex produces visual sensations as surely as shining a light in the eye, whereas electrical stimulation of the auditory cortex produces sensations experienced as sound. The stimulus may be the same—electrical current—but the pathways are different.

Coding for Intensity and Quality of the Stimulus For each sense, the brain codes sensory stimulation for intensity and quality. The neural code for **intensity,** or strength, of a sensation varies by sensory modality but usually involves the number of sensory neurons that fire, the frequency with which they fire, or some combination of the two. The neural code for **quality,** or nature, of the sensation (such as color, pitch, taste, or temperature) is often more complicated, relying on both the specific type of receptors involved and the pattern of neural impulses generated. For example, some receptors respond to warmth and others to cold, but a combination of both leads to the sensation of extreme heat. Remarkably, the brain synthesizes millions of simple on–off decisions (made by sensory neurons that receive information from receptors and either fire or do not fire) to perceive the lines and shapes of a Cezanne landscape or words on a printed page. It does this so quickly and automatically that we are unaware of anything but the end product.

INTERIM SUMMARY Sensation begins with an environmental stimulus; all sensory systems have specialized cells called **receptors** that respond to environmental stimuli and typically generate action potentials in adjacent sensory neurons. This process is called **transduction.** Within each sensory modality, the brain codes sensory stimulation for **intensity** and **quality.**

ABSOLUTE THRESHOLDS

Even if a sensory system has the capacity to respond to a stimulus, the individual may not experience the stimulus if it is too weak. The minimum amount of physical energy needed for an observer to notice a stimulus is called an **absolute threshold.** One way psychologists measure absolute thresholds is by presenting a particular stimulus (light, sound, taste, odor, pressure) at varying intensities and determining the level of stimulation necessary for the person to detect it about 50 percent of the time. A psychologist trying to identify the absolute threshold for sound of a particular pitch would present subjects with sounds at that pitch, some so soft they would never hear them and others so loud they would never miss them. In between would be sounds they would hear some or most of the time. The volume at which most subjects hear the sound half the time but miss it half the time is defined as the absolute threshold; above this point, people sense stimulation most of the time. The absolute thresholds for many senses are remarkably low, such as a small candle flame burning 30 miles away on a clear night (Table 4.1).

Despite the "absolute" label, absolute thresholds vary from person to person and situation to situation. One reason for this variation is the presence of **noise,** which technically refers to irrelevant, distracting information (not just to loud

TABLE 4.1 EXAMPLES OF ABSOLUTE THRESHOLDS

SENSE	THRESHOLD
Vision	A candle flame 30 miles away on a dark, clear night
Hearing	A watch ticking 20 feet away in a quiet place
Smell	A drop of perfume in a six-room house
Taste	A teaspoon of sugar in two gallons of water
Touch	A wing of a fly falling on the cheek from a height of one centimeter

Source: Adapted from Brown et al., 1962.

Whether a perceiver interprets an ambiguous stimulus as a meaningful signal or as noise can have extremely important ramifications.

sounds). Some noise is external; to pick out the ticking of a watch at a concert is far more difficult than in a quiet room. Other noise is internal, created by the random firing of neurons. Psychological events such as expectations, motivation, stress, and level of fatigue can also affect the threshold at which a person can sense a low level of stimulation (see Fehm-Wolfsdorf et al., 1993; Pause et al., 1996). Someone whose home has been burglarized, for example, is likely to be highly attuned to night-time sounds and to "hear" suspicious noises more readily, whether or not they actually occur.

▶ ONE STEP FURTHER

Signal Detection

Is the absolute threshold, then, really absolute? Or perhaps sensation at low levels of stimulation really involves the detection of a stimulus against a background of noise (Greene & Swets, 1966; Swets, 1992). According to **signal detection theory,** sensation is not a passive process that occurs when the amount of stimulation exceeds a critical threshold; rather, experiencing a sensation means making a *judgment* about whether a stimulus is present or absent.

Does a noise downstairs, a blip on a radar screen, or a small irregularity on a brain scan signal something dangerous? According to signal detection theory, two distinct processes are at work in detection tasks of this sort. The first is an initial sensory process, reflecting the observer's **sensitivity** to the stimulus—how well the person sees, hears, or feels the stimulus. The second is a decision process, reflecting the observer's **response bias** (or **decision criterion**), that is, the individual's readiness to report detecting a stimulus when uncertain.

To assess response bias, signal detection researchers present participants with stimuli at low intensities, as in the traditional procedure for measuring absolute thresholds, but they also add trials in which *no* stimulus is presented. What subjects experience on each trial is some mixture of stimulus energy (the signal), which may or may not be present, and noise, which randomly waxes and wanes. Sometimes the noise alone is enough to lead the person to say she heard or saw something because its effect crosses the decision criterion. At other times, the signal is present but too weak to be detected, and the noise level is too low to augment it. (At still other times, noise, when added to a signal, increases the intensity of the signal enough to lead the participant to report a sensation.)

Participants in signal detection experiments can make two kinds of errors. They may respond with a *false alarm*, reporting a stimulus when none was presented, or they may fail to report an actual stimulus (a *miss*). Similarly, they may give two kinds of correct response. They may *hit*, reporting an actual stimulus, or they may provide a *correct negative*, reporting no stimulus when none was presented. Accuracy in sensing a signal involves a trade-off between sensitivity to stimuli that are presented and vulnerability to reporting stimuli that have not been presented. Thus, an observer who tends to overreport sensations will have a high number of hits but also a high number of false alarms. An observer who tends to underreport will have a lower number of hits but also a lower number of false alarms.

Whether a person has a low or high response bias for reporting "yes" depends on many factors. One is expectations: If a patient complains of heart pain, shooting pain in his legs, and shortness of breath, his doctor is more likely to hear an irregular heartbeat. Another factor that influences response bias is motivation. Two neurologists who review the MRI scan of a woman who is experiencing blinding headaches may come to different conclusions about a possible irregularity. The neurologist who recently lost a patient by mistaking a tumor for noise will have a low threshold for reporting "yes" because the psychological cost of setting it higher is too great. The other, who recently performed exploratory surgery when in fact no tumor was present and accidentally left the patient with partial blindness, will have a much higher criterion for reporting a "hit."

To distinguish the relative contributions of sensitivity and response bias, psychologists experimentally manipulate the costs and benefits of over- or underreporting stimulation by paying participants different amounts for different types of correct or incorrect responses (Figure 4.4). These consequences can be described in a payoff matrix, which shows the costs and benefits of each type of response. Researchers then plot the proportion of hits against the proportion of false alarms on a *receiver operating characteristic (ROC)* curve, which literally shows the way the receiver of the signal operates at different signal intensities. This allows the researcher to determine how well the subject can actually sense the stimulus, independent of response bias. ◄

HERMAN®

11-15   © 1976 Jim Unger

"My mistake! I thought I heard a noise down here."

DIFFERENCE THRESHOLDS

Thus far, we have focused on absolute thresholds, the lowest level of stimulation required to sense a stimulus. Above this threshold, another kind of threshold is the **difference threshold**—the lowest level of stimulation required to sense that a *change* in stimulation has occurred. In other words, the difference threshold is the difference in intensity between two stimuli necessary to produce a **just noticeable difference** (or **jnd**), such as the difference between two light bulbs of slightly different wattage. (The absolute threshold is actually a special case of the difference threshold, in which the difference is between no intensity and a very weak stimulus.)

The jnd depends not only on the intensity of the new stimulus but also on the level of stimulation already present. The more intense the existing stimulus, the larger the change must be to be noticeable. A person carrying a two-pound backpack will easily notice the addition of a half-pound book, but adding the same book to a 60-pound backpack will not make the pack feel any heavier; that is, it will not produce a jnd.

CONDITION	SUBJECT'S RESPONSE	
	"Yes"	"No"
Stimulus presented	+ $10.00 (large gain)	– $10.00 (large loss)
Stimulus not presented	– $1.00 (small loss)	+ $1.00 (small gain)

(*a*) Matrix that will produce a "yes" bias

CONDITION	SUBJECT'S RESPONSE	
	"Yes"	"No"
Stimulus presented	+ $1.00 (small gain)	– $1.00 (small loss)
Stimulus not presented	– $10.00 (large loss)	+ $10.00 (large gain)

(*b*) Matrix that will produce a "no" bias

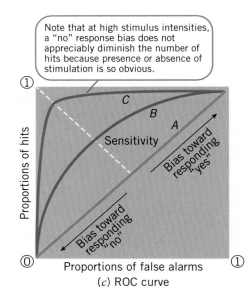

(*c*) ROC curve

FIGURE 4.4
Signal detection. Two payoff matrices, one that leads to a "yes" bias (*a*) and the other to a "no" bias (*b*). To assess sensitivity to a stimulus (*c*), researchers plot the proportion of hits against the proportion of false alarms on a ROC curve. If the signal is so low that it is imperceptible, the proportion of hits will equal the proportion of false alarms because the receiver's responses are essentially random (diagonal line *A*). At a somewhat higher stimulus intensity (line *B*), subjects have a better ratio of hits to false alarms because their responses are influenced by the presence of a detectable signal, so they are no longer just guessing. At very high signal intensities (line *C*), people rarely give wrong answers. The sensitivity of the observer to different signal intensities (e.g., how well the person can hear) is represented by the dotted line, which shows how far the receiver's ROC curve diverges from the diagonal, which represents random responding.

Weber's Law

In 1834, the German physiologist Ernst Weber recognized not only this lack of a one-to-one relationship between the physical and psychological worlds but also the existence of a consistent relationship between them. Regardless of the magnitude of two stimuli, the second must differ from the first by a constant proportion—for example, it must be a tenth larger—for it to be perceived as different. This relationship is called **Weber's law** (Figure 4.5*a*). That constant proportion—the ratio of change in intensity required to produce a jnd compared to the previous intensity of the stimulus—can be expressed as a fraction, called the **Weber fraction.**

The Weber fraction varies depending on the individual, stimulus, context, and sensory modality. For example, the Weber fraction for perceiving changes in heaviness is 1/50. This means that the average person can perceive an increase of one pound if added to a 50-pound bag, two pounds added to 100 pounds, and so forth. The Weber fraction for a sound around middle C is 1/10, which means that a person can hear an extra voice in a chorus of 10 but would require two voices to notice an increase in loudness in a chorus of 20.

Fechner's Law

Weber's brother-in-law, Gustav Fechner, took the field a noticeable step forward in 1860 with the publication of his *Elements of Psychophysics*. One of his major achievements was to broaden the application of Weber's law by linking the subjective experience of intensity of stimulation with the actual magnitude of a stimulus. In other words, using Weber's law, Fechner was able to estimate precisely how intensely a person would report experiencing a sensation based on the amount of stimulus energy actually present. He assumed that for any given stimulus, all jnds are created equal; that is, each additional jnd feels subjectively like one incremental (additional) unit in intensity. Using Weber's law, he then plotted these subjective units against the actual incremental units of stimulus intensity necessary to produce each jnd (Figure 4.5*b*). He recognized that at low stimulus intensities, only tiny increases in stimulation are required to produce subjective effects as large as those produced by enormous increases in stimulation at high levels of intensity.

As can be seen from Figure 4.5*b*, the result was a logarithmic function, which simply means that as one variable (in this case, subjective intensity) increases arithmetically (1, 2, 3, and etc.), the other variable (in this case, objective intensity) increases geometrically (1, 8, 64, etc.). This became known as **Fechner's law.** Fechner's law means, essentially, that people experience only a small percentage of actual increases in stimulus intensity but that this percentage is predictable. Knowing the Weber constant and the intensity of the stimulus, then, a psychologist can actually predict how strong a person's *subjective sensation* will be. This was a remarkable feat, since it demonstrated that aspects of our subjective experience can be predicted mathematically.

Stevens's Power Law

Fechner's law held up for a century but was modified by S. S. Stevens (1961, 1975) because it did not quite apply to all stimuli and senses. For example, the relation between perceived pain and stimulus intensity is the opposite of most other psychophysical relations: The greater the pain, the *less* additional intensity is required for a jnd. This makes adaptive sense, since increasing pain means increasing danger and therefore demands increased attention. In part on a dare from a colleague (Stevens, 1956), Stevens set out to prove that people can accurately rate subjective intensity on a numerical scale. He instructed participants to listen to a series of tones of differing intensity and asked them simply to assign numbers to the tones to indicate their relative loudness. What he discovered was a lawful relation between self-reports and stimulus intensity across a much wider range of sensory modes and intensities than Fechner's law could accommodate.

According to **Stevens's power law** (Figure 4.5*c*), as the perceived intensity of a stimulus grows arithmetically, the actual magnitude of the stimulus grows exponentially, that is, by some power (squared, cubed, etc.). The exponent varies, however, for different senses, just as the Weber fraction varies. Where the exponent is less than 1 (for example, for brightness it is .33), the results are generally similar to Fechner's law. Thus, to double the perceived brightness of a light, the physical stimulus has to increase by a factor of 8. Where the exponent is larger than 1, however, as for sensations produced by electric shock (where the exponent is 3.5), the magnitude of sensations grows quite rapidly as stimulation increases. Thus, Stevens's power law can predict subjective experiences of pain intensity as readily as brightness.

Although the formulas have become more precise, the message from Weber, Fechner, and Stevens is fundamentally the same: Sensation bears an orderly, predictable relation to physical stimulation, but psychological experience is not a photograph, tape recording, or wax impression of external reality.

INTERIM SUMMARY   The **absolute threshold** is the minimum amount of energy needed for an observer to notice a stimulus. The **difference threshold** is the lowest level of stimulation required to sense that a change in stimulation has occurred. According to **Weber's**

law, regardless of the magnitude of two stimuli, the second must differ by a constant proportion from the first for it to be perceived as different. According to **Fechner's law,** the magnitude of a stimulus grows logarithmically as the subjective experience of intensity grows arithmetically, so that people subjectively experience only a fraction of actual increases in stimulation. According to **Stevens' power law,** subjective intensity increases in a linear fashion as actual intensity grows exponentially.

FIGURE 4.5
Quantifying Subjective Experience: From Weber to Stevens

(a) Weber's Law

Weber's law states that regardless of the magnitude of two stimuli, the second must differ from the first by a constant proportion for it to be perceived as different. Expressed mathematically,

$$\Delta I / I = k$$

where I = the intensity of the stimulus, ΔI = the additional intensity necessary to produce a jnd at that intensity, and k = a constant. To put it still another way, the ratio of change in intensity to initial intensity required to produce a jnd—expressed as a fraction, such as one unit of change for every ten units—is a constant for a given sensory modality. This constant is known as a Weber fraction. This can be seen in the accompanying graph, where the constant is the slope of the line (in this case, $1/10$), plotting ΔI (the y-axis) as a function of I (the x-axis).

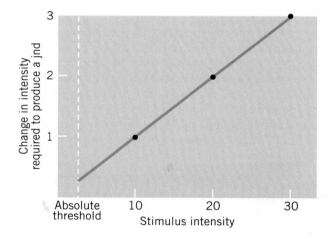

(b) Fechner's Law

Starting with Weber's law, Fechner realized that as the experienced sensation increases one unit of perceived intensity at a time, the actual intensity of the physical stimulus is increasing logarithmically. **Fechner's law** thus held that the subjective magnitude of a sensation (S) grows as a proportion (k) of the logarithm of the objective intensity of the stimulus (I), or

$$S = k \log I$$

This can be readily seen in the accompanying graph: Subjective units of sensation ($S1$, $S2$, etc.) increase by increments of one as objective units ($I1$, $I2$, etc.) increase geometrically (that is, by a factor of more than one). This leads to a logarithmic curve.
Source: Adapted from Guilford, 1954, p. 38.

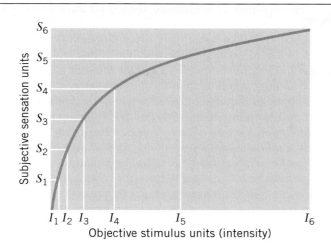

(c) Stevens' Power Law

Stevens' power law states that subjective intensity (S) grows as a proportion (k) of the actual intensity (I) raised to some power (b). Expressed mathematically,

$$S = k\,I^b$$

As the graph below shows, Stevens' power law plots subjective magnitude of stimulation as an exponential function of stimulus magnitude. Here, these functions are shown for brightness (where the exponent is .33), apparent length (where the exponent is 1.0, so the function is linear), and electric shock (where the exponent is 3.5). *Source:* Stevens, 1961, p. 11.

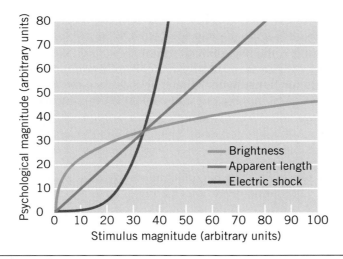

SENSORY ADAPTATION

A final process shared by all sensory systems is adaptation. You walk into a crowded restaurant, and the noise level is overwhelming, yet within a few minutes, you do not even notice it. Driving into an industrial city, you notice an unpleasant odor that smells like sulfur and wonder how anyone tolerates it; a short time later, you are no longer aware of it. These are examples of **sensory adapta-**

tion—the tendency of sensory receptors to respond less to stimuli that continue without change.

Sensory adaptation makes sense from an evolutionary perspective. Constant sensory inputs provide no new information about the environment, so the nervous system essentially ignores them. Given all the stimuli that bombard an organism at any particular moment, an animal that paid as much notice to constant stimulation as to changes that might be adaptively significant would be at a disadvantage. Sensory adaptation also performs the function of "turning down the volume" on information that would overwhelm the brain, by reducing its perceived intensity to a manageable level.

Although sensory adaptation generally applies across senses, the nervous system is wired to circumvent it in some important instances. For example, the visual system has ways to keep its receptors from adapting; otherwise, stationary objects would disappear from sight. The eyes are constantly making tiny quivering motions, which guarantees that the receptors affected by a given stimulus are constantly changing. The result is a steady flow of graded potentials on the sensory neurons that synapse with those receptors. Similarly, although we may adapt to mild pain, we generally do not adapt to severe pain (Miller & Kraus, 1990), again an evolutionarily sensible design feature of a sensory system that responds to body damage.

INTERIM SUMMARY   **Sensory adaptation** is the tendency of sensory systems to respond less to stimuli that continue without change. This makes adaptive sense, since changing stimuli provide more new information than those that are relatively constant.

VISION

Throughout this chapter we will use vision as our major example of sensory processes because it is the best understood of the senses. We begin by discussing the form of energy (light) transduced by the visual system. We then examine the organ responsible for transduction (the eye) and trace the neural pathways that take raw information from receptors and convert it into sensory knowledge.

THE NATURE OF LIGHT

Light is just one form of electromagnetic radiation, but it is the form to which the eye is sensitive. That humans and other animals respond to light is no accident, since cycles of light and dark have occurred over the course of five billion years of evolution. These cycles, and the mere presence of light as a medium for sensation, have shaped virtually every aspect of our psychology, from the times of day at which we are conscious to the way we choose mating partners (using visual appearance as a cue). Indeed, light is so useful for tracking prey, avoiding predators, and "checking out" potential mates that a structure resembling the eye has apparently evolved independently over 40 times in different organisms (Fernald, 1996). Other forms of electromagnetic radiation to which humans are blind include infrared, ultraviolet, radio, and X-ray radiation.

Electromagnetic energy travels in waves, created by the patterned movement, or *oscillation*, of electrically charged particles. Different forms of radiation have waves of different lengths, or **wavelengths.** This simply means that their particles oscillate more or less frequently, that is, with higher or lower *frequency*. Some of these wavelengths, such as gamma rays, are as short or shorter than the diameter

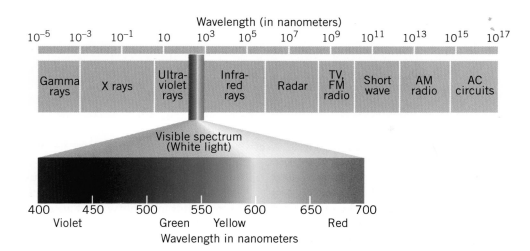

FIGURE 4.6
The electromagnetic spectrum. Humans sense only a small portion of the electromagnetic spectrum (enlarged in the figure), light. Light at different wavelengths is experienced as different colors.

of an atom; others are quite long, such as radio waves, which may oscillate once in a mile. Wavelengths are measured in **nanometers (nm),** or billionths of a meter (Figure 4.6).

The receptors in the human eye are tuned to detect only a very restricted portion of the electromagnetic spectrum, from roughly 400 to 700 nm. Other organisms are sensitive to different regions of the spectrum; for example, many insects (such as ants and bees) and some vertebrate animals (such as iguanas and some bird species) see ultraviolet light (Alberts, 1989; Goldsmith, 1994; Newman & Hartline, 1982).

The physical dimension of wavelength translates into the psychological dimension of color, just as the physical *intensity* of light is related to the subjective sensation of brightness. Light is a useful form of energy to sense for a number of reasons (see Sekuler & Blake, 1994). Like other forms of electromagnetic radiation, light travels very quickly (186,000 miles, or roughly 300,000 kilometers, per second), so sighted organisms can see things almost immediately after they happen. Light also travels in straight lines, which means that it preserves the geometric organization of the objects it illuminates; the image an object casts on the retina resembles its actual structure. Perhaps most importantly, light interacts with the molecules on the surface of many objects and is either absorbed or reflected. The light that is reflected reaches the eyes and creates a visual pattern. Objects that reflect a lot of light appear brighter, whereas those that absorb much of the light that hits them appear dark.

THE EYE

Two basic processes occur in the eyes (Figure 4.7). First, the cornea, pupil, and lens focus light on the retina. Next, the retina transduces this visual image into neural impulses that are relayed to and interpreted by the brain.

Focusing Light

Light enters the eye through the **cornea,** a tough, transparent tissue covering the front of the eyeball. Under water, people cannot see clearly because the cornea is constructed to bend (or *refract*) light rays traveling through air, not water. That is why a diving mask allows clearer vision: It puts a layer of air between the water and the cornea.

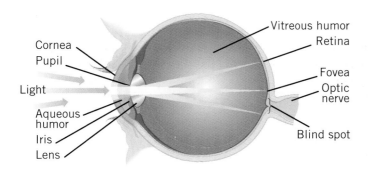

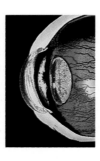

FIGURE 4.7
Anatomy of the human eye. The cornea, pupil, and lens focus a pattern of light onto the retina, which then transduces the retinal image into neural signals carried to the brain by the optic nerve.

From the cornea, light passes through a chamber of fluid called *aqueous humor*, which supplies oxygen and other nutrients to the cornea and lens. Unlike blood, which performs this function in other parts of the body, the aqueous humor is a clear fluid, so light can pass through it. Next, light travels through an opening in the center of the **iris** (the pigmented tissue that gives the eye its blue, green, or brown color); this opening is the **pupil.** Muscle fibers in the iris cause the pupil to expand (dilate) or constrict to regulate the amount of light entering the eye. The size of the pupil also changes with different psychological states, such as fear, excitement, interest, and sexual arousal. Experienced gamblers (and perhaps Don Juans) can use pupil size to read other people's emotions (Hess, 1965).

The next step in focusing light occurs in the **lens,** an elastic, disc-shaped structure about the size of a lima bean. Muscles attached to cells surrounding the lens alter its shape to focus on objects at various distances. The lens flattens for distant objects and becomes more rounded or spherical for closer objects, a process known as **accommodation.** The light is then projected through the *vitreous humor* (a clear, gelatinous liquid) onto the **retina,** a light-sensitive layer of tissue at the

The size of the pupils changes in different emotional states, which means that a skilled gambler may literally be able to read his opponents' hands from their eyes, although he may have no awareness of the mechanisms by which he can do this.

back of the eye. The retina receives a constant flow of images as people turn their heads and eyes or move through space.

Abnormalities in the eye sometimes make accommodation difficult, affecting **visual acuity,** or sharpness of the image. Since light waves normally spread out over a distance, the eye has to focus them on a single point in the retina to produce a clear image. **Nearsightedness** (or **myopia**) occurs when the cornea and lens focus this image in front of the retina; by the time rays of light reach the retina, they have begun to cross, leading to a blurred image (Figure 4.8). The opposite effect occurs in **farsightedness** (or **hyperopia**): The eye focuses light on a point beyond the retina, leading to decreased acuity at close range. Both abnormalities are common at all ages and usually are readily corrected with lenses that alter the optics of the eye. With advancing age, however, losses in visual acuity become more pronounced (Curcio and Drucker, 1993; Fukada et al., 1990; Matjucha and Katz, 1994). The lens becomes more opaque and loses some of its ability to accommodate, and the diameter of the pupil shrinks so that less light reaches the retina. Cataracts, which are common in older people, occur when the lens becomes so cloudy that the person may become almost blind. As a result of age-related changes, the retina of a normal 65-year-old receives only about one-third as much light as that of a 20-year-old (Kline & Schieber, 1985).

The Retina

The eye is like a camera, insofar as it has an opening to adjust the amount of incoming light, a lens to focus the light, and the equivalent of photosensitive film—

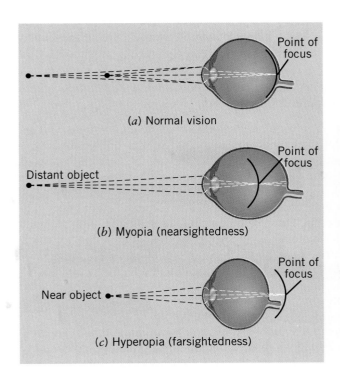

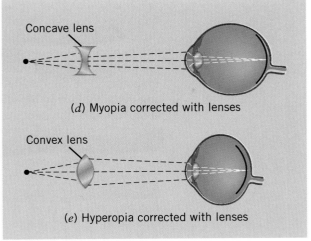

FIGURE 4.8
Normal vision (*a*), nearsightedness (*b*), and farsightedness (*c*). In (*a*), the cornea and lens focus the image on the retina, producing normal vision. The shape of the lens, of course, differs for optimal focus on objects nearby or at a distance. In (*b*), the image is focused in front of the retina (myopia), whereas in (*c*), it is focused behind the retina (hyperopia). In (*d*), a concave lens corrects vision by spreading out the light rays from distant objects. In (*e*), a convex lens has the opposite effect, bending light rays toward each other to focus them on the retina instead of behind it.

Light

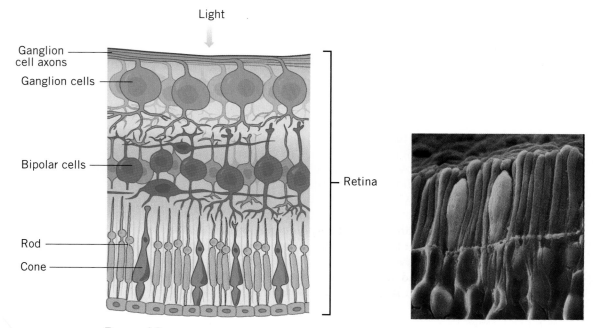

Ganglion cell axons

Ganglion cells

Bipolar cells

Retina

Rod

Cone

FIGURE 4.9

The retina. Light passes through layers of neurons to reach photoreceptors, called rods and cones, which respond to different wavelengths of light. These receptors in turn connect to bipolar cells, which pass information to the ganglion cells, whose axons form the optic nerve. The photo shows rods and cones magnified thousands of times. Above them are bipolar cells.

the retina. (The analogy is incomplete, of course, because the eye, unlike a camera, works best when it is moving.) The retina transduces light energy from illuminated objects into neural impulses, transforming a pattern of light reflected off objects into psychologically meaningful information.

Structure of the Retina   The retina is a multilayered structure about as thick as a sheet of paper (Figure 4.9). The innermost layer (at the back of the retina) contains two types of light receptors, or **photoreceptors** ("photo" is from the Greek word for light), called **rods** and **cones,** which were named for their distinctive shapes. Each retina contains approximately 120 million rods and 8 million cones. When a rod or cone absorbs light energy, it generates an electrical signal, stimulating the neighboring **bipolar cells.** These cells combine the information from many receptors and produce graded potentials on **ganglion cells,** which integrate information from multiple bipolar cells. The long axons of these ganglion cells bundle together to form the **optic nerve,** which carries visual information to the brain.

The central region of the retina, the **fovea,** is most sensitive to small detail, so vision is sharpest for stimuli directly in sight. In contrast, the point on the retina where the optic nerve leaves the eye, called the **optic disk** (or **blind spot**), has no receptor cells. People are generally unaware of their blind spots for several reasons. Different images usually fall on the blind spots of the two eyes, so one eye sees what the other does not. In addition, the eyes are always moving, providing information about the missing area. To avoid perceiving an empty visual space, the brain also automatically uses visual information from the rest of the retina to fill in the gap. (To see the effects of the blind spot in action, see Figure 4.10.)

Rods and Cones   Rods and cones have distinct functions. Rods are more sensitive to light than cones, allowing vision in dim light. Rods only produce visual sensations in black, white, and gray. Cones are, evolutionarily speaking, a

FIGURE 4.10
The blind spot. Close your left eye, fix your gaze on the plus, and slowly move the book toward and away from you. The circle will disappear when it falls in the blind spot of the right retina.

more recent development than rods and respond to color as well as black and white. They require more light to be activated, however, which is why we see little or no color in dim light. Nocturnal animals such as owls have mostly rods, whereas daytime animals and most other birds have mostly cones (Schiffman, 1996). Humans see both in black and white and in color, depending on the amount of light available.

Rods and cones also differ in their distribution on the retina and in their connections to bipolar cells. Rods are concentrated off the center of the retina. Thus, in dim light, objects are seen most clearly by looking slightly away from them. (You can test this yourself tonight by looking at the stars. Fix your eyes directly on a bright star and then focus your gaze slightly off to the side of it. The star will appear brighter when the image is cast away from the fovea.) Several rods may also provide input to a single bipolar cell. Since the bipolar cell can be activated by many different rods or combinations of them, it cannot transmit fine details to the brain. On the other hand, the sum of the energy collected by many rods can easily cause an action potential in sensory neurons excited by them, so these cells can fire in very dim light.

In contrast, cones are concentrated in the center of the retina in the fovea, although they are also found in smaller proportions in the periphery. Thus, in bright light an object is seen best if looked at directly, focusing the image on the fovea. Further, a single cone may connect with a single bipolar cell. This allows perception of fine detail, since precise information from each cone is preserved and passed on for higher processing.

Transforming Light into Sight   Both rods and cones contain photosensitive pigments that change chemical structure in response to light (Rushton, 1962; Wald, 1968). This process is called **bleaching** because the pigment breaks down when exposed to light, leading the photoreceptors to lose their characteristic color. When photoreceptors bleach, they create graded potentials in the bipolar cells connected to them, which may then fire.

Bleaching must be reversed before a photoreceptor is restored to full sensitivity. Pigment regeneration takes time, which is why people often have to feel their way around the seats when entering a dark theater on a bright day. Adjusting to a dimly illuminated setting is called **dark adaptation.** The cones adapt relatively quickly, usually within about five minutes, depending on the duration and intensity of light to which the eye was previously exposed. Rods, in contrast, take about 15 minutes to adapt. Since they are especially useful in dim light, vision may remain less than optimal in the theater for some time. **Light adaptation,** the process of adjusting to bright light after exposure to darkness, is much faster; readapting to bright sunlight upon leaving a theater takes only about a minute (Matlin, 1983).

Receptive Fields   Once the rods and cones have responded to patterns of light, the nervous system must somehow convert these patterns into a neural code to allow the brain to reconstruct the scene. This is truly a remarkable process: Waves of light reflected off, say, your friend's face, pass through the eye to the rods and cones of the retina. The pattern of light captured by those receptor cells translates your friend's face into a pattern of nerve impulses that the brain can "read" with such precision that you know precisely who you are seeing.

This process begins with the ganglion cells. Each ganglion cell has a *receptive field*. A **receptive field** is a region within which a neuron responds to appropriate stimulation (that is, in which it is *receptive* to stimulation), (Hartline, 1938). Neurons at higher levels of the visual system (in the brain) also have receptive fields, which means that at higher and higher levels of processing, the visual system keeps creating maps of the scenes the eye has observed. The same basic principles apply in other sensory systems, as when neurons from the peripheral nervous system all the way up through the cortex map precisely where a mosquito has landed on the skin.

Psychologists have learned about receptive fields in ganglion cells through a technique called single-cell recording. In **single-cell recording,** researchers insert a tiny electrode into the brain or retina of an animal, close enough to a neuron to detect when it fires. Then, holding the animal's head still, they flash light to different parts of the visual field to see what kind of stimulation leads the ganglion cell to fire. By placing electrodes in many places, psychologists can map the receptive fields of the ganglion cells of the retina.

Using this method, researchers discovered that the receptive fields of some ganglion cells have a center and a surrounding area, like a target (Figure 4.11). Presenting light to the center of the receptive field turns the cell "on" (that is, excites the cell), whereas presenting light within the receptive field but outside the center turns the cell "off." For other ganglion cells the pattern is just the opposite:

FIGURE 4.11
Single-cell recording. In (*a*), the neuron spontaneously fires (indicated by the thin vertical lines) randomly in darkness. In (*b*), it fires repeatedly when light is flashed to the center of its receptive field. In (*c*), firing stops when light is flashed in the periphery of its receptive field; that is, light outside the center inhibits firing. *Source:* Adapted from Sekuler & Blake, 1994, p. 68.

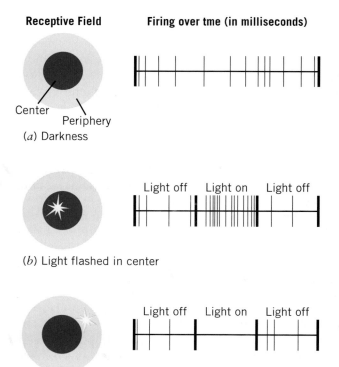

Receptive Field   **Firing over tme (in milliseconds)**

Center
          Periphery
(*a*) Darkness

Light off   Light on   Light off

(*b*) Light flashed in center

Light off   Light on   Light off

(*c*) Light flashed in periphery

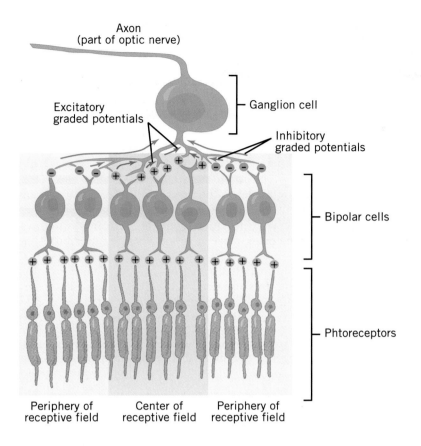

Axon
(part of optic nerve)

Ganglion cell

Excitatory
graded potentials

Inhibitory
graded potentials

Bipolar cells

Phtoreceptors

Periphery of
receptive field

Center of
receptive field

Periphery of
receptive field

FIGURE 4.12
Excitation and inhibition in receptive fields of a ganglion cell. In this example of a center-on/periphery-off ganglion cell, the process of transduction begins as photoreceptors that respond to light in the center of the ganglion cell's receptive field excite bipolar cells, which in turn generate excitatory graded potentials (represented here by a +) on the dendrites of the ganglion cell. Photoreceptors that respond to light in the periphery of the ganglion cell's receptive field excite bipolar cells that generate *inhibitory* action potentials (represented by a –). If enough light is present in the center, and little enough in the periphery, of the receptive field, the excitatory graded potentials will depolarize the ganglion cell membrane. The axon of the ganglion cell is part of the optic nerve, which will then transmit information about light in this particular visual location to the brain.

Light in the center inhibits neural firing, whereas light in the periphery excites the neuron. The process by which adjacent visual units inhibit or suppress each other's level of activity is called **lateral inhibition.** Figure 4.12 illustrates the way excitatory and inhibitory graded potentials from bipolar cells may be involved in this process.

Why do receptive fields have this concentric circular organization, with on and off regions that inhibit each other? As described at the beginning of the chapter, our sensory systems are attuned to changes and differences. The targetlike organization of ganglion cells allows humans and other animals to perceive edges and changes in brightness and texture that signal where one surface ends and another begins. A neuron that senses light in the center of its receptive field will fire rapidly if the light is bright and covers much of the center. To the extent that light is also present in the periphery of the receptive field, however, neural firing will be inhibited, essentially transmitting the information that the image is continuous in this region of space, with no edges.

Lateral inhibition appears to be responsible in part for the phenomenon seen in **Hermann grids** (Figure 4.13), in which the intersections of white lines in a dark grid appear gray and the intersections of black lines in a white grid appear gray (Spillman, 1994). Essentially, white surrounded by white on all four sides appears darker than white surrounded by black on two sides, and vice versa. The receptive fields of neurons in the fovea tend to be very small, allowing for high visual acuity, whereas receptive fields increase in size with distance from the center of the retina (Wiesel & Hubel, 1960). This is why looking straight at the illusory patches of darkness or lightness in Hermann grids makes them disappear: Receptive fields of neurons in the fovea can be so small that the middle of each line is surrounded primarily by the same shade regardless of whether it is at an intersection.

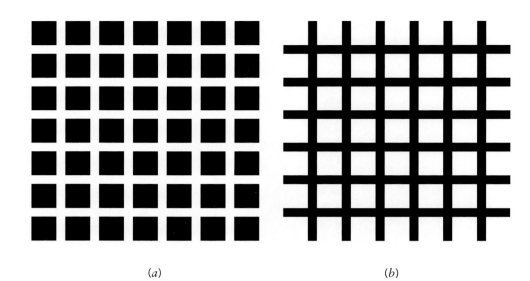

FIGURE 4.13
Hermann grids. White lines against a black grid appear to have gray patches at their intersections (*a*), as do black lines against a white grid (*b*).

(*a*)   (*b*)

INTERIM SUMMARY   Two basic processes occur in the eyes: light is focused on the **retina** by the **cornea, pupil,** and **lens;** and the retina transduces this visual image into a code that the brain can read. The retina includes two kinds of photoreceptors: **rods** (which produce sensations in black, white, and gray and are very sensitive to light) and **cones** (which produce sensations of color). Rods and cones excite **biopolar cells,** which in turn excite or inhibit **ganglion cells,** whose axons constitute the **optic nerve.** Ganglion cells, like sensory cells higher up in the nervous system, have **receptive fields,** in which sensory information can inhibit or excite them.

NEURAL PATHWAYS

Transduction in the eye, then, starts with the focusing of images onto the retina. When photoreceptors bleach, they excite bipolar cells, which in turn affect the firing of ganglion cells with particular receptive fields. The axons from these ganglion cells comprise the optic nerve, which transmits information from the retina to the brain.

From the Eye to the Brain

Impulses from the optic nerve first pass through the **optic chiasm** (*chiasm* comes from the Greek word for "cross"), where the optic nerve splits (Figure 4.14*a*). Information from the left half of each retina (which comes from the right visual field) goes to the left hemisphere, and vice versa. Once past the optic chiasm, combined information from the two eyes travels to the brain via the **optic tracts,** which are simply a continuation of the axons from ganglion cells that constitute the optic nerve. From there, visual information flows along two separate pathways within each hemisphere. (Figure 4.14*a*).

One small pathway projects to a clump of neurons in the midbrain known as the **superior colliculus,** which in humans is involved in controlling eye movements. Its neurons respond to the presence or absence of visual stimulation in parts of the visual field but cannot identify specific objects. Neurons in the superior colliculus also integrate input from the eyes and the ears, so that weak stimulation from the two senses together can orient the person toward a region in space that neither sense alone could detect (Stein & Meredith, 1990).

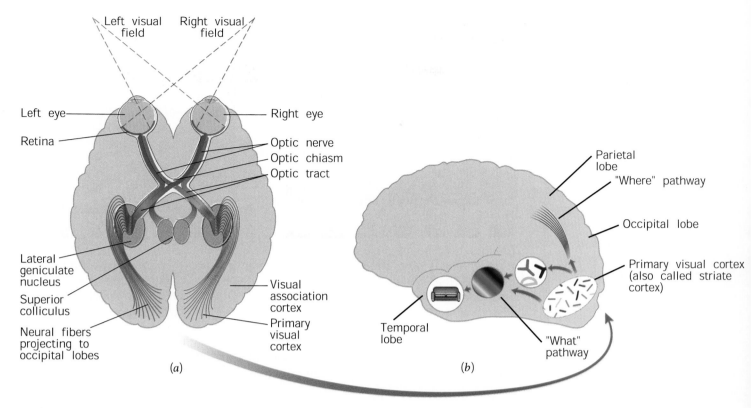

FIGURE 4.14

Visual pathways. The optic nerve carries visual information from the retina to the optic chiasm, where the optic nerve splits. The brain processes information from the right visual field in the left hemisphere and vice versa because of the way some visual information crosses and some does not cross over to the opposite hemisphere at the optic chiasm. At the optic chiasm, the optic nerve becomes the optic tract (because bundles of axons within the brain itself are called tracts, not nerves). A small pathway from the optic tract carries information simultaneously to the superior colliculus. The optic tract then carries information to the lateral geniculate nucleus of the thalamus, where neurons project to the primary visual cortex.

The second pathway projects to the **lateral geniculate nucleus** of the thalamus and then to the primary visual cortex in the occipital lobes. Neurons in the lateral geniculate nucleus preserve the map of visual space in the retina. That is, neighboring ganglion cells transmit information to thalamic neurons next to each other, which in turn transmit this retinal map to the cortex. Neurons in the lateral geniculate nucleus have the same kind of concentric (targetlike) receptive fields as retinal neurons. They also receive input from the reticular formation, which means that the extent to which an animal is attentive, aroused, and awake may modulate the transmission of impulses from the thalamus to the visual cortex (Burke & Cole, 1978; Munk et al., 1996).

The presence of two visual pathways from the optic nerve to the brain appears to be involved in an intriguing phenomenon known as **blindsight,** in which individuals are unaware of their capacity to see (Weiskrantz et al., 1974, 1997). Pursuing observations made by neurologists in the early part of the 20th century, researchers have studied patients with lesions to the primary visual cortex, which receives input from the second visual pathway (through the lateral geniculate nucleus). These patients are, for all intents and purposes, blind: If shown an object, they deny that they have seen it. Yet if asked to describe its geometrical form (e.g., triangle or square) or give its location in space (to the right or left, up or down),

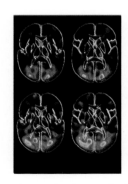

The primary visual cortex in the occipital lobes lights up on a PET scan when people actively view words, in contrast to when their eyes are closed or they stare continuously at a black dot.

they do so with accuracy far better than chance—frequently protesting all the while that they cannot do the task because they cannot see! Visual processing in the superior colliculus, and perhaps at the level of the lateral geniculate nucleus, apparently leads to visual experiences outside of awareness.

Visual Cortex

From the lateral geniculate nucleus, then, visual information travels to the primary visual cortex in the occipital lobes. The primary visual cortex is sometimes called the *striate cortex* because of its striped appearance; visual pathways outside the striate cortex to which its neurons project are thus called *extrastriate* cortex (because they are outside, or extra to, the striate cortex).

Primary Visual Cortex   The size of a brain region that serves a particular function (in this case, vision) is a rough index of the importance of that function to the organism's adaptation over the course of evolution. Once again this simply reflects the "logic" of natural selection: If vision was particularly useful for survival and reproduction in our primate ancestors, those animals with larger visual processing centers would be at an adaptive advantage, and larger and more sophisticated visual "modules" would be likely to evolve over time. In fact, in many monkey species whose visual systems resemble those of humans, over half the cortex is devoted to visual processing (Van Essen et al., 1992). Within a sensory system, such as the visual system, the same principle also holds true. For example, in humans as in other primates, the primary visual cortex does not give "equal time" to all regions of the person's visual field. Much of the striate cortex is devoted to information from the fovea (Drasdo, 1977), just as the somatosensory cortex in the parietal lobes overrepresents regions such as the hands, which have many receptors and transmit especially important information (Chapter 3).

The striate cortex is the "first stop" in the cortex for all visual information. Neurons in this region begin to "make sense" of visual information, in large measure through the action of neurons known as feature detectors. **Feature detectors,** discovered by Nobel Prize winners David Hubel and Thorsten Wiesel (1959, 1979), are neurons that fire only when stimulation in their receptive field matches a very specific pattern or orientation. **Simple cells** are feature detectors that respond most vigorously to lines of a particular orientation, such as horizontal or vertical, in an exact location in the visual field (Figure 4.15). **Complex cells** are feature detectors that generally cover a larger receptive field and respond when a stimulus of the proper orientation falls anywhere within their receptive field, not just at a particular location. They may also fire only when the stimulus moves in a particular direction. Still other cells, called **hypercomplex cells,** require that a stimulus be of a specific size or length to fire. Other neurons in the primary visual cortex respond selectively to color, contrast, and texture (Engel et al., 1997; Livingstone & Hubel, 1988).

The What and the Where Pathways   From the primary visual cortex, visual information appears to flow along two pathways, or *processing streams* (Figure 4.14*b*) (Shapley, 1995; Ungerleider & Haxby, 1994; Van Essen et al., 1992). Much of what we know about these pathways comes from the study of macaque monkeys, although recent imagining studies using PET and fMRI have confirmed researchers' suspicion that the neural pathways underlying visual perception in the human and the macaque are very similar. Researchers have labeled these visual streams the "what" and the "where" pathways.

The **what pathway,** which runs from the striate cortex in the occipital lobes through the lower part of the temporal lobes (or the *inferior temporal cortex*), is involved in determining *what* an object is. In this pathway, primitive features from

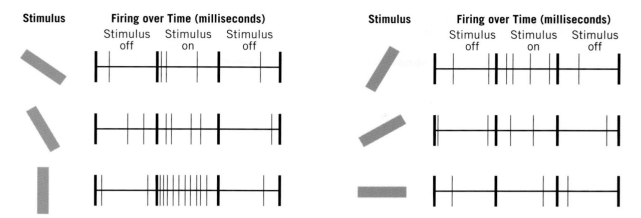

FIGURE 4.15

Feature detectors. A simple cell that responds to vertical lines will show more rapid firing the closer a visual image in its receptive field matches its preferred orientation. *Source:* Sekuler & Blake, 1994, p. 119.

the striate cortex (such as lines) are integrated into more complex combinations (such as cones or squares). At other locations along the pathway, the brain processes features of the object such as color and texture. All of these processes occur simultaneously, as the striate cortex routes shape information to a shape-processing module, color information to a color-processing module, and so forth. Although some "cross-talk" occurs among these different modules, each appears to create its own map of the visual field, such as a shape map and a color map. Not until the information has reached the front, or anterior, sections of the temporal lobes does a fully integrated percept appear to exist. At various points along the stream, however, polysensory areas bring visual information in contact with information from other senses. For example, when a person shakes hands with another person, he not only sees the other's hand but also feels it, hears the person move toward him, and feels his own arm moving through space. This requires integrating information from all of the lobes of the cortex. The second stream, the **where pathway,** is involved in locating the object in space, following its movement, and guiding movement toward it. This pathway runs from the striate cortex through the middle and upper (superior) regions of the temporal lobes and up into the parietal lobes.

Lesions that occur along these pathways produce disorders that would seem bizarre without understanding the neuroanatomy. For example, patients with lesions at various points along the what pathway show a variety of disorders, such as an inability to recognize or name objects, to recognize colors, or to recognize familiar faces (prosopagnosia). Patients with lesions in the where pathway, in contrast, typically have little trouble recognizing or naming objects, but they may constantly bump into things, have trouble grasping nearby objects, or fail to respond to objects in a part of their visual field, even including their own limbs (a phenomenon called *visual neglect*). Interestingly, this neglect may occur even when they are picturing a scene from memory: When asked to draw a scene, patients with neglect may simply leave out an entire segment of the scene and have no idea that it is missing.

Anatomically, the location of these two pathways makes sense as well. Recognition of objects ("what") is performed by modules in the temporal lobes directly below those involved in language, particularly in *naming* objects. Knowing where objects are in space and tracking their movements, on the other hand, is important for guiding one's own movement toward or away from them. The position of one's *own* body in space appears to be represented in the parietal lobes, adjacent to the "where" pathway.

The colors we perceive in a bouquet of flowers depend on the wavelengths of light the flowers reflect into our eyes.

INTERIM SUMMARY   From the optic nerve, visual information travels along two pathways. One is to a midbrain region called the **superior colliculus,** which in humans is particularly involved in eye movements. The other is to the **lateral geniculate nucleus** in the thalamus and on to the visual cortex. **Feature detectors** in the primary visual cortex respond only when stimulation in their receptive field matches a particular pattern or orientation. Beyond the primary visual cortex, visual information flows along two pathways, the **"what" pathway** (involved in determining what an object is) and the **"where" pathway** (involved in locating the object in space, following its movement, and guiding movement toward it).

PERCEIVING IN COLOR

"Roses are red, violets are blue." Well, not exactly. Color is a psychological property, not a quality of the stimulus. Grass is not green to a cow because cows lack color receptors; in contrast, most insects, reptiles, fish, and birds have excellent color vision (Nathans, 1987). As Sir Isaac Newton demonstrated in research with prisms in the sixteenth century, white light (such as sunlight and light from common indoor lamps) is composed of all the wavelengths that constitute the colors in the visual spectrum. A rose appears red because it absorbs certain wavelengths and reflects others, and humans have receptors that detect electromagnetic radiation in that range of the spectrum.

Actually, color has three psychological dimensions: hue, saturation, and lightness (Sewall & Wooten, 1991). **Hue** is what people commonly mean by color, that is, whether an object appears blue, red, violet, and so on. **Saturation** is a color's purity (the extent to which it is diluted with white or black or "saturated" with its own wavelength, like a sponge in water). **Lightness** is the extent to which a color is light or dark.

People of all cultures appear to perceive the same colors or hues, although cultures vary widely in the number of their color labels (Chapter 7). In the West, color also appears to be gendered (i.e., to differ between the two genders): Few men would pass a test requiring them to distinguish colors such as bone, taupe, and magenta, despite their mastery of the English language. (Males appear to improve considerably, however, after a few trips to the shoe store with a woman.)

Retinal Transduction of Color

How does the visual system translate wavelength into the subjective experience of color? The first step occurs in the retina, where cones with different photosensitive pigments respond to varying degrees to different wavelengths of the spectrum. In 1802, a British physician named Thomas Young proposed that human color vision is *trichromatic*, that is, the colors we see reflect blends of three colors to which our retinas are sensitive. Developed independently 50 years later by Hermann von Helmholtz, the **Young–Helmholtz** (or **trichromatic**) **theory of color** holds that the eye contains three types of receptors, each maximally sensitive to wavelengths of light that produce sensations of blue, green, or red.

Another century later, Nobel Prize winner George Wald and others confirmed the existence of three different types of cones in the retina (Brown & Wald, 1964; Dartnall et al., 1983; Schnapf et al., 1989). Each cone responds to a range of wavelengths but responds most persistently to waves of light at a particular point on the spectrum (Figure 4.16). Short-wavelength cones *(S-cones)* are most sensitive to wavelengths of about 420 nm, which are perceived as blue. Middle-wavelength cones *(M-cones),* which produce the sensation of green, are most sensitive to wavelengths of about 535 nm. Long-wavelength cones *(L-cones),* which produce red sensations, are most sensitive to wavelengths of about 560 nm (Brown & Wald, 1964). Mixing these three primary colors of light—red, green, and blue— produces the thousands of color shades humans can discriminate and identify.

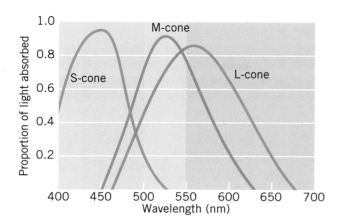

Figure showing cone response curves with wavelength (nm) on x-axis from 400 to 700, and proportion of light absorbed on y-axis from 0 to 1.0. Three curves labeled S-cone, M-cone, and L-cone.

FIGURE 4.16
Cone response curves. All three kinds of cones respond to a range of frequencies—that is, they absorb light waves of many lengths, which contributes to bleaching—but they are maximally sensitive at particular frequencies and thus produce different color sensations.

This list of primary colors differs from the list of primary colors children learn in elementary school from mixing paints (blue, red, and yellow). The reason is that mixing paint and mixing light alter the wavelengths perceived in different ways, one *subtracting* and the other *adding* parts of the spectrum. Mixing paints is called **subtractive color mixture** because each new paint added actually blocks out, or subtracts, wavelengths reflected onto the retina. For example, yellow paint appears yellow because its pigment absorbs most wavelengths and reflects only those perceived as yellow; the same is true of blue paint. When blue and yellow paints are mixed, only the wavelengths not absorbed by *either* the blue or yellow paint reach the eye; the wavelengths left are the ones we perceive as green.

Subtractive color mixture, then, mixes wavelengths of light before they reach the eye. In contrast, **additive color mixture** takes place in the eye itself, as light of differing wavelengths simultaneously strikes the retina and thus expands (adds to) the perceived section of the spectrum. Newton discovered additive color mixture by using two prisms to funnel two colors simultaneously into the eye. Color television works on an additive principle. A television picture is composed of tiny blue, green, and red dots, which the eye blends from a distance. When struck by an electron beam inside the set, the spots light up. From a distance, the spots combine to produce multicolored images, although the dots can be seen at very close range.

Processing Color in the Brain

The trichromatic theory accurately predicted the nature of retinal receptors, but it was not a complete theory of color perception. For example, the physiologist

The primary colors children learn in elementary school are not the same as the primary colors of the trichromatic theory—although learning the former tends to be more fun.

The Impressionists made heavy use of additive color mixture, as in this painting of Venice by the French painter Paul Signac.

Ewald Hering noted that trichromatic theory could not alone explain a phenomenon that occurs with **afterimages,** visual images that persist after a stimulus has been removed. Hering (1878, 1920) wondered why the colors of the afterimage were different in predictable ways from those of the original image (Figure 4.17). He proposed a theory, modified substantially by later researchers, known as opponent-process theory (DeValois, 1975; Hurvich & Jameson, 1957). **Opponent-process theory** argues that all colors are derived from three antagonistic color systems: black–white, blue–yellow, and red–green. The black–white system contributes to brightness and saturation; the other two systems are responsible for hue.

FIGURE 4.17
Afterimage. Stare at the yellow and red globe for three minutes, centering your eyes on the white dot in the middle, and then look at the white space on the page to the left of it. The afterimage is the traditional blue and green globe, reflecting the operation of antagonistic color-opponent cells in the lateral geniculate nucleus.

Hering proposed his theory in opposition to trichromatic theory, but subsequent research suggests that the two theories are actually complementary. Trichromatic theory applies to the retina, where cones are, in fact, particularly responsive to red, blue, or green. Opponent-process theory applies at higher visual centers in the brain. Researchers have found that some neurons in the lateral geniculate nucleus of monkeys, whose visual system is similar to that of humans, are **color-opponent cells,** excited by wavelengths that produce one color but inhibited by wavelengths of the other member of the pair (DeValois & DeValois, 1975). For example, some red–green neurons increase their activity when wavelengths experienced as red are in their receptive fields and decrease their activity when exposed to wavelengths perceived as green; others are excited by green and inhibited by red. The pattern of activation of several color-opponent neurons together determines the color the person senses (Abramov & Gordon, 1994).

Opponent-process theory neatly explains afterimages. Recall that in all sensory modalities the sensory system adapts, or responds less, to constant stimulation. In the visual system, adaptation begins with bleaching in the retina. Photoreceptors take time to resynthesize their pigments once they have bleached and thus cannot respond continuously to constant stimulation. During the period in which their pigment is returning, they cannot send inhibitory signals; this facilitates sensation of the opponent color. The afterimage of yellow therefore appears blue (and vice versa), red appears green, and black appears white.

Opponent-process and trichromatic theory together explain another phenomenon that interested Hering: *color blindness* (or, more accurately, *color deficiency*). Few people are entirely blind to color; those who are (because of genetic abnormalities that leave them with only one kind of cone) can only detect brightness, not color. Most color-deficient people confuse red and green (Figure 4.18). Red–green color blindness is sex linked, over ten times more prevalent in males than females. It generally reflects a deficiency of either M-cones or L-cones, which makes red–green distinctions impossible at higher levels of the nervous system (Vollrath et al., 1988; Weale, 1982; Wertenbaker, 1981).

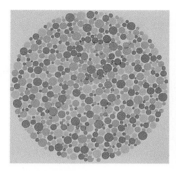

FIGURE 4.18
Color blindness. In this common test for color blindness, a green 3 is presented against a background of orange and yellow dots. The pattern of stimulation normally sent to the lateral geniculate nucleus by S-, M-, and L-cones allows discrimination of these colors. People who are red-green color blind see only a random array of dots.

INTERIM SUMMARY   Two theories together explain what is known about color vision. According to the **Young-Holmholtz,** or **trichromatic, theory,** the eye contains three types of receptors, which are most sensitive to wavelengths experienced as red, green, or blue. According to **opponent-process theory,** the colors we experience (and the afterimages we perceive) reflect three antagonistic color systems—a blue-yellow, red-green, and black-white system. Trichromatic theory is operative at the level of the retina, and opponent-process theory is more applicable at higher neural levels.

How the World Becomes Represented in the Mind

The processes by which objects in the external world become translated into an "internal" portrait of them in the mind should now be growing clear. At the lowest level of the nervous system, neurons collect highly specific information from receptor cells that would, by itself, be meaningless. At each subsequent stage, through the thalamus to the most complex modules in the cortex, information is combined to provide a progressively richer, more integrated picture of the bits and pieces of knowledge collected at the prior stage. Through this process, isolated units of stimulus energy gradually undergo a remarkable metamorphosis, in which the brain weaves sensory threads into complex and meaningful perceptual tapestries. As we will see, however, perceptions are not woven *exclusively* from sensory input, that is, from the simple threads. Our beliefs, expectations, and needs also exert an influence on what we perceive, so that knowledge is, from the very start, an interaction between an active perceiver and an environment that never stands still.

People see fireworks from a distance before they hear them because light travels faster than sound.

HEARING

If a tree falls in a forest, does it make a sound if no one hears it? To answer this question requires an understanding of hearing, or **audition,** and the physical properties it reflects. Like vision, hearing allows sensation at a distance and is thus of tremendous adaptive value. Hearing is also involved in the richest form of communication, spoken language. As with our discussion of vision, we begin by considering the stimulus energy underlying hearing—sound. Next we examine the organ that transduces it, the ear, and the neural pathways for auditory processing.

THE NATURE OF SOUND

When a tree falls in the forest, the crash produces vibrations in adjacent air molecules, which in turn collide with one another. A guitar string being plucked, a piece of paper rustling, or a tree falling to the ground all produce sound because they create vibrations in the air. Like ripples on a pond, these rhythmic pulsations of acoustic energy (sound) spread outward from the vibrating object as **sound waves.** Sound waves grow weaker with distance, but they travel at a constant speed, roughly 1130 feet (or 340 meters) per second.

Sound differs from light in a number of respects. Sound travels more slowly, which is why thunder often appears to follow lightening, or why fans in center field sometimes hear the crack of a bat *after* seeing the batter hit the ball; at close range, however, the difference between the speed of light and the speed of sound is imperceptible. Unlike light, sound also travels through most objects, which explains why sound is more difficult to shut out. Like light, sound waves can be reflected off or absorbed by objects in the environment, but the impact on hearing is different from the impact on vision. When sound is reflected off an object, it produces an echo; when it is absorbed by an object, such as carpet, it is muffled. Everyone sounds like the great Italian tenor Luciano Pavarotti in the shower (or like Bruce Springsteen if they have a sore throat) because tile absorbs so little sound, creating echoes and resonance that give fullness to even a mediocre voice.

Frequency

Acoustic energy has three important properties: frequency, complexity, and amplitude. When a person hits a tuning fork, the prongs of the fork move rapidly inward and outward, putting pressure on the air molecules around them, which collide with the molecules next to them. Each round of expansion and contraction of the distance between molecules of air is known as a **cycle.**

The number of cycles per second determines the sound wave's frequency. **Frequency** is just what it sounds like—a measure of how often (that is, how *frequently*) a wave cycles. Frequency is expressed in **hertz,** or **Hz** (named after the German physicist Heinrich Hertz). One hertz equals one cycle per second, so a 1500-Hz tone has 1500 cycles per second. The frequency of a simple sound wave corresponds to the psychological property of **pitch** (the quality of a tone, from low to high). Generally, the higher the frequency, the higher the pitch. When frequency is doubled—that is, when the number of cycles per second is twice as frequent—the pitch perceived is an octave higher.

The human auditory system is sensitive to a wide range of frequencies. Young adults can hear frequencies from about 15 to 20,000 Hz, but as with most senses, capacity diminishes with aging. Frequencies used in music range from the lowest note on an organ (16 Hz) to the highest note on a grand piano (over 4000 Hz). Human voices range from about 100 Hz to about 3500 Hz, and our ears are most sensitive to sounds in that frequency range. Other species are sensitive to different ranges. Dogs hear frequencies ranging from 15 to 50,000 Hz, which is why they are responsive to "silent" whistles whose frequencies fall above the range humans can sense. Elephants can hear ultralow frequencies over considerable distances.

So, does a tree falling in the forest produce a sound? It produces sound *waves*, but the waves only become perceptible as "a sound" if creatures in the forest have receptors tuned to them.

Complexity

Sounds rarely consist of waves of uniform frequency. Rather, most sounds are a combination of sound waves, each with a different frequency. The **complexity** of a sound wave—the extent to which it is composed of multiple frequencies—corresponds to the psychological property of **timbre,** or texture of the sound. People recognize each other's voices, as well as the sounds of different musical instruments, from their characteristic timbre. Timbre allows people to distinguish the middle C of a piano from the same pitch played on a flute. The dominant part of each wave produces the predominant pitch (in this case, middle C), but overtones (additional frequencies) give the instrument its distinctive sound. Synthesizers imitate conventional instruments by electronically adding the right overtones to pure frequencies (Hilts, 1980). Much of the music on popular radio stations today is synthesized; many of the sounds are actually played on a keyboard and mixed with special computer software. Adding instrumentation is as easy as saying, "Let's try adding some strings here."

The sounds instruments produce, whether in a rock band or a symphony, are music to our ears because we learn to interpret particular temporal patterns and combinations of sound waves as music. What people hear as music and as random auditory noise depends on their culture. The scales and harmonic structures that are standard in contemporary jazz would have been musically incomprehensible to Mozart, just as rock and roll was denounced by parents of teenagers in the 1960s as senseless noise.

Amplitude

In addition to frequency and complexity, sound waves have amplitude. **Amplitude** refers to the height and depth of a wave, that is, the difference between its maximum and minimum pressure level (Figure 4.19). The amplitude of a sound wave corresponds to the psychological property of **loudness;** the greater the amplitude, the louder the sound. Amplitude is measured in **decibels (dB).** Zero decibels is the absolute threshold above which most people can hear a 1000-Hz tone.

Like the visual system, the human auditory system has an astonishing range, handling energy levels that can differ by a factor of 10 billion or more (Bekesy & Rosenblith, 1951). The decibel scale is logarithmic, condensing a huge array of intensities into a manageable range, just as the auditory system does. A loud scream is 100,000 times more intense than a sound at the absolute threshold, but it is only 100 dB different. Conversation is usually held at 50 to 60 dB. Most people experience sounds over 130 dB as painful, and prolonged exposure to sounds over about 90 dB, such as subway cars rolling into the station or amplifiers at a rock concert, can produce permanent hearing loss or ringing in the ears (Figure 4.20).

INTERIM SUMMARY Sound travels in **waves,** which occur as a vibrating object sets air particles in motion. The sound wave's **frequency,** which is experienced as **pitch,** refers to the number of times those particles oscillate per second. Most sounds are actually composed of waves with many frequencies, which gives them their characteristic texture, or **timbre.** The loudness of a sound reflects the height and depth, or **amplitude,** of the wave.

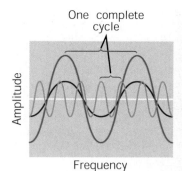

— High frequency, low amplitude (soft tenor or soprano)
— Low frequency, low amplitude (soft bass)
— Low frequency, high amplitude (loud bass)

FIGURE 4.19
Frequency and amplitude. Sound waves can differ in both frequency (pitch) and amplitude (loudness). A cycle can be represented as the length of time or distance between peaks of the curve.

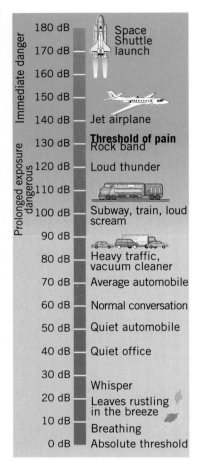

180 dB — Space Shuttle launch
170 dB —
160 dB —
150 dB —
140 dB — Jet airplane
130 dB — **Threshold of pain** Rock band
120 dB — Loud thunder
110 dB —
100 dB — Subway, train, loud scream
90 dB —
80 dB — Heavy traffic, vacuum cleaner
70 dB — Average automobile
60 dB — Normal conversation
50 dB — Quiet automobile
40 dB — Quiet office
30 dB —
20 dB — Whisper
            Leaves rustling in the breeze
10 dB — Breathing
0 dB — Absolute threshold

FIGURE 4.20
Loudness. Loudness of various common sounds at close range, in decibels.

THE EAR

Transduction of sound occurs in the ear, which consists of an outer, middle, and inner ear (Figure 4.21). The outer ear collects and magnifies sounds in the air; the middle ear converts waves of air pressure into movements of tiny bones; and the inner ear transforms these movements into waves in fluid that generate neural signals.

Transduction

The hearing process begins in the outer ear, which consists of the pinna and the auditory canal. Sound waves are funneled into the ear by the **pinna,** the skin-covered cartilage that protrudes from the sides of the head. The pinna is not essential for hearing, but its irregular shape is useful for locating sounds in space, which bounce off its folds differently when they come from various locations (Batteau, 1967). Just inside the skull is the **auditory canal,** a passageway about an inch long. As sound waves resonate in the auditory canal, they are amplified by up to a factor of 2.

   The Middle Ear   At the end of the auditory canal is a thin, flexible membrane known as the **eardrum, or tympanic membrane.** The eardrum marks the outer boundary of the middle ear. When sound waves reach the eardrum, they set it in motion. The movements of the eardrum are extremely small—0.00000001 centimeter, or about the width of a hydrogen molecule, in response to a whisper (Sekuler & Blake, 1994). The eardrum essentially reproduces the cyclical vibration of the object that created the noise, on a microcosmic scale. It is only able to do so, however, if air pressure on both sides of it (in the outer and middle ear) is roughly the same. When an airplane begins its descent and a person's head is blocked by a head cold, the pressure is greater on the inside, which blunts the vibrations of the eardrum. The normal mechanism for equalizing air pressure is the *Eustachian tube,* which connects the middle ear to the throat but can become blocked by mucous.
   When the eardrum vibrates, it sets in motion three tiny bones in the middle ear, called **ossicles.** These bones, named for their distinctive shapes, are called the *malleus, incus,* and *stapes,* which translate from the Latin into hammer, anvil, and

FIGURE 4.21
The ear. The ear consists of outer, middle, and inner sections, which direct the sound, amplify it, and turn mechanical energy into neural signals.

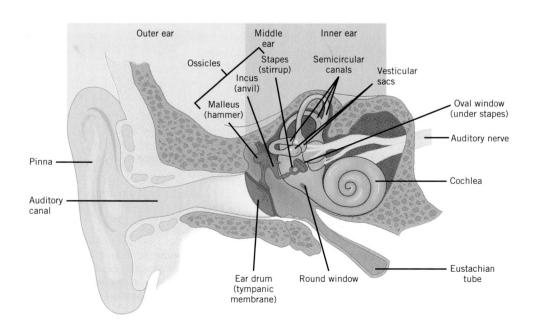

stirrup, respectively. The ossicles further amplify the sound two or three times before transmitting vibrations to the inner ear. The stirrup vibrates against a membrane called the **oval window,** which forms the beginning of the inner ear.

The Inner Ear The inner ear consists of two sets of fluid-filled cavities hollowed out of the temporal bone of the skull: the semicircular canals (involved in balance) and the cochlea (involved in hearing). The temporal bone is the hardest bone in the body and serves as natural soundproofing for its vibration-sensitive cavities. Chewing during a meeting sounds louder to the person doing the chewing than to those nearby because it rattles the temporal bone and thus augments the sounds from the ears.

The **cochlea** (Figure 4.22) is a three-chambered tube shaped like a snail. When the stirrup vibrates against the oval window, the oval window vibrates, causing pressure waves in the cochlear fluid. These waves disturb the **basilar membrane,** which separates two of the cochlea's chambers. Attached to the basilar membrane are the ear's 15,000 receptors for sound, called **hair cells** (because they terminate

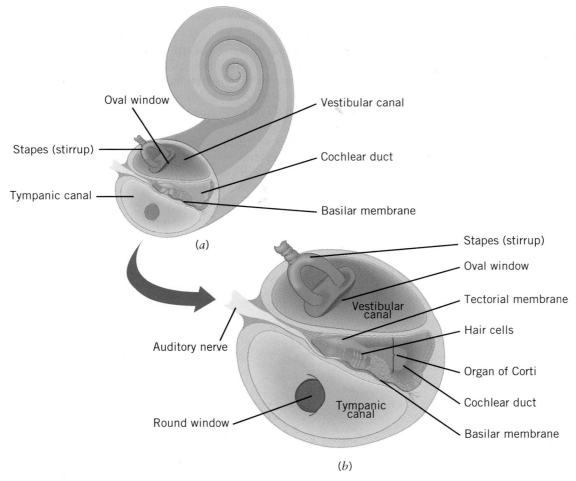

FIGURE 4.22
The cochlea. (*a*)The cochlea's chambers (the vestibular canal, the cochlear duct, and the tympanic canal) are filled with fluid. When the stirrup vibrates against the oval window, it vibrates, causing pressure waves in the fluid of the vestibular canal. These pressure waves spiral up the vestibular canal and down the tympanic canal, flexing the basilar membrane and, to a lesser extent, the tectorial membrane. (*b*)Transduction occurs in the organ of Corti, which includes these two membranes and the hair cells sandwiched between them. At the end of the tympanic canal is the round window, which pushes outward to relieve pressure when the sound waves have passed through the cochlea.

in tiny bristles, or **cilia**). Above the hair cells is another membrane, the **tectorial membrane,** which also moves as waves of pressure travel through the cochlear fluid. The cilia bend as the basilar and tectorial membranes move in different directions. This triggers action potentials in sensory neurons forming the **auditory nerve,** which transmits auditory information to the brain. Thus, mechanical energy—the movement of cilia and membranes—is transduced into neural energy.

Sensory deficits in hearing, as in other senses, can arise from problems either with parts of the sense organ that channel stimulus energy or with the receptors and neural circuits that convert this energy into psychological experience. Failure of the outer or middle ear to conduct sound to the receptors in the hair cells is called *conduction loss;* failure of receptors in the inner ear or of neurons in any auditory pathway in the brain is referred to as *sensorineural loss.* The most common problems with hearing result from exposure to noise or reflect changes in the receptors with aging; similar age-related changes occur in most sensory systems (Chapter 13). A single exposure to an extremely loud noise, such as a firecracker, an explosion, or a gun firing at close range, can permanently damage the hair cell receptors in the inner ear.

Sensing Pitch

Precisely how does auditory transduction transform the physical properties of sound frequency and amplitude into the psychological experiences of pitch and loudness? Two theories, both proposed in the nineteenth century and once considered opposing explanations, together appear to explain the available data. The first, called **place theory,** holds that different areas of the basilar membrane are maximally sensitive to different frequencies (Bekesy, 1959, 1960; Helmholtz, 1863). Place theory was initially proposed by Herman von Helmholtz (of trichromatic color fame), who had the wrong mechanism but the right idea. A Hungarian scientist named Georg von Bekesy discovered the mechanism a century after Helmholtz by recognizing that when the stapes hits the oval window, a wave travels down the basilar membrane like a carpet being shaken at one end (Figure 4.23). Shaking a carpet rapidly (i.e., at high frequency) produces an early peak in

FIGURE 4.23
Place theory. The frequency with which the stapes strikes the oval window affects the location of peak vibration on the basilar membrane. The lower the tone, the farther the maximum displacement on the membrane is from the oval window. *Source:* Sekuler & Blake, 1994, p. 315.

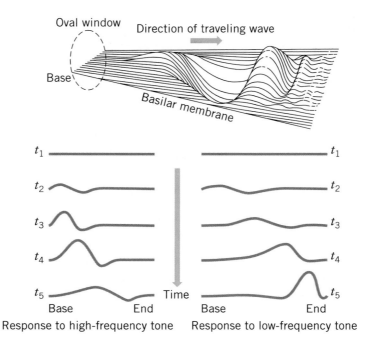

the wave of the carpet, whereas shaking it slowly produces a peak in the wave toward the other end of the carpet. Similarly, high-frequency tones, which produce rapid strokes of the stapes, produce the largest displacement of the basilar membrane close to the oval window, whereas low-frequency tones cause a peak in basilar movement toward the far end of the membrane. Peak vibration leads to peak firing of hair cells at a particular location. Hair cells at different points on the basilar membrane thus transmit information about different frequencies to the brain, just as rods and cones transduce electromagnetic energy at different frequencies.

Place theory has one major problem. At *very* low frequencies the entire basilar membrane vibrates fairly uniformly; thus, for very low tones, location of maximal vibration cannot account for pitch. The second theory of pitch, **frequency theory,** overcomes this problem, proposing that the more frequently a sound wave cycles, the more frequently the basilar membrane vibrates and its hair cells fire. Thus, pitch perception is probably mediated by two neural mechanisms: a place code at high frequencies and a frequency code at low frequencies. Both mechanisms likely operate at intermediate frequencies (Goldstein, 1989).

NEURAL PATHWAYS

Neurons in the auditory system are similar in many respects to those in the visual system. Firing depends on input from several hair cells, just as firing in ganglion cells reflects the total activity of many photoreceptors. Neurons comprising the auditory nerve also carry information specifying stimulus quality (pitch), as do fibers in the optic nerve (color). Thus, a neuron will respond to a range of frequencies if the sound is intense enough, but it will most readily respond to a characteristic frequency to which it is tuned. Neurons activated by hair cells near the oval window respond to high frequencies, whereas those activated by hair cells on the other end of the basilar membrane fire more readily for low tones. At each pitch, some neurons respond to relatively low intensities of sound, whereas others fire more at high sound levels. As with light, more intense sounds also cause more neurons to fire.

Information transmitted by the ears along the two auditory nerves ultimately finds its way to the auditory cortex in the temporal lobes, but it makes several stops along the way (Figure 4.24). The auditory nerve from each ear projects to the medulla, where the majority of its fibers cross over to the other hemisphere. (Recall that the medulla is where sensory and motor neurons cross from one side of the body to the other). Some information from each ear, however, does not cross over; thus, information from both ears is represented on both sides of the brain.

From the medulla, bundles of axons project to the midbrain (to the *inferior colliculus,* just below the superior colliculus, which is involved in vision) and on to the thalamus (to the *medial geniculate nucleus,* just toward the center of the brain from its visual counterpart, the lateral geniculate nucleus). The thalamus transmits information to the auditory cortex in the temporal lobes, which has sections devoted to different frequencies, much as sites in the primary visual cortex process different parts of the visual field. Some neurons in the auditory cortex also respond to the "movement" of sounds—whether frequency changes, moving up or down—similar to the way some complex cells in the visual cortex respond to movement in space. Just as the cortical region corresponding to the fovea is disproportionately large, so, too, is the region of the primary auditory cortex tuned to sound frequencies in the middle of the spectrum—the same frequencies involved in speech. Indeed, in humans and other animals, some cortical neurons in the left temporal lobe respond exclusively to particular sounds characteristic of the "language" of the species, whether monkey calls or human speech.

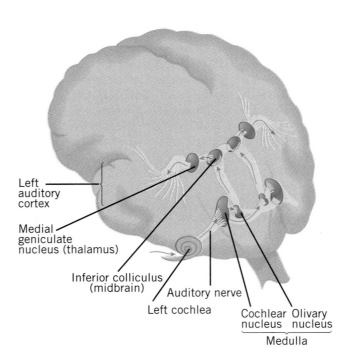

FIGURE 4.24
Auditory pathways. Axons from neurons in the inner ear project to the cochlear nucleus in the medulla. From there, most cross over to a structure called the olivary nucleus on the opposite side, although some remain uncrossed. At the olivary nucleus, information from the two ears begins to be integrated. Information from the olivary nucleus then passes to a midbrain structure (the inferior colliculus) and on to the medial geniculate nucleus in the thalamus before reaching the auditory cortex.

Sound Localization

Neurons in the thalamus and primary cortex are involved in identifying the location of a sound in space, or **sound localization.** In humans, sound localization requires the integration of information from both ears because the brain uses two main cues for localizing sound: differences between the two ears in loudness, and timing of the sound (King & Carlile, 1995; Middlebrooks & Green, 1991; Stevens & Newman, 1934). Particularly for high-frequency sounds, relative loudness in the ear closer to the source provides information about its location because the head blocks some of the sound from hitting the other ear (Figure 4.25).

Loudness is less useful for localizing lower frequency sounds because their waves are so long that the head does not effectively block them. For example, a 900-Hz sound (a relatively low tone) cycles about every 40 centimeters, which is twice the diameter of the average head, so it curves right around the head (Sekuler & Blake, 1994). Localization of sounds at low frequencies relies more on the difference in the arrival time of the sound at the two ears. A sound coming from the left reaches the left ear a split second before reaching the right, particularly if it is moving slowly (that is, at a low frequency). Timing differences are less useful for localizing sounds at high frequencies because they travel so quickly between the two ears. The ability to move the head toward sounds is also crucial for localizing sounds.

Neurologically, the basis for sound localization lies in neurons that respond to relative differences in the signals from the two ears. These *binaural neurons* (i.e., neurons that respond to information from both ears) exist at nearly all levels of the auditory system in the brain, from the brainstem up through the cortex (King & Carlile, 1995). At higher levels of the brain, this information is connected with visual information about the location and distance of objects, which allows a joint mapping of auditory and visual information. Researchers have studied this process extensively in the barn owl, an animal that localizes sound in the inferior colliculus (rather than the cortex) primarily through timing differences between the arrival of the sound at each ear (Feldman et al., 1996; Knudson et al., 1991; Konishi, 1995). When these animals are raised wearing glasses that use prisms to

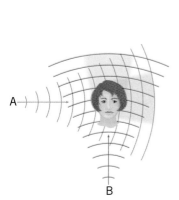

FIGURE 4.25
Sound localization. At high frequencies, sounds on one side of the head can be localized by relative intensity in the two ears because the head casts a "sound shadow" on one side but not the other, as in sound *A*. With sound *B*, the shadow is behind the head, so it does not lead to any relative differences between the ears. At low frequencies, the slight difference between the time a sound reaches one ear, as in *A*, provides a cue for sound localization.

distort the perceived location of objects, their auditory map essentially becomes linked to a visual map with different coordinates.

INTERIM SUMMARY   Sound waves travel through the **auditory canal** to the **eardrum,** which in turn sets the **ossicles** in motion, amplifying the sound. When the stirrup (one of the ossicles) strikes the **oval window,** it creates waves of pressure in the fluid of the **cochlea. Hair cells** attached to the **basilar membrane** then transduce the sound, triggering firing of the sensory neurons whose axons comprise the **auditory nerve.** Two theories, once considered opposing, explain the psychological qualities of sound. According to **place theory,** which best explains transduction at high frequencies, different areas of the basilar membrane respond to different frequencies. According to **frequency theory,** which best explains transduction at low frequencies, the rate of vibration of the basilar membrane transforms frequency into pitch. From the auditory nerve, sensory information passes through the inferior colliculus in the midbrain and the medial geniculate nucleus of the thalamus on to the auditory cortex in the temporal lobes. Neurons in both the thalamus and primary auditory cortex are involved in **sound localization,** which reflects the action of binaural neurons that respond to relative differences in the loudness and timing of sensory signals transduced by the two ears.

OTHER SENSES

Vision and audition are the most highly specialized senses in humans, occupying the greatest amount of brain space and showing the most cortical evolution. Our other senses, however, serve important adaptive functions as well. These include smell, taste, the skin senses (pressure, temperature, and pain), and the proprioceptive senses (body position and motion).

SMELL

Smell **(olfaction)** serves a number of functions in humans. It enables us to detect danger (e.g., the smell of something burning), discriminate palatable and unpalatable or spoiled foods, and recognize familiar others. Smell plays a less important role in humans than in most other animals, who rely heavily on olfaction to mark territory and track other animals. Many species communicate through **pheromones** (Chapter 10), scent messages that regulate the sexual behavior of many animals and direct a variety of behaviors in insects (Carolsfeld et al., 1997; Sorensen, 1996).

We humans, in contrast, often try to "cover our tracks" in the olfactory domain using perfumes and deodorants to mask odors that our mammalian ancestors might have found informative or appealing. Nevertheless, vestiges of this ancient reproductive mechanism remain. Humans appear both to secrete and sense olfactory cues related to reproduction. Experiments using sweaty hands or articles of clothing have shown that people can identify the gender of another person by smell alone with remarkable accuracy (Doty et al., 1982; Russell, 1976; Wallace, 1977). The synchronization of menstrual cycles of women living in close proximity also appears to occur through smell and may reflect ancient pheromonal mechanisms (McClintock, 1971; Preti et al., 1986; Stern & McClintock, 1998).

Transduction

The environmental stimuli for olfaction are invisible molecules of gas emitted by substances and suspended in the air. The thresholds for recognizing most odors are remarkably low—as low as one molecule per *50 trillion* molecules of air for some molecules (Geldard, 1972). Although the nose is the sense organ for smell, the vapors that give rise to olfactory sensations can enter the **nasal cavities**—the region hollowed out of the bone in the skull that contains smell receptors—through either the nose or the mouth (Figure 4.26). When food is chewed, vapors travel up the back of the mouth into the nasal cavity; this process actually accounts for much of the taste.

Transduction of smell occurs in the **olfactory epithelium,** a thin pair of structures (one on each side) less than a square inch in diameter at the top of the nasal cavities. Chemical molecules in the air become trapped in the mucus of the epithelium, where they make contact with olfactory receptor cells that transduce the stimulus into olfactory sensations. Humans have approximately 10 million olfactory receptors (Engen, 1982), in comparison with dogs, whose 200 million receptors enable them to track humans and other animals with their noses (Marshall & Moulton, 1981). Psychologists have long debated whether a small number of receptors coding different qualities combine to produce complex smells or whether the olfactory epithelium contains hundreds or thousands of receptors that bind only with very specific molecules. Recent research on the genes that produce proteins involved in smell transduction suggests that many receptors are responsive to chemicals with very specific molecular structures (Bartoshuk & Beauchamp, 1994; Breer et al., 1996; Buck & Axel, 1991).

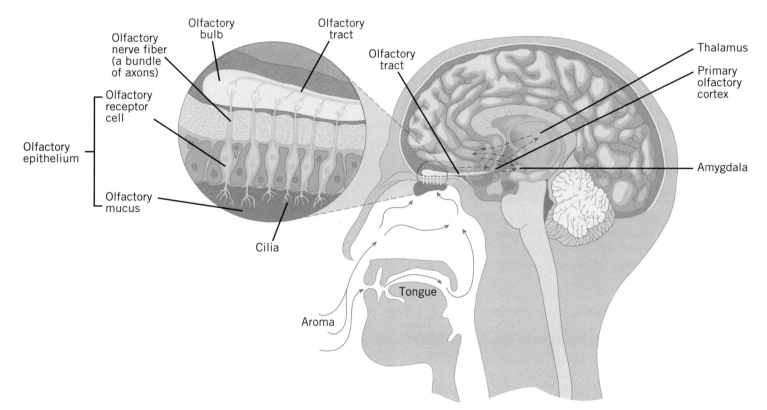

FIGURE 4.26
Olfaction. Molecules of air enter the nasal cavities through the nose and throat, where smell is transduced by receptors in the olfactory epithelium. Axons of receptor cells form the olfactory nerve, a relatively short nerve that projects to the olfactory bulb. From there, information passes through the olfactory tract to the primary olfactory cortex. This region connects with the thalamus and amygdala, which in turn connect with higher olfactory centers in a more evolutionarily recent region of the frontal lobe.

Neural Pathways

The axons of olfactory receptor cells form the **olfactory nerve,** which transmits information to the **olfactory bulbs,** multilayered structures that combine information from receptor cells. Olfactory information then travels to the primary olfactory cortex, a primitive region of the cortex deep in the frontal lobes. Unlike other senses, smell is not relayed through the thalamus on its way to the cortex; however, the olfactory cortex has projections to both the thalamus and the limbic system, so that smell is connected to both taste and emotion.

Many animals that respond to pheromonal cues have a second, or accessory, olfactory system, with its own olfactory bulbs and tracts, that projects directly to the amygdala and on to the hypothalamus, thus contributing to regulation of reproductive behavior. Although the data at this point are conflicting, some studies suggest that humans may have a similar secondary olfactory system, which, if operative, has no links to consciousness and thus influences reproductive behavior without our knowing it (Bartoshuk & Beauchamp, 1994; Stern and McClintock, 1998).

INTERIM SUMMARY The environmental stimuli for smell are gas molecules suspended in the air. These molecules flow through the nose into the **olfactory epithelium,** where they are detected by hundreds of different types of receptors. The axons of these receptor cells comprise the **olfactory nerve,** which transmits information to the **olfactory bulbs** and on to the primary olfactory cortex deep in the front lobes.

TASTE

The sense of smell is sensitive to molecules in the air, whereas taste **(gustation)** is sensitive to molecules soluble in saliva. At the dinner table, the contributions of the nose and mouth to taste are indistinguishable except when the nasal passages are blocked so that food loses much of its taste. From an evolutionary perspective, taste serves two functions: to protect the organism from ingesting toxic substances and to regulate intake of nutrients such as sugars and salt. For example, toxic substances often taste bitter, and foods high in sugar (which provides the body with energy) are usually sweet. The tendency to reject bitter substances and to ingest sweet ones is present even in newborns, despite their lack of experience with taste (Bartoshuk & Beauchamp, 1994).

Transduction of taste occurs in the **taste buds** (Figure 4.27). Roughly 10,000 taste buds are distributed throughout the mouth and throat (Miller, 1995), al-

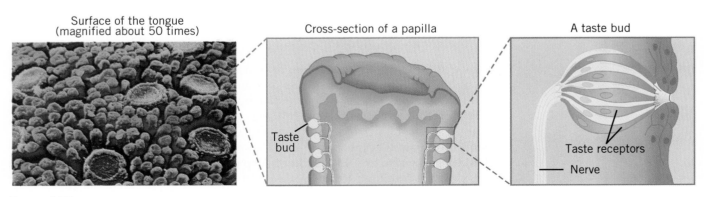

Surface of the tongue
(magnified about 50 times)

Cross-section of a papilla

A taste bud

Taste bud

Taste receptors

Nerve

FIGURE 4.27
The majority of taste buds are located on the papillae of the tongue. They contain receptor cells that bind with chemicals in the saliva and stimulate gustatory neurons.

though most are located in the bumps on the surface of the tongue called **papillae** (Latin for "pimple"). Soluble chemicals that enter the mouth penetrate tiny pores in the papillae and stimulate the taste receptors. Each taste bud contains between 50 and 150 receptor cells (Margolskee, 1995). Taste receptors, unlike sensory receptors in the eye or ear, wear out and are replaced every ten or 11 days (Graziadei, 1969). Regeneration is essential, or a burn to the tongue would result in permanent loss of taste.

Taste receptors stimulate neurons that carry information to the medulla and pons in the hindbrain. From there, gustatory information travels along one of two pathways. One leads to the thalamus and on to the primary gustatory cortex deep within a region between the temporal and parietal lobes. This pathway allows the identification of tastes. The second pathway, which has no access to consciousness, leads to the limbic system. This pathway allows immediate emotional and behavioral responses to tastes, such as spitting out bitter substances. It also appears to be involved in learned aversions to tastes that become associated through experience with nausea. As in blindsight, people with damage to the first (cortical) pathway cannot identify substances by taste, but they react with appropriate facial expressions to bitter and sour substances if this second, more primitive, pathway is intact.

The gustatory system responds to four basic tastes: sweet, sour, salty, and bitter. Different receptors are most sensitive to one of these tastes, at least at low levels of stimulation. This appears to be cross-culturally universal: People of different cultures diverge in their taste preferences and beliefs about basic flavors, but they vary little in identifying substances as sweet, sour, salty, or bitter (Laing et al., 1993). More than one receptor, however, can produce the same sensation, at least for bitterness. Apparently, as plants and insects evolved toxic chemicals to protect against predation, animals that ate them evolved specific receptors for detecting these substances. The nervous system, however, continued to rely on the same sensation, bitterness, to discourage snacking on them (Bartoshuk & Beauchamp, 1994).

INTERIM SUMMARY   Taste occurs as receptors in the **taste buds** transduce chemical information from molecules soluble in saliva into neural information, which is integrated with olfactory sensations in the brain. Taste receptors stimulate neurons that project to the medulla and pons in the hindbrain. From there, the information is carried along two neural pathways, one leading to the primary gustatory cortex, which allows identification of tastes, and the other leading to the limbic system, which allows initial gut-level reactions and learned responses to them. The gustatory system responds to four tastes: sweet, sour, salty, and bitter.

SKIN SENSES

The approximately 18 square feet of skin covering the human body constitutes a complex, multilayered organ. The skin senses help protect the body from injury, aid in identifying objects, help maintain body temperature, and facilitate social interaction through hugs, kisses, holding, and handshakes. What we colloquially call the sense of touch is actually a mix of at least three qualities: pressure, temperature, and pain. Receptors in the skin respond to different aspects of these qualities, such as warm or cold or light or deep pressure. The human body contains approximately 5 million touch receptors of various types (Figure 4.28). Although receptors are specialized for different qualities, most skin sensations are complex, reflecting stimulation across many receptors (Goldstein, 1989).

As with other sensory systems, several receptors in the skin typically transmit

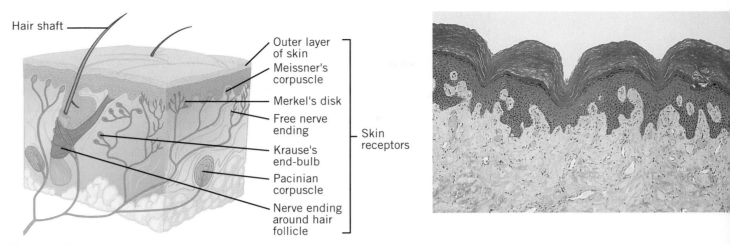

FIGURE 4.28
The skin and its receptors. Several different types of receptors transduce tactile stimulation, such as Meissner's corpuscles, which respond to brief stimulation (as when a ball of cotton moves across the skin); Merkel's disks, which detect steady pressure; and the nerve endings around hair follicles, which explain why plucking eyebrows or pulling tape off the skin can be painful.

information to a single sensory neuron, which in turn synapses with other neurons in the spinal cord. The qualities sensory neurons convey to the nervous system (such as soft pressure, warmth, and cold) depend on the receptors to which they are connected. Thus, when receptors reattach to the wrong nerve fibers, as appears to occur in some cases of painful neuropathy, sensory information can be misinterpreted. Like neurons in other sensory systems, those involved in touch also have receptive fields, which distinguish both where and how long the stimulation occurred on the skin.

Sensory neurons synapse with spinal interneurons that stimulate motor neurons, allowing animals to respond with rapid reflex actions. Sensory neurons also synapse with neurons that carry information up the spinal cord to the medulla, where neural tracts cross over. From there, sensory information travels to the thalamus and is subsequently routed to the primary touch center in the brain, the somatosensory cortex. The somatosensory cortex contains a map of the body (Chapter 3); neurons in the somatosensory cortex have receptive fields corresponding to different parts of the body. As in the visual system, the receptive fields of neurons become progressively larger as information passes to higher and higher processing centers. As a result, people can recognize the same shape (such as a pencil) pressing against different regions of the body, even though the stimulation is in entirely different places. Through experience, the brain represents more generalized tactile "pictures" of objects in association areas of the parietal lobes (Johnson et al., 1995).

People store information in this way about parts of their own bodies. People who have had a limb amputated often awaken from the operation disbelieving that the operation has occurred and only begin to believe it when they reach out to touch the missing limb (Katz and Melzack, 1990). Stored experiences of the limb's presence may continue for months or years, although they tend to change over time. For example, the "phantom limb" may begin to feel smaller and smaller, or the foot at the end of an amputated leg may come to feel like it is attached directly to the stump. Although the experience of a phantom limb tends to be most pronounced in people who have more recently lost a limb, phantom experiences of this sort can occur even in people who lost a limb very early in life or were even born without it (Melzack, 1993), suggesting that certain kinds of sensory "expectations" throughout the body may be partly innate. As we will see, phantom limbs may be the site of many "sensations," including intense pain, typically similar to pain experienced prior to amputation.

Each of the skin senses transduces a distinct form of stimulation. Pressure receptors transduce mechanical energy (like the receptors in the ear). Temperature receptors respond to thermal energy (heat). Pain receptors do not directly transform external stimulation into psychological experience; rather, they respond to a range of internal and external bodily states, from strained muscles to damaged skin.

Pressure

People experience pressure when the skin is mechanically displaced, or moved. Sensitivity to pressure varies considerably over the surface of the body (Weinstein, 1968). The most sensitive regions are the face and fingers; the least sensitive are the back and legs. These disparities in sensitivity are reflected in the amount of space taken by neurons representing these areas in the somatosensory cortex. The hands are the skin's foveas, providing tremendous acuity; they have small receptive fields that allow fine discriminations, and the primary cortex devotes substantial space to them (see Johnson & Lamb, 1981). The hands turn what could be a passive sensory process—responding to indentations produced in the skin by external stimulation—into an active process. As the hands move over objects, pressure receptors register the indentations created in the skin and hence allow perception of texture. Just as eye movements allow people to read written words, finger movements allow blind people to read the raised dots that constitute Braille. In other animals, the somatosensory cortex emphasizes other body zones that provide important information for adaptation, such as whiskers in cats (Kaas, 1987).

Temperature

When people sense the temperature of an object, they are actually sensing the difference between the temperature of the skin and the object, which is why a pool of 80-degree water feels warm to someone who has been standing in the cold rain but chilly to someone lying on a hot beach. Temperature sensation relies on two sets of receptors, one for cold and one for warmth (see Levine & Shefner, 1991; Spray, 1986). Cold receptors, however, not only detect coolness but are also involved in the experience of extreme temperatures, both hot and cold. Subjects who grasp two pipes twisted together, one containing warm water and the other cold, experience intense heat (Figure 4.29). As with pressure, the pattern of stimulation, rather than the activation of specific receptors alone, creates the sensation.

Pain

People spend billions of dollars a year fighting pain, but pain serves an important function: preventing tissue damage. Indeed, people who are insensitive to pain because of nerve damage or genetic abnormalities are at serious risk of injury and infection; young children with congenital (inborn) pain insensitivity have reportedly bitten off their tongues, chewed off the tips of their fingers, and been severely burned leaning against hot stoves or climbing into scalding bathwater (Jewesbury, 1951). On the other hand, persistent pain can be debilitating. Some

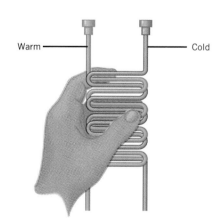

Warm ———   ——— Cold

FIGURE 4.29
Experiencing intense heat. Warm and cold receptors activated simultaneously produce a sensation of intense heat.

estimates suggest that as many as one-third of North Americans suffer from persistent or recurrent pain. The cost in suffering, lost productivity, and dollars is immense (Miller & Kraus, 1990).

In contrast to other senses, pain has no specific physical stimulus; the skin does not transduce "pain waves." Sounds that are too loud, lights that are too bright, pressure that is too intense, temperatures that are too extreme, and other stimuli can all elicit pain. Although pain transduction is not well understood, the most important receptors for pain in the skin appear to be the *free nerve endings*. According to one prominent theory, when cells are damaged, they release chemicals that stimulate the free nerve endings, which in turn transmit pain messages to the brain (Price, 1988). These chemicals can also activate pain receptors elsewhere in the body, such as in the muscles and teeth and in the spinal nerves that receive input from pain receptors throughout the body (see Cook et al., 1997; Liu et al., 1997; Lynn & Perl, 1996).

One such chemical is a neuropeptide (a string of amino acids that serves as a neurotransmitter) called **substance P** (for pain). In one study, researchers found that pinching the hindpaws of rats led to the release of substance P in the spinal cord (Beyer et al., 1991). The concentration of substance P increased with the amount of painful stimulation and returned to baseline when the stimulation stopped. In another study, rats injected with substance P responded with biting, scratching, and distress vocalizations, all of which are associated with painful stimulation (DeLander & Wahl, 1991).

A Japanese boy walks on fire at Mt. Takao. Pain is as much a state of mind as a state of receptors.

Experiencing Pain   Of all the senses, pain is probably the most affected by beliefs, expectations, and emotional state and the least reducible to level of stimulation (Sternbach, 1968). (The next time you have a headache or a sore throat, try focusing your consciousness on the minute details of the sensation, and you will notice that you can momentarily kill the pain by "reframing" it.) Anxiety can increase pain, whereas intense fear, stress, or concentration on other things can inhibit it (al Absi & Rokke, 1991; Melzack & Wall, 1983). Cultural norms and expectations also influence the subjective experience and behavioral expression of pain (Bates, 1987; Zatzick & Dimsdale, 1990). For example, on the island of Fiji, women of two subcultures appear to experience labor pain quite differently (Morse & Park, 1988). The native Fijiian culture is sympathetic to women in labor and provides both psychological support and herbal remedies for labor pain. In contrast, an Indian subculture on the island considers childbirth contaminating and hence offers little sympathy or support. Interestingly, women from the Indian group rate the pain of childbirth significantly lower than native Fijiians. Apparently, cultural recognition of pain influences the extent to which people can acknowledge it. Similarly, anecdotal evidence in the West suggests that people in subcultures that do not provide support for pain and encourage a "stiff upper lip" show fewer signs of pain and attend less to daily aches and pains than subcultures that dwell on pain.

Gate Control Theory   The phenomenological experience of pain is not always initiated by peripheral sensory stimulation. A striking example is phantom limb pain, experienced by a substantial number of amputees. **Phantom limb pain** is pain felt in a limb that no longer exists. The pain does not originate from severed nerves in the stump. Even if the stump is completely anesthetized, the pain persists, and medications that should ease it often fail to do so (Melzack, 1970).

One theory designed to account for phenomena such as phantom limb pain is **gate-control theory,** which emphasizes the role of the central nervous sytem (the brain and spinal cord, rather than the periphery) in regulating pain. According to gate control theory, when sensory neurons transmit information to the back (dorsal region) of the spinal cord, they do not automatically produce pain sensations because their actions can be inhibited or amplified by input from other nearby sensory neurons as well as from messages descending from the brain (Melzack, 1993; Melzack and Wall, 1965).

Gate control theory distinguishes two kinds of neural fibers (axons from sensory neurons) that open and close spinal "gateways" for pain. Large-diameter fibers (called L-fibers), which transmit neural information very quickly, carry information about many forms of tactile stimulation as well as sharp pain. Once they transmit a message, they close the pain gate by inhibiting the firing of the neurons with which they synapse. Small-diameter fibers (S-fibers) synapse with the same neurons, carrying information about dull pain and burning to the brain. Because their small axons transmit neural information more slowly, however, their messages may arrive at a closed gate (or, more accurately, a partially closed gate, since pain does not usually completely disappear) if competing sensory input from L-fibers has inhibited pain transmission. This may explain why rubbing the area around a burn or cut, or even pinching a nearby region of skin, can alleviate pain. These actions stimulate L-fibers, which close the gates to incoming signals from S-fibers. According to gate-control theory, messages from the brain to the spinal cord can also close or open the gates, so that calm or anxious mental states can increase or decrease pain sensations arising from the peripheral nervous system.

Gate-control theory offers one explanation of phantom limb pain (Melzack, 1973, 1995). If L-fibers are destroyed by amputation, the gates remain open, allowing random firing of neurons at the amputation site to trigger action potentials, leading to the experience of pain in the missing limb.

Pain Control   Because mental as well as physiological processes contribute to pain, treatment may require attention to both mind and matter—to both the psychology and neurophysiology of pain. The Lamaze method of childbirth, for example, teaches women to relax through deep breathing and muscle relaxation and to distract themselves by focusing their attention elsewhere. It also teaches the woman's "coach" (her partner) to stimulate L-fibers through gentle massage. These procedures can be quite effective: Lamaze-trained women tend to experience less pain during labor (Leventhal et al., 1989), and they show a general increase in pain tolerance. For example, experiments show that they are able to keep their hands submerged in ice water longer than women without the training, especially if their coach provides encouragement (Whipple et al., 1990; Worthington et al., 1983).

Many other techniques target the cognitive and emotional aspects of pain. Though not a panacea, distraction is generally a useful strategy for increasing pain tolerance (Christenfeld, 1997; McCaul & Malott, 1984; Weisenberg et al., 1995). Health care professionals often chatter away while giving patients injections in order to distract and relax them. Something as simple as a pleasant view can affect pain tolerance in hospitalized patients. In one study, surgery patients whose rooms overlooked lush plant life had shorter hospital stays and required less medication than patients whose otherwise identical rooms looked out on a brick wall (Ulrich, 1984). Environmental psychologists, who apply psychological knowledge to building and landscape design, use such information to help architects design hospitals (Saegert & Winkel, 1990). Hypnosis (Chapter 9) can also be useful in controlling pain (Evans, 1990; Hilgard & Hilgard, 1975). Research suggests that hypnotic procedures can help burn victims tolerate debriding (removing dead tissue and changing dressings on wounds), which can be so painful that patients writhe in agony even on the maximum dosage of medications such as morphine (Patterson et al., 1992).

FROM MIND TO BRAIN

PERSONALITY AND PAIN

If mental states can affect pain sensation, are some people vulnerable to chronic pain by virtue of their personalities? Despite long-standing controversy in this area, researchers have identified a personality style that appears to be shared by many chronic pain patients (Keller & Butcher, 1992). These patients often blame their physical condition for all life's difficulties and deny any emotional or interpersonal problems. They tend to have difficulty expressing anger and to be anxious, depressed, needy, and dependent. The difficulty in studying such patients, however, is distinguishing the causes from the effects of chronic pain, since unending pain could produce many of these personality traits (Gamsa, 1990).

A team of researchers addressed this methodological problem by studying patients *at risk* for developing chronic pain before they actually developed it (Dworkin et al., 1992). The patients suffered from herpes zoster (shingles), a viral infection that results from reactivation of chicken pox virus. The nature and duration of pain associated with herpes zoster vary widely, but some patients experience disabling chronic pain. To see if they could predict which patients would develop chronic pain, the investigators gave a sample of recently diagnosed herpes zoster patients a series of questionnaires and tests, including measures of depression, anxiety, life stress, attitudes toward their illness, and pain severity. Physicians provided data on the severity of the patients' initial outbreak of the disease.

The researchers recontacted the patients several times over the next year and distinguished those who reported ongoing pain three months after the acute outbreak from those who did not. Although these two groups did not differ in the initial severity of their symptoms, they did differ significantly on a number of psychological dimensions assessed *at the time of their initial diagnosis*. Fitting the description of the "chronic pain personality," those patients who would later experience continued pain were initially more depressed and anxious and less satisfied with their lives than patients without pain, and they were more likely to dwell on their illness and resist physicians' reassurances.

Chronic pain is by no means "all in the head." In many cases it likely reflects an interaction of psychological factors, physiological vulnerabilities, and disease or injury. But this research suggests that the way people experience themselves and the world affects their vulnerability to their own sensory processes.

INTERIM SUMMARY   Touch includes three senses: pressure, temperature, and pain. Sensory neurons synapse with spinal interneurons that stimulate motor neurons (producing reflexes) as well as with neurons that carry information up the spinal cord to the medulla. From there, nerve tracts cross over, and the information is conveyed through the thalamus to the somatosensory cortex, which contains a map of the body. The function of pain is to prevent tissue damage; the experience of pain is greatly affected by beliefs, expectations, emotional state, and personality.

PROPRIOCEPTIVE SENSES

Aside from the five traditional senses—vision, hearing, smell, taste, and touch— two additional senses, called **proprioceptive senses,** register body position and movement. The first, the **vestibular sense,** provides information about the position of the body in space by sensing gravity and movement. The ability to sense gravity is a very early evolutionary development, found in nearly all animals. The existence of this sense again exemplifies the way psychological characteristics have evolved to match characteristics of the environment that impact on adaptation. Gravity affects movement, so humans and other animals have receptors to transduce it, just as they have receptors for light.

The vestibular sense organs are in the inner ear, above the cochlea (see Figure 4.21, p. 160). Two organs transduce vestibular information: the semicircular canals and the vestibular sacs. The **semicircular canals** sense acceleration or deceleration in any direction as the head moves. The **vestibular sacs** sense gravity and the position of the head in space. Vestibular receptors are hair cells that register movement, much as hair cells in the ear transduce air movements. The neural pathways for the vestibular sense are not well understood, although impulses from the vestibular system travel to several regions of the hindbrain, notably the cerebellum, which is involved in smooth movement, and to a region deep in the temporal cortex.

The other proprioceptive sense, **kinesthesia,** provides information about the movement and position of the limbs and other parts of the body *relative to* one another. Kinesthesia is essential in guiding every complex movement, from walking, which requires instantaneous adjustments of the two legs, to drinking a cup of coffee. Some of the receptors for kinesthesia are in the joints; these cells transduce information about the position of the bones. Other receptors, in the tendons and muscles, transmit messages about muscle tension that signal body position (Neutra & LeBlond, 1969).

The vestibular and kinesthetic senses work in tandem, sensing different aspects of movement and position. Proprioceptive sensations are also integrated with messages from other sensory systems, especially touch and vision. For example, even when the proprioceptive senses are intact, walking can be difficult if tactile stimulation from the feet is shut off, as when a person's legs "fall asleep." (To see the importance of vision to balance, try balancing on one foot while raising the other foot as high as you can, first with your eyes closed and then with your eyes open.)

Without the capacity to sense position of the body in space and position of the limbs relative to each other, this skier would be on his way to the hospital rather than the lodge.

INTERIM SUMMARY   The **proprioceptive senses** register body position and movement. The **vestibular sense** provides information on the position of the body in space by sensing gravity and movement. **Kinesthesia** provides information about the movement and position of the limbs and other parts of the body relative to one another.

PERCEPTION

The line between sensation and perception is thin, and we probably have already crossed it in discussing the psychology of pain. The hallmarks of perception are organization and interpretation. (Many psychologists consider attention a third aspect of perception, but since attention is also involved in memory, thought, motivation, and emotion, we address it in Chapter 9 on consciousness.) Perception *organizes* a continuous array of sensations into meaningful units. When we speak we produce, on average, a dozen meaningful units of sounds (called phonemes) per second (such as "walk" and "-ing") and are capable of understanding up to *40* phonemes per second (Pinker, 1994). When we listen to a symphony or a popular song, we can easily follow the melody despite the presence of other instruments or voices. This requires organization of sensations. Beyond organization, we must *interpret* the information organized. A scrawl on a piece of paper is not just a set of lines of particular orientation but a series of letters and words. A melodic pattern in the middle of a song or symphony is not just a novel set of notes but a variation on an earlier theme.

In this final section, we again emphasize the visual system, since the bulk of work in perception has used visual stimuli, but the same principles largely hold across the senses. We begin by describing several ways in which perception is organized and then examine the way people interpret sensory experiences.

ORGANIZING SENSORY EXPERIENCE

If you put this book on the floor, it does not suddenly look like part of the floor; if you walk slowly away from it, it does not seem to diminish in size. These are examples of perceptual organization. **Perceptual organization** integrates sensations into **percepts** (meaningful perceptual units, such as images of particular objects), locates them in space, and preserves their meaning as the perceiver examines them from different vantage points. Here we explore four aspects of perceptual organization: form perception, depth or distance perception, motion perception, and perceptual constancy.

Form Perception

Form perception refers to the organization of sensations into meaningful shapes and patterns. When you look at this book, you do not perceive it as a patternless collection of molecules. Nor do you perceive it as part of your leg even though it may be resting on it or think a piece of it has disappeared simply because your hand or pen is blocking your vision of it.

Gestalt Principles   The first psychologists to study form perception systematically were the **Gestalt psychologists** of the early twentieth century. As noted in Chapter 1, *Gestalt* is a German word that translates loosely to "whole" or "form." Proponents of the Gestalt approach argued that in perception the whole (the percept) is greater than the sum of its sensory parts. Consider the ambiguous picture

FIGURE 4.30
An ambiguous figure. Whether the perceiver forms a global image of a young or an old woman determines the meaning of each part of the picture; what looks like a young woman's nose from one perspective looks like a wart on an old woman's nose from another. The perception of the whole even leads to different inferences about the coat the woman is wearing: In one case, it appears to be a stylish fur, whereas in the other, it is more likely to be interpreted as an old overcoat. *Source:* Boring, 1930, p.42.

in Figure 4.30, which some people see as an old woman with a scarf over her head and others see as a young woman with a feather coming out of a stylish hat. Depending on the perceiver's gestalt, or whole view of the picture, the short black line in the middle could be either the old woman's mouth or the young woman's necklace.

Based on experiments conducted in the 1920s and 1930s, the Gestalt psychologists proposed a small number of basic perceptual rules the brain automatically and unconsciously follows as it organizes sensory input into meaningful wholes (Figure 4.31). **Figure–ground perception** refers to the fact that people inherently distinguish between figure (the object they are viewing) and ground (or background), such as words in black ink against a white page. The second Gestalt principle is **similarity:** The brain tends to group similar elements together, such as the circles that form the letter R in Figure 4.31a. Another principle, **proximity** (nearness), means that the brain tends to group together objects that are close to one another. In Figure 4.31b, the first six lines have no particular organization, whereas the same six lines arranged somewhat differently in the second part of the panel are perceived as three pairs. The Gestalt rule of **good continuation** states that, if possible, the brain organizes stimuli into continuous lines or patterns rather than discontinuous elements. For example, in Figure 4.31c, the figure appears to show an X superimposed on a circle, rather than pieces of a pie with lines extending beyond the pie's perimeter. According to the principle of **simplicity,** people tend to perceive the simplest pattern possible. Most people perceive Figure 4.31d as a heart with an arrow through it because that is the simplest interpretation. Finally, the rule of **closure** states that, where possible, people tend to perceive incomplete figures as complete. If part of a familiar pattern or shape is missing, perceptual processes complete the pattern, as in the triangle shown in Figure 4.31e. The second part of Figure 4.31e demonstrates another type of closure (sometimes called *subjective contour*) (Albert, 1993; Kanizsa, 1976). People see two overlapping triangles, but in fact, neither one exists; the brain simply fills in the gaps to perceive familiar patterns. Covering the incomplete black circles reveals that the solid white triangle is entirely an illusion.

Although the Gestalt principles are most obvious with visual perception, they apply to other senses as well. For example, the figure–ground principle applies when people attend to the voice of a waitress in a noisy restaurant; her voice becomes figure and all other sounds, ground. In music perception, good continuation allows people to hear a series of notes as a melody; similarity allows them to

FIGURE 4.31
Gestalt principles of form perception. The Gestalt psychologists discovered a set of laws of perceptual organization, including (a) similarity, (b) proximity, (c) good continuation, (d) simplicity, and (e) closure. *Source:* Part (e) adapted from Kanizsa, 1976.

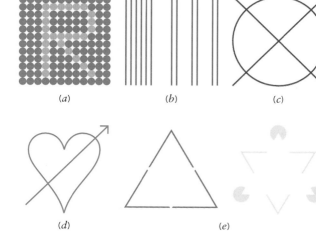

recognize a melody played on a violin while other instruments are playing; and proximity groups notes played together as a chord.

From an evolutionary perspective, the Gestalt principles exemplify the way the brain organizes perceptual experience to reflect the regularities of nature. In nature, the parts of objects tend to be near one another and attached. Thus, the principles of proximity and good continuation are useful perceptual rules of thumb. Similarly, objects often partially block, or occlude, other objects, as when a squirrel crawls up the bark of a tree. The principle of closure leads humans and other animals to assume the existence of the part of the tree that is covered by the squirrel's body.

Combining Features   More recent research has focused on the question of how the brain combines the simple features detected in primary areas of the cortex (particularly primary visual cortex) into larger units that can be used to identify objects. *Object identification* requires matching the current stimulus array against past percepts stored in memory to determine the identity of the object (such as a ball, a chair, or a particular person's face). Findings from imaging studies and research on patients and animals with temporal lobe lesions suggest that this process occurs along the "what" pathway, probably around the border between the occipital and temporal lobes.

One prominent theory of how the brain forms and recognizes images was developed by Irving Biederman (1987, 1990; Bar & Biederman, in press; Kirkpatrick-Steger & Biederman, 1998). Consider the following common scenario. It is late at night, and you are "channel surfing" on the television—rapidly pressing the remote control in search of something to watch. From less than a second's glance, you can readily perceive what most shows are about and whether they might be interesting. How does the brain, in less than a second, recognize a complex visual array on a television screen in order to make such a rapid decision?

Biederman and his colleagues have shown that we do not even need a *half* a second to recognize most scenes; 100 milliseconds—a tenth of a second—will typically do. To explain phenomena such as this, Biederman developed a theory called **recognition-by-components,** which asserts that we perceive and categorize objects in our environment by breaking them down into component parts and then matching the components and the way they are arranged against similar

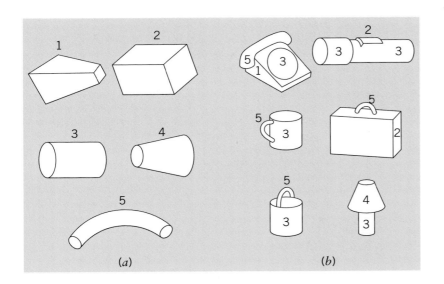

(a)   (b)

FIGURE 4.32
Recognition by components. The simple geons in (*a*) can be used to create thousands of different objects (*b*) simply by altering the relations among them, such as their relative size and placement. *Source:* Biederman, 1990, p. 49.

"sketches" stored in memory. In other words, the brain combines the simple features extracted by the primary cortex (such as lines of particular orientations) into a small number of elementary geometrical forms (called *geons*, for "geometric ions"). From this geometrical "alphabet" of 20 to 30 geons, Biederman argues, the outlines of virtually any object can be constructed, just as millions of words can be constructed from an alphabet of 26 letters in various combinations and orders. Figure 4.32 presents examples of some of these geons and the way most objects can be identified at a glance using only two or three of them.

Biederman argues that combining primitive visual sensations into geons not only allows rapid identification of objects but also explains why we can recognize objects even when parts of them are blocked or missing. The reason is that the Gestalt principles, such as good continuation, apply to perception of geons. In other words, the brain fills in gaps in a segment of a geon, such as a blocked piece of a circle. The theory predicts that failures in identifying objects should occur if the lines where separate geons connect are missing or ambiguous, so that the brain can no longer tell where one component ends and another begins (Figure 4.33). Experiments have supported this hypothesis: People can identify objects with parts missing only if the parts do not obscure the relations among the geons.

Recognition-by-components is not a complete theory of form perception. It was intended to explain how people make relatively rapid initial determinations

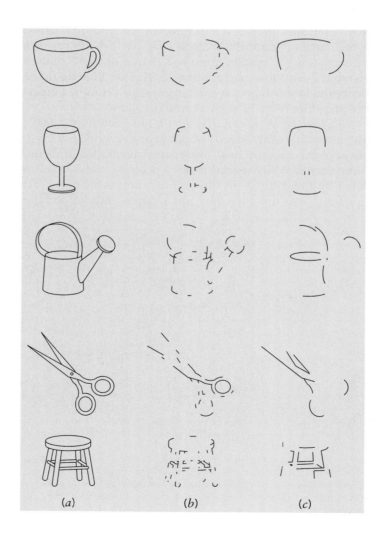

FIGURE 4.33
Identifiable and unidentifiable images. People can rapidly identify objects (*a*) even if many parts of them are missing, as long as the relations among their components, or geons, remain clear (*b*). When they can no longer tell where one geon ends and another begins (*c*), the ability to identify the objects will disappear. *Source:* Biederman, 1987, p. 135.

(*a*)   (*b*)   (*c*)

about what they are seeing and what might be worth closer inspection. More subtle discriminations—such as which type of poodle or which five-foot, ten-inch male is in view—require additional analysis of qualities such as color, texture, and characteristic motion (such as the way the dog walks or the man swaggers) (Ullman, 1995). These discriminations take considerably longer than 100 milliseconds because they require integration across a number of mental maps of visual space. Research shows, for example, that if people are asked to find a triangle amidst a large array of geometrical shapes, they can do so extremely quickly, and whether the triangle is in the midst of ten or 50 other shapes makes little difference in the length of time required to find it (Triesman, 1986). In contrast, if they are asked to find the *red* triangle, not only will their response time in finding it increase, but the length of time required to find it will be directly proportional to the number of other geometrical shapes in view. In other words, they will have to scan the objects one by one, which takes much more time. Apparently, making judgments about the *conjunction* of two attributes—in this case, shape and color—requires not only consulting two maps (one of shape and the other of color) but also superimposing one on the other. That we can nonetheless carry out such complex computations in seconds or hundreds of milliseconds is remarkable.

Perceptual Illusions   Sometimes the brain's efforts to organize sensations into coherent and accurate percepts fail. This is the case with **perceptual illusions,** in which normal perceptual processes produce perceptual misinterpretations. Impossible figures are one such type of illusion, which provide conflicting cues for three-dimensional organization, as illustrated in Figure 4.34. The second part of the figure shows a painting by M. C. Escher, an artist who made explicit use of psychological research on perception in his work (Ernst, 1976). Recognizing the impossibility of these figures takes time because the brain attempts to impose order by using principles such as simplicity on data that allow no simple solution. Each portion of an impossible figure is credible, but as soon as the brain organizes sensations in one way, another part of the figure invalidates it.

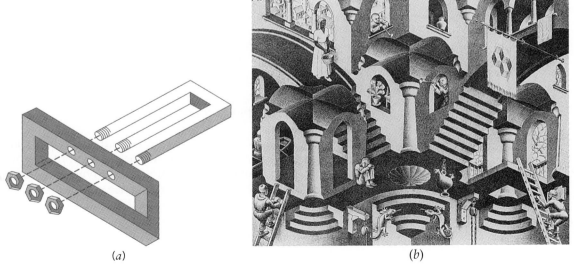

(a)   (b)

FIGURE 4.34
Impossible figures. The brain cannot form a stable percept because each time it does, another segment of the figure renders the percept impossible. Escher, who painted the impossible figure in (b), made use of perceptual research.

INTERIM SUMMARY   Perception involves the organization and interpretation of sensory experience. **Form perception** refers to the organization of sensations into meaningful shapes and patterns **(percepts).** The **Gestalt psychologists** described several principles of form perception; more recently, a theory called **recognition-by-components** has argued that people perceive and categorize objects by first breaking them down into elementary units. The brain's efforts to organize percepts can sometimes produce **perceptual illusions.**

Depth Perception

A second aspect of perceptual organization is **depth** or **distance perception,** the organization of perception in three dimensions. You perceive this book as having height, width, and breadth and being at a particular distance; a skilled athlete can throw a ball 15 yards into a tiny hoop not much bigger than the ball. These three-dimensional judgments arise from a two-dimensional retinal image—and do so with such rapidity that we have no awareness of the computations our nervous system must be making. Although we focus again on the visual system, other sensory systems provide cues for depth perception as well. Auditory cues are particularly important, but so are kinesthetic sensations about the extension of the body while touching an object and other kinesthetic sensations that occur as a person lifts and swivels an object (such as a pencil) held by the hands (Turvey, 1996). Two kinds of visual information provide particularly important information about depth and distance: **binocular cues** (visual input integrated from the two eyes) and **monocular cues** (visual input from one eye).

Binocular Cues   Because the eyes are in slightly different locations, all but the most distant objects produce a different image on each retina, or a **retinal disparity.** To see this in action, hold your finger about six inches from your nose and alternately close your left and right eye. You will note that each eye sees your finger in a slightly different position. Now, do the same for a distant object; you will note only minimal differences between the views. Retinal disparity is greatest for close objects and diminishes with distance.

How does the brain translate retinal disparity into depth perception? Most cells in the primary visual cortex are **binocular cells;** that is, they receive information from both eyes. Some of these cells respond most vigorously when the same input arrives from each eye, whether the input is a vertical line, a horizontal line, or a line moving in one direction. Other binocular cells respond to different sorts of disparities between the eyes. Like many cells receptive to particular orientations, binocular cells require environmental input early in life to assume their normal functions. Researchers have learned about binocular cells by allowing kittens to see with only one eye at a time, covering one eye or the other on alternate days. As adults, these cats are unable to use binocular cues for depth (Blake & Hirsch, 1975; Packwood & Gordon, 1975).

Another binocular cue, convergence, is actually more kinesthetic than visual. When looking at a close object (such as your finger six inches in front of your face), the eyes converge, whereas distant objects require ocular divergence. **Convergence** of the eyes toward each other thus creates a distance cue produced by muscle movements in the eyes.

Monocular Cues   Although binocular cues are extremely important for depth perception, people do not crash their cars whenever an eyelash momentarily gets into one eye because they can still rely on monocular cues. The photograph of the Taj Majal in Figure 4.35 illustrates the main monocular depth cues that arise even when looking at a nonmoving scene. **Interposition** occurs when one object blocks part of another; as a result, the obstructed object is perceived as

FIGURE 4.35
Monocular depth cues. The photo of the Taj Majal in India illustrates all of the monocular cues to depth perception: interposition (the trees blocking the sidewalk and the front of the building), elevation (the most distant object seems to be the highest), texture gradient (the relative clarity of the breaks in the walkways closer to the camera), linear perspective (the convergence of the lines of the walkways surrounding the water), shading (the indentation of the arches toward the top of the building), aerial perspective (the lack of the detail of the bird in the distance), familiar size (the person standing on the walkway who seems tiny), and relative size (the diminishing size of the trees as they get further away).

more distant. **Elevation** refers to the fact that objects farther away are higher on a person's plane of view and thus appear higher up toward the horizon. Another monocular cue is **texture gradient:** When looking at textured surfaces, such as cobblestones or grained wood, the pattern or texture appears coarser at close range and finer and more densely packed at greater distances. A similar mechanism is **linear perspective:** Parallel lines appear to converge in the distance. **Shading** also provides monocular depth cues, since two-dimensional objects do not cast shadows. The brain assumes that light comes from above and hence interprets shading differently toward the top or the bottom of an object. Another cue is **aerial perspective:** Since light scatters as it passes through space, and especially through moist or polluted air, objects at greater distances appear fuzzier than those nearby. Two other cues rely on the individual's knowledge of the size of familiar objects. **Familiar size** refers to the tendency to assume an object is its usual size; thus, people perceive familiar objects that appear small as distant. Closely related is **relative size:** When looking at two objects known to be of similar size, people perceive the smaller object as farther away.

Artists working in two-dimensional media rely on monocular depth cues to represent a three-dimensional world. Humans have used interposition and elevation to convey depth for thousands of years. Other cues, however, such as linear perspective, were not discovered until as late as the fifteenth century; as a result, art before that time appears flat to the modern eye (Figure 4.36). Although some monocular cues appear to be innate, cross-cultural research suggests that perceiving three dimensions in two-dimensional drawings is partially learned, influenced by artistic conventions and experience with different kinds of two-dimensional media. Some people in technologically less developed cultures who have never seen photography initially have difficulty recognizing even their own images in two-dimensional form (Berry et al., 1992).

A final monocular depth cue arises from movement. When people move, images of nearby objects sweep across their field of vision faster than objects farther away. This disparity in apparent velocity produces a depth cue called **motion parallax.** The relative motion of nearby versus distant objects is particularly striking when looking out the window of a moving car or train. Nearby trees appear to speed by, whereas distant objects barely seem to move.

(a)   (b)

FIGURE 4.36

Artistic use of monocular cues for depth perception has developed tremendously since Giotto's *Flight into Egypt* painted in the fifteenth century *(a)*. In the Cyclorama exhibit in Atlanta *(b)*, which depicts the Battle of Atlanta during the U.S. Civil War, the artists had such mastery of monocular cues for depth perception that visitors cannot easily tell where actual three-dimensional objects (soldiers, trees, etc.) end and a painted background begins.

Motion Perception

From an evolutionary perspective, just as important as identifying objects and their distance is identifying motion. A moving object is potentially a dangerous object—or, alternatively, a meal, a mate, or a friend or relative in distress. Thus, it is no surprise that humans, like other animals, developed the capacity for **motion perception**—the perception of movement in objects. Motion perception occurs in multiple sensory modes. People can perceive the movement of a fly on the skin through touch, just as they can perceive the fly's trajectory through space by the sounds it makes. We focus here again, however, on the visual system.

Neural Pathways   The visual perception of movement begins in the retina itself, with ganglion cells called **motion detectors** that are particularly sensitive to movement. These cells tend to be concentrated outside the fovea, to respond (and stop responding) very quickly, and to have large receptive fields. These characteristics make adaptive sense. An object in the fovea is one we are already "keeping a close eye on" through attention to it; motion detectors in the periphery of our vision, in contrast, provide an early warning system to turn the head or the eyes toward something potentially relevant. Relatively quick onset and offset of neurons that detect motion is also a useful characteristic; otherwise, many objects could escape detection by moving faster than these neurons could fire. In fact, the eyes cannot detect objects that move either too quickly (which appear blurry or cannot be seen at all) or too slowly (which do not "trip" the motion detectors). Large receptive fields are useful for motion detection because each cell receives input from many bipolar cells; the greater the number of bipolar cells that synapse with the ganglion cell, the greater the potential activation. A wider receptive field also covers more visual terrain in which motion might occur, maximizing the likelihood of detecting it (Schiffman, 1996).

With each new "stop" along the processing stream in the brain, the receptive fields of neurons that detect motion grow larger. Several ganglion cells project to each motion-detecting neuron in the thalamus (in the lateral geniculate nucleus); thus, these neurons are likely to respond to movement in a slightly larger area of space. Several of these thalamic neurons may then synapse with motion-sensitive neurons in the primary visual cortex. From there, information about the movement of objects travels along the "where" pathway through the upper temporal lobes and into the parietal lobes. One important "stop" along the way is a region in the middle of the temporal lobes called *area MT* (for *medial temporal*) (see Barinaga, 1997; Rodman et al., 1989; Tootell et al., 1995). In area MT, receptive fields are even larger than in the primary visual cortex; some neurons respond to movement across a very large part of the visual field or to any movement sensed at all. Like some neurons in the primary visual cortex, many neurons in area MT are also direction sensitive, so that when a human (or monkey) watches an object, these neurons will fire most vigorously only if it is moving in the direction to which the neuron is tuned.

Two Systems for Processing Movement   Tracking an object's movement is a tricky business because the perceiver may be moving as well; thus, perception requires distinguishing the motion of the perceiver from the motion of the perceived. Consider the perceptual task of a tennis player awaiting a serve. Most tennis players bob, fidget, or move from side to side as they await a serve, which means that the image on their retina is changing every second, even before the ball is in the air. Once the ball is served, its retinal image becomes larger and larger as it approaches, and somehow the brain must compute its distance and velocity as it moves through space. Making matters more complex, the perceiver is likely to be running, all the while trying to keep the ball's image on the fovea. And the brain must integrate these cues—the size of the image on the retina, its precise location on the retina, the movement of the eyes, and the movement of the body— all in a split second.

Two systems appear to be involved in motion perception (Gregory, 1977). The first computes motion from the changing image projected by the object on the retina; the second makes use of commands from the brain to the muscles in the eye that signal eye movements. (A third system, less well understood, likely integrates proprioceptive and other cues to offset the impact of body movements on the retinal image.) The first system operates when the eyes are relatively stable, as when an insect darts across the floor in the person's view so quickly that the eyes cannot move fast enough to track it. In this case, the image of the insect moves across the retina (Figure 4.37*a*). Motion detectors then fire as adjacent receptors in the retina bleach one after another in rapid succession.

The second system operates when people move their head and eyes to follow an object, as when fans watch a runner sprinting toward the finish line. In this case, the image of the object remains at roughly the same place on the retina; what moves is the position of the eyes (Figure 4.37*b*). This second system computes movement from a combination of the image on the retina and the movement of eye muscles. If the eyes are moving but the object continues to cast the same retinal image, the object must be moving. Essentially, the brain subtracts out muscle movements before computing movement from the retinal image. Interestingly, the movements of the eye must be intentional for this mechanism to work (although we are not typically conscious of the directives from the brain to the eye muscles). This is readily apparent by performing a simple experiment: Close one eye and then lightly push the other eyeball with your finger. You will perceive movement in the opposite direction in any object in front of you because the brain does not compensate for involuntary shifts in the position of the eye that do not occur through movement of the eye muscles (see Schiffman, 1996).

Perceptual Constancy

A fourth form of perceptual organization, **perceptual constancy,** refers to the perception of objects as relatively stable despite changes in the stimulation of sensory receptors. As your grandmother walks away from you, you do not perceive her as

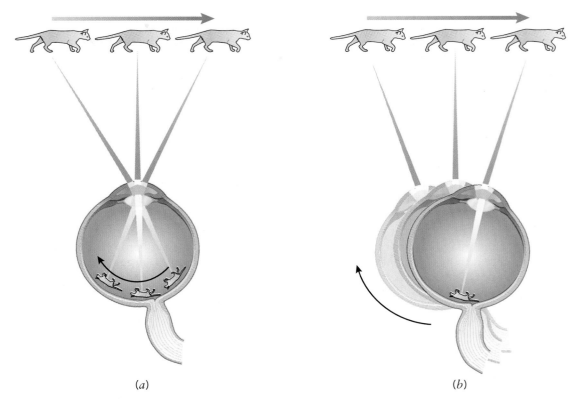

(a)   (b)

FIGURE 4.37
Two systems for processing movement. In (*a*), a stationary eye detects movement as an object moves across the person's visual field, progressively moving across the retina. In (*b*), the eye moves along with the object, which casts a relatively constant retinal image. What changes are the background and signals from the brain that control the muscles that move the eyes. *Source:* Adapted from Gregory, 1973, and Schiffman, 1996.

shrinking, even though the image she casts on your retina is steadily decreasing in size (although you may notice that she has shrunk a little since you last saw her). You similarly recognize that a song on the radio is still the same even though the volume has been turned down. Here we examine three types of perceptual constancy, again focusing on vision: color, shape, and size constancy.

Color Constancy   **Color constancy** refers to the tendency to perceive the color of objects as stable despite changing illumination. An apple appears the same color in the kitchen as it does in the sunlight, even though the light illuminating it is very different. A similar phenomenon occurs with achromatic color (black and white): Snow in moonlight appears whiter than coal appears in sunlight, even though the amount of light reflected off the coal may be greater (Schiffman, 1996). In perceiving the brightness of an object, neural mechanisms essentially adjust for the amount of light illuminating it. For chromatic colors, the mechanism is more complicated, but color constancy does not work if the light contains only a narrow band of wavelengths. Being in a room with only red lightbulbs causes even familiar objects to appear red.

Shape Constancy   A remarkable feat of the engineering of the brain is that we can maintain constant perception of the shape of objects despite the fact that the same object typically produces a new and different impression on the retina (or on the receptors in our skin) every time we encounter it. The brain has to overcome several substantial sources of noise to recognize, for example, that the unkempt beast in the mirror whose hair is pointing in every direction is the same person you happily called "me" the night before. When people see an object for the second time, they are likely to see it from a different position, with different lighting, in a different setting (e.g., against a different background), with different parts of it blocked from view (such as different locks of hair covering the face), and even in an altered shape (such as a body standing up versus on the couch) (see Ullman, 1995).

Recognition-by-components (geon) theory offers one possible explanation: As long as enough of the geons that define the form of the object remain the same, the object ought to be identifiable. Thus, if a person views a bee from one perspective and then from another as it flies around her face, she will still recognize the insect as a bee as long as it still looks like a tube with a little cone at the back and thin waferlike wings flapping at its sides.

Other theorists, however, have argued that this is not likely to be the whole story. Some have proposed that each time we view an object from a different perspective, we form a mental image of it from that point of view. Each new viewpoint provides a new image stored in memory. The next time we see a similar object, we rotate it in our minds so that we can "see" it from a previously seen perspective to determine if it looks like the same object or match it against a generalized image derived from our multiple "snapshots" of it. Recent research suggests, in fact, that the more a scene diverges the perspective from which a person has seen it before (e.g., if the image is 90 versus 15 degrees off from the earlier image), the longer the person will take to recognize it (DeLoache et al., 1997; Tarr et al., 1997; Ullman, 1989). This suggests that shape constancy does, to some extent, rely on the rotation of mental images (probably of both geons and finer perceptual details) and their comparison against perceptual experiences stored in memory.

Size Constancy   A third type of perceptual constancy is **size constancy:** Objects do not appear to change in size when viewed from different distances. The closer an object is, the larger an image it casts on the retina; a car ten feet away will cast a retinal image five times as large as the same car 50 feet away. Yet people do not wonder how the car 50 feet away can possibly carry full-sized passengers (Figure 4.38). The reason is that the brain essentially corrects for the size of the retinal image based on cues such as the size of objects in the background.

Helmholtz (1909) was the first to recognize that the brain adjusts for distance when assessing the size of objects, just as it adjusts for color and brightness. He called this process "unconscious inference" because people have no consciousness of the computations involved. Although these computations generally lead to accurate inferences, they can also give rise to perceptual illusions. A classic example is the moon illusion, in which the moon seems larger on the horizon than at its zenith (Figure 4.39). This illusion appears to result from depth cues such as relative size; the moon seems larger against a backdrop of large buildings than against a backdrop of stars that provide no depth cues.

INTERIM SUMMARY   **Depth perception** is the organization of perception in three dimensions, which utilizes **binocular** and **monocular visual cues. Motion perception,** the perception of movement, relies on **motion detectors** from the retina through the cortex. It appears to involve two systems, the first of which computes motion from the changing image on the retina, and the second of which uses information from eye muscles about the movements of the eyes. **Perceptual constancy** refers to the organization of changing sensations into percepts that are relatively stable in size, shape, and color. Three types of perceptual constancy are **color, shape,** and **size constancy.**

FIGURE 4.38
Size constancy. In (*a*), the man and the pyramids appear to be of normal size because the pyramids are off in the distance. The photo in (*b*) is perceptually confusing because the distance cues have been distorted by doctoring the photo.

(*a*)

(*b*)

FIGURE 4.39
The moon illusion. The moon appears larger against a city skyline than high in the sky, where, among other things, no depth cues exist. The retinal image is the same size in both cases, but in one case, depth cues signal that it must be further away.

A GLOBAL VISTA

CULTURE AND PERCEPTUAL ILLUSIONS

As this example suggests, size constancy, like other processes of perceptual organization, can sometimes produce perceptual illusions. This is likely the case with the **Müller–Lyer illusion,** in which two lines of equal length appear to differ in size (Figure 4.40). According to one theory, the angled lines provide linear perspective cues that make the vertical line appear closer or farther away (Gregory, 1978). The brain then adjusts for distance, interpreting the fact that the retinal images of the two vertical lines are the same size as evidence that the line on the right is longer.

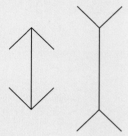

FIGURE 4.40
The Müller–Lyer illusion. The line on the right appears longer than the line on the left, when in fact they are exactly the same size.

If the Müller–Lyer illusion relies on depth cues such as linear perspective that are not recognized in all cultures, are people in some cultures more susceptible to the illusion than others? That is, does vulnerability to an illusion depend on culture and experience, or is it rooted entirely in the structure of the brain? Three decades ago, a team of psychologists and anthropologists set out to answer these questions in what has become a classic study (Segall et al., 1966).

Two hypotheses that guided the investigators are especially relevant. The first, called the *carpentered world* hypothesis, holds that the nature of architecture in a culture influences the tendency to experience particular illusions. According to this hypothesis, people reared in cultures lacking roads that join at angles, rectangular buildings, and houses with angled roofs lack experience with the kinds of cues that give rise to the Müller–Lyer illusion and hence should be less susceptible to it. Second, individuals from cultures that do not use sophisticated two-dimensional cues (such as linear perspective) to represent three dimensions in pictures should also be less vulnerable to perceptual illusions of this sort.

The researchers presented individuals from 14 non-Western and three Western societies with several stimuli designed to elicit perceptual illusions. They found that Westerners were consistently more likely to experience the Müller–Lyer illusion than non-Westerners, but they were no more likely to experience other illusions unrelated to angles and sophisticated depth cues. Subsequent studies have replicated these findings with the Müller–Lyer illusion (Pedersen & Wheeler, 1983; Segall et al., 1990). Teasing apart the relative impact of architecture and simple exposure to pictures is difficult, but the available data support both hypotheses (Berry et al., 1992).

(a)

People from this African village (a) are less susceptible to illusions involving straight lines than people who live in "carpentered worlds," such as Paris (b), who are familiar with angled buildings and streets.

(b)

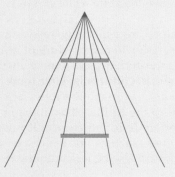

FIGURE 4.41
The Ponzo illusion. Converging lines lead to the perception of the upper red bar as larger since it appears to be farther away. The bars are actually identical in length.

Size constancy is involved in another famous illusion, the **Ponzo illusion,** which also appears to be influenced by culture and experience (Figure 4.41). Linear perspective cues indicate that the upper bar is larger because it seems farther away. Cross-culturally, people who live in environments in which lines converge in the distance (such as railroad tracks and long, straight highways) appear to be more susceptible to this illusion than people from environments with relatively few converging lines (Brislin & Keating, 1976).

INTERPRETING SENSORY EXPERIENCE

The processes of perceptual organization we have examined—form perception, depth perception, motion perception, and perceptual constancy—organize sensations into stable, recognizable forms. These perceptions do not, however, tell us what an object *is* or what its emotional or adaptive significance might be. Generating *meaning* from sensory experience is the task of **perceptual interpretation.** The line between organization and interpretation is not, of course, hard and fast. The kind of object identification tasks studied by Biederman, for example, involve both, and in everyday life, organizing perceptual experience is simply one step on the path to interpreting it.

Perceptual interpretation lies at the intersection of sensation and memory, as the brain interprets current sensations in light of past experience. This can occur at a very primitive level—reacting to a bitter taste, recoiling from an object coming toward the face, or responding emotionally to a familiar voice—without either consciousness or cortical involvement. Much of the time, however, interpretation involves classifying stimuli—a moving object is a dog; a pattern of tactile stimulation is a soft caress. In this final section, we examine how experience, expectations, and motivation shape perceptual interpretation.

The Influence of Experience

To what degree do our current perceptions rely on our past experience? This question leads back to the nature–nurture debate that runs through nearly every domain of psychology. The German philosopher Immanuel Kant argued that humans innately experience the world using certain categories, such as time, space, and causality. For example, when a person slams a door and the door frame shakes, she naturally infers that slamming the door caused the frame to shake. According to Kant, people automatically infer causality, prior to any learning.

Direct Perception   In psychology, the theory of **direct perception,** championed by James Gibson (1966, 1979), similarly holds that perceptual meaning requires little prior knowledge. Whereas Kant emphasized the way the mind orders perception of the world, Gibson emphasized the way the world organizes perception, so that we detect the order that exists in nature. Gibson argued that the senses evolved to respond to aspects of the environment relevant to adaptation, so that the meaning of stimuli is often immediate and obvious. An object coming rapidly toward the face is dangerous; food with a sweet taste affords energy; a loud, angry voice is threatening.

Laboratory evidence of direct perception comes from studies using the **visual cliff.** The visual cliff is a clear table with a checkerboard directly beneath it on one side and another checkerboard that appears to drop off like a cliff on the other (Figure 4.42). Infants are reluctant to crawl to the side of the table that looks deep even when they have recently begun crawling and have had little or no relevant experience with falling off of surfaces (E. Gibson & Walk, 1960). Once infants *need* to preceive the meaning of potentially dangerous actions, they rapidly becoming *able* to do so as they interact with the environment (see Bertenthal, 1996).

Nature and Nurture   Answers to the nature–nurture question have become more sophisticated as psychologists have come to recognize that the nervous system has certain innate potentials—such as seeing in depth or inferring distance from sound—but that these potentials require environmental input to develop. In one set of studies, researchers reared kittens in darkness for their first five months except for five hours each day, during which time they placed the kittens in a cylinder with either horizontal or vertical stripes (Blakemore & Cooper, 1970). The

FIGURE 4.42
The visual cliff. Infants are afraid to crawl over the "cliff" even when they have recently begun to crawl and therefore have little experience leading them to fear it.

FIGURE 4.43
Kittens reared in a vertical world lose their "innate" capacity to see horizontal lines.

kittens saw *only* the stripes, since they wore a big collar that kept them from seeing even their own bodies (Figure 4.43). As adults, kittens reared in horizontal environments were unable to perceive vertical lines, and they lacked cortical feature detectors responsive to vertical lines; the opposite was true of kittens reared in a vertical environment. Although these cats were genetically programmed to have both vertical and horizontal feature detectors, their brains adapted to a world without certain features to detect.

Other studies have outfitted infant kittens and monkeys with translucent goggles that allow light to pass through but only in a blurry, diffuse, unpatterned form. When the animals are adults and the goggles are removed, they are able to perform simple perceptual tasks without difficulty, such as distinguishing colors, brightness, and size. However, they have difficulty with other tasks; for example, they are unable to distinguish objects from one another or to track moving objects (Riesen, 1960, 1965; Wiesel, 1982). Similar findings have emerged in studies of humans who were born blind but subsequently obtained sight in adulthood through surgery (Gregory, 1978; Sacks, 1993; von Senden, 1960). Most of these individuals can tell figure from ground, sense colors, and follow moving objects, but many never learn to recognize objects they previously knew by touch and hence remain functionally blind. What these studies suggest, like studies described in Chapter 3, is that the brain has evolved to "expect" certain experiences, without which it will not develop normally.

Early experiences are not the only ones that shape the neural systems underlying sensation and perception. In one study, monkeys who were taught to make fine pitch discriminations showed increases in the size of the cortical regions responsive to pitch (Recanzone et al., 1993). Intriguing research with humans finds that practice at discriminating letters manually in Braille produces changes in the brain. A larger region of the cortex of Braille readers is devoted to the fingertips, with which they read (Pascual-Leone & Torres, 1993). Thus, experience can alter the structure of the brain, making it more or less responsive to subsequent sensory input.

Bottom-Up and Top-Down Processing

We have seen that experience can activate innate mechanisms or even affect the amount of cortical space devoted to certain kinds of sensory processing. But when we come upon a face that looks familiar or an animal that resembles one we have seen, does our past experience actually alter the way we perceive it, or do we only begin to categorize the face or the animal once we have identified its features? Similarly, does wine taste different to a wine connoisseur—does his knowledge about wine actually alter his perceptions—or does he just have fancier words to describe his experience after the fact?

Psychologists have traditionally offered two opposing answers to questions such as these, which now, as in many classic debates about sensation and perception, appear to be complementary. One view emphasizes the role of sensory data in shaping perception, whereas the other emphasizes the influence of prior experience. **Bottom-up processing** refers to processing that begins "at the bottom" with raw sensory data that feed "up" to the brain. A bottom-up explanation of visual perception argues that the brain forms perceptions by combining the responses of multiple feature detectors in the primary cortex, which themselves integrate input from neurons lower in the visual system. **Top-down processing,** in contrast, starts "at the top," with the observer's expectations and knowledge. Theorists who focus on top-down processing typically work from a cognitive perspective. They maintain that the brain uses prior knowledge to begin organizing and interpreting sensations as soon as the information starts coming in, rather than waiting for percepts to form based on sequential (step-by-step) analysis of

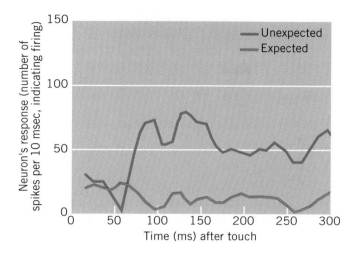

FIGURE 4.44
Expectations and neural firing. Expectations modulate the firing of a neuron in the macaque cortex. *Source:* Adapted from Mistlin & Perrett, 1990.

their isolated features. Thus, like Gestalt theorists, these researchers presume that as soon as the brain has detected features resembling eyes, it begins to expect a face and thus to look for a nose and mouth.

Studies Demonstrating Bottom-Up and Top-Down Processing   Both approaches have empirical support. Research on motion perception provides an example of bottom-up processing. Psychologists trained monkeys to report the direction in which a display of dots moved. The researchers then observed the response of individual neurons previously identified as feature detectors for movement of a particular speed and direction while the monkeys performed the task (Newsome et al., 1989). They discovered that the "decisions" made by individual neurons about the direction the dots moved were as accurate as—and sometimes even *more* accurate than—the decisions of the monkeys!

Perceptual decisions on simple tasks of this sort may require little involvement of higher mental processes. On the other hand, reading these words provides a good example of top-down processing, since reading would be incredibly cumbersome if people had to detect every letter of every word from the bottom up rather than expecting and recognizing patterns. A fascinating study demonstrates how expectations can have a top-down influence on cortical neurons that register sensory stimulation (Mistlin & Perrett, 1990). The researchers were studying a cortical region in macaque monkeys that responds to both visual and tactile stimulation when they noticed that neurons in this region responded differently to expected and unexpected stimuli. So they designed a study to compare the activation level of neurons when the monkey touched a familiar stimulus (part of its chair) or an unfamiliar one (a similar piece of metal not usually there). In both conditions, the monkey's vision was blocked, but its chair was in an expected location. As can be seen in Figure 4.44, touching the expected stimulus produced little neural activity. But when the monkey touched the unexpected object, the neuron fired repeatedly.

Other evidence of top-down processing has come from recent studies using PET technology while participants generated mental images. In one study, participants in one condition viewed block letters presented in a grid, as in Figure 4.45*a* (Kosslyn et al., in press). Following this, they were shown the same grid without the letter and asked to decide whether the letter would cover an X placed in one of the boxes of the grid. This task required that they create a mental image of the letter in the grid and locate the X on the imaginary letter. Next, they performed the same task, except this time the block letter was actually present in the grid, so they could perceive it instead of having to imagine it. Participants in a control

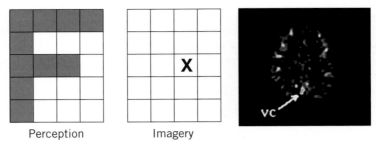

Perception   Imagery

FIGURE 4.45.

Visual imagery activates primary visual cortex. Participants viewed one of two stimulus patterns (left and center). In one, they actually saw a letter on a grid along with a black X. In another, they had to imagine the letter to decide whether the X would fall on the letter. In a control condition, they simply looked at the X come and go. As can be seen from the small area of bright activation (marked "vc") in the brain (right), the imaging condition activated primary visual cortex, just as looking at the actual letter did.

condition performed a simple task that essentially involved viewing the empty grid with and without an X.

The study relied on a "method of subtraction" used in many imaging studies: The investigators measured the amount of neuronal activity in the imagery and perception conditions and subtracted out the amount of brain activity seen in the control condition. The logic is to have the experimental and control conditions differ in as few respects as possible and subtract out the activation that occurs in the control condition; what is left in the computerized image of brain activity after subtraction is a picture of the regions of neural activity uniquely linked to the operation being investigated (in this case, mental imagery and perception).

Predictably, both perception and mental imagery activated many parts of the visual system, such as visual association cortex. However, the most striking finding was that the mental imagery condition activated the same areas of primary visual cortex activated by actual perception of the letters—normally believed to reflect bottom-up processing of sensory information (Figure 4.45b). In fact, the primary cortex was even *more* active during mental imagery than during actual perception! Although these findings are controversial (D'Esposito et al., 1997), if they hold up with future replications, they will suggest that when people picture an image in their minds, they actually create a visual image using the same neural pathways involved when they view a visual stimulus—a completely top-down activation of brain regions normally activated by sensory input.

Resolving the Paradox: Simultaneous Processing in Perception   Trying to explain perception by either bottom-up or top-down processes alone presents a paradox. You would not be able to identify the shapes in Figure 4.46a unless you knew they were part of a dog. Yet you would not recognize Figure 4.46b as a dog unless you could process information about the parts shown in the first panel. Without bottom-up processing, external stimuli would have no effect on perception; we would hallucinate rather than perceive. Without top-down processing, experience would have no effect on perception. How, then, do people ever recognize and classify objects?

According to current thinking, both types of processing occur simultaneously (Rumelhart et al., 1986). For example, features of the environment create patterns of stimulation in the primary visual cortex. These patterns in turn stimulate neural circuits in the visual association cortex that represent various objects, such as a friend's face. If the perceiver expects to see that face or if a large enough component of the neural network representing the face becomes activated, the brain essentially forms a "hypothesis" about an incoming pattern of sensory stimulation, even though all the data are not yet in from the feature detectors. It may even

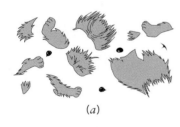

(a)

(b)

FIGURE 4.46

Top-down and bottom-up processing. In isolation (perceiving from the bottom up), the designs in (a) would have no meaning. At the same time, the broader design in (b), the dog, cannot be recognized without recognizing component parts.

entertain multiple hypotheses simultaneously, which are each tested against new incoming data until one hypothesis "wins out" because it seems to provide the best fit to the data. As we will see in later chapters, some of the most exciting recent research on human cognition suggests that most information processing, from sensation and perception through complex thinking, involves processes of this sort that occur in parallel, rather than one at a time from either the bottom up or the top down.

INTERIM SUMMARY   **Perceptual interpretation** means generating meaning from sensory experience. According to the theory of **direct perception,** the meaning or adaptive significance of a percept is often obvious, immediate, and innate. Trying to distinguish the relative roles of nature and nurture in perception may in some ways be asking the wrong question, since the nervous system has innate potentials that require environmental input to develop. Perception simultaneously involves **bottom-up processing,** which begins with raw sensory data that feeds "up" to the brain, and **top-down processing,** which begins with the observer's expectations and knowledge.

Expectations and Perception

Experience with the environment thus shapes perception by creating perceptual expectations, an important top-down influence on perception. These expectations, called **perceptual set** (i.e., the setting, or context, for a given perceptual "decision"), make certain interpretations more likely. Two aspects of perceptual set are the current context and enduring knowledge structures.

Context   Context plays a substantial role in perceptual interpretation. Consider, for example, how readily you understood the meaning of *substantial role* in the last sentence. Had someone uttered that phrase in a bakery, you would have

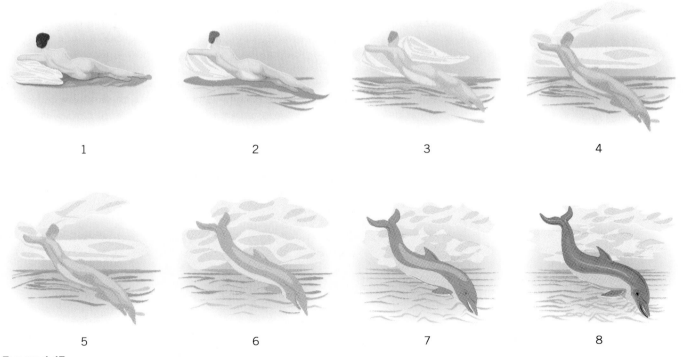

1   2   3   4

5   6   7   8

FIGURE 4.47
The impact of context on perception. Look at drawings 1, 2, 3, and 4, in that order (top row, left to right). Now look at drawings 5, 6, 7, and 8, in reverse order (bottom row, right to left). Drawing 4 most likely seems to be a woman's body and drawing 5, a porpoise, yet drawings 4 and 5 are identical. The same pattern of stimulation can be interpreted in many ways depending on context.

assumed they meant "substantial roll," unless the rest of the sentence provided a context suggesting otherwise. Context is just as important with tactile sensations (touch). A hug from a relative or from a stranger may have entirely different meanings and may immediately elicit very different feelings, even though the pattern of sensory stimulation may be identical. Figure 4.47 illustrates the importance of context in the visual mode. Context is especially important in perceiving spoken language (Chapter 7), since even the most careful speaker drops syllables, slurs sounds, or misses words altogether, and many words (such as *role* and *roll*) have the same sound but different meanings.

Schemas   Not only the immediate context but a person's enduring beliefs and expectations affect perceptual interpretation. One way knowledge is organized in memory is in **schemas**—patterns of thinking about a domain that render the environment relatively predictable (Neisser, 1976). We have schemas (organized knowledge) about objects (such as chairs and dogs), people (such as introverts and ministers), and situations (such as funerals and restaurants), which help us behave appropriately. The fact that people generally sit on chairs instead of on other people reflects their schemas about what chairs and people do.

Because schemas allow individuals to anticipate what they will encounter, they increase both the speed and efficiency of perception. For example, people process information extremely quickly when shown photographs of real-world scenes, such as a kitchen, a city street, or a desk top. In one study, subjects could recall almost half the objects in familiar scenes after viewing them for only one-tenth of a second (Biederman et al., 1973). In contrast, subjects who viewed the same scenes cut into six equal pieces and randomly reassembled had difficulty both identifying and remembering the objects in the picture (Figures 4.48*a* and *b*). Schemas can also induce perceptual errors, however, when individuals fail to notice what they do not expect to see (Figure 4.48*c*), such as an unfamiliar pothole on the street (see Biederman et al., 1981, 1982).

Motivation and Perception

As we have seen, expectations can lead people to see what they expect to see and hear what they expect to hear. But people also frequently hear the words they *want* to hear as well. In other words, motivation, like cognition, can exert a top-

Schemas produce expectations that can sometimes lead perception astray. Turn the book over and the abnormality in one photo of Bill Clinton is readily apparent.

  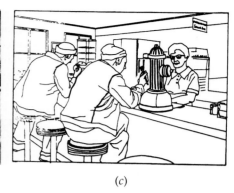

(a)   *(b)*   *(c)*

FIGURE 4.48

Schemas. Subjects had no trouble identifying and remembering objects in (*a*), a photo of a normal Chinatown street, because the scene activates a "city street schema" that guides perception and memory. In contrast, without a schema to help interpret what they were seeing (*b*), they had much more difficulty. Schemas can also lead to perceptual failures. Before reading further, look briefly at (*c*). People rarely notice the unexpected object in the upper right-hand corner (the fire hydrant) because it is incongruent with their activated "restaurant schema."

down influence on perception. This was the argument of a school of perceptual thought in the late 1940s called the *New Look* in perception, which focused on the impact of emotion, motivation, and personality on perception (Dixon, 1980; Erdelyi, 1985; Weinberger, in press). Many of the issues raised by New Look researchers are receiving renewed attention a half century later (see, e.g., Bargh, in press; Bruner, 1992; Uleman & Bargh, 1989).

One classic experiment examined the effects of food and water deprivation on identification of words (Wispe & Drambarean, 1953). The experimenters placed participants in one of three groups. Some went without food for 24 hours prior to the experiment; some ate nothing for ten hours; and others ate just beforehand. The researchers then flashed two kinds of words on a screen so rapidly that they were barely perceptible: neutral words (e.g., *serenade* and *hunch*) and words related to food (e.g., *lemonade* and *munch*). The three groups did not differ in their responses to the neutral words. However, both of the deprived groups perceived the need-related words more readily (i.e., when flashed more briefly) than nondeprived controls. A similar phenomenon occurs outside the laboratory: People are often intensely aware of the aroma of food outside a restaurant when they are hungry but oblivious to it when their stomachs are full.

New Look researchers were also interested in applying psychodynamic ideas to perception. For example, several studies presented participants with words on a screen so quickly that they could not report what they had seen (Broadbent, 1958; Dixon, 1970, 1980; Erdelyi, 1984). They noticed some striking differences when they presented subjects with neutral versus taboo words (such as sexual words). In one study, the researcher exposed participants to neutral and taboo words so quickly that they could barely recognize even a flash of light (Blum, 1954). Yet when asked which stimuli seemed more salient, participants consistently chose the taboo words—even though they had not consciously perceived that they had seen words at all! When similar words were presented at speeds that could just barely allow recognition of them, participants could "see" the neutral words but not the taboo ones. These findings suggest that more emotionally evocative taboo words attract attention even below the threshold of consciousness, but that they are harder to recognize consciously than neutral words. Subsequent research has confirmed and extended these findings (Erdelyi, 1984; Shevrin, 1980; Shevrin et al., 1996; Weinberger, in press).

INTERIM SUMMARY Expectations, based on both the current context and enduring knowledge structures (schemas), influence the way people interpret ongoing sensory experience. Motives can also influence perception, including motives to avoid perceiving stimuli with uncomfortable content.

SOME CONCLUDING THOUGHTS

As the examples in this chapter suggest, perception is not independent of our *reasons* for perceiving. Evolution has equipped humans with a nervous system remarkably attuned to stimuli that *matter*. If people did not need to eat or to worry about what they put in their mouths, they would not have a sense of taste. If they did not need to find food, escape danger, and communicate, they would not need to see and hear. And if their skin were not vulnerable to damage, they would not need to feel pain.

Sensation and perception are the gateway to the mind, and they provide much of the raw material for our thought. We think in words we have read and heard; we think in images we have seen. For centuries, philosophers have wondered whether learning, memory, and thought reflect anything *but* the mental manipulation and recombination of sensations—like the novel impressions formed by the turn of a kaleidoscope. In the next few chapters we explore what it means to learn, remember, and think. We then examine the motivational and emotional processes that ultimately provide the impetus for applying the knowledge delivered by our senses.

SUMMARY

BASIC PRINCIPLES

1. **Sensation** refers to the process by which sense organs gather information about the environment and transmit it to the brain for initial processing. **Perception** refers to the closely related process by which the brain selects, organizes, and interprets sensations.

2. Three basic principles apply across all the senses. First, there is no one-to-one correspondence between physical and psychological reality. Second, sensation and perception are active, not passive. Third, sensation and perception are adaptive.

SENSING THE ENVIRONMENT

3. Sensation begins with an environmental stimulus; all sensory systems have specialized cells called **receptors** that respond to environmental stimuli and typically generate action potentials in adjacent sensory neurons. This process is called **transduction.** Within each sensory modality, the brain codes sensory stimulation for intensity and quality.

4. The **absolute threshold** refers to the minimum amount of stimulation needed for an observer to notice a stimulus. The **difference threshold** refers to the lowest level of stimulation required to sense that a *change* in stimulation has occurred (a **just noticeable difference,** or **jnd**). **Weber's law** states that regardless of the magnitude of two stimuli, the second must differ by a

constant proportion from the first for it to be perceived as different. **Fechner's law** holds that the physical magnitude of a stimulus grows logarithmically as the subjective experience of intensity grows arithmetically; in other words, people only subjectively experience a small percentage of actual increases in stimulus intensity. **Stevens' power law** states that subjective intensity grows as a proportion of the actual intensity raised to some power, that is, that sensation increases in a linear fashion as actual intensity grows exponentially.

5. **Sensory adaptation** is the tendency of sensory systems to respond less to stimuli that continue without change.

VISION

6. The eyes are sensitive to a small portion of the electromagnetic spectrum called light. In vision, light is focused on the retina by the **cornea, pupil,** and **lens. Rods** are very sensitive to light, allowing vision in dim light; **cones** are especially sensitive to particular wavelengths, producing the psychological experience of color. Cones are concentrated at the **fovea,** the region of the retina most sensitive to detail. The **ganglion cells** of the retina transmit visual information via the **optic nerve** to the brain. Ganglion cells, like other neurons involved in sensation, have **receptive fields,** a region of stimulation to which the neuron responds. **Feature detectors** are specialized cells of the primary cortex in the occipital lobes that respond only when stimulation in their receptive field matches a particular pattern or orientation, such as horizontal or vertical lines.

7. From the primary visual cortex, visual information appears to flow along two pathways, or *processing streams*, called the "what" and the "where" pathways. The **what pathway** is involved in determining *what* an object is and runs from the primary visual cortex in the occipital lobes through the lower part of the temporal lobes (or the *inferior temporal cortex*). The second stream, the **where pathway,** is involved in locating the object in space, following its movement, and guiding movement toward it. This pathway runs from the primary visual cortex through the middle and upper regions of the temporal lobes and up into the parietal lobes.

8. The property of light that is transduced into color is **wavelength.** The **Young–Helmholtz,** or **trichromatic, theory** proposes that the eye contains three types of receptors, sensitive to red, green, or blue. **Opponent-process theory** argues for the existence of pairs of opposite primary colors linked in three systems: a blue–yellow system, a red–green system, and a black–white system. Both theories appear to be involved in color perception; trichromatic theory is operative at the level of the retina, and opponent-process theory at higher neural levels.

HEARING

9. Hearing, or **audition,** occurs as a vibrating object sets air particles in motion. Each round of expansion and contraction of the air is known as a **cycle.** The number of cycles per second determines a sound wave's **frequency,** which corresponds to the psychological property of **pitch. Amplitude** refers to the height and depth of the wave and corresponds to the psychological property of **loudness.** Sound waves travel through the auditory canal to the **eardrum,**

where they are amplified; transduction occurs by way of **hair cells** attached to the **basilar membrane** that respond to vibrations in the fluid-filled **cochlea.** This mechanical process triggers action potentials in the **auditory nerve,** which are then transmitted to the brain.

10. Two theories, once considered opposing, explain the psychological qualities of sound. **Place theory,** which holds that different areas of the basilar membrane respond to different frequencies, appears to be most accurate for high frequencies. **Frequency theory,** which asserts that the basilar membrane's rate of vibration reflects the frequency with which a sound wave cycles, explains sensation of low-frequency sounds.

OTHER SENSES

11. The environmental stimuli for smell, or **olfaction,** are invisible molecules of gas emitted by substances and suspended in the air. As air enters the nose, it flows into the **olfactory epithelium,** where hundreds of different types of receptors respond to various kinds of molecules, producing complex smells. The axons of olfactory receptor cells constitute the **olfactory nerve,** which transmits information to the **olfactory bulbs** under the frontal lobes and on to the primary olfactory cortex, a primitive region of the cortex deep in the frontal lobes.

12. Taste, or **gustation,** is sensitive to molecules soluble in saliva. Much of the experience of taste, however, is really contributed by smell. Taste occurs as receptors in the **taste buds** on the tongue and throughout the mouth transduce chemical information into neural information, which is integrated with olfactory information in the brain.

13. Touch actually includes three senses: pressure, temperature, and pain. The human body contains approximately 5 million touch receptors of at least seven different types. Sensory neurons synapse with spinal interneurons that stimulate motor neurons, allowing reflexive action, as well as with neurons that carry information up the spinal cord to the medulla, where nerve tracts cross over. From there, sensory information travels to the thalamus and is subsequently routed to the primary touch center in the brain, the somatosensory cortex, which contains a map of the body. Pain is greatly affected by beliefs, expectations, and emotional state. **Gate-control theory** holds that the experience of pain is heavily influenced by the central nervous system, through the action of neural fibers that can "close the gate" on pain, preventing messages from other fibers getting through.

14. The **proprioceptive senses** provide information about the body's position and movement. The **vestibular sense** provides information on the position of the body in space by sensing gravity and movement. **Kinesthesia** provides information about the movement and position of the limbs and other parts of the body relative to one another.

PERCEPTION

15. The hallmarks of perception are organization and interpretation. **Perceptual organization** integrates sensations into meaningful units, locates them in space, tracks their movement, and preserves their meaning as the perceiver observes them from different vantage points. **Form perception** refers to the organization of sensations into meaningful shapes and patterns **(percepts).**

The Gestalt psychologists described several principles of form perception, including figure–ground perception, similarity, proximity, good continuation, simplicity, and closure. A more recent theory, called **recognition-by-components,** asserts that we perceive and categorize objects in the environment by breaking them down into component parts, much like letters in words.

16. **Depth perception** is the organization of perception in three dimensions. Depth perception organizes two-dimensional retinal images into a three-dimensional world primarily through **binocular** and **monocular visual cues.**

17. **Motion perception** refers to the perception of movement. Two systems appear to be involved in motion perception. The first computes motion from the changing image projected by the object on the retina; the second makes use of commands from the brain to the muscles in the eye that signal eye movements.

18. **Perceptual constancy** refers to the organization of changing sensations into percepts that are relatively stable in size, shape, and color. Three types of perceptual constancy are size, shape, and color constancy, which refer to the perception of unchanging size, shape, and color despite momentary changes in the retinal image. The processes that organize perception leave perceivers vulnerable to **perceptual illusions,** some of which appear to be innate and others of which depend on culture and experience.

19. **Perceptual interpretation** involves generating meaning from sensory experience. Perceptual interpretation lies at the intersection of sensation and memory, as the brain interprets current sensations in light of past experience. Perception is neither entirely innate nor entirely learned. The nervous system has certain innate potentials, but these potentials require environmental input to develop. Experience can alter the structure of the brain, making it more or less responsive to subsequent sensory input.

20. **Bottom-up processing** refers to processing that begins "at the bottom," with raw sensory data that feeds "up" to the brain. **Top-down processing** starts "at the top," from the observer's expectations and knowledge. According to current thinking, perception proceeds in both directions simultaneously. Experience with the environment shapes perceptual interpretation by creating perceptual expectations called **perceptual set.** Two aspects of perceptual set are current context and enduring knowledge structures called **schemas.** Motives, like expectations, can influence perceptual interpretation.

Janet Fish, *Ruth Sewing*, 1983, D.C. More Gallery.

An experiment by John Garcia and his colleagues adds a new twist to all the stories ever told about wolves and sheep. The researchers fed a wolf a muttonburger (made of the finest sheep flesh) laced with odorless, tasteless capsules of lithium chloride, a chemical that induces nausea. Displaying a natural preference for mutton, the animal wolfed it down but half an hour later became sick and vomited (Garcia & Garcia-Robertson, 1985; Gustavson et al., 1976).

Several days later, the researchers introduced a sheep into the wolf's compound. At the sight of one of its favorite delicacies, the wolf went straight for the sheep's throat. But on contact, the wolf abruptly drew back. It slowly circled the sheep. Soon it attacked from another angle, going for the hamstring. This attack was as short-lived as the last. After an hour in the compound together, the wolf still had not attacked the sheep—and in fact, the sheep had made a few short

charges at the wolf. Lithium chloride seems to have been the real wolf in sheep's clothing.

Although the effects of a single dose of a toxic chemical do not last forever, Garcia's research illustrates the powerful impact of **learning,** which refers to any enduring change in the way an organism responds based on its experience. 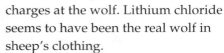 In humans, as in other animals, learning is central to adaptation because the environment does not stand still; it varies from place to place and from moment to moment. Knowing how to distinguish edible from inedible foods or to distinguish friends from enemies or predators is essential for survival. Although many animal species have natural preferences and aversions that guide their learning, such as young children's attraction to sweets (which provide energy) or fear of strangers, the range of possible foods or threats is simply too great to be prewired into the brain. The social environment, too, is complex and varied, particularly in humans. In some Islamic cultures, a woman who shows her legs may be beaten; in Western cultures, revealing skin can be a way to attract a mate. Even *within* a culture, the standards of appropriate behavior change across situations and over time. A skirt length that is acceptable in one context or during one era may be considered inappropriate or scandalous in another.

Theories of learning tend to share three assumptions. The first is that experience shapes behavior. Particularly in complex organisms such as humans, the vast majority of responses are learned rather than innate. The migration patterns of Pacific salmon may be instinctive, but the migration of college students to Daytona Beach during spring break is not. Second, learning is adaptive. Just as nature eliminates organisms that are not well suited to their environments, the environment naturally selects those behaviors in an individual that are adaptive and weeds out those that are not (Skinner, 1977). Behaviors useful to the organism (such as avoiding fights with larger members of its species) will be reproduced because of their consequences (safety from bodily harm). A third assumption is that careful experimentation can uncover laws of learning, many of which apply to human and nonhuman animals alike.

Learning theory is the foundation of the behaviorist perspective, and the bulk of this chapter explores the behavioral concepts of classical and operant conditioning (known together as *associative learning*). The remainder examines cognitive approaches that emphasize the role of thought and social experience in learning, although at many points we will also consider the links between learning and evolution.

Throughout, several questions are worth keeping in mind. First, to what extent are humans like other animals in the way they learn? To put it another way, how much difference does our expanded cortex really make to basic principles of learning observed across species? Second, what constraints and possibilities has evolution placed on what we can learn? As we saw in Chapter 4, our senses are only attuned to a subset of the physical stimuli around us; we obviously cannot learn to associate danger or reward with sound frequencies dogs can hear if our ears are not tuned to those frequencies. But even within the range of experiences available to our senses, are the possibilities for learning limitless? Or has natural selection "wired" us to learn some things more readily than others? And if so, to what degree can experience override innate tendencies?

Third, how complex must laws of learning be to explain most of human behavior? Twenty-five hundred years ago, Aristotle proposed a set of **laws of association**—conditions under which one thought becomes connected, or associated, with another—to account for learning and memory. The most important was the *law of contiguity*, which proposed that two events will become connected in the mind if they are experienced close together in time (such as thunder and lightning). Another was the *law of similarity*, which states that objects that resemble each other (such as two people with similar faces) are likely to become associated. The philosophical school of thought called *associationism* built upon the work of Aristotle, asserting that the most complex thoughts—which allow humans to create airplanes, understand laws of physics, or write symphonies—are ultimately nothing but elementary perceptions that become associated and then recombined in the mind. As we will see in the next few chapters, principles of association are fundamental to behaviorist theories of learning as well as to cognitive theories of memory, and neuroscientists have now begun to understand their neural basis—all the way down to changes at the synapse. The question, then, is the extent to which a relatively small set of fundamental principles such as these can explain most or all of what we do.

INTERIM SUMMARY   **Learning** refers to any enduring change in the way an organism responds based on its experience. Learning theories assume that experience shapes behavior, that learning is adaptive, and that only systematic experimentation can uncover laws of learning. Principles of **association** are fundamental to most accounts of learning.

CLASSICAL CONDITIONING

Classical conditioning (sometimes called *Pavlovian* or *respondent conditioning*) was the first type of learning to be studied systematically. In the late nineteenth century, the Russian physiologist Ivan Pavlov (1849–1936) was studying the digestive systems of dogs (research for which he won a Nobel Prize). During the course of his work, he noticed a peculiar phenomenon. Like humans and other animals, dogs normally salivate when presented with food, which is a simple reflex. A **reflex** is a behavior that is elicited automatically by an environmental stimulus, such as the knee-jerk reflex elicited by a doctor's rubber hammer. A **stimulus** is something in the environment that elicits a response. Pavlov noticed that if a stimulus, such as a bell or turning fork ringing, repeatedly occurred just as a dog was about to be fed, the dog would start to salivate when it heard the bell, even if food were not presented. As Pavlov understood it, the dog had learned to associate the bell with food, and because food produced the reflex of salivation, the bell also came to produce the reflex.

PAVLOV'S MODEL

An innate reflex such as salivation to food is an unconditioned reflex. **Conditioning** is a form of learning; hence, an **unconditioned reflex** is a reflex that occurs naturally, without any prior learning. The stimulus that produces the response in an unconditioned reflex—in this case, food—is called an **unconditioned stimulus, (UCS).** An unconditioned stimulus activates a reflexive response without any learning having taken place; thus, the reflex is unlearned, or unconditioned. An **unconditioned response (UCR)** is a response that does not have to be learned. In Pavlov's experiment, the UCR was salivation.

Pavlov's basic experimental setup is illustrated in Figure 5.1. Shortly before presenting the UCS (the food), Pavlov presented a *neutral stimulus*—a stimulus (in this case, ringing a bell) that normally does not elicit the response in question. After the bell had been paired with the unconditioned stimulus (the food) several times, the sound of the bell alone came to evoke a conditioned response, salivation (Figure 5.2). A **conditioned response (CR)** is a response that has been

FIGURE 5.1
Pavlov's dogs. Pavlov's research with dogs documented the phenomenon of classical conditioning. Actually, his dogs became conditioned to salivate in response to many aspects of the experimental situation and not just to bells or tuning forks; the sight of the experimenter and the harness, too, could elicit the conditioned response.

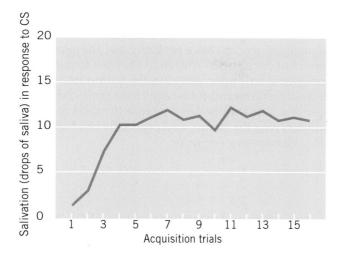

FIGURE 5.2
Acquisition of a classically conditioned response. Initially, the dog did not salivate in response to the sound of the bell. By the third conditioning trial, however, the conditioned stimulus (the bell) had begun to elicit a conditioned response (salivation), which was firmly established by the fifth or sixth trial. *Source:* Pavlov, 1927.

learned. By pairing the UCS (the food) with the sound of a bell, the bell became a **conditioned stimulus (CS)**—a stimulus that, through learning, has come to evoke a conditioned response. Figure 5.3 summarizes the classical conditioning process.

Why did such a seemingly simple discovery earn Pavlov a central place in the history of psychology? The reason is that classical conditioning can explain a wide array of learned responses outside the laboratory as well. For example, a house cat that was repeatedly sprayed with flea repellent squinted reflexively as the repellent got in its eyes. Eventually it came to squint and meow piteously (CR) whenever its owner used an aerosol spray (CS). The same cat, like many household felines, also came to associate the sound of an electric can opener with the opening of its favorite delicacies and would dash to the kitchen counter and meow whenever its owner opened any can, whether cat food or green beans. If you are beginning to feel somewhat superior to the poor cat wasting all those meows and squints on cans of deodorant and vegetables, consider whether you have ever been at your desk, engrossed in work, when you glanced at the clock and discovered that it was dinner time. If so, you probably noticed some physiological responses—feeling hungry, or perhaps mouth watering—that had not been present seconds earlier. Through repeated pairings of stimuli associated

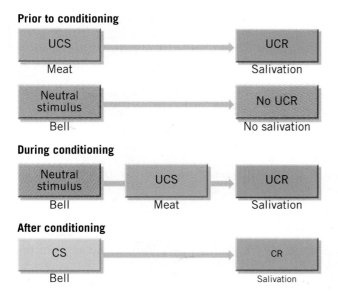

FIGURE 5.3
Classical conditioning. In classical conditioning, an initially neutral stimulus comes to elicit a conditioned response.

Drawing by John Chase

with a particular time of day and dinner, you have been classically conditioned to associate a time of day indicated on a clock (the CS) with food (the UCS). At the other end of the digestive system, most readers have probably had the experience of needing to go to the bathroom but deciding to wait until they get home. Upon arriving at the front door—and worse still upon entering the bathroom—the intensity of the urge seems to intensify a thousand-fold, requiring considerable self-control. This phenomenon, too, is a straightforward example of classical conditioning: Stimuli associated with entering the house, and especially the bathroom, are CSs that signal an impending eliminatory response.

CONDITIONED RESPONSES

Pavlov was heavily influenced by Darwin and recognized that the ability to learn new associations is crucial to adaptation. He also saw how learning could produce maladaptive patterns as well (Hollis, 1997; Windholz, 1997). Three cases in which classical conditioning generally fosters adaptation but can also lead to maladaptive responses are conditioned taste aversions, conditioned emotional responses, and conditioned immune responses.

Conditioned Taste Aversions

The case of the wolf and the muttonburger with which this chapter opened is an example of a *conditioned taste aversion*—a learned aversion to a taste associated with an unpleasant feeling, usually nausea. From an evolutionary perspective, the ability to connect tastes with nausea or other unpleasant visceral ("gut") experiences is crucial to survival; learning to avoid toxic foods can mean the difference between life and death for an animal that forages (that is, scrounges or hunts) for its meals. The capacity to learn taste aversions appears to be hundreds of millions of years old and is present in some very simple invertebrates, like certain species of slugs (Garcia et al., 1985; Schafe & Bernstein, 1996). As further evidence of its ancient roots, conditioned taste aversions do not require cortical involvement in humans or other vertebrates. Rats with their cortex removed can still learn taste aversions, and even animals *completely anesthetized* while nausea is induced can learn taste aversions, as long as they are conscious during presentation of the CS.

Although conditioned taste aversions normally protect the organism from ingesting toxic substances, anyone who has ever developed an aversion to a food eaten shortly before getting the flu knows how irrational these aversions can sometimes be. Cancer patients undergoing chemotherapy often develop aversions to virtually all food—and may lose dangerous amounts of weight—because a common side effect of chemotherapy is nausea. To put this in the language of classical conditioning, chemotherapy is a UCS that leads to nausea, a UCR; the result is an inadvertent association of any food eaten (CS) with nausea (the CR). This conditioned response can develop rapidly, with only one or two exposures to the food paired with nausea (Bernstein, 1991), much as Garcia's wolf took little time to acquire an aversion to the taste of sheep. Some patients even begin to feel nauseous at the sound of a nurse's voice, the sight of the clinic, or the thought of treatment, although acquisition of these CRs generally requires repeated exposure (Bovbjerg et al., 1990).

Conditioned Emotional Responses

One of the most important ways classical conditioning affects behavior is in the conditioning of emotional responses. Consider the automatic smile that comes to a person's face when hearing a special song or the fear of horses a person may de-

THE FAR SIDE   By GARY LARSON

"Zelda! Cool it! ... The Rothenbergs hear the can opener!"

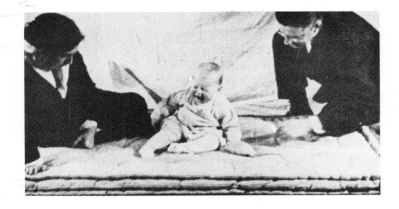

Through classical conditioning, little Albert developed a fear of rats and other furry objects—even Santa's face (a disabling phobia for a child, indeed). Courtesy of Benjamin Harris.

velop after falling off of one. *Conditioned emotional responses* occur when a formerly neutral stimulus is paired with a stimulus that evokes an emotional response (either naturally, as when bitten by an animal, or through prior learning). Conditioned emotional responses are commonplace in everyday life, such as the sweaty palms, pounding heart, and feeling of anxiety that arise after an instructor walks into a classroom and begins handing out a few printed pages of questions.

One of the most famous examples of classical conditioning was the case of little Albert. The study was performed by John Watson, considered the founder of American behaviorism, and his colleague, Rosalie Rayner (1920). The study was neither methodologically nor ethically beyond reproach, but its provocative findings served as a catalyst for decades of research. When Albert was nine months old, Watson and Rayner presented him with a variety of objects, including a dog, a rabbit, a white rat, masks (including a Santa Claus mask), and a fur coat. Albert showed no fear in response to any of these objects; in fact, he played regularly with the rat—a budding behaviorist, no doubt. A few days later, Watson and Rayner tested little Albert's response to a loud noise (the UCS) by banging on a steel bar directly behind his head. Albert reacted by jumping, falling forward, and whimpering.

About two months later, Watson and Rayner selected the white rat to be the CS in their experiment and proceeded to condition a fear response in Albert. Each time Albert reached out to touch the rat, they struck the steel bar, creating the same loud noise that had initially startled him. After only a few pairings of the noise and the rat, Albert learned to fear the rat.

Studies since Watson and Rayner's time have proposed classical conditioning as an explanation for some human **phobias,** that is, irrational fears of specific objects or situations (Merckelbach et al., 1991; Ost, 1991; Wolpe, 1958). For example, many people develop severe emotional reactions (including fainting) to hypodermic needles through exposure to injections in childhood. Knowing as an adult that injections are necessary and relatively painless usually has little impact on the fear, which is elicited automatically. Athletes such as football players often amuse nurses in student health centers with their combination of fearlessness on the field and fainting at the sight of a tiny needle. Many such fears are acquired and elicited through the activation of subcortical neural pathways between the visual system and the amygdala (LeDoux, 1995). Adult knowledge may be of little use in counteracting them because the crucial neural circuits are outside cortical control and are activated before the cortex even gets the message.

Conditioned Immune Responses

Psychologists have recently discovered that classical conditioning can even impact the **immune system,** the system of cells throughout the body that fight disease (e.g., Ader & Cohen, 1985, 1993). For example, aside from causing nausea, chemotherapy for cancer has a second unfortunate consequence: It decreases the activity of cells in the immune system that normally fight off infection. Can stimuli associated with chemotherapy, then, become CRs that suppress the activity of these cells? One study tested this by comparing the functioning of immune cells from the blood of cancer patients at two different times (Bovbjerg et al., 1990). The first time was a few days prior to chemotherapy. The second time was the morning of the day the patient would be receiving chemotherapy, after checking into the hospital. The investigators hypothesized that exposure to hospital stimuli associated with prior chemotherapy experiences (CS) would suppress immune functioning (CR), just as chemotherapy (UCS) reduces the activity of immune cells (UCR). They were right: Blood taken the morning of hospitalization showed weakened immune functioning when exposed to germs.

Researchers are now trying to see whether they can actually *strengthen* immune functioning using classical conditioning. One of the effects of exposure to potentially threatening substances such as bacteria or viruses is that the body develops *antibodies* for them (proteins that latch onto them and destroy them). To see whether antibody production can be classically conditioned, one research team allowed rats in one condition to drink water with saccharine (a sugar substitute) in it (the CS) just prior to injecting them with a substance (UCS) known to elicit antibodies (UCR) (Alvarez-Borda et al., 1995). Rats in a control condition received only water along with the injection. Several days later, after antibodies to this substance were no longer detectable in the rats' blood, rats in both conditions were given saccharine water, while rats in a third condition received another injection (along with water).

The experimenters hypothesized that rats in the first condition, for whom saccharine (CS) was associated with injection of the substance (UCS), would produce antibodies in response to the saccharine (CR), as would rats reexposed to the substance. In contrast, control rats, for whom saccharine was not a CS, should not show any renewed antibody production. As can be seen in Figure 5.4, this hypothesis was confirmed: Rats exposed to saccharine produced almost as much antibody as those given a fresh injection. Their immune systems seemed to anticipate

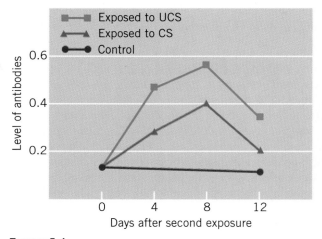

Figure 5.4

Conditioned immune response. The graph shows the density of antibodies seen in the blood of experimental rats reexposed to the CS (saccharine), rats reexposed to the UCS (injection of a substance that elicits antibody production), and control rats exposed to neither. Rats exposed to the UCS not surprisingly showed the most antibody production, but rats exposed to the CS also showed significant increases in antibodies. The impact of the experimental manipulation peaked for both groups at eight days after reexposure and dropped thereafter. *Source:* Alvarez-Borda et al., 1995.

an injection and prepare for it with antibodies, just as Pavlov's dogs prepared for meat with a mouth full of saliva when they heard a familiar tone.

INTERIM SUMMARY   In **classical conditioning,** an environmental stimulus leads to a learned response, through pairing of an **unconditioned stimulus** with a previously neutral **conditioned stimulus.** The result is a **conditioned response,** or learned reflex. *Conditioned taste aversions* are learned aversions to a taste associated with an unpleasant feeling (usually nausea). *Conditioned emotional responses* occur when a conditioned stimulus is paired with a stimulus that evokes an emotional response. *Conditioned immune responses* can occur when a conditioned stimulus is paired with a stimulus that evokes a change in the functioning of the **immune system** (the system of cells in the body that fight disease).

STIMULUS GENERALIZATION AND DISCRIMINATION

Once an organism has learned to associate a CS with a UCS, it may respond to stimuli that resemble the CS with a similar response. This phenomenon, predicted by Aristotle's principle of similarity, is called **stimulus generalization.** For example, you are at a sporting event and you stand for the national anthem. You suddenly well up with pride in your country (which you realize now, of course, is nothing but a classically conditioned emotional response). But the song you have heard, familiar as it may sound, is not *exactly* the same stimulus you heard the last time you were at a game. It is not in the same key, and this time the tenor took a few liberties with the melody. So how do you know to respond with the same emotion? Similarly, in Watson and Rayner's experiment, the pairing of the rat and the loud noise led little Albert to fear not only the rat but also other furry or hairy objects, including the rabbit, the dog, the fur coat, and even Santa's face. In other words, Albert's fear of the rat had *generalized* to other furry objects.

Many years ago researchers demonstrated that the more similar a stimulus is to the CS, the more likely generalization will occur (Hovland, 1937). In a classic study, the experimenters paired a tone (the CS) with a mild electrical shock (the UCS). With repeated pairings, participants produced a conditioned response to the tone known as a **galvanic skin response,** or **GSR**—an electrical measure of the amount of sweat on the skin, associated with arousal or anxiety. The experimenter then presented tones of varying frequencies that had not been paired with shock and measured the resulting GSR. Tones with frequencies similar to the CS evoked the most marked GSR, whereas dissimilar tones evoked progressively smaller responses (Figure 5.5).

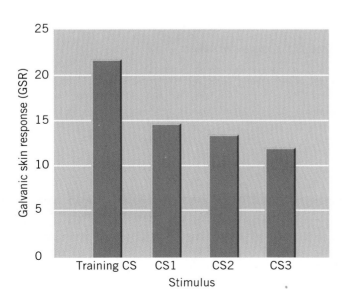

FIGURE 5.5
Stimulus generalization. Galvanic skin response (a measure of physiological arousal) varies according to the similarity of the CS to the training stimulus. In this case, the training stimulus was a tone of a particular frequency. CS-1 is most similar to the training stimulus; CS-3 is least similar to it. *Source:* Hovland, 1937.

A major component of adaptive learning is knowing when to generalize and when to be more specific or discriminating. Maladaptive patterns in humans often involve inappropriate generalization from one set of circumstances to others, as when a person who has been frequently criticized by a parent responds negatively to all authority figures. Much of the time, however, people are able to discriminate among stimuli in ways that foster adaptation. **Stimulus discrimination** is the learned tendency to respond to a restricted range of stimuli or only to the stimulus used during training. In many ways, stimulus discrimination is the opposite of stimulus generalization. Pavlov's dogs did not salivate in response to just *any* sound, and people do not get hungry when the clock reads four o'clock even though it is not far from six o'clock. Organisms learn to discriminate between two similar stimuli when these stimuli are not consistently associated with the same UCS.

EXTINCTION

In the **acquisition,** or initial learning, of a conditioned response, each pairing of the CS and UCS is known as a **conditioning trial.** But what happens later if the CS repeatedly occurs *without* the UCS? What would have happened if Watson and Rayner had, on the second, third, and all subsequent trials, exposed little Albert to the white rat without the loud noise?

Albert's learned fear response would eventually have been *extinguished*, or eliminated, from his behavioral repertoire. **Extinction** in classical conditioning refers to the process by which a CR is weakened by presentation of the CS without the UCS. If a dog has come to associate the sounding of a bell with food, it will eventually stop salivating at the bell tone if the bell rings enough times without the presentation of food. The association is weakened—but not obliterated. If days later the dog once more hears the bell, it is likely to salivate again. This is known as **spontaneous recovery**—the reemergence of a previously extinguished conditioned response. The spontaneous recovery of a CR is typically short-lived, however, and will rapidly extinguish again without renewed pairings of the CS and UCS.

INTERIM SUMMARY   **Stimulus generalization** occurs when an organism learns to respond to stimuli that resemble the CS with a similar response; **stimulus discrimination** occurs when an organism learns to respond to a restricted range of stimuli. **Extinction** occurs when a CR is weakened by presentation of the CS without the UCS.

FACTORS AFFECTING CLASSICAL CONDITIONING

Classical conditioning does not occur every time a bell rings, a baby startles, or a wolf eats some tainted lamb chops. Several factors influence the extent to which classical conditioning will occur. These include the interstimulus interval, the individual's learning history, and the organism's preparedness to learn (see Chase, 1988; Wasserman & Miller, 1997).

Interstimulus Interval

The **interstimulus interval** is the time between presentation of the CS and the UCS. Presumably, if too much time passes between the presentation of these two stimuli, the animal is unlikely to associate them, and conditioning is less likely to occur. For most responses, the optimal interval between the CS and UCS is very brief, usually a few seconds or less. The optimal interval depends, however, on the stimulus and tends to bear the imprint of natural selection (Hollis, 1997). A CS that occurs about a half a second before a puff of air blows on the eye will have the maximum power to elicit a conditioned eyeblink response in humans (Ross & Ross, 1971). This makes evolutionary sense because we usually have very little warning between the time we see or hear something and the time debris reaches our eyes. At the other extreme, conditioned taste aversions do not occur when the interstimulus interval is *less than* ten seconds, and learning often occurs with intervals up to several hours (Schafe & Bernstein, 1996). Given that nausea or stomach pain can develop hours after ingestion of a toxic substance, the capacity to associate tastes with feelings in the gut minutes or hours later clearly fosters survival. Just as in perception, our brains appear to be attuned to the patterns that exist in nature.

The temporal order of the CS and the UCS—that is, which one comes first—is also crucial (Figure 5.6). Maximal conditioning occurs when the onset of the CS precedes the UCS—called *forward conditioning.* Less effective is *simultaneous conditioning,* in which the CS and UCS are presented at the same time. A third pattern, *backward conditioning,* is the least effective of all. Here, the CS is presented after the UCS has occurred. These principles, too, make evolutionary sense, since a CS that consistently occurs after a UCS offers little additional information, whereas a CS that precedes a UCS allows the organism to prepare.

The Individual's Learning History

Another factor that influences classical conditioning is the individual's learning history. An extinguished response is usually easier to learn the second time around, presumably because the stimulus was once associated with the response. A previously extinguished nausea response to the taste of bacon is likely to be easily reinstated—and difficult to extinguish—if bacon and nausea ever occur together again. This suggests that neuronal connections established through learning may diminish in their strength when the environment no longer supports them but do not entirely disappear; later learning can build on old "tracks" that have been covered up but not obliterated.

In other circumstances, prior learning can actually *hinder* learning. Suppose a dog has learned to salivate at the sound of a bell (conditioned stimulus A, or CSA). The researcher now wants to teach the dog to associate food with a flash of light as well (CSB). If the bell continues to sound even occasionally in learning trials pairing the light (CSB) with food (the UCS), the dog is unlikely to produce a conditioned response to the flash of light. This phenomenon is known as blocking. **Blocking** refers to the failure of a stimulus (such as a flash of light) to elicit a CR when it is combined with another stimulus that already elicits the response (Kamin, 1969; Pearce, 1987). If a bell is already associated with food, a flashing light is of little consequence unless it provides additional, nonredundant information. Interestingly, if the CR to the bell (CSA) is subsequently extinguished, the animal will more quickly develop a CR to the CSB (the light) than control animals who have not undergone blocking trials. What this suggests is that the organism was in fact forming *associations* between the blocked CS (CSB) and the CR but that these were never expressed in *behavior* because they were blocked by prior associations (Wasserman & Miller, 1997).

A similar phenomenon occurs in **latent inhibition,** in which repeated exposure to a neutral stimulus without a UCS makes it less likely than a novel stimulus to become a CS; in other words, the familiar stimulus is less likely to produce a CR (Lubow & Gewirtz, 1995). Once again, this makes evolutionary sense, since it reduces the likelihood of accidental associations that do not mirror the natural co-occurrence of events in nature. A person who has drunk from water fountains 999 times and becomes sick two hours after the thousandth time is unlikely to associ-

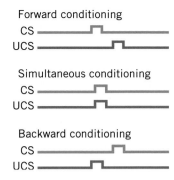

FIGURE 5.6

Forward, simultaneous, and backward conditioning. In forward conditioning, the onset of CS occurs before the UCS. In simultaneous conditioning, the CS is presented at the same time as the UCS. In backward conditioning, the CS is presented after the onset UCS.

ate water with nausea. If, however, she *repeatedly* gets sick after drinking from that fountain, she may start to associate water with nausea. Alternatively, she may learn to discriminate this fountain from others or may develop a more complex, compound association: The CSA (water) is associated with nausea only if the CSB (the fountain) precedes presentation of the water (CSA). Complex associations of this sort are extremely important in daily life (e.g., Schmajuk et al., 1998). For example, a child may normally feel happy (a conditioned emotional response) in the presence of her father (CSA) but learn over time to feel afraid (a different conditioned emotional response) if she hears her father slam the door when he enters the house (CSB).

Preparedness to Learn: An Evolutionary Perspective

A third influence on classical conditioning is the organism's readiness to learn certain associations. Many early behaviorists, such as Watson, believed that the laws of classical conditioning could link virtually any stimulus to any response. Yet subsequent research has shown that some responses can be conditioned much more readily to certain stimuli than to others.

This was demonstrated in a classic study by Garcia and Koelling (1966). The experimenters used three conditioned stimuli: light, sound, and taste (flavored water). For one group of rats, these stimuli were paired all at once with the UCS of radiation, which produces nausea. For the other group, the stimuli were paired with a different UCS, electric shock. The experimenters then exposed the rats to each of the three conditioned stimuli separately, rather than simultaneously, to test the strength of the conditioned response to each.

The results can be seen in Figure 5.7. Rats that experienced nausea after exposure to radiation developed an aversion to the flavored water but not to either the light or sound cues. In contrast, rats exposed to electric shock developed avoidance reactions to the audiovisual stimuli but not to the taste cues. In other words, the rats learned to associate sickness in their stomachs with a taste stimulus, and an aversive tactile stimulus (electrical shock) with audiovisual stimuli.

The phenomenon of **prepared learning**—the biologically wired *preparedness* to learn some associations more easily than others—is not limited to taste aversions (Seligman, 1971). Phobias of spiders, snakes, and similar animals are more common than phobias of flowers or telephones, and many snake phobics, such as people who are terrified of tarantulas, have never seen one up close, let alone been bitten by one (Kirby et al., 1995; Marks, 1969; Ohman et al., 1976; Seligman, 1971).

These findings once again suggest an evolutionary explanation: Natural selection has favored organisms that more readily associate stimuli that tend to be associated in nature and whose association is highly relevant to survival or reproduction. An animal lucky enough to survive after eating a poisonous caterpillar is more likely to survive if it can associate nausea with the right stimulus. For most land-dwelling mammals, taste cues are particularly useful for discriminating

FIGURE 5.7
Preparedness to learn. Garcia and Koelling's experiment examined the impact of biological constraints on learning in rats exposed to shock or X-rays. Rats associated nausea with a taste stimulus rather than with audiovisual cues; they associated an aversive tactile event with sights and sounds rather than with taste stimuli. The results demonstrated that animals are prepared to learn certain associations more readily than others in classical conditioning. *Source:* Adapted from Garcia & Koelling, 1966.

Unconditioned stimulus (ucs)	Conditioned stimulus (cs)		
	Light	Sound	Taste
Shock	Avoidance	Avoidance	No avoidance
X-rays	No avoidance	No avoidance	Avoidance

toxic from nontoxic substances; a preparedness to connect taste with nausea allows the animal to bypass irrelevant associations to the hundreds of other stimuli it might have encountered between the time it dined on the offending caterpillar and the time it got sick hours later. In contrast, most birds do not have well-developed gustatory systems and thus cannot rely heavily on taste to avoid toxic insects. In support of the evolutionary hypothesis, research on quail and other birds finds that, unlike rats, they are more likely to associate nausea with visual than gustatory stimuli (Hollis, 1997; Wilcoxon et al., 1991). Garcia and colleagues (1985) theorize that vertebrate animals have evolved two defense systems, one attending to defense of the gut (and hence favoring associations between nausea and sensory cues relevant to food) and the other attending to defense of the skin (and usually predisposing the animal to form associations between pain and sights and sounds that signal dangers such as predators).

Humans show some evidence of biological preparedness as well. Readers of this book, for example, are much more likely to have snake or spider phobias than automobile phobias, despite the fact that they are more than 10,000 times more likely to die at the wheel of a car than at the mouth of a spider—and to have experienced a car accident rather than a snakebite. Experimental data suggest that humans may also be biologically predisposed to associate aversive experiences more readily with angry faces than smiling ones (Dimberg, 1990).

Biological preparedness, of course, has its limits, especially in humans, whose associative capacities are *almost* limitless (McNally, 1987). One study, for example, found people equally likely to develop a fear of handguns as of snakes (Honeybourne et al., 1993). Where biological predispositions leave off, learning begins as a way of naturally selecting adaptive responses.

Snakes strike terror in the human psyche, even though most people have never had unpleasant encounters with them.

WHAT DO ORGANISMS LEARN IN CLASSICAL CONDITIONING?

In some ways, contrasting innate with learned responses is setting up a false dichotomy, because the capacity to learn—to form associations—is itself a product of natural selection. Precisely what organisms learn when they are classically conditioned, however, has been a topic of considerable debate. Some behavioral theorists have argued that in classical conditioning the organism learns to associate the CS with the UCS—a *stimulus–stimulus*, or *S–S*, association. Others have argued that what is learned is an association between the CS and the CR—a *stimulus–response*, or *S–R*, association. Both explanations are consistent with Aristotle's proposition that humans learn by associating events that tend to co-occur, and both probably occur in classical conditioning. For example, the S–S association may occur first, through repeated co-occurrence (contiguity) of the two stimuli; shortly thereafter, an S–R association forms as the CS begins to co-occur with the CR.

Pavlov (1927) was influenced by associationism and hypothesized that in classical conditioning the CS essentially becomes a *signal* to an organism that the UCS is about to occur. As a result, the organism responds to the CS as if it *were* the UCS. Pavlov proposed a neurological mechanism for this, hypothesizing that repeated pairings of the UCS and the CS lead to connections between them in the brain; as a result, the two stimuli eventually trigger the same response. Although Pavlov was probably right in broad strokes, subsequent research suggests that the CR and the UCR, though usually similar, are rarely identical. Dogs typically do not salivate as much in response to a bell as to the actual presentation of food, which means that the CS is not triggering the exact same response as the UCS.

Sometimes the CR is even the opposite of the UCR as in **paradoxical conditioning,** where the CR is actually the body's attempt to *counteract* the effects of a stimulus that is about to occur. For example, the sight of drug paraphernalia in heroin addicts can activate physiological reactions that reduce the effect of the heroin they are about to inject (Caggiula et al., 1991; Siegel, 1984). This produces a *conditioned tolerance*, or decreased sensitivity, to the drug with repeated use, as the body counteracts dosages that were previously effective. This conditioned response may be involved in the processes that force addicts to take progressively higher doses of a drug to achieve the same effect. One study of paradoxical conditioning in opiate addicts compared the effects of self-injection, which involved exposure to drug paraphernalia (the CS), with an intravenous injection provided by the researchers, which did not (Ehrman et al., 1992). Only the bodies of addicts who self-injected showed efforts to counteract the drug.

FROM MIND TO BRAIN

THE NEURAL BASIS OF CLASSICAL CONDITIONING

Research *has* however, confirmed Pavlov's speculation that classical conditioning alters the action of neurons that link stimuli with responses (Bailey & Kandel, 1995; Martinez & Derrick, 1996; Matthies, 1989). Eric Kandel and his colleagues have studied the cellular basis of learning in the marine snail, *Aplysia*, a simple organism ideally suited to the study of associative learning because reflex learning in *Aplysia* involves a very small number of large neurons. Thus, researchers can actually observe what is happening at all the relevant synapses as *Aplysia* learns. (In humans, in comparison, thousands or millions of neurons may be activated in a simple instance of classical conditioning.)

In *Aplysia*, classical conditioning and similar forms of learning occur through changes at synapses that link sensory neurons (activated by the CS) to neurons that trigger a motor reflex. Changes occur in both the presynaptic neuron, which releases neurotransmitters more readily with additional conditioning trials, and the postsynaptic neuron, which becomes more easily excited with additional trials (Kandel, 1989; Kandel & Schwartz, 1982). A small number of trials produces changes that last for minutes or hours, whereas a larger number of trials can produce changes that last for days.

Kandel and his colleagues have discovered some differences at the cellular level between short-term and longer term learning of this sort. For example, in short-term learning, the presynaptic neuron uses proteins already available within the cell to facilitate release of neurotransmitters. More frequent pairings of the CS and UCS, however, generate *new* proteins that lead to the sprouting of new dendritic connections between the presynaptic and postsynaptic neuron. This strengthens the connections between the two cells, creating a long-lasting neural association.

Other researchers have studied a similar phenomenon called *long-term potentiation (LTP)* in more complex animals (Bliss and Lomo, 1973; Jeffery et al., 1997; Laroche et al., 1995; Martinez & Derrick, 1996; McGaugh et al., 1995; Robertson et al., 1996). Long-term potentiation refers to the tendency of a *group of neurons* to fire more readily after consistent stimulation from other neurons, as presumably occurs in classical conditioning. Its name refers to a heightened potential for neural firing ("potentiation") that lasts much longer than the initial stimulus. Thus, even after the CS is no longer present, cellular changes at the synapse *are*.

Like the work on *Aplysia*, research on LTP supports a hypothesis proposed by the neurologist Donald Hebb (1949) years before the technologies existed to test it: "When an axon of cell A is near enough to excite cell B and repeatedly or persistently take part in firing it, some . . . process . . . takes

The marine snail, Aplysia, *has afforded researchers the opportunity to study the molecular basis of learning.*

place in one or both cells such that A's efficiency, as one of the cells firing B, is increased." In other words, when the activation of one set of neurons repeatedly leads to activation of another, the strength of the connection between the two neurons increases—a neural translation of the principles of association first formulated by Aristotle. The evidence linking LTP to learning and memory is not yet complete (see Eichenbaum, 1996). Nevertheless, in many respects LTP parallels processes seen in *Aplysia,* although it occurs in much larger networks of neurons.

INTERIM SUMMARY   Several factors influence classical conditioning, including the **interstimulus interval** (the time between presentation of the CS and the UCS), the individual's learning history (such as prior associations between the stimulus and other stimuli or responses), and **prepared learning** (the evolved tendency of some associations to be learned more readily than others). Precisely what organisms learn in classical conditioning is a matter of debate. Research on the marine snail Aplysia and on long-term potentiation in more complex animals suggests that learning occurs through changes in the strength of connections between neurons.

OPERANT CONDITIONING

In 1898, Edward Thorndike placed a hungry cat in a box with a mechanical latch and then placed food in full view just outside the box. The cat meowed, paced back and forth, and rubbed against the walls of the box. In so doing, it happened to trip the latch. Immediately, the door to the box opened, and the cat gained access to the food. Thorndike repeated the experiment, and with continued repetitions the cat became more adept at tripping the latch. Eventually, it was able to leave its cage almost as soon as food appeared.

Thorndike proposed a law of learning to account for this phenomenon, which he called the **law of effect:** An animal's tendency to reproduce a behavior depends on that behavior's effect on the environment and the consequent effect on the animal. If tripping the latch had not helped the cat reach the food, the cat would not have learned to keep brushing up against the latch. More simply, the law of effect states that *behavior is controlled by its consequences.*

The behavior of Thorndike's cats exemplifies a second form of conditioning, known as instrumental or operant conditioning. Thorndike used the term *instru-*

"Oh, not bad. The light comes on, I press the bar, they write me a check. How about you?"

mental conditioning because the behavior is instrumental to achieving a more satisfying state of affairs. B. F. Skinner, who spent years experimenting with and systematizing the ways in which behavior is controlled by the environment, called it **operant conditioning,** which means learning to operate on the environment to produce a consequence.

Although the lines between operant and classical conditioning are not always hard and fast, the major distinction between them is that in classical conditioning an environmental stimulus initiates a response, whereas in operant conditioning a *behavior* (or operant) produces an environmental response. **Operants** are behaviors that are emitted (spontaneously produced) rather than elicited by the environment. Thorndike's cat spontaneously emitted the behavior of brushing up against the latch, which resulted in an effect that conditioned future behavior. Skinner emitted the behaviors of experimenting and writing about his results, which brought him the respect of his colleagues and hence influenced his future behavior. Had his initial experiments failed, he would likely have been less likely to persist, just as Thorndike's cats did not continue emitting behaviors with neutral or aversive environment effects. In operant conditioning—whether the animal is a cat or a psychologist—the behavior *precedes* the environmental event that conditions future behavior. By contrast, in classical conditioning, an environmental stimulus (such as a bell) precedes a response.

The basic idea behind operant conditioning, then, is that behavior is controlled by its consequences. In this section, we explore two types of environmental consequence that produce operant conditioning: **reinforcement,** which increases the probability that a response will occur, and **punishment,** which diminishes its likelihood.

REINFORCEMENT

Reinforcement means just what the name implies: Something in the environment fortifies, or reinforces, a behavior. A **reinforcer** is an environmental consequence that occurs after an organism has produced a response and makes the response more likely to recur. Psychologists distinguish two kinds of reinforcement, positive and negative.

Positive Reinforcement

Positive reinforcement is the process whereby presentation of a stimulus (a reward or payoff) after a behavior makes the behavior more likely to occur again.

Old Psychological Testing Center

(a)   (b)

FIGURE 5.8
Apparatus for operant conditioning: (*a*) a pigeon is placed in a cage with a target on one side, which can be used for operant conditioning; (*b*) B. F. Skinner experiments with a rat placed in a Skinner box, with a similar design, in which pressing a bar may result in reinforcement.

For example, in experimental procedures pioneered by B. F. Skinner (1938, 1953), a pigeon was placed in a cage with a target mounted on one side (Figure 5.8). (Pigeons and rats were Skinner's favorite—that is, most reinforcing—subjects.) The pigeon spontaneously pecked around in the cage. This behavior was not a response to any particular stimulus; pecking is simply innate avian behavior. If, by chance, the pigeon pecked at the target, however, a pellet of grain dropped into a bin. If the pigeon happened to peck at the target again, it was once more rewarded with a pellet. The pellet is a **positive reinforcer**—an environmental consequence that, when presented, strengthens the probability that a response will recur. The pigeon would thus start to peck at the target more frequently since this operant became associated with the positive reinforcer.

Positive reinforcement is not limited to pigeons. In fact, it controls much of human behavior as well. Students learn to exert effort studying when they are reinforced with praise and good grades, salespeople learn to appease obnoxious customers and laugh at their jokes because doing so yields them commissions, and people learn to go to work each day because they receive a paycheck.

Negative Reinforcement

Eliminating something aversive can itself be a reinforcer or reward. This is known as **negative reinforcement**—the process whereby termination of an aversive stimulus makes a behavior more likely to occur. Just as the presentation of a positive reinforcer rewards a response, the removal of an aversive stimulus rewards a response. **Negative reinforcers,** then, are aversive or unpleasant stimuli that strengthen a behavior by their removal. Hitting the snooze button on an alarm clock is negatively reinforced by the termination of the alarm; cleaning the kitchen is negatively reinforced by the elimination of unpleasant sights and smells.

Negative reinforcement occurs in both escape learning and avoidance learning. In **escape learning,** a behavior is reinforced by the elimination of an aversive state of affairs that already exists; that is, the organism escapes an aversive situation. For example, a rat presses a lever and terminates an electric shock; an overzealous sunbather applies lotion to her skin to relieve sunburn pain; or a child cleans his room to stop his parents from nagging. **Avoidance learning** occurs as an organism prevents an *expected* aversive event from happening. In this case, avoidance of a potentially aversive situation reinforces the operant. For example, a rat presses a lever when it hears a tone that signals that a shock is about

"I would share my cookies, but I'm afraid I'll set up a cycle of dependency."

to occur; the sunbather puts on sunscreen before going out in the sun to avoid a sunburn; or the child cleans his room to avoid nagging.

PUNISHMENT

Reinforcement is one type of environmental consequence that controls behavior through operant conditioning; the other is punishment (Figure 5.9). Whereas reinforcement always *increases* the likelihood of a response, either by the presentation of a reward or the removal of an aversive stimulus, punishment *decreases* the probability that a response will recur. Thus, if Skinner's pigeon received an electric shock each time it pecked at the target, it would be less likely to peck again because this operant resulted in an aversive outcome. Parents intuitively apply this behavioral technique when they "ground" a teenager for staying out past curfew. The criminal justice system also operates on a system of punishment, attempting to discourage illicit behaviors by imposing penalties.

Like reinforcement, punishment can be positive or negative. ("Positive" and

Reinforcement strengthens behavior—such as hard work and practice in sports.

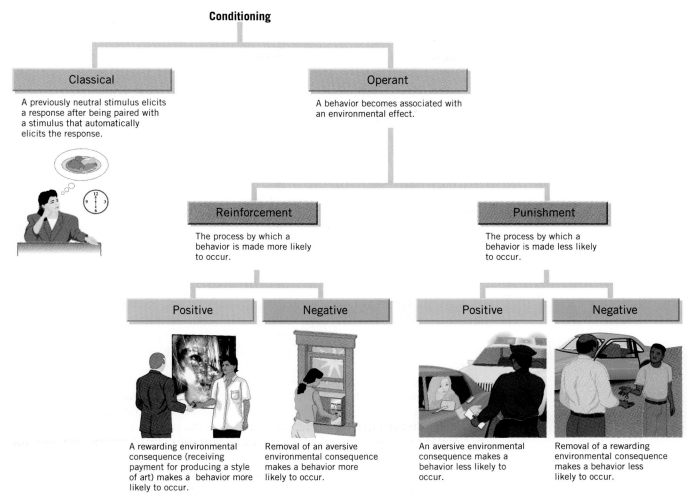

FIGURE 5.9
Conditioning processes. Behaviorists distinguish two kinds of conditioning, classical and operant. In operant conditioning, the environment influences behavior through reinforcement and punishment.

"negative" here do not refer to the feelings of the participants, who rarely consider punishment a positive experience. Positive simply means something is presented, whereas negative means something is taken away.) In positive punishment, such as spanking, exposure to an aversive event following a behavior reduces the likelihood of the operant recurring. Negative punishment involves losing, or not obtaining, a reinforcer as a consequence of behavior, as when an employee fails to receive a pay increase because of frequent lateness or absenteeism.

Punishment is commonplace and essential in human affairs, since reinforcement alone is not likely to inhibit many undesirable behaviors, but it is frequently applied in ways that render it ineffective (Chance, 1988; Laub & Sampson, 1995; Newsom et al., 1983; Skinner, 1953). One common problem in using punishment with animals and young children is that the learner may have difficulty distinguishing which operant is being punished. People who yell at their dog for coming after it has been called several times are actually punishing good behavior—coming when called. The dog is more likely to associate the punishment with its action than its inaction—and is likely to adjust its behavior accordingly, by becoming even less likely to come when called. A second and related problem associated with punishment is that the learner may come to fear the person meting out the punishment (via classical conditioning) rather than the action (via operant conditioning). A child who is harshly punished by his father may become afraid of his father instead of changing his behavior.

Third, people who rely heavily on punishment often fail to recognize that punishment may not eliminate existing rewards for a behavior. In nature, unlike the laboratory, a single action may have multiple consequences, and behavior can be controlled by any number of them. A teacher who punishes the class clown may not have much success if the behavior is reinforced by classmates. Sometimes, too, punishing one behavior (such as stealing) may inadvertently reinforce another (such as lying).

Fourth, people typically use punishment when they are angry, which can lead both to poorly designed punishment (from a learning point of view) and to the potential for abuse. An angry parent may punish a child for misdeeds just discovered but that occurred a considerable time earlier. The time interval between the child's action and the consequence may render the punishment ineffective because the child does not adequately connect the two events. Parents also frequently punish depending more on their mood than on the type of behavior they want to discourage, which can prevent the child from learning what behavior is being punished, under what circumstances, and how to avoid it.

Finally, aggression that is used to punish behavior often leads to further aggression. The child who is beaten typically learns a much deeper lesson: that problems can be solved with violence. In fact, the more physical punishment parents use, the more aggressively their children tend to behave at home and at school (Dodge et al., 1995, 1997; Kaplan, 1996; Larzelere, 1986; Larzelere et al., 1996; Weiss et al., 1993). Correlation does not, of course, prove causation; aggressive children may provoke punitive parenting. Nevertheless, the weight of evidence suggests that violent parents tend to create violent children. There is no evidence that the use of belts or paddles augments the painful effects of a swat with the hand of an adult who usually outweighs a child by a factor of at least 3 or 4. If parents who use such devices aim to teach their children self-control, they would do better to learn it themselves, since beating children tends to make them more likely as adults to have *less* self-control, lower self-esteem, more troubled relationships, and more depression and to be more likely to abuse their own children and spouses (Rohner, 1975, 1985; Straus & Kantor, 1994).

Punishment tends to be most effective when it is accompanied by reasoning—even in 2- and 3-year-olds (Larzelere et al., 1996)—and when the person being punished is also reinforced for an alternative, acceptable behavior. Explaining helps a child correctly connect an action with a punishment. Having other positively reinforced behaviors to draw on allows the child to generate alternative responses.

EXTINCTION

As in classical conditioning, learned operant responses can be extinguished. Extinction occurs if enough conditioning trials pass in which the operant is not followed by the consequence previously associated with it. A child may reduce effort in school if hard work no longer leads to reinforcers (such as "good work!" written on homework), just as a corporate executive may choose to stop producing a product that is no longer bringing in profits.

Knowing how to extinguish behavior is important in everyday life, particularly for parents. Consider the case of a 21-month-old boy who had a serious illness requiring around-the-clock attention (Williams, 1959). After recovering, the child continued to demand this level of attention, which was no longer necessary. His demands were especially troublesome at bedtime, when he screamed and

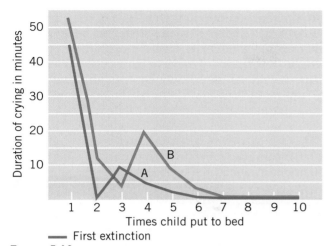

FIGURE 5.10

Extinction of tantrum behavior in a 21-month-old child. As shown in curve *A,* the child initially cried for long periods of time, but very few trials of nonreinforced crying were required to extinguish the behavior. In curve *B,* the behavior was again quickly extinguished following its spontaneous recovery. *Source:* Williams, 1959, p. 269.

cried unless a parent sat with him until he fell asleep, which could take up to two hours.

Relying on the principle that unreinforced behavior will be extinguished, the parents, with some help from a psychologist, began following a new bedtime regimen. In the first trial of the extinction series, they spent a relaxed and warm good-night session with their son, closed the door when they left the room, and refused to respond to the wails and screams that followed. After 45 minutes, the boy fell asleep, and he fell asleep immediately on the second trial (Figure 5.10). The next bedtimes were accompanied by tantrums that steadily decreased in duration, so that by the tenth trial, the parents fully enjoyed the sounds of silence.

As in classical conditioning, spontaneous recovery (in which a previously learned behavior recurs without renewed reinforcement) sometimes occurs. In fact, the boy cried and screamed again one night when his aunt attempted to put him to bed. She inadvertently reinforced this behavior by returning to his room; as a result, his parents had to repeat their extinction procedure.

INTERIM SUMMARY   **Operant conditioning** means learning to operate on the environment to produce a consequence. **Operants** are behaviors that are emitted rather than elicited by the environment. **Reinforcement** refers to a consequence that increases the probability that a response will recur. **Positive reinforcement** occurs when the environmental consequence (a reward or payoff) makes a behavior more likely to occur again. **Negative reinforcement** occurs when termination of an aversive stimulus makes a behavior more likely to recur. Whereas reinforcement increases the probability of a response, **punishment** decreases the probability that a response will recur. Punishment is commonplace in human affairs but is frequently applied in ways that render it ineffective. Extinction in operant conditioning occurs if enough condition trials pass in which the operant is not followed by the consequence previously associated with it.

OPERANT CONDITIONING OF COMPLEX BEHAVIORS

Thus far we have discussed relatively simple behaviors controlled by their environmental consequences—pigeons pecking, rats pressing, and people showing up at work for a paycheck. In fact, operant conditioning offers one of the most comprehensive explanatory accounts of the range of human and animal behavior ever produced. We will now ratchet up the complexity level by exploring four phenomena that substantially increase the breadth of the behaviorist account of learning: schedules of reinforcement, discriminative stimuli, context, and characteristics of the learner.

Schedules of Reinforcement

In the examples described so far, an animal is rewarded or punished every time it performs a behavior. This situation, in which the consequence is the same each time the animal emits a behavior, is called a **continuous reinforcement schedule** (because the behavior is *continuously* reinforced). A child reinforced for altruistic behavior on a continuous schedule of reinforcement would be praised every time she shares, just as a rat might receive a pellet of food each time it presses a lever. Such consistent reinforcement, however, rarely occurs in nature or in human life. More typically, an action sometimes leads to reinforcement but other times does not. Such reinforcement schedules are known as **partial** or **intermittent schedules of reinforcement** because the behavior is reinforced only part of the time, or intermittently. (These are called schedules of *reinforcement*, but the same principles apply with punishment.)

Intuitively, one would think that continuous schedules would be more effective. Although this tends to be true during the initial learning (acquisition) of a response (presumably because continuous reinforcement renders the connection between the behavior and its consequence clear and predictable), partial reinforcement is usually superior for maintaining learned behavior. For example, suppose you have a relatively new car, and every time you turn the key the engine starts. If one day, however, you try to start the car ten times and the engine will not turn over, you will probably give up and call a towing company. In contrast, if you are the proud owner of a rusted-out 1972 Chevy and are accustomed to ten turns of the ignition before the car finally cranks up, you may try 20 or 30 times before enlisting the help of a mechanic. Thus, behaviors maintained under partial schedules are usually more resistant to extinction.

Behaviorist researchers, notably Skinner and his colleagues, have categorized intermittent reinforcement schedules as either ratio schedules or interval schedules (Ferster & Skinner, 1957; Skinner, 1938). In **ratio schedules,** payoffs are tied to the number of responses emitted; only a fraction of "correct" behaviors receive reinforcement (such as one out of every five, for a ratio of 1 : 5). In **interval schedules,** rewards are delivered only after some interval of time. The organism can produce a response as often as it wants, but the response will only be reinforced (or punished) after a certain amount of time has elapsed.

Reinforcement schedules are often studied with a **cumulative response recorder,** an instrument that tallies the number of times a subject produces a response, such as pressing a bar or pecking a target. Figure 5.11 illustrates typical cumulative response recordings for the four reinforcement schedules we will now describe: fixed ratio, variable ratio, fixed interval, and variable interval.

Fixed-Ratio Schedules   In a **fixed-ratio (FR) schedule** of reinforcement, an organism receives reinforcement for a fixed proportion of the responses it emits. Piecework employment uses a fixed-ratio schedule of reinforcement: A person receives payment for every bushel of apples picked (an FR-1 schedule) or for every ten scarves woven (an FR-10 schedule). Workers weave the first nine scarves without reinforcement; the payoff occurs when the tenth scarf is completed. As shown in Figure 5.11, FR schedules are characterized by rapid responding, with a brief pause after each reinforcement.

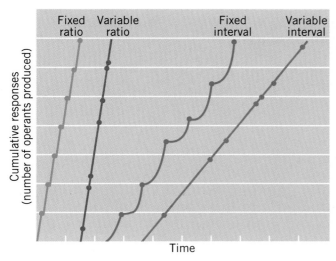

FIGURE 5.11
Schedules of reinforcement. The figure shows cumulative response records for fixed-ratio, variable-ratio, fixed-interval, and variable-interval reinforcement schedules. A cumulative response record graphs the total number of responses that have been emitted at any point in time. Different schedules of reinforcement produce different patterns of responding.

Variable-Ratio Schedules In **variable-ratio (VR) schedules,** the individual receives a reward for some percentage of responses, but the number of responses required before reinforcement is unpredictable (that is, variable). Variable-ratio schedules specify an *average* number of responses that will be rewarded. Thus, a pigeon on a VR-5 schedule may be rewarded on its fourth, seventh, 13th, and 20th responses, averaging one reward for every five responses. Variable-ratio schedules generally produce rapid, constant responding and are probably the most common in daily life. People cannot predict that they will be rewarded or praised for every fifth good deed, but they do receive occasional, irregular social reinforcement, which is enough to reinforce altruistic behavior in most people. Similarly, students may not receive a good grade each time they study hard for an examination, but many study nonetheless because they learn that the *average* rate of reinforcement is higher than if they do not study. The power of variable-ratio schedules can be seen in gambling, in which people may gradually lose their shirts if they are intermittently—and very irregularly—reinforced.

Fixed-Interval Ratios In a **fixed-interval (FI) schedule,** an animal receives reinforcement for its responses only after a fixed amount of time. For example, a rat that presses a bar is reinforced with a pellet of food every ten minutes. The rat may press the bar 100 times or one time during that ten minutes; doing so does not make a difference in the delivery of the pellet, just as long as the rat presses the bar at some point during each ten-minute interval.

An animal on an FI schedule of reinforcement will ultimately learn to stop responding except toward the end of each interval, producing the scalloped cumulative response pattern shown in Figure 5.11. Fixed-interval schedules affect human performance in the same way. For example, workers whose boss comes by only at two o'clock are likely to relax the rest of the day. Schools rely heavily on FI schedules; as a result, some students procrastinate between exams and pull "all-nighters" when reinforcement (or punishment) is imminent. Politicians, too, seem to resemble rats in their response patterns (Figure 5.12). Periodic adjournment of Congress on a fixed interval appears to reinforce bill passing (the congressional equivalent of bar pressing), producing precisely the same scalloped response record (Waldrop, 1972).

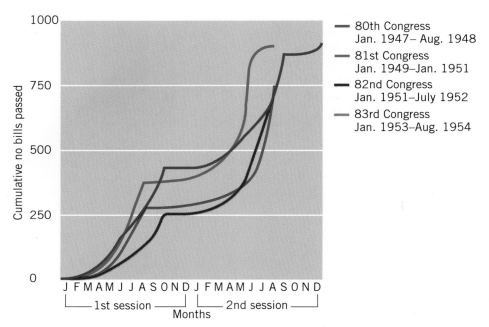

FIGURE 5.12

The effects of a fixed-interval schedule on the U.S. Congress. Adjournment serves as a powerful reinforcer for members of the U.S. House of Representatives, who seem to respond to this fixed-interval schedule of reinforcement with a flurry of last-minute activity before being reinforced. As the graph shows, the pattern looked the same over several years investigated. The scalloped curve is remarkably similar to the fixed-interval cumulative response recording derived from studying rats and pigeons in Figure 5.11. *Source:* Weisberg & Waldrop, 1972, p. 23.

Variable-Interval Schedules   A **variable interval (VI) schedule,** like a fixed-interval schedule, ties reinforcement to an interval of time after which the individual's response leads to reinforcement. In a VI schedule, however, the animal cannot predict how long that time interval will be. Thus, a rat might receive reinforcement for bar pressing, but only at five, six, 20, and 40 minutes (a VI-10 schedule).

Variable-interval schedules are more effective than fixed-interval schedules in maintaining consistent performance. Random, unannounced governmental inspections of working conditions in a plant are much more effective in getting management to maintain safety standards than inspections at fixed intervals. In the classroom, pop quizzes make similar use of VI schedules.

Discriminative Stimuli

In everyday life, then, rarely does a response receive continuous reinforcement in a given situation, such as work or school. Making matters even *more* complicated for learners is that a single behavior can lead to different effects in different situations. Professors receive a paycheck for lecturing to their classes, but if they lecture new acquaintances at a cocktail party, the environmental consequences will not be the same. Similarly, domestic cats learn that the dining room table is a great place to stretch out and relax—except when their owners are home.

In some situations, then, a connection might exist between a behavior and a consequence (called a response *contingency*, because the consequence is dependent, or *contingent*, on the behavior). In other situations, however, the contingencies might be different, so the organism needs to be able to discriminate circumstances under which different contingencies apply. A stimulus that signals the presence of particular contingencies of reinforcement is called a **discriminative stimulus (S^D).** In other words, an animal learns to produce certain actions only in the presence of the discriminative stimulus. For the professor, the classroom situation signals that lecturing behavior will be reinforced; for the cat on the dinner table, the presence of humans is a discriminative stimulus signaling punishment. In an experimental demonstration, rats were rewarded for turning clockwise when they were placed in one chamber and turning counterclockwise when placed in another; the chamber was the discriminative stimulus signaling different contingencies of reinforcement (Richards et al., 1990).

Stimulus discrimination is one of the keys to the complexity and flexibility of human and animal behavior. Behavior therapists, who apply behaviorist principles to maladaptive behaviors (Chapter 16), use the concept of stimulus discrimination to help people recognize and alter some very subtle triggers for maladaptive responses, particularly in relationships (Kohlenberg & Tsai, 1994). For example, one couple was on the verge of divorce because the husband complained that his wife was too passive and indecisive and the wife complained that her husband was too rigid and controlling. A careful analysis of their interactions suggested some complex contingencies controlling their behavior. The couple often engaged in mutually enjoyable conversation, in which each felt comfortable and relatively spontaneous. At times, however, the woman would detect a particular "tone" in her husband's voice (an S^D) that she had associated with his getting angry; upon hearing this tone, she would "shut down" and become more passive and quiet. Her husband, however, found her passivity (an S^D for him) infuriating and would then begin to push her for answers and decisions, which only intensified her "passivity" and his "controlling" behavior. She was not, in fact, always passive, and he was not always controlling. Easing the tension in the marriage thus required isolating the discriminative stimuli that controlled each of their responses.

INTERIM SUMMARY   In everyday life, **continuous schedules of reinforcement** (in which the consequence is the same each time an animal emits a behavior) are far less common than **intermittent schedules of reinforcement** (in which reinforcement occurs in some ratio or after certain intervals). A **discriminative stimulus** is a stimulus that signals that particular contingencies of reinforcement are in effect, so that the organism only produces the behavior in the presence of the discriminative stimulus.

Context

Thus far, we have treated operants as if they were isolated behaviors, produced one at a time in response to specific consequences. In fact, however, learning usually occurs in broader context (see Herrnstein, 1970; Premack, 1965).

The Costs and Benefits of Obtaining Reinforcement   In real life, reinforcement is not infinite, and attainment of one reinforcer may affect both its future availability and the availability of other reinforcers. Researchers studying the way animals forage in their natural habitats have noted that reinforcement schedules change because of the animal's own behavior: By continually eating fruit from one tree, an animal may deplete the supply, so that remaining fruit must be obtained with more work (Stephens & Krebs, 1986). Psychologists have simulated this phenomenon by changing contingencies of reinforcement based on the number of times rats feed from the same "patch" (Aparicio & Baum, 1997; Collier et al., 1998; Shettleworth, 1988). Thus, a rat may find that the more it presses one lever, the less reward it receives at that lever but not at another. Researchers using this kind of experimental procedure have found that rats make "choices" about how long to stay at a patch depending on variables such as its current rate of reinforcement, the average rate of reinforcement they could obtain elsewhere, and the amount of time required to get to a new "patch."

Obtaining one reinforcer may also adversely affect the chances of obtaining another. An omnivorous animal merrily snacking on some foliage must somehow weigh the benefits of its current refreshments against the cost of pursuing a source of protein it notices scampering nearby. Similarly, a person at a restaurant must choose which of many potential reinforcers to pursue, knowing that each has a cost and that eating one precludes eating the others. This recognition of the cost–benefit analysis involved in operant behavior has led to an approach called *behavioral economics*, which weds aspects of behavioral theory with economics (Bickel et al., 1995; Green & Freed, 1993; Rachlin et al., 1976). For example, some reinforcers, such as two brands of soda, are relatively substitutable for each other, so that as the cost of one goes down, its consumption goes up and the consumption of the other decreases. Other reinforcers are complementary, such as bagels and cream cheese, so that if the cost of bagels skyrockets, consumption of cream cheese will decrease.

Psychologists have studied principles of behavioral economics in some ingenious ways in the laboratory using rats and other animals as subjects. For example, they put animals on a "budget" by only reinforcing them for a certain number of lever presses per day; thus, the animals had to "conserve" their lever presses to purchase the "goods" they preferred (Rachlin et al., 1976). Decreasing the "cost" of Tom Collins mix (by reducing the number of bar presses necessary to obtain it) led rats to shift their natural preference from root beer to Tom Collins—a finding the liquor industry would likely find heartening. In contrast, decreasing the cost of food relative to water had much less effect on consumption. In the language of economics, the demand for water is relatively "inelastic"; that is, it does not change much, regardless of the price.

The Social and Cultural Context   We have spoken thus far as if reinforcement and punishment were unilateral techniques, in which one person (a trainer) conditions another person or animal (a learner). In fact, in human social interactions, each partner continuously uses operant conditioning techniques to mold the behavior of the other. When a child behaves in a way his parents find upsetting, the parents are likely to punish the child. But the parents' behavior is itself being conditioned: The operant of punishing the child will be *negatively reinforced* if it causes the child's bad behavior to cease. Thus, the child is negatively reinforcing the parents' use of punishment just as the parents are punishing the child's behavior. From this point of view, people give each other reinforcement and punishment in nearly all their interactions (Homans, 1961).

The reliance on different operant procedures varies considerably cross-culturally. In part, this reflects the dangers that confront a society. The Gusii of Kenya, with a history of tribal warfare, face threats not only from outsiders but also from natural forces, including wild animals. Gusii parents tend to rely more on punishment and fear than on rewards in conditioning social behavior in their children. Caning, food deprivation, and withdrawing shelter and protection are common forms of punishment. One Gusii mother warned her child, "If you don't stop crying, I shall open the door and call a hyena to come and eat you!" (LeVine & LeVine, 1963, p. 166). Death from wild animals is a real fear, so this threat gains compliance from Gusii children.

In contrast, the Mixtecan Indians of Juxtlahuaca, Mexico, are a highly cohesive community, with little internal conflict and social norms (expectations of appropriate behavior) that encourage cooperation. The Mixtecans do not generally impose fines or jail sentences or use physical punishment to deter aggression in either adults or children. They are more likely to rely on soothing persuasion. An anthropologist reported an incident of aggression that occurred among a group of Mixtecan males in which one man assaulted several others while intoxicated (Romney, 1963). Instead of retaliating, the victims worked together to calm him down. Social ostracism is the most feared punishment in Mixtecan culture, and social ties within the community are strong, so responses that reinforce these ties are effective in maintaining social order.

Characteristics of the Learner

An additional set of factors that increase the complexity of operant conditioning have to do less with the environment than with the learner. Current environmental contingencies operate on an animal that already has behaviors in its repertoire, enduring ways of responding, and species-specific learning patterns.

Shaping can introduce some unusual behaviors into an animal's repertoire.

Capitalizing on Past Behaviors: Shaping and Chaining   The range of behaviors humans and other animals can produce is made infinitely more complex by the fact that existing behaviors often serve as the raw material for novel ones. This occurs as the environment subtly refines them or links them together into sequences. For example, circus animals (and gymnasts) learn to do backflips and perform other behaviors not usually seen in their natural habitats. How does this occur?

A procedure used by animal trainers, called **shaping**, produces novel behavior by reinforcing closer and closer approximations to the desired response. Skinner (1951) described a shaping procedure that can be used to teach a dog to touch its nose to a cupboard door handle. The first step is to bring a hungry dog (in behavioral terms, a dog that has been deprived of food for a certain number of hours or until its body weight is a certain percent below normal) into the kitchen and immediately reward him with food any time he happens to face the cupboard; the dog will soon face the cupboard most of the time. The next step is to reward the dog whenever it moves toward the cupboard, then to reward it when it moves its head so that its nose comes closer to the cupboard, and finally to reward the dog only for touching its nose to the cupboard handle. This shaping procedure should take no more than five minutes, even for a beginner.

The same shaping techniques can be used to teach more complex behaviors. The key, as a trainer, is to begin by reinforcing a response the animal can readily produce. Gradually, the trainer reinforces only certain ways of performing the desired behavior, so that the animal eventually produces a very specific operant. With humans, shaping is common in all kinds of teaching. A tennis instructor may at first praise a student any time he holds the racquet in a way that resembles a good grip and gets the ball over the net. Gradually, however, the instructor compliments only proper form and well-placed shots, progressively shaping the student's behavior. Shaping does not require instruction and often occurs naturally as well. A tennis player may evolve a particular grip on the racket as his behavior is progressively reinforced toward a grip that originally would have felt completely unnatural and would never have been spontaneously produced.

Whereas shaping leads to the progressive modification of a specific behavior to produce a new response, **chaining** involves putting together a *sequence* of existing responses in a novel order. When I was a child, my brother Marc displayed a natural gift for applying a variant of this operant technique. Marc would awaken at four o'clock in the morning (who knows why), and while everyone else slept soundly, he devised a way to train the family cat to wake me by licking my face. This trick does not come naturally to most felines and required several steps to accomplish. The cat already knew how to climb, jump, and lick. Marc's goal was to get the cat to perform these behaviors in a particular sequence. First, Marc placed pieces of cat food on the stairs leading up to my bedroom. After several trials, the cat learned to climb the stairs on its own. The next step was to reinforce the operant of jumping onto my bed; again, a few judiciously placed bits of cat food did the trick. The same reward, placed gently in the proper location, was enough to train the cat to lick me on the face. Once this occurred enough times, the cat seemed to be reinforced simply by licking my cheek. (Marc seemed quite amused and was apparently reinforced for his little foray into behaviorism as well.)

Enduring Characteristics of the Learner   Not only do prior learning experiences influence operant conditioning, but so, too, do enduring characteristics of the learner. In humans as in other species, individuals differ in the ease with which they can be conditioned (Corr et al., 1995; Eysenck, 1990; Hooks et al., 1994). Individual rats vary, for example, in their tendency to behave aggressively or to respond with fear or avoidance in the face of aversive environmental events (e.g., Ramos et al., 1997). Rats can also be selectively bred for their ability to learn mazes (Innis, 1992; van der Staay & Blokland, 1996).

The role of the learner was especially clear in an experiment that attempted to teach three octopi (named Albert, Bertram, and Charles) to pull a lever in their saltwater tanks to obtain food (Dews, 1959). The usual shaping procedures worked successfully on Albert and Bertram, who were first rewarded for approaching the lever, then for touching it with a tentacle, and finally for tugging at it. With Charles, however, things were different. Instead of *pulling* the lever to obtain food, Charles tugged at it with such force that he broke it. Charles was generally a surly subject, spending much of his time "with eyes above the surface of the water, directing a jet of water at any individual who approached the tank" (p. 62).

Humans differ in their "conditionability" as well. Many individuals with antisocial personality disorder, who show a striking disregard for society's standards, tend to be relatively unresponsive to punishment (Eysenck, 1967, 1990; Magnusson, 1996). Their lack of anxiety when confronted with potential punishment renders them less likely to learn to control selfish, aggressive, or impulsive behaviors that other people learn to inhibit (Chapter 15). Similarly, genetic and environmental factors lead to differences among individuals in the ability to solve problems quickly and efficiently (Chapter 8).

Species-Specific Behavior and Preparedness   Operant conditioning is influenced not only by characteristics of the individual but also by characteristics of the species. Just as some stimulus–response connections are easier to acquire in classical conditioning, certain behaviors are more readily learned by some species in operant conditioning—or may be emitted despite learning to the contrary. This was vividly illustrated in the work of Keller and Marian Breland (1961), who learned operant conditioning techniques while working with Skinner. The Brelands went on to apply these procedures in their own animal training business but initially with mixed success. In one case, they trained pigs to deposit wooden coins in a large "piggy bank" in order to obtain food (p. 683):

> Pigs condition very rapidly. . . . [T]hey have ravenous appetites (naturally), and in many ways are among the most tractable animals we have worked with. However, this particular problem behavior developed in pig after pig, usually after a period of weeks or months, getting worse every day. At first the pig would eagerly pick up one dollar, carry it to the bank, run back, get another, carry it rapidly and neatly, and so on. . . . Thereafter, over a period of weeks the behavior would become slower and slower. He might run over ea-

gerly for each dollar, but on the way back, instead of carrying the dollar and depositing it simply and cleanly, he would repeatedly drop it, root it [nuzzle it with his snout], drop it again, root it along the way, pick it up, toss it up in the air, drop it, root it some more, and so on.

The Brelands observed that the pigs' "rooting" behavior eventually replaced the conditioned behavior of depositing coins in the bank so much that the hungry pigs were not getting enough food. The Brelands had similar experiences with porpoises that swallowed the balls they were supposed to manipulate, cats that would stalk their food slots, and raccoons that tried to wash the tokens they were supposed to deposit in banks. All these operants were more closely related to instinctive, species-specific behaviors than the operants the Brelands were attempting to condition. Species-specific behavior also influences the way animals respond to negative reinforcement. Conditioning a rat to press a lever to avoid an electric shock may be difficult because a rat's natural response to shock is either to crouch and freeze or to run away, both of which interfere with bar pressing. Species-specific behavioral tendencies, like prepared learning in classical conditioning, make sense from an evolutionary perspective: Pigs' rooting behavior normally allows them to obtain food, and a "frozen" rat is less likely to be noticed by a predator than a frenzied one searching for levers to press (Seligman, 1970, 1971).

INTERIM SUMMARY   Learning occurs in a broader context than one behavior at a time. Humans and other animals learn that attaining one reinforcer may affect attainment of others. Cultural factors also influence operant conditioning, since different cultures rely on different operate procedures. Characteristics of the learner influence operant conditioning, such as prior behaviors in the animal's repertoire, enduring characteristics of the learner (such as the tendency to respond with fear or avoidance in the face of aversive environmental events), and species-specific behavior (the tendency of particular species to produce particular responses).

SIMILAR PROCESSES IN CLASSICAL AND OPERANT CONDITIONING

As this discussion of preparedness in operant conditioning suggests, operant and classical conditioning share many features. Just as the interstimulus interval influences learning in classical conditioning, the interval between the operant and its environmental consequences is important as well. Parents intuitively recognize the advantage of shorter intervals: When a child misbehaves at the grocery store, parents rarely wait until the next day to address the problem. Concepts of discrimination and generalization also apply to operant conditioning. Animals can learn to make some surprisingly subtle discriminations and generalizations when access to food is at stake. For example, in one study, pigeons in one condition received access to a container of seed if they pecked at a pecking key when presented with paintings by Monet (projected from slides) (Watanabe et al., 1995). Pigeons in a second condition received reinforcement instead if they pecked at Picassos. Remarkably, the pigeons in each condition learned to peck at novel paintings (paintings they had not previously seen) by the same painter (stimulus generalization) but not at paintings by the other painter (stimulus discrimination). They even generalized from Monet to other impressionists (such as Cezanne) and from Picasso to other cubists (such as Matisse)! Apparently, pigeons can become impressive connoisseurs of art—if the price is right.

Further, just as humans and other animals can develop phobias by forming idiosyncratic associations, they can also erroneously associate an operant and an environmental event, a phenomenon Skinner (1948) labeled **superstitious behavior.**

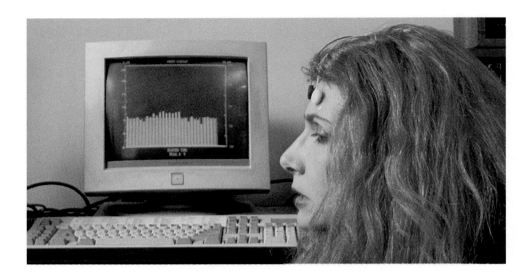

Biofeedback allows patients to gain operant control of autonomic processes.

In one study, he placed pigeons on a schedule in which grain was delivered at regular time intervals, no matter what behavior the pigeons happened to perform. As a result, each pigeon developed its own idiosyncratic response. One turned counterclockwise about the cage, another repeatedly thrust its head in an upper corner of the cage, and a third tossed its head as if lifting an invisible bar (1948, p. 168). Skinner compared these behaviors to human actions such as wearing a lucky outfit to a basketball game or tapping home plate three times when up to bat in baseball. According to Skinner, such behaviors develop because the delivery of a reinforcer strengthens whatever behavior an organism is engaged in at the time.

Are operant and classical conditioning really distinct processes? In some ways, yes. As we have seen, in classical conditioning the organism's behavior follows an environmental event (the stimulus), whereas in operant conditioning the environmental event (reinforcement or punishment) follows the behavior (operant). Furthermore, operant conditioning typically involves voluntary behavior, whereas classical conditioning involves involuntary behavior usually controlled by the autonomic nervous system.

The distinction is not, however, always so clear. In **biofeedback,** psychologists feed information back to patients about their biological processes, allowing them to gain operant control over autonomic responses such as heart rate, body temperature, and blood pressure (Nakao et al., 1997; Stroebel, 1985). As patients monitor their physiological processes on an electronic device or computer screen, they receive reinforcement for changes such as decreased muscle tension or heart rate. Biofeedback can help patients reduce or eliminate problems such as high blood pressure, headaches, and chronic pain (Arena & Blanchard, 1996; Gauthier, Ivers, & Carrier, 1996; Nakao et al., 1997). In one study, patients treated for chronic back pain with biofeedback showed substantial improvement in comparison to control subjects (Flor et al., 1986). They maintained these benefits at follow-up over two years later, reporting less need for treatment, less life disruption from pain, and fewer pain-related thoughts (Table 5.1).

In everyday life, operant and classical conditioning are often equally difficult to disentangle because most learned behavior involves both processes (Mowrer, 1947). A person who has a car accident, for instance, may develop a conditioned fear response to riding in cars, an example of classical conditioning. This typically leads to the operant response of avoiding cars, since doing so is negatively reinforced by avoidance of an aversive event (anxiety).

TABLE 5.1   THE EFFECTS OF BIOFEEDBACK ON CHRONIC BACK PAIN

(A) COMPARISONS OF BIOFEEDBACK AND CONTROL CONDITIONS AT END OF TREATMENT

DOMIAN DISRUPTED BY PAIN	BIOFEEDBACK CONDITION	CONTROL CONDITION
Sex	2.0	45.0
Work	19.9	48.6
Life in General	14.3[a]	38.9[a]

(B) CHANGES BETWEEN PRETREATMENT AND 2-YEAR FOLLOW-UP RATINGS FOR PARTICIPANTS WHO RECEIVED BIOFEEDBACK

PAIN RATINGS	PRETREATMENT	2-YEAR FOLLOW-UP
Hours in pain per day	15.5[b]	8.7[b]
Interference with life	35.0	15.0
Negative pain-related thoughts	40.7	29.0

Source: Adapted from Flor et al., 1986, pp. 198–199.

Note: Prior to and after treatment, patients made a number of ratings, such as the extent to which back pain interfered with their lives. As can be seen in (a), pain treated with biofeedback interfered substantially less in the lives of experimental subjects than in untreated controls. At follow-up (b), patients in the biofeedback condition continued to show substantial gains as compared with their initial pain reports prior to treatment.

INTERIM SUMMARY   Operant and classical conditioning share many features (such as extinction, prepared learning, discrimination, generalization, and the possibility of irrational associations) and are often intertwined in daily life.

▶ **ONE STEP FURTHER**

Why Are Reinforcers Reinforcing?

Behaviorists aim to formulate general *laws of behavior* that link behaviors with events in the environment. Skinner and others who called themselves "radical behaviorists" were less interested in theorizing about the mechanisms that produced these laws, since these mechanisms could not be readily observed. Other theorists within and without behaviorism, however, have asked, "What makes a reinforcer reinforcing or a punisher punishing?" No answer has achieved widespread acceptance, but three are worth considering.

Reinforcers as Drive Reducers

One theory relies on the concept of **drive**, a state that impels, or "drives," the organism to act. Clark Hull (1943, 1952) used the term to refer to unpleasant tension states caused by deprivation of basic needs such as food and water. He proposed a **drive-reduction theory**, which holds that stimuli that reduce drives are reinforcing. This theory makes intuitive sense and explains why an animal that is not hungry will not typically work hard to receive food as reinforcement. However, it requires additional principles to explain why behaviors related to basic needs may be learned even when drives are not currently activated. Lions can learn to hunt in packs, and humans to manipulate numbers on a computer, even when their stomachs are full (Smith, 1984). In fact, optimal learning does not typically occur under intense arousal.

Primary and Secondary Reinforcers

Drives help explain why some stimuli such as food, sex, and water are reinforcing. Hull and others called such stimuli **primary reinforcers** because they innately reinforce behavior without any prior learning. A **secondary reinforcer** is an originally neutral stimulus that becomes reinforcing by being paired repeatedly with a primary reinforcer. For example, children often hear phrases like "good girl!" while receiving other forms of reinforcement (such as hugs), so that the word "good" becomes a secondary reinforcer. Smiles are reinforcing in all cultures.

Most secondary reinforcers are culturally defined. Good grades, gold medals for athletic performance, thank-you notes, and cheering crowds are all examples of secondary reinforcers in many cultures. Children learn to associate coins and bills with *many* reinforcers in cultures that use money. In noncash economies, alternative forms of "currency" acquire secondary reinforcement value. In the Gusii community in Kenya, for example, cattle and other livestock are the primary form of economic exchange. Cattle, rather than cash, are thus associated with marriage, happiness, and social status (LeVine & LeVine, 1963), and the smell of the barnyard carries very different connotations than for most Westerners.

Gold medals are secondary reinforcers that reward skilled performance.

The Role of Feelings

A third explanation of reinforcement stresses the role of feelings. Consider the example of a student who cheats on a test and is lavishly praised for his performance by his unaware teacher. The more she praises him, the guiltier he feels. Paradoxically, the student may be *less* likely to cheat again following this apparent reinforcement. Why?

This third explanation harkens back to Thorndike's law of effect. It holds that feelings—including emotions such as sadness or joy as well as sensory experiences of pleasure or pain—provide a basis for operant conditioning (see Dollard & Miller, 1950; Mowrer, 1960; Wachtel, 1977; Westen, 1985, 1994). An operant that is followed by a pleasurable feeling will be reinforced, whereas one followed by unpleasant feelings will be less likely to recur. From this approach, the teacher's praise—normally a positive reinforcer—was punishing because it evoked guilt, which in turn decreased the probability of future cheating. This theory is incompatible with the goal of many behaviorists to avoid mentalistic explanations, but it fits with an intuitive understanding of operant conditioning: Positive reinforcement occurs because a consequence *feels good*, negative reinforcement occurs because termination of an unpleasant event *feels better*, and punishment occurs because a consequence *feels bad*.

Neuropsychological data support the proposition that feelings play a central role in operant conditioning. Gray (1987, 1990) has demonstrated the role of anatomically distinct pathways in the nervous system, each related to distinct emotional states, which lead to approach and avoidance (Figure 5.13). The **behavioral approach system (BAS)** is associated with pleasurable emotional states and is responsible for approach-oriented operant behavior. This system appears to be primarily involved in positive reinforcement. The **behavioral inhibition system (BIS)** is associated with anxiety and is involved in negative reinforcement and punishment. Dopamine is the primary neurotransmitter involved in transmitting information along BAS pathways (see also Schultz et al., 1997), whereas norepinephrine (known to be related to fear and anxiety) plays a more important role in the synapses involved in the BIS. (Gray also describes a third, more evolutionarily primitive system, the **fight–flight system**, which is related to rage and terror and leads to species-specific responses such as freezing in rats.)

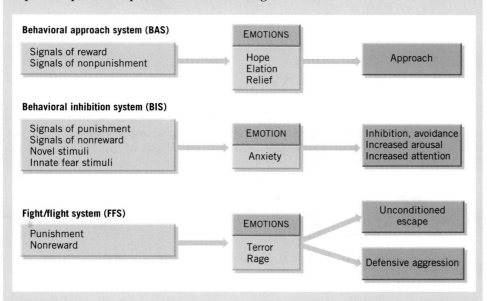

FIGURE 5.13

Gray's three behavioral systems. The behavioral approach system (BAS) orients the person (or animal) to stimuli associated with reward; approach is motivated by the positive emotions of hope, elation, and relief. The behavioral inhibition system (BIS) orients the person to avoidance and vigilance against threat. The BIS addresses potential dangers and involves anxiety. The fight–flight system (FFS) is a more evolutionarily primitive system that orients the person to escape currently punishing stimuli. It is associated with terror and rage. *Source:* Adapted from Gray, 1988, pp. 278–279.

Supporting this theory are studies showing that chemicals that reduce norepinephrine activity (and hence reduce anxiety) lead to poorer performance in avoidance learning tasks, that is, failure to learn from negative reinforcement. For example, dogs given antianxiety medications are less able to avoid behaviors associated with electric shock than dogs in control conditions (Scott, 1980), presumably because decreased fear leads to decreased behavioral inhibition. Further evidence for distinct pathways comes from experiments using EEG to measure electrical activity in the frontal lobes (Davidson, 1995; Sutton & Davidson, 1997). Left frontal activation tends to be more associated with pleasurable feelings and behavioral approach, whereas right frontal activation tends to be associated with unpleasant feelings and behavioral inhibition.

Psychodynamic conceptions have largely been aversive stimuli to learning theorists, but someday we may have an integrated account of learning that includes some psychodynamic concepts as well (Dollard & Miller, 1950; Wachtel, 1997). For example, one psychotherapy patient was unable to recall any events within a four-year period surrounding her parents' divorce, a phenomenon psychodynamic psychologists would call repression. A conditioning explanation would suggest that these memories are associated with emotions such as anxiety and sadness, so that recalling them elicits a conditioned emotional response. This CR is so unpleasant that it evokes avoidance or escape responses, one of which is to avoid retrieving the memories. If this mental "operant" reduces unpleasant emotion, it will be negatively reinforced—strengthened by the removal of an aversive emotional state— and hence likely to be maintained or used again. Similar ideas have recently been proposed by leading behavioral researchers to account for the "emotional avoidance" of unpleasant feelings (Hayes & Wilson, 1994).   ◄

COGNITIVE-SOCIAL THEORY

By the 1960s, many researchers and theorists had begun to wonder whether a psychological science could be built strictly on observable behaviors without reference to thoughts. Most agreed that learning is the basis of much of human behavior, but some were not convinced that classical and operant conditioning could explain *everything* people do. From behaviorist learning principles thus emerged **cognitive-social theory** (sometimes called *cognitive social learning* or *cognitive-behavioral theory*), which incorporated concepts of conditioning but added two new features: a focus on cognition and a focus on social learning.

LEARNING AND COGNITION

According to cognitive-social theory, the way an animal *construes* the environment is as important to learning as actual environmental contingencies. That is, humans and other animals are always developing mental images of, and expectations about, the environment that influence their behavior.

Latent Learning

Some of the first research to question whether a science of behavior could completely dispense with thought was conducted by the behaviorist Edward Tolman.

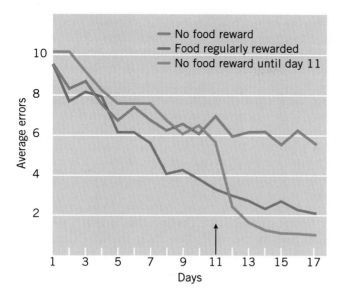

FIGURE 5.14
Latent learning. Rats that were not rewarded until the 11th trial immediately performed equally with rats that had been rewarded from the start. This suggests that they were learning the maze prior to reinforcement and were forming a cognitive map that allowed them to navigate it as soon as they received reinforcement. *Source:* Tolman & Honzik, 1930, p. 267.

In a paper entitled "Cognitive Maps in Rats and Men" (1948), Tolman described learning that occurred when rats were placed in a maze without any reinforcement, similar to the kind of learning that occurs when people learn their way around a city while looking out the window of a bus. In one experiment, Tolman let rats wander through a maze in ten trials on ten consecutive days without any reinforcement (Tolman & Honzik, 1930). A control group spent the same amount of time in the maze, but these rats received a food reinforcement on each trial.

The rats that were reinforced learned quite rapidly to travel to the end of the maze with few errors; not surprisingly, the behavior of the unreinforced rats was less predictable. On the 11th day, however, Tolman made food available for the first time to the previously unreinforced rats and recorded the number of errors they made. As Figure 5.14 shows, his findings were striking: These rats immediately took advantage of their familiarity with the maze and were able to obtain food just as efficiently as the rats who had previously received reinforcement. A third group of rats who still received no reinforcement continued to wander aimlessly through the maze.

To explain what had happened, Tolman suggested that the rats who were familiar with the maze had formed **cognitive maps**—mental representations or images—of the maze, even though they had received no reinforcement. Once the rats were reinforced, their learning became observable. Tolman called learning that has occurred but is not currently manifest in behavior **latent learning**. To cognitive-social theorists, latent learning was evidence that knowledge or beliefs about the environment are crucial to the way animals behave. And so began the effort to look inside the black box that lies between behaviors and environmental events while still maintaining a scientific, experimental approach to behavior.

Conditioning and Cognition

Many learning phenomena have been reinterpreted from a cognitive perspective. For example, in classical conditioning, why does an organism respond to a previously neutral stimulus (such as a particular taste) with a conditioned response (such as nausea)? A cognitive explanation suggests that the presence of the CS alerts the animal to prepare for a UCS that is likely to follow. In other words, the CS *predicts* the presence of the UCS. If a CS does *not* routinely predict a UCS, it will not likely draw a CR. In fact, experimental data show that when a UCS (such as electric shock) frequently occurs in the absence of a CS (a tone), rats are unlikely to develop a conditioned fear response to the CS, regardless of the number of times the CS has been paired with the UCS (Rescorla, 1988; Rescorla & Holland, 1982; Rescorla & Wagner, 1972). In cognitive language, rats will not become afraid of a stimulus unless it is highly predictive of an aversive event. This does not imply that rats are *conscious* of these predictions; it simply means that their nervous systems are making them. This was, in fact, an argument offered by Pavlov himself, who described these predictions as "unconscious" (see excerpts of Pavlov, 1997). From a cognitive point of view, stimulus discrimination and generalization similarly reflect an animal's formation of a concept of what "counts" as a particular type of stimulus, which may be relatively general (any furry object) or relatively specific (a white rat).

Operant conditioning phenomena can also be reinterpreted from a more cognitive framework. Consider the counterintuitive finding that intermittent reinforcement is more effective than continuous reinforcement in maintaining behavior. From a cognitive standpoint, exposure to an intermittent reinforcement schedule (such as an old car that starts after five or ten turns of the ignition) produces the expectation that reinforcement will only come intermittently. As a result, lack of reinforcement over several trials does not signal a change in environmental contingencies. In contrast, when the owner of a new car suddenly finds the engine will not turn over, he has reason to stop trying after only three or four attempts because he has come to *expect* continuous reinforcement.

Expectancies

Cognitive-social theory proposes that the expectations, or **expectancies,** an individual forms about the consequences of a behavior are what render the behavior more or less likely to occur. If a person expects a behavior to produce a reinforcing consequence, she is likely to perform it, as long as she has the competence or skill to do so (Mischel, 1973). Julian Rotter (1954), one of the earliest cognitive-social theorists, distinguished expectancies that are specific to concrete situations ("If I ask this professor for an extension, he will refuse") from those that are more generalized ("You can't ask people for anything in life—they'll always turn you down"). Rotter was particularly interested in **generalized expectancies** that influence a broad spectrum of behavior. He used the term **locus of control of reinforcement** (or simply **locus of control**) to refer to the generalized expectancies people hold about whether or not their own behavior can bring about the outcomes they seek (Rotter, 1954, 1990). Individuals with an **internal locus of control** believe they are the masters of their own fate; people with an **external locus of control** believe their lives are determined by forces outside (external to) themselves. Figure 5.15 shows some of the items included in Rotter's questionnaire for assessing locus of control. People who believe they control their own destiny are more likely to learn to do so, in part simply because they are more inclined to make the effort.

Learned Helplessness and Explanatory Style

The powerful impact of expectancies on the behavior of nonhuman animals was dramatically demonstrated in a series of studies by Martin Seligman (1975). Seligman harnessed dogs so that they could not escape electric shocks. At first the dogs howled, whimpered, and tried to escape the shocks, but eventually they gave up; they would lie on the floor without struggle, showing physiological stress responses and behaviors resembling human depression. A day later Seligman placed the dogs in a shuttlebox from which they could easily escape the shocks.

I more strongly believe that		
1. Promotions are earned through hard work and persistence.	**OR**	Making a lot of money is largely a matter of getting the right breaks.
2. In my experience I have noticed that there is usually a direct connection between how hard I study and the grades I get.	**OR**	Many times the reactions of teachers seem haphazard to me.
3. I am the master of my fate.	**OR**	A great deal that happens to me is probably a matter of chance.

FIGURE 5.15
Items from Rotter's locus-of-control questionnaire, called the Internal–External Scale. The scale presents subjects with a series of choices between two responses, one of which is internal and the other external.
Source: Rotter, 1971.

Unlike dogs in a control condition who had not been previously exposed to inescapable shocks, the dogs in the experimental condition made no effort to escape and generally failed to learn to do so even when they occasionally *did* escape. The dogs had come to expect that they could not get away; they had learned to be helpless. **Learned helplessness** consists of the expectancy that one cannot escape aversive events and the motivational and learning deficits that result from this belief.

Seligman argued that learned helplessness is central to human depression as well. In humans, however, learned helplessness is not an automatic outcome of uncontrollable aversive events. Seligman and his colleagues observed that some people have a positive, active coping attitude in the face of failure or disappointment, whereas others become depressed and helpless (Peterson & Seligman, 1984). They demonstrated in dozens of studies that **explanatory style**—the way people make sense of bad events—plays a crucial role in whether or not they become, and remain, depressed. Individuals with a depressive or **pessimistic explanatory style** blame themselves for the bad things that happen to them; in the language of helplessness theory, pessimists believe the causes of their misfortune are *internal* rather than external, leading to lowered self-esteem. They also tend to see these causes as *stable* (unlikely to change) and *global* (broad, general, and widespread in their impact). When a person with a pessimistic style does poorly on a biology exam, he may blame it on his own stupidity—an explanation that is internal, stable, and global. Most people, in contrast, would offer themselves explanations that permit hope and encourage further effort, such as "I didn't study hard enough," "The exam was ridiculous," or "I just had a bad day."

Whether optimists or pessimists are more *accurate* in these inferences is a matter of debate. Several studies suggest that pessimistic people are actually more accurate than optimists in recognizing when they lack control over outcomes; people who maintain *positive illusions* about themselves and their ability to control their environment are less accurate but tend to be happier and report fewer psychological symptoms such as depression and anxiety (Taylor, 1992; Taylor & Brown, 1988). Other researchers have challenged these findings, however, showing that people who deny their problems or substantially overestimate their positive qualities tend to be more poorly adjusted socially than people who see themselves as others see them (Colvin et al., 1995; Colvin & Block, 1995; Shedler et al., 1993). Optimism and positive illusions about the self are probably useful up to a point, since confidence can spur action. However, when optimism verges on denial of obvious realities, it is likely to be neither healthy nor useful.

Whether or not pessimists are more accurate in their beliefs, they clearly pay a price for their explanatory style: Numerous studies document that pessimists have a higher incidence of depression and lower achievement in school than optimists (Peterson & Seligman, 1984). As we will see (Chapter 11), pessimists are also more likely to become ill and to die earlier than those who do not attribute negative events to stable, internal, and global factors.

INTERIM SUMMARY   **Cognitive-social theory** incorporated concepts of conditioning from behaviorism but added a focus on cognition and on social learning. Many learning phenomena can be reinterpreted from a cognitive perspective. One example of this is the counterintuitive finding that intermittent reinforcement is more effective than continuous reinforcement, by considering the expectations, or **expectancies,** humans and other animals develop.

A GLOBAL VISTA

OPTIMISM, PESSIMISM, AND EXPECTANCIES OF CONTROL IN CROSS-CULTURAL PERSPECTIVE

Optimism and pessimism occur within a social and cultural context. Cultural belief systems offer individuals ways of interpreting experience that influence their reactions to unpleasant events. For example, in the United States, people from fundamentalist religious backgrounds (both Christian and Jewish) tend to have more optimistic explanatory styles than nonfundamentalists (Sethi & Seligman, 1993). They tend to believe their fate is in God's hands and that God will do what is right for them. This can be extremely comforting in the face of unpleasant events such as death or disease.

People who live in a society also share common experiences that lead to shared beliefs and expectancies. We often speak of "culture" as if it were a single variable; however, cultural beliefs and practices only influence individual thought and action through specific experiences (Matthews & Moore, in press; Sapir, 1949; Shore, 1995; Strauss & Quinn, 1998). For example, studies comparing people from East and West Berlin before the fall of the Berlin Wall have provided a window to understanding the impact of social, political, and cultural factors on expectancies of control and optimism (Oettingen & Seligman, 1990; Oettingen, Little, Lindenberger, & Baltes, 1994). Individuals from these two cities shared a common culture until 1945, at which point contact between them ceased. After 1945, the people of West Berlin lived in an affluent, thriving country, in which individual initiative was rewarded through free enterprise. Those in the East lived under Soviet domination, were much poorer, had fewer freedoms, and lived under the weight of inefficient bureaucracies that controlled many aspects of their lives, from the clothes that were available to the books they were allowed to read.

These realities were reflected in a more pessimistic explanatory style and more external locus of control among East Berliners. These patterns could be observed as early as the school years, probably reflecting not only the broader sociopolitical climate but also specific features of the school environment (Oettingen et al., 1994). In East Berlin, school curricula were much more rigid and lacked any room for tailoring learning to the individual child's strengths and weaknesses. The ideology taught to children also de-emphasized individualism, and feedback on school performance was largely delivered publicly, in front of peers, rather than privately on a report card.

Expectations of control and explanatory style differ cross-culturally in ways that reflect long-standing cultural differences as well. A classic study in the early 1960s examined value orientations in five North American groups: white Texans, Mormons, Hispanics, Zuni Indians, and Navaho Indians (Kluckhohn & Strodtbeck, 1961). The researchers presented subjects with short stories that posed a problem or dilemma and asked them to indicate which of several solutions was most appropriate. Individuals differed, of course, within each group; white Texans are not all alike, and neither are Hispanic or Navajo individuals. Nevertheless, some broad patterns emerged. For example, Hispanic participants, like members of most cultures in human history, tended to believe that humans should not tamper with nature. Most Navajo similarly did not view control over nature as a dominant value; rather, they tended to stress peaceful coexistence between humans and their natural environment.

In contrast, the white Texans, like most people in the West (that is, people from cultures of European descent—not the Wild West, although that heritage may have had an influence as well) preferred mastery over nature. For them, control was a core value, and lack of control would be associated with frustration and a sense of helplessness and failure. This value system makes sense in a highly competitive, individualistic, technologically advanced, capitalist society in which individual initiative is rewarded and mastery over nature—turning ores in the ground into metals for manufacturing, predicting earthquakes, and sending people to the moon—is commonplace. It is also adaptive for people who cannot count on help from others in the ways they did even a century ago, when most people in the West lived and died in small towns near family and close neighbors.

More recent studies document substantial cultural differences in the way people make sense of positive and negative events. One study compared explanatory style in white-American, Chinese-American, and mainland Chinese college students (Lee & Seligman, 1997). The mainland Chinese were much more pessimistic than white Americans; Chinese Americans were intermediate between the other two groups. White Americans tended to attribute their successes to themselves and their failures to others—a way of interpreting events that bolsters self-confidence but probably at the cost of accuracy. Mainland Chinese, in comparison, tended to attribute both positive and negative events to forces outside their control.

Some of the differences between white Americans and mainland Chinese may, like the differences between East and West Berliners, reflect the more recent history of mainland China, in which the communist government has actively promoted communal values and created communal work settings. However, the fact that Chinese Americans, who have grown up in the United States but share elements of culture with the mainland Chinese, showed similarities to both of the other groups suggests the impact of more long-standing cultural differences as well. For hundreds of years of Chinese history, people have lived with their families in densely populated agricultural areas. In such environments, as elsewhere in Asia, excessive pride and self-centeredness are disruptive and discouraged. Attributing successes to one's personal characteristics is likely to be neither adaptive nor accurate, since much of labor in agricultural societies is communal, and families and villagers tend to share much of their fate.

Much of human behavior reflects social learning processes such as modeling.

SOCIAL LEARNING

As this discussion suggests, learning does not occur in an interpersonal vacuum. Cognitive-social theory proposes that individuals learn many things from the people around them, with or without reinforcement, through **social learning** mechanisms other than classical and operant conditioning.

A major form of social learning is **observational learning**—learning by observing the behavior of others. The impact of observational learning in humans is enormous, from learning how to give a speech, to learning how to feel and act when someone tells an inappropriate joke, to learning what kind of clothes, haircuts, or foods are fashionable. Albert Bandura (1967), one of the major cognitive-social theorists, provides a tongue-in-cheek example of observational learning in the story of a lonesome farmer who bought a parrot to keep him company. The farmer spent many long hours trying to teach the parrot to repeat the phrase, "Say uncle," but to no avail. Even hitting the parrot with a stick whenever it failed to respond correctly had no effect. Finally, the farmer gave up; in disgust, he relegated the parrot to the chicken coop. Not long afterward, the farmer was walking by the chicken coop when he heard a terrible commotion. Looking in, he saw his parrot brandishing a stick at the chickens and yelling, "Say uncle! Say uncle!" The moral of the story is that the lesson intended in observational learning is not always the lesson learned.

Observational learning in which a human or other animal learns to reproduce behavior exhibited by a model is called **modeling** (Bandura, 1967). The most well-known modeling studies were done by Bandura and his colleagues on children's aggressive behavior (1961, 1963). In these studies, children observed an adult model interacting with a large inflatable doll named Bobo. One group of children watched the model behave in a subdued manner, while other groups observed the model verbally and physically attack the doll in real life, on film, or in a cartoon. A control group observed no model at all. Children who observed the model acting aggressively displayed nearly twice as much aggressive behavior as those who watched the nonaggressive model or no model at all (Figure 5.16).

The likelihood that a person will imitate a model depends on a number of factors, such as the model's prestige, likeability, and attractiveness. Whether an individual actually *performs* modeled behavior also depends on the behavior's likely outcome. This outcome expectancy is, itself, often learned through an observational learning mechanism known as vicarious conditioning. In **vicarious conditioning,** a person learns the consequences of an action by observing its consequences for someone else. For example, adolescents' attitudes toward high-risk behaviors such as drinking and having sex without a condom are influenced by their perceptions of the consequences of their older siblings' risk taking behavior (D'Amico and Fromme, 1997).

In a classic study of vicarious conditioning, Bandura and his colleagues (1963) had nursery school children observe an aggressive adult model named Rocky. Rocky took food and toys that belonged to someone named Johnny. In one condition, Johnny punished Rocky; in the other, Rocky packed all of Johnny's toys in a sack, singing, "Hi ho, hi ho, it's off to play I go" as the scene ended. Later, when placed in an analogous situation, the children who had seen Rocky punished displayed relatively little aggressive behavior. In contrast, those who had seen Rocky rewarded behaved much more aggressively. Because Rocky's aggressive behavior exemplified what the children had previously learned was bad behavior, however, even those who followed his lead displayed some ambivalence when they saw his behavior rewarded. One girl voiced strong disapproval of Rocky's behavior but then ended the experimental session by asking the researcher, "Do you have a sack?" More recent research shows that people who are empathic and

In Bandura's classic Bobo studies, children learned by observation.

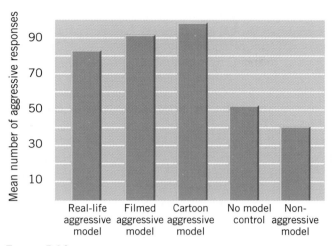

FIGURE 5.16

Social learning of aggressive behavior through modeling. This figure shows the average number of aggressive responses made by children after observing an adult model playing with an inflatable doll in each of five experimental conditions: real-life aggressive model, filmed aggressive model, cartoon aggressive model, no model control, and nonaggressive model. As can be seen, children tend to perform the behaviors of adult models. *Source:* Bandura, 1967, p. 45.

helpful to others tended to have parents who modeled similar behavior when they were children (Penner & Rioux, 1995).

Another form of social learning is direct **tutelage**—teaching concepts or procedures primarily through verbal explanation or instruction. This process is responsible for most formal education—and is occurring at this very moment. At times, conditioning processes, direct tutelage, and observational learning can influence behavior in contradictory ways. For example, most children receive the direct message that smoking is harmful to their health (tutelage). At the same time, they learn to associate smoking with positive images through advertising (classical conditioning) and may see high-status peers or parents smoking (modeling). In many cases, however, social learning processes, such as learning from a textbook (tutelage), work in tandem with conditioning processes. Most readers have been reinforced for completing reading assignments—and may also be reinforced by noticing that the chapter is just about over.

INTERIM SUMMARY **Social learning** refers to learning that occurs through social interaction. **Observational learning** occurs as individuals learn by observing the behavior of others. Learning to reproduce behavior exhibited by a model is called **modeling; vicarious conditioning** means learning by observing the consequences of a behavior for someone else. **Tutelage** occurs when people learn through direct instruction.

SOME CONCLUDING THOUGHTS

We began with wolves learning to avoid sheep and dogs salivating at bells and have somehow found our way to teenagers smoking and students reading a textbook. These widely disparate behaviors share one common denominator: They were all learned.

Psychologists' understanding of learning has changed over the course of the last century. Watson and many early behaviorists believed that *anything* could be learned. Subsequent research led to the recognition that evolutionary pressures have channeled the way humans and other animals learn, facilitating some associations and inhibiting others. Skinner probably put it best: Operant conditioning is nothing but a continuation of natural selection. Just as nature selects organisms whose characteristics are adaptive to their environment, the environment selects *responses* by organisms that have adaptive consequences. The link between these two forms of "natural selection" is crucial to a contemporary understanding of learning: Millions of years of evolution have selected *learning mechanisms* that themselves facilitate adaptation.

An even more fundamental shift has occurred in psychologists' conceptions of learning itself. Skinner and others who called themselves radical behaviorists argued that the best way to keep psychology scientific is to focus on what can be directly observed: behaviors and environmental events. Today, researchers from a more cognitive perspective view learning not primarily as a set of behavioral tendencies evoked by different situations but as the accumulation and mental organization of knowledge (see Canfield & Ceci, 1992). Psychologists now speak more freely of thoughts, emotions, motives, goals, and stresses that interact to produce behavioral outcomes

Skinner and other behaviorists wanted to avoid mentalistic explanations for a reason. Twenty-five hundred years of philosophical speculation about the mind had led to hundreds of great ideas—but no way to test them. Skinner's argument was simple and compelling: We cannot test what we cannot observe, and we cannot observe what is in other people's heads. In less than a century, behaviorally oriented researchers have, through systematic experimentation, produced a body of generalizations about conditioning processes that will undoubtedly be a permanent legacy to psychology. Researchers have now discovered some of the neural mechanisms that underlie these processes, and psychologists armed with principles of learning generated in the laboratory have been able to use them to improve people's lives, for example, by helping individuals overcome phobias or uncontrollable and sometimes debilitating panic attacks (Chapter 16). Perhaps as significant as its contributions to the understanding of learning is another important legacy of behaviorism: a hard-nosed attitude toward psychological observation and explanation and a skeptical attitude toward speculation without empirical support.

Psychologists may ultimately come to disagree with Skinner's belief that scientific explanation is incompatible with mentalistic explanation, particularly now that we can watch the brain in action as people look at objects, recall past experiences, or solve mathematical problems. But Skinner will no doubt be remembered as one of the greatest minds—or, as he might prefer, one of greatest emitters of scientifically important verbal behavior—in the history of the discipline.

SUMMARY

1. **Learning** refers to any enduring change in the way an organism responds based on its experience. Learning theories assume that experience shapes behavior, that learning is adaptive, and that uncovering laws of learning requires systematic experimentation.

CLASSICAL CONDITIONING

2. **Conditioning** is a type of learning studied by behaviorists. **Classical conditioning** refers to learning in which an environmental stimulus produces a re-

sponse in an organism. An innate reflex is an **unconditioned reflex.** The stimulus that produces the response in an unconditioned reflex is called an **unconditioned stimulus,** or **UCS.** An **unconditioned response (UCR)** is a response that does not have to be learned. A **conditioned response (CR)** is a response that has been learned. A **conditioned stimulus (CS)** is a stimulus that, through learning, has come to evoke a conditioned response.

3. Once an organism has learned to produce a CR, it may respond to stimuli that resemble the CS with a similar response. This phenomenon is called **stimulus generalization. Stimulus discrimination** is the learned tendency to respond to a very restricted range of stimuli or to only the one used during training. **Extinction** in classical conditioning refers to the process by which a CR is weakened by presentation of the CS without the UCS; that is, the response is *extinguished*.

4. Factors that influence classical conditioning include the **interstimulus interval** (the time between presentation of the CS and the UCS), the individual's learning history, and **prepared learning.**

5. Neuroscientists have begun to track down the neural processes involved in classical conditioning. Research on the marine snail *Aplysia* and on long-term potentiation in more complex animals suggests that learning involves an increase in the strength of synaptic connections through changes in the presynaptic neuron (which more readily releases neurotransmitters), changes in the postsynaptic neuron (which becomes more excitable), and probably an increase in dendritic connections between the two.

OPERANT CONDITIONING

6. Thorndike's **law of effect** states that an animal's tendency to produce a behavior depends on that behavior's effect on the environment. Skinner elaborated this idea into the concept of **operant conditioning,** which means learning to operate on the environment to produce a consequence. **Operants** are behaviors that are emitted rather than elicited by the environment. A consequence is said to lead to **reinforcement** if it increases the probability that a response will recur. A **reinforcer** is an environmental consequence that occurs after an organism has produced a response, which makes the response more likely to recur.

7. **Positive reinforcement** is the process whereby presentation of a stimulus (a reward or payoff) after a behavior makes the behavior more likely to occur again. A **positive reinforcer** is an environmental consequence that, when presented, strengthens the probability that a response will recur. Whereas the *presentation* of a positive reinforcer rewards a response, the *removal* of a negative reinforcer rewards a response. **Negative reinforcement** is the process whereby termination of an aversive stimulus (a negative reinforcer) makes a behavior more likely to recur. **Negative reinforcers** are aversive or unpleasant stimuli that strengthen a behavior by their removal. Whereas reinforcement always increases the probability that a response will recur, **punishment** decreases the probability. Punishment is commonplace in human affairs but is frequently applied in ways that render it ineffective. Extinction in operant conditioning occurs if enough conditioning trials pass in which the operant is not followed by its previously learned environmental consequence.

8. Four phenomena vastly increase the explanatory power of the concept of operant conditioning. These include schedules of reinforcement, **discriminative stimuli** (stimuli that signal to an organism that particular contingencies of re-

inforcement are in effect), the behavioral context, and characteristics of the learner.

9. In a **continuous schedule of reinforcement,** the environmental consequence is the same each time an animal emits a behavior. In an **intermittent schedule of reinforcement,** reinforcement does not occur every time the organism emits a particular response. In a **fixed-ratio (FR) schedule of reinforcement,** an organism receives reinforcement at a fixed rate, according to the number of operant responses emitted. As in the fixed-ratio schedule, an animal on a **variable-ratio (VR) schedule** receives a reward for some percentage of responses, but the number of responses required before each reinforcement is unpredictable. In a **fixed-interval (FI) schedule,** an animal receives reinforcement for its responses only after a fixed amount of time. In a **variable-interval (VI) schedule,** the animal cannot predict how long that time interval will be.

10. The operant conditioning of a given behavior occurs in the context of other environmental contingencies (such as the impact of obtaining one reinforcer on the probability of obtaining another) and broader social and cultural processes. Characteristics of the learner also influence operant conditioning, such as prior behaviors in the animal's repertoire, enduring characteristics of the learner (such as the tendency to respond with fear or avoidance in the face of aversive environmental events), and species-specific behavior.

11. Operant and classical conditioning share many common features, such as extinction, prepared learning, discrimination, generalization, and the possibility of irrational associations. Although operant conditioning usually applies to voluntary behavior, it can also be used in techniques such as **biofeedback** to alter autonomic responses, which are usually the domain of classical conditioning. In everyday life, operant and classical conditioning are often difficult to disentangle because most learned behavior involves both.

COGNITIVE-SOCIAL THEORY

12. **Cognitive-social theory** incorporated concepts of conditioning from behaviorism but added two additional features: a focus on cognition and a focus on social learning. Tolman demonstrated that rats formed **cognitive maps** or mental images of their environment and that these were responsible for **latent learning**—learning that has occurred but is not currently manifest in behavior. Many classic learning phenomena have been reinterpreted from a cognitive perspective, such as stimulus discrimination and generalization, which are taken as evidence that animals are able to classify stimuli as members of different categories.

13. According to cognitive-social theory, the way an animal *construes* the environment is as important to learning as actual environmental contingencies. Cognitive-social theory proposes that expectations or **expectancies** of the consequences of behaviors are what render behaviors more or less likely to occur. **Locus of control** refers to the generalized expectancies people hold about whether or not their own behavior will bring about the outcomes they prefer. **Learned helplessness** involves the expectancy that one cannot escape aversive events and the motivational and learning deficits that accrue from it. **Explanatory style** refers to the way people make sense of bad events. Individuals with a depressive or **pessimistic explanatory style** see the causes of bad events as internal, stable, and global. Expectancies such as locus of control and explanatory style differ across cultures, since cultural belief systems

offer people ready-made ways of interpreting events, and people who live in a society share common experiences (such as work and schooling) that lead to shared beliefs and expectancies.

14. Psychologists have studied several kinds of **social learning** (learning that takes place as a direct result of social interaction), including **observational learning** (learning by observing the behavior of others) and **tutelage** (direct instruction). Observational learning in which a human or other animal learns to reproduce behavior exhibited by a model is called **modeling.** In **vicarious conditioning,** a person learns the consequences of an action by observing its consequences for someone else.

Jan Sawka, "The Memories II," 1987.

CHAPTER 6

Memory

Jimmie was a fine-looking man, with a curly bush of gray hair, a healthy and handsome forty-nine-year-old. He was cheerful, friendly, and warm.

"Hi, Doc!" he said. "Nice morning! Do I take this chair here?" He was a genial soul, very ready to talk and to answer any question I asked him. He told me his name and birth date, and the name of the little town in Connecticut where he was born. . . . He recalled, and almost relived, his war days and service, the end of the war, and his thoughts for the future. . . .

With recalling, Jimmie was full of animation; he did not seem to be speaking of the past but of the present. . . . A sudden, improbable suspicion seized me.

"What year is this, Mr. G.?" I asked, concealing my perplexity in a casual manner.

"Forty-five, man. What do you mean?" He went on, "We've won the war, FDR's dead, Truman's at the helm. There are great times ahead."

"And you, Jimmie, how old would you be?"

Oddly, uncertainly, he hesitated a moment as if engaged in calculation.

"Why, I guess I'm nineteen, Doc. I'll be twenty next birthday."

Sachs, 1970, pp. 21–23

Jimmie was decades behind the times: He was nearly 50 years old. His **amnesia**, or memory loss, resulted from Korsakoff's syndrome, a disorder related to chronic alcoholism in which subcortical structures involved in memory deteriorate. Jimmie had no difficulty recalling incidents from World War II, but he could not remember anything since 1945, when he succumbed to Korsakoff's.

Curiously, though, amnesics like Jimmie are still able to form certain kinds of new memories (Schacter, 1995; Squire, 1986; Squire & Zola-Morgan, 1991). If asked to recall a seven-digit phone number long enough to walk to another room and dial it, they have no difficulty doing so. A minute after completing the call, however, they will not remember having picked up the phone. Or suppose Jimmie, who grew up before the days of computers, were to play a computer game every day for a week. Like most people, he would steadily improve at it, demonstrating that he was learning and remembering new skills. Yet each day he would likely greet the computer with, "Gee, what's this thing?"

Case studies of neurologically impaired patients and experimental studies of normal subjects have demonstrated that memory is not a single function that a person can have or lose. Rather, memory is composed of several systems. Just how many systems, and how independently they function, are questions at the heart of contemporary research.

The last chapter was dominated by the behaviorist perspective; this one and the next focus primarily on the cognitive perspective, which has offered a comprehensive model of thought and memory. We begin by describing some of the basic features of memory and an evolving model of information processing that has guided research on memory for over three decades. We then explore the memory systems that

allow people to store information temporarily and permanently, and examine why people sometimes forget and misremember. Along the way, we consider the implications of memory research for issues such as the accuracy of eyewitness testimony in court and the existence of repressed memories in victims of childhood sexual abuse.

MEMORY AND INFORMATION PROCESSING

Memory is so basic to human functioning that we take it for granted. Consider what was involved the last time you performed the seemingly simple task of remembering a friend's phone number. Did you bring to mind a visual image (a picture of the number), an auditory "image" (pronouncing a series of numbers out loud in your mind), or simply a pattern of motor movements as you punched the numbers on the phone? How did you bring to mind this particular number, given that you likely have a dozen other numbers stored in memory? (Try describing the process—and good luck.) Once a number was in your mind, how did you know it was the right one? And were you aware as you reached for the phone that you were remembering at that very moment how to use a phone, what phones do, how to lift an object smoothly to your face, how to push buttons, and who your friend is?

This example suggests how complex the simplest act of memory is. Memory involves taking something we have observed, such as a written phone number, and converting it into a form we can store, retrieve, and use. We begin by briefly describing the various ways the mind can preserve the past—the "raw material" of memory—and an evolving model of information processing that has guided psychologists' efforts to understand memory for the last quarter of a century.

MENTAL REPRESENTATIONS

For a sound, image, or thought to return to mind when it is no longer present, it has to be represented in the mind—literally, *re*-presented, or presented again—this time without the original stimulus. As we saw in Chapter 4, a *mental representation* is a psychological version or mental model of a stimulus or category of stimuli. In neuropsychological terms, it is the patterned firing of a network of neurons that forms the neural "code" for an object or concept, such as "dog " or "sister."

Representational modes are like languages that permit conversation within the mind (see Jackendoff, 1996). The content of our thoughts and memories—a bird, an angry friend, a beautiful sunset—can be described or translated into many "languages"—images, sounds, words, and so forth—but some languages cannot capture certain experiences the way others can. Fortunately, we are all "multilingual" and frequently process information simultaneously using multiple representational codes—an example of parallel processing of information by interdependent networks in the brain (Chapter 3).

Some kinds of representation are difficult to conceptualize and have received less attention from researchers. For example, people store memories of *actions*, such as how to press the buttons on a phone or how to squeeze the last drops of ketchup out of the bottle, which suggests the existence of *motoric representations*, or stored memories of muscle movements. The most commonly studied representations are sensory and verbal.

Sensory Representations

Sensory representations store information in a sensory mode, such as the sound of a dog barking or the image of a city skyline. The cognitive maps discovered in rats running mazes (Chapter 5) probably include visual representations. People rely on visual representations to recall where they left their keys last night or to catch a ball that is sailing toward them through the air. Visual representations are like pictures that can be mentally scrutinized or manipulated (Kosslyn, 1983). If asked, "How many light fixtures are in your home?" most people could answer, despite never having counted, by forming a mental image of the rooms in their house and simply counting the fixtures as they travel mentally from room to room.

Visual representations are not the only sensory representations. The auditory mode is also important for encoding information (Thompson & Paivio, 1994). Some forms of auditory information would be difficult to represent in any other mode. For instance, most readers would be able to retrieve pieces of Beethoven's Fifth Symphony or "Ironic" by Alanis Morrisette quite easily. In both cases, the representation that is retrieved is a series of patterned segments of sound, such as the *di-di-di-dah* that opens Beethoven's Fifth. Other types of sensory information have their own mental codes as well. People can identify many objects by smell, which suggests that they are comparing current sensory experience with olfactory knowledge (Schab & Crowder, 1995). Olfactory representations in humans are, however, far less reliable than visual representations in identifying even common objects (de Wijk et al., 1995). For example, if exposed to the smell of a lemon, people often misidentify it as an orange, whereas people with an intact visual system rarely confuse the two fruits visually.

Verbal Representations

Although many representations are stored in sensory modes, much of the time people think with words, using **verbal representations.** Try to imagine what "liberty" or "mental representation" means without thinking in words. Other experiences, in contrast, are virtually impossible to describe or remember verbally, such as the smell of bacon. In fact, using words to describe things about which one has little verbal knowledge can actually disrupt sensory-based memory: People who enjoy wine but have no formal training in it have more trouble identifying a wine they have just tasted if they try to describe it than if they just shut up and drink it (Melcher & Schooler, 1996).

Imaging studies confirm that verbal representations are in fact distinct from sensory representations. Consider what happens when researchers present subjects with a string of X's versus a word (Menard et al., 1996). Both stimuli lead to activation of the visual cortex, since both are processed visually. Presentation of the word, however, leads to additional activation of a region at the juncture of the left occipital, parietal, and temporal lobes that appears to be involved in transforming the visual representation into a verbal or semantic one.

INTERIM SUMMARY   For information to come back to mind after it is no longer present, it has to be represented. **Sensory representations** store information in a sensory mode; **verbal representations** store information in words. People also store knowledge about actions as *motoric representations*.

INFORMATION PROCESSING: AN EVOLVING MODEL

Psychologists began studying memory in the late nineteenth century, although interest in memory waned under the influence of behaviorism until the "cognitive revolution" of the 1960s. In 1890 William James proposed a distinction between

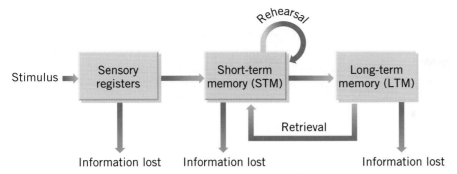

FIGURE 6.1

Standard model of memory. Stimulus information enters the sensory registers. Some information enters STM and is then passed on for storage in LTM. Information can be lost from any of the sensory stores, usually if it is not very important.

two kinds of memory, which he called primary and secondary memory. *Primary memory* is immediate memory for information momentarily held in consciousness, such as a telephone number. *Secondary memory* is the vast store of information that is unconscious except when called back into primary memory, such as the 10 or 20 phone numbers a person could bring to mind if he wanted to call various friends, family members, stores, and so forth. James's distinction is embodied in what we will call the *standard model of memory* (sometimes called the "modal model," since "modal" means most common or typical), which has guided research on memory and cognition since the 1960s (Atkinson & Shiffrin, 1968; Healy & McNamara, 1996).

The standard model is predicated on the metaphor of the mind as a computer, which places information into different memory stores (the system's "hardware") and retrieves and transforms it using various programs ("software"). According to this model (Figure 6.1), memory consists of three stores: sensory memory (or sensory registers), short-term memory (James's primary memory), and long-term memory (James's secondary memory). Storing and retrieving memories involves passing information from one store to the next and then retrieving the information from long-term memory.

Sensory Registers

Suppose you grab a handful of quarters (say, six or seven) from your pocket at the laundromat and, while looking away, stretch out your hand so that all of the coins are visible. If you then glance for a second at your hand but look away before counting the change, you are still likely to be able to report accurately the number of coins in your hand because the image is held momentarily in your visual sensory register. **Sensory registers** hold information about a perceived stimulus for a split second after the stimulus disappears, allowing a mental representation of it to remain in memory briefly for further processing (Sperling, 1960).

To date, most research has focused on visual and auditory sensory registration. The term **iconic storage** is used to describe visual sensory registration. For a brief period after an image disappears from vision, people retain a mental image (or "icon") of what they have seen (Figure 6.2). This visual trace is remarkably accurate and contains considerably more information than people can report before it fades (Baddeley & Patterson, 1971). The duration of icons varies from approximately half a second to two seconds, depending on the individual, the content of the image, and the circumstances (Neisser, 1976). Presenting another image or even a flash of light directly after the first image disappears erases the original

Display	Tone	Response
M Q T Z R F G A N S L C	High Medium Low	If low tone was sounded "N, S, L, C"

FIGURE 6.2

Visual sensory register. In a classic experiment, participants briefly viewed a grid of 12 letters and then heard a tone after a short delay. They had been instructed to report the top, middle, or bottom row, depending on whether a high, medium, or low tone sounded. If the tone sounded within half a second, they were 75 percent accurate, by reading off the image in their mind (iconic storage). If the tone sounded beyond that time, their accuracy dropped substantially because the visual image had faded from the sensory register. *Source:* From Sperling, 1960.

icon (Schiller, 1965), much as a new movie recorded on an old videotape erases prior material. The movie analogy is apt in another way: Motion pictures are really rapidly flashed sequences of still frames. The perception of movement relies in part on our capacity to hold the prior frame briefly in mind as the new one emerges. This leads to the illusion of continuity between frames and hence movement (rather than jerky replacement of one photo by another),

The auditory counterpart of iconic storage is called **echoic storage** (Battacchi et al., 1981; Darwin et al., 1972; Neisser, 1967). Most readers have probably had the experience of hearing a voice or a sound "echo" in their minds after the actual sound has stopped. Some researchers suggest that humans may have two types of echoic memory systems, one for nonspeech and the other for speech sounds, lateralized to the right and left hemispheres of the brain, respectively (Ardila et al., 1986; Deutsch, 1970; Kimura & Folb, 1970).

Take a quick glance at Renoir's Luncheon of the Boating Party *and try counting the number of people from momentary iconic memory.*

Short-Term Memory

According to the standard model, then, the first stage of memory is a brief sensory representation of a stimulus. Many of the stimuli people perceive in the course of a day register for such a short time that they drop out of the memory system without further processing, as indicated in Figure 6.1 ("information lost"). That is why people typically have trouble remembering details about objects their eyes quickly scanned for an instant, such as the wallpaper pattern they saw in the hallway while being escorted into a doctor's office or the license plate of a car that sped away from an accident. Other stimuli make a greater impression. Information about them is passed on to **short-term memory (STM)**, a memory store that holds a small amount of information in consciousness—such as a phone number—for roughly 20 to 30 seconds, unless the person makes a deliberate effort to maintain it longer by repeating it over and over (Waugh & Norman, 1965).

Like the counter at a diner, STM is rapidly accessed but limited in capacity.

Limited Capacity   Short-term memory has *limited capacity*; that is, it does not hold much information. On the average, people can remember about seven pieces of information at a time, with a normal range of from five to nine items (Miller, 1956). That phone numbers in most countries are five to seven digits is no mere coincidence. Hermann Ebbinghaus (1885) was the first to note the seven-item limit to STM. Ebbinghaus pioneered the study of memory using the most convenient and agreeable subject he could find—himself—with a method that involved inventing some 2300 nonsense syllables (such as *pir* and *vup*). Ebbinghaus randomly placed these syllables in lists of varying lengths and then attempted to memorize the lists; he used nonsense syllables rather than real words to try to control the possible influence of prior knowledge on memory. Ebbinghaus found that he could memorize up to seven syllables, but no more, in a single trial. The limits of STM seem to be neurologically based, as they are similar in other cultures, including those with very different languages (Yu et al., 1985).

Because of STM's limited capacity, psychologists have often likened it to a lunch counter (Bower, 1975). If only seven stools are available at the counter, some customers will have to get up before new customers can be seated. Similarly, new information "bumps" previous STMs from consciousness. Figure 6.3 illustrates this bumping effect: A person presented with seven digits stores them in STM. After 20 seconds, the memory of these digits begins to fade or decay, but it can probably still be retrieved. However, any new numbers that are presented will displace the numbers that first entered STM. With limited space at the counter, the waitress does not encourage customers to sip their coffee at their leisure when others are waiting to sit.

Rehearsal   Short-term memory is not, however, a completely passive process of getting bumped off a stool. People can control the information stored in STM. For example, after looking up a phone number, most people will repeat it over and over in their minds to prevent it from fading until they have dialed the number, a procedure known as **rehearsal**. This kind of rehearsal is called **maintenance rehearsal**, since its purpose is to *maintain* information in STM.

Rehearsal is also important in transferring information to long-term memory which will not surprise anyone who has ever memorized a poem, lines from a play, or a math formula by repeating it over and over. As we will see, however, maintenance rehearsal is not as useful for storing information in long-term memory as more actively thinking about the information while rehearsing, a procedure known as **elaborative rehearsal**. Remembering the words to a poem, for example, is much easier if the person really understands what it is about, rather than just committing each word to memory by rote.

(*a*) **7 6 3 8 8 2 6**

(*b*) 7 6 3 8 8 2 6 (20 seconds later)

(*c*) **9 1 8** 8 8 2 6 (25 seconds later)

FIGURE 6.3

Short-term memory. In an experimental task, the subject is presented with a string of seven digits (*a*). Without rehearsal, 20 seconds later, the representations of the digits have begun to fade but are likely still to be retrievable (*b*). At 25 seconds, however, the experimenter introduces three more digits, which "bump" the earliest of the still-fading digits (*c*).

INTERIM SUMMARY   The *standard model of memory* is predicated on the metaphor of the mind as a computer. It distinguishes three memory stores: sensory memory (or sensory registers), short-term memory, and long-term memory. **Sensory registers**, which can be **iconic** (visual) or **echoic** (auditory), hold information about a perceived stimulus for a split second after the stimulus disappears. From the sensory registers, information is passed on to a limited-capacity **short-term memory (STM)**, which holds up to seven pieces of information in consciousness for roughly 20 to 30 seconds unless the person makes a deliberate effort to maintain it longer by repeating it over and over (**maintenance rehearsal**).

Long-Term Memory

Just as relatively unimportant information drops out of memory after brief sensory registration, the same is true after storage in STM. An infrequently called phone number is not worth cluttering up the memory banks. More important information, however, goes on to **long-term memory (LTM)**, where representations of facts, images, thoughts, feelings, skills, and experiences may reside for as long as a lifetime. According to the standard model, the longer information remains in STM, the more likely it is to make a permanent impression in LTM. Recovering information from LTM, known as **retrieval**, involves bringing it back into STM (which is often used in information-processing models as a synonym for consciousness).

Why did researchers distinguish short-term from long-term memory? One reason was simple: Short-term memory is brief, limited in capacity, and quickly accessed, whereas LTM is enduring, virtually limitless, but more difficult to access (as anyone knows who has tried to recall a specific name or term on an exam without success). The difference between STM and LTM is like the difference between pulling a file from the top of the desk versus searching for it in a file drawer, or between searching for information in an open computer file versus first finding the file on the hard drive.

Another reason emerged as psychologists tested memory using free-recall tasks. In *free-recall tasks*, the experimenter presents subjects with a list of words, one at a time, and then asks them to recall as many as possible. When the delay is relatively short between presentation of the list and recall, participants are more likely to remember words toward the beginning and end of the list than those in the middle, a phenomenon known as the **serial position effect** (Figure 6.4).

Although researchers have offered many explanations for the serial position effect, one explanation proposed by advocates of the standard model involves the distinction between long-term and short-term storage (Atkinson & Shiffrin, 1968; Rundus, 1971). When people are trying to remember a list of words, they rehearse them in their minds. The first words on the list receive considerable rehearsal, but as the number of words steadily increases, the person has less opportunity to rehearse each one (Figure 6.5). Thus, words toward the beginning of the list are bet-

FIGURE 6.4
Serial position effect. Items earlier in a list and those at the end show a heightened probability of recall in comparison to those in the middle. *Source:* From Atkinson & Shiffrin, 1968.

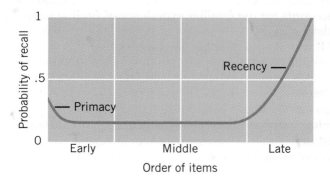

Item presented	Rehearsal
1. Reaction	Reaction, reaction, reaction, reaction
2. Hoof	Hoof, reaction, hoof, reaction
3. Blessing	Blessing, hoof, reaction
4. Research	Research, reaction, hoof, research
5. Candy	Candy, hoof, research, reaction
6. Hardship	Hardship, hoof, hardship, hoof
7. Kindness	Kindness, candy, hardship, hoof
8. Nonsense	Nonsense, kindness, candy, hardships
.	.
.	.
.	.
20. Cellar	Cellar, alcohol, misery, cellar

FIGURE 6.5
Rehearsal and the primacy effect. A subject rehearses aloud, demonstrating the way patterns of rehearsal produce a primacy effect. This partial listing of the items rehearsed by one subject shows that early items receive more rehearsal than later items and hence are more likely to be stored in LTM. *Source:* From Rundus, 1971.

ter remembered—a phenomenon called the *primacy effect*—because they are more likely to be stored in LTM.

Items at the end of a list are also remembered better than those in the middle. This phenomenon, known as the *recency effect*, was originally studied by Mary Calkins (1905), a pioneer in memory research (and the first female president of the American Psychological Association; see Madigan & O'Hara, 1992). Since STM has limited capacity, each successive word in the list bumps a previously presented word. The last words on the list are more likely to be remembered because they have not been displaced by any new words. In fact, if subjects are given a distracter task, such as counting, between initial presentation of a list of words and recall, the recency effect will disappear, suggesting that either decay of the memory or interference from this distracter task prevents retention of the most recent words in STM.

The Evolution of a Model

Although the standard model provides a basic foundation for thinking about memory, in the last decade it has evolved in four major respects. First, the standard model is a *serial processing model:* It proposes a series of stages of memory storage and retrieval that occur one at a time (serially) in a particular order, with information passing from the sensory registers to STM to LTM. For information to get into LTM, it must first be represented in each of the prior two memory stores, and the longer it stays in STM, the more likely it is to receive permanent storage in LTM.

Subsequent research casts doubt on this view. Most sensory information is never processed consciously (that is, placed in STM) but can nevertheless be stored and retrieved. This accounts for the familiar experience of finding oneself humming a tune that was playing in the background at a store without ever having noticed consciously that it was playing. Further, the process of selecting which sensory information to store in STM is actually influenced by LTM; that is, LTM may be activated *before* STM rather than after it. The function of STM is to hold important information in consciousness long enough to use it to solve problems and make decisions. But how do we know what information is important? The only way to decide which information to bring into STM is to compare incoming data with information stored in LTM that can provide some indication of its potential significance (Logie, 1996). Thus, LTM must actually be engaged *before* STM to figure out how to allocate conscious attention (Chapter 9).

A second major shift is that researchers have come to view memory as involving a set of **memory systems**—discrete but interdependent processing units responsible for different kinds of remembering. These memory systems operate simultaneously (that is, in parallel), rather than sequentially (one at a time) (Fodor, 1983; Rumelhart et al., 1986). This view fits with contemporary neuropsychological theories, which suggest that the central nervous system consists of *modules*—coordinated but autonomously functioning systems of neurons. For instance, when people simultaneously hear thunder and see lightning, they process the sound using auditory modules in the temporal cortex, identify the image as lightning using visual modules in the occipital and lower (inferior) temporal lobes, and pinpoint the location of the lightning using a visual–spatial processing module that runs from the occipital lobes through the upper (superior) temporal and parietal lobes (Chapter 4). When they remember the episode, however, all three modules are activated at the same time, so they have no awareness that these memory systems have been operating in parallel.

Similarly, researchers have come to question whether STM is really a single memory store. As we will see shortly, experimental evidence suggests, instead, that STM is part of a *working memory* system that can briefly keep at least three different kinds of information in mind simultaneously so that the information is available for conscious problem solving (Baddeley, 1986, 1995).

Third, researchers once focused exclusively on conscious recollection of word lists, nonsense syllables, and similar types of information. Cognitive psychologists now recognize other forms of remembering that do not involve retrieval into consciousness. An amnesic like Jimmie (whose case opened this chapter) who learns a new skill, or a child who learns to tie a shoe, is storing new information in LTM. When this information is remembered, however, it is expressed directly in skilled behavior rather than retrieved into consciousness or STM. Further, researchers are now paying closer attention to the kinds of remembering that occur in everyday life, as when people remember emotionally significant events or try to remember to pick up several items at the grocery store on the way back home from work.

The final change is a shift in the metaphor underlying the model. Researchers in the 1960s were struck by the extraordinary developments in computer science that were just beginning to revolutionize technology, and they saw in the computer a powerful metaphor for the most impressive computing machine ever designed: the human mind. Today, after a decade of similarly extraordinary progress in unraveling the mysteries of the brain, cognitive scientists have turned to a different metaphor: mind as brain. Thus, researchers are less likely to think of representations as located in a particular memory store than as distributed throughout a network of neurons whose simultaneous activation constitutes the memory.

In the remainder of this chapter we explore the major components of this evolving model in detail. We begin with working memory (the current version of STM) and then examine the variety of memory processes and systems that constitute LTM.

INTERIM SUMMARY   In **long-term memory (LTM)**, representations of facts, images, thoughts, feelings, skills, and experiences may reside for as long as a lifetime. Recovering information from LTM, known as **retrieval**, involves bringing it back into STM or consciousness. Although the standard model still provides a basic foundation for thinking about memory, in the last decade it has evolved in four major respects. First, the assumption that a *serial processing model* can account for memory no longer seems likely. Second and related, researchers have come to view memory as involving a set of **memory systems**—discrete but interdependent processing units responsible for different kinds of remembering that operate simultaneously (in parallel) rather than sequentially (one at a time). Third, the standard model overemphasized conscious memory for relatively neutral facts and underemphasized other forms of remembering, such as skill learning and everyday remembering. Fourth, the underlying metaphor has changed, from *mind as computer* to *mind as brain*.

WORKING MEMORY

Because people use STM as a "workspace" to process new information and to call up relevant information from LTM, many psychologists now think of STM as a component of working memory. **Working memory** refers to the temporary storage and processing of information that can be used to solve problems, respond to environmental demands, or achieve goals (see Baddeley, 1986, 1995; Richardson et al., 1996). Working memory is *active* memory: Information remains in working memory only so long as the person is consciously processing, examining, or manipulating it. Like the older concept of STM, working memory includes both a temporary memory store and a set of strategies, or *control processes*, for mentally manipulating the information momentarily held in that store. These control processes can be as simple as maintenance rehearsal—such as repeating a phone number over and over until we have finished dialing it—or as complex as trying to solve an equation in our heads.

Researchers initially believed that these two components of working memory—temporary storage and mental control—competed for the limited space at the lunch counter. In this view, rehearsing information is an active process that itself uses up some of the limited capacity of STM. Researchers also tended to view STM as a single system that could hold a maximum of about seven pieces of information of *any* kind, whether numbers, words, or images. More recent research suggests, instead, that working memory consists of multiple systems and that its storage and processing functions do not compete for limited space. According to one prominent model, working memory consists of three memory systems: a visual memory store, a verbal memory store, and a "central executive" that controls and manipulates the information these two short-term stores hold in mind (Baddeley, 1992, 1995). We begin by discussing the central executive and then examine the memory stores at its disposal.

PROCESSING INFORMATION IN WORKING MEMORY: THE CENTRAL EXECUTIVE

In 1974, Alan Baddeley and Graham Hitch challenged the view of a single all-purpose working memory by presenting subjects with two tasks simultaneously, one involving recall of a series of digits and the other involving some kind of thinking, such as reasoning or comprehending the meaning of sentences. They reasoned that if working memory is a single system, trying to remember seven or eight digits would fill the memory store and eliminate any further capacity for thinking.

The investigators *did* find that performing STM and reasoning tasks simultaneously slowed down subjects' ability to think; in one study, holding a memory load of four to eight digits increased the time participants took to solve a reasoning task (Figure 6.6). However, a memory load of three items had no effect at all on reasoning speed, despite the fact that it should have consumed at least three of the "slots" in STM. Further, performing the two tasks simultaneously had no impact on the number of *errors* subjects made on the thinking task, suggesting that carrying out processes such as reasoning and rehearsal does not compete with storing digits for "workspace" in a short-term store.

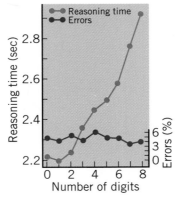

FIGURE 6.6
Speed and accuracy of reasoning as a function of number of digits to remember. Having to remember up to eight digits slowed the response time of participants as they tried to solve a reasoning task, but it did not lead to more errors. Keeping one to three digits in mind had minimal impact on reasoning time or speed. *Source:* From Baddeley, 1995.

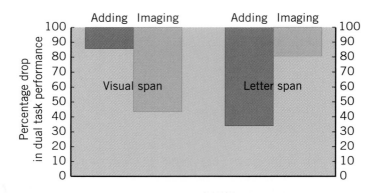

These and other data led Baddeley and his colleagues to propose that storage capacity and processing capacity are two separate aspects of working memory. Processes such as rehearsal, reasoning, and making decisions about how to balance two tasks simultaneously are the work of a *central executive* system that has its own limited capacity, independent of the information it is storing or holding momentarily in mind. Other researchers have found that working memory as a whole does seem to have a limited capacity—people cannot do and remember too many things at the same time—but working memory capacity varies across individuals and is probably related to their general intellectual ability (Daneman & Merikle, 1996; Just & Carpenter, 1992; Kyllonen, 1993, Logie, 1996).

VISUAL AND VERBAL STORAGE

Most contemporary models of working memory distinguish between at least two kinds of temporary memory: a visual store (also called the *visuospatial sketchpad*) and a verbal store (Baddeley, 1995; Baddeley et al., 1998). The visual store, or visuospatial sketchpad, is like a temporary image the person can hold in mind for 20 or 30 seconds. It momentarily stores visual information such as the location and nature of objects in the environment, so that, for example, a person turning around to grab a mug at the sink will remember where she placed a teabag a moment before. Images in the visual store can be mentally rotated, moved around, or used to locate objects in space that have momentarily dropped out of sight.

The verbal (or *phonological*) store is the familiar short-term store studied using tasks such as digit span. Verbal working memory is relatively shallow: Words are stored in order, based primarily on their sound (*phonology*), not their meaning. Researchers learned about this "shallowness" of verbal memory by studying the kinds of words that interfere with each other in free-recall tasks (Baddeley, 1986). A list of similar-sounding words (such as *man, mat, cap,* and *map*) is more difficult to recall than a list of words that do not sound alike. Similarity of meaning (e.g., *large, big, huge, tall*) does not similarly interfere with verbal working memory, but it *does* interfere with LTM. This suggests that verbal working memory and LTM have somewhat different ways of storing information.

Several lines of evidence suggest that visual and verbal storage are indeed distinct components of working memory. For example, researchers have reported cases of brain-damaged individuals who have normal verbal working memory but impaired visual working memory; others can store visual information but have difficulty with verbal storage (De Renzi & Nichelli, 1975). Researchers have produced compelling data for the independence of these two systems in experiments with normal individuals as well (Figure 6.7).

INTERIM SUMMARY   Many psychologists now refer to STM as **working memory**—the temporary storage and processing of information that can be used to solve problems, respond to environmental demands, or achieve goals. Working memory includes both a *storage capacity* and a *processing capacity*. According to the model proposed by Baddeley and his colleagues, processes such as rehearsal, reasoning, and making decisions about how to balance two tasks simultaneously are the work of a limited-capacity *central executive* system. Most contemporary models distinguish between at least two kinds of temporary memory: a visual store (also called the *visuospatial sketchpad*) and a verbal store.

▶ ONE STEP FURTHER

The Neuropsychology of Working Memory

Recently researchers have begun tracking down the neuropsychology of working memory, confirming many aspects of Baddeley's model while refining others. The emerging consensus is that when information is temporarily stored and manipulated, a region of the frontal lobes called the *prefrontal cortex* is activated along with whichever posterior regions (that is, regions toward the back of the brain) normally process the kind of information being held in memory, such as words or images (D'Esposito et al., 1995; Frith & Dolan, 1996; Goldman-Rakic, 1996). Working memory appears to be "directed" by the prefrontal cortex, a region of the brain long known to be involved in the most high-level cognitive functions. When people hold information in mind temporarily and manipulate it, the prefrontal cortex appears to provide conscious activation to representations in cortical regions normally involved in perception and memory whether or not they are conscious.

Working Memory and the Prefrontal Cortex

The first psychologists to use the term "working memory" actually speculated about its likely basis in the frontal lobes (Miller et al., 1960). Evidence of the pivotal role of the prefrontal cortex began to accumulate when researchers designed working memory tasks for monkeys and observed the activity of neutrons in this region (Friedman & Goldman-Rakic, 1994; Fuster, 1989, 1996; Goldman-Rakic, 1995). Similar studies have now been conducted with humans. In one study, the researchers used fMRI to study the activation of different cortical regions while participants tried to remember faces or scrambled faces (a meaningless visual stimulus) (Courtney et al., 1997). The results were striking (Figure 6.8). Relatively meaningless visual information activated posterior regions of the occipital lobes involved in the early stages of processing visual stimuli. Facial stimuli activated areas of the visual cortex in the occipital and temporal lobes involved in processing and identifying meaningful visual stimuli (and perhaps faces in particular). Anterior regions of the frontal lobes, that is, the prefrontal cortex, were most active during the delay period in which the faces and scrambled faces were removed and had to be held in working memory.

Distinct Components of Working Memory

Other research demonstrates the independence of different components of working memory. Imaging studies confirm that verbal and visual working memory activate different cortical regions. In one study, verbal working memory (recalling letters) primarily activated areas of the left prefrontal cortex along with left temporal and frontal regions involved in speech and language (Jonides et al., 1996). In contrast, a visuospatial working memory task

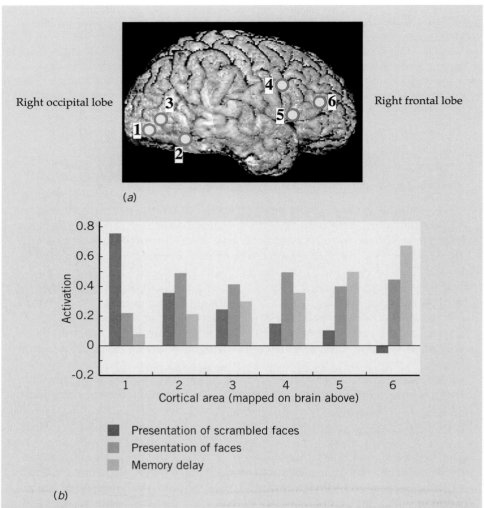

Right occipital lobe

Right frontal lobe

(a)

(b)

FIGURE 6.8

Working memory for faces and scrambled faces. Researchers used fMRI to study working memory for meaningful stimuli, in this case faces. The top part of the figure (a) shows the parts of the brain that were activated at different times by presentation of a meaningless stimulus (scrambled faces), a meaningful stimulus (faces), and the delay period in which participants had to hold images in working memory. As can be seen in (b), different regions of the brain showed distinct functions, with the prefrontal cortex involved in holding images in mind after they were no longer present. *Source:* From Courtney et al., 1997.

(remembering the location of three dots on a screen) activated right prefrontal cortex along with regions of the right visual cortex that process spatial location. Studies also demonstrate the existence of two distinct kinds of visual working memory processed in different areas of the prefrontal cortex: memory for location and memory for objects (Courtney et al., 1998). This makes sense in light of research described in Chapter 4 that distinguished between two visual pathways involved in perception, the "what" pathway (involved in identifying what objects are) and the "where" pathway (involved in identifying where they are in space).

In real life, when people briefly hold visual information in mind, they usually need to know both what it is and where it is. A recent study used single-cell recording techniques to monitor the activity of 195 neurons in the prefrontal cortex of monkeys to try to see how working memory integrates information about what and where (Rao et al., 1997). The researchers pre-

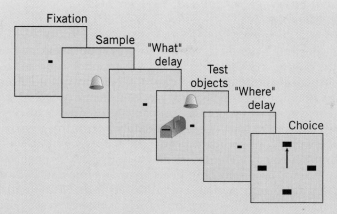

FIGURE 6.9

Procedure for distinguishing what from where. Monkeys were trained to fix their gaze first on a dot in the center of the screen. The experimenters then presented an object (a bell), which disappeared from sight, during which time the monkey had to retain its image in working memory. Next, the bell appeared in a different location along with another object, followed by another delay period. To receive a reward, the monkey had to hold both "what" and "where" information in working memory in order to point its eyes in the direction that the bell had been last. *Source:* From Rao et al., 1997.

sented the monkey with a sequence of working memory tasks. In a typical example, they trained the monkey (using operant conditioning techniques, rewarding it for moving its eyes to particular locations) to fix its gaze on a dot in the middle of a screen (Figure 6.9). Then an image of an object was presented, in this case a bell. The bell then disappeared, replaced again by the dot. During this first delay, the monkey had to remember *what* the object was. A few seconds later, the bell appeared in a new location along with a second object. The objects then disappeared again, replaced once more by the dot. During this delay, the monkey now had to remember *where* the object was, because to receive a reward, it had to move its eyes toward the location in which the bell had last appeared.

The results were quite remarkable. One set of neurons became active only during the first delay, holding information in mind about *what* the object was. Another set of neurons was active only during the second delay, holding information in mind about *where* the object was. A third set of neurons, however, which the researchers dubbed "what-and-where" neurons, were activated during both delays, integrating information about both the identity and location of the bell.

Researchers have thus located specific regions and specific neurons of the prefrontal cortex involved in different kinds of visual and verbal tasks. But what about the central executive? Using fMRI, researchers have recently located a region of the prefrontal cortex that may be involved in "executive" functions such as managing the demands of two simultaneous tasks (D'Esposito et al., 1995). The researchers presented subjects with two tasks that do not involve short-term storage, one verbal (making simple decisions about some words) and the other visual (mentally rotating images). As expected, the verbal task activated left temporal cortex, whereas the visual task activated occipital and parietal cortex. Neither task alone activated prefrontal cortex. However, when subjects had to complete both tasks at the same time, regions of the prefrontal cortex became active, suggesting that prefrontal working memory circuits are indeed activated when people have to make "executive decisions" about how to manage the limited workspace in working memory. ◄

THE RELATION BETWEEN WORKING MEMORY AND LONG-TERM MEMORY

What can we conclude from these various studies about working memory? First, in line with the original concept of STM, working memory appears to be a system for temporarily storing and processing information, a way of holding information in mind long enough to use it. Second, working memory includes a number of limited-capacity component processes, probably a central executive system, a verbal storage system, and at least one and probably two or three visual storage systems (one for location, one for identification of objects, and perhaps another that stores both simultaneously). Third, working memory is better conceived as a conscious workspace for accomplishing goals than as a way-station or gateway to storage in LTM, since information can be stored in LTM without being represented in consciousness and information in LTM is often accessed prior to its representation in working memory (Logie, 1996).

How Distinct Are Working Memory and Long-Term Memory?

Are working memory and LTM really distinct? In one sense, yes. As we have seen, working memory is rapidly accessed and severely limited in capacity. Imagine if our LTM only allowed us to remember seven pieces of verbal information, seven objects or faces, and seven locations! Perhaps the strongest evidence for a distinction between working memory and LTM is neurological. Patients like Jimmie with severe amnesia can often store and manipulate information for momentary use with little trouble. They may be able, for example, to recall seven digits and keep them in mind by rehearsing them. The moment they stop rehearsing, however, they may forget that they were even trying to recall digits, indicating a severe impairment in LTM. Researchers have also observed patients with the opposite problem: severe working memory deficits (such as a memory span of only two digits) but intact LTM (Caplan & Waters, 1990; Shallice & Warrington, 1970).

Interactions of Working Memory and LTM   Working memory and LTM may be distinct, but much of the time they are so intertwined that they can be difficult to distinguish. For example, when people are asked to recall a sequence of words after a brief delay, their performance is better if the words are semantically related (such as *chicken* and *duck*), presumably because they recognize the link between them and can use the memory of one to cue the memory of the other from LTM (Wetherick, 1975). Similarly, words are more easily remembered than nonsense syllables (Hulme et al., 1991). This suggests that working memory involves the conscious activation of knowledge from LTM, since without accessing LTM, the person could not tell the difference between words and nonwords.

Indeed, from a neuroanatomical standpoint, working memory appears to occur as neural networks in the frontal lobes become activated along with and linked to networks in the occipital, temporal, and parietal lobes that represent various words or images. These mental representations of words or images themselves reflect an interaction between current sensory data and stored knowledge from LTM, such as matching a visual pattern with a stored image of a particular person's face. In this sense, working memory in part involves a special kind of activation of information stored in LTM (see Cowan, 1994; Erickson & Kintsch, 1995).

Chunking   Perhaps the best example of the interaction between working memory and long-term memory in daily life is a strategy people use to expand the capacity of their working memory in particular situations (Erickson & Kintsch, 1995). We have spoken thus far of the brain holding a certain number of units of information in consciousness at a time. But what constitutes a unit? A letter? A word? Perhaps an entire sentence or idea?

Consider the working memory capacity of a skilled waiter or waitress. How can a person take the order of eight people without the aid of a notepad, armed only with a *mental* sketchpad and a limited-capacity verbal store? One way people increase their mental workspace in situations such as this is to use knowledge stored in LTM to group information in larger units than single words or digits, a process known as **chunking**. (Yes, the term arose just as it sounds, reflecting the process of sticking memory units into "chunks.") Chunking is essential in everyday life, particularly in cultures that rely upon literacy, because people are constantly called upon to remember telephone numbers, written words, and lists.

Consider the following sequence of letters: DJIBMNYSEWSJSEC. This string would be impossible for most people to hold in working memory, unless they are interested in business and recognize some meaningful chunks: *DJ* for Dow-Jones, *IBM* for International Business Machines, *NYSE* for New York Stock Exchange, *WSJ* for *Wall Street Journal*, and *SEC* for Securities and Exchange Commission. In this example, chunking effectively reduces the number of pieces of information in working memory from 15 to six, by putting two or three customers on each stool. People tend to use chunking most effectively in their areas of expertise, such as waiters who know a menu like the back of their hands. Similarly, knowledge of area codes allows people to store ten or 11 digits at a time, since 202 (the area code for Washington, D.C.) or 212 (the area code for Manhattan in New York City) can become a single chunk rather than three "slots" in verbal working memory.

The value of chunking as a memory aid was demonstrated in a remarkable study done with an undergraduate student of average intelligence called SF (Ericsson & Chase, 1982; see also Ericsson, 1985). The goal was to increase SF's capacity to memorize strings of digits. SF was a long-distance runner, and early in the study he noticed that he could group some of the digits to resemble running times for races. For instance, SF remembered the number 3492 as "3 minutes and 49.2 seconds," close to the world record at that time for running a mile. Not all of the numbers he was asked to memorize lent themselves to running times, however, so he also incorporated ages and dates into his system. Thus, the number 893 became "89.3 years old, a very old person," and 1944 became "near the end of World War II." The next step was to group the running times, ages, and dates into larger "supergroups," consisting of three groups of three- or four- digit numbers (Figure 6.10). Any number SF could not organize meaningfully he remembered by simple

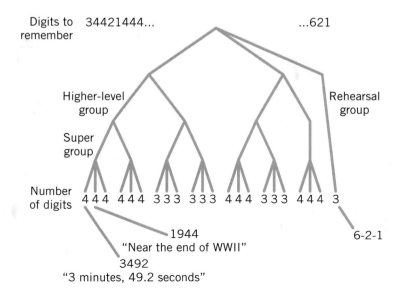

Digits to remember   34421444...   ...621

Higher-level group

Super group

Rehearsal group

Number of digits   4 4 4   4 4 4   3 3 3   3 3 3   4 4 4   3 3 3   4 4 4   3

1944
"Near the end of WWII"   6-2-1
3492
"3 minutes, 49.2 seconds"

FIGURE 6.10
Chunking. An ordinary subject (SF) demonstrates extraordinary control of information in STM. SF grouped sequences of digits into hierarchically organized groups. Except for the group of three digits at the end that he rehearsed mentally, SF coded sequences of digits into groups of three or four digits, which, in turn, he combined into supergroups. These supergroups were then combined into higher-level groups. *Source:* Adapted from Ericsson & Chase, 1982.

rehearsal. SF began the study with unexceptional memory abilities; after about 20 months of practice (one hour a day, three to five days a week), he had increased the number of digits he could remember in one presentation from seven to 80. By calling upon information in LTM, SF was able to increase his temporary memory for digits more than ten times the widely believed upper limit for STM.

INTERIM SUMMARY   Working memory and LTM appear to be distinct from one another, since patients with brain damage can show severe deficits on one but not the other. Working memory appears to occur as frontal lobe neural networks become activated along with and linked to networks in the occipital, temporal, and parietal lobes that represent various words or images. Working memory clearly interacts with LTM systems, as occurs in **chunking**—using knowledge stored in LTM to group information in larger units than single words or digits and hence to expand working memory capacity in specific domains.

VARIETIES OF LONG-TERM MEMORY

Most readers are now probably sufficiently impressed with how much actually went on in their brains the last time they looked up a phone number and remembered it long enough to get to the phone. Now imagine how complex the processes must be that allow people to store 20 or 30 phone numbers and retrieve the right one at the right time. Or consider how we manage to store the images of several hundred faces distinguished by what are actually miniscule anatomical differences (vanity aside, we all look alike to a squirrel); to retrieve the right name with the right face; and to recognize a person's face after many years even when the face has changed with age!

The terrain of LTM is only partly charted. Researchers do not yet agree on precisely how many independent systems constitute LTM. In this section, we explore some of the major types of memory distinguished by researchers and consider whether these different types of memory are really distinct by tracing their paths in the brain. We then examine everyday memory, such as the way people remember to stop off after work to pick up groceries or the way they remember emotional events.

DECLARATIVE AND PROCEDURAL MEMORY

In general, people store two kinds of information, declarative and procedural. **Declarative memory** refers to memory for facts and events, much of which can be consciously stated or "declared" (Squire, 1986). **Procedural memory** refers to "how to" knowledge of procedures or skills.

Declarative Memory

When we think of memory, we usually mean declarative memory: knowledge of facts and events. Remembering a happy memory from the past or retrieving the name and location of the store where we found a particular brand of cat food requires access to declarative memory.

Declarative memory can be semantic or episodic (Tulving, 1972, 1987). **Semantic memory (or generic memory)** refers to general world knowledge or facts, such as the knowledge that summers are hot in Katmandu or that NaCl is the chemical formula for table salt (Tulving, 1972). The term is somewhat misleading because *semantic* implies that general knowledge is stored in words, whereas people know many things about objects, such as their color or smell, that are encoded as sensory representations. (For this reason, some psychologists now refer to it as generic memory.)

Episodic memory consists of memories of particular events, rather than general knowledge. Episodic memory allows people to travel mentally through time, to remember thoughts and feelings (or in memory experiments, word lists) from the recent or distant past or to imagine the future (Wheeler et al., 1997). In everyday life, episodic memory is often *autobiographical*, as when people remember what they did on their 18th birthday or what they ate yesterday. It is also closely linked to semantic memory, since when people experience similar episodes over time (such as 180 days a year in school or hundreds of thousands of interactions with their father), they gradually develop generic memories of what those situations were like (e.g., "I used to love weekends with my father").

Procedural Memory

Declarative memory is the most obvious kind of memory, but another kind of memory is equally important in daily life: procedural memory, or memory for skills. People are often astonished to find that even though they have not skated for 20 years, the skills are reactivated easily, almost as if their use had never been interrupted. When people tie their shoes, put a back-spin on a tennis ball, speak grammatically, or drive a car, they are drawing on procedural memory. Other procedural skills are less obvious, such as reading, which involves a set of complex procedures for decoding strings of letters and words.

EXPLICIT AND IMPLICIT MEMORY

For much of the last century psychologists studied memory by asking subjects to memorize word lists, nonsense syllables, or connections between pairs of words and then asking them to recall them. These tasks all tap **explicit memory**, or conscious recollection. Recently, however, psychologists have recognized another kind of memory: implicit memory (Graf & Schacter, 1987; Roediger, 1990; Schacter, 1992, 1995; Schacter & Buckner, 1998). **Implicit memory** refers to memory that is expressed in behavior but does not require conscious recollection, such as tying a shoe, which people do effortlessly without consciously retrieving the steps involved.

Some psychologists use explicit and implicit memory as synonyms for declarative and procedural memory. Although the terms clearly overlap, the declarative/procedural dichotomy refers more to the *type of knowledge* stored (facts versus skills), whereas the explicit/implicit distinction refers more to the *way this knowledge is retrieved and expressed* (with or without conscious awareness). As we will see, people's knowledge of facts (declarative knowledge) is often expressed without awareness (implicity).

Explicit Memory

Explicit memory involves the conscious retrieval of information. Researchers distinguish between two kinds of explicit retrieval: recall and recognition. **Recall** is the spontaneous conscious recollection of material from LTM, as when a person brings to mind memories of her wedding day or the name of the capital of Egypt. **Recognition** refers to the explicit feeling or remembrance that something currently perceived has been previously encountered or learned (as when a researcher asks a subject to identify a word on a list that was on a different list the previous day) (see Hirshman & Henzler, 1998; Mandler, 1980; Rajaram, 1993).

An expert guitarist like Eric Clapton can improvise much faster than he can consciously think.

Recent PET data suggest that recall and recognition rely on similar networks in the frontal lobes. However, recall requires more "effort" from neural circuits below the cortex (see Cabeza et al., 1997), presumably because it involves actually *generating* the memory rather than simply matching currently perceived information against information stored in memory. The greater difficulty of recall over recognition is illustrated by the **tip-of-the-tongue phenomenon**, the experience of trying to remember a piece of information and knowing that "it's in there" but not being quite able to call it to mind (Brennan et al., 1990; Brown & McNeill, 1966).

Implicit Memory

Implicit memory is evident in skills, conditioned learning, and associative memory (that is, associations between one representation and another). It can be seen in skills such as turning the wheel in the right direction when the car starts to skid in the snow, which skilled drivers in cold regions do before they have even formed the thought "I'm skidding," as well as in responses learned through classical and operant conditioning, such as avoiding a food that was once associated with nausea even when the person has no explicit recollection of the event.

Implicit associative memory emerges in experiments on **priming effects**, in which prior exposure to a stimulus (the *prime*) facilitates or inhibits the processing of new information. Participants in memory experiments show priming effects even when they do not consciously remember being exposed to the prime (Bowers & Schacter, 1990; Tulving et al., 1982). For example, they might be exposed to a list of words that are relatively rarely used in everyday conversation, such as *assassin*. A week later, they may have no idea whether *"assassin"* was on the list (a test of explicit recognition memory), but if asked to fill in the missing letters of a word fragment such as *A–A–IN*, they are more likely to complete it with the word *"assassin"* than control subjects who studied a different list the week earlier. Priming effects appear to rely on activation of information stored in LTM, even though the person is unaware of what has been activated.

INTERIM SUMMARY   Researchers do not yet agree on precisely how many independent systems constitute LTM. Types of memory can be distinguished by *kind of knowledge stored* (facts versus skills) and the *way this knowledge is retrieved and expressed* (with or without conscious awareness). People store two kinds of information, declarative and procedural. **Declarative memory** refers to memory for facts and events. Declarative memory can be **semantic** (general world knowledge or facts) or **episodic** (memories of particular events). **Procedural memory** refers to "how to" knowledge of procedures or skills. Knowledge can be retrieved explicitly or implicitly. **Explicit memory** refers to conscious recollection, whereas **implicit memory** refers to memory that is expressed in behavior. Researchers distinguish between two kinds of explicit retrieval: **recall** (the spontaneous retrieval of material from LTM) and **recognition** (memory for whether something currently perceived has been previously encountered or learned). Implicit memory is evident in skills, conditioned learning, and associative memory (that is, associations between one representation and another).

FROM MIND TO BRAIN

THE NEUROPSYCHOLOGY OF LONG-TERM MEMORY

How distinct are these varieties of LTM? Are researchers simply splitting hairs, or are they really "carving nature at its joints," making distinctions where distinctions truly exist?

Some of the most definitive evidence comes from neurological data demonstrating that different neural pathways underlie distinct kinds of memory (Gabrieli, 1998; Gluck & Myers, 1997; Squire, 1992, 1995). Researchers have begun to track down the neural structures involved in LTM using a combination of methods, including case studies of patients with neurological damage, brain imaging with normal and brain-damaged patients, and experimental studies with animals.

Explicit and Implicit Memory

One of the ways researchers discovered the distinction between implicit and explicit memory was by observing amnesic patients like Jimmie, who have trouble storing and retrieving new declarative information (such as their age or the name or face of their doctor) but show minimal impairment on implicit tasks (Schacter, 1995). Recall the case of H.M. (Chapter 3), who had most of his *medial temporal lobes* (the region in the middle of the temporal lobes, including the hippocampus and amygdala) removed because of uncontrollable seizures (Figure 6.11). Following the operation, H.M. had one of the deepest, purest cases of amnesia ever recorded, leading to the conclusion that medial temporal structures play a central role in the *consolidation* (that is, solidification) of new explicit memories. Despite his inability to store new memories, however, H. M. was able to learn new procedural skills, such as writing words upside down. Each new time H. M. was asked to perform this task his speed improved, but he had no recollection that he had ever performed it before.

Over the last decade, lesion research with monkeys and imaging research with humans have demonstrated that the hippocampus and adjacent anatomically related regions of the cortex are central to the consolidation of

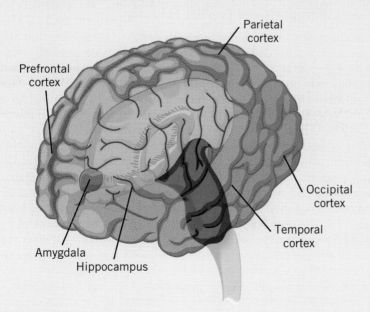

FIGURE 6.11

Anatomy of memory. The medial temporal region (inside the middle of the temporal lobes), particularly the hippocampus, plays a key role in consolidation of explicit, declarative information. The frontal lobes play a more important role in working memory, procedural memory, and aspects of episodic memory, such as dating memories for the time at which they occurred. Posterior regions of the cortex (occipital, parietal, and temporal cortex) are involved in memory just as they are in perception, by creating mental representations.

explicit memories (Eichenbaum, 1997; Squire, 1992, 1995; Squire et al., 1991). The fact that amnesics like H.M. and Jimmie often show normal skill learning and priming effects suggests, however, that the hippocampus is not central to implicit memory.

In daily life, of course, implicit and explicit memory are often intertwined. For example, people learn through conditioning to fear and avoid stimuli that are painful, but they are also frequently aware of the connection between various stimuli or behaviors and their effects. Thus, a child might learn by touching a stove that doing so is punishing (conditioning) but also be able explicitly to recall the connection between the two events: "If I touch the stove, I get an ouchie!"

Neurologically speaking, however, implicit and explicit memory rely on separate mechanisms (Bechara et al., 1995). For example, fear conditioning and avoidance learning require an intact amygdala. In a classical conditioning procedure in which a particular sound (the conditioned stimulus) is paired with an electric shock, patients with an intact hippocampus but a damaged amygdala can explicitly state the connection between the CS and the UCS—they consciously know that the tone is associated with shock—but their nervous system shows no signs of autonomic reactivity or fear when exposed to the CS. They can *know* the connection but not *feel* it. In contrast, patients with an intact amygdala but a damaged hippocampus may have no conscious idea that the CS is associated with electric shock—in fact, they may have no recollection of ever having encountered the stimulus before—but they show a conditioned fear response to it nonetheless.

Subsystems of Implicit and Explicit Memory

Implicit and explicit memory are themselves broad categories that appear to include neurologically distinct subsystems. Studies of patients with brain damage suggest that the two kinds of explicit memory, semantic and episodic, may rely on different neural mechanisms. Patients with damage to the frontal lobes do not generally have trouble retrieving semantic knowledge, but they often show several kinds of deficit in episodic memory (Shimamura, 1995; Wheeler et al., 1995, 1997). They may, for example, have difficulty *dating* episodic memories, such as remembering which of two events in their lifetime came first, or have trouble remembering the order in which words are presented (Swain et al., 1998). Patients with frontal damage are also more likely to have trouble distinguishing true from false memories, often producing detailed and vivid recollections of events that did not occur (Schacter, 1997). Supporting the distinction between semantic and episodic memory, PET studies with neurologically intact subjects have shown greater activation of prefrontal (anterior frontal) regions when people are recalling episodic rather than semantic information (Nyberg, 1998).

Implicit memory is also likely comprised of at least two systems, one involving procedural memory and the other involving the kinds of associative memory processes observed in priming studies. For example, patients with damage to the cortex caused by Alzheimer's disease may have normal procedural memory but impaired performance on priming tasks. In contrast, many patients with Huntington's disease, a fatal, degenerative illness that affects the basal ganglia, show normal priming but impaired procedural learning (Butters et al., 1990). This makes sense since the basal ganglia are involved in learning to produce actions, whereas cortical regions are more involved in forming associations. Recent brain imaging data on normal subjects suggest that procedural learning of skills such as mirror-reading leads to increased activity in some regions and decreased activity in others, as the brain essentially transfers the processing of the task from one network to another as efficiency increases (see Poldrack et al., 1998). For example, after practice at reading words backward in a mirror, people show *decreased* activity in visual pathways but *increased* activity in verbal pathways in the left temporal lobe. This suggests that they are more rapidly moving from the visual task of mentally turning the word around to the linguistic task of understanding its meaning.

INTERIM SUMMARY The hippocampus and adjacent regions of the cortex are central to the consolidation of explicit memories. Amnesics with hippocampal damage often show normal skill learning, conditioning, and priming effects, suggesting that the hippocampus is not central to implicit memory. Neuroanatomical data also support the distinction between episodic and semantic memory. Different kinds of implicit memory appear to have distinct neural pathways as well.

EVERYDAY MEMORY

In designing studies, researchers always have to strike a balance between the often conflicting goals of maximizing internal validity—creating a study whose methods are sound, rigorous, and can lead to unambiguous conclusions—and external or ecological validity—making sure the results generalize to the real world (Chapter 2). Since Ebbinghaus's studies in the late nineteenth century, memory research has tended to emphasize internal validity, measuring subjects' responses as they memorize words, nonsense syllables, and pairs of words, to try to learn about basic memory processes. Increasingly, however, researchers have begun to argue for the importance of studying **everyday memory** as well, that is, memory as it occurs in daily life (Banaji & Crowder, 1989; Ceci & Bronfenbrenner, 1991; Herrmann et al., 1996; Koriat & Goldsmith, 1996; Neisser, 1978; Rogoff & Lave, 1985; Stein et al., 1997).

In the laboratory, the experimenter usually supplies the information to be remembered, the reason to remember it (the experimenter asks the person to), and the occasion to remember it (immediately, a week later, etc.). Often the information to be remembered has little intrinsic meaning, such as isolated words on a list. In contrast, in daily life, people store and retrieve information because they need to for one reason or another, the information is usually meaningful and emotionally significant, and the context for retrieval is sometimes a future point in time that itself must be remembered, as when a person tries to remember to call a friend later in the day. Thus, researchers have begun to study everyday memory in its naturalistic setting—such as people's memory for appointments (Andrzejewski et al., 1991)—as well as to devise ways to bring everyday memory into the laboratory.

Everyday Memory Is Functional Memory

In their daily lives, people typically remember for a purpose, to achieve some goal (Anderson, 1996; Gruneberg et al., 1978; Stein et al., 1997). Memory, like all psychological processes, is *functional*; of all the things we could commit to memory over the course of a day, we tend to remember those that bear on our needs and

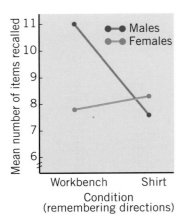

FIGURE 6.12
Gender and everyday memory. The figure shows men and women's memory, following a distracter task, for a list of directions that they thought were either for making a workbench or a shirt. Women recalled slightly more items when they thought they were remembering sewing instructions. Men's performance was dramatically different in the two conditions: Men were much more likely to remember "manly" instructions. *Source:* From Herrmann et al., 1992.

People who survive an event like a powerful earthquake often report that the scene is indelibly etched in memory.

interests. This was demonstrated experimentally in a study in which participants read a passage about the contents of a house under one of two conditions (Anderson & Pitchert, 1978). In one condition, the investigators instructed participants to take the perspective of a potential home buyer; in the other, participants were to read the passage from the point of view of a potential burglar. When asked to recall the passage, participants in the first condition were more likely to remember attributes relevant to buying a house (such as leaks in the roof), whereas participants in the burglar condition were more likely to recall valuable items that could be easily stolen, such as television sets!

Similar findings emerged in a set of studies that examined whether men and women would have better recall for stereotypically masculine and feminine memory tasks (Herrmann et al., 1992). In one study, the investigators asked participants to remember a shopping list and a list of travel directions. As predicted, women's memory was better for the shopping list, whereas men had better memory for the directions.

So does this mean that women are born to shop and men to navigate? A second study suggested otherwise. This time, some participants received a "grocery list" to remember whereas others received a "hardware list." Additionally, some received directions on "how to make a shirt" whereas others received directions on "how to make a workbench." In reality, the grocery and hardware lists were identical, as were the two lists of "directions." For example, the shopping list included items such as *brush, oil, chips, nuts,* and *gum* that could just as easily be interpreted as goods at a grocery store as hardware items. The "directions" were so general that they could refer to almost anything (e.g., "First, you rearrange the pieces into different groups. Of course, one pile may be sufficient . . .").

As predicted, women were more likely to remember what women are "supposed" to remember. The biases in recall for men were particularly strong (Figure 6.12). Apparently, "real men" do not make shirts. These findings demonstrate the importance of noncognitive factors such as motivation and interest in everyday memory: What men define as not relevant, not interesting, or threatening to their masculinity does not make a lasting impression on their memory.

Emotional Memory

Another characteristic of memory in everyday life is its emotional significance. One of the major functions of emotion is to draw attention, thought, and memory to objects and events that are relevant to our goals (Chapter 11). When people recall events in their lives, they typically recall, and in some cases reexperience, many of the emotions they felt at the time. In fact, people's most vivid memories tend to be emotional memories (Reisberg & Heuer, 1995).

Researchers have known about two aspects of the relation between emotion and memory for many years. The first is that emotionally arousing events are more easily recalled, but only up to a point; above that optimal level of arousal, strong feelings interfere with storing the information in a form that will later be retrievable (see McGaugh, 1989). This makes evolutionary sense, since events that lead to minimal arousal are not likely to be very significant, whereas events that are extremely frightening or painful can be overwhelming, as people either "freeze" or spend their mental energy trying to escape. Second, emotional arousal tends to lead to a narrowing of cognitive focus, as the person turns attention to the most relevant features of the environment associated with the memory (Easterbrook, 1959). Thus, when people recall emotionally significant incidents, they are likely to have highly accurate recollections of central aspects of the memory, such as who did what to whom, but less complete and accurate recall of minor details (Burke et al., 1992; Reisberg & Heuer, 1995).

Recent research suggests that emotional memories are qualitatively distinct from more neutral ones and rely on different neural mechanisms (Cahill et al., 1994). The amygdala plays a crucial role in emotion, and damage to the amygdala leads to impaired ability to associate emotions with stimuli or behaviors (Hugdahl et al., 1995). Drugs injected into the amygdala in rats that block the action of neurotransmitters involved in fear reactions also impair emotional memory (Gold, 1995; McGaugh, 1997).

Prospective Memory

Most studies of memory have examined **retrospective memory**, that is, memory for things from the past, such as a list of words encountered 20 minutes earlier. In everyday life, an equally important kind of memory is **prospective memory**, or memory for things that need to be done in the future, such as picking up some items at the store after work (Brandimonte et al., 1996; Einstein & McDaniel, 1990; McDaniel et al., 1998). Prospective memory has at least two components: remembering *to* remember ("be sure to stop at the store after work") and remembering *what* to remember (e.g., a loaf of bread and a sponge). In other words, prospective memory requires memory of *intent* as well as *content* (Kvavilashvili, 1987; Marsh et al., 1998).

Prospective Memory and Heightened Activation   Experimental studies suggest that intending to carry out certain acts in the future leads to their heightened activation in LTM. In one set of studies, researchers instructed participants to read two passages describing a simple set of actions (called a "script") such as setting the table, which included four elements (e.g., lighting the candles). In the prospective memory condition, they were told that they would later have to carry out the script, whereas in a simple memory condition they were told they would later watch the experimenter perform the scripted behaviors and check for mistakes (Goschke & Kuhl, 1993, 1997). Next, the investigators presented participants with a list of words that included words such as *candles* that were part of the scripts they had just been instructed to remember; their task was to press a key on the computer as soon as they knew whether the word had or had not been presented earlier.

The investigators hypothesized that forming a prospective memory (in this case, to carry out the script) should lead to heightened activation of the contents of the script (such as lighting the candles). They tested the hypothesis by seeing whether the two conditions would differ in the time participants took to recognize words from the script, on the assumption that words that are at a higher level of activation should be recognized more quickly. In fact, that is precisely what they found: When participants were told that they would have to execute the script, they recognized the words faster than when they were simply instructed to remember it. Similar findings emerged using an implicit memory task, completion of word fragments (e.g., *T-BL-* for *table*): When participants formed a prospective memory, they were more likely to complete the fragments with words from the script than when they simply tried to remember the items. These findings make adaptive sense, since keeping to-be-remembered information at a high level of activation increases the likelihood that it will be triggered at the appropriate time.

Is Prospective Memory a Distinct Kind of Memory?   Although prospective memory is probably not itself a memory "system" with its own properties, it does have elements that distinguish it from other kinds of memory (see Ellis, 1997). One is its heavy emphasis on time. Part of remembering an intention is remembering *when* to remember it—that is, getting the attention to spring to mind at the right time and in the right place—such as at a specific time (e.g., right after work or at ten o'clock) or an interval of time (tonight, tomorrow, sometime over the next few days).

Another unique feature of remembered intentions is that the person has to remember whether they have been performed so they can be "shut off." Personally, I seem to have a specific deficit with this aspect of prospective memory when I rent movies: I often remember at the rental store that I want to see a particular movie, rent it, and then realize in the first five minutes that I had fulfilled the same intention a week ago! In my case, this reflects poor LTM for movie names, which I rarely connect with plots unless they are so obvious that I cannot forget them (such as *Titanic*, which I think I have seen).

INTERIM SUMMARY   In recent years researchers have begun to focus on **everyday memory**, memory as it occurs in daily life. Everyday memory is *functional*, focused on remembering information that is meaningful, particularly information that is *emotionally* significant. Up to a point, emotional arousal generally enhances memory, through the action of hormones and neurotransmitters that make emotional memories more vivid and easily remembered. Another kind of everyday memory is **prospective memory**, memory for things that need to be done in the future.

ENCODING AND ORGANIZATION OF LONG-TERM MEMORY

We have now completed our tour of the varieties of memory. But how does information find its way into LTM in the first place? And how is information organized in the mind so that it can be readily retrieved? In this section we explore these two questions. We focus on the storage and organization of declarative knowledge, since it has received the most empirical attention.

ENCODING

For information to be retrievable from memory, it must be **encoded**, or cast into a representational form, or "code," that can be readily accessed. The manner of encoding—how, how much, and when the person tries to learn new information—has a substantial influence on its *accessibility* (ability to be retrieved, or *accessed*).

Levels of Processing

Anyone who has ever crammed for a test knows that rehearsal is important for storing information in LTM. As noted earlier, however, the simple, repetitive rehearsal that maintains information momentarily in working memory is not optimal for LTM. A more effective strategy is usually to attend to the *meaning* of the stimulus and form mental connections between it and previously stored information. Some encoding is deliberate, such as studying for an exam, learning lines for a play, or trying to remember a joke. However, much of the time encoding simply occurs as a byproduct of thought and perception, which is why people can remember incidents that happened to them ten years ago even though they were not trying to commit them to memory.

Deep and Shallow Processing   The degree to which information is elaborated, reflected upon, and processed in a meaningful way during memory storage is referred to as the depth or **level of processing** (Craik & Lockhart, 1972; Lockhart & Craik, 1990). Information may be processed at a shallow, structural level (focusing on physical characteristics of the stimulus); at a somewhat deeper, phonemic level (focusing on simple characteristics of the language used to describe it); or at the deepest, semantic level (focusing on the meaning of the stimulus). For example, at a shallow, structural level, a person may walk by a restaurant and notice the typeface and colors of its sign. At a phonemic level, she may read the sign to herself and notice that it sounds Spanish. Processing material deeply, in contrast, means paying attention to its meaning or significance, noticing, for instance, that this is the restaurant a friend has been recommending for months.

Different levels of processing activate different neural circuits. As one might guess, encoding that occurs as people make judgments about the meaning of words (such as whether they are concrete or abstract) leads to greater activation of the left temporal cortex, which is involved in language comprehension, than attending to qualities such as whether they are printed in upper- or lowercase letters (Gabrieli et al., 1996). *Deliberate* use of strategies to remember (such as remembering to buy bread and bottled water by thinking of a prisoner who is only fed bread and water) activates regions of the prefrontal cortex involved in other executive functions such as manipulating information in working memory (Kapur et al., 1996).

Encoding Specificity   Advocates of depth-of-processing theory originally thought that deeper processing is always better. Although this is *generally* true, subsequent research has shown that the best encoding strategy depends on what the person later needs to retrieve (see Anderson, 1995). If a person is asked to recall shallow information (such as whether a word was originally presented in capital letters), shallow encoding actually tends to be more useful. The fact that ease of retrieval depends on the match between the way information is encoded and later retrieved is known as the **encoding specificity principle** (Tulving & Thompson, 1973). For example, a student who studies for a multiple-choice test by memorizing definitions and details without trying to understand the underlying concepts may be in much more trouble if the professor decides to include an essay question, since the student has encoded the information at too shallow a level.

Why does the match between encoding and retrieval influence the ease with which people can access information from memory? According to several theorists, memory is not really a process distinct from perception and thought; rather, it is a byproduct of the normal processes of perceiving and thinking, which automatically lay down traces of an experience as it is occurring. When people remember, they simply reactivate the same neural networks that processed the information in the first place (Crowder, 1993; Lockhart & Craik, 1990). If the circumstances at encoding and retrieval are similar, the memory is more easily retrieved because more of the neural network that represents it is activated. To put it another way, a new thought, feeling, or perception is like a hiker who has to create a new trail through the woods. Each time another traveler takes that path, that is, each time a similar event occurs, the trail becomes more defined and easier to locate.

Context and Retrieval   According to the encoding specificity principle, the *contexts* in which people encode and retrieve information can also affect the ease of retrieval. One study presented scuba divers with different lists of words, some while the divers were under water and others while they were above (Godden & Baddeley, 1975). The divers had better recall for lists they had encoded under water when they were under water at retrieval; conversely, lists encoded above water were better recalled above water. Similarly, recalling material from lectures is easier if students are sitting in the same lecture room when they take the examination. The same may also be true of the emotional state at encoding and re-

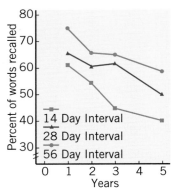

FIGURE 6.13

Impact of spacing on memory retention over five years. As can be seen, longer intervals between rehearsal sessions for English–foreign language word pairs predicted higher long-term retention of the information one, two, three, and five years after the last training session. *Source:* From Bahrick et al., 1993.

trieval, a phenomenon called *state-dependent memory:* Being in a similar mood at encoding and retrieval (e.g., angry while learning a word list and angry while trying to remember it) can facilitate memory, as long as the emotional state is not so intense that it inhibits memory in general (see Bower, 1981; Kenealy, 1997). Having the same context during encoding and retrieval facilitates recall because the context provides **retrieval cues**, stimuli or thoughts that can be used to facilitate recollection.

Spacing

Another encoding variable that influences memory is of particular importance in educational settings: the interval between study sessions. Students intuitively know that if they cram the night before a test, the information is likely to be available to them when they need it the next day. They also tend to believe that *massed* rehearsal (that is, studying in one long session or several times over a short interval, such as a day) is more effective than *spaced,* or *distributed,* rehearsal over longer intervals (Zechmeister & Shaughnessy, 1980). But is this strategy really optimal for long-term retention of the information?

In fact, it is not (Bruce & Bahrick, 1992; Dempster, 1996; Ebbinghaus, 1885). Massed rehearsal *seems* superior because it makes initial acquisition of memory slightly easier, since the material is at a heightened state of activation in a massed practice session. Over the long run, however, research on the **spacing effect**—the superiority of memory for information rehearsed over longer intervals—demonstrates that spacing study sessions over longer intervals tends to double long-term retention of information. In one study, the Bahrick family (which includes four psychologists—a frightening thought!) tested the long-term effects of spaced rehearsal by teaching themselves 300 pairs of words: an English word and an unfamiliar foreign word with the same meaning. Memory was tested at one, two, three, or five years after the conclusion of these practice sessions. The major finding was that, over a five-year period, 13 training sessions at intervals of 56 days apart produced memory retention rates comparable to 26 sessions spaced at 14-day intervals (Figure 6.13).

These and related findings have important implications for students and teachers (Bruce & Bahrick, 1992; Dempster, 1996; Rea & Modigliani, 1988). Students who want to remember information for more than a day or two after an exam should space their studying over time and avoid cramming. (Medical students, law students, and others who intend to practice a profession based on their coursework should be particularly wary of all-nighters.) Much as students might protest, cumulative exams over the course of a semester are superior to exams that only test the material that immediately preceded them because they require students to relearn material at long intervals and because tests themselves constitute learning sessions in which memory is retrieved and reinforced. In fact, research on spacing is part of what led me to include both interim summaries and a general summary at the end of each chapter, since learning occurs best with a combination of immediate reviews and spaced rehearsal.

Representational Modes and Encoding

The ability to retrieve information from LTM also depends on the modes used to encode it. In general, the more ways a memory can be encoded, the greater the likelihood that it will be accessible for later retrieval. Storing a memory in multiple representational modes—such as words, images, and sounds—provides more retrieval cues to bring it back to mind (see Paivio, 1991). For instance, many people remember phone numbers not only by memorizing the digits but also by forming a mental map of the buttons they need to push and a motoric (procedural) representation of the pattern of buttons to push that becomes automatic and is expressed implicitly. When pushing the buttons, they may even be alerted that they have dialed the wrong number by hearing a sound pattern that does not match the expected pattern, suggesting auditory storage as well.

INTERIM SUMMARY   For information to be retrievable from memory, it must be **encoded**, or cast into a representational form that can be readily accessed from memory. The degree to which information is elaborated, reflected upon, and processed in a meaningful way during memory storage is referred to as the depth or **level of processing**. Although deeper processing tends to be more useful for storing information for the long term, ease of retrieval depends on the match between the way information is encoded and later retrieved, a phenomenon known as the **encoding specificity principle**. Similar contexts during encoding and retrieval provide **retrieval cues**—stimuli or thoughts that can be used to facilitate recollection. Aside from level of processing, two other variables related to encoding that influence accessibility of memory are the **spacing** of study sessions and the use of multiple and redundant representational modes

MNEMONIC DEVICES

The principles of encoding we have just been describing help explain the utility of many **mnemonic devices**—systematic strategies for remembering information (named after the Greek word *mneme*, which means "memory"). People can use external aids (such as note taking or asking someone else) to enhance their memory, or they can rely on internal aids, such as rehearsal and various mnemonic devices (Harris, 1980; Intons-Peterson & Fournier, 1986). Most mnemonic devices draw on the principle that the more retrieval cues that can be created, and the more vivid these cues are, the better memory is likely to be.

Method of Loci

One mnemonic strategy is the **method of loci**, which uses visual imagery as a memory aid. Cicero attributed this technique to the ancient Greek poet Simonides, who was attending a banquet when he was reportedly summoned by the gods from the banquet hall to receive a message. In his absence, the roof collapsed, killing everyone. The bodies were mangled beyond recognition, but Simonides was able to identify the guests by their physical placement around the banquet table. He thus realized that images could be remembered by fitting them into an orderly arrangement of locations (Bower, 1970).

To use the method of loci, you must first decide on a series of "snapshot" mental images of locations with which you are very familiar. For instance, locations in your bedroom might be your pillow, your closet, the top of your dresser, and under the bed. Now, suppose that you need to do the following errands: pick up vitamin C pills, buy milk, return a book to the library, and make plans with one of your friends for the weekend. You can remember these items by visualizing each in one of your loci, making the image as vivid as possible to maximize the likelihood of retrieving it. Thus, you might picture the vitamin C pills spilled all over your pillow, a bottle of milk poured over the best outfit in your closet, the book lying on top of your dresser, and your friend hiding under your bed until Friday night. Often, the more ridiculous the image, the easier it is to remember. While you are out doing your errands, you can mentally flip through your imagined loci to bring back the mental images.

Peg Method

A second mnemonic technique, called the **peg method**, uses imagery as well as an auditory cue, rhyming. Here, people "hang" information to be remembered on mental pegs such as numbers. For example, you might create a number rhyme that you cannot possibly forget, such as "One is a bun, two is a shoe, three is a tree, four is a door," and so forth. Note that each number in this rhyme is associated with an object that can easily be visualized.

Like the various locations in the method-of-loci approach, these images then act as mental pegs with which you can associate the items that you need to remember. To return to the list of errands, you might hang the first item, vitamin C, on the "one is a bun" image by visualizing a hamburger bun full of vitamin C pills. You might likewise visualize a shoe full of milk, your library book caught in the branches of a tree, and your friend coming to the door on the way out for the evening.

SQ3R Method

The method of loci and the peg method can lead to dramatic increases in memory performance, but people who learn them in memory improvement courses tend to stop using them after a few months, in part because the most effective mnemonic strategies tend to apply to a specific task or situation (Herrmann et al., 1988). A task-specific strategy developed to help students remember the information they read in textbooks is called the **SQ3R method**, for the five steps involved in the method: survey, question, read, recite, and review (Martin, 1985; Robinson, 1961). The SQ3R method fosters active rather than passive learning while reading. The first step is to *survey*, or glance through the organization of the chapter, looking at headings and the summary, so that you know the gist of it and therefore organize the material more efficiently as you encode. *Questioning* refers to turning the headings into questions; this orients you to the content of each section and makes reading more interesting. For example, for the subheading Long-Term Memory Systems, you might ask yourself, "What evidence could demonstrate the existence of separate memory systems? Could patients with different brain lesions have one kind of LTM intact and another disrupted?" The third step is to *read*, trying to find answers to the questions that you posed. Fourth, *recite* the answers to these questions as well as other relevant information in each section before going on to the next section. Finally, when you have finished the chapter, *review* the material by recalling your questions and answers and actively thinking about the material, relating the new material you have learned to things that you know about and that interest you. (The only catch is that you may need a mnemonic to help you remember the acronym SQ3R.)

INTERIM SUMMARY   **Mnemonic devices** are systematic strategies for remembering information. The **method of loci** associates new information with a visual image of a familiar place; the **peg method** associates new information with a rhyme that also helps create a visual image; and the **SQ3R method** helps students study textbook material efficiently by inducing them to survey, question, read, recite, and review.

NETWORKS OF ASSOCIATION

One of the reasons mnemonics can be effective is that they connect new information with information already stored and organized in memory. This makes the new information easier to access because a "trail" blazed in the neural woods by prior knowledge can be more easily spotted than a new, barely worn path. As William James proposed over a century ago (1890, p. 662, italics deleted):

> The more other facts a fact is associated with in the mind, the better possession of it our memory retains. Each of its associates becomes a hook to which

it hangs, a means to fish it up by when sunk beneath the surface. Together, they form a network of attachments by which it is woven into the entire tissue of our thought. The "secret of a good memory" is thus the secret of forming diverse and multiple associations with every fact we care to retain.

James's comments bring us back once again to the concept of *association*, which, as we saw in Chapter 5, is central to many accounts of learning. Associations are crucial to remembering because the pieces of information stored in memory form **networks of association**, clusters of interconnected information. For example, for most people the word *dog* is associatively linked to characteristics such as barking and fetching (Figure 6.14). It is also associated, though less strongly, with *cat* because cats and dogs are both household pets. The word or image of a dog is also linked to more idiosyncratic personal associations, such as an episodic memory of being bitten by a dog in childhood.

Each piece of information along a network is called a **node**. Nodes may be thoughts, images, concepts, propositions, smells, tastes, memories, emotions, or any other piece of information. One node may have connections to many other nodes, leading to tremendously complex networks of association. As we will see in Chapter 7, a node may itself really be nothing more than a set of neurons distributed throughout the brain that, when they fire together, represent an object or category such as *dog*, integrating visual, tactile, auditory, verbal, and other information stored in memory.

To search through memory, then, means to go from node to node until locating the right information. In this sense, nodes are like cities, which are connected to each other (associated) by roads (Reisberg, 1997). Not all associations are equally strong; *dog* is more strongly connected to *barks* than to *cat* or *animal*. To return to the cities analogy, some cities are connected by superhighways, which facilitate rapid travel between them, whereas others are connected only by slow, winding country roads. Other cities have no direct links between them at all, which means that travel between them requires an intermediate link. The same is true of associative networks: In Figure 6.14, *cat* is not directly associated to *cold weather*, but it is through the intermediate link of *my cat Mittens*, which is semantically related to *wear mittens*, which is in turn linked to the *cold weather* node.

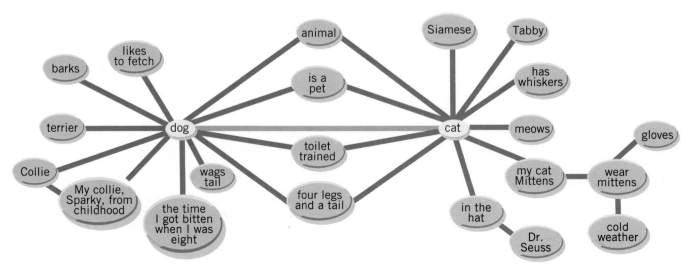

FIGURE 6.14

Networks of association. Long-term knowledge is stored in networks of association, ideas that are mentally connected with one another other by repeatedly occurring together.

From a neuropsychological perspective, if two nodes without a direct link become increasingly associated through experience, a "road" between them is built, and if the association continues to grow, that road will be "widened" to ensure rapid neural transit between one and the other. If, on the other hand, a neural highway between two nodes falls into disuse because the two objects or events stop occurring together (such as the link between the word *girlfriend* and a particular girlfriend months after the relationship has ended and a new woman has stepped into that role), the highway will fall into disrepair and be less easily traveled. The old road will not likely disappear completely: Occasionally a traveler may wander off the main road down the old highway, as when a person accidentally calls his new girlfriend by his old girlfriend's name.

Spreading Activation

One theory that attempts to explain the workings of networks of association is called spreading activation (Collins & Loftus, 1975; Collins & Quillian, 1969). According to **spreading activation theory,** activating one node in a network triggers activation in closely related nodes. In other words, presenting a stimulus that leads to firing in the neural circuits that represent that stimulus spreads activation, or energy, to related information stored in memory.

Spreading activation does not always start with a stimulus such as a spoken word. Activation may also begin with a thought, fantasy, or wish, which in turn activates other nodes. For example, a psychotherapy patient trying to decide whether to divorce his wife found the song "Reunited and It Feels So Good" coming to mind on days when he leaned toward reconciliation. On days when he was contemplating divorce, however, he found himself inadvertently singing a different tune, "Fifty Ways to Leave Your Lover."

Considerable research supports the theory of spreading activation. For example, in one study the experimenters presented participants with word pairs to learn, including the pair "*ocean–moon*" (see Nisbett & Wilson, 1977). Later, when asked to name a laundry detergent, participants in this condition were more likely to respond with *Tide* than control subjects, who had been exposed to a different list of word pairs. (For readers outside North America, Tide is a popular American laundry detergent.) The researchers offered an intriguing explanation (Figure 6.15): The network of associations that includes *ocean* and *moon* also includes *tide*. Priming with *ocean–moon* thus activated other nodes on the network, spreading activation to *tide*, which was associated with another network of associations (laundry detergents).

According to many contemporary models, each time a thought or image is

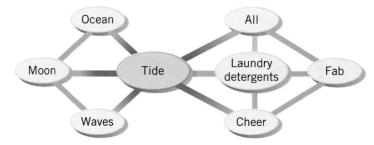

Figure 6.15

Spreading activation. Tide stands at the intersection of two activated networks of association and is thus doubly activated. In contrast, other brands only receive activation from one network. (This experiment, of course, only works in North America and other places where Tide has a substantial market share. I once tried demonstrating it in a lecture in Australia, where the only thing I demonstrated was my ethnocentrism.)

perceived, primed, or retrieved from memory, the level of activation of the neural networks that represent it increases. This essentially means that two kinds of information are likely to be at a high state of activation at any given moment: *recently activated* information (such as a news story seen a moment ago on television) and *frequently activated* information (such as a physician's knowledge about disease). Thus, a person who has just seen a documentary on cancer is likely to identify the word *leukemia* faster than someone who tuned in to a different channel; a doctor is similarly likely to identify the word quickly because *leukemia* is at a chronically higher state of activation.

Hierarchical Organization of Information

Although activating a *dog* node can trigger some idiosyncratic thoughts and memories, networks of association are far from haphazard jumbles of information. Efficient retrieval requires some degree of organization of information so that the mind can find its way through dense networks of neural trails. Some researchers have compared LTM to a filing cabinet, in which important information is kept toward the front of the files and less important information is relegated to the back of our mental archives, or to a box in the attic.

The filing cabinet metaphor also suggests that some information is filed **hierarchically:** Broad categories are composed of narrower subcategories, which in turn consist of even more specific categories. For example, a person could store information about *animals* under the subcategories *pets, farm animals,* and *wild animals* (Figure 6.16). Under *farm animals* are *cows, horses,* and *chickens.* At each level of the hierarchy, each node will have features associated with it (such as knowledge that chickens squawk and lay eggs) as well as other associations to it (such as roasted chicken, which is associated with being tasty).

Hierarchical storage is generally quite efficient, but it can occasionally lead to errors. For instance, when asked, "Which is farther north, Seattle or Montreal?" most people say Montreal (Stevens & Coupe, 1978). In fact, Seattle is farther north. People mistakenly assume that Montreal is north of Seattle because they go to their general level of knowledge about Canada and the United States and remember that Canada is north of the United States. In reality, some parts of the United States are farther north than many parts of Canada. A better strategy in this case

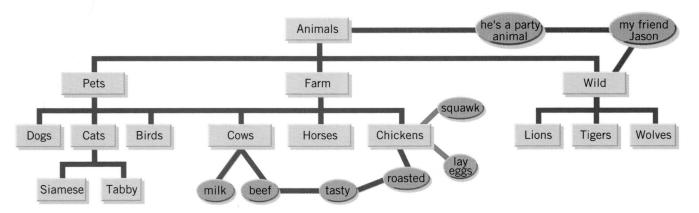

FIGURE 6.16

Hierarchical organization of information in LTM. Information about animals may be hierarchically organized, although nodes at each level of the network have their own associations. Blue lines indicate hierarchical connections. Green lines indicate features closely associated with nodes at each level that are not hierarchically organized. Purple lines indicate simple associative connections (such as visual, gustatory, or olfactory representations of baked chicken associated with chickens).

would be to visualize a map of North America and scan it for Seattle and Montreal.

INTERIM SUMMARY   Knowledge stored in memory forms **networks of association—** clusters of interconnected information. Each piece of information along a network is called a **node**. According to **spreading activation theory,** activating one node in a network triggers activation in closely related nodes. Some parts of networks are organized **hierarchically**, with broad categories composed of narrower subcategories, which in turn consist of even more specific categories.

SCHEMAS

▶ *Now is the time for all good men to to come to the aid of their countrymen.*

The extra "to" at the beginning of the third line is easily overlooked because of the schema-based expectation that it is not there. Students often fail to notice typographical errors in their papers for the same reason.

The models of associative networks and spreading activation we have been discussing go a long way toward describing the organization of memory, but they have limits. For example, psychologists have not yet agreed on how to represent propositions like "The dog chased the cat" using network models, since if *dog* and *cat* are nodes, how is the link between them (*chased*) represented? Further, as we will see in the next chapter, activation of one node can actually either increase or *inhibit* activation of associated nodes, as when a person identifies an approaching animal as a dog and not a wolf and hence "shuts off" the *wolf* node.

Psychologists have argued for a century about the adequacy of principles of association in explaining memory (Bahrick, 1985). Some have argued that we do not associate isolated bits of information with each other but instead store and remember the *gist* of facts and events. They note that when people remember passages of prose rather than single words or word pairs, they typically remember the general meaning of the passage rather than a verbatim account.

According to this view, when confronted with a novel event, people match it against *schemas* stored in memory. As discussed in Chapter 4, schemas are patterns of thought, or organized knowledge structures, that render the environment relatively predictable. When students walk into a classroom on the first day of class and a person resembling a professor begins to lecture, they listen and take notes in a routine fashion. They are not surprised that one person has assumed control of the situation and begun talking because they have a schema for events that normally transpire in a classroom.

Proponents of schema theories argue that memory is an active process of *reconstruction* of the past. Remembering means combining bits and pieces of what we once perceived with general knowledge that helps us fill in the gaps. In this view, memory is not like taking snapshots of an event; it is more like *taking notes*.

Consider the following passage (Rumelhart, 1980, p. 43)

> Business had been slow since the oil crisis. Nobody seemed to want anything really elegant anymore. Suddenly the door opened and a well-dressed man entered the showroom floor. John put on his friendliest and most sincere expression and walked toward the man.

Most readers gradually realize that this paragraph is about selling cars through a process of generating and rejecting or confirming hypotheses. The first sentence suggests that the passage is somehow related to the economy and that it probably has something to do with the auto or gas industry. The second sentence narrows the choices: The word "elegant" relates to cars but not generally to gas stations. The phrase "showroom floor" in the third sentence supports the hypothesis that the passage relates to the auto industry. Finally, John's reaction in the fourth sentence confirms this interpretation because our general knowledge structures, that is, schemas, about car salesmen often include "insincere."

Schemas affect the way people remember in two ways: by influencing the information they encode and by shaping the way they reconstruct data that they have already stored (Rumelhart, 1980; Rumelhart & Ortony, 1977).

Schemas and Encoding

Schemas influence the way people initially understand the meaning of an event and thus the manner in which they encode it in LTM. Harry Triandis (1994) relates an account of two Englishmen engaged in a friendly game of tennis in nineteenth-century China. The two were sweating and panting under the hot August sun. As they finished their final set, a Chinese friend sympathetically asked, "Could you not get two servants to do this for you?" Operating from a different set of schemas, their Chinese friend encoded this event rather differently than would an audience at Wimbledon.

A brief experiment illustrates the influence of schemas on encoding (Bransford & Johnson, 1977, p. 400):

> The procedure is actually quite simple. First you arrange things into different groups. Of course, one pile may be sufficient depending on how much there is to do. If you have to go somewhere else due to lack of facilities, that is the next step, otherwise you are pretty well set. It is important not to overdo things. That is, it is better to do too few things at once than too many. . . . After the procedure is completed, one arranges the materials into different groups again. Then they can be put into their appropriate places. Eventually they will be used once more and the whole cycle will then have to be repeated.

Most readers have difficulty comprehending this paragraph, let alone remembering its component parts five minutes later. But try rereading the passage with the title, "Washing Clothes." The title activates a schema that organizes the information and allows it to be stored efficiently, so that its parts can later be more readily retrieved.

Schemas and Retrieval

Titling a paragraph also aids memory because of the influence of schemas on retrieval. Schemas not only provide hooks on which to hang information during encoding, but they also provide hooks for fishing information out of LTM. Many schemas have "slots" for particular kinds of information (Minsky, 1975). A person shopping for stereo equipment who is trying to recall the various compact disk players she saw that day is likely to remember the names Sony and Pioneer but not Frank Sylvester (the salesman at one of the stores). Unlike Sony, Frank Sylvester does not fit into the slot "brand names of compact disk players." The slots in schemas often have **default values,** or standard answers, that fill in missing information the person did not initially notice or bother to store. When asked if the cover of this book gives the author's name, you are likely to report that it does (default value = *yes*) even if you never really noticed because the author's name normally appears on a book cover. In fact, people are generally unable to tell which pieces of information in a memory are truly remembered and which reflect the operation of default values.

One classic study demonstrated the reconstructive role of schemas using a visual task (Brewer & Treyens, 1981). The experimenter instructed college student subjects to wait (one at a time) in a "graduate student's office" similar to the one depicted in Figure 6.17 while he excused himself to check on something. The experimenter returned in 35 seconds and led the student to a different room. There, he asked the subject either to write down a description of the graduate student's

FIGURE 6.17
Influence of schemas on memory. Subjects asked to recall this graduate student's office frequently remembered many items that actually were not in it but were in their office schemas. *Source:* From Brewer & Treyens, 1981.

office or to draw a picture of it, including as many objects as could be recalled. The room contained a number of objects (e.g., bookshelves, coffee pot, desk) that would fit most subjects' schema of a graduate student's office. Several objects, however, were conspicuous—or rather, inconspicuous—in their absence, such as a filing cabinet, a coffee cup, books on the shelves, a window, pens and pencils, and curtains. Many subjects assumed the presence of these default items, however, and "remembered" seeing them even though they had not actually been present.

Without schemas, life would seem like one random event after another, and efficient memory would be impossible. Yet as the research just described shows, schemas can lead people to misclassify information, to believe they have seen what they really have not seen, and to fail to notice things that might be important.

INTERIM SUMMARY   Another way psychologists describe the organization of LTM is in terms of *schemas*, organized knowledge about a particular domain. Proponents of schema theories argue that memory involves *reconstruction* of the past, by combining knowledge of what we once perceived with general knowledge that helps fill in the gaps. Schemas influence both the way information is encoded and the way it is retrieved.

A GLOBAL VISTA

CROSS-CULTURAL VARIATION IN MEMORY— BETTER, WORSE, OR JUST DIFFERENT?

The account of memory presented thus far is based almost exclusively on studies of subjects in Western, technologically advanced societies. Do the general principles of memory from these samples apply cross culturally, or do memory and thought differ depending on the cultural, historical, and ecological context?

Memory and Adaptation

One way to find out how much memory differs across cultures is to run versions of the same experiments in multiple cultures. Studies comparing memory processes across cultures (such as large industrial versus small tribal societies) have often produced inconsistent findings, largely because people tend to do better on tasks that resemble the demands of their everyday lives (see Cole et al., 1968; Doob, 1964). Members of hunter-gatherer societies who must remember the location of edible berries tend to be very skilled at doing so, just as people who need to remember phone numbers tend to have superior recall for seemingly meaningless strings of digits.

Cultures are not, however, homogeneous, nor are the ecological or environmental demands on different subgroups within a culture. Just as men and women in the West appear to differ in their capacity for remembering instructions for driving versus sewing, the same is likely to be true of men and women in hunter-gatherer societies, who begin to specialize in childhood in either tracking animals or locating patches of edible vegetation.

One study compared rural Zambian women with urban Zambian schoolboys in their ability to recall information relevant to *time* from a story (Deregowski, 1970). The daily life of rural Zambian women is regulated primarily by cycles of night and day and is free of references to time. In contrast, the day of a Zambian schoolboy is highly time structured, as in the West. The experimenters found no differences between the two groups in their ability to recall information unrelated to time. However, the schoolboys were significantly more likely to recall information about time. Across and within cultures, people tend to remember information that matters to them, and they organize information in memory to match the demands of their environment.

A particularly important influence on memory that varies across cultures is literacy. On the one hand, literacy increases the role played by verbal representations, since it converts many visual experiences to verbal experi-

In preliterate societies, oral tradition shapes the way people think and serves as an archive for collective memories.

ences. In preliterate societies, the human brain is the only memory device on which people can rely, and collective knowledge is preserved primarily through oral history and tradition, such as story telling. Literate societies possess a number of ways of storing information that can extend the limits of memory, from magazines and textbooks to simple devices such as lists that can expand memory capacity exponentially (Goody, 1977).

Cultural Models

Throughout this chapter, we have described memory as if it occurs in isolated information processors (see Cole, 1975; Middleton & Edwards, 1990). However, shared cultural concepts—what anthropologists call **cultural models**—organize knowledge and hence shape the way people think and remember in their daily lives (D'Andrade, 1992; Mathews & Moore, in press; Strauss & Quinn, 1997). Some aspects of these models are taught explicitly or through guided participation with adults (Rogoff, 1995). Others arise through experience, often implicitly, as when children learn to associate particular forms of dress, such as a coat and tie, with status or authority.

Years ago, Frederic Bartlett (1932), one of the first psychologists to talk about schemas, demonstrated the impact of cultural models on retrieval. British subjects read a North American Indian folk tale, waited 15 minutes, and then attempted to reproduce it verbatim. Their errors were systematic. At times subjects omitted details that did not make sense given their own cultural conceptions of what was logical and conventional; at other times they elaborated or reworked details to make them consistent with their own culturally shaped schemas. Thus, they drew upon their schemas to reconstruct the story, and when these schemas differed from the schemas of members of the culture that generated the story, the story changed dramatically.

Cultural models shape individuals' schemas about nearly every aspect of their lives, from the way they interact with family members to their beliefs about the nature of personality, the supernatural, and the meaning of life (Baumeister, 1991; Tyler, 1969; Price-Williams, 1975; Shweder, 1991).

INTERIM SUMMARY   Across and within cultures, people tend to remember information that matters to them, and they organize information in memory to match the demands of their environment. Shared cultural concepts, or **cultural models,** also shape the way people think and remember.

REMEMBERING, MISREMEMBERING, AND FORGETTING

The flipside of memory is **forgetting**, the inability to remember. Ebbinghaus (1885) documented over a century ago a typical pattern of forgetting that occurs with many kinds of declarative knowledge, beginning with rapid initial loss of information after initial learning and only gradual decline thereafter (Figure 6.18). Researchers have recently refined Ebbinghaus's forgetting curve, finding that the relation between memory decline and length of time between learning and retrieval is logarithmic, which essentially means that the rate of forgetting is initially very high but eventually becomes very low (Wixted & Ebbesen, 1991). Interestingly, this forgetting curve seems to apply whether the period of time is hours or years. The same curve emerged when researchers studied people's ability to remember the names of old television shows: They rapidly forgot the names of shows canceled within the last seven years, but the rate of forgetting trailed off after that (Squire, 1989).

HOW LONG IS LONG-TERM MEMORY?

When people forget, does this mean that the information is no longer stored or simply that it is no longer easy to retrieve? And is some information permanent, or does the mind eventually throw away old boxes in the attic if the person does not use them for a number of years?

The first question is more difficult to answer than the second. Psychologists often distinguish between the *availability* of information in memory—whether it is still "in there"—and its *accessibility*—the ease with which it can be retrieved. The tip-of-the-tongue phenomenon, like the priming effects shown by amnesics, is a good example of information that is available but inaccessible. In large part, accessibility reflects level of activation, which diminishes over time but remains for much longer than most people would intuitively suppose. Memory for a picture flashed briefly on a screen a year earlier continues to have some amount of activation, which is expressed implicitly even if the person has no conscious recollection of it (Cave, 1997). And most people have vivid recollections of incidents from their childhood that occurred once, such as the moment they heard the news that a beloved pet died when they were six. But what about the other hundreds of millions of incidents that cannot be retrieved? To what degree these memories may now be unavailable, and not just inaccessible, is unknown.

Studies of very long term memory suggest, however, that if information is consolidated through spacing over long learning intervals, it will last a lifetime, even if the person does not rehearse it for half a century (Bahrick et al., 1991). Eight years after having taught students for a single semester, college professors will forget the names and faces of most of their students (sorry!), but 35 years after graduation, people still recognize 90 percent of the names and faces from their high school yearbook. The difference is in the spacing: The professor only teaches a student for a few months, whereas high school students typically know each other for at least three or four years. Similarly, people who take college mathematics courses that require them to use the knowledge they learned in high school algebra show nearly complete memory for algebra 50 years later even if they work as artists and never balance their checkbook, whereas people who stop at high school algebra remember nothing of it decades later.

HOW ACCURATE IS LONG-TERM MEMORY?

Aside from the question of *how long* people remember is the question of *how accurately* they remember. The short answer is that if memory is both functional and reconstructive, most of the time it will serve us well, but it is subject to a variety of errors and biases. For example, the normal associative processes that help people remember can also lead to memory errors (see Robinson & Roediger, 1997; Schacter et al., 1998, in press). In one set of studies the researchers presented participants with a series of words (such as *slumber*, *nap*, and *bed*) that were all related to a single word that had *not* been presented (*sleep*), which essentially primed that word repeatedly (Roediger & McDermott, 1995). Not only did most participants "remember" having heard the multiply-primed word, but the majority even "remembered" which of two people had read the word to them. Some participants

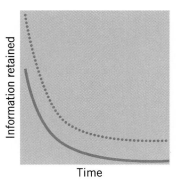

FIGURE 6.18
Forgetting follows a standard pattern, with rapid initial loss of information followed by more gradual later decline. Increasing initial study-time (the dotted line) increases retention, but forgetting occurs at the same rate. In other words, increased study shifts the curve upward but does not change the rate of forgetting or eliminate it.

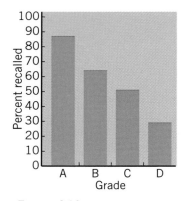

FIGURE 6.19
Distortion in memory for high school grades. The lower the grade, the less memorable it seems to be, demonstrating the impact of motivation and emotion on memory. *Source:* Adapted from Bahrick et al., 1996.

refused to believe that the word had not been presented even after hearing an audiotape of the session!

Emotional factors can also bias recall. The investigators in one study asked college student participants to recall their math, science, history, English, and foreign language grades from high school and then compared their recollections to their high school transcripts (Bahrick et al., 1996). Students recalled 71 percent of their grades correctly. More interesting, however, was the pattern of their errors (Figure 6.19). Participants rarely misremembered their A's, but they rarely *correctly* remembered their D's. In fact, D's were twice as likely to be remembered as a B or a C than as a D. Approximately 80 percent of participants tended to inflate their remembered grades, whereas only 6 percent reported grades lower than they had actually achieved. The remaining 14 percent remembered correctly.

Flashbulb Memories

If remembering is more like consulting an artist's sketch than a photograph, what do we make of **flashbulb memories**, that is, vivid memories of exciting or highly consequential events (Brown & Kulik, 1977; Conway, 1995; Pillemer, 1995; Winograd & Neisser, 1993)? Many people around the world can recall precisely where and when they heard the news of the death of Princess Diana of England in 1997, almost as if a camera had recorded that moment in time. People report similarly vivid memories of the assassination of Martin Luther King in 1968 as well as personal events such as the death of a loved one or a romantic encounter (Pillemer, 1984; Rubin & Kozin, 1984).

Flashbulb memories are so clear and vivid that we tend to think of them as totally accurate; however, considerable evidence suggests that flashbulb memories are often not of snapshot clarity or accuracy and can even be entirely incorrect (Neisser, 1991). For people whose lives are directly affected, such as Princess Diana's children, flashbulb memories tend to be extremely accurate, especially for the central details of the episode. People who are only affected from afar, in contrast, tend to have much more confidence in their memories of vivid events than they should.

Eyewitness Testimony

Research on the accuracy of memory has an important real-life application in the courtroom: How accurate is eyewitness testimony (see Schacter, 1995; Sporer et al., 1996)? Numerous studies have explored this question experimentally, usually by showing participants a short film or slides of an event such as a car accident (Loftus, 1979; Wells & Loftus, 1984; Wells & Turtle, 1987; Zaragosta & Mitchell, 1996). The experimenter then asks subjects specific questions about the scene, sometimes introducing information that was not present in the actual scene, asking leading questions, or contradicting what participants saw.

Even seemingly minor variations in the wording of a question can determine what participants "remember" from a scene. One study simply substituted the definite article "the" for the indefinite article "a" in the question "Did you see the/a broken headlight?" Using the definite article increased both the likelihood that participants would recall seeing a broken headlight and their certainty that they had, even if they never actually observed one (Loftus & Palmer, 1974; Loftus & Zanni, 1975).

These findings have clear implications both in the courtroom and in the way police interrogate witnesses, although some researchers have been unable to replicate these results or have qualified them on a number of grounds (e.g., Gruneberg & Sykes, 1993; Kohnken & Maass, 1988; McCloskey & Egeth, 1983; Smith & Ellsworth, 1987; Yuille, 1980). For instance, individuals vary in their sus-

An accident can become more severe if a lawyer asks the right questions, such as "How fast were the cars going when they smashed [rather than "hit"] each other?"

ceptibility to misleading information. People with poor memories are especially susceptible to misinformation (Loftus et al., 1992). Further, some aspects of a memory may be more reliable than others. The emotional stress of witnessing a traumatic event can lead to heightened processing (and hence better memory) of core details of the event but less extensive processing of peripheral details (Christianson, 1992). A sharp attorney could thus attack the credibility of a witness's entire testimony by establishing that her memory of peripheral details is faulty even though she clearly remembers the central aspects of the event.

INTERIM SUMMARY   The flipside of memory is **forgetting**. Many kinds of declarative knowledge show a similar forgetting curve, which is initially steep and then levels off. Psychologists often distinguish between the *availability* of information in memory—whether it is still "in there"—and its *accessibility*—the ease with which it can be retrieved. People tend to make memory errors for a variety of reasons, some cognitive and some emotional (such as remembering what they want to remember). **Flashbulb memories**—vivid memories of exciting or highly consequential events—are sometimes highly accurate but sometimes completely mistaken. Eyewitness testimony is also subject to many biases and errors, although people are more likely to remember central, emotionally significant details.

WHY DO PEOPLE FORGET?

The reconstructive nature of remembering—the fact that we have to weave together a memory from patches of specific and general knowledge—leaves memory open to a number of potential errors and biases. But why do people sometimes forget things entirely? Psychologists have proposed several explanations, including decay, interference, and motivated forgetting.

Decay Theory

The **decay theory** explains forgetting as a result of a fading memory trace. Having a thought or perception produces changes in synaptic connections, which in turn creates the potential for remembering if the neural circuits that were initially activated are later reactivated. According to decay theory, these neurophysiological changes fade with disuse, much as a wilderness path grows over unless repeatedly trodden. The decay theory is difficult to corroborate or disprove empirically, but some studies show a similar pattern of rapid and then more gradual deactivation of neural pathways in the hippocampus, which is involved in memory consolidation, suggesting a possible physiological basis for decay (see Anderson, 1995).

Interference Theory

A second theory points to **interference** as the prime culprit in memory failure: Memories of similar information or events tend to interfere with one another, as when students confuse two theories they learned about around the same time or two similar-sounding words in a foreign language. Finding the right path in the neural wilderness is difficult if two paths are close together and look alike. Or to use the filing cabinet metaphor, storing too many documents under the same heading makes finding the right one difficult.

Cognitive psychologists distinguish two kinds of interference. **Proactive interference** refers to the interference of previously stored memories with the retrieval of new information, as when a person calls a new romantic partner by the name of an old one (a common but dangerous memory lapse). In **retroactive interference**, new information interferes with retrieval of old information, as when

... AND, AS YOU GO OUT INTO THE WORLD, I PREDICT THAT YOU WILL, GRADUALLY AND IMPERCEPTIBLY, FORGET ALL YOU EVER LEARNED AT THIS UNIVERSITY."

Drawing by Sidney Harris

people have difficulty recalling their home phone numbers from past residences. One reason children take years to memorize multiplication tables, even though they can learn the names of cartoon characters or classmates with astonishing speed, is the tremendous interference involved, because every number is paired with so many others (Anderson, 1995).

Motivated Forgetting

Another cause of forgetting is **motivated forgetting**, or forgetting for a reason. People often explicitly instruct themselves or others to forget, as when a person stops in the middle of a sentence and says, "Oops—forget that. That's the wrong address. The right one is . . ." (Bjork & Bjork, 1996). At other times, the "intention" to forget is implicit, as when a person who parks in the same garage everyday implicitly *remembers to forget* where she parked the day before so it does not interfere with memory for where she parked today (Bjork, et al., 1998). Experimental evidence suggests that this kind of goal-directed forgetting requires active inhibition of the forgotten information, which remains active but inaccessible. Researchers have demonstrated this using *directed forgetting* procedures, in which participants learn a list of words but are told midway through to forget the words they just learned and just remember the last part of the list. This procedure reduces recall for the words in the first part of the list and decreases proactive interference from them, so that words in the last half of the list are more easily remembered. This suggests that the procedure is in fact inhibiting retrieval of the to-be-forgotten words. On the other hand, this procedure does *not* decrease recognition of, or implicit memory for, the to-be-forgotten words, suggesting that they remain in an activated state.

Other studies show that instructing a person not to think about something can effectively keep the information from consciousness but that doing so creates an automatic, unconscious process that "watches out" for the information and hence keeps it active (Wegner, 1992). For example, when people are instructed to suppress an exciting thought about sex, they remain physiologically aroused even while the thought is outside awareness. In fact, they remain just as aroused as subjects instructed to *think about* the sexual thought (Wegner et al., 1990). In a sense, goal-directed forgetting is like a form of prospective memory, in which the intention is to forget something in the future rather than to remember it.

In real life, people often try to inhibit unpleasant or anxiety-provoking thoughts or feelings. When they do this consciously, as when they tell themselves not to worry about a medical procedure they are about to undergo, it is called *suppression*. When they do this unconsciously, it is called *repression* (Chapter 12). People often forget things they do not want to remember, such as "overlooking" a dentist appointment. If dentists were handing out $100 bills instead of filling teeth, few people would forget their appointments.

COMMENTARY
Repressed Memories of Sexual Abuse

The concept of repression has always been controversial in psychology, with many psychologists doubting the evidence for its existence (Holmes, 1990), but it is now the centerpiece of controversy for social and political reasons: It is at the heart of claims of childhood sexual abuse and counterclaims of false memories (Pezdek & Banks, 1996). The controversy stems from the outrage of alleged perpetrators who maintain that charges of sexual abuse against them have been fabricated in psychotherapy by unscrupulous, poorly trained clinicians. A group of these individuals has formed and financed a False Memory Syndrome Foundation and has enlisted the support of many prominent experimental psychologists dubious about the concept of repression and concerned about the limitations of memories reconstructed in psychotherapy (e.g., Loftus, 1997).

Actually, most victims of repeated or severe sexual abuse in childhood have at least some memories of the abuse prior to psychotherapy, although their memories are often fragmented (Herman, 1992). Their recollection of childhood events tends to have gaps of months or years, and the memories they do recall of traumatic experiences frequently come to them in flashbacks, in physical forms (such as the sensation of gagging that initially attended the experience of being forced to perform oral sex), or in nightmares. One patient interviewed for research purposes had such severe amnesia for childhood events that she could not recognize herself in childhood pictures.

The question of false memories is exceedingly difficult to address scientifically for a number of reasons. First, distinguishing true from false allegations is difficult under any circumstances (see Schacter, 1995). Different people often remember the same incident very differently. Second, a cardinal feature of sexual abuse is the perpetrator's insistence on secrecy and the attempt to discredit victims who tell their story. Discrediting the victim is as characteristic of childhood sexual abuse as it is of political torture, persecution, and genocide (Herman, 1992). Complicating matters, however, is that for every hundred genuine perpetrators of sexual abuse who are exposed for their crimes, some number of innocent people are unfairly accused. Unfortunately, we do not know what that number is. Some divorcing parents make accusations against their former spouses as a tactic in custody disputes. And some poorly trained therapists look for abuse whenever an adult female patient steps into their office complaining of anxiety or depression and may convince nontraumatized patients that their symptoms reflect a history of childhood abuse that never existed (Loftus, 1993). Fourth, the controversy over repressed versus fabricated memories of abuse cannot be divorced from the larger context of gender. Most abuse victims are female, and most perpetrators are male. The power differential between men and women has undoubtedly contributed to the extent to which abuse victims have historically been silenced and no doubt contributes to the sympathetic hearing that alleged abusers are currently receiving from the public and many psychological researchers.

EVIDENCE OF FALSE MEMORIES

Data from numerous laboratory studies suggest that people can sometimes be led to create subjectively compelling memories of things that did not happen (Loftus, 1997; Payne et al., 1997). As we have seen, presenting participants with a series of words semantically related to a target word that was *not* presented can produce high rates of false recognition of the target, and people can be quite firm in their beliefs about these false memories.

In another experimental design, researchers obtain detailed information from parents of college students about events that actually occurred to them in childhood and then present the students in the laboratory with several real memories and one false one, such as getting lost in the mall at age five and being found by an elderly woman (Loftus, 1997). The investigators then interview participants about each event, ask them if they remember it, and ask them to recall what they remember. In these studies, roughly 15 to 25 percent of participants can be induced to recall a false memory over the course of two or three interviews.

Researchers are now beginning to study the characteristics of people who are likely to do so (Hyman & Billings, 1998). Interestingly, however, when one researcher tried to induce memories more like those of sexual abuse victims, in this case, memory of a rectal enema in childhood, none of the subjects created a false memory (Pezdek, cited in Loftus, 1997). This suggests the need for caution in extending the findings of these studies to the creation of false memories of highly traumatic, evocative events such as sexual abuse.

EVIDENCE OF REPRESSED MEMORIES

Empirical evidence for the existence of repressed traumatic memories has begun to accumulate. Among a large sample of adults reporting histories of childhood sexual abuse, roughly 60 percent identified some period during childhood in which they were amnesic for the abuse (Briere & Conte, 1993). The earlier and more severe the trauma, the more likely were subjects to have repressed it at some point. Another study found that 19 percent of women treated for substance abuse who acknowledged a history of childhood abuse similarly reported a period of amnesia for the events (Loftus et al., 1994). Other traumatic events, such as combat or rape, also frequently produce periods of amnesia (Arrigo & Pezdek, 1997).

Perhaps the clearest empirical evidence for repressed memories comes from a study that tracked down women who had been treated at a hospital for sexual molestation when they were children (Williams, 1992, 1994). Seventeen years after their documented abuse, 38 percent were amnesic for the incident, even though many reported other traumas, including later incidents of sexual abuse. When asked if any family members had ever gotten into trouble for their sexual behavior, one subject, who denied sexual abuse, reported that before she was born an uncle had apparently molested a little girl and was stabbed to death by the girl's mother. Examination of newspaper reports 17 years earlier found that the subject herself had been one of the uncle's two victims and that the mother of the other victim had indeed stabbed the perpetrator.

THE NEED FOR CAUTION ON BOTH SIDES

My own clinical experience suggests the need for caution on both sides of this issue. About 15 years ago, like many clinicians, I began to see cases in which patients gradually retrieved memories of abusive childhood experiences through flashbacks, dreams, and careful examination of gaps in their memories. This occured before television coverage of the controversy and before I knew to assess abuse histories more systematically. It is therefore highly unlikely that the return of these memories reflected anything other than my patients' painful and courageous efforts to come to terms with their past.

A few years later, however, when I had become sensitized to issues of abuse and had conducted research on its effects, I treated a woman who had many signs of abuse, such as long gaps in her memory and violent images that occasionally came to mind like pictures on a screen. During one session, I repeatedly probed some very suspicious memories and their possible links to her violent imagery. With some exasperation, she finally chided, "You know, I wasn't sexually abused, if that's what you're looking for."

Perhaps the moral of the story is that psychologists should always attend both to the phenomenon they are studying—in this case repressed memories—and to their own needs, fears, and cognitive biases. Clinicians need to be aware of the research on the limits of reconstructive memory, not to mention the influence of their own emotional processes on the way they understand their patients. Research demonstrates that people with abuse histories are more likely to see or hear themes of abuse in ambiguous situations (Nigg et al., 1992), so that clinicians who have not come to terms with painful childhood histories of their own might have a low threshold for believing their patients have been abused and subtly or explicitly coaxing them to create false memories. On the other hand, cognitive researchers who may have had little or no exposure to real sexual abuse victims should be very circumspect before overstepping the limits of their own vantage point. In matters of public policy, experimental psychologists, like clinicians, need to examine carefully their own psychologies before trying to write—or write off—the life histories of others. ■

INTERIM SUMMARY   The **decay theory** explains forgetting as a result of a fading memory trace; disuse of information leads to a gradual decrease in the strength of neural connections. **Interference** of similar information is another cause of forgetting. **Proactive interference** refers to the interference of previously stored memories with the retrieval of new information, whereas **retroactive interference** refers to the interference of new information with retrieval of old information. Another cause of forgetting is **motivated forgetting**, or forgetting for a reason, as occurs in directed forgetting, suppression, and repression. The final word has not yet been written about repressed memories of childhood sexual abuse, although the data suggest caution on both sides: Memories recovered in therapy cannot be assumed to be accurate, but they also cannot be routinely dismissed as false.

SOME CONCLUDING THOUGHTS

As we saw in Chapter 1, the 1960s witnessed a cognitive revolution in psychology, as many experimental psychologists began to turn their attention to questions about thought and memory. In writing this chapter for the second edition of this book, and discarding about 80 percent of what I had written in the first edition, it became clear to me that we are in the midst of a second cognitive revolution, one that is rewriting our understanding of memory and probably of the mind as a whole. As the philosopher of science Thomas Kuhn argued, a paradigm (or perspective in psychology) includes a set of propositions that constitute a model, an underlying metaphor, and a set of agreed-upon methods. In the last few years, all of these have changed, as the standard model that has guided research for three decades has begun to change. We have moved from three sequential memory stores to multiple memory systems operating in parallel; from a computer metaphor to a brain metaphor; and from a set of methods (such as memorizing word pairs) that productively guided research for a century but tended to study memory divorced from meaning to a more diverse array of methods that can elucidate memory in its natural habitat.

Although we have focused in this chapter almost exclusively on the cognitive perspective, this second cognitive revolution may actually foster integration with other perspectives. For years I wondered whatever happened to classical and operant conditioning in the standard cognitive model, since behaviorists emphasized that these forms of learning do not require conscious attention and often involve emotional learning (as when a rat learns to avoid situations associated with fear-inducing stimuli). A preliminary answer has begun to emerge: Conditioning is a form of associative learning that is expressed implicitly rather than retrieved as explicit, declarative memory.

The gulf between cognitive and psychodynamic approaches was also once seemingly insurmountable. The standard model assumed that information had to be processed consciously (in STM) before being stored in LTM and that remembering required conscious retrieval. Psychoanalysis, in contrast, proposed that most mental processes occur outside of awareness, are processed in parallel, and can be expressed in behavior without ever becoming conscious. Freud, like most contemporary cognitive theorists, was schooled in classical associationist thought, and he proposed a network theory of the mind and a mechanism similar to spreading activation a century ago (see Erdelyi, 1985; Freud, 1895; Pribram & Gill, 1976). He argued that networks of association operate unconsciously, leading people to think, feel, and behave in ways they may not understand. Freud and later psychodynamic theorists thus developed an approach to psychotherapy that involved mapping these networks, so that a person with authority problems, for example, might come to recognize how aspects of his relationship with his boss were triggering feelings and behavior patterns that developed in his relationship with earlier authority figures, such as his father.

Finally, the standard model viewed the capacity for memory and thought as essentially independent of their content, that is, as applying to any kind of information. The mind was a general information-processing machine that could take almost any input, manipulate it, and remember it with appropriate encoding and rehearsal. But an increasingly modular conception of the brain and memory systems has made contemporary cognitive models more compatible with a view of cognition emerging in evolutionary circles. This view maintains that the mind has evolved content-specific mechanisms that facilitate the remembering and processing of very particular kinds of information (Tooby & Cosmides, 1992).

Few would doubt that the taste buds evolved to detect qualities such as bitter and salty that allow humans and other animals to recognize and remember foods that cause illness or supply essential nutrients. And as we have seen, the human mind is attuned to certain kinds of information and is more likely to form some types of associations than others. Areas of the visual cortex are specialized for facial recognition. In human evolution, the ability to recognize faces would certainly have conferred an adaptive advantage, facilitating investment of resources in one's own offspring or genetically related individuals and permitting our ancestors to make very quick judgments about who they needed to fear and who they could trust.

Could the human mind be similarly designed to process and remember subtle social cues that indicate a person's position in a status hierarchy or his willingness to respond altruistically in the face of threats to the community? Humans, like other primates, are universally attuned to status. Although the indices of status differ across cultures (clothing, physical appearance, and so forth), adolescents everywhere spontaneously rank themselves and their peers by their position in social hierarchies and tend to agree on their relative ranks. People everywhere also attend to two salient dimensions of personality—agreeableness and conscientiousness—that reflect on their peers' ability to be good social partners (Buss, 1991). Research is just beginning in these areas, but the evidence that does exist suggests that evolution may have created a brain designed by natural selection to solve specific problems of adaptation.

The symbols differ, but everywhere people attend to status cues.

These areas of potential integration among cognitive, behavioral, psychodynamic, and evolutionary perspectives were unthinkable just a decade ago, but research in cognitive neuroscience has dramatically altered the psychological landscape. In the next chapter we extend our investigation of information processing to the mechanisms by which people transform and manipulate information stored in memory in the process of thinking, making decisions, and trying to meet their goals. In the process, we discuss the pivotal role of language in human thought, itself a remarkable product of millions of years of evolution.

SUMMARY

MEMORY AND INFORMATION PROCESSING

1. Case studies of neurologically impaired patients and experimental studies of normal subjects have demonstrated that memory is composed of several systems.

2. For information to return to mind after it is no longer present, it has to be put into a mental code, or *representation*. The major forms of representations studied by psychologists are **sensory representations** and **verbal representations**. People also store memory for actions as *motoric representations*.

3. The *standard model of memory* views the mind as a computer, which stores, transforms, and retrieves information processing. It includes three sequential memory stores or stages of memory. The first is the **sensory register,** the split-second mental representation of a perceived stimulus that remains very briefly after that stimulus disappears. **Iconic storage** describes visual sensory registration; and **echoic storage** describes auditory sensory registration.

4. **Short-term memory (STM)** stores information for roughly 20 to 30 seconds, unless the information is maintained through **rehearsal** (repeating the information again and again). This form of rehearsal, which merely maintains information in STM, is called **maintenance rehearsal. Elaborative rehearsal**—thinking about and elaborating on the information's meaning—tends to be superior for storing information in long-term memory.

5. Important information is passed along to **long-term memory (LTM)**, where representations may last as long as a lifetime. Recovering information from LTM, or **retrieval**, brings it back into STM, or consciousness.

6. In the last decade this model has been changing substantially. Instead of viewing memory in terms of *serial processing* (which assumes that information passes through a series of stages, one at a time and in order), researchers now view memory as involving a set of **memory systems** that operate simultaneously (in parallel) rather than sequentially (one at a time). Researchers now recognize that not all remembering is expressed by retrieving information into consciousness, or STM, and they rely less on the metaphor of the *mind as a computer* than the *mind as a brain*.

Working Memory

7. Many psychologists now refer to STM as **working memory**, which refers to the temporary *storage* and *processing* of information that can be used to solve problems, respond to environmental demands, or achieve goals. According to one prominent model, *control processes* such as rehearsal, reasoning, and making decisions about how to balance two tasks simultaneously are the work of a limited-capacity *central executive* system, whereas storage involves at least two limited-capacity systems, a visual store (also called the *visuospatial sketchpad*) and a verbal store.

8. The existence of neurological patients who show deficits in either working memory or LTM but not both suggests that these memory systems are neurologically distinct, although in everyday life they work together, as frontal working memory networks provide a special form of activation to networks in the posterior parts of the cortex that represent current perceptions and information stored in LTM. One way to expand the capacity of working memory in particular domains is **chunking**, that is, grouping information in larger units than single words or digits, which means that the roughly seven pieces of information stored in visual or auditory working memory can represent larger, more meaningful pieces of information.

Varieties of Long-Term Memory

9. Types of memory can be distinguished by the *kind of knowledge stored* and the *way this knowledge is retrieved and expressed*. People store two kinds of information, declarative and procedural. **Declarative memory** refers to memory for facts and events and is subdivided into **semantic** or **generic memory** (general world knowledge or facts) and **episodic memory** (memories of particular events). **Procedural memory** refers to "how to" knowledge of procedures or skills.

10. Information can be retrieved either explicitly or implicitly. **Explicit memory** refers to conscious recollection, expressed through **recall** (the spontaneous retrieval of material from LTM) or **recognition** (memory for whether something currently perceived has been previously encountered or learned). **Implicit memory** is expressed in behavior rather than consciously retrieved.

11. Neurological data suggest that different kinds of memory form discrete memory systems. The hippocampus and adjacent regions of the cortex are central to the consolidation of explicit memories but do not appear to play an important role in either implicit memory or working memory.

12. **Everyday memory**—memory as it occurs in daily life—tends to be *functional*—focused on remembering information that is meaningful—and emotionally significant. Emotional memories tend to be more easily remembered than neutral memories and to involve activation of the amygdala. **Prospective memory** is memory for things that need to be done in the future.

ENCODING AND ORGANIZATION OF MEMORY

13. For information to be retrievable from memory, it must be **encoded**, or cast into a representational form, or "code," that can be readily accessed from memory.

14. Among the factors that influence later accessibility of memory are the degree to which information is elaborated, reflected upon, and processed in a meaningful way during encoding (**level of processing**); the presence of **retrieval cues** (stimuli or thoughts that can be used to facilitate recollection); the **spacing** of study sessions (with longer intervals between rehearsal sessions tending to be more effective); and the use of multiple and redundant representational modes to encode the information, which provides more cues for its retrieval. **Mnemonic devices,** or systematic strategies for remembering information, can also be useful for remembering, as can external memory aids such as notes.

15. Information stored in memory forms **networks of association**—clusters of interconnected units of information called **nodes**. According to **spreading activation theory,** activating one node in a network triggers activation in closely related nodes. Some information is organized **hierarchically**, with broad categories composed of narrower subcategories, which in turn consist of even more specific categories.

16. *Schemas* are organized knowledge about a particular domain. According to schema theory, memory is an active, *reconstructive* process that involves reactivation of both the initial representations of an event and general knowledge that helps fill in the gaps. Schemas facilitate memory by organizing information at both encoding and retrieval.

17. Many schemas are shaped by culture, from beliefs about foods that are appropriate to eat to beliefs about the meaning of life. Across cultures, people tend to remember what matters to them, although literacy affects aspects of memory such as the use of verbal representations.

REMEMBERING, MISREMEMBERING, AND FORGETTING

18. Ebbinghaus discovered a forgetting curve that applies to many kinds of declarative memory, in which considerable information is initially lost but forgetting then tapers off.

19. Memory is a reconstructive process that mingles representations of actual experiences with general knowledge. Although memory is functional and tends to work well most of the time, misremembering is common, even in **flashbulb memories** (vivid memories of exciting or highly consequential events) and eyewitness testimony, which can be biased by even seemingly minor changes in the way questions are asked.

20. Three theories attempt to account for forgetting: **decay theory** (which explains forgetting as a result of a fading memory trace); **interference** of new and old information with retrieval of the other; and **motivated forgetting** (forgetting for a reason, which leads to inhibition of retrieval).

SOME CONCLUDING THOUGHTS

21. Psychology may be in the midst of a second cognitive revolution that may allow greater integration across perspectives, as models, metaphors, and methods have all begun to shift in cognitive science.

R. B. K. Kitaj, "I and Thou," 1990–92, Marlborough Fine Art, London.

Thought and Language

Y̶ou are sitting in a café with your closest friend, and she tells you tearfully, "I think my relationship with Brett has hit a dead-end. Things have been pretty bumpy for a while, but I had no idea how bad. He says he loves me, but I can tell he's really putting on the brakes, and I think he just wants to bail out. Every time we try to talk about it, we just end up spinning our wheels. It's hard to see how we can move forward."

You have no trouble understanding your friend. You are not confused by her metaphors—the relationship hitting a *dead-end*, things being *bumpy*, her boyfriend *putting on the brakes* and wanting to *bail out*, the two of them *spinning their wheels* and having trouble *moving forward*. Your friend is not a poet, yet she communicates her problem through a single controlling metaphor that you understand implicitly: Lovers are like travelers on a journey trying to reach a common destination, and their relationship is the vehicle for this journey. With the exception of *bailing out* (an aeronautical metaphor), your friend is describing her

relationship as a car traveling on a bumpy road and reaching a dead-end, and she is unsure whether the vehicle can go forward under these circumstances (Lakoff, 1980, 1989, 1997).

Several features of this scenario in the café are striking. First, your friend is not Shakespeare—"love is a car" would probably not have played well at the Globe Theatre—yet the two of you both understand what she is saying because you share a metaphor rooted in your culture. Second, in transforming her experience into words, she is manipulating representations—knowledge about cars and relationships—and mapping one knowledge domain onto another (a rough time in a relationship is a bumpy road; feeling "stuck" in a relationship despite efforts to talk is like spinning your wheels trying to get out of a snow bank). Third, she is essentially speaking in highly evocative poetry—and you are able to understand it—without a second's thought and without any likely awareness on your part or hers of the metaphor guiding your thinking. Finally, through words, a set of thoughts and feelings in one person's mind enter another's.

This chapter is about thought and language—how we transform and manipulate mental representations to navigate our way through life (another journey metaphor) and interact with others using words. We begin by exploring the basic units of thought, such as mental images and concepts, and the way people manipulate these units to reason, solve problems, and make decisions. Next we examine implicit and everyday thinking, exploring how people solve problems and make judgments outside of awareness, often relying as much on emotion as on rationality. Then we turn to language, the system of symbols that forms the medium for much of human thought and communication. Could we think in metaphor without language? When we have an idea, do we *translate* it into language, or are complex thoughts inherently linguistic? Finally, we examine the way children learn to provide and comprehend language, and address the question of whether evolution has created a brain specifically attuned to linguistic information.

UNITS OF THOUGHT

In many ways, thought is simply an extension of perception and memory. When we perceive, we form a mental representation. When we remember, we try to bring that representation to mind. When we think, we use representations to try to solve a problem or answer a question. **Thinking** means manipulating mental representations for a purpose.

MANIPULATING MENTAL REPRESENTATIONS

People can manipulate virtually any kind of representation in their minds. You may not have realized it, but the last time you sniffed the milk and decided it was spoiled, you were thinking with your nose (actually, with olfactory representations). Or consider what happens when people harmonize while singing along with the radio. Although their companions in the car may not appreciate it, they are engaged in an impressive act of musical thinking, unconsciously manipulating auditory representations and using sophisticated rules of harmonic structure, probably with no awareness whatsoever.

Thinking in Words and Images

Much of the time people think using words and images. When people try to figure out whether they have enough money with them to buy an extra bag of pretzels, how to tell an unwanted suitor they are not interested, or how to reorganize their department at the office to increase efficiency, they usually think in words. At other times they rely on **mental images**, visual representations such as the image of a street or a circle.

Psychologists once disagreed about whether people actually think in images or whether they convert visual questions into verbal questions in order to solve them. For example, to figure out how to carry a large desk through a narrow doorway, do people somehow rotate a visual image of the desk in their minds, or do they convert the problem into statements (e.g., "the desk won't fit if it isn't turned sideways")?

One study addressed this question by showing subjects pictures of a stimulus such as a capital R, rotated between 0 and 360 degrees (Figure 7.1). The subject had to decide whether the letter was shown normally or in mirror image. The results were clear: The amount of time subjects took to answer varied directly with the degree of rotation from upright. In other words, the more the rotation, the longer the reaction time. This indicated that subjects were actually mentally rotating an image of the letter to come to a conclusion (Cooper, 1976; Cooper & Shepard, 1973). Supporting these findings, PET studies show that perceiving, remembering, and mentally manipulating visual scenes all involve activation of the visual cortex and that people typically solve problems of this sort without activating left-hemisphere language centers (Kosslyn et al., 1993, in press).

As we saw in Chapter 5, humans are not the only animals that use mental images or mental maps. Recent research shows that other animals are even aware of geometric relationships! In one study, the investigators consistently hid birdseed

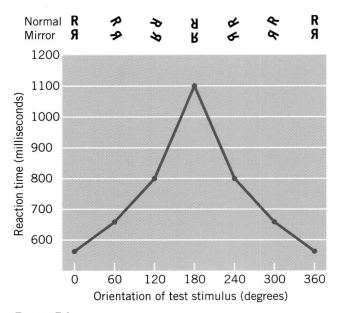

FIGURE 7.1

The manipulation of visual representations. The investigators asked participants to determine whether the "R" they saw at different degrees of rotation was forward or backward. The dependent variable was the amount of time required to accomplish the task. The figure graphs reaction time as a function of degrees of rotation. As can be seen, the more subjects had to rotate the letter mentally, the longer they took to complete the task. Peak reaction time was at 180 degrees, which requires the furthest rotation. *Source:* Adapted from Cooper & Shepard, 1973.

midway between two pipes on a wall, but they moved the pipes different distances from each other so that nutcrackers flying around the room had to keep finding the new midpoint (Kamil & Jones, 1997). Remarkably, the birds were consistently able to locate the midpoint to find the seed. They also appeared to be mentally drawing a straight line between the two pipes, which were always placed one above the other, since they tended to land right on the line that intersected them rather than to the right or left.

Mental Models

People also frequently think using **mental models**, representations that describe, explain, or predict the way things work (Johnson-Laird, 1995). Mental models may be quite simple, like most people's understanding of automobiles ("If the car doesn't start, there's a problem somewhere under the hood") or a child's understanding of what a "cavity" is (a bad thing in the mouth that requires a trip to the dentist). On the other hand, they can be quite complex, such as the mental models used by mechanics to troubleshoot a car or a dentist's conception of the processes that produce cavities.

Although mental models often include visual elements (such as the dentist's visual representations of different kinds of teeth and what erosion in a tooth looks like), they always include descriptions of the *relations* among elements. For example, the dentist may have a *causal* model of how build-up of food residues leads to bacterial action that eats away at a tooth. Mental models are often guided in part by the kinds of metaphors described in the opening to this chapter. One common metaphor for trying to get information from a reluctant source—"it's like pulling teeth"—is modeled on how difficult it is to yank teeth out of "reluctant" bone (and how equally difficult it can be to get someone who needs a tooth pulled into the dentist's chair).

INTERIM SUMMARY: **Thinking** means manipulating mental representations for a purpose. Much of the time people think using words, **mental images** (visual representations), and **mental models** (representations that describe, explain, or predict the way things work).

CONCEPTS AND CATEGORIES

Before people can think about an object, they usually first have to *classify* it so that they know what it is and what it does. An approaching person is a friend or a stranger; a piece of fruit on the table is an apple or an orange; a political commentator on television is a conservative or a liberal.

People and things fall into groupings based on common properties called **categories**. A **concept** is a mental representation of a category, that is, an internal portrait of a class of objects, ideas, or events that share common properties (Murphy & Medin, 1985; Smith, 1995). Some concepts can be visualized, but a concept is broader than its visual image. For example, the concept *car* stands for a class of vehicles with four wheels, seating space for at least two people, and a generally predictable shape. Other concepts, like *honest*, defy visualization or representation in any other sensory mode, although they may have visual associations (such as an image of an honest face).

The process of identifying an object as an instance of a category—recognizing its similarity to some objects and dissimilarity to others—is called **categorization**. Categorization is essential to thinking because it allows people to make inferences about objects. For example, if I classify the drink in my glass as an alcoholic beverage, I am likely to make assumptions about how many I can drink, what I will feel like after drinking it, and so forth.

Defining Features and Prototypes

For years, philosophers and psychologists have wrestled with the question of how people categorize objects or situations (Huttenlocher & Hedges, 1994; Medin & Smith, 1985; Smith & Medin, 1981). How do they decide that a crab is an animal rather than an insect, even though crabs look like big spiders?

Defining Features   One possibility is that they compare the features of the objects with a list of **defining features**—qualities that are essential, or necessarily present in order to classify the object as a member of the category. For some concepts this strategy could work. Concepts like salt, water, or triangle are **well-defined concepts** which have properties that clearly set them apart from other concepts. A triangle can be defined as a two-dimensional geometric figure with three sides and three angles, and anything that does not fit this definition is not a triangle.

Most of the concepts used in daily life, however, are not easily defined by a precise set of features; rather, they are **fuzzy concepts** (Holland et al., 1986; Malt, 1993; Rosch, 1978). Consider the concept *good*. This concept takes on different meanings when applied to a meal or a person: Few of us look for tastiness in a person or honesty and sensitivity in a meal. Similarly, the concept *adult* is fuzzy around the edges, at least in Western cultures: At what point does a person stop being an adolescent and become an adult? Is a person an adult at voting age? At drinking age? At marriage?

Prototypes   Even where concepts are well defined, consulting a list of defining features is, in psychological time (that is, milliseconds), a rather slow procedure. As we saw in Chapter 3, a person flipping through television stations with a remote control can recognize scenes and classify the objects in them far faster than

At what point does a creature be-come categorized as "human"?

People readily recognize robins as birds. Categorizing penguins takes a little more thought—and hence measurably more time.

anyone could possibly go through a list of defining features. People typically classify objects rapidly by judging their *similarity* to concepts stored in memory (Estes, 1994; Tversky, 1977). For example, if asked whether Windsor, Ontario, is a city, most people compare it with their image of a crowded, bustling, typical example of a city, such as New York City, or with a generalized portrait extracted from experience with several cities, such as Los Angeles, Toronto, New York, and London.

Researchers have learned how people use similarity in classification by using both visual and verbal categorization tasks. In visual categorization tasks, the experimenter states the name of a target category (e.g., *bird*) and then presents a picture and asks whether it is a member of the category. In verbal categorization tasks, the target category is followed by a word instead of a picture (e.g., *sparrow*); the task for the subject is to judge whether the second word is an instance of the category.

Psychologists have learned about the role of similarity in classification by measuring the time subjects take to respond in tasks such as these. For example, people rapidly recognize that a robin is a bird but take 100 to 200 milliseconds longer to classify a penguin (see Smith, 1995). The reason is that a robin is a more *prototypical* bird, that is, it shares more of the characteristic features of the concept (Rosch, 1978). A **prototype** is an abstraction across many instances of a category (such as robins, bluebirds, and sparrows). When people construct a prototype in their minds, they essentially abstract out the most important common features of the objects in a category. Thus, the prototype of a bird does not look exactly like any particular bird the person has ever seen; it is more like an airbrushed photograph that smoothes out idiosyncratic features.

When people judge similarity in visual tasks, they rely primarily on shape. When they judge similarity verbally, they tend to rely on **characteristic** or **prototypical features**, that is, qualities typically found in members of a category. For example, most birds fly, sing, and lay eggs. People classify robins quickly because they do all three. Penguins take longer to classify because they lay eggs but do not share many other features of birds, except for having wings (see Malt & Smith, 1984). Most concepts include both visual information and information about characteristic features, so that in everyday categorization, people often use some combination of the two. In judging similarity, people may also compare an object to an

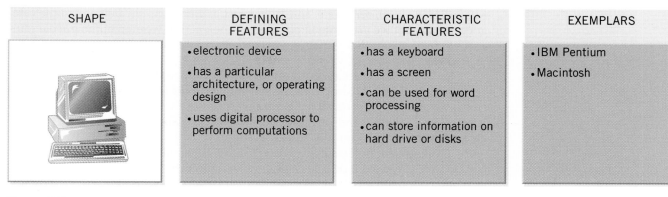

SHAPE	DEFINING FEATURES	CHARACTERISTIC FEATURES	EXEMPLARS
	• electronic device • has a particular architecture, or operating design • uses digital processor to perform computations	• has a keyboard • has a screen • can be used for word processing • can store information on hard drive or disks	• IBM Pentium • Macintosh

FIGURE 7.2
Concepts can represent information in multiple ways that aid categorization.

exemplar, or a prototypic example of the category, rather than an abstract proto-type (Lamberts, 1996; Medin & Schaffer, 1978).

Implicit and Explicit Categorization Are these two views of categorization—one based on defining features and the other on similarity—irreconcilable? In everyday life, concepts probably represent information in multiple ways that are used flexibly in different categorization tasks (Figure 7.2). Rapid, implicit categorization usually relies primarily on similarity. If a person has difficulty implicitly classifying a novel object based on similarity or if the classification task is complex, she may switch to explicit categorization based on defining features (or on features that may not be defining but are nevertheless *definitive* or *diagnostic.* Complex classification tasks generally require careful, explicit evaluation of the data. A doctor will not diagnose appendicitis in a patient whose symptoms appear similar to a textbook case of appendicitis (a prototype) or cases she has seen before (exemplars) unless a laboratory test shows an abnormal white blood cell count, particularly since the symptoms of appendicitis are similar to those of food poisoning and the flu.

Hierarchies of Concepts

Many concepts are hierarchically ordered at multiple levels of abstraction. We categorize all pets that pant, slobber, and bark as dogs, but we can further subdivide the concept *dog* into more specific categories such as *collie* and *poodle.* Similarly, *dog* is itself an instance of larger, more general categories such as *mammal* and *vertebrate* (Figure 7.3). Efficient thinking requires choosing the right level of abstraction. A woman walking down the street in a bright purple raincoat belongs to the

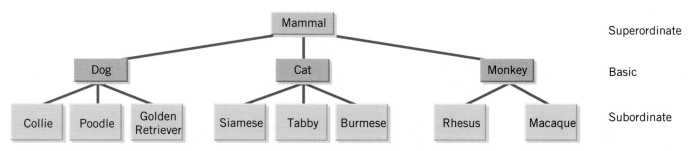

FIGURE 7.3
Superordinate, basic, and subordinate levels of categorization.

categories *mammal, vertebrate,* and *human* just as clearly as she belongs to the category *woman.* Yet we are more likely to say "Look at that woman in the purple raincoat" than "Look at that vertebrate in brightly colored apparel."

The Basic Level of Categorization   The level people naturally tend to use in categorizing objects is known as the **basic level**. This is the broadest, most inclusive level at which objects share common attributes that are distinctive of the concept—that is, that "stand out" (Rosch, 1978). It is also the level at which people categorize most quickly; it is thus the "natural" level to which the mind gravitates. Thus, *woman* is a basic-level category; so are *dinner, car,* and *bird.*

At times, however, people categorize at a more specific or **subordinate level,** as when people on a nature hike distinguish between robins and wrens. Actually, the natural level (sometimes called the *entry level*) at which people tend to classify an *unusual* instance of a category, such as penguin, is often the subordinate level (Jolicoeur, 1984). For these atypical cases, a more subordinate level than the basic level maximizes similarity of objects within the category and minimizes similarity with objects outside the category, which is what the basic level does for most concepts. People also sometimes classify objects at the larger or **superordinate level,** as when a farmer asks, "are the animals in the barn?" rather than running down a list including chickens, horses, and so forth. The superordinate level is one level more abstract than the basic level, and members of this class share fewer common features (Figure 7.3).

Interestingly, the metaphors people use tend to be mapped at the superordinate, rather than the basic, level (Lakoff, 1997). In the example that opened this chapter, the underlying metaphor was that *love is a journey,* and hence a *relationship is a vehicle.* Since the richest, most evocative information is stored at the basic level, using the superordinate level allows the mapping of *multiple* rich concepts onto the current situation. Thus, the listener was not surprised when the woman talking about her relationship seemingly mixed metaphors in likening her relationship to a car but throwing in a metaphor based on a different kind of vehicle, an airplane ("he just wants to *bail out*"). She could also have based the metaphor of her relationship on a boat: Initially it had been *smooth sailing,* but now it is *on the rocks* or has gotten *off course.*

Imaging research suggests that categorizing at different levels actually activates different cognitive processes and neural networks. In one study the experimenters presented participants with line drawings of objects, such as a shirt, followed by a word (Kosslyn et al., 1995). The participant's task was to decide whether the object was an instance of the category. Some of the words were at the basic level (such as *shirt*), whereas others were subordinate (*dress shirt*) or superordinate (*clothing*). The authors reasoned that identifying an object at the superordinate level requires a memory search using language (e.g., mentally "looking up" whether a shirt is a kind of clothing). In contrast, identifying an object at a subordinate level requires a perceptual search of the object to see if it has the specific features of the specific type of object (e.g., whether the shirt has the characteristic collar of a dress shirt). The results were as the researchers hypothesized. Deciding whether a shirt was an article of clothing activated a region of the *left* prefrontal cortex involved in verbal memory retrieval. In contrast, deciding whether a shirt was a dress shirt led to activation of search mechanisms in the *right* prefrontal cortex along with circuits involved in shifting visual attention to aspects of the picture.

One Person's Basic May Be Another's Subordinate   Although the basic level shows surprising similarity across people and cultures, the more a person knows about a particular domain, the more likely she is to use more specific rather than basic-level terms (Geoghehan, 1976; Mervis & Rosch, 1981; Tanaka & Taylor, 1991). For example, clinical psychologists and psychiatrists do not use words like "nut" to describe a psychotic patient or say that a person "has problems," as people do in everyday discourse. Instead, they make a more specific diagnosis that identifies precisely what the problem is.

The basic level of categorization also changes according to the situation. During the workday, furniture makers may refer to chairs according to specific types (for instance, an oak ladder-back reproduction), but when the day ends and they are ready to rest their feet, "chair" will suffice (Holland et al., 1986). Basic-level categories also vary to some extent across cultures. While *love* is a basic-level concept for most Westerners, the Native American Utku distinguish love-for-those-who-need-protection and love-for-those-who-are-charming-or-admired at the basic level (Russell, 1991).

A GLOBAL VISTA

CULTURE AND CATEGORIZATION

To a large extent, culture shapes not only the categories people consider basic but also the way they group things (Lopez et al., 1997; Mishra, 1997). One tribe of Australian aborigines includes women, fire, and dangerous things in one category (Lakoff, 1985). This category would make little sense to members of other societies, but to the aborigines it seems perfectly natural. In their mythology, the sun—a woman—is the wife of the moon. Because the sun gives off heat, it is associated with fire, and since fire is dangerous, both the sun and women are linked to dangerous things. A Papuan from New Guinea included the crested dove, the black cockatoo, and a particular iguana as members of his tribe (Kitagawa, 1962, pp. 42–43). Although these ways of classifying may seem peculiar to the Western ear, consider the difficulty a Christian might have explaining to a Papuan how Jesus could simultaneously be a man, a god, a spirit, and the Son of God.

One study examined the influence of culture on categorization, compar-

In her tribe in Australia, this little girl, by virtue of her gender, will one day find herself in a category that includes "dangerous things."

ing 100 college students from New Mexico with 80 illiterate Manu farmers from a small village in Liberia, Africa (Irwin et al., 1974). To assess people's ability to categorize and think abstractly, psychologists in the West often use card sorting tasks. The psychologist presents participants with a deck of cards showing different geometric forms (squares, triangles, etc.). The geometric forms vary in color and number. The subject is to figure out the three dimensions on which the cards vary and sort them by category, that is, by form, color, and number. The subject has a certain amount of time (in this study, five minutes) in which to sort the cards in all three correct ways.

Previous research had found that many preliterate people did poorly on this task, which was often attributed to inferior cognitive skills caused by a lack of formal education. The experimenters in this study wondered, however, whether the apparent superiority of Western-educated subjects would disappear if the task involved materials more familiar to the Manu. An extremely familiar object in the Manu culture is rice, which comes in different forms that the Manu readily distinguish. Thus, the experimenters adapted the sorting task to fit Manu experience by presenting subjects with bowls of rice. The bowls varied in amount, type (long-grain and short-grain), and texture (polished versus unpolished). The task, then, was to sort the rice using each of these three categories. The researchers hypothesized that the Manu would do better on the rice task, whereas North American subjects would do better on the card sort task.

The results generally supported the hypothesis: North American subjects performed much better and faster on card sorting, which is more familiar to them, than rice sorting (Table 7.1). The opposite was true for the Manu farmers. Interestingly, however, the Western subjects were faster on both tasks than the Manu, and their performance was generally superior. Whether this reflects the difference between educated and uneducated or Western and non-Western populations cannot be determined from this study. What is clear, however, is that people in different cultures categorize objects in different ways depending on their use and familiarity. In other words, categorization is constrained by the nature of reality, which leads to cross-cultural universals: We group some things together simply because that is the way they are. Like most cognitive processes, however, categorization is also *functional*, so that people tend to categorize in ways that help them solve problems (Medin et al. 1997).

TABLE 7.1   SORTING PERFORMANCE OF U.S. AND MANU SUBJECTS USING CARDS AND RICE

SAMPLE	MEAN NUMBER OF CORRECT SORTS		MEAN TIME (IN SECONDS) TAKEN TO PERFORM SORTS		
	CARDS	RICE	CARDS	RICE	
U.S.	2.92	1.82	11.42	27.80	U.S. subjects were faster than Manus, even on the rice task.
Manu	1.42	2.10	49.40	42.43	

U.S. subjects performed better with cards, a familiar stimulus.

Manu subjects performed better with rice, a familiar stimulus.

Source: Adapted from Irwin et al., 1974.

INTERIM SUMMARY: A **concept** is a mental representation of a class of objects, ideas, or events that share common properties. **Categorization** is the process of identifying an object as an instance of a category. Although people sometimes categorize objects by comparing them with a list of **defining features**, or essential characteristics, of a concept, people typically classify objects rapidly by judging their *similarity* to **prototypes** (abstract representations of a category) stored in memory. Many concepts are hierarchically ordered. The level people naturally tend to use in categorizing objects is known as the **basic level**. One level up is the **superordinate** level, and one level down is the **subordinate** level. Culture shapes not only the categories people consider basic but also the way they group things together. Categorization, like most cognitive processes, is *functional*, so that people tend to categorize in ways that help them solve problems.

REASONING, PROBLEM SOLVING, AND DECISION MAKING

Mental images, mental models, and concepts are the building blocks of thought. In the next several pages, we explore how people manipulate these elementary units of thought to reason, solve problems, and make decisions.

REASONING

Reasoning refers to the process by which people generate and evaluate arguments and beliefs (Anderson, 1985; Holyoak & Spellman, 1993). Philosophers have long distinguished two kinds of reasoning: inductive and deductive. We examine each separately here, although as we shall see, psychologists have begun to question whether induction and deduction are really distinct processes *psychologically* (Rips, 1990). We then explore one of the most powerful mechanisms people use to make inferences, particularly about novel situations: reasoning by analogy.

Inductive Reasoning

After taking a new medication for three days, a woman finds she has developed a rash on her chest. She cannot think of any new foods she has eaten in the past few days, so she concludes that she is probably allergic to the medication. This type of thinking is called **inductive reasoning**—reasoning from specific observations to more general propositions that seem likely to be true (Holland et al., 1986). The inductive logic that led to the woman's conclusions might be summarized as follows:

> Today I have a rash.
> For the past three days I have been taking a new medication.
> For the past three days I have not eaten any foods to which I am allergic.
> Therefore, I must be allergic to the new medication.

Inductive reasoning relies on probabilities. An inductive conclusion is not *necessarily* true because its underlying premises are only probable, not certain. For example, the woman with the rash may have been exposed to chicken pox, so that the symptoms appeared coincidentally with her new medication schedule. Similarly one four-year-old child's inductive reasoning reinforced her fear of the bogeyman: If Santa can come down the chimney, she reasoned, so can the bogeyman!

Although inductive reasoning is fallible, it is essential in daily life. In fact, every time we categorize an object, we are using a form of inductive reasoning.

When we classify a novel animal as a cat, we assume that a particular body shape, whiskers, and feline body movements imply "cat-hood," although the animal could turn out to be an unusual rabbit or a species with which we are unfamiliar.

If induction relies on probabilities, how well do people intuitively use probability theory and the statistical principles derived from it when they reason inductively (Nisbett & Ross, 1980)? Most of us are not very astute intuitive statisticians, but instruction in statistical rules and probability theory can improve our ability to reason inductively in everyday life (Fong & Nisbett, 1991; Lehman et al., 1988; Nisbett, 1993). For example, one study investigated the extent to which undergraduate training improves everyday reasoning (Lehman & Nisbett, 1990). The researchers tested undergraduates in the first semester of their freshman year and again in the second semester of their senior year. Among other tasks, they asked participants questions that required statistical reasoning and an understanding of scientific method, such as the importance of large samples and control groups (Figure 7.4a). After four years of college, the statistical-methodological reasoning abilities of students majoring in the natural sciences and the humanities improved only slightly, while the abilities of psychology and other social science majors improved dramatically (Figure 7.4b). (This may be something to write home about.)

Deductive Reasoning

Deductive reasoning is logical reasoning that draws a conclusion from a set of assumptions, or premises. In contrast to inductive reasoning, it starts with an idea rather than an observation. In some ways, deduction is the flipside of induction: Whereas induction starts with specifics and draws general conclusions, deduction starts with general principles and makes inferences about specific instances. For example, if you understand the general premise that all dogs have fur and you know that Barkley is a dog, then you can deduce that Barkley has fur, even though you have never made Barkley's acquaintance. Unlike inductive reasoning, deductive reasoning can lead to *certain* rather than simply *probable* conclusions, as long as the premises are correct and the reasoning is logical.

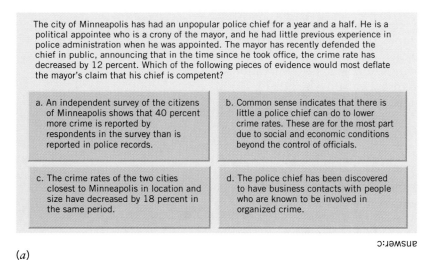

(a)

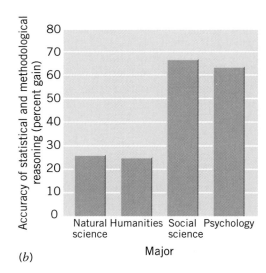

(b)

FIGURE 7.4

Statistical and methodological reasoning. With training, students improve in their reasoning abilities in college on questions such as those found in (a). As seen in (b), undergraduates who majored in subjects placing a premium on statistical and methodological reasoning showed substanially higher gains in reasoning than subjects in other majors. *Sources: (a)* Lehman et al., 1988; *(b)* Lehman & Nisbett, 1990.

Syllogisms   One form of deductive argument studied extensively by psychologists is the syllogism. A **syllogism** consists of two premises that lead to a logical conclusion. A classic example of a syllogism is the following, first stated in abstract form (*a*) and then more concretely (*b*):

(*a*)	(*b*)
Premise: All *A*s are *B*.	All men are mortal.
Premise: *C* is an *A*	Socrates is a man.
Therefore: *C* is a *B*.	Socrates is mortal.

Making accurate deductions requires preserving the meaning of each proposition in the syllogism while mentally manipulating it or testing its implications. This requires substantial working memory resources and can often lead to mistakes, particularly when the propositions are stated formally (in terms of *A*s and *B*s). Consider the following syllogism, expressed both formally (*a*) and concretely (*b*). Try to assess the validity of (*a*) before reading (*b*).

(*a*)	(*b*)
Premise: All *A*s are *B*.	All men are mortal
Premise: *C* is an *A*.	Socrates is a man.
Therefore: All *A*s are *C*.	All men are Socrates.

As this example suggests, deductive reasoning is often more difficult when the propositions are presented as highly abstract propositions. On the other hand, consider the following syllogism, presented in three different forms. Again, try evaluating the formal syllogism before looking at the specific examples of it.

(*a*)	(*b*)	(*c*)
Premise: All *A*s are *B*.	All men are human.	All birds have wings.
Premise: Some *C*s are *A*.	Some artists are men.	Some animals are birds.
Therefore: All *C*s are *B*.	All artists are human.	All animals have wings.

As example (*b*) illustrates, a valid conclusion does not imply that a person has applied logic correctly. People can sometimes be lulled into accepting bad logic if they know the conclusion is correct.

Factors That Influence Deductive Reasoning   Both the form (abstract or concrete) and content of deductive reasoning problems influence how easily people solve them (Cosmides, 1989; Wilkins, 1982). This can be seen in the card problem presented in Figure 7.5. Participants in this study are shown four cards and told that each card has a letter on one side and a number on the other. They are also told that the cards conform to the following rule: *If a card has an A on one side, then it has a 3 on the other side.* The task: Turn over only those cards necessary to discover whether the rule is true or false (Johnson-Laird et al., 1972; Wason, 1968).

While most people correctly conclude that they must turn over the card with the *A* on it (a number other than 3 would falsify the rule), few also realize that they must turn over the 2 card: Finding an *A* on the opposite side of this card would disprove the rule just as surely as would turning over the *A* card and finding something other than a 3. Most subjects also think they have to turn over the 3 card, which is irrelevant: If an *A* is not on the other side, it has no bearing on the rule *If A, then 3*. (If your self-esteem has just plummeted, take heart, I did not get this right on the first try, either.) If the same problem is posed with more familiar contents, deductive reasoning is much easier (Figure 7.6).

FIGURE 7.5
Card selection task. If each card has a number on one side and a letter on the other, which cards must be turned over to verify or disprove the rule "If a card has an *A* on one side, then it has a 3 on the other"? *Source:* Wason, 1968.

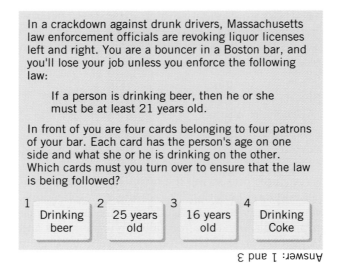

Figure 7.6
Card selection task with familiar content. *Source:* Adapted from Griggs & Cox, 1982.

If deductive reasoning depends in part on the content of the premises, do people really solve deductive problems by mentally manipulating abstract propositions? According to one theory, deduction is actually less about formal rules of inference (about As and Bs) than about forming mental models of each of the premises that allow the person to draw reasonable judgments about the conclusion (Johnson-Laird, 1995). For example, if asked to solve a syllogism of the form, "If A is on the left of B, and B is on the left of C, then . . ." people typically *visualize* the scene, creating a mental model that combines the premises. In this view, people make both inductive and deductive inferences by imagining scenarios or scenes and the relations among their elements, and then imagining what they are like, could be like, or could not be like.

Are Deduction and Induction Really Distinct Processes? Since the content of a syllogism can influence the ability to solve it, some psychologists now question whether induction and deduction are really different forms of reasoning (Rips, 1990, 1995). If people can reason more accurately about the properties of men and Socrates than about As and Bs, perhaps they are really intermingling deduction and induction—using mental models about the world that emerged inductively to draw deductive conclusions, or at least using their inductive knowledge about reality to check their logical deductions (Johnson-Laird, 1995, 1996; Oakhill et al., 1989). And where do the premises of deductive logic come from, such as the proposition that all dogs have fur? Usually from induction—from seeing several dogs and realizing they all have fur.

Some fascinating neurological data may help resolve some of these questions. In a series of studies, researchers studied syllogistic reasoning in psychiatric patients just before and after treatment with electroconvulsive therapy (ECT, or "shock therapy") (Deglin & Kinsbourne, 1996). Electroconvulsive therapy is typically used to treat depression when other methods have proven ineffective (Chapter 16). Because jarring the brain with electric shocks temporarily disrupts cognitive functioning, the procedure is typically applied to only one hemisphere. Researchers compared the disruptive effects on deductive reasoning of momentarily disabling either the right or the left hemisphere.

Patients with right-hemisphere ECT, who had to rely on their left-hemisphere (the "analytical" side of the brain), solved syllogisms using formal, theoretical reasoning. In contrast, patients with left hemisphere ECT, who had to rely on their right hemispheres, tried to reason from their knowledge and personal experience.

When given syllogisms with false premises, patients whose right hemispheres were disabled did not seem to notice the problem and continued to test the logic of the syllogism. Patients whose left hemispheres were disabled, in contrast, often refused to respond to syllogisms whose content was unfamiliar or whose premises were obviously false. These data suggest that the right and left hemispheres may contribute differently to deductive reasoning, with the left hemisphere evaluating the "pure" logic and the right hemisphere responding to the content.

Reasoning by Analogy

When people encounter a novel situation, they often rely on *analogies* to make inferences about what it is and what to do. Reasoning by analogy, or **analogical reasoning**, is the process by which people understand a novel situation in terms of a familiar one (Gentner & Holyoak, 1997). Thus, to a cognitive psychologist, the mind is like a computer or a network of neurons; to a premedical student primarily studying physics, biology, and organic chemistry, a literature course may be "a breath of fresh air."

People use analogies to categorize novel situations, make inferences, and solve problems. They also try to influence the inferences other people will make and the conclusions they will reach by using analogies that suit their own goals. During the Gulf War, U.S. President George Bush compared Saddam Hussein to Hitler. If one accepts this premise, then Iraq's invasion of Kuwait was like Germany's invasion of its neighbors at the start of World War II, which implied that Saddam must be stopped immediately before becoming a danger to the world (Spellman & Holyoak, 1992). Similarly, Saddam compared Bush and the United States to Satan, which implied that fighting the enemy was a holy war.

A key aspect of analogies of this sort is that the familiar situation and the novel situation must each contain a system of elements that can be mapped onto one another (Gentner, 1983; Gentner & Markman, 1997). For an analogy to take hold, the two situations need not *literally* resemble each other; Saddam did not look much like Hitler (although each sported a distinctive mustache), and Iraq was not a mighty power like Germany. However, the *elements* of the familiar situation must relate to one another in a way that explains how the elements of the novel situation are related. Thus, it did not matter that Hitler was European and Saddam was Middle Eastern. If one accepted the analogy that Saddam was like Hitler, then his behavior could be understood as the actions of a ruthless, power-hungry megalomaniac who must be stopped before he took over any more of his neighbors.

To reason from analogies, the person must first activate one or more relevant *analogs*—mental models of familiar situations—from long-term memory. Selecting the best-fitting analog involves meeting three sets of constraints (Holyoak & Thagard, 1989, 1995, 1997). First, the current situation must, at some level, be similar enough to the familiar situation to activate the analog. Thus, Iraq's occupation of Kuwait did not activate the analog of one team defeating another in a soccer match because the situation involved bloodshed and Kuwait was not a willing participant in the "game." Second, as described above, the elements of the novel situation and the analog must be readily mapped onto one another in a way that seems to make sense. If Kuwait had itself been aggressive prior to Iraq's attack, the analogy *Iraq : Kuwait :: Germany : Czechoslovakia* would not have worked because the first countries Germany occupied before World War II had not been aggressive and thus had not provoked Hitler's attack. Third, the choice of an analog depends on the reasoner's goals. Had President Bush not wanted to intervene after the Iraqi takeover of Kuwait, he could easily have chosen a different analog, such as a *family dispute* that the participants must settle on their own.

The analogies people use can play a crucial part in the actions they take and are highly influenced by emotionally powerful experiences. World War II played a central role in determining the analogies that shaped foreign policy in the West for three decades. When communist governments began coming to power in Asia in the late 1940s and 1950s, policymakers in the West had the analogy of prewar Germany squarely in mind: To "lose" another country to communism was like letting another country fall to Hitler. Thus, in the 1960s, the United States entered into a war against the communists in North Vietnam. That war, however, led to disastrous consequences for the United States—60,000 dead soldiers and nothing to show for it—and created a new analog as powerful to a younger generation of Americans as World War II had been to their elders. Thus, whenever an aggressor nation attacked one of its neighbors, opponents of intervention likened the situation to "another Vietnam." It is probably no accident that George Bush chose the analog of World War II instead of Vietnam in responding to the Iraqi invasion of Kuwait, since he had fought in World War II, and its memory was etched in his mind.

INTERIM SUMMARY: **Reasoning** is the process by which people generate and evaluate arguments and beliefs. **Inductive reasoning** means reasoning from specific observations to more general propositions that seem likely to be true. **Deductive reasoning** means drawing a conclusion from a set of assumptions that is true if the premises are true. Both the form (abstract or concrete) and content of deductive reasoning problems such as syllogisms influence how easily people solve them. **Analogical reasoning** is the process by which people understand a novel situation in terms of a familiar one. Analogical reasoning is influenced by the similarity of the situations, the ease of mapping of their elements, and the reasoner's goals.

PROBLEM SOLVING

Life is a series of problems to solve. How much should you tip the waiter? How are you going to afford a new car? What can you do to get your boyfriend to be more responsive? Syllogisms might momentarily seem insightful ("All men are trouble, Bob is a man, therefore Bob is trouble"), but they have their limits. **Problem solving** refers to the process of transforming one situation into another to meet a goal (Gilhooly, 1989; Greeno, 1978). The aim is to move from a current, unsatisfactory state (the *initial state*) to a state in which the problem is resolved (the *goal state*) (Figure 7.7). To get from the initial state to the goal state, the person uses *operators*, mental and behavioral processes aimed at transforming the initial state until it eventually approximates the goal (Anderson, 1993; Miller et al., 1960; Newell & Simon, 1972).

Some problems are **well-defined**; the initial state, goal state, and operators are easily determined. The math problems that students confront countless times in their school careers are examples of well-defined problems (Kintsch & Greeno, 1985). In real life, however, few problems are so straightforward; rather, most are **ill-defined**, since both the information needed to solve them and the criteria for determining whether the goals have been met are vague (Schraw et al., 1995; Simon, 1978). For example, a manager trying to raise morale among his employees faces an ill-defined problem, since he may not know the extent of the problem, or how to be sure whether his efforts to solve it have really worked.

Solving a problem, once it has been clarified, can be viewed as a four-step process (Holland et al., 1986; Newell, 1969; Reiman & Chi, 1989). The first step is to compare the initial state with the goal state to identify precise differences between the two. Thus, if the initial state is that the person sitting next to you on a flight from Chicago to Melbourne, Australia, has decided that you are the perfect

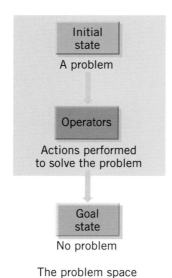

FIGURE 7.7
The problem-solving process. Problem solving means transforming an initial problem state, using operators, to attain a goal state.

person to hear his life story (the problem), the goal state is to be free of his charming discourse. The second step is to identify possible operators and select the one that seems most likely to reduce the differences. One possible strategy is to pull out a book and start reading; another is to tell him how much you enjoy talking with people about your profession, theoretical mathematics. (I have a friend who does this, and he assures me that it works every time.) The third step is to apply the operator or operators, responding to challenges or roadblocks by establishing **subgoals**—minigoals on the way to achieving the broader goal. For example, if your seatmate does not take the hint when you pull out a book and announce with great fanfare that you have to finish reading it by the end of the trip, you may determine that your only means of escape is to change seats. This subgoal then creates a search for operators (and flight attendants) that might help you attain it. The final step is to continue using operators until all differences between the initial state and the goal state are eliminated.

Problem-Solving Strategies

Problem solving would be impossible if people had to try every potential operator in every situation until they found one that worked. Instead, they employ **problem-solving strategies**, techniques that serve as guides for solving a problem (Demorest, 1986; Mayer, 1983; Reimann & Chi, 1989). One type of problem-solving strategy, called **algorithms,** employs systematic procedures that inevitably produce a solution (Anderson, 1995). Computers use algorithms in memory searches, as when a spell-check command compares every word in a file against an internal dictionary. Humans also use algorithms to solve problems, such as counting the number of guests coming to a barbeque and multiplying by 2 to determine how many hot dogs to buy. Algorithms are guaranteed to find a solution as long as one exists, but they are generally only practical for solving relatively simple problems. Imagine solving for the square root of 16,129 by methodically squaring 1, then 2, then 3, and so forth, each time checking to see if the answer is 16,129. (You would eventually arrive at the right answer, but only on your 127th try.)

Another common problem-solving strategy is **hypothesis testing**, or formulating an educated guess about what might solve the problem and then testing it (Klayman & Ha, 1989). One study examined the relationship between medical students' hypothesis-testing skills and their cost-effectiveness in ordering diagnostic tests (Durand et al., 1991). Researchers presented third-year medical students with case studies and asked them to generate hypotheses about possible diagnoses and list the tests they would order. Students whose hypotheses were logically organized suggested fewer and less expensive tests than their peers who did not systematically rule in and rule out possible disorders.

One of the most important problem-solving strategies is **mental simulation**— imagining the steps involved in solving a problem mentally before actually undertaking them. People conduct mental simulations of this sort every day, such as imagining precisely how they will tell their boss about the vacation they want to take during the busy season or picturing alternative routes they could take to make it to three different stores after work before the stores close.

Although many self-help books encourage people to visualize desired outcomes (the "power of positive thinking"), mentally simulating the steps to *achieving* that outcome is usually more beneficial (Taylor et al., 1998). One study demonstrated this with introductory psychology students facing a midterm examination. Students in one condition were told to visualize in detail the things they needed to do to get a good grade—picturing themselves on their beds reviewing lecture notes, and so forth. Students in the "positive-thinking" condition were instructed, instead, to visualize themselves receiving the grade they wanted and how good they would

Outcome	CONDITION		
	Mental simulation	Positive thinking	Control
Number of hours studying	16.07	11.57	14.50
Grade (% of questions correct)	80.60	72.57	77.68

FIGURE 7.8
Effects of mental simulation on exam performance. Students who mentally simulated the steps involved in solving the problem of getting a good grade studied harder and were more successful than students who either visualized success without the steps or did not imagine anything.

feel. Students who imagined the steps to achieving a good grade studied harder and scored better on the exam than students in the positive thinking group, who actually did worse than students in a control condition who did not visualize anything (Figure 7.8).

Problem Solving Gone Awry

Most of us muddle through our lives solving problems relatively well. However, human problem solving is far from perfect. One common problem is **functional fixedness**, the tendency for people to ignore other possible functions of an object when they have a fixed function in mind. In one experiment, participants were asked to mount a candle on a wall so that, when lit, no wax would drip on the floor (Duncker, 1946). On a table lay a few small candles, some tacks, and a box of matches (Figure 7.9a, p. 315). The tendency, of course, was to see a matchbox as only a matchbox. If the matches were *out* of the box, however, subjects solved the problem more easily (Figure 7.9b, p. 316).

Another common error in problem solving is **confirmation bias**, the tendency for people to search for confirmation of what they already believe (see Klayman & Ha, 1989; Oakhill & Garnham, 1993). In one study, the experimenters presented participants with three numbers (2, 4, and 6) and asked them to discover the rule used to construct this sequence of numbers by generating their own sets of numbers (Wason, 1960). Each time, the experimenters told participants whether or not their response correctly illustrated the rule. In fact, the rule was quite simple: any three numbers, arranged from smallest to largest. However, the way most people tried to solve the problem kept finding the rule. Instead of testing a variety of sequences—such as *3, 12, 428,* or *7, 4, 46*—until only one rule remained plausible, most participants did just the opposite. Early on, they formed a hypothesis such as "add 2 to each number to form the next number" and repeatedly generated one sequence after another that confirmed this rule until they were satisfied they were right. Confirmation bias can be a particular problem for experts in a field; for example, scientists studying a topic may only test hypotheses and use methods that fit with current thinking (Sternberg, 1996).

Solving Problems with Numbers

In literate societies, people are constantly called upon to think in numbers. Consider the following examples from two very different places—a box of brownie mix and an income tax form (McCloskey & Macaruso, 1995):

> Grease bottom of 13 × 9-inch pan. Mix brownie mix, water, oil, and egg in large bowl. Beat 50 strokes by hand. . . . Bake at 350 degrees F for 35 to 37 minutes.

If line 32 is $81,350 or less, multiply $2,350 by the total number of exemptions claimed on line 6e. If line 32 is over $81,350, see the worksheet on page 25.

How do people translate numbers on a page into a form with which they can think and solve problems? According to one theory, the first step in solving a numerical problem is to translate a visual image or a pattern of sound (as when someone asks, "Did you say that was three dollars or four?") into an abstract representation of the number and its meaning. Indeed, if people did not first make this "translation," children would have to learn their multiplication tables twice, once for problems presented on paper and once for problems presented verbally (McCloskey & Macaruso, 1995).

Solving mathematical problems, like most problem solving, involves a combination of declarative and procedural knowledge (Anderson, 1996). People store information in declarative units, such as the knowledge that 4+4=8. To solve more difficult problems, they apply procedures that use this knowledge. For example, suppose an eight-year-old child is given this addition problem:

$$422$$
$$+514$$

FIGURE 7.9
(*a*) The candle problem. Use the objects on the table to mount a candle on the wall so that when it is lit, no wax drips on the floor. [Solution is on next page.]

Through experience in school, the child will begin with the procedure of starting on the right-hand side and activating the knowledge that 2+4=6. Once this knowledge comes to mind, the next procedure activated is to write a 6 in the bottom right-hand column, followed by the procedure of moving over one column to the left and starting again.

The way people solve arithmetic problems depends on the kind of problem. Consider the example from the tax form, which involves two steps: deciding whether the amount on one line is greater than another and then multiplying two numbers. Deciding whether one number is larger than another involves activating stored information about both numbers, bringing this information into working memory, and comparing it. Multiplication of small numbers (e.g., 2 x 9) requires little more than activating a simple, well-learned fact and should require less effort. However, multiplication of large numbers, like those on an income tax form (hopefully), places heavy loads on working memory: The person has to multiply a digit from two columns, momentarily store the product, add one digit from this to the product of the next set of digits while retaining the other digit in memory, and repeat the process until arriving at a solution. (This is why people typically have trouble multiplying long numbers in their heads and instead rely on shortcuts in everyday life, such as calculating a 15 percent tip by calculating 10 percent, dividing that amount in half to arrive at the other 5 percent, and then adding the two amounts.) Imaging research on mathematical problem solving is just beginning, but preliminary studies suggest that tasks such as comparing the size of two numbers and multiplying numbers draw on somewhat different neural circuits (Dehaene et al., 1996)—or a sheet of paper!

Humans are not alone in the need to solve numerical problems. When a lion responds to the presence of other lions about to intrude into her territory, she is more cautious if she hears *three* approaching lions roaring than one, and she is more likely to mount an aggressive response if more of her kin and companions are present (McComb et al., 1994). From an evolutionary perspective, being able to "count" friends and enemies in such situations is essential to survival. So do lions actually have a concept of number? And how does a rat that is rewarded in a learning experiment for pressing a bar every 20th time know when the 20th time is approaching?

Although psychologists are still unraveling the mechanisms by which animals "count" (e.g., Roberts, 1995), research suggests that those of us who have

FIGURE 7.9
(*b*) Solution to the candle problem. *Source:* Duncker, 1946.

trouble balancing our checkbooks might learn a few things from even the lowly rat (Davis, 1996; Davis & Perusse, 1988). For example, in one study, rats were punished if they ate more than a certain number of pieces of food (e.g., three pellets) out of 20 pieces in front of them. Showing not only a talent for math but also some impressive self-restraint, the rats learned to eat the right number of pellets and leave the rest. In other studies, rats have even demonstrated an "understanding" that if $A<B<C$, then $A<C$!

INTERIM SUMMARY: **Problem solving** means transforming an *initial state* into a more satisfying *goal state* using *operators*. People frequently rely on **problem-solving strategies** that serve as guides for solving problems, such as **algorithms** (systematic procedures that inevitably produce a solution), **hypothesis testing** (trying out solutions based on hypotheses), and **mental simulations** (imagining the steps involved in solving a problem before actually trying them out).

DECISION MAKING

Just as life is a series of problems to solve, it is also a series of decisions to make, from the mundane ("Should I buy the cheaper brand or the one that tastes better?") to the consequential ("What career should I choose?"). **Decision making** is the process by which an individual weighs the pros and cons of different alternatives in order to make a choice.

Calculating Expected Utilities

According to one information-processing model, when people make decisions, they consider two things: the *utility*, or value to them, of the outcomes of different options and the *probability*, or estimated likelihood, of each outcome. For example, if you have found three apartments near campus and must choose one, you are likely to consider rent, proximity to campus, attractiveness, availability of parking, and permission to keep pets. According to this model, a rational decision maker would begin by assigning a weight to each attribute according to its importance (Edwards, 1977). Thus, if budget is the most important factor, rent would receive the highest weight. Then, for each apartment, you would assign a **utility value** to each attribute, which represents the extent to which the potential choice (the apartment) meets each criterion (such as affordable price).

The next step is to multiply the weight of the attribute (how important it is) by its utility value (how well the option fulfills the criterion) for each option (apartment) (Table 7.2). This yields to a **weighted utility value**, a combined measure of the importance of an attribute and the extent to which a given option satisfies it. Suppose, for example, the attribute of parking has a weight of 2, and parking at 1010 California Street is inconvenient enough to have a utility value of -2; then its weighted utility value will be 2 x -2, or -4. Once you have rated and weighted all the attributes, determining which alternative has the highest overall weighted utility value is simply a matter of adding up the totals.

In reality, of course, as the noted psychologist Mick Jagger pointed out, "You can't always get what you want," and shooting for an unattainable goal may carry heavy costs. For example, the Green Street apartment may have so many applicants that no matter how high a rating it earns, it may be a poor selection if you have only a slight chance of getting it and must have a place to live by a certain date. Making a rational decision, then, involves integrating information about both the value and probability of different options; this combined assessment is called **expected utility**. The expected utility of an alternative is obtained by multi-

TABLE 7.2 CALCULATING WEIGHTED UTILITY VALUE

ATTRIBUTES (IN ORDER OF IMPORTANCE)	IMPORTANCE (NUMERICAL WEIGHT)	ALTERNATIVE APARTMENTS					
		216 GREEN ST.		16 CEDAR ST.		1010 CALIFORNIA ST.	
		UTILITY VALUE	WEIGHTED UTILITY VALUE	UTILITY VALUE	WEIGHTED UTILITY VALUE	UTILITY VALUE	WEIGHTED UTILITY VALUE
Rent	5	+10	×5 = 50	+ 8	×5 = 40	+ 5	×5 = 25
Location	4	0	×4 = 0	+ 3	×4 = 12	+10	×4 = 40
Livability	3	+ 8	×3 = 24	+ 3	×3 = 9	+ 1	×3 = 3
Parking	2	+10	×2 = 20	+10	×2 = 20	− 2	×2 = −4
Pets	1	+10	×1 = 10	−10	×1 = −10	+10	×1 = 10
			104		**71**		**74**

Source: Adapted from Edwards, 1977. Copyright © 1977 IEEE.

Note: Multiplying the utility value of each of several attributes by their importance yields weighted utility values for three apartments on five dimensions. Adding together the weighted utilities leads to a preference for the apartment at 216 Green Street.

plying the weighted utility by the expected probability of that outcome (Table 7.3). If you have a 10 percent chance of getting the Green Street apartment, the expected utility of that choice is .10 × 104, or 10.4. By comparison, if you have a 50 percent chance of getting the Cedar Street apartment and a 90 percent chance of getting the California Street apartment, the expected utilities of those alternatives are 35.5 and 66.6, respectively. If you need to make a decision quickly, then the one to choose is 1010 California.

INTERIM SUMMARY: **Decision making** is the process by which an individual weighs the pros and cons of different alternatives in order to make a choice. According to one information-processing model, when people make decisions, they consider both the *utility* of the outcomes of different options and their *probability*. A **weighted utility value** is a combined judgment of the importance of an attribute and the extent to which a given option satisfies it. **Expected utility** is a combined judgment of the weighted utility and the expected probability of obtaining an outcome.

TABLE 7.3 CALCULATING EXPECTED UTILITY

	ALTERNATIVE APARTMENTS		
	216 GREEN ST.	16 CEDAR ST.	1010 CALIFORNIA ST.
Weighted utility value	104	71	74
Probability of getting apartment	×.10	×.50	×.90
Expected utility =	10.4	35.5	66.6

Source: Adapted from Edwards, 1977. Copyright © 1977 IEEE.

Note: Although the apartment on Green Street has the highest weighted utility value, its improbability makes it the worst choice among the three options.

IMPLICIT AND EVERYDAY THINKING

The models of problem solving and decision making we have just described largely follow a classical model of rationality that guided Western philosophers for centuries. It is the same model assumed by economists who view people as maximizing the utility of the goods they buy and by political scientists who view voters as rationally choosing the leaders who best reflect their interests. In this view, rationality means considering potential paths to solving a problem or the relevant data for making a judgment and then consciously manipulating this information to come to the most reasonable conclusion.

These models are both *descriptive* and *prescriptive*: They attempt to *describe* the way people think but also to *prescribe* the way rational people *should* think. These models emerged in the 1960s, when cognitive scientists compared the human mind to the "mind" of a computer and assumed that cognition, like memory, involves explicit, step-by-step activation of information, as in the sequential steps involved in problem solving.

As we saw in Chapter 6, however, the models and metaphors used by cognitive psychologists have shifted dramatically in the last decade, and as will see, this shift is changing our understanding not only of memory but also of thinking. Critics argued that computers, unlike people, lack feelings and consciousness, and although computers can provide *analogs* of thought processes, they cannot literally understand the subjective meaning of events, which is crucial to human mental life (Dreyfus & Dreyfus, 1986; Searle, 1987).

Some hints about what might be missing from these models of **explicit cognition**—cognition that involves conscious manipulation of representations—actually came from behaviorist and psychodynamic models, which are becoming increasingly compatible with more contemporary cognitive models. From a behaviorist perspective, the pros and cons of different courses of action—their environmental consequences—determine the decisions people make, whether or not they think about these consequences. People learn, generalize, and discriminate stimuli all the time without conscious thought. For instance, in one study participants who had a single, brief, unfriendly encounter with an experimenter later avoided a confederate who physically resembled the experimenter (Lewicki, 1985). In behavioral terms, they generalized a conditioned emotional response, which in turn motivated avoidance behavior. Control subjects who did not have the initial aversive encounter with the experimenter did not avoid the confederate. When the investigators asked participants in the experimental condition why they felt and behaved as they did, they came up with every explanation but the real one. They were unaware that their behavior with one person had influenced their behavior with the other.

From a psychodynamic perspective, most problem solving and decision making involve motivation and emotion. A child with a learning disability who suffers repeated setbacks in school might "solve" this problem by convincing himself that he does not care about success or failure and hence stop making any effort. Further, according to psychodynamic psychologists, some of the motives that underlie decisions are unconscious or implicit (Chapter 8). For example, many adults who had an alcoholic parent gravitate toward alcoholic mates, despite the misery that their parent's alcoholism caused them as children. Although they may have strong *explicit* motives to avoid getting involved with a drinker, cues associated with alcoholism seem to be important *implicit* criteria in their mate selection, presumably because these cues are associated with the affection they received as children from the only parents they had.

HOW RATIONAL ARE WE?

In recent years, cognitive psychologists have begun to wonder just how rational we humans really are. Some have pointed to the cognitive shortcuts people use that can lead them to make less than optimal decisions, whereas others have suggested that the concept of rationality itself may be limited (Mellers et al., 1998).

Heuristics

The assault on human rationality in psychology began when researchers started to notice the extent to which people rely on cognitive shortcuts, or **heuristics**, that allow them to make rapid, but sometimes irrational, judgments (Dawes, 1997; Nisbett & Ross, 1980). One example is the **representativeness heuristic**, in which people categorize by matching the similarity of an object or incident to a prototype but ignore information about its probability of occurring. Consider the following personality description (Tversky & Kahneman, 1974, p. 1124):

> Steve is very shy and withdrawn, invariably helpful, but with little interest in people or in the world of reality. A meek and tidy soul, he has a need for order and structure and a passion for detail.

Is Steve most likely a farmer, a salesman, an airline pilot, a librarian, or a physician? Most people think he is probably a librarian, even if they are told that librarians are much less common in the population from which Steve has been drawn than the other occupations. Although Steve's attributes seem typical or representative of a librarian, if the population has 50 salesmen for every librarian, the chances are high that Steve is a salesman, even though he fits the prototype of a librarian.

Using the **availability heuristic,** people infer the frequency of a class of events or the likelihood of something happening on the basis of its availability in memory (that is, how readily it comes to mind) (Tversky & Kahneman, 1973). People essentially assume that events or occurrences they can recall easily are common and typical. For example, in one study, participants were presented with a list of 26 names, half male and half female (McKelvie, 1996). Some of the names were famous, whereas others were not. When asked how many of the names were male or female, participants overestimated the gender that had more famous names because famous names were more salient and hence cognitively available.

The availability heuristic is generally adaptive because things that "stick in our minds" tend to be important; familiar or vivid occurrences come to mind more readily than less familiar or less striking events. Availability can, however, lead to biased judgments when striking or memorable events are in fact infrequent. For instance, most people in the United States, Canada, and Europe believe that driving to a family holiday gathering a few hours away is safer than flying to the Middle East, with its history of terrorist activity. Statistically, however, the chances of fatality are much greater driving on a holiday. In large part, the error in judgment occurs because the mass media, especially television, vividly portray isolated examples of violence in the Middle East, making these incidents more available in memory (Wober, 1987).

Bounded Rationality

Researchers studying heuristics challenged the rational models described earlier by suggesting that human thought is highly susceptible to error. An alternative and emerging perspective takes this critique of pure reason one step further, arguing that because people rarely have complete information and limitless time, they are often better off using strategies for making inferences and decisions that might seem less than optimal to a philosopher (Gigerenzer & Goldstein, 1996). This view essentially places thought in its ecological context: People tend to do the best they can given the demands of the task and the cognitive resources they have available (Simon, 1990).

A conclusion is the place where you got tired of thinking.

—AUTHOR UNKNOWN

Underlying this view is the notion of **bounded rationality**: People are rational *within bounds*, and those bounds depend on the environment, their goals, and their abilities. In this view, instead of making *optimal* judgments, people typically make *good-enough* judgments. Herbert Simon (1956) called this *satisficing*, a combination of *satisfying* and *sufficing*. When we choose a place to have dinner, we do not go through every restaurant in the phone book; rather, we go through a list of the restaurants that come to our minds and choose the one that seems most satisfying at the moment.

According to one theory, when people are called upon to make rapid inferences or decisions, they often use the strategy "take the best, ignore the rest" (Gigerenzer & Goldstein, 1996). Thus, instead of weighing all the information possible, they begin with a quick yes/no judgment; if that works, they stop and assume their inference is good enough. If it does not work, they go on to the next quickest judgment, and down the list until they get a "satisficing" answer. For example, when people are asked, "Which city is larger, Toronto or Columbus, Ohio?" the first judgment they make is whether they have heard of them both. If they have only heard of Toronto, they assume Toronto is bigger (since, presumably, they would have heard about a large city). If they have heard of both, they go to the next judgment. For a hockey fan, it might be "Do both have a major league team?" In this case, the answer is no: Toronto has the Maple Leafs, whereas Columbus is on thinner ice for a hockey fan. Thus, the conclusion is "Toronto."

INTERIM SUMMARY: **Explicit cognition** (cognition that involves conscious manipulation of representations) is only one form of thinking. Much of the time people rely on cognitive shortcuts, or **heuristics**, that allow them to make rapid judgments but can sometimes lead to irrational choices. Some psychologists argue that the classical model of rationality that has guided much research on explicit cognition needs to be amended to recognize the extent to which people do, and should, practice a **bounded rationality** constrained by their goals, their cognitive resources, and environmental demands.

IMPLICIT COGNITION

The classical model of rationality emphasizes conscious reflection. Yet many of the judgments and inferences people make occur outside of awareness. Try to recall the last time you said to yourself, "I think I'd like Chinese food for dinner." How did you come to that conclusion? Did you scan long-term gustatory memory, weigh various potential tastes, calculate the expected utility of each one, and reflect on the probability of making it to The Szechuan Palace in time for dinner? Most of the time judgments like this just "come to us," which is a shorthand for saying that they are a form of **implicit cognition**, or cognition outside of awareness.

Implicit Learning

Much of learning occurs outside awareness, as people implicitly register regularities in their environment or learn to behave in particular ways with little or no explicit instruction (Reber, 1992; Seger, 1994). For example, men in many cultures turn their eyes away from an attractive woman if her mate notices them looking. No one ever *teaches* boys the rule, "You have to stop looking at an attractive woman if her boyfriend catches you," yet they learn it nonetheless. Generally, rules of gaze (such as how long to look someone in the eye while speaking before breaking eye contact or where to look in a crowded elevator) are rarely taught explicitly, yet people implicitly learn to follow them and notice immediately if someone does not understand "the rules."

One way researchers study implicit learning is to create strings of letters according to an artificial "grammar," which specifies the way letters should be arranged in a word (much as English words typically include a vowel between consonants) (Reber, 1989). Although people can rarely articulate many of these rules verbally, after a few trials they tend to learn novel word strings that fit the grammar more quickly than word strings that do not, and they can generally judge whether a word string is grammatical—even though they cannot describe the rules they are using to make the judgment! Other studies show that people make many complex inferences, such as judging a person's social class from subtle facial, gestural, linguistic, or clothing cues, even though they frequently cannot articulate the principles of inference they are implicitly using (Lewicki, 1986).

Implicit Problem Solving

Another form of implicit cognition can be seen in "aha" experiences, when people set aside a seemingly insoluble problem only to find hours or days later that the answer suddenly comes to them (as in, "Aha! I know the answer!"). Implicit problem solving of this sort probably occurs through the implicit activity of associational networks, as information associated with unresolved problems remains active outside awareness (Bowers et al., 1990; Butterfield, 1964; Dorfman et al., 1996; Ziegarnik, 1927). For example, researchers in one study presented participants with definitions of uncommon words, such as the following (Yaniv & Meyer, 1987):

> Large bright colored handkerchief; brightly colored square of silk material with red or yellow spots, usually worn around the neck.

If participants could not name the word, it was then presented to them in a list of words (in this case, including the word *bandana*) and nonwords (incorrectly spelled words, such as *dascribe*). Participants were instructed to read each item on the list and quickly decide whether or not it was a (correctly spelled) word. Although they had initially been unable to name the word and were moving on to another task, participants nevertheless showed priming effects, responding more rapidly to words whose definitions they had just read. The unsolved problem had activated a network of associations even though the person had been unable to locate the key word on the network.

Information related to unsolved problems appears to remain active for extended periods. Over time, other cues in the environment or thoughts that occur during the day are likely to spread further activation to parts of the network. If enough activation reaches a potential solution, it will "jar" the answer free, catapulting it into consciousness (Yaniv & Meyer, 1987). This might explain what happens when people wake up from a dream with the answer to a problem, since elements of the dream can also spread activation to networks involving the unsolved problem.

EMOTION, MOTIVATION, AND DECISION MAKING

Another shift in psychologists' understanding of rationality is the recognition of the substantial role played by motivation and emotion in everyday judgments, inferences, and decisions.

When choosing a mate, people often have criteria in mind, but their choices are guided as much by their heart and gut as by their head.

Reason and Emotion

For two thousand years philosophers have bemoaned the way reason can be derailed by emotion (Chapter 11). Numerous studies have documented that emotional processes can, in fact, produce seemingly illogical responses. For example, people are much more likely to be upset if they miss a winning lottery ticket by one digit than by all six because they feel like they *just missed* it (Kahneman & Tversky, 1982). In reality, missing by one digit has exactly the same consequences as missing every digit.

On the other hand, *thinking* can sometimes interfere with sound judgment. In one study, participants looked at five art posters and rated the extent to which they liked each. The investigators asked participants in the experimental group to list their reasons for liking or disliking each poster before rating them; participants in the control group simply rated the posters. Afterwards, participants were allowed to choose a poster to take home. A few weeks later, the experimenters contacted them and asked how satisfied they were with their choice. Participants who had analyzed the reasons for their preferences were significantly less satisfied with their choice of poster than subjects who had chosen without reflection (Wilson et al., 1993). Conscious thinking appears to have overridden automatic, unconscious reactions, which proved to be a better guide.

Assessing Risk

Many of the decisions people make in everyday life stem from their emotional reactions and their *expected* emotional reactions. This is often apparent in the way people assess risks (Kahneman & Tversky, 1979; Mellers et al., 1997, 1998; Shapira, 1995). Judging risk is a highly subjective enterprise. What are the chances of an accident at a nuclear plant? The answer depends on how one chooses to frame the question. Compared to the number of automobile accidents, the risk of nuclear melt-down is exceedingly low. But how many nuclear disasters or near-disasters constitute an acceptable risk? And in the worst such accident in history, at Chernobyl, how does one calculate the damage? The number of people killed? The number of likely cancers to result in the thousands of people exposed to the radiation? Or does one try to calculate what *could* have happened if the winds had been different at the time of the blast or if the melt-down could not have been contained even as well as it was?

Risk assessment leads to some intriguing questions about precisely what constitutes "rational" behavior—and whether researchers can really assume that any given choice is the "right answer" in many judgment tasks. For example, many experiments have assessed the risks people are willing to take in gambling situations when the probabilities of success and failure and the size of the potential gains or losses vary. In Western samples, at least, losses tend to influence people's behavior more than gains, even where paying equal attention to the two would yield the highest average payoff (Coombs & Lehner, 1984). People differ substantially, however, in their willingness to take risks—and in their enjoyment of risky behavior (Zuckerman, 1994). Some people are motivated more by fear, whereas others are motivated more by pleasure; these differences may in part be rooted in the extent to which their nervous systems are responsive to norepinephrine, which regulates many fear responses, or dopamine, which is involved in pleasure-seeking behavior (Chapter 11).

Given the ambiguity of risk, it is not surprising that motivational and emotional factors play an important role in the way people assess it. Scientists who work in corporate research laboratories tend to find the risk of potential cancer-causing agents much smaller than scientists who work at universities (Kraus,

Malmfors, & Slovic, 1992). The difference depends upon who pays their salaries and hence what they are motivated to find. Other research finds that people are more likely to take risks when the chips are down than when they are up (Tversky & Kahneman, 1981). For example, in a simulated tax collection experiment, participants who expected to receive a tax refund were less likely to write off questionable expenses than those who thought their deductions would not cover their taxes. These findings have practical implications for policy makers: If the government deducted more from people's paychecks during the year and gave it back to them in refunds, taxpayers would write off fewer questionable expenses (Robben et al., 1990).

INTERIM SUMMARY: **Implicit cognition** refers to cognition outside of awareness. Much of learning is implicit, as people implicitly recognize patterns in the environment but cannot articulate these patterns explicitly. Problem solving can also occur implicitly, as in "aha" experiences. Motivation and emotion also play a substantial role in everyday cognition. Although emotion can disrupt cognition, it can also sometimes be a better guide for behavior. Motives and emotions substantially influence the way people assess risks; given the ambiguity involved in risk assessment, there may be no single "rational" assessment that is free of emotional influences.

CONNECTIONISM

As we saw in Chapter 6, psychology is in the midst of a "second cognitive revolution," which has challenged the notion of the mind as a conscious, one-step-at-a-time information processor that functions like a computer. One of the major contributors to this revolution is an approach to perception, learning, memory, thought, and language called **connectionism**, or **parallel distributed processing (PDP)** (Holyoak & Thagard, 1995; Read et al., 1997; Rumelhart et al., 1986; Smolensky, 1988). Unlike traditional models that emphasize serial processing, connectionist approaches assert that most cognitive processes occur simultaneously through the action of multiple activated networks. Like traditional cognitive psychologists, connectionists use computer models to test their theories, but their explicit metaphor for cognitive processing is the mind as a set of neurons that activate and inhibit one another, rather than the mind as a computer with memory stores.

Parallel Distributed Processing

The easiest way to get a grasp of PDP models is to understand what is meant by the terms *parallel* and *distributed*. First and foremost, PDP models emphasize *parallel* rather than serial processing. Human information processing is simply too fast and the requirements of the environment too instantaneous for serial processing to be our primary mode of information processing. For example, in typing the word *vacuum*, the right hand does nothing until the first *u*, yet high-speed videotapes of skilled typists find that the right hand has moved into position to hit the *u* by the time the left hand is typing the *v*. This happens so quickly that the typist cannot possibly be aware of it. Thus, even while the typist is focusing on the action of the left hand, recognition of the word "vacuum" has activated parallel systems that prepare the right hand for action (Rumelhart et al., 1986).

Second, according to PDP models, the meaning of a representation is not contained in some specific locus in the brain. Rather, it is spread out, or *distributed*, throughout an entire network of processing units (*nodes* in the network) that have become activated together through experience. Each node attends to some small aspect of the representation, and none alone "stands for" the entire concept. For instance, when a person comes across a barking dog, her visual system will simultaneously activate networks of neurons that have previously been activated by animals with two ears, four legs, and a tail. At the same time, auditory circuits previously "turned on" by barking will become active. The simultaneous activation of all these neural circuits identifies the animal with high probability as a dog. The person is not aware of any of this; all she consciously thinks is that she has come upon a dog.

This is how connectionist models explain categorization based on similarity. Current perceptions activate neural networks. A concept stored in memory is nothing but a series of nodes that become activated together and hence constitute a network. If current perceptual experience (such as seeing the shape of a dog and hearing barking) activates a large enough number of those nodes, the stimulus will be classified as an instance of that concept. However, several concepts may be activated simultaneously since many animals have four legs and a tail. According to connectionist models, the concept that "wins out" is the one that best matches current perceptions, that is, the one with the most nodes in common with current perceptual input. The connectionist model offers a deceptively simple and compelling explanation of memory as well: Remembering a visual scene, such as a sunset, entails activation of a substantial part of the visual network that was active when the sunset was initially perceived.

The Brain Metaphor

According to the connectionist view, then, the brain represents knowledge through the interaction of hundreds, thousands, or millions of neurons, which constitute nodes in a neural network. Perception, memory, categorization, and inference lie in the *connections* among these nodes. Hence the term *connectionism*.

When neurons interact, they may either excite or inhibit other neurons, through the action of excitatory and inhibitory neurotransmitters (Chapter 3). Connectionist models postulate similar cognitive mechanisms. Consider the simple perceptual problem posed in Figure 7.10. Although the letters are ambiguous, either because they are slanted or because pieces are blotted out, you were probably unaware that your brain was performing some complex "computations" to determine what the letters and words were. Instead, the meaning of the words just seemed obvious.

The incomplete letters shown in Figure 7.10 are actually the norm in handwriting, where letters are never perfectly drawn. But people can read handwriting rapidly because they simultaneously process information about the letters and the words. For example, in the top line of Figure 7.10, the second letter of each word could either be an *a* or an *h*. Both letters are thus activated by information-processing units whose job is letter recognition. At the same time, however, a word recognition processing unit recognizes that an *a* would render the first word a nonword and an *h* would do the same for the second word. The two processing modules interact, so that extra activation spreads to the *h* option in *the*, and the impossibility of *tae* as a word leads to inhibition of *a* as an option in that word. On an even broader level, the phrase *the cat* is also being processed, and because no other phrase is possible using that configuration of letters, the brain is even more likely to come to the "decision" that the first word is *the* (because what else would precede *cat* and has three letters?), further spreading activation to the *h* in *the*. Similar processes account for the fact that we decode the second word in the figure as *RED*, even though substantial pieces of the letters are covered.

Parallel Constraint Satisfaction

As Figure 7.10 suggests, categorizing, making inferences, reading, and other cognitive processes actually require substantial "decision making" at an implicit

FIGURE 7.10
Parallel distributed processing. People are able to decipher ambiguous or distorted messages by simultaneously processing parts (such as letters) and wholes (words and phrases). *Source:* Rumelhart, 1984, p.8.

level. The brain has to decide whether a letter is an *a* or an *h* or whether a four-legged animal with a tail is a dog or a cat. According to connectionist models, implicit desision-making of this sort happens rapidly, automatically, and without awareness through a process of parallel constraint satisfaction. **Constraint satisfaction** refers to the tendency of the mind to settle on a cognitive solution that satisfies as many constraints as possible in order to achieve the best fit to the data. A four-legged creature with a tail could be a dog or a cat, but if it starts barking, barking will further activate the *dog* concept and inhibit the *cat* concept because the neurons representing barking spread activation to networks associated with dogs and spread inhibition to networks associated with cats. Similarly, in reading the words in Figure 7.10, the brain has to satisfy constraints imposed by the structure of the word t_e as well as by the structure of the phrase t_e c_t), which will increase the activation of some possibilities and decrease the activation of others. To put it slightly differently, the nodes in a PDP network are like *hypotheses* about the presence or absence of a given feature, such as whether a letter is an *a* or an *h* (Read et al., 1997). Parallel distributed processing is an implicit everyday form of hypothesis testing, in which the brain weeds out hypotheses that data do not support and converges on hypotheses that best fit the data in light of multiple constraints processed in parallel.

The connections between nodes in a connectionist network are weighted according to the strength of the association between them and whether they excite or inhibit one another. The presence of barking is strong negative evidence for the "cat" hypothesis and strong positive evidence that the animal is a dog. Thus, the weight between *barks* and *cats* is strongly negative, whereas the weight that connects barking with dogs is strongly positive. These weights simply reflect the extent to which the two nodes have been activated together in the past. These weights increase and decrease with experience, which accounts for learning. Thus, if a person bought an unusual species of cat that made a barking sound, the weight between *bark* and *cat* would become more positive, at least for this particular type of cat.

Connectionist models can also be used to explain some complex phenomena, such as analogies and inferences (Golden & Rumelhart, 1993; Holyoak & Thagard, 1995). Consider the vignette with which this chapter began, in which a woman was beginning to infer that her boyfriend wanted to end their relationship. Figure 7.11 presents a simplified connectionist model of how she might have come to that judgment. Suppose she observed two things: He says he loves her, but he seems to be avoiding her. Direct observations carry a lot of weight when making inferences and hence receive high activation values (as indicated by the heavy blue lines, which indicate strong positive weights) (Kunda & Thagard, 1996). His saying "I love you," however, could have two interpretations: Either he wants to stay with her or he is trying to let her down easy; thus, "I love you" has a positive connection to both hypotheses. Wanting to let her down easy is associated with wanting to split up, which is also strongly associated with his avoiding her. Thus, the *wants to split up* node is doubly activated—directly by the *avoiding me* node and indirectly by the *"I love you"* node—through its connection to the *wants to let me down easy* node. The *wants to stay together* node is relatively weakly activated in comparison because its only positive input is from the *"I love you"* node. Thus, the system is likely to settle on the solution with the highest activation: He wants to leave.

INTERIM SUMMARY: According to **connectionist** or **parallel distributed processing (PDP)** models, most cognitive processes occur simultaneously through the action of multiple activated networks; the meaning of a representation is *distributed* throughout a network of processing units (*nodes*) that are activated together through experience. Knowledge thus lies in the connections between these nodes—in the extent to which they are positively or negatively associated with one another. When perceiving, remembering, categorizing, or

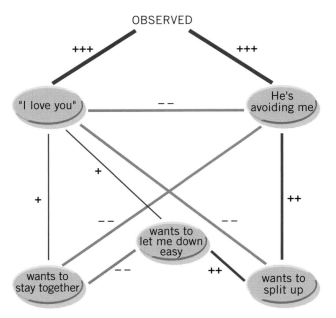

FIGURE 7.11
A connectionist model of inference. Positive weights are indicated in blue, whereas negative weights (inhibitory associations) are indicated in red. Strength of the associative connection (either positive or negative) is indicated by the width of the lines. Observed behavior has the strongest weights, since it is most certain. In this case, the woman has observed two behaviors by her boyfriend that are mutually incompatible (indicated by the thick red line connecting them): He says he loves her, and he is avoiding her. Each of these nodes is connected to multiple other nodes. Simultaneous processing of all of these connections leads to the conclusion that he wants to split up, since it has higher activation than the *wants to stay together* node.

performing other cognitive tasks, the mind settles on a cognitive solution that satisfies as many constraints as possible in order to achieve the best fit to the data through a process of parallel **constraint satisfaction**.

FROM MIND TO BRAIN

THE NEUROPSYCHOLOGY OF THINKING

Connectionist models treat the brain as a powerful metaphor. Other cognitive scientists are studying the brain itself to try to uncover the mysteries of thought.

Thinking requires mental representations and virtually every region of the cortex participates in creating representations. In this sense, the whole brain is involved in thought. Like other psychological functions, however, thought processes are both distributed—spread out through large networks of neurons—as well as localized—carried out through specialized processing units in particular regions of the brain. For explicit reasoning, problem solving, and decision making, those regions largely lie in the frontal lobes. Unlike the other lobes, the frontal lobes receive no direct sensory input. Instead, they receive their input from other parts of the brain. Just as the other lobes combine sensations into perceptions, the frontal lobes combine perceptions into complex ideas.

Patients with frontal lobe damage show a variety of cognitive impairments. They may have trouble making decisions, planning, paying atten-

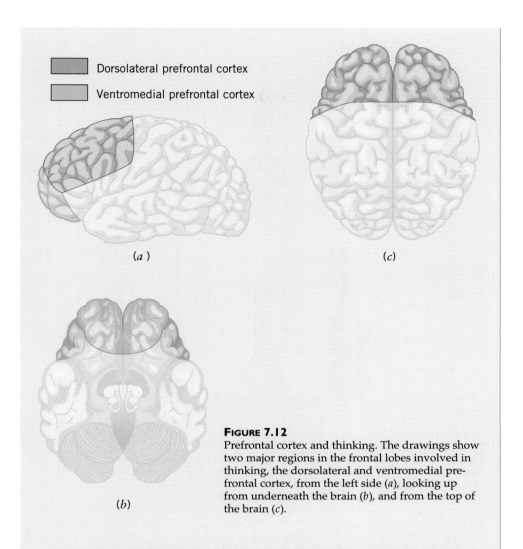

Dorsolateral prefrontal cortex

Ventromedial prefrontal cortex

(a)

(c)

(b)

FIGURE 7.12
Prefrontal cortex and thinking. The drawings show two major regions in the frontal lobes involved in thinking, the dorsolateral and ventromedial prefrontal cortex, from the left side (a), looking up from underneath the brain (b), and from the top of the brain (c).

tion, stopping themselves from doing things that will get them in trouble, or holding information in working memory. Researchers distinguish two broad regions of the prefrontal cortex that perform different cognitive functions: the dorsolateral and ventromedial prefrontal cortex (Figure 7.12) (Damasio, 1994; Fuster, 1989; Frith & Dolan, 1996; Robin & Holyoak, 1995).

Dorsolateral Prefrontal Cortex

The **dorsolateral prefrontal cortex** has many connections to regions of cortex (occipital, temporal, and parietal) as well as to the basal ganglia. (Recall that *dorsal* means toward the top of the brain, and lateral means to the sides; thus, this region encompasses the upper and side regions of the prefrontal cortex.) The connections to posterior cortical regions allow the person to integrate information from multiple senses and to hold multiple kinds of information in mind while solving problems. The links to the basal ganglia allow people to form and carry out complex sequences of behavior and to develop skills. Skill acquisition (such as learning to type, read, or fly an airplane) at first requires considerable conscious attention and prefrontal activity. However, once a skill is well learned and becomes automatic, performance requires minimal involvement of dorsolateral prefrontal circuits; instead, the mental work is largely carried out without attention or con-

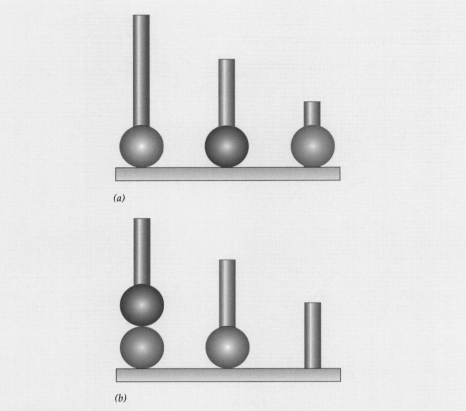

FIGURE 7.13
The Tower of London problem. Participants are presented with pegs holding one, two, or three balls (*a*) and have to manipulate the placement of the balls in their minds so that they can produce the desired solution (*b*). They can only move one ball at a time, which means that they have to figure out which ball to move in what order to solve the problem. In this example, five moves are required. While mentally performing these manipulations, subjects show activation of dorsolateral prefrontal circuits in the same region involved in "central executive" working memory tasks, such as managing multiple simultaneous tasks. The reason appears to be that the Tower of London problem requires the person to hold visual information in memory while mentally arranging a sequence of behaviors. *Source:* Frith & Dolan, 1996.

sciousness by neurons in the motor cortex of the frontal lobes and in subcortical circuits in the basal ganglia (Frith & Dolan, 1996).

Dorsolateral prefrontal circuits appear to be involved in associating complex ideas, allocating attention, making plans, and forming and executing intentions. Damage to this region is associated with impaired planning, distractability, and deficits in working memory (Fuster, 1989). The effect of dorsolateral prefrontal damage can be seen in the way patients with damage to this area respond to the "Tower of London" task (Figure 7.13). In this task, subjects have to think out a sequence of moves in their heads before taking any kind of action. Patients with prefrontal damage find this task very difficult because they cannot seem to hold all the information in mind or to think systematically about how to solve it.

Ventromedial Prefrontal Cortex

Another part of the cortex crucial to judgment and decision making is the **ventromedial prefrontal cortex** (*ventral* meaning toward the bottom of the

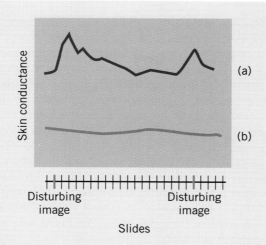

FIGURE 7.14

Physiological reactivity in patients with ventromedial prefrontal damage. The experimenters presented a series of slides to patients with and without ventromedial prefrontal damage. Interspersed among the neutral slides were occasional disturbing scenes of death or destruction. In (*a*), a patient without damage to this region shows spikes in skin conductance immediately after presentation of the disturbing slides, indicating autonomic arousal. In (*b*), a patient with damage to this region of the prefrontal cortex shows no difference in emotional response to neutral and disturbing slides. *Source:* Damasio, 1994.

brain, and *medial* meaning toward the middle). The ventromedial prefrontal cortex has dense connections with the limbic system. People with damage to this region show difficulty inhibiting thoughts and actions, mood swings, loss of social skills, deficits in moral behavior, and disturbances in personality functioning. Phineas Gage, the railroad foreman whose brain was pierced by an iron rod in 1848 (Chapter 3), suffered damage to this region of the brain.

Neurologist Antonio Damasio (1994) has studied many patients with damage to this region. Like Gage, these patients often seem cognitively intact: They can solve problems, manipulate information in working memory, and recall events from the recent and distant past. However, damage to this region demonstrates the importance of *feeling*—and of the ability to connect feelings with thoughts—in making sound decisions (Damasio, 1994).

Ventromedial prefrontal damage can disrupt the neural links between frontal circuits involved in decision making and limbic circuits that establish the emotional significance of stimuli and events. In one study, Damasio and his colleagues showed patients with damage to this region a set of images. Interspersed among a series of neutral slides were disturbing pictures that normally lead to emotional arousal, which can be assessed by measuring skin conductance (autonomic arousal measured by release of sweat in the skin). Unlike normal controls and patients with damage to other parts of the brain, who show spikes in skin conductance directly after viewing of the upsetting images, patients with lesions to the ventromedial prefrontal cortex showed no emotional reaction at all (see Figure 7.14). When asked about the pictures, one patient acknowledged that they *looked* distressing but said that did not make him *feel* distressed.

Damasio relates another incident with one of these patients that supports the notion that reason is not independent of emotion or motivation. The patient came in for testing on a cold winter day, when the roads were so icy that cars were skidding and crashing at an alarming rate. When the patient arrived, Damasio asked him how his ride in had been. The patient responded, casually, that it was no different than usual, except that he had had to take proper procedures to avoid skidding. The patient mentioned that on one especially icy patch, the car ahead of him had spun around and skidded off the road. Unperturbed, the patient simply drove through the same patch with no particular concern. The next day, Damasio and the patient were scheduling their next appointment, and the patient had the choice of two days. For the next *30 minutes* the patient performed a careful cost–benefit analysis of every possible reason for choosing one day over the other, ranging from possible other engagements to potential weather conditions! He seemed unable to *satisfice*: Without the emotional input that would have told him that this decision was not worth 30 minutes, he behaved like a "rational problem solver" trying to optimize weighted utility. Emotion may be the "on/off switch" for explicit thought, letting us know when we can simply settle on a good-enough decision.

INTERIM SUMMARY: The frontal cortex plays a substantial role in explicit thought. Circuits in the **dorsolateral prefrontal cortex** appear to be involved in associating complex ideas, allocating attention, making plans, and forming and executing intentions. The **ventromedial prefrontal cortex** is involved in emotional control over decision making, and many aspects of social functioning.

LANGUAGE

So much thinking is done with words that understanding thought is impossible without understanding language. Try, for instance, to solve an arithmetic problem without thinking with words or symbols or to think about the concept *justice* without relying on words. Beyond its role in thinking, language is fundamental to one of the most basic activities of people in literate societies: reading. Without the ability to manipulate and comprehend the written word, we would be unable to carry out the simplest activities, from selecting items from a menu to filling out a form. And nothing is as potent as language in bridging our separateness from one another, for language allows people to share intimate thoughts and resolve disagreements. Conversely, the lack of a shared language can be frustrating and alienating, contributing to the perception of "otherness" that fuels ethnic strife.

The remainder of this chapter discusses **language,** the system of symbols, sounds, meanings, and rules for their combination that constitutes the primary mode of communication among humans. We begin by considering the ways language and thought shape each other. We then examine the elements of language, how people use language in everyday life, and how children acquire the capacity to think and communicate with words. In so doing, we enter into one of the most intriguing debates in all of psychology: the extent to which the capacity to acquire language is innate. We conclude by considering whether we are alone among species in the capacity to use symbols to think.

LANGUAGE AND THOUGHT

The Hanunoo people of the Philippines have 92 names for rice (Anderson, 1985). Does this mean that the Hanunoo can think about rice in more complex ways than

North Americans, who are hard pressed to do much better than "white rice" and "brown rice"? This line of reasoning led Benjamin Whorf (1956) and others to formulate what came to be called the **Whorfian hypothesis of linguistic relativity**, the idea that language shapes thought (Gumperz & Levinson, 1996; Maffi & Hardin, 1997). According to the Whorfian hypothesis, people whose language provides numerous terms for distinguishing subtypes within a category actually *perceive* the world differently from people with a more limited linguistic repertoire. In its most extreme version, this hypothesis asserts that what people can even think is constrained by the words and grammatical constructions in their language.

Does Language Shape Thought?

Although Whorf's hypothesis has grains of truth, subsequent research has not supported it, at least in its more extreme forms. For example, young children's ability to categorize objects is independent of their vocabulary for them; thus, at least for toddlers, categorization does not depend on language (Gershkoff-Stowe et al., 1997). A particularly strong test of Whorf's hypothesis comes from cross-cultural research on color perception. Color is universal in all cultures, but the number of words for colors is not constant. The English language uses at least 11 words to describe commonly perceived colors: blue, red, yellow, black, white, gray, green, brown, orange, pink, and purple. Yet the Dani people of New Guinea have only two basic color words: *mola* for bright, warm shades and *mili* for dark, cold hues (Anderson, 1985). To what extent does the presence or absence of linguistic labels affect the way people perceive or think about colors?

A series of experiments with Dani and English-speaking subjects explored this question (Rosch, 1973). In one, researchers briefly showed participants a color chip (Figure 7.15) and then asked them 30 seconds later to select a chip of the same color from an array of 160 chips. The hypothesis was that English-speaking subjects would perform better if the chip were one of the basic colors for which their language provides a primary name (for instance, a clear, bright red) than if it were an in-between shade, such as magenta or taupe—and indeed they did. Contrary to the Whorfian hypothesis, however, the Dani subjects, too, correctly selected basic colors more often than less distinctive shades, even though their language had no names for them. (Dani subjects were, however, outperformed overall by the Westerners.)

With complex concepts, however, language does appear to play a role in shaping thought. Having certain concepts, such as *freedom* or *capitalism*, would seem impossible without language. Reasoning deductively would certainly be difficult if people could not construct propositions verbally (such as *all men are mortal* and *Socrates is a man*). Different languages also call attention to different information. For example, the English language draws attention to a person's gender. English speakers cannot avoid specifying gender when using possessive pronouns; if someone asks, "Whose car is that?" the answer is either "his" or "hers." Many languages have different words for *you* that indicate the relative status of the person being addressed. The more polite, formal form is *usted* in Spanish, *vous* in French, and *Sie* in German. The Japanese have many more gradations of respect, and Japanese professionals often exchange business cards immediately upon meeting so they will know which term to use (Triandis, 1994).

Although language is an important medium for thought and can sometimes influence it, thought can certainly occur independent of language. Consider the common experiences of starting to say something and then correcting it because it did not accurately convey the intended thought, or remembering the "gist" of what was said in a conversation without remembering the exact words (Pinker, 1994). Patients with strokes that damage left-hemisphere language centers can become very frustrated trying to get ideas and intentions across without words, as

FIGURE 7.15
Language and color. Although the Dani can remember the hue of different-colored chips, they will call the first three chips *mola* and the last three *mili*.

can young toddlers. In all these cases, the thought appears to be independent of any particular words.

Does Thought Shape Language?

The converse of Whorf's hypothesis—that thought shapes language—is at least as valid. Because rice is critically important to the Hanunoo, it is no accident that their language provides words to describe distinctions in its appearance, texture, and use. The same evolution in vocabulary can be seen in the West, where words such as *yuppie* and *VCR* have emerged to describe what previously did not exist. Conversely, words describing phenomena that are no longer part of everyday life (such as *flapper, speakeasy, hippie,* and *flower child*) fall into disuse.

The interaction of thought and language can be seen in political discourse. At times, language signals that a change in thinking has occurred. For example, politicians once used the plural in referring to "these United States." The nation was originally founded as a confederation of relatively independent states, but the increasing role of the federal government and commercial interdependence of the states rendered that usage obsolete. People with political agendas certainly believe language can influence thinking. In the 1960s and 1970s, feminists attempted to raise consciousness about condescending attitudes toward women by objecting to the use of the word *girl* to describe an adult female. Groups for and against abortion rights try to take the moral high ground by referring to themselves as *pro choice* and *pro life,* respectively.

INTERIM SUMMARY: **Language** is the system of symbols, sounds, meanings, and rules for their combination that constitutes the primary mode of communication among humans. According to the **Whorfian hypothesis of linguistic relativity,** language shapes thought; what people can even think is constrained by the words in their language. Subsequent research has not generally supported the hypothesis—people often seem to have ideas about things that can only inadequately be expressed in words—although language is central to some abstract categories and some forms of reasoning. Thought also shapes language, and language evolves to express new concepts.

TRANSFORMING SOUNDS AND SYMBOLS INTO MEANING

One of the defining features of language is that its symbols are arbitrary. The English language could just as easily have called cats *dogs* and vice versa. In this next section, we examine how sounds and symbols are transformed into meaningful sentences, beginning with the elements of language: phonemes, morphemes, phrases, and sentences. We then explore the grammatical rules people implicitly follow as they manipulate these elements to produce meaningful utterances.

Elements of Language

Language is processed hierarchically, from small units of sound people produce through their mouths and noses to the complex combinations of words and sentences that are produced to convey meaning (Table 7.4). The smallest units of sound that constitute speech (as opposed to grunts or sniffles), called **phonemes,** are strung together to create meaningful utterances. In the English language, phonemes include not only vowels and consonants but also the different ways of pronouncing them (such as the two pronunciations of the letter *a* in *at* and *ate*).

A string of randomly connected phonemes, however, does not convey any message. To be meaningful, strings of phonemes must be combined into **morphemes,** the smallest units of meaning in language. Words, suffixes, and prefixes

TABLE 7.4   ELEMENTS OF LANGUAGE

ELEMENT	DEFINITION	EXAMPLES
Phonemes	Smallest units of sound that constitute speech	th, s, ē, ĕ
Morphemes	Smallest units of meaning	anti-, house, the, -ing
Phrases	Group of words that act as a unit and convey a meaning	in the den, the rain in Spain, ate the candy
Sentences	Organized sequences of words that express a thought or intention	The house is old. Did you get milk?

are all morphemes, such as *pillow, horse, the, pre-*, and *-ing*. The word *cognition*, for example, consists of two morphemes: *cognit-*, from the Latin *cogito* ("to know") and *-ion*, meaning "the act of."

Morphemes are combined into **phrases**, groups of words that act as a unit and convey a meaning. In the sentence *When people speak, they make many sounds*, the words *when people speak* and *many sounds* are phrases. Morphemes and phrases are combined into **sentences**, organized sequences of words that express a thought or intention. Some sentences are intended as statements of fact or propositions; others ask questions or make requests (e.g., "Bill, come here!").

Syntax: The Rules for Organizing Words and Phrases

Speakers of a language intuitively know that they cannot place words or phrases wherever they want in a sentence. An English speaker would never ask, "Why you did come here today?" because it violates implicit rules of word placement. Consider, in contrast, the pseudo-sentence *The sten befted down the flotway*. Although the individual words have no meaning, readers will intuitively recognize it as grammatical: *Sten* is clearly a noun and the subject of the sentence; *befted* is a verb in the past tense (as indicated by the morpheme *-ed*), and *flotway* is the direct object. This pseudo-sentence "feels" grammatical to an English speaker because it conforms to the **syntax** of the language, that is, to the rules that govern the placement of words and phrases in a sentence.

Linguists (people who study languages) and *psycholinguists* (psychologists who study the way people use and acquire language) map the structure of sentences using diagrams such as the one presented in Figure 7.16, which maps the simple sentence *The young woman kissed her anxious date*. Two aspects of this mapping are worth noting. The first is the extent to which rules of syntax determine the way people create and comprehend linguistic utterances. Much of the way psychologists think about syntax in sentences like this reflects the pioneering work of the linguist Noam Chomsky (1957, 1965). Chomsky views **grammar** (which includes syntax) as a system for generating acceptable language utterances and identifying unacceptable ones. According to Chomsky, the remarkable thing about language is that by acquiring the grammar of their linguistic community, people can generate an infinite number of sentences they have never heard before; that is, grammar is *generative*. People can also readily transform one sentence into another with the same *underlying meaning* despite a very different apparent syntactic construction, or *surface structure*, of the sentence. For example, instead of stating "The young woman kissed her anxious date," a speaker could just as easily say, "The anxious date was kissed by the young woman."

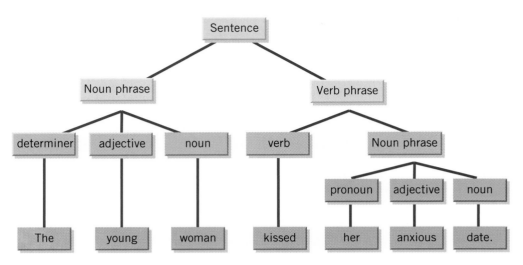

FIGURE 7.16

A syntactic analysis of sentence and phrase structure. Sentences can be broken down through treelike diagrams, indicating noun phrases and verb phrases and their component parts. One of the regularities in language that makes learning syntax easier is that the same principles apply to phrase structures anywhere in the sentence; thus, the same syntactical rules apply to noun phrases whether the phrase describes the subject (*the young woman*) or the direct object (*her anxious date*).

A second aspect of this mapping worth noting is the interaction of syntax and **semantics** (the rules that govern the *meanings*, rather than the order, of morphemes, words, phrases, and sentences) in understanding what people say. For example, the word *date* has multiple meanings; perhaps the woman who kissed the date could really love fruit. The presence of *anxious* as a modifier, however, constrains the possible interpretations of *date* and thus makes the fruity interpretation unlikely. But to recognize this semantic constraint, the reader or listener has to recognize a syntactic rule, namely that an adjective preceding a noun typically modifies the noun.

The interaction between syntax and semantics—between grammatical information processed heavily in Broca's area in the prefrontal cortex and Wernicke's area of the temporal lobes (Chapter 3)—is particularly useful in resolving the meaning of ambiguous sentences, as in the following sentence from *TV Guide*: "On tonight's show Dr. Ruth will discuss sex with Dick Cavett" (Pinker, 1994). Each morpheme in this sentence is clear and unambiguous, yet the sentence can be construed either to mean that Dr. Ruth will discuss sex *in general* as she talks with a talk show host or that she will discuss her experience of having sex *with him*.

The remarkable thing about this interaction of semantic and syntactical knowledge is how quickly and unconsciously it takes place. People do not consciously break sentences down into their syntactic structures and then scan memory for the meanings of each word. Rather, both syntactic and semantic analysis proceed simultaneously, in parallel, and create a set of constraints that lead the reader or listener to settle on the most likely meaning of the sentence. Even this last sentence understates the role of parallel constraint satisfaction in language comprehension, since the person is simultaneously breaking the stream of sound down into phonemes, morphemes, words, phrases, and sentences; processing each level of meaning; and using information at one hierarchical level to inform decisions at other levels. We tend to become aware of one level or another only if we have trouble coming to an implicit solution (for example, if a word does not

Noam Chomsky

seem to fit or a phrase has multiple potential meanings that cannot be resolved without conscious attention). As with induction, understanding language probably relies on a combination of formal rules (in this case, of syntax) and general knowledge (semantics, or the meanings of words).

INTERIM SUMMARY: Language is processed hierarchically. The smallest units of sound that constitute speech are **phonemes**, which are combined into **morphemes,** the smallest units of meaning. Morphemes, in turn, are combined into **phrases**, groups of words that act as a unit and convey a meaning. Morphemes and phrases are combined into **sentences**, organized sequences of words that express a thought or intention. The rules that govern the placement of words and phrases within a language are called its **syntax**. Syntax is an aspect of **grammar**, the system for generating acceptable language utterances and identifying unacceptable ones. To understand what people are saying, people often use information about both syntax and **semantics**—the rules that govern the *meanings* of morphemes, words, phrases, and sentences.

THE USE OF LANGUAGE IN EVERYDAY LIFE

Two people catch each others' eyes at a party. Eventually, one casually walks over to the other and asks, "Enjoying the party?" A linguist could easily map the syntax of the question: It is a variant of the proposition *You are enjoying the party*, constructed by using a syntactic rule that specifies how to switch words around to make a question (and dropping the *you*, which is the understood subject). But that would completely miss the point. The sentence is not a question at all, and its meaning has nothing to do with the party. The real message is, "We've caught each other's eyes several times and I'd like to meet you." Psychologists interested in the **pragmatics** of language—the way language is used and understood in everyday life—are interested in how people decode linguistic messages of this sort.(e.g., Fussel & Krauss, 1992; Gibbs, 1981).

For years, Chomsky was such a towering figure in linguistics that his research, much of it on grammar and syntax, set the agenda for psychologists studying language. More recently, however, some researchers have begun to focus on levels of linguistic processing broader than the isolated sentence. Rather than studying the elements of language from the bottom up, they have turned to the analysis of **discourse**—the way people ordinarily speak, hear, read, and write in interconnected sentences (Carpenter et al., 1995; Graesser et al., 1997; McKoon & Ratcliff, 1998; Rubin, 1995). Much of our time is spent, in fact, telling and hearing stories—news stories, gossip, events in our lives. Discourse analysts point out that the meaning (and even the syntactic structure) of every sentence reflects the larger discourse in which it is embedded. The question *Enjoying the party?* made sense to both people involved in the conversation because it came in the context of a party and some significant nonverbal communication. The move away from an exclusive focus on processing at the level of individual sentences reflects a growing sense that language is about conveying *meaning*, not just about constructing and interpreting grammatically correct sentences.

Multiple Levels of Discourse

According to many discourse analysts, people mentally represent discourse at multiple levels (Graesser et al., 1997; van Dijk & Kintsch, 1983). At the lowest level is the *surface code,* which refers to the exact wording of the phrases and sentences written or spoken. When people read or hear a sentence, they generally retain a surface code—a memory for precisely what was said—only briefly, while they process the rest of the sentence or the next few phrases. When later called upon to remember a sentence such as *Bill took the car into the shop*, people generally remember the gist but cannot recall the exact wording (e.g., they are just as likely to remember the sentence as *Bill took the car into the* auto *shop*). This gist is called the *textbase*, which includes the general meaning of the sentence along with some inferences about it (e.g., that the "shop" was an auto shop). These inferences, which are largely automatic and implicit, influence both what people "hear" and what they remember (Bransford et al., 1972). Consider the inferences involved when a person reads the familiar instructions "Wet hair, apply shampoo, lather, rinse, repeat" (Pinker, 1994). If the person did not think beyond the words on the bottle, she would wet her hair again after each rinse cycle and repeat endlessly (since the instructions never say to stop).

Above the level of the gist or textbase is the *situation model*, the miniworld into which the speaker or narrator wants the reader or listener to enter. Consider the vignette with which this chapter opened, which began with the words "You are sitting in a café with your closest friend, and she tells you tearfully, 'I think my relationship with Brett has hit a dead-end.'" The aim is to bring readers into the scene, to paint an evocative picture that allows them to suspend reality and enter into a different time and place.

One step above the situation model is the *communication* level, which reflects what the communicator is trying to do, such as impart ideas in a textbook or tell a story. At an even broader level of discourse is the *text genre*—the type of communication the text is, whether a story, a news report, a textbook, a joke, or a comment at a party intended to start a conversation. From a cognitive perspective, the simple act of "getting" a joke is an extraordinary feat that requires parallel processing at multiple levels, from distinguishing phonemes and morphemes up through using knowledge of the genre (that is, what jokes are) to figure out that a punch line is coming and recognizing it when it hits.

When people read a sentence or larger text, two kinds of long-term memories are evoked (McKoon & Ratcliff, 1998). The first are memories for earlier sentences, passages, or parts of the text that may have occurred many pages earlier. Memory for what has come before is crucial in following the action of a novel; it is what allows readers to catch inconsistencies that may lead them to generate hypotheses about "whodunnit" in a murder mystery. Second, a passage evokes ideas, images, and emotions that lead readers to "resonate" with a text (see Albrecht & Myers, 1995). Activated associations from the past are what make a piece of fiction or a powerful speech compelling.

Principles of Communication

When people converse or write, their communications are guided not only by syntactic rules that shape the way they put words together but also by a set of shared rules of conversation that are implicit in the minds of both participants (Grice, 1975). For example, people keep track of what their listener knows, and when they introduce a new term or idea, they typically signal it with a change in syntax and embellish it with examples or evocative language. They also use various cues to signal important information. In writing, people usually put the topic sentence of a paragraph first so that readers know what the main point is. In public speaking, people often use *intonation* (tone of voice) to make particular points forcefully or use phrases such as "the point to remember here is. . ."

These "literary devices" of everyday life may seem obvious, but what is remarkable is how effortlessly people use them and how individuals who share a culture (and even many who do not, such as contemporary theater-goers watching a Shakespearean play written in the sixteenth century) pick up on these cues automatically. Consider again the opening line of the vignette with which this chapter began: "You are sitting in a café with your closest friend, and she tells you

HERMAN®

© 1976 Jim Unger/dist. by LaughingStock Licensing Inc.   5-19

**"That's just his way of saying
he wants you to stay!"**

tearfully, 'I think my relationship with Brett has hit a dead-end.'" By switching to a narrative mode more characteristic of fiction, I was signaling to the reader that something different was happening—namely that we were "setting the stage" for a chapter and a new set of ideas. I also introduced a second-person construction ("You are. . ."), which I seldom use in this book, which again served as a syntactic cue that this material was somehow different and required special attention. I suspect, however, that most readers were no more aware of the "rules" I was using to direct their attention than I was in using them.

Nonverbal Communication

People communicate verbally through language, but they also communicate nonverbally, and aspects of speech other than nouns and verbs often speak louder than words. When a parent calls a child by her whole name, it may be to chastise or to praise, depending on the inflection and intonation. ("Jennifer Marie Simp*son* [rising tone on last syllable]? *Stop teasing your brother,*" versus "Jennifer Marie Simp*son* [lowering tone on last syllable]. You are *so cute.*") Even when no words are spoken, clenched fists and a tense look convey a clear message.

    Nonverbal communication includes a variety of signals: intonation, body language, gestures, physical distance, nonverbal vocalizations (such as sighs or throat clearings), facial expressions, and touch (Dil, 1984; Feldman & Rime, 1991). Being conversant in the grammars of nonverbal communication can be just as important in interpersonal relations as understanding the grammar of verbal language. When a person sits too close to you on a bus or stands too close when talking, the effect can be very unsettling. Like other grammars, this one is largely unconscious, encoded as procedural knowledge.

    Just how important is nonverbal communication? One study addressed this question by showing participants 30-second video clips of graduate-student teaching assistants (TAs) at the beginning of a term. Participants rated the TAs using a number of adjectives, such as *accepting, active, competent,* and *confident.*

The grammar of nonverbal communication differs by culture. What feels uncomfortably close in one culture may signal friendship in another.

The investigators wanted to know whether these brief ratings from a single lecture would predict student evaluations of the teacher at the end of the term. The investigators added one extra difficulty: They turned off the audio on the videotapes, so that participants could rely only on nonverbal behavior (Ambady & Rosenthal, 1993).

The findings were extraordinary. Many of the correlations between initial nonverbal ratings and eventual student evaluations were as near perfect as one finds in psychology, in the range of .75 to .85. Teaching assistants who appeared confident, active, optimistic, likable, and enthusiastic in their nonverbal behavior were rated much better teachers. Correlations remained substantial (though of course lower) when judges were asked to rate *two-second* film clips!

Nonverbal communication also contributes to language learning. How, for example, does a child of 12 to 18 months figure out which of the hundreds of objects in sight is connected with a new word, as when a parent just says, "Birdie!" Research suggests that children spontaneously recognize very early that they need to follow the gaze of the speaker to figure out the object to which the speaker is referring. This does not appear to be the case for *autistic* children, who in many ways are isolated in their own mental worlds and often use their own private languages to refer to objects (Baron-Cohen et al., 1997). Autistic children, who have trouble understanding the concept that other people have their own mind and subjective experience, appear to be unable to recognize that the speaker's gaze is an index of the speaker's *intention* to refer to something; instead, these children often associate the word with the object in their *own* gaze.

INTERIM SUMMARY: Psychologists interested in the **pragmatics** of language study the way language is used and understood in everyday life. Rather than studying the elements of language from the bottom-up, many researchers have turned to the analysis of **discourse**, the way people ordinarily speak, hear, read, and write in interconnected sentences. People mentally represent and discourse simultaneously at multiple levels, from the *surface code* that records the exact sentences and phrases of a text all the way up to the text's *genre* or narrative type. When people converse or write, their communications are guided not only by syntactic rules that shape the way they put their words together but also by a set of shared rules of conversation that are implicit in the minds of both participants. People also use **nonverbal communication** (such as intonation, body language, gestures, physical distance, nonverbal vocalizations, facial expressions, and touch).

LANGUAGE DEVELOPMENT

For most people who have ever studied a foreign language and then visited a country where that language is the native tongue, watching five-year-olds speak is a humbling experience. Without benefit of years of course work, hours of rote memorization and drilling, and seemingly endless hours of grammatical instruction, these tiny creatures with their half-baked cortexes can typically run linguistic circles around their fumbling foreign elders. How do they do it?

In this final section we consider the mystery of how children acquire language so quickly and effortlessly. We begin by exploring the roles of nature and nurture in language development and then examine the way children acquire language. We conclude by inquiring into the linguistic abilities of our nearest neighbors on the evolutionary tree.

NATURE AND NURTURE IN LANGUAGE DEVELOPMENT

Children develop linguistic competence with astonishing speed. For the first year of life, most babies are lucky if they can rattle off *dadadadada*, but four years later, children have mastered the basics of verbal communication. By young adulthood, the average person knows the meaning of around 60,000 words. To what extent does this remarkable capacity for language acquisition depend on genetic programs as opposed to learning, on nature versus nurture?

The Case for Nurture

The behaviorist B. F. Skinner explained verbal behavior using the same conditioning principles that apply to other forms of behavior, notably reinforcement, punishment, generalization, and discrimination (Skinner, 1957; see also MacCorquodale, 1970; Moerk, 1992). Thus, language development requires no special principles. A baby who happens to gurgle *Muh* after his mother says "Say Mommy" will receive tremendous positive reinforcement from his delighted mother. Consequently, the baby will be more likely to say *Muh* in the future and to imitate the sounds his mother produces and subsequently reinforces. Later, his mother will be pickier about what she reinforces, shaping the baby's verbal responses to approximate adult speech more closely. She and other adults will also reinforce the child for grammatical constructions, which he will then generalize to create new sentences. He will also learn to respond appropriately to the verbal behavior of others. According to behaviorists, the most complex linguistic achievements result from these relatively simple principles.

Children clearly do learn language in part by imitation, suggesting a substantial role for social learning in language acquisition (see Bohannon & Bonvillian, 1997). In addition, parents frequently "recast" their children's nongrammatical statements into more grammatical forms (Bohannon & Stanowitz, 1988; Farrar, 1992). However, empirical data do not generally support an operant conditioning approach to language acquisition. Parents tend to focus on the *content* of their young children's speech rather than the grammar, providing negative feedback largely when they are entirely unable to understand their children's utterances. (Brown & Hanlon, 1970; Hoff-Ginsberg & Shatz, 1982; Marcus, 1993). In addition, some children who have never spoken a word are nevertheless able to comprehend language and understand complex rules of syntax (Stromswold, 1995). This is difficult to explain using a model that presumes that language use and comprehension reflect the same processes of shaping and reinforcement as other learning.

The Case for Nature

Whereas Skinner championed nurture, Chomsky took the side of nature. According to Chomsky (1959, 1986), children could not possibly learn the rules of grammar and thousands of words within such a few short years simply through reinforcement mechanisms. Children effortlessly use grammatical rules far earlier than they can learn less complicated mental operations, such as multiplication, or even less complicated behaviors, such as turning a door knob. Further, they acquire language in similar ways and at a similar pace across cultures, despite very different learning environments; deaf children show similar developmental patterns in learning sign language as well (Bonvillian, in press).

An Innate Grammar?   The similarities of grammar that appear in languages across cultures led Chomsky instead to propose an innate **universal grammar**—a shared set of linguistic principles—that underlies the grammatical forms found in all cultures. In this view, to get from the universal grammar to any particular language is like flipping a series of "switches." For example, in English, the switch that indicates whether to include a pronoun before a verb (such as *I have*) is set to "yes." In contrast, in Spanish, the same switch is set to "no" (e.g., *tango*), since the form of the verb (in this case, first person singular) already indicates the subject, and a pronoun would be redundant.

According to Chomsky, humans are born with a **language acquisition device (LAD),** or innate set of neural structures for acquiring language. Through the operation of this language acquisition device, children are born knowing the features that are universal to language, and language learning in childhood "sets the switches" so that children speak their native tongue. Children routinely follow implicit rules of grammar to produce utterances they have never heard before. For example, most English-speaking four-year-olds use the pronoun *hisself* instead of *himself,* even though this usage has never been reinforced (Brown, 1973). Children essentially invent "hisself" by applying a general rule of English grammar.

In fact, children exposed to language without proper grammar will infuse their language with grammatical rules they have never been taught. This has been demonstrated in research with deaf children exposed to sign language by their hearing-unimpaired parents, whose ability to sign is often very limited (Goldin-Meadow & Mylander, 1984, 1998; Newport, 1990). These children typically become much better speakers than their parents even before they enter school, using grammatical constructions their parents do not know. These data strongly support Chomsky's view of a universal grammar, or, to use the more recent term proposed by the linguist Steven Pinker (1994), a "language instinct."

Some equally striking evidence for a language instinct comes from a "natural experiment" that recently occurred when the Sandinista government came to power in Nicaragua in 1979 and opened schools for the deaf a year later (Senghas, 1996; cited in Bonvillian, in press). Although their efforts to teach lip reading instead of sign language largely failed, the schools brought together for the first time a group of children who had never spent much time with other deaf children. Outside their classrooms, these children learned to communicate with each other through gestures, most of which involved pantomiming actions rather than the more symbolic gestures of American Sign Language (ASL).

Something remarkable, however, occurred when the next generation of deaf children arrived: They effortlessly transformed the primitive sign language of the playground into a real language, introducing grammatical constructions such as distinctions between nouns and verbs, "speaking" more fluidly and quickly, and developing a system of symbols that were arbitrary rather than pantomimic. In fact, this new Nicaraguan Sign Language was similar in many ways to existing sign languages. Perhaps these children had flipped some switches in a novel way on Chomsky's universal grammar.

Specialized Neural Circuits   The presence of specialized neural circuits for processing grammar and word meaning in the left frontal and temporal lobes, respectively, further suggests that the tendency to follow syntactic rules and to learn word meanings is an innate potential in humans (Chapter 3). At birth, language regions of the temporal cortex are already larger in the left than the right hemisphere, and neurons in the left hemisphere are more sensitive to speech sounds than neurons in corresponding regions on the right (Stromswold, 1995). Further evidence comes from individuals with *dyslexia,* a language-processing impairment that makes tasks such as spelling and arithmetic difficult. The specific left-hemisphere regions activated during certain linguistic tasks (such as rhyming) in non-dyslexic people are not activated in people with the disorder (Paulesu et al., 1996; Shaywitz et al., 1998).

From an evolutionary perspective, the brain evolved modules to process specialized linguistic information just as the visual system developed specialized cells in the occipital cortex that respond to particular features of the physical world such as angles (Tooby & Cosmides, 1992). In other words, the brain adapted to regular features of the linguistic environment, just as it gradually changed its structure to match the structure of nature. The only difference is that the evolution of language capacities fed its own development, as increasing linguistic capacities allowed progressively more complex communication, which required further neural adaptation (see Deacon, 1996; Kimura, 1993).

Interactions of Nature and Nurture: An Emerging View

Can we conclude that Chomsky was right, that language is innate? In one sense, yes. Today, no one can make a credible case that language is completely learned, any more than one can argue that the organization of other organs, such as the kidney, results completely from experience (Chomsky, 1980; Pinker, 1994). On the other hand, some contemporary researchers suggest that the concept of a language acquisition device is not well fleshed out. What is the nature of this device, and how do children actually learn to flip the switches so that they speak the language of their parents? Are children literally born with knowledge of syntax? And if so, how could rules of syntax be encoded in DNA?

An alternative view suggests that humans are, indeed, born with a particular *sensitivity* to certain properties of speech, such as intonation, duration of syllables, and so forth, but that connectionist principles used to explain other aspects of thought and memory can account for language given these innate tendencies (MacWhinney, 1998; Prince & Smolensky, 1997; Seidenberg, 1997). Chomsky argued that rules of language are so perfect and abstract that children could never learn them given the imperfections of the actual sentences they have heard spoken. Recently, however, connectionist models have shown how people can implicitly learn abstractions from very imperfect cases: Categories (in this case, syntactic categories, such as nouns or verbs) share certain properties, which are encoded in neural networks. When enough of a network representing a syntactic category (such as *verb*) is activated by a given word, the word will be classified as that part of speech. Qualities associated with that part of speech (such as the fact that the past tense of most verbs in English is constructed by adding *-ed*) will then be assumed to apply to a novel word that fits into the category. This could explain both how children learn to apply grammatical rules correctly to new words as well as why they overgeneralize (e.g., *he goed away*) until they learn rules that apply only to specific cases.

INTERIM SUMMARY   How children acquire language so quickly has been a matter of considerable debate. Skinner argued that verbal behavior, like all behavior, is selected by its consequences, although empirical data have not generally supported an operant conditioning approach to language learning. Chomsky argued that the speed and similarity of language acquisition around the world suggest a shared set of linguistic principles, or **universal grammar**, that is innate. When children converse with others, they spontaneously develop linguistic constructions that resemble other languages even if their parents do not provide them. The existence of specialized neural circuits for language also supports a strong innate component to language acquisition. Recent connectionist thinking is producing an interactionist view that attempts to describe the way language emerges in children from the interaction of innate tendencies and implicit learning.

A CRITICAL PERIOD FOR LANGUAGE DEVELOPMENT?

The interplay of nature and nurture in language development has led to a hotly debated question among psychologists and linguists: Does a *critical period* exist for language learning; that is, is the brain maximally sensitive to language acquisition at a certain point in development (Lenneberg, 1967)?

Readers who have tried to learn a foreign language as teenagers or young adults have probably found that language acquisition is not so easy at later stages of life. As we have seen (Chapter 3), the development of the brain depends on certain kinds of environmental enrichment, and neurons and neuronal connections

The movie Nell *is about a young woman who grows up in extreme isolation. She develops her own language, based on her mother's speech defect and imaginary conversations with a twin who died at age six. After Nell is rescued, she, in effect, becomes bilingual. The story is fiction. Isolated children in real life do not fare so well linguistically.*

not used at age-appropriate times may die or disappear (Cowan, 1979). Exposure to language may be necessary for normal lateralization of linguistic processes to the left hemisphere, which is typically completed between ages 2 and 5 (Kinsbourne & Smith, 1974; Marcotte & Morere, 1990). Exposure to particular phonemes in the first three years may be required in order to attain native fluency in a second language, particularly if that language is very different from one's own (such as Chinese and English). Learning a second language becomes steadily more difficult after age three, up until at least age 12. After that point, people are seldom able to attain even near-native fluency, and the brain appears to recruit different neural circuits to carry out linguistic tasks than it uses to process first languages (McDonald, 1997).

Most late learners of language are learning a second language, but some limited data exist on individuals who learned their first language late. Perhaps the most convincing evidence of critical periods comes from the study of deaf children whose parents did not know sign language and who did not become exposed to sign language until enrolled in schools for the deaf as late as adolescence (Mayberry & Eichen, 1991; McDonald, 1996). Late learners generally do not catch up to early learners in their ability to use sign language, particularly if they begin in adolescence. They have more trouble learning to comprehend the language fluently and to produce signs as rapidly and effortlessly, suggesting that they "speak with an accent," much like adults who try to learn a second language. Even after 30 years of using sign language, native signers outperform people who learned to sign later in childhood, who in turn outperform later learners (Newport, 1990).

Researchers have also examined a handful of cases of children who were not exposed early to language because they were raised in extreme isolation. The most famous case was a child known as Genie. Authorities found Genie at age 13; she had been living in a tiny room tied to a chair from the time she was 20 months. Her abusive father rarely spoke to her except for occasional screaming. After she was discovered, linguists and psychologists worked with her intensively. Genie acquired a reasonable vocabulary and learned to combine words into meaningful phrases, but she never progressed beyond sentences like "Genie go" (Curtiss, 1977, 1989). She also did not appear to have the normal left-hemisphere lateralization for language.

These findings fit with data on patients with massive brain damage (Stromswold, 1995). Infants who have their entire left hemisphere removed often develop normal linguistic abilities, as language shifts to the right hemisphere. Left-hemisphere lesions that occur after age five typically leave at least some signs years later, and damage to language circuits on the left in adolescents and adults often produce permanent and severe linguistic deficits.

INTERIM SUMMARY: For many years psychologists have debated the existence of a *critical period* for language learning. The first three years of life seem to be the optimal time to attain native fluency; after age 12, even near-native fluency is difficult to achieve, and language appears to be processed using different neural circuits than in native speakers. Data from individuals with left-hemisphere damage also suggest that early transfer of language functions to the non-damaged right hemisphere produces few if any impairments, whereas later attempts are much less successful.

WHAT INFANTS KNOW ABOUT LANGUAGE

Although psychologists disagree about the relative roles of nature and nurture in language development, no one doubts that children learn language with extraordinary speed. Language acquisition is not, however, just about memorizing meanings of words or rules of syntax. Before infants can even start to acquire vocabulary or syntax, they have to learn to *segment* the continuous streams of speech they hear into units so they can distinguish one phoneme, morpheme, word, or phrase from another. As anyone knows who has ever traveled to a country with an unfamiliar language, this is no easy task because native speakers talk rapidly and do not typically "brake" for learners.

Infants use a number of cues to segment speech, such as pauses, pitch, and duration. Remarkably, by the time they are nine months old, they already show a preference for speech interrupted at the boundaries of phrases, even though they have not yet learned the meanings of any of the words that constitute those phrases (McDonald, 1997). By nine months, when infants hear a string of uninterrupted syllables (such as *badigotabitabadigo*), they can also recognize recurring patterns (in this case *badigo*), suggesting that they can register the frequency with which commonly used morphemes occur in everyday language (Saffran et al., 1996).

Although infants have to learn to segment speech into meaningful units, innate factors appear to give them a head start in recognizing cues for segmenting and distinguishing speech sounds. Long before they begin speaking, human infants display a sensitivity to distinctions among the phonemes that make up human languages, including languages they have not heard (Cohen et al., 1992; Miller & Eimas, 1995). Researchers have documented this ability by measuring the rate at which one- and four-month-old infants suck on a pacifier as they listen to various sounds (Eimas et al., 1971, 1985). Infants will suck faster on a specially wired pacifier to look at a novel stimulus, allowing psychologists to learn how infants think and perceive (Chapter 13). One study investigated whether infants would respond differently to novel linguistic sounds, such as the phonemic change between *bah* and *pah,* than to other novel sounds (Eimas, 1985). In fact, a change in phonemic sound produced a much greater increase in sucking rate than a similar change that carried no potential meaning (Figure 7.17).

Once infants learn to segment speech, one of the next tasks is to learn to classify words into syntactic categories, such as nouns, verbs, and noun phrases (McDonald, 1997). That young children implicitly classify words into parts of speech by noticing regularities in their use can be seen in the tendency of preschoolers to *overgeneralize*, that is, to generalize rules that normally apply to irregular instances. For example, just as they create words such as *hisself,* they also create sentences such as *She hitted me!*

FROM BABBLING TO BANTERING

Babies begin **babbling** (making utterances such as "lalala" or "baba") sometime between six months and one year. By the end of this period, even before they speak their first words, their language development bears the imprint of their culture. Toward the end of this period, babies' babbling sounds start to resemble the sounds of their parents' language. Further, the baby's innate attention to phonemic distinctions becomes markedly limited during this period, so that infants are soon sensitive only to phonemes in the language to which they are habitually exposed (Eimas, 1985; Miller & Eimas, 1995). One study showed that at six months, infants of English-speaking families could discern phonemic distinctions typical of both the Hindi language and a Native American language called Salish. By 12 months, however, their ability to discriminate phonemes from these foreign languages had virtually disappeared (Werker & Tees, 1984).

Using Words

Sometime between about one and one and a half years, babbling gives way to a stage in which children utter one word at a time. Children's first words refer to concrete things or action, such as "mama," "ball," or "go." At about 18 to 20

Sometime after the first year of life, children utter a single word at a time, often pointing to things.

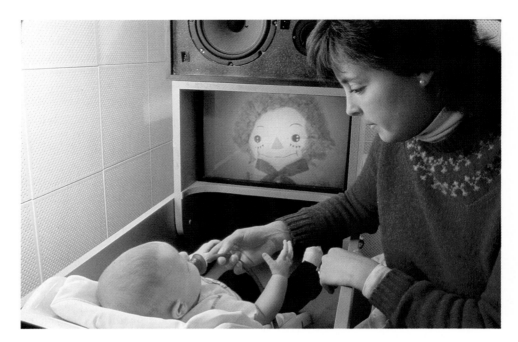

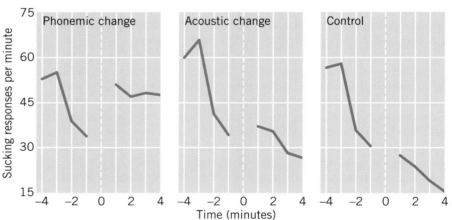

FIGURE 7.17

Infant response to phonemic change. A four-month-old infant sucks on a pacifier connected to recording instruments while synthetic speech syllables are played through a loudspeaker. The graphs show the mean sucking rate under three conditions: phonemic change (e.g., *bah* to *pah*), acoustic change (new sound but same consonant), and control (no change). Sucking rate increases with the presentation of a syllable and then decreases as the stimulus becomes familiar (time –5 to –1). The sucking rate for infants in the phonemic change group increased sharply when the change occurred (time 0), whereas the sucking rate for infants in the acoustic change group increased only slightly. *Source:* Eimas, 1985.

months, they begin to form two-word phrases. From that point, the number of morphemes they combine in their utterances steadily increases. The use of grammatical niceties such as articles, prepositions, and auxiliary verbs expands as well.

Young children characteristically use **telegraphic speech**, leaving out all but the essential words (as in a telegram), producing phrases such as "Dog out" for "The dog is outside." The words they tend to omit are words like *if, the,* and *under.* Although young children tend not to use these words in speech, children as young as two actually *comprehend* some of these words, responding more accurately to sentences that include them (Gerken & McIntosh, 1993). By age four, the vast majority of their sentences are fully grammatical (Stromswold, 1995). Table

TABLE 7.5 PROGRESSION FROM TELEGRAPHIC SPEECH TO COMPLETE SENTENCES IN CHILDREN AGES 25^1/$_2$ TO 35^1/$_2$ MONTHS

	IMITATIONS OF SPOKEN SENTENCES				
MODEL SENTENCE	EVE, 25^1/$_2$	ADAM, 28^1/$_2$	HELEN, 30	IAN, 31^1/$_2$	JUNE, 35^1/$_2$
1. It goes in a big box.	Big box.	Big box.	In big box.	It goes in the box.	C
2. Read the book.	Read book.	Read book.	—	Read a book.	C
3. I will not do that again.	Do again.	I will that again.	I do that.	I again.	C
4. I do not want an apple.	I do apple.	I do a apple.	—	I do not want apple.	I don't want apple.
5. Is it a car?	't car?	Is it car?	Car?	That a car?	C
6. Where does it go?	Where go?	Go?	Does it go?	Where do it go?	C

Source: Brown and Fraser, 1963.

Note: — indicates no intelligible imitation was obtained; C indicates imitation was correct

7.5 illustrates the progression from telegraphic to grammatical speech in five children whose language was studied intensively.

Children's vocabulary increases exponentially after they achieve their first 50 to 100 words. Their repertoire of words blossoms to several thousand by the time they are six years old (Bloom, 1993; MacWhinney, 1998).

Influences on Language Development

Although the stages of language development are virtually universal, children acquire language at widely different rates (Goldfield & Snow, 1989; Richards, 1990). These differences in part stem from genetic predispositions, but they also reflect environmental influences. Probably the most important environmental factor is the day-to-day input and feedback that children get from their caregivers. One way caregivers facilitate infants' language development is by speaking "Motherese." Everyone is familiar with the dialect, as it is nearly irresistible when talking to a baby. Motherese is characterized by exaggerated intonation, a slow rate of speech, and high pitch (Fernald & Kuhl, 1987). The exaggerated style of Motherese may help infants recognize where phrases and sentences begin and end, a skill essential for future language learning (Gleitman et al., 1988; Morgan, 1986).

The content of the primary caregiver's speech is also important in language acquisition. When parents repeat themselves ("Shall we go to the store? Let's go to the store") and expand on their children's telegraphic utterances (for instance, responding to "dog out" with "Is the dog out?"), their children tend to develop earlier in their ability to use verbs correctly. In contrast, merely acknowledging what the child has said without adding any new information ("That's right") is associated with delayed syntax development (Hoff-Ginsberg, 1990; Hoff-Ginsberg & Shatz, 1982; Newport et al., 1977).

Studies of children who do not receive normal feedback offer insight into the role of experience in shaping language development. One study investigated the language development of three- and four-year olds whose hearing was normal but whose parents were deaf and therefore could not provide normal feedback (Murphy & Slorach, 1983). Tape recordings of these children's speech indicated that their language development was well behind other aspects of their cognitive development, characterized by incorrect syntax and poor vocabulary. Thus, while language development follows a universal schedule, the precise timing and course depend on many environmental factors.

INTERIM SUMMARY: Language progresses through a series of stages. Before infants can start to acquire vocabulary or syntax, they have to learn to *segment* the continuous streams of speech they hear into units; they then have to learn to classify words into syntactic categories. Babies' first recognizable speech sounds occur as **babbling** in the first year; sometime in the second year they begin to speak in one-word utterances. Young children use **telegraphic speech**, leaving out all but the essential words. By age four, most of the sentences children produce are grammatical. Although the stages of language development are virtually universal, children acquire language at widely different rates depending on environmental input.

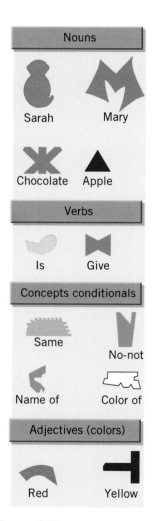

FIGURE 7.18
Sarah's plastic symbols. Researchers provided Sarah, a chimpanzee, with plastic symbols that varied in color, shape, and size. The symbols were backed with metal so that Sarah could arrange them on a magnetic board. Each symbol stood for a single word or concept. (Sarah preferred to write her sentences vertically from top to bottom.) *Source:* Premack & Premack, 1972.

▶ ONE STEP FURTHER

Is Language Distinctly Human?

TIM: Lana want apple.
LANA: Yes. (Thereupon Tim went to the kitchen and got one.) You give this to Lana.
TIM: Give what to Lana.
LANA: You give this which-is red.
TIM: This. (Tim held up a red piece of plastic as he responded.)
LANA: You give this apple to Lana.
TIM: Yes. (And gave her the apple.)
                        (Rumbaugh & Gill, 1977, p. 182)

This conversation is not between two humans but between a human and a chimpanzee named Lana. Apes lack the physiological equipment to speak as humans do, but several chimpanzees and other primates (such as bonobos, another close relative of humans) have been trained to use nonverbal symbols to communicate with human researchers. Lana learned a computer language called "Yerkish" (named for the Yerkes Regional Primate Research Center in Atlanta where the research took place), which uses geometric symbols, or *lexigrams*, to represent concepts and relationships. Other apes have learned to use signs from American Sign Language or other systems using lexigrams.

Teaching Language to Apes

The impressive accomplishments of simian linguists have taught researchers a great deal about the language capabilities of nonhuman primates. One of Ann and David Premack's (1972) chimpanzees, Sarah, learned a vocabulary of about 130 plastic symbols, which she used with 75 to 80 percent accuracy (Figure 7.18). Another chimpanzee, named Nim Chimpsky, has reportedly expressed feelings through signs, saying "angry" or "bite" instead of actually committing those acts (Terrace, 1979). Language-trained chimpanzees have also proven capable of communicating with each other (Figure 7.19), although in a very limited fashion, using symbols taught to them by their trainers (Savage-Rumbaugh et al., 1978, 1983). Another chimpanzee who learned to use signs from American Sign Language was observed teaching signs to her son (Fouts et al., 1982).

Do such findings mean that the chimpanzee is, as one researcher put it, "a creature with considerable innate linguistic competence who has, by accident of nature, been trapped inside a body that lacks the proper [structure for] vocal output" (Savage-Rumbaugh et al., 1983)? Although some researchers have compared the linguistic abilities of chimpanzees and other

(a)   (b)   (c)

FIGURE 7.19

Two chimpanzees communicating. Sherman and Austin learned to communicate with each other using symbols taught to them by their trainers. In this sequence, Sherman requests M&Ms using his symbol board (a), while Austin watches (b). Austin then hands the M&Ms to Sherman (c).

apes to human children at the stage of telegraphic speech (Gardner & Gardner, 1975; Nelson, 1987), others do not consider language to be monkey business. After five years of working with Nim Chimpsky, H. S. Terrace (1979) remained skeptical about both the ability of chimpanzees to use language and the analogy to child language. While human children combine progressively more words as they get older, the average length of Nim's utterances never rose above 1.1 to 1.6 signs. Furthermore, children frequently use language as an end in itself, to draw attention to objects or events, or to announce their intentions. Chimpanzees, Terrace observed, tend to use symbols either for purely pragmatic purposes (to request objects they want) or to imitate their trainers' communications (Seidenberg & Petitto, 1987).

Other psychologists are more convinced by the accomplishments of our primate brethren (Fouts et al., 1982; Gardner & Gardner, 1975). For example, some researchers have observed chimps signing in solitude and even videotaped them signing to other chimps. Researchers from the Yerkes Regional Primate Research Center describe a bonobo named Kanzi who spontaneously began to use symbols to communicate with humans without any special training (Rumbaugh, 1992; Savage-Rumbaugh, 1990; Savage-Rumbaugh et al., 1986). Kanzi was born in captivity at Yerkes and was sent to the Language Research Center at six months with his mother. His mother was the subject of language training and was encouraged to communicate by pushing geometric symbols on a keyboard. Kanzi remained with her until he was two and a half years old, observing her training sessions and often interfering by leaping on her or the keyboard, snatching food treats, and generally being a nuisance.

When Kanzi was two and a half, his mother was sent to the Yerkes breeding colony. To the researchers' surprise, Kanzi suddenly began using the keyboard to communicate, asking for specific fruits. When presented with apples, bananas, and oranges, he would choose the fruit he had requested, demonstrating that he did indeed know what he was asking. Kanzi's human observers noted that Kanzi differed in many ways from Nim Chimpsky and suggested that Nim may have been a bit dim, so that his limited accomplishments did not adequately reflect the language capacities of apes. Unlike Nim, over 80 percent of Kanzi's communications occurred

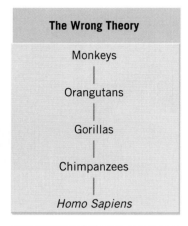

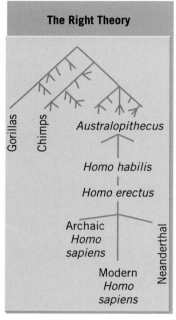

FIGURE 7.20
Two models of the evolution of language. *Source:* Adapted from Pinker, 1994.

spontaneously. Kanzi also used language differently from Nim: He pointed out objects to the researchers, and he announced his intentions (for example, by pushing "ball" and then searching for his ball).

Swinging on the Evolutionary Tree

Psychologists who study language in nonhuman primates continue to disagree as to whether apes are capable of human language (although no one has definitively shown that humans can be taught to comprehend and use chimpanzee communication systems, either). Chimps apparently have the capacity to use symbolic thought under the right conditions, and recent data suggest that lowland gorillas may use some forms of symbolic gesture to communicate (Tanner & Byrne, 1996). Perhaps the most distinctive feature of human language, however, is not the capacity to use symbols to stand for objects but the creation of a *system* of symbols whose meaning lies primarily in their relation to *one another*, not to any concrete realities (Deacon, 1996). This is what allows people to imagine what *could* be and to create objects in their minds that they then create in the world. And in this, we are essentially alone.

Linguist Steven Pinker (1994) suggests that the question of whether other primates possess language has actually been badly framed, based on the misconception that humans are the highest and latest rung on an evolutionary ladder that runs from orangutans to gorillas to chimpanzees to *Homo sapiens*. Rather than a ladder, the proper analogy is a bush, with a common trunk but multiple branches (Figure 7.20). Gorillas, chimps, humans, and other living primates shared a common ancestor five to ten million years ago, at which point their evolutionary paths began to diverge like branches on a bush. Somewhere after that point, language began to evolve in the now-extinct ancestors of *Homo sapiens*, such as *Homo erectus*. Natural selection has pruned the bush dramatically—roughly 99 percent of all species become extinct—so that the bush is now quite sparse, leading to the misconception that the species left on the bush are close relatives rather than distant cousins. Pinker's (1994) conclusion to the debate about language in other primates is concise: "Other species undoubtedly have language. Unfortunately, they're all dead." ◄

SOME CONCLUDING THOUGHTS

It has been said that humankind has suffered four major blows to its exalted conception of itself. First, Copernicus showed that we are not at the center of the universe, that we are just one species on one planet revolving around the sun. When humans persisted in seeing themselves as a privileged species separate from all other animals, Darwin suggested that we are little more than hairless monkeys—remarkable ones, but nonetheless continuous with other species. After Darwin, humans prided themselves on being distinguished from other animals by reason and consciousness—until Freud argued that reason and consciousness are a thin veneer and that below the surface we are primarily motivated by the same drives that direct the behavior of other animals (Freud, 1925). After Freud, what is left to defend as uniquely human? An apologist for the species might argue that the way we *think* still makes us special. Who else can create a syllogism, solve differential equations, or send a vessel into space? No one—except, of course, a computer.

Perhaps we will ultimately find that what is distinctly human is neither the passions we share with other animals nor the capacity for complex computations we share with computers. The ability to link passion and reason in pursuit of our goals may be the crowning achievement of the human intellect.

SUMMARY

UNITS OF THOUGHT

1. **Thinking** means representing mental representations for a purpose. Much of the time people think using words, **mental images** (visual representations), and **mental models** (representations that describe, explain, or predict the way things work).

2. A **concept** is a mental representation of a category, that is, an internal portrait of a class of objects, ideas, or events that share common properties. The process of identifying an object as an instance of a category—recognizing its similarity to some objects and dissimilarity to others—is called **categorization**. Concepts that have properties that clearly set them apart from other concepts are relatively **well defined**; **fuzzy concepts** are not easily defined by a precise set of features. People typically classify objects rapidly by judging their *similarity* to concepts stored in memory. They often do this by comparing the observed object they are trying to classify with a **prototype**, an abstraction across many instances of a category. When people rapidly categorize, they probably rely heavily on prototype matching; complex, deliberate classification tasks often require more explicit evaluation of the data, such as consulting lists of **defining features**.

3. In categorizing objects, people naturally tend to use the **basic level,** the broadest, most inclusive level at which objects share common attributes that are distinctive of the concept. The way people categorize is partially dependent on culture, expertise, and their goals.

REASONING, PROBLEM SOLVING, AND DECISION MAKING

4. **Reasoning** refers to the process by which people generate and evaluate arguments and beliefs. **Inductive reasoning** means reasoning from specific observations to more general propositions that seem likely to be true. **Deductive reasoning** is logical reasoning that draws conclusions from premises and leads to certainty if the premises are correct. **Analogical reasoning** is the process by which people understand a novel situation in terms of a familiar one.

5. **Problem solving** is the process of transforming one situation into another to meet a goal, by identifying discrepancies between the initial state and the goal state and using various *operators* to try to eliminate the discrepancies. **Problem-solving strategies** are techniques that serve as guides for solving a problem. One of the most important problem-solving strategies is **mental simulation**—imagining the steps involved in solving a problem mentally before actually undertaking them.

6. **Decision making** is the process by which people weigh the pros and cons of different alternatives in order to make a choice. According to one information-processing model, making a rational decision involves a combined as-

sessment of the value and probability of the different options, known as **expected utility**.

IMPLICIT AND EVERYDAY THINKING

7. Psychologists have recently begun to question whether the kind of rationality seen in **explicit cognition** (cognition that involves conscious manipulation of representations models) is always optimal. In everyday life, people make use of cognitive shortcuts, or **heuristics**, that allow them to make rapid judgments. Because people rarely have complete information and limitless time, they often practice **bounded rationality**, or rationality *within limits* that depend on the environment, their goals, and their abilities.

8. Much of human behavior reflects **implicit cognition**, or cognition outside of awareness, including implicit learning and implicit problem solving.

9. Another shift in psychologists' understanding of rationality is the recognition of the role played by motivation and emotion in everyday judgments, inferences, and decisions. Motives and emotions substantially influence the way people assess risks; people's values also influence their decisions, as they weigh their own interests and those of others.

10. **Connectionist**, or **parallel distributed processing (PDP)**, models propose that many cognitive processes occur simultaneously (in parallel) and are spread (distributed) throughout a network of interacting neural processing units. Connectionist models differ from traditional information-processing models by minimizing the importance of serial processing and shifting from the metaphor of mind as computer to mind as brain. These principles assert that perception, memory, and thought occur through processes of **constraint satisfaction**, in which the mind settles on a solution that satisfies as many constraints as possible in order to achieve the best fit to the data.

11. The frontal lobes play a particularly important role in thinking. Two regions of the frontal lobes involved in thinking are the **dorsolateral prefrontal cortex**, which is involved in associating complex ideas, allocating attention, making plans, and forming and executing intentions, and the **ventromedial prefrontal cortex,** which is involved in emotional control over decision making, inhibiting actions that lead to negative consequences, and many aspects of social functioning.

LANGUAGE

12. **Language** is the system of symbols, sounds, meanings, and rules for their combination that constitutes the primary mode of communication among humans. Thought and language shape one another, but thought and language are to some extent separable.

13. The smallest units of sound that constitute speech are **phonemes**; phonemes are combined into **morphemes,** the smallest units of meaning. Morphemes are combined into **phrases**, groups of words that act as a unit and convey a meaning. Morphemes and phrases are combined into **sentences**, organized sequences of words that express a thought or intention. The rules of **syntax** govern the placement of words and phrases within a language.

14. Psychologists interested in the **pragmatics** of language are interested in the way language is used and understood in everyday life. **Discourse**—the way people ordinarily speak, hear, read, and write in interconnected sentences—occurs at multiple levels, such as the *surface code* (the exact wording of the

phrases and sentences) and the *textbase* (the gist of a sentence along with some inferences about it). **Nonverbal communication** relies on tone of voice, body language, gestures, physical distance, facial expressions, and so forth.

LANGUAGE DEVELOPMENT

15. Language development reflects an interaction of nature and nurture, although Chomsky appears to be right that the brain is constructed to make language learning easy. According to Chomsky, all language derives from an innate **universal grammar**, or shared set of linguistic principles. Chomsky explains the speed with which children develop language by arguing that the human brain includes a **language acquisition device (LAD)**, an innate set of neural structures for acquiring language.

16. Data from a variety of sources support the *critical period* hypothesis for language learning. The first three years of life seem to be the optimal time to attain native fluency; after age 12, even near-native fluency is difficult to achieve.

17. Cross-culturally, children go through similar stages of language development. They begin by **babbling** in the first year and then begin producing one-word utterances toward the beginning of the second year. Young children's speech is **telegraphic speech**, omitting all but the essential words. By age four, children's sentences largely conform to the grammar of their language. The stages of language development are virtually universal; however, the precise timing and course of individual language development depends on both nature and nurture.

Tsing-Fang Chen, "Human Achievement," Lucia Gallery, New York City / Super Stock.

CHAPTER 8

Intelligence

eter Franklin, a historian by training, had spent many years of his academic career as the dean of a prestigious liberal arts college. He was also a talented amateur musician and athlete who enjoyed good food and lively conversation. In 1971, while vacationing in Maine, he suffered a stroke. He had been at dinner with a longtime friend, Natalie Hope, and had gone to bed early with a slight headache. He next recalled waking up on the floor with clothing strewn around him, dragging himself outside, and being discovered by Mrs. Hope. He was drooling, disheveled, and confused.

When psychologist Howard Gardner met Mr. Franklin two years later at the hospital where he was being treated, Gardner asked what brought him there. Mr. Franklin replied (Gardner, 1975, pp. 6–7):

Now, listen here. Now listen here. Well, I'll tell you. I said, sit down, strewn with clothes, sit, sit down, thank you, thank you. Oh goodness gracious, goodness gracious. Mrs. Hope, thank God, Mrs. Hope, going to bed. Sleeping. All right, all right. . . . I said and, by the way. Dead. All right and two days. Sick. . . . And doctors, doctors. Boys, boys, tip fifty dollars, tip, tip boys."

Recognizing this to be a version of what had happened around the time of Mr. Franklin's stroke, Gardner asked, "Could you tell me what's bothering you now?" Mr. Franklin lashed out, shaking his fist,

"Now listen here. Irritate. Irritate. Irritate, irritate, irritate, irritate, irritate, irritate! Questions, questions. Stupid doctors. No good, no good. Irritate. Irritate. Dean, dean, yes sir, yes sir. . . . That's all, that's all, forget it, forget it.

Mr. Franklin's linguistic abilities were impaired in many ways. He could not converse in a straightforward manner, express himself in writing, or follow complex commands. Standard measures of intelligence showed that he had lost much of his mental capacity, yet many of his abilities remained intact. He could easily hum familiar tunes and startled Gardner with his renditions of show tunes on the piano. He even maintained a sense of humor, kidding Gardner about doctors and their Saturday golf games when Gardner once stopped by on a Saturday.

Mr. Franklin's case points to a number of questions that are central to understanding intelligence. First, what is intelligence? Can a man who cannot speak coherently but can play show tunes flawlessly be described as intelligent? Second, how accurate are commonly used measures of intelligence? Mr. Franklin scored very poorly on IQ tests, yet he maintained a sense of humor as well as other capacities reflecting intelligent thinking. Third, is intelligence a general trait, or do people possess different kinds of intelligence, such as one that facilitates verbal conversation and another that allows a person's fingers to dance deftly across the ivories? Finally, to what extent is intelligence biologically or environmentally determined?

This chapter explores each of these questions in turn. We begin by discussing the nature of intelligence and the methods psychologists have devised to assess it, notably IQ tests. Next, we examine theoretical approaches to intelligence, from those that center on the kinds of abilities that best predict school success to those that include aptitudes in domains such as music and sports. We then address the controversial question of the heritability of intelligence—the extent to which differences between people reflect differences in their genetic endowment. We conclude with the extremes of intelligence—mental retardation and giftedness—and explore the relations among giftedness, creativity, and madness.

THE NATURE OF INTELLIGENCE

The concept of intelligence has so successfully eluded definition that long ago one psychologist somewhat sarcastically defined intelligence as "what intelligence tests measure" (Boring, 1923). When asked what intelligence means, most people emphasize problem-solving abilities and knowledge about the world; they also sometimes distinguish between academic intelligence ("book smarts") and social intelligence or interpersonal skill (Berg, 1992; Sternberg & Wagner, 1993; Sternberg et al., 1981). In recent years, psychologists have come to recognize that intelligence is many-faceted, functional, and culturally defined.

INTELLIGENCE IS MULTIFACETED AND FUNCTIONAL

Intelligence is multifaceted; that is, aspects of it can be expressed in many domains. Most readers are familiar with people who excel in academic and social tasks and are equally adept at changing spark plugs and concocting an exquisite meal (without a cookbook, of course). Yet other people excel in one realm while amazing those around them with their utter incompetence in other domains. One psychologist with a national reputation in his field is equally well known among his friends and students as the prototypical absent-minded professor. He once drove to a conference out of town, forgot he had driven, and accepted a ride home with a colleague. As we will see, speaking of "intelligence" may be less useful than speaking of "intelligences."

Intelligence is also functional. Intelligent behavior is always directed toward accomplishing a task or solving a problem. According to one definition, intelligence is "the capacity for goal-directed adaptive behavior" (Sternberg & Salter, 1982, p. 3). From an evolutionary perspective, intelligent behavior solves problems of adaptation and hence facilitates survival and reproduction. From a psychodynamic perspective, people use their intelligence to satisfy wishes and avoid things they fear. From a cognitive perspective, intelligence is applied cognition, that is, the use of cognitive skills to solve problems or obtain desired ends.

Intelligence comes in different forms.

A Global Vista

The Cultural Context of Intelligence

Intelligence is also culturally defined. If the function of intelligence is to help people manage the tasks they confront in their lives, then intelligent behavior is likely to vary cross-culturally, since the circumstances that confront members of one society differ markedly from those that face another. In fact, the kinds of thinking and behavior recognized as intelligent vary considerably. Among the Kipsigi of Kenya, for example, the word *ng'om* is the closest approximation to the English word *intelligent*. The concept of *ng'om*, however, carries a number of connotations that Westerners do not generally associate with intelligence, including obedience and responsibility (Super & Harkness, 1980). The Cree Indians of northern Ontario consider someone a "good thinker" if she is wise and respectful, pays attention, thinks carefully, and has a good sense of direction. The Cree also emphasize taking time (proceeding slowly and thoroughly) and self-sufficiency (not being a burden to others) (Berry & Bennet, 1992).

The attributes a culture considers intelligent are not arbitrary. The personal qualities, skills, and cognitive style cultures value and foster tend to be related to their ecology and social structure (see Mistry & Rogoff, 1985). Cultural practices teach people efficient ways of solving everyday problems, and these strategies become part of the way individuals think (Miller, 1997; Vygotsky, 1978; Wertsch & Kanner, 1992). Western views of intelligence emphasize verbal skills (such as the ability to comprehend a written passage) and the kinds of mathematical and spatial abilities useful in engineering or manufacturing, which makes sense in a literate, technologically developed capitalist society. In most African cultures, intelligence tends to be defined in terms of practical abilities and competences (Serpell, 1989). For example, observers have commented on the almost encyclopedic knowledge of animal behavior possessed by some members of the !Kung tribe of Africa's Kalahari Desert, knowledge that is adaptive for a people who must hunt and avoid dangerous animals (Blurton-Jones & Konner, 1976). Cultural groups who depend on the sea for their livelihood often show an extraordinary ability to remember relevant landmarks or calculate locations in navigating the ocean (Gladwin, 1970). Sir Francis Galton, a pioneer in research on intelligence, described one Eskimo (Werner, 1948, p. 147, in Berry & Irvine, 1986):

> With no aid except his memory . . . [the Eskimo] drew a map of a territory whose shores he had but once explored in his kayak. The strip of country was 1100 miles long as the crow flies, but the coast line was at least six times this distance. A comparison of the Eskimo's rude map with an Admiralty chart printed in 1870 revealed a most unexpected agreement.

In a recent study, researchers asked immigrants to the United States from Cambodia, Mexico, the Phillipines, and Vietnam, as well as Anglo-American and Mexican-American natives, to describe their conceptions of intelligence in children (Okagaki & Sternberg, 1993). Only the Anglo-American parents described cognitive skills as more central to intelligence than motivation, social skills, and practical school skills.

Is intelligence, then, a property of individuals, or is it simply a social construction or value judgment? To put it another way, is intelligence solely

Navigational skills are essential for survival and hence highly developed among the Truk Islanders in Micronesia.

in the eye of the beholder? Probably not. Some attributes, such as mental quickness or the ability to generate solutions when confronted with novel problems, are valued in any culture. Moreover, among cultures at a similar level of technological development, concepts of intelligence tend to share many elements because demands on individuals are similar. An intelligent Norwegian is not very different from an intelligent American, although the Norwegian is likely to know more languages—itself an aspect of intelligence in a small country surrounded by countries with many languages. As the United States increasingly depends on powerful trading partners around the world, particularly to its south, the lack of fluency in other languages characteristic of most Americans will probably be increasingly defined as unintelligent.

We can thus provisionally define **intelligence** as the application of cognitive skills and knowledge to learn, solve problems, and obtain ends that are valued by an individual or culture (see Gardner, 1983). As we will see in the following section, intelligence was not always so broadly defined; only in recent years has the concept been expanded to include much more than what intelligence tests measure.

INTERIM SUMMARY **Intelligence** refers to the application of cognitive skills and knowledge to learn, solve problems, and obtain ends that are valued by an individual or culture. Intelligence is multifaceted and functional, directed at problems of adaptation. It is also to some extent culturally shaped and culturally defined, since cultural practices tend to support and recognize intellectual qualities that are useful in the social and ecological context.

INTELLIGENCE TESTING

Measuring psychological qualities such as intelligence is not as straight-forward as stepping on a bathroom scale. Psychologists use **psychometric instruments**—psychological tests that compare individuals in a population—to determine how people differ on dimensions such as personality attributes or intellectual abilities. Although scientists usually design measures to fit the construct they are trying to quantify (such as scales to measure weight or mass), almost the opposite has occurred with the Western concept of intelligence, which has largely evolved along with the measures devised to assess it. **Intelligence tests** are measures designed to assess an individual's level of cognitive capabilities compared to other people in a population.

Historians credit Sir Francis Galton (1822–1911) of England with the first systematic effort to measure intelligence. A relative of Charles Darwin and a member of his society's aristocracy, Galton set out to evaluate the implications of the theory of evolution for human intelligence (Berg, 1992). He was convinced that intelligence and social preeminence were products of the evolutionary process of "survival of the fittest," and that intelligence runs in families. Galton believed that the building blocks of intelligence are simple perceptual, sensory, and motor abilities. Like his German contemporary Wilhelm Wundt, Galton argued that by studying the "atoms" of thought one could make inferences about the way they combine into larger intellectual "molecules."

To prove his theory, Galton set up a laboratory at London's 1884 International Exposition, where, for threepence, some 10,000 people underwent tests of reaction time, memory, sensory ability, and other intellectual tasks. To his surprise, performance on these elementary tasks did not correlate with much of anything, including social class. Nevertheless, Galton will be remembered not only as the first to attempt to test mental abilities but also as a pioneering statistician who first expressed the relationship between two variables using the correlation coefficient (Chapter 2), a fundamental statistical tool for understanding intelligence and many other aspects of psychological functioning.

BINET'S SCALE

The most direct ancestor of today's intelligence tests was developed in 1905 in France by Alfred Binet (1857–1911). Unlike Galton, Binet believed that a true measure of intelligence is an individual's performance on *complex* tasks of memory, judgment, and comprehension (Berg, 1992; Kail & Pellegrino, 1985). Binet was also less interested in comparing intellectual functioning in adults than in measuring intellectual potential in children.

Binet's purpose was in fact quite practical. In 1904, an education commission in France recommended the establishment of special schools for retarded children. This project required some objective way of distinguishing these children from their intellectually normal peers (Kail & Pellegrino, 1985; Tuddenham, 1962). Binet and his associate, Theodore Simon, noted that problem-solving abilities increase with age, so they constructed a series of tasks ranging in difficulty from simple to complex to capture the ability of children at different ages. A seven-year old could explain the difference between paper and cardboard, for instance, whereas a typical five-year old could not (Peterson, 1925).

To express a child's level of intellectual development, Binet and Simon (1908) introduced the concept of mental age. **Mental age (MA)** is the average age at which children achieve a particular score. A child with a chronological (or actual)

Alfred Binet

age of 5 who can answer questions at a seven-year-old level has a mental age of 7. A five-year old who can answer the questions expected for her own age but not for higher ages has a mental age of 5. Thus, for the average child, mental age and chronological age coincide. From this standpoint, a mentally retarded child is just what the term implies: retarded, or slowed, in cognitive development. A mentally retarded seven-year-old might miss questions at the seven- and six-year-old levels and be able to answer only some of the five-year-old items.

INTELLIGENCE TESTING CROSSES THE ATLANTIC

Binet's scale was translated and extensively revised by Lewis Terman of Stanford University, whose revision was known as the **Stanford-Binet Scale** (1916). Perhaps the most important modification was the **intelligence quotient**, or **IQ**, a score meant to quantify intellectual functioning to allow comparison among individuals. To arrive at an IQ score, Terman relied on a formula for expressing the relation between an individual's mental age and chronological age developed a few years earlier in Germany. The formula derives a child's IQ by dividing mental age by chronological age (CA) and multiplying by 100:

$$IQ = (MA/CA) \times 100.$$

Thus, if an eight-year-old performs at the level of a 12-year-old (that is, displays a mental age of 12), the child's IQ is $12/8 \times 100$, or 150. Similarly, a 12-year-old-child whose test score is equivalent to that expected of an eight-year-old has an IQ of 66; and a 12-year-old who performs at the expected level of a 12-year-old has an IQ of 100. By definition, then, a person of average intelligence has an IQ of 100.

When intelligence testing crossed the Atlantic, another modification occurred that was at once more subtle and profound in its implications than the intelligence quotient. Binet had developed intelligence testing for a purpose—to predict

Drawing by Sidney Harris

school success—and for that purpose intelligence testing was, and is, highly successful. But in North America, particularly in the United States, IQ became synonymous with "smarts" rather than "school smarts." People became preoccupied with IQ as a measure of general intellectual ability that could predict their children's success in life, like a deck of psychological tarot cards.

Group Tests

Terman's adaptation of Binet's scale gained rapid use, for the intelligence test filled a number of pressing social needs. One of the most important was military (Weinberg, 1989). At the time of Terman's 1916 revision of his test, the United States was involved in World War I, and the army needed to recruit hundreds of thousands of soldiers from among millions of men, many of them recent immigrants. Testing IQ promised a way of determining quickly which men were mentally fit for military service and, of those, which were likely to make good officers.

The army appointed a committee that included Terman to adapt mental testing to these needs. The result was two tests, the Army Alpha for literate adults and the Army Beta for men who were either illiterate or did not speak English (Figure 8.1). Unlike the Stanford-Binet, which required one-on-one administration by trained personnel, the army tests were **group tests**, paper-and-pencil measures that can be administered to a roomful of people at a time. Between September 1917 and January 1919, over 1.7 million men took the Army Alpha test. Group tests are widely used today to assess IQ and related attributes. A modern group test with which most North American students are familiar is the Scholastic Assessment Test, or SAT, which was designed to predict college performance.

The Wechsler Intelligence Scales

Although the Army Beta tried to circumvent the problem of language, the intelligence tests used early in this century were linguistically and culturally biased toward native-born English speakers. David Wechsler attempted to minimize these biases by creating a new instrument, the Wechsler-Bellevue tests (Wechsler, 1939). The latest renditions of these tests are the **Wechsler Adult Intelligence Scale—Third Edition**, or **WAIS-III** (1997), and the child version (appropriate through age 16), the **Wechsler Intelligence Scale for Children**, or **WISC-III** (1991). As measured by the WAIS-III, IQ is a composite score derived from 11 of 14 subtests; six of these subtests depend on verbal ability and the other five do not. The verbal subtests require facility at symbolic thought and language, such as knowledge of general information, arithmetic skills, ability to hold and manipulate numbers in

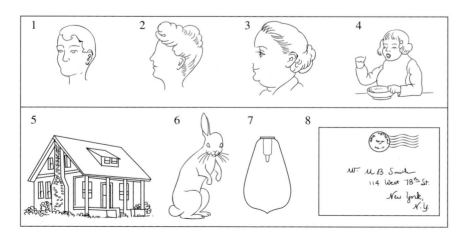

FIGURE 8.1
Selected items from the Army Beta test for nonliterate adults. In this task, subjects are asked to name the part of each picture that is missing.

TABLE 8.1 SAMPLE ITEMS SIMILAR TO THOSE ON SELECTED WAIS-III VERBAL AND PERFORMANCE SUBTESTS

Verbal Subtests	Performance Subtests
Comprehension: "What does this saying mean: 'A rolling stone gathers no moss'?"	Picture completion: Tests speed and accuracy of finding missing parts of picture, e.g., the laces on a boot
Arithmetic: "A boy ran 50 yard in 10 seconds. How many yards did he run per second?"	Block design: Tests speed and accuracy in matching a design with red and white blocks, e.g.,
Similarities: "How are fast and slow alike?"	Picture arrangement: Tests speed and accuracy in putting cartoon frames in the right order to tell a story, e.g., frames depicting (1) a robber running from a bank, (2) a robber at a teller's window, and (3) a robber in handcuffs should be ordered by the subject 2–1–3
Digit span: "Repeat the following numbers backward: 8–4–2–1–9."	

Source: Items similar to those in the Wechster Adult Intelligence Scale, Third ed. Copyright © 1997, 1981, 1955 by The Psychological Corporation. Reproduced by permission. All rights reserved.

working memory, and vocabulary. The nonverbal subtests present tasks such as picture arrangement (arranging a series of out-of-order cartoon frames into their correct order to make a story) and picture completion (finding missing elements in a picture) that do not depend as heavily on verbal thinking (Table 8.1).

In addition to a single, overall IQ score, the WAIS-III yields separate scores for each of the 14 subtests and overall scores for verbal and performance (nonverbal) IQ. It also yields more specific subscales of verbal comprehension (how well the person thinks using language, a predominantly left-hemisphere function), perceptual organization (how well the person thinks using visual images, a predominantly right-hemisphere function), working memory (which relies substantially on functioning of the frontal lobes), and processing speed (which probably is not localized to any particular region of the brain). This allows psychologists to identify specific problem areas or strengths. Peter Franklin, the historian from the opening vignette, would probably not receive an abnormally low score on the picture arrangement subtest, since his visual processing appeared to be intact and his understanding of social scenarios did not seem impaired except when language problems interfered. On the similarities subtest, however, which requires abstract verbal reasoning (e.g., how is a cup similar to a saucer?), the effects of the stroke would be more be apparent.

Frequency Distribution of IQ Scores

Wechsler was responsible for another important innovation in IQ testing. The formula originally devised for deriving IQ (MA/CA × 100) was useful in assessing children's test performance, but it was logically inconsistent when applied to adult test scores. As people grew older, the denominator (chronological age) in the formula grew larger, while the numerator (mental age) remained relatively constant. Thus, subjects seemed to become less intelligent with age. Although this supports the intuitive theories held by many teenagers about their parents, as we will see in Chapter 13, it is not really true. Further, the differences between a 26-year-old and a 29-year-old are not comparable to the differences between a 7-year-old and a 10-year-old, whose abilities are developing at a rapid pace. Wechsler remedied these problems by abandoning the concept of mental age and calculating IQ as an individual's position relative to peers of the same age on a frequency distribution.

A frequency distribution (Chapter 2 Supplement) describes the frequency of various scores in the population. Like the distributions for weight, height, and many other human traits, the distribution for IQ takes the form of a normal, bell-shaped curve (Figure 8.2). A normal curve is a frequency distribution in which the vast majority of subjects receive scores close to the mean, resulting in the bell-shaped curve. Extremely high IQ scores, such as 150, are relatively rare, as are extremely low scores, such as 50. Most people's scores fall within the average range (between about 85 and 115), while a progressively smaller percentage fall within ranges that deviate farther from the norm.

INTERIM SUMMARY   **Intelligence tests** are psychometric instruments designed to assess an individual's cognitive capabilities relative to others in a population. Binet developed the ancestor of modern intelligence tests for the purpose of identifying retarded children. His scale assigned an individual child a **mental age (MA),** which refers to the average age at which children can be expected to achieve a particular score. Terman brought intelligence testing to North America, adapted the concept of the **intelligence quotient (IQ),** and expanded the meaning of IQ from a predictor of school success to a broader index of intellectual ability. IQ was initially calculated by dividing mental age by chronological age and multiplying by 100, but Wechsler abandoned the concept of mental age and calculated IQ as an individual's position relative to peers of the same age by using a frequency distribution. The Wechsler scales (the **WAIS-III** and the **WISC-III** for children) yield an overall full-scale IQ score as well as specific scores, such as verbal and nonverbal (performance) IQ.

VALIDITY AND LIMITATIONS OF IQ TESTS

As we have seen (Chapter 2), the validity of a psychological test refers to its ability to assess the construct it is attempting to assess. If by "intelligence" one means

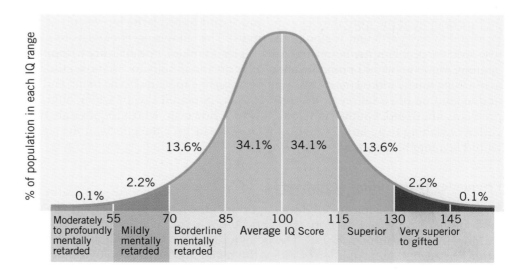

FIGURE 8.2
Frequency distribution of IQ scores. The frequency distribution for IQ takes the form of a bell-shaped curve. *Source:* Anastasi & Urbina, 1997.

the kind of mental ability that allows people to succeed in school, then intelligence tests have considerable validity. Recall from Chapter 2 that one way of determining a test's validity is to correlate its results with a relevant external measure. IQ, as determined by intelligence tests, is strongly related to school grades, showing a correlation coefficient between .60 and .70 (where 1.0 is a perfect correlation and 0 is no correlation at all) (Brody, 1992; Wilkinson, 1993). In psychological research, this is as strong a correlation as can be found. It is far higher than the ability of any test of a personality trait (such as conscientiousness) to predict any class of behavior (such as the tendency to come to work or class on time).

Nevertheless, IQ testing has drawn criticism and controversy for many years, largely for two reasons: the lack of a theoretical basis and the potential for culture bias.

Lack of a Theoretical Basis

In many respects, IQ tests have been tests in search of a construct. As one psychologist has noted, "social needs have seemed to lead, and theoretical developments to follow, the changes in mental tests over the last half century" (Tuddenham, 1962, p. 515). Most IQ tests only partially address the domains of memory, reasoning, problem solving, and decision making studied by cognitive scientists. Only in its most recent version has the Wechsler scale, for example, begun to reflect developments in the scientific study of cognition, such as the recognition of the importance of working memory.

One question raised by this lack of theoretical clarity is whether the kinds of abilities required for academic performance, which IQ assesses with considerable validity, can be equated with general intellectual ability. In contrast to current popular conceptions of IQ, Binet himself never considered his test a measure of native ability but only a means of diagnosing performance deficits in school (Fass, 1980). Critics argue that intelligence tests and tests such as the SAT provide little insight into the type of practical intelligence involved in achieving goals in everyday life (Atwater, 1992; Scribner, 1986; Sternberg & Wagner, 1993; Sternberg & Williams, 1997); nor do they assess creativity, interpersonal skill, or, as in Mr. Franklin's case, the ability to play a tune (Gardner, 1983). Intelligence tests and similar measures (including many exams in school) focus on problems that are often of little interest to the test taker, in which the problem is well defined, the data necessary for solving the problem are all presented without requiring any creative effort, and only one answer is usually correct (Neisser, 1976; Sternberg et al., 1995). This bears little resemblance to the kinds of adaptive tasks that face people in their everyday lives.

Are IQ Tests Culturally Biased?

A second concern frequently raised about IQ tests is their vulnerability to cultural biases. Consider the following questions from the Army Alpha test administered in the early part of this century (reprinted in Gould, 1981, p. 200):

> Crisco is a: a) patent medicine, b) disinfectant, c) toothpaste, d) food product.
> The number of a Kaffir's legs is: a) 2, b) 4, c) 6, d) 8.
> Christy Mathewson is famous as a: a) writer, b) artist, c) baseball player, d) comedian.

The knowledge that Crisco is a food product, that a Kaffir (like any other human) has two legs, or that Christy Mathewson was a baseball player demonstrates a familiarity with early twentieth-century U.S. culture more than basic intelligence.

Since the days of the Army Alpha, intelligence tests have undergone considerable revision to minimize cultural bias. How successful these efforts have been is

"WE REALIZE YOU DO BETTER ON YOUR IQ TESTS THAN YOU DO IN ANYTHING ELSE, BUT YOU JUST CANNOT MAJOR IN IQ."

Drawing by Sidney Harris

a matter of debate (see Helms, 1997). Some psychologists argue that intelligence and aptitude tests continue to favor the dominant white middle class (Darou, 1992; Elliott, 1988; Schiele, 1991). Indeed, some opponents of IQ testing contend that IQ tests, like other standardized tests such as the SAT, are *designed* to favor the white middle class, in order to justify the perpetuation of social inequality (Garcia, 1979; Putnam, 1973; Weinberg, 1989). Of particular concern is the 15-point difference that has separated the average IQ scores of white Americans and African Americans for decades (Loehlin et al., 1975). IQ is also associated with socioeconomic status; poor and working-class people tend to receive lower scores than their wealthier peers (see Williams & Ceci, 1997). According to critics, reliance on IQ and similar tests can thus perpetuate inequalities.

How do these charges hold up against the evidence? Some cultural bias is unavoidable in IQ tests, despite the best of intentions. Tests that may intuitively seem *culture free* (i.e., independent of a particular cultural experience) often carry hidden biases. For example, many standardized intelligence tests ask the person to categorize geometric stimuli according to color or shape. At first glance, this task seems culture free: It requires no language and does not seem to depend on familiarity with cultural artifacts that are typically North American. As we saw in Chapter 7, however, this task can be quite confusing to nonliterate people, such as the Liberians, who have no experience with abstract geometric figures taken out of context and reproduced on paper (Irwin & McGlaughlin, 1970). When the shoe is on the other foot, cultural bias becomes readily apparent. North American undergraduates asked to categorize leaves according to whether they come from vines or trees perform much more poorly than nonliterate Liberians (Cole et al., 1971).

Other seemingly culture-free elements of intelligence tests may also carry hidden biases, such as the use of timed tests. IQ and achievement tests impose strict time limits in answering questions. Although this may in part tap a universal feature of intelligence—how quickly a person can think—it also reflects the cultural emphasis on speed characteristic of the advanced capitalist societies that created intelligence testing. The ability to work quickly is essential to a manufacturing economy, where sluggish workers hold up an assembly line and profit margins depend on rapid production. In contrast, many traditional cultures place less value on quick and independent thinking and instead prefer slow deliberation and collective decision making (see Berry et al., 1992).

IQ tests may be equally problematic in assessing subcultures within multicultural societies such as the United States and Canada, in part because many questions rely on knowledge that is more familiar to some groups than to others, such as "Who wrote *Macbeth*?" or "On what continent is France?" Psychologists have raised particular concerns about the validity of IQ tests in assessing African Americans, many of whom are raised in low-income neighborhoods and have little exposure to Shakespeare or travel. Further, the Black English spoken in many of these homes differs substantially from the language assessed in standardized intelligence tests (see Stewart, 1969).

A case in point was African-American psychologist Robert L. Williams, who was advised to become a bricklayer after receiving an IQ score of 82 at the age of 15. He declined the advice and later illustrated the linguistic bias in IQ tests—after receiving his Ph.D.—by developing the Black Intelligence Test of Cultural Homogeneity. The test drew from a vocabulary more familiar to African Americans than to whites (e.g., asking the meaning of terms like *running a game*); not surprisingly, blacks tended to outperform whites on the test (Williams, 1974).

A more recent rendition of this controversy occurred in the United States in the mid-1990s when a school board in California tried to elevate black English (also called Ebonics) to the status of a language. The question was whether African-American students should learn to speak standard English, and, if so, whether they were being asked to learn to "talk right" or "talk white."

Are IQ Tests Valid?

Are IQ tests, then, invalid, useless, and dangerous? The answer is not black or white: IQ tests are some of the most valid, highly predictive tests psychologists have ever devised, and they can be useful in targeting children on both ends of the bell curve who require special attention. Comparing members of markedly different cultures or subcultures can be problematic, but IQ tests *do* tend to be valid when comparing two people with similar backgrounds. IQ and SAT scores are just as predictive of school success within African-American samples as within white samples; that is, an African-American student with a high IQ is likely to fare much better in school than an African-American student with a low IQ (Anastasi & Urbina, 1997). Controlling for dialect (such as translating questions into Black English) does not generally eliminate black/white differences (Quay, 1974); in fact, items on standard IQ tests that show the strongest ethnic differences are not the ones that seem most obviously culturally biased (Jensen, 1998).

Furthermore, despite their biases, IQ tests do evaluate areas of intelligence that are important in a literate industrial society, such as the ability to think abstractly, to reason with words, and to perceive spatial relations quickly and accurately. For many years, psychologists accepted the conclusion that intelligence tests predicted very little outside of the classroom, but more recent evaluations of the evidence suggest that intelligence tests can be powerful predictors of job performance and occupational achievement (Barrett & Depinet, 1991). All ideology and academic controversies aside, few critics of IQ testing would probably choose a doctor with a low IQ if their child needed treatment for leukemia.

Asking whether IQ tests are valid is in some ways the wrong question. Validity only has meaning in relation to a goal, and it is always enhanced by matching the test to the goal and adding additional measures that can enhance prediction. If the aim is prediction of school success, IQ tests, SATs, and the like are highly valid. Nevertheless, all tests include a substantial component of error, so that they will overpredict some people's performance and underpredict others'; that is why admissions committees should never use *only* standardized test scores in making admissions decisions. If the goal is to predict something like occupational performance, the tester would do well to combine a measure of intelligence, which has *some* predictive value, with other measures that more closely mirror the requirements of the job, such as measures of social skills when selecting salespeople or managers.

INTERIM SUMMARY   Critics charge that IQ tests lack a theoretical basis, fail to capture other kinds of intelligence such as practical intelligence and creativity, and have cultural biases. Intelligence tests and similar instruments are highly predictive of school performance and, to a lesser degree, occupational success, although they should always be supplemented by other methods when used for selecting applicants for jobs or universities.

APPROACHES TO INTELLIGENCE

IQ tests place individuals on a continuum of intelligence but do not explain what intelligence is. Three approaches to understanding the nature of intelligence are the psychometric approach, the information-processing approach, and a theory of multiple intelligences.

THE PSYCHOMETRIC APPROACH

The **psychometric approach** tries to identify groups of items in a test that correlate highly with one another in order to identify underlying skills or abilities. If subjects perform multiple tasks, strong performance on some of tasks is likely to predict strong performance on others. Subjects who have good vocabularies, for example, usually have strong verbal reasoning skills (such as figuring out the meaning of unfamiliar proverbs) as well. Because vocabulary and verbal reasoning are highly correlated, usually a person's score on one will predict her score on the other.

The primary tool of the psychometric approach is **factor analysis**, a statistical procedure for identifying common elements, or **factors** (in this case, primary mental abilities), that underlie performance across a set of tasks. Using factor analysis, researchers set up a table, or matrix, that shows how scores on tests of different abilities correlate with one another. Their aim is to reduce ten, 50, or 100 scores to a few combined variables (factors). Once they identify a factor empirically, they examine the various items that comprise it to try to discover the underlying attribute it is measuring, such as verbal intelligence or arithmetical ability.

For example, if a diverse sample were tested on four kinds of athletic ability and the scores for each measure were correlated, the result might look something like the matrix presented in Table 8.2. The correlations between each pair are moderate to strong: People who are good sprinters tend to be good at weightlifting (a correlation of +.35), and so forth. A common factor shared by all these variables that accounts for the positive correlations may be physical conditioning or athletic ability. The extremely high correlation between weightlifting ability and number of pullups probably reflects a more specific factor, muscle strength.

TABLE 8.2 IDENTIFYING A COMMON FACTOR

	SPRINT	WEIGHTS	PULLUPS	SIT-UPS
Sprint	—	.35	.45	.41
Weights		—	.70	.52
Pullups			—	.57
Pulse				—

Spearman's Two-Factor Theory

The English psychologist Charles Spearman (1863–1945) was the first to apply factor analysis to intelligence tests. Spearman (1904, 1927) set up a matrix of correlations to see how children's test scores on various measures were related to their academic ranking at a village school in England. His analysis formed the basis for his **two-factor theory,** so named because Spearman believed the correlations he found were the result of two types of factors or abilities.

Spearman called the first factor the **g-factor**, or **general intelligence**. Children with the highest academic ranking tended to score well on such measures as arithmetic ability, general knowledge, and vocabulary, suggesting a general intelligence factor. Spearman believed the g-factor explained why almost any two sets of items assessing intellectual functioning will tend to correlate with one another.

Yet Spearman also noted that subjects who performed well or poorly on math tests did not necessarily score equally well or poorly on other measures, such as vocabulary or general knowledge. The correlations among different subtests on a correlation matrix were far from uniform, just as the correlation between weightlifting and number of pullups was far higher than the correlation between weightlifting and sprinting speed in Table 8.2. Spearman therefore proposed another type of factor, called an s-factor ("s" for *specific*), to explain the differences in correlations between different pairs of measures. According to Spearman, **s-factors** reveal specific abilities unique to certain tests or shared only by a subset of tests. Individuals vary in overall intellectual ability (the g-factor), but some people are adept at some kinds of reasoning (such as mathematical, spatial, or verbal) while mediocre at others.

Other Factor Theories

Factor analysis has proven useful in identifying common factors among the mountains of statistical data produced by intelligence tests. However, both the number of factors and the types of mental abilities revealed through factor analysis can vary depending on who is doing the analysis. To illustrate why this happens, return to the matrix of correlations of physical skills presented in Table 8.2. We noted a somewhat stronger correlation between weightlifting and pullups and suggested that the factor common to the two might be muscle strength. Alternatively, however, one might have concluded that *upper body* strength is the s-factor—since we have not directly assessed strength of lower body muscles, except in sprinting—or perhaps even motivation to develop strong upper body muscles, which we have not assessed either. Factor analysis can yield many varying interpretations of the same findings, and it cannot rule out the possibility that different factors might have emerged if other tasks had been included.

Different Interpretations In fact, when other psychologists applied Spearman's factor analytic technique, they arrived at different interpretations. For example, L. L. Thurstone (1938, 1962) argued against the existence of an overriding g-factor, finding instead seven primary factors in intelligence: word fluency, comprehension, numerical computation, spatial skills, associative memory, reasoning, and perceptual speed. The most comprehensive re-analysis of data from over 400 data sets collected from 1927 to 1987 (Carroll, 1993) produced a hierarchical, three-level solution that in some ways resembles a compromise between Spearman's and Thurstone's models. At the highest level is a g-factor shared by all lower level abilities. At the middle level are more specific factors similar to those Thurstone discovered. At the bottom level of the hierarchy are simple processes, such as speed of recognizing objects, that are ultimately necessary for producing any intelligent action.

Gf–Gc Theory   Another major approach, called **Gf–Gc theory**, also proposes a hierarchical model (Cattell, 1957; Horn, 1968; Horn & Noll, 1997). Instead of encompassing all lower order factors under a *single* g-factor, however, this model distinguishes two general intelligence factors, rather than one, at the highest level: fluid and crystallized intelligence. **Fluid intelligence** refers to intellectual capacities that have no specific content but are used in processing information and approaching novel problems, such as the ability to draw inferences or recognize patterns. **Crystallized intelligence** refers to people's store of knowledge, much of it learned from their culture, such as vocabulary and general world knowledge. At a lower hierarchical level are seven more specific factors: short-term memory, long-term memory, visual processing, auditory processing, processing speed on simple tasks, correct decision speed (processing speed on tasks that are much more difficult, such as solving problems), and quantitative knowledge (mathematical reasoning).

Although considerable controversy remains about whether the data support abandonment of a single g-factor, Gf–Gc theory has two advantages. First, many of its dimensions make theoretical sense in light of research in cognitive science on the components of information processing, such as the distinction between long-term and short-term (working) memory. Second, as we will see in Chapter 13 on cognitive development, the theory can distinguish components of intelligence that change independently over the life span. Figure 8.3 provides a striking example of age-related differences on several of the factors identified by the model. In general, crystallized intelligence—general knowledge—continues to increase through at least age 60, whereas fluid intelligence declines gradually but steadily in adulthood. The capacity to consolidate and retrieve long-term memories increases until age 30 and then levels off; processing speed and visual processing ability decline steadily after about age 25. By way of comparison, the figure shows what happens to a measure of "g" over time—namely, nothing. Proponents of Gf–Gc theory suggest that relying solely on "g" thus considerably understates the complexity of cognitive changes through the life span and fails to distinguish components of intelligence that have different developmental trajectories.

Limitations of the Psychometric Approach

The psychometric approach provides a set of measures that can accurately predict school performance from as early as the preschool years and can show how different abilities correlate with one another. This is a very impressive achievement. Because psychometrics is purely a descriptive tool, however, it cannot *explain* the way people think intelligently; it can only identify dimensions of intelligent functioning, such as verbal or mathematical ability.

In some ways, a strictly psychometric approach illustrates the problem of trying to study a domain without a theoretical perspective. Without solid theory, psychologists have no way to decide whether they have organized the data sensi-

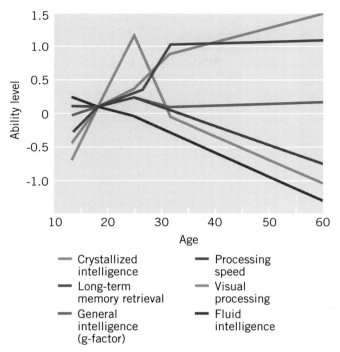

FIGURE 8.3
Intellectual functioning over the life span. Whereas general intelligence does not appear to differ across the life span, analysis of specific types of intelligence suggests otherwise. In particular, crystallized intelligence increases in adulthood, whereas fluid intelligence declines. That is, knowledge continues to increase, but ability to respond quickly and to novel tasks decreases with aging. Adapted from J. Horn & J. Noll (1997). Human cognitive capacities: Gf-Gc theory. In D. P. Flanagan, J. L. Gershaft, & P. L. Harrison (eds.), *Contemporary Intellectual Assessment,* New York: Guilford, p. 72.

bly (such as how many factors, and which ones) or even whether they have collected the right data in the first place.

INTERIM SUMMARY   The **psychometric approach** tries to shed light on the nature of intelligence by determining empirically which tasks tend to correlate with one another. The primary tool of the psychometric approach is **factor analysis**, a statistical technique for identifying common **factors** that underlie performance across a variety of tasks. Spearman's **two-factor theory** distinguishes a **g-factor**, or general intelligence, from **s-factors**, or specific abilities. **Gf–Gc theory** is another hierarchical model of intelligence that argues for the presence of two overarching types of intelligence and several subordinate factors, such as short-term and long-term memory. The two broad types of intelligence in Gf–Gc theory are **fluid intelligence** (intellectual capacities that have no specific content but are used in processing information) and **crystallized intelligence** (people's store of knowledge, much of it learned from their culture).

THE INFORMATION-PROCESSING APPROACH

In contrast to the psychometric approach, which tries to quantify basic abilities, the information-processing approach tries to understand the *processes* that underlie intelligent behavior (Sternberg, 1985, 1997). In other words, the information-processing approach looks at the "how" of intelligence and not just the "how much." It defines intelligence as a process rather than a measurable quantity, and it posits that individual differences in intelligence reflect differences in the cognitive operations people use in thinking (Brody, 1992; Ceci, 1990).

FIGURE 8.4

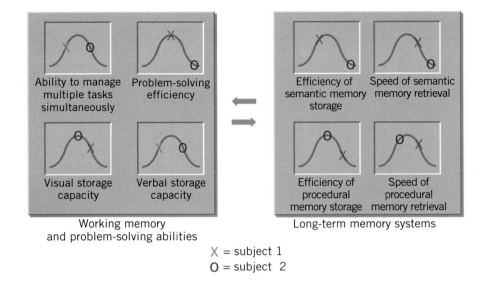

FIGURE 8.4
Multiple components of information processing. People have different degrees of ability and hence fall on different points of a bell-shaped curve on various components of information processing. Subject 2 is generally superior to subject 1 in problem-solving ability and verbal information processing (semantic memory), although the first subject can store more information in visual working memory and has a faster and more efficient procedural memory system.

In principle, a cognitive psychologist interested in intelligence would test the abilities of subjects on various information-processing abilities, such as working memory capacity, efficiency of various long-term memory systems, and ability to apply strategies for manipulating mental representations to solve problems and make decisions. He would present subjects with tasks such as repeating digits to measure aspects of working memory or memorizing word lists to test explicit memory. For each process, a subject's score would be plotted on a frequency distribution (Figure 8.4). The cognitive psychologist might then try to see which of the many bell curves best predicted some criterion of achievement, such as academic performance or success at engineering, and whether some combination of these abilities is necessary for success in particular endeavors.

Researchers from this perspective have found that three variables are particularly important in explaining individual differences as assessed by intelligence tests: speed of processing, knowledge base, and ability to acquire and apply mental strategies.

Speed of Processing

We commonly use the adjective *slow* to describe people who perform poorly in school or on similar tasks and describe more skilled performers as *quick*. In fact, processing speed appears to be an important aspect of intelligence and a strong correlate of IQ (Deary & Stough, 1996; McGeorge et al., 1996; Vernon & Weese, 1993). One experimental design presents participants with pairs of letters and measures the amount of time they take to decide whether the letters are identical physically (as are the letters *AA* in Figure 8.5) or identical in name (as is the pair *Aa*). Identifying letters with the same name but different physical appearance is the more complicated of the two tasks; to judge whether two letters have the same name even though they do not look alike, the subject must perform an additional step, searching long-term memory for the name of each letter form before comparing the two symbols. The difference in response times between these two types of task reflects the speed of memory search (Posner et al., 1969).

Research shows that differences in response time in tasks such as this correlate with measures of academic achievement: Children with above-average scholastic abilities tend to perform this kind of task more rapidly than average-ability children, as do college students with higher IQs than their peers (Campione et al., 1982; Lindley & Smith, 1992). Conversely, individuals who are mentally

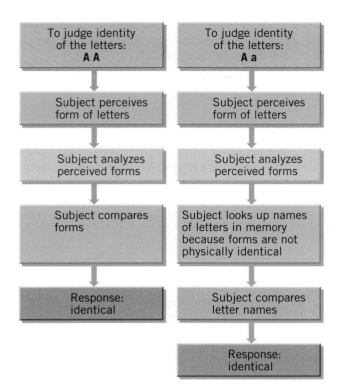

FIGURE 8.5
Speed of processing. In this study of speed of processing, investigators measured the time subjects took to decide whether pairs of letters were physically identical (AA) or identical in name (Aa). Judging name identity when physical identity is absent requires an extra processing step and hence takes longer. *Source:* Based on Posner et al., 1969.

retarded respond much more slowly on a variety of tasks (Nettelbeck & Wilson, 1997). Studies using geometric figures (Figure 8.6) document a similar correlation between achievement and visual processing speed (Mumaw & Pellegrino, 1984).

Knowledge Base

Variation among individuals in intellectual functioning also reflects variation in their **knowledge base**—the information stored in long-term memory. Differences in knowledge base that affect performance include not only the amount of knowledge a person has but the way it is organized and its accessibility for retrieval (Glaser & Schauble, 1990). People who have expertise in a particular knowledge domain have well-developed schemas that facilitate encoding, retrieval, and mental manipulation of relevant information. Florists, for example, can generally recognize and classify flowers more quickly than people with less exposure to (and interest in) flowers (see Chi et al., 1982). People with a broad knowledge base are likely to appear more intelligent simply because they have a ready way of categorizing and retrieving information, like the baseball afficionado who can rattle off World Series scores from decades ago.

Ability to Acquire and Apply Cognitive Strategies

A third variable that correlates with many measures of intelligence is the ability to acquire mental strategies (such as mnemonic devices and formulas for solving math problems) and apply them to new situations. Cognitive strategies are essential for many everyday tasks, from remembering grocery lists to calculating a server's tip. Their efficient use distinguishes children from adults and individuals with differing IQ levels from their peers. Children are less likely than adults to apply mnemonic strategies such as rehearsal in memorizing information (Flavell & Wellman, 1976), although their performance improves considerably when they

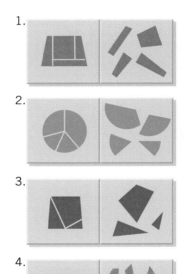

FIGURE 8.6
Spatial transformation problems. Can the figure on the left be constructed from the pieces on the right? *Source:* Mumaw & Pellegrino, 1984. *Answers: 1—yes; 2—no; 3—yes; 4—yes; 5—no.*

are taught and encouraged to use them (Best, 1993). In contrast to their peers, retarded children require more explicit instruction in mnemonic and problem-solving strategies (Campione et al., 1982; Niedalman, 1991).

Limitations of the Information-Processing Approach

Unlike the psychometric approach, the information-processing approach begins with a theory as well as a set of observations and uses the theory to explain the data. Although some researchers have begun exploring differences among individuals in the way they apply cognitive processes to real-world problems (Sternberg et al., 1995; Wagner, 1987), the major limitation of information-processing approaches is that many remain tied to the kind of intelligence used in academic situations and measured on IQ tests. As the study of intelligence moves into areas such as leadership ability or musical composition, traditional models and tasks may require revision.

INTERIM SUMMARY   Information-processing approaches to intelligence attempt to describe and measure the specific cognitive *processes* that underlie intelligent behavior; they tend to be more interested in "how" than "how much" in studying intelligence. Three variables on which people differ, and which correlate with IQ and achievement, are speed of processing, knowledge base, and the ability to learn and apply mental strategies.

A THEORY OF MULTIPLE INTELLIGENCES

In recent years, a more radical approach to intelligence has emerged that has greatly expanded the scope of thinking about intelligence. Intelligence tests may measure the kinds of intellectual abilities that foster success in school, but what about practical intelligence (the ability to put plans into action in real life), emotional intelligence (the ability to read people's emotions and use one's own emotional responses adaptively), or creativity (Mayer & Geher, 1996; Mayer & Salovey, 1997; Sternberg, 1985; Sternberg et al, 1995)?

A third view of intelligence that addresses questions such as these is Howard Gardner's **theory of multiple intelligences** (Chen & Gardner, 1997; Gardner, 1983). Gardner views intelligence as "an ability or set of abilities that is used to solve problems or fashion products that are of consequence in a particular cultural setting" (Walters & Gardner, 1986, p. 165). He identifies seven intelligences: musical, bodily/kinesthetic (such as the control over the body and movement that distinguishes great athletes and dancers), spatial (the use of mental maps), linguistic or verbal, logical/mathematical, intrapersonal (self-understanding), and interpersonal (social skills). Gardner would map a person's intelligence on seven different bell curves, one for each type of intelligence, rather than on a single IQ curve. Someone could be a brilliant mathematician but inhabit the lowest percentiles of musical or interpersonal intelligence.

Some of the intelligences on Gardner's list may surprise readers accustomed to equating intelligence with the logical and linguistic abilities assessed by IQ tests, but Gardner argues that defining intelligence only by the abilities assessed on IQ tests is problematic for several reasons. Although conventional IQ tests have some capacity to predict later occupational success, they are much better at predicting grades in school. A person with high interpersonal intelligence may become a superb salesperson despite having only average logical/mathematical abilities, or a brilliant composer may have poor linguistic skills. Furthermore, the emphasis on verbal and logical/mathematical intelligence in IQ measures reflects a bias toward skills valued in technologically advanced societies. Over the broad sweep of human history, musical, spatial, and bodily intelligences have tended to be more valued.

Musician Melissa Etheridge and golf sensation Tiger Woods display forms of intelligence not measured on standard tests.

Selecting Intelligences

To recognize the existence of multiple forms of intelligence, Gardner recommends a simple exercise: Instead of asking "How smart are you?" try asking "How are you smart?" (Chen & Gardner, 1997). The answer is likely to be a list of intellectual strengths and weaknesses, such as "I'm a really good writer, but I'm terrible at math," that will include some of the intelligences he has isolated.

Gardner acknowledges that one can never develop "a single irrefutable and universally acceptable list of human intelligences" (1983, p. 60). On what basis, then, did he choose each of his seven intelligences? One criterion was whether an intelligence could be isolated neuropsychologically. According to Gardner's view, people have multiple intelligences because they have multiple neural modules. Each module has its own modes of representation, its own rules or procedures, and its own memory systems. As in the case of Mr. Franklin in the opening vignette, brain damage may impair one system without necessarily damaging others. An intellectual skill that can be specifically affected or spared by brain damage qualifies as an independent intelligence. The modularity of intelligences means that a person's ability in one area does not predict ability in another (Gardner, 1983).

Another criterion emerged from savant and prodigy studies. **Savants** are individuals with extraordinary ability in one area but comparatively low functioning in others. For example, a young man with an IQ in the mentally retarded range was able to memorize lengthy and complex piano pieces in only a few hearings (Sloboda et al., 1985). Similarly, schizophrenic patients often have difficulty with tasks involving interpersonal intelligence—such as reading emotions from people's faces (Bryson et al., 1997)—yet they can be brilliant in realms such as mathematics. The existence of **prodigies**—individuals with extraordinary and generally early-developing genius in one area but normal abilities in others—also supports the notion of separate, modular intelligence systems. Indeed, creative geniuses in fields such as music generally require strikingly little time to master their fields.

A third criterion for selecting an intelligence is its distinctive developmental course from childhood to adulthood. The fact that one domain may develop more quickly or slowly than others supports the notion of multiple intelligences. Children learn language and mathematics at very different paces. The existence of prodigies is again instructive. If a Mozart could write music before he could even read, then the neural systems involved in musical intelligence must be separate from those involved in processing language.

Limitations of the Theory of Multiple Intelligences

Gardner presents a refreshing view of intelligence that draws on a far broader range of data than other approaches. It takes into account dimensions of behavior that are not commonly assessed in IQ tests but clearly require intelligence, from writing music to managing a crew of workers. His theory also firmly grounds intelligence in both its neurological and cultural context.

Nevertheless, like all theories, Gardner's has its limitations. One is that it underestimates the possibility of some kinds of general intelligence, such as the mental quickness across different domains that characterizes many highly intelligent people. A second limitation of Gardner's theory is that it lacks measures of most of the intelligences, such as intrapersonal and musical, that would allow it to be tested empirically, although Gardner and his colleagues are now beginning to focus more on assessment. A third problem is the potential proliferation of intelligences. If bodily intelligence is a distinct domain of intellectual functioning, can one similarly distinguish dance intelligence, football intelligence, and tennis intelligence? If not, can one assume that someone with a talent for football could equally have turned that talent to ballet? Similarly, the concept of musical intelligence conceals differences between the intelligence required to write a symphony and that required to play precisely or expressively from a musical score. Differences even exist between the ability to play various instruments, such as the African marimba and the concert violin. The marimba requires considerable spontaneity, with musical improvisations and almost perpetual give-and-take with both the audience and other musicians. By contrast, the violin demands an ability to read a musical score and to produce a highly controlled performance cued by the conductor (Judd, 1988).

INTERIM SUMMARY   Gardner's theory of **multiple intelligences** proposes that intelligence is not one capacity but many. Gardner argues that intelligences can be isolated based on a number of criteria, including their neurological independence (each with its own neural modules, which can be independently affected by brain damage), the presence of savants (who are severely deficient in major intellectual respects but have pockets of giftedness), and their different developmental courses. The theory distinguishes seven kinds of intelligence: musical, bodily/kinesthetic, spatial, linguistic or verbal, logical/mathematical, intrapersonal, and interpersonal.

HEREDITY AND INTELLIGENCE

Having some concept of what intelligence is and how to measure it, we are now prepared to address the most controversial issue surrounding the concept of intelligence: its origins. The question of the degree to which intelligence is inherited or learned is another incarnation of the nature–nurture controversy and one that is emotionally loaded. We begin by examining research on the roots of differences among individuals in IQ and then turn to the thorny issue of differences among groups.

INDIVIDUAL DIFFERENCES IN IQ

The influence of both nature and nurture on individual differences in intelligence is well established (see Sternberg, 1997). With respect to environmental effects, as we saw in Chapter 3, early enrichment of the environments of rats not only makes them better learners but actually increases their brain mass (see Bors & Forrin, 1996). In humans, an enriched home environment, positive mother–child interactions that foster interest and exploration, and maternal knowledge about child rearing and child development are among the best predictors of a child's performance on tests of IQ and language in the toddler and preschool years (Bee, 1982; Benasich & Brooks-Gunn, 1996; Hart & Risley, 1992; Landau & Weissler, 1993).

Environmental effects such as these persist into adolescence. In one *longitudinal study* (a study following individuals over time), the investigators examined the relation between the number of risk factors to which the child was exposed in early childhood and the child's IQ at age four and 13 (Sameroff et al., 1993). Among these risk factors were maternal lack of education, maternal mental illness, minority status (associated with, among other things, low standard of living and inferior schools), and family size. As can be seen from Figure 8.7, the child's IQ varied inversely with the number of risk factors: the more risk factors, the lower the child's IQ. Furthermore, low maternal IQ and multiple risks at age four

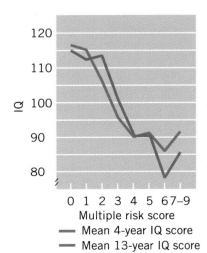

FIGURE 8.7
The impact of the environment on IQ. The figure shows the correlation between number of risk factors and child IQ at ages 4 and 13. By and large, each of several risk factors was highly predictive of IQ on its own, but the combination predicted IQ with a correlation near –.70 at both ages 4 and 13. *Source:* Sameroff et al., 1993, p. 89.

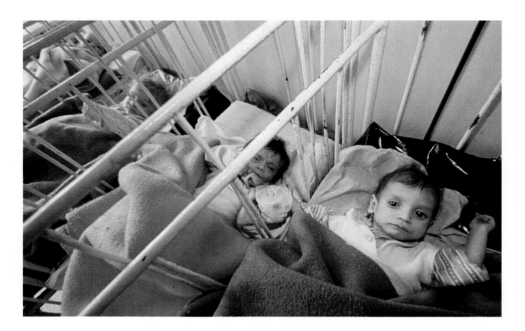

Children reared in unstimulating institutional environments, such as this Rumanian orphanage during the reign of dictator Nicolai Ceaucescu, often suffer permanent intellectual damage.

were highly predictive of IQ at age 13, with each correlation exceeding –.60, which is extraordinarily large.

The results of this study are striking, but they cannot definitively tease apart the relative contributions of heredity and environment. Maternal IQ could influence the child's IQ genetically or environmentally, and it could indirectly influence some environmental risk factors, such as low maternal education level. Other methods—notably twin, family, and adoption studies—can, however, more clearly distinguish some of the influences of nature and nurture. The logic of these studies is to examine subjects whose approximate degree of genetic relatedness is known and then to see whether degree of genetic relatedness predicts the size of the correlation between their IQs. If the size of the correlation varies with the degree of relatedness, this suggests a genetic effect. As described in Chapter 3, siblings, dizygotic (DZ) twins, and parent–offspring pairs are all related by .50. Monozygotic (MZ) twins are genetically identical (degree of relatedness 1.0), whereas adoptive relatives are unrelated (degree of relatedness 0). Thus, if genetic factors are important in IQ, MZ twins should be more alike than DZ twins, siblings, and parents and their offspring; and biological relatives should be more alike than children and their adoptive parents or siblings.

Results of Twin, Family, and Adoption Studies

The data across dozens of studies suggest that IQ, like nearly every psychological trait on which individuals differ, reflects a combination of heredity and environment (Table 8.3). On the one hand, the data clearly suggest an environmental impact: Being born at the same time (and presumably being treated more alike than siblings who are not twins) produces a higher correlation between DZ twins (.62) than between siblings (.41), even though both are related by .50.

On the other hand, the data on MZ twins suggest a strong genetic effect. The higher correlation between MZ than DZ twins reared together does not in itself prove a genetic effect; parents tend to treat identical twins more similarly than fraternal twins, which could also influence the size of the correlations between their IQs (Beckwith et al., 1991; Kamin, 1974). However, most data suggest that the genetic effect is more powerful (Kendler et al., 1993; Plomin et al., 1976; Scarr & Carter-Saltzman, 1982). For example, identical twins reared apart show an average IQ correlation

TABLE 8.3 CORRELATIONS IN INTELLIGENCE BETWEEN PAIRS OF PEOPLE WITH VARYING DEGREES OF RELATEDNESS REARED TOGETHER OR APART

RELATIONSHIP	REARING	DEGREE OF RELATEDNESS	CORRELATION	NUMBER OF PAIRS
Same individual		1.0	.87	456
Monozygotic twins	Together	1.0	.86	1417
Dizygotic twins	Together	.50	.62	1329
Siblings	Together	.50	.41	5350
Siblings	Apart	.50	.24	203
Parent-child	Together	.50	.35	3973
Parent-child	Apart	.50	.31	345
Adoptive parent-child	Together	0	.16	1594
Unrelated children	Together	0	.25	601
Spouses	Apart	0	.29	5318

Interestingly, the IQ of adoptive parents has little association with the IQ of their adopted children.

Identical twins score as similarly as the same person taking the test on two occasions.

The environment appears to have a substantial impact, as dizygotic twins and siblings have the same degree of relatedness but different IQ correlations.

Source: Adapted from Henderson, 1982.

Note. The table summarizes the results from family studies comparing IQs among multiple pairs of individuals, contrasting the degree of relatedness with correlation of intelligence scores. For "same individuals," the correlation refers to the same person taking the test at two different times.

of about .75, which is even stronger than DZ twins reared together (Bouchard et al., 1990; Newman et al., 1937; Plomin & DeFries, 1980; Shields, 1962).

Adoption studies provide a particularly important source of information on the relative impact of heredity and environment. Most of these studies compare the IQs of adopted children with those of other members of their adoptive family, their biological family, and a control group matched for the child's age, sex, socioeconomic status, and ethnic background. Beginning with the earliest adoption studies conducted in the first half of this century (Burks, 1928, 1938; Leahy, 1935; Skodak & Skeels, 1949), the results have identified genetic influences as the primary determinant of differences between individuals on IQ, with environmental circumstances substantially limiting or augmenting the effects of native ability (Cardon et al., 1992; Coon et al., 1990; Loehlin et al., 1989; Scarr & Carter-Saltzman, 1982; Turkheimer, 1991; Weiss, 1992).

In a classic study, researchers tested the IQ of each biological mother in the sample at the time of delivery and found an average IQ of 86 (Skodak & Skeels, 1949). Years later, they tested the children, who were reared by adoptive parents (often of higher socioeconomic status), using the same test (the Stanford-Binet). At age 13, these children scored an average of 107, over 20 points higher than their

Studies of monozygotic (identical) and dizygotic (fraternal) twins provide a way of studying the impact of genetics on intelligence.

biological mothers, providing strong evidence for the environmental component of intelligence. Subsequent studies have similarly shown increases in both IQ scores and school performance among children adopted into families of higher socioeconomic status (Dumaret, 1985; Schiff et al., 1982) and among members of twin pairs who attended better schools (Dudley, 1991).

However, in this classic adoption study, as in others, the correlation between the IQ of adopted children and their biological parents was considerably larger than the correlation with their adoptive parents' IQ. In other words, blood runs thicker than adoption papers in predicting IQ. More recent research similarly finds that the correlation between the IQs of biologically unrelated (adopted) siblings reared together is only .17, compared with .50 for biological siblings reared together (Segal, 1997). Further, in this study and several others, the correlation between the IQ of children and their adoptive relatives diminished over the years (Loehlin & Horn, 1997; Scarr & Weinberg, 1974, 1976; Scarr & Yee, 1980), with older adolescents resembling one another "only if they share genes" (Scarr & Weinberg, 1983).

In another large adoption study, the Texas Adoption Project, the investigators administered IQ and other tests to 1230 members of 300 Texas families that adopted one or more children from a home for unwed mothers (Horn et al., 1979, 1982; Loehlin & Horn, 1997). The researchers tested the adopted child, the adoptive parents, and other adopted and biological children in the family. Many of the birth mothers had taken IQ tests while at the home during their pregnancy, and the researchers had access to these scores as well.

At the time the project began, the adopted children were between three and 14 years old. At this initial assessment, the correlations between the IQ of the adoptive parents and their adopted children were similar to the correlations between the IQ of the adoptive parents and their biological children (Table 8.4), suggesting relatively equal contributions of heredity and environment. Approximately ten years later, the researchers located and retested many of the participants (Loehlin et al., 1989). This time the data presented a very different picture: As Table 8.4 shows, the only correlations that remained above .20 were between biological relatives. The results of the Texas Adoption Project support the findings of other studies that both genes and environment influence IQ in child-

---

TABLE 8.4   CORRELATIONS AMONG IQs OF PARENTS AND CHILDREN IN THE TEXAS ADOPTION PROJECT

RELATIONSHIP	INITIAL ASSESSMENT	FOLLOW-UP
Adoptive father/adopted child	.19	.10
Adoptive mother/adopted child	.13	.05
Adoptive father/biological child[a]	.29	.32
Adoptive mother/biological child[a]	.04	.14
Biological mother[b]/Adopted child	.23	.26
Adopted child/biological child	.20	.05
Biological child/biological sibling	.27	.24

[a]Biological child of parents who adopted other children.

[b]Biological mother of child who was adopted out.

Source: Adapted from Loehlin et al., 1990.

Note. The initial assessment data provide evidence for substantial contributions to IQ by both family environment and heredity. The 10-year follow-up data, however, suggest that the impact of the family environment decreases with age, since the only substantial correlations at follow-up were between biological relatives.

hood, but the impact of the family environment decreases with age as the impact of genetics increases. Similarities among the IQs of family members are apparently a greater reflection of their shared genes than their shared environment (Brody, 1992).

Are Differences Between Individuals in IQ Largely Genetic? Two Caveats

Before leaving this discussion, two caveats are important. First, the formulas used to assess heritability were developed 60 years ago, in the field of "agricultural eugenics," for the purpose of breeding high-quality cattle, and built into them are some assumptions that do not hold in any of the data sets discussed here (Hirsch, 1997). One important assumption is that cows do not choose their environments or their mates. Humans are very different. If people choose mates whose IQs and cultural experience are similar to their own, and if they choose environments that fit their talents and interests, heritability coefficients will be inflated. In fact, in the West, where these studies have largely been conducted, people do both.

Second, heritability coefficients apply only to a particular population, and they cannot be generalized outside that population. The most decisive studies of the heritability of IQ—twin studies—have nearly all used middle-class samples (Neisser et al., 1996). Their results are thus only generalizable to individuals from middle-class homes. If these studies were to include people from an urban ghetto—or from Liberia or Guatemala—heritability estimates would probably drop substantially because the environments would be so much more varied. The more varied the environment, the more environmental influences are likely to show up when calculating heritability. We know, for example, that schooling plays a crucial role in shaping intellectual skills, such as the ability to think abstractly. To the extent that twin studies have only included literate people, they have eliminated a substantial environmental effect before calculating heritability.

These comments are not intended to suggest that the findings of these studies should be dismissed. The point is simply that nature and nurture interact from birth in complex ways, and any attempt to separate them out in a definitive way is likely to be unsuccessful.

GROUP DIFFERENCES: RACE AND INTELLIGENCE

The 15-point discrepancy between the average IQ scores of blacks and whites in the United States has raised the question of the extent to which IQ differences among *groups* reflect genetic or environmental factors. Arthur Jensen created a storm of controversy over two decades ago when he concluded, based on the available data, that "between one-half and three-fourths of the average IQ difference between American Negroes and whites is attributable to genetic factors" (1973, p. 363; see also 1969; Jensen & Reynolds, 1982). Many denounced Jensen's interpretation of the data as blatantly racist, questioning both his science and his politics. The potential implications of Jensen's hypothesis made it among the most passionately debated in the history of psychology.

Several pieces of evidence militate against a primarily genetic explanation for group difference in IQ. One study of black children whose families had moved north to Philadelphia between World Wars I and II found that subjects gained between 0.5 and 0.7 IQ points for each year they were enrolled in Philadelphia schools, suggesting a clear environmental effect (Lee, 1951). Of particular importance in addressing this controversy was the Minnesota Adoption Study, which examined the IQ of children of various races adopted by white middle-class families (Scarr & Weinberg, 1976, 1983). Black children who had been adopted in the first year of life scored an average IQ of 110, at least 20 points higher than that of comparable children raised in the black community, where economic deprivation was much more common. When the researchers retested as many of the adoptees as they could locate ten years later, the IQ scores of black adoptees remained above the average IQ of blacks raised in the black community, although their mean IQ was somewhat below the mean IQ for whites in the sample (Weinberg et al., 1992).

Another study (Scarr et al., 1977) used an entirely different approach to test Jensen's hypothesis. Because a substantial proportion of American blacks have mixed ancestry, one of the measures the researchers used was the chemical composition of blood samples. If a substantial portion of racial IQ differences is attributable to genetics, then IQ levels should rise and fall in direct proportion to the degrees of African and European ancestry in a subject's blood. In fact, the researchers found no correlation between IQ and racial ancestry, refuting the genetic hypothesis.

Other research suggests that the average difference in standardized achievement test scores between blacks and whites in the United States has diminished in recent decades as educational opportunities have expanded and African Americans have climbed up the socioeconomic ladder (Williams & Ceci, 1997). Further, across all the industrialized countries, IQ appears to be rising about three points a decade, so that a person who is of only average IQ today would have been above average in comparison to other people 50 years ago (Flynn, 1987). Although the reasons for this are unclear, this steady increase probably reflects the greater complexity of the occupational and technical tasks required of people today than in their grandparents' day (Neisser et al., 1996). In any case, these data suggest that social and environmental conditions can lead to changes in IQ as large as the average difference between blacks and whites. As a leading researcher in the area concludes, "it is highly unlikely that genetic differences between the races could account for the major portion of the usually observed differences in the performance levels of [blacks and whites]" (Scarr & Carter-Saltzman, 1982, p. 864).

How can genetic factors be so important in accounting for individual differences in intelligence while environmental factors play such an important role in group differences (see Gould, 1981, 1994)? The answer becomes clear through an analogy. Anyone who has ever visited a war museum notices immediately how small the uniforms were even a century ago. If researchers were to measure skeletal remains, they might find that most men who fought in the civil war ranged from 5 feet 2 inches to 5 feet 6 inches, with an average of 5 feet 4 inches. Then, as now, tall fathers tended to beget tall sons, although "tall" in the 1860s would be short or average today. Were the same researchers to assess men who fought in the Vietnam War 100 years later, they would similarly find high heritability, but the average height would be several inches taller. In both samples—from the same country, a mere century apart—heritability is high, but the difference between the average height in 1865 and 1965 is entirely environmental, largely resulting from nutritional differences. Similarly, genetic differences could account for many of the observed differences between individuals in IQ, while environmental effects could account for observed differences between groups.

COMMENTARY

The Science and Politics of Intelligence

It is tempting to conclude, then, that group differences in intelligence can be explained in terms of environmental differences, such as social disadvantage, nutrition, and quality of education. Although research projects such as the Minnesota and racial ancestry studies seem to refute genetic explanations for racial differences in intelligence, a few words of caution are in order.

The question of genetic versus environmental components of intelligence is a highly emotional issue, particularly with respect to racial differences. The notion that a mental attribute as highly valued in the West as intelligence could be genetically influenced goes against the grain of many of our most fundamental beliefs and values, including the view that we are all created equal (see Fletcher, 1990). Furthermore, claims of racial superiority have a long and sordid history in human affairs, certainly in the twentieth century. Hence, any psychologist who argues for a genetic basis to any racial differences is immediately suspect, and the psychological community has, by and large, been much less critical of studies that claim to refute genetic or racial differences.

A case in point concerns published reports of an intervention program that took place in the late 1960s and early 1970s. This program, known as the Milwaukee Project, provided an intellectually enriched environment for children at high risk for mental retardation. The program's results seemed impressive. The investigators reported an average difference of 24 IQ points between the program's children and a control group. The findings were described in every introductory psychology textbook for nearly two decades to illustrate the decisive impact of environment, as opposed to heredity, on IQ. Unfortunately, the study had never been published by a journal, which means it had never been subjected to normal peer review processes and examined for its scientific merit (Sommer & Sommer, 1983). We have no idea whether or not the study had any validity.

At the other end of the political spectrum, Richard Herrnstein and Charles Murray (1994) more recently created a political storm rivaling Jensen's with their publication of *The Bell Curve*. Most of their argument is not about race; rather, they argue that as the United States increasingly approximates a meritocracy, in which people rise in their professions because of their merits, a great divide is emerging between the intellectual "haves" and "have nots." Because individual differences reflect to some large measure variation in genetic endowment and because people of similar intellectual levels tend to marry each other, the result, they argue, is an increasing concentration of cognitive resources in a small elite and a concentration of low intellect in a rapidly expanding underclass. People with low IQ are disproportionately represented among welfare recipients, prison inmates, mothers of illegitimate babies, drug abusers, and high school dropouts; this finding emerges regardless of whether the subjects in these studies are black or white.

The intertwining effects of genetics and environment on intelligence are difficult to tease apart.

In response to *The Bell Curve*, the American Psychological Association commissioned a distinguished task force to prepare a report on the state of the evidence with respect to intelligence and intelligence testing, including the question of the causes of group differences. The ultimate document was published with the unanimous support of the entire task force (Neisser et al., 1996). Some of its major conclusions were as follows. First, intelligence tests are highly predictive of school success; the average correlation is about .50, which is strong, but leaves much of the variance in academic success unaccounted for. Other variables, such as persistence, interest in school, and supportive attitudes of parents or peers also contribute to academic success. Intelligence tests only capture some of what we think of as intelligent behavior, although some general intelligence, or g-factor, appears to exist. Intelligence tests are not, however, biased against particular groups, since they are equally predictive of outcomes such as school performance within groups. Second, the heritability of IQ in children is about .45 but reaches about .75 in adulthood, which means that a substantial percentage of the difference in IQ between most individuals is genetic. Third, heritability does not imply immutability. Every genetic effect acts within an environmental circumstance, and changing the environment, such as placing a poor child in a middle-class home, can have a substantial impact on IQ. Fourth, whites and Asian Americans tend to have higher IQs than Hispanics, whose IQs are higher, on average, than African Americans. The lower average IQ of African Americans could potentially reflect some combination of causes, including poverty and related environmental risk factors, test-taking attitudes and motivational patterns shaped by generations of discrimination, or aspects of African American culture and genetics. There is no empirical support for genetic explanations, but the evidence for environmental explanations is also weak; thus, at present, no one knows what causes the difference in black and white IQ scores.

As the task force also points out, only a single generation has passed in the United States since the passage of civil rights legislation that has made discrimination illegal; Martin Luther King died in the height of the civil rights movement only 30 years ago. A definitive study of the relative roles of various environmental and genetic factors in group differences in IQ will probably have to wait until psychologists can assess African Americans whose families have been middle or upper class for four or five generations and who have attended schools comparable to those of whites of similar socioeconomic status. Such a study is many years away.

A final conclusion to be drawn from the debate regarding the causes of group differences in IQ may be equally important and is reflected in my own struggle to write this commentary. I rewrote this section of the chapter many times. I would come upon a new article and suddenly decide that the position I had taken in the last draft was badly flawed. With each new revision, I would wonder whether my ideological biases were interfering with my attempt to provide a balanced discussion of the topic. My training as a scientist reminded me at every step to look at the data. But my training as a clinician equally reminded me to look at myself, for data are always interpreted by a mind with motives, attitudes, and ideological commitments. No position is the final word on any important issue in psychology. However, the only way to get closer to the truth is to respect the scientific method—and the impediments to it imposed by our own imperfect and passionate intellects. ■

INTERIM SUMMARY   IQ reflects a combination of nature and nurture. Twin, family, and adoption studies suggest that genetic factors are likely more important in explaining differences between individuals. Studies of the influence of home environment and socioeconomic status suggest that racial differences are likely primarily environmental, although at this point no firm conclusions can be drawn.

THE EXTREMES OF INTELLIGENCE

Having explored the nature of intelligence and the factors that contribute to it, we now turn to the extremes of intelligence—mental retardation and giftedness—and to the relationship between creativity and intelligence.

MENTAL RETARDATION

Roughly 2 percent of the American population is **mentally retarded,** that is, significantly below average in general intellectual functioning (IQ less than 70), with deficits in adaptive functioning that appear in more than one realm (such as communicating with others, living autonomously, interacting socially, functioning in school or work, and maintaining safety and health) and are first evident in childhood (American Association on Mental Retardation, 1992; American Psychiatric Association, 1994). IQ is easier to quantify than adaptive functioning, which includes a broad range of skills such as social judgment and self-care abilities, but IQ scores alone are not enough to diagnose retardation (Greenspan & Granfield, 1992; Wechsler, 1997).

This definition encompasses a wide spectrum of disabilities, ranging from mild to moderate retardation (IQ between 50 and 70) to more severe conditions (IQ below 50). By far the largest number (about 75 to 90 percent) of people classified as retarded fall into the mild to moderate category. Individuals in this range can learn academic skills at an elementary school level, and as adults they are capable of self-supporting activities, although often in special, supervised environments (Tyler, 1965). Their retardation is frequently not diagnosed until they reach school age, when teachers notice not only their difficulty with academic demands but also troubles they may experience on the playground, at lunch, and in extracurricular activities (Richardson & Koller, 1996). Only about 10 percent of retarded individuals are classified as severely to profoundly retarded; in these cases, retardation is often accompanied by physiological handicaps and a mortality rate three or more times the norm.

Causes of Mental Retardation

Many individuals, particularly in the "severe to profound" category, are diagnosed early because of obvious neurological or medical symptoms. Wide-set eyes, flattened facial features, and stunted body shape characterize individuals with **Down syndrome**, a disorder caused by the presence of an extra 21st chromosome. Doctors can now diagnose Down syndrome during pregnancy through genetic testing of the amniotic fluid that surrounds the fetus.

Severe forms of retardation are often related to a genetic abnormality, as with Down syndrome and **phenylketonuria (PKU)**. Phenylketonuria reflects the presence of a recessive gene that causes the body to produce insufficient quantities of an enzyme that normally converts the amino acid phenylalanine into another

Children with Down syndrome have characteristic facial features as well as mental retardation.

amino acid. Without the appropriate enzyme, phenylalanine is converted instead into a toxin that damages the infant's developing central nervous system, resulting in severe mental retardation. If detected early, PKU is treatable by minimizing phenylalanine in the child's diet (Pavone et al., 1993; Wurtman & Ritter-Walker, 1988).

Retardation may also have environmental causes, including brain damage before birth (e.g., as a result of the mother's exposure to diseases), during delivery (as when oxygen to the brain is cut off by the umbilical cord), or after birth (through head injury, disease, or other environmental insult). In addition, retardation may also result from exposure in utero to alcohol and other drugs, such as cocaine (Jacobson et al., 1993; Lewis & Bendersky, 1995; Miller, 1992).

Although hundreds of biological factors have been linked to mental retardation, most cases cannot be tied to any specific biological cause (Bregman & Hodapp, 1991). As a result, more than 70 percent of cases, mostly those in the mild to moderate range, are not diagnosed at birth (Scott & Carran, 1987). Unlike severely or profoundly retarded individuals, children in this group often have parents and siblings with low IQs, and they come disproportionately from families who live in poverty (Abramowicz & Richardson, 1975; Richardson & Koller, 1996). Genetics are likely to play some role in the development of low IQ in mildly mentally retarded individuals, but environmental circumstances are probably more influential.

The prevalence of more severe forms of retardation is fairly constant around the world; in contrast, rates of mild retardation vary considerably from country to country (Grunewald, 1979; Stein & Susser, 1975). Whereas about 1 to 2 percent of the U.S. population is mildly retarded, this condition appears to be much less common in the People's Republic of China (Robinson, 1978). There, intellectually "slow" individuals tend to be more productively engaged and integrated into extended family networks (Landesman-Dwyer & Butterfield, 1983). Thus, cultural factors alter not only the social conditions that predispose some individuals to retardation but also the way people define and respond to retardation.

Treating Mental Retardation

Some forms of retardation, such as those caused by nutritional or other environmental deficits, may be prevented or treated if diagnosed in time. However, most forms are not curable in the sense of restoring the person to normality. Nevertheless, recent decades have seen an emphasis on **normalization** of mentally retarded individuals, taking them out of institutions whenever possible and providing either home care or living arrangements in small community-based centers (Birenbaum & Cohen, 1993; Zigler et al., 1990; Wolfe et al., 1995). In 1967, nearly 200,000 mentally retarded people lived in institutions in the United States. By 1984, this number had been reduced by more than half (Landesman & Butterfield, 1987). Another aspect of normalization is "mainstreaming" children, enrolling them in public schools in regular or special-education classes (Gottlieb, 1990; Ittenbach et al., 1993).

Normalization policies have been highly controversial. Supporters consider institutional care degrading and stress the enrichment that comes from living in less restrictive environments. The reality of normalization, however, is often very different from the ideal. Mainstreaming has placed extra strain on schools, which have not always been prepared to handle the special needs of mentally handicapped children (Schroeder et al., 1987). Mentally retarded children are frequently teased and ridiculed by "normal" peers; they may not be socially accepted even after years of mainstreaming (Brewer & Smith, 1989). The discrepancy between the goals and realities of normalization shows why changes in social policy based on theory or prior data should always be accompanied by research on outcome, to see whether the change is really beneficial.

GIFTEDNESS

Mental retardation occupies the extreme left-hand side of the bell-shaped IQ distribution. People whose IQs fall on the extreme right-hand side are generally classified as **gifted**. Like definitions of intelligence, definitions of giftedness depend on whatever skills or talents a society labels as gifts (Becker, 1978; Goodnow, 1976; Mistry & Rogoff, 1985). Balinese culture emphasizes artistic expression in music and visual symbolism (Belo, 1955), whereas Eastern European Jewish communities traditionally emphasized literary analysis in studying the scriptures (Zborowski & Herzog, 1952). In the West, with its emphasis on academic aptitude as measured by psychometric tests, giftedness is often equated with an IQ exceeding 130.

Definitions of giftedness depend on definitions of intelligence. In accord with Gardner's theory of multiple intelligences, many psychologists consider giftedness at least partially domain specific or limited to particular abilities (Read, 1982). The prodigy who can mentally multiply two three-digit numbers in 30 seconds may be gifted in mathematics but have only normal abilities in other areas (Smith, 1988). A broader definition of giftedness, proposed by psychologist Robert Sternberg, identifies domains of special talent, ranging from intellectual skills (such as verbal, mathematical, spatial, and memory skills) to artistic and physical abilities (Sternberg & Davidson, 1985).

Are Gifted People Maladjusted?

However giftedness is defined, people of unusual intelligence have been viewed with a mixture of awe and suspicion over the centuries. The ancient Greek and Roman civilizations associated uncommon intelligence with divine power, but the Roman philosopher Seneca postulated that "there is no great genius without a touch of madness." Indeed, for much of the history of Western civilization, at least until the Renaissance, giftedness was seen as an aberration or abnormality that was unhealthy at best and heretical at worst. (From a statistical point of view, of course, gifted people *are* abnormal; that is, they are outside the norm as defined by the middle region of the bell curve.) The common notion persists that extreme intelligence is associated with unhappiness or social maladjustment.

Is this simply wishful thinking on the part of the rest of us? In 1921, Lewis Terman began a longitudinal study of over 1000 California children with IQs above 140 that still continues today (Terman, 1925; Tomlinson-Keasey & Little, 1990; Vaillant & Vaillant, 1990). The primary finding is that gifted individuals tend to have average or above-average personality adjustment, slightly better chances of marital success, and far greater likelihood of achieving vocational success than the general population (Terman & Oden, 1947). Other studies have produced similar findings (Janos & Robinson, 1985), although a subset of the gifted population—children with very high IQs in the range of 180—have higher than normal rates of adjustment difficulties (Hollingworth, 1926, 1942).

CREATIVITY AND INTELLIGENCE

A quality related to both intelligence and giftedness is **creativity**, which can be defined as the ability to produce valued outcomes in a novel way. Creativity is moderately correlated with intelligence (Sternberg & Lubart, 1996), but not all people who are high in "g" are high in creativity. In general, intelligence in a particular area seems necessary but not sufficient for creativity. A person who has little ability in mathematics or architecture would be hard pressed to solve problems in those fields creatively, but many competent mathematicians and architects have no flare for innovation. Individuals with IQs below 120 are less likely to display creative thinking than those with a higher IQ, but above 120, the correlation between intelligence and creativity is essentially zero (Feldman, 1980; Keating, 1983; Wallach, 1970, 1985). Interestingly, in the 40-year follow-up of Terman's study of children with superior levels of intelligence, none had produced highly creative works (Terman & Oden, 1959).

Because people do not express creativity in any uniform way (otherwise, they would not be creative), creativity can be extremely difficult to measure. Thus, some researchers have turned to the study of eminent people, such as Einstein and Darwin, to learn about the nature and origins of creativity (Simonton, 1994, 1997). Others have attempted to devise measures of creativity that can be administered in the laboratory. One strategy is to measure **divergent thinking**, the ability to generate multiple possibilities in a given situation, such as describing all the possible uses of a paper clip. At face value, divergent thinking seems to be related to creativity because it involves finding unusual or unconventional ways of solving a problem. (As an iced tea drinker, I have my own test of diverged thinking. When a waiter informs me that he does not serve iced tea, I ask for a hot tea and a very large cup of ice. The longer it takes him to recognize that I am getting my ice tea, the less capacity for divergent thinking he is demonstrating!) Whether Mozart or Einstein would have distinguished themselves in finding uses for a paper clip will, however, never be known.

The best-known creativity tests measure either the thought processes involved in creativity or the personality characteristics of creative people (Khatena, 1982; Torrance, 1966; Ward et al., 1997). Evaluating creativity by examining attributes of the person instead of the process reflects the view that creativity is as much a personality trait as a cognitive trait or aspect of intelligence (Eysenck, 1983, 1993). Indeed, research has linked creativity to such personality traits as high energy, intuitiveness, independence, self-acceptance, a willingness to take risks, and an intensely passionate way of engaging in certain tasks for the sheer pleasure of it (Amabile, 1996; Barron & Harrington, 1981). Creative activity also depends in part on environmental conditions. Social and economic circumstances, such as exposure to role models and access to financial resources, can also foster or hinder creative activity (Simonton, 1994).

FROM MIND TO BRAIN

CREATIVITY AND MENTAL DISORDERS

Writers since the time of Plato have proposed an association between creativity and madness. Many famous creative geniuses, including Vincent Van Gogh, Isaac Newton, Michelangelo, and William Blake, have had some form of mental disorder (Karlsson, 1978; Prentky, 1980). An association between creativity and abnormality may not be incidental. The ability to suspend one's normal cognitive structures momentarily and to associate concepts in novel ways is basic to creativity. In their extreme form, these tendencies also characterize severe mental disorders.

Research on creativity and mental illness has recently focused on bipolar disorder, otherwise known as manic-depression (Chapter 15). Bipolar disorder is marked by extreme mood swings, from euphoria and grandiosity to paralyzing depression. Heritability of the disorder is high, and although environmental factors appear to influence its course and development, virtually no one develops the illness who does not have a family history of it. Roughly 4 percent of the population have either the disorder or some milder condition genetically related to it (Richards, 1994).

A number of studies have examined the association between bipolar disorder and creativity in writers, especially poets (Andreasen & Glick, 1988; Holden, 1987; Jamison, 1989, 1994). These studies have found similarities between the intense creative episodes during which writers accomplish some of their best work and the highly energized manic phase of bipolar disorder (Richards & Kinney, 1990; Richards et al., 1992). At the very least, manic periods appear to be associated with tremendous productivity in some creative individuals, such as the classical composer Robert Schumann (Weisberg, 1994). Prominent among twentieth-century American poets with bipolar disorder are Theodore Roethke, Robert Lowell, and Sylvia Plath (who committed suicide in her early 30s).

Composer Cole Porter, writer Sylvia Plath, and writer Ernest Hemingway all appear to have suffered from bipolar disorder, cyclothymia, or a related condition.

One study of 47 of the top writers and artists in England found that fully 38 percent had sought treatment for mood disorders (including bipolar disorder), with poets and writers reporting the highest rates of psychiatric intervention (Jamison, 1989). Other investigations have taken the reverse approach, studying creativity in bipolar patients and their relatives. The relatives of bipolar patients, as well as patients with a mild form of the disorder (called *cyclothymia,* meaning cycles of shifting moods that do not reach psychotic levels), appear to have unusually high rates of creativity and occupational achievement (Coryell et al., 1989; Richards et al., 1988). The findings of one such study are depicted in Figure 8.8. As the figure shows, cyclothymic individuals and first-degree relatives of bipolar and cyclothymic patients manifest higher rates of creativity than bipolars, normals, or other people with psychiatric disorders.

Why relatives of bipolar patients and people with a mild version of the disorder show high rates of creativity is unclear. As we will see (Chapter 15), relatives of schizophrenic patients are more prone than other people to exhibit peculiar ways of thinking, but these are not linked to creativity. They are more likely to report odd perceptual experiences and magical ideas, and they frequently have idiosyncratic associations to words (Meehl, 1962, 1989). On questionnaires they tend to endorse items such as "Sometimes I have had a passing thought that my body was rotting away," "It has seemed at

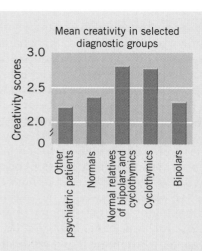

FIGURE 8.8
Creativity and mental illness. The highest rates of creativity occurred in cyclothymic individuals and relatives of cyclothymic or bipolar individuals. *Source:* Richards et al., 1988, p. 286.

times as if my body was melting into my surroundings," and "I have occasionally had the silly feeling that a TV or radio broadcaster knew I was listening to him" (Chapman & Chapman, 1980; Chapman et al., 1993). We usually assume that a "close cousin" of a disorder must be dysfunctional, as in the milder syndromes genetically related to schizophrenia. This may not always be the case, however. People who receive the gene that causes sickle cell anemia from both parents develop the fatal disease, but individuals who receive the gene from only one parent are immune to malaria. In fact, the sickle cell gene appears to have been favored by natural selection in regions of Africa in which malaria is common. Something similar may be true of the genes that produce a vulnerability to bipolar disorder, which may predispose their bearers either to madness or to creativity, depending on their other genes and the environmental circumstances that activate genetic tendencies (see Richards, 1994).

INTERIM SUMMARY   About 2 percent of the population is characterized by **mental retardation,** defined as significantly subaverage general intellectual functioning with deficits in adaptive behavior manifested during childhood. Milder forms of retardation appear to be more environmentally influenced, whereas the severe forms primarily reflect genetic and other physical causes. **Giftedness** refers to the extremes at the other end of the bell curve, although most psychologists recognize that "gifts" do not all come in the form of an IQ above 130. **Creativity** refers to the ability to produce valued outcomes in a novel way; it is correlated with IQ but not reducible to it.

SOME CONCLUDING THOUGHTS

All the approaches to intelligence explored in this chapter have been, broadly speaking, cognitive. Intelligence is, after all, applied cognition. Yet intelligence cannot be defined entirely without reference to the uses to which individuals put it. Consider the case of a sociopath or antisocial personality, who lacks a mature sense of right and wrong. Many psychologists now argue that **social intelligence**—the ability to store, retrieve, and understand social information—is an important form of intelligence (Bye & Jussim, 1993; Cantor & Kihlstrom, 1987; Gardner, 1983; Salovey & Sluyter, 1997). But is a sociopath defective in social intelligence?

In some cases, decidedly not. Many sociopaths are extremely successful con artists, with an extraordinary capacity to lie convincingly and manipulate people to achieve their goals. The words "successful" and "convincingly" convey the *intelligent* aspects of the sociopath's behavior. Sociopaths may thus be quite socially intelligent, at least in certain respects, but their social *motivation* is clearly abnormal. They may *know* social rules; they just lack the desire to obey them. The question, then, is whether intelligence and motivation can be clearly distinguished, especially if intelligence is defined in terms of meeting culturally accepted standards.

Intelligence is always at the service of goals; it is thus inherently embedded in a psychological context that includes motivation and emotion. A person's IQ score reflects not only her intellectual abilities but also her motivation to achieve, her ability to manage anxiety and frustration, and her feelings and beliefs about her abilities. The IQ score of a person who is distracted by intense anxiety while taking the test may reflect emotional factors as much as cognitive ability, and a person with a history of learning disabilities or failures in school may give up quickly on items that he could answer if he were not afraid to make the effort and risk failing.

The next three chapters explore this broader context of cognition. We turn first to consciousness, which has loomed increasingly large over the last decade in studies of cognition. We then examine the motives and emotions that give purpose and meaning to our most elegant cognitive processes.

Summary

The Nature of Intelligence

1. **Intelligence** is the application of cognitive skills and knowledge to learn, solve problems, and obtain ends that are valued by an individual or culture. Intelligence is multifaceted, functional, and culturally defined. Some aspects of intelligence are universal, whereas others depend on the tasks of adaptation in a particular society.

Intelligence Testing

2. **Intelligence tests** represent a type of psychometric instrument designed to assess an individual's cognitive capabilities compared to others in a population. The ancestor of modern IQ tests was invented by Binet for the specific purpose of identifying retarded children. Binet developed the concept of **mental age (MA)**, the average age at which children can be expected to achieve a particular score.

3. The **intelligence quotient**, or **IQ**, is a score meant to represent an individual's intellectual ability, which permits comparison with other individuals. It was initially calculated by dividing mental age by chronological age and multiplying by 100.

4. Wechsler abandoned the concept of mental age and calculated IQ as an individual's position relative to peers of the same age by using a frequency distribution. The Wechsler scales (the **WAIS-III** and the **WISC-III** for children) include verbal and nonverbal (performance) tests.

5. Intelligence tests are highly predictive of scholastic success, and they also predict occupational success. Critics argue that they lack a theoretical basis, are culturally biased, and fail to capture other kinds of intelligence.

APPROACHES TO INTELLIGENCE

6. The **psychometric approach** derives the components and structure of intelligence empirically from statistical analysis of psychometric test findings. The primary tool of the psychometric approach is **factor analysis**, a statistical technique for identifying common **factors** that underlie performance on a wide variety of measures. Spearman's **two-factor theory** distinguishes the **g-factor**, or general intelligence, from **s-factors**, or specific abilities. Other models derived from factor analysis have provided different lists of factors, such as **Gf–Gc theory**, which distinguishes between content-free **fluid intelligence** and knowledge-based **crystallized intelligence**.

7. The information-processing approach tries to understand the specific cognitive processes that underlie intelligent behavior. Three of the most important variables on which people differ are speed of processing, a knowledge base, and ability to learn and apply mental strategies. Unlike the psychometric approach, the information-processing approach is theory driven, drawing on research in cognitive science.

8. Gardner's **theory of multiple intelligences** distinguishes seven kinds of intelligence that are relatively independent, neurologically distinct, and show different courses of development. These include musical, bodily/kinesthetic, spatial, linguistic or verbal, logical/mathematical, intrapersonal, and interpersonal intelligences.

HEREDITY AND INTELLIGENCE

9. A central question in the study of intelligence is the extent to which environment and heredity each shape intelligence. To examine the heritability of IQ, studies have correlated the IQ scores of subjects with differing degrees of genetic relatedness and of biological and adoptive family members. Twin, family, and adoption studies suggest that heredity, environment, and their interaction all contribute to IQ but that individual differences in IQ are highly heritable. Research does not, however, support the hypothesis that differences among racial or ethnic groups are primarily genetic.

THE EXTREMES OF INTELLIGENCE

10. **Mental retardation** refers to significantly subaverage general intellectual functioning with deficits in adaptive behavior manifested during childhood. **Giftedness** refers to the other extreme of the intellectual spectrum, although theorists differ in the extent to which they focus on the kind of intelligence assessed by IQ tests.

11. **Creativity** is the ability to produce valued outcomes in a novel way. Creativity is correlated with IQ but distinct from intelligence as assessed by IQ tests. Highly intelligent people do not tend to be maladjusted, although creativity seems to be particularly high in relatives of people with bipolar disorder (manic-depression) and people with a mild variant of the disorder.

Josh Goshfield, "Girl and a Clock," 1990. Private collection.

CHAPTER 9

Consciousness

lmost a century ago, a Swiss psychologist named Claparede shook hands with a patient suffering from Korsakoff's disorder, which produces amnesia for recent events. Claparede had concealed a pin between his fingers, which pricked the patient as their hands clasped. At their next meeting, the patient had no memory of having met Claparede, but she found herself inexplicably unwilling to shake his hand (Cowey, 1991). What the patient knew (that the good doctor was not so good) and what she knew *consciously* (that she was meeting a doctor, whom she need not fear) were two very different things.

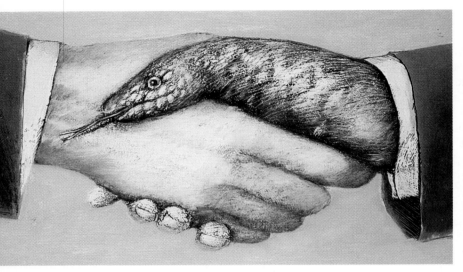

Amnesics are not the only people who can respond to a stimulus at different levels of consciousness. As we shall see, we all do, but the signs are often more subtle. We begin this chapter by discussing the nature and functions of consciousness, examining the way attention focuses consciousness at any given time on a narrow subset of the thoughts and feelings of which a person could be aware. We then examine multiple perspectives on consciousness and explore the neural basis of consciousness. The remainder of the chapter is devoted to **states of consciousness**—qualitatively different patterns of subjective experience, including ways of experiencing both internal and external events. We start with the most basic distinction, between waking and sleeping, exploring the stages of sleep and the nature of dreaming. We conclude by examining several altered states of consciousness—deviations from the normal waking state—including meditation, religious experiences, hypnosis, and drug-induced states.

THE NATURE OF CONSCIOUSNESS

Consciousness, the subjective awareness of mental events, may be easier to describe than to define. William James (1890) viewed consciousness as a constantly moving stream of thoughts, feelings, and perceptions. Shutting off consciousness in this sense is probably impossible, as anyone knows who has ever tried to "stop thinking" to escape insomnia. Following in the footsteps of the French philosopher René Descartes, who offered the famous proposition *"cogito ergo sum"* (I think, therefore I am), James also emphasized a second aspect of consciousness, the consciousness of self. James argued that part of being conscious of any particular thought is a simultaneous awareness of oneself as the author or owner of it.

FUNCTIONS OF CONSCIOUSNESS

Why do people have consciousness at all? Two of its functions are readily apparent: Consciousness monitors the self and the environment and controls thought and behavior (Kihlstrom, 1987). *Consciousness as a monitor* is analogous to a continuously moving video camera, surveying potentially significant perceptions, thoughts, emotions, goals, and problem-solving strategies. The *control function of consciousness* allows people to initiate and terminate thought and behavior in order to attain goals. People often rehearse scenarios in their minds, such as asking for a raise or confronting a disloyal friend. Consciousness is frequently engaged when people choose between competing strategies for solving a problem (Mandler & Nakamura, 1987).

These two functions of consciousness—monitoring and controlling—are intertwined, since consciousness monitors inner and outer experience in order to prevent and solve problems. For example, consciousness often "steps in" when automatized processes (procedural knowledge) are not successful. In this sense, consciousness is like the inspector in a garment factory: It does not make the product, but it checks to make sure the product is made correctly. If it finds an imperfection, it institutes a remedy (Gilbert, 1989, p. 206). In typing this sentence, for example, I paid no conscious attention to the keys on my terminal, but when I made a mistake—hitting an *m* instead of a comma, the adjacent key—I looked at the keys and corrected the error.

From an evolutionary standpoint, consciousness probably evolved as a mechanism for directing behavior in adaptive ways that was superimposed on more primitive psychological processes such as conditioning (Reber, 1992). Indeed, William James was heavily influenced by Darwin, and he explained consciousness in terms of its function: fostering adaptation. Consciousness is often "grabbed" by things that are unexpected, unusual, or contrary to expectations— precisely the things that could affect well-being or survival. Much of the time people respond automatically to the environment, learning and processing information without conscious awareness. Important choices, however, require more consideration, and consciousness permits heightened reflection on significant events and the likely consequences of alternative choices.

INTERIM SUMMARY **Consciousness** refers to the subjective awareness of mental events. **States of consciousness** are qualitatively different patterns of subjective experience, including ways of experiencing both internal and external events. Consciousness plays at least two functions: monitoring the self and the environment and controlling thought and behavior. Consciousness probably evolved as a mechanism for directing behavior in adaptive ways that was superimposed on more primitive psychological processes that today continue outside awareness.

CONSCIOUSNESS AND ATTENTION

At any given time, people are dimly aware of much more than what is conscious. For example, while reading the newspaper a person may have some vague awareness of the radiator clanking, voices in the next room, and the smell of breakfast cooking, although none of these is at the center of awareness or consciousness. At some point, however, certain olfactory sensations may unconsciously be given enough perceptual meaning (smoke or danger) to shift attention. Paradoxically, the monitoring and controlling functions of consciousness are thus to a considerable degree regulated *outside* of consciousness, by unconscious or implicit attentional mechanisms that focus conscious awareness.

Attention

Attention refers to the process of focusing conscious awareness, providing heightened sensitivity to a limited range of experience requiring more extensive information processing. *Selection*—of a particular object, a train of thought, or a location in space at which something important might be happening—is the essence of attention (Rees et al., 1997). Attention is generally guided by some combination of external stimulation—which naturally leads us to focus on relevant sensory information—and activated goals—which lead us to attend to thoughts, feelings, or stimuli relevant to obtaining them.

Filtering in and Filtering Out   Some psychologists have likened attention to a filtering process through which only more important information passes (Broadbent, 1958). For example, people frequently become so engrossed in conversation with one person that they tune out all the other conversations in the room—an important skill at a loud party. However, if they hear someone mention their name across the room, they may suddenly look up and focus attention on the person who has just spoken the magic word. This phenomenon, called the *cocktail party phenomenon* (Cherry, 1953), suggests that we implicitly process much more information than reaches consciousness.

On the other hand, people also sometimes divert attention from information that may be relevant but emotionally upsetting, a process called **selective inattention**. This can be highly adaptive, as when students divert their attention from the anxiety of taking a test to the task itself. It can also be maladaptive, as when people ignore something as small as a darkening birthmark on the arm or as global as nuclear proliferation and hence fail to devote adequate cognitive resources to them (Lifton, 1980).

Components of Attention   Attention actually consists of at least three functions: *orienting* to sensory stimuli, *controlling the contents* of consciousness and voluntary behavior, and *maintaining alertness* (see Posner, 1995). Different neural networks (using different neurotransmitter systems) appear to be involved in these three functions (Robbins, 1997). Orienting, which has been studied most extensively in the visual system (Rafal & Robertson, 1995), involves turning sensory organs such as the eyes and ears toward a stimulus. It also involves spreading extra activation to the parts of the cortex that are processing information about the stimulus and probably inhibiting activation of others. When we attend to a stimulus, such as a mosquito buzzing around the room, the brain uses the same circuits it normally uses to process information that is not the focus of attention. For example, watching the mosquito leads to activation of the "what" and "where" visual pathways in the occipital, temporal, and parietal lobes. Attention enhances processing at those cortical locations as soon as a person (or monkey) has been signaled to watch or listen for particular stimuli or stimuli in a specific location. Recent PET data suggest that attentional mechanisms may generally increase the activation of a particular region of the brain when a person or monkey is signaled to watch for a stimulus; attentional mechanisms may also spread extra activation to objects once detected so they can be examined more carefully (Rees et al., 1997).

Controlling the contents of consciousness (such as deciding how much to listen to something someone is saying) and controlling voluntary behavior involve different neural pathways than orienting to stimuli. These "executive" control functions typically involve areas of the frontal lobes and basal ganglia, which are known to be involved in thought, movement, and self-control. In contrast, orienting to stimuli tends to require the involvement of neural circuits in the midbrain (such as the superior colliculus, which helps control eye movements), thalamus (which directs attention to particular sensory systems), and parietal lobes (which, among other functions, direct attention to particular locations).

Maintaining alertness is crucial in tasks ranging from paying attention to items on a test—and ignoring distractions such as anxiety or the sounds of traffic outside—to staying alert enough to notice a small change while keeping an eye on a radar screen for hours. A whole network of neurons from the reticular formation (which is involved in regulating states of alertness) through the frontal lobes appear to regulate alertness (Posner, 1995).

Divided Attention

Everyone has had the experience of trying to pay attention to too many things at once—and consequently not understanding or competently performing any of them. Psychologists have tried to determine the extent to which whether people can split attention between two complex tasks, such as following two conversations simultaneously; this is known as **divided attention** (see Craik et al., 1996). One way researchers study divided attention is through **dichotic listening** tasks (Figure 9.1): Subjects are fitted with earphones, and different information is directed into each ear simultaneously. They are instructed to attend only to the information from one ear by repeating aloud what they hear in that ear for a period of time, a process called *shadowing*. Attending to one channel or the other is difficult at first; it is easier if the two channels differ in topic, voice pitch, and so forth (Hirst, 1986).

Subjects can become so adept at shadowing that they are completely unable to recognize information in the unattended channel, performing no better than chance when asked whether a word presented in the unattended channel had been presented. Nevertheless, the information does appear to be processed to some degree, much as the smell of smoke is processed while reading a newspaper. This has been clearly demonstrated in research on priming (Chapter 6), the process by which exposure to a stimulus (such as a word) affects performance on tasks involving related stimuli (Nisbett & Wilson, 1977; Schacter, 1992). For example, a subject who hears "England" in the unattended channel may have no recollection of having heard the name of any country. When compared to a control subject who has not been similarly primed, however, the individual is more likely to say "London" if asked to name a capital city, and he will more quickly fill in the missing letters when asked for the name of a city when presented with

LO_ _ _ N.

The data from many dichotic listening studies of divided attention actually suggest that subjects may not be dividing their attention at all: Failing to show recognition memory for the prime suggests that participants never consciously attended to it. In other cases, however, people do appear to divide their attention, performing two complex tasks simultaneously. Listening to a lecture while taking notes requires a student to hear and process one idea while simultaneously writing, and even paraphrasing, a previous idea or sentence. This is remarkable because both tasks are verbal and the content of each is highly similar; hence, one would expect heavy interference between the two. Psychologists have even trained subjects to take dictation while reading (Spelke et al., 1976).

Sometimes people accomplish such feats by rapidly shifting attention back and forth between the two tasks. Much of the time, however, people solve attentional dilemmas by automatizing one task or the other (Chapter 6). Automatization develops through practice, as actions previously performed with deliberate conscious effort are eventually processed automatically. While students listen to a lecture, their primary focus of consciousness is on the lecturer's current words, while a largely automatic process, perhaps drawing on some subset of attentional processes, allows note taking. Precisely how much consciousness is involved in divided attention is not well understood. Students can generally recount what they have just written even while listening to a lecture, suggesting *some* involvement of conscious attention, although their primary allocation of attentional resources is to the lecturer.

FIGURE 9.1
A dichotic listening task. Subjects are fitted with earphones, and different information is transmitted into each ear simultaneously. Subjects often show awareness of information in the unattended channel, even when they have no conscious recognition of it.

A portrait of divided attention.

INTERIM SUMMARY **Attention** refers to the process of focusing conscious awareness, providing heightened sensitivity to a limited range of experience requiring more extensive information processing. Attention consists of at least three functions: orienting to sensory stimuli, controlling the contents of consciousness and voluntary behavior, and maintaining alertness. **Divided attention**, which often involves automatizing one or more tasks or rapidly shifting attention between them, refers to the capacity to split attention or cognitive resources between two or more tasks.

THE NORMAL FLOW OF CONSCIOUSNESS

A major component of the normal flow of consciousness is **daydreaming**—turning attention away from external stimuli to internal thoughts and imagined scenarios. Some daydreams are pleasurable fantasies, whereas others involve planning for future actions, particularly involving people in important relationships. In one large-scale study of daydreaming, all subjects reported daydreaming daily (Singer, 1975). Another research team found that college students daydream about half the time they are conscious, if daydreaming includes thoughts about something other than what is currently happening in the person's environment, such as thinking about a paper that needs to be written while watching a basketball game or engaging in a less than captivating conversation (Klinger, 1992).

Psychologists study the normal flow of consciousness through **experience-sampling** techniques (Larsen, 1997; Singer & Kolligian, 1987; Wong & Csikszentmihalyi, 1991). In one design, subjects talk aloud, sometimes while performing a task, simply reporting the contents of their consciousness. Psychologists then code their verbal responses into categories, such as emotional tone, relevance to the task at hand, or content.

Beeper Studies

An experience-sampling technique that has provided a more natural window to the flow of consciousness in everyday life is used in **beeper studies**, in which participants carry pagers and report their experience when "beeped" at various points during the day. In one study, researchers sampled the experience of 75 adolescents from a Chicago high school (Csikszentmihalyi & Larson, 1984). They randomly selected students within each of several categories, including sex, grade, and social class (a stratified random sample; Chapter 2). For one week, participants were beeped at some point during every two-hour period (except, of course, at night), at which time they filled out a brief form reporting what they were doing and with whom, what they were thinking and feeling, and how intensely they were feeling it.

Some of the results were quite unexpected. When subjects were with their families, their negative thoughts outnumbered their positive thoughts by about 10 to 1. When they were asked, "As you were beeped, what were you thinking about?" their responses included "my aunt talks too much" or "how incompetent my mom is" (p. 139). Using this method, the investigators were also able to explore the subjective experience of individual subjects (Figure 9.2).

Culture and Consciousness

We are accustomed to thinking of consciousness as a realm of experience that is uniquely private, but consciousness is in part culturally constructed. Cultural practices and beliefs shape the way people organize their subjective world, including the way they conceive of time and space (Hallowell, 1955; Shore, 1996). In most preindustrial cultures, consciousness is organized into broad units of time, such as sunup and sundown, rather than into the tiny units of time that organize consciousness in cultures ruled by the clock.

Cultural processes also shape the phenomena to which people turn their attention. People in the industrialized West are constantly making inferences about other people's mental states, listening carefully to their words and actions to try to

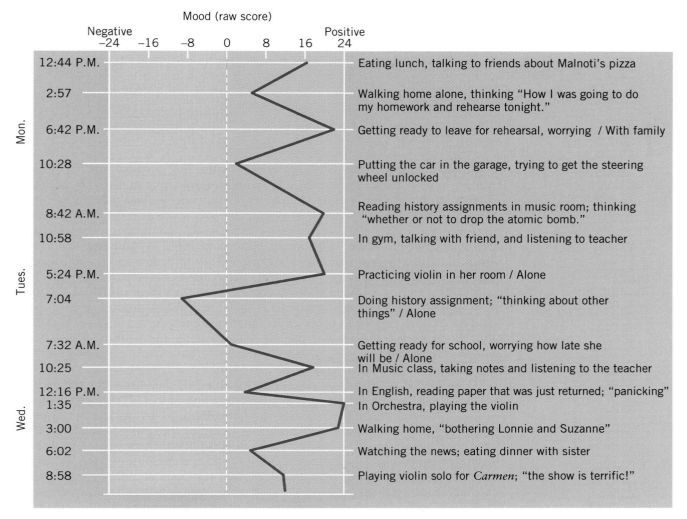

FIGURE 9.2

Three days in the life of Katherine. In this experience-sampling study, Katherine reported what she was doing and thinking about whenever she was paged by a beeper. *Source:* Csikszentmihalyi & Larson, 1984, p. 117.

figure out, for example, whether they are sincere—that is, whether they really *mean* what they are saying. In contrast, the Ifaluk of Micronesia, like many preindustrialized peoples, are not so concerned with the inner meanings of social actions (Lutz, 1992). Their moral code revolves around harmony within the group, which is essential for people who must live together on a small island. When people are behaving in ways that maintain this harmony, no one is concerned about whether or not they mean it, since the Ifaluk assume that people behave morally because that is the right thing to do. Further, the kind of introspection valued in many segments of contemporary Western culture, which involves self-reflection for the purpose of self-knowledge, is not encouraged by Ifaluk values and practices. In fact, the Ifaluk perceive it as a sign of self-absorption (Lutz, 1992).

INTERIM SUMMARY Prominent in the normal flow of conscious experience are **daydreams**, in which the person turns attention away from external stimuli to internal thoughts and imagined scenarios, often for pleasure or for problem solving. Psychologists learn about the normal flow of consciousness through **experience-sampling** techniques, such as **beeper studies**, in which participants carry pagers and report on aspects of consciousness when they are paged at random intervals. Cultural practices and beliefs shape the way people organize their conscious experience, including the way they conceive of time and space and the extent to which they focus on their own and others' internal states.

PERSPECTIVES ON CONSCIOUSNESS

Consciousness occupied a central role in the first textbook on psychology, written by William James in 1890, and figured prominently in the work of Freud, who expanded the focus of psychology to include unconscious processes as well. When behaviorism came into ascendance, consciousness as a focus of investigation receded from the consciousness of the scientific community and remained that way until the 1980s. Behaviorists wanted to avoid explaining behaviors in terms of mental events that cannot be observed scientifically, since people's introspective reports are impossible to verify. Behaviorists also rejected the idea of a conscious mind as an agent that chooses, intends, or makes decisions (Skinner, 1974, p. 169). Organisms as primitive as snails respond to environmental contingencies, yet no one would propose that snails therefore have consciousness. Further, according to Skinner, to explain a person's action on the basis of an unconscious process is simply to admit that we have not yet observed the environmental stimuli controlling the behavior.

Until about a decade ago, cognitive psychologists paid little attention to consciousness, either. But as we saw in Chapters 6 and 7, that all changed with the surge of research on implicit memory and cognition. In the last decade, spurred by developments in neuroscience and neuro-imaging that provide a new window on consciousness, cognitive scientists—as well as philosophers, neurologists, biologists, and even physicists—have begun rethinking consciousness (e.g., Edelman, 1989; Cohen & Schooler, 1997). In this section we examine psychodynamic and cognitive perspectives on consciousness and explore ways they converge. We then consider what can be learned about normal consciousness by observing neuropsychological patients like Claparede's, who manifest a dissociation between what they know consciously and unconsciously.

THE PSYCHODYNAMIC UNCONSCIOUS

Freud (1900) defined consciousness as one of three mental systems called the conscious, preconscious, and unconscious (Figure 9.3). **Conscious** mental processes are those of which a person is subjectively aware (such as the sentence you just read—if you were paying attention!). **Preconscious** mental processes are not presently conscious but could be readily brought to consciousness if the need arose, such as the smell of bacon cooking in the background or the name of a city that is not currently in mind but could easily be retrieved. **Unconscious processes** are inaccessible to consciousness because they would be too anxiety provoking to acknowledge; that is, they are repressed.

Freud likened repression to a censor: Just as a repressive government censors ideas or wishes it considers threatening, so, too, does the mind censor threatening thoughts from consciousness (Figure 9.3). Thus, a person may remember an abusive father with love and admiration and have little access to unhappy memories because admitting the truth would be painful. Unconscious processes of this sort are *dynamically unconscious*—that is, kept unconscious for a reason, requiring psychological effort or energy (dynamic force) to keep them out of awareness. Freud

Conscious

Preconscious

Repression

Wishes, fears, memories, emotions

Unconscious

FIGURE 9.3
Freud's model of consciousness. Conscious mental processes are those of which a person is subjectively aware. Preconscious mental processes are not presently conscious but could readily be brought to consciousness. Unconscious mental processes are inaccessible to consciousness because they have been repressed.

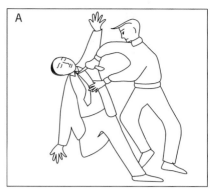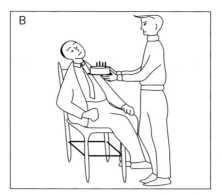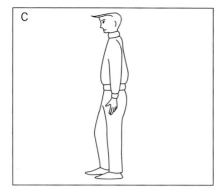

FIGURE 9.4
Subliminal perception. Participants were presented subliminally with either slide A, a boy behaving aggressively, or B, a boy behaving altruistically. Participants were then shown a neutral picture of the boy and asked to judge his personality. Participants who had seen slide A described the boy as aggressive, whereas those who had seen slide B described him as altruistic. *Source:* Eagle, 1959.

(1915) recognized that many other psychological processes are *descriptively unconscious*—that is, not conscious even though they are not threatening, such as the processes by which depletion of glucose levels in the blood lead to hunger.

Subliminal Perception

In the 1940s and 1950s, as part of the New Look in perception (Chapter 4), researchers tested hypotheses derived from Freud's theory of consciousness. Studies of **subliminal perception**—the perception of stimuli below the threshold of consciousness—used a device called a *tachistoscope* to flash images too quickly for conscious recognition but slowly enough to be registered outside awareness (Dixon, 1971, 1981; Erdelyi, 1985; Weinberger, in press). For example, in one study the experimenter flashed one of two pictures subliminally (Figure 9.4). The first depicted a boy behaving aggressively toward a man; the second depicted the boy presenting a man with a birthday cake. Participants were then shown a neutral picture of the boy and asked to judge the boy's personality. Participants exposed to the aggressive picture tended to judge the boy negatively, whereas those who had been flashed the altruistic picture rated him positively.

This line of research drew considerable fire, in part because of methodological concerns, but also in part because the field was still dominated by behaviorism and was not yet ready for the concept of unconscious processes. In recent years, however, both psychodynamic and cognitive researchers have breathed new life into subliminal research, demonstrating that subliminal presentation of stimuli can indeed influence thought and emotion (Bowers, 1984; Neidenthal & Cantor, 1986; Shevrin et al., 1996; Weinberger & Hardaway, 1990). For instance, subliminal presentation of a happy or sad face directly prior to exposure to a novel visual stimulus (such as a Chinese letter) affects the extent to which subjects like it (Murphy & Zajonc, 1993). Subliminal presentation of the face seems to "tag" the stimulus with an emotional connotation.

In one study, the investigator subliminally presented participants with either a word or a blank field (Marcel, 1983). The stimulus was followed immediately by a masking stimulus to prevent it from lingering as a visual memory (Figure 9.5). Participants were then given one of two tasks. One task was to indicate whether a word or a blank had been flashed. On this task, participants were wrong half the time, demonstrating that they were never conscious of the stimulus. The second

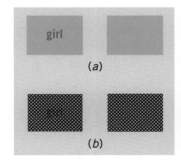

FIGURE 9.5
Subliminal priming. Participants were presented with either a word or a blank field (*a*). This stimulus was followed by a mask, a stimulus that would prevent the word or blank field from lingering as a visual memory (*b*). Participants were then asked to indicate whether a word or a blank had been flashed. Results showed that subliminally presented stimuli can influence thought. *Source:* Marcel, 1983.

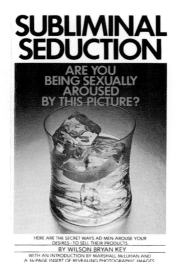

SUBLIMINAL SEDUCTION

ARE YOU BEING SEXUALLY AROUSED BY THIS PICTURE?

HERE ARE THE SECRET WAYS AD MEN AROUSE YOUR DESIRES–TO SELL THEIR PRODUCTS.
BY WILSON BRYAN KEY
WITH AN INTRODUCTION BY MARSHALL McLUHAN AND A 16-PAGE INSERT OF REVEALING PHOTOGRAPHIC IMAGES.

Ideas about subliminal influence have often captured the popular imagination.

task was to identify a string of letters as either a word or a nonword. Some of the words were semantically related to the original word (the prime) presented subliminally; thus, the participant might be subliminally exposed to a word like *pea* and then be asked whether the letters *p-o-d* formed a word. The dependent variable was reaction time, that is, how quickly participants could decide whether the letters formed a word. The results documented the influence of the subliminal prime on thought: Participants more quickly recognized words that were semantically related to the prime, even though they had never consciously registered it.

Psychologists have not been the only people interested in subliminal processing. Several years ago, rumors flew that movie theaters were manipulating consumers by subliminally presenting messages like "eat popcorn" and "buy Coke." More recently, parents have expressed fears about subliminal messages in rock music, such as backward messages encouraging violence. Subliminal effects, however, tend to be more subtle and relatively weak motivators of consumer behavior; backward messages have no effect whatsoever, since they cannot be perceived (Kirk & Rogers, 1994; Trappey, 1996; Vokey & Read, 1985). A person who is already thirsty may become slightly more likely to buy a soft drink after a subliminal message, but a person whose stomach is full is unlikely to make a run for the popcorn.

Unconscious Emotion and Motivation

The proposition that unconscious cognitive and perceptual processes can influence behavior is no longer controversial. Historically, however, the most distinctively psychodynamic hypothesis is that motivational and emotional processes can be unconscious as well. As we will see in the next two chapters, this proposition is also gaining experimental support (see Epstein, 1994; Westen, in press). Research on motivation suggests a distinction between conscious and unconscious motive systems similar to the distinction between implicit and explicit memory in cognitive science (Bargh & Barndollar, 1996; McClelland et al., 1989). Numerous studies have shown that when people are not consciously attending to their goals and values, their unconscious or implicit motives tend to control their behavior. Further, priming people with words associated with motives (such as the word *success* to prime the need for achievement) influences their tendency to act on those motives, even when they are unaware that they have been primed.

Experimental data also show that emotional processes can influence thought and behavior without being conscious. Patients with hippocampal lesions, who have difficulty consolidating new explicit memories, may be entirely unable to tell whether they have seen a stimulus before, yet they may respond with a conditioned emotional response to the stimulus nonetheless (such as fear when presented with a conditioned stimulus previously paired with electric shock) (Bechara et al., 1995). Patients with Korsakoff's disorder, like the woman whose case began this chapter, can learn to prefer a person who was described a week earlier as having positive traits over someone who was described more negatively, even though they have no recollection of ever having seen either face before (Johnson et al., 1985).

Similar findings emerge in studies of people without neurological damage. In one study, the investigators paired nonsense syllables (the conditioned stimulus) with a mild electric shock (the unconditioned stimulus). They then presented the conditioned stimuli to subjects subliminally (Lazarus & McCleary, 1951). Nonsense syllables previously paired with shock elicited a galvanic skin response (GSR) indicating anxious arousal even when presented below the threshold of conscious recognition. Thus, a conditioned stimulus can elicit an emotional response even when the person has no idea it has been presented. A host of recent studies have produced similar results using other measures such as facial muscle movements indicating distress and brain wave activity assessed by EEG (see

Ohman, 1994; Wong, et al., 1994). Findings such as these are of particular relevance to the psychodynamic hypothesis that individuals can respond emotionally to people or situations without knowing why. One of the major aims of psychodynamic forms of therapy is to try to uncover these patterns of emotional arousal so the person can take more conscious control over them (Chapter 16).

Other researchers have found that people can regulate their emotions outside of awareness by keeping distressing thoughts, feelings, and memories out of consciousness (Paulhus et al., 1997; Vaillant, 1992). This can sometimes be adaptive, particularly if nothing can be done to change an uncomfortable situation. However, several research teams have found that people who chronically keep themselves unaware of their emotions pay a physical toll: They are more likely to suffer from asthma, heart disease, and other illnesses than people who are more aware of their unpleasant feelings and can therefore take steps to try to deal with the things that are distressing them (Asendorph & Sherer, 1983; Newton & Contrada, 1992; Pennebaker, 1992; Shedler et al., 1993; Singer, 1990; D. Weinberger, 1990).

THE COGNITIVE UNCONSCIOUS

By the mid–1980s, cognitive scientists began to take much more interest in consciousness (Kihlstrom, 1987). Although they have recently begun to attend to emotional and motivational processes, the **cognitive unconscious** primarily includes information-processing mechanisms that operate outside of awareness (such as implicit memory) rather than information the person is *motivated* to keep from awareness. In other words, the cognitive unconscious includes what Freud called *descriptively* unconscious but not *dynamically* unconscious processes. Freud was not ignorant of these processes—he proposed a theory of association that mirrored many aspects of contemporary cognitive theory—but he did not elaborate a comprehensive model of unconscious cognitive processes or try to examine them experimentally.

Information-processing models often use the terms *consciousness* and *working memory* interchangeably, viewing consciousness as an "on-line" workspace for focusing attention on perceptions, memories, and skills relevant for solving current problems. As we saw in Chapters 6 and 7, most models also distinguish explicit (conscious) and implicit (unconscious) memory and cognition, such as conscious problem-solving strategies versus automatic, unconscious heuristics. Parallel distributed processing models (Chapter 7) further propose that information processing occurs simultaneously in multiple, relatively separate neural networks, most of which are unconscious. The brain synthesizes a unitary conscious experience from the various activated unconscious networks—giving us the impression of a flow of coherent conscious experiences over time—by selecting for conscious attention networks that are most immediately relevant (Baars, 1988, 1997; Mandler, 1997; Mandler & Nakamura, 1987).

Distinguishing Unconscious Cognitive Processes

John Kihlstrom (1987, 1996), a cognitive theorist of consciousness, distinguishes unconscious from preconscious cognitive processes, both of which occur outside of awareness. *Unconscious cognitive processes* are skills or procedures that operate without awareness and are not accessible to consciousness under any circumstance. *Preconscious cognitive processes* refer to associations and schemas (declarative knowledge) activated below the threshold of consciousness that influence conscious thought and behavior. Preconscious processes can be seen experimentally in subliminal priming procedures as well as in everyday life, as when a person cannot get a song "out of his head" because it is preconsciously activated.

Kihlstrom adds a third distinction to account for two more unusual phenomena. The first is that people given hypnotic suggestions to do certain actions may perform them without any sense of having chosen to do so. The second is that people with *dissociative disorders* (in which memories or feelings are literally disassociated from consciousness), such as the classic cases of multiple personality disorder described in many media accounts, may carry out seemingly conscious actions but later have no recollection of them or may only recollect them under particular circumstances (Chapter 15). According to Kihlstrom, these phenomena suggest, as William James asserted, that part of normal consciousness involves consciousness of self, that is, an activated representation of self that is linked with the thought or action, so that the person sees her thoughts or actions as *hers*.

The Functions of Conscious and Unconscious Processes

Other cognitive theorists have used a knowledge of cognitive processes to further our understanding of the functions of consciousness and the complementary roles of conscious and unconscious processes in everyday behavior. Unconscious processes, notably skills and associative processes such as priming and classical conditioning, are extremely fast and efficient (Baars & McGovern, 1996; Mandler, 1997). Since they are usually based on considerable learning, they tend to lead to adaptive responses that make sense in light of observed regularities in the environment (such as avoiding actions or stimuli that would lead to pain or danger). Another advantage of unconscious processes is that they can operate simultaneously. When solving a problem, for example, multiple networks can "collect data" at the same time and come up with independent and well-"researched" potential solutions. Consciousness, in contrast, has limited capacity: We can only form one "scene" at a time in our conscious minds; we cannot, for example, see the classic ambiguous gestalt figure as both two faces and a vase simultaneously. We can switch rapidly back and forth between two views of a scene or among tasks that require attention, but ultimately, each will draw conscious cognitive resources from the other.

On the other hand, conscious processes are more flexible than unconscious processes, and because consciousness is not limited to quasi-independent networks operating in parallel in their own small domains, consciousness can survey the landscape and consider the "big picture." The unconscious processes that operate in parallel are like independent teams of "experts," each offering its own advice on how to solve a problem or make a decision. According to one view, consciousness is like a blackboard on which each team of experts fights to present its solution or several of these teams brainstorm "at the board" to develop novel answers that none alone could produce (Baars, 1988, 1997). If a network manages to get its "message" on the blackboard, its "solution" is advertised throughout the system and leads other experts to begin trying to find solutions along those lines.

In more technical terms, the role of consciousness in this sense is to redistribute activation among the tens, hundreds, or thousands of networks active at any given time (Mandler, 1997). When conscious goals are active, they spread extra activation to networks associated with goal attainment. If a person is trying to make a decision or solve a problem, the "leading contenders" activated below consciousness all vie for conscious access. Those that seem to provide the best potential solutions become represented in consciousness; becoming conscious in turn spreads further activation to them and inhibits activation of less compelling alternatives.

INTERIM SUMMARY   Freud distinguished types of mental activities: **conscious** processes, of which the person is currently subjectively aware; **preconscious** processes, which are not presently conscious but could be readily brought to consciousness; and **unconscious**

processes, which are dynamically kept from consciousness because they are threatening. Studies of **subliminal perception** have shown that perception of stimuli below the threshold of consciousness can indeed have an impact on conscious thought and behavior. Recent research has also confirmed the psychodynamic contention that emotional and motivational processes can also occur outside of awareness. From a cognitive perspective, researchers have been studying the **cognitive unconscious**, which focuses on information-processing mechanisms that operate outside of awareness, such as procedural knowledge and implicit memory.

COMMENTARY
An Integrated View of Consciousness

Fifteen years ago, summarizing psychologists' views of conscious and unconscious processes was easy: Psychoanalysts believed in them, behaviorists did not, cognitive scientists were indifferent to them, and evolutionary psychology was just getting off the ground and had not yet weighed in on the subject. Today, we are beginning to see a rare convergence of views. The state of the art might be summarized as follows.

In humans, as in other animals, most behavior is controlled through implicit processes. Conscious processing is too limited in capacity to regulate and monitor the range of stimuli and goals confronting a person at any given time. Associative learning mechanisms, such as those studied by behaviorists, are generally rapid and efficient, and they served our pre-human ancestors well, long before consciousness arrived on the scene (Reber, 1992). The vast majority of perceptual, cognitive, emotional, and motivational processes are implicit and are thus not available to introspection. We can see the *impact* of our own implicit processes and form conscious representations of them (recognizing, for example, the kinds of people or situations that "push our buttons" and make us angry), but our minds are not constructed to give us direct access to them.

Some processes to which we *could* have access, such as thoughts, fantasies, or motives of which we are ashamed, can also become inaccessible to consciousness if we learn that keeping them from consciousness reduces our discomfort. The mechanisms for keeping uncomfortable material outside of awareness or transforming it into conscious representations that are not threatening (e.g., "I'm not a competitive person; I'm only competitive with *myself*") are themselves a form of procedural knowledge or skill, and these procedures are learned like any other: Those that reduce uncomfortable feelings are reinforced.

Consciousness is a specialized function that monitors our current state in relation to the environment for the purpose of maximizing adaptation. Consciousness is particularly attentive to *news*; that is, it is most likely to shine its spotlight on information that is novel or unexpected or on procedures that are not working optimally (Baars & McGovern, 1996). Its control function involves overriding procedures that are ineffective or bringing together quasi-independent "experts" to help provide flexible solutions that cannot be obtained while running on automatic pilot.

While specialized processing units operate in parallel to track various stimuli, feelings, motives, and memories, attentional mechanisms operate outside awareness to prioritize cognitive resources and spread extra activation to those that might be adaptively significant or help solve current goals. Once a perception, thought, goal, or motive enters consciousness, it further spreads activation to those neural networks that are most relevant. Much of the time this increases the likelihood that aspects of those neural networks will become conscious, although activated networks can influence behavior outside of awareness, and threatening information can be inhibited from consciousness even while it is maximally active.   ■

FROM MIND TO BRAIN

THE NEUROPSYCHOLOGY OF CONSCIOUSNESS

Having explored the nature of consciousness, we now examine its underlying neuroanatomy. Subjectively, consciousness is the seat of who we are; to lose consciousness permanently is to lose existence as a psychological being. So what neural structures produce conscious awareness and regulate states of consciousness?

Insights from Neurological Disorders

One way to learn about the neural pathways involved in consciousness is to examine neurological conditions that disrupt it. People with split brains, whose two hemispheres function independently following severing of the corpus callosum, provide one window to the neuropsychology of consciousness. An instructive case described in Chapter 3 concerned a ten-year-old boy who could only answer written questions orally when inquiries were made to the left hemisphere but who could answer by spelling words with letter tiles with the left hand when questions were addressed to the right hemisphere (LeDoux et al., 1977). The feelings spelled by his nonverbal right hemisphere were consistently more negative than those of his left hemisphere, raising questions about the unity of consciousness across the hemispheres.

Blindsight   Another phenomenon that bears on the neural underpinnings of consciousness is blindsight. Pursuing observations made by neurologists in the early part of the twentieth century, researchers have examined patients about whom Hamlet might have asked, "To see or not to see?" These patients are, in one sense, totally blind; if shown an object, they deny having seen it. They have lesions to the primary visual cortex in the occipital lobes, which is responsible for visual sensation, so their inability to see makes neurological sense. Yet if asked to describe its geometric form (e.g., triangle or square) or give its location in space (to the right or left, up or down), they do so with accuracy far better than chance—frequently protesting all the while that they cannot do the task because they cannot see! As noted in Chapter 4, researchers call this phenomenon *blindsight* (Weiskrantz, 1997; Weiskrantz et al., 1974).

The neural basis for blindsight is not entirely clear (see Wessinger et al., 1997), but one hypothesis, derived in part from animal research, points to the presence in the visual system of two neural pathways involved in vision (Figure 9.6). In the evolutionarily more recent pathway, neurons of the optic nerve carrying sensory information project to the thalamus via the optic tract; the information is subsequently transmitted to the primary visual cor-

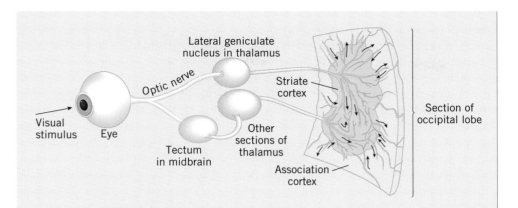

FIGURE 9.6
Blindsight. In blindsight, the neural pathway from the lateral geniculate nucleus in the thalamus to the primary visual cortex, which allows consciousness of visual images, is inoperative. However, a second, evolutionarily older pathway through the midbrain remains intact, permitting the implicit ability to locate visual stimuli.

tex in the occipital lobes. This pathway is responsible for conscious visual perception and for determining the precise nature of stimuli. The other pathway is evolutionarily older: Neurons carrying information from the retina project to a midbrain structure responsible for vision in animals such as frogs and birds that lack the highly specialized visual cortex of humans. From there the information passes through the thalamus and eventually on to the cortex. In blindsight, this second pathway appears to allow some visual processing at the midbrain level, even though the first pathway is rendered inoperative by damage to the visual cortex. Thalamic processing may also permit some recognition of what an object is even though this thalamic knowledge cannot be consciously accessed.

Amnesia   Studies with amnesics have shown that people can remember things implicitly even while lacking explicit memory. In one series of studies (Squire, 1986), amnesic and normal subjects were shown a word list and asked to recall the words with and without cues. When later tested for explicit memory, amnesic subjects were considerably impaired on both free recall (without cues) and cued recall tasks using word fragments (in which the first three letters of the word were presented) (Figure 9.7). However, amnesics were as likely as neurologically intact subjects to use words from the list when shown word fragments and asked to complete them with the first words that came to mind. Thus, although the amnesic subjects had no recollection of seeing the list of words, priming effects were just as pronounced as for normal subjects.

Priming studies like these suggest that some forms of amnesia may represent as much a failure of consciousness as of memory; the information has been encoded in some form but cannot be consciously accessed. Similarly, a psychologist told a joke to a Korsakoff's patient whose ability to remember new experiences was virtually nonexistent (Jacoby & Kelley, 1987). Predictably, the man laughed, but the next time he heard the joke, he was stonefaced. He had no recollection of having heard it before but thought the joke was "dumb." The patient had apparently anticipated the punch line unconsciously, even though he had no conscious recollection of it.

Where Is Consciousness Located?

So where is consciousness located in the brain? Research over the past two decades has made increasingly clear that this is probably not the right question to ask about any psychological phenomenon. Consciousness, like most psychological functions, involves a distributed network of neurons rather

FIGURE 9.7
Priming effects in amnesia. Participants were shown word lists including words like *absent, income,* and *motel* and asked to recall the words. Amnesic patients were impaired on both unaided recall and cued recall (where the first three letters of the word were given) (*a*). However, amnesic patients exhibited normal priming effects when they completed three-letter fragments (e.g., *ABS—*) with the first word that came to mind (*b*). *Source:* Squire, 1986.

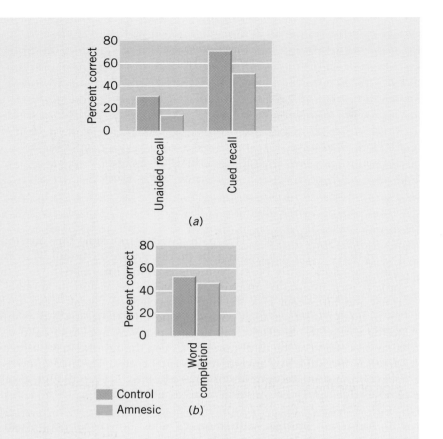

than a single "center." The better question then, is, "What neural structures are involved in the experience of consciousness?"

The answer to this question, too, has a twist: It depends on which meaning of consciousness one has in mind. If one means simply the state of being conscious (as opposed to being unconscious or asleep), then hindbrain and midbrain structures, especially the reticular formation, are particularly important (Bogen, 1995; Franklin et al., 1988; Szymusiak et al., 1989). Damage to the reticular formation through head injury in humans or lesioning in animals can lead to coma or loss of consciousness. The pons and medulla are also involved in regulating states of conscious arousal (Figure 9.8). In contrast, we can lose an entire cerebral hemisphere and remain conscious.

But consciousness has another meaning, which has been our focus thus far in this chapter: consciousness as the center of subjective awareness. In this sense, consciousness is distributed across a number of neural pathways, most of them found in the reticular formation, the thalamus, and the cortex (Newman, 1995). The reticular formation extends throughout much of the hindbrain and sends axons through the midbrain (in the tegmentum). These fibers then synapse with nuclei in the thalamus, which in turn activate parts of the cortex. A region of particular importance is the prefrontal cortex (Goldman-Rakic, 1995), which is involved in momentarily storing, manipulating, or calling up information from various senses into working memory and hence making them conscious (Chapter 6).

Recent PET data have in fact confirmed that when subjects are consciously attending to stimuli, a pathway from the midbrain sections of the reticular formation through the region of the thalamus to which it projects

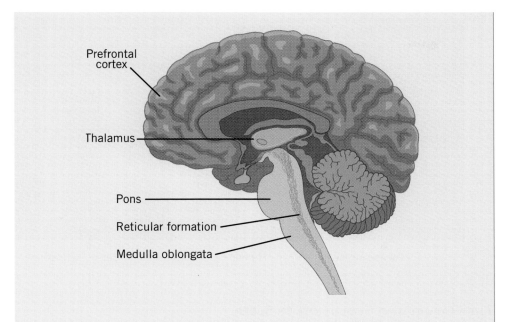

FIGURE 9.8
Neuropsychological basis of consciousness. The hindbrain and midbrain structures involved in conscious arousal and shifts from waking to sleep include the reticular formation, the pons, and the medulla. Midbrain reticular regions, the thalamus, and the prefrontal cortex play a particular role in shining a conscious "spotlight" on thoughts, feelings, or perceptions.

becomes activated (Kinomura et al., 1996). Once the cortex is activated and the person attends to a stimulus, it sends messages back down to another region of the thalamus that signals the first region to limit its activation to the most relevant details of the stimulus, "shining a spotlight" on information that needs to be highlighted and inhibiting attention to irrelevant details (see Crick & Koch, 1990). Thus, the thalamus and cortex appear to have a feedback loop, in which the thalamus and reticular formation "illuminate" a large terrain, the cortex sends messages back to narrow the focus, and the thalamus in turn helps the cortex focus its conscious spotlight on a more specific target (Newman, 1995).

INTERIM SUMMARY   An integrated view suggests that consciousness is a specialized processing function that monitors and controls current states for the purpose of maximizing adaptation, which highlights or inhibits information based on its relevance to adaptation and its emotional consequences. Consciousness involves a network of neurons distributed throughout the brain. Damage to hindbrain structures, particularly the reticular formation, can lead to a complete loss of consciousness. The neural networks that "shine a spotlight" on perceptions, thoughts, emotions, or goals at any moment appear to involve the prefrontal cortex, the thalamus, and midbrain regions of the reticular formation.

SLEEP AND DREAMING

We have focused thus far on waking consciousness. We now turn to the major series of changes that regularly occur in consciousness every 24 hours: the sleep and waking cycle. Those who lament that life is too short would be horrified to realize that they will sleep away roughly a third of their time on the earth, about 25 years. Infants sleep two-thirds of each day, and elderly people, about one-fourth.

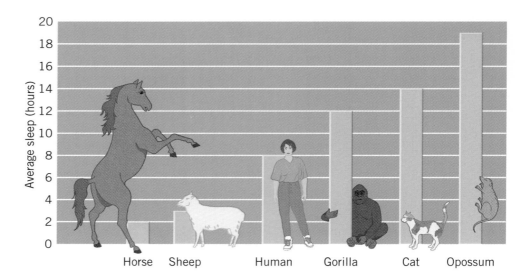

FIGURE 9.9
Average hours of sleep per night. Animals vary according to the amount of sleep they need; humans lie somewhere in the middle.

THE NATURE AND EVOLUTION OF SLEEP

Sleep evolved over three billion years ago in some organisms, and the mechanisms that govern the biological clock in humans are apparently over 500 million years old (Lavie, 1996). Although not all animals show the characteristic EEG signs of sleep (described below), nearly all animals show behavioral signs of sleeping: minimal movement, a stereotyped posture, and a high degree of stimulation needed to arouse them.

Animals differ in aspects of their sleep in ways that make evolutionary sense. For example, animals that are readily eaten by predators tend to sleep lightly. Large animals also tend to sleep less than small animals (Campbell & Tobler, 1984), presumably because they need to be awake longer hours to find food to sustain their larger bodies (Figure 9.9).

During sleep, responsiveness to external, and particularly visual, stimulation is diminished, but it is not entirely absent (see Antrobus, 1991). From an evolutionary perspective, some degree of responsiveness during sleep is essential for survival, as when a person wakes upon hearing a loud noise. The processing of external sensory information is sometimes apparent in dreams, which may incorporate elements of sensory experience into the ongoing story. Sleep researchers who sprayed a mist of cold water on subjects who were dreaming received dream reports such as the following:

> "Children came into the room and came over to me asking for water. I had a glass of ice water and I tipped the glass to give it to them. I was sitting, and I spilled the water on myself. . . . Then I got out of the chair and was going to change my pants" (Dement & Wolpert, 1958, p. 550).

Individuals differ widely in the amount of sleep they both need and get. Most people left on their own (such as on weekends) would sleep about eight hours. In terms of actual hours slept, people fall on a bell-shaped curve, ranging averaging from 4.5 to 10.5 hours a night, with most people sleeping between 6.5 and 8.5 hours (Lavie, 1996). Researchers have documented rare cases of people who require minimal sleep, such as a 70-year-old English nurse who was observed to sleep only one hour every night with no adverse consequences (Borbély, 1986). Interestingly, from the late 1960s to the early 1990s, college students reported sleeping about an hour less on the average per night (Hicks & Pelligrini, 1991). (This

Dreaming of catnip?

probably reflects the increasing length of textbooks, a trend that is costing at least one textbook author sleep at this very moment.)

Circadian Rhythms

The cycle of sleep and waking in humans and other animals, like the ebb and flow of body temperature, hormones, and other life support processes, is a circadian rhythm. A **circadian rhythm** (from the Latin, *circa*, meaning "about," and *diem*, meaning "day") is a cyclical biological process that evolved around the daily cycles of light and dark. Circadian rhythms akin to sleep–wake cycles may exist in daytime as well. Research supports the distinction between "day people" and "night people," finding that people peak in their alertness, arousal, and even hypnotizability at different times of the day (Wallace, 1993). Researchers studying mice have just tracked down the genes responsible for creating their internal "clock" by examining mutant mice whose clocks do not tick correctly (Antoch et al., 1997).

Human circadian rhythms are controlled by the hypothalamus, but they are influenced by the presence of light and dark. A special neural tract projects from the retina to the hypothalamus which responds only to relatively intense light, such as sunlight. During periods of darkness, the pineal gland in the middle of the brain produces a hormone called *melatonin*; melatonin levels gradually diminish during daylight hours. Melatonin influences not only sleep but sexual arousal. Thus, during the winter months, when the number of daylight hours diminishes, so, too, does sexual arousal. The old saying that "a young man's fancy turns to thoughts of love" in the springtime thus has more than a grain (or gram) of hormonal truth (see Lavie, 1996).

Circadian rhythms account for the difficulties people experience when they cross time zones (jet lag) or have frequently changing work shifts. Nurses, medical residents on call, police, pilots, and flight attendants, whose shifts change from day to day or week to week, suffer greater incidence of health problems, in part because of disrupted circadian rhythms (Monk, 1997; Tan, 1991). Although some people seem to function well despite these frequent disruptions in their sleep cycle, others become irritable and inefficient—not particularly comforting traits to see in pilots or young doctors.

Sleep Deprivation

No one knows precisely what function sleep serves. Some researchers emphasize its role in energy conservation, since sleep turns down the body's "thermostat" at night (Berger & Phillips, 1995). Others emphasize functions of restoring the body and mind to a "fresh" or rejuvenated state, while still others point to a potential role in consolidating memory (see Karni et al., 1994; Walsh & Londblom, 1997). The number of hours people sleep is related to mortality rates, although the reasons for this are unclear. People who report sleeping for unusually long *or* unusually short durations are prone to die earlier than people whose reported sleep is in the middle of the bell curve (Figure 9.10). Long-term sleep deprivation reduces the functioning of the immune system and makes the body more vulnerable to diseases ranging from common colds to cancer (Everson, 1997). Rats deprived of sleep die after two or three weeks; researchers tracking down the cause of death have found that sleep deprivation throws off homeostatic mechanisms that maintain energy and temperature (Rechtscaffen et al., 1989).

People have known of the ill effects of extreme sleep deprivation for at least 2000 years. In Roman times and during the Middle Ages, sleep deprivation was used as a form of torture. About a century ago psychologists published a study of three men deprived of sleep for 90 hours, or about four days (Patrick & Gilbert,

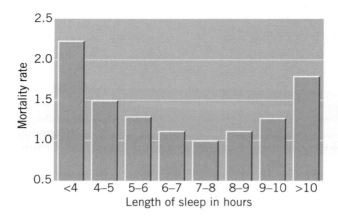

FIGURE 9.10
Sleep duration and mortality. Mortality rates are highest among those at the extremes, who report sleeping less than five or more than ten hours per night. (Mortality rate is scaled against the group with the lowest mortality rate, those who sleep eight hours.) *Source:* Adapted from Kripke et al., 1979.

1896). After their second sleepless night, the subjects began to experience disturbances in perception, including hallucinations. The hallucinations disappeared once the subjects were able to sleep. Decades ago, Soviet and Chinese experts in thought reform (brainwashing) discovered that depriving people of sleep makes them more susceptible to major alterations in belief and value systems (Lifton, 1963).

In 1959, a New York disk jockey, Peter Tripp, stayed awake for 200 hours, or about eight days, as part of a "wakeathon" for charity (Luce, 1966). As time went on, Tripp deteriorated considerably, developing hallucinations (such as the belief that his bureau drawer was on fire), delusions, and paranoid thinking, all of which disappeared after a good night's sleep. Extreme sleep deprivation does not generally produce such dramatic symptoms, however. One 17 year old who stayed awake 264 hours impressed a sleep researcher by beating him in a game of basketball at 3 a.m. on the last night (Lavie, 1996)!

Not surprisingly, the time required to fall asleep is dramatically lowered after even a single sleepless night (Carskadon & Dement, 1982). Researchers have recently discovered a neurotransmitter substance (actually, a neuromodulator, which regulates the impact of other neurotransmitters) in the thalamus and in structures deep within the cerebrum that increases with each additional hour an animal is awake (Porkka-Heiskanen et al., 1997). This neuromodulator, called *adenosine*, plays an inhibitory role, shutting down the systems that normally lead to arousal and hence fostering sleep when an animal has been awake too long.

INTERIM SUMMARY   People spend roughly one-third of their lives asleep. The sleep cycle is governed by **circadian rhythms**, the internal "clocks" that regulate biological processes that evolved in relation to the daily cycles of light and dark. The functions of sleep are not yet known, although sleep appears to be involved in restoration and maintenance of bodily processes such as homeostasis and immune functioning and in consolidation of memory.

STAGES OF SLEEP

Sleep proceeds through a series of stages (Dement & Kleitman, 1957). To study these stages, researchers use an EEG, attaching electrodes to subjects' heads to measure brain waves. (They also use electrodes at the corners of the eyes to track eye movements.) In general, as people move from a waking state through deeper stages of sleep, their brain waves become slower and more rhythmic, decreasing from over 14 cycles per second in the waking state to as little as one-half cycle per second in deep sleep. (The number of cycles per second is a gross measure of rate of neural firing and hence of mental activity.)

A subject in a sleep laboratory is outfitted with electrodes on the forehead and scalp for the EEG to measure brain waves. Electrodes are applied next to the eyes for a similar instrument, an electro-oculogram, to measure eye movements.

Early Stages of Sleep

As Figure 9.11 shows, normal waking brain activity has an irregular pattern with a high mental activity level, evidenced in a large number of cycles per second (known as beta waves). As people close their eyes and relax in bed, alpha waves (eight to 12 cycles per second) emerge, signaling a slowing of mental activity and a transition into sleep. Stage 1 sleep is brief (only a few minutes), marked by the appearance of slower theta waves (three to seven cycles per second). Physiological changes accompany this shift from drowsiness into sleep as eye movements slow, muscles relax, and blood pressure drops, bringing the body into a calm, quiet state.

Stage 2 sleep is marked by an EEG pattern of slightly larger waves interrupted by bursts of low-amplitude activity (called sleep spindles) and slow, high-amplitude waves called K complexes (Halasz, 1993). During Stage 2, sleep deepens, as alpha activity disappears. Stage 3 sleep is marked by the emergence of large, slow, rhythmic delta waves (less than one cycle per second). When delta waves comprise more than 50 percent of recorded brain activity, the person has entered Stage 4 sleep. Together, Stages 3 and 4 constitute what is called **delta sleep**. Delta sleep is a deep sleep characterized by relaxation of muscles and decreased rate of respiration and body temperature. People aroused from delta sleep are groggy and disoriented. During delta sleep, muscles apparently rest and rejuvenate, since people deprived of it frequently complain of muscle aches and tension.

Rapid Eye Movement (REM) Sleep

The first indication that something is about to change usually comes when the person rolls over or changes position. Stage 4 sleep is interrupted, and the sleep

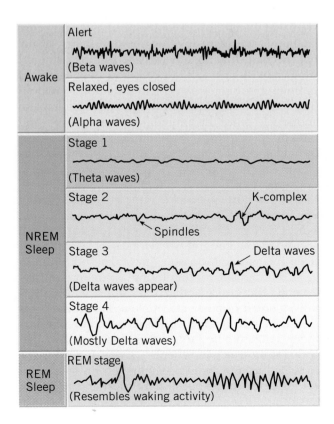

FIGURE 9.11
Stages of sleep. As people move from a waking state through deeper stages of sleep, their brain waves become slower and more rhythmic, decreasing from over 14 cycles per second in the waking state to as little as one-half cycle per second in deep sleep.

stages occur in reverse order, through Stages 3 and 2. Then, suddenly, the eyes begin to dance, darting around as if the sleeper were watching a play. Instead of returning to Stage 1, the person instead moves into a new stage called **rapid eye movement** (or **REM**) **sleep**, named for the bursts of darting eye movement that occur throughout this period. Qualitatively, REM sleep is so different that the other stages are often collectively called simply **non-REM** (or **NREM**) **sleep**.

In REM sleep, autonomic activity increases: Pulse and blood pressure quicken, respiration becomes faster and irregular, and both males and females evidence signs of sexual arousal that may last for several minutes. The EEG during REM sleep resembles the irregular, faster pattern of waking life, suggesting that, although the body is not moving, the brain is quite active. In addition, people aroused from REM sleep become alert very quickly, unlike those aroused from deep sleep. No one is entirely sure what the function of REM sleep is, but if a person is repeatedly awakened from it, the brain will return to it with increasing persistence.

The mental activity that occurs during REM sleep is dreaming. Roughly 80 percent of the time when people are awakened from REM sleep, they report dream activity. Although many people believe they do not dream, the evidence suggests that everyone dreams several times a night. Contrary to popular belief, dreaming also occurs during NREM sleep; however, dreams occur somewhat less frequently during NREM sleep and tend to be less rich and developed than REM dreams, often consisting of a simple experience, such as, "I dreamed I smelled fish" (Antrobus, 1991; Foulkes, 1995).

Recent data using PET scans find that a network of neurons, beginning from the pons and extending through the thalamus and amygdala, are active during REM sleep (Maquet et al., 1996). Visual association areas in the occipital and temporal lobes, which are active when people form mental images and identify objects, are also activated during REM sleep, but the primary visual cortex is not (Braun et al., 1998). Areas of the frontal cortex involved in consciousness and attention are also inactive or inhibited during REM sleep. These findings are particularly interesting in light of the fact that watching an event in normal waking consciousness (as opposed to "watching" a dream) involves both primary visual cortex and prefrontal attentional mechanisms. Together, these findings suggest that dreaming involves a neurologically distinct kind of consciousness that does not rely on normal waking attentional mechanisms and that attention to real visual stimuli is suspended during REM sleep. These findings may also explain why dreams are often highly emotional—since the amygdala is very active—and why dreamers can uncritically accept bizarre story lines—because the frontal circuits involved in critical thinking and social judgment are shut off during dreaming.

Perhaps the most paradoxical aspect of REM sleep is that the mind is quite active but the body is immobile; the only motor activity that typically occurs during REM sleep is occasional twitching. Brain damage, however, can change this. Cats with damage to midbrain structures involved in sleep and consciousness thrash around violently and perform seemingly meaningful behaviors, such as attacking imaginary prey, during REM sleep (Henley & Morrison, 1974). The midbrain in intact animals appears to have a mechanism for inhibiting voluntary muscle movement during REM sleep—a good thing, since otherwise people would literally act out their dreams. Actually, a small number of people suffer from a syndrome called REM behavior disorder: Their motor behavior is not inhibited during REM sleep, which makes them dangerous to both themselves and their bed partners, whom they may attack (Mahowald & Schenck, 1989). Interestingly, much of the REM sleep in babies is also accompanied by small motor movements, such as facial expressions and jerking of the limbs, because the mechanisms for inhibiting action during sleep do not mature until the end of the first year of life (Lavie, 1996).

After a period of REM sleep, the person descends again through Stage 2 and on to delta sleep. A complete cycle of REM and NREM sleep occurs about every 90 minutes (Figure 9.12). However, as the night progresses, the person spends less of the 90 minutes in delta sleep and more in REM sleep. Rapid eye movement sleep recurs four or five times a night and accounts for about 25 percent of all time asleep (on the average, two hours per night). Thus, over the course of a lifetime, the average person spends an estimated 50,000 hours—2000 days, or six full years—dreaming (Hobson, 1988).

INTERIM SUMMARY   Sleep proceeds through a series of stages that can be assessed by EEG. The major distinction is between **rapid eye movement (REM)** and **non-REM (NREM) sleep**. Most dreaming occurs in REM sleep, in which the eyes dart around and the EEG takes on an active pattern resembling waking consciousness. Perception of external stimuli and the capacity to move are substantially curtailed during REM sleep.

THREE VIEWS OF DREAMING

For thousands of years, humans have speculated about the nature and significance of dreams. Some cultures view dreams as actions carried out by the dreamer's soul. Others regard dreams as indices of the dreamer's deepest desires, revelations from the spiritual world, or sources of supernatural power (Bourguignon, 1979).

In the West in the late nineteenth century, dream interpretation was considered the realm of "primitives" and charlatans. Freud, however, argued that dream interpretation is a legitimate scientific and psychological pursuit. Versions of his psychodynamic theory are among the major approaches to dreaming. The other approaches are cognitive and biological.

A Psychodynamic View

Freud (1900) believed that dreams, like all mental events, have meaning but must be deciphered by someone skilled in dream interpretation. As communications spoken in the language of the unconscious, which is irrational and wishful, dreams are often vague, illogical, or bizarre and thus require translation into the

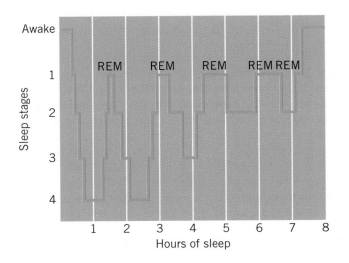

FIGURE 9.12
REM sleep. The stages of sleep follow a cyclical pattern that occurs about every 90 minutes, from Stage 1 through delta sleep and back again. As the night progresses, the person spends less time in deeper sleep and more time in REM sleep. *Source:* Cartwright, 1978.

language of rational waking consciousness. For example, in dreams two people are often condensed into one, or thoughts about one person are displaced onto someone else (that is, ascribed to the wrong person). According to Freud, unconscious processes are associative processes; thus, ideas are connected by their relationship to one another along networks of association, not by logic. During sleep, a person is not using conscious, rational processes to create or monitor the story, so one thought or image can easily be activated in place of another.

In this sense, Freud saw dreams as "the insanity of the night," where associative thinking replaces logical thought. For example, a man who was angry at his father had a dream of murdering his father's best friend, presumably because anger and murder were associatively linked, as were his father and his father's friend. According to Freud, people often rapidly forget their dreams upon awakening because dreams contain elements of unconscious mental life that would be anxiety provoking and are repressed during normal waking consciousness.

Freud distinguished between the **manifest content**, or story line of the dream, and the **latent content,** or its underlying meaning. He proposed that the underlying meaning of every dream is an unconscious wish, typically a forbidden sexual or aggressive desire. The empirical data do not support this hypothesis (see Fisher & Greenberg, 1997), and today, most psychodynamic psychologists believe, rather, that the latent content can be a wish, a fear, or anything else that is emotionally pressing. To uncover the latent content of a dream, the dreamer free-associates to each part of the dream (that is, simply says aloud whatever thoughts come to mind about it), while the dream analyst tries to trace the networks of association involved in the dream's construction. Probably the most central aspect of the psychodynamic approach is its view of dreams as *associative thought* laden with *emotional concerns.*

A Cognitive View

A cognitive perspective suggests that dreams are cognitive constructions that reflect the concerns and metaphors people express in their waking thought (Antrobus, 1991; Domhoff, 1996; Foulkes, 1978; Hall, 1951). In this view, dreams are simply a form of thought. At times, they may even serve a problem-solving function, presenting dreamers with potential solutions to problems they are facing during the day (e.g., Cartwright, 1996). Dreams rely on the same metaphors people use in everyday thinking; however, conscious monitoring is deactivated during dreaming, so metaphoric thinking is relatively unconstrained, leading to images or events that may seem bizarre to the conscious mind (Lakoff, 1997). Dreams also show cognitive development: Children's dreams lack the sophistication of adult dreams (Foulkes, 1982).

A Grammar of Dreams   One cognitive viewpoint that shares many points with Freud's theory was proposed by dream researcher David Foulkes (Cavallero & Foulkes, 1993; Foulkes, 1978, 1995). Like many contemporary psychodynamic psychologists, Foulkes takes issue with the contention that the latent meaning of every dream is an unconscious wish. He proposes instead that dreams simply express current concerns of one sort or another in a language with its own peculiar grammar. The manifest content is constructed from the latent content through rules of transformation, that is, rules for putting a thought or concern into the "language" of dreaming.

Decoding dream language thus requires a knowledge of those rules of transformation, just as a transformational grammar allows linguists to transform surface structure into deep structure (Chapter 7). In everyday language, the sentence "The boy threw the ball" can be transformed into "The ball was thrown by the boy." In dream language, the thought "I am worried about my upcoming exam" can be translated into a dream about falling off a cliff.

Dreams and Current Concerns   Evidence that dreams are related to current concerns—whether wishes, fears, or preoccupations of other sorts—comes not only from the clinic but also from empirical research (Domhoff, 1996). A study of dreams of Israeli medical students five weeks into the Gulf War, when Saddam Hussein was threatening Israel with Scud missile attacks, found that over half the dream reports of students dealt with themes of war or attack (Lavie, 1996). Other research finds that the extent to which people's dreams express wishes for intimacy correlates with their desires for intimacy by day (Evans & Singer, 1994).

Gender and cross-cultural differences also support the view that dreams express concerns similar to those that people experience in their waking consciousness (Domhoff, 1996). Just as males tend to be more aggressive than females by day, their dreams show a greater ratio of aggressive to friendly interactions than do women's dreams. Similarly, the Netherlands and Switzerland are two of the least violent technologically developed societies, whereas the United States is the most violent. Strikingly, incidents involving physical aggression are about 20 percent more prevalent in the dreams of U.S. males and females than among their Dutch and Swiss counterparts.

Although the evidence is sketchy and inconsistent, some research suggests that dreams may not only reflect but even influence conscious experience and concerns. For example, one study compared dream reports in migraine headache sufferers before and after the day of a migraine attack (Heather-Greener et al., 1996). Strikingly, pre-migraine dreams were characterized by a greater incidence of anger, aggressive interactions, themes of misfortune, and apprehension. Whether these worries revealed at night played a role in *causing* the headaches or simply provided an index of an impending migraine attack is unclear. In another study, women undergoing divorce who dreamed more about their ex-spouse and had more dream interactions depicting efforts to deal with and get over the divorce were less depressed a year later (Cartwright, 1996). Again, whether the dream served a problem-solving function or simply reflected the progress of the women's grieving is unknown.

A Biological View

Some dream researchers argue that dreams are biological phenomena with no meaning at all (e.g., Crick & Mitchison, 1983). According to one such theory (Hobson, 1988; Hobson & McCarley, 1977), dreams reflect cortical interpretations of random neural signals initiated in the midbrain during REM sleep. These signals are relayed through the thalamus to the visual and association cortex, which tries to understand this information in its usual way, namely, by using existing knowledge structures (schemas) to process the information. Because the initial signals are essentially random, however, the interpretations proposed by the cortex rarely make logical sense. Many dream researchers have, however, criticized this view, arguing that the presence of dreams during NREM sleep and the absence of any clear evidence linking specific patterns of midbrain activation with specific patterns of dream content suggest that it is at least incomplete (Foulkes, 1995; Squier & Domhoff, 1997).

Integrating the Alternative Models

Are these three models of dreaming really incompatible? The psychodynamic and cognitive views converge on the notion that dreams express current ideas and

▶ *You would wish to be responsible for everything except your dreams! What miserable weakness, what lack of logical courage! Nothing contains more of your own work than your dreams! Nothing belongs to you so much! Substance, form, duration, actor, spectator—in these comedies you act as your complete selves!*

NIETZSCHE,
Thus Spake Zarathustra

concerns in a highly symbolic language that requires decoding. They differ over the extent to which those concerns involve deep-seated or repressed wishes and fears. In reality, dreams probably express motives (wishes and fears) as well as ideas. Many motives have cognitive components, such as representations of wished-for or feared states (Chapter 10). Thus, a fear of failing an examination includes a representation of the feared scenario and its possible consequences. What applies to cognition, then, probably applies to many aspects of motivation as well, so dreams are as likely to express motives as beliefs.

Moreover, the biological explanation of dreaming is not necessarily incompatible with either the psychodynamic or the cognitive view. The interpretive processes that occur at the cortical level involve the same structures of meaning—schemas, associational networks, and emotional processes—posited by Freud and Foulkes. Hence, even random activation of these structures would produce dreams that reveal something about the organization of thoughts and feelings in the person's mind, particularly those that have received chronic or recent activation.

INTERIM SUMMARY   Freud viewed dreams as a window to the language of unconscious associative thoughts, feelings, and wishes. He distinguished the **latent content**, or underlying meaning, from the **manifest content**, or story line. Although Freud believed that the latent content of every dream is an unconscious wish that has been repressed, empirical data do not support this view, and most psychodynamic theorists and clinicians instead believe that the latent content can be a wish, a fear, or anything else that is emotionally pressing. The cognitive perspective suggests that dreams are the outcome of cognitive processes and that their content reflects the concerns and metaphors people express in their waking cognition. A biological view of dreaming proposes that dreams reflect cortical interpretations of random neural signals arising from the midbrain during REM sleep. These three views are probably not incompatible.

SLEEP DISORDERS

Most people have experienced occasional bouts of **insomnia** (inability to sleep), tossing and turning from anxiety or excitement. More enduring sleep disturbances, or **sleep disorders**, result from a number of biological and psychosocial causes (see Rothenberg, 1997). Insomnia and **hypersomnia** (sleeping too much) are frequent symptoms of depression, since the neurotransmitter systems that mediate mood are also involved in the regulation of circadian rhythms. Anxiety and depression can also impair sleep even when the causes are not primarily biological (see Ware, 1997). Trauma survivors show an elevated incidence of sleep disorders, including nightmares and insomnia (Ross et al., 1989; Yehuda & McFarlane, 1997). Following the massive earthquake that struck San Francisco in 1989, the incidence of nightmares in general, as well as nightmares about earthquakes in particular, rose dramatically (Wood et al., 1992).

Sleep disturbances may persist for years, even decades, after a traumatic experience, particularly if the trauma was prolonged. Survivors of the Nazi Holocaust, now primarily in their sixties and seventies, continue to have significantly more sleep disturbances than comparison subjects—over five decades after the experience (Rosen et al., 1991). The longer subjects spent in the camps, the more sleep disturbance they currently report.

No single treatment is effective for all patients with sleep disorders. Some respond better to psychological treatments, others to biological treatments (such as medications), and others to combination therapies (Buysee et al., 1995). "Sleeping pills," however, should always be taken with caution, since they can have paradoxical effects: They can sometimes lead to more, rather than less, trouble sleeping, as the person becomes dependent on them or the brain develops a tolerance for them, requiring higher doses to achieve the same effect (Lavie, 1996).

Insomnia

The most common sleep disorder is insomnia, which may take one of several forms: initial insomnia (difficulty falling asleep), middle insomnia (typically, frequent awakenings during the night), and early morning insomnia (waking up consistently around four o'clock and being unable to return to sleep) (Reynolds et al., 1991). As prevalent as insomnia is, researchers often find a substantial discrepancy between patients' self-reports of insomnia and their actual sleep patterns when assessed in the laboratory. People who claim to have severe insomnia frequently do sleep several hours, but they think they have not slept at all.

Insomnia often results from stress, but it can become a source of stress as well if it becomes chronic (Rosch, 1996). Insomnia can create a vicious cycle, in which the insomniac starts to worry that she will not be able to sleep as soon as she gets into bed. Essentially, the bed becomes a conditioned stimulus that elicits anxiety, which in turn fuels the insomnia. Sleeping pills can exacerbate the sleep disturbance by interfering with natural sleep processes (Hindmarch, 1991). A better strategy is to establish a regular bedtime, avoid activities that activate the sympathetic nervous system before bedtime (such as exercising or drinking beverages containing caffeine), and get up rather than roll around restlessly in bed (Bootzin et al., 1991). Table 9.1 lists some suggestions by a major sleep researcher for reducing or avoiding insomnia.

Nightmares, Night Terrors, Sleep Apnea, and Narcolepsy

Other sleep disorders include nightmares, night terrors, sleep apnea, and narcolepsy. **Nightmares** are vivid, frightening dreams typically associated with fears like falling, death, or calamity (see Bearden, 1994). About 5 percent of the general population suffers from chronic nightmares (Bixler et al., 1979); not surprisingly, sufferers of chronic nightmares tend to have other emotional problems or histories of trauma (Berquier & Ashton, 1992). Nightmares typically occur during REM

TABLE 9.1   SUGGESTIONS FOR AVOIDING OR REDUCING INSOMNIA

1. Avoid spending too much time in bed. If you are awake, get out. Do not let the bed become a conditioned stimulus associated with insomnia and anxiety.
2. Do not try to force sleep. Go to bed when you are ready, and get out if you are not.
3. Do not keep a brightly lit, ticking clock near the bed.
4. Avoid physical activity late at night. It activates the autonomic nervous system, which is incompatible with sleep.
5. Avoid coffee, chocolate, or alcohol before bedtime. Caffeine will keep you up, even if you do not think it affects you, and alcohol often causes people to wake up in the middle of the night.
6. Keep a regular sleep schedule. If you have insomnia, you need more of a routine than most people.
7. Do not eat a large meal before bedtime. If you wake up, do not visit the refrigerator.
8. Avoid sleeping during the day if you have insomnia.

Source: Adapted from P. Lavie, *The Enchanted World of Sleep* (A. Berris, Trans.), Yale University Press, New Haven, CT, 1996, pp. 176–177.

sleep and thus can take place at any time during the night. In contrast, **night terrors**—dramatic experiences of intense terror or panic during sleep—typically occur during delta sleep and hence tend to take place in the first two or three hours of sleep. Unlike nightmares, which people usually vividly recall, individuals seldom remember the contents of night terrors upon wakening. Instead, they may scream and awaken, feeling very confused.

Another disorder is **sleep apnea**, which usually produces symptoms of chronic sleepiness because the person is awakened as many as several hundred times during the night. In sleep apnea, breathing typically stops for more than ten seconds at a time, leaving the person gasping for air. People with sleep apnea often do not know the cause of their distress; they are aware only of feeling as if they have not slept. Their bed partners, however, may be quite aware of their loud snoring and restless sleep. Sleep apnea typically occurs in overweight men.

Narcolepsy is a sleep disorder of the day rather than the night. Narcoleptics are subject to sudden sleep attacks, falling into REM sleep in the middle of talking, driving, laughing, or other activities. Narcolepsy is often genetically transmitted, although the incidence varies cross-culturally. In Japan, one in 600 people suffers from the disorder, whereas in North America the prevalence is more on the order of one in 10,000 (Aldrich, 1990). Narcoleptics often find themselves continuously battling the urge to sleep and hence experience a constant state of fatigue and sleepiness. As with some of the other sleep disorders, medications can often be useful in controlling the symptoms of narcolepsy, although a cure has not been developed (see Buysse et al., 1995).

INTERIM SUMMARY Sleep disorders reflect a variety of biological and psychosocial causes, ranging from neurotransmitter dysfunction in depression to conditioned emotional responses that impede sleep in people who have come to associate bedtime with anxiety. The most common sleep disorder is **insomnia**, or the inability to sleep.

ALTERED STATES OF CONSCIOUSNESS

Sleep is the most common example of a psychological state in which normal waking consciousness is suspended, but it is not the only one. **Altered states of consciousness,** in which the usual conscious ways of perceiving, thinking, and feeling are modified or disrupted, are culturally patterned and occur through meditation, hypnosis, ingestion of drugs, and religious experiences.

MEDITATION

In **meditation**, which is practiced by many religions, the meditator develops a deep state of tranquility by altering the normal flow of conscious thoughts. Many religions, such as Buddhism, believe that meditation leads to a deepened understanding of reality (Ornstein, 1986). By focusing attention on a simple stimulus or by concentrating on stimuli that are usually in the background of awareness (such as one's breathing), meditation shuts down the normal flow of self-conscious inner dialogue (J. Weinberger, personal communication, 1992). In all types of meditation, the usual goal-directed flow of consciousness is disrupted as the procedures that normally direct conscious attention are de-automatized. Meditators and theologians often describe the experience as liberation from the self or an expansion of conscious awareness.

Meditation can produce a state of serenity that is reflected in altered brain wave activity. Some forms of meditation facilitate the alpha waves characteristic of the relaxed state of falling into sleep; others even produce theta waves, which are rarely observed except in subjects who are fully asleep (Jangid et al., 1988; Matsuoka, 1990). As a result, some experienced meditators in the East can perform remarkable feats, such as meditating for hours in the bitter cold. Meditation can be highly therapeutic, decreasing stress and physiological symptoms (Collings, 1989). Research suggests that introducing meditation in the workplace as a stress management technique can be useful for both employee health and worker productivity (Murphy, 1996).

HYPNOSIS

Another type of altered state, hypnosis, was named after Hypnos, the Greek god of sleep, because of the superficial resemblance between the hypnotic state and sleep. **Hypnosis** is characterized by deep relaxation and suggestibility (proneness to follow the suggestions of the hypnotist). The subject is likely to experience a number of changes in consciousness, including an altered sense of time, self, volition (voluntary control over actions or muscle movements), and perception of the external world. For instance, if the hypnotist directs the subject's arm to float in the air, the individual may have no sensation that she herself is causing the arm to rise; she may feel as if the arm has a mind of its own (Bowers, 1976).

As a skeptic taking a weekend workshop on clinical hypnosis a couple of years ago, I was personally shocked when, after two unsuccessful attempts at being hypnotized, I found my arm suddenly rising when instructed that I would feel like my wrist was tied to a helium balloon. Two weeks later, having learned to control mild pain under hypnosis, I decided to try the same technique on myself on an airplane, playing the roles of both hypnotist and hypnotic subject, when I could not shake a nasty headache (a procedure called *self-hypnosis*). The procedure worked—a throbbing sinus headache transformed itself into a vague, dull pain—

A subject responds to a hypnotic suggestion that his hand is tied to a helium-filled balloon.

but I still wonder what the person sitting next to me thought when my arm began to head for the ceiling as I sat motionless with my eyes closed at 30,000 feet!

Not everyone can be hypnotized. People differ in their **hypnotic susceptibility**, or capacity to enter into deep hypnotic states (Hilgard, 1965, 1986). People who are highly hypnotizable tend to be able to form vivid visual images and to become readily absorbed in fantasy, daydreams, movies, and the like (see Kunzendorf et al., 1996). They can also be discriminated from nonhypnotizable people by patterns of brain wave activity while under hypnosis as assessed by EEG (De-Pascalis & Perrone, 1996).

Hypnotic Effects

Hypnosis can produce an array of unusual effects, although, as we will see, researchers disagree on the extent to which many of these effects are either genuine or unique to hypnosis. As a result of hypnotic suggestions, people can experience amnesia or its opposite, **hypermnesia** (the recall of forgotten memories). A hypnotist can induce **age regression**, leading the subject to feel like he is reliving an incident he experienced at a prior age or to speak a language he does not consciously remember but which was spoken in his home when he was a very young child (Nash, 1988). Hypnotized subjects often demonstrate **hypnotic analgesia**, an apparent lack of pain despite pain-inducing stimulation. For example, if told they are about to smell a beautiful flower, subjects will smile placidly rather than reflexively turn their heads when ammonia is placed under their noses.

Hypnosis has clear and well-documented therapeutic effects (Kirsch et al., 1995). Some hypnotic subjects have undergone surgery without anesthesia and shown no signs of conscious pain. Hypnosis can, in fact, be useful in minimizing the experience of pain in many situations, ranging from the dentist's chair to the treatment of burn injuries (Mulligan, 1996; Patterson & Ptacek, 1997). Controlled scientific studies have even shown hypnotized subjects to be able to rid themselves of warts (Noll, 1994; Sinclair-Gieben & Chalmers, 1959; Surman et al., 1983) and stop blood from flowing profusely from lacerated skin (Bowers, 1976; Kihlstrom, 1985; Ornstein, 1986).

The Hidden Observer

Ernest Hilgard (1986) has experimented extensively with hypnotic phenomena, including hypnotic analgesia and hypnotically induced deafness. In one class demonstration, he hypnotized a student to become deaf, telling him he could hear nothing until his instructor touched his right shoulder. To prove the extent of the subject's deafness, Hilgard banged together large wooden blocks near the subject's ears and even fired off a starter pistol, to which the subject did not respond. A student in the room wondered whether "some part" of the subject could still hear him, so Hilgard, confident this was not the case, told the subject, "Perhaps there is some part of you that is hearing my voice . . . If there is, I should like the index finger of your right hand to rise."

To the surprise of both instructor and students, the finger rose. The hypnotized student then asked Hilgard to restore his hearing to tell him what had just happened, explaining, "I felt my finger rise in a way that was not a spontaneous twitch, so you must have done something to make it rise, and I want to know what you did" (Hilgard, 1986, p. 186). Hilgard then instructed the subject, "When I place my hand on your arm . . . I can be in touch with that part of you that listened to me before and made your finger rise. . . . But this hypnotized part of you, to whom I am now talking, will not know what you are saying." The *hidden observer*—the part of the subject's consciousness that raised the finger—then fully described what had happened, including hearing the slamming wooden blocks. When Hilgard lifted his hand and again asked what had happened in the last few minutes, the subject had no idea (pp. 187–188).

Hilgard's discovery of the hidden observer led him to conduct some fascinating experiments on hypnotic analgesia. In the basic design, the subject places her hand and forearm in ice water and reports the degree of pain produced, from 0 (no pain) to 10 (pain so severe that she wants to pull out her hand). In a normal waking state, the person usually hits 10 in less than a minute. When given a suggestion for hypnotic analgesia, subjects often report no pain and in fact keep their arm in the water indefinitely. However, when given the suggestion for the hidden observer to rate the pain (writing with the other hand kept out of sight) using the same 0 to 10 scale, subjects report steadily increasing pain (Figure 9.13).

Hypnosis and Memory

A controversial claim made by advocates of hypnosis is that hypnosis can restore forgotten memories. In the late 1970s, for example, a busload of children and their driver were kidnapped at gunpoint. Later, under hypnosis, the driver relived the experience from beginning to end and was able to recall the kidnappers' license plate number with enough clarity to lead to their apprehension. Police detectives have used hypnosis to solve other cases as well (Geiselman et al., 1985).

One researcher found that subjects under hypnosis could recall events that occurred under anesthesia (Levinson, 1965). While a surgeon was removing a small lump from the lower lip of a patient, the doctor made the comment, "Good gracious . . . it may be a cancer!" For the next three weeks, the patient was inexplicably depressed. The investigator then hypnotized the woman and induced hypnotic regression to the day of the operation. She remembered the exclamation "Good gracious" and then, crying profusely, recalled, "He is saying this may be malignant" (p. 201). The researcher subsequently demonstrated the capacity for recall of similar events experimentally with a sample of dental patients. Since then, a number of memory researchers have demonstrated both implicit and explicit memory for events occurring during anesthesia, such as later recognition of word lists presented while surgery patients were completely unconscious (Bonebakker, 1996; Cork, 1996).

Although these examples suggest that hypnosis may sometimes be useful in retrieving forgotten memories, many psychologists have expressed concern about its overenthusiastic use to retrieve memories of sexual abuse or crime scenes, and others have questioned the scientific validity of hypnosis as an aid to memory enhancement for legal purposes (Lynn et al., 1997; Smith, 1983). The limits of hypnosis are substantial enough that many states now outlaw the use of hypnotically induced memories in court testimony. One of the major problems is that people under hypnosis are highly suggestible and hence are likely to report more than they actually know (Wagstaff, 1984). A subtle inflection or leading question can lead a hypnotized eyewitness to believe he remembers things that are simply not true (although this is applicable, to a lesser degree, to nonhypnotized subjects as well, as we saw in Chapter 6). Hypnosis may also lower the threshold for feeling confident enough to report a memory, which can increase the capacity to recall actual memories *but also* increase the tendency to mistake beliefs, hypotheses, fantasies, or suggestions for true memories (Malpass & Devine, 1980). Controversy continues over the conditions under which hypnosis leads to genuine or distorted memories and is likely to do so for some time (Appelbaum et al., 1996; McConkey, 1995).

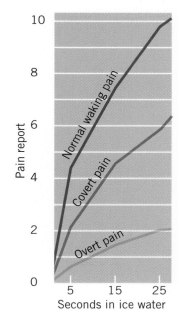

FIGURE 9.13
Hidden observer. The figure shows overt and covert pain following hypnotic suggestion for analgesia, as compared with normal waking pain, when the hand is immersed in ice water. *Source:* Hilgard, 1986, p. 190.

▶ ONE STEP FURTHER

Is Hypnosis Real?

Hypnosis has drawn considerable skepticism since it first received scientific attention in the nineteenth century, in part because of a history of charlatans using stage hypnosis mixed with liberal doses of deception (such as planting subjects). Although many researchers have come to some minimal consensus on the attributes of hypnotic states (Kirsch & Lynn, 1995), a substantial number of scientists remain unconvinced that hypnosis reflects anything other than subjects' desires to produce the behavior they think the hypnotist or investigator wants to see.

As we will see in Chapter 17, research over many decades has demonstrated that social pressure can lead people to perform peculiar, deviant, or destructive behavior, even in a normal state of consciousness. Several researchers have produced evidence to suggest that hypnotic subjects are simply playing the role they believe they are expected to play (Murrey et al., 1992; Spanos et al., 1992; Spanos et al., 1996). Others contend that aspects of hypnotic suggestion that are not *unique* to hypnosis, such as heavy reliance on imagery, actually account for hypnotic effects. For example, people instructed to use vivid visual images can often accomplish the same feats as hypnotized subjects, such as eliminating warts (Spanos et al., 1988).

The validity of hypnosis, however, is bolstered by findings from studies in which subjects are given **posthypnotic suggestions**—commands to perform a behavior on demand once they are out of the hypnotic trance. In a study designed to test the hypothesis that hypnotized subjects are simply role playing, the investigators compared the behavior of subjects instructed to act *as if* they were hypnotized with the behavior of true hypnotized subjects (Orne et al., 1968). When both groups of subjects were distracted from assigned tasks and thus diverted from thinking about what they were supposed to do, hypnotized subjects were three times as likely to carry out the posthypnotic suggestion as simulators. Findings of distinct EEG patterns in hypnotized subjects also bolster the claims for hypnosis as an altered state.

Another compelling source of evidence comes from studies in which hypnotic subjects have been able to endure painful medical procedures, including surgery, without anesthesia. Although some skeptics have argued that these patients must be "faking it," it is difficult to imagine undergoing an operation without anesthesia simply to please an experimenter (Bowers, 1976). (I wish the participants in my own studies were so compliant!) At this juncture, perhaps the safest conclusion is that hypnosis is an altered state of consciousness, at least in highly hypnotizable subjects, but that some or many of the phenomena produced under this condition can be produced under others, such as use of imagery, relaxation, or social pressure.   ◀

INTERIM SUMMARY   **Altered states of consciousness**, in which the usual conscious ways of perceiving, thinking, and feeling are modified or disrupted, are culturally patterned and occur through meditation, hypnosis, ingestion of drugs, and religious experiences. **Meditation** creates a deep state of tranquility by altering the normal conscious flow of conscious thoughts. **Hypnosis** is an altered state characterized by deep relaxation and suggestibility. Hypnosis can produce a wide range of effects, including some that foster medical and physical health, such as pain relief. Considerable controversy surrounds the conditions under which hypnosis leads to heightened memory retrieval versus memory distortion and fabrication. Another question concerns the extent to which hypnosis has unique features not observable under other conditions.

DRUG-INDUCED STATES OF CONSCIOUSNESS

The most common way people alter their state of consciousness (other than by going to sleep) is by ingesting **psychoactive substances**—drugs that operate on the nervous system to alter mental activity. In the West, people use many psychoactive substances, ranging from caffeine in coffee and nicotine in tobacco to drugs that seriously impair functioning, such as cocaine and heroin. Some psychoactive drugs resemble the molecular structure of naturally occurring neurotransmitters and thus have similar effects at synapses. Others alter the normal processes of synthesis, release, reuptake, or breakdown of neurotransmitters (Chapter 3) and consequently affect the rate of neural firing in various regions of the brain.

The action of psychoactive substances cannot, however, be reduced entirely to their chemical properties; their impact also depends on cultural beliefs and expectations. Native Americans who use peyote (a potent consciousness-altering drug) in religious rituals typically experience visions congruent with their religious beliefs, feelings of reverence or religious awe, and relief from physical ailments. In contrast, Anglo-Americans using the same drug often experience frightening visions, extreme mood states, and a breakdown in normal social inhibitions (Wallace, 1959).

Cross-culturally, the most widely used psychoactive substance is alcohol. In moderate doses—wine with dinner or a drink after work—alcohol can enhance experience and even have positive health consequences, but the social costs of abuse of alcohol and other substances are staggering. In the United States, approximately one in seven people abuse alcohol, and another one in 20 misuse other psychoactive substances. The number of people killed in alcohol-related accidents in the United States every year surpasses the total number killed in the entire Vietnam War (GAP, 1991). A Swedish study found that reported alcohol consumption in 1973 predicted mortality rates in a large sample followed up over the next 20 years (Andreasson & Brandt, 1997).

The major types of psychoactive substances in widespread use include alcohol and other depressants, stimulants, hallucinogens, and marijuana. We briefly examine each in turn.

Alcohol and Other Depressants

Depressants are substances that depress, or slow down, the nervous system. Common depressants include **barbiturates** (often called "downers") and benzodiazepines (tranquilizers, or anti-anxiety agents) such as Valium and Xanax. These drugs provide a sedative or calming effect, and higher doses can be used as sleeping pills. Unfortunately, they can also produce both psychological and physical dependence.

Contrary to what many people who rely on alcohol to elevate their mood believe, alcohol is a sedative. Researchers are still tracking down the precise neural mechanisms by which alcohol slows down central nervous system activity, but like other sedatives, alcohol appears to enhance the activity of the neurotransmitter GABA (gamma-aminobutyric acid), which normally inhibits transmission of neural impulses (Buck, 1996). For example, GABA inhibits norepinephrine, which is involved in anxiety. Thus, by increasing the neural inhibition of anxiety reactions, alcohol can reduce anxiety. Alcohol also enhances the activity of dopamine and endorphins (natural opiates in the brain) that normally provide pleasurable feelings that reinforce behavior (De Witte, 1996; Di Chiara et al., 1996). Thus, alcohol derives its powerful effects from its capacity to both diminish unpleasant feelings and heighten pleasurable ones.

▶ *O God, that men should put an enemy in their mouths to steal away their brains; that we should, with joy, pleasance, revel and applause, transform ourselves into beasts!*

SHAKESPEARE,
Othello *(II, iii)*

Alcohol and Expectations   As with psychoactive substances in general, expectations about alcohol's effects, shaped by culture and personal experience, can have as much impact on behavior as the drug's direct effects on the nervous system (see Collins et al., 1990; Hittner, 1997). This appears to be true cross-culturally; for example, similar findings have emerged in both mainland U.S. and Puerto Rican college student samples (Velez-Blasini, 1997).

Several studies have sought to distinguish the causal roles of two independent variables: whether subjects are drinking alcohol and whether they *think* they are drinking alcohol. Subjects are placed in one of four groups. In one, they drink an alcoholic beverage and are told they are drinking alcohol; in another, they drink alcohol but are told they are not. (The flavor of the drink makes alcohol detection impossible.) In the other two groups, subjects drink a nonalcoholic beverage and are either informed or misinformed about what they are drinking.

The results of these investigations elucidate the relative contributions of biology and beliefs to the effects of alcohol. For example, male subjects who think they are drinking alcohol report greater sexual arousal and less guilt when exposed to sexually arousing stimuli, whether or not they have actually been drinking alcohol. This is even more likely to occur if they have strong beliefs about the impact of alcohol on arousal (see Abrams & Wilson, 1983; Hull & Bond, 1986). More generally, people are more likely to behave in ways that may be deviant, dangerous, or antisocial if they can attribute their behavior to alcohol.

Consequences of Alcohol Use and Abuse   Alcohol abuse is involved in many violent crimes, including assault, rape, spouse abuse, and murder, but precisely how alcohol contributes to aggression is not entirely clear (see Bushman, 1997; Bushman & Cooper, 1990; Ito et al., 1996). One theory suggests that it disengages normal prohibitions; that is, alcohol contributes to aggression "not by 'stepping on the gas' but rather by paralyzing the brakes" (Muehlberger, 1956, cited in Bushman & Cooper, 1990, p. 342). A related theory suggests that alcohol facilitates aggression by derailing other psychological processes that normally decrease the likelihood of aggression, such as the ability to assess risks accurately. A third theory suggests that violence-prone individuals drink so that they can have an excuse for aggression, particularly since they tend to believe that alcohol makes them aggressive. All three processes can operate together, since an angry, violent person may drink in part in order to dull his conscience and provide himself an excuse for anything he does while intoxicated.

Long-term ingestion of alcohol produces physical changes in the brain that can seriously affect cognitive functioning, sometimes to the point of dementia (confusion and disorientation) or Korsakoff's syndrome. Imaging techniques such as CT scans reveal that roughly half of alcoholics show cerebral atrophy, and many show subcortical damage as well. Some of the behavioral changes associated with these physiological changes appear to be reversible, however, if the person stops drinking (Bowden, 1990).

Stimulants

Stimulants are drugs that increase alertness, energy, and autonomic reactivity (such as heart rate and blood pressure). These drugs range from commonly used substances like nicotine and caffeine to more potent ones such as amphetamines and cocaine. Nicotine increases heart rate and blood pressure while often decreasing emotional reactivity. Thus, cigarette smokers often report that smoking increases their arousal and alertness while also providing a soothing effect. Caffeine is found in coffee, tea, chocolate, soft drinks, and some nonprescription drugs such as aspirin products, decongestants, and sleep suppressants. Whereas moderate amounts of caffeine can help a person stay awake, high doses can produce symptoms indistinguishable from anxiety disorders, such as "the jitters" or even panic.

Amphetamines (sometimes called "uppers" or "speed") lead to hyperarousal and a feeling of "speeding," where everything seems to move quickly. The molecular structure of amphetamines is similar to that of the neurotransmitters dopamine and norepinephrine. Stimulation of norepinephrine receptors appears to produce alertness, while stimulation of dopamine receptors produces euphoria and increased motor activity (Ray & Ksir, 1987). Amphetamines can produce psychosis in vulnerable individuals, death by overdose, or ill health in chronic users, who essentially circumvent the normal signals sent by the brain to protect the body from fatigue and overuse.

Cocaine has held an attraction for people since about 500 A.D., when it was used by the Inca in Peru. The coca leaf, which contains cocaine, was used in religious ceremonies and even treated as money to compensate laborers. In the late 1800s, physicians discovered cocaine's anesthetic properties; soon many medicines and elixirs were laced with cocaine, as was Coca-Cola. Like other stimulants, cocaine appears to increase the activity of norepinephrine and dopamine, leading to a "rush" that can last a few minutes to two or three hours, depending on the form of ingestion and the potency of the drug. Chronic use depletes these neurotransmitters and can cause chronic depression similar to the crash that occurs when the initial high is over (GAP, 1991). Cocaine is one of the most potent pleasure-inducing substances, as well as one of the most addictive, ever discovered. Experimental animals will press a lever thousands of times to receive a single dose (Siegel, 1990).

Cocaine produces momentary distortions in thinking, such as diminished judgment and an inflated sense of one's own abilities. Regular cocaine use commonly produces paranoid thinking, which is usually temporary but can become chronic with continued use. One study found that 68 percent of cocaine-dependent men in a rehabilitation program reported paranoid experiences on cocaine that lasted several hours, long after the cocaine high was over (Satel et al., 1991). Moreover, 38 percent of the patients who reported paranoia actually responded by arming themselves with guns or knives. A recent study found that two-thirds of the assailants in domestic violence cases had consumed both cocaine and alcohol on the day they beat their spouse or children (Brookoff et al., 1997).

Hallucinogens

Hallucinogens derive their name from their capacity to create **hallucinations**—sensations and perceptions that occur in the absence of any external stimulation. While under the influence of hallucinogens, people may experience time as speeding up or slowing down or sense colors bursting from the sky, walls moving, or ants crawling under the skin.

Humans have used hallucinogens for thousands of years, but their impact and cultural meaning differ dramatically. In many cultures, people have used hallucinogens largely during cultural rituals, as when Australian aboriginal boys ingest hallucinogenic plants during ceremonies initiating them into manhood (Grob & Dobkin de Rios, 1992). In these settings, the meaning of hallucinations is established by the elders, who consider the drugs essential for bringing the young into the community of adults. In the contemporary West, individuals ingest these substances for recreation and with minimal social control, so the effects are more variable.

Hallucinogenic drug use in Europe and North America dramatically increased in the 1960s with the discovery of the synthetic hallucinogen **lysergic acid**

In the nineteenth century, cocaine was an ingredient of many elixirs, including Coca-Cola.

diethylamide (LSD). By the late 1970s, concern over the abuse of LSD and other hallucinogens, such as PCP ("angel dust") and hallucinogenic mushrooms ("shrooms"), intensified, and with good scientific reason: Chronic use of LSD, for example, is associated with psychotic symptoms, depression, paranoia, lack of motivation, and changes in brain physiology (Kaminer & Hrecznyj, 1991; King & Ellison, 1989; Smith and Seymour, 1994). Some chronic users develop a syndrome in which they repeatedly experience strange visual phenomena, such as seeing trails of light or images as they move their hands. Even when they are not experiencing these symptoms, their EEGs show a pattern of abnormal firing of neurons in visual pathways of the brain (Abraham & Duffy, 1996). The long-term effects of even occasional use of LSD are not entirely clear, although tragic events have occurred with LSD use, such as people walking out of windows and falling to their death.

Marijuana

The use of **marijuana** has been a subject of controversy for decades. Marijuana use among young people peaked in 1979 in the United States, with 60.4 percent of high school seniors reporting having tried the drug at least once. That number dropped to 35.3 percent in 1993, with the percentages fluctuating slightly throughout the 1990s (Hansen & O'Malley, 1996). Marijuana produces a state of being high, or "stoned," during which the individual may feel euphoric, giddy, unself-conscious, or contemplative. During a marijuana high, judgment is moderately impaired, problem solving becomes less focused and efficient, and attention is more difficult to direct; some people report paranoia or panic symptoms.

For decades, people have speculated about the detrimental effects of marijuana. It has been said to lead to moral depravity, impotence, the development of breasts in males, and an inevitable progression to harder drugs. By and large, these concerns tend more to reflect political and ideological agendas than scientific evidence. No credible scientific studies have documented the negative effects of occasional recreational use of the drug (Castle & Ames, 1996; Massachusetts General Hospital Bulletin, 1986), and research does not support previously alleged long-term negative effects on reproductive functioning (Block et al., 1991). As discussed in Chapter 15 on mental disorders, the most definitive study in this area, a longitudinal follow-up of young adults observed since early childhood, actually found occasional marijuana users and experimenters to be healthier psychologically than either abusers *or* abstainers (Shedler & Block, 1990). Other research finds that marijuana abuse, but not occasional use, is a risk factor for use of harder drugs (Kouri et al., 1995).

Nevertheless, marijuana, like harder drugs, artificially manipulates dopamine reward circuits in the brain (Wickelgren, 1997), and it can produce unwanted consequences. Memory for incidents that occur under the influence of the drug can be impaired, as reflected in temporary decreases in hippocampal functioning while high (see Heyser et al., 1993). Residual effects of the drug on attention, working memory, and motor abilities can also be detected for 12 to 24 hours after ingestion, which means that users may not be aware of subtle impairment at work, school, or at the wheel because the high has worn off (Pope et al., 1995). Chronic or heavy use, particularly beyond adolescence, is also a symptom of psychological disturbance (Chapter 15) and can contribute to deficits in social and occupational functioning. As with other drugs, smoking during pregnancy should be avoided, since studies have produced conflicting results on the impact of prenatal exposure (Chandler et al., 1996; Fried, 1995). In sum, like alcohol, the extent to which marijuana has negative psychological consequences probably depends on whether or not it is abused.

INTERIM SUMMARY   The most common way people alter their state of consciousness is by ingesting **psychoactive substances**, drugs that operate on the nervous system to alter mental activity. Drugs have their effects not only physiologically but also through cultural beliefs and expectations. The most widely used psychoactive substance cross-culturally is alcohol, which is also a major contributor to violence worldwide. **Depressants** such as alcohol slow down, or depress, the nervous system. **Stimulants**, such as amphetamines and cocaine, increase alertness, energy, and autonomic reactivity. **Hallucinogens** such as LSD produce **hallucinations**, sensations and perceptions that occur without external sensory stimulation. **Marijuana** is a controversial drug that produces a temporary "high" during which the person may have a number of different, largely pleasurable feelings, although it can also temporarily produce panic, paranoia, and attentional problems.

A GLOBAL VISTA

RELIGIOUS EXPERIENCES IN CROSS-CULTURAL PERSPECTIVE

Religious experiences are subjective experiences of being in contact with the divine. They range from relatively ordinary experiences, such as listening passively to a sermon, to altered states of consciousness in which a person feels at one with nature or the supernatural. In his classic work, *The Varieties of Religious Experience* (1902), William James described the state of contact with the divine that characterizes more dramatic forms of religious experience. During this state, the person experiences a sense of peace and inner harmony, perceives the world and self as having changed dramatically in some way, and has "the sense of perceiving truths not known before" (p. 199). James quotes the manuscript of a clergyman (1902, p. 67):

> I remember the night, and almost the very spot on the hilltop where my soul opened out, as it were, into the Infinite, and there was a rushing together of the two worlds, the inner and the outer. . . . The ordinary sense of things around me faded. . . . It was like the effect of some great orchestra when all the separate notes have melted into one swelling harmony.

In most societies, dramatic religious experiences tend to occur in the context of ritualized religious practices. A common example is known as a possession trance. In a *possession trance*, the soul is believed to be entered by another person or a supernatural being—that is, the person is "possessed." Induction into this altered state typically occurs through drumming, singing, dancing, and crowd participation (Bourguignon, 1979). Many born-

Humans seem predisposed to be moved by collective experiences. Left, a Balinese ritual; right, a spontaneous "ritual" at a rock festival in North America.

again Christian churches include possession trances as part of their regular religious practices (see, e.g., Griffith et al., 1984).

The use of ritualized altered states dates back at least to the time of the Neanderthals. Material found near prehistoric human remains in northern Iraq contains medicinal substances that are still used today to induce trance-like states in Europe and Asia. The "vision quest" of some Native American tribes frequently included religious trance states. During these states, a young person being initiated into adulthood would come in contact with ancestors or a personal guardian and emerge as a full member of adult society (Bourguignon, 1979). John Lame Deer, a Sioux medicine man, describes an experience that in certain respects resembles that of the Western clergyman quoted by James (Lame Deer & Erdoes, 1972, pp. 14–15):

> I was still lightheaded and dizzy from my first sweatbath in which I had purified myself before going up the hill. Even now, an hour later, my skin still tingled. But it seemed to have made my brain empty. . . . Blackness was wrapped around me like a velvet cloth. It seemed to cut me off from the outside world, even from my own body. It made me listen to voices within me. I thought of my forefathers, who had crouched on this hill before me. . . . I thought I could sense their presence. . . . I trembled and my bones turned to ice.

Like James's clergyman, Lame Deer describes a breakdown in the normal boundaries of the inner and outer worlds. Both men also describe a sense of being touched by a presence beyond themselves and an altered experience of reality, perception, and consciousness.

Ritualized religious experiences are simultaneously cultural and psychological phenomena. For individuals, they offer a sense of security, enlightenment, and oneness with something greater than themselves. For the group, they provide a sense of solidarity, cohesiveness, and certainty in shared values and beliefs. The individual is typically swept away in the experience, losing the self-reflective component of consciousness and experiencing a dissolution of the boundaries between self and nonself. The French sociologist Emile Durkheim (1915) described this phenomenon as "collective effervescence," in which the individual's consciousness seems dominated by the "collective consciousness." Most readers have probably experienced collective effervescence, either during religious ceremonies or in less profound circumstances, such as rock concerts and sporting events. Collective events of this sort, many of which involve chanting or rhythmic movement and speech, seem to tap into a basic human capacity for this kind of altered state.

Some Concluding Thoughts

Like the attentional mechanisms that direct the consciousness of individuals, scientific communities have mechanisms that bring phenomena in and out of focus at various times. In the heyday of behaviorism, consciousness was relegated to the periphery of psychological awareness. Recent developments in cognitive science have generated renewed interest in the roles of conscious and unconscious processes in human information processing.

This renewed interest may actually contribute to integration across the theoretical perspectives in psychology. Interest in unconscious processes brings the field squarely back to one of the central tenets of psychoanalytic theory, that much of mental life is unconscious, including thoughts, feelings, and motivations. Paradoxically, the growing literature on unconscious processes has also produced new interest in learning that occurs without awareness, a central focus of behavioral research. We may discover that the conditioned emotional responses of the behaviorist and the unconsciously triggered emotional reactions of the psychoanalyst are not as far apart as they once seemed—and that they may have much in common with associations between emotions and memories studied by the cognitive psychologist. Psychologists studying consciousness have also relied to some extent on a functionalist approach common to both William James and current evolutionary psychologists: Consciousness serves the functions of monitoring and controlling the self and the environment. It allows us to examine and sometimes override automatic procedures, unconscious motives, dysfunctional conditioned emotional responses, and operant responses normally triggered outside awareness.

The study of conscious and unconscious processes has also focused the attention of the psychological community on two areas of psychological functioning that had previously been relatively neglected: motivation and emotion. To these we now turn.

SUMMARY

THE NATURE OF CONSCIOUSNESS

1. **Consciousness** refers to the subjective awareness of percepts, thoughts, feelings, and behavior. It performs two functions: monitoring the self and environment and controlling thought and behavior. **Attention** is the process of focusing awareness, providing heightened sensitivity to a limited range of experience requiring more extensive information processing. **Divided attention** means splitting attention between two or more stimuli or tasks.

2. Psychologists study the flow of consciousness through **experience-sampling** techniques, such as **beeper studies**. Even such a private experience as consciousness is in part shaped by cultural practices and beliefs, which influence aspects of subjective awareness, such as the experience of time and the focus on internal psychological states.

PERSPECTIVES ON CONSCIOUSNESS

3. Freud distinguished among conscious, preconscious, and unconscious processes. **Conscious** mental processes are at the center of subjective awareness. **Preconscious** processes are not presently conscious but could be readily brought to consciousness. *Dynamically unconscious processes*—or the system of mental processes Freud called the **unconscious**—are thoughts, feelings, and memories that are inaccessible to consciousness because they have been repressed, or kept from awareness because they are threatening or anxiety provoking. Research over several decades has demonstrated that subliminal pre-

sentation of stimuli can influence conscious thought and behavior. Emotional and motivational processes can also be unconscious or implicit.

4. The **cognitive unconscious** refers to information-processing mechanisms that occur outside of awareness, notably unconscious procedures or skills and preconscious associational processes such as those that emerge in priming experiments. Cognitive theorists have argued that consciousness is a mechanism for flexibly bringing together quasi-independent processing modules that normally operate in relative isolation, and for solving problems that automatic processes cannot optimally solve.

5. Hindbrain and midbrain structures, notably the reticular formation, play a key role in regulating states of wakefulness and arousal. Like most psychological functions, consciousness appears to be distributed across a number of neural pathways, involving a circuit running from the reticular formation through the thalamus, from the thalamus to the cortex (particularly the prefrontal cortex), and back down to the thalamus and midbrain regions of the reticular formation.

SLEEP AND DREAMING

6. The sleep–wake cycle is a **circadian rhythm**, a cyclical biological process that evolved around the daily cycles of light and dark. Sleep proceeds through a series of stages that cycle throughout the night. Most dreaming occurs during **REM** sleep, named for the bursts of darting eye movements.

7. Freud distinguished between the **manifest content,** or story line, and the **latent content,** or underlying meaning, of dreams. Freud believed the latent content is always an unconscious wish, although most contemporary psychodynamic psychologists believe that wishes, fears, and current concerns can underlie dreams. Cognitive theorists suggest that dreams express thoughts and current concerns in a distinct language with its own rules of transformation. Some biological theorists contend that dreams have no meaning; in this view, dreams are cortical interpretations of random neural impulses generated in the midbrain. These three approaches to dreaming are not necessarily incompatible.

8. Common **sleep disorders** include **insomnia, nightmares, night terrors, sleep apnea,** and **narcolepsy.**

ALTERED STATES OF CONSCIOUSNESS

9. In **altered states of consciousness**, the usual conscious ways of perceiving, thinking, and feeling are changed. **Meditation** is an altered state in which the person narrows consciousness to a single thought or expands consciousness to focus on stimuli that are usually at the periphery of awareness. **Hypnosis,** characterized by deep relaxation and suggestibility, appears to be an altered state, but many hypnotic phenomena can be produced under other conditions. In altered states that occur during **religious experiences**, the person feels a sense of oneness with nature, others, or the supernatural and experiences a breakdown in the normal boundaries between self and nonself.

10. **Psychoactive substances** are drugs that operate on the nervous system to alter patterns of perception, thought, feeling, and behavior. **Depressants,** the most widely used of which is alcohol, slow down the nervous system. **Stim-**

ulants (such as nicotine, caffeine, amphetamines, and cocaine) increase alertness, energy, and autonomic reactivity. **Hallucinogens** create **hallucinations**, in which sensations and perceptions occur in the absence of any external stimulation. **Marijuana** leads to a state of being high—euphoric, giddy, unself-conscious, or contemplative. Psychoactive substances alter consciousness biologically, by facilitating or inhibiting neural transmission at the synapse, and psychologically, through expectations shaped by cultural beliefs.

Peter Malone, "Dreams."

CHAPTER 10

Motivation

*S*ince 1981, when an article in the *New York Times* informed the world of a new "gay cancer," knowledge about AIDS in the general population has increased tremendously. Researchers eventually discovered that heterosexuals were at risk as well. In fact, 75 percent of HIV-positive people in the world were infected through heterosexual transmission (Miller et al., 1993).

Although AIDS is a deadly, contagious disease, the risk of contracting the HIV virus is substantially diminished in people who use condoms. Thus, one would expect condom use to be nearly universal among sexually active people who are not in exclusive relationships. Remarkably, this is not the case. In one study, only 17 percent of heterosexuals with multiple sexual partners reported using condoms regularly (Catania et al., 1992), and physicians in San Francisco, a city whose gay population has been decimated by the virus, report that condom use among young gay males has returned to pre-AIDS levels (Hamilton, 1994).

The more sexual partners you have, the greater your risk of contracting AIDS. Use condoms and limit your sexual partners.

In light of all the knowledge about AIDS transmission and prevention, why do people continue to engage in unsafe sexual practices? One explanation is cognitive: People simply do not understand the risks. However, research has not consistently shown any relation between AIDS knowledge and high-risk behavior (Moatti et al., 1997; Winslow et al., 1992). For example, college students who engage in high-risk sexual behavior tend to be fully aware of the protective value of condoms and the dangers of unprotected sex with multiple partners (Lewis et al., 1997).

An alternative hypothesis is that the problem lies less in cognition than in motivation. A person who is afraid of contracting AIDS might cope with the fear by downplaying the probability that he could contract it and hence behave in ways that actually maximize his danger. For someone else, the motivation to please a partner who dislikes condoms—and thereby to avoid rejection—may supersede the goal of avoiding AIDS (Miller et al., 1993), especially since the probability of rejection may seem higher and momentarily more salient than of infection. In fact, research shows that individuals high in sensation seeking (the motivation to experience new and exciting activities) are less likely than others to practice safe sex (Stein et al., 1994).

The last few chapters have focused primarily on thought and behavior—how people learn to act as they do, how they think and remember, how they solve problems, and how conscious and unconscious processes interact to produce complex responses. An understanding of these processes explains many of the *hows* of human behavior but few of the *whys*, such as why people ignore what they know about AIDS and risk contracting a fatal infection.

This chapter addresses the whys as it explores motivation. After examining the major perspectives on motivation, we consider some of the most important motives that energize human behavior across cultures. Developing an adequate taxonomy, or system of classification, for motives is no easy task, but we follow one of the first and most successful efforts, proposed by Henry Murray (1938).

Murray distinguished biological needs from nonbiological, or "psychogenic," needs. Psychogenic needs, more commonly called *psychosocial motives*, are needs for order, dominance, achievement, autonomy, aggression, nurturance, and so forth that people find satisfying.

We first examine two major biological motives, eating and sex, and then the major psychosocial needs, focusing on the needs for relatedness and achievement. Throughout, however, we will see that human nature is not as straightforward as our attempts to describe it: The most biological of needs are shaped by culture and experience, and the most psychogenic draw on innate tendencies. As Sir Francis Bacon wisely warned, the subtlety of nature is far greater than the subtlety of any mind trying to comprehend and categorize it.

PERSPECTIVES ON MOTIVATION

The word **motivation** derives from the Latin *to move* (*movere*) and refers to the moving force that energizes behavior. Motives cannot be directly observed but are inferred from behavior. Motivation has two components: what people want to do and how strongly they want to do it. The first component refers to the *direction* in which activity is motivated, namely, which goals the person is pursuing or avoiding. The range of goals humans can be motivated to pursue is truly extraordinary, from going to the library, to parachuting out of a plane, to murdering a lover in a fit of rage. Motives also vary in their *strength*. People may have dozens of motives available to them at any given point, but they only act on those that currently "move" them.

Throughout this chapter, several basic issues repeatedly emerge. The first is the extent to which people are driven by internal needs or pulled by external goals or stimuli. Does the presence of a condom in a nearby drawer increase the likelihood of its use, or must the goal be internal to matter in a moment of passion? A second and related issue is the extent to which human motivation is rooted in biology or influenced by culture and environment. Do the motives of a Western corporate executive and a tribal chief in the Sudan differ dramatically, or did both individuals rise to their position out of similar needs for power or achievement? A third issue is the relative importance of thoughts, feelings, and arousal in motivation. Can a person simply be motivated by a thought or goal? Or must goals be connected with feeling or arousal to be motivating? In other words, what transforms a thought or daydream into an intention that directs behavior? Once again, the ways psychologists answer these questions depend on the perspectives they take.

INTERIM SUMMARY   **Motivation** refers to the moving force that energizes behavior. Two components of a motive are its aim, direction, or goal and its strength. Motives can be divided into biological needs and psychosocial needs (such as needs for dominance, power, achievement, and relatedness to others), although nature and nurture contribute to both.

EVOLUTIONARY PERSPECTIVE

In the early part of this century, psychologists assumed that humans, like other animals, had **instincts**—relatively fixed patterns of behavior produced without learning (Tinbergen, 1951). An example is the mating ritual of the ring dove,

Many animals have elaborate courting rituals that precede mating.

which must perform an elaborate, stereotyped sequence of behaviors in exactly the right manner to attract a mate. If the male does not bow and coo at the proper point in the ritual, the female will not be receptive (Lehrman, 1956). (Male humans whose dancing is less than elegant may feel some kinship with the poor ring dove.) However, most psychologists eventually abandoned instinct theory, arguing that learning, not instinct, directs human behavior.

Maximizing Inclusive Fitness

Contemporary evolutionary psychologists rarely speak of instinct in humans, but they contend that human motivational systems, like other psychological attributes, have been selected by nature for their ability to maximize reproductive success (survival and reproduction). For some motives, this is an unremarkable claim. Organisms that do not replenish their energy by eating or fail to regulate their temperature to preserve their cells do not survive and reproduce. Nature has thus designed humans and other animals with intricate systems for maintaining basic life-support processes.

Some evolutionary explanations, however, are much more controversial. As we saw in Chapter 1, evolutionary theorists have argued that evolution selects animals that maximize their inclusive fitness, which refers to their own reproductive success plus their influence on the reproductive success of genetically related individuals (Hamilton, 1964). This theory makes mathematical sense. Fifty percent of the genes of an individual who protects only his own child will be available in the next generation because his child shares half his genes. In contrast, 75 percent of the genes of someone who protects his child *plus* his niece will be present in the gene pool (one-half from his child and one-fourth from his niece). Over many generations, this difference becomes substantial. Applied to other species, such as ants, the theory of inclusive fitness has produced some stunningly accurate predictions about the way organisms behave toward kin of varying degrees of relatedness (e.g., Anderson & Ricklefs, 1995; Sundstrom et al., 1996).

Evolutionary psychologists are generally careful to distinguish the theory that evolution *favors* organisms that maximize their inclusive fitness from the assumption that organisms deliberately *seek* to maximize their inclusive fitness, as if they carry inclusive fitness calculators in their pockets. Nevertheless, some basic motivational mechanisms presumably evolved to help organisms select courses

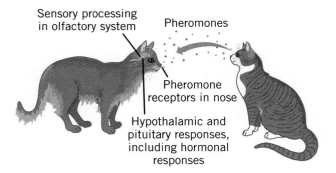

Sensory processing in olfactory system

Pheromones

Pheromone receptors in nose

Hypothalamic and pituitary responses, including hormonal responses

FIGURE 10.1
Pheromonal communication. Pheromones activate sexual and other responses much as hormones do, except that they are secreted by other animals instead of by the animal's own endocrine system.

of action that foster survival, reproduction, and the care and protection of kin. These mechanisms should guide their behavior so that their degree of investment is roughly proportional to their degree of relatedness.

So how do organisms—whether ants or humans—know who their sons, brothers, or cousins are? Recent research suggests that some species are actually endowed with chemical mechanisms (pheromones) for kin recognition. Pheromones are similar to hormones, except that they allow intercellular communication *between* rather than *within* organisms (Figure 10.1). They are typically detected by specialized neural circuits in the olfactory system (Chapter 4) and may have the same or similar effects as hormones (Sorenson, 1996).

Whether pheromonal communication leads to increased investment in close relatives in some species is unknown, but it does help members of some species avoid mating with members of other species (which wastes precious mating time) and avoid incest, which can produce genetically defective offspring and hence reduce reproductive success (Blaustein & Waldman, 1992; Wilson & Bossert, 1996). In one study, the experimenter allowed female crickets to choose where they would spend their time (Simmons, 1990). Potential male mates were not present, but the experimenter created four territories, marked with the scent (from droppings) of a male who was a full sibling, a half sibling, a cousin, or an unrelated cricket. Thus, the females could spend time in the territory of male crickets related to them by .5, .25, .125, or 0, respectively. The amount of time the females spent in each territory was inversely proportional to degree of relatedness; that is, the more distant the relation, the more time spent in the neighborhood (Figure 10.2). The mechanism for kin recognition proved to be chemical, since female crickets whose pheromone receptors were covered with wax showed no preference for unrelated males.

Humans probably do not rely on pheromones for kin recognition; however, as suggested in Chapter 1, they probably make use of other mechanisms, such as degree of familiarity, particularly from childhood. Throughout the course of much of human evolution, people who grew up together were more than likely family members, so longtime familiarity, particularly from childhood, would be a rough index of degree of kinship, if an imperfect one. And in fact, just as crickets avoid sexual contact with other crickets with the scent of family, marriage among children who grow up together in Israeli communal living arrangements, or *kibbutzim*, is almost nonexistent (Shepher, 1978).

If familiarity evolved in humans as an index of degree of relatedness, it should not only be associated with sexual avoidance but also with investment of resources in others. The mechanism has likely been partially derailed in technically advanced societies, where extended families often live at great distances from one another, unlike the small band and tribal units in which our ancestors lived. In Western cultures, in which children are reared in nuclear families, this familiarity mechanism probably fosters investment primarily in close relations but

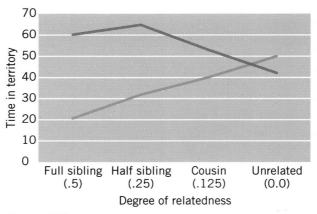

FIGURE 10.2

Pheromonal mechanisms for kin recognition in crickets. In normal females (blue line), the smaller the degree of relatedness, the more time spent in the territory of a male cricket. Females whose pheromone receptors were covered with wax (red line) did not show the same inverse relationship between degree of relatedness and amount of time in the territory. *Source:* Adapted from Simmons, 1990, p. 194.

does not activate secondary investment in cousins and other extended family members. In contrast, in much of the Third World, such as rural parts of India, Pakistan, Thailand, and Nigeria, numerous members of an extended family live in the same house and hence develop affection based on familiarity. Not surprisingly, the investment in extended kin is much stronger outside the industrialized West.

Multiple Motivational Systems

> ▶ *"Nearly all men can stand adversity, but if you want to test a man's character, give him power."*
> ABRAHAM LINCOLN

Evolutionary psychologists have begun to distinguish multiple processes necessary for reproduction and survival that could have evolved independently through natural selection (Buss, 1991, 1993, 1995; Cosmides & Tooby, 1995). The primary motivations that emerge in cross-cultural research are power and love, which is not surprising from an evolutionary perspective (Buss, 1991). Power is related to the ability to dominate potential rivals, to establish status (which females tend to find attractive in males), and to protect one's "turf." Love is related to caring for offspring, mates, kin, and friends who can be counted on "like a brother" or "like a sister." The fact that we use phrases like these to describe close friends may not be accidental.

Reproduction involves many motives. People want sex, but their choice of partners is not indiscriminate. Same-sex members of a species compete for access to desirable partners. From an evolutionary perspective, the number of poems, novels, and movies involving love triangles is no accident. At the same time, motives for sexual competition are likely to conflict with motives for friendship and coalition building (Tooby & Cosmides, 1990) that allow groups of humans (and individuals within those groups) to protect themselves and their kin. Reproduction also involves motives for parental care, which exist in nearly every animal species.

Homeostasis

Survival involves basic motives such as eating, drinking, and sleeping, which are regulated by a biological process called homeostasis. **Homeostasis** refers to the body's tendency to maintain a relatively constant state that permits cells to live and function; it literally means "same state." Since cells live within a fairly narrow range of conditions, the body monitors such variables as temperature and nutrient levels through specialized receptors. These receptors provide **feedback,** information about a variable in relation to its **set point**, or biologically optimal level (e.g., 98.6 degrees Fahrenheit for temperature). The hypothalamus and other central nervous system structures use this feedback to determine whether the nervous system needs to respond with autonomic responses (such as shivering or sweating) or voluntary responses (putting on or taking off a jacket) to prevent body heat from diverging too far in either direction from its set point (Roscoe & Myers, 1991).

The body's self-regulating systems work much like a thermostat in a house (Figure 10.3). If the thermostat is set at 70 degrees (the set point), the furnace remains off whenever the house temperature meets or exceeds 70 degrees. When the temperature falls below the set point, however, a circuit running from the system's thermometer switches on the furnace long enough to restore the temperature to 70 degrees. Once feedback from the thermostat signals that the goal is attained, the furnace is again deactivated.

INTERIM SUMMARY   According to evolutionary theory, evolution selects animals that maximize their inclusive fitness (their own reproductive success plus their influence on the reproductive success of genetically related individuals). Maximizing inclusive fitness entails a range of motives, such as selecting and competing for mates, taking care of offspring, caring about other genetically related individuals, forming useful alliances, and maintaining one's own survival through eating, drinking, keeping the body warm, and so forth. Many motives that lead to survival involve homeostatic mechanisms. **Homeostasis** refers to the body's tendency to maintain a relatively constant state that permits cells to live and function.

PSYCHODYNAMIC PERSPECTIVE

The psychodynamic perspective also emphasizes the biological basis of motivation. Humans are animals, and their motives reflect their animal heritage. According to Freud, humans, like other animals, are motivated by internal tension states, or **drives,** that build up until they are satisfied. Freud proposed two basic drives: sex and aggression. The sexual drive includes desires for love, lust, and intimacy, whereas the aggressive drive includes not only blatantly aggressive or sadistic impulses but desires to control or master other people and the environment. These drives may express themselves in subtle ways. Aggression, for example, can underlie sarcastic comments or enjoyment of violent movies.

Changing Views of Motivation: What Are Our Basic Motives?

Freud initially proposed self-preservation and sex as the two basic drives, much like the contemporary concept of reproductive success. His decision to change

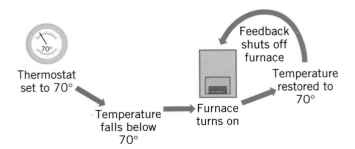

Thermostat set to 70°

Temperature falls below 70°

Furnace turns on

Feedback shuts off furnace

Temperature restored to 70°

FIGURE 10.3
A common homeostatic device is a household thermostat.

Observing the immense destruction perpetrated by allegedly civilized nations in one world war and the beginning of another, Freud changed his view of human motivation.

from self-preservation to aggression stemmed in part from living through one world war and witnessing the beginning of another. If aggression on such a massive scale kept breaking through in the most "civilized" societies, he reasoned, it must be a basic motivational force. Although few psychologists (or even psychoanalysts) now accept Freud's theory of aggression as an instinct that builds up until discharged, the ethnic warfare in Eastern Europe, the Middle East, and Africa in our own times should perhaps give us pause before we discard the notion altogether (Chapter 18).

Psychodynamic views of motivation have advanced considerably in the half century since Freud's death. In addition to sexual and aggressive desires, psychodynamic theorists now emphasize two other motives: the need for relatedness to others (independent of any sexual desires) and the need for self-esteem (feeling good about oneself) (Aron, 1996; Fairbairn, 1954; Kohut, 1977; Mitchell, 1988). Most contemporary psychodynamic theorists and clinicians also write less about drives than about wishes and fears as primary motivational units (Brenner, 1982; Holt, 1976; Westen, 1997). **Wishes** include a representation of a desired state (such as being promoted at work, beating out a rival in a competition, or having a romantic encounter) that is associated with some kind of energy, emotion, or arousal. Once a wish is achieved, it is often temporarily deactivated or becomes less intense. **Fears** are representations of undesired states that are similarly associated with feelings.

From a psychodynamic perspective, people's wishes and fears can often conflict with one another. For example, one patient wanted to leave a very unhappy relationship of many years and had fantasies about what it would be like to be free to date whomever he wanted, but he felt guilty and feared he would be a bad person if he left his wife. He eventually did move out, but he chose to live in an

"I can't explain it. I see that guy coming up the walkway and I go postal."

apartment far below his means in an undesirable area of town. Exploration of his conflicting motives led to the hypothesis that he had chosen a compromise between two motives, moving out and being free but choosing a place that would likely decrease his success at dating and more generally make him uncomfortable, allowing him to atone for his "sin."

Unconscious Motivation

Perhaps the most distinctive aspect of the psychodynamic theory of motivation is the view that motives can be unconscious. An individual may be tremendously competitive in school or sports but vehemently assert that "I'm only competitive with myself." The child of an abusive alcoholic parent may desperately want to avoid an alcoholic mate but just keeps "finding" herself in relationships with abusive alcoholic men. Until recently, the evidence for unconscious motivation was largely clinical and anecdotal. However, laboratory evidence has begun to confirm the distinction between unconscious motives and the conscious motives people can self-report (Bargh & Barndollar, 1996; Koestner et al., 1991; McClelland et al., 1989).

To study unconscious motives, researchers for many years have relied on the **Thematic Apperception Test**, or **TAT** (Morgan & Murray, 1935). The TAT consists of a series of ambiguous pictures about which subjects make up a story. Researchers then code the stories for motivational themes: Do the stories describe people seeking success or achievement? Power? Affiliation with other people? Intimacy in a close relationship? The motives a subject attributes to characters in stories are highly predictive of long-term behavioral trends. For example, in samples from both the United States and India, the number of achievement themes a person produces predicts entrepreneurial success over time (McClelland et al., 1989). Similarly, the number of intimacy themes expressed in stories at age 30 predicts the quality of marital adjustment almost 20 years later (McAdams & Vaillant, 1982).

Another way to measure motives is simply to ask people: "Is achievement important to you? Is power? Is intimacy?" Interestingly, the correlation between con-

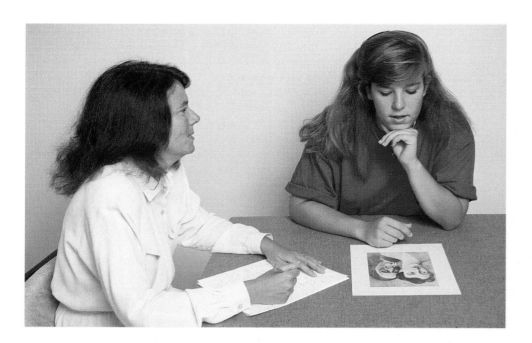

A person taking the Thematic Apperception Test (TAT)

scious, self-reported motives and the motives expressed in TAT stories is typically zero. People who demonstrate high achievement motivation in their stories, for example, do not necessarily report high motivation to achieve. Although this could simply mean that one of the two assessment methods is invalid, in fact, each type of measure predicts different kinds of behavior. For instance, achievement motivation assessed by the TAT is far more predictive of long-term entrepreneurial success than is the same motive assessed by self-report. However, if subjects in a laboratory are told they must do well on a task they are about to undertake, self-reported achievement motivation is far more predictive of effort and success than TAT-expressed motivation. How can both types of measure predict achievement behavior but not predict each other?

David McClelland and his colleagues (1989) suggest that the answer lies in a distinction similar to that between implicit and explicit memory. The TAT taps implicit (unconscious) motives, whereas self-reports reflect explicit (conscious) motives. Implicit or unconscious motivation is expressed over time without conscious effort or awareness, whereas explicit or self-reported motivation becomes activated when people focus conscious attention on tasks and goals. Conscious motives, which are more flexible and controllable, can override unconscious motives but often only temporarily, as anyone knows who has ever made—and broken—a New Year's resolution.

The two kinds of motives, implicit and explicit, appear to have different developmental antecedents. One study examined the motives implicit in stories told by 31 year olds whose mothers had been extensively interviewed about their childrearing practices 26 years earlier (McClelland & Pilon, 1983). The researchers found that several childrearing variables that predicted implicit motives did not predict self-reported motives, and vice versa. For example, rigidly scheduled feeding in infancy and severe early toilet training correlated with need for achievement assessed by the TAT but not by self-report. Thus, parental demands for mastery in early life (in this sample, largely before much language development, since the majority of children were toilet trained by 19 months) appear to shape unconscious needs for achievement but have little effect on conscious motives and values, which are shaped more by later verbal instruction.

Recent research by John Bargh and his colleagues has documented the existence of unconscious or implicit motivational processes experimentally. Bargh has extended research on automatization of cognitive processes to motives, arguing that just as well-learned cognitive procedures can become automatized and run their course without conscious awareness, so, too, can well-learned goals. Drawing upon principles of association, Bargh argues that if an individual frequently chooses the same goal in a given situation (such as competition in school), that goal will become associated with the situation. As a result, whenever that situation arises (as when a teacher or professor asks a question in class), the goal state will be activated and may guide behavior in the absence of any conscious intention (Bargh & Barndollar, 1996, p. 8).

In a series of studies, Bargh and his colleagues tested this hypothesis using priming techniques usually used to assess implicit memory (see Bargh, in press). They primed subjects with words related to either achievement (e.g., "strive") or affiliation (e.g., "friend") by having them make words out of scrambled letters. Shortly thereafter, the experimenters informed participants that the study was over but asked if they could help an experimenter down the hall who was allegedly conducting an entirely separate experiment. In this "second experiment," subjects found themselves in a situation of motivational conflict: They worked with an incompetent partner (a confederate of the experimenters) on a puzzle task and were informed that they would receive a joint score reflecting their work as a team. This meant that either they could succeed—by essentially ignoring what the partner had to say but risk making the partner feel humiliated and stupid—or they could be more interpersonally sensitive but receive a lower score. As predicted, subjects who had been primed with achievement words outperformed both subjects primed with affiliation words and control subjects. When debriefed at the end of the study, none of the subjects had any idea of the connection between the two "experiments."

INTERIM SUMMARY Freud argued that humans are motivated by two **drives**—internal tension states that build up until they are satisfied—sex and aggression. Contemporary psychodynamic theorists emphasize other needs as well, notably self-esteem and relatedness, and conceptualize motives in terms of **wishes** and **fears**. The most distinctive aspect of the psychodynamic approach is the distinction between conscious and unconscious motives, which has recently received empirical support.

BEHAVIORIST PERSPECTIVE

Although behaviorists usually prefer to avoid terms such as *motivation* that suggest a causal role for internal states, the theory of operant conditioning offers (if only implicitly) one of the clearest and most empirically supported views of motivation: Humans, like other animals, are motivated to produce behaviors rewarded by the environment and to avoid behaviors that are punished. Learning theorists recognized many years ago, however, that the internal state of the organism influences reinforcement; a pellet of food will reinforce a hungry rat but not a sated one.

Clark Hull (1943, 1952) and other behaviorists dealt with this issue through the concept of drive. All biological organisms have needs, such as those for food, drink, and sex. Unfulfilled needs lead to *drives*, defined by those theorists as states of arousal that motivate behavior. **Drive-reduction theories**, which were popular in the 1940s and 1950s, propose that motivation stems from a combination of drive and reinforcement. Deprivation of basic needs creates an unpleasant state of tension; as a result, the animal begins emitting behaviors. If the animal in this state happens to perform an action that reduces the tension (as when a hungry dog finds food on the dinner table), it will associate this behavior with drive reduction. Hence, the behavior will be reinforced (and the family may have to set another plate).

This conditioning process occurs with innate drives, such as hunger, thirst, and sex, which are called **primary drives**. Most human behaviors, however, are not directed toward fulfilling primary drives. Especially in wealthier societies, people spend much of their waking time in activities such as earning a living, playing, or studying. The motives for these behaviors are secondary, or acquired, drives. **Secondary drives** are learned through classical conditioning and other mechanisms such as modeling. An originally neutral stimulus comes to be associated with drive reduction and thus itself becomes a motivator. In many cultures, the desire for money is a secondary, or acquired, drive, which ultimately permits the satisfaction of many other primary and secondary drives.

Although drive-reduction theories explain a wide range of behaviors, they leave others unexplained. Why, for instance, do people sometimes stay up until 3:00 A.M. to finish a riveting novel, even though they are exhausted? And why are some people unable to refuse dessert, even after a filling meal? Such behaviors seem motivated more by the presence of an external stimulus or reward—called an **incentive**—than by an internal need state. Incentives control much of human behavior, as when a person not previously hungry is enticed by the smells of a bakery or an individual not previously sexually aroused becomes excited by an attractive, scantily clad body on a beach. In these cases, stimuli *activate* drive states rather than eliminate them. Drive-reduction theories also have difficulty explaining the motivation to create stimulation, encounter novelty, or avoid boredom, which is present to varying degrees in different individuals (Zuckerman, 1994) and even in other animal species (Premack, 1962).

INTERIM SUMMARY   A powerful theory of motivation implicit in the theory of operant conditioning is that humans and other animals are motivated to repeat behaviors that lead to reinforcement and avoid behaviors associated with punishment. Some behavioral theorists have proposed **drive-reduction theories**, which assert that deprivation of basic needs creates an unpleasant state of tension; if the animal produces a behavior that reduces that tension, the behavior is reinforced. Some drives, called **primary drives**, are innate, whereas others, called **secondary drives**, are learned, through their association with primary drives.

COGNITIVE PERSPECTIVE

If evolutionary and biological approaches to motivation start with nature, cognitive perspectives start with nurture. They often focus on **goals**—desired outcomes established through social learning—such as finding a mate or getting good grades (Cantor, 1990). Some theorists use the homeostat or thermostat analogy to describe the way people set goals, monitor their progress, and respond to feedback by adjusting their performance (Miller et al., 1960; Powers, 1973).

A cognitive theory of motivation used widely by organizational psychologists interested in worker motivation is **goal-setting theory** (Locke, 1996; Locke & Latham, 1990). The core proposition of goal-setting theory is that conscious goals regulate much of human behavior, especially performance on work tasks (Locke, 1991, p. 18). People establish goals, which specify desired outcomes that differ in some way from their current situation. A salesperson may set a goal of selling ten computers next month, which is ten more than she has currently sold. Goals activate old solutions that have worked before and encourage efforts to create new solutions if the old ones fail.

According to this theory, maximum job performance occurs only under certain conditions (Locke, 1991). The first condition is a discrepancy between what the person has and wants. If a salesperson's income is tied to the number of computers she sells, she will be most motivated to boost her sales figures is she is is dissatisfied with her income. Second, the person must receive continuing feedback about her progress toward achieving the goal. Without feedback, goals have minimal motivational value because people do not know whether they are succeeding or failing; consequently, they do not know when they need to work harder. Specific goals tend to be much more useful than goals like "do your best"—in sports as well as the workplace—because they allow more concrete feedback (see Smith et al., 1996). Third, the individual must believe she has the ability to attain the goal. Fourth, the person must set a high enough goal. A computer salesperson is not likely to perform optimally if she sets a goal of ten computers per month when she could reasonably expect to sell 20; when people set their goals too low, they tend to lose their motivation once they have attained the goal. Finally, the person must have a high degree of commitment to the goal. In a work setting, commitment tends to stem from the perception that a legitimate authority values the goal, from peer influence, from the goal being public, and from rewards or punishments contingent upon its attainment or nonattainment.

How might behaviorist, evolutionary, psychodynamic, and cognitive psychologists explain the self-inflicted pain people endure in order to sport a tattoo or pierced body parts? How would Maslow account for such behavior?

Other cognitive theorists employ **expectancy-value theories** to account for motivation. These theories, like theories of decision making (Chapter 7), view motivation as a joint function of the value people place on an outcome and the extent to which they believe they can attain it. Becoming a rock star may be my wildest dream, but if I know I am tone-deaf and unable to play any instrument, I am unlikely to be motivated to grow my hair and abandon a tenured faculty position (unless I hear of an opening in Hole or Green Day).

Several factors influence the value of an outcome or goal to a person (Geen, 1985). One, of course, is the extent to which the individual needs a goal object for a specific purpose; a student who is not taking organic chemistry is unlikely to buy an organic chemistry text. Another is the amount of effort required to attain the goal. Goals that are impossibly difficult or too easy to attain tend to be less attractive than moderately challenging goals.

INTERIM SUMMARY   Cognitive theorists often account for motivation in terms of **goals**, which are valued outcomes often established through social learning. According to **goal-setting theory**, conscious goals regulate much of human action. According to **expectancy-value theories,** people are motivated to perform a behavior to the extent that they value the potential outcome and believe they can attain it.

A HIERARCHY OF NEEDS

An alternative approach to motivation was advanced by Abraham Maslow (1962, 1970), who proposed a **hierarchy of needs**—from needs that take precedence when they are active because they are basic to survival, to needs that guide behavior only once the person has fulfilled needs lower down the hierarchy (Figure 10.4). At the most basic level are physiological needs, such as those for water and food. Next are safety needs, for security and protection. Having satisfied physiological and safety needs to some extent, people are motivated to pursue closeness and affiliation with other people, or what Maslow calls belongingness needs. Next in the hierarchy are esteem needs, including both self-esteem and the esteem of others. Finally, at the highest level are **self-actualization needs**, the need to express oneself and grow, or to actualize one's potential. Self-actualization needs differ from all the previous levels in that they are not *deficiency needs*; that is, they are not generated by a lack of something (food, shelter, closeness, the esteem of others). Rather, they are *growth needs*, motives to expand and develop one's skills and abilities.

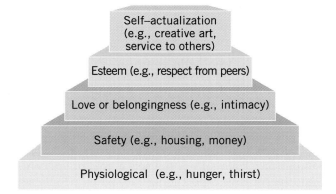

Self–actualization
(e.g., creative art,
service to others)

Esteem (e.g., respect from peers)

Love or belongingness (e.g., intimacy)

Safety (e.g., housing, money)

Physiological (e.g., hunger, thirst)

FIGURE 10.4
Maslow's hierarchy of needs.
Except for self-actualization, all
of Maslow's needs are generated by a lack of something,
such as food or shelter.

According to Maslow, people can spend their lives focused on motives at one
level and not develop beyond it. People who are starving are unlikely to think
much about art, and motives for self-expression may take a back seat in people
who desperately need the esteem of others. In contrast, self-actualized individuals are no longer preoccupied with where they will get their dinner or who will
hold them in esteem and are thus free to pursue moral, cultural, or aesthetic concerns. Maslow offered prominent examples of self-actualizers—Gandhi, Martin
Luther King, Jr., and Eleanor Roosevelt—but believed that few people reach this
level.

Maslow's theory of self-actualization has proven difficult to test (Neher,
1991). However, one organizational psychologist, Clayton Alderfer, refined and
applied aspects of Maslow's model to motivation in the workplace (Alderfer,
1972, 1989). Alderfer was a consultant to a small manufacturing company that
was having trouble motivating its workers. In interviewing the employees, he noticed that their concerns seemed to fall into three categories: material concerns
such as pay, fringe benefits, and physical conditions in the plant; relationships
with peers and supervisors; and opportunities to learn and use their skills on the
job. His observations led to **ERG theory**, which, among other things, condenses
Maslow's hierarchy to three levels of need: existence, relatedness, and growth

*To what extent does factory work
on this frozen food production line
match the motives described by
Maslow and ERG theory?*

(hence ERG). According to ERG theory, worker satisfaction and motivation vary with the extent to which a job matches a given worker's needs. Workers whose primary concern is pay are unlikely to appreciate attempts to give them more training to expand their skills. In general, however, the best job is one that provides good pay and working conditions, a chance to interact with other people, and opportunities to develop one's skills, thus satisfying the major needs. This theory offers testable hypotheses, although the empirical evidence for it remains sketchy.

INTERIM SUMMARY   Maslow proposed a **hierarchy of needs**—from needs that take precedence when they are active because they are basic to survival to needs that guide behavior only once the person has fulfilled needs lower down the hierarchy. The hierarchy includes physiological needs, safety needs, belongingness needs, esteem needs, and **self-actualization needs** (needs to express oneself and grow). **ERG theory**, which applied Maslow's model to the workplace, proposes that workers are motivated by three kinds of needs: existence, relatedness, and growth.

APPLYING THE PERSPECTIVES ON MOTIVATION

How might the different approaches to motivation explain the puzzling scenario with which this chapter began—the apparent lack of motivation for protection against HIV infection many people demonstrate in sexual situations?

From an evolutionary perspective, one answer lies in the discrepancy between the current environment and the circumstances in which our ancestors evolved. Humans have neural programs for sexual arousal that were engineered over millennia, but AIDS, like other deadly venereal diseases (notably syphilis), is a new disease in evolutionary time. Thus, these neural programs do not include momentary breaks for condoms. Distaste for condoms should be particularly high among males, who can lose erections while searching for or wearing condoms, whose reproductive success may be compromised by their application, who face less risk of AIDS transmission than females from heterosexual intercourse, and who in many cultures attract females through apparent bravery ("Nothing scares me, babe").

From a psychodynamic perspective, sex is a basic human motivation, and people are prone to self-deception and wishful thinking; the fact that people frequently deny the risk to themselves of unprotected sex should thus come as no surprise. Furthermore, any sexual encounter reflects multiple motives, and the balance of these motives can sometimes override good judgment. For example, people have casual sex for many reasons beyond biological drive. These include self-esteem motives (to feel desirable), wishes to feel physically or emotionally close to someone, and motives for dominance (the feeling of conquest). Casual, unprotected sex may also reflect blatantly self-destructive motives, as was the case with a suicidal young gay man who regularly attended bath houses at the height of media attention to the epidemic.

From a behaviorist perspective, sexual behavior, like all behavior, is under environmental control. If condom use is punishing (because it "breaks the mood," decreases genital sensations, or leads to whining by male partners), it will diminish over time. Partners who consent to unsafe sex may also be negatively reinforced for doing so by the cessation of complaining or cajoling and rewarded by praise or enjoyable sex.

From a cognitive perspective, people's expectancies about the probable outcomes of high-risk behavior can simply be wrong because of misinformation or inattention to media messages. Moreover, because HIV may not lead to symptoms of AIDS for many years, unprotected sexual contact produces no immediate feedback to deter its continued practice. In fact, the absence of consequences probably bolsters erroneously optimistic expectancies.

From Maslow's perspective, sexual behavior can satisfy both physiological and belongingness needs, so it is likely a powerful source of motivation. When the behavior is life threatening, safety needs should be activated, although the absence of any obvious negative impact of high-risk behavior for several years could provide a false sense of safety and allow other motives to be expressed in behavior. Further, as we will see in the next chapter, one mechanism for judging the strength of a need and how much to attend to it is the intensity of feeling it generates. If people do not *feel* scared, they will not focus on their safety needs.

A GLOBAL VISTA

CULTURAL INFLUENCES ON MOTIVATION

Although the major approaches to motivation take the individual as their starting point, cross-cultural work suggests that culture plays a substantial role in shaping motivation (Benedict, 1934). Some societies, such as the United States, view the personal accumulation of material wealth as a worthy end of individual endeavor and even celebrate wealthy people (achievers of the American Dream). In contrast, other cultures disapprove of accumulating material goods for oneself or one's family, considering it a crime against the community or a mark of poor character. The Kapauka Papuans of New Guinea strictly punish individual wealth (Pospisil, 1963). Disapproval or sanctions against individual consumption are common in

"I HATE THE WAY THESE COMMERCIALS EXPLOIT US KIDS AND SUBTLY IMPLANT DESIRES IN US FOR NONESSENTIAL MATERIAL GOODS."

agricultural or peasant societies, where resources tend to be limited and communalistic sentiments prevail (Foster, 1965).

Psychologist Erich Fromm (1955) argued that a culture's socioeconomic system shapes people's motivations so that they *want* to act in ways that the system *needs* them to act. In other words, for an economic system to work, it must create individuals whose personal needs match the needs of the system. A capitalist economy such as our own depends on workers and consumers to be materialistic. If advertisements for VCRs or the latest compact disk system did not motivate people, entrepreneurs would not create them, and ultimately the economy would stagnate.

In stark contrast to the materialism of contemporary capitalist societies is a ritual called the *potlatch*, practiced by some of the original peoples of the northwest coast of North America, such as the Kwakiutl and the Tlingit. The potlatch is a ceremony of song, dance, and gift giving that commemorates various occasions, such as a naming, marriage, coming of age, or death. Perhaps the most distinctive feature of the potlatch is that the host typically gives away tremendous quantities of food, possessions, and other resources to his guests. Leaders of neighboring groups may even become caught up in competitive gift-giving "contests," each trying to outshine the other with his generosity.

A potlatch among the Kwakiutl.

The potlatch apparently serves a number of functions. Among the most important are maintaining mutual ties and good relations among neighbors and redistributing wealth (Cole, 1991; Kan, 1986). These functions are probably similar to the original functions of the lavish events following such Western rituals as marriages, funerals, and bar mitzvahs.

INTERIM SUMMARY Social and cultural practices play a substantial role in shaping motives. People in technologically developed capitalist societies are much more materialistic than people in most societies in human history, where individuals often demonstrate their commitment to the community by redistributing wealth through rituals such as the potlatch.

EATING

The motivation to eat is biologically based, but the story is not that simple. Even as I write these words, I am struggling, as many readers undoubtedly do while writing term papers, to keep my mind from drifting into the refrigerator where it does not belong. In general, however, the function of eating is not to relieve anxiety, frustration, or boredom but to convert what were once the cells of other living organisms into energy. **Metabolism** refers to the processes by which the body transforms food into energy for moving muscles, maintaining body heat, operating the nervous system, and building and maintaining organ tissue.

Metabolism has two phases (Figure 10.5): absorptive and fasting. In the **absorptive phase**, the person is ingesting food. The simple carbohydrate **glucose** (sugar) is a primary source of fuel for the body and the nervous system. At the same time the digestive system is filling short-term reservoirs with glucose and more complex sugars, it is also filling long-term energy tanks located under the skin and in the abdomen: fat cells. These cells are capable of expanding enormously when reserves are high. From an evolutionary perspective, the ability to

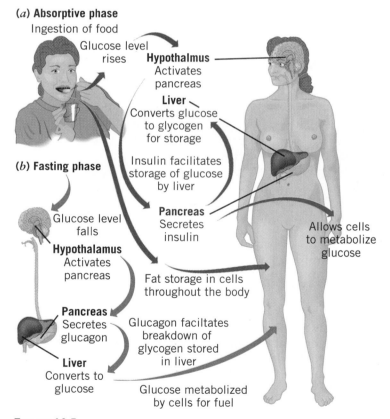

(a) Absorptive phase
Ingestion of food
Glucose level rises
Hypothalmus
Activates pancreas
Liver
Converts glucose to glycogen for storage
Insulin facilitates storage of glucose by liver
Pancreas
Secretes insulin
Allows cells to metabolize glucose

(b) Fasting phase
Glucose level falls
Hypothalamus
Activates pancreas
Pancreas
Secretes glucagon
Glucagon faciltates breakdown of glycogen stored in liver
Liver
Converts to glucose
Fat storage in cells throughout the body
Glucose metabolized by cells for fuel

FIGURE 10.5
Metabolism. During the absorptive phase (*a*), the person ingests food. The hypothalamus detects rising glucose rates in the bloodstream and activates the pancreas, which secretes insulin. Insulin allows cells to absorb and convert glucose into energy for their use. Insulin also is required for the liver to convert glucose into glycogen to provide a short-term energy reservoir. In the fasting phase (*b*), when the individual is not eating, the hypothalamus detects falling glucose levels and activates the pancreas. The pancreas now secretes glucagon, which converts the glycogen in the liver into glucose, which the cells in the body can metabolize.

HERMAN®

© 1990 Jim Unger/dist. by LaughingStock Licensing Inc.   8-9

**"I think you've had enough.
Why don't I call you a cab?"**

store fat served our ancestors well. When winter came and food was scarce, they had both extra reserves of body fuel and an extra layer of warmth. The second phase of metabolism, the **fasting phase**, occurs when a person is not eating, as the body converts its short- and long-term stores into energy.

HUNGER AND SATIETY

Eating is part of a complex homeostatic process: Energy reserves become depleted, and the person becomes hungry and eats. As the fuel tanks become full, ingestion stops, until reserves again become depleted. So how do these biological processes (nutrient depletion and restoration) become translated into a psychological motive (hunger), and how is this motive switched off?

Homeostatic Mechanisms

The hypothalamus plays a key role in homeostatic processes, and hunger is no exception. For several years, psychologists believed the "on" switch for hunger was in the lateral hypothalamus and the "off" switch, signaling satiety (being sated, or "full"), in the ventromedial hypothalamus (Figure 10.6) (Anand & Brobeck, 1951; Teitelbaum, 1961). This conclusion was based on experiments in which researchers either lesioned or electrically stimulated these two sections of the hypothalamus in experimental animals. Lesioning the lateral hypothalamus led to undereating, sometimes to the point of starvation. In contrast, destruction of the ventromedial hypothalamus led to an insatiable, obese animal (Hernandez & Hoebel, 1989; Hetherington & Ransom, 1940). Electrical stimulation of the lateral hypothalamus also produced eating even when the animal was satiated (full), whereas stimulation of the ventromedial hypothalamus inhibited eating even if the animal was starved (Wyricka, 1976). Damage to the hypothalamus in humans through tumors and infections can lead to gross obesity, which no treatment has yet been able to address (Jordaan et al., 1996).

More recent research suggests that eating behavior, like virtually every other psychological function, reflects the action of neural circuits running through mul-

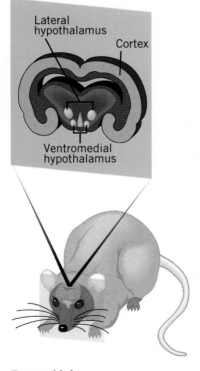

Cross section of
rat's hypothalamus

Lateral
hypothalamus

Cortex

Ventromedial
hypothalamus

FIGURE 10.6
Role of the hypothalamus in hunger. This cross section of a rat's brain shows the lateral and ventromedial hypothalamus.

Obese rat after destruction of the ventromedial hypothalamus.

tiple parts of the brain, in this case with the hypothalamus playing a central role (Sakurai et al., 1998; Winn, 1995). One contemporary hypothesis is that a more central (that is, medial, or middle) region of the hypothalamus is actually involved in monitoring the state of nutrients in the body and hence turning hunger "on" (Gerald et al., 1996), whereas the lateral hypothalamus may provide a line of communication between this region of the hypothalamus and regions of the frontal cortex that control motor behavior (such as seeking food). The role of the ventromedial hypothalamus in eating is less clear.

The Subjective Experience of Hunger   What causes the subjective experience of hunger? The intuitive answer to this question is simple: an empty stomach. A classic experiment performed in the early 1900s by W. B. Cannon and A. L. Washburn supported this notion (1912). Washburn fasted on the days of the experiment and inserted a narrow rubber tube into his esophagus. At the end of the tube was a small balloon that could be inflated in his stomach just enough to register a change in pressure when the stomach walls contracted. (Some people will do almost anything to get tenure.) Washburn's reports of hunger pangs occurred consistently toward the end of each measured contraction of the stomach.

Other findings indicate, however, that hunger is more complicated than that. People whose stomachs have been removed because of cancer nonetheless report feeling hunger (Janowitz & Grossman, 1949; Wagensteen & Carlson, 1931). The presence or absence of food in the stomach is only a rough indicator of the biological need for food because the stomach can be filled with foods or liquids that do not provide the body with energy. Dieters try to "trick" their stomachs into feeling full by eating quantities of celery and drinking diet cola, but this trick does not last very long because the body has a second, and probably more important, measure of the need to eat: the amount of glucose in the bloodstream.

The Glucostatic Theory of Hunger   The **glucostatic theory** of hunger proposes that hunger arises when glucose "thermostats" in the nervous system (or *glucostats*) detect low levels of glucose in the bloodstream (Hoebel & Teitelbaum, 1966; Mayer, 1955). Both the liver and the hypothalamus contain **glucoreceptors**, cells that monitor glucose levels (Karadi et al., 1990; Russek, 1970; Shimizu et al., 1983). When glucose levels drop, a subjective feeling of hunger arises and initiates eating.

Considerable evidence supports the glucostatic theory. In rats, injecting small amounts of glucose into the bloodstream when glucose levels begin to drop delays feeding behavior (Campfield et al., 1985). In humans, who can report how hungry they feel, hunger increases as glucose levels decrease. Figure 10.7 compares the reported sensations of hunger in two groups of well-fed subjects. The experimental group received injections of a drug that suppresses blood glucose levels, while the control group received an inert injection of salt water (that is, an injection with no significant physiological effect). Subjects whose glucose level had been artificially lowered felt hungrier than control subjects, even after a meal (Thompson & Campbell, 1977). In another study, the investigators continuously recorded participants' glucose levels, subjective ratings of hunger, and requests for food (Campfield et al., 1996). Just after momentary decreases in glucose levels, subjects tended to feel hungry and ask for food.

Satiation   The processes that terminate eating behavior are similar to those that initiate it. Sensations in the stomach and levels of nutrients in the body, especially glucose, regulate the subjective experience of satiety that causes a person or an animal to leave the table or the trough. The stomach wall has stretch receptors that send emergency messages to the brain signaling that enough is enough, but these receptors probably play less of a role than glucoreceptors in the stomach

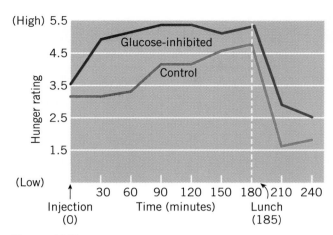

FIGURE 10.7

Hunger and glucose levels. The blue line depicts data from the experimental group, who received injections of a drug that suppresses blood-sugar levels. The red line illustrates data from the control group, who received a saline-solution injection. As the figure illustrates, subjects whose blood-sugar level had been artificially lowered (the glucose-inhibited group) felt considerably more hunger than the control group, even after a meal. *Source:* Thompson & Campbell, 1977.

and liver (Carlson, 1994). Rats will eat more when their stomachs are full of saline solution than of a high-calorie liquid, suggesting that glucoreceptors are involved in feelings of satiety as well as hunger (Angel et al., 1992; Deutsch & Gonzalez, 1980).

External Cues and Eating Behavior

Hunger is the prime motivator for eating, but external factors, such as palatability (the tastiness or appeal of food), also influence the inclination to eat. In fact, desire for a food can be motivated either by hunger or simply by its taste, and these two sources of eating motivation are mediated by different neural pathways and neurotransmitters (Berridge, 1996). Palatability plays an important role in eating even in animals not known for their gourmet tastes (Capaldi & VandenBos, 1991; Warwick et al., 1993). Rats, like humans, like variety in their diets, and as pet owners can attest, dogs and cats may grow tired of a brand of food and walk away from a delightful and nutritious bowl of horse meat or tuna innards even if they are hungry. Some taste preferences are inborn, such as the preference of human infants and baby rats for sweet tastes, while others depend on exposure and learning.

Another external factor that influences the motive to eat is the presence of other people. One study gave subjects pocket-sized cards on which they were to record both their food intake and dining companions for seven consecutive days (deCastro & Brewer, 1992). The more people present, the more subjects ate. Meals eaten with a large group of people were 75 percent larger than meals eaten alone.

INTERIM SUMMARY **Metabolism,** the processes by which the body transforms food into energy, has two phases: the **absorptive phase,** in which the person is ingesting food, and the **fasting phase,** during which the body converts its short- and long-term stores into energy. Various regions of the hypothalamus are involved in the homeostatic processes that regulate eating. According to the **glucostatic theory,** hunger arises when glucose "thermostats" in the nervous system detect low levels of glucose in the bloodstream. Hunger and satiety also reflect other processes, such as registration of other nutrients in the bloodstream, fullness of the stomach, and the presence of external cues, such as palatable food.

TABLE 10.1 WEIGHT AND OBESITY CHARACTERISTICS BY RACE AND SEX				
	MALE		**FEMALE**	
CHARACTERISTIC	**WHITE**	**BLACK**	**WHITE**	**BLACK**
Weight (lbs.)	174.5	175.6	139.9	162.5
Ideal weight (lbs.)	162.1	158.3	138.3	138.2
Pounds overweight (%)				
20 or more	34.2	41.4	22.1	49.2
50 or more	7.0	12.1	8.8	20.0
100 or more	0.4	1.4	0.6	4.1
Obesity (%)				
Moderate	16.3	27.7	18.2	46.5
Severe	6.2	12.8	5.6	20.1

Source: Rand & Kuldau, 1990, pp. 333–334.

Note: This survey collected data on a stratified random sample of 2115 U.S. adults, aged 18–96.

OBESITY

Obesity is defined as body weight 15 percent or more above the ideal for one's height and age (Metropolitan Life Insurance Co., 1984). By this criterion, about one-third of the adult population of the United States is obese, and the percentage is growing. The rates of obesity vary among different races, cultures, subcultures, and social classes. One example is shown in Table 10.1.

In industrialized countries, fatness tends to be inversely correlated with socioeconomic status; that is, people in lower social classes tend to be more obese. In developing nations, the direction of this correlation is reversed: the richer, the fatter, at least for women (Sobal & Stunkard, 1989). The situation in the developing world probably approximates the state of affairs through most of human evolution. Particularly for women, whose pregnancies could extend into times of scarcity, larger *internal* food reserves were adaptive in the face of variable *external* reserves.

Obesity places people at increased risk for a number of medical problems, such as heart disease, high blood pressure, and diabetes (Manson et al., 1990; National Research Council, 1989). The mortality rates of overweight people are up to four times higher than in people of normal weight (Foreyt, 1987; Garrison & Castelli, 1985). Many of these risks are well established (Brownell & Rodin, 1994); however, some researchers suggest they may be somewhat exaggerated, in part because health experts share negative cultural stereotypes about fat people (Garner & Wooley, 1991).

Cultural Conceptions of Weight and Obesity

Although obesity may sound like an objective phenomenon, it is to some degree culturally relative. When participants in the study shown in Table 10.1 were asked if they had a weight problem, white women complained about their weight even when they were under their ideal body weight, whereas the other groups did not. In a study of undergraduates, African-Americans, and especially African-American females, were heavier than whites, but they were more satisfied with their weight and less likely to find weight on other people (particularly women) unattractive (Harris et al., 1991). Men were more concerned about the weight of their dates than women were, but African-American men were less likely than white

CLOSE TO HOME JOHN McPHERSON

© 1992 Universal Press Syndicate

NO SMOKING

12-26

"I wish you'd renew your membership
at the health club."

men to refuse to date a woman because of her weight. Another study similarly found that white women rate heavier women (especially other white women) negatively on multiple dimensions (such as attractiveness, intelligence, and popularity), whereas African-American women do not (Hebl and Hetherton, 1998).

Contemporary North American culture is preoccupied with thinness, particularly for women. Compared to the Rubenesque view of beauty of just a few centuries ago, expressed in the art and culture of that period, the prototypes of feminine beauty portrayed in the mass media today look emaciated. The standards have even changed considerably since the 1950s, when the ideal was the voluptuous beauty of Marilyn Monroe, replete with large breasts and slightly protruding abdomen. A study of *Playboy* centerfolds and Miss America Pageant contestants found a 10 percent decrease in the ratio of weight to height in both groups from the late 1950s to the late 1970s, paralleled by a dramatic increase in the number of articles on dieting in popular women's magazines (Garner et al., 1980, cited in Hsu, 1989).

Ironically, one hypothesis links these changed standards to the women's movement: "As women have moved into previously male-dominated activities, the 'traditional' female body shape has developed negative connotations while the masculine shape has come to symbolize self-discipline and competency" (Garner & Wooley, 1991, p. 731). In fact, curvaceousness went out of fashion in both the 1920s and the 1970s–1980s, periods in which women vigorously sought political and economic equality with men (Silverstein et al., 1986). Whatever the causes, females in our society are obsessed with dieting, and the obsession begins early. At any given moment, two-thirds of high school girls report that they are trying to lose weight (Rosen & Gross, 1987). Unlike contemporary Western societies, soci-

Cultures set standards for body types that are considered attractive and unattractive. In Renoir's time, beautiful meant bountiful. Even in the 1950s and 1960s, the standard of beauty was considerably plumper than it is now. Marilyn Monroe, for example, would probably be considered chubby today — and might well have difficulty making it on television.

eties in which food is scarce tend to associate beauty with bulk, since women who are healthy and have more resources tend to be heavier (Triandis, 1994).

In Western culture, stereotypes about the obese are extremely negative (Crandall, 1994) and contribute to discrimination in education, jobs, and housing. Anti-fat attitudes are much less common not only among African Americans but in countries such as Mexico, where cultural attitudes do not link fatness with personal irresponsibility (Crandall & Martinez, 1996). Negative stereotypes about obese people in the West begin as early as kindergarten (Garner & Wooley, 1991; Hsu, 1989; Rothblum, 1992). Children who are overweight are teased and often develop both lowered self-esteem and negative expectations about the way others will treat them. These expectations and the way others behave toward them may actually lead obese people to behave less attractively. In one study testing this hypothesis, obese and nonobese women conversed on the phone with other subjects who did not know them and could not see them (Miller et al., 1991). College student raters, unaware of the subjects' weights (or even of what the study was about), then listened to the recorded conversations and rated the women on their social skills, likability, and probable physical attractiveness. Not only did the raters view the obese women more negatively on all dimensions, but the correlations between pounds overweight and each dimension were strongly negative. In other words, the heavier the subject, the less socially skilled, likable, and physically attractive she was perceived to be. Remarkably, coders seemed to be able to judge appearance from purely auditory cues.

Causes of Obesity

Obesity likely has many causes, which differ in different individuals. Both nature and nurture appear to play a role, but as with IQ, biology appears to be the more substantial contributor across individuals.

Biology and Obesity   Twin studies reveal that both body weight and the amount of fat in a person's body are highly heritable; body weight of adoptees correlates with the weight of their biological parents but not with their adoptive parents (Allison et al., 1994; Bouchard, 1989; Stunkard et al., 1986). The correlation between the amount of fat in the bodies of monozygotic twins is in the range of .72 to .83, whereas the correlation for dizygotic twins is in the range of .34 to .49 (Brook et al., 1975, summarized in Katahn & McMinn, 1990). Heritability for obesity is estimated to range from .50 to .88, which is extremely high (Borjeson, 1976). Even the amount a person eats is highly heritable: One twin study found that roughly half of differences among individuals in the amount of food they eat is attributable to genetics (De Castro, 1993).

Two physiological factors seem especially important in creating obesity, both of which show substantial heritability. The first is the number and size of fat cells in the body. Obese people have many more fat cells than average-weight individuals, and the cells they do have tend to be larger (Hirsch & Knittle, 1970). Unfortunately, fat cells that develop early in life do not disappear when a person later attempts to lose weight; they only shrink.

The second physiological factor is the body's tendency to maintain a relatively constant weight, or set point. **Set-point theory** suggests that each person has a natural weight to which his body gravitates, which is regulated by the hypothalamus. If a person starts to gain weight above the set point, his metabolism will increase; thus, even though the person consumes more calories, the body burns these more efficiently than before, making further weight gain difficult. Conversely, if the person starts to lose weight, the body compensates by slowing down metabolism, requiring fewer calories to maintain the same weight (Keesey & Corbett, 1984; Keesey & Powley, 1986; Williams & Thompson, 1993).

Studies of both humans and other animals suggest that metabolism does, in fact, rise and fall with changes in food consumption and body weight. One study examined the metabolism of obese women enrolled in a weight-loss program. Although subjects ate radically less than usual, their bodies compensated by slowing down the metabolic rate disproportionately to the decrease in caloric intake. Conversely, subjects instructed to *overeat* by 1600 calories a day for ten days in another study showed a 22 percent increase in their metabolic rate by the end of the study, making weight gain harder (Garrow & Warwick, 1978).

The implication of this homeostatic process is probably painfully clear to dieters: The more you lose, the harder losing becomes. As weight drops, so, too, does metabolic level, so that even maintaining the loss becomes difficult. Setpoint theory may explain why the long-term success rate of almost every diet ever devised—no matter how impressive its advertised short-term gains—is dismal. In the long run, the vast majority of dieters gain back every ounce of weight they took off (Garner & Wooley, 1991; Katahn & McMinn, 1990). Those who succeed in keeping it off may need to live with a metabolism rate that has slowed by about 15 percent, requiring food intake forever lower than their previous maintenance-level consumption (see Geissler et al., 1987). Despite many discouraging statistics, however, studies suggest that weight control through diet and exercise seems to be possible for a subset of people who want to lose weight, but researchers do not yet know who that subset is (Brownell & Rodin, 1994).

Environmental and Psychological Factors in Obesity Biological factors alone do not control weight. The fact that obesity rates in the United States have doubled since 1900 points to the significance of environmental influences and the possibility of reversing them (Brownell & Rodin, 1994). As noted, women of higher socioeconomic status in technologically developed countries are substantially less obese than women of lower socioeconomic status. The difference between the two groups appears to reflect diet, efforts to restrain eating, and trips to the gym (Garner & Wooley, 1991). In fact, the amount of fat a person consumes is strongly related to the amount of fat deposited in the body (Capaldi & VandenBos, 1991; Drewnowski, 1991). Exercise plays a key role in weight control (Katahn & McMinn, 1990) and is strongly linked to decreased mortality (Blair et al., 1989).

Psychological factors also likely contribute to obesity, although studies have generally led to conflicting results, in part because different people become obese for different reasons (Brownell & Wadden, 1992; Friedman & Brownell, 1995; Rodin et al., 1989). For example, if conflicts about sexuality lead some sexual-abuse survivors to gain weight (to avoid being attractive), this would not likely be detected in a broad study of obesity, since it applies only to a subset of the obese population. One frequent psychological correlate of obesity is low self-esteem (Bruch, 1970; Williams et al., 1993). The extent to which self-esteem problems are a cause or a consequence of obesity is not entirely clear; the relationship probably runs in both directions.

Another potentially important psychological variable is anxiety (Greeno & Wing, 1994). Both clinical and experimental evidence suggests that some people overeat to control anxiety (Ganley, 1989; McKenna, 1972; Slowchower, 1987). People who are morbidly obese, that is, at least 100 pounds or 100 percent over ideal body weight, are more likely than nonobese people to suffer from depressive, anxiety, and personality disorders (Black et al., 1992), although this could also in part result from, rather than cause, obesity. Another set of psychological variables that have not been explored systematically are the motivational processes that lead dieters to stay on or go off diet and exercise regimens. Exercising is strongly predictive of weight control, but only 15 percent of dieters continue their exercise regimens after reaching their goal weight (Katahn & McMinn, 1990).

EATING DISORDERS

Dieters in the United States spend as much per year on weight loss programs and products as the entire federal budget for education, training, employment, and social services combined (Garner & Wooley, 1991). The obsession with thinness in many Western industrialized countries is no doubt related to the prevalence of two eating disorders, anorexia nervosa and bulimia. These disorders are most common in young, white females and are rarely reported outside the West (Mumford, 1993; Wakeling, 1996).

In **anorexia nervosa** the individual refuses to eat (and often exercises excessively), starving herself until she is below 85 percent of her ideal body weight (e.g., a 120-pound woman who drops to 102). Anorexia is a life-threatening illness that can lead to permanent physiological changes (such as brittle bones) and death, usually through heart attack. Anorexics generally have a distorted body image, seeing themselves as fat even as they are wasting away. The disorder is about ten times more prevalent in women than in men (Hsu, 1989), and it typically begins in adolescence or the early adult years. Some variant of the disorder appears to have existed for at least seven centuries—mostly in the form of "holy fasting" to escape the flesh in the name of God—and clear cases were described in the medical literature in the nineteenth century; however, the incidence appears to have skyrocketed in the late twentieth century (Bell, 1985; Bemporad, 1996; Bynum, 1987). The disorder only emerges in cultures and historical periods of relative affluence; people who are starving never develop anorexia (Bemporad, 1996). The causes of anorexia are still poorly understood, and the outcome of treatment ranges from complete cure to complete failure.

Anorexics are often bright, talented perfectionists who are preoccupied with feeling in control (Bruch, 1973; Casper et al., 1992). Controlling food intake seems to be a way of maintaining control in general, particularly over impulses (Strauss & Ryan, 1987). Psychotherapists who work with anorexic females commonly report that a wish to avoid becoming a physically mature woman often underlies anorexic symptoms. In this objective, anorexics are successful: Severely restricted food intake can stop the development of secondary sex characteristics such as breasts, halt menstruation, and make the body look like a prepubescent girl's. By restricting food intake, anorexics may be triggering mechanisms that evolved to prevent pregnancy and perhaps to discourage sexual interest from males during famine, when food was scarce and reproduction was secondary to survival.

Bulimia is characterized by a binge-and-purge syndrome; the person gorges on food (typically massive amounts of carbohydrates such as bags of Oreos or potato chips) and then either induces vomiting or uses laxatives (purging). The typical result is a feeling of relief, but it is often accompanied by depression and a sense of being out of control. Like anorexia, bulimia is almost exclusively a female disorder; some 90 percent of reported cases are female (Halmi et al., 1977; Pyle et al., 1983). About 3 to 5 percent of the female population has bulimia (Hoek, 1993; Kendler et al., 1991).

Unlike anorexics, bulimics are not characterized by any particular or consistent set of personality traits (Keel, 1997; Striegel-Moore et al., 1986), although depression, impulsivity, low self-esteem, poor coping skills, alcoholism, and distorted body image are more common in bulimic patients than their nonbulimic peers (Hinz & Williamson, 1987; Striegel-Moore et al., 1986). Some research suggests that bulimia may be related genetically to depression and anxiety, sharing a common problem with serotonin regulation (Brewerton, 1995). Bulimic symptoms can sometimes be reduced by medications designed for the treatment of depression and anxiety (Bulik et al., 1996; Jimmerson et al., 1996; Kendler et al., 1991).

INTERIM SUMMARY   Obesity—having a body weight more than 15 percent above the ideal for one's height and age—is highly prevalent in some countries, particularly the United States. Attitudes about weight vary considerably by culture, class, ethnic group, and level of affluence of a society. The causes of obesity lie in both nature and nurture: Differences among individuals in body fat are highly heritable, although dietary factors and exercise can also strongly influence weight. **Set-point theory** suggests that lost weight is difficult to maintain because of homeostatic processes that keep body fat in some relatively narrowly specified goal range. Two eating disorders are **anorexia nervosa**, in which the individual drops below 85 percent of ideal body weight because of refusal to eat, and **bulimia**, in which the person binges and then purges.

SEXUAL MOTIVATION

Like hunger, sex is a universal drive based in biology, but its expression varies considerably from culture to culture and from person to person. In fact, sexual motivation is even more variable than hunger. Most people eat two or three meals a day, whereas sexual appetites defy generalizations. Sexual behavior is driven as much by fantasies as by hormones; indeed, the primary sexual organ in humans is arguably not the genitals but the brain.

Although psychoanalysis broke down many of the Victorian taboos against discussing sexuality, sex did not become a respectable area of scientific research until Alfred Kinsey and his colleagues published two massive volumes on the sexual behavior of the human male and female (Kinsey et al., 1948, 1953). Many of Kinsey's findings, based on interviews with thousands of adults, provoked shock and outrage. For instance, some 37 percent of males and 13 percent of women reported having engaged in homosexual activity at some time in their lives. More recent research finds slightly lower rates of male homosexual activity but otherwise paints a similar picture; rates of lesbian contact remain unchanged (Seidman & Reider, 1994). The average sexually active person reports having intercourse between one and three times a week and becomes sexually active between ages 17 and 19 (although many start earlier or later).

Since the time of the Kinsey report, and especially since the sexual revolution of the 1960s and 1970s, sexual attitudes and practices have become much more liberal. For example, in a recent study that used the original Kinsey data for comparison, both white and black women reported earlier age at first intercourse, a wider range of sexual practices, a larger number of sexual partners, and reduced likelihood of marrying their first lover (Wyatt et al., 1988a,b).

THE SEXUAL RESPONSE CYCLE

After Kinsey, the next quantum leap forward in the scientific study of sex was William Masters and Virginia Johnson's book, *Human Sexual Response* (1966). Masters and Johnson studied the physiological changes that take place during sexual activity by observing several hundred women and men in the laboratory. Their best known finding is that similar physiological changes take place in both women and men and follow a general pattern that Masters and Johnson called the **sexual response cycle** (Figure 10.8).

The sexual response cycle begins with a phase of **excitement**, characterized by increased muscle tension, engorgement of blood vessels in the genitals causing erection of the penis and lubrication of the vagina, and often a skin flush. Maximum arousal occurs during the second, or **plateau**, phase. During this stage, heart rate, respiration, muscle tension, and blood pressure reach their peak. The third phase, **orgasm**, is characterized by vaginal contractions in females and expulsion

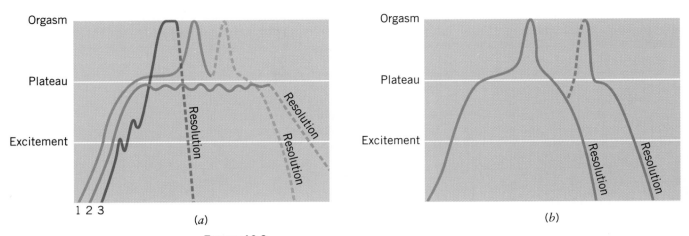

FIGURE 10.8

Sexual response cycles. Part (*a*) depicts the variations of sensation in women's sexual response. Part (*b*) illustrates the typical male sexual response cycle. The two are practically indistinguishable, except for the greater variability in women's experience. *Source:* Masters & Johnson, 1966, p. 5.

of semen in males. During the fourth phase, **resolution**, the person's physiological and psychological functioning gradually returns to normal.

The subjective experience of orgasm is very similar in men and women. When given written descriptions of orgasms, psychologists, medical students, and gynecologists are unable to distinguish men's from women's if not told the writer's gender (Vance & Wagner, 1976). However, the female sexual response cycle does seem to be more variable. Women describe a few different types of orgasm, from mild pulsations to a sharp climax to repeated sensations of orgasm (Bardwick, 1971). In addition, many women do not reach orgasm with every sexual encounter (Table 10.2), but they do report a sense of sexual release even without experiencing orgasm (Butler, 1976). Women are capable of experiencing multiple orgasms, although contrary to popular myths and male fantasies, not always or primarily by sexual intercourse (Darling et al., 1991).

NATURE AND NURTURE IN SEXUAL MOTIVATION

In many animal species, females and males are genetically programmed to follow very specific, stereotyped mating rituals, with attraction and mating behavior

TABLE 10.2   PERCENTAGE OF WOMEN REPORTING ATTAINING ORGASM FROM SEXUAL RELATIONS

FREQUENCY ACHIEVING ORGASM	AGE 29 AND UNDER	AGE 30 AND OVER	TOTAL
Never	10	7	9
Less than 50% of the time	28	21	25
More than 50% of the time but not always	59	48	52
Always	3	24	14

Source: Butler, 1976, p. 42.

Human sexuality differs substantially from sexuality in other animal species—or does it?

often controlled by pheromones. In the American cockroach, pheromone detection leads the male to touch its antennae to the female's antennae, spread its wings, and turn 180 degrees in a courtship dance (Seelinger & Schuderer, 1985). Even in species less reliant on pheromonal communication, mating behavior is often rigidly instinctive. Humans do not have the same kinds of genetically based mating rituals or mating seasons as other animals. However, one need only think of the plumage displayed by both sexes at a fraternity mixer, scents with names like "Passion" and "Musk," and the simple fact that most humans choose to mate only with members of their own species to recognize the biological influences on human dating and mating.

Biology and Sexual Motivation

Much of sexual behavior in humans and other animals is under hormonal control. Hormones have two effects on the nervous system and behavior: organizational and activational.

Organizational Effects **Organizational effects** influence the circuitry, or "organization," of the brain. In humans, these effects occur prenatally. All human fetuses begin female and develop into females unless male hormones called androgens are present. Androgens and other substances initiate the development of male genitalia, reproductive systems, and neural circuitry. In rodents, the organizational effects of hormones continue postnatally; thus, psychologists can study these effects by surgically removing the testes in males (castration) or the ovaries in females (ovariectomy). Male rats castrated at birth become sexually receptive to males if given female hormones in adulthood, manifesting the characteristic female mating behavior of hunching over and exposing the hindquarters (Blaustein & Olster, 1989; Edwards & Einhorn, 1986).

Although researchers cannot similarly experiment on humans, certain natural "experiments" provide insight into the organizational effects of hormones on be-

Are most males innately wired to find the female form appealing, or is such attraction primarily learned behavior?

havior and sexual orientation (Money, 1987; Money & Ehrhardt, 1972; Money et al., 1984). In **adrenogenital syndrome**, the adrenal glands secrete too much androgen, which masculinizes the genitals in females, producing an enlarged clitoris and labia that may resemble a scrotum. Among a sample of women with this very rare disorder who would discuss their sexual orientation, roughly half reported that they were homosexual or bisexual (Money et al., 1984).

In **androgen insensitivity syndrome**, androgens are secreted in utero, but a genetic defect leads to an absence of androgen receptors. Thus, even though the hormone is released, the body responds as if no androgen is present. As a result, a genetic male develops female genitalia (and will be reared as a girl, usually leading a perfectly normal life except for sterility). Interestingly, people with this disorder, who are by all outward appearances female, are rarely attracted to other females, even though they have testes instead of ovaries. (Their testicles are not externally visible.) Attraction to females among humans may thus require masculinization of the brain in utero.

Activational Effects   Hormones also have **activational effects**; that is, once the brain circuitry is in place, hormones activate these circuits, leading to psychobiological changes such as the development of secondary sex characteristics (e.g., breasts in adolescent females and facial hair in males). In males, hormones produce fluctuations in sexual arousal. Studies have shown a direct association between levels of testosterone in the bloodstream and sexual activity, desire, and arousal in men (Schiavi et al., 1991; Udry et al., 1985). One study demonstrated the relationship experimentally by administering doses of testosterone to adult males (Alexander et al., 1997). During the period in which their testosterone levels were chemically inflated, the men reported more sexual desire and enjoyment when presented with erotic auditory stimulation. They also showed increased attention to sexual words presented in the unattended channel in a dichotic listening task. The data are much less clear for women. Some women experience greater arousal at particular points in the menstrual cycle, but how much this reflects the influence of biology, culture, or personal feelings about sexuality and menstruation is unclear (see Hedricks, 1994; Regan, 1996; Slob et al., 1996).

Culture and Sexual Behavior

Although biology plays an important role in sexual motivation, anthropological studies show enormous cultural diversity in both the ways people carry out sexual acts and the types of behaviors they consider acceptable (Davis & Whitten, 1987). Among the Basongye people of the Congo, for instance, the conventional position for intercourse is for partners to lie facing each other with the woman on her left side and the man on his right; the woman lifts her right leg to allow the man to enter (Merriam, 1971). In many parts of Australia, Melanesia, and India, the woman typically lies on her back as the man squats between her legs (Gebhard, 1971), whereas in Western culture the male lying prone on top of the female is more typical. Cultures also differ in their conceptions of male and female sexuality; some, such as our own, view men as having greater sexual needs, whereas others believe just the opposite (Gordon & Shankweiler, 1971; Griffitt, 1987; Scully & Bart, 1973).

INTERIM SUMMARY   Sexual motivation and behavior are highly variable across cultures and individuals. Masters and Johnson discovered a common pattern of physiological changes that takes place in both women and men during sex called the **sexual response cycle.** Hormones influence sexual behavior through both **organizational effects**, which influence the circuitry, or "organization," of the brain, and **activational effects**, in which hormones activate those circuits.

SEXUAL ORIENTATION

Sexual orientation refers to the direction of a person's enduring sexual attraction: to members of the same sex, the opposite sex, or both. Determining a person's sexual orientation is not as easy as it may seem. Many people report having occasional homosexual fantasies or encounters even though they are not homosexual. Stigma, discrimination, religious values, and violence directed against homosexuals lead some people whose sexual motives and fantasies are primarily homosexual to behave heterosexually or to abstain from sex, to deny their homosexuality to themselves, or to take on the trappings of a heterosexual life-style such as marriage to a member of the opposite sex.

Prevalence of Homosexuality   An exclusive homosexual orientation is rare among animals, but homosexual behaviors occur frequently among many species, from lizards to chimpanzees (Ellis & Ames, 1987; Money, 1987; Srivastava et al., 1991). The incidence of homosexuality varies substantially among human cultures, largely reflecting cultural attitudes (Herdt, 1997). In some parts of the world, homosexuality is reportedly rare (Marshall, 1971). In contrast, in seventeenth-century Japan, homosexual liaisons among samurai warriors were common (Adams, 1985), as they were among educated men in ancient Greece. In a large part of the world, stretching from Sumatra throughout Melanesia, males almost universally participate in homosexual activities several years before they reach marriageable age (Herdt, 1984, 1997; Money & Ehrhardt, 1972). Yet even in some of these cultures, in which homosexual activity is normative during a particular time in life, the concept of homosexuality as a permanent state does not exist (Herdt, 1997).

In contemporary Western societies, approximately 2 to 7 percent of men and 1 percent of women consider themselves homosexual, although the numbers vary depending on how researchers phrase the questions (see Ellis & Ames, 1987; Pillard et al., 1981). Until relatively recently, both laypeople and the psychiatric community considered homosexuality a disorder; in fact, the official diagnostic manual of the American Psychiatric Association classified it as a disorder until 1973. People harbor many misperceptions about homosexuality, such as the idea that homosexuals are unfit to teach because they will invariably molest children. In fact, homosexuals are no more likely to be child molesters than are heterosexuals. Psychologist John Money (1987), who has conducted some of the best-known research on homosexuality (and on sexuality in general), points out that one of the most pervasive misconceptions is the notion that homosexuality is a sexual *preference*, which implies voluntary choice. Money argues that people no more choose their sexual orientation than they select their native language or decide to be right-handed.

Early Markers of Homosexual Orientation   An accumulating body of research demonstrates that children who prefer to dress or act in ways typically associated with the opposite sex are more likely to become homosexual than other children; this is especially true in males (Bailey, 1995). In fact, the best predictor of male homosexuality in adulthood is the presence in childhood of marked behavioral characteristics of the opposite sex, sometimes called "sissy" behavior (Bell et al., 1981; Green, 1987). Although this pattern applies only to a subset of homosexual men, and cross-gender behavior is present in some boys who do not become homosexual, it is a strong predictor nonetheless. Consider an example described in an interview with the mother of an eight-year-old boy (Green, 1987, pp. 2–3):

Mother: He acts like a sissy. He has expressed the wish to be a girl. He doesn't play with boys. He's afraid of boys, because he's afraid to play boys'

TABLE 10.3   CHILDHOOD CROSS-GENDER BEHAVIOR OF HOMOSEXUAL AND HETEROSEXUAL FEMALES IN FOUR CULTURES

BEHAVIOR	BRAZIL	PERU	PHILIPPINES	UNITED STATES	TOTAL SAMPLE
Interest in boys' toys					
Heterosexual (% "yes")	39.3	39.5	24.4	64.5	47.8
Homosexual (% "yes")	75.4	83.3	87.9	91.9	85.1
Interest in girls' toys					
Heterosexual	78.7	93.6	96.9	86.2	87.3
Homosexual	50.8	51.2	42.3	40.4	46.9
Regarded as "tomboy"					
Heterosexual	1.6	8.5	9.8	39.1	20.1
Homosexual	23.0	16.7	27.3	77.9	43.7
Dressed in men's clothes or pretended with pipes, shaving cream, etc.					
Heterosexual	16.4	4.5	24.4	15.5	15.2
Homosexual	42.6	38.1	75.8	44.2	47.3

Source: Adapted from Whitam & Mathy, 1991.

Note: Being a tomboy as a child is much more common in heterosexual girls in the United States than in the other countries sampled, where it is a stronger predictor of later homosexuality.

games. He used to like to dress in girls' clothing. He would still like to, only we have absolutely put our foot down. And he talks like a girl, sometimes walks like a girl, acts like a girl.

Interviewer: What was the very earliest thing that you noticed?

Mother: Wanting to put on a blouse of mine, a pink and white blouse which if he'd put it on it would fit him like a dress. And he was very excited about the whole thing, and leaped around and danced around the room. I didn't like it and I just told him to take it off and I put it away. He kept asking for it.

Interviewer: You mentioned that he's expressed the wish to be a girl. Has he ever said, "I am a girl"?

Mother: Playing in front of the mirror, he'll undress for bed, and he's standing in front of the mirror and he took his penis and he folded it under, and he said, "Look, Mommy, I'm a girl."

A cross-cultural study reported the same finding in females: The distinguishing characteristic between homosexual and heterosexual females in Brazil, Peru, the Philippines, and the United States was cross-gender childhood behavior (Whitam & Mathy, 1991). Lesbians in all four cultures were more interested in "boy things" and less interested in "girl things" as defined by their cultures than were their heterosexual peers (Table 10.3).

FROM MIND TO BRAIN

THE BIOLOGY OF MALE HOMOSEXUALITY

If sexual orientation is not a matter of conscious choice, what are its causes? Homosexuality is probably the end result of many causes, some environmental and some biological; however, most environmental hypotheses (such as absent or weak fathers and dominant mothers) have received little empirical support (see Bell et al., 1981; Blanchard & Zucker, 1994; Freud, 1922; Friedman & Stern, 1980; Gagnon & Simon, 1973; Lewes, 1988). Researchers who emphasize the nature side of the nature-nurture continuum have had more success, particularly in explaining male homosexuality. The causes of female homosexuality have received much less attention, although a first study has now appeared documenting a physiological difference between homosexual and heterosexual women in a pattern of functioning of the ear that typically distinguishes males from females (McFadden & Pasanen, 1998).

Do Homosexual and Heterosexual Males Differ in their Neurobiology?

One line of intriguing research suggests a possible biochemical factor in sexual orientation in males (Gladue et al., 1984). In one study, homosexual men, heterosexual men, and heterosexual women received injections of an estrogen preparation called Premarin. Premarin is known to increase concentrations of luteinizing hormone (LH) in women but not in men; LH is responsible for, among other things, stimulating the ovaries in women and producing testosterone in men. As one would expect, Premarin injections increased concentrations of LH in women but not in heterosexual men. The response of homosexual male subjects, however, was intermediate between the two, suggesting some hormonal similarity between homosexual men and heterosexual women (Figure 10.9).

Another study found differences in the neuroanatomy of homosexual and heterosexual men (LeVay, 1991). Based on research with nonhuman primates, the investigator hypothesized that two specific nuclei (sets of neurons) in the anterior hypothalamus (the front portion) would be larger in individuals who are sexually attracted to women than in individuals attracted to men. He compared the brains of homosexual men (who died of AIDS complications) with men and women presumed to be heterosexual, and found that one of the two nuclei of interest was twice as large in heterosexual men as in women and homosexual men.

A recent study compared the EEG patterns of heterosexual and homosexual men and women while undergoing a mental rotation task (on which men usually excel relative to women) and a verbal task (on which women usually outperform men). Straight and lesbian women did not differ substantially from each other on either task. However, gay men's EEG patterns looked more like those of heterosexual women than heterosexual men on the mental rotation task (Wegesin, 1998).

Explanations

What accounts for physiological differences between homosexuals and heterosexuals? Two biological theories have received attention, one focusing on prenatal maternal stress, the other on genetics. The maternal stress theory stems from the experimental observation that stress during pregnancy in rats leads to more feminine and less masculine sexual behavior, apparently because it interferes with androgenization (Ward, 1984). One researcher studied human males born in Germany over the 20-year period from 1934 to 1953, a time of considerable stress (Dorner et al., 1980). He found a much higher proportion of homosexual males born during World War II and the few years directly after the war than in other years of the study (Dorner et

FIGURE 10.9

Hormonal response in male homosexuals. This figure depicts the changes in luteinizing hormone (LH) in response to injections of Premarin in homosexual men, heterosexual men, and heterosexual women. Heterosexual men and women showed very different hormonal responses. The responses of homosexual males, however, were intermediate between the heterosexual men and women. *Source:* Gladue et al., 1984, p. 1496.

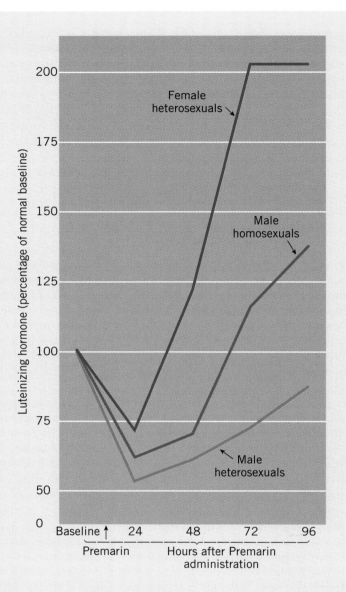

al., 1980). A second study asked homosexual, bisexual, and heterosexual men to report on stresses (such as a death in the family or a divorce) that their mothers experienced while pregnant. Less than 10 percent of mothers of heterosexual sons were reported to have experienced moderate to severe levels of stress, in contrast with two-thirds of the mothers of homosexuals; the bisexual group was intermediate (Dorner et al., 1983).

Again, these two studies are suggestive, but neither can rule out alternative explanations. For example, the mothers of homosexuals may have been generally more stress prone and hence may have interacted differently with their children, or these mothers may have differed genetically in other ways from mothers of heterosexuals. Subsequent research in which mothers directly reported on their stress levels while pregnant has not supported the theory (Bailey et al., 1991).

A second explanation is genetic. Several studies have found a higher incidence of homosexuality among relatives of male homosexuals than in the general population (Buhrich et al., 1991). Whereas rates of homosexuality in the general population are estimated at 2 to 7 percent, nearly 25 percent of brothers of male homosexuals in one study were reportedly homosexual (Pillard et al., 1981, 1982). The most definitive study to date found concordance rates for homosexuality much higher among identical than fraternal twins and adoptive brothers. In other words, if one identical twin is homosexual, the other has a high probability of being homosexual (Bailey & Pillard, 1991). Concordance for homosexuality was 52 percent for monozygotic twins, 22 percent for dizygotic twins, and 11 percent for adoptive brothers, with heritability estimated somewhere between .31 and .74. The same research group conducted one of the only studies of heritability of homosexuality in women and found a similar pattern of results. Concordance for homosexuality was 48 percent for monozygotic twins, 16 percent for dizygotic twins, and 6 percent for adoptive sisters, with heritability estimates ranging from .27 to .76 (Bailey et al., 1993).

Another large study of heterosexual and homosexual men over 40 used legal records to ascertain whether homosexual men would have more unmarried male siblings than heterosexuals (Blanchard & Bogaert, 1997). Since the vast majority of heterosexual men are married by that age, the investigators reasoned that marital status might prove a useful proxy for homosexuality. As predicted, homosexual men had significantly more unmarried brothers but not sisters. (As in other research, the investigators also found that homosexual men tend to have more older brothers than heterosexuals, although the explanation for this is not entirely clear.)

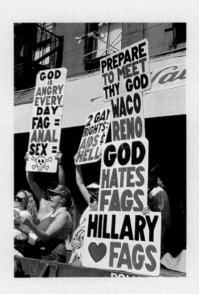

If homosexuality is substantially influenced by genetics, attacking homosexuality as immoral or unnatural would be as indefensible as persecuting people with blue eyes.

Recently, researchers have begun to investigate the genetics of homosexuality experimentally. One team of investigators *created* male homosexuality in fruitflies in the laboratory using techniques that insert genetic material in ways that cause mutations (Yamamoto et al., 1996). These "gay" fruitflies all showed mutations at precisely the same chromosomal locus that has been shown to distinguish heterosexual fruitflies from a bisexual breed. Although generalizations from fruitflies to humans obviously require caution, the fact that genetic alteration in any organism can predictably alter sexual orientation is clearly of importance.

Can we conclude, then, that homosexuality is genetic? Not yet. First, some research groups studying twins have failed to find convincing genetic effects (Eckert et al., 1986; King & McDonald, 1992). Second, even if heritability is 50 percent, that leaves the rest of the variance in sexual orientation explained by other factors. Nevertheless, if sexual orientation is in part a preference exercised by our genes instead of our souls, this would have enormous implications for public policy and attitudes toward homosexuals. No humane person could disparage an individual for his sexual orientation, any more than one would discriminate against someone who is brown eyed or near sighted.

SEXUAL DYSFUNCTIONS

Sexual dysfunctions are problems that impair sexual functioning. The most common are inhibited orgasm in women, premature ejaculation in men, and inhibited sexual excitement or desire in both men and women (Metz et al., 1997; Nathan, 1986; Rosen, 1993). Sexual problems are quite common, especially in mild forms and for periods in a couple's relationship (Spector & Carey, 1990). The widespread nature of sexual dysfunction was underscored by reaction to the recent release of the male erectile "wonder drug," Viagra, which sent millions of men scurrying to their doctors' offices and even led to a black market for the drug in countries where it was not yet available!

Sexual dysfunctions can result from both physiological and psychological causes (Metz et al., 1997; Rosen, 1996). For example, excessive alcohol use, fatigue, hypertension, and kidney disease all contribute to male difficulties in achieving erection (Shrom et al., 1979). In most cases, however, the causes are primarily psychological, with anxiety a prime culprit (see Patterson & O'Gorman, 1989; Tugrul & Kabakci, 1997). People often fear they will not perform adequately (Masters & Johnson, 1970), are self-critical or perfectionistic (DiBartolo & Barlow, 1996), or are anxious about losing control during intercourse (Kaplan, 1981). Others may not feel comfortable sharing intimacy with another person (Beck & Barlow, 1984) or may have developed anxiety-provoking fantasies, feelings, or ideas about sexuality during childhood. Dissatisfaction with a mate in general also can translate into difficulty in bed (Spence, 1997).

INTERIM SUMMARY   **Sexual orientation** refers to the direction of a person's enduring sexual attraction to members of the same or opposite sex. Attitudes toward homosexuality differ substantially across cultures. In the West, between 2 and 7 percent of men and 1 percent of women report a primary homosexual orientation. The causes of homosexuality are likely numerous, but particularly for males, mounting evidence suggests that homosexuality is highly heritable and does not likely reflect a "choice." **Sexual dysfunctions** are problems that impair sexual functioning. Although biological factors sometimes contribute, most sexual dysfunctions result from anxiety.

PSYCHOSOCIAL MOTIVES

Unlike sex, **psychosocial motives** (personal and interpersonal motives for achievement, power, self-esteem, affiliation, intimacy, and the like) are less obviously tied to biology, but they are not independent of it either. Human infants, like the young of other species, have an inborn tendency to form intense social bonds with their primary caretakers, and toddlers spontaneously exhibit joy at their achievements and frustration at their failures. Once again, nature and nurture jointly weave even the most socially constructed fabrics.

Two major clusters of goals pursued cross-culturally are **relatedness** (sometimes called "communion") and **agency** (achievement, autonomy, mastery, power, and other self-oriented goals) (Bakan, 1966; McAdams, 1996).

NEEDS FOR RELATEDNESS

Humans have a number of interpersonal needs (Baumeister & Leary, 1995; Weiss, 1986). The earliest to arise in children are related to attachment (Chapter 14). **Attachment motivation** refers to the desire for physical and psychological proximity (closeness) to another person, so that the individual experiences comfort and pleasure in the other person's presence. Attachment motives form the basis for many aspects of adult love (Hazan & Shaver, 1987, 1994; Main et al., 1985). A related need common among adults and older children in some cultures is **intimacy**, a special kind of closeness characterized by self-disclosure, warmth, and mutual caring (McAdams, 1986; McAdams et al., 1996; Reis & Shaver, 1988). Intimacy needs are often satisfied in adult attachment relationships and deep friendships.

Another social motive is the need for **affiliation**, or interaction with friends or acquaintances. Most people need to be with and communicate with other people, whether that means obtaining support after an upsetting experience, sharing good news, or playing sports together. Unfulfilled affiliative needs, like frustrated desires for attachment or intimacy, lead to loneliness. In one survey of college students, 26 percent reported feeling lonely within the previous two weeks (Stokes, 1985). Individuals differ in the extent to which they seek intimate versus affiliative relationships. Some people have many friends and acquaintances but have little need for intimacy, whereas others desire one or two intimate friends and have little need for a broad social network (Reis & Shaver, 1988; Weiss, 1986).

Social relationships, particularly with people in whom one can confide, are important for both physical and mental health. For example, women who report having at least one confidante are 10 times less likely to suffer depression following a stressful event than women who do not have someone in whom they can confide (Brown et al., 1975). Lack of supportive relationships is a risk factor for mortality as well (Farmer et al., 1996; House et al., 1988).

INTERIM SUMMARY Two clusters of **psychosocial needs** pursued cross-culturally are **relatedness** and **agency** (achievement, autonomy, mastery, power, and other self-oriented goals). Needs for relatedness include attachment, intimacy, and affiliation. Although relatedness needs are psychosocial, the failure to fulfill them can have powerful biological effects, such as sickness or mortality.

ACHIEVEMENT AND OTHER AGENCY MOTIVES

Motives for power, competence, achievement, autonomy, and self-esteem form another cluster of motives common to humans throughout the world. The psychoanalyst Robert White (1959) argued that humans have innate impulses to deal competently and effectively with their surroundings. Indeed, as early as the second year of life, infants seem to desire to be competent and effective, even when they are not rewarded by their parents (Kagan et al., 1978). This can

Pride at mastery appears to emerge spontaneously in the second year of life.

The need for achievement was undoubtedly a contributing motive to the success of novelist Toni Morrison, computer magnate Bill Gates, and actress Jodie Foster.

be clearly seen in the persistence and pride shown by young children as they learn to walk.

Some theorists suggest that humans have a related motive to know and understand the world around them (Epstein, 1990). Pleasure in knowing and displeasure in feeling uncertain may have evolved as mechanisms that foster exploration of the environment. Another self-oriented motive is self-esteem. Theorists of many theoretical persuasions—psychodynamic (Kohut, 1971), humanistic (Rogers, 1959), and cognitive-social (Higgins, 1990), among others—view self-esteem motivation—the need to view oneself in a positive light—as a fundamental motivator of behavior (Chapter 17).

Need for Achievement

The **need for achievement**—to do well, to succeed, and to avoid failure—is the best researched psychosocial motive. This is not surprising in view of our own culture's emphasis on personal achievement in school, sports, careers, and practically every domain in which our actions can be described in terms of success and failure. In general, people high in achievement motivation tend to choose moderately difficult tasks (those with about a 50/50 chance of success) over very easy or very difficult tasks (Atkinson, 1977; Slade & Rush, 1991). They enjoy being challenged and take pleasure in accomplishing a difficult task but are often motivated to avoid failure. In one study, subjects played a ring-toss game and were free to choose their own distance from the target (Atkinson & Litwin, 1960). Those who scored high in achievement motivation selected distances that were challenging but not impossible. In contrast, subjects who scored low in achievement motivation and had a high fear of failure stood either very close to the target or impossibly far, which guaranteed either success or a good excuse for failing.

How do experimental findings such as these translate into everyday behaviors? People with a high need for achievement tend to work more persistently than others to achieve a goal, and they take more pride in their accomplishments when they succeed (Atkinson, 1977). Not surprisingly, they are consequently more likely to succeed. They also tend to attribute their past successes to their abilities and their past failures to forces beyond their control, which increases confidence and persistence in the face of adverse feedback (Dweck, 1975; Meece et al., 1990; Weiner, 1974). A student with high achievement motivation is likely to select a major that suits his abilities, commit to a study schedule that is rigorous but not impossible, and work hard to succeed within those limits.

The consequences of achievement motivation extend far beyond the classroom or the laboratory. In an economically depressed area of India, where government programs had been ineffective in raising the standard of living, psychologist David McClelland undertook an interesting experiment. He taught local businessmen to fantasize about high achievement and to problem-solve ways to succeed (McClelland, 1978; McClelland & Winter, 1969). Over time, they began new businesses and employed new workers at a much higher rate than businessmen in a comparable town in the same region. In Western cultures, achievement motivation also predicts occupational success, such as how well a car salesperson can move cars off the lot (Barling et al., 1996).

Components of Achievement Motivation

As with other motives, people do not express achievement motivation in every domain. For example, an achievement-oriented premedical student may place little value in succeeding in literature courses or may be undisturbed by her failure to bake a tasty soufflé. From a cognitive perspective, motives may be expressed

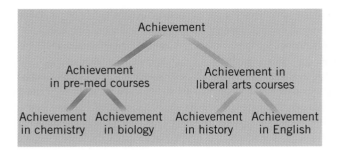

Achievement

Achievement
in pre-med courses

Achievement in
liberal arts courses

Achievement
in chemistry

Achievement
in biology

Achievement
in history

Achievement
in English

FIGURE 10.10
Cognitive structure of achievement motivation. A premedical student attaches different motivational weights to different sections of the hierarchy. Red lines indicate strong motivation; blue lines indicate weaker motivation.

selectively because they are hierarchically organized, with some sections of the hierarchy carrying more motivational weight than others (Figure 10.10).

Achievement goals themselves appear to reflect a blend of at least three motives (Elliott & Church, 1997; Elliott & Harackiewicz, 1996). When people set a goal—doing well in a class, becoming a doctor, or running a marathon—they may be motivated by the desire to meet a socially defined standard (such as a good grade), to avoid failure, or to master the skill. These are called performance-approach, performance-avoidance, and mastery goals.

Performance goals are motives to achieve at a particular level, usually one that meets a socially defined standard, such as getting an A in a class (Dweck, 1986). The emphasis of performance goals is on the *outcome*, that is, on success or failure in meeting a standard. Some people are more motivated to *attain* a goal, whereas others are more motivated by the fear of *not* attaining it. When performance goals center on approaching or attaining a standard, they are called **performance-approach goals**. If I am spending a weekend skiing, for example, I may be motivated by the desire to say I skiied a black-diamond slope—a slope of considerable difficulty. When performance goals center less on achieving a high standard than on avoiding failure, particularly publicly observable failure, they are called **performance-avoidance goals**. I may, for example, stay on the baby slopes to avoid skiing down the hill on my buttocks.

Performance goals, whether for approach or avoidance, are about achieving a concrete outcome—obtaining success or avoiding failure. In contrast, **mastery goals** are motives to increase one's competence, mastery, or skill. If I am motivated by mastery goals, my interest is in developing my skill or technique—enjoying the sheer pleasure of skiing more quickly or competently—not in being able to brag about my exploits on the slopes or avoid the snickers of even little children passing by. (My own goals in skiing are probably now apparent.)

Parenting, Culture, and Achievement

The need for achievement is primarily a learned motive, which numerous studies have linked to patterns of childrearing. Children with high achievement motivation tend to have parents who encourage them to attempt new tasks slightly beyond their reach, praise success when it occurs, encourage independent thinking, discourage complaining, and prompt their children to try new solutions when they fail (McClelland, 1985; Weiss & Schwarz, 1996; Winterbottom, 1953).

Parenting always occurs within a cultural context, and motivation for achievement varies considerably across cultures and historical periods. McClelland and his colleagues (1953) have explored some of the links among culture, childrearing, and achievement. In several studies, they rated the extent of achievement imagery in stories and folktales, particularly those told to children. They then examined the correlation between achievement imagery in these stories

When stories told to children become filled with achievement themes, entrepreneurship rises.

on the one hand and childrearing practices and entrepreneurial activity in each society on the other. They focused on folktales and other stories on the assumption that these would reflect the motives and concerns members of a society find compelling and thus transmit to their children. For instance, a prominent children's story in our own achievement-oriented society is *The Little Engine that Could*. From a psychological standpoint, the moral of this story is simple: Those who expect success and strive for it despite adversity will succeed ("I think I can, I think I can....").

In one study, McClelland and his colleagues (1953) collected the folktales of eight Native American cultures and rated them for degree of achievement motivation expressed. Another set of coders independently rated the cultures for independence training, noting the age at which training began and the strength and frequency of punishment for failure to behave autonomously. The findings documented a clear relationship between achievement motivation and independence training (Table 10.4). Navaho and Central Apache cultures, which stress independence in their child training, showed the strongest need for achievement in their folktales.

In another set of studies, McClelland (1961) found that the achievement orientation expressed in children's stories rose dramatically shortly before periods of rapid economic growth. According to McClelland, as parents in less economically developed countries increasingly value achievement, they transmit this value in the stories they tell their children. Their children, in turn, are more likely to become entrepreneurs, which spurs economic growth.

Western cultures tend to view achievement as a particularly positive motive, but it may not always be the most important motive for success. One intriguing study assessed motivation for power, affiliation, and achievement as reflected in the inaugural addresses of U.S. presidents from George Washington to Ronald Reagan (Spangler & House, 1991). Power motivation, particularly the motive to use power for institutional rather than personal purposes, was the strongest predictor of presidential success (assessed by historians' ratings). Surprisingly, affiliation and achievement motivation were *inversely* correlated with historians' ratings of presidential greatness. Apparently, needing to be loved and having a

TABLE 10.4   RANKING OF CULTURES ON NEED FOR ACHIEVEMENT AND INDEPENDENCE TRAINING

	RANK	
CULTURE	NEED FOR ACHIEVEMENT MEASURED FROM FOLKTALES	INDEPENDENCE TRAINING (AGE AND SEVERITY)
Navajo	1	1
Central Apache	2	2
Hopi	3	4
Comanche	4	3
Sanpoil	5	5.5
Western Apache	6	5.5
Paiute	7	7
Flatheads	8	8

Source: Adapted from McClelland et al., 1953, p. 294.

burning agenda of goals to achieve ultimately inhibit effective presidential leadership.

INTERIM SUMMARY   Agency needs include self-oriented motives for power, competence, achievement, autonomy, and self-esteem. The **need for achievement**—to do well, to succeed, and to avoid failure—has a strong impact on the goals people pursue in everyday life, the tasks they choose to tackle, and the extent to which they persist in the face of difficulty. Achievement goals themselves reflect a blend of at least three motives: **performance-approach goals** (the desire to meet a socially defined standard, **performance-avoidance goals** (the desire to avoid failure, particularly when it is publicly observable), and **mastery goals** (the desire to master the skill). Parenting practices, which themselves reflect cultural values and social and economic circumstances, have a substantial impact on achievement motivation.

▶ **ONE STEP FURTHER**

Distinguishing the Motives Underlying Achievement

All three of these underlying motives can produce what look like similar efforts at achievement. Under certain conditions, however, the differences in the underlying motivation become apparent. To demonstrate this, one team of investigators studied students taking a class on personality psychology (Elliott & Church, 1997). They were interested in predicting two dependent variables: grades and intrinsic motivation. **Intrinsic motivation** refers to enjoyment of, and interest in, an activity for its own sake rather than for some kind of external (or "extrinsic") reward (Deci & Ryan, 1985; Deci et al., 1998; Leeper, 1981; Vallerand, 1993). The researchers wanted to know how well the three types of goals assessed early in the term could predict students' grades and intrinsic interest in personality at the end of the term. Thus, during the second week of class they administered questionnaires to assess students' performance-approach goals (with items such as "It is important to me to do well compared to others in this class"), performance-avoidance goals ("I'm afraid that if I ask my TA or instructor a 'dumb' question, they might not think I'm very smart"), and mastery goals ("I hope to have gained a broader and deeper knowledge of psychology when I am done with this class").

The researchers had three hypotheses. First, high mastery goals at the beginning of the term should predict high intrinsic motivation at the end of the term but should not be particularly associated with grades, since students whose primary motivation is learning may or may not be motivated to demonstrate their knowledge on tests. Second, high performance-approach goals should be associated with high grades at the end of the term but not necessarily with intrinsic motivation. Focusing on the goal of doing well can just as easily stifle as promote interest in the material. Third, students with high performance-avoidance goals should have both worse grades and less intrinsic motivation than other students at the end of the course because their worries about their performance should interfere with both their enjoyment and their ability to study and manage their anxiety during tests.

As can be seen in Figure 10.11, all three predictions were borne out. The figure shows the results of what is called a *path analysis*, which simply shows the paths by which one set of variables (in this case, goals) influences another (in this case, grades and intrinsic motivation). The numbers on the fig-

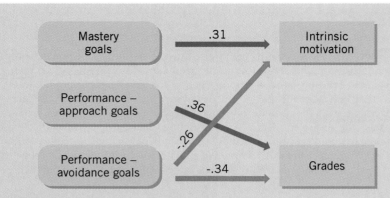

FIGURE 10.11
Predicting intrinsic motivation and grades from achievement-related goals. The figure shows a path analysis, which indicates the ability of one set of variables to predict another. Blue lines indicate a positive relation between variables (that is, higher scores on one predict higher scores on the other), whereas red lines indicate a negative relationship. Missing paths (such as the lack of a path from mastery goals to grades) indicate the absence of any association between the variables. In this case, as predicted, mastery goals did not predict grades, and performance-approach goals did not predict intrinsic motivation. Adapted from A. J. Elliott & M. A. Church (1997). A hierarchical model of approach and avoidance achievement motivation. *J. Personality & Social Psych., 72,* 218–232, p. 227.

ure are similar to correlation coefficients and show the strength of the association between the variables along different pathways.

Researchers are likely someday to make even more fine-grained distinctions regarding the motives that underlie achievement goals. A competitive childhood relationship with a sibling may fuel high performance-approach goals in some people, whereas a loving relationship with a parent may motivate performance-approach goals in others. For the former, a competitive workplace may spur success, whereas the latter may thrive under the wing of a good mentor. Further, a blend of motives probably underlies most behavior. Few people who succeed in their fields are motivated purely by *either* performance or mastery goals; even Einstein, presumably, enjoyed to some degree the acclaim he received for his work, though he was obviously motivated by an intrinsic pleasure in understanding nature. Similarly, asking someone out for dinner may reflect multiple motives, including affiliation, attachment, hunger, sex, altruism, and self-esteem.   ◄

SOME CONCLUDING THOUGHTS

Having explored a variety of motives from multiple perspectives, we return to the basic questions with which we began. First, to what extent are people driven by internal needs or pulled by external stimuli? Examination of the most biological of needs—hunger and sex—makes clear that even where a motive is undeniably rooted in biology, its strength depends in part on whether an appropriate stimulus presents itself, whether the stimulus is a sundae or a sexual partner. A stimulus by itself, however, never motivates behavior unless the person has acquired some motivational tendency toward it. A hot fudge sundae that calls one person's name will have no effect on another who is indifferent to ice cream or chocolate.

A second and related question concerns the extent to which human motivation is rooted in biology or in culture and experience. As in nearly every other discussion of nature and nurture in this book, the answer is an intellectually unsatisfying "yes." Humans are creatures of both biology and culture. Belonging to communities channels their innate motivational tendencies so that their expressed motives fit local social and economic conditions.

The third pertains to the relative importance of thought, feeling, and arousal in motivation: Do people act on the basis of cognition? Emotion? Generalized arousal? The most likely answer is that motivation typically requires both cognition and some form of emotional energy or arousal. To put it another way, cognitive representations or thoughts provide the direction or goals of a motive, and feelings provide the strength or force behind it, but neither alone is likely to move anyone anywhere. In neuropsychological terms, the cortex provides the map for life's journeys, but the hypothalamus and limbic system largely provide the fuel. In the next chapter, we continue to examine the fuel as we explore emotion—and consider what happens if the vehicle begins to sputter under stress.

SUMMARY

PERSPECTIVES ON MOTIVATION

1. **Motivation** refers to the moving force that energizes behavior. It includes two components: what people want to do (the direction in which activity is motivated) and how strongly they want to do it (the strength of the motivation). Although some motives (e.g., eating and sex) are more clearly biologically based and others (e.g., relatedness to others and achievement) are more psychogenic or psychosocial, both types of motives have roots in biology and are both shaped by culture and experience.

2. Evolutionary psychologists argue that basic human motives derive from the tasks of survival and reproduction. They have expanded the concept of reproductive success to include inclusive fitness, which means that natural selection favors organisms that survive, reproduce, and foster the survival and reproduction of their kin. Natural selection has endowed humans and other animals with motivational mechanisms that lead them to maximize their inclusive fitness.

3. Many survival motives involve **homeostasis**, the body's tendency to maintain a relatively constant state, or internal equilibrium, that permits cells to live and function.

4. Freud believed that humans, like other animals, are motivated by internal tension states, or **drives**, for sex and aggression. Contemporary psychodynamic theorists focus less on drives than on wishes and fears. They emphasize motives for relatedness and self-esteem, as well as sex and aggression, and contend that many human motives are unconscious. Recent research supports the distinction between implicit and explicit, or unconscious and conscious, motivation.

5. Behavioral theorists use the term *drive* to refer to motivation activated by a need state (such as hunger). According to **drive-reduction theories**, deprivation of basic needs creates an unpleasant state of tension that leads the animal to act. If an action happens to reduce the tension, the behavior is rein-

forced. Innate drives such as hunger, thirst, and sex are **primary drives**; with **secondary drives**, an originally neutral stimulus that comes to be associated with drive reduction itself becomes a motivator.

6. Cognitive theorists often speak of **goals**, valued outcomes established through social learning. **Expectancy-value theories** assert that motivation is a joint function of the value people place on an outcome and the extent to which they believe they can attain it. **Goal-setting theory** proposes that conscious goals regulate much of human action, particularly in work tasks.

7. According to Maslow's **hierarchy of needs**, basic needs must be met before higher level needs become active. Maslow's hierarchy includes physiological, safety, belongingness, esteem, and **self-actualization needs.**

EATING

8. **Metabolism** refers to the processes by which the body transforms food into energy. The **glucostatic theory** of hunger proposes that hunger motivation arises as **glucose** levels drop in the bloodstream. Sensations in the stomach walls also seem to influence hunger motivation, as may levels of other nutrients.

9. **Obesity** is a condition characterized by a body weight over 15 percent above the ideal for one's height and age. Genetic factors and dietary fat intake are strong predictors of body fat. **Anorexia nervosa** is an eating disorder in which the individual becomes dangerously underweight because of a refusal to eat. **Bulimia** is characterized by a binge-and-purge syndrome, in which the person gorges and then feels the need to get rid of the food she has just consumed.

SEXUAL MOTIVATION

10. Sexual motivation is driven by both fantasies and hormones and is shaped by culture. Hormones control sexual behavior in humans and other animals through **organizational effects** (influencing the structure of neural circuitry) and **activational effects** (activating physiological changes that depend on this circuitry).

11. **Sexual orientation** refers to the direction of a person's enduring sexual attraction—to members of the same sex, the opposite sex, or both. Although the data on female homosexuality are less numerous, accumulating evidence on male homosexuality suggests a substantial biological influence.

12. **Sexual dysfunctions** are problems that impair sexual functioning, such as inhibited orgasm and premature ejaculation.

PSYCHOSOCIAL MOTIVES

13. **Psychosocial motives** are personal and interpersonal motives for such ends as mastery, achievement, power, self-esteem, affiliation, and intimacy. Across cultures, the two major clusters of motives are **agency** (self-oriented goals, such as mastery or power) and **relatedness** (interpersonal motives for connection, or communion, with others).

14. The **need for achievement** refers to a motive to succeed and to avoid failure, which is heavily influenced by cultural and economic conditions. Underlying

achievement motivation may be **performance goals** (to approach or achieve a socially visible standard) or **mastery goals** (to master the skill).

15. Even for needs undeniably rooted in biology, such as hunger and sex, the strength of a motive depends in part on whether appropriate stimuli impinge on the organism. Motives also often reflect a subtle blend of innate factors (nature) and learning and culture (nurture). Motivation usually requires both cognition (representations that provide the direction of motivation) and emotional energy or arousal (providing the "fuel," or strength, of motivation).

Robert Birmelin, "The Telephone Rings," 1994, Hackett-Freedman Gallery.

CHAPTER 11

Emotion, Stress, and Coping

*I*n March of 1998, the media in the United States were aflurry with reports of a Presidential sex scandal. For years, allegations of affairs had surrounded President Clinton, but they had taken on new intensity since January when a story broke suggesting an affair between the President and a 21-year-old White House intern named Monica Lewinsky. The public, however, had already begun to forgive the popular President, as evidenced in record-high approval ratings, assuming that even if he had dallied with the intern, the relationship was seedy but consensual.

But in March, a new story broke when Kathleen Willey, a former supporter of the President, alleged in front of a television audience of 20 million that the President had forced himself on her in the Oval Office—kissing her, fondling her, and

putting her hand on his body. Her televised performance was, in the words of many commentators, "mesmerizing." She spoke with a combination of pain and composure, speaking articulately with emotional pauses that seemed to indicate a compelling story. Perhaps even more compelling was the lack of a motive for anything but honesty. After all, she had been in the Clinton camp for years.

A day later, however, another side of the story began to emerge. The White House released copies of letters she had written the President many times after the alleged incident, in which she asked for private appointments with him, sent him birthday and other congratulatory cards, and described herself as his "number one fan." More damning still was the presence of a possible motive: Her lawyer had been busy arranging a $300,000 book deal, an amount that would virtually cancel out a debt with which her deceased husband had left her.

In the days surrounding the incident, after watching the dozens of "talking heads" on television, my graduate student Ali Feit and I were struck by how much the inferences these commentators made about the case seemed to depend on their political preferences. Republicans described Willey's emotional testimony as highly credible; Democrats pointed to the book negotiations as clear evidence of her motive for lying. How could people vary so widely in their inferences after seeing exactly the same interview?

To try to answer that question, in the next three days we distributed questionnaires to roughly 120 people in Boston and New York asking them about what they thought had happened between the President and Mrs. Willey, as well as assessing their feelings toward Democrats, Republicans, feminists, Clinton, and infidelity. We also assessed their knowledge of Clinton's life and the current scandal, so that we could test the hypothesis that people's inferences in ambiguous, emotionally charged incidents of this sort reflect a combination of cognitive processes (based on their prior knowledge) and emotional pulls.

That was just what we found. We used a statistical procedure (called *multiple regression*) that can determine how much of one variable (in this case, the extent to which participants believed Clinton had forced himself on Willey) can be accounted for by other variables (in this instance, feelings about Republicans and Democrats, knowledge about Clinton, etc.). The best predictor of beliefs about what happened between the President and Mrs. Willey was people's feelings toward the two political parties: The more strongly people liked Republicans, the more strongly they believed the President had sexually harassed Willey. The second strongest predictor was feelings about high-status philandering men: People who strongly disliked unfaithful, charismatic men also tended to believe Willey's account. A somewhat distant third was people's knowledge about Clinton's life: The more they knew, the more they thought he did it.

This example raises many of the questions that will emerge in this chapter on emotion, stress, and coping. What emotional cues help us decipher whether a person is lying or telling the truth? Is our ability to read those cues inborn? How does emotion affect cognition? And how do people cope with stressful events, such as unwanted sexual advances or public attacks on their character? We begin by exploring the nature of emotion, starting with components and types of emotion and different perspectives on emotional experience. Next, we turn to the related phenomenon of stress, from major stresses like the death of a spouse, to catastrophes like earthquakes, to daily hassles like traffic and sloppy roommates. After examining stress and its effects on health, we explore the strategies people use to cope with stress, as well as the role of culture in patterning responses to experiences ranging from loss and unemployment to discrimination and torture.

EMOTION

Everyone has an intuitive sense of what an emotion is, but emotion can be exceedingly difficult to define. Imagine explaining the concept of emotion to someone who has never experienced one (like a tax collector). **Emotion**, or **affect** (a synonym for emotion, pronounced with the accent on the first syllable), is an evaluative response (a positive or negative feeling) that typically includes some combination of physiological arousal, subjective experience, and behavioral or emotional expression. We examine each component of emotion in turn.

PHYSIOLOGICAL COMPONENTS

Over a century ago, William James (1884) argued that emotion is rooted in bodily experience. According to James, an emotion-inducing stimulus elicits visceral, or gut, reactions and voluntary behaviors such as running or gesturing. The physical experience in turn leads the person to feel aroused, and the arousal stimulates the subjective experience of fear. In this view, confronting a bear on a camping trip causes a person to run, and running produces fear.

James thus offered a counterintuitive proposition: We do not run because we are afraid; rather, we become afraid because we run (Figure 11.1*a*). James's theory is sometimes called the *peripheral theory of emotion* because it sees the origins of emotion in the peripheral nervous system. Recall that the peripheral nervous system controls both muscle movements and autonomic responses such as racing heart and shortness of breath in the face of fear-eliciting stimuli. Because the Danish physiologist Carl Lange (1885) proposed a similar view at about the same time as James (which no doubt made both of their hearts pound and fists clench, lead-

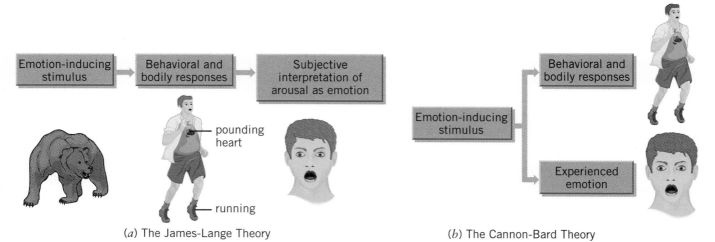

(a) The James-Lange Theory   (b) The Cannon-Bard Theory

FIGURE 11.1

The James–Lange and Cannon–Bard theories of emotion. In the James-Lange theory (a), a stimulus leads to a peripheral nervous system response, which in turn is interpreted as an emotion. In the Cannon–Bard theory (b), the stimulus produces simultaneous peripheral responses and subjective experience.

ing them to feel angry), this view of emotion is known as the **James-Lange theory** (see Lang, 1994).

As the theory would predict, some emotional experiences—particularly sexual arousal, fear, and anger—do appear to be blunted in individuals with spinal cord lesions that prevent them from moving or experiencing gut feelings (Hohmann, 1966; Jasmos & Hakmiller, 1975). One man with a cervical lesion (a lesion near the neck, which cuts off almost all autonomic signals) compared his feelings of sexual arousal before and after the accident:

> Before I got hurt . . . I would get a hot, tense feeling all over my body. I've got out and necked a few times since I was hurt, but it doesn't do anything for me. I daydream once in a while about it, and when I'm around a bunch of guys I talk big, but I just don't get worked up anymore. (Hohmann, 1966, p. 148)

Not all evidence on spinal injuries, however, supports the James-Lange theory (Bermond et al., 1991), and the theory was challenged on other grounds over a half century ago by Cannon (1927) and Bard (1934). Cannon and Bard noted that autonomic responses are typically slow, occurring about one to two seconds after presentation of a stimulus. In contrast, emotional responses are immediate and often precede both autonomic reactions and behaviors such as running. Cannon and Bard argued further that many different emotional states are linked to the same visceral responses, so that arousal is too generalized to translate directly into discrete emotional experiences. For instance, muscle tension and quickened heart rate accompany sexual arousal, fear, and rage, which people experience as very different emotional states. Cannon and Bard offered the alternative view (known as the **Cannon-Bard theory**) that emotion-inducing stimuli simultaneously elicit both an emotional experience, such as fear, and bodily responses, such as sweaty palms (Figure 11.1b).

Cannon and Bard's first criticism (about the relative speed of autonomic and emotional responses) continues to be valid. However, their second criticism, that visceral arousal is general, has been challenged by more recent research. In fact, different emotions appear to be associated with distinct patterns of autonomic arousal (Ekman, 1992; Levenson, 1992; Levenson et al., 1990). Different clusters of emotions show modest but consistent differences on variables such as heart rate acceleration, finger temperature, and skin conductance (a measure of sweat on the palms related to arousal or anxiety, also known as galvanic skin response, or GSR). Anger and fear, for example, produce greater heart rate acceleration than happiness. This makes evolutionary sense, because anger and fear are related to fight-or-flight responses, which require the heart to pump more blood to the muscles. Anger and fear are also distinguishable from each other autonomically. The language we use to describe anger ("hot under the collar") appears to be physiologically accurate: People who are angry do get "heated" in their surface skin temperatures. Moreover, psychologists have found the same links between emotional experience and physiology among men from the island of Sumatra in Indonesia, as in the West, suggesting that the connection is wired into the brain (Levenson et al., 1992).

SUBJECTIVE EXPERIENCE

The most familiar component of emotion is **subjective experience**, or what it feels like to be happy, sad, angry, or elated. Individuals differ tremendously in the intensity of their emotional states (Bryant et al., 1996; Larsen et al., 1996; Larsen & Diener, 1987), and these differences already begin to be apparent in preschool children (Cole et al., 1997). At the extreme high end of the bell curve of emotional intensity in adults are people with severe personality disorders (Chapter 15), whose emotions spiral out of control (Linehan, 1987). At the other end of the bell curve are people with a psychological disorder called **alexithymia** (Sifneos, 1973; Taylor and Taylor, 1997), which literally means "no language for emotions." Alexithymics have difficulty telling one emotion from another and often report what seem to be meaningful, painful, or traumatic experiences with bland indifference. One alexithymic patient told his therapist about a "strange event" that had occurred the previous day. He had found himself shaking and felt his eyes tearing and wondered if he had been crying. The patient showed no recognition that his tears could have been related to frightening news he had received that morning about the results of a biopsy on a suspicious growth on his skin (D. Hulihan, personal communication, 1992). Alexithymics appear to pay a toll for their inability to feel: They are more likely to suffer from stress-related illnesses such as chronic pain and ulcers (Fukunishi et al., 1997).

Emotional Disclosure

As we saw in Chapter 2, acknowledging and examining one's feelings can have a positive impact on health (Pennebaker, 1997). For example, in one study, Holocaust survivors talked for one to two hours about their experiences during World War II while the investigators measured the extent to which they disclosed emotionally about traumatic events (Pennebaker et al., 1989). The more the survivors disclosed, the better their health for over a year later. Another study assessed the impact of emotional disclosure on an ongoing stressful event in college students, such as an academic or a relationship problem (Taylor et al., 1998). The experimenters first asked college student participants to identify an ongoing stressful event. In the emotional disclosure condition, they were instructed to visualize what led up to the problem, what happened step by step, what they did to cope with it, and so forth. In a second condition, students were asked to imagine the problem resolving, to experience the satisfaction they would feel when it was over, and so forth ("positive thinking"). A control group did not visualize anything. A week later, participants in the emotional disclosure condition had taken positive steps to resolve the problem and had sought advice from people about it, whereas participants in the "positive thinking" condition were indistinguishable from controls. This suggests that emotional disclosure may not only directly affect feelings and health but indirectly affect it by helping the person address the ongoing problem directly.

The effects of disclosure are not always immediate. In fact, disclosure can initially be quite difficult but have positive consequences down the road. In one study, patients with painful arthritis were assigned to one of two groups (Kelley et al., 1997). In one condition, they spoke into a tape recorder for 15 minutes a day about stressful events in their lives. In the other, they talked about trivial topics. Disclosure led to more negative mood initially. Three months later, however, both the physical and emotional condition of the patients in the disclosure group was higher, and the more unpleasant emotion patients had experienced initially, the better the condition of their joints.

Researchers have been tracking down some of the precise mechanisms through which disclosure affects health (Pennebaker, 1997). Writing about stressful unpleasant events has been shown to increase the functioning of specific cells in the immune system (the system of cells in the body that fight off disease) against various viruses. Disclosure also decreases autonomic reactivity that keeps the body on red alert (or chronically yellow alert) and gradually takes its toll over time. Perhaps most importantly, disclosure permits a change in cognitive functioning that signals a reworking of the traumatic experience in thought and memory: People who benefit from disclosure tend to begin with disorganized, disjointed narratives about the event, suggesting emotional disruption of their thinking, but after writing, their narratives become more coherent. The narratives of people whose health improves also show a higher level of cognitive complexity relative to people who remain less well (Suedfeld & Pennebaker, 1997). It seems likely that people who are either afraid to think about their experiences and put them into words, or those who ruminate on negative events rather than really coming to some kind of resolution, are least affected by disclosure.

Feeling Happy

Although psychologists tend to focus most on unpleasant emotions such as anxiety and depression, a growing body of research has examined the subjective experience of happiness (Myers & Diener, 1995). On average, men and women are equally happy, as are the young and old. In contrast, some of the largest differences in self-reported happiness are cultural. The percentage of people who describe themselves as "very happy" ranges from a low of 10 percent in Portugal to a high of 40 percent in the Netherlands. One predictor of happiness is the extent to which a culture is more individualist or collectivist: People in individualistic cultures, which focus on the needs and desires of individuals, tend to be happier than people in collectivist cultures, which emphasize the needs of the group. Another predictor is political: The correlation between life satisfaction and the number of uninterrupted years of democracy in a country is .85, which is one of the largest observed correlations ever produced in psychology between two seemingly dissimilar variables (Inglehart, 1990).

Does money buy happiness? The answer appears to be yes and no. Across cultures, the correlation between self-reported happiness and economic prosperity is substantial (Figure 11.2). Interestingly, however, within cultures, happiness and income are not highly correlated. Apparently, a decent income is necessary but not sufficient for happiness. Other variables that predict happiness are a large network of close friends and strong religious faith.

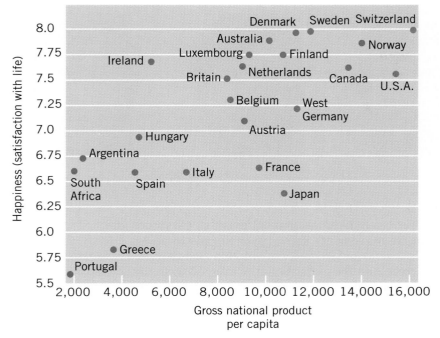

FIGURE 11.2
Happiness in 24 nations. Happiness is strongly correlated with gross national product (GNP), a measure of economic prosperity. Adapted from D. Myers and E. Diener (1995). Who is Happy? *Psychological Science*, p. 13.

INTERIM SUMMARY   **Emotion**, or **affect**, is an evaluative response that typically includes physiological arousal, subjective experience, and behavioral or emotional expression. The **James–Lange theory** asserts that emotions originate in peripheral nervous system responses, which the central nervous system then interprets. The **Cannon–Bard theory** argues that emotion-inducing stimuli simultaneously elicit both an emotional experience and bodily responses. Although people likely experience some forms of general arousal that require interpretation, different emotions are associated with distinct patterns of emotional activation. The **subjective experience** of an emotion refers to what the emotion feels like to the individual. People differ tremendously in emotional intensity. Acknowledging, talking about, and thinking about feelings can have a positive impact on health. The extent to which people experience happiness is relatively stable across age and gender lines but differs substantially across cultures. A certain amount of economic security appears necessary but not sufficient to buy happiness.

EMOTIONAL EXPRESSION

A third component of emotion is **emotional expression**, the overt behavioral signs of emotion. People express feelings in various ways, including facial expressions, posture, gestures, and tone of voice.

Facial Expression and Emotion

In a twist on William James's peripheral hypothesis of emotion, some theorists argue that the face is the primary center of emotion (Tomkins, 1962, 1980). Whereas James asserted that we feel afraid because we run, these theorists argue that we feel afraid because our face shows fear. In this view, emotion consists of muscular responses located primarily in the face (and secondarily of muscular and glandular responses throughout the body).

Different facial expressions are, in fact, associated with different emotions (Ekman, 1992; Izard, 1971, 1997). Terror is marked by eyes that are open wide "in a fixed stare or moving away from the dreaded object to the side" (Tomkins, 1980, p. 142). The relationship between emotion and facial muscle movements is uni-

Then imitate the action of the tiger:
Stiffen the sinews, summon up the blood,
Disguise fair nature with hard-favored rage;
Then lend the eye a terrible aspect;
Let it pry through the portage of the head
Like the brass cannon…
Now set the teeth and stretch the nostril wide,
Hold hard the breath and bend up every spirit
To his full height!
    SHAKESPEARE,
    Henry V, (III. i.)

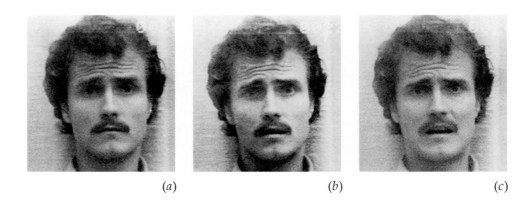

(a)   (b)   (c)

FIGURE 11.3
Creating fear in the face. Participants instructed to (a) raise their eyebrows and pull them together, (b) then raise their upper eyelids, and (c) stretch their lips back toward their ears showed physiological changes consistent with fear.

form enough across individuals and cultures that electrodes attached to the face to detect muscle movements allow psychologists to assess directly the *valence* (positive or negative) and intensity of emotion (Tassinary & Cacioppo, 1992). Interestingly, across cultures some similarity even exists in the colors people use to describe emotions, such as the association of anger with seeing red—perhaps because anger is associated with facial flushing and an increase in temperature (see Hupka et al., 1997).

Facial expressions not only indicate a person's emotional state, but they also influence its physiological and subjective components. In a classic study, researchers gave participants specific directions to contract their facial muscles in particular ways (Ekman et al., 1983). For instance, as shown in Figure 11.3, they instructed participants to raise their eyebrows and pull them together, then raise their upper eyelids, and finally stretch their lips horizontally. The result was an expression of fear, even though the participants (actors) had not been instructed to show a particular emotion. The experimenters similarly created expressions characteristic of anger, sadness, happiness, surprise, and disgust. Participants held these expressions for 10 seconds, during which their heart rate and finger temperature were measured.

The researchers found a striking causal relation between the simple act of changing facial expression and patterns of autonomic response (Figure 11.4). Although some research has challenged this finding (Boiten, 1996), other research has found that when people imitate positive and negative expressions in photographs, their own emotions tend to change accordingly (Kleinke et al., 1998). (These effects may not be limited to the face: People who receive positive feedback about their appearance experience more pride when they receive the feedback while standing upright rather than hunching over [Stepper & Strack, 1993]!) Still other studies document distinct EEG activity associated with the different posed emotions as well as changes in subjective experience that accompany changes in the face (Ekman & Davidson, 1993; Izard, 1990; Lanzetta et al., 1976). Whoever wrote the lyric about letting a smile be your umbrella on a rainy day may have been a savvy psychologist.

Furthermore, true and fake smiles appear to be physiologically different and rely on different sets of muscles (Ekman, 1992; Ekman and Keltner, 1997). "True" smiles use eye muscles as well as cheek muscles. Interestingly, children have some capacity to detect these differences as early as the preschool years, which allows them to distinguish between "real" and "fake" emotions (Banerjee, 1997). Perhaps an analysis of Kathleen Willey's facial expressions during her videotaped interview will someday reveal whether her emotional pain was genuine.

The flipside of emotional expression is *suppression* of the overt expression of emotion, as when people try to hide their feelings from others or decrease the intensity of an emotion by "keeping a stiff upper lip." Suppressing the behavioral

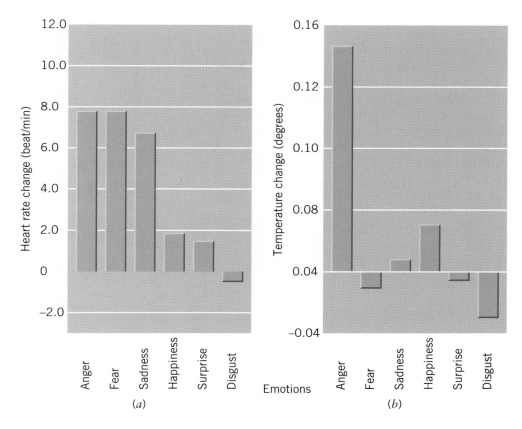

FIGURE 11.4
Facial expression and physiological response. The figure shows changes in heart rate and finger temperature associated with certain emotional expressions. Anger, fear, and sadness elevate heart rate, but of these three emotions, only anger also increases temperature. People presumably learn to distinguish these affects based on subtle physiological cues such as these. *Source:* Ekman et al., 1983, p. 1209.

expression of emotion is not, however, without its costs. In one study, participants instructed to inhibit emotional expression while watching sad, amusing, and neutral films showed diminished enjoyment of both the sad and amusing videos (Gross & Levenson, 1997). In addition, emotional suppression had the paradoxical effect of increasing sympathetic nervous system activity, particularly in the cardiovascular system. Thus, trying to shut off emotional expression can heighten arousal, leading to increased heart rate (see also Chapter 9).

Culture and Emotional Display Rules

Prior to research documenting the physiological and anatomical differences among emotions, psychologists and sociologists hotly debated whether people across cultures ascribe the same meaning to a smile or a frown. In fact, some facial expressions are universally recognized (see Ekman & Oster, 1979; Frick, 1985; Scherer & Wallbott, 1994). Participants in one classic study viewed photographs showing the faces of North American actors expressing fear, anger, happiness, and other emotions. Participants from diverse cultural groups, ranging from Swedes and Kenyans to members of a preliterate tribe in New Guinea with minimal Western contact, all recognized certain emotions (Ekman, 1971). Cross-cultural studies have identified six facial expressions recognized by people of every culture examined (Figure 11.5): surprise, fear, anger, disgust, happiness, and sadness (Ekman & Oster, 1979). Shame and interest also may have universal facial expressions (Izard, 1977). These findings suggest that some emotions are biologically linked not only to distinct autonomic states but also to certain facial movements, which people in all cultures can decode.

Not all facial expressions, however, are the same from culture to culture. People learn to control the way they express many emotions, using patterns of emotional expression considered appropriate within their culture or subculture, called

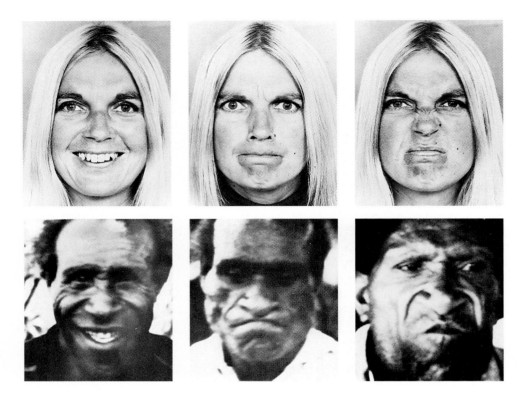

FIGURE 11.5
Universal facial expressions. Members of the remote Fore tribe of New Guinea recognize Western facial expressions, just as Western college students recognize the expressions on Fore faces.

display rules (Ekman & Friesen, 1975; Ekman et al., 1982b). Some of these differences appear to reflect such simple variables as geography: A study of a large sample of participants from 26 countries found, as many observers and travelers had long believed, that both within and across countries, southerners tend to be more emotionally expressive than northerners (Pennebaker et al., 1997). Other studies have assessed more strictly cultural differences. In one study, Japanese and North American participants viewed a film depicting a painful initiation rite. As long as they were unaware that they were being observed, participants from the two cultures showed the same facial responses. When participants believed they might be observed, however, their reactions were quite different. The North Americans still showed revulsion, but the Japanese, socialized to show far less emotion, masked their expressions (Ekman, 1977). Whether the Japanese experienced the emotion differently as a result is unknown.

Gender and Emotional Expression

Display rules differ not only by culture but also by gender. Whether men and women actually experience their emotions differently is difficult to ascertain, but the best evidence suggests that women probably experience emotion more intensely, are better able to read emotions from other people's faces and nonverbal cues, and express emotion more intensely and openly than men (Brody & Hall, 1993). A recent study found that women and men differed in both emotional expression and autonomic arousal while watching emotional films, suggesting that men and women do, in fact, differ in their experience of emotion (Kring & Gordon, 1998). These distinctions apply to children as well. While watching videotapes of emotional interactions, girls not only show facial expressions that more closely match those of the people on the videos, suggesting greater emotional empathy, but they are also more accurate in verbally describing the emotions of the people on the films (Strayer and Roberts, 1997). Interestingly, even children as young as 3 years old recognize that females are more likely to express fear, sadness, and happiness, and that males are more likely to express anger (Birnbaum, 1983).

The reasons for gender differences in emotion are a matter of debate. On the one hand, they likely reflect adaptation to the roles that men and women have historically tended to occupy. Women are generally more comfortable with emotions such as love, happiness, warmth, shame, guilt, and sympathy, which foster affiliation and caretaking. Men, on the other hand, are socialized to compete and to fight; hence, they avoid "soft" emotions that display their vulnerabilities to competitors and enemies or discourage them from asserting their dominance when the need arises (Brody & Hall, 1993). Parents talk to their children differently about emotion from at least the time they are toddlers—for example, talking more about feelings with girls—implicitly teaching them how, and how much, to think about and express their emotions (Cervantes & Callahan, 1998; Dunn et al., 1987; Kuebli et al., 1995). From the time they are little, boys also receive repeated messages that only "sissies" cry, and that feeling scared and showing signs of emotional vulnerability are unmanly.

On the other hand, gender differences make sense from an evolutionary perspective. In particular, nurturing children requires attention to feelings. Attention to feelings—particularly empathy and fear—can be dysfunctional for males when they are fighting, defending territory, or competing with other males for mates. This is not, of course, absolute: Men who understand others well, which means being able to read their emotions, are likely to be more socially successful and to compete more successfully for females. Thus, males may have countervailing pressures to feel and not to feel.

INTERIM SUMMARY   **Emotional expression** refers to the overt behavioral signs of emotion. Different facial muscles are associated with different emotions. Facial expressions not only indicate but can actually influence the subjective experience of emotion. Display rules are patterns of emotional expression considered appropriate within a culture or subculture. Display rules differ not only by culture but also by gender. Women also appear to experience emotions more intensely and to show greater competence in reading people's emotions.

A TAXONOMY OF EMOTIONS

Some aspects of emotion, then, are universal, whereas others vary by culture and gender (see Lutz, 1988; Mesquita, 1997; Russell, 1994). How many emotions do humans experience, and how many of these are innate?

Basic Emotions

Psychologists have attempted to produce a list of **basic emotions**, emotions common to the human species, similar to primary colors in perception, from which all other emotions and emotional blends are derived. An emotion is basic if it has characteristic physiological, subjective, and expressive components (Izard & Buechler, 1980).

Although theorists generate slightly different lists, and some even argue against the existence of basic emotions (Ortony & Turner, 1990), most classifications include five to nine emotions (Russell, 1991). All theorists of basic emotions list anger, fear, happiness, sadness, and disgust. Surprise, contempt, interest, shame, guilt, joy, trust, and anticipation sometimes make the roster (Plutchik, 1980; Russell, 1991; Shaver et al., 1987; Tomkins, 1980). Similar lists of basic emotions have been compiled in India (Lynch, 1990) and in China, where an encyclopedia from the 1st century B.C. contained the following entry:

Can complex emotions be read from the face?

What are the feelings of men? They are joy, anger, sadness, fear, love, disliking, and liking. These seven feelings belong to men without their learning
them. (The Li Chi, cited in Russell, 1991, p. 426)

Beyond these basic emotions, cultures vary in the extent to which they elaborate and distinguish emotional states (Kitayama & Markus, 1994; Mesquita, 1997;
Russell, 1991). The Tahitian language has 46 different words for anger (much as
English has several terms, such as annoyance, frustration, and rage) but no word
for sadness. The Tahitians do not even have a word for *emotion*. In some African
languages, the same word denotes both anger and sadness; members of these cultures seldom seem to distinguish between the two.

Positive and Negative Affect

Perhaps a distinction even more fundamental than differences among the basic
emotions is between **positive affect** (pleasant emotions) and **negative affect** (unpleasant emotions). Factor analysis of data from several cultures suggests that
these two factors underlie people's self-reported emotions (see Watson & Clark,
1992; Watson & Tellegen, 1985) and are in fact distinct in infancy (Belsky et al.,
1996). (Recall from Chapter 8 that factor analysis combines variables that are
highly correlated with each other into superordinate variables, or factors.) Within
these two factors, emotions are substantially intercorrelated. In other words, people who frequently experience one negative emotion, such as guilt, also tend to
experience others, such as anxiety and sadness.

Positive and negative affect are negatively correlated with one another but
not very highly; that is, people who often feel anxious or guilty may also frequently feel happy (see Diener et al., 1995). Brain imaging studies suggest that
positive and negative affect are largely neurologically distinct but share *some*
neural pathways that lead to feelings of emotional arousal regardless of emotional
valence (Lane et al., 1997).

Approach and Avoidance   The distinction between positive and negative affect is congruent with behaviorist and neuropsychological data distinguishing a
pleasure-seeking, approach-oriented behavioral system driven by positive affect,
from an aversive or avoidance-oriented system driven by negative affect (Chapter
5; see also Davidson, 1992; Gray, 1994; Lang, 1995). Approach-oriented feelings
and motives are processed to a greater extent in the left frontal lobe, whereas
avoidance-oriented feelings and motives are associated with right frontal activation. Discovery of this distinction has allowed researchers to predict mood and
other related variables from the difference in activation levels of the two frontal
lobes using EEG recordings. For example, among four-year-olds, those with
greater relative activation on the left tend to be more socially competent and less
isolated interpersonally than those who show little difference between the hemispheres or greater right frontal activation (Fox et al., 1995).

A growing body of research suggests not only that people differ substantially
in the extent to which they experience positive and negative affect, but that these
differences play a central role in the way they live their lives (Chapters 10, 12, and
15). People who are particularly prone to negative affect may organize their lives
around preventing potentially aversive events from occurring. In contrast, people
who are more driven by positive affect tend to seek novel and exciting events. For
most people, positive and negative affect provide an internal set of checks and
balances, leading them to pursue things they enjoy but putting on the brakes
when they are about to get themselves into trouble. People who are high on one
and low on the other, in contrast, are at risk for psychological problems: They may
be vulnerable to depression and anxiety on the one hand, or excessive risk taking
and antisocial behavior on the other.

Positive and negative affect are regulated by different neurotransmitter systems, suggesting that individual differences in the tendency to experience one or the other are related to individual differences in neurotransmitter functioning (Cloninger, 1998). According to one hypothesis, people who are fear-driven have an abundance of, or strong reactivity to, norepinephrine. In contrast, people who are reward- or pleasure-driven are more reactive to dopamine. Part of the tendency to experience positive and negative emotions is heritable. For positive affectivity, estimated heritability based on studies of twins reared together and apart is .40; for negative affectivity, heritability is even higher, at .55 (Tellegen, cited in Gabbay, 1992; Watson & Tellegen, 1985).

Anger The one emotion that does not fit cleanly into this distinction is anger. Subjectively, anger can feel unpleasant, but anger and aggression can also have pleasurable components—as anyone knows who has ever fantasized about revenge. Anger can sometimes lead to withdrawal, as when people regulate their anger by "swallowing it" and not saying anything about it, but more often it is an approach-oriented emotion, because it leads people to approach the object of their anger and attack. Interestingly, recent EEG research finds that people who tend to be angry show greater relative activity in the left versus the right frontal lobe, the standard pattern for positive affect (Harmon-Jones & Allen, 1998). This suggests either that anger is more akin to positive affect, or that the asymmetry between left and right frontal functioning has less to do with emotional valence than with approach versus avoidance tendencies.

An Emotion Hierarchy

How can the various views of emotion be reconciled, with their competing claims about the number of emotions and the relative importance of biology and culture? One solution (Figure 11.6) is to organize emotions hierarchically (Fischer et al., 1990). The most universal categories are positive and negative affect. All cultures make this distinction, and it is the first drawn by young children, who use words such as *nice, mean, good, bad, like,* and *don't like.* The basic emotions at the next level

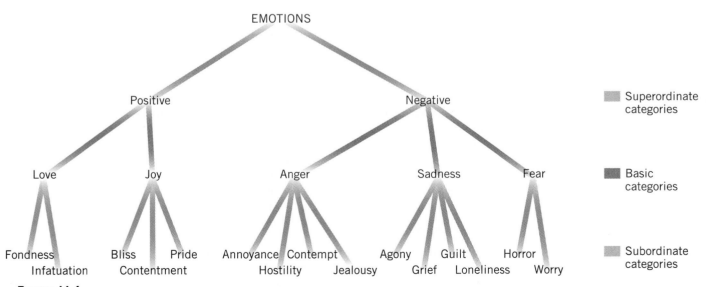

FIGURE 11.6
An emotion hierarchy. Emotions may be arranged hierarchically, with universal categories at the superordinate and basic levels, and categories that vary by culture at the subordinate level. *Source*: Fischer et al., 1990, p. 90.

of the hierarchy also apply across cultures. Below this level, however, most emotion concepts are culturally constructed. Western culture, for example, distinguishes different forms of love, such as infatuation, fondness, sexual love, nonsexual love, and puppy love. Indian culture, in contrast, distinguishes only two forms of love: *vatsalya bhava*, a mother's love for her child, and *madhurya bhava*, erotic love (Lynch, 1990). Children recognize these culture-specific distinctions much later than the basic emotions.

INTERIM SUMMARY   Basic emotions—such as anger, fear, happiness, sadness, and disgust—are common to the human species and include characteristic physiological, subjective, and expressive components. Beyond the basic emotions, different cultures elaborate and distinguish different emotional states. Probably the most fundamental distinction is between **positive affect** (pleasant emotions) and **negative affect** (unpleasant emotions), with positive affect associated with approach-oriented motives and negative affect associated with avoidance-oriented emotions. These emotional systems are to a substantial degree neurologically distinct. People also differ in the extent to which they experience, and their behavior tends to be driven by, one or the other. Emotions appear to be organized hierarchically, with positive and negative affect at the superordinate level, followed by basic emotions, and then more culture-specific emotions at subordinate levels.

FROM MIND TO BRAIN

THE NEUROPSYCHOLOGY OF EMOTION

Poets often locate emotion in the heart, whereas theorists with a less romantic bend of mind locate it in the face or the peripheral nervous system. Still other researchers have searched for the neural circuits underlying emotion in the central nervous system. They have found that affects, like cognitions, are distributed throughout the nervous system and are not located in any particular region (Derryberry & Tucker, 1992). Three areas of the brain, however, are particularly important: the hypothalamus, the limbic system, and the cortex.

The Hypothalamus

Since the 1930s, psychologists have recognized the role of the hypothalamus in emotion. Electrical stimulation of this region can produce attack, defense, or flight reactions, with corresponding emotions of rage or terror. Papez (1937) considered the hypothalamus a crucial component of a circuit or "loop" involved in the generation of emotion. Figure 11.7*a* shows a modified version of the Papez circuit.

Papez argued that when the hypothalamus receives emotionally relevant sensory information from the thalamus (which functions as a sensory relay station), it instigates activity in a circuit of neurons higher up in the brain. These neurons, which include what is now referred to as the limbic system as well as the cortex, process the information more deeply to assess its emotional significance. Once the circuit is completed, it feeds back to the hypothalamus, which in turn activates autonomic and endocrine responses.

The Limbic System

Many aspects of Papez's theory have turned out to be anatomically correct, although contemporary theories (LeDoux, 1989, 1995) place more emphasis on the limbic system (Figure 11.7). In some species, motivation is largely controlled by the hypothalamus, and hence by instinct. However, the

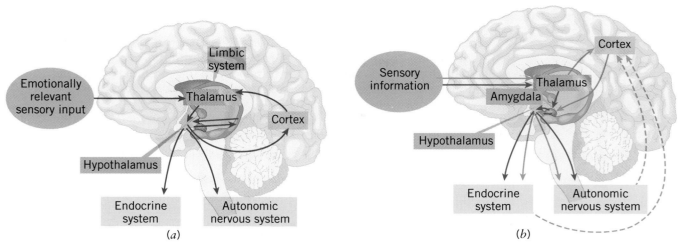

FIGURE 11.7

Neural and endocrine pathways involved in emotion. (*a*) A modified version of the Papez circuit. According to Papez, sensory information is transmitted from the thalamus to the hypothalamus. If that information is emotionally relevant, it activates the cortex and limbic system, which in turn assess the emotional relevance of the information and influence subsequent hypothalamic response. (b) Two circuits for emotion processing in the brain. Emotionally relevant information is relayed from the thalamus simultaneously to the amygdala and the cortex. The initial emotional response from the amygdala may produce autonomic and endocrine changes (such as those indicative of fear and anger), which the cortex must interpret. The second (cortical) pathway allows the person to evaluate the stimulus on the basis of stored knowledge and goals. *Source:* Adapted from LeDoux, 1986, p. 329.

evolution of the limbic system meant that in other species, especially humans, behavior is controlled less by instinct than by learning, and particularly by emotional responses to stimuli.

Perhaps the most important limbic structure for emotion is the amygdala. The amygdala is the brain's "emotional computer" for calculating the emotional significance of a stimulus (LeDoux, 1989). In 1937, researchers discovered that lesioning a large temporal region (which later turned out primarily to involve the amygdala) produced a peculiar syndrome in monkeys (Kluver & Bucy, 1939). The monkeys no longer seemed to understand the emotional significance of objects in their environment, even though they had no trouble recognizing or identifying them. The animals showed no fear of previously feared stimuli and were generally unable to use their emotions to guide behavior. They would, for example, eat feces or other inedible objects that normally elicited disgust or indifference.

Researchers have subsequently found that lesioning the neurons connecting the amygdala with a specific sense, such as vision or hearing, makes the monkey unable to register the emotional significance of objects perceived by that sense (LeDoux, 1989). In other words, the amygdala (together with the hippocampus, which is involved in memory) plays a crucial role in associating sensory and other information with pleasant and unpleasant feelings (see Derryberry & Tucker, 1992). This allows humans and other animals to adjust their behavior based on positive and negative emotional reactions to objects or situations they encounter.

The mechanism through which this occurs appears to involve changes in the way neurons in the amygdala respond to stimuli that have previously been associated with reward or punishment. For example, in one study, the experimenters classically conditioned a fear response in rats by pairing a tone with an aversive stimulus (Rogan et al., 1997). Following acquisition of a conditioned emotional response (fear when hearing the tone), neurons in the region of the amygdala that receives auditory information showed enduring changes in the way they responded to the conditioned stimulus (the tone) that were not present in control rats that had not learned to associate the tone with electric shocks.

In humans, the amygdala also plays a crucial role in detecting other people's emotions, particularly from observing their facial expressions (Scott et al., 1997). Supporting the role of the amygdala specifically in fear responses, PET imaging research has found that the amygdala is more responsive to facial expressions of fear than of happiness (Morris et al., 1996). In fact, the more fear a face shows, the more activated the amygdala becomes.

Two Systems for Processing Emotion

The amygdala is in many respects the neuronal hub of emotion because of its connections with both the cortex and the hypothalamus. The amygdala also receives some sensory information directly from the thalamus. This information is relatively simple, based on neurons in the thalamus that process primitive sensory patterns (Chapter 4), but it can elicit an immediate emotional response (such as to a snake approaching). Conditioning can also occur through this thalamo-limbic circuit even when links between the amygdala and the cortex have been severed, as long as the neural connections between the amygdala and the hippocampus are intact. (The reason is that the hippocampus allows memory of associations between stimuli and emotional reactions.) For primitive vertebrates, this simple circuit was probably the sole basis of emotional reaction.

In primates such as humans and chimpanzees, however, the amygdala is also connected to higher processing centers in the cortex. Thus, when the thalamus sends sensory information to the amygdala, it simultaneously routes information to the cortex for more thorough examination. Once the cortex has processed the information, it transmits information down to the amygdala. A second emotional response may then occur, based on this more complex information processing.

The emotional reaction to a stimulus, then, may pass through two stages (LeDoux, 1992, 1995), reflecting two somewhat independent processes (Figure 11.7b). One is a quick response based on a cursory reaction to gross stimulus features, involving a circuit running from the thalamus to the amygdala. (A dark shadow in the water frightens a bather.) The second process is slower, based on a more thorough cognitive appraisal, involving a thalamus-to-cortex-to-amygdala circuit. (The bather realizes that the dark shadow is a buoy.) The initial thalamus-to-amygdala process typically occurs faster because it involves fewer synaptic connections; that is, the circuit is shorter. The endocrine and autonomic responses it triggers will in turn produce sensations that are processed by the cortex, which must interpret their significance.

The existence of two circuits for emotional processing raises fascinating questions about what happens when the affective reactions generated by these two circuits are in conflict. For example, a cancer patient may have an immediate aversive conditioned response to the room in which she receives chemotherapy but also recognize that what happens in this room may be key to her survival. She therefore overrides the avoidance behavior that would ordinarily be elicited by the conditioned emotional response and keeps appearing for her treatments.

The Cortex

The cortex plays several roles with respect to emotion. As noted above, it allows people to consider the implications of a stimulus for adaptation or well-being. People with damage to the regions of the frontal cortex that receive input from the amygdala have difficulty making choices guided by their emotions and often behave in ways that are socially inappropriate (Chapter 7) (Damasio, 1994). The cortex is also involved in interpreting the meaning of peripheral responses, as when a person's experience of shaky knees and a dry throat while speaking in front of a group shows her that she is anxious (Pribram, 1980). In addition, the frontal cortex plays an important part in the social regulation of the face (Rinn, 1984), such as the ability to amplify, minimize, or feign an emotion.

Finally, the right and left hemispheres appear to be specialized, with the right hemisphere dominant in processing emotional cues from others and producing facial displays of emotion (Borod, 1992). Further, as noted above, approach-related emotions are associated with activation of the left frontal cortex, whereas avoidance-related emotions are associated with activation of the right frontal lobe (Davidson, 1992; Sutton & Davidson, 1997). People who show strong asymmetries in activation of regions of the left versus the right hemisphere tend to report corresponding asymmetries in their experience of positive and negative affect (Figure 11.8). In other words, participants who tend toward more left than right hemisphere activation report that they experience more positive than negative affect.

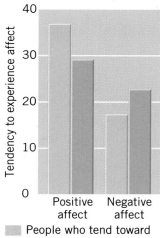

People who tend toward left hemisphere activation

People who tend toward right hemisphere activation

FIGURE 11.8
Emotional experience and hemisphere activation. The figure shows mean positive and negative affect scores for participants with a strong tendency toward left versus right midfrontal activation. As can be seen, participants with a bias toward left relative to right hemisphere activation reported more positive and less negative affect than those with less or no asymmetry toward the left. *Source*: Adapted from Tomarken et al., 1992, p. 681.

EMOTION REGULATION

Because emotions feel good or bad and can draw positive or negative responses from other people, from early in life people learn to regulate their emotions. **Emotion regulation** (or *affect regulation*) refers to efforts to control emotional states (Baumeister et al., 1994; Gross, in press; Kopp, 1989; Westen, 1994). People can regulate emotions before or after they occur. For example, they can avoid placing themselves in distressing situations, or deliberately undertake activities associated with pleasure. Alternatively, once an emotion has occurred, they can try to "reframe" an unpleasant situation ("Losing that job was probably a blessing in disguise") or attempt to escape the emotion directly (e.g., by drinking or distracting themselves).

People use similar strategies to try to regulate **moods**, which are relatively extended emotional states. Unlike emotions, moods typically do not shift attention or disrupt ongoing activities (Oatley & Jenkins, 1992.) Nevertheless, their subjective experience as painful or pleasurable makes them, like emotions, targets for affect-regulation strategies.

Emotion regulation strategies are a form of procedural knowledge (Chapter 6); that is, they are strategies people use to try to alter their emotional states in desired directions. Many of these strategies are conscious, as when people exercise when they are angry or depressed to "blow off steam" or "take their mind off" whatever is bothering them. One study examined gender differences in regulation of mood by asking participants to describe what they typically do when they feel tense or anxious (Thayer et al., 1994). Women were more likely to call or talk to someone, go shopping, and tend to chores, whereas men were more likely to have sex, engage in a hobby, or take a nap.

Much of the time, however, people learn what regulates their emotions in everyday life implicitly. Some people, for example, regularly handle distress by avoiding awareness of unpleasant emotions (Weinberger, 1990). This affect-regulatory style involves a complex set of processes, including selective inattention to negative feelings and inhibition of encoding and retrieval of unpleasant memories (see Cutler et al., 1996). Stable styles of emotion regulation are already observable by the time children enter preschool (Cole et al., 1996).

INTERIM SUMMARY   Emotional processes are distributed throughout the nervous system. The amygdala is the brain's "emotional computer" for calculating the emotional significance of a stimulus. It is also involved in detecting other people's emotions from their facial expression and vocal tone. The emotional reaction to a stimulus appears to involve two distinct neural pathways: a quick response based on a circuit running from the thalamus to the amygdala, and a slower response, based on a more thorough cognitive appraisal, involving a thalamus-to-cortex-to-amygdala circuit. In both cases, the amygdala then passes information on to the hypothalamus, which is involved in regulating autonomic responses. The cortex plays multiple roles with respect to emotion, such as interpreting the meaning of events and translating emotional reactions into socially desirable behaviors. **Emotion regulation** (or **affect regulation**) refers to efforts to control emotional states.

PERSPECTIVES ON EMOTION

We have now examined the components of emotion and its basis in the nervous system and now turn to *perspectives* on emotion. We have already explored the behavioral account of emotion in some detail in Chapter 5. As we have seen, behaviorist research points to approach and avoidance systems associated with positive and negative affect, respectively. Behaviorist researchers have studied conditioned emotional responses in classical conditioning as well, such as fear upon seeing a doctor approaching with a hypodermic needle. The psychodynamic, cognitive, and evolutionary perspectives offer additional insights into the nature and function of emotion.

Psychodynamic Perspectives

A growing body of evidence supports a central, and somewhat counterintuitive, contention of psychodynamic theory: that people can be unconscious of their own emotional experience and that unconscious emotional processes can influence thought, behavior, and even health (Singer, 1990; Westen, 1985, 1998). In one study (see Moray, 1969), the experimenter repeatedly paired previously neutral words with electric shock in a classical conditioning procedure, eventually producing a conditioned emotional response to them (anxiety or fear). The experimenter then exposed participants to the fear-inducing words using a dichotic listening procedure (Chapter 9). Thus, the researcher presented the words in the unattended channel of a pair of headphones as participants attended to the other channel, and measured anxious arousal physiologically by assessing skin conductance (Chapters 5 and 9). The conditioned stimuli elicited physiological reactivity (a GSR), even though participants had no conscious awareness of their presentation. Thus, participants reacted emotionally to stimuli perceived unconsciously.

Psychodynamic theory asserts that people regularly delude themselves about their own abilities and personality attributes as a way of avoiding unpleasant emotion, and a considerable body of experimental data supports this view (see Vaillant, 1992; Greenwald & Pratkanis, 1984). A recent set of studies tested the hypothesis that such defensive self-deception about emotions takes its toll physiologically (Shedler et al., 1993). The experiments focused on participants who are prone to disavowing negative thoughts and feelings about themselves. Participants were asked to fill out a questionnaire about their mental health and were then asked to describe in detail their earliest memories (a common procedure used by clinicians to assess degree of psychological health or disturbance; Mayman, 1968). Participants who self-reported themselves as happy and healthy on the questionnaire but who were judged by a clinician (in one study) or a team of undergraduates (in another) as emotionally troubled were categorized as having "illusory mental health." All subjects then underwent a potentially anxiety-provoking task, such as making up TAT stories or answering items from an IQ test.

During the task, subjects with illusory mental health could be distinguished from other subjects on numerous physiological indices of psychological distress. Notably, they had elevated heart rate and blood pressure, which are related to heart disease. These subjects also consistently scored highest on various indirect measures of anxiety, such as sighing and stammering, during the experimental procedure. All the while, however, they consciously reported the least anxiety, suggesting the presence of unconscious anxiety (Figure 11.9). Several other research groups have presented similar data on people who tend to keep themselves unaware of their emotions (see Asendorph & Sherer, 1983; Newton & Contrada, 1992; Singer, 1990; D. Weinberger, 1990).

Cognitive Perspectives

Throughout much of the history of Western culture, beginning at least with Plato in the 5th century B.C., emotion has been viewed as a disruptive force in human affairs. Plato asserted that reason must rein in the passions, which otherwise distort rational thinking. Today cognitive theorists empirically study the impact of feelings on cognitive processes such as memory and judgment, as well as the reverse—the influence of cognition on emotion (Power & Dalgleish, 1997; Dalgleish and Power, in press).

Interpretation and Emotion   You have just climbed four flights of stairs to your apartment on a frigid day, to be confronted by a roommate complaining about dirty dishes in the sink. Your heart is racing, and your face feels flushed.

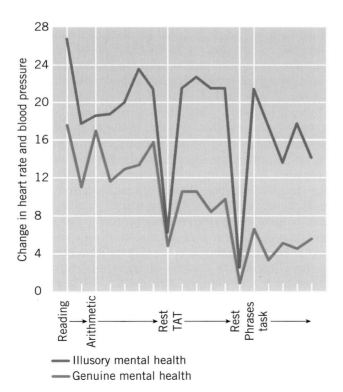

Illusory mental health
Genuine mental health

FIGURE 11.9
Illusory mental health. Participants judged high, but who self-reported themselves low in distress, showed substantially larger heart rate and blood pressure increases while performing such mildly stressful tasks as solving arithmetic questions and making up stories in response to TAT cards. Note, however, that during resting periods participants who deluded themselves showed as little reactivity as genuinely healthy participants, suggesting that their unconscious anxiety comes out only when performing a potentially threatening task. *Source:* Shedler et al., 1993.

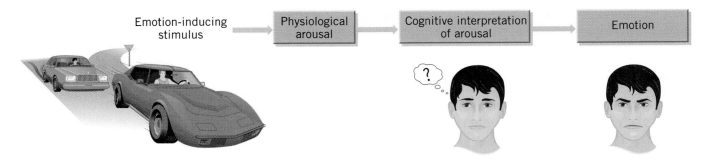

FIGURE 11.10

The Schachter-Singer theory of emotion. According to Schachter and Singer, people must interpret their arousal (for example, when cut off by a speeding car) in order to experience a specific emotion.

Are you angry? Or is your body simply registering the impact of four flights of stairs and a sudden change in temperature? The way you react may well depend on the **attributions** (inferences about causes) you make about these bodily sensations.

In a classic paper, Stanley Schachter and Jerome Singer (1962) argued that a cognitive judgment or attribution is crucial to emotional experience. That is, when people experience a state of nonspecific physiological arousal, which could be anger, happiness, or any other feeling, they try to figure out what the arousal means. If situational cues suggest that they should be afraid, they interpret the arousal as fear; if the cues suggest excitement, they interpret their arousal as excitement. Thus, according to the **Schachter-Singer theory**, emotion involves two factors: physiological arousal and cognitive interpretation (Figure 11.10).

To test their hypothesis, Schachter and Singer injected subjects with either adrenalin or an inert placebo and then placed them in a waiting room. Participants were either correctly informed, misinformed, or told nothing about the possible effects of the injection, in order to see whether their emotional state would be influenced by knowing they had been physiologically aroused. Next, participants in each condition were joined by a presumed participant (actually a confederate of the experimenter), who either behaved angrily and stormed out of the room (designed to elicit anger) or assumed a playful and euphoric attitude, throwing paper wads into the wastebasket, flying paper airplanes, and generally enjoying himself (designed to elicit euphoria).

Schachter and Singer predicted that participants who knew they had been injected with an arousing drug would attribute their arousal to the drug, whereas those who became aroused but did not know why would think they were either angry or euphoric, depending on the condition. The results were as predicted, suggesting that emotional experience is not simply the subjective awareness of arousal. Rather, it is a complex cognitive-affective state that includes inferences about the meaning of the arousal.

Schachter and Singer's conclusions have drawn criticism on a number of grounds (see Leventhal & Tomarken, 1986). For example, people can experience emotions without arousal. Even when physiological arousal is inhibited pharmacologically, people sometimes report feeling as anxious or angry as control subjects (Cleghorn et al., 1970; Erdmann & van Lindern, 1980). Thus, while arousal may intensify emotional experience, it may not be necessary for an emotion to occur (Reisenzein, 1983). Moreover, as the research reviewed earlier suggests, different emotions do, in fact, have distinct physiological correlates; thus, emotion is not simply the interpretation of general arousal. Finally, studies using experimental designs similar to Schachter and Singer's have often failed to replicate the original findings (Marshall & Zimbardo, 1979; Maslach, 1979). Nevertheless, numerous studies support the view that some degree of interpretation is involved in the experience of many emotional states. For instance, distinguishing between being tired (or fatigued) and being depressed requires interpretation because the two physiological states share many common features.

Cognition and Appraisal   In Schachter and Singer's study, participants initially became aroused by a shot of adrenalin. In normal life, however, people typically become aroused by their experiences rather than by injection. According to many cognitive theorists, people's emotions reflect their judgments and appraisals of the situations or stimuli that confront them (Lazarus, 1993; Roseman et al., 1996; Smith & Ellsworth, 1985; Weiner, 1985). Anger results from a judgment that a perceived punishment is caused by another person and is unfair (Roseman et al., 1990). (Presumably, Bill Clinton became furious at Kathleen Willey's actions, whether or not he made an improper advance, because he made the inference that her choosing to go on national television after staying friendly with him for years after the incident was a deliberate attempt to harm him.) An event that affects a person's well-being in the present leads to joy or distress, whereas an event that influences the person's potential well-being in the future leads to hope or fear (Ortony et al., 1988).

Many of these cognitive principles operate the same way cross-culturally (Mauro, Sato, & Tucker, 1992; Scherer, 1997). Judgments underlying emotion may, however, take some very different twists, depending on cultural conceptions of causality. Some preliterate societies believe that prolonged illness is the result of sorcery (Whiting & Child, 1958). Hence, the ill person or his loved ones may direct anger about the illness toward an accused sorcerer. The increased incidence in the United States of malpractice suits against physicians may reflect a similar process, as people respond to their anger and frustration by accusing a doctor of being negligent or incompetent.

Cognitive processes also play a central role in interpreting *other* people's emotions. Research from a cognitive perspective has, in fact, recently suggested that facial expressions provide only one source of information about people's emotions, and that knowledge about the situation can shape or even override information from the face. In one study, the researchers showed participants the face of a woman that had been unambiguously interpreted in prior studies as expressing fear (Carroll & Russell, 1996). Along with the photograph, however, they were also told the following story that led up to it: She had made a reservation at a fancy restaurant and was kept waiting for over an hour as celebrities and others walked in and were seated immediately. When she reminded the maitre d' of her reservation after the last couple was seated ahead of her, he told her that the tables were now full and the wait would likely be over an hour. With this information about the circumstances that led to her facial expression, the vast majority of participants interpreted the expression as anger, not fear.

These findings suggest that not only emotions but interpretations of emotion reflect cognitive appraisals. From a cognitive perspective, they could also could be readily interpreted from a connectionist point of view (Chapter 7): Facial expressions provide a powerful, "hard-wired" set of constraints that influence the interpretation of another person's emotion, but they provide only one of the sets of constraints that influence interpretation of emotion; in everyday life, knowledge about the situation also constrains inferences and may color the way a person interprets another's facial expression.

Although cognitive appraisals often underlie emotions, they do not always do so. Indeed, emotional responses can sometimes precede complex cognitive evaluations of a stimulus—or as psychologist Robert Zajonc (1980) has put it, "preferences need no inferences." Zajonc and his colleagues made use of the **mere exposure effect**, which shows that people become more positive about stimuli the more times they are exposed to them. The experimenters briefly exposed participants several times to Japanese ideographs (written characters). When later asked about their preferences for particular characters, as expected from the mere exposure effect, participants preferred characters they had previously seen—even when they did not consciously recognize having seen them. Zajonc concluded that the subjective sense of liking or disliking a stimulus may occur independently of cognitions about that stimulus. At the very least, affect may precede the *conscious* cognitive appraisals proposed by many theorists.

The Influence of Emotion and Mood on Cognition   Just as cognition can influence emotion, so, too, can emotion and mood influence ongoing thought and memory. As we saw at the beginning of the chapter, people often interpret ambiguous social or political situations in line with what they want to believe or what they feel rather than objectively weighing the facts.

Emotion can affect memory and thought in multiple ways. For example, anxiety can reduce working memory capacity and explicit problem solving by distracting the person from focusing on the task at hand (Eysenck, 1982; Richardson, 1996). Mood can also influence the way people make judgments, inferences, or predictions (see Basso et al., 1994; Mayer et al., 1992). People who are depressed, for example, tend to underestimate the probability of their own success and overestimate the probability of bad events occurring in the future (Beck, 1976, 1991).

Numerous studies have documented the influence of emotional states on both the encoding and retrieval of information in long-term memory (Bower, 1989; Kenealy, 1997; Mathews & Macleod, 1994). Individuals in a positive mood tend both to store and to retrieve more positive information (Isen, 1984, 1993). Thus, subjects exposed to a list of words are more likely to remember positive words from that list a week later if they were in a positive mood during encoding or if they are in a positive mood during retrieval. Positive mood also tends to facilitate memory more generally: Being in a good mood increases overall recall of information, independent of its emotional quality (Levine & Burgess, 1997).

Negative moods also affect encoding and retrieval, but the mechanisms are more complex. Negative mood at retrieval facilitates recall of negative words, since they are associatively linked in memory by the feeling common to both of them. However, people actively fight negative moods because they are aversive, so they try to retrieve more positive information (Josephson et al., 1996; Boden and Baumeister, 1997). Thus, a motivational process (regulating a negative mood) may counteract an automatic cognitive process (recall of information congruent with current thought and mood).

Emotional processes can also have a direct physiological effect on memory: Stressful emotional experiences can alter the structure of the brain (Gould et al., 1998). In one study, monkeys in one condition were exposed to an emotionally threatening encounter—being placed in another monkey's cage, who attacked until the "intruder" cowered in the corner. In comparison to monkeys in a control condition, these traumatized monkeys showed reduced production of neural cells in the hippocampus, a neural structure that plays a crucial role in memory (Chapter 6).

Evolutionary Perspectives

The evolutionary perspective on emotion derives from Charles Darwin's (1872) view that emotions serve an adaptive purpose. Darwin stressed their communicative function: Animals, including humans, signal their readiness to fight, run, or attend to each other's needs through a variety of postural, facial, and other nonverbal communications (see Buck, 1986). A baby's cry and a dog's raised hackles send signals to other members of the species. These communications regulate social behavior and increase the individual's chances of survival. The expression people display when angry—bared teeth and clenched jaws—shares the same evolutionary roots as the expression of other animals prepared to attack and bite an adversary. Darwin's theory explains why basic emotional expressions are wired into the organism and recognized cross-culturally.

Darwin's theory has received support from brain imaging studies demonstrating the existence of hard-wired neural circuits whose function is recognition of emotion in other people. As we have seen, the amygdala includes specific regions that allow people to recognize emotions such as fear and anger from other people's faces. Interestingly, damage to the same regions does not impair recognition of people's faces—that is, knowing who a particular person is—but does impair the capacity to read emotions from people's voices (Scott et al., 1997).

Emotion and Motivation Evolutionary theorists also view emotion as a powerful source of motivation—an internal communication that something must be done (Izard, 1977; Lang, 1995; Plutchik, 1980, 1997; Tomkins, 1962). In fact, the words "motivation" and "emotion" share the same Latin root, *movere*, which means to move. For example, when people are threatened, they feel fear, which in turn leads them to deal with the threatening situation through either fight or flight. Table 11.1 shows how emotional reactions motivate behaviors that promote survival and reproduction (Plutchik, 1980). Emotions and drives may also operate in tandem to motivate action, as when excitement accompanies sexual arousal (Tomkins, 1986). From an evolutionary perspective, different emotions serve different functions. Fear facilitates flight in the face of danger; disgust prevents ingestion of potentially toxic substances such as rotting meat.

Jealousy: An Evolutionary View An emotion that is less well understood is jealousy. Why do people become jealous in intimate sexual relationships? One series of studies tested evolutionary hypotheses about differences in the concerns men and women have about their partners' fidelity (Buss et al., 1992). Since females can have only a limited number of children during their lifetimes, to maximize their reproductive success they should be motivated to form relationships with males who have resources and will contribute them to their offspring. Indeed, cross-cultural evidence demonstrates that one of the main mate selection criteria used by females around the world is male resources, whether cattle or Corvettes (Chapter 18). From a female's point of view, then, infidelity accompanied by emotional commitment to the other woman is a major threat to resources. A man is unlikely to divert resources from his mate and her offspring to a casual fling, but the risk increases dramatically if he becomes emotionally involved and

The similarities of facial expressions of emotions such as anger show their common evolutionary roots.

TABLE 11.1	EVOLUTIONARY LINKS BETWEEN EMOTION AND BEHAVIOR IN HUMANS AND OTHER ANIMALS	
STIMULUS EVENT	**EMOTION**	**BEHAVIOR**
Threat	Fear, terror, anxiety	Fight, flight
Obstacle	Anger, rage	Biting, hitting
Potential mate	Joy, ecstasy, excitement	Courtship, mating
Loss of valued person	Sadness, grief	Crying for help
Group member	Acceptance, trust	Grooming, sharing
New territory	Anticipation	Examining, mapping
Sudden novel object	Surprise	Stopping, attending

Source: Adapted from Plutchik, 1980, p. 16.

perhaps considers switching long-term partners. Hence, a woman's jealousy would be expected to focus on her mate's emotional commitment to another female.

For males, the situation is different. If a male commits himself to an exclusive relationship with a female, he must be certain that the offspring in whom he is investing are his own. Because he cannot be sure of paternity, the best he can do is prevent his mate from copulating with any other males. In males, then, jealousy would be expected to focus less on the female's emotional commitment or resources and more on her tendency to give other males sexual access. Indeed, in species ranging from insects to humans, males take extreme measures to prevent other males from inseminating their mates (Hasselquist & Bensch, 1991). Male birds in some species refuse to let a female out of their sight for days after insemination. In humans, male sexual jealousy is the leading cause of homicides and of spouse battering cross-culturally (Daly & Wilson, 1988).

To test the evolutionary hypothesis that males and females differ in their reasons for jealousy, male and female college students were asked to "imagine that you discover that the person with whom you've been seriously involved became interested in someone else" (Buss et al., 1992). In the first study, participants were to choose which of two related scenarios would upset them more: "imagining your partner forming a deep emotional attachment to that person," or "imagining your partner enjoying passionate sexual intercourse with that person." They were then asked a second question involving similar scenarios contrasting love and sex: "imagining your partner falling in love with that other person," or "imagining your partner trying different sexual positions with that other person." As Figure 11.11 shows, 60 percent of males reported greater distress at the thought of sexual infidelity in response to the first question, compared to only 17 percent of the females, who were more concerned about emotional attachment. The second question yielded similar results.

In a second study, the investigators tested male and female students' physiological reactions to these questions to see whether these large gender differences would similarly appear if they assessed people's gut reactions rather than simply their words. Physiological distress was assessed using indices such as pulse rate and electronic detection of subtle facial muscle movements, particularly furrowing the brow, which is associated with unpleasant emotion. The findings were striking: Men showed increased distress as measured by multiple indices when imagining sexual infidelity, whereas females reacted more strongly to the emotional attachment scenario. A third study, recognizing that many college students may not have had intimate sexual relationships, employed the same design as the first study but asked participants whether or not they had had a physical relation-

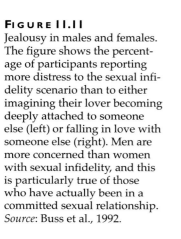

FIGURE 11.11
Jealousy in males and females. The figure shows the percentage of participants reporting more distress to the sexual infidelity scenario than to either imagining their lover becoming deeply attached to someone else (left) or falling in love with someone else (right). Men are more concerned than women with sexual infidelity, and this is particularly true of those who have actually been in a committed sexual relationship.
Source: Buss et al., 1992.

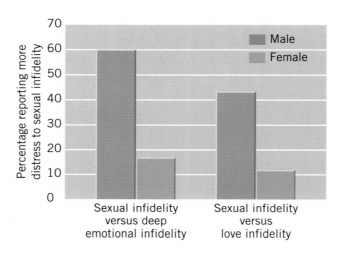

ship. Males who had actually had a sexual relationship, who were not just imagining an abstract scenario, were particularly concerned about sexual infidelity. The investigators theorized that having sexual experiences activates or amplifies an innate sexual jealousy mechanism in males.

The evolutionary interpretation of these findings has not gone unchallenged (DeSteno and Salovey, 1996; Harris and Christenfeld, 1996). For example, cultural explanations cannot be ruled out on the basis of these studies because they were conducted in a single culture. More recently, however, cross-cultural researchers have found similar sex differences in countries as diverse as Germany and China, although these differences were slightly less pronounced than in the U.S., suggesting both cultural and evolutionary influences on feelings of jealousy (Buunk et al., 1996; Geary et al., 1995).

INTERIM SUMMARY   Psychodynamic theorists argue that people can be unconscious of their emotional experience and can act on affects even when they lack subjective awareness of them. Often people do not know what they feel because doing so would be anxiety-provoking or otherwise unpleasant. According to the **Schachter–Singer** theory, a cognitive approach to emotion, emotion occurs as people interpret their physiological arousal. Subsequent research suggests that cognitive judgments and appraisals generate specific emotions. Mood and emotion can also influence cognition through its impact on working memory, encoding and retrieval of information in long-term memory, and thinking. From an evolutionary perspective, emotion serves an important role in communication between members of a species. It also serves as a powerful source of motivation.

▶ **ONE STEP FURTHER**

Integrating the Perspectives on Emotion

The various perspectives on emotion clearly focus on different parts of the fabled elephant (Chapter 1), and one would hope that ultimately a more fully elephantine portrait might emerge. As a step in that direction, we briefly explore a model of emotion that attempts to integrate aspects of the evolutionary, behavioral, psychodynamic, and cognitive perspectives (Westen, 1985, 1994). According to this model, feelings—including both emotions and sensory experiences of pleasure and pain caused by tactile stimulation—are mechanisms for selecting behavioral and mental responses. In other words, feelings regulate thought and behavior.

From an evolutionary perspective, the model suggests that emotions perform a central function in animals whose behavior is not rigidly controlled by instinct: They select behavior that enhances survival and reproduction by associating specific responses and stimuli to pleasant and unpleasant feelings. This evolved function can also provide the basis for dysfunctional behavior. For example, evolutionary theorists have recently cast a new light on drug abuse by suggesting that using drugs to regulate emotional states can "hijack" mechanisms that evolved through natural selection to alert us to danger or lead us to approach stimuli that are normally useful for survival and adaptation (Nesse & Berridge, 1997). Drugs that "trick" the brain into believing that all is well can derail mechanisms that have helped humans and other animals adapt to the natural and social environment for millenia.

From a behaviorist perspective, the model proposes that the consequences of an action determine whether or not it is maintained or produced again. Those consequences typically involve feelings (Bolles, 1975; Rachman, 1978). When a baby discovers that crying brings its caretaker and alleviates physical or emotional discomfort, crying behavior is reinforced; that

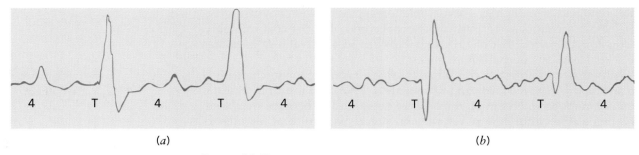

(a)   (b)

FIGURE 11.12

Classical conditioning of a thought. Part (a) shows the GSR of a participant to electric shock presented along with the letter T. Part (b) shows the GSR that occurred each time the participant thought about a T following acquisition of the conditioned response. *Source*: Miller, 1992.

is, crying behavior is selected for continued use out of all the baby's other past and potential behaviors. Similarly, when a rat is punished with an electric shock each time it presses a lever, it is motivated to avoid pressing the lever by fear (Chapter 5). Behavior is also influenced by expectancies about the likely positive or negative impact of an action or event, as in expectancy-value theories of motivation (Chapter 10).

From a psychodynamic perspective, mental processes, like behaviors, can also be conditioned—that is, selectively retained—by their association with emotion. Dollard and Miller (1950) argued many years ago that repression is essentially an internal flight mechanism—flight from a thought that would bring on an unpleasant feeling. Integrating behaviorist and psychodynamic thinking, Miller published an ingenious study showing that a conditioned emotional response could be transferred from a stimulus to a thought (see Miller, 1951, 1992). Participants initially underwent several trials in which they saw a 4 and a T. Presentation of the T was followed by an electric shock. Not surprisingly, this led to a large GSR (indicating anxious arousal) upon presentation of the T, even when it was no longer followed by a shock. Participants were then shown a series of dots and asked to think of a 4 on the first dot, a T on the second, a 4 on the third, and so on. The thought became a conditioned stimulus: Merely thinking of a T led to measurable anxiety (Figure 11.12). In real life, avoiding consciousness of thoughts associated with unpleasant emotions is reinforced by the elimination of the aversive emotion.

From a cognitive perspective, emotions often reflect a person's judgment about the extent to which current or potential realities match representations of desired states (wishes) or feared states (fears). For example, an individual may worry that his lover is going to leave. Discrepancies between cognitions about reality (his lover's presence is comforting) and desired or feared states (his lover might leave) produce emotional feedback (anxiety, sadness, guilt, shame, and so forth), much as in homeostatic models of motivation (see also Bowlby, 1969; Carver & Scheier, 1981; Menninger et al., 1963; Miller et al., 1960). These emotional signals in turn activate behavioral and mental responses (such as pleading, or convincing himself that the relationship really does not matter) designed to minimize negative feelings and maximize positive ones.

Any number of goal-states can energize human thought and behavior, such as desired closeness to a loved one (Bowlby, 1969), values and ideals (e.g., fighting poverty), ideals for oneself such as behaving morally or competently in some domain (see Higgins, 1990; Rogers, 1959), or hoping for

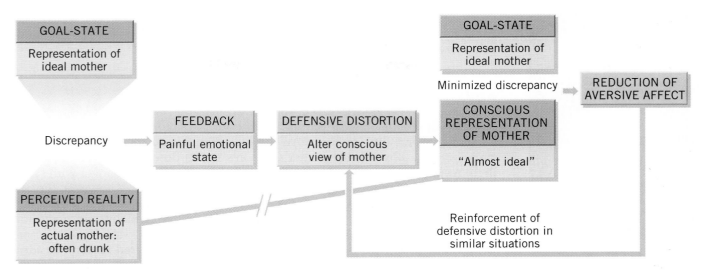

FIGURE 11.13

An integrated model of emotion. In this application of the model, the discrepancy between the son's view of his ideal and real mother produces a painful emotional state that elicits a defensive distortion. The result is that his real view of his mother, which is now unconscious (mother as often drunk), is cut off from his conscious view of his mother (mother as "almost ideal"), as shown by the break in the line. *Source*: Adapted from Westen, 1991.

snow during an upcoming ski trip. Over the long run, the goal-states people pursue tend to promote survival and reproduction, and they are influenced by innate preferences (such as worries about infidelity). Violation of goal-states produces unpleasant emotions and can initiate either mental or behavioral responses. A student who arrives at college and feels lonely (violation of goal-states regarding affiliation or intimacy) may respond behaviorally (joining organizations) or mentally (telling herself that things will get better). If these responses reduce the loneliness, they will be reinforced; that is, they will be maintained and more likely used in similar situations in the future.

Figure 11.13 illustrates how this integrated model might account for the behavior of a teenage boy with an alcoholic mother. The mother had often been grossly negligent in her caretaking, yet the son claimed he did not resent her "little drinking problem" and described her as "almost an ideal mother." According to the model, confronted with the painful discrepancy between his wished-for or ideal mother and the mother he really had, the boy distorted his view of his mother in a positive direction. His conscious view (mother as "almost ideal") then became cognitively cut off from more realistic memories of her.   ◀

STRESS

Emotion and stress are closely related concepts. Kathleen Willey's interview in front of 20 million viewers, like President Clinton's experience watching the interview on television with his wife beside him, were not only stressful events but emotional events. **Stress** refers to a challenge to a person's capacity to adapt to inner and outer demands, which may be physiologically arousing and emotionally taxing and call for cognitive or behavioral responses. This definition points to two important aspects of stress: that stress is a psychobiological process, and that stress entails a transaction between people and their environments. We begin by

Four years of stress can take a remarkable toll on the body. President Jimmy Carter, like Bill Clinton, appeared to age tremendously during his years in the White House.

discussing these two aspects of stress and then consider the major sources of stress and the impact of stress on health. Afterward, we explore the cognitive and behavioral strategies people use to cope with stress.

STRESS AS A PSYCHOBIOLOGICAL PROCESS

Stress is a psychobiological process, with both physiological and psychological components and consequences. An early contribution to the understanding of stress was the physiologist Walter Cannon's (1932) description of the fight-or-flight response (Chapter 3), in which the organism prepares for danger with sympathetic and endocrine activation. If the danger does not abate, however, the organism remains perpetually aroused, which leads to deteriorating health as the body continues to divert its resources away from everyday maintenance and toward emergency readiness.

Another major contribution to the study of stress occurred several decades ago when a young Canadian scientist made an accidental discovery (Selye, 1936, 1976). Hoping to discover a new sex hormone, Hans Selye injected rats with extracts of ovarian tissue. At first he thought he had discovered a new substance because the injections consistently produced specific effects: bleeding ulcers, an enlarged adrenal cortex, and a shrinking thymus gland (which contains white blood cells responsible for fighting disease). However, when he injected tissue from other parts of the body, it produced exactly the same syndrome, suggesting that the effects were not caused by a sex hormone.

At first, the reaction baffled Selye, but eventually he realized he had uncovered something very important about the physiology of stress. Experiments with a wide range of stressful events, from injections to fatigue to extreme cold, revealed that the body responds to stressful conditions with a **general adaptation syndrome** consisting of three stages: alarm, resistance, and exhaustion. The first stage, *alarm*, involves the release of adrenalin and other hormones such as cortisol, and activation of the sympathetic nervous system. This is what occurs biologically in fight-or-flight responses. Blood pressure, heart rate, respiration, and blood sugar rise as blood is diverted from the gastrointestinal tract to muscles and other parts of the body that may be called upon for an emergency response.

The alarm stage cannot last indefinitely, however, and the parasympathetic nervous system soon comes into play, returning levels of respiration and heart rate to normal. This second stage is what Selye calls the *resistance* stage. At this stage, all systems may appear to have returned to normal. However, the blood still has elevated levels of glucose (for energy) and some hormones (including adrenalin and the pituitary hormone ACTH), and the body continues to use its resources at an accelerated rate. Essentially, the organism remains on red alert, with heightened energy and arousal, but it has begun to adapt to a higher level of stress. Remaining on red alert, however, is not without its costs. During this stage the organism is especially vulnerable to illness, which is why Selye's rats developed many of their symptoms. It is also why overworked college students become susceptible to influenza, mononucleosis, and whatever garden-variety colds happen to be making the rounds. The situation is analogous to a country that deploys all its military troops to one border to protect against an invasion, leaving its other borders unprotected.

If the resistance phase lasts long enough, the body eventually wears down, and the organism enters a third stage, *exhaustion*. In this stage, physiological defenses break down, resulting in greatly increased vulnerability to serious or even life-threatening disease. Organs such as the heart that are vulnerable genetically or environmentally (from smoking, too much lifelong cholesterol intake, etc.) are the first to go during the exhaustion stage.

STRESS AS A TRANSACTIONAL PROCESS

In daily life, injection of ovarian tissue is not a major source of stress, and people do not respond to the same events with uniform stress responses. Richard Lazarus, who developed the most widely used model of stress, views normally occurring stress as a *transaction* between the individual and the environment rather than a property of either the person or the environment alone (Lazarus, 1981, 1991, 1993). Just as the amount of stress on a rope is jointly determined by the quality of the rope and the amount of weight pulling on it, so, too, is the amount of stress a person experiences a joint function of the individual's internal resources and the external situations "tugging" at the person.

Stress entails an individual's perception that demands of the environment tax or exceed her available psychosocial resources. Thus, in this view, stress depends on the meaning of an event to the individual: An event that fills one person with excitement, such as a new business opportunity, can make another feel overwhelmed and anxious. The extent to which an event is experienced as stressful therefore depends on the person's appraisal of both the situation and her ability to cope with it.

Lazarus's model identifies two stages in the process of stress and coping, neither of which is entirely conscious. In a **primary appraisal** of the situation, the person decides whether the situation is benign, stressful, or irrelevant. If the situation is appraised as stressful, she must determine what to do about it. This second stage, during which the person evaluates the options and decides how to respond, is called **secondary appraisal**. For instance, when President Clinton learned that Kathleen Willey was about to take her embarrassing allegations to the public on a nationally televised show, his primary appraisal was probably that this could further erode if not destroy his credibility with the public, which likely led to anxiety (and probably shame or humiliation). He then presumably reappraised the situation in light of possible coping strategies, such as getting his side of the story out, attacking her credibility, making some kind of public statement, talking to close confidantes, or praying.

Lazarus distinguishes three types of stress: *harm* or *loss*, as when a person loses a loved one or something greatly valued, such as a job; *threat*, which refers to perceived anticipated harm; and *challenge*, which refers to opportunities for growth that may nonetheless be fraught with disruption and uncertainty. Stress, then, is not always negative. Positive forms of stress, or challenges, include events such as getting married or entering college. These events can be exceedingly stressful—that is, psychologically and physiologically taxing—because of all the changes and adjustments they entail. Thus, while stress is often associated with anxiety, sadness, and anger, it can also entail pleasure, excitement, and interest.

Researchers study stress in individuals, but stress is often related to broader social and economic forces. Stress levels rise as unemployment levels rise; so, too, do rates of child abuse, violence against spouses, alcoholism, and disease (Hoffman et al., 1991; Jones, 1990). With every 1 percent increase in the unemployment rate, deaths from heart disease and cirrhosis of the liver (associated with drinking) increase approximately 2 percent, suicides increase 4 percent, and first-time mental hospital admissions increase 2 to 4 percent (see Taylor, 1991). Lower social status is also associated with stress and illness. One study found higher rates of cardiovascular disease in low-ranking civil servants, as compared with their higher status co-workers (Kessler, 1979, cited in Taylor, 1991).

INTERIM SUMMARY   **Stress** refers to a challenge to a person's capacity to adapt to inner and outer demands. Stress is a psychobiological process, with both physiological and psychological components and consequences. The **general adaptation syndrome** consists of three stages: alarm, resistance, and exhaustion. Stress is also a transactional process—a transaction between the individual and the environment—that entails the individual's perception that demands of the environment tax or exceed her available psychosocial resources. In a **primary appraisal** of the situation, the person decides whether the situation is benign, stressful, or irrelevant. During **secondary appraisal**, the person evaluates the options and decides how to respond.

SOURCES OF STRESS

Stress is an unavoidable part of life. Events that often lead to stress are called **stressors**, and they range from the infrequent, such as the death of a parent, to the commonplace, such as a demanding job or a noisy neighbor. Research on stressors has focused on life events, catastrophes, and daily hassles.

Life Events

One of the most significant sources of stress is change. Virtually any event that requires someone to make a readjustment can be a stressor. Thirty years ago, researchers devised a scale to measure the stress of various *life events* that require change and adaptation (Holmes & Rahe, 1967). To create the scale, they asked 394 participants to complete a questionnaire that listed 43 life events drawn from earlier clinical work. Participants rated the extent to which each event would require readjustment in their lives. By taking the mean score for each item, the investigators produced a life events rating scale that has been used in thousands of studies (Table 11.2). An individual's total stress score is the sum of all the life change units experienced within a period of 12 months. Although this scale offers a good rough

TABLE 11.2   TOP 25 STRESSORS ON THE HOLMES-RAHE LIFE EVENTS RATING SCALE

RANK	LIFE EVENT	MEAN VALUE
1	Death of spouse	100
2	Divorce	73
3	Marital separation	65
4	Jail term	63
5	Death of a close family member	63
6	Personal injury or illness	53
7	Marriage	50
8	Fired at work	47
9	Marital reconciliation	45
10	Retirement	45
11	Change in health in family member	44
12	Pregnancy	40
13	Sex difficulties	39
14	Gain of new family member	39
15	Business readjustment	39
16	Change in financial state	38
17	Death of close friend	37
18	Change to different line of work	36
19	Change in number of arguments with spouse	35
20	Mortgage over $10,000 (1964 dollars)	31
21	Foreclosure of mortgage or loan	30
22	Change in responsibilities at work	29
23	Son or daughter leaving home	29
24	Trouble with in-laws	29
25	Outstanding personal achievement	28

Source: Holmes & Rahe, 1967.

Even very positive events can be a substantial source of stress.

estimate of the amount of stress a person is encountering, it does not take into account the different meanings of various experiences for different individuals. Consequently, some researchers have turned, instead, to measures of *perceived stress*—that is, the extent to which participants *consider* the experiences they have undergone stressful.

Major Stressors   One of the most stressful events any individual can experience is the death of a spouse or child. Some early studies suggested that the effects of such a loss were relatively transitory and that the grieving process could take as little as four to six months (Clayton et al., 1968, 1972). However, the weight of research now points toward longer-lasting effects. A study of people who had lost a spouse or child in a car accident indicated that, for many bereaved persons, distress lasts as long as four to seven years after a sudden loss. Symptoms of prolonged distress included depression, sleep disturbances, fatigue, panic attacks, loneliness, and higher mortality rate. Among parents who had unexpectedly lost a child, divorce rates were also higher than among a comparison group (Lehman et al., 1987).

Striking findings on the relation between loss and mortality emerged in a study of over 1 million people from Finland, which examined the mortality rates of those who had lost a spouse over a five-year period (Martikainen and Valkonen, 1996). Deaths related to accidents, violence, and alcohol generally increase by a factor of two or more in the bereaved group. Deaths from heart disease doubled, perhaps confirming the popular view that people can "die of a broken heart." The relative risk of dying was particularly high within six months of the death of a spouse, and was highest in younger people (Figure 11.14). As we will see, loss takes a toll on physical health in two ways: by leading people to behave in ways that are more self-destructive, and by affecting the capacity of the body to fight off disease.

Another major stressor, unemployment, can also lead to impairments in both physical and mental health, although the effects are generally not as dramatic (Jahoda, 1988; Kessler et al., 1987). For example, another large Finnish study followed workers for several months after a plant lay-off (Viinamaki et al., 1996). Those who remained unemployed were at heightened risk for depression, subjective distress, and stress-related illnesses as the months wore on.

Major stressors such as loss or unemployment actually include many specific sources of stress, and the effect of these life events on a given person depends on

Cause of Death	Men		Women	
	Age 35-64	Age 65-74	Age 35-64	Age 65-74
All causes	1.66	1.16	1.25	1.10
All Diseases	1.56	1.21	1.19	1.10
Cancer	1.31	1.26	1.04	1.10
Lung cancer	1.49	1.37	1.56	.98
Stomach cancer	1.49	.94	1.13	.98
Chronic heart disease	2.08	1.31	1.71	1.22
Alcohol-related illness	3.08	1.69	2.91	1.27
Motor vehicle accidents	1.52	1.05	1.52	1.22
Other accidents and violence	3.05	1.62	2.45	1.47
Suicide	3.02	2.03	2.30	.92

Source: Adapted from P. Martikainen and T. Valkenen. (1996). Mortality after the death of a spouse: Rates and causes of death in a large Finnish cohort. *American Journal of Public Health*, 86, p.1090.

FIGURE 11.14
Relative risk of death following death of a spouse. The data show the relative risk of mortality by various causes (such as disease and suicide) associated with death of a spouse for men and women aged 35–64 and 65–74. A relative risk of 1.0 means no increased risk compared with people who have not lost a spouse. As can be seen, death of a spouse leads to substantially increased risk for younger people and tends to have a greater impact on men, although both sexes show elevated risk of mortality following death of a spouse. *Source:* Martikainen & Valkonen, 1996, p. 1090.

the individual's vulnerabilities to these specific stressors (Monroe & Simons, 1991). For example, unemployment can be devastating because of the financial strain on an individual or family. It can also produce other forms of stress, including marital strain, forced relocation, and loss of social contact with friends from work (Bolton & Oakley, 1986; Kessler et al., 1989). Even a person who has other sources of income, such as unemployment compensation or savings, may nevertheless experience lowered self-esteem, loneliness, or anxiety.

Acculturative Stress   A severe form of life stress that is increasingly confronting people throughout the world is **acculturative stress** (Berry, 1989, in press; Nwadiora and McAdoo, 1996; Rogler et al., 1991). Acculturation means coming into contact with a new, typically dominant culture. Thus, acculturative stress refers to the stress people experience in trying to adapt to a new culture, whether they willingly emigrate for better opportunities or flee as refugees from persecution. Acculturative stress is associated with anxiety, depression, uncertainty and conflict about ethnic identity, and alcohol abuse, although individual responses vary widely.

Like other major life stresses, acculturative stress includes many specific stresses. People entering new cultures frequently encounter difficulty communicating (because of language differences), racial or ethnic prejudice, lower socio-economic status than they enjoyed at home (such as Russian doctors working in North America as paramedics because of licensing requirements), separation from loved ones, total disruption of familiar routines, loss of familiar surroundings, and new values and beliefs. Many refugees must also come to terms with the torture or murder of loved ones back home and may themselves have encountered political repression or inhuman experiences en route to their new lands. The

A refugee camp during the civil war in Rwanda.

"boat people" who fled Vietnam, for example, not only suffered from lack of food and water but also faced robbery, kidnapping, rape, and murder at the hands of pirates (Gong-Guy et al., 1991). Immigrants also typically face tremendous conflicts over the extent to which they preserve their old values or adopt the values of their new culture. Such conflicts are often played out across the generations, as children of immigrants shun their parents' Old World attitudes.

Catastrophes

Catastrophes are stressors of massive proportions—rare, unexpected disasters such as earthquakes, floods, or other traumatic events that affect many people. Catastrophes may be caused by nature, but they may also be caused by humans, as were the Holocaust, the bombing of London during World War II, the exodus of the Vietnamese boat people, recent civil wars in Somalia, Rwanda, and the Balkan states, and the terrorist bombing attack that left nearly 200 dead in an Oklahoma City federal building in 1995.

Catastrophes sometimes lead to post-traumatic stress disorder (PTSD), which includes symptoms such as nightmares, flashbacks to the traumatic event, depression, anxiety, and intrusive thoughts about the experience (Chapter 15). Most severe life events, including losses, do not elicit PTSD. The major exception is rape, which leads to PTSD 80 percent of the time (Breslau et al., 1991).

One natural catastrophe studied by psychologists was the 1980 eruption of the Mount St. Helens volcano, which spewed a heavy covering of ash over a large area of Washington State (Adams & Adams, 1984). Unlike most natural disasters, the Mount St. Helens ash fall was predictable, which enabled researchers to compare people's predisaster and postdisaster functioning. Among residents of the small agricultural town of Othello, for example, reactions included significant increases in emergency room visits, court cases, crisis hotline calls, and mental health appointments for months after the eruption (Figure 11.15). The research also documented an 18.6 percent increase in the death rate, a 198 percent increase in stress-aggravated illness, and a 235 percent increase in diagnoses of mental illness in the local mental health clinic.

A man-made (and seldom woman-made) stress of catastrophic proportions, practiced by dozens of countries, is torture (Basoglu, 1997). In any given year,

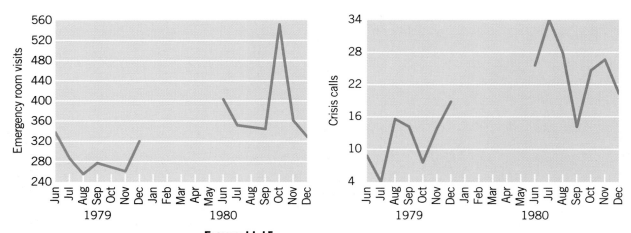

FIGURE 11.15

Impact of catastrophic stress. The number of emergency room visits and crisis calls jumped dramatically after the Mount St. Helens eruption, demonstrating the powerful effects of catastrophic stress. *Source*: Adams & Adams, 1984, p. 257.

over 150 countries in the world practice torture, and between 5 and 35 percent of the world's 14 million refugees have been subjected to at least one episode of torture. The most common psychological effects of torture include emotional symptoms such as anxiety and depression, social withdrawal, problems with memory and attention, sexual dysfunction, nightmares, insomnia, and personality changes. A study of torture victims in Turkey found that years later nearly half the survivors continued to suffer from nightmares and other symptoms of post-traumatic stress (Basoglu et al., 1994). The average subject was tortured 291 times over four years in captivity, with forms of torture including beating, electric shock, being stripped naked, prevention of urination or defecation, hanging by the wrists, rape, and twisting of the testicles. Perhaps the most remarkable finding, however, was how many victims did not suffer emotional distress years later. Less than 20 percent actually met the criteria for post-traumatic stress disorder, and the mean ratings of anxiety and depression were only slightly higher than for a matched group of people with similar backgrounds who had not been subjected to torture. The low rate of PTSD in this group may perhaps be explained by the fact that the torture victims were political activists, many of whom knew their actions could lead to imprisonment and torture. The researchers speculated, as others have about survivors of the Nazi Holocaust, that people with particularly

An Iranian torture victim.

TABLE 11.3   TEN MOST COMMON DAILY HASSLES

ITEM	PERCENTAGE OF TIMES CHECKED
1. Concerns about weight	52.4
2. Health of a family member	48.1
3. Rising prices of common goods	43.7
4. Home maintenance	42.8
5. Too many things to do	38.6
6. Misplacing or losing things	38.1
7. Yard work or outside home maintenance	38.1
8. Property, investment, or taxes	37.6
9. Crime	37.1
10. Physical appearance	35.9

Source: Kanner et al., 1981, p. 14.

Note: The numbers represent the mean percentage of people checking the item each month averaged over nine monthly administrations.

strong political or religious convictions show the most resilience to torture. Another study found that two variables—humiliation and being forced to watch other people tortured—predicted the tendency to develop PTSD in Asian torture survivors (Cunningham and Cunningham, 1997).

Daily Hassles

Although the concept of stressors tends to bring to mind major events such as death, unemployment, and catastrophes, more mundane but nonetheless potent sources of stress are **daily hassles**, "the irritating, frustrating, distressing demands that to some degree characterize everyday transactions with the environment" (Kanner et al., 1981, p. 3). Daily hassles range from interpersonal conflicts to commuting during rush hour; the most common daily hassles are listed in Table 11.3. Daily hassles are correlated with self-reports of distress and stress-related illnesses (Affleck et al., 1994; deJong et al., 1996), although it is not entirely clear whether hassles cause stress-related problems or whether people who are distressed notice daily hassles more and find minor complaints more upsetting.

INTERIM SUMMARY   Events that often lead to stress are called **stressors**. **Life events** are stressors that require change and adaptation. **Perceived stress** refers to the extent to which people consider the experiences they have undergone stressful. **Acculturative stress** refers to the stress people experience in trying to adapt to a new culture. **Catastrophes** are stressors of massive proportions, including both natural and man-made disasters. **Daily hassles** are minor annoyances of everyday life that contribute to stress.

STRESS AND HEALTH

Stress has a considerable impact not only on psychological well-being but also on health and mortality (Adler & Matthews, 1994; Miller, 1997; O'Leary, 1997). People under stress often suffer from headaches, depression, and other health problems such as influenza, sore throat, and backache (Cohen et al., 1991; DeLongis et al., 1988). Several studies have also linked stress to vulnerability to cancer, and studies have shown that psychotherapy can substantially increase life expectan-

*It's not the large things that send a man to the madhouse....
no, it's the continuing series of small tragedies that send a man to the madhouse ...
not the death of his love but a shoelace that snaps with no time left ...*

C. BUKOWSKI,
"The Shoelace," 1980

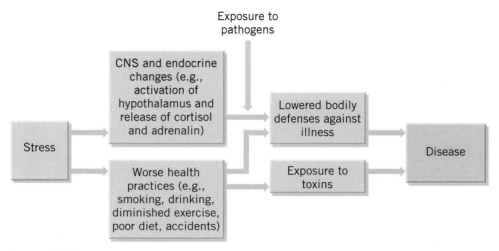

FIGURE 11.16

Pathways linking stress to infectious diseases. Stress can influence the onset of infectious disease in a number of ways. It can lead to CNS (central nervous system) and endocrine responses that diminish immune system functioning, leaving the person vulnerable to infection and illness from random exposure to pathogens such as airborne viruses. Alternatively, stress can lead to nonrandom exposure to toxins through poor health practices such as smoking. *Source:* Adapted from Cohen & Williamson, 1991, p. 8.

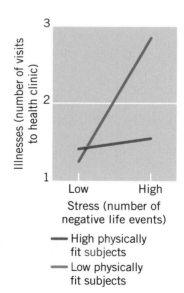

FIGURE 11.17

Interaction between stress and physical fitness. Students who were physically fit did not become sick when confronted with stress. Less fit participants, however, became ill when confronted with negative life events. *Source:* Brown, 1991, p. 559.

cies in some cancer patients (Jacobs & Charles, 1980; Levenson & Bemis, 1991; Spiegel & Kato, 1996).

Stress can have a direct effect on health by decreasing the body's capacity to fight illness. It can also affect health indirectly by instigating behaviors and coping responses that weaken the body's defenses or lead to exposure to pathogens, toxic agents that can produce physical illness (Figure 11.16). People under stress tend to drink more alcohol, smoke more, sleep less, and exercise less than their peers (Cohen & Williamson, 1991; O'Leary, 1992).

Other variables can exacerbate or minimize the impact of stress on health. Stress is more likely to affect people's health, for example, if they do not have adequate social support (Baron et al., 1990; Cohen & Williamson, 1991). Similarly, exercise can moderate the impact of stress on health. One study compared the number of visits to the health clinic of college students who were either high or low in physical fitness (Brown, 1991). Physically fit participants made fewer visits to the health clinic even when reporting many negative life events, whereas participants who were less physically fit became ill when stressed (Figure 11.17).

Exercise is an example of a preventive measure that can directly reduce both stress and illness. Unfortunately, people frequently fail to carry out health-promoting behaviors for a variety of reasons (Taylor, 1991). They may, for example, lack the knowledge or resources, or be unrealistically optimistic about their chances for avoiding major health problems (such as believing that others, not themselves, will develop heart disease from smoking). They may also face institutional incentives for waiting until the machinery is broken before fixing anything, such as health plans that cover visits to the doctor but not to the nutritionist, the gym, or the smoking clinic.

Stress and the Immune System

The **immune system** is the body's surveillance and security system, responsible for detecting and eliminating disease-causing agents in the body such as bacteria and viruses. Three important types of cells in the immune system are **B cells**, **T** cells, and **natural killer cells**. B cells produce **antibodies**, protein molecules that attach themselves to foreign invaders and mark them for destruction. Some T cells search out and directly destroy invaders, while others (T-helper cells) stimulate immunological activity. T-helper cells are the primary target of HIV, the virus that causes AIDS. Natural killer cells fight viruses and tumors (Weisse, 1992). Both acute and chronic stress can affect the efficiency and availability of cells in the immune system and hence the body's capacity to fight off disease (O'Leary et al., 1997).

When a group of people are exposed to an infectious disease, such as respiratory illness, only some of them actually become sick. Consequently, one way to explore the effects of stress on the immune system is to see whether people under stress are more likely to suffer from infectious diseases. The evidence suggests that they are. One study (Jemmott et al., 1983) investigated the relationship between academic pressure and immunologic functioning (specifically, the secretion of an antibody called Immunoglobin A, or IgA). During periods of the academic calendar rated by both the researchers and participants as most stressful, the secretion rate of IgA was lower—that is, the immune response was reduced.

Perhaps the most conclusive study yet of the influence of stress on both immune functioning and illness assessed 394 healthy participants for degree of life stress and then administered nasal drops containing one of five different viruses (Cohen et al., 1991). Participants reporting higher stress showed greater rates of infection for all five viruses (Figure 11.18).

Similar findings emerged in another study that has followed up a huge sample of gifted children since 1921 (Friedman et al., 1995). In this study, conscientiousness, as assessed by their teachers, predicted disease and mortality over their lifespans. Children rated as low in conscientiousness were somewhat more likely to die a violent death, but the more important finding was that being highly conscientious seemed to protect against diseases such as cancer and heart disease, even when statistically controlling for behaviors such as smoking (that is, essen-

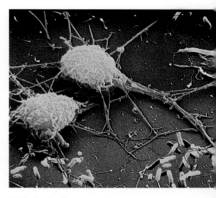

Cells in the immune system attacking E. coli bacteria.

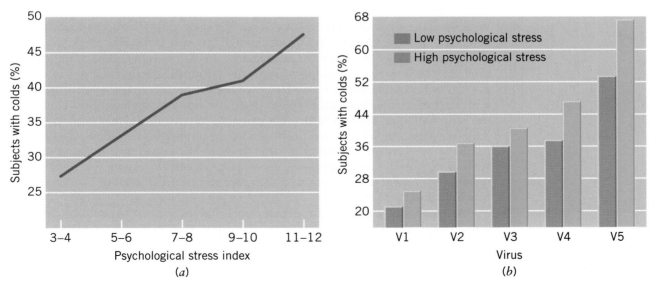

FIGURE 11.18
The relation between stress and illness following viral exposure. Part (*a*) shows the relation between amount of self-reported psychological stress and the percentage of participants judged by a physician to have a clinical cold after exposure to a virus. As can be seen, the more stress, the more colds. Part (*b*) presents data from a biological test of participants' blood for presence of infection. For each of five viruses, participants reporting higher stress showed higher rates of infection. *Source*: Cohen et al., 1991, pp. 609–610.

tially comparing smokers high and low on conscientiousness and nonsmokers high and low on this personality trait). Precisely how conscientiousness is good for the body and not just the soul is not yet clear.

Stress and Health-Seeking Behavior

Stress can influence health in a more subtle way by influencing the way the person interprets bodily symptoms (Cameron et al., 1995; Leventhal & Leventhal, 1993). When symptoms are unambiguous and ominous, such as severe stomach pain accompanied by bloody stools, people tend to seek help immediately. However, many symptoms of physical illness are ambiguous. This ambiguity can lead to several alternative responses. The person may ignore symptoms such as chest pains or take a "wait and see attitude." In some instances, this reflects an effort to cope with the emotion that would be generated if the person took the symptom seriously (in this case, as a possible sign of a failing heart). By deciding that "it's probably nothing," the person essentially reduces his distress—but may ultimately be sealing his fate if indeed the symptom was a warning of an impending heart attack. In other instances, this "wait and see" approach can reflect the inferences people make in the context of recent stressors. For example, a person who has lost a job within the last few months may decide that "it's just stress" and hence fail to seek medical attention.

At other times, and for other people, stress can have precisely the opposite effect, causing people to seek medical care for one minor complaint after another, and leading them to fear that each new bodily complaint could be a sign of a serious disease. In fact, people who are depressed, anxious, or recently stressed by experiences such as job loss tend not only to *have* more physical illnesses but also to interpret their illnesses more seriously and to experience the pain as greater. Thus, stress can lead people either to take their health too seriously or not seriously enough.

Stress, Health, and Personality

Whether a person under stress remains healthy or becomes ill also depends on the person's enduring personality dispositions (O'Brien & DeLongis, 1996; Suls et al, 1996). Personality can influence stress and health through the motives the person pursues, the way the individual chronically appraises circumstances (for example, easily becoming angry or sad), or the way the person characteristically copes with stress (such as through drinking, cigarette smoking, avoiding doctors, suppressing emotions, and so forth). For example, in one study, participants kept a daily diary of their moods and the events of the day (Suls et al., 1998). The higher participants were in neuroticism—the tendency to experience negative affects such as depression or anxiety—the more daily problems they reported, the more reactive they were to stressors, and the more they were distressed by bad things that happened to them.

A recent study powerfully demonstrates the impact of personality on both stress and health (Caspi et al., in press). The investigators have been following up the entire group of people born in Dunedin, New Zealand during one year in the early 1970s—a total sample of about a thousand people—and have assessed them repeatedly beginning at age three. At age 18, researchers assessed aspects of their personalities by questionnaire. At age 21, they assessed four high-risk behaviors associated with stress and health: alcohol dependence, violent crime, unprotected sex with multiple partners, and dangerous driving habits. Personality at age 18 was a powerful predictor of these behaviors three years later: Those who tended to engage in all of them were lower on traditionalism, harm avoidance (concern about avoiding danger), control (ability to regulate impulses), and social closeness. They were also higher on aggression. Perhaps more striking, risk behaviors at age 21 were predictable from the initial assessment of participants at age three: Those who were classified in preschool as undercontrolled—impulsive, poorly behaved, and aggressive—were more likely to engage in all four high-risk behaviors than their better-controlled (and particularly overcontrolled) peers.

An understanding of the relation between stress and personality reinforces an important point: Stress is not something that happens to a person; it reflects an interaction between the person and the situation. Recent research on the genetics of personality and stress highlights some of the complexities involved in the relations among stress, environmental events, and genes (Kendler, 1995). Genetics can influence stress in two ways: by influencing the probability a person will place herself in stressful situations, and by influencing her vulnerability to the stressors she encounters. For example, comparisons of monozygotic and dizygotic twins find that the likelihood of being robbed, assaulted, or confronted with financial difficulties is moderately heritable, with heritability estimated between 30 and 40 percent. For example, the correlation between monozygotic (identical) twins' reports of financial difficulties is .44, whereas for dizygotic (fraternal) twins the correlation is only .12. As we will see (Chapter 12), the tendency to take risks is itself heritable—in large part because people who are fearful take fewer risks, and those who are more pleasure-driven take more—which could account for findings such as this. Once a person experiences a stressful event, the tendency to experience negative affect, which is also heritable, can then amplify the individual's distress.

Type A Behavior Pattern and Hostility   One of the most thoroughly researched links between personality and health is between heart disease and the **Type A behavior pattern**. Type A individuals, first identified by two cardiologists (Friedman & Rosenman, 1959), are impatient, hard-driving, ambitious, competitive, and hostile. Type B individuals are more relaxed, easy-going, and less easily angered. One psychologist illustrated the differences between Type A and Type B behavior in describing a fishing trip he took with a colleague:

> I baited the hook and dropped the line over in a relaxed fashion, watched the gulls, and swayed with the swells. But what really struck [my colleague] was my talking to the fish when they bit the hook: "That's nice" or "Take your time, I'm in no rush." (Schwartz, 1987, p. 136)

In contrast to his own Type B pattern, a man fishing in a boat nearby exhibited Type A behavior:

> He was fishing with two poles, racing back and forth between them, and tangling his lines while cursing the fish that happened to be on the line beyond his reach. If the fish eluded him while others caught them, he would pull up the anchor in frustration, start the engine with a roar, and race to another part of the bay. (p. 136)

A comparison of bus drivers in North America and India suggests that these behavioral patterns occur cross-culturally, at least in some form (Evans et al., 1987). In both samples, Type A bus drivers reported greater job stress, had more accidents, and had more absences per month than Type B drivers. In addition, in India, Type A bus drivers braked, blew their horns, and passed more frequently than Type B drivers.

More recent research suggests that the Type A pattern has subcomponents that may be differentially related to heart disease (Dembroski & Costa, 1987; Siegman, 1994). In particular, hostility, or the combination of defensiveness, negative affect, and disavowed hostility, has been implicated in coronary atherosclerosis, or narrowing of the arteries leading to the heart. Hostility is more generally re-

Type A and Type B behavior on the tennis court.

lated to mortality; that is, angry people tend to die slightly younger (Miller et al., 1996).

Optimism/Pessimism   Another personality dimension related to immune functioning and health is optimism/pessimism (Peterson, 1995; Scheier and Bridges, 1995). One study found that coronary artery bypass patients who reported higher levels of optimism on a questionnaire recovered more quickly and returned to normal life more easily than pessimistic participants (Scheier et al., 1989). Another study found that college students with a pessimistic explanatory style (a tendency to explain bad events in negative, self-blaming ways; see Chapter 5) experienced more days of illness and visited physicians more frequently than other students (Peterson, 1988).

Even more striking results emerged in a 35-year study of 99 graduates of Harvard University. Participants with a pessimistic explanatory style at age 25 were more likely to be in poor health or dead at ages 45–50, even when controlling statistically for physical and mental health at age 25 (Peterson et al., 1988). People who are pessimistic do not take as good care of themselves, do not cope as well, and appear to have depressed immune functioning, all of which lead to greater illness (Kamen & Seligman, 1987; Lin & Peterson, 1990).

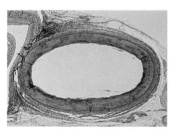

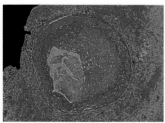

Type A behavior appears to contribute to the blocking of arteries. The top photo shows a normal artery. The bottom photo shows an artery severely narrowed.

INTERIM SUMMARY   Stress can affect physical health in two ways: directly, by weakening the **immune system** (the system of cells that detects and destroys disease-causing agents), and indirectly, by leading to behaviors and coping responses that weaken the body's defenses or lead to exposure to pathogens (toxic agents). Personality factors also affect stress levels and health, such as the tendency to experience negative affect (or neuroticism), hostility and inhibited hostility, and pessimism.

COPING

That people get sick or experience unpleasant emotions in response to stress should come as no surprise. What may seem more surprising is that most people who experience life crises remain healthy (Moos & Schaefer, 1986). This resiliency in the face of stress reflects the ways people deal with stressful situations, or ways of **coping**.

COPING MECHANISMS

Researchers often distinguish two or three basic types of coping strategies (Folkman & Lazarus, 1980; Moos & Billings, 1982). Strategies aimed at changing the situation are called *problem-focused*, because they try to deal with the stressor itself. Two other types of strategy—efforts to alter thoughts about the situation, and efforts to alter the unpleasant emotional consequences of stress—are called *emotion-focused*, because their aim is to regulate the emotions generated by a stressful experience. In other words, if a person cannot change a stressful situation directly, he can try to change his perception of it or the emotions it produces.

Efforts to cope by changing the situation typically involve problem solving (Chapter 7). The individual may try to remove the stressor, plan ways of resolving the situation, seek advice or assistance from others to change the situation, or try to avoid the stressor altogether by planning ahead (Aspinwall & Taylor, 1997; Carver et al., 1989). People high in problem-solving ability and who have a problem-solving orientation (a tendency to define potential problems as challenging and to confront them directly) tend to report less stress and fewer psychological symptoms than other participants (D'Zurilla & Sheedy, 1991; Epstein & Katz, 1992). Individuals with a problem-focused orientation tend to endorse questionnaire statements such as, "I am the kind of person who takes action rather than just thinks or complains about a situation" (Epstein, 1992, p. 828). Children whose mothers have a problem-focused coping style tend to be better adjusted and more socially skilled than their peers (Eisenberg et al., 1996).

Coping by changing one's cognition or appraisal of the situation often involves reframing an event mentally to make it seem less threatening. For example, a person who is anxious about giving a speech may say to himself, "Come on now, this is ridiculous. You are just talking to a bunch of people who are interested in what you have to say." An example of reframing a more tragic situation is the way a man dying of AIDS combined cognitive restructuring with a sense of humor: "I made a list of all the other diseases I would rather not have than AIDS. Lou Gehrig's disease, being in a wheelchair; rheumatoid arthritis, when you are in knots and in terrible pain. So I said, you've got to get some perspective on this, and where you are on the Great Nasty Disease List" (Reed, 1989, in Taylor, 1991, p. 243).

A number of studies suggest that religious faith often helps people cope with stressful events, such as contracting a terminal disease or losing a child, by allowing them to ascribe meaning to the event or strengthening their sense of closeness to the divine (Pargament & Park, 1995). For example, one study found that people who used their religion to cope with a major life stress—a kidney transplant—tended to have better outcomes 3 and 12 months later, as did their significant others who relied on faith to help them through the experience (Tix & Frazier, 1998).

When a stressful situation cannot be avoided, people often try to relieve the associated emotional state, as when a person smiles nervously to try to regulate anxiety. Alcohol and drug use are common mechanisms for escaping emotional distress, as is distraction. Another AIDS patient, in describing his efforts to cope with distressing emotions, confided, "I used to depend on drugs a lot to change my mood. Once in a while, I still find that if I can't feel better any other way, I will take a puff of grass or have a glass of wine, or I use music. There are certain recordings that can really change my mood drastically. I play it [music] loud and I dance around and try to clear my head" (Reed, 1989, in Taylor, 1992, p. 242).

A GLOBAL VISTA

THE IMPACT OF CULTURE ON COPING STYLES

The way people respond to stress, as well as the situations they consider stressful, are in part culturally patterned. One study found significant cultural differences in the coping styles of children in the United States and Mexico, with U.S. participants more likely to attempt to master stressful situations actively (Diaz-Guerrero, 1979). Mexican children are socialized to adopt a more passive style of coping with events, modifying themselves rather than confronting obstacles in the environment, while U.S. children are encouraged to take an active approach, modifying their physical, social, and interpersonal environments. Mexican children, for example, were more likely to be compliant and to work slowly than U.S. children when given tasks to perform.

This cultural difference is not surprising in the light of psychological and anthropological research on value orientations in different cultures (Kluckhohn & Strodtbeck, 1961). The emphasis on mastering the environment, characteristic of highly technologically developed societies, is an anomaly in human history. Most cultures instead believe humans should live harmoniously with nature and recognize their place in the natural order. These value differences may limit the applicability of Western theories and research which argue that a sense of personal control or efficacy is important for mental health and that active coping styles are preferable to passive ones. In a society based on entrepreneurship, technological development, wage labor, and individual productivity, active mastery and a strong belief in one's own ability are highly adaptive traits. In a society organized around family, community, or tribal ties, in which development of new technologies is neither expected nor particularly encouraged, such traits may be unrelated to mental and physical health. Coping is always relative to its cultural context, and coping strategies considered useful in one society (such as wailing at a funeral) may engender disapproval, and hence additional stress, in another.

Low-Effort Syndrome

Understanding patterns of culture and coping may also lead to a better understanding of the dilemmas facing African-American and other minority adolescents, particularly in regard to achievement (Ogbu, 1991). For years educators, social scientists, and policymakers have wrestled with the question of why a large gap exists between the educational performance of whites and some minority groups in the U.S., such as African- and Mexican-Americans, while no such gap exists for other immigrant groups, such as Arabs, Chinese, and West Indian blacks. John Ogbu (1991) argues that, throughout the world, minority groups who for generations experience a ceiling on their economic prospects because of job discrimination develop a **low-effort syndrome** that is not present in new immigrants who voluntarily move to a culture in search of a better life. The school performance of Koreans in Japan, who have been an underclass there for many years, is very poor, whereas Korean immigrants to North America tend to excel. When social barriers make effort and achievement fruitless, low-effort syndrome is an adaptive coping strategy because hard work and academic success would only increase frustration and anger.

Low-effort syndrome is an example of a coping strategy that solves one problem (minimizing frustration in the face of racism and barriers to success) but creates another, particularly if opportunities and social attitudes toward race change faster than coping styles developed over several generations. Because African-Americans for years faced impassable barriers to upward mobility, scholastic achievement became defined in many black communities as "white" behavior. Thus, for many black adolescents today the fear of being ridiculed for "acting white," together with a subcultural ambivalence toward achievement, inhibits scholastic achievement. Even high-achieving African-American students from disadvantaged areas may respond with low effort when they enter college and their prior schooling places them at a sudden disadvantage. Although increased effort would actually be the most useful strategy at that point, effort can ironically threaten self-esteem: If increased effort does not immediately bring success, the lack of success cannot be attributed to lack of effort. As we will see (Chapter 17), efforts at achievement can lead to anxiety in even the most accomplished African-American students because of associations they, like their white peers, have formed over years between blacks and lack of success (Steele, 1997).

John Henryism

Low-effort syndrome among people who historically faced external limits on what they could hope to achieve can be understood as an adaptation to a social and political system that eliminated rewards for effort. Recent research suggests another way in which, paradoxically, low effort among African-Americans for years made adaptive sense: Those who tried harder died earlier.

A legend is told (and a song sung) of a "steel-drivin' man" named John Henry, a black man known among railroad workers in the late 19th century for his extraordinary strength and endurance. As the legend goes, in a famous steel-driving contest, after an extraordinary battle of man versus machine, Henry beat a mechanical steam drill with mighty blows from his nine-pound hammer. Moments later, however, he died from exhaustion (Sherman, 1994).

This may not have been an isolated incident. Physicians have been puzzled for years by the increased rates of high blood pressure in African-Americans, which is associated with greater rates of stroke (because high blood pressure puts pressure on blood vessels in the brain, which eventually burst). Genetics may explain some of the difference between blacks and whites in blood pressure. However, researchers have recently identified a coping style among some African-Americans called **John Henryism**—defined by a tendency to work hard and cope actively despite difficult circumstances—that may also account for a substantial part of the difference (Sherman, 1994; Wright et al., 1996). Individuals with this coping style show a single-minded determination to succeed despite the odds, as evident in their endorsement of statements such as "When things don't go the way I want them to, that just makes me work even harder."

Several studies have shown that individuals high in John Henryism are vulnerable to high blood pressure, particularly when they are black, and particularly when they are of low socioeconomic status. In other words, African-Americans who are poor who try to better themselves are especially at risk. In some sense, then, low-effort syndrome may have been an adaptive solution to a system that psychologically put a noose around the neck of those who tried to better themselves. To what extent the physiological consequences of John Henryism will change as opportunities continue to expand for African-Americans is as yet unknown.

INTERIM SUMMARY   **Coping mechanisms** are the ways people deal with stressful events. *Problem-focused* coping involves changing the situation. *Emotion-focused* coping aims to regulate the emotion generated by a stressful situation. The way people respond to stress, as well as the situations they consider stressful, are in part culturally patterned. Members of minority groups who, for generations, experience a ceiling on their economic prospects because of job discrimination sometimes develop a **low-effort syndrome** in which they seemingly stop making the kinds of active efforts that might alleviate some of their hardships. In African-Americans, **John Henryism**—the tendency to work hard and cope actively despite difficult circumstances—is associated with high blood pressure and early death.

SOCIAL SUPPORT

An important resource for coping with stress is **social support**, the presence of others in whom one can confide and from whom one can expect help and concern (Strobe & Strobe, 1996). Social support is as important for maintaining physical as mental health (Salovey et al., 1998). A high level of social support is associated with protection against a range of illnesses, from hypertension and herpes to cancer and heart disease (Cohen, 1996; Sarason et al., 1997; Spiegel, 1996). In rhesus monkeys, immune functioning is suppressed when adult monkeys are separated from their social group but alleviated if they are given a companion (Gust et al., 1994; Landenslager & Boccia, 1996).

In humans, the number of social relationships a person has, and the extent to which the individual feels close to other people, is a powerful predictor of mortality (House et al., 1988). In fact, the evidence supporting the beneficial effects of social relationships on health is as strong as the evidence for the negative relationship between smoking and health in the Surgeon General's 1964 report. For example, in a large Swedish study, workers who had little control over their jobs were over one and one-half times more likely to die of heart disease over a 14-year

Social support protects against stress and illness in humans and other animals.

period than those with greater control, suggesting that lack of control is not only psychologically but physically damaging (Johnson et al., 1996). But those who had low control plus low social support were at even greater risk: They were two and one-half times more likely to die of heart disease.

Two hypotheses have been advanced to explain the beneficial effects of social support, both of which have received empirical support (Cohn & Wills, 1985; Taylor, 1991). The *buffering hypothesis* proposes that social support is a buffer or protective factor against the harmful effects of stress during high-stress periods. In a classic study, urban women who experienced significant life stress were much less likely to become depressed if they had an intimate, confiding relationship with a boyfriend or husband (Brown & Harris, 1978). The alternative hypothesis views social support as a continuously positive force that makes the person less susceptible to stress in the first place. In this view, people with supportive relationships are less likely to make a primary appraisal of situations as stressful, and they are more likely to perceive themselves as able to cope. Taking a new job is much more threatening to a person who has no one in whom to confide and no one to tell her, "Don't worry, you'll do well at it." In either case, an important aspect of social support is likely to be the opportunity for emotional disclosure, which, as we saw earlier in this chapter, promotes physical health at least in part by strengthening the immune system.

The relations between social support and stress are not, however, simple or uniform. For example, stress can erode social support, leading to a vicious cycle, particularly if the person under stress responds with anger or helplessness (Lane & Hobfoll, 1992). Further, severely stressful life events, such as getting cancer, can overwhelm significant others, who may actually withdraw in response to the person's emotional distress, because they, too, feel helpless and distressed (Bolger et al., 1996). More enduring aspects of a person's relationships can also be problematic. As we shall see in Chapter 14 on children's friendships, quantity is nice, but quality matters as well. High-conflict or unsupportive relationships can have detrimental effects on health and psychological well-being (e.g., Major et al., 1997). Further, supportive friends are helpful in times of crisis, but they cannot make up for the loss of a person to whom an individual is deeply emotionally attached, such as a spouse (Stroebe et al., 1996). Individuals have different kinds of social needs (Chapter 10) that are not interchangeable. Coping with death, for example, requires time to adjust to the loss of a particular person, not a quantity of social support.

INTERIM SUMMARY   Social support refers to the presence of others in whom a person can confide and from whom the individual can expect help and concern. In humans and other primates, lack of social support predicts disease and mortality. The *buffering hypothesis* proposes that social support buffers people against the harmful effects of acute stress. An alternative hypothesis suggests that social support is a continuously positive force that makes the person less susceptible to stress. Social support is not, however, uniformly beneficial. Bad relationships do not promote health, and significant others often have difficulty themselves being supportive at times of crisis.

SOME CONCLUDING THOUGHTS

Having spent several chapters on the more calm, cool aspects of psychology—perception, memory, thought, and language—in this chapter and the last we have explored the "hotter" sides of mental life and behavior—motivation, emotion, stress, and coping. In this chapter, we began to see some of the ways these two sides of human mental life are related: Just as political commentators interpret the events of the day through lenses distorted by their feelings, so, too, do people in everyday life remember and think in the context of their moods and emotions. In the next chapter, we more systematically explore psychologists' efforts to understand the varied ways thought, memory, emotion, and motivation interact in the complex phenomenon we call personality.

SUMMARY

EMOTION

1. **Emotion**, or **affect**, is an evaluative response (a positive or negative feeling state) that typically includes subjective experience, physiological arousal, and behavioral expression.

2. The **James–Lange theory** asserts that the subjective experience of emotion results from bodily experience induced by an emotion-eliciting stimulus. According to this theory, we do not run because we are afraid; we become afraid because we run (and our hearts pound). In contrast, the **Cannon-Bard theory** proposes that emotion-inducing stimuli simultaneously elicit both emotional experience and bodily responses. Although both theories have their strengths and limitations, recent research suggests that different emotions are, as James believed, associated with distinct, innate patterns of autonomic nervous system arousal.

3. **Emotional expression** refers to facial and other outward indications of emotion, such as body language and tone of voice. Many aspects of emotional expression, particularly facial expression, are innate and cross-culturally universal. Culturally variable patterns of regulating and displaying emotion are called **display rules**.

4. Psychologists have attempted to produce a list of **basic emotions**, emotions common to the human species from which all other emotions and emotional blends can be derived. Anger, fear, happiness, sadness, and disgust are listed by all theorists as basic. An even more fundamental distinction is between **positive affect** and **negative affect**, which is related, as well, to approach-oriented versus avoidance-oriented motives.

5. Emotions are controlled by neural pathways distributed throughout the nervous system. The hypothalamus activates sympathetic and endocrine responses related to emotion. The limbic system, and particularly the amygdala, is part of an emotional circuit that includes the hypothalamus. The amygdala is the brain's "emotional computer" for calculating the affective significance of a stimulus. The cortex plays several roles with respect to emotion, particularly in the appraisal of events.

6. The behaviorist perspective on emotion points to approach and avoidance systems associated with positive and negative affect, respectively. According to the psychodynamic perspective, people can be unconscious of their own emotional experience, which can nonetheless influence thought, behavior, and even health.

7. From a cognitive perspective, the way people respond emotionally depends on the **attributions** they make—that is, their inferences about causes of the emotion and their own bodily sensations. According to the **Schachter-Singer theory**, emotion involves two factors: physiological arousal and cognitive interpretation of the arousal. Emotion and **mood** (relatively extended emotional states which, unlike emotions, typically do not disrupt ongoing activities) have an impact on encoding, retrieval, judgment, and decision making.

8. The evolutionary perspective on emotion derives from Charles Darwin's view that emotions serve an adaptive purpose. Emotion has both communicative and motivational functions.

STRESS

9. **Stress** refers to a challenge to a person's capacity to adapt to inner and outer demands, which may be physiologically arousing and emotionally taxing and call for cognitive and behavioral responses. Stress is a psychobiological process that entails a transaction between a person and her environment. Selye proposed that the body responds to stressful conditions with a **general adaptation syndrome** consisting of three stages: alarm, resistance, and exhaustion.

10. From a psychological standpoint, stress entails a person's perception that demands of the environment tax or exceed his available psychosocial resources. Stress, in this view, depends on the meaning of an event to the individual. Lazarus's model identifies two stages in the process of stress and coping: **primary appraisal**, in which the person decides whether the situation is benign, stressful, or irrelevant; and **secondary appraisal**, in which the person evaluates the options and decides how to respond.

11. Events that often lead to stress are called **stressors**. Stressors include life events, catastrophes, and daily hassles.

12. Stress has a considerable impact on health and mortality, particularly through its effects on the **immune system**. Whether a person under stress remains healthy or becomes ill also depends in part on the person's enduring personality dispositions. **Type A behavior pattern**, and particularly its hostility component, has been linked to heart disease. Neuroticism (tendency to experience negative affective states), power motivation, hardiness, and optimism/pessimism are other personality traits linked to stress and health.

COPING

13. People cope by trying to change the situation directly, changing their perception of it, or changing the emotions it engenders. The ways people deal with stressful situations are known as strategies for **coping**; coping mechanisms are in part culturally patterned.

14. A major resource for coping with stress is **social support**, which is related to health and longevity.

Diana Ong, "Parts Equal the Whole, IV," 1940/SUPERSTOCK.

CHAPTER *12*

Personality

Oskar and Jack were identical twins who shared dozens of idiosyncrasies. They dressed alike (both wore wire-rimmed glasses and two-pocket shirts), read magazines from back to front, and wrapped rubber bands around their wrists. Their personalities were similar, from their basic "tempo," or speed of activity, to the way they responded to stress, their sense of well-being, and their style of interacting socially. None of this may seem unusual; they were, after all, identical twins. What makes this remarkable, however, is that Oskar Stohr was raised as a Catholic and a Nazi by his mother in Germany, while his twin brother Jack Yufe was raised as a Jew by his father and lived part of his life on an Israeli kibbutz. Separated shortly after birth, the men did not meet again until they were adults, when they participated in a study of twins (Holden, 1980).

Francis Picabia, "Aello," 1930. Collection Jean-Jacques Lebel, Paris.

The term *personality* is a part of everyday speech. When people make statements such as "Jim isn't the best-looking, but he has a nice personality," they typically use the term to denote the manner in which a person acts across a variety of situations. Psychologists use the term to describe not only an individual's *reputation*— the way the person acts and is known socially—but also the *internal processes* that create that reputation (Hogan, 1983, 1987). **Personality** refers to the enduring patterns of thought, feeling, motivation, and behavior that are expressed in different circumstances.

Personality psychologists have two aims. The first is to construct general theories that describe the **structure of personality**, that is, the organization of enduring patterns of thought, feeling, motivation, and behavior. The second task is to study **individual differences** in personality—the way people vary from one another in their personality characteristics. Thus, personality psychologists study both how people resemble one another and how they differ.

The approach psychologists use to carry out this dual mission depends, once again, on their theoretical perspective. We begin by exploring Freud's models of the mind and the evolution of psychodynamic thinking about personality since Freud's time. We then consider cognitive-social approaches, which derive from theories of learning and cognition, which we have already examined in some detail. Next, we examine trait theories, which use everyday language to describe personality, and examine the extent to which personality traits are inherited, as suggested by the case of Jack and Oskar. We then turn to humanistic theories, which focus on the way people wrestle with fundamental human concerns, such as mortality and meaning in life. We conclude by considering the extent to which personality differs across cultures.

INTERIM SUMMARY   **Personality** refers to the enduring patterns of thought, feeling, motivation, and behavior that are expressed in different circumstances. Personality psychologists construct general theories of the **structure of personality** (the way personality processes are organized) and **individual differences** (the way people vary from one another in their personality characteristics).

PSYCHODYNAMIC THEORIES

Sigmund Freud developed the first comprehensive theory of personality. As a neurologist practicing in the 1880s before the advent of psychiatry and clinical psychology, Freud encountered patients with a wide range of psychological disturbances. A particularly perplexing disorder was *hysteria,* in which a number of patients, most of them women, suffered from paralysis, numbness, and fainting spells, with no apparent biological origin. In seeking a treatment for the disorder, Freud was particularly influenced by the work of Jean Martin Charcot. Charcot, a French neurologist, demonstrated that hysterical symptoms could be produced—and alleviated, at least temporarily—through hypnosis. Paralyzed patients could walk again under the influence of a hypnotic suggestion, but the symptoms usually returned before long. These patients *wanted* to walk, but something seemed to override their conscious determination or will, much as many individuals today with bulimia cannot stop binging and purging.

Freud reasoned that if a symptom is not of physiological origin and the patient is consciously trying to stop it but cannot, then opposing the conscious will must be an unconscious counter-will of equal or greater magnitude. This basic assumption was the centerpiece of Freud's theory of **psychodynamics,** analogous to dynamics among physical forces. According to Freud, psychological forces such as wishes, fears, and intentions have a direction and an intensity. When several such motives collide and conflict, the balance of these forces determines the person's behavior, as in the case of a patient suffering from a hysterical paralysis, whose will to move her leg is unconsciously overridden (Figure 12.1).

FREUD'S MODELS

Why would a counter-will be unconscious? And what balance of unconscious forces could lead to paralysis or to a need to starve or drink oneself to death? Freud tried to answer these questions throughout his career by developing a series of models, which he never entirely reconciled with one another. Before turning to Freud's models and those of later psychodynamic theorists, a brief comment about method is in order. The data presented in the next several pages are not the same kind of laboratory data to which the reader is by now accustomed. Although we will explore some of the laboratory evidence for psychodynamic theories, the basis for these theories has largely been observations during clinical sessions with patients. Many critics have rightfully pointed to the problems with case study data of this sort: They cannot easily be observed by other scientists, they are filtered through the biases of the investigator, and they do not easily permit generalization from one subject to another. Nevertheless, clinical observation has led to the discovery of many important phenomena, such as unconscious processes, that were ignored or rejected by advocates of other perspectives for up to a century for want of reliable methods to study them (Chapter 2).

Topographic Model

Freud's first model, the **topographic model** (1900), used a spatial metaphor (the mind as split into sectors) that divided mental processes into three types: con-

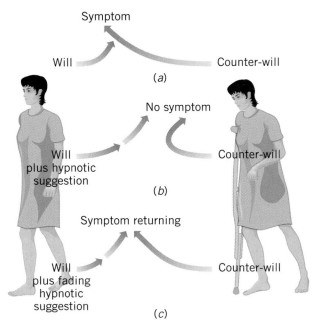

FIGURE 12.1

Psychodynamics. This figure depicts the conflicting forces involved before, during, and after treatment of hysterical symptoms (such as paralysis) with hypnosis. Originally *(a)*, the conscious will ("I will be able to walk") is overpowered by the stronger unconscious counter-will ("I will not be able to walk"). With hypnosis *(b)*, the conscious desire is strengthened and "bends back" the unconscious counter-will. Note that the counter-will is not lessened; it is simply temporarily overpowered by the extra force added by hypnosis. Eventually, as the hypnotic suggestion begins to wear off *(c)*, the counter-will, which was dormant during the period of maximal hypnotic action, once again begins to overpower the will.

scious, preconscious, and unconscious (Chapter 9). **Conscious mental processes** are rational, goal-directed thoughts at the center of awareness. **Preconscious mental processes** are not conscious but could become conscious at any point, such as knowledge of the color of robins. Finally, **unconscious mental processes** are irrational, organized along associative lines rather than by logic. They are inaccessible to consciousness because they have been repressed, that is, kept from consciousness to avoid emotional distress.

Unconscious processes, while barred from consciousness, are not inert. Because they are not consciously acknowledged, they may leak into consciousness and affect behavior in unexpected and often unwelcome ways, as in slips of the tongue. For example, a woman in her late thirties who was dating a man several years her junior was asked about the age difference. She replied, "Oh, I don't think it really mothers." Apparently, a part of her was not so sure.

Freud used the topographic model to understand dreams, distinguishing between their story line—the manifest content—and their underlying message—the latent content (Chapter 9). For example, a 30-year-old male virgin considering having his first sexual encounter reported in psychotherapy a recurring dream of dipping his feet into a polluted river. From a psychodynamic perspective, the dream appeared to express conflicting feelings and wishes about sexuality—will and counter-will. He wanted to get his feet wet, so to speak, but he was reluctant because he considered sex unclean. The connection of sexuality, wetness, and pollution, in this view, is not accidental and was supported by many statements the patient made in this and other sessions.

Conflict and Ambivalence   Freud postulated that such **ambivalence**—conflicting feelings or motives—is the rule, rather than the exception in human experience. The reason is simple: From childhood on, we constantly interact with people who are important to us, but those interactions include both pleasant and unpleasant experiences. We learn to love where we learn to hate.

For example, a patient named Bill was terrified that he would someday marry a woman who would treat him in the same harsh and belittling way that he felt his mother had treated his father. Unfortunately, Bill's most ingrained (and unconscious) models of femininity and marital interaction were profoundly shaped by observing his parents as a child. Years later, Bill and his friend Pete were in a bar, where they noticed two attractively dressed women. Pete thought they looked somewhat severe, that their gestures and facial expressions seemed harsh or angry, and that they were sending clear signals that they had no interest in being disturbed. Bill laughingly disagreed and insisted that he and Pete introduce themselves. Within ten minutes, both men felt, in Bill's words, like "bananas in a blender"; the women spoke to them with sarcasm and barely veiled hostility for about five minutes and then simply turned back to each other and ignored them. Shortly afterward, Bill asked his friend, "How could you tell they'd treat us that way?" Pete replied, "The more interesting question is, how could you *not* tell?"

Bill's behavior reflects a classic psychodynamic **conflict**, that is, a tension or battle between opposing motives. On the one hand, he is consciously determined to avoid women like his mother; on the other, he is unconsciously compelled to provoke hostility or to pursue hostile women, which he did on many occasions. Bill may not recall incidents from his childhood in which he came to associate excitement, love, sensuality, and sexuality with a woman's scorn, but his behavior nonetheless reflects those unconscious associations.

Freud proposed that our minds are always to some degree in conflict. However, excessive conflict among competing motives can exact a toll in psychological symptoms, negative emotions, and even ill health. One study asked students to list 15 of their "personal strivings" or goals, defined as objectives "that you are typically trying to accomplish." Participants then rated the extent to which each striving conflicted with every other striving; that is, they examined every possible pair of strivings and rated them for conflict, allowing the researchers to compute an average level of conflict score for each subject. They also reported how *unhappy* they would be if they were successful at each striving (a measure of ambivalence). Dependent variables included participants' daily mood reports taken twice a day over 21 consecutive days; reports of bodily ailments such as headaches, coughing, and acne; and visits to the health service (Table 12.1). The results show that conflict and ambivalence are related to emotion and illness (Emmons & King, 1988).

TABLE 12.1 RELATIONS AMONG PHYSICAL AND MENTAL WELL-BEING, CONFLICT, AND AMBIVALENCE

WELL-BEING	CONFLICT	AMBIVALENCE
Positive affect	−.11	**−.34**
Negative affect	.21	.18
Anxiety	.17	**.27**
Depression	.19	**.34**
Physical complaints	**.24**	.19
Health center visits	**.27**	.12
Number of illnesses	**.31**	.21

Source: Adapted from Emmons & King, 1988, p. 1044.

Note: Conflict and ambivalence in personal strivings are related to emotional and physical indices of well-being. Statistically significant correlations are in bold.

Compromise Formations   According to Freud, a single behavior, or a complex pattern of thought and action as in Bill's case, typically reflects compromises among multiple and often conflicting forces. The solutions people develop to maximize fulfillment of conflicting motives simultaneously, such as Bill's unconscious pursuit of difficult women while consciously failing to recognize his motive, are called **compromise formations** (Brenner, 1982).

Compromise formations occur in normal as well as abnormal functioning. For example, people are constantly faced with the conflicting motives of seeing themselves accurately and maintaining their self-esteem. Understanding ourselves has obvious adaptive value, since it allows us to know what we can and cannot accomplish, what strategies we can use that will likely succeed, and so forth. On the other hand, few of us can withstand too close a look in the mirror. Thus, a psychodynamic theorist would predict that when faced with a conflict between accuracy and self-enhancement, people compromise, creating a distorted self-portrait that allows them a balance of satisfaction of both motives. Empirical research supports this view (see Chapter 17). For example, when extroverted people are induced to believe that introversion is a predictor of academic success, they come to view themselves as less extroverted, but they will not completely deny their extroversion (see Kunda, 1990).

INTERIM SUMMARY   Freud's **topographic model** divided mental processes into **conscious** (rational, goal-directed thoughts at the center of awareness), **preconscious** (not conscious but could become conscious at any point), and **unconscious** (irrational, organized along associative lines, and repressed). In this view, **ambivalence** (conflicting feelings or motives) and **conflict** (a tension or battle between opposing forces) are the rule in mental life. People resolve conflicts through **compromise formations**, which try to maximize fulfillment of conflicting motives simultaneously.

Drive Model

Freud's topographic model addressed conflict between conscious and unconscious motives. His second model, the **drive model**, tried to explain why people pursue the motives they do. Influenced by the work of Charles Darwin, Freud stressed the continuity of human and nonhuman behavior. He hypothesized that humans are motivated by drives, or instincts, like other animals. Freud (1933) proposed two basic drives: sex and aggression. He defined the sexual drive, or **libido**, more broadly than its colloquial usage. Libido refers as much to pleasure seeking, sensuality, and love as it does to desires for sexual intercourse. Expressions of libido may be as varied as daydreaming about sex or romance, dressing to attract romantic partners, or selecting a career likely to attract a potential spouse because of its status or income potential.

People also express aggression in various ways, some socially acceptable and others not. We see aggression on the sports field, in the corporate boardroom, and in just about every video game on the market. Freud would not have been surprised by the two criteria used to determine whether television shows and movies are acceptable for general viewing—the amount of sex and the amount of aggression—because these are the same things that individuals regulate and censor in themselves.

Developmental Model

Freud (1933) considered the development of the libidinal drive the key to personality development, and hence proposed a **developmental model**, or theory of **psychosexual stages** (Table 12.2). The psychosexual stages reflect the child's evolving quest for pleasure and growing realization of the social limitations on this quest. At each stage, libido is focused on a particular bodily region, or **erogenous zone**.

A scene from the erotic thriller Basic Instinct. *Freud would not have been surprised by the symbolism, since he believed our basic instincts, sex and aggression, go hand in hand.*

TABLE 12.2   FREUD'S PSYCHOSEXUAL STAGES

STAGE	AGE	CONFLICTS AND CONCERNS
Oral	0–18 months	Dependency
Anal	2–3 years	Orderliness, cleanliness, control, compliance
Phallic	4–6 years	Identification with parents (especially same sex) and others, Oedipus complex, establishment of conscience
Latency	7–11 years	Sublimation of sexual and aggressive impulses
Genital	12+ years	Mature sexuality and relationships

To understand these stages, one must view them both narrowly and broadly. That is, the stages describe specific bodily experiences, but they also represent broader psychological and psychosocial conflicts and concerns (Erikson, 1963). Freud's psychosexual stages may sound preposterous at first, but if you try to imagine yourself a child at each stage—sucking your mother's breast for nourishment, fighting with your parents about toilet training (a fight that can go on for a year), or sobbing and shrieking as your parents leave you alone in your room at night—the broader issues may seem less absurd than at first glance.

Oral Stage   During the **oral stage** (roughly the first 18 months of life), children explore the world through their mouths. Many parents are aghast to observe that their infants literally put anything that is not nailed down into their mouths. During the oral stage, sucking the breast or bottle is the means by which infants gain nourishment, but it is also a prime avenue for *social* nourishment, that is, warmth and closeness.

From a broader standpoint, in the oral stage children develop wishes and expectations about *dependence* because they are totally dependent on their caretakers. Difficulties (such as chronic dissatisfaction or discomfort) during the oral stage—or any of the stages—can lead to **fixations**, conflicts or concerns that persist beyond the developmental period in which they arise. People with fixations at the oral stage may be extremely clingy and dependent, with an exaggerated need for approval, nurturance, and love. More concretely, the soothing and pleasure associated with mouthing and sucking during this stage may lead to fixated behavior such as thumb sucking and cigarette smoking.

An infant in the oral stage (and perhaps a future Olympic gymnast).

Although many people at first doubt Freud's depiction of the anal region as an erogenous zone, the buttocks are clearly an object of desire, at least in Western culture.

Anal Stage   The **anal stage** (roughly ages 2 to 3) is characterized by conflicts with parents about compliance and defiance, which Freud linked to conflicts over toilet training. Freud argued that these conflicts form the basis of attitudes toward order and disorder, giving and withholding, and messiness and cleanliness. Imagine a toddler, who has scarcely been told "no" to anything, who finds himself barraged by rules during his second year, with the ultimate insult of being told to control his own body. This is the age during which the child learns to do unto others what they are now constantly doing unto him: saying *no*.

More concretely, Freud proposed that in the anal stage the child discovers that the anus can be a source of pleasurable excitation. If this seems preposterous, ask any child care worker or parent about the way young children seem to enjoy this part of the body and its warm, squishy contents. Within a few short years the anal region is experienced as so disgusting that we cannot even touch it without the intervention of a piece of paper. Paradoxically, however, anal elements often enter into adult sexual interest and arousal ("Nice buns!"), foreplay (looking at or touching the buttocks or anus), and intercourse. Freud would suggest that apparent contradictions of this sort—is it disgusting or erotically arousing?—point to the presence of intrapsychic conflict, between impulses for pleasure and prohibitions against them.

People with anal fixations exhibit a variety of behavioral tendencies. On the one hand, they may be overly orderly, neat, and punctual or, on the other, extremely messy, stubborn, or constantly late. They may have conflicts about giving and receiving or about compliance versus noncompliance with other people's demands. Interestingly, in support of Freud's theory, research finds that people with these character traits tend to find anal humor particularly compelling (O'Neill et al., 1992)! Children can also regress to anal issues, particularly in times of stress. **Regression** means reverting to conflicts or modes of managing emotion characteristic of an earlier stage, as when young children whose parents are undergoing a divorce suddenly start soiling themselves again (an anal regression) or sucking their thumbs (regression to the oral stage).

Phallic Stage   During the **phallic stage** (roughly ages 4 to 6), children enjoy the pleasure they can obtain from touching their genitals and even from masturbating. Preschool teachers can attest that children commonly masturbate while rocking themselves to sleep at naptime, and during bathroom visits little boys can be seen comparing the size of their penises. During this stage children also become very aware of differences between boys and girls and mommies and daddies.

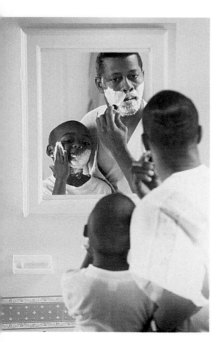

Identification is a powerful force in the life of a child.

More broadly, during the phallic stage the child identifies with significant others, especially the same-sex parent. **Identification** means making another person part of oneself: imitating the person's behavior, changing the self-concept to see oneself as more like the person, and trying to become more like the person by adopting his or her values and attitudes. Much of adult personality is built through identification, as the child internalizes motives, behaviors, beliefs, and ideals—from the importance of achieving in school to the proper way to hold a fork. A longitudinal study of children's attitudes toward themselves provides empirical support for Freud's theory of identification (Koestner et al., 1991). The extent to which girls were self-critical at age 12 correlated with observer ratings of their mothers as restrictive and rejecting at age 5. For boys, self-criticism correlated with these same behaviors manifested by their fathers, not their mothers. This suggests that boys' and girls' attitudes toward themselves reflect identification with the same-sex parent (although, of course, children identify with both parents).

Identification has many roots. Freud emphasized its link to the **Oedipus complex**, named after the character in Greek tragedy who unknowingly slept with his mother. According to Freud, little boys want an exclusive relationship with their mothers, and little girls want an exclusive relationship with their fathers. From a young boy's perspective, for example, "Why should Mommy spend the night alone with Daddy? Why can't I go in there instead?" (Many children manage a compromise by finding ways to spend the night in the middle.) Children sometimes make astoundingly Oedipal comments. For example, one colleague's three-year-old boy exclaimed, "Daddy, I'm going to have to eat you all up so I can have Mommy to myself!" Another four-year-old matter-of-factly declared to his mother, "Mommy, Daddy has to leave. I don't like him anymore." When the child's mother asked why, the boy baldly acknowledged, "He has a bigger penis than I do!"

Freud argued that because children learn about love and sensual gratification from their parents, they desire an exclusive sexual relationship with the parent of the opposite sex (bearing in mind the broad meaning of "sexual" in Freud's theory). At the same time, these wishes are so threatening that they are quickly repressed or renounced (consciously given up). Boys unconsciously fear that their father, their ultimate rival, will castrate them because of their desires for their mother (the **castration complex**). The fear is so threatening that they repress their Oedipal wishes and identify with their father. In other words, they internalize a moral prohibition against incest as a way of preventing themselves from acting on their wishes, which would be dangerous, and they instead become like their father in the hopes of someday obtaining someone like their mother. Girls, too, renounce their secret wishes toward their fathers and identify with their mothers because they fear losing her love.

During the phallic stage, according to Freud, **penis envy** emerges in girls, who feel that because they lack a penis they are inferior to boys. Taken on a metaphorical level, penis envy refers to the envy a girl develops in a society in which men's activities seem more interesting and valued (Horney, 1956). Given the concreteness of childhood cognition, that a five-year-old might symbolize this in terms of having or not having a penis would not be surprising. Parents often report that their daughters cry when bathing with brothers, who have "one of those things." Therapists working with women frequently hear stories about the way male children were preferentially treated in their families, which is hardly unusual in our culture (or almost any other, for that matter). Clinically, this may lead to deep-seated rage at men, but it may also lead to underlying fears and unconscious attitudes about male superiority, which may conflict with conscious beliefs. An avowedly feminist patient, for instance, refused to work with female mentors because she did not respect them. Hearing female patients describe childhood ideas of their vaginas as wounds or physical defects is also not uncommon.

Latency Stage   During the **latency stage** (roughly ages 7 to 11), children repress their sexual impulses and continue to identify with their same-sex parent. They also learn to channel their sexual and aggressive drives into socially acceptable activities such as school, sports, and art. Whereas people fixated at the phallic stage may be preoccupied with attracting mates or take on stereotypical characteristics of their own or the opposite gender, individuals fixated at the latency stage may seem totally asexual.

Genital Stage   During the **genital stage** (approximately age 12 and beyond), conscious sexuality resurfaces after years of repression, and genital sex becomes the primary goal of sexual activity. At this stage, people become capable of relating to and loving others on a mature level and carrying out adult responsibilities such as work and parenting. Prior elements of sexuality do not disappear—most people's foreplay continues to have oral and anal components—but these "pregenital" elements become integrated into patterns of sexual activity involving genital satisfaction. This stage was probably least elaborated by Freud, who be-

▶ *So be sweet and kind to mother, now and then have a chat Buy her candy and some flowers or a brand new hat But maybe you had better let it go at that*

　　—TOM LEHRER, *"Oedipus Rex"*

Some people appear to take the Oedipus complex literally.

lieved that the major aspects of personality become firmly established in child-hood and may require considerable effort to change thereafter.

Freud's Developmental Model: Erotic or Erroneous?   Some of the more sexual aspects of Freud's theory may seem dubious, and many psychologists have reasonably questioned the extent to which Freud emphasized the sexual sides of personality or the ubiquity of the castration complex or penis envy. Nevertheless, Freud's psychosexual theory suggests explanations for a number of perplexing phenomena that are not easily explained by other theories. Some men and women *do* recurrently seem to "find" themselves in love triangles involving "another man" or "another woman," which psychodynamic psychologists explain as a fixation on wishes and conflicts from the Oedipal period (the phallic stage). Therapists often see prominent dynamics of this sort in adults whose parents divorced when they were children, whose relationship with the opposite-sex parent seemed to them almost illicit because the other parent envied or detested it. Most readers will also know women who seem to be attracted only to much older men, drawing such casual remarks as, "She's looking for a daddy."

Experimental data provide surprising support for some of Freud's psychosexual theories, such as his theory of the Oedipus complex (see Fisher & Greenberg, 1985, 1996). For example, in one study researchers asked parents of children age 3 to 6 to record the number of affectionate and aggressive acts the children displayed toward their same- and opposite-sex parents over a seven-day period (Watson & Getz, 1990). As predicted by Freud, affection toward the opposite-sex parent and aggression toward the same-sex parent were significantly more common than the reverse pattern. This Oedipal pattern was strongest at age 4 and began to decline by age 5. Other studies have used a dart-throwing procedure to test the effects of subliminal presentation of messages such as "Beating dad is OK" versus "Beating dad is wrong" on the performance of college-age males (see Palumbo & Gillman, 1984; Weinberger & Silverman, 1988). Remarkably, participants exposed to "Beating dad is OK" tend to outperform control subjects exposed to messages such as "Beating him is wrong." In contrast, participants exposed to "Beating dad is wrong" have more trouble hitting the bull's eye than control subjects.

Even the notion of castration anxiety, perhaps Freud's most seemingly outlandish concept, may account for certain observations. In the men's dressing room of a department store, two boys around age 5 were struggling with a curtain that would not quite close—pulling the curtain one way only seemed to open up the other side—when one of them was overheard saying, "You've got to make sure it closes so no one can come in and steal your ding." Surely no one had warned the child to protect his "ding" at J. C. Penney's. Similarly, running down a list of obscenities—verbally taboo words—one will find that most reflect one or another of Freud's stages. Indeed, perhaps the most vulgar thing someone can call another person in our society has a distinctly Oedipal ring (you can figure this one out on your own), and its originators were surely not psychoanalysts. How did these terms acquire such strong connotations?

INTERIM SUMMARY   According to Freud's **drive** or **instinct model**, people have two instincts, sex and aggression. His **developmental model** proposes a series of **psychosexual stages**. During the **oral stage**, pleasure is focused on the mouth, and children wrestle with dependence. During the **anal stage**, children derive pleasure from the anus and wrestle with issues of compliance, orderliness, and cleanliness. During the **phallic stage**, children's personalities develop through **identification** with others. They also experience the **Oedipus complex**, in which they want an exclusive relationship with their opposite-sex parent. In the **latency stage** children repress their sexual impulses; in the **genital stage** they develop mature sexuality and a capacity for emotional intimacy.

Structural Model

The final model Freud developed was his **structural model** (Freud, 1923, 1933). In it, he shifted his understanding of conflict, from conflict between conscious and unconscious forces, to conflict between desires on the one hand and the dictates of conscience or the constraints of reality on the other.

   Id, Ego, and Superego   The structural model posits three sets of mental forces, or structures: id, ego, and superego. The **id** is the reservoir of sexual and aggressive energy. It is driven by impulses and, like the unconscious of the topographic model, is characterized by wishful, illogical, and associative thought (called **primary process thinking**). To counterbalance the "untamed passions" of the id (Freud, 1933, p. 76), the **superego** acts as a conscience and source of ideals. The superego is the parental voice within the person, established through identification. The **ego** is the structure that must somehow balance desire, reality, and morality, a task Freud described in terms of serving three masters: the id, the external world, and the superego. Unlike the id, the ego is capable of **secondary process thinking**, which is rational, logical, and goal directed. The ego is thus responsible for cognition and problem solving (Hartmann, 1939). It is also responsible for managing emotions (Chapter 11) and finding compromises among competing demands.

   To demonstrate how conflict among these forces plays out, consider an example taken from the therapy of an angry, somewhat insecure junior partner at a law firm who felt threatened by a promising young associate. The partner decided to give the associate a poor job performance evaluation, even though the associate was one of the best the firm ever had. The partner convinced himself that he was justified because the associate could be working harder, and he wanted to send a message that laziness would get the young barrister nowhere—an admirable goal indeed! From the perspective of the structural model (Figure 12.2), the perceived threat activated aggressive wishes (id) to hurt the associate (give him a poor evaluation). The partner's conscience (superego), on the other hand, would not permit such a blatant display of aggression and unfairness. Hence, he unconsciously forged a compromise (ego): He satisfied his aggression by giving the poor evaluation, but he cloaked his action in the language of the superego, claiming to be helping the young associate by discouraging his laziness, and hence satisfying his own conscience.

   Defense Mechanisms   When people confront problems in their lives, they typically draw on problem-solving strategies that have worked for them in the past, rather than inventing new solutions to every problem (Chapter 7). The same is true of emotional problem solving. According to psychodynamic theory, people regulate their emotions and deal with their conflicts by employing **defense mechanisms**—unconscious mental processes aimed at protecting the person from unpleasant emotions (particularly anxiety) or bolstering pleasurable emotions (see Cramer, 1996; A. Freud, 1936; Perry & Cooper, 1987; Vaillant, 1977, 1992).

   One defense is **repression**, an unconscious mechanism that keeps thoughts or memories that would be too threatening to acknowledge from awareness. A similar mechanism is **denial**, in which the person refuses to acknowledge external realities (such as having cancer) or emotions (such as anxiety) rather than thoughts. Denial is at work when an individual notices a peculiar skin growth but concludes that "it's nothing." Much of the time it *is* nothing, but this defense can lead to failure to seek a potentially life-threatening treatment (see Strauss et al., 1990; Zervas et al., 1993).

   In **projection**, a person attributes his own unacknowledged feelings or im-

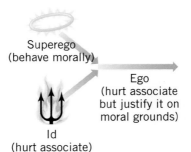

FIGURE 12.2
Freud's structural model. Conflict among various forces leads to a compromise forged by the ego.

Reaction formation was apparently a primary defense mechanism used by televangelist Jimmy Swaggart, here shown confessing his sins to the faithful after his misdeeds were exposed.

pulses to others. The hard-driving businessman who thinks his competitors, suppliers, and customers are always trying to cheat him may in fact be the one with questionable ethics. To recognize his own greed and lack of concern for others would conflict with his conscience, so instead he sees these traits in others. Recent research suggests a cognitive mechanism through which projection may occur (Newman et al., 1997). Paradoxically, keeping a thought out of awareness keeps it chronically activated at an implicit level; to stop a thought from attaining consciousness, the mind essentially sets up an automatic mechanism to "keep a lookout" for the thought, but this process has the unintended byproduct of keeping the thought active (Wegner, 1992). Thus, when a person is trying not to see himself as dishonest, the concept of *dishonesty* remains active implicitly. When someone else then behaves in a way that could be interpreted as either accidental or dishonest, the concept of *dishonesty* is already activated and is thus more likely to be used to interpret the person's behavior. As a result, the individual sees in others what he is trying hard not to see in himself.

Another defense is **reaction formation**, in which the person turns unacceptable feelings or impulses into their opposites. For example, at the same time that televangelist Jimmy Swaggart was preaching the evils of sex to millions, he was regularly seeing a prostitute. His conscious repulsion toward sexuality, and particularly illicit sexuality, apparently masked a tremendous need for it.

Sublimation involves converting sexual or aggressive impulses into socially acceptable activities. A young boy may turn his feelings of competition with his father or brother into a desire to excel in competitive sports or to succeed in business when he is older. **Rationalization** means explaining away actions in a seemingly logical way to avoid uncomfortable feelings, especially guilt or shame. A student who plagiarizes her term paper and justifies her actions by saying that passing the course will help her earn her public policy degree and serve the community is using rationalization to justify her dishonesty. **Passive aggression** is the indirect expression of anger toward others. One administrator frustrated everyone around her by "sitting on" important documents that required a fast turnaround. To be actively aggressive would run afoul of her moral standards and potentially lead to reprimand from her boss, so she accomplished the same goal—frustrating co-workers and thus satisfying her aggressive impulses—in a way that allowed her to disavow any intention or responsibility.

Just as people tailor their problem-solving efforts to specific situations, so too do people typically use defense mechanisms flexibly and creatively. Thus, any taxonomy of defenses is by definition incomplete. Using defenses is neither abnormal nor unhealthy. In fact, some degree of defensive distortion may be useful, such as the tendency for people to see themselves more positively than is warranted by reality (Taylor & Armor, 1996; Taylor & Brown, 1988). A bit of denial can also be essential to surmounting seemingly insurmountable odds, as when an aspiring novelist persists despite repeated rejection and suddenly gets a break. Defenses become dysfunctional when they inhibit adaptive functioning rather than foster it.

Defense mechanisms are generally considered properties of individuals, but they often require collusion from other people. An alcoholic who denies his alcoholism will have a much easier time maintaining his defense if his wife and children adopt a code of silence. Some defenses are even patterned at a cultural level (Spiro, 1965). In the Kerala province of India, where cows are considered sacred and cannot be killed, an anthropologist observed that the mortality rate for male cows was twice as high as for females (Harris, 1979). Although all the farmers espoused the Hindu prohibition against slaughtering cattle, they were essentially starving the males to death because males cannot give milk and were a drain on scarce economic resources. A single whistle-blower would have challenged this collective denial.

INTERIM SUMMARY Freud's **structural model** focuses on conflict among the **id** (the reservoir of instincts or desires), **superego** (conscience), and **ego** (the structure that tries to balance desire, reality, and morality). People regulate their emotions and deal with their conflicts by employing **defense mechanisms**, unconscious mental processes aimed at protecting the person from unpleasant emotions (particularly anxiety) or bolstering pleasurable emotions.

NEO-FREUDIANS

From the start, Freud's theories drew a wide range of responses, from admiration to repulsion and derision. A group who came to be known as **neo-Freudians** accepted the notion of unconscious processes and conflicts among psychological forces but rejected Freud's drive theory, particularly the central role of sexuality. Swiss psychiatrist Carl Jung (1875–1961) and Austrian psychiatrist Alfred Adler (1870–1937) were the first psychodynamic theorists to defect from the Freudian camp; in some ways, they were less neo-Freudians (that is, people who developed a new Freudian-inspired approach) than dissenters who went their own separate ways and started their own schools of thought.

Jung split with Freud over Freud's emphasis on libido because he felt that Freud viewed the brain as "an appendage of the genital glands" (Jung, 1961, p. 213). Furthermore, although Jung accepted the existence of unconscious processes, he proposed that people also have a **collective unconscious**, a repository of ideas, feelings, and symbols shared by all humans and passed genetically from one generation to another. According to Jung, certain basic symbols arise in all cultures because they reflect innate tendencies originating from the collective unconscious. These **archetypes**, or mythological motifs that emerge in dreams and cultural practices, express basic human needs, such as the image of a mother or a wise elder (Jung, 1923, 1968). Within all men, he argued, is a feminine archetype, or **anima**, just as women possess an unconscious masculine side, or **animus**.

Adler also took issue with Freud's libido theory, eventually replacing it with a theory based on the "will to power" and "social interest"—loosely analogous to the distinction between motives for agency and relatedness (Chapter 10) According to Adler, mature, well-adjusted people have needs for power, control, mastery, and personal growth as well as needs to participate in a larger community. Adler maintained that people are motivated by a lifelong need for superiority in order to overcome feelings of inferiority developed in childhood (Adler, 1929). He also paid more attention to people's conscious goals and values than Freud, who emphasized unconscious determinants of behavior.

Many neo-Freudians focused on the role of culture, along with biology and childhood experience, in shaping psychodynamics and basic human strivings. Erich Fromm (1947, 1955) proposed that competitiveness, materialism, and self-involvement are common personality traits in capitalist societies because of economic and social pressures to compete, buy, and focus on oneself (Chapter 10). According to Karen Horney (1937), the neurotic patterns seen in a society, such as endless striving after material goods or difficulty committing to intimate relationships, are similarly shaped by cultural forces. Harry Stack Sullivan (1953) argued that the ways people relate to others, and their deepest views of themselves, are shaped by both cultural norms and their interactions with caregivers during infancy and childhood. Children will do whatever they must to maintain closeness with their parents and to avoid interpersonal anxiety. Abused children often cling to abusive parents and see *themselves* as bad and unworthy in order to maintain even a tenuous tie. Erik Erikson (1963) proposed a psychosocial model of development, which stressed the interpersonal nature of human development, to complement Freud's psychosexual theory (Chapter 14). For example, alongside

Freud's oral stage, Erikson proposed a more interpersonal stage, in which the child wrestles with how much she can trust people. Similarly, adolescence is a time of discovery of a sense of self, or *identity*, and not just mature sexuality. Common to all of these thinkers was a focus on the social, rather than primarily the biological, foundations of personality.

OBJECT RELATIONS THEORIES

Perhaps the most important theoretical development in psychoanalysis since Freud's death has been the emergence of object relations theories. When once asked what the healthy person should be able to do, Freud responded, "to love and to work." **Object relations theories** attempt to account for the difficulties of people who are highly impaired in both domains, who may show an extreme inability to maintain commitment or trust in relationships, a disavowal of any wish for intimate human contact at all, or an inability to sustain employment because of chronic interpersonal conflicts with co-workers and employers.

Object relations refers both to enduring patterns of behavior in intimate relationships and to the motivational, cognitive, and affective processes that produce those patterns. (The term comes from Freud's view that an instinct has an aim, which is some kind of gratification, and an object, which is usually a person. Thus, object relations theories are about people's relationships with others.) Of particular importance are representations of self, significant others, and relationships (Bowlby, 1982; Jacobson, 1964; Sandler & Rosenblatt, 1962). People who have difficulty maintaining relationships tend to represent themselves and others mentally in more negative ways, frequently expecting abuse or malevolence in relationships (Nigg et al., 1992). They also have trouble maintaining *constancy* of their representations; that is, they have difficulty holding in mind positive representations of people they love during the inevitable interpersonal conflicts that friends, family members, and lovers experience (Baker et al., 1992; Kernberg, 1984). As a result, they may break off or irreparably damage their relationships while angry.

Instead of explaining such behavior in terms of neurotic compromise solutions to unconscious conflicts, object relations theorists explain severe interpersonal problems in terms of maladaptive interpersonal patterns laid down in the first few years of life. Whereas Freud described development as a sequence of psychosexual stages, object relations theorists describe it as a progressive movement toward more mature relatedness to others. Like studies of defensive processes (e.g., Cramer & Block, 1998; Shedler et al., 1993; Vaillant, 1992; Westen et al., 1997), many aspects of object relations theory have been tested and corroborated empirically (Blatt, 1996; Hadley et al., 1993; Masling and Bornstein, 1994; Porcerelli et al., 1995; Stricker & Healey, 1990; Westen, 1991).

A recent outgrowth of object relations theories, called **relational theories**, extends this line of thinking to people who are less troubled, arguing that for all individuals adaptation is primarily adaptation to other people (Aron, 1996; Mitchell, 1988). According to relational theorists, the need for relatedness is a central motive in humans, and people will distort their personalities (such as denying anger) to maintain ties to important people in their lives. Like object relations theorists, relational theorists also argue that many of the ways adults interact with one another, particularly in intimate relationships, reflect patterns of relatedness learned in childhood.

INTERIM SUMMARY   **Neo-Freudians** accepted the notion of unconscious processes and conflicts among psychological forces but rejected Freud's drive theory. Many focused on the role of culture in shaping personality. **Object relations theories** focus on interpersonal disturbances and the mental processes that underlie the capacity for relatedness to others.

Relational theories argue that for all individuals adaptation is primarily adaptation to other people.

► ONE STEP FURTHER

Assessing Unconscious Patterns

A core assumption of all psychodynamic approaches—that many personality processes are unconscious—raises a difficult question: How can one assess what one cannot directly *access*? This dilemma led to a number of methods of personality assessment, including life history methods and indirect methods called projective tests.

LIFE HISTORY METHODS

Life history methods aim to understand the whole person in the context of his life experience and environment (see Alexander, 1990; McAdams, 1992; McAdams & West, 1997; Runyan, 1984). They are the bread and butter of psychodynamic investigation, typically involving case studies in which the psychologist studies an individual in depth over an extended time. Information may be gathered through psychotherapy, historical or biographical sources, or research interviews.

In one creative study, researchers turned this method on none other than B. F. Skinner! On the assumption that enduring personality dynamics influence an individual's personal and professional lives, the researchers took the opening paragraph from Skinner's first major work and from his autobiography and mapped out the underlying themes in each (Demorest & Siegel, 1996). They then randomly interspersed these two "maps" of Skinner's dynamics with similar thematic maps taken from other people and asked undergraduate coders to rate the resemblance between the various pairs of thematic maps, to test for a resemblance between Skinner's underlying themes expressed in such different contexts. Despite the fact that one passage described the way rats entered a chamber and the other described the geography of his home town, coders rated Skinner's two productions as substantially more similar to each other than to any of the other thematic maps included in the sample.

PROJECTIVE TESTS

Projective tests present subjects with an ambiguous stimulus and ask them to give some kind of definition to it, or to "project" a meaning into it. The assumption is that in providing definition where none exists in reality, people will "fill in the gaps" in a way that expresses some of their characteristic ways of thinking, feeling, and regulating emotions, that is, aspects of their personalities.

In the **Rorschach inkblot test**, developed by Swiss psychiatrist Hermann Rorschach in 1921, a subject views a set of inkblots and tells the tester what each one resembles. For example, a teenager whose parents were divorcing and battling for custody of her was shown the inkblot reproduced in Figure 12.3. The subject saw a girl being torn apart down the middle, "with feelings on each side," just as she felt torn by her parents' conflict.

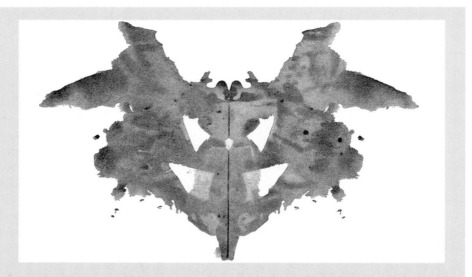

FIGURE 12.3
The Rorschach inkblot test. Subjects' responses provide insight into their unconscious perceptual, cognitive, and emotional processes. Reproduced with permission.

In the Thematic Apperception Test, or TAT (Chapter 10), the subject is asked to make up a story about each of a series of ambiguous drawings, most of which depict people interacting. The assumption is that in eliminating the ambiguity, the individual will create a story that reflects her own recurring wishes, fears, and ways of experiencing relationships. Consider the response of a subject with a borderline personality disorder, which typically manifests itself in unstable relationships, repeated suicide attempts, and difficulty controlling rage, anxiety, and sadness (Chapter 15). When shown a TAT card depicting a man and woman similar to Figure 12.4, the subject responded:

This guy looks a lot like my father—my father going off the handle, ready to beat one of us kids. My mother was trying to control him;

FIGURE 12.4
Thematic Apperception Test (TAT). Psychodynamic psychologists often use projective tests like the TAT to assess object relations and personality dynamics. (This is an artist's rendering of a TAT-like image. The actual card is not reproduced to protect the valid use of the test.)

she'd get beaten along with the rest of us. Did you choose these pictures by what I told you? The woman in the picture is feeling fear for her kids, thinking of ways to stop him—thinking and feeling fear for herself. What this man is thinking or feeling is beyond me. I don't like this picture—as you can tell—it bothers me bad. (She flips the card over.) The resemblance between this and pictures of my father and me when I was younger is uncanny (from Westen et al., 1991).

The subject brings in themes of abuse, which is typical of the stories of borderline patients, many of whom were abused as children (Herman et al., 1989; Ogata et al., 1989; Zanarini, 1997). Further, while most people generate stories that are independent of themselves, this subject cannot keep herself out of the cards, a sign of egocentricism or self-preoccupation characteristic of the TAT responses of patients with this disorder (Westen et al., 1990). After another card also reminded her of herself, the subject later wondered whether these cards were chosen just for her, demonstrating a degree of paranoia consistent with her personality disorder.

Psychologists have criticized projective tests for years, citing various inadequacies (Mischel, 1968). Projective tests are often less useful in predicting behavior than simple demographic data such as the subject's age, sex, and social class (Garb, 1984); they are frequently used idiosyncratically by clinicians, who may offer very different interpretations of the same response; and they have sometimes been misused to make predictions about behaviors for which the tests are not valid, such as potential job performance.

"MR. KILGORE, I HAVE REASON TO BELIEVE YOUR LACTOSE INTOLERENCE IS PSYCHOLOGICAL."

More recent evidence, however, suggests that projective tests can be reliable and valid for assessing disturbances in thinking and in object relations and can effectively distinguish patients with different diagnoses (see Blatt & Lerner, 1991; Coleman et al., 1996; Loevinger, 1976, 1985; Stricker & Healey, 1990). For example, one study asked four- and five-year-olds to complete ten story stems, stories that the investigators started and asked children to finish (Oppenheim, 1997). The more a child's stories included themes of positive interaction and nonabusive discipline, the less depressed, misbehaving, and aggressive their mothers reported them to be; conversely, presence of negative themes (such as physical or verbal abuse) strongly predicted maternal reports of the child's troubles with aggression and misbehavior. From a cognitive perspective, projective tests essentially tap implicit processes (Chapter 6), such as implicit associational networks, particularly those in which emotional elements are prominent (Westen et al., in press).   ◄

CONTRIBUTIONS AND LIMITATIONS OF PSYCHODYNAMIC THEORIES

Although many of Freud's original formulations are, as one might expect, somewhat dated a century after he began his work, the tradition he initiated emphasizes five aspects of personality that have now received widespread empirical support. These include the importance of (1) unconscious cognitive, emotional, and motivational processes; (2) ambivalence, conflict, and compromise; (3) childhood experiences in shaping adult interpersonal patterns; (4) mental representations of the self, others, and relationships; and (5) the development of the capacity to regulate impulses and to shift from an immature dependent state in infancy to a mutually caring, interdependent interpersonal stance in adulthood (Westen, in press). Perhaps most importantly, psychodynamic approaches offer a way of interpreting what people mean by their communications and actions. Proponents maintain that the brief questionnaire studies with college students that constitute the bulk of research in personality cannot compare to the richness of clinical observation or generate sophisticated theories about personality functioning in complex real-life events.

At the same time, perhaps the major limitation of psychodynamic theory is its inadequate basis in scientifically sound observation (see Mischel, 1973; Grunbaum, 1984; Wallerstein, 1988). Some aspects of the theory seem particularly problematic, such as Freud's theory of female development (especially the concept of penis envy). Indeed, many feminist scholars reject Freud's thought entirely as misogynist, or derogatory toward women. (Although Freud's thinking on women was certainly influenced by the gender stereotypes of his time, the charge of misogyny is actually not well founded. Psychoanalysis was one of the few disciplines that elevated women to positions of prominence in the early twentieth century, and it arguably remained more progressive in this respect than the rest of psychology until the 1960s.)

The most recurrent criticism of psychodynamic theory regards Freud's theory of drives (Holt, 1985). Aggression does not appear to be a bodily need in the same way as sex or hunger, and the theory generally overemphasizes sexual motivation. Still other critics charge that psychodynamic theory pays too much attention to childhood experiences and not enough to adult learning.

In evaluating psychodynamic theory, the reader should keep in mind what it is *not*. Psychodynamic theory is no longer a single theory forged by a single thinker, Sigmund Freud. Most contemporary psychodynamic psychologists think about motivation in terms of wishes and fears, not sexual and aggressive drives, although they agree with Freud that many motives, such as sex and love, are biologically rooted and fundamentally shaped in childhood. Contemporary psychodynamic psychologists also tend to rely on concepts like conflict, compromise, mental representation, and self-esteem, rather than id, ego, and superego.

Although Freud developed psychoanalysis as a method of exploring and interpreting meaning, and not predicting behavior, there can be little doubt that psychodynamic theories would be much farther along today if psychoanalysts had taken more interest in testing and refining their ideas empirically. On the other hand, prediction and interpretation should both be central aims of any approach to personality. Just as psychodynamic theorists have failed to refine their theories empirically, most alternative theories of personality have failed to offer principles that would facilitate the interpretative understanding of behavior. We would likely do well to develop theories that integrate the best of both clinical and empirical approaches to personality (Pervin, 1996; Westen, in press).

COGNITIVE-SOCIAL THEORIES

Cognitive-social theories offered the first comprehensive alternative to psychodynamic theories of personality. First developed in the 1960s, these theories go by several names, including social learning theory, cognitive-social learning theory, and social cognitive theory (Chapter 5). Cognitive-social theories developed from behaviorist and cognitive roots (Chapter 1); we have already examined several aspects of these theories in some detail (Chapter 5).

From a behaviorist perspective, personality consists of learned behaviors and emotional reactions that are relatively specific and tied to particular environmental stimuli. These behaviors are selected through operant conditioning on the basis of their rewarding or aversive consequences. Cognitive-social theories share the behaviorist belief that learning (rather than instinct, conflict, or defense) is the basis of personality and that personality dispositions tend to be relatively specific and shaped by their consequences. However, they also focus on beliefs, expectations, and information processing.

According to this approach, personality reflects a constant interplay between environmental demands and the way the individual processes information about the self and the world. Thus, people's actions reflect an interaction between the requirements of the situation (e.g., in school people are expected to work hard, come to class on time, and follow the directives of teachers) and the person's learned tendencies to behave in particular ways under particular circumstances, which reflect their knowledge and beliefs. As Albert Bandura (1986) argues, people are not driven by inner forces, as proposed by many psychodynamic theories, nor are they automatically shaped and controlled by external stimuli, as asserted by radical behaviorists such as B. F. Skinner. Rather, people's actions reflect the schemas they use in understanding the world, their expectations of what will happen if they act in particular ways, and the degree to which they believe they can attain their goals. Whereas psychodynamic theory centers on the irrational, cognitive-social theories tend to be eminently rational; and whereas behaviorists downplay the role of thought in producing behavior, cognitive-social theorists emphasize it.

According to cognitive-social theories (Bandura 1977b, 1986; Mischel, 1990; Mischel et al., 1996; Rotter 1954, 1966; Shoda and Mischel, 1996), several conditions must be met for a behavior to occur. As can be seen in Figure 12.5, the person must encode the current situation as relevant to her goals or current concerns, and the situation must have enough personal meaning or value to initiate goal-driven behavior. The individual must believe that performing the behavior will lead to the desired outcome and that she has the ability to perform it. She must also actually have the ability to carry out the behavior or it cannot occur. Finally, the person must be able to regulate her ongoing activity in a way that leads to goal fulfillment. This may mean monitoring her behavior at each step of the way until the goal is fulfilled, as in decision-making theories, or changing the goal if she cannot fully achieve it. If any of these conditions are not met, the behavior will not occur.

To illustrate these stages before examining each in more detail, imagine you have just been stood up for a date (the stimulus). When you realize what has happened (encoding as personally relevant), your self-esteem plummets, you see that

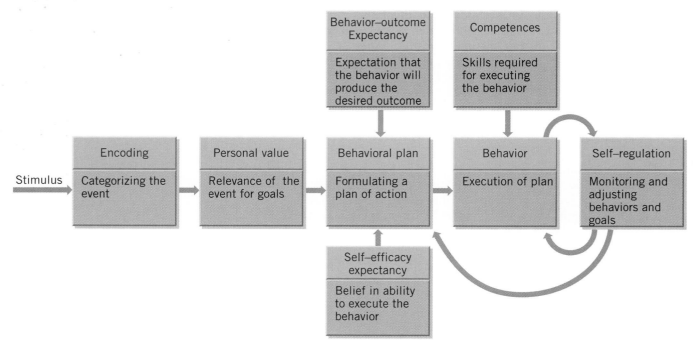

Figure 12.5
A cognitive-social model of behavior. This figure depicts the conditions that must be met for a behavior to occur according to cognitive-social theories.

your plans for the evening are ruined, and you would like to make the person feel bad and think twice before doing that again (personal value). You therefore decide to confront your date (behavioral plan). In formulating a behavioral plan, however, you must decide whether any action you take will actually achieve the desired result (expectation of link between behavior and outcome). Will your date simply ignore you and make up an excuse? On top of that, your expectations and beliefs must be accurate: You must actually be able to respond quickly (competence) or you will emit the wrong behavior, such as saying, "Oh, that's OK. I found something else to do. Do you want to get together some other time?" Finally, as you begin to execute the action, you will need to monitor progress toward your goal—is your "date" squirming enough yet?—as you go along.

Interim Summary   Cognitive-social theories developed from behaviorist and cognitive roots and consider learning, beliefs, expectations, and information processing central to personality. For a behavior to occur, several conditions must be met: The person must encode the current situation as relevant, endow the situation with personal meaning or value, believe performing the behavior will lead to the desired outcome, believe she has the ability to perform it, have the ability to carry out the behavior, and regulate ongoing activity in a way that leads toward fulfilling the goal.

Encoding and Personal Relevance

For people to respond to a situation, they must first encode its meaning and determine its relevance to them. Responding to a situation is difficult if we cannot categorize it, and responding is unnecessary if it is not demanded by the situation or relevant to our goals.

10-27   © 1978 Jim Unger/dist. by LaughingStock Licensing Inc.

"You can't blame TV if you're dumb enough to walk up to a 300-lb. truck driver and say, 'Ring around the collar.'"

Cognitive-social theorists propose that social learning processes such as modeling (chapter 5) are central to personality.

Encoding

If a delinquent or maladjusted boy is accidentally bumped by a peer, he may punch his unwitting assailant because he encoded the bump as deliberate (Crick & Dodge, 1994). George Kelly (1955) developed an early cognitive approach to personality that focused on **personal constructs**—mental representations of the people, places, things, and events that are significant to a person. According to Kelly, people can construe the world in many different ways, which defines their personality. Kelly looked for the roots of behavior not in motivation, as in psychodynamic theory, but in cognition. For example, an individual who believes someone will always step in to take care of him may act in a manner that appears dependent (see Walker, 1996).

People are not always able to articulate their personal constructs when asked directly. Thus, Kelly and his colleagues developed a technique for assessing them indirectly, called the **repertory grid technique** (Blowers and O'Connor, 1996; Brown & Chiesa, 1990; Sewell et al., 1992). Subjects are asked to describe the dimensions on which important people in their lives resemble and differ from one another (e.g., "How is your father like your sister? In what ways are they unlike your mother?"). By eliciting enough comparisons, the psychologist can discover the constructs that the subject implicitly uses in thinking about people. Experimental research using very different methods confirms that the idiosyncratic categories individuals tend to use to describe themselves and others influence their behavior, such as what draws their attention and what they remember (Higgins, 1990).

Nancy Cantor and John Kihlstrom (1987) combined Kelly's emphasis on personal constructs with information-processing theory to create a cognitive theory of personality. They argue that the way people conceive of themselves and others and encode, interpret, and remember social information defines both their personality and their social intelligence. In this view, individuals who have more accurate and well-organized schemas about people and relationships have greater social intelligence and should be more effective in accomplishing their interpersonal goals, such as making friends and getting desirable jobs.

Personal Value and Goals

Individuals have elaborate schemas about people and situations that have relevance or personal value to them. **Personal value** refers to the importance individuals attach to various outcomes or potential outcomes (Mischel, 1979). Whether a situation or anticipated action has a positive or negative value for an individual often depends on the person's goals. Cantor and Kihlstrom (1987) define motivation in terms of **life tasks**, the conscious, self-defined problems people attempt to solve. For a college student, salient life tasks may involve establishing independence from parents, getting good grades, or making and keeping friends (Cantor, 1990; Cantor & Blanton, 1996; Harlow & Cantor, 1994).

> **INTERIM SUMMARY**   For people to respond to a situation, they must first encode it as relevant. George Kelley proposed that **personal constructs**—mental representations of the people, places, things, and events that are significant to a person—substantially influence their behavior. People tend to focus on and select behaviors and situations that have **personal value** to them, which are relevant to their goals or **life tasks** (conscious, self-defined problems people try to solve).

EXPECTANCIES AND COMPETENCES

Whether or not people carry out various actions depends substantially on both their **expectancies,** or expectations relevant to desired outcomes (Chapter 5), and their competence to perform the behaviors that would solve their problems or achieve their goals.

Expectancies

Of particular importance are behavior–outcome expectancies and self-efficacy expectancies. A **behavior–outcome expectancy** is a belief that a certain behavior will lead to a particular outcome. A **self-efficacy expectancy** is a person's conviction that she can perform the actions necessary to produce the desired outcome. For example, a person will not start a new business unless she believes both that starting the business is likely to lead to desired results (such as wealth or satisfaction) *and* that she has the ability to get a new business off the ground.

Bandura (1977a, 1982, 1995) argues that self-efficacy expectancies are generally the most important determinant of successful task performance. Research in a number of areas clearly documents that people who are confident in their abilities are more likely to act, and ultimately succeed, than those plagued by self-doubts. James Joyce weathered 22 rejections when trying to publish *Dubliners*, and a prominent psychologist was once told that "one is no more likely to find the phenomenon [that he eventually discovered and documented] than bird droppings in a cuckoo clock" (Bandura, 1989, p. 1176).

Competences

Believing in one's abilities is one thing, but truly having them is another. Thus, another crucial variable that impacts behavior is **competences**, that is, skills and abilities used for solving problems. Social intelligence includes a variety of competences that help people navigate interpersonal waters that can sometimes be turbulent, such as social skills that allow them to talk comfortably with strangers at a cocktail party, the ability to end an argument to maintain a friendship, or the ability to find ways of solving problems that impede attainment of their goals (see Cantor & Harlow, 1994; Cantor & Kihlstrom, 1987; Kosmitzki & John, 1993; Mischel, 1990). Individuals develop highly specific skills for handling particular tasks through operant conditioning, observational learning, practice, and deliberate conscious effort.

SELF-REGULATION

The final variable required to execute a behavior successfully is self-regulation. **Self-regulation** refers to setting goals, evaluating one's performance, and adjusting one's behavior to achieve these goals in the context of ongoing feedback (Bandura, 1986, 1991; Mischel, 1990). Cognitive-social theorists take a problem-solving or decision-making approach to personality, much like information-processing approaches to cognition (Chapter 7) and goal-setting and expectancy–value theories of motivation (Chapter 10). In other words, people are constantly setting goals, applying their skills to achieve them, and monitoring their thoughts and actions until their goals are reached or modified.

In this view, personality is nothing more or less than the problem-solving efforts of people trying to fulfill their life tasks (Harlow & Cantor, 1994). Successful problem solving requires constant feedback, which people use to self-regulate. Feedback on performance can help people solve problems better if it focuses their attention on the problem and ways to achieve a solution; however, feedback can also diminish performance if it leads people to focus on themselves with self-doubt or anxiety (Kluger & DeNisi, 1996).

One study applied a cognitive-social approach to organizational decision making (Wood & Bandura, 1989). Using a computer simulation, graduate business students were asked to allocate workers and resources to maximize efficient production. The simulation involved 18 decision-making trials, with each trial followed by performance feedback useful for the next. Half the participants (the acquirable skill group) were told that in "acquiring a new skill, people do not begin with faultless performance. However, the more they practice, the more capable they become." Essentially, these participants were encouraged to use the task to develop their skills rather than to evaluate their ability. The other half (the fixed-ability group) were led to believe that the simulation would test their underlying ability as a manager, a basic competence they either did or did not have.

The researchers wanted to know how this manipulation would affect participants' perceived self-efficacy, goal setting, efficiency in problem solving, and managerial success in running the simulated company. Self-efficacy was assessed by regularly asking participants how confident they were of achieving production goals following feedback on their performance. Performance goals were assessed by asking them after each trial what performance level they were striving for on the next trial. The researchers also measured the efficiency of participants' problem-solving strategies as well as their actual level of performance on the task (Figure 12.6).

Participants who believed they could learn from the task showed consistent increases in perceived self-efficacy, unlike those who believed their ability was fixed. The fixed-ability group showed a steady decline in self-efficacy performance goals, efficiency of problem solving, and actual performance. Essentially, in confronting a difficult task, the group that believed their skills were fixed steadily lowered their estimates of their efficacy and their level of aspiration, and their performance steadily declined. Statistical analysis showed that the declines in self-efficacy expectancies particularly affected performance. In other words, managers are much more likely to be successful if they *believe* they can be successful.

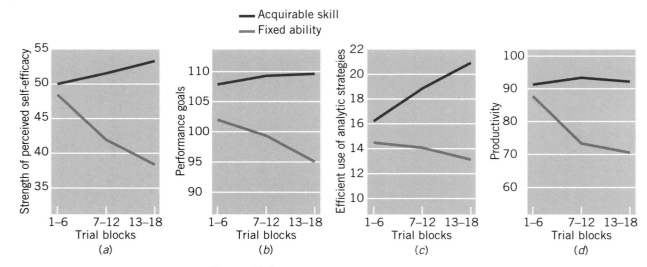

FIGURE 12.6

An experimental study of self-regulation. Participants who believed they could learn from the task showed consistent increases in perceived self-efficacy, unlike participants who believed their ability to be fixed (*a*). The latter showed a steady decline in performance goals (*b*), efficiency of problem solving (*c*), and actual performance (*d*). *Source:* Wood & Bandura, 1989, pp. 411–413.

INTERIM SUMMARY   People's **expectancies**, or expectations relevant to desired outcomes, influence the actions they take. A **behavior–outcome expectancy** is a belief that a certain behavior will lead to a particular outcome. A **self-efficacy expectancy** is a person's conviction that she can perform the actions necessary to produce the desired outcome. A **competence** is a skill used for solving problems. **Self-regulation** refers to setting goals, evaluating one's performance, and adjusting one's behavior to achieve these goals in the context of ongoing feedback.

CONTRIBUTIONS AND LIMITATIONS OF COGNITIVE-SOCIAL THEORIES

Cognitive-social theories have contributed substantially to the study of personality, particularly by bringing into focus the role of thought and memory in personality. The way people behave clearly reflects the expectations and skills they have developed, which are encoded in memory and activated by particular situations. Furthermore, unlike psychodynamic theory, which is difficult to test, cognitive-social theory is readily testable through experimentation.

Cognitive-social approaches are limited, however, in at least two respects. First, they overemphasize the rational side of life and underemphasize the emotional, motivational, and irrational. If personality is really reducible to cognitive processes (Cantor, 1990), one would have difficulty accounting for the psychological abnormalities of a man like Adolph Hitler. Because Hitler was tremendously adept at getting people to follow him and had an extraordinary sense of self-efficacy, one would have to rate him high on several dimensions of social intelligence. Yet his social motives, and his ways of dealing with his emotions, were clearly disturbed. If the image one gets from reading Freud is of people who do little more than find sublimated ways to satisfy their sexual urges, the image one gets from reading cognitive-social theory is of individuals who spend their days reading and thinking.

A related problem stems from the attempt of cognitive-social theorists to avoid explanations that resemble anything psychodynamic, such as defenses. Rather, they tend to assume that people consciously know what they want and hence can report it. But would most of us accept Hitler's self-report of his life task of bettering the world by creating a master race? Or would we suspect that his dreams of world domination and his program of genocide reflected thoughts, feelings, and motivations that he could not easily have described?

In some ways, psychodynamic and cognitive-social approaches each offer what the other lacks. Psychodynamic theory is weak in its understanding of cognition and conscious problem solving; cognitive-social theory is weak in its understanding of emotion, motivation, and personality processes that occur outside awareness. We are, however, beginning to see some important areas of convergence, as psychodynamic theorists have become interested in developments in cognitive science (e.g., Bucci, 1997; Horowitz, 1988; Shevrin et al., 1996) and cognitive-social researchers have become interested in implicit processes and interactions of emotion and cognition (Mischel & Shoda, 1995). Further, integrative approaches have begun to emerge that focus on the construct of *emotional intelligence,* the ability to adapt to the environment, particularly the social environment, in flexible ways that allow fulfillment of goals and satisfying social relationships (e.g., Block & Kremen, 1996; Goleman, 1995; Mayer & Salovey, 1997).

TRAIT THEORIES

Psychodynamic approaches to personality emerged from the clinic, whereas cognitive-social approaches stemmed from laboratory observation. Trait theories, in contrast, were largely derived from the words people use to describe themselves and others in their everyday lives, beginning with adjectives like *shy, devious, manipulative, open,* or *friendly.* **Traits** are emotional, cognitive, and behavioral tendencies that constitute underlying personality dimensions on which individuals vary.

According to Gordon Allport (1937; Allport & Odbert, 1936), who developed the trait approach to personality, the concept of trait has two separate but complementary meanings. On the one hand, a trait is an observed tendency to behave in a particular way. On the other, a trait is an inferred underlying personality disposition that generates this behavioral tendency. Presumably, a tendency to be cheerful (an observed trait) stems from an enduring pattern of internal processes, such as a tendency to experience positive affect, to think positive thoughts, or to wish to be perceived as happy (an inferred disposition).

How does one measure traits? The most straightforward way is the same way people intuitively assess other people's personalities: Observe their behavior over time and in different situations. Because extensive observation of this sort can be very cumbersome and time consuming, however, psychologists often use two other methods. One is to ask people who know the subject well to fill out questionnaires about the person's personality. The second, more commonly used method is to ask subjects themselves to answer self-report questionnaires.

To describe personality from a trait perspective, one must know not only how to measure traits but also which ones to measure. The case of Oskar and Jack, which opened this chapter, described twins who dressed alike and were similar in their sense of well-being. Are these central personality traits?

With literally thousands of different ways to classify people, choosing a set of traits that definitively describe personality seems like a Herculean task. Allport and Odbert (1936) compiled a list of some 18,000 words from Webster's unabridged dictionary that could be used to distinguish one person from another. Many of these words denote similar characteristics, however, so over the years trait psychologists have collapsed the list into fewer and fewer traits. Raymond Cattell (1957, 1990) reduced the list to just 16 traits, such as warm, emotionally stable, intelligent, cheerful, suspicious, imaginative, sensitive, and tense. To select

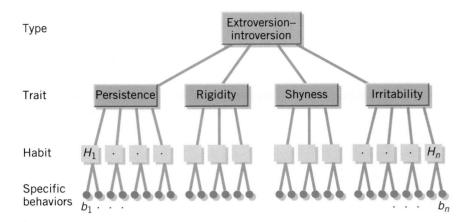

FIGURE 12.7
Eysenck's model of personality. Extroversion–introversion is a type, a group of traits that correlate highly with one another. Persistence, rigidity, and so forth are traits—groups of correlated behavioral tendencies (habits). Habits are abstractions derived from observations of specific instances of behavior. *Source:* Adapted from Eysenck, 1953, p. 13.

these key traits, Cattell relied on factor analysis (Chapter 8) to group adjectives on Allport's and Odbert's list that were highly correlated with each other; adjectives that appeared to be measuring similar qualities were thus grouped into overarching factors.

EYSENCK'S THEORY

One of the best-researched trait theories was developed by Hans Eysenck (1953, 1990). Eysenck distinguishes traits and types, with *types* representing a higher order organization of personality (Figure 12.7). In his view, individuals produce specific behaviors, some of which are frequent or habitual (that is, they are habits). A trait is a group of correlated habits; that is, a person who has one of these habits tends to have the other habits that constitute the trait. For example, avoiding attention in a group, not initiating conversation, and avoiding large social gatherings are habitual behaviors of people with the trait of shyness. A type is a group of correlated traits. People who are shy, rigid, and inward looking are introverts.

On the basis of thousands of studies conducted over the last half century, Eysenck identified three overarching psychological types: extroversion–introversion, neuroticism–emotional stability, and psychoticism–impulse control. **Extroversion** refers to a tendency to be sociable, active, and willing to take risks. Introverts, who score at the low end of the extroversion scale, are characterized by social inhibition, seriousness, and caution. **Neuroticism** defines a continuum from emotional stability to instability. It is closely related to the construct of negative affect (Chapter 11). People high on neuroticism report feeling anxious, guilty, tense, and moody, and they tend to have low self-esteem. **Psychoticism** is an oddly named scale whose opposite pole is impulse control. People high on psychoticism are aggressive, egocentric, impulsive, and antisocial. People low on psychoticism are empathic and able to control their impulses.

THE FIVE FACTOR MODEL

Most theorists who have used factor analysis to arrive at a taxonomy of traits have found that their long lists boil down to five superordinate traits, known as the **Big Five factors,** or the **Five Factor Model (FFM)** (Goldberg, 1981, 1993; John, 1990; McCrae & Costa, 1990, 1997; Norman, 1963). Different studies yield slightly different factors, and theorists label them in different ways, but the lists are strikingly consistent. Costa & McCrae (1990, 1997) use the labels openness to experience, conscientiousness, extroversion, agreeableness, and neuroticism. (A good acronym to remember them is OCEAN.).

Each of the five factors represents an amalgam of several more specific traits. For example, as Table 12.3 shows, people high on neuroticism tend to be anxious, depressed, impulsive, and so forth. These lower order traits are called "facets" of the FFM. The FFM provides a comprehensive assessment of the personality traits that most people perceive in themselves and others. (To demonstrate this for yourself, rate yourself or someone you know well on each of these factors, including the lower order traits, and see if the profiles that emerge leave out anything important.)

The delineation of basic factors in personality initially arose from the assumption that important individual differences are likely to show up in language, so that classifying hundreds of adjectives into a small group of higher order trait descriptions would generate an adequate taxonomy of traits (Goldberg, 1981). Interestingly, the same five factors seem to appear almost regardless of the specific data used, including adjectives, antonym pairs, or statements such as "I often feel that. . ." (Goldberg, 1993; John, 1990). The five factors even emerged in a cross-cultural study using a *nonverbal* personality test (Paunonen et al., 1992). Subjects in Canada, Finland, Poland, and Germany viewed drawings of people engaged in behaviors related to various traits and rated how often they engage in similar behaviors. Once again, five traits seemed to encompass the spectrum of personality dispositions that they ascribed to themselves.

Is the FFM cross-culturally universal? Research in multiple countries has produced remarkably similar results (see John, 1990; McCrae & Costa, 1997; McCrae et al., 1998; Stumpf, 1993). This is particularly impressive because of the wide array of languages from different linguistic families that have reproduced the FFM, from English and German to Korean. This has led advocates to assert that they have uncovered "general laws of personality structure" that are applicable everywhere, either because people are biologically similar across cultures or because the requirements of living together in groups makes certain traits salient (such as agreeableness) regardless of the culture.

The strongest cross-cultural confirmations of the FFM occur when researchers translate Western instruments into other languages. Findings are not so clear when researchers draw adjectives from the native language, as in a study of university students in Taiwan (Kuo-shu & Bond, 1990). In this study, participants described people they knew well using two sets of adjectives: adjectives included in Cattell's inventory (reflecting Western concepts), and adjectives culled from Chinese newspapers, (to represent indigenous, that is, native, conceptions of person-

TABLE 12.3 THE FIVE FACTOR MODEL AND ITS FACETS

NEUROTICISM	EXTROVERSION	AGREEABLENESS	CONSCIENTIOUSNESS	OPENNESS
Anxiety	Warmth	Trust	Competence	Fantasy (active fantasy life)
Angry hostility	Gregariousness	Straightforwardness	Order	Aesthetics (artistic interests)
Depression	Assertiveness	Altruism	Dutifulness	Feelings (emotionally open)
Self-consciousness	Activity	Compliance	Achievement striving	Actions (flexible)
Impulsivity	Excitement seeking	Modesty	Self-discipline	Ideas (intellectual)
Vulnerability	Positive emotion	Tenderness	Deliberation	Values (unconventional)

Source: Adapted from McCrae & Costa, 1997, p.513.

Note: These are the higher order and lower order traits ("facets") that constitute the Five Factor Model. Within each factor, traits are highly correlated; across factors, they are not.

ality). Factor analysis of the Western words produced the FFM; factor analysis of the Chinese-derived words produced only three of five factors with some similarity to the FFM. A study that factor-analyzed personality descriptions taken from interviews and open-ended questionnaires in the Philippines similarly produced a factor structure that only partially mapped onto the FFM (Katigbak et al., 1996); factors resembling conscientiousness, agreeableness, and openness emerged, but the other factors could not be mapped onto neuroticism and extroversion.

INTERIM SUMMARY: **Traits** are emotional, cognitive, and behavioral tendencies that constitute underlying personality dimensions on which individuals vary. Eysenck identified three overarching psychological types, or constellations of traits: **extroversion** (tendency to be sociable, active, and willing to take risks), **neuroticism** (emotional stability or negative affect), and **psychoticism** (tendency to be aggressive, egocentric, impulsive, and antisocial). According to the **Five Factor Model (FFM)**, personality can be reduced to five factors—openness to experience, conscientiousness, extroversion, agreeableness, and neuroticism—each of which includes several lower order factors or *facets*. Many of these factors appear to be cross-culturally universal.

FROM MIND TO BRAIN

THE GENETICS OF PERSONALITY

Why is one person extroverted and another introverted? While few would doubt the influence of learning and environment on personality dispositions, a considerable body of evidence supports the somewhat counterintuitive position that a substantial part of personality is inherited, an idea first proposed by the Greek physician Galen 2000 years ago.

The case of Oskar and Jack is not unusual in finding strong similarities among people with shared genes (Beer et al., 1998; Jang et al., in press; Lykken et al., 1993; McGue et al., 1993; Saudino, 1997). Despite the fact that adopted children may have lived with their adoptive family from birth, biological relatives tend to be more similar than adoptive relatives, even if they have had no contact with one another (Loehlin et al., 1987, 1988; Plomin et al., 1990). For example, in comparing the court convictions of 14,427 adoptees, researchers found the conviction rates of the adopted children related to the conviction rates of their biological, rather than their adoptive, parents (Mednick et al., 1984). Some heritable personality traits emerge quite early in development. Extroversion, task orientation, and activity level already show high heritability in one- and two-year-olds (Braungart et al., 1992).

The most definitive studies in this area compare twins reared together and twins reared apart, a procedure that can distinguish cleanly between genetic and environmental influences (Chapter 8). Two studies have yielded somewhat discrepant findings. A Minnesota study (Tellegen et al., 1988) examined 217 monozygotic (MZ) and 114 dizygotic (DZ) adult twin pairs who had been reared together and 44 MZ and 27 DZ adult twin pairs who had been reared apart (average age 22). Table 12.4 displays the correlations between MZ and DZ twins reared together and apart on a personality test measuring such traits as well-being, achievement, aggression, and traditionalism. The MZ twins showed substantially higher correlations than DZ twins on almost every trait, even when they were reared apart. The differences in the correlations between MZ twins reared together and MZ twins reared apart were also not particularly large, suggesting that heredity accounts for more of the variance in personality than environment.

TABLE 12.4 CORRELATIONS BETWEEN MINNESOTA TWINS REARED TOGETHER AND APART ON A MULTIDIMENSIONAL PERSONALITY MEASURE

	REARED APART		REARED TOGETHER	
	MZ	DZ	MZ	DZ
Primary traits				
Well-being	.48	.18	.58	.23
Social potency	.56	.27	.65	.08
Achievement	.36	.07	.51	.13
Social closeness	.29	.30	.57	.24
Stress reaction	.61	.27	.52	.24
Alienation	.48	.18	.55	.38
Aggression	.46	.06	.43	.14
Control	.50	.03	.41	−.06
Harm avoidance	.49	.24	.55	.17
Traditionalism	.53	.39	.50	.47
Absorption in fantasy	.61	.21	.49	.41
Higher order traits				
Positive emotionality	.34	−.07	.63	.18
Negative emotionality	.61	.29	.54	.41
Constraint	.57	.04	.58	.25

Substantial differences between MZ and DZ twins suggest a genetic effect

Substantial differences between MZ twins reared apart and together suggest an environmental effect

Source: Tellegen et al., 1988, p. 1035.

A series of studies of Swedish adoptees with a much larger sample but a higher mean age of subjects (in their fifties rather than their twenties) also found considerable evidence for genetic influences but yielded much lower heritability estimates, averaging about .27 (see Plomin et al., 1990). As Table 12.5 shows, the correlations for MZ twins reared together are considerably larger than those reared apart, demonstrating substantial environmental influences on personality. Some traits show greater genetic effects, while others show stronger environmental influence. For example, two Big Five factors, agreeableness and conscientiousness, appear to have minimal heritability (low correlations for MZ twins reared apart) but substantial environmental influence (contrastingly high correlations for MZ twins reared together). Openness is largely heritable, while extroversion and neuroticism show substantial genetic *and* environmental impact (see also McCrae, 1996; Viken et al., 1994).

The evidence thus points to heritability estimates in the range of .15 to .50 for most personality traits, with the balance attributable to the environment. Interestingly, despite this strong environmental influence, the same family does not necessarily produce children with similar personalities. Adoptive siblings, for example, tend to share few personality traits, and even natural siblings show great variations. While this may be surprising in one sense, in another, it may simply attest to the flexibility with which human beings can respond to similar circumstances. In a family with erratic alcoholic parents, one sibling may cope by turning inward, becoming introverted and studious, while another may cope by becoming wild, poorly con-

TABLE 12.5   CORRELATIONS BETWEEN SWEDISH TWINS REARED TOGETHER AND APART

	REARED APART		REARED TOGETHER		
SCALE	MZ	DZ	MZ	DZ	
Extroversion	.30	.04	.54	.06	Substantial differences between MZ twins reared together and apart suggest an environmental effect
Neuroticism	.25	.28	.41	.24	
Openness	.43	.23	.51	.14	
Conscientiousness	.15	−.03	.41	.23	
Agreeableness	.19	.10	.47	.11	
Emotionality—distress	.30	.26	.52	.16	Substantial differences between MZ and DZ twins suggest a genetic effect
Emotionality—fear	.37	.04	.49	.08	
Emotionality—anger	.33	.09	.37	.08	

Source: Adapted from Plomin et al., 1990, p. 231.

trolled, and eventually alcoholic. In both cases, their personalities have been shaped by a similar environment, but for reasons that can only be understood by examining their individual life histories, they took different roads. Each sibling in a family also has different experiences within that family and outside of it, and these unshared experiences can be as important in shaping personality as shared environment. Further, some inherited traits may only find behavioral expression if each sibling has *several* genes that interact to produce it or if both siblings have the same dominant gene (see Saudino, 1997). Some genes that control personality may, for example, be dominant, like genes for brown eyes; thus, identical twins with the gene will be highly similar, whereas nonidentical twins or other siblings will be entirely different if they do not both inherit the dominant gene.

IS PERSONALITY CONSISTENT?

The concept of personality traits described thus far implies that personality has some degree of consistency. If John is an honest person, one assumes he is likely to behave honestly in various situations and to be honest two years from now. No one is honest all the time, however, and people do change. Thus, two questions arise: Is personality consistent from one situation to another? And is personality consistent over time?

Consistency Across Situations

In 1968, Walter Mischel touched off a 30-year debate by arguing that people's behavior largely reflects **situational variables**—the circumstances in which they find themselves—rather than enduring aspects of their personalities. In an influential book, he marshaled considerable evidence of the inconsistency of people's behavior across situations and showed that most personality tests had only modest correlations with behaviors in the real world. For example, trait measures tended to be far less predictive of whether a psychiatric patient would require future hospitalization than the weight of the patient's psychiatric chart!

Mischel almost single-handedly slew the mighty field of personality. If personality is not consistent, psychologists have nothing to measure, so they might as

TABLE 12.6 INFLUENCE OF CONSISTENCY AND RELEVANCE OF TRAITS ON THE CORRELATIONS BETWEEN SELF-REPORTS AND PEER REPORTS

TRAIT	SELF-REPORTED CONSISTENCY		SELF-REPORTED RELEVANCE	
	HIGH	LOW	HIGH	LOW
Emotional—calm	.44	.25	.47	.24
Reserved—outgoing	.48	.47	.60	.34
Assertive—mild-mannered	.37	.34	.45	.25
Self-assured—worrying	.41	.13	.38	.16

The influence of self-reported consistency primarily occurred for this variable.

Note how much higher the correlations are for participants reporting high rather than low relevance.

Source: Adapted from Zuckerman et al., 1988, pp. 1013–1014.

well pack up their questionnaires and go home. Indeed, the field of personality languished for years after Mischel's critique. Several psychologists, however, challenged Mischel's arguments. Seymour Epstein (1979, 1986, 1997) pointed out that any single behavior has multiple causes, so that trying to predict a single behavior from a personality trait is virtually impossible. No measure of "honesty," for example, can predict whether a child will cheat on an exam on a *particular* occasion. However, averaging across multiple occasions, measures of honesty *do* predict whether or not a child will cheat.

Other psychologists argued, further, that psychologists cannot predict all of the people all of the time, but they *can* predict some of the people some of the time (Bem & Allen, 1974; Kenrick & Stringfield, 1980). The key is to figure out which people tend to be consistent on which traits and which traits are relevant for which people. For example, people's self-descriptions tend to be highly predictive of the way others see them on traits on which they consider themselves consistent and traits they view as relevant or central to their personality (Table 12.6) (Zuckerman et al., 1988). Further, some people are more open and easy to "read"; their behavior is thus easier for people who know them well to predict (Colvin, 1993).

Consistency over Time

Researchers have now also documented considerable consistency in many aspects of personality over long periods of time (Caspi, 1998; Mischel & Shoda, 1995). One example is *inhibition to the unfamiliar,* a cluster of attributes in children that includes shyness and anxiety in the face of novelty (Gest, 1997; Kagan, 1989; Kagan & Snidman, 1991). Inhibition to the unfamiliar appears to be an aspect of **temperament**, that is, a basic personality disposition heavily influenced by genes (Chess & Thomas, 1987). Infants who are inhibited (roughly 10 percent of the population) show a distinct pattern of crying and motor behavior as early as four months when confronted with unfamiliar stimuli. In fact, infants classified as inhibited at four months show more fear responses than uninhibited children at nine, 14, and 21 months when confronted with novel stimuli (such as an unfamiliar room, application of painless electrodes to the skin, or application of liquid through a dropper to the mouth or eye). At seven and a half years of age, inhibited children also have significantly more fears outside the laboratory about attending summer camp, public speaking, remaining alone at home, and so forth.

An infant in Kagan's laboratory shows little inhibition to the unfamiliar.

Psychologists have also documented consistency from childhood through early adulthood. One group of investigators reanalyzed data from a longitudinal project that assessed every third birth in Berkeley, California, in 1928 to 1929 (Caspi et al., 1990). The most striking finding was that eight-, nine-, and ten-year-old boys characterized as ill-tempered, who had repeated temper tantrums, were characterized at age 30 by maladaptive personality traits, poor occupational performance, and disrupted marriages. As adults they were also rated as undercontrolled, irritable, moody, unethical, and undependable. In another study, children described as inhibited at age 3 were more likely than others to be depressed at age 21, whereas children described at age 3 as impulsive were more likely to be diagnosed as antisocial (aggressive, lacking guilt, and so forth) at age 21 (Caspi et al., 1996). A Swedish study similarly found that children (particularly boys) rated as aggressive at ages 10 and 13 by their teachers were disproportionately represented among criminals (especially perpetrators of violent crime) at age 26 (Stattin & Magnusson, 1989).

Personality also shows considerable stability throughout adulthood (Block, 1977; Conley, 1985; Costa & McCrae, 1990). A study of the FFM in a sample of adults ages 30 to 96 found that personality stabilizes by age 30 and remains consistent thereafter (Costa & McCrae, 1988, 1990).

One of the most important studies to document consistency over time examined the childhood personality antecedents of depressive tendencies in 18-year-olds (Block et al., 1991). Several preschool teachers rated aspects of the children's behavior and personality at ages 3 and 4; the same subjects were then observed in depth at ages 7, 11, 14, and 18 by various teachers and psychologists.

The investigators offered a more complex hypothesis than simply that depression in childhood would predict depression in adulthood. Their previous research suggested that an important variable that could influence the results was gender: Based on their knowledge of research on the way boys and girls are socialized (boys to be autonomous and girls to be more attuned to social demands), they hypothesized that the personality antecedents of depression in males and females might be quite different. The results supported their hypothesis. Boys who later showed depressive tendencies were characterized when young as aggressive, self-aggrandizing, and unable to control their impulses. Girls who later became depressed, in contrast, showed almost the opposite attributes in childhood: They were shy, obedient, conscientious, and unassuming. Boys who were less bright were also more prone to depression at age 18, whereas girls who were *more* intelli-

TABLE 12.7 GENDER DIFFERENCES IN SELECTED ITEMS THAT CORRELATE WITH DEPRESSIVE SYMPTOMS AT AGE 18		
	CORRELATION	
ITEM	FOR BOYS	FOR GIRLS
AGES 3–4		
Can admit to own negative feelings	–.34	.28
Tends to be judgmental of others	–.26	.26
Is attentive and able to concentrate	–.04	.37
High intellectual capacity	–.14	.25
AGE 7		
Characteristically stretches limits	.37	–.22
Teases other children	.25	–.32
Tries to be center of attention	.30	.29
Is empathic	–.30	.29
Can be trusted; is dependable	–.37	.20
Is obedient and compliant	–.22	.30
AGE 11		
Is stubborn	.34	–.19
Characteristically stretches limits	.29	–.27
Is unable to delay gratification	.19	–.37
Has high intellectual capacity	–.19	.24
Is eager to please	–.37	.00
High standards of performance	–.33	.24

Source: Adapted from Block et al., 1991.

Note: The table reports the correlations between personality dimensions assessed at ages 3–4, 7, and 11 with degree of depression reported at age 18. As can be seen, on many dimensions, predictors of depression in males and females differed considerably.

gent were more likely to report depression at age 18. Some of the differences in childhood personality antecedents of depression in boys and girls are reproduced in Table 12.7. Although the pattern is not consistent at ages 3 to 4, by age 7 a clear picture emerges of the kind of boy or girl who is likely to be depressed in late adolescence.

A More Complex View of Personality and Consistency

If personality shows substantial consistency across situations and over time, was Mischel simply wrong? Yes and no. He clearly overstated the case for the role of situations in behavior and understated the case for personality variables. A 21-year-old man who was impulsive and undercontrolled at age 3 is more likely to be aggressive when someone accidentally bumps into him on the street and to steal from a store than a similar man who was better adjusted in preschool. In many respects, that is quite remarkable.

On the other hand, Mischel forced personality psychologists to move beyond simple statements such as "John is an aggressive person" to more complex statements about the *circumstances* under which John will be aggressive. In other words, Mischel's critique of traits led to a recognition of **person-by-situation interactions**, which simply means that people express particular traits in particular situations. In fact, in his most recent statements of his approach, Mischel argues that personality lies in *if–then* patterns—stable ways in which particular situations trigger specific patterns of thought, feeling, and behavior (Mischel & Shoda, 1995). For example, one man may become aggressive when another man appears to be threatening or humiliating him; another may become aggressive when he feels vulnerable with his wife, which leads him to feel unmasculine. Both men may be equally aggressive when their behavior is averaged across situations, but the difference between them lies in the circumstance (the "if") that elicits the response (the "then"). One of the things that is exciting about this approach is that Mischel explicitly attempts to integrate his own cognitive-social approach with both trait theory (arguing for enduring personality dispositions) and psychodynamic theory (focusing on personality dynamics that get activated under particular conditions, often outside of awareness).

Mischel's recent research, like that of a line of other psychologists who have been tracking down the nature of person-by-situation interactions (e.g., Funder & Colvin, 1993), supports a contention of early trait theorists that seemed to get lost for many years: Consistency is most likely to emerge in similar situations (Allport, 1937; Rotter, 1990). Like Spearman's distinction between s-factors and g-factors in intelligence (Chapter 8), some personality traits are specific to particular situations, whereas others are probably general or global in some individuals. A person who is generally quite low on neuroticism may nevertheless tend to become extremely distressed after a loss. Her difficulty in coping with loss is just as much a part of her personality as her generally placid nature; the only difference is that the circumstances that activate neurotic behavior are much more specific than those that activate its opposite.

INTERIM SUMMARY   Data from studies of behavioral genetics suggest that most personality variables are 15 to 50 percent heritable. Personality demonstrates many consistencies across time and situations. The debate over the extent to which personality is consistent led to a recognition of the importance of **person-by-situation interactions**—ways in which people express personality dispositions only under specific circumstances. According to Mischel, personality lies in *if–then* patterns—stable ways in which particular situations trigger specific patterns of thought, feeling, and behavior.

CONTRIBUTIONS AND LIMITATIONS OF TRAIT THEORIES

The trait approach to personality has several advantages. Traits lend themselves to measurement and hence to empirical investigation through questionnaires. Without the trait approach, we would not have been able to assess the heritability or consistency of personality. Further, trait theories are not committed to theoretical assumptions that may be valid for some people but not for others. Psychodynamic and cognitive-social theories offer universal answers to questions such as "Are humans basically aggressive?" or "Are people basically rational?" Trait theories, in contrast, offer a very different answer: "Some people are, some aren't, and some are in between" (see McCrae & Costa, 1990, pp. 20–21).

Trait approaches, however, have a number of limitations (see Block, 1995; McAdams, 1992; Westen, 1995). First, they rely too heavily on self-reports; people often cannot or will not give an accurate assessment of themselves. For example, people who consider themselves psychologically healthy may deny statements about themselves that are true but threaten their self-concept (Shedler et al., 1993). Correlations between self-reports and peer reports tend to be in the range of .40 to .50 (Costa & McCrae, 1990; McCrae, 1993). These are substantial correlations, but for a hefty percentage of subjects, either their peers do not know them very well or they do not know themselves.

Second, trait theories can be no more sophisticated than the theories of personality held by lay people and particularly by college students, who serve as subjects for most studies, because the basic terms of trait theory come from everyday language (see Block, 1995). Trait theory may be less a theory of personality than a theory of the way *everyday people* think about personality. Where do concepts developed by experts such as defenses or expectancies fit in? One could argue that relying almost exclusively on self-reports is like asking a physicist to depend on the observations of untrained observers who report, "Yeah, I think that apple fell pretty fast."

Third, as in factor-analytic studies of intelligence, the factor structure that emerges depends in part on the items that are included and a number of highly subjective decisions made by the factor analyst (see, for example, Katigbak et al., 1996). Although most personality researchers have converged on the FFM, others have repeatedly found three or four factors (e.g., Cloninger et al., 1993; Eysenck, 1990; Stallings et al., 1996), and some have found seven (e.g., Benet-Martinez & Waller, 1997).

Finally, trait theories often provide more insight into the *how much* of personality than the *how* or the *why* (Block, 1995). They describe and even predict behavior but do not explain it. A person may rank high in aggressiveness, but this says little about the internal processes that occur when the person is behaving aggressively or why he behaves aggressively in some circumstances but not in others. Some approaches, however, attempt to provide causal mechanisms, linking traits to underlying biology. For example, one approach ties neuroticism and extroversion to the neural pathways and neurotransmitter systems that underlie avoidance and negative affect on the one hand, and approach and positive affect on the other (Chapter 11).

HUMANISTIC THEORIES

During the 1950s and especially during the 1960s, an approach to personality emerged as an alternative to psychoanalysis and behaviorism. **Humanistic** approaches to personality hold that within each individual is an active, creative force, or "self," that seeks expression, development, and growth. Thus, the aim of the psychologist should not be to search for unconscious processes or environmental contingencies but to understand how individuals experience themselves, others, and the world and to help them actualize their potential. Thus, many humanistic psychologists argue that scientific methods borrowed from the natural sciences are inappropriate for studying people, whose actions reflect the way they understand and experience themselves and the world.

Although humanistic psychology has its roots in European philosophical thinking from the late nineteenth century, the humanistic approach to personality emerged during the 1960s, a decade that challenged traditional values. People were tired of fitting into roles others set for them and instead sought ways to be true to themselves and their personal beliefs (see Smith, 1978, 1988, 1994). Here we examine two humanistic theories: the person-centered approach of Carl Rogers and existential theories of personality.

ROGERS'S PERSON-CENTERED APPROACH

The most widely used humanistic theory of personality is Carl Rogers's **person-centered approach** (1951, 1959). Philosophically, Rogers descended from the

French philosopher Jean-Jacques Rousseau, who two centuries earlier wrote that "man is born free but everywhere he is in chains." Rousseau meant that people are innately free and compassionate to their fellows, but somehow in the course of growing up, they become mean-spirited, selfish, and trapped by convention. Rogers similarly believed that human beings are basically good but their personalities become distorted by interpersonal experiences, especially in childhood. In his view, psychology should try to understand individuals' **phenomenal experience**—that is, the way they conceive of reality and experience themselves and their world. According to Rogers and other humanistic psychologists, we should not be studying people as *objects* of our investigations but as *subjects* who construct meaning. Thus, the fundamental tool of the psychologist is not a projective test, an experiment, or a questionnaire, but **empathy**, the capacity to understand another person's experience cognitively and emotionally.

Rogers, like other humanistic theorists, postulated that individuals have a **true self**—a core aspect of being, untainted by the demands of those around them—but that they often distort this into a **false self**—a mask they wear and ultimately mistake to be their true psychological "face." According to Rogers, the false self emerges because of people's natural desire to gain the positive regard of other people. As children develop, they learn that to be loved they must meet certain standards. In the process of internalizing these **conditions of worth**, they distort themselves into being what significant others want them to be.

Rogers defines the self, or **self-concept,** as an organized pattern of thought and perception about oneself. When the self-concept diverges too much from the **ideal self** (the person's view of what she *should* be like), the individual may distort her behavior or the way she sees herself to avoid this painful state. Thus, people's internalized expectations of what others want them to be may lead them to abandon their own talents or inclinations and ignore their own needs and feelings. The artistic student who becomes an accountant because that is what his father always wanted him to be is, in Rogers's view, sacrificing his true self to meet internalized conditions of worth.

Rogers proposed that the primary motivation in humans is an **actualizing tendency**, a desire to fulfill the range of needs that humans experience, from the basic needs for food and drink to the needs to be open to experience and to express one's true self. These needs were similarly described by Maslow, another humanistic psychologist (Chapter 10). Opposing the actualizing tendency, however, are the needs for positive regard from others and for positive self-regard, which often require distorting the self to meet imposed standards.

▶ *No one of us can help the things life has done to us. They're done before you realize it, and once they're done, they make you do other things until at last everything comes between you and what you'd like to be, and you've lost your true self forever.*

—EUGENE O'NEILL,
Long Day's Journey into Night

INTERIM SUMMARY   **Humanistic** approaches to personality hold that within each individual is an active, creative force, or "self," that seeks expression, development, and growth. According to Carl Rogers's **person-centered approach,** psychology should try to understand individuals' **phenomenal experience**—the way they conceive of reality and experience themselves and their world—through **empathy**. Rogers defines the self, or **self-concept,** as an organized pattern of thought and perception about oneself, which can diverge from the **ideal self**, leading to distortions in personality.

EXISTENTIAL APPROACHES TO PERSONALITY

Existentialism is a school of modern philosophy that similarly focuses on subjective existence. According to many existentialist philosophers, the individual is alone throughout life and must confront what it means to be human and what values to embrace. According to the existential philosopher Jean-Paul Sartre (1971), unlike other animals and physical objects, people have no fixed nature and must essentially *create themselves*.

Existential Questions

Sartre argued that the meaning we find in life is essentially our own invention and dies along with us. The paradox inherent in the human condition is that we must find meaning in our lives by committing ourselves to values, ideals, people, and courses of action while simultaneously recognizing that these things are finite and have no intrinsic meaning, that we have simply endowed them with meaning in order to make our lives seem worthwhile.

Sartre would object to the idea that we have a personality at all, if personality implies a static or unchanging set of traits. What distinguishes humans, he asserts, is that we are ever-changing and free to alter our course of action at any time. Thus, we *have* no essence, no personality, except if we choose to delude ourselves into believing that we have no choice.

According to Sartre, people often sacrifice their autonomy and freedom in order to avoid the anxiety that accompanies it. Someone who works for the same company for 20 years makes a new decision every day to go to work, although he may not conceptualize this as a choice. People who act as if they are not making these continuous choices are practicing what Sartre termed bad faith. **Bad faith** is a form of self-deception in which people convince themselves that their actions are determined—that they must stay with a job or in an unfulfilling marriage—even when doing so feels stifling or false.

According to existential psychologists, the dilemmas at the heart of existential philosophy are central to personality. Although many different theoretical perspectives have developed within existential psychology (Frankl, 1959; May, 1953; May et al., 1958), they converge on several key issues: the importance of subjective experience; the centrality of the human quest for meaning in life; the dangers of losing touch with one's own inner feelings; and the hazards of conceiving of oneself as thinglike, rather than as a changing, ever-forming, creative source of will and action. Chief among the problems humans face is **existential dread**, the recognition that life has no absolute value or meaning and that, ultimately, we all face death. People spend their lives denying their mortality and the nothingness hidden behind their values and pursuits (Brown, 1959; Becker, 1973).

Members of cults often share a desperate need for an ideology and community to provide meaning to their lives. Marshall Applewhite and his 38 followers in the Heaven's Gate cult committed mass suicide, hoping to catch a ride on a UFO they believed was traveling behind the Hale-Bopp comet.

Experimental Investigations of Death Anxiety

Existential psychologists, like other humanistic psychologists, have generally avoided testing their hypotheses or developing methods of personality assessment because they distrust psychological techniques that turn people into objects to be studied rather than subjects to be understood. Nevertheless, a team of researchers has been systematically testing Ernest Becker's (1973) theory that cultural beliefs and values serve to protect people from facing the reality of their mortality. According to Becker's theory, an unfortunate by-product of the evolution of human intelligence is that people can imagine possible futures, including those that are painful and tragic. To avoid the potentially debilitating anxiety that could result, they create and embrace cultural beliefs and values that symbolically deny death and allow hope in the face of mortality and meaninglessness. Cultural values and worldviews thus "imbue the world with meaning, order, stability, and permanence, and by so doing, buffer the anxiety that results from living in a terrifying and largely uncontrollable universe in which death is the only certainty" (Solomon et al., 1991, p. 96).

The researchers testing Becker's theory have demonstrated across a series of studies that when confronted with experimental procedures designed to stimulate death anxiety (such as a questionnaire asking participants to think about their own death), people cling more tenaciously to their cultural values (Greenberg et al., 1994; Solomon et al., 1991). In one study, municipal court judges served as subjects (Rosenblatt et al., 1989). Half the judges received the mortality salience manipulation (the death questionnaire), whereas the other half (the control group) did not. The experimenters then asked the judges to set bond for a prostitute in a hypothetical case. Prostitution was chosen as the crime because of its culturally defined moral overtones. As predicted, judges who filled out the mortality questionnaire were significantly more punitive, setting bond substantially higher than judges in the control group, whose death anxiety had not been activated.

In another study, the experimenters presented Christian college students with information on two people, one identified as Christian and the other as Jewish (Greenberg et al., 1990). The researchers hypothesized that inducing death anxiety would lead participants to prefer people who share their cultural beliefs, in this case, other Christians. As predicted, participants induced to think about their death evaluated the Christian more favorably than the Jew, while participants in the control condition showed no preference for the Christian or the Jew. More recent research finds that priming participants with the word *death* outside of awareness (through rapid, subliminal presentation) produces the same kinds of effects, suggesting that people can indeed defend against death unconsciously (Arndt et al., 1997).

INTERIM SUMMARY   According to **existential** approaches to psychology, people have no fixed nature and must essentially create themselves. Sartre argued that people must find meaning in their lives by making commitments while recognizing that these commitments have no intrinsic meaning. **Bad faith** is a form of self-deception people use to escape the anxiety associated with freedom to choose. **Existential dread** is the recognition that life has no absolute value or meaning and that we all face death. Research supports Becker's theory that people deny death by committing to cultural worldviews that give them a sense of meaning and immortality.

CONTRIBUTIONS AND LIMITATIONS OF HUMANISTIC THEORIES

Humanistic psychology has made a number of contributions to the study of personality. Perhaps the most important is its unique focus on the way humans strive to find meaning in life, a dimension that other approaches have failed to address. In day-to-day life this need may not be readily observable because culture confers meaning on activities, relationships, and values. The salience of this aspect of personality emerges, however, in times of personal crisis or loss (Janoff-Bulman, 1992), when life may seem capricious and meaningless. The search for meaning also becomes apparent in times of rapid cultural change (Wallace, 1956), when a culture's values and worldview are breaking down and no longer fulfill their function of making life predictable and meaningful (see also Baumeister, 1991).

The humanistic approach has at least two major limitations. First, it does not offer a comprehensive theory of personality in the same way that psychodynamic and cognitive-social theory do. It does not, for example, offer a general theory of cognition, emotion, behavior, and psychological disorder, although different theorists at times address many of these. Second, with some notable exceptions (Rogers, 1959), humanistic psychology has largely failed to develop a body of testable hypotheses and research, although this failure reflects its rejection of empiricism as a philosophy of science.

PERSONALITY AND CULTURE

The theories we have explored in this chapter represent our own culture's most sophisticated attempts to understand personality. Other cultures, however, have alternative views. In fact, every culture has some implicit, commonsense conception of personality.

The Cheyenne of North America, for example, distinguish several aspects of personhood (Straus, 1977). The individual's basic nature and identity reside in the heart. The person's power, called *omotome*, is distinguished from spirit, which is the storehouse of learning, experience, and memory. To some degree, the Cheyenne believe in behavioral genetics, holding that certain behaviors run in families and that children are born predisposed to behave in particular ways. Theirs is also a somewhat psychodynamic view of childhood as an extremely important period of life, crucial for learning and spiritual development. Unlike contemporary Western theories, however, the Cheyenne do not believe personality resides entirely or even primarily in individuals. Rather, they believe, like many preliterate societies, that the innermost parts of the soul or personality are in part communal, shared by kin and community (see Geertz, 1973; Markus & Kitayama, 1991; Shweder & Bourne, 1982; Triandis et al., 1989; Westen, 1985).

LINKING PERSONALITY AND CULTURE

Although most Western theories of personality have been constructed with Western subjects in mind, the complex interactions of personality and culture have intrigued psychologists and anthropologists since the early part of the century (see Church & Lonner, in press; LeVine, 1982) Do cultures with harsh childrearing practices create hostile or paranoid personalities? And how do cultural practices help individuals satisfy psychological needs, such as escaping from death anxiety? We briefly consider four approaches to culture and personality: Marx's, Freud's, the culture pattern approach, and interactionist approaches.

Marx's Approach

One of the earliest theories of personality and culture was proposed by the social philosopher Karl Marx (although Marx is not generally considered a personality theorist). Marx (1972) disputed the idea of a common human nature and instead proposed that people's needs, wishes, beliefs, and values are products of the conditions under which they live and work. According to Marx, the materialistic, competitive, individualistic personality style of people in Western, industrialized, capitalist nations reflects underlying economic realities, such as competition for scarce jobs and the breakdown of extended family work units (such as family farms) that occurred with the rise of capitalism.

An orientation toward individual liberty, materialism, and achievement seems like human nature to us, but Marx was indeed correct that human nature looks very different in other societies. Research consistently shows that individualism and competitiveness correlate highly with the extent of industrialization in an economy. For example, Machiavellianism—the belief that manipulating other people is acceptable and even desirable—is highly correlated with the degree of technological development (Christie & Geis, 1980; Geis, 1978). People in industrial societies tend to rear their children to compete and achieve, whereas those in less technologically advanced societies stress obedience and cooperation (see Werner, 1979). Marx further argued that the conditions under which individuals labor play a fundamental role in shaping the kind of people they are. He would not have been surprised to find high rates of drug abuse among automobile factory workers in America, who may spend much of their day performing tasks that have no personal meaning and provide little personal satisfaction.

Freud's Approach

Whereas Marx essentially reduced personality and culture to economic factors, Freud reduced culture to personality, seeing cultural phenomena as reflections of individual psychodynamics. The Freudian method of analyzing cultures is the

A holy mother is a motif that recurs in religious imagery throughout the world.

same method applied to dreams, neurotic symptoms, and conscious beliefs in individuals: Look beneath manifest content to find latent content (see Spain, 1992).

Freud viewed cultural phenomena such as myths, moral and religious beliefs, and games as expressions of the needs and conflicts of individuals. For example, my friends are all aghast to find that I am a devotee of boxing. Because I do not appear to be a very aggressive person, they cannot understand how I can enjoy watching two grown men dancing around on a piece of canvas, trying to destroy each other's cerebellum with flurries of punches. The function of boxing for me, no doubt, is to express aggressive impulses that I would not permit myself in my daily life.

Freud (1928) similarly argued that institutions such as religion can be understood in terms of their functions for individuals. Should one be surprised to find representations in Western culture of a Holy Father and a sacred Mother? The monotheistic concept of God in many religions is remarkably similar to a young child's conception of his father: a strong, masculine, frightening figure who can be both loving and vengeful. (Interestingly, empirical research suggests that people's concepts of God actually tend to resemble their descriptions of their *mothers*, particularly when they are closer to their mother than to their father; see Wulff, 1997.) A Freudian might also note that the virgin mother of Christian theology is a perfect resolution of Oedipal conflict: No child wants to think that his parents have sex, and the best way of keeping mother pure is to imagine that she could have had a virgin birth.

The Culture Pattern Approach

A third approach asserts that individual psychology reflects cultural practices, not the other way around. The **culture pattern approach** sees culture as an organized set of beliefs, rituals, and institutions that shape individuals to fit its patterns. Some cultures stress community and pursuit of the common good, and their members generally internalize these values. Others foster a paranoid attitude, which individuals express in their relations with neighbors or outsiders, such as the Nuer of the Sudan (Evans-Pritchard, 1956) or the Aymaya of South America (LaBarre, 1966). As Ruth Benedict put it, "The life history of the individual is first and foremost an accommodation to the patterns and standards traditionally handed down in the community" (1934, p. 2).

From the standpoint of the culture pattern approach, culture is a great sculptor that chisels the raw biological material of an individual from infancy on until it conforms to the sculptor's aesthetic ideal. Some slabs of humanity, however, are very difficult to chisel and are labeled deviant or thrown back into the quarry after being deformed by the hand of the frustrated artist. Those whose temperament and personality patterns do not readily conform to culture patterns may thus find themselves ostracized or incarcerated, viewed in various societies as sinners, criminals, dissidents, or mentally ill.

A GLOBAL VISTA

INTERACTIONIST APPROACHES TO PERSONALITY AND CULTURE

Each of the approaches described thus far essentially reduces one broad set of variables to another: personality to economics, culture to personality, or personality to culture. While each has considerable merit, more complex **interactionist** approaches, which view causality as multidirectional, combine many of their virtues (LeVine, 1982; Whiting & Whiting, 1975). Personality must certainly accommodate to economic and cultural demands, but

FIGURE 12.8
An interactionist approach to personality and culture. Interactionist models attempt to address the mutual influences of culture, personality, and economics, rather than reducing one to another. In this view, cultural beliefs and economic forces shape individual needs, which in turn give rise to new economic and cultural forces.

cultural and economic processes themselves are in part created to fulfill psychological needs. These in turn are shaped by cultural and economic practices, so that causality runs in more than one direction (Figure 12.8).

For example, societies that treat children more abusively tend to have more aggressive myths and religious beliefs (Rohner, 1975). From an interactionist perspective, this should not be surprising. On the one hand, the schemas or representations that children develop about relationships in childhood color their understanding of supernatural relationships. Thus, children with hostile or abusive parents are likely to respond emotionally to images of evil or sadistic gods when they grow older. Indeed, one could

The Western conception of God was once much more frightening and judgmental, as in Michelangelo's depiction of God creating the world (from the Sistine Chapel).

argue that in the West, as childrearing practices have become less harsh since the Middle Ages, the image of God has shifted from a vengeful, angry father to a loving, nurturant one.

On the other hand, causality runs in the opposite direction as well, from aggressive myths to abusive childrearing practices. Societies use myths and religious beliefs to train people to behave in ways valued by the culture. People reared on a steady diet of myths depicting aggressive interactions are likely to treat their children more aggressively, which in turn produces children who resonate with the aggression in the myths they will teach their own children.

Other interactionist approaches consider historical as well as cultural factors. The psychoanalyst Erik Erikson (1969) examined the lives of powerful leaders like Gandhi and Hitler and explored the intersection of their personality dynamics, the needs of their followers, and cultural and historical circumstances. Erikson argued, for example, that Hitler's strong need for power and his grandiosity, sensitivity to humiliation, and disgust for anyone he saw as weak contributed to the development of Nazi ideology, which stressed the greatness of Germany (with which Hitler identified) and the need to destroy groups Hitler perceived as either powerful (and hence threatening) or powerless. This ideology appealed to a nation that had been humiliated in World War I and forced to pay reparations to its adversaries as well as to members of a culture whose childrearing patterns left them vulnerable to feeling humiliated and unable to express their rage (Chapter 17).

INTERIM SUMMARY   Marx disputed the idea of a common human nature and instead proposed that people's needs, wishes, beliefs, and values are products of the conditions under which they live and work. Freud reduced culture to personality, seeing cultural phenomena as reflections of individual psychodynamics. The **culture pattern approach** sees culture as an organized set of beliefs, rituals, and institutions that shape individuals to fit its patterns. **Interactionist approaches** view causality as multidirectional, with personality, economics, and culture mutually influencing one another.

SOME CONCLUDING THOUGHTS

We began the chapter with the case of Oskar and Jack, whose shared genes seemed to contribute to remarkable similarities in their personalities, and end with the powerful impact of culture. Had Oskar and Jack grown up among the Nuer of the Sudan, they both would likely have been fierce and hostile compared to most Westerners, but this would have little to do with their genes. How, then, do we understand the complex forces that produce an individual personality?

Some aspects of personality are clearly heritable, others reflect the conflicts and concerns of childhood, while still others reflect the daily impact of social interaction. A person is the handiwork of both nature and nurture, of chromosomes and culture.

Precisely how do biology, culture, and experience interact to produce a person? To this question we now turn, as we explore the nature of human development.

SUMMARY

1. **Personality** refers to the enduring patterns of thought, feeling, and behavior that are expressed in different circumstances. Personality psychologists study both the **structure of personality** (the organization or patterning of thoughts, feelings, and behaviors) and **individual differences** in dimensions of personality.

PSYCHODYNAMIC THEORIES

2. Freud's theory of **psychodynamics** holds that psychological forces such as wishes, fears, and intentions determine behavior. His **topographic model** distinguished among **conscious, preconscious,** and **unconscious mental processes.** Freud argued that mental **conflict** is ubiquitous and that **ambivalence**—conflicting feelings or intentions—is the rule rather than the exception in human experience. The solutions people develop in an effort to maximize fulfillment of conflicting motives simultaneously are called **compromise formations**.

3. Freud's **drive,** or instinct, **model** views sex **(libido)** and aggression as the basic human motives. His **developmental model** proposed a series of **psychosexual stages**—stages in the development of personality and sexuality. These include the **oral, anal, phallic, latency,** and **genital stages**. Problematic experiences during a stage can lead to **fixations**—prominent conflicts and concerns that are focused on wishes from a particular period—or **regressions,** in which issues from a past stage resurface. During the phallic stage, the child must resolve the **Oedipus complex,** the desire for an exclusive, sensual/sexual relationship with the opposite-sex parent.

4. Freud's **structural model** distinguished among **id** (the reservoir of sexual and aggressive energy), **superego** (conscience), and **ego** (the rational part of the mind that must somehow balance desire, reality, and morality). Unconscious strategies aimed at minimizing unpleasant emotions or maximizing pleasant emotions are called **defense mechanisms**. Common defense mechanisms include **repression, denial, projection, reaction formation, sublimation, rationalization,** and **passive aggression**.

5. The **neo-Freudians** accepted the influence of unconscious processes and conflicts among psychological forces but rejected Freud's drive theory and focused more on the role of culture. **Object relations theories** stress the role of representations of self and others in interpersonal functioning and the role of early experience in shaping the capacity for intimacy and chart the development of the capacity for mature love.

6. Psychodynamic approaches usually assess personality using life history and projective methods, such as the **Rorschach inkblot test** and **Thematic Apperception Test (TAT),** though they also use experimental procedures to test hypotheses.

7. The psychodynamic perspective has contributed a number of fundamental insights about unconscious processes, defenses, conflict, and so forth; however, it is weaker in its empirical base than other theories.

COGNITIVE-SOCIAL THEORIES

8. Cognitive-social theories argue for the importance of encoding, personal value, expectancies, competencies, and self-regulation in personality. The

schemas people use to encode and retrieve social information play an important role in personality. **Personal value** refers to the importance individuals attach to various outcomes or potential outcomes. **Expectancies** are expectations relevant to desired outcomes. A **behavior-outcome expectancy** is a belief that a certain behavior will lead to a particular outcome. **Self-efficacy expectancies** are people's beliefs about their ability to perform actions necessary to produce a desired outcome. **Competences** are skills and abilities used to solve problems. **Self-regulation** means setting goals, evaluating one's own performance, and adjusting one's behaviors to achieve goals in the context of ongoing feedback. Cognitive-social theories view personality as problem solving to attain goals.

9. Cognitive-social theory can explain a wide spectrum of behavior and has considerable empirical support; however, it tends to be overly rational and to assume that people can report on the most important aspects of their personality.

TRAIT THEORIES

10. Trait theories are based on the concept of **traits**, emotional, cognitive, and behavioral tendencies that constitute underlying dimensions of personality on which individuals vary. Using factor analysis, different theorists have proposed different theories of the major factors that constitute personality. Eysenck considers the major factors (which he calls *types*) to be extroversion, neuroticism, and psychoticism. The current consensus among trait psychologists is that personality consists of five traits, known as the **Big Five factors** or **Five Factor Model** (FFM) (openness to experience, conscientiousness, extroversion, agreeableness, and neuroticism).

11. The heritability of personality traits varies considerably; most are influenced by nature and nurture, but some are highly heritable. A debate about the consistency of personality has raged for the past 30 years, sparked by Mischel's arguments against consistency. Mischel's work sensitized researchers to the complexities of **person-by-situation interactions,** in which personality processes become activated only in particular situations.

12. Trait theories lend themselves to empirical measurement and heritability studies; however, they tend to describe, rather than explain, personality.

HUMANISTIC THEORIES

13. **Humanistic** theories of personality suggest that within each individual is an active, creative force, or "self," seeking expression, development, and growth. Rogers's **person-centered approach** aims at understanding individuals' **phenomenal experience,** that is, how they conceive of reality and experience themselves and their world. According to Rogers, individuals have a **true self** (a core aspect of being, untainted by the demands of those around them), which is often distorted into a **false self** by the desire to conform to social demands. When the self-concept diverges too much from the individual's **ideal self** (the person's view of what she should be like), she may distort the way she behaves or the way she sees herself to avoid this painful state of affairs. Psychological understanding requires **empathy.**

14. **Existential** personality theories stress the importance of subjective experience and the individual's quest for meaning in life. Chief among the prob-

lems human beings face is **existential dread,** the recognition that life has no absolute value or meaning and that death is inevitable. The ways people handle issues of meaning, mortality, and existential dread are central aspects of personality.

15. Humanistic theories contribute to the understanding of some fundamental aspects of personality, like the quest for meaning; however, they tend not to be as comprehensive as other approaches.

PERSONALITY AND CULTURE

16. Some aspects of personality are probably universal, whereas others are culturally specific. Marx's theory reduces personality to economics, while Freud's reduces culture to personality. The culture pattern approach sees personality primarily as an accommodation to culture. According to interactionist approaches, personality is shaped by economic and cultural demands, but cultural and economic processes themselves are in part created to fulfill psychological needs.

Suzy Kitman, "Flying Baby: Ellie #3," 1997.

CHAPTER 13

Physical and Cognitive Development

Dear God,
   I saw Saint Patrick's Church last week when we went to New York. You live in a nice house.

                              Frank

*F*rank is a young child who wrote this letter as part of a research project studying children's developing ideas about God (Heller, 1986, p. 16). As Frank's letter suggests, young children translate cultural concepts like God into their own "language." Frank converted the idea of the church as God's

home into his own concrete notion of what constitutes a "nice house." Children's drawings similarly reveal the way they translate adult spiritual beliefs into "childese" (Figure 13.1).

In religious belief as in other areas, children frequently wrestle with concepts beyond their grasp, and their efforts reveal much about childish thought. Consider the mighty task faced by a six-year-old trying to make sense of the relation between Jesus and God in Christian theology: "Well, I know Jesus was a president and God is not . . . sort of like David was a king and God is not" (Heller, 1986, p. 40).

Whether children are reared Jewish, Baptist, Catholic, or Hindu, their views of God, like their understanding of most objects of thought, are initially concrete (Heller, 1986). By the time they move into adolescence, they are likely to offer abstract conceptions, such as "God is a force within us all." If cultural conditions permit, they may also express considerable skepticism about religious notions, since they are able to imagine and reflect on a variety of possible realities.

Changes in the way children understand reality and cultural beliefs are a central focus of **developmental psychology**, which studies the way humans develop and change over time. For years, psychologists focused largely on childhood and adolescence and tended to consider development complete by the teenage years. More recently, however, psychologists have adopted a *lifespan developmental perspective* that considers both constancy and change, and gains and losses in functioning, that occur at different points over the entire human life cycle (Baltes et al., 1998).

In this chapter, we first consider some basic issues in developmental psychology and the ways researchers study development. Then we examine physical development and its bearing on psychological functioning throughout the lifespan. For example, how does an individual adapt to a changing body during puberty, menopause, or old age? Next, we describe cognitive development, beginning with the question of what infants know. We conclude by describing cognitive changes in adulthood, addressing myths and realities of aging, such as the view that "senility" is the inevitable endpoint of development.

BASIC ISSUES IN DEVELOPMENTAL PSYCHOLOGY

Throughout this chapter and the next, three major issues repeatedly emerge: How do genetic and environmental influences interact to shape development? To what extent do capacities such as language or morality depend on early experiences? And is development characterized by leaps and plateaus or by continuous growth?

NATURE AND NURTURE

For almost as many years as psychologists have been interested in development, they have wrestled with the extent to which changes in individuals over time reflect the influence of genetically programmed maturation or of experience, that is, of nature or nurture. **Maturation** refers to biologically based changes that follow an orderly sequence, each step setting the stage for the next step according to an age-related timetable (Wesley & Sullivan, 1986). Infants crawl before they walk, and they utter single syllables and words before they talk in complete sentences. Unless reared in a profoundly deprived environment, virtually all human infants follow these developmental patterns in the same sequence and at roughly the same age, give or take a few months.

Most psychologists believe that development, like intelligence or personality, reflects the interaction of genes and environment (Loehlin et al., 1997; Plomin, 1990; Plomin et al., 1994). Nature provides a fertile field for development, but this field requires cultivation. Thus, the question is not *which* is more important, nature or nurture, or even *how much* each contributes, but rather *how* nature and nurture contribute interactively to development (Anastasi, 1958). In fact, in many respects the contrast of nature *versus* nurture is misplaced, since genetic blueprints do not express themselves without environmental input (Bors & Forrin, 1996; Gottlieb, 1991). For example, sensory stimulation is necessary for some genes even to become activated (Gottlieb et al., 1998). To try to quantify the relative contribution of genes and environment in this case makes little sense, because the action of the gene itself depends on the environmental stimulation.

THE RELATIVE IMPORTANCE OF EARLY EXPERIENCE

> Before dawn on January 9, 1800, a remarkable creature came out of the woods near the village of Saint-Sernin in southern France . . . He was human in bodily form and walked erect. Everything else about him suggested an animal. He was naked except for the tatters of a shirt and showed . . . no awareness of himself as a human person . . . He could not speak and made only weird, meaningless cries. Though very short, he appeared to be a boy of about eleven or twelve, with a round face under dark matted hair. [From Shattuck, 1980, p. 5]

The "Wild Boy of Aveyron" created an immediate sensation in Europe. To scientists, the child was a unique laboratory for exploring the question of **critical periods** in human development, periods of special sensitivity to specific types of learning that shape the capacity for future development. Would a boy who was raised, at best, by wolves be able to develop language, interact with other people, and develop a conscience? A young doctor named Jean-Marie Itard became the

FIGURE 13.1
Children translate cultural beliefs into their own "language." In this picture, God is a man with a halo wearing a white smock. Another child, a preschooler, attributed the origins of the universe to "God, Mother Nature, and Mother Goose."

boy's tutor. Itard's efforts met with limited but nonetheless substantial success: The boy became affectionate and learned to respond to some verbal instructions, but he never learned to talk.

Evidence for Critical Periods

The concept of critical periods initially came from embryology, as researchers discovered that toxic substances could affect the developing fetus, but only if the fetus were exposed at very specific points in development. Critical periods in psychological development have been demonstrated in many animal species. The first few hours after hatching are a critical period for goslings, which are biologically prepared to follow whatever moving object they see, usually their mother (Lorenz, 1935). The concept of critical periods in humans is more controversial. Can a child who does not experience nurturant caretaking in the first five years of life ever develop the capacity to love?

Human development is more flexible than development in other animals, but the brain is particularly sensitive to certain kinds of environmental input at certain times (see Bornstein, 1989). We saw in Chapter 7 that language acquisition is more difficult in adulthood than childhood and that the language spoken in a culture shapes an infant's sensitivity to particular linguistic sounds even before the end of the first year of life. Similarly, in Chapter 10 we discussed the organizational effects of prenatal hormones, which appear to shape psychological characteristics such as sexual motives and behavior as well as physical characteristics.

The neuropsychological basis for critical periods probably lies in the connections among neurons. During some periods, the nervous system is most sensitive to sprouting particular connections among neurons, given the right environmental stimulus. Equally important is the pruning of neurons: Infants are born with an abundance of neural connections, and those that are not used or activated by the environment are gradually lost (Greenough, 1991; Greenough et al., 1987).

Research on nonhuman animals has documented the importance of early environmental experience on the developing brain. In one study, researchers surgically closed the eyelids of newborn monkeys, depriving them of visual experience for their first 12 months (S. Carlson, 1990). Then, over the following 12 months, they were tested on a number of visual tasks. Although the monkeys were able to perform some tasks, including following a large object with their eyes, they showed a number of abnormal behaviors in trying to explore their environment, such as relying heavily on their hands to compensate for visual deficits (Figure 13.2).

The Impact of Early Abuse or Deprivation

As we saw in Chapter 3, the human brain, like that of other mammals, appears to have evolved with many innate potentialities that require environmental imput to activate. Given appropriate stimulation, most children will learn to speak, think, solve problems, love and hate in ways accepted and encouraged by their culture.

In this view, the brain has essentially been "programmed" by natural selection to expect a range of input. That range is wide, but it is not infinite. What happens to children whose experience is outside that range?

As we saw in Chapter 7, a famous case was of a girl named Genie, who received almost no exposure to language after the age of 1 or 2 (Fromkin et al., 1974; Rymer, 1993). Genie's father was emotionally ill and locked her in a small room, where she was frequently bound and unable to move. She was discovered at age

  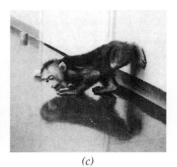 

(a)   *(b)*   *(c)*   *(d)*

Figure 13.2

The importance of early environmental experience. Visually deprived monkeys showed a number of peculiarities in the way they explored their environments in the year following deprivation. Photo (*a*) shows a monkey carefully moving about the floor, in a "spider walk"; (*b*) shows a monkey anchoring itself to a chair while exploring with one hand; (*c*) shows similar anchoring to the wall; and (*d*) shows a monkey exploring the wall with its hands. Lacking early perceptual experience, these monkeys could not navigate their world visually.

13. Like the Wild Boy of Aveyron, Genie was subsequently able to learn some aspects of language; however, her use of syntax never reached normal levels, and she remained severely handicapped socially (Fromkin et al., 1974).

Other psychologists, however, question whether the impact of early deprivation is so indelible (Kagan, 1984, 1996; Lerner, 1991). In one study, children who spent their first 19 months in an overcrowded and understaffed orphanage experienced average IQ gains of 28.5 points after being moved to an environment that provided individual care (Skeels, 1966). Even the case of Genie can be used to counter the notion of critical periods, since she demonstrated remarkable progress in social and intellectual skills in just a few short years (Kagan, 1984). On the other hand, after those initial gains her functioning stabilized and never approached the levels of a normal adolescent or adult.

Sensitive Periods

Does the evidence, then, support the notion of critical periods in humans? The conservative answer is that humans have **sensitive periods**—times that are more important to subsequent development than others but are not absolute gatekeepers for future psychological growth. In some domains, such as language, these sensitive periods may actually be critical; appropriate environmental input at certain points may be required or further development is permanently impaired. In most domains, however, sensitive periods are simply sensitive—particularly important but not decisive.

Stages or Continuous Change?

The third basic issue in development concerns the nature of developmental change. According to one view, development occurs in **stages**, relatively discrete steps through which everyone progresses in the same sequence. Behavior in one stage is not just *quantitatively* different from the next, involving a little less or more of something, such as slightly more rebelliousness at age 13 than at 11 or a gradually increasing capacity to think abstractly. Rather, stages are *qualitatively* different from one another. For example, a stage theorist would suggest that adolescent rebelliousness is qualitatively different from the rule breaking of younger children because it rests on a rejection of parental authority and a new way of experiencing the self. The point is not that 13-year-olds break the rules 20 or 30 percent more than 11-year-olds but that they have passed from one stage of life to another and their assumptions and values have changed.

An alternative perspective sees development as **continuous**, characterized less by major transformations than by steady and gradual change. From this point of view, what may look like a massive change, such as becoming literate between the ages of 5 and 8 or rebellious at 13, may actually reflect a slow and steady process of learning at school or increased reinforcement for independent behavior. Actually, many theorists suggest that development involves both stages and continuous processes (Fischer, 1992; Fischer & Bidell, 1998; Piaget, 1972). Stagelike phenomena are much more obvious in childhood, when the nervous system is maturing. As individuals move into adulthood, they are likely to develop in a number of alternative directions, and stages become especially difficult to recognize across cultures.

INTERIM SUMMARY   **Developmental psychology** studies the way humans develop and change over time. Since the origins of the discipline, psychologists have wrestled with the nature–nurture question, trying to discover the extent to which psychological changes reflect experience or **maturation** (biologically based changes that follow an orderly sequence). Most agree that genes and environment interact in complex ways in nearly all aspects of development. Another question is the extent to which development is characterized by **critical periods**—periods of special sensitivity to specific types of learning that shape the capacity for future development. At the very least, humans have **sensitive periods**—times that are more important to subsequent development than others but are not absolute gatekeepers for future psychological growth. An additional question is whether development occurs in **stages**—relatively discrete steps through which everyone progresses in the same sequence—or is better characterized as **continuous**—involving steady and gradual change.

STUDYING DEVELOPMENT

At first glance, studying development might seem relatively straightforward: To find out how 5- and 10-year-olds differ in working memory, skill at throwing a ball, or relationships with peers, simply collect a sample at each age and see how differently children at the two ages respond. In fact, however, matters are more complex. Psychologists primarily use three types of research designs to study development: cross-sectional, longitudinal, and sequential.

CROSS-SECTIONAL STUDIES

Cross-sectional studies compare groups of subjects of different ages at a single time to see whether differences exist among them. For example, a research group in Georgia is currently studying centenarians—people who have reached 100 years of age—to compare them on a number of dimensions with people in their 60s and 80s (Poon et al., 1992). Cross-sectional studies are useful for providing a snapshot of **age differences**, or variations among people of different ages.

The major limitation of cross-sectional studies is that they do not directly assess **age changes**, the ways *individuals* change over time. As a result, they are vulnerable to confounding variables such as cultural changes. For example, the centenarian researchers note that one of their groups of subjects grew up in the early years of Reconstruction in the South following the Civil War, another during World War I, and the third during the Great Depression and World War II. These different historical experiences could profoundly influence observed differences between the three **cohorts** (groups of people born around the same time) (Elder, 1998). Cultural changes in education, mass communication, and nutrition could also have a profound impact on subjects' later ways of thinking and acting. Cross-sectional studies are most useful when **cohort effects**—differences among age groups associated with differences in the culture—are minimal, as when assessing differences in the self-concepts of 4-and 6-year olds.

LONGITUDINAL STUDIES

Longitudinal studies follow the same individuals over time, providing the opportunity to assess age changes rather than age differences. The advantage of longitudinal over cross-sectional studies is their ability to reveal differences *among* individuals as well as changes *within* individuals over time.

Like cross-sectional designs, however, longitudinal designs are vulnerable to cohort effects. Because they investigate only one cohort, they cannot rule out the possibility that people born at a different time might show different developmental paths or trajectories. For example, the data from four longitudinal studies of gifted women at midlife showed that gifted women born after 1940 scored higher on all measures of psychological well-being than gifted women born before that time (Schuster, 1990). The impact of giftedness on women's well-being appears to depend in part on cultural attitudes toward women's intelligence and on opportunities for achievement.

SEQUENTIAL STUDIES

Sequential studies minimize cohort effects by studying multiple cohorts longitudinally. In an ideal sequential design, a group of people at one age is studied and followed up over time. As the study progresses, a new, younger cohort is added to the study, beginning at the same age at which the first cohort began. Essentially, a sequential design combines cross-sectional and longitudinal comparisons, allowing researchers to distinguish between age effects (differences associated with age) and cohort effects.

Figure 13.3 illustrates the differences among the three designs in hypothetical studies of attitudes toward parents at ages 8, 18, and 28; the sequential design yields the most useful and precise information but takes 30 years to yield its returns. The moral of the story is that, ideally, psychologists should live a long time, find successors to carry on their research after they are dead, and conduct sequential studies, preferably in several cultures. Short of that, researchers should, and do, try to use the best methods at their disposal and remain aware of the methodological limitations on the generalizability of their results.

INTERIM SUMMARY   **Cross-sectional studies** compare groups of subjects of different ages at a single time to provide a picture of **age differences**. **Longitudinal studies** follow the same individuals over time, providing the opportunity to assess **age changes** rather than age differences. **Sequential studies** minimize **cohort effects** by studying multiple cohorts longitudinally.

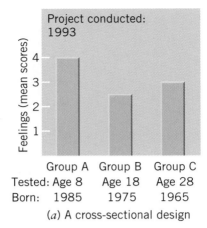

(a) A cross-sectional design

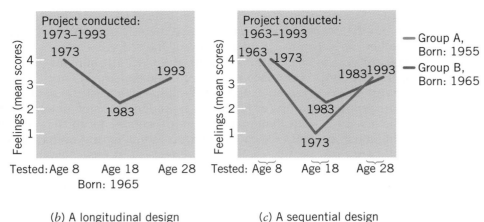

(b) A longitudinal design

(c) A sequential design

FIGURE 13.3

Cross-sectional (a), longitudinal (b), and sequential (c) designs. The figure illustrates the way three designs might assess feelings toward parents at three ages. In these hypothetical studies, feelings are rated on a 1–5 scale, where 1 = extremely negative and 5 = extremely positive. Results from the cross-sectional study (a) suggest that between ages 8 and 18, feelings become more negative (from 4.0 to 2.5) and then improve again (to 3.0) at age 28. The longitudinal study (b) finds a slightly larger drop at age 18 (to 2.0). The sequential study (c) suggests an interaction between age effects and cohort effects: Children begin with very positive attitudes toward their parents at age 8 and become relatively positive again by age 28. They also tend to become more negative in adolescence, but the extent to which they do so depends on their cohort. 18- year-olds in 1973 grew up during the social upheaval of the 1960s and were thus more negative toward their parents than children who grew up in the next decade.

PHYSICAL DEVELOPMENT AND ITS PSYCHOLOGICAL CONSEQUENCES

Having examined some of the basic issues and methods of developmental psychology, we turn now to physical development and its impact on psychological functioning. From an evolutionary perspective, the timing of physical changes has evolved as a series of adaptations that maximize survival and reproduction. Humans have much to learn before taking on the responsibilities of parenthood; not surprisingly, we have longer childhoods than any other animal, and our physical capacity to reproduce occurs only in the second decade of life, after considerable learning.

Many changes associated with physical development are obvious even to the untrained eye. Children develop rapidly during the early years, outgrowing clothes before wearing them out. Some of the most dramatic aspects of physical development cannot be observed directly, however, because they take place before birth.

PRENATAL DEVELOPMENT

One of the most remarkable aspects of development is that a single cell, forged by the union of a sperm and an egg, contains the blueprint for an organism that will emerge—complete with billions of specialized cells—several months later. Substantial development occurs during the period of **gestation** (between conception and birth). This **prenatal** (before birth) period is divided into three stages (Figure 13.4). During the **germinal period** (approximately the first two weeks after conception), the fertilized egg becomes implanted in the uterus. The second stage, the **embryonic period** (from the beginning of the third week to about the eighth week of gestation), is the most important period in the development of the central nervous system and of the organs. By the end of this stage, the features of the embryo become recognizably human, the rudiments of most organs have formed, and the heart has begun to beat. During the third or **fetal period** (from about nine weeks to birth), muscular development is rapid. By about 28 weeks, the fetus is capable of sustaining life on its own. (The term *fetus* is often used more broadly to refer to the organism between conception and birth.) Birth usually occurs at 38 weeks, or 9 months.

Mothers often sense that their child is "willful" or has a "personality" even before birth. In part this undoubtedly reflects vivid maternal imagination (as in the case of a friend of mine—a psychologist, no less—who routinely tells me of the latest antics of Danny, her five-month-old fetus!). Recent research suggests, however, that fetuses of many species can actually behave and even learn in utero (Smotherman & Robinson, 1996). In some ways this should not be surprising. By the time a child of any species is born, it has to be ready to respond to features of its environment (so that it can eat, for example), and Mother Nature is not such a procrastinator that she would wait until the day of birth to assemble the capacities necessary for survival. Inserting a nipple into the mouth of a rat fetus produces the same sucking responses seen in newborns; rat fetuses can also be classically conditioned.

The ways children "behave" *in utero* (prenatally) are also highly predictive of the ways they will behave once they are born (DiPietro et al., 1996). In one study, researchers measured fetal heart rate and movement beginning around the fifth month of gestation and tried to predict mothers' ratings of the baby's temperament during the first 6 months of life. Individual differences in fetal behavior were remarkably predictive of infant temperament, particularly when measured about two weeks before birth. For example, fetuses that were more active in the womb were more active and difficult babies at 6 months.

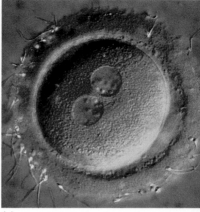

(a)

(b)

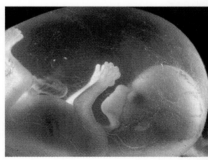

(c)

FIGURE 13.4
Prenatal development. The photo in (*a*) shows a fertilized egg surrounded by sperm. Photo (*b*) shows a 6-week-old embryo. Only 8 weeks later (c), the fetus is recognizably human.

CLOSE TO HOME   JOHN McPHERSON

The staff at Wilmont Obstetrics just couldn't resist pulling the fake sonogram trick.

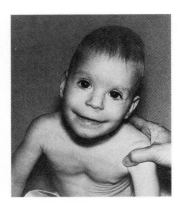

A child born with fetal alcohol syndrome. Facial and other physical abnormalities often occur alongside intellectual deficits.

Environmental Influences on Prenatal Development

The stages of prenatal development provide perhaps the clearest example in humans of the process of maturation. They follow a timetable so closely that a doctor can usually tell when the child was conceived and predict within a matter of days when a fetus's heartbeat will be audible. At the same time, prenatal development provides a dramatic example of the influence of environment, particularly hazardous environmental toxins, on the developing psyche.

The embryonic stage is the period of greatest vulnerability to **teratogens**—harmful environmental agents such as drugs, radiation, and viruses that cause maternal illness, such as rubella (German measles)—although toxic chemicals or vitamin deficiencies throughout gestation and infancy can have lasting effects. Infants who do not receive enough iron in their diets, for example, not only show lower energy as children but also show less pleasure and more wariness than normal infants, and many of these effects last into adulthood (see Lozoff et al., 1998).

One of the most widespread teratogens is alcohol. In the 1970s researchers identified **fetal alcohol syndrome (FAS)**, a serious condition affecting up to half the babies born to alcoholic mothers (Jones et al., 1973). Babies with FAS are born with numerous physical defects: deformed limbs, faces, ears, and genitals. They also show a wide range of mental abnormalities, including learning disabilities, behavior problems, and attention difficulties (Larsson et al., 1985; Steinhausen et al., 1993; Streissguth et al., 1985, 1989). Precisely when the damage occurs to the fetus is unclear, but the syndrome has been observed in the offspring of mothers who had occasional binges as well as mothers who chronically abused alcohol.

Whether *any* amount of maternal alcohol ingestion is dangerous or whether alcohol use must cross some threshold is a matter of controversy (see Knupfer, 1991; Passaro & Little, 1997). Recent research with rhesus monkeys finds that even moderate exposure to alcohol (the monkey equivalent of one to two drinks a day) during pregnancy produces subtle deficits in attention and motor abilities in infant monkeys (Schneider et al., 1997). In fact, the effect is exacerbated if the mother is also exposed to stressful experiences, as occurs with many human mothers who drink excessively. Women who are trying to conceive should probably minimize their alcohol consumption because the teratogenic effect appears to be highest in the early weeks of pregnancy (often before the woman knows she is pregnant) and increases with greater consumption (Barr et al., 1990). The most recent research suggests that women who know they are pregnant would do well to abstain from alcohol as much as possible (Braun, 1996).

Another increasingly prevalent teratogen is crack cocaine (Inciardi et al., 1997). Prenatal cocaine exposure carries risk of premature birth, malformed internal organs, withdrawal symptoms, respiratory problems, delayed motor development, difficulty regulating arousal level (such as positive and negative affect), and death (Arendt et al., 1996; Bendersky & Lewis, 1998; Griffith et al., 1994). "Crack babies" tend to be triply exposed: to cocaine prenatally (the teratogenic effect of the drug), to neglectful parenting postnatally, and to poverty and environmental hazards throughout childhood.

FROM MIND TO BRAIN

THE DEVELOPMENT OF THE NERVOUS SYSTEM

The development of the nervous system provides an extraordinary example of nature–nurture interaction (Johnson, 1998). Most of the neurons people use during their lifetimes develop within the first seven months of gestation; this means that neuron formation takes place at the staggering rate of hundreds of thousands per minute (Cowan, 1979). In fact, the brain overproduces neurons by as much as a factor of two and then trims them back by about 50 percent, weeding out those that are not used (Kolb, 1989). The process of weeding and trimming continues through adolescence and contributes to the flexibility, or **plasticity**, of the brain in meeting environmental demands (Barnes, 1990).

In many respects, the environment is like a building contractor working with a genetic blueprint: The contractor follows the general plan but makes modifications based on experience and availability of materials. The brain itself is therefore a collaboration of heredity and environment (Rosenzweig, 1966, 1984; Shapiro & Vukovich, 1970). From an evolutionary perspective, the brain is wired to adapt to a wide array of environmental circumstances and is prepared to compensate for some degree of damage or faulty wiring.

Although the formation of new neurons is virtually complete at birth, neural development continues in other ways for several years. The brain grows from about 350 grams at birth to about 1250 grams at 4 years, which is nearly 80 percent of its adult size (Spreen et al., 1984). The increase in size is due primarily to two processes: continuing myelination (growth of the fatty myelin sheath that surrounds neural axons) and sprouting of new synaptic connections between existing neurons.

Different regions of the nervous system become myelinated at different periods of development. Some neurons involved in hearing and balance are fully myelinated at birth; others, especially those in the association areas that govern higher cortical functions like abstract thinking, may not become myelinated for months or years (Benes, 1989; Bjorklund & Harnishfeger, 1990). The amount of myelin in some areas of the brain doubles between the first and second decades of life, and considerable myelination occurs for decades throughout adulthood (Benes et al., 1994; Cotman, 1990).

Another important aspect of neural development after birth involves the formation of new dendrites (the branchlike projections from the cell body of one neuron that allow it to form many synapses with others) and dendritic connections between neurons. The ability to create new dendritic connections appears to underlie the brain's ability to compensate in the face of injury in adulthood (Bondareff, 1985; Cotman, 1990; Kolb & Gibb, 1991; O'Leary et al., 1994).

INTERIM SUMMARY   The **prenatal,** or **gestational,** period is a time of rapid physical and neurological growth that can be disrupted by exposure to **teratogens,** harmful environmental agents that damage the embryo or fetus. One of the most prevalent teratogens is alcohol. Maternal alcohol abuse can lead to **fetal alcohol syndrome,** but increasing evidence suggests that even moderate levels of drinking can impair the developing child. During gestation, neurons develop at the rate of hundreds of thousands per minute. Development continues for years thereafter and also involves considerable pruning of potential neural connections that are not strengthened by environmental input.

INFANCY

When asked about their babies, parents almost uniformly begin with motor milestones, such as "Jennifer can sit up now by herself" or "Now that Brandon is crawling, I have to babyproof everything in the house" (Thelen, 1995). How infants move from flailing bundles of flesh to willful little creatures with radar for breakable objects reflects a complex interaction of nature and nurture.

At birth, an infant possesses many adaptive reflexes. For example, the **rooting reflex** helps ensure that the infant will get nourishment; when touched on the cheek, an infant will turn her head and open her mouth, ready to suck. The **sucking reflex** is similarly adaptive: Infants suck rhythmically in response to stimulation 3 or 4 centimeters inside their mouths. Many early reflexes disappear within the first six or seven months, as infants gain more control over their movements. In general, motor skills progress from head to toe. Infants first master movements of the head, then the trunk and arms, and finally the legs (Rallison, 1986).

Motor development in infancy follows a universal sequence, from smiling, turning the head, and rolling over to creeping, walking with support, and ultimately standing alone and walking unaided (Figure 13.5). Nevertheless, cross-cultural evidence suggests that environmental stimulation can affect the *pace* of development. The Kipsigis of Kenya teach their infants to sit, stand, and walk at an early age. At 5 or 6 months, infants are placed in a specially constructed hole in the ground that supports them while they sit upright, and at 7 or 8 months, their mothers hold them either under the arms or by the hands to help them practice walking. As a result, Kipsigi infants walk at a considerably earlier age than North American infants (Super, 1981).

For many years psychologists believed that the universality of stages of motor development implied that these movement patterns were innately programmed. In some respects they were right; regardless of environmental circumstances, infants will not crawl off the delivery table. A more careful analysis of movement, however, challenges the view that movement patterns could be completely "wired." Once infants begin walking, they can toddle across terrain that slopes upward or downward, provided the hill is not too steep. But walking up or down a hill requires the coordination of *very different* combinations of muscles. If walking involves the innate patterning of muscle movements at a particular age, how could the brain be programmed with the infinite number of possible muscle movements required for walking on different surfaces? The same is true for reaching for objects and virtually every other kind of movement infants learn to produce.

Such observations have led researchers to recognize the extent to which motor development reflects an inseparable mixture of brain maturation, muscle

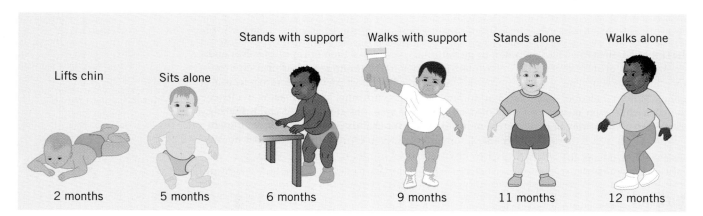

FIGURE 13.5
Milestones in infant motor development. The maturational sequence of motor development is universal, although the age at which skills are acquired varies. This figure shows average ages at which children reach these milestones. *Source:* Adapted from Frankenburg & Dodds, 1967.

maturation, environmental input, and simple biomechanics, such as the fact that the legs are springy or that moving the legs is much more difficult when standing upright because of gravity than when lying flat in a crib (Bertenthal & Clifton, 1998; Thelen, 1995; Thelen & Smith, 1994, 1998). Beginning in infancy, the development of motor control reflects the gradual coordination of movements of an infant exploring its environment, preferring certain kinds of stimulation, and responding to environmental feedback (such as whether the fingers managed to grasp the rubber ducky). Similar to connectionist models in cognitive science, contemporary models suggest that movement involves the coordination of multiple processes simultaneously outside of awareness, as the brain settles on solutions that solve problems, such as how to sip from a cup, and adapts preexisting procedures to new situations.

CHILDHOOD AND ADOLESCENCE

Some of the most important maturational changes that influence psychological development involve changes in the size and shape of the body. A remarkable aspect of human development is the extent to which children can maintain the sense that they are the same person over time despite massive changes in the sheer size of their bodies and the shape of their faces. Growth rates for girls and boys are roughly equal until about age 10. At that point, girls begin a growth spurt that usually peaks at age 12, and boys typically follow suit about two or three years later. Girls and boys usually grow very little after the ages of 16 and 18, respectively, although in some cases, growth may actually continue for a decade (Garn, 1980).

Individuals vary in the age at which they enter **puberty**, the stage during which they become capable of reproduction. Girls usually experience the onset of menstruation (known as *menarche*) at about age 11 to 13, preceded by the growth of breasts and the appearance of pubic hair (Frisch et al., 1980). For boys, enlargement of the genitals begins at about 11 to $13^1/_2$ years, with the first ejaculations of live sperm occurring somewhat later at about $14^1/_2$ years (Rallison, 1986). The onset of menarche or ejaculation often precedes the presence of eggs or live sperm by a few months (Tanner, 1978). Girls under 15 still have immature reproductive systems, putting their infants at risk for prematurity and low birth weight (Garn, 1980). Most teenagers rank the onset of puberty very high among important life events (Eme et al., 1979).

The effects of unusually early or late maturation tend to differ for boys and girls (Gross & Duke, 1980; Jones & Mussen, 1958; Simmons & Blythe, 1987). Boys whose growth spurt comes early are more likely to excel at athletics, to be more popular, and to appear more poised and relaxed than late-maturing boys. For girls, early onset of puberty tends to be more stressful and associated with greater psychological distress and delinquency than later maturation (Caspi et al., 1993; Ge et al., 1996). Parents report more conflict with early-maturing than late-maturing daughters but *less* conflict with early-maturing than late-maturing sons (see Savin-Williams & Small, 1986; Steinberg, 1988). Presumably, this gender difference in parent–child conflict reflects, in part, a different level of parental concern about their teenagers' sexuality. Fathers of early-maturing girls tend to have more hostile feelings toward them (Ge et al., 1996), whether because of their concerns about the child's sexual behavior or because of their own difficulty watching their daughter turn into a woman. In fact, a poor relationship with the father predicts the development of disordered eating patterns in adolescence, perhaps in part because the girl senses that her father is uncomfortable with her emerging sexuality and body shape (Swarr & Richards, 1996).

A profile of middle age?

INTERIM SUMMARY   At birth, infants possess many adaptive reflexes, such as the **rooting reflex**, which helps ensure that the infant will get nourishment. Motor development in infancy reflects an inseparable mixture of brain maturation, muscle maturation, environmental input, and simple biomechanics, as the brain coordinates multiple components of movement and perception to create smooth, efficient solutions to everyday problems. Individuals vary in the age at which they enter **puberty**, the stage during which they become capable of reproduction. Early pubertal development tends to be associated with positive outcomes for boys but negative outcomes for girls.

ADULTHOOD AND AGING

By the end of adolescence, physical growth is virtually complete, and the changes that occur thereafter tend to be gradual and less dramatic. People often gain a few centimeters in height and several more centimeters in fat between ages 18 and 28 (Garn, 1980) and many more centimeters in fat with middle age. Indeed, someone once described middle age as the period during which a person's broad mind and narrow waist trade places (although, as we shall see, maturity may broaden the mind as well).

With aging comes a gradual decline in physical abilities (see Spence, 1989; Spirduso & MacRae, 1990). Muscular strength, sensory acuity, and reaction time all peak by the 20s or early 30s. Lung capacity and cardiac output also begin to decline in the 30s, although many people do not feel a change until their 40s, 50s, or 60s, when the rate of decline accelerates. Individuals differ tremendously in the extent and pace of these changes, ranging from the frail elderly person in a nursing home who cannot dress herself or walk without assistance to the 80-year-old who lives independently and runs marathons in seniors' track meets (Spirduso & MacRae, 1990). Whether the variable is muscle strength or intellectual ability, the rule of thumb is *use it or lose it*: Mental and physical capacities atrophy with disuse.

Menopause

For women, the most dramatic physical change of middle adulthood is **menopause**, the cessation of the menstrual cycle. Menopause usually occurs in the 40s or 50s; in Western cultures the average age is 51 (Riley, 1991). Since most women now live into their 70s or 80s, the postmenopausal period encompasses roughly a third of their lives.

Until fairly recently, menopause was considered traumatic for women because of the psychological loss of the capacity for childbearing (Deutsch, 1945) and symptoms such as "hot flashes," aching joints, and irritability. However, research over the last three decades suggests that most women neither expect nor experience menopause to be traumatic (Matthews, 1992). Many women enjoy the increased freedom from monthly periods and birth control. Moreover, most of the uncomfortable symptoms of menopause can be alleviated medically with hormone replacement therapy, which compensates for the ovaries' reduced estrogen production (Sherwin, 1993; Steward & Robinson, 1997).

Sexuality does not end following menopause, although it does change (Frock & Money, 1992; Gibson, 1996). Decreased vaginal lubrication, for example, can indirectly affect sexual desire and interest because women may gauge their own arousal from the amount of lubrication and mistakenly conclude they are not aroused. The evidence on whether a woman's sexual interest declines during menopause is conflicting. Several studies across cultures ranging from the United States to Nigeria have documented decreases in both interest and sensory sensitivity (Hallstrom, 1973; Riley, 1991), but changes in sexual feelings, like most sensory changes, are usually more gradual than dramatic. Women, like men, continue to enjoy and desire sex until death unless physical, psychological, or cultural barriers interfere.

A GLOBAL VISTA

MENOPAUSE IN A MAYAN VILLAGE

Because menopause is both a physiological and a psychological event, its impact on a woman reflects an interaction of biological processes and personal expectations (Robinson, 1996). Women who expect menopause to be very distressing tend to have more symptoms (Matthews, 1992). Many of these expectations depend on culture. In Western technologically developed societies, which value youth and beauty, menopause tends to be viewed as a negative event, a milestone along the path to aging, diminished sexuality, and ultimately death.

Cultures with different beliefs and values about aging, menstruation, and the role of older women view the psychological experience of menopause differently. Many societies consider menstruation unclean and contaminating and hence impose strict taboos and sanctions on menstruating women (Douglas, 1966). Consequently, cessation of menstruation means greater freedom for women in these cultures. In some Islamic and African cultures with strict taboos on menstruating women, women do not appear to manifest many of the physical and psychological symptoms associated with menopause in the West (Beyenne, 1986).

One researcher studied 100 pre-, peri - (that is, during), and postmenopausal women in a rural Mayan Indian village in Yucatan, Mexico (Beyenne, 1986). In addition to interviewing the women themselves, the investigator interviewed local physicians, midwives, and traditional healers to explore more fully the psychological and cultural aspects of menopause. Mayan women marry and begin having children in their teens. They are frequently grandmothers in their 30s, and the onset of menopause typically occurs in the 30s or early 40s. As in many traditional societies, old age is a period of power and respect, particularly for women, who become the head of the extended family households of their married sons.

The Mayans believe that menstruating women carry danger. Women therefore stay home during their menstrual periods to avoid contaminating other people, particularly newborn babies. Not surprisingly, Mayan women are pleased to gain the freedom from restrictions and taboos that comes with the cessation of menstruation. Premenopausal women reported looking forward to menopause and did not expect any adverse physical or psychological effects. Peri - and postmenopausal women, like others in the community, were unfamiliar with the concept of hot flashes and denied ever experiencing anything of the sort. These reports were corroborated by medical personnel, who had never treated any of the women of the village for menopause-related symptoms.

The absence of a common physical symptom of menopause, hot flashes, could be attributed to many causes, from the psychological to the physical (such as bearing a large number of babies and early onset of menopause). Crosscultural research suggests that the presence of hot flashes varies tremendously from culture to culture; 50 to 80 percent of European and

North American women report hot flashes, whereas these experiences are unusual in Japan and India (Hulka & Meirik, 1996; Robinson, 1996). The dramatically different experience of menopause among the Mayans and women in other cultures underscores the role of culture in shaping what, to us, may have seemed a universal stage driven by biological maturation.

Midlife Changes in Men

The term *male menopause* is part of the American vernacular, although male reproductive ability does not undergo any specific or dramatic period of physical change. Healthy men can produce sperm and engage in sexual activity as long as they live, although male sexuality does change gradually with age. One study found strong negative correlations between age and a number of sexual variables in a sample of healthy married men aged 45 to 74. For example, age correlated -.61 with frequency of sexual thoughts and -.49 with number of orgasms per month. These results suggest that, at least in terms of quantity, sexual functioning in males declines substantially from midlife to later life, although individuals differ considerably in the extent to which they experience such declines (Schiavi et al., 1990). Decreasing sexual interest in men appears in part to reflect lower levels of testosterone in the bloodstream (Chapter 10). The ability to sense touch and vibration in the penis also diminishes with age and is correlated with reduced sexual activity (see Johnson & Murray, 1992).

As with women, however, men can enjoy sexuality through their 90s if they live that long and if they have an available partner. Sex also appears to be like riding a bicycle: People frequently resume sexual activity after a period of even years after the loss of a partner when a new one comes on the scene, and although they may initially experience some anxiety about whether the parts will work, they typically find them quite functional. Contrary to youthful stereotypes, masturbation is also a lifelong affair in many men and women (Gibson, 1996).

Later Life

As in childhood, some of the most apparent signs of aging are in physical appearance. The body loses its youthful shape as fat redistributes itself to the middle of the body; the skin wrinkles; and the hair loses its characteristic color. The impact of these and other physical changes depends considerably on their meaning to the aging individual, who may cope better or worse depending on his investment in particular aspects of his appearance or performance (Whitbourne, 1996). Loss of muscle, weakening of the bones, and decreasing functioning of the joints are also inevitable aspects of aging, although life-style factors (such as regular exercise) can minimize discomfort or disability.

Sensory-Perceptual Changes   Some of the most obvious changes associated with advanced aging in men and women are declines in sensory-perceptual functioning. Older adults have a reduced sensitivity to contrasts, as when climbing stairs (see Scialfa et al., 1992), and their ability to see at night declines (Fozard, 1990). Older adults take longer to adapt to the dark, which can cause problems driving at night, as oncoming headlights may create temporary flashes of brightness (*AARP News Bulletin*, 1989; Perlmutter, 1983). Hearing loss is also common; many older people experience **presbycusis**, the inability to hear high-frequency sounds (Fozard, 1990; Spence, 1989). Presbycusis can make hearing the telephone ring or understanding high-pitched voices more difficult.

In China, attitudes toward the elderly, who tend to be respected and revered, influence every aspect of their functioning.

The inability to understand what others are saying can have disturbing psychological consequences. People often lose patience with older people who constantly ask them to repeat what they have said. Younger people may also inadvertently treat older individuals with hearing loss condescendingly, simplifying their communications instead of speaking more loudly or distinctly.

Ageism   Deterioration in certain areas of functioning is an inevitable part of aging, but development throughout the life span is characterized by gains as well as losses (Baltes, 1997). Many Western images of the elderly stem from negative cultural myths and stereotypes, such as the idea that sexuality ends in the 40s or 50s or that senility is inevitable. **Gerontologists**—scientists who study the elderly—refer to such images as examples of **ageism**, or prejudice against old people (Butler, 1969; Schaie, 1988; Whitbourne & Hulicka, 1990). Ageism can lead not only to condescending treatment of the elderly ("How are *we* today, Mrs. Jones?") but also to discrimination in employment and access to medical care.

Experimental evidence suggests that people in the West process information about the aged in a negatively biased way automatically, without conscious awareness (Perdue & Gurtman, 1990). Using a priming procedure (Chapter 6), investigators in one study presented college students with 18 positive adjectives (such as *skillful* and *helpful*) and 18 negative adjectives (such as *clumsy* and *impolite*) on a computer screen. Immediately prior to presenting each adjective, the computer screen randomly flashed the word *old* or *young* briefly enough to register but too briefly to be recognized consciously. The investigators measured participants reaction time (in milliseconds) in identifying whether each word was positive or negative.

If people differentially associate old and young with positive and negative traits, then flashing "young" should facilitate responding about positive words, while "old" should reduce reaction time in identifying negative words. In fact, participants were slightly quicker to identify negative traits when presented with "old" and substantially faster in identifying positive traits when presented with "young" (Figure 13.6). Apparently, people (or at least college students) are prejudiced in favor of the young without a moment's thought.

Negative stereotypes about aging can actually affect the way older people behave. In one study, six groups of participants (old and young Chinese, deaf North Americans, and hearing North Americans) completed various memory tasks (Levy & Langer, 1994). The investigators hypothesized that Chinese and deaf North Americans, whose cultures have fewer negative stereotypes about the el-

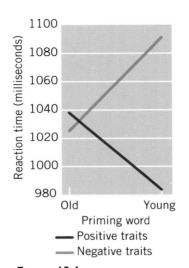

FIGURE 13.6
Implicit ageism. Priming subjects with "old" led to slightly decreased reaction time in identifying negative words. In contrast, priming with "young" markedly facilitated identification of positive traits in comparison to negative ones.
Source: Perdue & Gurtman, 1990, p. 21.

derly than the North American hearing culture, would perform better in old age than would nondeaf North Americans. The results supported the hypothesis. The three young groups did not differ, but among the old groups, the Chinese performed the best, followed by deaf and then by hearing North Americans. In fact, older Chinese subjects performed similarly to young Chinese subjects. If older people become physically, cognitively, or sexually inactive, the causes may lie in cultural beliefs that amplify biological declines.

INTERIM SUMMARY   With aging comes a gradual decline in physical abilities, including muscular strength, sensory functioning, and reaction time. People differ tremendously, however, in their physical competence throughout life; the rule of thumb is *use it or lose it*. For women, the most dramatic physical change of middle adulthood is **menopause**; for men, sexuality changes more gradually. Deterioration in certain areas of functioning is an inevitable part of aging, but the extent of deterioration in part reflects internalization of **ageist** stereotypes.

COGNITIVE DEVELOPMENT IN INFANCY, CHILDHOOD, AND ADOLESCENCE

In a study performed three decades ago, 3- and 6-year-old children petted a good-natured cat named Maynard (DeVries, 1969). When asked what kind of animal Maynard was, every child responded correctly. In plain sight of the children, the researcher then put a dog mask on Maynard and again asked whether Maynard was a dog or a cat. Unlike the older children, the younger children were confused: Most of them said Maynard was now a dog!

How do children learn that physical entities, such as their pets, parents, or teddy bears, remain constant over time? This is the kind of question explored by psychologists who study cognitive development. We begin by describing perceptual and cognitive development in infancy and then examine the ways psychologists have conceptualized cognitive development through adolescence.

PERCEPTUAL AND COGNITIVE DEVELOPMENT IN INFANCY

For many years, psychologists underestimated the cognitive capacities of infants (Bower, 1982). With neither motor control nor the ability to describe what they are thinking, newborn infants do not appear to be a particularly impressive lot. Infants also have notoriously short attention spans, falling asleep so frequently that a researcher must schedule two hours of laboratory time for every five minutes of useful experimental time (Butterworth, 1978).

New Methods, New Discoveries

A very different picture of infancy has emerged, however, as methods to study it have become more sophisticated. Three decades ago, psychologists discovered that they could learn about infant perception and cognition by taking advantage of the **orienting reflex**, the tendency of humans, even from birth, to pay more attention to novel stimuli than to stimuli to which they have become habituated, or grown accustomed (Fantz, 1966; Fantz et al., 1975). Thus, even though a picture of a face might hold an infant's attention at first, after repeated exposures the infant will no longer show interest in it. This finding is useful because it means that researchers can tell when an infant is discriminating between two stimuli, such as the face of its mother and the face of another woman. If the infant is presented with a photograph of its mother's face, it will gradually habituate to it. When the photograph is switched to the other woman's face, if the infant shows interest in the new face, then the experimenter knows that the infant has perceived the difference between the two. The orienting reflex allows psychologists to study infant perception and cognition by recording the amount of time an infant looks at visual stimuli, called *fixation* time (eye fixation, not psychosexual fixation), by using special equipment to observe the reflection in the infant's cornea.

Researchers have subsequently found other ways of assessing infants' knowledge, such as measuring brain wave activity when presented with novel stimuli and stimuli to which they have habituated; certain waveforms indicate that the child recognizes the difference between an old stimulus and a new one. Another behavioral response used to assess infants' knowledge is sucking. Because infants prefer novelty, they can be conditioned to suck in response to novel stimuli using a simple operant conditioning procedure. Sucking rate decreases as the infant habituates to a stimulus and increases with the presentation of a new stimulus.

Measuring behavioral and physiological responses associated with the orienting reflex has enabled researchers to answer some very subtle questions about perception, memory, and cognition, such as whether infants can form abstractions of concepts such as "ball": Will they habituate to a red ball they have never seen if they have previously habituated to a blue ball and a green ball?

What Can Infants Sense and Perceive?

Infants are born with many sensory capabilities, some better developed than others. The sense of hearing is in working order quite early. Even before birth, fetal heart rate and movements increase in response to loud sounds, and studies of habituation in newborns show that infants actually hear and recognize their mother's voices before they are born, despite a wall of flesh and an earful of amniotic fluid.

Vision is not as well developed at birth as hearing; the visual cortex, retina, and some other structures are still immature (Kellman & Banks, 1998). At birth, visual acuity is estimated to be approximately 20/500 (that is, an object 20 feet away looks as clear as an object 500 feet away would look to an adult), but it improves to about 20/100 by 6 months (Banks & Salapatek, 1983; Dobson & Teller, 1978). Infants focus best on objects between 7 and 8 inches away—approximately the distance between a nursing infant and its mother's face. As early as 1 week after birth, infants can discriminate colors, although their color perception is limited (Adams, 1989, 1994).

The attention infants pay to various objects in their environment is not arbitrary. Infants pay particular attention to human faces and objects with qualities similar to faces—objects that move, are complex, are skin colored, and produce sounds (Siegler, 1991). This tendency is innate and likely evolved because of the important emotional information carried by the face. Infants prefer progressively more complex visual stimuli as they develop, which reflects and stimulates their growing cognitive capacities (Banks & Salapatek, 1983). Whereas 3-week-olds prefer to look at simple checkerboards with only four squares, 14-week-olds prefer 8-by-8 boards (Brennan et al., 1966).

Intermodal Understanding   Sensory processing occurs in anatomically discrete neural modules (Chapter 4). To what extent can infants integrate information across these different neural systems? When they see their mothers talking, do they connect the sound with the visual image, or is the world like a dubbed movie, with lips moving and people talking out of sync? And do infants *learn* to make connections across different modes or between what they observe and what they do, or are these capacities innate?

Intermodal (or **cross-modal**) **processing** allows infants to associate sensations of an object from different senses or to match their own actions to behaviors they have observed visually. Infants show some recognition of the relation between sights and sounds even minutes after birth, turning their eyes toward the direction of a sound (Bower, 1982; Wertheimer, 1961). By three months, they attend more to an experimenter if the sound of her speech is synchronized with her lip movements than if it is not (Dodd, 1979; Kuhl & Meltzoff, 1988). By four to five months, they follow a conversation by shifting visual attention between two adults as they speak to one another (Horner & Chethik, 1986).

Over the last 20 years, Andrew Meltzoff and his colleagues have demonstrated that infants are capable of much more intermodal integration than anyone had expected. In an initial study, Meltzoff and Moore (1977) found that newborns between 12 and 21 days old were able to imitate the facial gestures of an adult. Infants who observed an adult sticking out his tongue were more likely to stick out their own tongues, while those who observed other facial movements, such as opening the mouth, were more likely to perform those behaviors (Figure 13.7). How does an infant—who has no idea what a tongue is—recognize that she can move her own as an adult model does? Such capacities appear to be innate, since they have been demonstrated in children as young as *42 minutes* old.

Subsequent research documents that infants can know something by sight when they have explored it by touch (Meltzoff, 1990). Getting young infants to explore an object with their hands is no easy trick because they tend to grasp it rigidly. Researchers therefore designed an experiment in which infants could explore an object with their mouths. One-month-old infants sucked on one of two

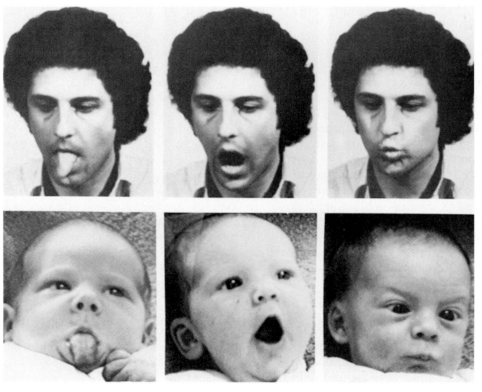

FIGURE 13.7
Imitation in infants. These photographs, published in 1977, show 2- to 3-week-old infants imitating the facial gestures of an adult. (They were, however, unable to imitate the hairstyle.)

pacifiers, exploring them with their lips and tongues (Figure 13.8). One of the pacifiers was a sphere and the other a sphere-with-nubs. To test whether infants could recognize these shapes visually, the experimenters presented them with similar objects constructed out of orange styrofoam. The investigators reasoned that if the infants visually recognized the shape they had been sucking, they would fixate on the two visual stimuli for different lengths of time. In fact, of 32 infants tested, 24 stared longer at the shape they had sucked, demonstrating that they knew with their eyes what they had felt with their mouths.

FIGURE 13.8
Stimuli used for tactile exploration. One-month-old infants sucked on one of two pacifiers like those depicted above. Later, they explored similar objects with their eyes. Most stared longer at the shape they had sucked, demonstrating that they knew with their eyes what they had felt with their mouths. *Source:* From Meltzoff, A. N., & Borton, R. W. (1979). Intermodal matching by human neonates. *Nature*, 282, 403–404.

Perceiving Meaning   The research described thus far suggests that infants perceive more than psychologists, and probably most laypeople, imagined. But do they attribute meaning to the objects they perceive? According to *ecological* theorists, who understand perception in its environmental, adaptive context, they do (Gibson, 1984; Gibson & Gibson, 1966, 1969). Ecological theorists argue that the nervous system is wired to recognize certain dangers and to perceive the potential utility of some stimuli without prior learning, as with the visual cliff (Chapter 4).

Ecological researchers have used looming-object studies to demonstrate that infants can in fact attach meaning to their perceptions (Figure 13.9). As an alert infant sits in a seat, an object suddenly begins moving directly toward the infant at a constant rate. The object may be real, such as the box shown in the figure, or it may be an expanding shadow. As early as two weeks after birth, infants show a defensive response to the looming object, drawing their heads back, jerking their hands in front of their faces, and showing distress (Bower, 1971).

What Can Infants Remember?

Most people completely lack explicit memory for any events before the age of three or four, a phenomenon known as **infantile amnesia**. This does not imply, however, that experience is lost on infants and young children. Infants' memory capacity varies considerably depending on the task and reflects in large part the maturation of neural circuits mediating different kinds of memory (Nelson, 1995).

Infants actually remember far more than people would ever have guessed (Mandler & McDonough, 1997; Meltzoff, 1995; Newcombe et al., 1995). For example, various forms of implicit memory are present from birth. In one study, six-month-olds exposed once to a stimulus responded faster to it *two years later* than peers not previously exposed to it, demonstrating implicit memory for a single event that occurred in infancy (Perris et al., 1990). Infants as young as 3 months old who have been conditioned to kick their legs to make a mobile move will begin kicking their legs before control infants up to several weeks later, suggest-

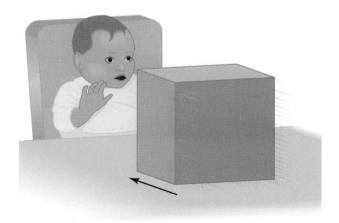

FIGURE 13.9
The looming object. Infants show distress and defensive responses to looming objects as early as two weeks of age. Because they would not yet have had the opportunity to associate a looming object with the risk of being hit, many psychologists consider their response evidence of innate knowledge. *Source:* Adapted from Bower, 1971.

ing implicit memory about the relation between the behavior and its consequence (Rovee-Collier, 1990).

The rudiments of explicit memory are also present from birth, although more complete development of explicit memory depends on maturation of the hippocampus and connected tissue in the temporal lobes sometime between eight and 18 months (Nelson, 1995). In the earliest days of life, infants appear to have recognition memory for stimuli they have seen or heard for at least a day; for example, when given a choice, they prefer novel words to those to which they habituated a day before (Swain et al., 1993). EEG recordings suggest that five-month-olds can even tell the difference between tones of two different pitches—preferring the novel one—a day later (Thomas & Lykins, 1995).

Clear evidence of explicit memory can be seen in the ability of 11-month-old infants to store and then retrieve a representation of events a year later (McDonough & Mandler, 1994). Shortly before their first birthday, infants were shown a series of actions in the laboratory, such as "feeding" a novel object that looked like a teddy bear with another novel object that resembled a bottle. A year later, infants who had been exposed to this action (along with an accompanied "yum, yum"!) were more likely to do the same than infants who had not similarly witnessed this event a year earlier.

The rudiments of working memory can be seen by 6 months of age, when measurement of eye movements suggests that infants can hold spatial information in mind for 3 to 5 seconds (Gilmore & Johnson, 1995). However, working memory appears to be the slowest-developing memory system, relying on the maturation of the prefrontal cortex (Chapter 6).

INTERIM SUMMARY   Although infants have various sensory deficits compared to adults, they are able to perceive subtle differences, such as the sound of their mothers' and another woman's voice, from birth. They are also able to associate sensations of an object from different senses and match their own actions to behaviors they have observed visually, a phenomenon called **intermodal processing**. Research by psychologists with an *ecological* orientation to perception suggests that infants innately appreciate the meaning of some experiences that are important to adaptation. Various forms of implicit memory are present from birth. The rudiments of explicit memory can also be seen in early infancy, although explicit memory requires maturation of the hippocampus over at least the first 18 months of life. Working memory is the slowest-developing memory system, requiring the maturation of the prefrontal cortex.

PIAGET'S THEORY OF COGNITIVE DEVELOPMENT

Cognitive development begins in infancy and proceeds at a rapid pace through adolescence. The first theorist to trace cognitive development systematically was the Swiss psychologist Jean Piaget (1896–1980). The philosopher of science Thomas Kuhn (1970) observed that major innovations often come from outsiders who have not yet been indoctrinated into the discipline, and this was the case with Piaget. Piaget began his career as a biologist, publishing his first paper at the age of 11. He was offered the curatorship of a Geneva museum's mollusk collection while still in high school (the offer was rescinded when the museum realized he was a child) and received his doctorate in biology at the age of 21. How, then, did a biologist become a world-famous psychologist by age 30?

A Philosophical Question and a Psychological Answer

Piaget had a keen interest in *epistemology*, the branch of philosophy concerned with the nature of knowledge. The empiricist philosophers, such as John Locke,

Jean Piaget developing his own schemas by studying the development of schemas in children.

argued that all knowledge comes from experience. To know what a dog is like, a person has to examine a number of dogs, experience them with the senses, and come to some conclusions about their common properties. In contrast, the German philosopher Immanuel Kant argued that some forms of knowledge do *not* come from observation. People impose certain categories of thought—such as space, time, and causality—on the data of their senses, but these categories are not derived from experience. Similarly, the rules of logic and mathematics seem to work in the world, yet they are not mere summaries of sensory information: No one has ever seen the *square root of 2* or *pi*, but these concepts have real-world applications, as any engineer or architect can attest. Kant argued that the human propensity for mathematical thinking, like the tendency to use certain categories of thought, is innate.

Kant's ideas were the starting point for Piaget's life's work. His hunch was that Kant was both right and wrong: Kant was right that people's understanding of time, space, and logic is not simply derived from experience but wrong that people are born with this knowledge. Piaget therefore decided to look into the way children develop an understanding of these categories of thought—a "temporary" intellectual foray that occupied the next 60 years of his life.

Piaget began his study in Paris, working in Alfred Binet's intelligence-testing laboratory. There he noticed that children of the same age tended to make the same types of mistakes. They not only gave the same kinds of wrong answers, but when questioned about their reasoning, they provided similar explanations. Piaget concluded that children of different ages think in qualitatively different ways and that understanding these differences might hold the key to understanding the origins of knowledge. This led him to a stage theory of cognitive development.

Piaget (1970) proposed that children develop knowledge by inventing or *constructing* reality out of their own experience, mixing what they observe with their own ideas about how the world works. Thus, the preschooler who sees a dog's mask placed on Maynard the cat applies her own rules of logic—"When things look different, they are different"—to conclude that Maynard is a dog. Similarly, a toddler who notices that a shadow is attached to his feet no matter where he is on a sunny playground may use his own logic to conclude that the shadow is following him. These cognitive constructions are creative, but they are not arbitrary, since they are constrained by both physical realities (such as the fact that cats and dogs usually do not change into one another) and brain development (Brainerd, 1996).

Assimilation and Accommodation

Piaget viewed intelligence as the individual's way of adapting to new information about the world. He argued that children cognitively adapt to their environment through two interrelated processes, assimilation and accommodation (Piaget & Inhelder, 1969). **Assimilation** involves interpreting actions or events in terms of one's present schemas, that is, fitting reality into one's existing structures of knowledge. According to Piaget, a **schema** is an organized, repeatedly exercised pattern of thought or behavior (Flavell, 1985), such as an infant's propensity to suck anything that will fit into its mouth—a nipple, a finger, or a pacifier. All of these objects can be assimilated—taken in without modifying the existing schema or pattern—by sucking. Similarly, a person with a cognitive schema about "police" can drive into a crowded intersection and immediately understand the role of the person directing traffic.

If humans only assimilated information into existing schemas, no cognitive development would take place. The second process of adaptation, **accommodation**, is the modification of schemas to fit reality. At the behavioral level, accommodation takes place when an infant with a sucking schema is presented with a cup: She must modify her existing schema to drink from this new device. At the thought level, accommodation is likely to occur if the reader looks carefully at the spelling of *accommodation*—it has two *c*'s and two *m*'s, which is highly unusual. The word "accommodation" requires revision of the implicit schema most people hold that would lead them to double only one consonant or the other.

For Piaget, the driving force behind cognitive development is **equilibration**, which means balancing assimilation and accommodation to adapt to the world. When a child comes across something she does not understand, she finds herself in a state of cognitive disequilibrium that motivates her to try to make sense of what she has encountered. She may attempt to fit it into existing schemas (assimilation) or she may combine schemas or construct an entirely new schema to fit the new reality (accommodation).

INTERIM SUMMARY   Piaget argued that children develop knowledge by *constructing* reality out of their own experience, mixing what they observe with their own ideas about how the world works. They do this through a process of **equilibration**, which means balancing two interrelated processes: **assimilation** (fitting reality into their existing structures of knowledge) and **accommodation** (modifying schemas to fit reality).

Stages of Cognitive Development

According to Piaget, people assimilate and accommodate when confronted with new information throughout their lives. At each stage of development, however, children use a distinct underlying logic, or **structure of thought**, to guide their thinking. The same four stages—sensorimotor, preoperational, concrete operational, and formal operational—occur in the same sequence for everyone, although the ages may vary somewhat (Table 13.1). A fundamental principle of Piaget's developmental theory is that every stage builds on the next, as children wrestle with problems their old structures will not resolve and work their way toward new solutions by trying out and adjusting schemas in their repertoire (Siegler & Ellis, 1996).

Sensorimotor Stage   For Piaget, to *know* an object is to operate or act on it. **Operations** are internalized (i.e., mental) actions the individual can use to manip-

TABLE 13.1   PIAGET'S STAGES OF COGNITIVE DEVELOPMENT

STAGE	APPROXIMATE AGES (YEARS)	CHARACTERISTICS
Sensorimotor	0–2	Thought and action are virtually identical, as the infant explores the world with its senses and behaviors; object permanence develops; the child is completely egocentric.
Preoperational	2–7	Symbolic thought develops; object permanence is firmly established; the child cannot coordinate different physical attributes of an object or different perspectives.
Concrete operational	7–12	The child is able to perform reversible mental operations on representations of objects; understanding of conservation develops; the child can apply logic to concrete situations.
Formal operational	12 +	The adolescent (or adult) can apply logic more abstractly; hypothetical thinking develops.

ulate, transform, and return an object of knowledge to its original state (Piaget, 1972). Alphabetizing a list of names is an operation; so is imagining what one could have said to someone who behaved rudely.

According to Piaget, such mental operations are beyond the capability of very young, preverbal children, who are in the **sensorimotor stage**. The sensorimotor stage lasts from birth to about 2 years of age, when toddlers become more thoroughly verbal. Sensorimotor thought primarily takes the form of action, as infants learn about the world by mouthing, grasping, watching, and manipulating objects. According to Piaget, the practical knowledge infants develop during this period forms the basis for their later ability to represent things mentally. The label "sensorimotor" emphasizes that infants are bound by their sensations and actions and are capable of very little reasoning beyond what they are sensing and doing. They know about an object, such as a toy duck, only in terms of the sensations and actions associated with it, not as an objective reality "out there" that exists when they are not touching or looking at it.

A major achievement of the sensorimotor stage is the development of **object permanence**, the recognition that objects exist in time and space independent of their actions on, or observation of, them. According to Piaget, before the age of about 8 to 12 months, an object such as a ball exists for an infant only when it is in sight. If it is hidden from view, it no longer exists, as illustrated by Piaget's description of his own son, Laurent (1954, p. 39):

> At age 7 months, 28 days, I offer him a little bell behind a cushion. So long as he sees the little bell, however small it may be, he tries to grasp it. But if the little bell disappears completely, he stops all searching . . . I then resume the experiment, using my hand as a screen. Laurent's arm is outstretched and about to grasp the little bell at the moment I make it disappear behind my hand . . . He immediately withdraws his arm, as though the little bell no longer existed. I then shake my hand. . . . Laurent watches attentively, greatly surprised to rediscover the sound of the little bell, but he does not try to grasp it. I turn my hand over and he sees the little bell: he then stretches his hand toward it. (Piaget, 1954, p. 39)

A few months later, when Laurent has acquired object permanence, he will look for the bell even when it is hidden from view and will be delighted to find it. Once infants recognize the permanence of objects in this way, they have a seemingly endless fascination for games such as peek-a-boo, which affirm their new-

During the sensorimotor stage, children learn through doing.

found understanding. Subsequent research suggests that children acquire *aspects* of object permanence much earlier than Piaget supposed (Baillargeon & DeVos, 1991), even by 4 or 5 months, but a comprehensive understanding of the permanence of objects evolves gradually during infancy (Halford, 1989).

During the sensorimotor stage children are extremely **egocentric**, or thoroughly embedded in their own point of view. When an infant closes her eyes, the whole world becomes dark; when a bell is no longer in Laurent's view, it ceases to exist. For Piaget, development entails a gradual movement away from egocentrism toward a recognition of alternative points of view (see Flavell, 1985; Selman, 1980).

Preoperational Stage   The **preoperational stage** begins roughly around age 2 and lasts until ages 5 to 7. It is characterized by the emergence of *symbolic* thought—the ability to use arbitrary symbols, such as words, to represent concepts. As children learn to manipulate symbols and mental images, thought becomes detachable from action. They no longer have to think exclusively with their hands or mouths.

Symbolic thought allows preschool children to converse with other people and imagine solutions to problems before actually doing anything. Preoperational thought continues, however, to have a number of limitations. Preschool children remain egocentric in many respects; they still tend to think about the external world primarily from their own point of view. A classic demonstration of egocentrism at this stage occurs in the **three-mountain task**. A child is seated at a table displaying three model mountains (Figure 13.10), with a teddy bear or doll seated at another chair at the same table. The child is shown a number of pictures of the table from different perspectives and is asked which view the teddy bear would see.

Preschool children often answer that the bear would see their own view of the table (Piaget & Inhelder, 1956). Preschoolers are not egocentric in every situation and can even solve simplified versions of the three-mountain task (Burke, 1975; Ford, 1979; Lempers et al., 1977). Nevertheless, they are much more likely to make egocentric cognitive errors than older children, like the 3-year-old who covers her eyes and declares, "You can't see me!"

Another limitation of preoperational thought is the tendency to focus, or *center*, on one perceptually striking feature of an object without considering other features that might be relevant. Piaget calls this process **centration**. When asked which of two candy bars is bigger, a long, thin one or a short, thick one, the

FIGURE 13.10
The three-mountain task. Preoperational children typically do not recognize that the stuffed animal "sees" the mountain from a perspective different from their own, although they can do so if the stimulus is very simple.

preschooler is likely to pick the longer one and ignore thickness, even though the amount of chocolate is identical.

Preoperational thinking also tends to be fairly literal. The mother of a 3-year-old tried to teach her son the meaning of "compromise" when he wanted her to read him three bedtime stories instead of the usual one, suggesting that they compromise on two. A few days later, they were debating his bedtime, and the mother asked, "Billy, do you remember what 'compromise' means?" "Yes," he replied, earnestly, "*two*."

INTERIM SUMMARY   Piaget argued that cognitive development occurs through a series of stages. During the **sensorimotor stage**, infants "think" with their hands and eyes. A major achievement of the sensorimotor stage is **object permanence**, when infants recognize that objects exist in time and space. During the sensorimotor stage children are extremely **egocentric**. The **preoperational stage** is characterized by the emergence of *symbolic* thought, which allows preschool-age children to imagine solutions to problems mentally rather than through action. Children at this stage remain egocentric; they have difficulty imagining reality from other viewpoints, and they have a tendency to center on one perceptually striking feature of an object.

Concrete Operational Stage   Piaget called the third stage of cognitive development the **concrete operational stage**. At this point (roughly ages 7 to 12) children are capable of operating on, or mentally manipulating, internal representations of concrete objects in ways that are reversible. In other words, children can imagine performing mental manipulations (operations) on a set of objects and then mentally put them back the way they found them (Piaget, 1972).

This achievement of the concrete operational stage is demonstrated in Piaget's classic experiments with conservation problems. According to Piaget, once children reach this third stage, they are able to understand the concept of **conservation**—that basic properties of an object or situation remain stable (or are *conserved*) even though superficial properties may be changed. For example, if preoperational children are shown the three beakers in part (a) of Figure 13.11, they easily recognize that the two same-sized beakers contain the same amount of liquid. They will not realize, however, that the tall and short beakers contain the same amount of liquid even if they watch the experimenter pour the liquid from the short to the tall beaker. In contrast, concrete operational children understand that the amount of liquid remains unchanged even though it has been poured into a beaker of a different shape. If asked to justify their answers, they usually say something like, "You just poured it from one container to another!" Whereas preoperational thought is characterized by *centration* on one dimension, concrete operational thinkers are able to *decenter*, that is, to hold in mind multiple dimensions at once.

Two other types of conservation problems, conservation of number and conservation of mass, are shown in parts (b) and (c), respectively, of Figure 13.11. Children typically master different kinds of conservation at slightly different ages. Many children understand conservation of number by age 6 but do not understand conservation of mass until about age 8 (Elkind, 1981; Katz & Beilin, 1976).

Concrete operational children also understand *transitivity*—that if $a < b$ and $b < c$, then $a < c$. Although preoperational children can be trained to make some transitive inferences (Bryant & Trabasso, 1971), they have difficulty keeping enough information in mind to solve transitive thinking problems. One transitivity problem asks, "If Henry is taller than Jack, and Jack is taller than Claude, which boy is the shortest?" Preschoolers are equally likely to pick Jack or Claude because each one is shorter than someone else; they fail to put together the two pieces of information about relative height into a single transitive proposition.

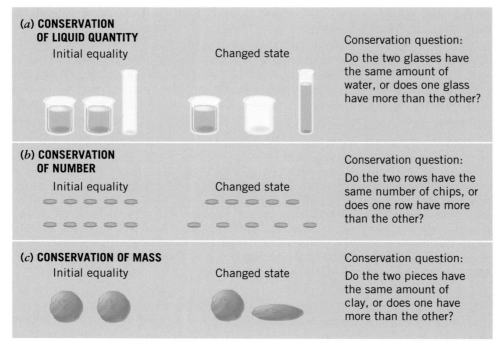

(a) CONSERVATION OF LIQUID QUANTITY

Initial equality   Changed state

Conservation question:

Do the two glasses have the same amount of water, or does one glass have more than the other?

(b) CONSERVATION OF NUMBER

Initial equality   Changed state

Conservation question:

Do the two rows have the same number of chips, or does one row have more than the other?

(c) CONSERVATION OF MASS

Initial equality   Changed state

Conservation question:

Do the two pieces have the same amount of clay, or does one have more than the other?

FIGURE 13.11

Conservation. *(a)* Conservation of liquid quantity: Unlike preoperational children, concrete operational children understand that the amount of liquid remains unchanged even though it has been poured into a beaker of a different shape. *(b)* Conservation of number: Preoperational children believe that altering the physical configuration changes the number of objects present. *(c)* Conservation of mass: Preoperational children fail to realize that mass is conserved despite changing the shape of a ball of clay.

Formal Operational Stage Piaget's fourth stage, formal operations, begins at about ages 12 to 15, when children start to think more abstractly. The **formal operational stage** is characterized by the ability to manipulate abstract as well as concrete objects, events, and ideas mentally, that is, to reason about formal propositions rather than concrete events. Teenagers are less likely to argue that the two beakers in the conservation task contain the same amount of liquid because they saw the liquid being poured back and forth. They may instead discuss the law of conservation or argue that surface appearances do not always reflect the underlying reality.

In planning their curricula, school systems commonly recognize this new ability to reason with abstractions. Schools typically wait until the eighth or ninth grade to teach algebra, which requires abstract reasoning. Another hallmark of formal operational reasoning, commonly applied in high school chemistry classes, is the ability to frame hypotheses and figure out how to test them systematically (Inhelder & Piaget, 1958).

Putting Piaget in Perspective

Piaget's theory literally defined cognitive development for several decades, and it continues to have a profound influence. Contrary to the approaches that prevailed when he began writing, Piaget argued that children are not blank slates upon which experience writes itself but active construers of their world. Aside from generating literally hundreds of hypotheses, one of Piaget's greatest accomplishments was his invention of one after another ingenious experimental procedure for testing them, such as the three-mountain task or the beaker experiments (Brainerd, 1996; Flavell, 1996).

In recent years, however, Piaget's theory has come under fire. One criticism is that Piaget focused too heavily on the kind of thinking typical of scientific or philosophical pursuits and underplayed the extent to which people's thinking is biased, irrational, or influenced by motives or emotions (Cohen, 1983; see Wason & Johnson-Laird, 1972). For example, whereas Piaget emphasized the increasing rationality of the formal-operational teenager, a considerable body of research suggests that by the teenage years, people are already using the same kinds of biases in weighing arguments against their pet theories that have been observed in adult scientists (see Klaczynski, 1997).

Another criticism concerns Piaget's assumption that as children progress through the stages of cognitive development, they apply the same underlying logic in most of the things they do. In fact, cognitive development often progresses unevenly and proceeds at different paces in different domains (Case, 1992; Flavell, 1982). Just as people have varying intellectual abilities in different domains (Chapter 8), children progress differently in different areas depending on their abilities and their familiarity with the domain. They also provide a range of responses to any task, some reflecting higher levels of functioning than others (Siegler & Ellis, 1996).

Piaget also underestimated the capacities of infants and preschool children (Gelman & Baillargeon, 1983). For example, Piaget maintained that object permanence does not begin to develop until about 8 months. Subsequent research suggests, however, that even by the age of 20 days infants are aware, at least for a few seconds, that a hidden object still exists, and by 2 months they can distinguish between an object moved out of sight and one that ceases to exist (Breuer, 1985). Numerous studies also suggest that children can sometimes accomplish conservation tasks by age 5 or even earlier. By age 5, children recognize that some substances may dissolve into tiny pieces that can no longer be seen but still preserve their qualities, such as sweet taste (Rosen & Rozin, 1993). Preoperational children are most likely to fail at conservation tasks under particular circumstances, as when the task is unfamiliar and the answer is quantitative (Siegler & Ellis, 1996).

Piaget also underestimated the role of culture in development. A number of cross-cultural studies have found that stages of development typically do occur in the sequence described by Piaget, but the age at which children attain particular stages often varies greatly and depends on the task (Mishra, 1997; Price-Williams, 1981). By and large, these studies have found indications of slower cognitive development in preliterate societies, except when a cultural group is particularly familiar with the task materials used in cognitive tests. Mexican children of potters show delayed development on the conservation task using beakers, but they demonstrate a relatively early understanding of conservation when asked if a ball of clay has the same volume when it is stretched into an oblong shape (Price-Williams et al., 1969). Children's abilities tend to reflect cultural and environmental pressures (Dasen, 1975; Dasen & Heron, 1981). Children in nomadic societies, which travel from location to location for their survival, tend to outperform other children on spatial tasks.

The bulk of research suggests that Piaget was correct in many of the broad strokes he used to describe cognitive development: Children become less egocentric, increasingly able to think symbolically, and increasingly able to reason abstractly as they develop (Halford, 1989). At the same time, many of the specific strokes, hues, and textures of his portrait require revision. Development is less uniform and unitary than his model suggests, and infants and young children appear to be more competent—and adults less competent—than Piaget believed (Flavell, 1992).

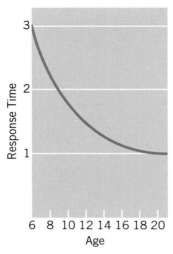

FIGURE 13.12
Processing speed and age. Here, processing speed (scaled as the ratio of children's speed relative to adult speed) follows an exponential function—and can in fact be predicted with mathematical precision (Kail, 1991). In other words, speed increases rapidly from about ages 6 to 12 and starts to level off by age 15. *Source:* Adapted from Fry & Hale, 1996.

INTERIM SUMMARY   During the **concrete operational** stage, children can mentally manipulate representations of concrete objects in ways that are reversible, as can be seen in their understanding of **conservation** (that basic properties of an object or situation remain stable even though superficial properties change). The **formal operational stage** is characterized by the ability to manipulate abstract as well as concrete representations, to reason about formal propositions rather than concrete events. Many of Piaget's broad principles have withstood the test of time, but many specifics of the theory no longer appear accurate.

THE INFORMATION-PROCESSING APPROACH TO COGNITIVE DEVELOPMENT

The information-processing approach is well suited to sketching some of the finer details of cognitive development. It examines the component processes involved in thinking and focuses on continuous, quantitative changes rather than the broad, qualitative stages studied by Piaget. Information-processing researchers have tried to track down the specific processes that account for cognitive development.

Processing Speed

One of the variables that appears to account most for cognitive development is surprisingly simple: processing speed (Fry & Hale, 1996; Kail, 1991; Miller & Vernon, 1997). As we saw in Chapter 8, mental quickness is a central aspect of intelligence. As children get older, they get faster on a range of cognitive tasks, from categorizing objects to making decisions (Figure 13.12). This allows them, among other things, to hold more information in working memory at any given moment and hence to solve problems more effectively. Speed of processing across a wide array of simple and complex tasks increases throughout childhood and levels off around age 15 (Kail, 1991).

Knowledge Base

Another factor that influences children's cognitive efficiency is accumulated knowledge already in long-term memory, or their **knowledge base**. Compared to adults, children's knowledge bases are obviously limited because of their comparative inexperience with life (Chi, 1976, 1978). To what extent, then, does the size of children's knowledge base, rather than some other factor, account for their relative cognitive inefficiency?

One study explored this question by reversing the usual state of affairs, selecting children who were *more* knowledgeable than their adult counterparts (Chi, 1978). The cognitive task was to remember arrangements of pieces on a chessboard. Child participants (averaging age 10) were recruited from a local chess tournament, whereas adult participants had no particular skill at chess. The children easily outperformed the adults at remembering the arrangement of pieces on the board, demonstrating that knowledge base was more important than age-related factors in this cognitive task. Other studies have corroborated this finding using stimuli such as cartoon characters with which children are more familiar than adults (Lindberg, 1980).

Automatic Processing

A third factor that influences children's cognitive skill is their increasing ability to perform cognitive tasks automatically (Anderson, 1985; Sternberg, 1984). **Automatization** refers to the process of executing mental processes with increasing efficiency so that they require less and less attention. In many tasks, from performing addition problems to driving a car, increased competence involves shifting from conscious, controlled processing to automatic, or implicit, processing.

Cognitive Strategies

Children's use of cognitive strategies also develops throughout childhood and adolescence (Siegler, 1996). In memory tasks, young children tend to rely on simple strategies such as rote repetition; older children learn to use increasingly sophisticated, elaborative rehearsal strategies (Chapter 6), such as arranging lists into categories or using imagery (see Alexander & Schwanenflugel, 1994; Brown et al., 1983; Hasselhorn, 1990). In many respects, cognitive development reflects a process akin to evolution: Children try out new "mutations" (different problem-solving strategies), weed out those that do not work as well, and gradually evolve new strategies depending on changes in the situation (Siegler, 1996).

Children can remember the names and personalities of dozens of cartoon characters that "all look alike" to their parents.

One early study demonstrated differences in the way children of various ages spontaneously use memory strategies (Flavell et al., 1966). The experimenter showed 5-, 7-, and 10-year-old children seven pictures and pointed to three they should remember. Between the time the children saw the pictures and the next phase, when their memory was tested, the experimenter carefully watched them to see whether they used any verbalizations to "think aloud" as an aid to memory. (The researcher was trained at lip reading.) Whereas only 10 percent of the 5-year-olds talked to themselves to help remember the pictures, 60 percent of the 7-year-olds and 85 percent of the 10-year-olds did so.

Metacognition

A final variable involved in cognitive development is **metacognition**—thinking about thinking (Flavell, 1979; Reeve & Brown, 1985; Metcalfe & Shimamura, 1994). To solve problems effectively, people often need to understand how their mind works—how they perform cognitive tasks such as remembering, learning, and solving problems. When young children are asked if they understand something, they typically have difficulty discriminating whether they do or not, so they may fail to ask other people or seek information that could inform them (Brown, 1983). Similarly, although preschoolers can recognize under certain circumstances that other people have thoughts or desires (Chapter 14), they do not assume that much is going on in their own and other people's minds when people solve problems, read, write, and so forth (Flavell et al., 1997). For example, they fail to recognize the importance of "inner speech"—using words inside one's head—while performing tasks such as mental arithmetic.

Simply knowing what one does and does not know can be crucial for accurately performing various skills. But how do we know when we really know something or when we are simply guessing or making it up? Knowing something involves a *feeling* of knowing (Conway et al., 1996; Kamas & Reder, 1995). Consider an incident in which a friend and I struggled to recall the name of a famous maker of fine crystal while buying a wedding gift. My friend suggested that the name was something like "Stanford." Somehow "feeling" that she was on the right track, I at first guessed, based, presumably, on my intuitive knowledge of the way memory works, that the name must begin with "St" but then suddenly changed my mind, concluding that the name ended with "-ford." She said it had a British sound to it, I said it had three syllables like "Rutherford," and then she retrieved the name—*Waterford*. Although our exchange may sound more like an example of senile dementia, it illustrates the complex processes involved in knowing what one does and does not know, processes that develop with age.

An important aspect of metacognition is *metamemory*— knowledge about one's own memory and about strategies that can be used to help remember. Metamemory is impaired in many patients with frontal lobe damage (Shimamura, 1995). Not surprisingly, it is also less developed in children, whose frontal lobes remain immature for many years. As they mature, children develop a better understanding of what they can and cannot remember and of the types of strategies useful for approaching different kinds of memory tasks (Flavell & Wellman, 1977; O'Sullivan et al., 1996; Schneider & Pressley, 1989; Yussen & Levy, 1975). For example, in one study researchers showed pictures to younger and older children and asked them to predict how many they could remember. The older children's predictions were much more accurate than those of younger children, who often predicted total recall (Flavell et al., 1970)! Although metamemory, like metacognition in general, often involves explicit processes, many metamemory processes are implicit, such as knowing how, where, and how long to search memory (Reder & Schunn, 1996).

> **INTERIM SUMMARY**   Many aspects of information processing change with age. Among the most important are processing speed, children's **knowledge base** (store of accumulated knowledge), **automatization** (executing mental processes automatically and relatively effortlessly, with increasing efficiency and decreased attention), more efficient use of cognitive strategies, and **metacognition** (knowledge about how one's mind works—or cognition about cognition).

INTEGRATIVE THEORIES OF COGNITIVE DEVELOPMENT

Piaget's theory views cognitive development as a progression through qualitatively different stages, whereas the information-processing approach focuses on small-scale, quantitative refinements in the child's ability to encode, remember, and process different kinds of information. As different as these viewpoints are, they are not mutually exclusive: Cognitive development may be characterized by both qualitative and quantitative changes and general and specific processes (Fischer, 1980; Fischer & Bidell, 1998).

Theorists who attempt to integrate these views (sometimes called **neo-Piagetian theorists**) agree with several fundamental tenets of Piagetian theory: that children actively structure their understanding, that knowledge progresses from a preconcrete to a concrete and then to an abstract stage, and that all of this occurs in roughly the order and ages reported by Piaget (Bidell & Fischer, 1992; Case, 1992; Fischer, 1980). Like information-processing theorists, however, the neo-Piagetians pay more attention to discrete components of cognitive processing than Piaget, and they stress the way cognition develops within specific domains.

Case's Theory

One theory that attempts to wed Piagetian and information-processing models was developed by Robbie Case. Case (1985, 1992, 1998) holds that cognitive development progresses within a general stage framework similar to Piaget's, from a sensorimotor period to an abstract, complex, highly symbolic, formal operational stage. Each stage differs qualitatively from the others in the way children represent problems and strategies for solving them (Case, 1984). Unlike Piaget, Case believes that cognitive progress within each stage is possible because humans are innately motivated to engage in certain types of behaviors, including problem solving, exploration, imitation, and social interaction. Cognitive development occurs within each stage as children set goals, formulate problem-solving strategies, and evaluate the results of those strategies. They then integrate existing problem-solving strategies to create more elaborate strategies as new situations arise, and they practice those new strategies until they become automatic.

According to Case, development from one stage to another depends on cultural input, but the factor most responsible for qualitative changes in cognitive development is an increasing capacity for working memory (Chapter 6). Working memory expands with increased automaticity and more efficient use of cognitive strategies, allowing children to keep progressively more things in mind simultaneously and to coordinate previously separate actions and ideas. Attending to both length and width in a conservation task is much easier if a child has large enough working memory capacity to hold both dimensions in mind simultaneously while imagining how, for example, a ball of clay might look if those dimensions changed. Recent research suggests that the central executive function of working memory, which is involved in allocating attention, coordinating different kinds of information held in short-term storage, and handling multiple tasks at once, does in fact continue to develop, at least through age 10 (Hale et al., 1997).

An example of how expanded working memory allows for more complex cognition can be seen in Figure 13.13. In this study, children ages 10 to 18 were asked to draw a picture of a mother looking out the window of her home to see her son playing peek-a-boo with her in the park across the street (Dennis, 1992, cited in Case, 1992). The youngest subjects could not simultaneously coordinate the two scenes. They could keep in mind the image of the mother in the house and the image of the boy in the park, but they could not integrate the two images.

This study illustrates the advantages of Case's neo-Piagetian model over classical Piagetian theory. Certain broad processes, notably limitations in working memory, *constrain* the thinking of the child, providing an upper limit on what a child within a given age range can achieve. This leads to qualitative differences in thought at different stages that appear across a variety of domains (such as art, language, and mathematics), just as Piaget postulated. At the same time, the neo-Piagetian model, like similar theories about the way children acquire and coordinate skills (Fischer, 1980), recognizes that development occurs in specific domains and is influenced by culture and experience. By ages 8 to 10, children in Western cultures incorporate artistic conventions developed over the past several centuries for depicting perspective (Chapter 4), such as representing closer objects as

FIGURE 13.13
Artistic skill and working memory. Subjects ages 10 to 18 were asked to draw a picture of a mother looking out the window to see her son playing peek-a-boo with her in the park. The 10-year-old who drew this picture accurately depicted both *parts* of the scene but failed to integrate them, drawing the mother and son both facing the artist instead of each other.

larger, but a 4-year-old with a crayon is unlikely to outperform an adult regardless of culture or experience.

An important question that remains is why development follows any broad stages at all, particularly if learning always occurs in specific situations. From North American suburbs to villages in West Africa, children develop basic skills such as counting at approximately the same age, despite wide variations in experience (Case, 1985). Even with extensive practice in counting, young children seem to reach a maximum level of efficiency beyond which they cannot progress at their stage of development (Kurland, 1981). Case proposes a maturational explanation: the myelination of the prefrontal cortex, which plays a central role in working memory and continues to develop through at least early adolescence.

INTERIM SUMMARY   Integrative theories, often called **neo-Piagetian**, attempt to integrate an understanding of the broad stages of Piaget's theory, which suggests progressive ability to coordinate mental representations and think abstractly, with an information processing approach. According to Case's theory, the main variable responsible for cognitive development *across* stages is expansion of working memory capacity.

COGNITIVE DEVELOPMENT AND CHANGE IN ADULTHOOD

All cultures consider adolescents and adults better decision makers than children, but they differ dramatically in their beliefs about cognition and aging. Many cultures associate age with wisdom. In contrast, Western cultures tend to associate it with decline, although they are ambiguous about when this decline begins and whether middle age confers cognitive advantages over youth. In the United States, for example, people can vote at 18, but the minimum age to run for the presidency is 35. Apparently, the framers of the Constitution held some implicit theory of cognitive development in adulthood, even though most contemporary North Americans believe that some cognitive functions, such as memory, decline by the 40s (see Ryan, 1992).

Experimental data are similarly ambiguous about cognition in middle age. Many measures of memory show steady declines in adulthood, with young adults performing better than both middle-aged and older adults (Figure 13.14). On other tasks, however, people in their early 20s and 40s perform equally well, and both groups outperform their elders (Lavigne & Finley, 1990).

John Kennedy and Bill Clinton were "youngsters" when they assumed the United States presidency—in their fifth decade.

Unlike cultural concepts of intelligence in middle age, views of cognition in the elderly in contemporary Western societies are unambiguously negative. In part, the stereotype of the slow, forgetful senior citizen reflects real changes in speed of processing and capacity for learning and memory that occur cross-culturally (see Crook et al., 1992). In other respects, however, the negative view of cognition in later life is idiosyncratic and culture specific. Unlike most periods in human history, in times of rapid technological change, as occurred in the last century, the knowledge and strategies used by one generation may be irrelevant or even unproductive 20 or 30 years later. To younger individuals, an older person's reliance on accumulated wisdom may thus look like a sign of cognitive rigidity or failure to accommodate, rather than maturity. As we shall see, the extent to which cognition declines in old age varies not only across cultures but also across individuals within a single culture.

STUDYING COGNITION AND AGING: SOME CAUTIONS

Almost any method of studying cognition and aging has its limitations. Cohort effects render cross-sectional data problematic. Older people have generally had less exposure to experiences such as higher education, computers, television, and standardized tests, and IQ has risen steadily over the last several decades, so comparing current young people with current old people can confound age changes and age differences (see Schaie, 1994). In contrast, longitudinal and sequential designs suffer from subject attrition, as elderly participants are not always available to return for the final assessments.

Another problem is that the psychometric tests used to measure intelligence were developed to predict school performance. Some researchers question whether these youth-oriented tests are appropriate measures of intelligence in older people (Labouvie-Vief, 1985; Willis & Baltes, 1980). For example, older people may simply not be as motivated to jump through cognitive hoops as younger people, who are likely either to be in school or recently out of it (Blanchard-Fields & Chen, 1996; Kausler, 1990).

An additional problem in studying aging and cognition is that both factors— aging and cognition—are multifaceted. The body ages, the brain ages, social roles shift, the social environment changes, and beliefs about the self alter. Understanding how aging affects cognitive capabilities requires determining precisely *which* aspects of aging are responsible for any observed changes. Anyone who has taken an important examination while feeling ill knows that poor health interferes with cognitive performance. Because older people are more likely than the general population to be in poor health, cognitive studies that use random samples may show declines with age simply because a greater proportion of their older subjects are ill (see Perlmutter & Nyquist, 1990).

To further complicate matters, different aspects of aging may produce gains or losses in different cognitive processes. Most people would trust their legal work more readily to a senior partner in a law firm than to a young associate, even though, at 60, the senior partner may suffer some of the memory declines illustrated in Figure 13.14. Despite aging neural hardware, years of experience enable the older lawyer to solve problems more efficiently—enough, at times, to justify the cost of a senior partner at $300 an hour versus an associate at $150.

A final problem in considering the relationship between aging and cognition is that culturally constructed *beliefs* about lifespan development affect the way people actually think and remember. Researchers studying metamemory have documented that what people believe about their capacity to remember influences both the strategies they use and their ultimate ability to retrieve information

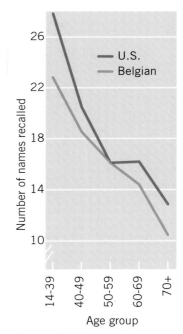

FIGURE 13.14
Age differences in recall in the United States and Belgium. The experimenters taught participants to associate pictures of faces with names, as might occur at a party. They subsequently showed participants pictures of the faces and asked them to retrieve the names. In both societies, performance showed steady decline with age. *Source:* Crook et al., 1992, p. 133.

(Devolder & Pressley, 1989; Hertzog et al., 1990). People who think they are suffering memory losses are more likely to suffer them.

INTERIM SUMMARY   Studying cognitive changes with aging is difficult for several reasons: Cohort effects confound age differences with true age changes in cognition; psychometric tests may be more appropriate for assessing school functioning than everyday cognitive ability; aging is easily confounded with disease; different aspects of aging may affect different aspects of functioning; and beliefs about age-related changes can effect performance.

COGNITIVE CHANGES ASSOCIATED WITH AGING

Within these methodological constraints, experimental investigations suggest that cognition does change as people age.

Changes in Psychomotor Speed

One of the clearest changes that accompanies aging is **psychomotor slowing**, an increase in the time between sensory input and motor output and a general increase in the time required for processing (Park et al., 1996; Rabbitt, 1996; Salthouse, 1996). This deceleration actually begins early, around the mid-20s. Psychomotor slowing can be observed both on tasks of simple reaction time, such as pushing a button in response to a flash of a light, and on more complex reaction-time tasks, such as typing or writing (Era et al., 1986; Spirduso & McCrae, 1990; Wilkinson & Allison, 1989). Semantic information processing, assessed by priming studies, takes approximately 1.5 times as long in adults in their 60s and 70s as in younger adults (Myerson et al., 1992).

For most people, psychomotor slowing is so gradual that it goes unnoticed until the 50s or 60s. However, increased reaction time can be a devastating problem for professional athletes, like tennis players, who make their living respond-

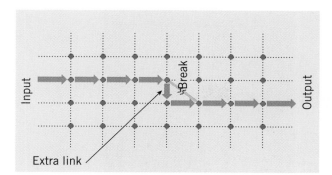

FIGURE 13.15
Connectionist model of psycho-motor slowing with aging. A neural circuit that is broken with aging forces a detour that adds an extra step and hence increased reaction time. *Source:* Adapted from Cerella, 1990, p. 203.

ing deftly to balls coming at them in rapid succession. This explains why most athletes are considered has-beens by their early 30s. Middle-aged athletes such as George Foreman, who shocked the world in 1994 by winning back the heavy-weight championship in his late 40s, know their days are numbered. Even so, they can stage temporary comebacks through extra practice and increased skill and compensatory strategies.

Why do declines in processing speed matter? We have seen that processing speed is an essential component of intelligence as measured by IQ tests and that it is one of the prime movers behind cognitive development in children. But the reasons are not intuitively obvious; if a person takes longer to get to an answer, why is the answer less likely to be correct?

Researchers are just beginning to tease apart the reasons, but two explanations may help explain the link between speed and ability (Salthouse, 1996). The first is limited time. If complex mental operations rely on the execution and coordination of many simpler mechanisms, then in the brief period of time people have to make most decisions, especially implicit decisions—such as how to categorize an object—the person will simply have less time to process multiple pieces of information and combine them in complex ways. From a connectionist perspective, if people categorize, perceive, and remember through processes of parallel constraint satisfaction, finding the solution that best fits all the constraints active at the moment, then people who think quickly can weigh a greater number of constraints and hence come to a more accurate conclusion. A second way decreased processing speed can affect cognitive performance is its influence on working memory: If cognitive processes take longer to execute, less information is available simultaneously in working memory and relevant information may no longer be available by the time the person needs to think about it.

Why psychomotor processes take longer as people age is not entirely clear. A connectionist model (Chapter 7) suggests that if a mental process or representation is distributed across a number of neurons that form a circuit, any small break that occurs with aging will require additional steps to recomplete the circuit (Cerella, 1990). Because every synaptic connection adds processing time, the more broken connections that amass over the years, the more time required to find alternative routes to carry out psychological processes (Figure 13.15).

Changes in Memory

A common stereotype is that older people are constantly forgetting things—names of people they have just met, what they did yesterday, and where they put their house keys. This stereotype has grains of truth but is far too sweeping. Understanding declines in memory requires distinguishing different types of memory (Chapter 6).

Which tasks involved in obtaining a college education would be most difficult for older people who decide to get their degree following retirement? At which tasks would they more likely excel?

Working Memory Older people show minimal impairment on simple short-term storage tasks, such as remembering a string of digits (Hultsch & Dixon, 1990; Labouvie-Vief & Schell, 1982). However, they show much more substantial deficits in complex working memory tasks, such as repeating a list of digits *backward*, or when they have to deal with more than one task at a time (Einstein et al., 1997; Kirasic et al., 1996; Park et al., 1996). Elderly people tend to have difficulty performing divided attention tasks (Ponds et al., 1988), such as keeping the actions of multiple cars in mind at an intersection with a four-way stop. If neo-Piagetian theorists such as Robbie Case are right that the key to cognitive development in childhood is increased working memory capacity, then advanced aging means development in reverse.

Encoding Long-Term Memories As for long-term memory, some aspects remain intact throughout the life span, whereas others show clear decline. Older people tend to take more time to learn new information than younger people; however, when given ample encoding time, their performance level approaches that of younger subjects (Perlmutter, 1983). Where older people show encoding deficits is in their use of strategies that will later facilitate retrieval.

Long-term memory storage, on the other hand, seems to give older people little difficulty. Healthy people continue to add to their knowledge base until the day they die (Horn & Hofer, 1992; Light, 1990; Salthouse, 1992). One way researchers know that the memory losses of later life do not primarily reflect problems with storage is that older subjects show few declines in recognition memory. For example, if shown a list of words and subsequently asked which words in a new list were in the old one, older subjects are as likely as younger subjects to recognize words they had previously seen. Similarly, implicit memory, as assessed by tasks such as the tendency to complete a word stem (e.g., *per—*) with a previously primed word (e.g., perfume), is not typically impaired with age (see Russo & Parkin, 1993; Schacter et al., 1992).

Retrieving Long-Term Memories The problems older people have with long-term memory appear to lie more in retrieval than in encoding. Compared to their unimpaired performance on recognition tasks ("Did you see the word *dove*?"), older people show relative deficits in free recall ("What words did you see?") and cued recall ("Did you see the name of a bird?"). As people age, they have more difficulty with such tests of explicit memory than with implicit memory tasks.

In part, declines in retrieval (and in the kinds of complex encoding strategies that facilitate retrieval) reflect changes in the use of cognitive strategies. Although older subjects still have the capacity to use chunking, imagery, and deep processing strategies (Chapter 6), they tend not to employ these strategies spontaneously (Perlmutter, 1983). When trained to use mnemonic devices and encouraged to organize learning materials, they show significant improvements in memory performance (Greenberg & Powers, 1987). However, older subjects often do not transfer these skills to other situations and do not continue to apply them months later (Baltes et al., 1986; Labouvie-Vief & Gonda, 1976).

If older people have trouble retrieving new information, do they "live in the past"? Interestingly, the years between 10 and 30 seem to be peak years for storing significant autobiographical memories (Rubin et al., 1998). When older adults are asked to recall significant episodic memories (memories of events they have experienced), they tend to remember memories from that period more than other memories, and the memories they produce are more vivid. They also show greater semantic knowledge for facts such as current events and who won an Oscar or the World Series during that period. The extent to which this selective memory for events during adolescence and early adulthood reflects cognitive or motivational factors is not yet clear.

Everyday Memory   As in the study of memory more generally (Chapter 6), many researchers have become interested in everyday memory and cognition in the lives of older people, wondering whether the gloomy picture of decline painted by many studies may not adequately assess adaptive functioning (see Blanchard-Fields & Chen, 1996). Older people also have difficulty with some forms of problem solving, such as the strategic questioning required in the game "Twenty Questions," which laboratory researchers have adapted to assess problem-solving ability. In these studies, the person is shown several pictures and told that the researcher is thinking of one of them. The individual then asks the researcher questions to narrow the field and eliminate all but the selected picture. Older subjects tend to ask many more redundant and unnecessary questions than younger ones (Denney & Denney, 1973; Denney & Palmer, 1981).

In contrast, when presented with more familiar everyday problems, older people appear to make better use of their cognitive "software" (such as making grocery lists rather than relying strictly on memory) to compensate for deteriorating neural "hardware" (see Martin, 1986). In fact, an analysis of nearly one hundred studies with a combined total of more than 38,000 subjects found that the correlation between worker productivity and age is essentially zero (McEvoy & Cascio, 1989). Most workers apparently compensate for declines in processing power with increases in their knowledge base and with alternative strategies for carrying out tasks (see Baltes, 1987; Perlmutter et al., 1990; Salthouse, 1985).

The tests used to assess cognitive functioning may mask some ways in which the cognition of older people is actually *superior* to that of their children and grandchildren. Most memory tests assess the kind of rote memory—for lists of words, numbers, or propositions in an essay—that is frequently required of students but less relevant for complex thought and decision making throughout the life span. One researcher examined the way four groups of subjects recalled the events of a story: early adolescents (aged 12 to 15), late adolescents (aged 16 to 19), middle-aged adults (aged 39 to 56), and older adults (aged 60 to 78) (Adams, 1991). Whereas the younger participants were somewhat more likely to recall the details of the story, the older participants were more likely to "get it"—to elaborate on the underlying meaning of the story. In summarizing the story, only 15 to

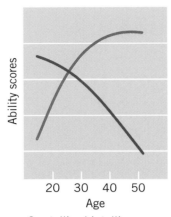

— Crystallized intelligence
— Fluid intelligence

FIGURE 13.16
Fluid and crystallized intelligence throughout the lifespan. Unlike fluid intelligence, crystallized intelligence increases through at least the 40s and 50s and then levels off. *Source:* Horn & Hofer, 1992, p. 79.

20 percent of early and late adolescents offered an interpretation of its main theme or moral, compared with 70 percent of middle-aged and 60 percent of older subjects. Thus, changes in cognition probably involve both gains and losses (Baltes, 1987).

Fluid and Crystallized Intelligence

Intelligence has many facets, and different aspects of intelligence change in different ways as people age. An important distinction is between fluid and crystallized intelligence (Cattell, 1941; Horn & Cattell, 1967; Horn & Hofer, 1992). As we saw in Chapter 8, **fluid intelligence** refers to intellectual capacities that have no specific content but are used in processing information, particularly novel information. Measures of fluid intelligence assess speed of processing, the capacity to spot missing elements in a picture, the ability to solve analogies or form concepts quickly, and similar abilities. Fluid intelligence peaks in young adulthood and then levels off and begins declining by mid-adulthood, largely because of a decline in speed of processing.

Unlike fluid intelligence, **crystallized intelligence** (people's store of knowledge) increases throughout most of life, showing declines only in very old age (Horn, 1979, in Labouvie-Vief, 1985). These declines appear to occur, if at all, only when the "machinery" for processing information breaks down to such a degree that new memories, strategies, and ways of categorizing information can no longer be processed by an aging neural assembly line. Figure 13.16 shows the different developmental trajectories of fluid and crystallized intelligence in adulthood.

COMMENTARY
Intelligence and Aging

The picture painted thus far of intelligence in adulthood is one of selective decline. Recent research suggests, however, that this is only part of the picture. First, to the extent that psychomotor speed decreases with aging, older people show deficits compared with younger people on a host of variables, such as memory (because they take longer to encode and retrieve) and problem solving (because selecting strategies takes time). Whether timed tests translate to real-life deficits, however, depends on the individuals involved and their occupations. If their jobs require rapid performance, they will either show declines or have to find ways to compensate; if they have time to think and work at their own pace, they are unlikely to show declines (see Salthouse, 1996).

Second, most of the studies showing declines with aging have been cross-sectional. Aside from the possibility of cohort effects, the major problem with cross-sectional studies is that they do not show the *proportion* of people whose cognitive capacities decline. Statistically, if a sizable minority of older people show evidence of substantial cognitive deterioration, mean scores for their age group will be lower than for younger groups; the apparent conclusion is that intelligence declines with age. But longitudinal studies can ask a different question: What *percentage* of people in different age groups shows deterioration?

The most extensive longitudinal study, the Seattle Longitudinal Study (Schaie, 1990, 1994), provides an important corrective to the view of inevitable cognitive decline through middle and old age. The investigators followed a large sample ranging in age from 25 to 81 over a 7-year interval.

The first forty years of life furnish the text, while the remaining thirty supply the commentary; without the commentary we are unable to understand aright the true sense and coherence of the text, together with the moral it contains.

SCHOPENHAUER
(cited in Adams, 1991, p. 323)

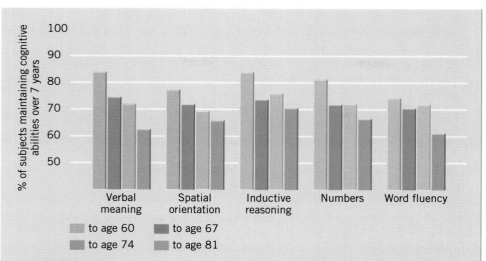

FIGURE 13.17

Cognitive stability over seven years. On five tests of mental ability, less than 25 percent of subjects tested at seven-year intervals showed any decline prior to age 60. Even by age 81, over 60 percent of all subjects showed stable cognitive functioning rather than decline. *Source:* Adapted from Schaie, 1990, p. 297.

They administered a battery of tests of mental abilities such as verbal meaning (vocabulary) and facility with numbers (arithmetic). The findings are striking (Figure 13.17): Most people do not show significant mental declines. Even on the average, intellectual functioning does not decline until the 60s and 70s.

The Seattle study shows that people differ tremendously in the way they age. People who are healthy and mentally active experience fewer mental declines than those who are not (Diamond, 1978; Horn & Meer, 1987). The "use it or lose it" theory applies to mental functioning as much as to physical. B. F. Skinner, Pablo Picasso, Sigmund Freud, Eleanor Roosevelt, Jean Piaget, and a host of other septuagenarians and octogenarians have shown remarkable cognitive longevity in diverse fields.

Third, teaching strategies for memory or problem solving can dramatically increase people's functioning, so that skilled older people can outperform less skilled younger people (Sharpts & Price-Sharps, 1996). Both the promise of such training and the limitations imposed by an aging nervous system are illustrated in a study that taught old and young adults mnemonic strategies for remembering words and numbers (Baltes, 1987). Older subjects improved dramatically, outperforming untrained younger subjects, but younger subjects with training were far superior to their trained elders.

There is no doubt that aging brings with it inevitable declines across a number of domains, including memory and cognition. Particularly as the frontal lobes begin to function less effectively, explicit memory and decision making decline or at best hold steady if the person finds alternative ways to compensate (see Parkin et al., 1995; West, 1996). Although most people actually continue to function well for most or all of their lives, cognitive decline generally escalates in the mid 80s as the brain's hardware begins to wear out (Korten et al., 1997). Interestingly, among people older than 75, cognitive decline, particularly in explicit memory, appears to be an early warning sign of impending death (Small & Backman, 1997).

> In many respects, changes in the brain, and particularly the prefrontal cortex, lead to "development in reverse" in aging. Some researchers call this the "last in, first out" theory, which means that the latest developing capacities in adolescence are the first to go in adulthood. On the other hand, intelligence is multifaceted, and cumulative—we do not lose much of our crystallized intelligence—and most of us would do well to be half as productive or creative at 20 or 30 as Picasso was at 90. ■

AGING AND "SENILITY"

One of the most pervasive myths about aging is that in old age people lose their memory, their intellectual capacity, and their ability to think and reason; that is, they become "senile" (Butler, 1975, 1984). In fact, only about 5 percent of the population suffer progressive and incurable **dementia**, a disorder marked by global disturbance of higher mental functions (Morris & Baddeley, 1988). Another 10 to 15 percent experience mild to moderate memory loss, whereas the majority of people retain sharp mental functioning even through old age (Butler, 1984; Schaie, 1990). Although organic brain disease, or what people often call senility, is far more prevalent among people in their 80s and 90s than among those in their 60s and 70s, even in the ninth decade, only about 20 percent of people are affected by senile dementia (Roth, 1978). Rates of dementia show slight variability across cultures, although they are everywhere linked to advancing age (van Duijn, 1996).

Senile dementia has a variety of causes including reduced blood supplies to the brain and neurological syndromes brought on by exposure to toxins such as alcohol. Roughly 10 to 20 percent of dementias are curable by diagnosing and eliminating an environmental toxin (Elias et al., 1990). Well over half the cases, however, are caused by **Alzheimer's disease**, a progressive and incurable illness that destroys neurons in the brain, severely impairing memory, reasoning, perception, language, and behavior (see Ashford et al., 1996). Although onset can occur in middle adulthood, as early as the 40s, Alzheimer's disease most commonly occurs later in life.

Characteristic changes in brain tissue include tangled neurons and protein deposits that destroy the functioning of cortical cells (Figure 13.18). Alzheimer's patients also have abnormally low levels of several neurotransmitters (Winblad et al., 1985), most importantly acetylcholine, which plays a central role in memory functioning. The acetylcholine deficit is linked to an insufficient quantity of an enzyme necessary for its production (Price et al., 1985); levels of this enzyme are 60 to 90 percent lower in patients with Alzheimer's disease than in the normal population of the same age (Coyle et al., 1983). Recent imaging research has found a direct correlation between the extent of damage in the medial temporal lobes and the degree of cognitive impairment in Alzheimer's patients, which makes sense in light of the pervasive effects of the disease on explicit memory (Schroder et al., 1997). Of particular importance may be regions of the medial temporal lobes that connect the hippocampus with other areas of the neocortex (Bierer et al., 1995).

Alzheimer's disease may have several different causes, some of them viral, but at least one major form of the disorder is genetic (Coyle, 1991). Researchers have isolated genes on at least three chromosomes that are implicated in the genetic transmission of Alzheimer's. One form of the disease has been linked to a defect on chromosome 21 (Holland & Oliver, 1995), the chromosome implicated in Down syndrome, a form of mental retardation (Chapter 8). Down syndrome patients who live into late middle age often develop symptoms and neurological changes similar to Alzheimer's disease.

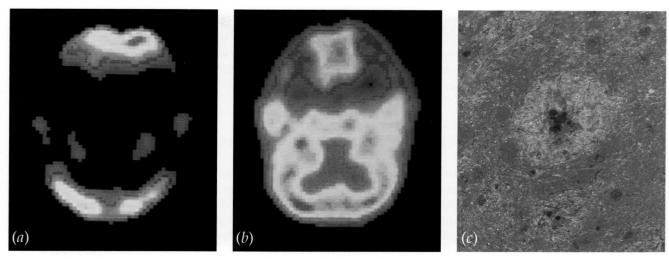

FIGURE 13.18
PET scans of a brain with Alzheimer's (*a*) and a normal brain (*b*). Note the comparative inactivity of the Alzheimer's brain. The brains of Alzheimer's patients (*c*) show abnormal chemical deposits (called plaques) and tangled neural fibers.

INTERIM SUMMARY   Cognitive declines in later life tend to be selective rather than global. Processing speed decreases; working memory capacity declines; explicit memory retrieval becomes more difficult; problem-solving strategies become less efficient; and fluid intelligence declines. Other functions show little or no noticeable decline, including encoding processes, many aspects of everyday memory, and crystallized intelligence. People also show tremendous variability in the way their minds change with aging. About 5 percent of the population suffer progressive and incurable **dementia**, a disorder marked by global disturbance of higher mental functions. The most common cause of dementia is **Alzheimer's disease**.

SOME CONCLUDING THOUGHTS

This chapter began with three questions about development: What are the relative contributions of nature and nurture? To what extent is development characterized by critical or sensitive periods? And to what extent is development stage-like or continuous? All three questions address the way maturational, cultural, and environmental forces interact over time to create an organism capable of responding adaptively to its social and physical environment.

Maturational factors provide both the possibilities and limits of physical and cognitive development. Young children cannot think in the abstract ways that adolescents can about justice, God, or conservation of matter, and old people cannot think as quickly as their younger counterparts. In both cases, the nervous system determines the range within which people can function. Except in cases of congenital mental retardation or neural degeneration, however, that range is extraordinarily large. Moreover, the nervous system that establishes the parameters of cognitive functioning is itself partially a product of its environment. Experience can enrich the developing brain, increasing the connections among neurons that underlie the capacity for complex thought. At the same time, it can constrain psychological functioning by limiting the processing power of the brain.

Understanding development thus means living with ambiguities. Perhaps that is a developmental achievement in itself.

SUMMARY

1. **Developmental psychology** studies the way humans develop and change over time. A *life-span developmental perspective* examines both constancy and change, and gains and losses in functioning, that occur at different points over the human life cycle.

BASIC ISSUES IN DEVELOPMENTAL PSYCHOLOGY

2. Three basic issues confront developmental psychologists. The first concerns the relative roles of nature (genetically programmed **maturation**) and nurture. The second is the relative importance of early experience and whether human development is characterized by **critical periods** (periods of special sensitivity to specific types of learning that shape the capacity for future development) or **sensitive periods** (periods of special, but not definitive, importance). The third issue is whether development occurs in **stages**—relatively discrete steps through which everyone progresses in the same sequence—or whether it is **continuous**, or gradual.

STUDYING DEVELOPMENT

3. Developmental psychologists rely on three types of research designs. **Cross-sectional studies** compare groups of different-aged subjects at a single time to see if differences exist among them. **Longitudinal studies** follow the same individuals over time and thus can directly assess age changes rather than age differences. **Sequential studies** minimize the confounding variable of cohort by studying multiple cohorts longitudinally.

PHYSICAL DEVELOPMENT AND ITS PSYCHOLOGICAL CONSEQUENCES

4. **Prenatal** (before birth) development is divided into three stages: the **germinal**, **embryonic**, and **fetal periods**. Prenatal development can be disrupted by harmful environmental agents known as **teratogens**, such as alcohol.

5. Neural development, both prenatally and throughout childhood, proceeds through progressive myelination, trimming back of neurons, and increasing dendritic connections. Throughout life the brain demonstrates considerable **plasticity**, or flexibility, in meeting environmental demands.

6. Physical development and psychological development are intertwined. At birth, an infant possesses many adaptive reflexes. Motor development follows a universal maturational sequence, although cross-cultural research indicates that the environment can affect the pace of development. By the end of adolescence, physical growth is virtually complete. With aging comes a gradual decline in physical and sensory abilities with which people must cope psychologically. Women experience a dramatic physical change in middle adulthood during **menopause**, the cessation of the menstrual cycle.

COGNITIVE DEVELOPMENT IN INFANCY, CHILDHOOD, AND ADOLESCENCE

7. For many years psychologists underestimated the substantial abilities of infants; researchers now know they are capable of **intermodal** understanding—the ability to associate sensations about an object from different senses

and to match their own actions to behaviors they observe visually—in the earliest days of life.

8. Piaget proposed that children develop knowledge by inventing or *constructing* reality out of their own experience. According to Piaget, people cognitively adapt to their environment through two interrelated processes. **Assimilation** means interpreting actions or events in terms of one's present schemas, that is, fitting reality into one's previous structures of knowledge. **Accommodation** involves modifying schemas to fit reality.

9. Piaget proposed a stage theory of cognitive development. During the **sensorimotor stage**, thought primarily takes the form of perception and action. Gradually, children acquire **object permanence**, recognizing that objects exist in time and space independent of their actions on, or observation of them. Sensorimotor children are extremely **egocentric**, or thoroughly embedded in their own point of view. The **preoperational stage** is characterized by the emergence of symbolic thought. **Operations** are internalized, or mental, actions the individual can use to manipulate, transform, and return an object of knowledge to its original state. Piaget called the third stage the **concrete operational stage** because at this point children can operate on, or mentally manipulate, internal representations of concrete objects in ways that are reversible. The concrete operational child understands **conservation**—the idea that basic properties of an object or situation remain stable even though superficial properties may change. The **formal operational stage** is characterized by the ability to reason about formal propositions rather than concrete events.

10. In its broadest outlines, such as the movement from concrete, egocentric thought to abstract thought, Piaget's theory appears to be accurate. Psychologists have, however, criticized Piaget for underestimating the capacities of younger children, assuming too much consistency across domains, and downplaying the influence of culture.

11. The information-processing approach to cognitive development focuses on the development of different components of cognition. Several variables that develop over time are children's **knowledge base**, their **automatization** of processing, their ability to use **cognitive strategies,** and their **metacognitive abilities** (understanding their own thinking processes).

12. Integrative or **neo-Piagetian theories** attempt to wed stage conceptions with research on information processing and domain-specific knowledge; they also focus more heavily than either approach on the roles of emotion and motivation in shaping thought.

COGNITIVE DEVELOPMENT AND CHANGE IN ADULTHOOD

13. As with muscle strength, the rule of thumb with intellectual ability is *use it or lose it*: Mental capacities atrophy with disuse.

14. **Fluid intelligence** (intellectual capacities that have no specific content but are used in processing information) begins to decline gradually in midlife, whereas **crystallized intelligence** (a person's store of knowledge) continues to expand over the life span. One of the clearest changes that accompanies aging is a general **psychomotor slowing**. Substantial intellectual decline occurs in only a minority of people.

15. Senile **dementia** is a disorder marked by global disturbance of higher mental functions. Well over half the cases of senile dementia result from **Alzheimer's disease**, a progressive and incurable illness that destroys neurons in the brain, severely impairing memory, reasoning, perception, language, and behavior.

Diana Ong, "Faces 1"/SuperStock

Social Development

Kate was 2½ years old when her mother was hospitalized for 27 days with a complicated delivery. Long hospital stays for mothers giving birth were not unusual in the 1960s, and fathers often felt unable to care for young children. Kate's parents placed her temporarily in the home of psychologists James and Joyce Robertson (1971), who were studying the way infants and young children respond to prolonged separation from their mothers. Kate was well prepared for the event: Her parents had discussed it with her for weeks and had taken her for several long visits to the Robertsons' home. Kate knew her parents loved her and would take her back home eventually and that her father would visit regularly.

On the day her mother was to be hospitalized, Kate left home saying, "Kate come back soon." During the first week in her new home, she was cooperative and cheerful but in an exaggerated, somewhat unnatural way, as if to reassure herself and her caretakers that she felt safe and happy. At one point she said, "Look, I'm a good girl, I'm laughing." She would sometimes repeat to herself her parents' instructions: "Be a good girl, don't cry," "Eat up your potatoes," and "Don't make a mess."

During the second week, the Robertsons began to observe a paradoxical combination of behaviors. On the one hand, Kate seemed more natural and spontaneous; on the other, she showed signs of increasing sadness and listlessness. When Kate's mother came up in conversation, the child would sometimes point to her psychologist surrogate mother and insist, "*You* are my Mummy." After her first visit with her real "Mummy" in the hospital, her behavior changed markedly. She became negative, aggressive, and difficult to console and readily flew into tears or tantrums.

When Kate returned home, she generally reverted to her good-natured self, but she slept restlessly, wet her bed, and was much more defiant than prior to the separation. Two weeks after returning home, Kate's mother took her to register for nursery school. That night Kate screamed in her sleep, presumably from nightmares, and awoke with an acute asthma attack, a symptom seen more frequently in children whose bonding with their mothers is problematic (Madrid & Schwartz, 1991). When the doctor inquired about recent stresses, Kate's mother realized that she and a school official had talked that day about Kate being "taken"—meaning "accepted"—but Kate had apparently misunderstood what they meant.

Children react to separations very differently at different ages. At age 2½, separation can be devastating for a child; by age 6, a few weeks away may only result in occasional homesickness. The difference reflects **social development**, changes in interpersonal thought, feeling, and behavior throughout the lifespan.

Social and cognitive development can be placed in separate chapters of a book, but in reality they are intertwined. On the one hand, children's cognitions—their constructions of reality—are in part social constructions; implicitly and explicitly, parents and others offer children ways of thinking about themselves and the world (see Cole, 1997; Nelson, 1997). On the other hand, the way children enter into relationships depends on the way they perceive and think about them. A child who can represent time, keep a stable mental image of her mother despite a prolonged period of separation, and remember soothing images of her mother when she becomes distressed will have a much easier time with a separation than Kate did.

We begin with the earliest relationships—between an infant and her caregivers—and consider how, and how much, these relationships lay the groundwork for later relationships. Next, we examine the way children learn the ways of their culture. For example, how and when do children take on the attributes expected of their gender? Then we explore children's relationships with friends and siblings, their changing conceptions of themselves and others, and their developing capacity for moral judgment and action. We conclude by expanding the focus to the entire lifespan, with a discussion of social development from infancy to the final days of life.

ATTACHMENT

In the middle of the 20th century, psychoanalysts observed that children reared in large institutional homes, with minimal stimulation and no consistent contact with a loving caretaker, often became emotionally unstable, lacking in conscience, or mentally retarded. These observations led to recognition of the importance of **attachment**, the enduring affectional ties that children form with their primary caregivers (Ainsworth & Bell, 1970; Ainsworth & Bowlby, 1991; Bowlby, 1969). Attachment includes a desire for proximity to an attachment figure, a sense of security derived from the person's presence, and feelings of distress when the person is absent. Attachment is not unilateral; rather, it involves an interaction between two people who react to each other's signals.

ATTACHMENT IN INFANCY

For many years, psychoanalysts and behaviorists were in rare agreement on the origins of attachment behavior, both linking it to feeding. Psychoanalysts assumed that the gratification of oral needs led infants to become attached to people who satisfy those needs; according to behaviorists, mothers became secondary reinforcers through their association with food, which is a primary (innate) reinforcer (Chapter 5). Both theories, however, proved to be wrong. Definitive evidence came from a series of classic experiments performed by Harry Harlow (Harlow & Zimmerman, 1959).

Harlow reared infant rhesus monkeys in isolation from their mothers for several months and then placed them in a cage with two inanimate surrogate mothers (Chapter 2). One, a wire monkey that provided no warmth or softness, held a bottle from which the infant could nurse. The other was covered with terrycloth to provide softness, but it had no bottle, so it could not provide food. Baby monkeys spent much of their time clinging to the softer mother. They would also run to the softer surrogate when they were frightened, but they virtually ignored the wire surrogate except when hungry. Harlow's findings established the notion that perceived security, not food, is the crucial element in forming attachment relationships in primates; he referred to the ties that bind an infant to its caregivers as *contact comfort*.

Bowlby's Theory

John Bowlby (1969, 1973, 1983), who developed attachment theory, linked Harlow's findings to the psychodynamic literature on children reared in institutional settings. Bowlby was both a psychoanalyst and an ethologist (a psychologist interested in comparative animal behavior), and he proposed an evolutionary theory of attachment. He argued that attachment behavior is prewired in humans, as is similar behavior in other animal species, to keep immature animals close to their parents.

Bowlby noted the relation between human attachment behavior and a phenomenon studied by the ethologist Konrad Lorenz (1935) called imprinting. **Imprinting** is the tendency of young animals of certain species to follow an animal to which they were exposed during a sensitive period early in their lives (Figure 14.1). According to Lorenz, imprinting confers an evolutionary advantage: A gosling that stays close to its mother or father is more likely to be fed, protected from predators, and taught skills useful for survival and reproduction than a gosling that strays from its parents (Hess, 1959; Lorenz, 1937). Bowlby argued that attachment behavior in human infants, such as staying close to parents and crying loudly in their absence, evolved for the same reasons.

Bowlby proposed a model of attachment that relies on the concept of homeostasis (Chapters 10 and 11). The child's goal is to remain physically close to the attachment figure. When this goal is threatened, as when a toddler's mother leaves the room for a few minutes, the child experiences a feedback signal: distress. Distress motivates the child to cry or search for his mother. If either crying or searching is successful, the child receives new feedback—a sense of security—that deactivates the attachment system, temporarily switching off attachment-related motives and thoughts. The child is then free to play or explore the environment.

The attachment figure thus becomes a safe base from which the child can explore (Ainsworth, 1979) and to whom he can periodically return for "emotional refueling" (Mahler et al., 1975). Toddlers who are playing happily often suddenly look around to establish the whereabouts of their attachment figures. Once they

FIGURE 14.1
Imprinting. Normally, imprinting leads young animals to follow an adult member of their species. At times, however, Mother Nature may lead her children astray. Here, geese trail Lorenz, on whom they imprinted when young.

locate their caregiver or even run to a comforting lap, they return to play, refueled for the next period of time. Later in life, a college student's phone calls home may serve a similar function.

The Origins of Attachment

Attachment behavior emerges gradually over the first several months of life, peaking some time during the second year and then diminishing in intensity as children become more confident in their independence (Ainsworth, 1967). Among the first precursors of attachment is a general preference for social stimuli (such as faces) over other objects in the environment. Visual recognition of mother (the primary caregiver studied in most research) occurs at about 3 months (Olson, 1981); by 5 or 6 months, infants recognize and greet their mothers and other attachment figures from across the room.

At 6 to 7 months, infants begin to show **separation anxiety,** distress at separation from their attachment figures. In 9-month-olds, a 30-minute separation from the mother leads to hormonal as well as behavioral changes such as crying and fretting (Gunnar et al., 1992). Separation anxiety emerges at about the same time in children of different cultures (Figure 14.2), despite widely different child-rearing practices (Kagan, 1976). Similarly, blind children show a comparable pattern (although the onset is a few months later), becoming anxious when they no longer hear the familiar sounds of their mother's voice or movements (Adelson & Fraiberg, 1974; Fraiberg, 1975). These data suggest a maturational basis for separation anxiety. In fact, separation anxiety emerges about the same time infants begin to crawl, which makes sense from an evolutionary perspective. As one anthropologist noted, "When a child knows it *can* [physically] get away, then it is afraid it *could* get away" (Konner, in Greenberg, 1977, p. 75).

INTERIM SUMMARY   **Social development** involves changes in interpersonal thought, feeling, and behavior throughout the lifespan. **Attachment** refers to the enduring ties that children form with their primary caregivers; it includes a desire for proximity to an attachment figure, a sense of security derived from the person's presence, and feelings of distress when the person is absent. John Bowlby, who developed attachment theory, argued that attachment, like **imprinting** (the tendency of young animals to follow another animal to which they were exposed during a sensitive period), evolved as a mechanism for keeping infants close to their parents while they are immature and vulnerable.

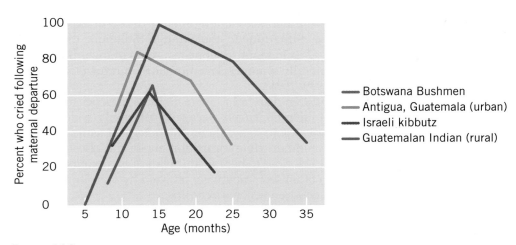

FIGURE 14.2
Separation anxiety (as measured by the percentage of children who cry when separated from their mother) tends to peak at approximately the same time across various cultures. *Source:* Kagan, 1983, p. 198.

Basic attachment mechanisms appear very similar in human and other primates, such as rhesus macaque.

INDIVIDUAL DIFFERENCES IN ATTACHMENT PATTERNS

Bowlby observed that young children typically exhibit a sequence of behaviors in response to separations from their attachment figures. Like 2½-year-old Kate, they initially *protest* by crying or throwing tantrums. Unlike Kate, they may ultimately become *detached* and indifferent to the attachment figure if she is gone too long.

Attachment Patterns

Bowlby's colleague Mary Ainsworth recognized that children vary in their responses to separation: While some seem secure in their relationship with their attachment figure, others seem perpetually stuck in protest or detachment. Ainsworth demonstrated these differences among infants using an experimental procedure called the **Strange Situation**. In the Strange Situation, the mother leaves her young child (aged 12 to 18 months) alone in a room of toys. The child is joined for a brief time by a friendly stranger. The mother then returns and greets the child (Ainsworth, 1973, 1979, 1991).

Ainsworth found that children respond to their mothers' absence and return in three basic ways. Some infants (called **securely attached**) welcome the mother's return and seek closeness to her. Others, characterized as *insecurely attached*, either ignore her (an **avoidant** style) or exhibit anger and rejection while also indicating a clear desire to be close to her (an **ambivalent** or **anxious-ambivalent** style). Avoidant children often seem relatively unfazed by their mother's departure, whereas ambivalent children become very upset.

More recent research with infants in high-risk samples, such as those who have been maltreated, has uncovered a fourth style of attachment, a variant of insecure attachment called **disorganized** (Lyons-Ruth et al., 1997; Main & Solomon, 1986). Disorganized children behave in contradictory ways, such as approaching the mother while simultaneously gazing away. They also appear disoriented, a response manifested in stereotyped rocking and dazed facial expressions. Whereas the other attachment patterns seem organized and predictable, the disorganized child's behavior is difficult to understand, and typically comes in the context of parenting that is itself unpredictable and difficult to understand from the infant's point of view.

Secure attachment is the most commonly observed attachment pattern around the world (see Main, 1990; van IJzendoorn & Kroonenberg, 1988). Nevertheless, the frequency of different styles of attachment differs substantially across cultures. For example, infants reared on Israeli kibbutzim (collective living arrangements) are much more likely to have ambivalent attachments to their mothers than infants in the West (Sagi, 1990; Sagi et al., 1994). Interestingly, the quality of an infant's attachment to its daytime mother surrogate on the kibbutz, not to its parents, predicts later social adjustment in childhood, unlike in Europe and North America.

Internal Working Models of Relationships

Attachment does not just refer to a pattern of behavior. Bowlby proposed that infants develop **internal working models,** or mental representations of attachment relationships, which form the basis for expectations in close relationships (Bowlby, 1969, 1982; Bretherton, 1990; Main, 1995; Main et al., 1985). For example, a child whose early attachment to her mother is marked by extreme anxiety resulting from inconsistent or abusive caretaking may form a working model of herself as unlovable or unworthy. She may also see significant others as hostile or unpredictable. Her behavior will appear disorganized or disoriented because she cannot form a coherent working model or representation of her relationship with her mother that both makes sense and provides a feeling of security.

The concept of internal working models may help explain why infants and toddlers who are secure with one caretaker may not be secure with another (Howes & Hamilton, 1992). A child's experience with one person, such as the mother, may feel secure, while another relationship (such as with a father or preschool teacher) may feel less comfortable or predictable because the child has different internal working models of the relationships. This concept may also help explain why attachment classification in infancy predicts not only social but cognitive variables years later, such as ability to sustain attention. Attachment in infancy should lay the groundwork for later social experience. Attachment also provides a secure base for exploration; infants who feel safe and secure will have more freedom to explore their environment than insecure infants, whose time and attention are more likely to be consumed by attachment-related thoughts, feelings, and motivations.

FROM MIND TO BRAIN

TEMPERAMENT AND EXPERIENCE IN ATTACHMENT STYLE

Why do infants differ in their patterns of attachment? Some researchers emphasize temperament; others emphasize the way caregivers respond to the infant. Both appear to influence attachment security, along with an important interaction between the two: the fit between the child and parent (Belsky & Isabella, 1988; Goldsmith & Harman, 1994; Rosen & Rothbaum, 1993).

Biological Contributions

Like all psychological processes, attachment can be understood in part at a psychobiological level. Attachment-related behavior such as protest at separation probably does not occur in the first six months of life because myelination of neurons has not sufficiently progressed in limbic structures that regulate emotional distress, particularly fear and anxiety (Konner, 1991). Protest, distress, and despair at separation after that time appear mediated by several neurotransmitter systems, notably dopamine, norepinephrine, and serotonin, which are involved in arousal, anxiety, and depression (Kraemer, 1992). For example, monkeys separated from their mothers show elevated norepinephrine levels, which is consistent with behavioral responses indicating distress. (Attachment is a two-way affair: Rhesus monkey *mothers* separated from their newborn infants similarly show elevated stress hormones for days; Champoux & Suomi, 1994.)

These normal neurotransmitter responses to separation can be altered in monkeys either pharmacologically, using chemicals that disrupt neural transmission, or through abnormal rearing, in which the infant is removed from the mother at birth and reared in isolation or with peers. Abnormal rearing conditions alter neuronal development in the cortex, cerebellum, and limbic system in monkeys, suggesting that even environmental events can produce lasting biological changes in the systems that mediate attachment behavior. These monkeys are particularly vulnerable to despair responses upon later separations.

The relation between attachment style and temperament is a matter of controversy. In humans, researchers have identified three infant temperaments—easy, difficult, and slow-to-warm-up—which correspond in certain respects to secure, ambivalent, and avoidant attachment styles (Chess & Thomas, 1986). Some researchers have, therefore, argued that attachment security largely reflects temperament (see Kagan, 1984; Manglesdorf et al., 1990). An inborn tendency to be timid or fearful, for example, could produce anxious behavior in the Strange Situation (Goldsmith & Alansky, 1987). The temperamental variable most highly predictive of attachment status across several studies is negative emotion. The correlation, however, is only .30 (Vaughn et al., 1992), which suggests that temperament is only one determinant of attachment style.

Caregiver Responsiveness

The variable that appears to have the biggest impact on security of attachment is environmental: the mother's sensitivity to her baby's signals (Ainsworth, 1979; Bowlby, 1969; Sroufe & Fleeson, 1986; Sroufe & Waters, 1977). Mothers who are sensitive to their infants tend to enjoy interacting with their babies, to provide warmth and nurturance, and to stimulate and encourage them (De Wolff & van IJzendoorn, 1997); their interactions with their babies tend to be mutually rewarding. When mothers are sensitive and attuned to their children's communications, are psychologically accessible, and convey a sense of acceptance and enjoyment, infants are more likely to feel secure. In contrast, infants whose mothers do not respond to their needs form less secure attachment bonds and display more anger, fear, and avoidance (Bretherton, 1985; Erickson et al., 1985; De Wolff & van IJzendoorn, 1997; Pederson et al., 1990; Ricks, 1985). The role of the father in attachment is an area of continued debate (see van IJzendoorn & De Wolff, 1997), although paternal sensitivity is an important predictor of the parent–child relationship as well.

Personality characteristics, such as warmth and empathy, can heavily influence parental sensitivity, but so can cultural factors (Richman et al., 1992). Mothers of 10-month-olds in the United States tend to talk to and look at their infants, particularly when the infants vocalize, look at them, or cry. In contrast, among the Gusii of East Africa, mothers generally avert their gaze when they hold their infants. Differences exist not only between but within cultures. Within a society, more educated mothers tend to be more responsive to their infants.

Nature-Nurture Interaction

Although both biology and experience affect individual differences in attachment, the interaction of the two—such as the match between children and their caregivers—is equally important. For example, infants who are temperamentally prone to distress may be more likely to become insecurely attached if their caretakers are rigid and emotionally controlled (Mangelsdorf et al., 1990). Similarly, infants with an easy temperament may be more likely to become securely attached despite an unresponsive caregiver than infants with a more difficult temperament.

IMPLICATIONS OF ATTACHMENT FOR LATER DEVELOPMENT

Attachment patterns that begin in infancy can persist and find expression in a wide range of social behaviors throughout the lifespan. Children rated as disorganized, particularly those who are also below average intellectually, are disproportionately represented among 7-year-olds rated by their teachers as impulsive, disruptive, and aggressive (Lyons-Ruth et al., 1997). Children rated avoidant in infancy tend to be described by their teachers as relatively insecure and detached in nursery school and to have difficulty discussing their feelings about separation at age 6. In contrast, securely attached preschoolers studied in longitudinal research have higher self-esteem, are more socially competent, show greater sensitivity to the needs of their peers, and are more popular (LaFreniere & Sroufe, 1985; Main et al., 1985; Waters et al., 1979).

Security of attachment in infancy also predicts a range of behaviors in the elementary-school years, from self-control and peer acceptance to competent behavior in the classroom (Bretherton, 1990; Howes et al., 1998; Olson et al., 1989). Security of attachment measured at age 7 in turn predicts social and intellectual variables such as insecurity and school grades in adolescence (Jacobsen & Hofmann, 1997).

The theory of internal working models helps make sense of why attachment security with parents would predict the quality of peer relationships years later (Cassidy et al., 1996). Children who are secure with their parents have more positive expectations about what they can expect from relationships. This leads them to be more trusting and engaging with peers, who are then more likely to respond to them positively. As a result, they then form more positive representations of peer relationships—creating a self-reinforcing cycle, in which positive initial working models foster good relationships, which maintain those models.

INTERIM SUMMARY   Researchers have discovered four patterns of infant attachment: **secure, insecure-avoidant, insecure-ambivalent,** and **disorganized.** Whereas secure infants are readily comforted by their attachment figures, insecure infants tend to shut off their needs for attachment (avoidant) or have difficulty being soothed (ambivalent). Disorganized infants behave in contradictory ways and appear to have difficulty predicting or understanding the way their attachment figures will behave. Infant attachment patterns reflect a combination of temperament, parental responsiveness, and the interaction of the two. Attachment security in infancy predicts social competence as well as school grades from preschool through adolescence.

Adult Attachment

Some of the infants assessed in longitudinal Strange Situation research studies are just reaching adulthood, and evidence suggests that early attachment patterns remain influential in adult life. Researchers studying **adult attachment** have examined the way individuals describe and recall their relationships with their parents (Main, 1995; Main et al., 1985) or the way they report interacting with attachment figures in adulthood such as spouses (Brennan et al., 1998).

Patterns of Adult Attachment   Adults with secure adult attachment styles speak freely and openly about their relationships with their parents. People with ambivalent styles appear preoccupied with, and ambivalent about, their parents. Avoidant adults dismiss the importance of attachment relationships or offer idealized generalizations about their parents but are unable to back them up with specific examples. Individuals with an **unresolved/disorganized** style have difficulty speaking coherently about attachment figures from their past and appear to have been unable to cope with painful and traumatic experiences from their past. As a result, their narratives are often confused and confusing, and they send conflicting signals to their own children, particularly when their own unmet attachment needs get activated under stress.

How common are these attachment patterns? Data from multiple sources find similar rates of each type of attachment pattern in adults as in infants. A large stratified random sample of over 8000 individuals in the United States using a self-report measure of the first three adult attachment patterns found that roughly 60 percent of people reported a secure attachment pattern, whereas 25 percent were classified as avoidant and about 10 percent anxiously attached (Mickelson et al., 1997). Interview studies across several cultures have similarly classified roughly 60 percent of people as securely attached in relation to their own parents, with varying numbers placed in the other three categories (van IJzendoorn & Bakermans-Kranenburg, 1996).

Predicting Behavior from Adult Attachment Patterns   Attachment patterns in adults predict a range of phenomena, from whether people want to have children (Rholes et al., 1997) to how they cope with stressful life events (Mikulincer & Florian, in press). Perhaps most importantly, adults' attachment patterns in relation to their own parents, as assessed by interview, predict their own children's attachment styles with remarkable accuracy (Main, 1995; Steele et al., 1996; van IJzendoorn, 1995). For example, mothers who are uncomfortable or avoidant in describing their own attachment to their mothers tend to have avoidant infants and children (Fonagy et al., 1991; Main et al., 1985). Considerable evidence suggests that mothers whose early attachment experiences were disrupted—through death of a parent, divorce, abuse or neglect, or long-term separation from their parents—are more likely to have difficulty forming close attachment relationships with their own infants and to have infants with a disorganized attachment pattern (Lyons-Ruth et al., 1997; Ricks, 1985; Rutter et al., 1983; Zeanah & Zeanah, 1989). Mothers who have insecure attachment relationships with their own mothers are less responsive and have more difficulty maintaining physical proximity to their infants and young children (Crowell & Feldman, 1991). Other studies find a continuity between relationship patterns of college students and the security of their attachment to their parents (Kobak & Sceery, 1988).

Attachment patterns also predict physiological responses. Avoidant adults, like avoidant infants, apparently shut off attachment feelings to avoid distress. Physiological evidence of this *deactivating* process comes from a study that monitored electrodermal response (a measure of anxiety or conflict) as subjects recalled memories involving separation, rejection, and threat from their parents (Dozier & Kobak, 1992). As can be seen in Table 14.1, more secure subjects are slightly less reactive. The picture is quite different with avoidance: The more avoidance, the more physiological reactivity. This is particularly striking given that avoidance was measured by, among other things, subjects' claims during these interviews that they were not at all distressed by separations, rejections, or parental threats.

Stability of Early Attachment Patterns

Is history destiny? Can a person ever overcome a bad start in childhood or infancy? Research certainly suggests that problematic early attachments substantially increase vulnerability to subsequent difficulties. Disturbances in childhood attachment relationships predict later difficulties in childhood and adolescence (Bowlby, 1969; Ricks, 1985; Spitz, 1945). Disrupted attachments are associated with severe personality disturbances (Ludolph et al., 1990; Zanarini et al., 1989), depression (Brown et al., 1986), antisocial behavior and adjustment problems (Tizard & Hodges, 1978), and difficulty behaving appropriately as a parent (Ricks,

---

TABLE 14.1 CORRELATIONS BETWEEN PHYSIOLOGICAL REACTIVITY AND ATTACHMENT

INTERVIEW QUESTIONS	SECURITY OF ATTACHMENT	TENDENCY TO USE AVOIDANT (DEACTIVATING) STRATEGIES
1. Background information	.11	−.07
2. Memories of separation from parents	−.27	.43
3. Memories of parental rejection	−.18	.34
4. Memories of parental threat	−.28	.39

Note that avoidant subjects were only physiologically reactive during threatening questions—precisely the questions they claimed to find nonthreatening.

Source: Dozier & Koback, 1992.

Note: The table shows the correlations between physiological reactivity (assessed by increases in electrodermal activity) and two dimensions of attachment (security and use of avoidant strategies).

1985). Negative childhood interpersonal experiences such as divorce of parents and parental neglect or mistreatment make people more vulnerable to insecure attachment in adulthood (Mickelson et al., 1997).

Nevertheless, early attachment style is not the only determinant of later functioning. Some children are remarkably resilient in the face of neglectful or abusive life experiences (Anthony & Cohler, 1987). Furthermore, as circumstances change, so may patterns of attachment. Internal working models, like the schemas described in previous chapters, are inherently conservative, but they are not immutable (see Belsky & Nezworski, 1987; Lamb, 1987). Many forms of psychotherapy are predicated on the notion that exploring experiences and feelings in a therapeutic relationship can help people change basic patterns of relatedness (Chapter 16). Indeed, some of Harlow's monkeys who had been raised in isolation and were extremely socially maladapted showed marked improvement in social interactions after developing a close relationship with a normal monkey who served as a simian "therapist" (Chamove, 1978; Novak & Harlow, 1975).

One study provides dramatic evidence of the possibilities for altering problematic patterns of attachment. The investigators provided a group of high-risk infants and mothers with a weekly home visitor. The mothers were poor, often depressed, and exhibited enough signs of inadequate caretaking to warrant referrals from health, educational, or social service professionals (Lyons-Ruth et al., 1990). The home visitor offered support and advice, modeled positive and active interactions with the infant, and provided a trusting relationship for the mother. The results were compelling: Compared to an untreated control group, infants in the intervention group scored 10 points higher on an infant IQ measure and were twice as likely (roughly 60 versus 30 percent) to be classified as securely attached at 18 months.

The Impact of Day Care on Children's Welfare

If early attachment experiences shape later emotional health, does a working mother's daily routine of leaving her child with surrogate caregivers adversely affect the child's emotional and cognitive development? In the United States, the number of employed women with children under age 6 has doubled over the last two decades and tripled over the last three. Roughly two-thirds of mothers with infants and toddlers are now employed outside the home (see Silverstein, 1991).

Some people, like poet Maya Angelou, are resilient in the face of even highly traumatic childhood experiences.

We have essentially embarked on a massive social experiment, whose impact is a matter of considerable debate (see Scarr, 1997, 1998).

Findings across studies are inconsistent. One large-scale study found an association between maternal employment in the first year of life and relatively poor intellectual functioning and greater behavioral problems in preschool (ages 3 to 4). This was true across race, gender, and social class. Delaying maternal employment until even the fourth quarter of the first year, and involving a grandmother in childcare, proved to be highly advantageous, particularly for poor children (Baydar & Brooks-Gunn, 1991). Another study found a correlation between length of maternity leave in the first few months and positive mother–child interactions; in other words, mothers who took off more time had better relationships with their infants (Clark et al., 1997).

Whereas some studies find a negative impact of day care on a range of variables such as social competence and security of attachment (e.g., Belsky & Rovine, 1988; Goldberg et al., 1996), others find just the opposite (e.g., Field, 1991; Scarr & Eisenberg, 1993). Outside the United States, day care is often associated with positive outcomes. For example, a Swedish study found that children in day care had higher math and verbal test scores than children reared at home or in other family settings at age 8, and that the longer they were in day care, the better the outcome (Broberg et al., 1997).

Researchers are beginning to tease apart the factors that determine whether day care leads to positive or negative outcomes. One of the most important factors is socioeconomic status. For children of poor families, day care is generally associated with more positive cognitive, social, and emotional outcomes than maternal care at home. Equally important at all socioeconomic levels are parents' attitudes about parenthood, the amount of time they spend with their children, and the quality of that time (Campos et al., 1983; Easterbrooks & Goldberg, 1985). Women who stay at home to care for their infants when they really want to be working outside the home may not be doing their children any favors (Farel, 1980). These mothers report higher levels of depression than mothers whose lifestyles more closely match their preferences (Hock & DeMeis, 1990). Depression, in turn, is related to poorer child outcomes. Another variable is attachment status: At least among relatively poor children, day care appears to be beneficial for insecurely attached children but detrimental to those who are securely attached (Egeland & Hiester, 1995).

Quality of day care—nutritious meals, carefully designed curricula, low staff turnover, and so forth—is also important (Scarr & Eisenberg, 1993). This is particularly true for infants whose mothers are relatively insensitive to their needs or feelings (NICHD Early Child Care Research Network, 1997). Early entry into low-quality day care is particularly detrimental to children's later adaptation in kindergarten (Bates et al., 1994; Howes, 1990), whereas early entry into high-quality day care may confer advantages that last many years (Andersson, 1992; Howes et al., 1992; McCartney et al., 1982). Unfortunately, the children most likely to benefit from quality day care—poor children—are most likely to get low-quality care. Thus far, the moral of the story appears to be that for middle class children, decent day care is unlikely to have much of an impact either way on child welfare, whereas for poor children, it can be beneficial (see Scarr, 1997).

INTERIM SUMMARY   Researchers studying **adult attachment** examine the way individuals describe and recall their relationships with their parents or the way they report interacting with attachment figures in adulthood. Roughly 60 percent of people appear to have a secure attachment style. Parents tend to produce children with an attachment style similar to their own. Attachment patterns have considerable stability because internal working models tend to change slowly, but as life circumstances change, so can attachment styles. The effects of day care on attachment, social competence, and cognitive performance are highly variable.

SOCIALIZATION

Attachment relationships provide the child's first social experiences and serve as a model for many future relationships, but they are only one avenue for initiating the child into the social world. To function as adults, children must learn the rules, beliefs, values, skills, attitudes, and behavior patterns of their society, a process called **socialization**. Children learn from a variety of **socialization agents** (individuals and groups that transmit social knowledge and values to the child).

Before describing research on socialization, several caveats are in order. First, socialization is not a unidirectional process in which adults fill children's minds with values and beliefs. Rather, it is interactive, or *transactional*. Children are active participants in their own socialization who must construct an understanding of social rules and gradually come to experience cultural beliefs and values as their own (Bell, 1968; Kochanska, 1997; Maccoby, 1992; Sapir, 1949). Children also have innate temperamental dispositions that influence attempts to shape them. Inherited tendencies tend to increase in their expression throughout adolescence, so that the quality of parent–child relationships continues to be shaped, not just by infant temperament but by genetic dispositions for many years afterward (Elkins et al., 1997). Further, the way children behave shapes the way their parents respond; parents can create impulsive, poorly controlled adolescents through poor parenting, but children who are impulsive and poorly controlled in turn elicit less effective parenting (Stice & Barrera, 1995).

Second, although our focus is on socialization during childhood, socialization is a lifelong process. People are socialized throughout their lives to play different roles, such as student, parent, friend, wage-earner, or retiree, and these roles change from one phase of life to the next.

Third, although we tend to think of socialization as a process through which parents and other adults "leave their mark" on children, from an evolutionary perspective, children are *biologically prepared* to be socialized (Bugental & Goodnow, 1998). From early in life, children pay special attention to the words directed at them. They come prepared to experience emotions such as shame and guilt that render them readily shaped by parents into the kinds of people who will one day be accepted in their society.

A fourth caveat is that socialization always occurs within a broader social and economic context (Bronfenbrenner, 1998; Elder, 1998; McLoyd, 1989; Parke & Buriel, 1998). Cultural beliefs and economic conditions have a substantial impact on the way parents respond to their children (Harkness & Super, 1996; Harwood et al., 1996). Adults who are economically stressed, for example, are less likely to parent effectively than financially secure parents (Conger et al., 1993). Similarly, low-income African-American mothers who parent children without the help of the child's father are more likely to use controlling, harsh, and less child-centered disciplinary techniques than their counterparts in intact families (Kelley et al., 1992). Further, some of the most important socialization experiences occur within the family, and the state of a marriage—the extent to which the parents are satisfied with the marriage and loving toward each other—has a considerable impact on the parenting children receive (e.g., Fincham, 1998).

Finally, socialization is not *one* process; in fact, it involves the dovetailing of many cognitive, affective, and motivational processes in both the child and socialization agents (Bugental & Goodnow, 1998). For example, for parents' moral lessons to "stick," children must attend to them, understand them, and learn to *feel* what their parents feel about certain values and behaviors. Parents must also be motivated to teach these lessons through words and behavior and must intuitively know how to communicate them in a way that will be heard and internalized. Socialization involves deliberate teaching, but as anthropologists have increasingly come to stress, much of socialization is implicit, as when children learn about the importance of being on time by the regular sounding of school bells between classes (see Mathews & Moore, in press; Shore, 1996; Strauss & Quinn, 1998).

THE ROLE OF PARENTS

Parents are particularly important socialization agents, and their methods vary widely. Diana Baumrind (1967, 1971, 1991) discovered three styles of parenting, distinguished by the extent to which parents control their children's actions and respond to their feelings. **Authoritarian** parents place high value on obedience and respect for authority. They do not encourage discussion of why particular behaviors are important or listen to the child's point of view. Rather, authoritarian parents impose a rigid set of standards to which they expect their children to adhere; they are likely to punish their children frequently and physically. **Permissive** parents, in contrast, impose virtually no controls on their children, allowing them to make their own decisions whenever possible. Permissive parents tend to accept their children's impulsive behaviors, including angry or aggressive ones, and rarely dole out punishments. **Authoritative** parents, the third group, set standards for their children and firmly enforce them, but they also encourage verbal give-and-take, explaining their views and showing respect for their children's opinions.

Each parenting style tends to produce children with different characteristics. Preschool studies have found that the most self-controlled, independent, inquisitive, and sociable children usually have authoritative parents. Studies of grade school children and adolescents have similarly found authoritative parenting associated with social, intellectual, and academic competence (Baumrind, 1987; Dornbush et al., 1987; Sternberg et al., 1994; Weiss & Schwarz, 1996). Authoritarian parenting, on the other hand, has been linked to low independence, vulnerability to stress, low self-esteem, and an external locus of control (a sense that one has little control over what happens in life) (Buri et al., 1988; Loeb et al., 1980; Steinberg et al., 1994). Children with permissive parents tend to be low in self-reliance and control over their aggressive impulses (Olweus, 1980; Maccoby & Martin, 1983; Yarrow et al., 1971) and to have more trouble with substance abuse in adolescence (Baumrind, 1991).

INTERIM SUMMARY   **Socialization** is the process by which children learn the rules, beliefs, values, skills, attitudes, and behavior patterns of their society. Socialization is *transactional*, lifelong, biologically prepared, and multifaceted. Socialization also always occurs in a broader social context. **Authoritarian** parents place high value on obedience and respect for authority. **Permissive** parents impose minimal controls on their children. **Authoritative** parents enforce standards but explain their views and encourage verbal give-and-take.

A Mayan mother and her children.

THE ROLE OF CULTURE

Over two decades of research on parenting styles indicate that the authoritative style most effectively produces traits valued in Anglo-European culture. However, this parenting style is rare or nonexistent in many cultures and is probably not the most adaptive pattern everywhere (Whiting & Whiting, 1973, 1975). Agricultural societies usually value obedience far more than autonomy or independence. Among the Mayan Zinacanteco Indians of Mexico, for example, an entire family shares a single-room 20-square-foot hut, and every member contributes to the family's survival by farming (Brazelton, 1972). In this culture, where people have no real choice in the roles they will fill, socialization for independence and free choice would often prove frustrating or counterproductive.

Training for independence or for embeddedness in kin or clan begins in the first days of life. Infants in most cultures sleep in the same beds, or at least the same rooms, as their mothers (Whiting, 1964). In contrast, North American pediatricians discourage parents from bringing the child into their bed, and most middle-class parents give infants their own rooms by 3 to 6 months at the latest, fostering independence from the start.

In a study comparing the sleeping patterns of Mayan and North American infants, Mayan infants tended simply to fall asleep when they were tired, whereas American families had elaborate bedtime rituals that might begin with a bath and toothbrushing and include reading bedtime stories, singing lullabies, and providing the baby with a special object (Morelli et al., 1992). One North American mother jokingly reported, "When my friends hear that it is time for my son to go to bed, they teasingly say, 'See you in an hour.'" Mayan parents were generally aghast to hear that parents could separate infants from their mothers at night and seemed to consider it tantamount to child neglect. One horrified Mayan mother asked, "But there's someone else with them there, isn't there?" The Mayan children typically slept with their mothers until another child was born, at which time they joined their fathers or siblings.

Parents implicitly convey attitudes toward collective values in what they say to young children as well. For example, when Chinese parents recount stories to their toddlers about the child's past behavior, they are more likely than European-American parents to describe times when the child did something bad and use the opportunity to convey moral and social standards. Western parents, in contrast, are more likely to use such stories to entertain their children's and boost the child's self-esteem (Miller et al., 1997).

A GLOBAL VISTA

PARENTAL ACCEPTANCE AND REJECTION IN CROSS-CULTURAL PERSPECTIVE

One of the most important ways parents vary across and within cultures is the extent to which they are accepting or rejecting of their children (Rohner, 1975, 1986). Parents can express acceptance verbally through praise, compliments, or support, or nonverbally through hugging, approving glances, smiling, and caressing. Like acceptance, rejection can be expressed verbally (bullying or harsh criticism) or nonverbally (hitting, beating, shaking, or simply neglecting). Parental acceptance and rejection were once considered polar opposites of a single dimension, and they are clearly related. However, like positive and negative affect, they can be measured independently and have somewhat independent effects; a parent who is often loving can also sometimes be harsh or even abusive (Pettit et al., 1997).

Whether a specific behavior is accepting or rejecting depends in part on shared cultural meanings. Parents in India do not praise their children openly, particularly in front of other people. Instead, a mother may express positive feelings by peeling an orange for her child and removing the seeds. A North American child who received no praise from his mother but plenty of seedless oranges would likely look on the oranges much differently than his Indian counterpart (Rohner, 1986). Even the meaning of physical discipline may vary within and between cultures (Deater-Deckard et al., 1996). In European-American samples, the more parents use harsh physical discipline, the more their children (particularly boys) are likely to be impulsive, aggressive, and poorly controlled. The same correlation does not hold for African-American children: Up to a point, the more discipline, the fewer behavior problems children tend to have. Severe parenting that is clearly abusive, however, appears to have the same meaning regardless of cultural circumstances, and predicts poorer outcomes in children.

In general, findings both within the West and across cultures show that parental acceptance is quite consistently associated with high self-esteem, independence, and emotional stability. Parental rejection, on the other hand, is associated with a wide range of problems, including delinquency, difficulty maintaining intimate relationships, poorly controlled aggression, unpredictable mood, and lower intelligence (Rohner, 1986). Studies using Western samples have clearly documented these patterns (e.g., MacKinnon-Lewis et al., 1997). One longitudinal study found that individuals who had a warm or affectionate parent or father are more likely, 35 years later, to have a long and happy marriage, children, and close friendships in middle age (Franz et al., 1991). Other studies found that abused children and adults with childhood histories of abuse are more likely than their nonabused peers to view the world as a dangerous place, have poor self-esteem, and have difficulty maintaining close relationships (see Finkelhor, 1994; Gelinas, 1983; Nigg et al., 1992).

A large cross-cultural study correlating parental acceptance–rejection

Alorese children are fed at their parents' convenience and frequently have temper tantrums when they are frustrated.

TABLE 14.2   CORRELATIONS BETWEEN PARENTAL ACCEPTANCE AND PERSONALITY CHARACTERISTICS

PERSONALITY CHARACTERISTIC	CORRELATION WITH DEGREE OF ACCEPTANCE IN PARENTING	
	CHILDREN	ADULTS
Hostility	−.48	−.31
Dependence	−.30	−.39
Self-esteem	.72	.38
Emotional stability	—	.62
Generosity	—	.41
Nurturance	—	.39

The more accepting the parents in a culture are, the less dependent and higher in self-esteem their children tend to be.

Source: Adapted from Rohner, 1975, p. 260.
Note: Dashes indicate missing data.

with personality traits in children and adults demonstrated that these patterns are indeed universal (Rohner, 1975): Cultures in which parents were more rejecting (as rated from anthropological reports) produced children who were more hostile and dependent, and adults who were less emotionally stable, than cultures with more benign parenting practices (Table 14.2).

The Alorese, who inhabit a Pacific island off Java, exemplify a culture with highly rejecting parenting practices (see DuBois, 1944; Rohner, 1975). Alorese women return to the fields within two weeks of childbirth—if they have not had an abortion, which is common because they tend to find children intensely burdensome. After a brief initial period of benign and playful caretaking, Alorese infants receive very inconsistent care, such as sporadic feeding. Alorese children are constantly teased, ridiculed, and frightened for sport by older children and adults. Mothers may tease young children they are weaning by nursing the neighbor's baby. Parents threaten children with abandonment and send them to live with relatives if they are too difficult. As young children, the Alorese are left for the day without food unless they can get some by begging or screaming at their elders.

Generalizations about an entire people are, of course, always overgeneralizations, because individual differences exist in all cultures. Nevertheless, anthropologists describe Alorese adults as hostile, aggressive, and distrustful, characteristics that make sense in the context of Alorese child-rearing. The Alorese are intensely sensitive to insults and humiliation, and adult relationships are fraught with discord. Males strive to amass as much wealth as they can, always expecting others to cheat and deceive them. Marital affairs are common in both sexes, divorce is rampant, and men often beat their wives in jealousy or anger. Direct aggression between males is strongly discouraged, although women at times may openly brawl. Even the supernatural world of the Alorese is hostile and unstable, with the Good Beings under constant attack in their myths. In Alor, as elsewhere, patterns of child-rearing reflect cultural beliefs and values, and parents tend to harvest what they sow.

SOCIALIZATION OF GENDER

Among the most powerful roles into which people are socialized are **gender roles**, which specify the range of behaviors considered appropriate for males and females (see Ruble & Miller, 1998). Unlike sex (a biological categorization based on genetic and anatomical differences), **gender** (the psychological meaning of being male or female) is influenced by learning. When a new baby is born, people greet its arrival with one of two announcements: "It's a girl!" or "It's a boy!" This response rests on a relatively small anatomical feature, but it has important consequences for the way the person will come to think, feel, and behave (Archer & Lloyd, 1985). The process by which children acquire personality traits, emotional responses, skills, behaviors, and preferences that are culturally considered appropriate to their sex is called **sex typing** (Perry & Bussey, 1979).

Differential treatment of boys and girls begins at the very beginning. In one study, first-time mothers of young infants were asked to play with a 6-month-old baby (not their own) for 10 minutes (Smith & Lloyd, 1978). Several toys were available. Some, like a squeaky hammer and a stuffed rabbit wearing a bow-tie and trousers, were typical masculine toys; others, like a doll and a squeaky Bambi, were more feminine. The mothers did not know the babies were cross-dressed—that the 6-month-old in the little boy's outfit was actually a little girl, and that the baby in the pink dress, was a boy. The mothers tended to offer the infants "gender-appropriate" toys and to encourage more physical activity in the "boy."

Similar findings emerge from studies of socialization in slightly older children. In experimental settings, adults tend to compliment and encourage girls more, particularly in nurturance play, such as taking care of dolls. They hold higher expectations for boys and provide them with more goal-directed reinforcements (Day, cited in Block, 1979). Naturalistic investigations of parents' behavior with their own children indicate that sons and daughters receive different treatment, especially after the first year of life, as children's activities become more sex-typed (O'Brien & Huston, 1983). Throughout early childhood, parents (especially fathers) tend to encourage traditional sex-typed behavior, discouraging play with toys that are typical of the opposite gender (Langlois & Downs, 1980). Boys in Europe and North America receive more encouragement to compete, more punishment, and more pressure not to cry or express feelings; girls receive more warmth, affection, and trust, although they are kept under closer surveillance (presumably for their protection) than boys (Block, 1978). Mothers tend to talk more, and speak in more supportive ways, with their daughters than their sons (Leaper et al., 1998). Peers, too, enforce gender roles and become distressed and often ridiculing when others violate them (Fagot & Patterson, 1969; Lamb & Roopnarine, 1979).

INTERIM SUMMARY   Cultural practices affect virtually every aspect of socialization, such as the relative importance placed on independence and autonomy. Parental acceptance and rejection also differ substantially across cultures. Rejection and abuse appear to have similar negative effects on children everywhere, although whether a specific behavior (such as a type of punishment) is experienced as accepting or rejecting depends in part on shared cultural meanings. Among the most powerful roles into which people are socialized are **gender roles**, which specify the range of behaviors considered appropriate for males and females.

PEER RELATIONSHIPS

We have focused thus far primarily on children's relationships with their parents and other adults. These relationships are *vertical*, characterized by a substantial power differential (Hartup, 1986). In contrast, children's relationships with peers are more likely to be *horizontal*, or relatively equal. Pure equality, of course, probably exists in few relationships; in children's friendships, one partner may be more submissive or eager to please, just as partners in a marriage differ in their power over one another. Although horizontal authority relationships persist throughout life—as people interact with bosses, institutional officials, or police officers—much of adult life is spent with peers. Childhood peer relations are a training ground for adult peer relationships, just as early attachment relationships establish the initial prototypes for adult attachments. The two major kinds of peer relationships in childhood are with friends and siblings.

FRIENDSHIPS

Researchers have extensively studied the development of children's friendships. They have also focused on children who are rejected or neglected by their peers.

The Development of Friendship

Children's friendships are almost exclusively same-sex friendships; children simply like same-sex peers better (Bukowski et al., 1994). Cross-sex relationships account for only about 5 percent of friends in childhood (Hartup, 1989); in one large study, only .3 percent of children had a best friend of the opposite sex (Kovacs et al., 1996)!

Friendships begin to emerge around the third year of life and are marked by the same kind of commitment, reciprocity (sharing and mutuality), and relative equality that characterize friendships throughout the lifespan (see Hartup, 1989). Even preschool friendships have some stability. Young children tend to maintain their friendships unless one member of the pair moves away (see Collins & Gunnar, 1990).

The meaning of friendship, however, changes throughout childhood (Damon, 1977; Selman, 1980). Young children focus on the gratification they expect from relationships, describing friends as people who give them things or let them play with their toys. By middle childhood, children recognize the longer-term payoffs of specific friendships. When asked why one girl was her friend, an 8-year-old responded, "Because she helps when I'm getting beat up, she cheers me up when I'm sad, and she shares.... I share so she'll share" (Damon, 1977, pp. 159–160). Adolescents are more concerned than children with *intimacy* in friendships, that is, mutual self-disclosure and feeling understood (Buhrmester, 1990). Girls tend to self-disclose more than boys; when boys self-disclose, they generally do so with girls (Youniss & Haynie, 1992).

The role of friends, siblings, and parents changes over the course of social development. Between the fifth and twelfth grades (roughly ages 10 to 18), the amount of time North American children spend with their families drops by more than half, from 35 to 14 percent (Larson et al., 1996). By mid-adolescence (roughly ages 14 to 16) peer conformity is at its peak, but it diminishes by late adolescence (ages 17 to 22) (Youniss & Haynie, 1992). The experience of relationships as sources of conflict and support also changes during this period (Blos, 1967; Sullivan, 1953). One large cross-sectional study asked children, adolescents, and college students to rate the degree of support and conflict they experienced in several relationships (Furman & Buhrmester, 1992). Mothers and fathers are the primary sources of support for fourth graders, but this wanes during the adolescent years, when conflict with parents is at a peak. Friends loom much larger as sources of support in seventh grade but are gradually replaced by romantic partners by college age. Romantic relationships, like relationships with parents, are emotionally intense. They are experienced as most supportive at the same time as they are most conflictual, suggesting that they represent a battleground for both love and hate, as psychodynamic theory asserts.

The way children experience their parents, siblings, and peers at different times in their lives varies from culture to culture. In less individualistic, more collectivistic cultures, such as Costa Rica, elementary school children report higher satisfaction across the board with their families (and with their teachers, who do not change from year to year as they do in the United States). The shift toward greater satisfaction and intimacy with friends occurs later, if at all, in Costa Rica, perhaps because the task of becoming separate and autonomous from one's family is not central, as in the United States and much of the West (DeRosier & Kupersmidt, 1991).

Peer Status

Most primates are hierarchical animals, and humans are no exception. From preschool onward, children begin to assume different positions in status hierarchies. Most readers could probably remember and pinpoint their peers' relative positions in status hierarchies in high school with remarkable accuracy. In fact, researchers rely on peer reports of "who is in" and "who is out" to study peer status in children. From an evolutionary perspective, the fact that people can locate themselves and others on various status hierarchies from the time they are very young—and remember these rankings for years—reflects the importance of status in primate societies. A person who could not "read" social hierarchies would not know who might be a useful ally, a dangerous person with whom to pick a fight, or a potential mate. Peer relationships provide fertile ground for the development of what may well be an innate tendency to attend to status.

Children differ substantially in the way they form relationships and are accepted by their peers (Rubin et al., 1998). Children who are disliked by their peers, called **rejected children**, are often teased and ostracized. Others are bullies. **Neglected children**, on the other hand, are ignored. Researchers study peer acceptance using peer nomination methods: They ask students in a class, for example, to write down the names of children they really like and dislike. Rejected children are those whose names frequently show up on the "disliked" list; neglected children receive no mention at all. Most research to date has focused on rejected boys.

Children develop reputations among their peers by the time they are in preschool, and these reputations affect the way other children behave toward them (Denham & Holt, 1993). Not all children who develop early negative reputations maintain this status throughout the rest of their school careers, but boys who are aggressive and impulsive by kindergarten and first grade have a much harder time "growing out of" their rejected status than other rejected boys (Cillessen et al., 1992). Being actively disliked by peers tends to be associated with low self-esteem and difficulties later in life, such as higher incidence of school dropout and delinquency in adolescence and more troubles at work and in relationships in adulthood (Dunn & McGuire, 1992; Parker & Asher, 1987; Richards et al., 1998).

However, matters are actually not quite so simple. Neglected children often perform better academically than more popular peers, as they sink themselves into their school work; rejected children tend to do poorly in school but only if they are also aggressive (Wentzel & Asher, 1995).

Quality of Friendship

Children's friendships differ not only in the quantity—in how many friends a child has and how readily other children "take" to him—but in their quality (Hartup, 1996; Hartup & Stevens, 1997). Whereas having friends is typically a good thing, research supports the commonsense notion that having the wrong kinds of friends—alienated, angry, and delinquent—can be detrimental to development, particularly for children who are vulnerable by virtue of their temperament, attachment history, or own aggressive or delinquent tendencies (Vitaro et al., 1997).

Beyond the *type* of company they keep, another important dimension of children's friendship is the way they interact with one another (Bukowsky et al., 1997; Hartup, 1996). Some children tend to have relatively negative, hostile, contentious interactions with their friends. Others have much more positive, supportive interactions. As in the study of emotion, these aspects of children's friendships are surprisingly independent: As in adult relationships, people can have passionate friendships that are high on both positive and negative affect.

SIBLING RELATIONSHIPS

Until the 1980s, relationships with siblings received almost no attention from researchers. This is rather remarkable as many children spend as much time with siblings as with parents. Sibling relationships involve rivalry and conflict as well as warmth and companionship (Collins & Gunnar, 1992).

From an evolutionary perspective, one would expect both conflict and love between siblings. On the one hand, siblings are genetically related by half, so the welfare of each influences the inclusive fitness of the other. Thus, natural selection should have selected mechanisms encouraging humans and other animals to care for their siblings. On the other hand, particularly in childhood, siblings compete for precious parental resources, which can mean the difference between life and death when conditions are scarce (see Trivers, 1972). As they mature, they may compete for familial resources that attract mates; squabbling over an estate is, in fact, a major source of conflict among adult siblings. This appears to be true cross-culturally. For example, among the Gabbra of Kenya, a nomadic people, the number of camels in a household predicts reproductive success for males but not females (Mace, 1996). Not surprisingly, sibling competition for resources is much higher in Gabbra society among males.

The birth of a sibling can be a difficult event. Parents report a wide range of behavioral disturbances in their children when a new child is born, such as increased dependency, anxiety, bedwetting, toilet "accidents," and aggressiveness (Dunn & McGuire, 1992). The younger the child's age at the birth, the more difficulty the child has with being displaced (Kramer & Gottman, 1992). Not knowing whether to express hostility or nurturance, the young child may alternate between the two. Parents commonly report the heartwarming experience of watching their child happily sidle up to the crib to play with the baby—only to find their hearts beating faster and less warmly as their ambivalent offspring tries to tip the crib.

Love, hate, care and rivalry are all part of the sibling experience.

Closeness is as integral a part of the sibling relationship as conflict and rivalry. Childhood experiences as playmates, confidants, nurturers, or objects of nurturance plant the seeds for adult sibling relationships that may be warm and intimate. The majority of Western adults report being close to their siblings, with pairs of sisters the closest and pairs of brothers the least close (Cicirelli, 1991). Only 20 percent report apathy or hostility toward their adult siblings.

INTERIM SUMMARY   Friendship patterns develop substantially in childhood and adolescence, from largely same-sex experiences involving mutual play and gratification to more intimate interactions in adolescence. **Rejected children** are teased, ostracized, or disliked by their peers. **Neglected children** are ignored. Children develop reputations among their peers by preschool. Children also differ in both the company they keep and in the extent to which their friendships are characterized by positive and negative interactions. Sibling relationships involve rivalry and conflict as well as warmth, both of which make sense from an evolutionary standpoint.

DEVELOPMENT OF SOCIAL COGNITION

The changing nature of children's friendships results in part from children's emotional and motivational development, such as an increasing concern with intimacy and an expanding capacity to commit to relationships despite momentary ups and downs. Children's friendships also change as their understanding of themselves, others, and relationships—that is, their **social cognition**–develops.

THE EVOLVING SELF-CONCEPT

One of the initial tasks of social-cognitive development is acquiring a sense of self as a distinct entity with its own physical qualities and psychological processes (Stern, 1985). As adults, we tend to assume that we have always had a **self-concept**, an organized view of ourselves or way of representing information about the self. However, children are not born knowing that other people have thoughts and feelings or that their own experience is not the center of the universe.

Self-Concept in Infants and Young Children

Because infants cannot talk about themselves, researchers have had to devise indirect methods to learn how the self-concept develops in the first few years. Some evidence suggests that the rudiments of self-recognition come by the middle of the first year, when children prefer the voices and facial images of infants other than themselves, based on their preference for novelty (Legerstee et al., 1998). Whether this means that infants actually know who they are or have just habituated to their own sounds and images is not entirely clear.

One of the most reliable ways to learn about the developing self-concept in very young children, originally devised as a way of determining whether chimpanzees have a self-concept (Gallup, 1972), is to assess visual self-recognition by putting rouge on the child's nose and observing the way the child responds to its image in a mirror (Amsterdam, 1972; Asendorpf & Baudonniere, 1993; Lewis & Brooks-Gunn, 1979). Infants of different ages respond very differently to the image they see. Children younger than 15 months rarely touch their noses, unlike the vast majority of 2-year-olds, who recognize a discrepancy between the way they look and the way they should look. Thus, infants appear to develop a visual self-concept between 15 and 24 months. Interestingly, development in this respect is not complete even by 2 years: When presented with a videotape of themselves from a week or a few minutes earlier in which a sticker was secretly placed on their foreheads, 3-year-olds do not touch their foreheads, suggesting a lack of awareness that the sticker that was on their heads 3 or 4 minutes earlier is likely still there. Four- and five-year-olds, in contrast, only touch their foreheads after watching the tape of themselves a few minutes earlier, suggesting that they form more general representations of themselves over time (Povinelli & Simon, 1998).

During the toddler years, children begin to categorize themselves on various dimensions, especially age and gender (Damon & Hart, 1988; Lewis & Brooks-Gunn, 1979). Throughout early childhood, the categories they use are largely concrete. When asked to describe themselves, they refer to their membership in groups ("I live with my mommy and my daddy and my sister Jenny and my cat, Sneakers"), material possessions ("I have a pretty room"), things they can do ("I can tie my shoes"), and appearance. That is not to say the self-concept of young children is entirely devoid of subtlety; even preschoolers can sometimes observe consistencies in their own behaviors that resemble adult categories of personality, like extroversion ("I usually play with my friends" versus "I usually play by myself"). However, they have difficulty making generalizations about their enduring feelings, such as "I get mad a lot" versus "I don't usually get mad," or "I like myself" versus "I don't like myself" (Eder, 1990).

Self-Concept in Childhood and Adolescence

Around age 8, children begin to define themselves based on internal, psychological attributes as much as on the obviously perceptible qualities or appearances that dominate all cognition in early childhood (Broughton, 1978; Damon & Hart, 1988). In other words, they start to think about their aptitudes, their likes and dislikes, and the ways they tend to feel and think—namely, their personality. Conceiving the self at this point often involves comparisons with other children ("I'm good at math," or "I'm the best skateboarder in my school"). Once again this suggests an interaction of cognitive and social development: As children center less on salient, observable attributes of themselves and others, they begin to look inside, making inferences about mental processes; they are also more able simulta-

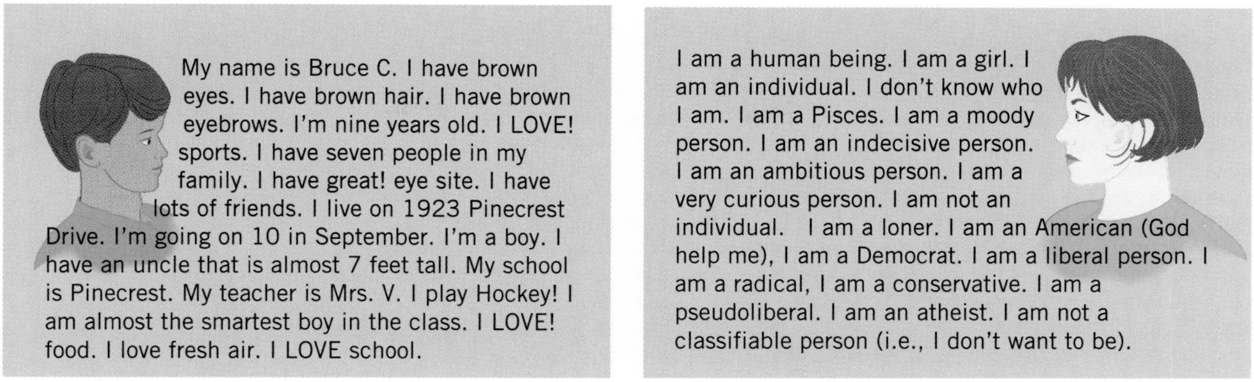

My name is Bruce C. I have brown eyes. I have brown hair. I have brown eyebrows. I'm nine years old. I LOVE! sports. I have seven people in my family. I have great! eye site. I have lots of friends. I live on 1923 Pinecrest Drive. I'm going on 10 in September. I'm a boy. I have an uncle that is almost 7 feet tall. My school is Pinecrest. My teacher is Mrs. V. I play Hockey! I am almost the smartest boy in the class. I LOVE! food. I love fresh air. I LOVE school.

I am a human being. I am a girl. I am an individual. I don't know who I am. I am a Pisces. I am a moody person. I am an indecisive person. I am an ambitious person. I am a very curious person. I am not an individual. I am a loner. I am an American (God help me), I am a Democrat. I am a liberal person. I am a radical, I am a conservative. I am a pseudoliberal. I am an atheist. I am not a classifiable person (i.e., I don't want to be).

FIGURE 14.3

Self-concept in childhood and adolescence. School-age children most frequently mention activities, significant others, and attitudes when describing themselves, as in this excerpt from an interview with a 9-year-old boy. With age, the self-concept becomes more abstract and complex, as in the response by a 17-year-old girl. *Source:* Montemayor & Eisen, 1977, pp. 317–318.

neously to coordinate information about themselves and other children, probably reflecting their expanded working memory capacity.

In adolescence, representations of the self become much more subtle (Figure 14.3) (Harter, 1998; Harter & Monsour, 1992). For example, a 17-year-old interviewed for a research project on the development of children's representations of self and others described herself, "I seem really shy on the outside, but *inside* I'm really involved when I'm with people, thinking a lot about what they are saying and doing. And with people I'm comfortable with, I probably don't seem shy at all" (Westen et al., 1991). As children move into adolescence, they also recognize that they are not the same kind of person with everyone or in every situation (Harter & Monsour, 1992).

CONCEPTS OF OTHERS

Coming to understand other people, like coming to understand the self, is a lengthy developmental process (Flavell & Miller, 1998). An accomplishment of infancy is recognizing that social interactions are reciprocal—that other people's actions depend on one's own. Infants learn, for instance, that smiling brings playful responses from caregivers, whereas crying usually means being picked up and held. Infants also come to read emotions in people's faces. As early as 12 months of age, infants "consult" their mothers by looking to them for reassurance when introduced to a new toy. If their mother's face shows concern, infants approach their mother rather than the toy (Klinnert et al., 1983; Saarni et al., 1998). If they receive a smile from one parent but a fearful look from the other, infants become confused and distressed (Hirshberg, 1990).

From early childhood until about age 8, children tend to focus on relatively simple, concrete attributes of other people, such as the way they look or the roles they perform (Shantz, 1983). For instance, a typical 7-year-old described a neighbor she liked as follows: "She is very nice because she gives my friends and me toffee. She lives by the main road . . . She sometimes gives us flowers" (Livesley & Bromley, 1973, p. 214). Around age 8, however, children's schemas about others begin to change. Figure 14.4 illustrates the changes that occur in children's understanding of people and relationships between ninth and twelfth grades.

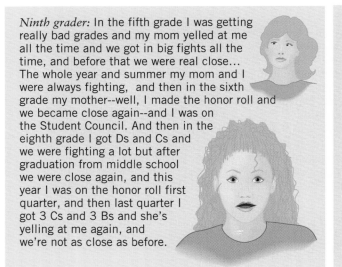

Ninth grader: In the fifth grade I was getting really bad grades and my mom yelled at me all the time and we got in big fights all the time, and before that we were real close... The whole year and summer my mom and I were always fighting, and then in the sixth grade my mother--well, I made the honor roll and we became close again--and I was on the Student Council. And then in the eighth grade I got Ds and Cs and we were fighting a lot but after graduation from middle school we were close again, and this year I was on the honor roll first quarter, and then last quarter I got 3 Cs and 3 Bs and she's yelling at me again, and we're not as close as before.

Twelfth grader: As I'm getting older we argue more, disagree on more--disagree on a lot more things. But I think we're getting closer now, more on the same level than when I was a little girl. Like, one time I was getting ready for a competition--we had a lot of misunderstanding, beforehand--I didn't feel she understood. She'd been in so many of these competitions and won, and I didn't feel she really cared about this one I was in. She hadn't felt I was serious about it. I didn't think she cared, and she didn't think I was serious. So finally we talked about it--realized it was a misunder- standing. I think we're closer now-- I realized we do have to talk about things when we have misunderstandings.

FIGURE 14.4

The development of views of relationships in adolescence. These are excerpts from interviews with a ninth and a twelfth grader who were asked to describe their relationship with their mothers. The twelfth grader provided a rich account of a developing relationship, pointing out the different perspectives she and her mother held. The ninth grader, in contrast, saw her mother just as "mom," who scolds or praises, not as a separate person with whom she is in- volved in an ongoing relationship. *Source:* Westen et al., 1991.

PERSPECTIVE-TAKING AND THEORY OF MIND

An important social-cognitive skill that develops throughout childhood and ado- lescence, and probably beyond, is **perspective-taking**, the ability to understand other people's viewpoints or perspectives. As we saw in Chapter 13, young chil- dren have difficulty taking another person's *visual* perspective in Piaget's three- mountain task, in which they have trouble imagining how a person from the other side of a table might perceive a scene. Taking other people's perspectives— from simple visual perspectives to complex emotional perspectives (as when a person can imagine, in the midst of an argument, why the other person is angry)—involves moving out of egocentrism and representing the other person's mind in one's own.

A prerequisite to perspective-taking is the development of a **theory of mind**—an implicit set of ideas about the existence of mental states, such as beliefs and feelings, in oneself and others (Gopnik, 1993). Researchers have argued about precisely when children develop a coherent theory of mind, but it appears to arise somewhere in the toddler years, between ages 2 and 4. Before that time, children have trouble understanding, for example, that people can hold false beliefs, be- cause they have trouble recognizing that thought and reality can differ. Precursors can be seen, however, as early as the middle of the second year, as when children can infer from the face an experimenter makes after eating a food that the experi- menter does not want it—even if the child likes that food (Repacholi & Gopnik, 1997).

One ingenious technique researchers have devised for assessing perspective- taking involves observing the way children play games of strategy (Flavell et al., 1968; Selman, 1980). In a game called "Decoy and Defender" (Selman, 1980),

"How would you feel if the mouse did that to you?"

which is played on a checkerboard, each player has two "flag carriers" as well as several less valuable tokens. The object is to move one's flag carriers to the opponent's side of the board. From the opposite side of the table, all the pieces look alike, so players must figure out which pieces to block by observing their opponents' moves.

The strategies used by children of different ages illustrate the stagelike development of perspective-taking ability. Consistent with a lack of a clear understanding that other people have minds and that their mental processes *matter*, children aged 3 to 6 have an egocentric perspective, totally failing to take their opponent's perspective into account. Typical of this age is the "rush for glory" strategy: The child simply moves her flag carrier as quickly as possible across the board. By ages 6 to 8, children become craftier but in a transparent fashion: They often announce, "I'm moving my *flag carrier* now" while moving an unimportant token. (They may even clear their throat first for effect.) They are beginning to recognize that to win they must influence the *beliefs* of their opponents. Other research similarly indicates that by age 5 children start to recognize the value of trying to influence other people's mental states in order to alter their behavior (Peskin, 1992).

By ages 8 to 10, children show more sophistication. For example, in the "double take" strategy, they might advance their flag carrier with considerable fanfare, expecting that the other player would not think they would be so stupid. Behind this strategy is a more complex perspective-taking process: "He's thinking that I'm thinking. . . ." The subtlety and complexity of this kind of back-and-forth thinking expands throughout adolescence.

INTERIM SUMMARY   Children develop in their **social cognition**, their understanding of themselves, others, and relationships. Researchers studying children's **self-concept** have found that children are not born with self-knowledge; even learning to store and maintain in memory a visual image of themselves is an achievement of the toddler years. Throughout early childhood, children tend to think of themselves and others in relatively concrete ways, such as their age, gender, group membership, and possessions. Around age 8, they begin to think more about enduring personality attributes. By adolescence, social cognition, like all cognition, is much more subtle and abstract. **Perspective-taking** also increases steadily throughout childhood and adolescence, beginning with children's development of a **theory of mind**—an implicit set of ideas about the existence of mental states in the self and others.

CHILDREN'S UNDERSTANDING OF GENDER

Children's social cognition thus develops in complexity and abstractness, much as cognition does in nonsocial domains (Chapter 13). The same is true of children's understanding of what gender is and how it applies to them, which changes dramatically over the first several years of life and continues to evolve throughout the lifespan.

One cognitive-developmental theory proposes that children progress through three stages in understanding gender (Kohlberg, 1966). First, they acquire **gender identity**, categorizing themselves as either male or female. Usually by age 2 they can correctly label themselves as a boy or girl and identify other children of the same sex (Slaby & Frey, 1975). Precursors to gender knowledge of this sort can be seen as early as 6 to 9 months of age, when habituation studies show that infants can discriminate males and females (see Ruble & Martin, 1998).

In the second stage, **gender stability**, children come to understand that their gender remains constant over time. Girls learn that they will never grow up to be Batman, Superman, or even a garden-variety father, and boys learn that they will not become Wonder Woman, Madonna, or a mommy. Even after they recognize that they will never change their sex, however, children are not absolutely certain that this is also true of other people. Before age 6 or 7, some children believe that boys who wear dresses may eventually become girls and girls may metamorphose into boys if they do enough boyish things (Marcus & Overton, 1978; McConaghy, 1979; Slaby & Frey, 1975). For example, when a 4-year-old saw his father dressed as a woman for Halloween, he exclaimed, "Two mommies!"

Thus, in the third stage, **gender constancy**, children learn that a person's gender cannot be altered by changes in appearance or activities (except, of course, in exceptional circumstances). This last stage is related to a major cognitive achievement of this age: understanding conservation of physical properties such as mass (Chapter 13). Gender constancy may seem a simple achievement to us, but it does not necessarily come easily. One psychologist tells the story of a 4-year-old boy who wore a barrette to nursery school. When another little boy called him a girl, the first child pulled down his pants to demonstrate that he was indeed still a boy. The other child, however, found this unconvincing. In a you-can't-fool-me tone of voice, he responded, "Everyone has a penis; only girls wear barrettes" (Bem, 1983, p. 607).

Gender Schemas

While cognitive developmentalists focus on the cognitive *structure* of children's thinking about gender (such as the conservation or constancy of gender), other researchers have turned their attention to the *content* of children's knowledge. Cross-culturally, children begin to show an awareness of their culture's beliefs about gender by the age of 5; by middle childhood they share many of the stereotypes common in their society (Best et al., 1977; Huston, 1983). They encode and organize information about their culture's definitions of maleness and femaleness in **gender schemas,** mental representations that associate psychological characteristics with one sex or the other (Bem, 1985).

Gender schemas can be quite persistent across the lifespan. Consider the following scenario, familiar to any female doctor, that was reported by a colleague:

"Is Dr. Williams in?"

"Yes, speaking."

"I'm calling regarding one of the doctor's patients. May I speak with the doctor please?"

"This is the doctor."

"No, I need to speak with the doctor, Dr. Williams."

"This is Dr. Williams."

Because the caller's gender schema associates doctors with masculinity, the person has difficulty recognizing that the doctor is, indeed, on the phone. (Interestingly, my colleagues uniformly report that callers who do this are usually female.)

Gender schemas across the globe show both remarkable similarities but also considerable differences. One team of researchers gave an adjective checklist with 300 items (e.g., aggressive, arrogant, artistic, bossy) to university students in 25 countries and asked them to rate whether the words were more characteristic of men, women, or neither (Best & Williams, in press; Williams & Best, 1982). Although many adjectives were categorized differently in different countries, a number were almost universally associated with men or with women. Broadly speaking, people everywhere consider men more active, strong, dominant, and aggressive, and perceive women as more passive, weak, and nurturant (Table 14.3).

Although the consistency of these findings is striking, two qualifications are in order. First, technological change is reducing the distinctions between the sexes. In a followup to their initial investigation (1990), the researchers examined **sex-role ideology** (beliefs about appropriate behaviors of the sexes) in 14 countries using a similar adjective checklist method. Technologically developed, urban, individualistic societies tended to have more egalitarian sex roles, with less divergent views of appropriate behaviors for men and women. Protestant countries were also more likely to be egalitarian, while people in predominantly Muslim countries tended to believe men should be dominant and women, submissive.

A second qualification is that gender differences are only *average* differences (Williams, 1983). The only differences that are absolute—on which males categorically differ from females—are primary and secondary sex characteristics, such as the genitals and breasts. For most traits, such as aggressiveness or sensitivity, the bell-shaped curves for males and females overlap substantially; thus within a cul-

---

TABLE 14.3 ADJECTIVES ASSOCIATED WITH MALES AND FEMALES ACROSS CULTURES

MALE		FEMALE	
Active (23)	Egotistical (21)	Affectionate (24)	Gentle (21)
Adventurous (25)	Forceful (25)	Attractive (23)	Sensitive (24)
Aggressive (24)	Hardhearted (21)	Charming (20)	Sentimental (25)
Clear-thinking (21)	Lazy (21)	Dependent (23)	Sexy (22)
Coarse (21)	Rational (20)	Emotional (23)	Submissive (25)
Courageous (23)	Self-confident (21)	Fearful (23)	Weak (23)
Cruel (21)	Unemotional (23)		
Dominant (25)	Wise (23)		

Source: Williams & Best, 1982, p. 77.

Note: The numbers in parentheses represent the number of countries sharing the stereotype, out of a sample of 25 cultures.

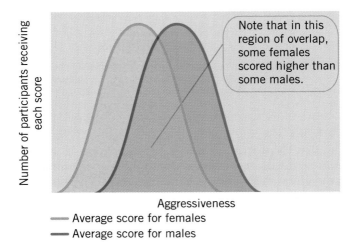

FIGURE 14.5
Aggressiveness in men and women. In this hypothetical distribution of scores on a measure of aggressiveness, one for men and one for women, the male curve is shifted to the right, signifying that most men are more aggressive than most women. Note the significant region of overlap, however, in which many women score higher than many men.

ture, some women score higher than some men even on "masculine" traits, and vice versa (Figure 14.5).

Cross-Cultural Gender Stereotypes

Why are gender stereotypes so similar cross-culturally? As early as age 2, Western boys prefer blocks and transportation toys such as trucks and cars, and girls prefer dolls and soft toys. Boys play more actively at manipulating objects and are more likely to engage in forbidden activities (Fagot, 1985; Smith & Daglish, 1977), whereas girls are more likely to play dress-up and dance. Girls also tend to talk earlier than boys (Schachter et al., 1978). Cross-cultural research with a large sample of preindustrial societies shows that the vast majority socialize boys from early childhood to be brave and self-reliant and girls to be responsible, self-restrained, obedient, and sexually restrained (Low, 1989). Why do so many cultures socialize children in similar ways?

As we saw in exploring the links between gender differences and brain structures in Chapter 3, where nature lays a foundation, culture tends to adorn, embellish, and reshape it. This is likely to be the case with the most well-documented difference between the sexes, that males are more aggressive and females more nurturant (see Archer & Lloyd, 1985; Jacklin, 1989; Maccoby & Jacklin, 1974, 1980). These differences occur across cultures and species and are evident well before children begin school. Boys display higher rates of aggression in virtually every society and are far more likely to engage in rough-and-tumble play (Edwards & Whiting, 1983; Whiting & Pope, 1973). Girls have never been found to be more prone to initiate aggressive encounters in any society (Maccoby & Jacklin, 1980).

Biology and Evolution   The male hormone testosterone appears to be related to aggression in both males and females (Chapter 18). Highly suggestive data come from studies of girls with **adrenogenital syndrome (AGS),** a malfunction of the adrenal glands that exposes the female fetus to unusually high levels of male hormones (Erhardt & Baker, 1974; Money & Erhardt, 1972). The result is not only an increase in aggressiveness but also a general increase in "tomboy" behavior during childhood.

According to the evolutionary perspective, sex differences in aggression and nurturance are products of natural selection. In many species, including most primates, males compete for sexual access to females, often physically establishing dominance over other males by fighting. Hence, males' greater tendency to exhibit aggressive behavior and to practice such behavior in childhood would optimize reproductive success. Behavioral differences would likely have been selected alongside physical differences such as greater body mass in males of most species, including humans. Females, in contrast, have no choice but to invest their resources heavily in their offspring because they carry the fetus for 9 months. In the context of these sex differences, a division of labor may have evolved in which males tend to fight for status and protect the group and females tend to care for infants and young children.

Fathers are much more capable of nurturance toward infants and children than was once believed.

Culture and Social Learning   The most stridently biological version of this hypothesis about sex differences is difficult to sustain because research finds that males are quite capable of nurturant behavior but are often discouraged from it by socialization practices (Fogel et al., 1986; Williams, 1983). In fact, changing gender roles now allow fathers to care for infants and young children in ways that would have been considered "unnatural" decades ago.

A social learning interpretation of sex differences holds that most behavioral differences observed between women and men result not from innate differences but from expectancies, which in turn reflect social structure (Eagly, 1983). Women and men consistently find themselves in hierarchical relationships in which men are in positions of power and status and women are subordinate (e.g., doctor/nurse, executive/secretary). Because this occurs so frequently, people see it as natural and generalize to other situations, even where status is presumably equal, such as dinner-table discussions of politics.

Nature and Nurture: An Integrative View   Although the social learning theory is compelling and can certainly help explain the maintenance of gender stereotypes, it does not account for the fact that such similar social structures have emerged throughout history and across cultures. It also does not account for the recent finding that boys are more active in utero than girls, even before their parents have begun to push them toward more rough and tumble play (DiPietro et al., 1996). Perhaps a more balanced account would consider the interaction among biological evolution, cultural evolution, and the learned expectations described by social learning theory. In this view, biological evolution produced motivational proclivities that diverge somewhat for the two sexes, such as a tendency toward aggressive behavior in males and toward nurturant behavior in females, along with physical differences such as body size and strength. Based on these biological differences, nearly all cultures create a division of labor between the sexes and amplify innate tendencies through socialization that maximizes safety of offspring and efficient food gathering. Simply noting the differences in size and strength between the average man and woman, for example, most cultures would be expected to enlist men and not women in warfare.

As ecological conditions shift (such as the disappearance of hand-to-hand combat), cultural ideology changes, and so do socialization practices. In fact, cross-cultural data document that where women have more power (where they control resources such as property), girls are taught to be less submissive and more aggressive, although they still remain less aggressive than males (Low, 1989).

The Politics and Science of Gender   One of the great difficulties of drawing conclusions about gender differences—both perceived and real—is the extent of passion and politics involved (Eagly, 1995). The systematic study of gender differences emerged in the 1970s with the rise of the feminist movement, which attempted to use psychological findings to discredit pervasive stereotypes that devalued women. Yet more recent research challenges the view that gender differences tend to be small; men and women differ substantially in a number of ways, particularly in their relative affinity for verbal versus mathematical tasks and their tendency to be nurturant or aggressive (e.g., Feingold, 1994). Whereas the first wave of feminist influence on the understanding of gender attempted to show that gender differences are really negligible, more recent thinking suggests that men and women do differ in some important respects, but that the problem lies less in those differences than in our tendency to devalue the things at which women excel.

INTERIM SUMMARY   Children's understanding of their own and other people's gender begins in the toddler years, when they can classify themselves and others according to gender. Over time, they develop **gender constancy**, the knowledge that gender cannot be altered by changes in appearance or activities. Children encode and organize information about their culture's definitions of maleness and femaleness in **gender schemas**. People everywhere consider men more active, strong, dominant, and aggressive, and perceive women as more passive, weak, and nurturant. Many of these stereotypes are based, at least in part, in actual differences.

MORAL DEVELOPMENT

INTERVIEWER:	Should boys get more? Why should they get more?
FOUR-YEAR-OLD BOY:	Because they always need more.
INTERVIEWER:	Why do they need more?
BOY:	Because that's how I want it.

(DAMON, 1977, P. 121)

Thankfully, children's thinking about what is fair (and why) changes dramatically over the years, so that older children and adults do not operate at the same level of morality as the 4-year-old above. The development of **morality**—the set of

"DON'T YOU REALIZE, JASON, THAT WHEN YOU THROW FURNITURE OUT THE WINDOW AND TIE YOUR SISTER TO A TREE, YOU MAKE MOMMY AND DADDY VERY SAD?"

rules people use to balance the conflicting interests of themselves and others—is a richly researched area (see Rest, 1983; Turiel, 1998). One of the central questions concerns the relative roles of cognition and emotion in the child's evolving sense of right and wrong.

THE ROLE OF COGNITION

Several theories focus on cognition in moral development. These include cognitive-developmental, cognitive-social, and information-processing theories.

Cognitive-Developmental Theories

The cognitive-developmental models of Jean Piaget and Lawrence Kohlberg focus on moral *reasoning*. These models propose that moral development proceeds through a series of stages that reflect cognitive development.

Piaget's Theory   Piaget observed a simple occasion—games of marbles among children—and noted important differences in the way younger and older children thought about the rules (Piaget 1932/1965). The youngest children, who were essentially pre-moral, arbitrarily altered the rules so they could win. Once children had accepted the notion of rules, however, they would stick staunchly to them, and if asked where the rules for playing marbles came from, they would reply with answers like, "They just are," "From Daddy," or "From God!"

This stage of moral judgment, which Piaget called the **morality of constraint**, is typical of school children before the age of 9 or 10. Piaget described this morality as one "of duty pure and simple," of conformity to societal rules, which are viewed as unchanging and immutable (1932/65, p. 335). When judging the actions of others, children in this stage tend to center on the most salient characteristic of the act—its severity—and have difficulty simultaneously keeping in mind other aspects of the act, such as the intention behind it. Consider what happens when a child is asked to decide who is more blameworthy, a boy who went to steal a cookie from the kitchen and broke a glass while reaching into the cookie jar, or another boy who accidentally slipped and broke five glasses. In line with the tendency of preoperational children to focus on only one salient attribute (Chapter 13), a 5-year-old is likely to reason that the boy who broke more glasses has committed the worse offense, even though his "crime" was accidental.

Older children and adults not only attend more to inferences about others' intentions, but they tend to view rules as means to ends, as strategies for regulating social interactions that keep people safe and comfortable. In this **morality of cooperation**, moral rules can be changed if they are not appropriate to the occasion, as long as the people involved agree to do so. Older children playing marbles may thus change the rules by mutual consent without believing they are violating something sacred.

Kohlberg's Theory   Kohlberg shared two of Piaget's central convictions about moral development. The first is that changes in moral reasoning result from basic changes in cognitive structures—that is, changes in ways of thinking. For example, as children's thinking becomes more abstract, so, too, does their moral reasoning. Second, Kohlberg conceptualized children as active constructors of their own moral reality, not passive recipients of social rules.

Kohlberg (1976; Kohlberg & Kramer, 1969) proposed a sequence of three levels of moral development, each comprised of two stages. He assessed moral development by presenting subjects with hypothetical dilemmas and asking them

According to Kohlberg, moral development is not about what *people* believe, *but about how they derive their beliefs. Try generating examples of reasoning at each of Kohlberg's levels for pro-life and pro-choice positions on abortion.*

how these dilemmas should be resolved and why. An example is the dilemma of Heinz and the druggist:

> In Europe a woman was near death from a special kind of cancer. There was one drug that the doctors thought might save her. It was a form of radium that a druggist in the same town had recently discovered. The drug was expensive to make, but the druggist was charging ten times what the drug cost him to make. He paid $200 for the radium and charged $2,000 for a small dose of the drug. The sick woman's husband, Heinz, went to everyone he knew to borrow the money, but he could only get together about $1,000, which is half of what it cost. He told the druggist that his wife was dying and asked him to sell it cheaper or let him pay later. But the druggist said, "No, I discovered the drug and I'm going to make money from it." So Heinz got desperate and broke into the man's store to steal the drug for his wife. Should the husband have done that? (Kohlberg, 1963, p. 19)

The level of moral development a person shows in answering this question depends not on the particular answer (to steal or not to steal) but on the reasoning behind the response (Table 14.4). At the first level, **preconventional morality**, children follow moral rules either to avoid punishment (Stage 1) or to obtain reward (Stage 2). A preconventional child might conclude that Heinz should steal the drug "if he likes having his wife around." At the second level, **conventional morality**, individuals define what is right by the standards they have learned from other people, particularly respected authorities. People with conventional morality justify their choice of moral actions on the basis of their desire to gain the approval or avoid the disapproval of others (Stage 3), or on the need to maintain law and order (e.g., "if everyone stole whenever he wanted to, what would this world come to?") (Stage 4).

The third level, **postconventional morality**, is a morality of abstract, self-defined principles that may or may not match the dominant morals of the times. A postconventional adult, like a preconventional child, might condone stealing the drug but for a very different reason, such as, "The value of a human life far ex-

Kohlberg's theory emerged in the 1960's, when the Vietnam War led many to question the wisdom of authorities and moral legitimacy of conventional beliefs about war, patriotism, and duty.

TABLE 14.4 KOHLBERG'S STAGES OF MORAL DEVELOPMENT

LEVEL	REASONS TO STEAL THE DRUG	REASONS NOT TO STEAL THE DRUG
Preconventional: Morality centers on avoiding punishment and obtaining reward.	"He should steal it if he likes her a lot"; "If he gets caught, he won't get much of a jail term, so he'll get to see her when he gets out."	"He'll get caught"; "He shouldn't have to pay with jail time for his wife's problem."
Conventional: Morality centers on meeting moral standards learned from others, avoiding their disapproval, and maintaining law and order.	"If he doesn't steal it, everyone will think he's a terrible person"; "It's his duty to care for his wife."	"If he steals it, everyone will think he's a criminal"; "He can't just go stealing things whenever he wants to—it isn't right."
Postconventional: Morality centers on abstract, carefully considered principles.	"If he has to run from the police, at least he'll know he did the right thing"; "Sometimes people have to break the law if the law is unjust."	"If he steals it, he'll lose all respect for himself"; "Other people might say it was okay, but he'll have to live with his conscience, knowing he's stolen from the druggist."

Source: Adapted from Kohlberg, 1969.

ceeds any rights of ownership or property." Kohlberg developed his theory during the 1960s, a time of social turbulence in which people questioned the norms and values of their parents and the larger society. He argued that people who never question their parents' moral beliefs are less developed in their moral reasoning than people who consider alternative ways of thinking about morality. (Distinctions between the two postconventional stages originally outlined by Kohlberg have not proven useful and will thus not be described here.)

The basic logic of Kohlberg's theory is that at the preconventional level, the person accepts moral standards only if doing so is personally advantageous; this is an ethic of hedonism or self-interest. The child is *pre*conventional in the sense that he has not yet come to accept society's conventions in their own right as rules that good people should follow. At the conventional level, the individual believes in the moral rules he has learned. The person with postconventional morality, in contrast, views the values of the time as conventions—rules established by social contract rather than by any absolute or divine power—and hence as both potentially fallible and changeable.

Virtually all normal children progress to Stage 3 by the age of 13. Beyond stages 3 and 4, however, the development of moral reasoning is not related to age and is more a matter of individual differences. Only about 5 percent of people reach the postconventional level (Colby & Kohlberg, 1984). Cross-cultural studies largely support the general sequence Kohlberg discovered in Western subjects (Chiu, 1990; Kuhn, 1976; Rest, 1983).

Cognitive-Social Theories

Cognitive-social theories focus less on moral reasoning than on moral *behavior*. According to behaviorist and cognitive-social theories, moral behaviors, like other behaviors, are learned through processes such as conditioning and modeling (Bandura, 1977; Mischel & Mischel, 1976). Cognitive-social approaches measure moral development in terms of **prosocial behavior**—behavior that benefits other individuals or groups (Eisenberg & Fabes, 1998; Mischel & Mischel, 1976).

From this point of view, morality develops as children come to discover through trial and error, as well as through deliberate instruction, that certain actions are reinforced and others are punished. Thus, children learn that stealing is wrong because they are punished for it, see someone else punished (vicarious conditioning), or are told they will be punished (direct tutelage). They acquire expectancies about the outcome of their behaviors under different circumstances (whether they will, or will not, be punished), and they develop conditioned emotional responses (such as anxiety) to behaviors that are regularly punished. They also generalize from one situation to the next, recognizing, for example, that talking in the library is no more acceptable than talking while a teacher is speaking.

Information-Processing Theories

An alternative cognitive view of moral development is an information-processing approach (Darley & Schultz, 1990; Grusec & Goodnow, 1994). Information-processing theories do not postulate broad stages of moral development; rather, they break moral thinking down into component processes and examine the way each changes during childhood.

According to one such view (Schultz & Schliefer, 1983), when adults make decisions about whether an act is immoral and whether it deserves punishment, as in jury deliberations, they make a series of sequential judgments (Figure 14.6). The first question concerns cause: Did the person cause the damage? If so, the next question is whether the individual was morally responsible. Did the person intend to do harm? Should the person have foreseen the results of his actions? Was the person grossly negligent in not taking measures to prevent the harm?

If the individual is morally responsible, the next question is whether he is blameworthy. Did someone else suffer significant harm from his action? If so, did the perpetrator have reasonable justification for his actions? Finally, if the person is to blame, the last judgment involves assigning appropriate punishment. People in the West make determinations about appropriate punishment, whether in a jury trial or in the discipline of their children, according to three criteria: the extent of the damage, whether the perpetrator has already made appropriate restitution (e.g., by apologizing), and whether the perpetrator has suffered as a result of his actions.

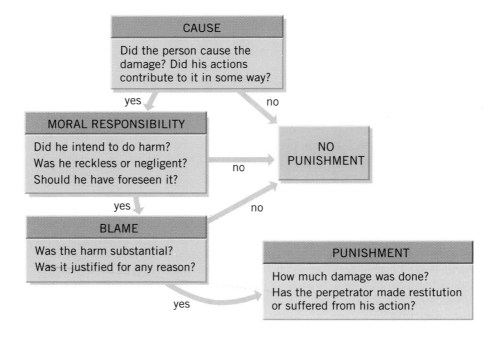

FIGURE 14.6
An information-processing model of moral decision making. According to this model, when people make decisions about whether an act is immoral and whether it deserves penishment, they make a series of sequential judgments, such as whether the person caused the event, was morally responsible, is blameworthy, and deserves punishment. *Source:* Adapted from Darley & Schultz, 1990, p. 532.

From an information-processing view, then, understanding moral development means understanding changes in the way children answer these multiple questions. For example, when do children come to understand the difference between directly causing someone to suffer (e.g., taking something from them) as opposed to taking an action that, combined with what someone else has done, produces suffering (e.g., forgetting to lock a door, which contributed to a theft)? According to this view, global stage theories cannot capture developmental changes in the multiple components of moral reasoning, and the problem is compounded because these components vary independently of one another.

INTERIM SUMMARY   Cognitive theories stress the role of thought and learning in moral development. According to Piaget, children at first believe moral rules are immutable but ultimately come to understand that they are the product of convention. Young children also tend to center on consequences rather than intentions in making moral judgments. Kohlberg distinguished three levels of moral development: **preconventional morality** (children follow moral rules either to avoid punishment or obtain rewards); **conventional** (individuals define what is right by the standards they have learned from other people, particularly respected authorities), and **postconventional** (people reason using abstract, self-defined moral principles that may not match conventional moral beliefs). Cognitive-social approaches measure moral development in terms of **prosocial behavior.** Information-processing approaches examine changes in the component processes involved in moral thinking.

THE ROLE OF EMOTION

The theories of moral development discussed thus far emphasize the role of cognition—judgment and decision making—in moral development. Other approaches, however, focus on the emotional side. Prominent among these are psychodynamic theories and research on childhood empathy.

Psychodynamic Theories

The psychodynamic view of moral development proposes that children start out relatively **narcissistic**—self-centered and interested in gratifying their own needs—as when the young child who wants an extra piece of cake simply grabs it. This orientation begins to change with the development of a conscience or superego between ages 2 and 5 (Chapter 12).

Moral development stems from identification: Children take in the values of their parents, which are at first external, and gradually internalize them by adopting them as their own. The way very young children begin to internalize their parents' values and edicts was illustrated by Kate, who opened this chapter, as she repeated her parents' commands in their absence ("Be a good girl, don't cry," or "Eat up your potatoes"). Empirically, parents and their children do tend to think similarly about moral questions (Speicher, 1994).

From a psychodynamic perspective, guilt is the primary moral emotion that motivates people to obey their conscience. Guilt arises from discrepancies between what people feel they should do and what they contemplate or observe themselves doing. When toddlers are learning about morals they may feel anxious or ashamed at being caught. Yet they do not experience genuine guilt until they actually internalize their parents' values as their own—that is, until they not only *know* them but also *believe in* them.

Young children's moral beliefs are very concrete and specific and are often tied directly to a mental image or representation of a parent. Toddlers may thus be observed telling themselves, "No!" even as they follow a forbidden impulse, or, as

Moral values tend to be highly similar in fathers and sons. A prime example: Governor George W. Bush of Texas and his father, President George Bush.

in the opening vignette, repeating their parents' admonitions as a way of stopping themselves from doing something they have been told is wrong ("Don't make a mess"). As children get older, they rely less on an internalized parent "sitting on their shoulder" and more on abstract moral demands integrated from their parents and the wider culture (see Williams & Bybee, 1994).

Empathy

Unpleasant emotions such as guilt, anxiety, and shame are not the only emotions involved in moral behavior. Some theorists emphasize the motivational role of **empathy**, or feeling for another person who is hurting (see Eisenberg & Fabes, 1998). Empathy has both a cognitive component (understanding what the person is experiencing) and an emotional component (experiencing a similar feeling). Research supports the view that empathy contributes to prosocial behavior, although empathizing too much in an emotional way can actually make people self-focused and hence *less* helpful (Strayer, 1993).

According to one view (Hoffman, 1978, 1990; Strayer, 1993), the ability to respond empathically changes considerably over the course of development. During the first year, infants experience global empathy; that is, they feel the same distress as the other person but cannot separate whose distress is whose. An 11-month-old who witnesses another child fall and cry may put her thumb in her mouth and bury her head in her mother's lap as if she were hurt herself.

As children become better able to distinguish their own thoughts and feelings from those of others, they begin to experience genuine **empathic distress**—feeling upset for another person—which motivates moral or prosocial behavior. As early as the second year of life, children can recognize when someone is hurting, feel bad for that person, and try to take action to make the person feel better (Zahn-Waxler et al., 1992). The response may nonetheless be egocentric: A 13-month-old may give a sad-looking adult his own favorite stuffed animal or bring his own mother over to comfort a crying playmate. This behavior reflects the immature perspective-taking ability of the young child.

As children get older, they respond more accurately to cues about what other people are feeling. By adolescence, a more mature form of empathy emerges, as individuals begin to think about suffering that exists beyond the immediate moment and hence become concerned about broader issues such as poverty or famine.

COMMENTARY
Making Sense of Moral Development

Cognitive and emotional approaches to moral development each present part of the picture, but none alone covers the entire landscape.

Cognitive Approaches

The strength of the cognitive-social approach is its emphasis on precisely what is missing from most other approaches, namely, moral or prosocial *behavior*. People may think as abstractly about moral questions as they like, but thinking is irrelevant if it does not affect their actions. Research does not, in fact, show particularly strong correlations between moral reasoning and prosocial behavior, at least in older children and adults; correlations between empathy and prosocial behavior tend to be relatively small as well (see, e.g., Eisenberg et al., 1991; Miller et al., 1996).

On the other hand, the cognitive-social approach assumes that certain behaviors are moral or prosocial and offers little insight into situations that require choosing between imperfect options. During the Vietnam War, people agonized over the question of what was moral or "prosocial." Was it moral to answer the draft, even though many considered the war immoral or nonsensical? Evade the draft and let other people die instead? Protest the war? These kinds of questions are what moral decision making is about.

Cognitive-developmental models have their advantages and disadvantages as well. Kohlberg's theory highlights a significant phenomenon that no other theory addresses—that moral development may go beyond the internalization of society's rules. This has been the principle of many moral leaders, from Jesus to Gandhi to Martin Luther King, Jr., who believed they were obeying higher laws than those of their particular country.

At the same time, Kohlberg's theory has drawn considerable criticism. People at the higher stages of moral reasoning do not necessarily behave any differently from people who are conventional in their moral reasoning. The philosopher Martin Heidegger, who reflected deeply and abstractly on a range of human experiences, found ways to rationalize cooperation with the Nazi regime, which many more "ordinary" Europeans did not.

Other critics, including Carol Gilligan (1982), contend that Kohlberg's theory is biased against women. In Kohlberg's early studies, women rarely transcended Stage 3 morality, in which goodness is equated with pleasing or helping others; men more often reached Stage 4, which is oriented toward maintaining the social order. Does this mean women are morally inferior? Gilligan thinks not—and a glance around the globe at the perpetrators of violence supports her view.

According to Gilligan, women and men follow divergent developmental paths, with one no less mature than the other. Women's moral concerns, she argues, are more likely to center on care and responsibility for specific individuals then on duty, law and order, and formal procedures for resolving moral and legal questions. Both Gilligan's and Kohlberg's theories may require modification when applied to other cultures where concepts of duty and caring can be quite different, and less gender-based, then in the West (Miller, 1994).

As for the information-processing approach to moral development, its greatest contribution is that, like similar approaches to cognitive development, it fills in and clarifies many of the broad strokes painted by stage theories. Nevertheless, an information-processing account leaves many questions unanswered, particularly about the way motivation influences moral reasoning and behavior. Why do children accept values in the first place, when doing so produces guilt, and why are they willing to control their impulses at all? Why do children make excuses when they have committed a transgression? How do they adjudicate conflicts between their own needs and those of others, and how do their judgments about their own culpability differ from their judgments about others'? Asking people to make judgments about what other people have done is very different from understanding their own struggles to remain faithful to their lover, to report their income honestly to the Internal Revenue Service, or to resist saying something unkind behind a friend's back.

Emotional Approaches

Perspectives that focus on the emotional side of morality fare better in answering these questions. Because morality so often requires self-sacrifice and self-restraint, an emotional counterweight such as anxiety or guilt seems essential to balance out the net losses in gratification. Empathy adds a further source of motivation for moral behavior: Helping other people leads to a sense of satisfaction and reduces the empathic distress that comes from observing someone else's suffering (Chapter 18).

Affective approaches, however, also have their pitfalls. Why children internalize moral values is unclear. Freud linked identification with the father to the fear of castration in boys. This seems a rather unlikely impetus for the development of morality and cannot account for moral development in females. Moreover, research indicates that mothers are largely responsible for moral training in most Western families (Hoffman & Saltzstein, 1967), and that internalization of values is associated with the extent to which mothers engage in an emotionally responsive, reciprocal relationship with their children (Kochanski, 1997). Identification with the father is probably not as central as Freud supposed, although research on moral reasoning does show particularly strong links between fathers' level of moral reasoning and the moral reasoning of both their sons and daughters (Speicher, 1994).

Empathy theories do not provide insight into specifically *moral* questions, which arise when people's needs are in conflict. Prosocial responses are common by 18 to 20 months when infants witness other people's distress but *not* when they cause the distress themselves (Zahn-Waxler et al., 1992). Infants as young as 12 to 18 months often share toys with other children or with their parents, but by age 2 they are less likely to share if it means giving up their toys (Hay et al., 1991). Perhaps not incidentally, by this age most children have mastered the word "mine." Prosocial responses aimed at making up for a transgression emerge at around 2 years, precisely when psychodynamic and other theorists argue for the beginnings of moral conscience fueled by guilt.

Recent research suggests that the roots of conscience may lie in both the fear emphasized by Freud and the empathy emphasized by more recent thinkers (Kochanska, 1997). For children who have a fearful temperament, gentle discipline by mothers predicts conscience at age 4. For children who have a fearless temperament and are less responsive to discipline, *positive* mother–child interactions appear to predict conscience development. These data make sense in light of research suggesting that some people are more driven by fear, whereas others are more pulled by rewards (Chapter 11).

What is interesting is the possibility that these basic temperamental variables may affect the way children internalize moral values as well.

An Integrated View

An integrated account of moral development would need to spell out more carefully the interactions of cognition, affect, and motivation involved when children and adults wrestle with moral questions. Infants and toddlers have many selfish impulses, but they also have prosocial impulses based on their innate capacity for empathy. When self-centered and other-centered motives clash, young children tend to opt for the most gratifying course of action.

This probably changes over time for a number of reasons. Children mature in their capacity to love and care about other people and to understand the perspective of others. They also become more able to regulate their impulses as neural circuits in the frontal lobes mature and as expanding cognitive abilities allow them to transform situations in their minds. Furthermore, through social learning, children come to associate actions such as sharing with positive reinforcement, and hitting and lying with punishment. By identifying with people they fear and admire, children's fear of punishment gradually becomes transformed into fear of their own internal monitor of right and wrong—and hence into guilt. Eventually, they reflect more abstractly about moral questions and try to integrate the moral feelings and beliefs they have accrued over the course of their development. ■

INTERIM SUMMARY   Psychodynamic theories emphasize the role of emotions, particularly guilt, in moral development, and argue that conscience arises through identification with parents. Other theories emphasize **empathy**, or feeling for another person who is hurting. Moral development probably reflects an interaction of cognitive and affective changes that allow children to understand and feel for other people as well as to inhibit their own wishes and impulses.

SOCIAL DEVELOPMENT ACROSS THE LIFESPAN

In discussing social development, we have thus far focused on the first quarter of the lifespan. Like physical and cognitive development, however, social development continues throughout life. The most widely known theory of lifespan development was formulated by Erik Erikson (1963). We use Erikson's theory as the basis for organizing our discussion of lifespan development in the remainder of the chapter.

Erikson's is not the only model of adult development, but it has two particularly important features. First, it is culturally sensitive, emerging not only from Erikson's experience as a psychoanalyst but also from his having lived in, and observed, several cultures, from Denmark and Germany to a Sioux reservation. Research since Erikson's time suggests that when and where people develop are crucial to the way they develop throughout their lives, even within a single culture (Elder, 1998). For example, people who were young children during the Great Depression never forgot the lessons of poverty and hunger they learned, even when they were financially secure years later.

Second, Erikson's theory integrates biology, psychological experience, and culture by grounding development simultaneously in biological maturation and

Cultures initiate adolescents into society in a variety of ways, from the rites of passage of Xhosa tribe of South Africa, to the rituals intended to install discipline in a western military school, to the less structured "rituals" of teenagers in a mall.

changing social demands. For example, like his mentor, Anna Freud (1958), Erikson noted the connection between adolescents' questions about who they are and what they believe with the surge of new feelings and impulses they experience as they wrestle with puberty and emerging sexuality. Reconstituting a self-concept that now includes the self as a sexual being is a major task spurred by biological maturation, but the extent to which adolescents find this conflictual depends on the beliefs, values, rituals, and sexual practices of their culture (Mead, 1928). Aspects of Erikson's developmental model have also received empirical support in cross-sectional, longitudinal, and sequential studies (Marcia, 1987; McAdams & de St. Aubin, 1992; Whitbourne et al., 1992).

Erikson intended his model of **psychosocial stages**—stages in the development of the person as a social being—to supplement Freud's psychosexual stages. Thus, the toddler years are not only a time of toilet training (and hence dealing with feelings in the anus) but, more generally, of learning what it means to submit to authority, to control impulses, and to assert one's own autonomy. At each of eight stages, the individual faces a **developmental task**, a challenge that is normative for that period of life (Table 14.5). Each successive task provides a *crisis*—an opportunity for steaming ahead or a danger point for psychological derailment—that influences subsequent development. These alternative "tracks" at each juncture are not, of course, absolute. No infant, for example, ever feels *totally* trusting or mistrusting, and people have many opportunities over the course of development to backtrack or take a new route.

CHILDHOOD

Four of the eight stages in Erikson's theory take place in childhood. During the first stage, **basic trust versus mistrust**, infants come to trust others or to perceive the social world as hostile or unreliable. This stage comprises roughly the first 18 months of life; during this period infants develop their earliest internal working models of relationships. In the language of attachment theory, the task for the child in this period is to establish attachment security given the constraints of her own temperament and her caregivers' responsiveness.

The second stage, **autonomy versus shame and doubt**, occurs during the second and third years as maturation allows children to walk and talk and hence to experience themselves as independent sources of will and power. Toddlers learn to feel secure in their independence, or they doubt their newfound skills and feel shame at their failures. During the second year, children spontaneously set standards for themselves and experience pride in their accomplishments (Kagan, 1984). This is also the time of the "terrible twos," in which toddlers regularly as-

TABLE 14.5 ERIKSON'S PSYCHOLOGICAL STAGES IN RELATION TO OTHER MODELS OF DEVELOPMENT

LIFE PERIOD	ERIKSON'S PSYCHOSOCIAL STAGE	FREUD'S PSYCHOSEXUAL STAGE	PIAGET'S COGNITIVE STAGE
Infancy	*Basic trust versus mistust*: Development of interpersonal expectations and hope	Oral	Sensorimotor
Toddlerhood	*Autonomy versus shame and doubt*: Development of will and self-control	Anal	Preoperational
Preschool and early school years	*Initiative versus guilt*: Development of conscience and purpose	Phallic	
Late childhood	*Industry versus inferiority*: Development of competence	Latency	Concrete operational
Adolescence	*Identity versus identity confusion*: Development of commitment and sense of integration	Genital	Formal operational
Young adulthood	*Intimacy versus isolation*: Development of adult love		
Midlife	*Generativity versus stagnation*: Development of care for the next generation and for one's legacy		
Old age	*Integrity versus despair*: Development of wisdom		

Note: Erikson's model describes psychosocial development, which is not independent of either the development of pleasure-seeking motives, as described by Freud, or cognition, as described by Piaget. Among the major theories we have discussed, however, Erikson's is the only one that posits development through adulthood.

sert their authority. A danger of this stage is that the child may be afraid to explore and challenge, and never develop a secure sense of autonomous selfhood. Long or repeated separations from attachment figures during this period can threaten the child's growing autonomy. This occurred temporarily with 2½-year-old Kate, who became somewhat clinging and fearful for a while after separation from her parents.

In the third stage, roughly between 3 and 6 years of age, children struggle with **initiative versus guilt**. Initiative refers to a sense of planfulness and responsibility that enables a child to follow through with ideas and goals. Initiative adds purpose to the willfulness of the toddler years. The opposite pole is the guilt that accompanies the emergence of a conscience and heightened control over impulses. Children who have difficulty with this stage may develop a tyrannical conscience that is always berating them, or they may become rigid and constricted as a way of dealing with impulses they have come to view as bad.

The next stage, which occurs roughly between ages 7 and 11, is **industry versus inferiority**. Children develop a sense of industry, or competence, as they begin to practice skills they will use for a lifetime in productive work. During this period, **social comparison** processes become important as children size up themselves and others on intelligence, athletic ability, popularity, and so on. The vulnerability of this stage reflects the dangers inherent in learning and social comparison: feelings of incompetence or inferiority. In literate cultures, children enter school during this age, and their experiences of academic and social success or failure shape both their self-concepts and the strategies they use to protect their self-esteem. Some children become caught in a vicious cycle, in which a sense of inferiority leads them to give up quickly on tasks, which, in turn, increases the probability of further failure. In nonliterate societies children learn skills that prepare them for adulthood, such as hunting, gathering, and caring for infants.

INTERIM SUMMARY   Erikson proposed a lifespan model of **psychosocial stages**—stages in the development of the person as a social being. In **basic trust versus mistrust**, infants come to trust others or perceive the social world as hostile or unreliable. In **autonomy versus shame and doubt**, toddlers come to experience themselves as independent sources of will and power or feel insecure in their newfound skills. In **initiative versus guilt**, young children develop the capacity to form and carry out plans, but their emerging conscience can render them vulnerable to guilt. In **industry versus inferiority** school-age children develop a sense of competence but may suffer from feelings of inferiority as they compare themselves to others.

ADOLESCENCE

According to Erikson, the developmental crisis of adolescence is **identity versus identity confusion**. **Identity** refers to a stable sense of who one is and what one's values and ideals are (Erikson, 1968). **Identity confusion** occurs when the individual fails to develop a coherent and enduring sense of self and has difficulty committing to roles, values, people, or occupational choices. Empirically, individuals differ in the extent to which they explore and maintain commitments to ideologies, occupational choices, and interpersonal values (Marcia, 1987). Some establish an identity after a period of soul-searching, while others commit early without exploration, foreclosing identity development. Still others remain perpetually confused, or put off identity consolidation for many years while trying on various roles throughout their 20s.

These different paths to identity depend heavily on culture. Many traditional cultures have **initiation rites** in adolescence, ceremonies that initiate the child into adulthood and impose a socially bestowed identity. A period of identity confusion occurs primarily in technologically more advanced societies or in cultures that are undergoing rapid changes, as in much of the contemporary world.

Sometimes adolescents have trouble establishing a positive identity; they may be doing poorly in school or lack models of successful adulthood with whom to identify. As a result, they may develop a **negative identity**, taking on a role society defines as bad but that nevertheless provides them with a sense that they are *something*. This is a path often taken by gang members and chronic delinquents, who may seemingly revel in their "badness."

Failure to form a cohesive identity beyond adolescence can signify problems later on. Girls who have difficulty forming an identity in late adolescence are more likely than their peers to experience marital disruption at midlife; boys with late-adolescent identity problems are more likely to remain single and be unsatisfied with their lives in middle age (Kahn et al., 1985).

As adolescents grow less dependent on their parents and try out new values and roles, they may become rebellious and moody, shifting from compliance one moment to defiance the next. According to the **conflict model** put forth at the turn of the century (Hall, 1904) and later elaborated by psychodynamic theorists (Blos, 1962; A. Freud, 1958), conflict and crisis are normal in adolescence. Indeed, conflict theorists argue that adolescents *need* to go through a period of crisis to separate themselves psychologically from their parents and carve out their own identity. Beeper studies (Chapter 9) show that adolescents do, in fact, experience a wider range of moods over a shorter period of time than adults (Csikszentmihalyi & Larson, 1984). Longitudinal studies find decreases in hostility and negative emotionality and increases in diligence, self-control, and congeniality as teenagers move into early adulthood (see McGue et al., 1993).

Other theorists argue, however, that the stormy, moody, conflict-ridden adolescent is the exception rather than the rule (Compas et al., 1995; Douvan & Adelson, 1966; Offer et al., 1990). According to the **continuity model,** adolescence for most individuals is essentially continuous with childhood and adulthood, undistinguished by turbulence. Research supporting this view finds that roughly 80 percent of adolescents show no signs of severe storm and stress and that some of the remaining 20 percent are emotionally troubled (Offer & Offer, 1975). Probably the most accurate conclusion is that adolescence is a time of enormous individual differences, with many alternative paths that vary according to the individual, culture, and historical period (see Hauser et al., 1994).

EARLY ADULTHOOD

Erikson was one of the first theorists to take seriously the notion of development after adolescence. While his stages of childhood and adolescence correspond loosely to Freud's psychosexual stages (Table 14.5), Freud's stages have no parallel in adulthood. Erikson describes the developmental task confronting young adults as **intimacy versus isolation**. Intimacy, for Erikson, means establishing enduring, committed relationships, including friendships and romantic relationships. The danger of this period is isolation—the tendency to withdraw from relationships or avoid commitment.

Establishing intimacy does not mean simply getting married. In Western cultures, marital distress actually increases over the first 3 years of marriage. Maintaining intimate relationships in the face of conflict and disillusionment is a challenge that requires continuous negotiation and compromise. Marital conflict is at its peak when children are young, housework doubles, financial pressures mount, and intimate time alone is difficult to find (Belsky & Pensky, 1988; Berman & Pedersen, 1987). For women, motherhood usually involves a redefinition of roles and reallocation of time. For men, fatherhood means that they are no longer the primary recipients of their wives' attention and love; at the same time, they incur new financial and domestic responsibilities (Lamb, 1987). The stresses of early parenthood are lessened when the marital relationship is supportive and the couple is financially comfortable (Schaie & Willis, 1986).

MIDDLE AGE

Erikson describes the crisis of midlife as **generativity versus stagnation. Generativity** means concern for the next generation as well as an interest in producing (generating) something of lasting value to society. People express their generative impulses through rearing children, participating in culturally meaningful institutions such as churches or civic organizations, mentoring younger workers, or creating something that will last beyond them, such as a work of art. The opposite of generativity is **stagnation**, which may be expressed as dissatisfaction with a marital partner, alienation from one's children, or a feeling that the promise of one's youth has gone unfulfilled. Empirically, people in midlife express more generative themes than younger adults when describing their lives, and they report more generative activities (McAdams & de St. Aubins, 1992; McAdams et al., 1993). As Erikson hypothesized, individuals also differ in the extent to which they maintain an active, generative stance during middle age (Bradley & Marcia, 1998).

Some observers have described this period as a time of **midlife crisis** (Jacques, 1965; Levinson et al., 1978; Sheehy, 1976). One researcher found that roughly 80 percent of the men he interviewed were in a state of crisis around age 40, as they began to think of themselves as middle-aged instead of young and to question the basic structure of their lives (Levinson, 1978). In Western culture, people are frequently at the height of their careers in their 40s and 50s, enjoying leadership positions at work or in the community. At the same time, however, the death of parents, the occasional jarring death of siblings or contemporaries, and an aging body inevitably lead people to confront their mortality and to consider how they will live their remaining years.

As with adolescence, some psychologists challenge the view of midlife as a time of crisis. Only a minority of people report experiencing a midlife crisis, and in these cases, the crisis usually occurs along with a specific interruption in the normal rhythm of life, such as loss of a job or divorce (Neugarten, 1968, 1977). Women report feeling more independent, more competent, more generative, and better about themselves in midlife than they did at age 30 (Helson & Moane, 1987). For men, across many cultures, the 50s and 60s often bring a gradual decrease in aggressiveness and a blossoming of nurturant impulses (Guttman, 1974; Hyde et al., 1991; Neugarten, 1972). For many people the changes of midlife are gradual, not cataclysmic.

OLD AGE

The meaning of old age changed dramatically over the course of the 20th century. The average lifespan increased 26 years (Labouvie-Vief, 1985), and the proportion of people over age 65 in North America has grown from 1 in 30 in 1900 to a projected 1 in 5 by the year 2020 (Eisdorfer, 1983). People over 85 currently account for nearly 10 percent of the population and are expected to constitute roughly 20 percent by 2040 (Verbrugge, 1989, cited in Von Dras & Blumenthal, 1992). These demographic shifts have produced substantial changes in perceptions of old age. Even three decades ago, people were considered "old" in their 60s; today, no one is surprised to play tennis next to a court full of active 70-year-olds.

In Erikson's final stage, **integrity versus despair**, individuals look back on their lives with a sense of satisfaction that they have lived it well or with despair, regret, and loss for loved ones who have died. In many respects, the balance between integrity and despair is fluid, as individuals must inevitably cope with losing people who have made their lives meaningful.

Technologically developed and Western cultures tend to devalue the elderly and emphasize the despairing end of the continuum. William Shakespeare's characterization of old age, from *As You Like It* (Act II, Scene vii), presents a grim picture that is not far from the contemporary Western conception of life's final phase:

> Last scene of all,
> That ends this strange eventful history,
> Is second childishness and mere oblivion,
> Sans teeth, sans eyes, sans taste, sans every thing.

Fortunately, Shakespeare took some poetic license; reality is nowhere near this bleak. For example, contrary to stereotypes, only about 5 percent of the population over 65 have physical or mental impairments serious enough to require continuous nursing care (Tolliver, 1983). In fact, most people report having more positive and less negative affect as they move toward the end of middle age (Helson & Klohnen, 1998). Why, then, are our stereotypes so negative?

A prime culprit appears to be technological development. Ironically, the same factor that has prolonged life by decades has undermined the status of the aged by making their jobs obsolete, limiting the applicability of their beliefs and values in a radically changed social and cultural milieu, and eroding the traditional structure of the extended family. Furthermore, the geographical mobility associated with economic development means that children may live hundreds of miles from their aging parents. In contrast, in more traditional societies, the aged are by definition the most knowledgeable because they have lived the longest and accumulated the most information, and mutual ties of affection between the generations are reinforced by daily interaction.

In the face of physical decline, negative stereotypes, and the loss of spouse, friends, and social roles, what allows an individual to find satisfaction, or what Erikson describes as integrity, in the final years of life? In one study of 1000 people aged 65 to 72, several variables predicted life satisfaction: close relationships, an active social and community life, continuing recreation, good health, and sufficient income (Flanagan, 1981). Other studies have pointed to similar factors, particularly community involvement (Harlow & Cantor, 1996).

Longitudinal studies suggest that *earlier* factors predict happiness and physical and mental health in later life, including marital and career fulfillment as a younger adult, sustained family relationships, and long-lived ancestors; risk factors from young and middle adulthood include defense mechanisms such as projection that grossly distort reality, alcoholism, and depression before age 50 (Sears, 1977; Vaillant & Vaillant, 1990). The quality of old age thus appears to depend to a substantial degree on the quality of youth.

Shakespeare would be surprised by the way senior citizens have responded to changing views of "appropriate" behavior in old age.

INTERIM SUMMARY   Erikson described adolescence as a period of **identity versus identity confusion** in which the task is to establish a stable sense of who one is and what one values. Some researchers adopt a **conflict model** of adolescence, arguing that conflict and struggle are normal in adolescence, whereas others propose a **continuity model**, arguing that adolescence is essentially continuous with childhood and adulthood. Each model probably applies to a subset of adolescents. Erikson describes the developmental task of young adulthood as **intimacy** (establishing enduring, committed relationships) **versus isolation**. In **generativity versus stagnation**, middle-aged individuals attempt to pass something on to the next generation. In Erikson's final stage, **integrity versus despair**, individuals look back on their lives with a sense of satisfaction that they have lived it well or with despair, regret, and loss for loved ones who have died. The realities of older age appear far better than the negative stereotypes seen in technologically developed societies.

SOME CONCLUDING THOUGHTS

This chapter and the previous one have focused on pathways through development. Psychological development through the lifespan involves continuous adaptation to a changing brain and body within a social and cultural context. A toddler upset by the absence of her mother, an adolescent trying to make sense of a body that looks and feels increasingly unfamiliar, a person whose spouse has died and whose time on life's stage is drawing to an end—in each case, psychological experience reflects a social animal wrestling with biological givens.

In the next chapter we examine what happens when development goes awry, as we explore psychological disorders. Then, in the following chapter, we consider approaches to helping people return to more satisfying pathways through psychological treatment.

SUMMARY

1. **Social development** refers to predictable changes in interpersonal thought, feeling, and behavior over the lifespan.

ATTACHMENT

2. **Attachment** refers to the enduring emotional ties children form with their primary caregivers. **Separation anxiety**—distress at separation from attachment figures—occurs around the same time in all human cultures and peaks in the second year of life. Harlow's experiments with monkeys showed that security, not food, is the basis for attachment. Integrating psychodynamic and evolutionary theory, Bowlby proposed that attachment is a mechanism to keep immature animals close to their parents.

3. Using a procedure called the **Strange Situation,** researchers have identified four styles of attachment: secure, avoidant, ambivalent, and disorganized. Early attachment patterns have a powerful impact on later social functioning and form the basis of **adult attachment** styles. Infants develop **internal working models**, or mental representations of attachment relationships, which form the basis for their expectations in later close relationships.

SOCIALIZATION

4. **Socialization** refers to the processes through which individuals come to learn the rules, beliefs, values, skills, attitudes, and behavior patterns of their society. Socialization is transactional (interactive), lifelong, and multifaceted. Like all psychological processes, it also occurs within constraints imposed by biology and the broader economic and cultural context.

5. Parents are particularly important **socialization agents**. Research distinguishes authoritarian, permissive, and authoritative parenting styles. Each parenting style tends to produce children with different characteristics. Parents vary across and within cultures in the extent to which they are accepting and rejecting of their children. Parental warmth and sensitivity are associated with self-esteem, independence, and emotional stability.

6. Among the most powerful roles into which people are socialized are **gender roles**, the range of behaviors considered appropriate for males and females. Unlike sex (a biologically based categorization), **gender** (the psychological meaning of being male or female) is influenced by learning, although evolutionary pressures have probably led to gender differences that cultures embellish and magnify. Gender socialization begins in the first days of life.

PEER RELATIONSHIPS

7. Friendships with other children begin to emerge around the third year. Children differ in the extent to which they are accepted by their peers. **Rejected children** are often teased and ostracized, although they may also elicit dislike because they are bullies. **Neglected children** are less likely to draw a positive or negative response from their peers, and are more likely to be friendless or ignored. Sibling relationships have many dimensions, including both rivalry and closeness.

DEVELOPMENT OF SOCIAL COGNITION

8. As with cognitive development in nonsocial domains, children develop in their **social cognition**—the way they conceptualize themselves, others, and relationships. The **self-concept** refers to a person's organized way of representing information about the self. Initially, children lack a distinct concept of self. Their views of themselves, like their views of others, begin concrete and gradually become more abstract; by adolescence, they are much more likely to think about their own and others' internal psychological processes such as feelings and personality traits. An important social-cognitive skill that develops gradually is **perspective-taking**, the ability to understand other people's viewpoints.

9. Children's understanding of what gender is and how it applies to them develops substantially throughout the first several years of life. Children develop **gender schemas**—mental representations that associate psychological characteristics with one sex or the other—by integrating cultural beliefs with their personal experiences. Gender schemas share striking similarities across cultures, which appear to reflect an interaction between biology and social learning.

MORAL DEVELOPMENT

10. Researchers have concentrated considerable effort on **moral development**, the acquisition of values and rules for balancing the potentially conflicting interests of the self and others. Behaviorist and cognitive-social theories assert that **prosocial behavior** (behavior that benefits others), like other behaviors, is learned through processes such as conditioning and modeling. Cognitive-developmental models focus less on moral behaviors than on moral reasoning. Kohlberg's stage theory distinguishes three levels of moral reasoning: **preconventional** (following moral rules to avoid punishment or obtain reward), **conventional** (defining right and wrong according to learned cultural standards), and **postconventional** (applying abstract, self-defined principles). Information-processing approaches break down moral development into component processes and examine the way each changes during childhood.

11. According to psychodynamic theories, children internalize their parents' values, and guilt motivates people to obey their conscience. Other theorists emphasize the role of **empathy** (feeling for someone who is hurting) in motivating prosocial behavior. Recent research suggests that the paths to internalization of conscience in children depend an interaction of temperament and parenting styles. Undoubtedly, moral development reflects an interaction of cognitive and emotional development.

SOCIAL DEVELOPMENT ACROSS THE LIFESPAN

12. The most widely known theory of lifespan development is Erik Erikson's eight **psychosocial stages: basic trust versus mistrust, autonomy versus shame and doubt, initiative versus guilt,** and **industry versus inferiority** in childhood; **identity versus identity confusion** in adolescence; and **intimacy versus isolation, generativity versus stagnation,** and **integrity versus despair** during adulthood. Psychologists disagree on the extent to which adolescents and people in midlife experience crises, but in general, there does not appear to be any single path to "successful aging."

Freshman Brown, "Loss," 1996/SuperStock.

CHAPTER *15*

Psychological Disorders

*L*ate on a blustery February night, a woman we will call Mary sat crying in the corner of a shelter for battered women. Her eyes blackened, her ribs badly bruised, and sobbing with pain and betrayal, she told a staff member her story: Her boyfriend of two years, drunk and enraged, had kicked and beaten her.

This was not the first time Mary had told this story. Twice before she had sought the safe confines of the shelter because of her boyfriend. Each time, over the objections of shelter staff, she returned home, seduced by his promises that he would change. Her ex-husband had also abused her, as had her father when she was a child.

This vignette challenges our notions of normality and abnormality, sickness and sin. Until very recently, police officers intervened only minimally in cases of domestic violence, doctors treated broken noses and ribs in obviously battered

women without addressing their equally broken spirits, and laws allowed angry, jealous men to stalk and terrorize their ex-lovers under the guise of civil liberties. Apparently, our society has not considered battering abnormal. Rather, violence against women has been deemed "a domestic affair."

Yet few readers would disagree that something is wrong with the violent men in Mary's life. They are bad or mad, criminal or disturbed. They are unlikely, however, to serve time for their crimes or to receive psychiatric diagnoses. And what about Mary? Is she simply a victim of circumstance, accidentally finding herself over and over again at the mercy of abusive men? Or does the abuse she suffered at her father's hands influence her choice of partners and her choice to stay or leave the abusive situation? As this vignette suggests, classifying a particular pattern of psychological functioning as disordered is not always clear. It also reflects cultural values, beliefs, and attitudes, such as cultural views of the rights of men and women.

In this chapter, we examine **psychopathology** (literally, sickness, or *pathology*, of the mind), which refers to problematic patterns of thought, feeling, or behavior that disrupt an individual's sense of well-being or social or occupational functioning. We begin with the cultural context of psychopathology, considering how people like Mary and the men in her life become classified as normal or disordered. Next we examine the often starkly contrasting ways psychodynamic, cognitive-behavioral, biological, and systems theorists understand psychopathology as well as a descriptive approach that focuses on diagnosis. Then we describe the major psychopathological syndromes, from those that first manifest themselves in childhood, to those characterized by specific symptoms such as depression and anxiety, to disorders of the entire personality. We conclude by asking three questions: Do mental disorders really fit into discrete categories as medical syndromes do? Have we identified the right syndromes? And can the causes of these disorders be neatly categorized as the result of either nature or nurture?

THE CULTURAL CONTEXT OF PSYCHOPATHOLOGY

Every society has its concept of "madness," and what a society considers normal or abnormal is constantly changing. The kind of competitive, every-person-for-himself stance taken for granted in many large cities would have been a sign of bad character—or in today's language, personality pathology—by the rural grandparents of many city-dwellers.

Some of the psychopathological syndromes clinicians encounter today were identified and classified as early as 2500 BC by the ancient Sumerians and Egyptians. Over the centuries Western culture has attributed mental illness to a variety of causes, such as demon possession, supernatural forces, witches, and Satan. To what extent does culture shape and define mental illness? And are diagnoses anything but labels a culture uses to brand its deviants?

CULTURE AND PSYCHOPATHOLOGY

Cultures differ in both the disorders they spawn and the ways they categorize mental illness (see Kleinman, 1988; Leff, 1988). The concept of "crazy" among one Alaskan Eskimo group is somewhat similar to our own, encompassing talking to oneself, screaming at people who do not exist, or making peculiar grimaces. Their concept of mental illness, however, also includes some symptoms unusual in the rest of North America, such as believing that a loved one was murdered by witchcraft when no one else thought so, believing oneself to be an animal, drinking urine, and killing dogs (Murphy, 1976). In rural Ireland, which is almost uniformly Catholic, people with schizophrenia are more likely than North Americans with the same disorder to have bizarre religious beliefs, such as the conviction that their body has become inhabited by the Virgin Mary (Scheper-Hughes, 1979). As these examples illustrate, when people fall ill psychologically, they tend to do so in a cultural idiom, that is, to draw on culturally shared meanings and symbols but in idiosyncratic ways (see Fabrega, 1989, 1994).

Psychopathology differs within as well as across cultures (Table 15.1). For example, prevalence rates of alcoholism, schizophrenia, and severe depression vary depending on cultural and demographic factors (such as city size), although the reasons for these variations are not entirely clear (Compton et al., 1991). Conceptions of psychopathology also differ within cultures, especially in multicultural societies. The Amish, who value humility, moderation, and self-control, consider a

TABLE 15.1 CULTURE AND MENTAL ILLNESS

	PERCENT OF SAMPLE WITH THE DISORDER		
COMMUNITY	ALCOHOLISM	SCHIZOPHRENIA	MAJOR DEPRESSION
Metropolitan Taipei	5.17	0.34	0.94
Small Taiwan towns	9.96	0.23	1.61
Rural Taiwan villages	7.58	0.17	1.01
Urban North Carolina	8.97	1.36	5.13
Rural North Carolina	9.60	1.21	2.44
West Los Angeles	14.37	0.46	7.03

Source: Adapted from Compton et al., 1991, pp. 1700–1701.

person who races a horse too hard, treats livestock too harshly, or buys and consumes in excess to have an emotional disturbance (Draguns, 1986). Cuban Americans who practice a religion called *santeria* believe that people can be possessed by spirits and communicate with deceased ancestors. Individuals who report this belief to clinicians unfamiliar with their religious beliefs can be misdiagnosed as psychotic (Alonso & Jeffrey, 1988). Thus, diagnosis of psychiatric illness always requires knowledge of the patient's culture or subculture.

Social change can also lead to changes in prevalent forms of psychopathology. In times of rapid social change, when people do not know what norms to follow and have lost the sense of meaning in life that an intact culture provides, drug abuse, suicide, and aggressive behavior tend to rise dramatically (Berry, 1989; Wallace, 1956). At the same time, the extended family may buffer children against some of the negative effects of rapid social change. In Khartoum, the capital of the Sudan, children reared in extended families have considerably fewer emotional problems than those reared in nuclear families; children with a grandmother involved in parenting are especially likely to be psychologically healthy (El Hassan Al Awad & Sonuga-Barke, 1992).

IS MENTAL ILLNESS NOTHING BUT A CULTURAL CONSTRUCTION?

If definitions of abnormality vary by culture, can we really speak of mental illness at all, or is mental illness simply a construct used by a society to brand and punish those who fail to respect its norms? In the 1960s and 1970s, several prominent researchers and social critics suggested that this is the case. Psychiatrist Thomas Szasz (1974) proposed that mental illness is a myth used to make people conform to society's standards of normality. In his view, which was highly influential in changing laws for commitment to mental institutions, people should only be treated for mental illness if *they* consider their symptoms a problem.

A variation of this view, called labeling theory, focuses on the disadvantages of categorizing mental disorders at all (Scheff, 1970). According to **labeling theory,**

According to labeling theory, once people take on the label of "patient," they may be forced into the role by others and may actually become helpless and dysfunctional.

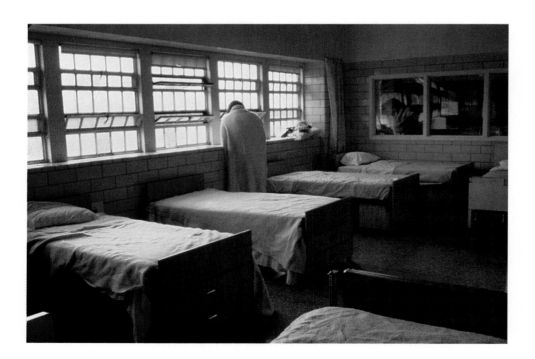

diagnosis is simply a way of labeling individuals whom a society considers deviant. Labeling can be dangerous because it stigmatizes and stereotypes "patients," whose subsequent actions are interpreted as part of their "craziness" and who may face discrimination based on their diagnoses. Labeled individuals may also take on the role of a sick or crazy person and hence actually begin to play the part into which they have been cast.

A Case of Misdiagnosis?   A classic study raised some of these issues in a dramatic way. David Rosenhan had himself and seven other normal persons around the United States admitted to various psychiatric hospitals by faking symptoms of schizophrenia, complaining of hearing voices that said "empty," "hollow," or "thud" (Rosenhan, 1973). All but one of these "patients" was subsequently diagnosed schizophrenic. Once on the psychiatric wards, however, the pseudopatients behaved as they normally would and told staff they no longer heard voices. Psychiatric staff nonetheless interpreted their behavior as evidence of disturbance. For example, when the pseudopatients took copious notes while on the unit, hospital personnel commented in their psychiatric records about their "peculiar note-taking behavior." When these pseudopatients were finally discharged, which took an average of 19 days, they were given the label "schizophrenia, in remission."

Rosenhan's study set off a wave of controversy, for it appeared to demonstrate that psychiatric illness is in the eye of the beholder and that even trained eyes are not very acute. Others argued, however, that the study led to some very dramatic but largely incorrect conclusions (see Spitzer, 1985). Behavior is meaningful only when it is understood in context. Singing is normal in a chorus but would be very peculiar during a lecture. Similarly, taking notes *does* appear to be abnormal for a patient in a psychiatric hospital who has complained of hallucinations; had the pseudopatients not lied about their initial symptoms, this would have been an appropriate inference. Furthermore, in medical terminology "in remission" means simply that a patient has previously reported symptoms that are no longer present. One critic concluded that the study did little more than illustrate that people can fool a clinician if they try hard enough (Spitzer, 1985), just as they can trick a neurologist by complaining of all the symptoms of stroke, or a potential employer by creating a false resume.

Mental Illness Is More Than Just a Label   Empirical investigations have not supported labeling theory either, at least not in its more sweeping forms (see Gove, 1982; Phillips & Dinitz, 1982). Many disorders occur and are recognized as problems cross-culturally, suggesting that they are not just ways of labeling deviants (Draguns, 1990). This is the case, for example, with schizophrenia, in which people lose touch with reality and may hold bizarre beliefs (e.g., that their thoughts are being broadcast on the radio). The negative consequences of labeling can indeed be profound. Without diagnosis, however, mental health professionals would be in the same helpless and confused position as physicians in the early 1980s were when confronted with patients exhibiting the strange set of symptoms that turned out to be AIDS. One cannot research and treat a problem without distinguishing those who have it from those who do not.

The idea that psychopathology is a myth or an arbitrary label also tends to romanticize illness. Would anyone in his "right mind" really want to take on the problems that accompany schizophrenia, such as loss of contact with reality and the profound sense of loneliness and isolation that arises from chronically misunderstanding and feeling misunderstood or shunned? In light of the tremendous suffering that accompanies this illness, the view that schizophrenia is simply an alternative way of seeing the world appears rather naive. It is also contradicted by an accumulating body of evidence documenting that schizophrenia is an illness of the brain, much like Alzheimer's disease, which no one would similarly describe as an alternative way of seeing the world.

INTERIM SUMMARY   **Psychopathology** refers to problematic patterns of thought, feeling, or behavior that disrupt an individual's sense of well-being or social or occupational functioning. Cultures differ in both the disorders to which their members are vulnerable and the ways they categorize mental illness. Szasz proposed that mental illness is a myth used to make people conform to society's standards of normality. Similarly, **labeling theory** argues that diagnosis is a way of stigmatizing deviants. Both approaches have some validity but are substantially overstated.

CONTEMPORARY APPROACHES TO PSYCHOPATHOLOGY

Although few contemporary psychologists view mental illness as a myth or ascribe its causes to demon possession, they differ considerably in the way they conceptualize the nature and causes of psychological disorders. Consider the case of Charlie, a 24-year-old business school student with an intense fear of being in groups. This symptom is particularly difficult since his program (and future occupation) requires him to participate in many group situations. Socially, his fear of groups is also distressing: Whenever Charlie is at a party, he feels tremendously anxious and usually ends up leaving shortly after he arrives. He worries that people will laugh at and ostracize him and that he will be mortally embarrassed. His mouth becomes dry, his hands become clammy, and his stomach knots. Paradoxically, he feels most anxious when he should feel most confident, as when he has expertise in the topic being discussed. Charlie's problem has intensified since he began business school. His father, who never attended college, ridiculed him for his decision to enter graduate school ("Why don't you just get a job?").

The way a psychologist would understand Charlie's anxiety depends on the psychologist's theoretical orientation. We first examine psychodynamic and cognitive-behavioral perspectives. Next we consider two very different approaches—biological and systems theories—and then consider what evolutionary theory might have to offer the understanding of psychopathology.

PSYCHODYNAMIC PERSPECTIVE

Psychodynamic theorists distinguish among three broad classes of psychopathology: neuroses, personality disorders, and psychoses. **Neuroses** are problems in living, such as phobias, constant self-doubt, and repetitive interpersonal problems (e.g., trouble with authority figures). They occur in most, if not all, people at different points in their lives and usually do not stop them from functioning reasonably well. **Personality disorders** are chronic and severe disturbances that substantially inhibit the capacity to love and to work. People with personality disorders often have difficulty maintaining meaningful relationships and employment, interpret interpersonal events in highly distorted ways, and are chronically vulnerable to depression or despair. **Psychoses** are gross disturbances involving a loss of touch with reality; a psychotic person may hear voices telling him to kill himself or believe (without good reason) that the CIA is trying to assassinate him.

From a psychodynamic perspective, these three broad classes of disorders form a continuum of functioning (Figure 15.1). People in the normal to neurotic range may have a variety of neurotic problems, but they are generally able, as Freud put it, "to love and to work." Pathology becomes more severe as people move down the continuum, with the most troubled individuals being those who are chronically psychotic (Kernberg, 1984).

LEVEL OF DISTURBANCE	CAPACITIES		
	Love	Work	Relation to Reality
Normal to neurotic	Able to maintain relationships.	Able to maintain employment.	Able to see reality clearly.
	May have minor difficulties such as conflicts with significant others or a tendency to be competitive.	May have difficulties such as rigidity, defensiveness, underconfidence, workaholism, overambition, or underachievement.	May have minor defensive distortions, such as seeing the self and significant others as better than they really are.
Personality disordered	Unable to maintain relationships consistently.	Difficulty maintaining employment.	Generally able to see reality with clarity (i.e., with no hallucinations or delusions).
	May avoid relationships, jump into them too quickly, or end them abruptly.	May be grossly underemployed, extremely unable to get along with bosses, or likely to terminate employment abruptly.	Prone to gross misinterpretations in interpersonal affairs. (A subset suffers from chronically idiosyncratic thinking.)
Psychotic	Tremendous difficulty maintaining relationships.	Unable to maintain employment anywhere near intellectual level.	Unable to distinguish clearly between what is real and what is not.
	May be socially peculiar.	Large percentage are chronically unemployed.	Has delusions, hallucinations, or other psychotic thought processes.

FIGURE 15.1

Continuum of psychopathology. Psychodynamic theorists place disorders on a continuum of functioning, reflecting the maturity and strength of the person's underlying personality structure.

These three levels of pathology also lie along a continuum in terms of the **etiology** (origins) of psychological disturbance. Psychoses result primarily from biological abnormalities, with some environmental input, although psychodynamic clinicians emphasize that even people with debilitating mental disorders have wishes, fears, conflicts, defenses, hopes for their lives that they must often grieve losing, and patterns of thinking, feeling, and behaving in close relationships that are not all reducible to biological illness. Neuroses and personality disorders stem more from environmental (particularly childhood) experiences, sometimes interacting with biological vulnerabilities (Figure 15.2). In general, people tend to function consistently at one level or another. However, neurotic symptoms (such as phobias) also occur in more severely disturbed patients, and psychotic states can occur episodically (that is, periodically, in discrete episodes) in people who are otherwise relatively healthy, such as many patients with bipolar disorder (manic-depression) who are largely unimpaired between episodes.

FIGURE 15.2
Heredity and experience in psychopathology. From a psychodynamic point of view, neuroses are primarily environmental in origin, although they may reflect some genetic vulnerabilities. Personality disorders stem either from extreme childhood experiences or from an interaction of genetic and environmental vulnerabilities. Psychoses are primarily genetic in origin, although childhood and adult experiences shape their expression.

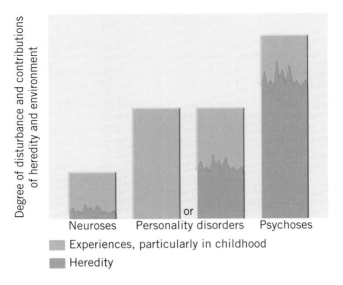

To assess psychopathology, a psychodynamic psychologist gathers information about the patient's current level of functioning and life stresses, the origins and course of the symptom, and salient events in the person's developmental history. The clinician uses all of this information to make a **psychodynamic formulation,** a set of hypotheses about the patient's personality structure and the meaning of the symptom. This formulation attempts to answer three questions: What does the patient wish for and fear? What psychological resources does the person have at his disposal? And how does he experience himself and others (Westen, 1995, 1998)?

The first question focuses on the person's dominant motives and conflicts. Psychodynamic clinicians view neurotic symptoms as expressions of, or compromises among, various motives. In this view, symptoms typically reflect unconscious conflicts among wishes and fears and the defensive efforts used to resolve them. Symptoms may also result from beliefs, often forged in childhood (such as the belief that anger is "wrong"), which lead to conflicts and defenses (such as efforts to avoid feeling or acknowledging anger). The second question is about ego functioning—the person's ability to function autonomously, make sound decisions, think clearly, and regulate impulses and emotions (see Bellack et al., 1973). The third question addresses the patient's object relations (Chapter 12), that is, the person's ability to form meaningful relationships with others and to maintain self-esteem.

Any competent psychologist would require more data before arriving at a formulation of Charlie's case. Nevertheless, a psychodynamic psychologist might hypothesize that Charlie's symptoms reflect a conflict over success, since his anxiety is strongest when he is in a position to shine and increases as he gets closer to achieving his goals. Charlie wants to be successful and display his abilities, but this desire evokes old feelings of ridicule by his father. Charlie might also unconsciously equate success with outdoing his father, who had minimal education; hence he feels anxious and guilty. A psychodynamic psychologist would want to assess whether Charlie's ability to function and adapt to the environment is impaired in other ways or whether his social phobia is a relatively isolated symptom (ego functioning). The clinician would also assess whether Charlie's interpersonal problems are specific to groups or are part of a more serious underlying difficulty in forming and maintaining relationships (attachment and object relations).

INTERIM SUMMARY Psychodynamic theorists distinguish among three broad classes of psychopathology that form a continuum of functioning: **neuroses** (enduring problems in living that cause distress or dysfunction), **personality disorders** (chronic, severe disturbances that substantially inhibit the capacity to love and to work), and **psychoses** (gross disturbances involving a loss of touch with reality). A **psychodynamic formulation** is a set of hypotheses about the patient's personality structure and the meaning of the symptom, focusing on the person's motives and conflicts, adaptive functions, and ability to form meaningful relationships and maintain self-esteem.

COGNITIVE-BEHAVIORAL PERSPECTIVE

In clinical psychology, many practitioners consider themselves **cognitive-behavioral,** integrating an understanding of classical and operant conditioning with a cognitive-social perspective (Turner et al., 1992). They focus not on a hypothesized underlying personality structure but on discrete processes, such as thoughts that precede an anxiety reaction or physiological symptoms (e.g., racing heart) that accompany it.

From a more behavioral perspective, many of the problems that require treatment involve conditioned emotional responses (Chapter 5), in which a previously neutral stimulus has become associated with an emotionally arousing stimulus. For example, a person like Charlie might have had bad experiences in school when he would speak and thus came to associate speaking in groups with anxiety. This anxiety might then have generalized to other group situations. Making matters worse, his fear of groups would then likely lead him to avoid them, resulting not only in continued social anxiety but in poor social skills. Thus, a behaviorally oriented clinician carefully assesses the conditions under which symptoms such as depression and anxiety arise and tries to discover the stimuli that elicit them (see Hersen, 1988). What stimuli have become associated with depressed feelings through classical conditioning? What behaviors is the person engaging in that increase depression, such as negative interactions with a spouse (see Gottman, 1998)? Under what circumstances does the individual become so distressed that she becomes suicidal or tries to hurt herself as a way of controlling the feeling (Koerner & Linehan, 1996)?

From a more cognitive perspective, psychopathology reflects dysfunctional cognitions, such as low self-efficacy expectancies, a tendency to believe that situations are hopeless, and negative views of the self (Alloy et al., 1989; Beck, 1976, 1991). The clinician thus focuses on irrational beliefs and maladaptive cognitive processes that maintain dysfunctional behaviors and emotions. For example, a number of studies show that patients with different kinds of disorders show attentional biases that may perpetuate their psychopathology (Gilboa & Gotlib, 1997). Depressed people tend to be "on the lookout" for negative information about themselves; patients with anxiety disorders tend to notice potentially threatening stimuli that would not catch other people's attention, or they interpret ambiguous information in a threatening way (such as a random comment by a friend that could be interpreted as subtly rejecting).

From a behavioral point of view, Charlie's phobia is a conditioned emotional response (classical conditioning). Unfortunately, the more he avoids the phobic situation, the more his avoidance behavior is negatively reinforced; in other words, avoidance reduces anxiety, which reinforces avoidance (operant conditioning). Further, Charlie's anxiety may actually *make* him less socially competent; as a result, others respond less positively to him, which in turn makes him more anxious and avoidant. To try to unravel the conditions eliciting his anxiety, the behaviorally oriented clinician would ask precisely where and when Charlie becomes anxious. Are there group situations in which he does not become anxious? Does he become anxious only when he is expected to talk or even when he can remain silent?

Working more cognitively, the cognitive-behavioral clinician would assess the thoughts that run through Charlie's mind as his anxiety mounts. For instance, Charlie may erroneously believe that if people laugh at him, he will "die" of embarrassment or some other calamity will befall him. The clinician would examine the way such irrational ideas maintain the phobia. For example, Charlie might feel anxious in any situation that requires him to speak articulately because he does not believe he can do so. Alternatively, he may hold the irrational belief that he must excel in all situations if people are to like and respect him and consequently become terrified at the possibility of failure.

INTERIM SUMMARY   **Cognitive-behavioral** clinicians integrate an understanding of classical and operant conditioning with a cognitive-social perspective. From a behavioral perspective, many psychological problems involve conditioned emotional responses, in which a previously neutral stimulus has become associated with unpleasant emotions. Irrational fears in turn elicit avoidance, which perpetuates them and may lead to secondary problems, such as poor social skills. From a cognitive perspective, many psychological problems reflect dysfunctional attitudes, beliefs, and cognitive processes, such as a tendency to interpret events negatively.

BIOLOGICAL APPROACH

To understand psychopathology, mental health professionals often move from a mental to a physiological level. Practitioners from all theoretical perspectives operate at this level of analysis when they evaluate patients for potential biological contributions to their symptoms, as when they take a family history to assess possible genetic contributions or inquire about head injuries and serious viral infections in childhood to assess possible influences on the developing brain. However, some practitioners believe a biological approach can explain all or most psychopathology.

Understanding and Assessing Psychopathology

The biological approach looks for the roots of mental disorders in the brain's circuitry. For example, normal anxiety occurs through activation of neural circuits involving, among other structures, the amygdala and frontal lobes (Chapter 11). Thus, one might expect pathological anxiety to involve heightened or easily triggered activation of those circuits, and, indeed, neuroimaging studies confirm this hypothesis for many anxiety disorders (Reiman, 1997).

Biological researchers have focused much of their attention on neurotransmitter dysfunction, since too much or too little neurotransmitter activity could disrupt normal patterns of neural firing. To return to the example of anxiety, if normal anxiety reactions involve the neurotransmitter norepinephrine, then individuals whose genes predispose them to produce too much of this neurotransmitter or whose receptors are overly sensitive in circuits involving the amygdala are likely to experience pathological anxiety. Because psychopathology runs in families, biologically oriented clinicians are likely to assess carefully for family history of various disorders that could suggest genetic vulnerability.

Aside from family (genetic) history, clinicians considering biological contributions to mental disorders often assess the patient's mental status. **Mental status** refers to the intactness of memory, orientation to reality (whether the patient knows who he is, what day of the week it is, and so forth), state of consciousness (whether the person is clear and alert), reasoning ability, and ability to think abstractly. For example, if the patient tends to use words idiosyncratically, the clinician might suspect psychosis. The clinician might then inquire whether she ever hears voices or sees things that are not there or ask her to explain the meaning of a proverb like "A stitch in time saves nine." A patient whose thinking is disordered may produce a very concrete response such as "You have to sew things now or they will fall apart again" or a response filled with idiosyncratic elaborations such as "A stitch now could save your life—nine lives, like a cat."

Integrating Nature and Nurture: The Diathesis–Stress Model

The biological approach is not incompatible with the perspectives described thus far. Charlie's anxiety may indeed be associated with his conflicts about achieving success, or he may be caught in a spiral of negatively reinforced avoidance of social situations. Nevertheless, his tendency to become anxious in the first place could reflect a biological predisposition.

Theorists of various persuasions often adopt a **diathesis-stress model**, which proposes that people with an underlying vulnerability (called a diathesis) may exhibit symptoms under stressful circumstances. The diathesis may be biological, such as a genetic propensity for anxiety symptoms caused by overactivity of norepinephrine. Alternatively, the diathesis can be environmental, stemming from events such as a history of neglect, excessive parental criticism, or loss in childhood. Upsetting events in adulthood, such as the loss of a lover or a failure at work, might then activate the vulnerability.

INTERIM SUMMARY The biological approach looks for the roots of mental disorders in the brain's circuitry, such as neurotransmitter dysfunction. Clinicians operating from a biological viewpoint assess the patient's family history for genetic contributions as well as the patient's **mental status**, including memory, orientation to reality, state of consciousness, reasoning ability, and ability to think abstractly. Theorists of various persuasions often adopt a **diathesis-stress model**, which proposes that people with an underlying vulnerability (called a diathesis) may exhibit symptoms under stressful circumstances.

SYSTEMS APPROACH

A social systems approach looks for the roots of psychopathology in the broader social context. That is, a **systems approach** explains an individual's behavior in the context of a social group, such as a couple, family, or larger group. An individual is part of a **system**, a group with interdependent parts; what happens in one part of the system influences what happens in others. From this standpoint, diagnosing a problem in an individual without considering the systems in which he operates is like trying to figure out why a car is getting poor gas mileage without considering traffic conditions.

Like the biological approach, a systems approach is not incompatible with other perspectives, since it operates at another level of analysis. For example, a child who has problems with aggressive behavior at school may be part of a broader family system in which violence is a way of life. Nevertheless, in clinical practice, practitioners who take a systems approach frequently consider it their primary theoretical orientation, much as some psychiatrists (medical doctors trained in psychiatry) view most psychopathology in terms of biological dysfunction.

Family Systems

Most systems clinicians adopt a **family systems model**, which views an individual's symptoms as symptoms of dysfunction in the family (Hoffman, 1981, 1991). In other words, the **identified patient** (the person identified as the one who needs help) is the **symptom bearer** (the person displaying the family's difficulties); however, the problem lies in the family, not primarily in the individual. For instance, a couple brought their child to see a therapist because he was disruptive at school and punishment had been ineffective. The psychologist inquired about the parents' marriage and found that it had been very shaky until the child began having difficulties at school. Once the child became symptomatic, the parents worked together to help him, and their marital problems subsided. Thus, the problem was not so much a disruptive child as a disruptive marriage. The child not only *expressed* his parents' marital problems through his symptom but also helped preserve their marriage by becoming symptomatic.

Systems theorists refer to the methods family members use to preserve equilibrium in a family (such as preserving a marriage) as **family homeostatic mechanisms**. These mechanisms operate much like the homeostatic mechanisms discussed in Chapter 10 on motivation. In the case above, marital tension evoked a set of behaviors in the child, which in turn reduced the marital tension, much as a furnace turns on until the temperature in a room reaches the temperature set on the thermostat. Thus, psychological symptoms are actually dysfunctional efforts to cope with a disturbance in the family.

Family systems theorists also focus on the ways families are organized, including family roles, boundaries, and alliances (see Boszormenyi-Nagy & Spark, 1973; Haley, 1976; Minuchin, 1974). **Family roles** are the parts individuals play in repetitive family "dramas"—typical interaction patterns among family members—much like actors in a play. Playing roles is not in itself pathological; it occurs in every social group (Chapter 18). For example, one child may take on the role of mediator between two siblings who are often in conflict. In some families, however, a child may become a *scapegoat* who is blamed for anything bad that happens (Bermann, 1973). In other families, a child and parent may switch roles, a phenomenon known as **role reversal**, in which the child takes care of the parent, attends to the parent's needs, and takes on the parent's responsibilities (see Alexander, 1992; Burkett, 1991).

Assessing the Family System

In assessing a family, a psychologist with a systems orientation examines the marital subsystem (the relationship between the parents) and the roles people play. The clinician may want to explore the **boundaries**, or physical and psychological limits, of the family system and its subsystems (see Finkelhor, 1984; Friedman et al., 1987; Goldstein, 1988; Ryder & Bartle, 1991). Some families are *enmeshed*, that is, too involved with each other's business, making privacy and autonomy impossible. Others are *disengaged*, with minimal contact among family members (see Olson, 1985). Some families have rigid boundaries with the outside world, punishing their members if they disclose too many family secrets or spend too much time away from home; others seem to lack internal boundaries, as when a parent refuses to allow a child any privacy.

The systems-oriented psychologist assesses other interaction patterns, such as **family alliances,** or who sides with whom in conflicts. A child who begins abusing drugs, for example, may be expressing frustration at feeling excluded from or consistently attacked by an alliance between a parent and a sibling who is seen as the "good" child. The clinician also looks for problematic **communication patterns**, as when a couple communicates primarily by fighting.

A psychologist working from a systems approach might evaluate Charlie first in one session by himself and then in another with his father or family. Although systems theorists differ considerably in their specific approaches, the clinician might assess the extent to which Charlie is bringing issues from his family of origin into his new relationships (Bowen, 1978, 1991). The systems clinician would likely observe the way Charlie and his father communicate, looking for mutually unsatisfying patterns in their interactions. The clinician might also try to understand these patterns in the context of the family's subculture, which may have particular ways of regulating emotional expression and communication between the generations. For example, Charlie's conflicts about success may be heightened by the fact that his father is an immigrant who does not approve of Charlie's occupational choice and believes that a son should follow his father's directives.

INTERIM SUMMARY   A **systems approach** explains an individual's behavior in the context of a social group, such as a couple, family, or larger group. Most systems clinicians adopt a **family systems model**, which views an individual's symptoms as symptoms of family dysfunction. The methods family members use to preserve equilibrium in a family are called **family homeostatic mechanisms**. Family systems theorists focus on the ways families are organized, including **family roles** (the parts individuals play in the family), **boundaries** (physical and psychological limits of the family and its subsystems, including individual members), and **alliances** (patterns in which family members side with one another).

EVOLUTIONARY PERSPECTIVE

Although the evolutionary perspective does not offer the kind of comprehensive system for understanding (and treating) psychopathology as the approaches described above, evolutionary psychologists are likely to provide insight into psychopathology in the years ahead. In one sense, psychopathology is a paradox from an evolutionary perspective, since psychopathology is maladaptation, and evolution is about natural selection of adaptive traits. Nevertheless, an evolutionary perspective could explain psychopathology in at least three ways.

First, nothing in the nature of evolution requires that every organism is well adapted to its environment. In fact, natural selection acts on random variation in genotypes by weeding out those that lead to less adaptive phenotypes. As in all evolutionary analyses, it is important to remember that evolutionary pressures are always relative to a specific environment. In some circumstances, a tendency to be anxious could confer an evolutionary advantage by making individuals vigilant to potential dangers; in others, a tendency to be anxious could be socially stigmatizing and hence reduce reproductive success.

A challenging question for evolutionary psychologists is how to explain the presence, over several generations, of a stable percentage of the population that has a debilitating mental disorder. How, for example, can an evolutionary theorist explain the worldwide presence of schizophrenia, a disease that clearly diminishes an individual's capacity for both survival and reproduction? A second evolutionary explanation, though still speculative at this point, uses the analogy of sickle cell anemia (Chapter 8). Sickle cell anemia is common only in people whose ancestors came from parts of the world where malaria was prevalent. The reason is that people who inherit the sickle cell gene from one parent are immune to malaria; however, if they inherit the gene from both parents, they will die from sickle cell anemia. Over time a population will evolve a stable percentage of sickle cell genes: If the presence of the gene gets too high in the population, more people die of sickle cell, which reduces its prevalence; if the percentage gets too low, more people die of malaria, and those who survive are more likely to carry the gene.

A similar phenomenon could explain genes for mental disorders such as anxiety disorders or schizophrenia. The mechanisms in some cases may be obvious and intuitive, whereas in others they may be completely unexpected. An obvious example might occur in the evolution of anxiety disorders, which are to some degree heritable. As we will see, having too little anxiety (a central component of neuroticism) can contribute to antisocial personality traits and reckless behavior that lead to premature death; in contrast, having too much anxiety can lead to anxiety disorders. The levels of anxiety in the population attributable to genes could thus reflect a relatively simple mechanism of natural selection that, across the *population,* maximizes survival and reproduction but produces dysfunction in *individuals* whose genetic inheritance places them at one extreme or another.

The evolutionary "trade-offs" that produce a stable percentage of disordered individuals could actually be much less obvious because a single gene or set of genes could act on two very different traits. For example, the genes that predispose individuals to schizophrenia could also render nondisordered bearers of the gene less vulnerable to some kind of deadly viral infection such as smallpox. The result would be a stable percentage of the population with schizophrenia, just as is the case for sickle cell.

A third evolutionary explanation for psychopathology centers on the interaction of genes and environments. Psychopathology could reflect normal processes gone awry because of abnormal circumstances. Fear is a highly adaptive, inborn mechanism that keeps people away from circumstances associated with danger. However, if those circumstances cannot be avoided, or if the person is traumatized by them, he may become preoccupied with fear and less able to function adaptively.

INTERIM SUMMARY   Evolutionary psychologists could explain psychopathology in at least three ways: as random variation likely to be weeded out by natural selection; as the result of broader population pressures that select rates of genes in the population that can be either functional or dysfunctional depending on the other genes an individual inherits; and as the maladaptive "tuning" of psychological mechanisms that are normally adaptive.

DESCRIPTIVE DIAGNOSIS: DSM-IV AND PSYCHOLOGICAL SYNDROMES

The approaches discussed thus far all assume a particular point of view about the nature and origins of psychopathology. A *descriptive* approach, in contrast, attempts to be *atheoretical*, that is, not wedded to any particular theoretical perspective on etiology. In **descriptive diagnosis**, mental disorders are classified in terms of **clinical syndromes**, or constellations of symptoms that tend to occur together. For example, in a depressive syndrome, depressed mood is often accompanied by loss of interest in pleasurable activities, insomnia, loss of appetite, poor concentration, and decreased self-esteem.

DSM-IV

Until the early 1950s, psychologists and psychiatrists lacked a standard set of diagnoses. Psychologists from each school of thought used their own preferred terms, and systematic empirical investigation of most psychiatric disorders was impossible (see Nathan, 1998). That changed when the American Psychiatric Association published the first edition of a manual of clinical syndromes that clinicians use to make diagnoses, called the *Diagnostic and Statistical Manual of Mental Disorders (DSM)*, now in its fourth edition **(DSM-IV)** (1994). DSM-IV aims to identify mental disorders on the basis of readily observable signs or symptoms to minimize idiosyncratic diagnoses. The major diagnostic categories of DSM-IV are listed in Table 15.2.

Descriptive diagnosis allows researchers and clinicians in many different settings to diagnose patients in a similar manner, regardless of their theoretical orientation (see Spitzer et al., 1992). In reality, however, not even a descriptive approach can be entirely atheoretical. The descriptive approach embodied in DSM-IV tends to be most compatible with a **medical model** of psychopathology, which presumes that psychological disorders fall into discrete categories, much like medical disorders such as tuberculosis or melanoma. Not surprisingly, then, psychiatrists tend to emphasize descriptive diagnosis more than psychologists, although nearly all mental health professionals use descriptive diagnoses when initially evaluating a patient.

DSM-IV uses a **multiaxial system of diagnosis,** placing symptoms in their biological and social context by evaluating patients along five axes (Table 15.3). These axes cover not only symptoms and personality disturbances but also relevant information such as medical conditions and environmental stressors. Axis I lists the clinical syndromes for which a patient seeks treatment, such as depression or schizophrenia. Axis II lists personality disorders and mental retardation. The assumption behind the distinction between the two axes is that Axis I describes *state* disorders—the patient's current condition, or state—whereas Axis II describes *trait* disorders—enduring problems with the person's functioning, such as level adaptive capacity and problematic ways of thinking, feeling, and behaving. Thus, a person who is severely depressed (a state disorder, coded on Axis I) may have an enduring personality disorder that renders him vulnerable to depression, or he may simply have had difficulty coping with the death of a spouse (and hence receive no Axis II diagnosis). Although Axis II also includes mental retardation, as a shorthand most researchers treat "Axis II" and "personality disorders" as synonyms, since personality disorders are much more prevalent in psychiatric populations.

Axis III lists any general medical conditions that may be relevant to under-

TABLE 15.2   SELECTED DIAGNOSTIC CATEGORIES OF DSM-IV

CATEGORY	DESCRIPTION
Disorders usually first diagnosed in infancy, childhood, or adolescence	Disorders involving deviations from normal development, such as mental retardation, attention deficit/hyperactivity disorder, and conduct disorder
Substance-related disorders	Disorders associated with drug abuse (including alcohol), as well as side effects of medication and exposure to toxins
Schizophrenia and other psychotic disorders	Disorders characterized by loss of contact with reality, marked disturbances of thought and perception, and bizarre behavior
Mood disorders	Disorders characterized by disturbances of normal mood, notably depression, mania (elation), or alternating periods of each
Anxiety disorders	Disorders in which anxiety is the main symptom (such as generalized anxiety, panic, phobic, posttraumatic stress disorders, and obsessive-compulsive disorder)
Somatoform disorders	Disorders involving physical symptoms that lack an organic basis, such as hypochondriasis (excessive preoccupation with health and fear of disease without a realistic basis for concern)
Dissociative disorders	Disorders characterized by temporary alterations or disruptions in consciousness, memory, identity, or perception, such as psychologically induced amnesia
Sexual and gender identity disorders	Disorders of sexuality and gender identity, including sexual dysfunctions, paraphilias (sexual urges, fantasies, or behaviors involving unusual objects, nonconsenting partners, or pain or humiliation, which cause significant distress or dysfunction), and gender identity disorders (such as cross-dressing that leads to considerable distress or impairment in functioning)
Eating disorders	Disorders characterized by severe disturbance in eating behavior, including anorexia nervosa and bulimia nervosa
Adjustment disorders	Disorders that are usually relatively mild and transient, in which clinically significant emotional or behavioral symptoms develop as a consequence of some identifiable stressor
Personality disorders	Disorders characterized by long-standing patterns of maladaptive behavior that deviate from cultural expectations and are pervasive and inflexible, such as borderline and antisocial personality disorders

Source: Adapted from *Diagnostic and Statistical Manual of Mental Disorders,* 4th ed., American Psychiatric Association, Washington, DC, 1994.

standing the person's psychopathology (such as diabetes or hypothyroidism, which can affect mood). Axis IV is reserved for psychosocial and environmental stressors (life events such as the death of a family member that could be contributing to emotional problems). Axis V rates the patient's current level of functioning (on a scale of 0 to 100) and the highest level of functioning the patient has attained during the past year. Table 15.4 shows how Charlie might be diagnosed using this multiaxial system.

In the sections that follow, we examine some of the major clinical syndromes, starting with disorders that usually become evident in childhood and working our way through substance-related disorders, schizophrenia, mood disorders, anxiety disorders, dissociative disorders, and personality disorders. (The order is arbitrary; we simply follow the order in which the disorders are described in DSM-IV.)

First, however, a brief warning is in order. You may have experienced some of these symptoms at one time or another and may start to worry that you have one

TABLE 15.3 AXES OF DSM-IV

AXIS	DESCRIPTION
Axis I	Symptoms that cause distress or significantly impair social or occupational functioning
Axis II	Personality disorders and mental retardation—chronic and enduring problems that impair interpersonal or occupational functioning
Axis III	Medical conditions that may be relevant to understanding or treating a psychological disorder
Axis IV	Psychosocial and environmental problems (such as negative life events and interpersonal stressors) that may affect the diagnosis, treatment, and prognosis of psychological disorders
Axis V	Global assessment of functioning—the individual's overall level of functioning in social, occupational, and leisure activities

Source: Adapted from *Diagnostic and Statistical Manual of Mental Disorders*, 4th ed., American Psychiatric Association, Washington, DC, 1994.

(or all) of the disorders. This reaction is similar to the "first-year medical student syndrome" experienced by many medical students, who imagine they have whichever disease they are currently studying. Thus, you may recognize yourself or someone you know in many of the symptoms or syndromes described, in part because these disorders are in fact highly prevalent in the population and in part because we all experience anxiety, sadness, and interpersonal difficulties at various points in our lives, often appropriately (as at the death of a loved one). Further, bear in mind that only when symptoms disrupt a person's functioning or sense of well-being would a trained mental health professional actually diagnose a disorder, and that most forms of psychopathology can be treated (Chapter 16).

INTERIM SUMMARY In **descriptive diagnosis**, mental disorders are classified into **clinical syndromes**, constellations of symptoms that tend to occur together. The descriptive approach embodied in DSM-IV tends to be most compatible with a **medical model** that presumes psychological disorders fall into discrete categories. DSM-IV uses a **multiaxial system of diagnosis,** placing symptoms in their biological and social context by evaluating patients along five axes: clinical syndromes, personality disorders (and mental retardation), medical conditions, environmental stressors, and global level of functioning.

DISORDERS USUALLY FIRST DIAGNOSED IN INFANCY, CHILDHOOD, OR ADOLESCENCE

Several mental disorders typically arise during infancy, childhood, or adolescence, ranging from disturbances of eating and feeding (such as eating rocks and other

TABLE 15.4 MULTIAXIAL DIAGNOSIS OF CHARLIE

AXIS	DESCRIPTION
Axis I	**Social phobia** (disorder marked by fear that occurs when the person is in a social situation)
Axis II	Rule out (possible) **avoidant personality disorder** (disorder marked by avoidance of interpersonal situations, fear of being disliked or rejected, and view of self as inadequate or inferior)
Axis III	None (no medical conditions)
Axis IV	Business school, father's criticism (current stressors)
Axis V	Global assessment of functioning: 55 (*moderate symptoms*, on a scale from 0 to 100)

inedible objects) to severe separation distress upon leaving home for school. Two of the most common disorders are attention-deficit hyperactivity disorder and conduct disorder.

Attention-Deficit Hyperactivity Disorder

Many children and adolescents are brought to mental health professionals because of behavioral difficulties at school or at home. Consider the case of Jimmy, a 6-year-old whose teacher reports that he cannot sit still, does not pay attention, and is constantly disturbing his classmates. Jimmy fidgets in his chair, and when his teacher directs him to do work, he can only concentrate for a few seconds before becoming disruptive, making noises or throwing paper wads across the room. Jimmy's teacher may suspect that he has **attention-deficit hyperactivity disorder (ADHD)**, characterized by inattention, impulsiveness, and hyperactivity inappropriate for the child's age. Children with this disorder have disturbances in each of these areas to differing degrees. In the extreme case, a child may be in perpetual motion—running, jumping, disrupting activities, or picking fights with other children.

Although children with ADHD may exhibit symptoms by age 4, the disorder often goes unrecognized until they enter school, since children are not usually required to comply with stringent social demands before that time (Campbell, 1985). Setting a standard for hyperactive behavior in preschoolers is difficult; in fact, as many as 50 percent of mothers of 4-year-old boys believe their son is hyperactive (Varley, 1984)! The prevalence of ADHD is estimated at 3 to 5 percent of school-aged children (Cantwell, 1976; Whalen & Henker, 1991). The disorder is four to nine times more prevalent in males than females.

Attention-deficit hyperactivity disorder runs in families: 20 to 30 percent of children with ADHD have a parent or sibling with a history of the disorder (Brunstetter & Silver, 1985). Moreover, families of children with ADHD have a higher incidence of alcoholism and personality disorders in both parents, especially fathers (Cantwell, 1972; Pihl et al., 1990). Although many cases probably stem from central nervous system dysfunction, the more risk factors a child experiences (such as severe marital discord between parents, low social class, maternal psychopathology, and paternal criminality), the more likely he is to develop the disorder (Biederman et al., 1995).

To what extent children "grow out of" this disorder is unclear. One longitudinal study found that *half* of adults who were hyperactive as children exhibited residual signs of the disorder in adulthood, such as difficulty sustaining attention; in contrast, another study found clear evidence of ADHD in only 4 percent of adults diagnosed with the disorder in childhood (Mannuzza et al., 1998; Weiss et al., 1985). Children with ADHD are, however, at increased risk for other psychiatric and social problems in adolescence and adulthood, particularly antisocial behavior and substance abuse (Biederman et al., 1996; Mannuzza et al., 1998).

Conduct Disorder

Another relatively common disturbance of childhood is **conduct disorder**, in which a child persistently violates societal norms and the rights of others. Symptoms include physical aggression toward people or animals, chronic fighting, vandalism, persistent lying, and stealing. Such children are obstinate, resent taking direction, lack empathy and compassion, and seldom express remorse for their destructive behavior. Roughly 6 to 16 percent of boys and 2 to 9 percent of girls have this disorder.

Researchers offer varying explanations for conduct disorders. Some children with conduct disorders are difficult to condition, that is, they have trouble learning from their experience, because they are physiologically less responsive to rewards and especially punishments (Kruesi et al., 1992; Raine & Venables, 1984). Their autonomic nervous systems are less reactive, so they lack the anxiety that motivates other children to adjust their behavior to avoid threatening consequences. The extent to which their behavior reflects biological abnormalities is unclear, since ineffectively lax or excessively punitive parenting can also lead to delinquent behavior (see Eysenck, 1983; Patterson & Bank, 1986). Recent research suggests, however, that poor parenting may itself be partly genetic, reflecting the same genes in the parents that predispose their children to develop conduct disorders (Slutske et al., 1997).

The evidence is clear that genetic and environmental factors, as well as their interaction, contribute to the etiology of conduct disorder and delinquent behavior more generally (Biederman, 1995; O'Connor et al., 1998; Wooten et al., 1997). For example, one study compared adopted children who either had or did not have a biological parent with a history of criminality (Cardoret et al., 1995). Genetic and environmental variables each contributed to the likelihood of the child to have conduct and other disorders, but so did their interaction: An unstable home environment was particularly dangerous to children who were genetically vulnerable.

INTERIM SUMMARY   **Attention-deficit hyperactivity disorder (ADHD)** is characterized by inattention, impulsiveness, and hyperactivity inappropriate for the child's age. It is more prevalent in boys and runs in families, apparently for both genetic and environmental reasons. The same is true of **conduct disorder**, in which a child persistently violates societal norms and the rights of others.

SUBSTANCE-RELATED DISORDERS

The disorders discussed thus far begin in childhood and often continue in one form or another into adulthood. Both ADHD and conduct disorders predispose individuals to one set of adult disorders, **substance-related disorders**, which are characterized by continued use of a substance (such as alcohol or cocaine) that negatively affects psychological and social functioning.

Alcoholism

The most common substance-related disorder is **alcoholism**. In the United States, for example, an estimated 13 million people are alcoholics. Alcoholism appears in

Alcoholism occurs in all social classes and can produce different degrees of social dysfunction.

every social class. A longitudinal study of Harvard undergraduates over 50 years found that 21 percent met criteria for alcohol abuse at some point in their lives, and nearly 60 percent of these were still abusing alcohol in their 60s (Vaillant, 1996). As in other Western countries, alcoholism is the third largest health problem in the United States, following heart disease and cancer, and the most common psychiatric problem in males (Kessler et al., 1994). Alcoholism also appears to be steadily rising in the United States since World War II, with more adolescents becoming alcohol dependent (Nelson et al., 1998).

Why would someone use and abuse alcohol when the effects are clearly destructive to relationships, professional ambitions, and health? As in much research on psychopathology, the major controversy concerns the relative contributions of genetics and environment. Perhaps the best predictor of whether someone will become alcoholic is a family history of alcoholism (Cadoret et al., 1985; Marlatt & Baer, 1988). Children of alcoholics are four times as likely to develop alcoholism as children of nonalcoholics (Peele, 1986; Schuckit, 1987). Family history, however, supports both genetic and environmental hypotheses.

The influence of heredity on alcoholism is well established (Kendler et al., 1997). Children whose biological parents are alcoholic may be predisposed to respond differently to alcohol physiologically than children of nonalcoholic parents (Gordis, 1996; Schuckit, 1984, 1994). They may, for example, be predisposed to like the taste, to find alcohol rewarding, or to find alcohol emotionally soothing. Alternatively, children could inherit a predisposition to other emotional disorders, which indirectly lead to alcoholism. For example, an inherited vulnerability to depression or anxiety could lead both parents and their children to medicate themselves with alcohol. In this case, a predisposition to alcoholism itself is not inherited, but the effect is the same.

Research has clearly demonstrated both genetic and environmental routes to alcoholism (Cadoret et al., 1985; Kendler et al., 1994). According to one model, severe, early-onset alcoholism associated with delinquency, antisocial personality disorder, and other forms of substance abuse is highly heritable in males; if it is heritable in females, its heritability is low (Kendler et al., 1994; McGue et al., 1992). The more common form of alcoholism, which is less severe and not associated with such significant psychopathology, stems largely from environmental factors shared by family members, such as parents who model alcoholic behavior or whose parenting leads to poor self-esteem in their children, who are then vulnerable to alcohol as self-medication for depression (Babor et al., 1992; Cloninger et al., 1981; Pickens et al., 1991).

Another model based on studies of children adopted away from their biological parents applies to other kinds of drug abusers as well. This model distinguishes *two* heritable paths to substance abuse, in addition to the environmental pathway (Cadoret et al., 1985, 1995). In the first genetic route, a genetic tendency to alcoholism in the biological parent leads directly to the same genetic vulnerability in the child. A second pathway is less direct: A parent with a history of criminality transmits his genes to the child, who is more likely to develop conduct disorder and antisocial traits. Later, the delinquent child becomes involved in substance abuse. This model suggests that some people may be genetically vulnerable to the drug itself, whereas others are vulnerable to becoming antisocial and aggressive, which leads *socially* to substance-related disorders, since drug abuse can be a form of antisocial behavior.

When Substance Use Is Pathological

A large national sample of individuals age 15 to 54 in the United States found that slightly over half had used illegal drugs at some point in their lives, 15 percent had used within the last year, and 7.5 percent had been drug dependent at some point in their lives (Warner et al., 1995). Substance abuse can be a crippling psychological disorder, but the relation between substance use and abuse is not always clear. Most people drink alcohol, but this does not mean that most people are alcoholics. Similarly, is minor, occasional, or experimental use of drugs such as marijuana a sign of mental disorder?

Contrary to popular wisdom, the most definitive study in the area found that late teenagers (age 18) who experimented with marijuana in moderate amounts actually tended to be healthier psychologically than those who either used marijuana frequently or abstained (Shedler & Block, 1990). Abstainers were more anxious, emotionally inhibited, and lacking in social skills than "experimenters" (defined as individuals who used marijuana no more than once a month and had tried no more than one other illicit drug). Conversely, frequent users were more impulsive and alienated than experimenters (see Figure 15.3). The study suggests that experimentation may be a relatively normal expression of adolescent rebellion and the desire to try new experiences.

The study also found that interactions between subjects and their mothers when subjects were 5 years old could be used to predict future substance use. The most positive, mutually pleasurable mother–child interactions occurred in the group who later experimented with marijuana but did not abuse it. The mother–child interactions of both abstainers and frequent users at age 5 were rated as more hostile, more critical, less spontaneous, less relaxed, and less enjoyable to the child than those of the experimenters.

These findings have important implications for the potential effectiveness of anti-substance abuse campaigns that encourage teenagers and young adults to "Just Say No." As the investigators point out, such campaigns may unnecessarily frighten parents of normal teenagers who experiment with marijuana and underplay the deep-seated personality disturbances that give rise to substance abuse in heavy users. With marijuana as with alcohol, substance *use* and *abuse* are not synonymous, although for vulnerable individuals, use will more likely lead to abuse, which can in turn grossly disrupt functioning. It is important to note that the find-

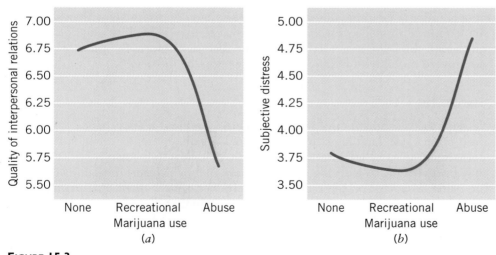

FIGURE 15.3

Relation between marijuana use and adjustment. The two graphs show the relations between level of marijuana use and two composite variables of psychological adjustment: quality of interpersonal relations (a) and subjective distress (b). The relation between marijuana use and these variables is clearly not linear; that is, more marijuana use does not uniformly predict worse mental health. Abstention, mild use, and frequent use are qualitatively different, not on a continuum of abuse. *Source:* Shedler & Block, 1990, p. 624.

ings of this study did not apply to use of hard drugs such as cocaine or heroin. Marijuana use and hard drug use in this sample appeared to mean very different things (Block et al., 1988). In girls, for example, marijuana use was not correlated with depression, but hard drug use was. Hard drug use also correlated with mood swings and identity confusion.

INTERIM SUMMARY   **Substance-related disorders** are characterized by continued use of a substance (such as alcohol or cocaine) that negatively affects psychological and social functioning. The most common substance-related disorder is **alcoholism**. Research has clearly demonstrated both environmental and genetic contributions to alcoholism, although researchers are still trying to track down precisely how genetic transmission occurs in different individuals. With marijuana as with alcohol, substance *use* and *abuse* are not synonymous, although for vulnerable individuals, use will more likely lead to abuse.

SCHIZOPHRENIA

Of all the mental disorders that can afflict a human being, schizophrenia is probably the most tragic. **Schizophrenia** is an umbrella term for a number of psychotic disorders that involve disturbances in nearly every dimension of human psychology, including thought, perception, behavior, language, communication, and emotion. Most forms of schizophrenia begin in the late teens and early 20s. Although estimates vary, only 10 to 20 percent of individuals with schizophrenia ever fully recover (Breier et al., 1991; Carone et al., 1991), and less than half show even moderate improvement after falling ill (Hegarty et al., 1994). Most people with schizophrenia periodically experience acute phases of the illness and otherwise suffer residual (continuing) impairment in social and occupational functioning throughout life. This pattern appears to hold true cross-culturally (Marengo et al., 1991), although relapse rates and severity of the illness tend to be higher in the industrialized West (Jenkins & Karno, 1992).

In the United States, between 1.2 and 6 million people suffer from schizophrenia, or roughly 0.5 to 2.5 percent of the population. Some studies have found the rate of schizophrenia higher among economically impoverished groups. The higher incidence among the poor may reflect the detrimental effect of poverty on people vulnerable to the illness. On the other hand, individuals with schizophrenia tend to plummet socioeconomically because they have difficulty holding employment; thus, the increased rates of the disorder among the poor may reflect downward mobility of individuals who develop the disease.

Symptoms

Perhaps the most distinctive feature of schizophrenia is a disturbance of thought, perception, and language. Individuals with schizophrenia often suffer from **delusions**—false beliefs firmly held despite evidence to the contrary. The person may believe the CIA is trying to kidnap him, that he is Jesus, or that his thoughts are being broadcast on the radio so that others can hear them. **Hallucinations**—sensory perceptions that occur without an external stimulus—are also common; auditory hallucinations (hearing voices) are the most frequent kind of hallucinations in schizophrenia.

Schizophrenic thinking is also frequently characterized by a **loosening of associations**, the tendency of conscious thought to move along associative lines rather than to be controlled, logical, and purposeful. One patient with schizophrenia was talking about her sister April: "She came in last night from Denver, in like a lion, she's the king of beasts." Whereas a poet might use a similar metaphor deliberately to express the sentiment that a person is angry or hostile, the individual

Disorganized thoughts and perceptions are apparent in the artwork of many schizophrenic patients (though in much of contemporary art as well).

with schizophrenia often has minimal control over associative thinking and intersperses it with rational thought. In this case, the patient's associations apparently ran from April to March, to a proverb about March coming in like a lion, and then to another network of associations linked to lions. People with schizophrenia may thus speak what sounds like gibberish, as they substitute one word for another associatively connected to it or simply follow a train of associations wherever it takes them.

In many respects, schizophrenia is a disorder of consciousness, in which the normal monitor and control functions of consciousness (Chapter 9) are suspended. People with schizophrenia have trouble keeping irrelevant associations out of consciousness and controlling the contents of their consciousness so that consciousness is useful for problem solving. In line with this hypothesis, numerous studies have documented deficits in working memory (Gold et al., 1997; Granholm et al., 1997) as well as in focusing and maintaining attention (Cornblatt & Kelip, 1994; Elkins et al., 1992).

Schizophrenic symptoms can be categorized into positive and negative symptoms (Crow, 1980; Strauss et al., 1974). **Positive symptoms**, such as delusions, hallucinations, and loose associations, are most apparent in acute phases of the illness and are often treatable by antipsychotic medications. They are called positive symptoms because they reflect the presence of something not usually or previously there, such as delusions. Recent research suggests a further distinction between two kinds of positive symptoms: *disorganized* (inappropriate emotions, disordered thought, and bizarre behavior) and *psychotic* (delusions and hallucinations) (Andreasen et al., 1995).

Negative symptoms, so named because they signal something missing (like normal emotions), are relatively chronic and less responsive to most medications. Negative symptoms include *flat affect* (blunted emotional response), lack of motivation, socially inappropriate behavior and withdrawal from relationships, and intellectual impairments such as *impoverished thought* (lack of complex thought in response to environmental events). The distinction between positive and negative symptoms may be important for recognizing different neural systems involved and for designing medications that target particular symptoms (Chapter 16).

Types of Schizophrenia

DSM-IV delineates three main subtypes of schizophrenia: paranoid, catatonic, and disorganized (Table 15.5). It also adds an *undifferentiated* category to describe mixed cases and a *residual* category for people who have had at least one episode

---

TABLE 15.5 MAJOR SUBTYPES OF SCHIZOPHRENIA

TYPE OF SCHIZOPHRENIA	MAJOR SYMPTOMS
Paranoid	Delusions or auditory hallucinations
Catatonic	Motor immobility, rigid posture, or excessive motor activity, including parrotlike repetition of what someone else says or does
Disorganized	Disorganized speech, bizarre behavior, and flat or inappropriate affect
Undifferentiated	Mixed symptoms that do not meet criteria for any of the above subtypes
Residual	Partial recovery after an acute episode of schizophrenia, characterized primarily by negative symptoms, such as lack of affect, poverty of speech (nothing to say), or lack of motivation

Source: Adapted from *Diagnostic and Statistical Manual of Mental Disorders*, 4th ed., American Psychiatric Association, Washington, DC, 1994.

and are not currently floridly psychotic but remain chronically affected by the disease, typically experiencing primarily negative symptoms.

Paranoid schizophrenia is marked by delusions of persecution. People with paranoid schizophrenia are tense, suspicious, and guarded. They may believe people are trying to harm them or are plotting against them, as the following example illustrates (Lehmann & Cancro, 1985):

> Well, I started for my sister's home and on the streetcar again there were two women talking. I did not know them at all. They were looking in my direction and one woman said to the other, "She is always looking for a fight." They changed their seats to the same side as I was on, and I heard one of them say, "He will never marry her." One of the women followed me into the grocery store. The man at the counter said, "Maybe they will put your heart on a platter." Saying that out loud to no one in particular. . . . I seemed to be known wherever I went.

Paranoid schizophrenia has a much better **prognosis** (that is, a better likely outcome) than other kinds of schizophrenia and a substantially later age of onset, usually the late 20s (Fenton & McGlashan, 1991).

Catatonic schizophrenia is marked by peculiar motor behavior, such as an extended period of frozen posture and stupor, in which the individual is minimally responsive to the external world. Catatonic patients may assume peculiar poses for long periods of time (Figure 15.4) or may echo or mirror the words or actions of people in their company.

Disorganized schizophrenia is characterized by extremely poor contact with reality, disheveled appearance, and bizarre behavior such as breaking into explosive laughter at inappropriate times. One 17-year-old girl with schizophrenia described the futility of continuing to live and her sense of emotional isolation in a monotone, occasionally looking up and chuckling. Another woman with disorganized schizophrenia stated that she heard voices, that a popular singer was chasing her with a knife, and that she was pregnant because she hugged a psychiatrist.

INTERIM SUMMARY   Schizophrenia is an umbrella term for a number of psychotic disorders that involve disturbances in thought, perception, behavior, language, communication, and emotion. **Positive symptoms** include disorganized (e.g., disordered thought and bizarre behavior) and psychotic (e.g., delusions and hallucinations) symptoms. **Negative symptoms** are relatively chronic and include flat affect, lack of motivation, peculiar or withdrawn interpersonal behavior, and impoverished thought. The main subtypes of schizophrenia are **paranoid** (marked by delusions of persecution), **catatonic** (marked by peculiar motor behavior), and **disorganized** (marked by bizarre behavior and poor contact with reality).

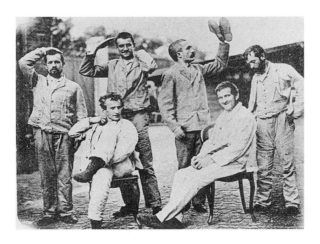

FIGURE 15.4
A group of patients photographed in 1896 showing symptoms associated with the condition now called schizophrenia, catatonic type.

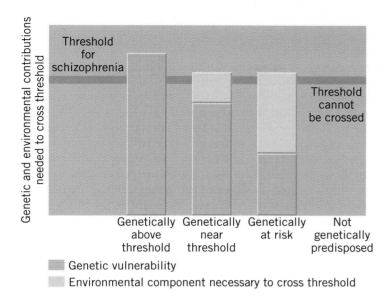

Genetic vulnerability

Environmental component necessary to cross threshold

FIGURE 15.5
Diathesis–stress model of schizophrenia. Some individuals probably have a genetic makeup above threshold for schizophrenia. For others, differing degrees of environmental stress activate the vulnerability or diathesis. People who are not biologically at risk will not develop the disorder, regardless of environmental circumstances.

Theories of Schizophrenia

Over the last century, researchers have advanced several theories to explain the causes of schizophrenia. Most contemporary theorists adopt a diathesis–stress model, hypothesizing that people with an underlying biological vulnerability develop the disorder or fall into an episode under stress (Rosenthal, 1970; Walker & Diforio, 1997). Most of the time this diathesis is genetic, but other cases of schizophrenia probably reflect early damage to the brain (Garver, 1997).

Some individuals are probably genetically above threshold for the illness, meaning that they will develop schizophrenia regardless of environmental circumstances (Figure 15.5). Others are near threshold, requiring only a small environmental contribution. Still others, simply at risk, will not develop the disorder without exposure to substantial pathogenic (disease-causing) experiences (Fowles, 1992). Whether the vulnerability to schizophrenia reflects a single gene or multiple genes is a matter of controversy; the disorder may be the end result of multiple disruptions in neural functioning, carried on several genes, which different affected individuals may have to varying degrees (see Carpenter, 1992).

TABLE 15.6   RISK OF SCHIZOPHRENIA AND DEGREE OF GENETIC RELATEDNESS

RELATIONSHIP	DEGREE OF RELATEDNESS	RISK (%)
Identical twin	1.0	48
Fraternal twin	.5	17
Sibling	.5	9
Parent	.5	6
Child	.5	13
Second-degree relatives	.25	2–6

Source: Adapted from Gottesman, 1991, p. 96.

Each of these identical quadruplets later developed schizophrenia.

Genetics   Genetics undoubtedly plays a primary role in the etiology of schizophrenia (Fowles, 1992; Gottesman, 1991; Kendler & Diehl, 1993). By most estimates, heritability is around 50 percent. A recent study of all monozygotic and dizygotic twins born in Finland between 1940 and 1957, however, found an estimated heritability of 83 percent (Cannon et al., 1998).

Table 15.6 shows the risk of developing schizophrenia in people with differing degrees of relatedness to a person with schizophrenia. The table is based on data pooled across over 40 studies conducted over nearly 60 years (Gottesman, 1991). As one would expect for a disorder with a genetic basis, concordance rates between individuals with schizophrenia and their relatives increase with the degree of relatedness; that is, people who share more genes are more likely to share the diagnosis. Also supporting the role of genetics is the fact that the offspring of the healthy twin in a discordant pair of monozygotic twins are just as likely as the offspring of the twin with schizophrenia to develop the disorder (Gottesman & Bertelsen, 1989).

Dopamine and Glutamate   Precisely how a genetic defect produces schizophrenia is not entirely clear. The most widely held view, called the **dopamine hypothesis**, implicates dopamine imbalance in schizophrenia. Several lines of evidence have long suggested that the brain of schizophrenic individuals produces too much of the neurotransmitter dopamine (Davis et al., 1991). Amphetamines increase dopamine activity, and high doses of amphetamines induce psychotic-like symptoms such as paranoia and hallucinations in normal people (Angrist et al., 1974; Kleven & Seiden, 1991). An amphetamine-induced psychosis is even more likely to occur in individuals with a predisposition to schizophrenia. Further, postmortem studies of brains of people with schizophrenia have shown abnormally high amounts of dopamine in a the neural regions (Kahn et al., 1996).

The strongest evidence for the dopamine hypothesis is the response of schizophrenic patients to medications that decrease dopamine activity in the brain (Pickar, 1988; Seeman & Lee, 1975). These antipsychotic medications block dopamine from binding with postsynaptic receptors, thus preventing neural transmission. The result is a reduction or elimination of positive symptoms such as hallucinations, suggesting that overactivity of neurons excited by dopamine is related to psychotic symptoms. An excess of dopamine cannot, however, account for several important pieces of data. Not all patients respond to medicines that block dopamine activity; different types of dopamine receptors control different psychological processes; and other neurotransmitters, particularly serotonin, appear to be involved in ways that are not yet well understood (perhaps in modulating the effects of dopamine).

The most current formulation of the dopamine hypothesis suggests that different neural circuits underlie the positive and negative symptoms of schizophrenia (Kahn et al., 1996; Tamminga et al., 1992). Subcortical circuits projecting from the midbrain to the limbic system and basal ganglia have *excess* dopamine and seem to be responsible for positive symptoms. Another circuit that projects from the midbrain to the prefrontal cortex, in contrast, seems to be characterized by too *little* dopamine transmission. This circuit is thought to be responsible for negative symptoms and many of the cognitive deficits seen in schizophrenia (such as problems reining in associations), since frontal activation is necessary for emotion, attention, and social judgment. This may explain why most antipsychotic medications, which reduce positive symptoms by diminishing the action of dopamine, do not alleviate negative symptoms and may even exacerbate them.

Although the dopamine hypothesis is well established, researchers have recently implicated another neurotransmitter, glutamate, in schizophrenia (Kim et al., 1980; Olney et al., 1995; Tsai et al., 1995). As we have seen, one of the primary pieces of evidence for the dopamine hypothesis is amphetamine-induced psychosis, in which amphetamines produce positive symptoms of schizophrenia by

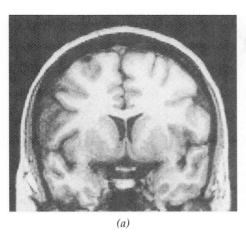 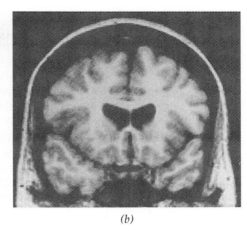

(a)   *(b)*

FIGURE 15.6
Ventricular enlargement in patients with schizophrenia. Magnetic resonance imaging shows a biological basis for schizophrenia: (*a*) shows the brain of a 30-year-old woman with normal ventricles; (*b*) shows the enlarged ventricles of a 36-year-old woman with schizophrenia.

increasing dopamine activity. Researchers have now discovered, however, that phencyclidine hydrochloride (PCP, or "angel dust"), which reduces the responsivity of a particular glutamate receptor, can produce both positive *and* negative symptoms of schizophrenia. Precisely how dopamine and glutamate may both be involved is not yet clear. Dopamine can inhibit glutamate, so that too much dopamine could lead to too little glutamate activity. Another possibility is that some cases of schizophrenia reflect a primary dopamine dysfunction, whereas others reflect decreased glutamate activity, which can lead to similar symptoms.

Neural Atrophy and Dysfunction   Other data implicate abnormalities in the structure and function of the brains of people with schizophrenia. One such abnormality is brain atrophy or neuronal loss, reflected in enlargement of the fluid-filled cavities in the brain called **ventricles**, indicating that the neural regions surrounding them have atrophied or degenerated (Figure 15.6). The brain appears to degenerate over the course of the illness, with larger ventricles seen in patients with chronic schizophrenia (Zipursky et al., 1998). Ventricular enlargement does not appear to be exclusive to schizophrenia, however, as it has been observed in patients with other psychotic disorders (Andreason et al., 1990; Weiner, 1985) and even in patients with recurring depression (Elkis et al., 1995).

Atrophy appears to be most apparent in the temporal and frontal lobes (Gur et al., 1998). One study found that severity of symptoms (particularly auditory hallucinations) correlated strongly with the degree of atrophy in a region of the left temporal cortex specialized for auditory processing of language (Barta et al., 1990). Analysis of dopamine receptors and EEG response in the same region has detected abnormalities in patients with schizophrenia (Goldsmith et al., 1997; Salisbury et al., 1998).

Atrophy and other cellular abnormalities have also been repeatedly confirmed in the prefrontal cortex (that is, the most anterior regions of the cortex) of patients with schizophrenia (Park & Holzman, 1993; Selemon et al., 1995). The prefrontal cortex is a particularly likely site for pathology in schizophrenia, since one section is involved in working memory (Chapter 6) and another in social and emotional functioning (Chapter 7).

Relatives of Patients with Schizophrenia   Several studies have shown a variety of subtle impairments in the perceptual and cognitive functioning of nonschizophrenic relatives of patients with schizophrenia. These impairments resemble the more blatant disturbances in individuals with the disorder, such as deficits in working memory and attention (e.g., Faraone et al., 1995; Green et al., 1997; Park et al., 1995). One study examined the presence of disordered thinking in adoptive and biological relatives of people with schizophrenia by recording speech samples and later coding them for idiosyncrasies of thinking (Kinney et al., 1997). Biological relatives of patients diagnosed with schizophrenia, particularly their siblings and half-siblings, showed elevated rates of thought disorder compared to relatives of control subjects.

Environmental Contributions   Although a biological vulnerability appears to be essential for the development of schizophrenia, environmental variables play an important role in the onset and course of the disorder. A large body of research focuses on patterns of communication and expression of emotion within the families of schizophrenic patients (Doane et al., 1981; Hooley & Hiller, 1998; Wynne et al., 1963). Adoption studies show that biological children of schizophrenics are likely to become schizophrenic if their adoptive families have hostile or confusing communication patterns that involve many mixed messages but not if the adoptive family functions normally (Kety et al., 1975; Tienari, 1991).

A particularly important variable is **expressed emotion**, a family interaction style characterized by criticism, hostile interchanges, and emotional overinvolvement or intrusiveness by family members. Researchers study expressed emotion by asking family members to talk about the patient and then coding their responses for comments that indicate criticism, hostility, and so forth. Roughly 65 to 75 percent of patients with schizophrenia who return to homes high in expressed emotion relapse relatively quickly, compared to roughly 25 to 35 percent of those whose homes have less intense and negative emotional climates (Brown, 1962, 1985; Butzlaff & Hooley, 1998; Jenkins et al., 1986). Precisely how stressors such as family hostility could interact with the neural abnormalities that provide the underlying vulnerability to schizophrenia is just beginning to be explored. According to one hypothesis, stress actually leads to increased dopamine activity, which increases psychotic symptoms (Walker & Diforio, 1997).

Culture and the Course of Schizophrenia   These findings on expressed emotion have been replicated cross-culturally, particularly the link between criticism and relapse. High expressed emotion, however, is much less common in families of people with schizophrenia outside the West (Jenkins & Karno, 1992). Although the incidence of schizophrenia is similar across cultures (Jablensky, 1989), the relapse rate tends to be lower, and the course of the illness more benign, in cultures low in expressed emotion (such as India).

One explanation for this is that Third World cultures tend to be less individualistic and committed to concepts of personal responsibility than Western cultures; thus, they are less likely to assign blame to people with schizophrenia for their actions. Western family members high in expressed emotion tend to have an internal locus of control; that is, they believe they control their own destiny. They also tend to believe their schizophrenic relatives could fight their symptoms if they just exercised more willpower (Hooley, 1998). Theorists in Western cultures generally consider an internal locus of control a sign of positive adjustment, but this view is not universal and probably understates the negative side effects of an individualistic worldview. Believing that people can control their destiny may be destructive when it is not true.

Although the term *environmental* typically connotes something nonbiological, researchers have considered other possible environmental causes of schizophrenia such as birth complications and viruses. Perinatal (at birth) complications are slightly more common among individuals who develop schizophrenia, and some of the brain abnormalities discovered in schizophrenic patients are similar to changes in the brain resulting from viral infections (Jones et al., 1998; Mirsky & Duncan, 1986). Recent studies suggest, more generally, that events that affect the developing nervous system in utero can later lead to a vulnerability to schizophrenia, particularly if they occur during the second trimester of pregnancy (Venables, 1996; Wyatt, 1996). For example, a Dutch study found that people exposed in utero to famine during World War II showed a twofold increase in rates of schizophrenia decades later compared to control subjects born at the same time (Susser et al., 1996).

INTERIM SUMMARY   Most theorists adopt a diathesis–stress model of schizophrenia. Heritability of schizophrenia is at least 50 percent. According to the **dopamine hypothesis**, positive symptoms of schizophrenia reflect too much dopamine activity in subcortical circuits involving the basal ganglia and limbic system, whereas negative symptoms reflect too little dopamine activity in the prefrontal cortex. Glutamate may also play a role, at least in some individuals with schizophrenia. Other data implicate abnormalities in the structure and function of the brain, such as enlarged **ventricles** and corresponding atrophy (degeneration) in the frontal and temporal lobes. Environmental variables, notably **expressed emotion** (criticism, hostile interchanges, and emotional overinvolvement by family members), play an important role in the onset and course of the disorder. Prenatal and perinatal events that affect the developing nervous system may also be involved in some cases of schizophrenia.

MOOD DISORDERS

Whereas the most striking feature of schizophrenic disorders is disordered thinking, **mood disorders** are characterized by disturbances in emotion and mood. In most cases the mood disturbance is negative, marked by persistent or severe feelings of sadness and hopelessness, but a mood disturbance can also be dangerously positive, as in manic states. Individuals who are **manic** feel excessively happy or euphoric and believe they can do anything. As a consequence, they may undertake unrealistic ventures such as starting a new business on a grandiose scale.

Types of Mood Disorders

Depression has been recorded as far back as ancient Egypt, when the condition was called melancholia and treated by priests. Occasional blue periods are a common response to life events such as loss of a job, end of a relationship, or death of a loved one. In a depressive disorder, however, the sadness may emerge without a clear trigger or *precipitant*, continue long after one would reasonably expect, or be far more intense than normal sadness, including intense feelings of worthlessness or even delusions.

Major Depressive Disorder   The most severe form of depression is **major depressive disorder**, characterized by depressed mood and loss of interest in pleasurable activities (**anhedonia**). It also includes disturbances in appetite, sleep, energy level, and concentration. People in a major depressive episode may be so fatigued that they sleep day and night or cannot go to work or do household chores because of intense sadness and lethargy. They often feel worthless, shoulder excessive guilt, and are preoccupied with thoughts of suicide. Major depressive episodes typically last about five months (Solomon et al., 1997).

At any given moment, 2 to 3 percent of males and 5 to 9 percent of females suffer from major depression. The lifetime risk for major depressive disorder is 5 to 12 percent in men and 10 to 26 percent in women (APA, 1994). Major depression is a progressive disorder, with episodes gradually increasing in severity. Roughly 75 percent of patients who experience a major depressive episode will have a recurrence within five years (Maj et al., 1992).

Dysthymic Disorder   A less severe type of depression is dysthymic disorder. **Dysthymic disorder** (or **dysthymia**) refers to a chronic low-level depression lasting more than 2 years, with intervals of normal moods that never last more than a few weeks or months. Dysthymic disorder may include symptoms found in major depression (such as disturbances in sleep, energy, and self-esteem), but they are not debilitating. The effects of dysthymic disorder on functioning are more subtle, as when people who are chronically depressed choose professions that underuse their talents because of a lack of confidence, self-esteem, or motivation.

Bipolar Disorder   A manic episode, or **mania**, is characterized by a period of abnormally elevated or expansive mood. While manic, a person usually has an inflated sense of self that reaches grandiose proportions. During a manic episode people generally require less sleep, experience their thoughts as racing, and feel a constant need to talk. Individuals with **bipolar disorder** have manic episodes but often experience both emotional "poles," depression and mania (in contrast with **unipolar depression**, which involves only depression). About 15 to 20 percent of patients who have manic episodes also develop psychotic delusions and hallucinations (Lehmann, 1985).

The lifetime risk for bipolar disorder in the general population is low—somewhere between 0.5 and 1.6 percent—but it can be one of the most debilitating and lethal psychiatric disorders, with a suicide rate between 10 and 20 percent (Goodwin & Ghaemi, 1998; MacKinnon et al., 1997). Less severe variants of the disorder, in which the individual experiences *hypomanic* episodes (with similar features except less intense), make disorders on the bipolar "spectrum" more common. As we saw in Chapter 8, patients with cyclothymia, or *cyclothymic disorder,* have intense mood fluctuations but do not develop full-blown mania. Bipolar disorder appears to occur more frequently in the upper social classes. People with bipolar disorder and their relatives tend to achieve higher levels of education and are disproportionately represented among creative writers and other professionals (Chapter 8).

INTERIM SUMMARY   **Mood disorders** are characterized by disturbances in emotion and mood, including both depressed and **manic** states (characterized by symptoms such as abnormally elevated mood, grandiosity, and racing thoughts). The most severe form of depression is **major depressive disorder**, characterized by depressed mood and loss of interest in pleasurable activities. **Dysthymic disorder** refers to a chronic low-level depression lasting more than two years, with intervals of normal moods that never last than a few weeks or months. In **bipolar disorder**, individuals have manic episodes and may also experience intense depression.

Theories of Depression

Depression can arise for many different reasons. As in schizophrenia, biological and psychological processes often interact, with environmental events frequently triggering a biologically based vulnerability. However, unlike schizophrenia, depression is common even among people without a genetic vulnerability.

Genetics   Heredity clearly plays a major role in some cases of depression, particularly severe forms of major depression, although heritability is considerably lower than in schizophrenia (Lyons et al., 1998; McGuffin et al., 1996; Kendler et al., 1992). Estimated heritabilities for major depression range from about .30 to .50; for dysthymia they are lower. A family history of depression doubles or triples an individual's risk of a mood disorder. An estimated 50 percent of individuals with unipolar depression have a family history of depression (Winokur et al., 1978).

Bipolar disorder, like schizophrenia, probably requires a biological predisposition; roughly 80 to 90 percent of individuals with bipolar disorder have a family history of some mood disorder (Andreasen et al., 1987; Winokur et al., 1969). First-

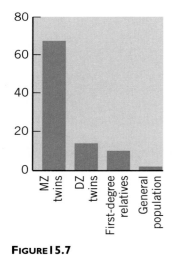

FIGURE 15.7
Genetics of bipolar disorder. Monozygotic twins have a highly elevated concordance rate for bipolar disorder relative to dizygotic twins and other relatives, suggesting substantial heritability. *Source:* Primarily based on D.F. MacKinnon, K.R. Jamison, and J.R. DeDavlo (1997). Genetics of manic depressive illness. *Annual Review of Neuroscience, 20,* 355–373.

degree relatives of bipolar patients have an 11.5 percent risk of developing the disease, which is 15 to 20 times higher than in the general population (Schlesser & Alshuler, 1983). Twin studies provide strong support for the role of genetic factors in the development of the disorder as well (Figure 15.7) (Bertelson, 1979). Some promising genetic data have linked at least some forms of the disorder to specific chromosomes, particularly chromosome 18 (MacKinnon et al., 1997). Bipolar disorder appears to be genetically distinct from unipolar depression, since relatives of bipolar patients are more likely to have bipolar illness than relatives of either unipolar depressives or control subjects without psychiatric illness (Winokur et al., 1995).

Neural Transmission   Serotonin and norepinephrine have been implicated in both major depression and bipolar disorders (e.g., Bellivier et al., 1998). This makes neurobiological sense because these same neurotransmitters are involved in the capacity to be aroused or energized and in the control of other functions affected by depression such as sleep cycles and hunger (Delgado et al., 1990; Stokes et al., 1987). Drugs that alter the activity of these neurotransmitters decrease the symptoms of depression (and hence are called antidepressants).

Environmental Factors   Early childhood and familial experiences also play an important role in the etiology of depression (Kendler et al., 1992). Depressed adults are more likely than other people to have been raised in disruptive, hostile, and negative home environments (Brown & Harris, 1989). Depressed children report a greater incidence of negative life events (such as family deaths and divorce) than their nondepressed peers (Nolen-Hoeksema et al., 1992). Children of depressed mothers who themselves become severely depressed tend to do so shortly after the onset of their mother's depression (Hammen et al., 1991).

Adult experiences also play a significant role. Severe stressors (such as loss of a job or loss of a significant other) tend to occur within six to nine months prior to the onset of depression in roughly 90 percent of people who become depressed (Brown & Harris, 1978, 1989; Brown et al., 1994; Frank et al., 1994). High levels of expressed emotion (especially criticism) in the families of patients with major depression predict relapse, much as in schizophrenia; this finding has been replicated cross-culturally (Hooley & Teasdale, 1989; Okasha et al., 1994). Lack of an intimate relationship is also a high-risk factor for depression, particularly in women (Brown & Harris, 1989). Adult experiences influence the course of bipolar illness as well. In one study, bipolar patients with high life stress were over four times more likely to relapse than those with few significant stressors (Ellicott et al., 1990). In another study, bipolar patients who experienced severe negative life events took three times as long to recover from an episode than patients with less severe stressors (Johnson & Miller, 1997).

The negative environments of depressed people are not always independent of their actions, however. A lack of intimate relationships is often a byproduct of personality patterns that also generate depression, and depression itself can be hard for another person to tolerate day after day. Remarkably, experimental research also finds that depressed people seek out partners who view them negatively, and they prefer negative to positive feedback (Giesler et al., 1996; Swann et al., 1992). In one study, depressed, mildly dysphoric (unhappy), and nondepressed college students were allowed to choose to interact with someone they were led to believe viewed them in a negative, neutral, or positive manner. Depressed participants, unlike the others, preferred the partner who perceived them negatively (Figure 15.8). Like their nondepresseed peers, depressed individuals apparently seek others who verify their self-concept (Chapter 17), even when this means being surrounded by people who view them negatively instead of positively.

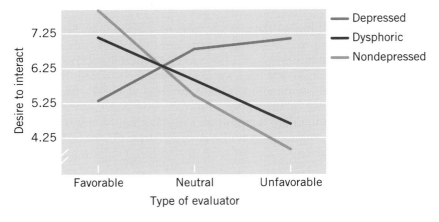

FIGURE 15.8
Partner choice in depression. The figure graphs the desire to interact with people believed to hold positive, neutral, and negative views of self. Depressed subjects, unlike mildly dysphoric and nondepressed subjects, preferred to interact with people who viewed them negatively. *Source:* Swann et al., 1992, p. 296.

Cognitive Theories   Cognitive theories look for the roots of depression in dysfunctional patterns of thinking. Learned helplessness theory ties depression to expectancies of helplessness in the face of unpleasant events (Chapter 5). According to helplessness theorists, the way people feel depends on the way they explain events or outcomes to themselves, particularly aversive events (Abramson et al., 1978; Peterson & Seligman, 1984). People with a pessimistic explanatory style, who interpret the causes of bad occurrences as internal (their own fault), stable (unchanging), and global (far-reaching), are more likely to become depressed. Upon being jilted by a lover, for example, a person who is vulnerable to depression may conclude that he is inherently unlovable.

Depressed people differ both in the *content* of their thinking—how negative their ideas about themselves and the world are—and in their cognitive *processes*—the ways they manipulate and use information (Hollon, 1988). Aaron Beck (1976, 1991), who developed the major cognitive theory of depression, proposes that depressed people interpret events unfavorably, do not like themselves, and regard the future pessimistically. Beck calls this negative outlook on the world, the self, and the future the **negative triad** (Figure 15.9). Research suggests that depressed individuals process information about themselves in a negative way automatically and implicitly, perceiving even neutral or positive information negatively (Bargh & Tota, 1988; Mineka & Sutton, 1992). An outgrowth of learned helplessness theory, called *hopelessness theory,* draws on Beck's observation that depressed people view the future negatively (Alloy et al., 1989). According to this view, depression in some people reflects the loss of hope that things in the future will improve.

Beck calls the cognitive mechanisms by which a depressed person transforms neutral or positive information in a depressive direction **cognitive distortions** (Beck, 1976). Consider the following interaction between a therapist and a highly intelligent patient who was afraid to go back to school to pursue a career in law:

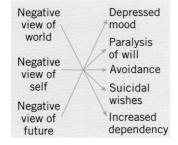

FIGURE 15.9
Beck's negative triad. Beck believes that a negative outlook on the world, the self, and the future—the negative triad—affects mood, motivation, and behavior. *Source:* Beck, 1976, p. 256.

PATIENT: I can't go back to school. I'm just not smart enough.
THERAPIST: How did you do the last time you were in school?
PATIENT: Um … I got mostly As. But that was a long time ago. And what have I ever done career-wise that suggests I could handle being a lawyer?
THERAPIST: That's not really a fair question is it? Don't you think your low image of yourself has something to do with why you haven't done anything "spectacular" career-wise?
PATIENT: I guess you're right. I'm as smart as my sister, and she's a lawyer.
THERAPIST: Right.
PATIENT: But what have I ever done career-wise that says I could handle being a lawyer?

The patient repeatedly doubts herself, ignores her past successes, and generalizes in ways that do not fit the "data." At the end, she simply repeats a self-doubting question that she has just admitted is based on a faulty premise.

Beck (1976, 1985) has identified a number of cognitive errors typical of depressed patients. In *arbitrary inference*, the person draws a conclusion in the absence of supporting evidence or in the presence of contradictory evidence. The patient above used arbitrary inference when she concluded with little reason that she could not succeed at school despite prior success. Similarly, when faced with contradictory evidence (her prior grades), she arbitrarily dismissed that as "a long time ago." *Magnification* and *minimization* are biases in evaluating the relative importance of events. For example, a man reacted to storm damage to his house by thinking, "The side of the house is wrecked. . . . It will cost a fortune to fix it." In fact, the damage was minor and cost only about fifty dollars to fix (Beck, 1976). *Personalization* occurs when depressed people relate external events to themselves without good reason, as when a student with the highest grades in a class assumed the teacher had a low opinion of him whenever she called on or complimented another student. *Overgeneralization* occurs when a person draws a general conclusion on the basis of a single incident. For example, one depressed patient, after a disagreement with his parents, concluded, "I can't get along with anybody" (Beck, 1985).

Psychodynamic Theories   Psychodynamic theorists argue that depression may have a number of roots, such as identification with a depressed or belittling parent or an attachment history that predisposes the person to fear of rejection or abandonment (Blatt & Homann, 1992). For instance, Mr. B, whose father was very critical of him, never allowed himself to feel pleasure when he accomplished something. Instead, he would say to himself, much as his father had said to him when he was a child, "You could have done better." Unlike cognitive theories, which focus on faulty cognition, psychodynamic explanations focus on motivation. Mr. B may have been motivated to deny the reality of his successes. Acknowledging a success might raise his hopes that he could succeed and win other people's esteem in the future; because that wish had been frustrated so often in childhood, he may have been motivated to avoid putting himself in that position again. If one does not wish, one cannot be disappointed.

From a psychodynamic perspective, depression cannot be isolated from the personality structure of the individual experiencing it (see Kernberg, 1984). A person who has poor object relations (difficulty investing in relationships and ideals and maintaining a constant view of the self) may experience depression because he is prone to feeling abandoned, empty, and alone. Such patients frequently report feeling that they are totally evil and not just helpless or incompetent. Similarly, a person who is so self-centered and narcissistic that he cannot form deep attachments to other people is likely to become depressed in middle age, when he becomes more aware of his mortality and realizes that the grandiose dreams of his youth are not likely to be actualized. In contrast, a depressed person with a greater capacity for relationships may feel that he is a failure at meeting standards and consequently be vulnerable to feeling guilty or inadequate (Blatt & Zuroff, 1992; Gunderson, 1984; Wixom et al., 1993).

Psychodynamic and cognitive theorists have recently converged on a distinction between depression related to interpersonal distress versus depression related to feelings of inadequacy or failure to meet standards. People whose depression focuses on interpersonal issues tend to develop depression in the face of rejection or loss, whereas people whose depression focuses on autonomy and achievement issues tend to become depressed by failures (Hammen et al., 1989; Peselow et al., 1992).

A GLOBAL VISTA

DEPRESSION ON A HOPI RESERVATION

Depression, like most mental disorders, has equivalents in every culture, but the way people view and experience depression varies considerably. Shiite Muslims in Iran consider the ability to feel depressed at tragedy and injustice a sign of personal depth. Buddhists believe that pleasure is the basis of all suffering and perceive willful dysphoria as a step toward salvation (Kleinman & Good, 1985).

People from diverse cultures describe depression in very different terms. Depressed Nigerians complain that "ants keep creeping in parts of my brain," while Chinese complain that they feel "exhaustion of their nerves" and that their hearts are being "squeezed and weighed down" (Kleinman & Good, 1985, p. 4). While people in Western society tend to view depression as originating within themselves, the Maori believe that distressing emotional states such as sadness are inflicted from the outside, often by angry spirits (Smith, 1981).

Do these differences imply that the actual subjective experience of depression differs cross-culturally? The answer appears to be yes. Members of less individualistic societies tend to focus more on the behavioral dimensions of depression (such as lethargy, fatigue, loss of appetite, and slowness of movement) than on the subjective experience. In contrast, contemporary Westerners are far more attuned to their internal psychological states than people in most cultures in human history. When they suffer from depression, they typically focus on their inner sense of helplessness, hopelessness, guilt, and low self-esteem.

Guilt is a common component of depression in the contemporary West, unlike much of the Third World (Kleinman & Good, 1985) or the West of previous epochs. When the Greek physician Hippocrates described depression 2500 years ago, he listed symptoms such as irritability, sleeplessness, and despondency. Not until the sixteenth to seventeenth centuries did physicians note a relationship between depression and guilt (Jackson, 1985). That this occurred at the same time as the beginning of the Industrial Revolution is probably no accident, since technological development brings with it social changes that lead to increased individualism and put a premium on personal responsibility (Chapter 18). The shift to urban living may also have played a role in heightening vulnerability to guilt. As people moved to cities and lost the constant interpersonal surveillance of smaller groups, parents began to socialize their children to monitor themselves more closely, to bring significant others *inside* themselves psychologically to watch over their behavior (Piers & Singer, 1953).

Spero Manson and his colleagues (1985) studied the Hopi of northeastern Arizona, whose culture was disrupted by the conquest by white settlers in the nineteenth century. Like many contemporary Native American peoples who live on reservations, the Hopi suffer from disproportionate rates of depression, alcoholism, suicide, and antisocial behavior. Instead of assuming that Western categories apply to the Hopi, the investigators began by asking their Hopi informants, "What are the sicknesses or things that can be wrong with people's minds or spirits?" With further probing, the researchers identified several categories of illness recognized by their subjects: worry sickness, unhappiness, heartbrokenness, drunkenlike craziness with or without alcohol, and disappointment or "turning one's face to the wall" (pouting). When the participants were asked if they knew of any Hopi word

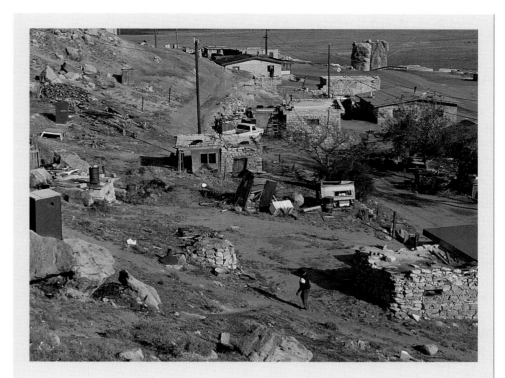

A Hopi reservation, where depression, alcoholism, and suicide are common emotional problems.

or phrase that corresponds to the English term "depression," 93 percent indicated that they did not. The nearest equivalent seems to be "heartbrokenness" the illness ascribed to most Hopi people diagnosed in Western terms with major depression. Thus, the Western concept of depression can be translated into Hopi culture, but some of the nuances of experience that depressed Hopi verbalize often get lost.

Another finding of Manson's study was an alarmingly high incidence of depression in the Hopi community. Depression appears to be on the rise cross-culturally, as documented by a study of 39,000 people across the world, in societies from North America and Western Europe to Puerto Rico, Asia, and the Middle East (Cross-National Collaborative Group, 1992). Depression typically increases in periods of crisis such as civil wars, but it has apparently been steadily increasing and afflicting people at an earlier age in this century. The causes of this trend are unclear, but the enormous social changes that have occurred in the modern era likely play a role. These changes include disruption of family, social relationships, cultural values, and ways of understanding the world that have, throughout human history, allowed people to experience the world and their lives as meaningful.

INTERIM SUMMARY   Genetic factors increase the vulnerability to depressive disorders, particularly major depression, and play a central role in the etiology of bipolar disorder. Serotonin and norepinephrine have been implicated in both major depression and bipolar disorder. Both childhood and adult experiences also play a significant role in the etiology and course of mood disorders. According to cognitive theories, dysfunctional thought patterns play a crucial role in depression. Depressed people transform neutral or positive information into depressive cognitions through **cognitive distortions**. According to psychodynamic theory, depressive symptoms, like other psychological symptoms, can only be understood in the context of the individual's personality structure. Depression has equivalents in all cultures, but the way people view and experience it varies considerably.

ANXIETY DISORDERS

Anxiety, like sadness, is a normal feeling. Anxiety typically functions as an internal alarm bell that warns of potential danger. In **anxiety disorders**, however, the individual is subject to false alarms that may be intense, frequent, or even continuous. These false alarms may lead to dysfunctional avoidance behavior, as when a person refuses to leave the house for fear of a panic attack.

Anxiety disorders are the most frequently occurring category of mental disorders in the general population (American Psychiatric Association, 1994). Women are twice as likely as men to be afflicted; this gender difference already exists by age 6 (Lewinsohn et al., 1998). Although many anxiety disorders are triggered under particular circumstances, some people (about 2 percent of the population) have a **generalized anxiety disorder**, characterized by persistent anxiety at a moderate but disturbing level and excessive and unrealistic worry about life circumstances (Rapee, 1991).

Types of Anxiety Disorders

In this section we review the symptoms of some other common anxiety disorders. Although we discuss them separately, people with one anxiety disorder often have others (Barlow et al., 1998; Kendler et al., 1992).

Phobia   At any given time, about 5 percent of the population have at least one irrational fear, or **phobia**, and more than twice that percent have a phobia at some point in their lifetimes (Magee et al., 1996). For most people, mild phobic responses to spiders or snakes have minimal effect on their lives; for others with diagnosable phobias, irrational fears can be extremely uncomfortable, such as fear of riding in airplanes.

A common type of phobia is **social phobia**, a marked fear that occurs when the person is in a specific social or performance situation, such as intense public speaking anxiety. The lifetime prevalence for this disorder is almost 15 percent (Magee et al., 1996). Recent research suggests the potential importance of distinguishing two kinds of social phobias: public speaking phobias, which often occur in people without any other psychiatric problems, and other social phobias, such as intense anxiety at interacting with other people, which typically suggest greater disturbance (Kessler et al., 1998).

Panic Disorder

I was 25 when I had my first attack. It was a few weeks after I'd come home from the hospital. I had had my appendix out. The surgery had gone well, and I wasn't in any danger, which is why I don't understand what happened. But one night I went to sleep and I woke up a few hours later . . . with this vague feeling of apprehension. Mostly I remember how my heart started pounding. And my chest hurt; it felt like someone was standing on my chest. I was so scared, I was sure that I was dying. [Patient cited in Barlow, 1988]

Panic disorder is characterized by attacks of intense fear and feelings of doom or terror not justified by the situation. The attacks typically include physiological symptoms such as shortness of breath, dizziness, heart palpitations, trembling, and chest pains (Barlow, 1988). Psychological symptoms include fear of dying or going crazy. Lifetime prevalence for panic disorder is in the range of 1.4 to 2.9 percent cross-culturally, in countries as diverse as Canada, New Zealand, and Lebanon (Weissman et al., 1997).

Agoraphobia   A related disorder is **agoraphobia**, a fear of being in places or situations from which escape might be difficult, such as crowded grocery stores or elevators. Between 6 and 7 percent of the population suffer from agoraphobia at some point in their lives (Magee et al., 1996). Agoraphobia can be extremely debilitating; the person may not leave the house because of intense fears of being outside alone, in a crowd, on a bridge, or traveling in a train, car, or bus. Agoraphobia is often instigated by a fear of having a panic attack; ultimately the individual suffering from this disorder may avoid leaving home for fear of having a panic attack in a public place.

Obsessive-Compulsive Disorder

Mrs. C is a 47-year-old mother of six children who are named in alphabetical order. For 10 years she had been suffering with a compulsion to wash excessively, sometimes 25 to 30 times a day for five- to ten-minute intervals. Her daily morning shower lasts two hours, with rituals involving each part of her body. . . . If she loses track of her ritual, she must start at the beginning. Mrs. C's compulsions affect her family as well. She does not let family members wear a pair of underwear more than once and prohibits washing them. The family spends large sums of money buying new underwear for daily use. Mrs. C has hoarded various items such as towels, sheets, earrings, and her own clothes for the past two decades. [From Prochaska, 1984.]

Obsessive-compulsive disorder is marked by recurrent obsessions and compulsions that cause severe distress and significantly interfere with an individual's life. **Obsessions** are persistent thoughts or ideas, such as the notion that a terrible accident is about to occur to a loved one or that underwear is filled with germs. **Compulsions** are intentional behaviors or mental acts performed in response to

Many Vietnam veterans with untreated posttraumatic stress disorder cannot extricate themselves from the past.

an obsession and in a stereotyped fashion, often as a magical way of warding off the obsessive thought. Washing every part of the body over and over in the shower in a prescribed order is a compulsion. People with obsessive-compulsive disorder experience their compulsions as irresistible acts that must be performed even though they generally recognize them as irrational.

Common compulsions include counting, hand-washing, and touching; common obsessions are repetitive thoughts of contamination, violence, or doubt (Jenike, 1983). Typically, obsessive-compulsive people experience intense anxiety or even panic if they are prevented from performing their rituals. Obsessive-compulsive disorders typically begin during childhood, adolescence, or early adulthood.

Posttraumatic Stress Disorder   An anxiety disorder that began receiving wide attention following the Vietnam War is **posttraumatic stress disorder (PTSD)**. This disorder is marked by flashbacks and recurrent thoughts of a psychologically distressing event outside the range of usual human experience. Typically, the traumatic event is of horrific proportions, such as seeing someone murdered, surviving torture or imprisonment in a concentration camp, being raped, or losing one's home in an earthquake or some other natural disaster. One study examined Cambodian refugees who escaped massive genocide during the 1980s but experienced multiple losses, uprooting from their homes, torture, rape, as well as immigration to a new country with a new language. Over 80 percent were diagnosable with PTSD (Carlson & Rosser-Hogan, 1991). Even in countries such as the United States that have not had war on their soil for over a century, lifetime prevalence of PTSD is near 8 percent, with men typically traumatized by combat exposure and women by rape or childhood sexual molestation (Kessler et al., 1995).

Posttraumatic stress disorder has a number of symptoms: nightmares, flashbacks, deliberate efforts to avoid thoughts or feelings about the traumatic event, diminished responsiveness to the external world, and psychological numbness. Other symptoms that may occur are hypervigilance (constant scanning of the environment), an exaggerated startle response (such as screaming when tapped on the shoulder), and autonomic activation when exposed to stimuli associated with the traumatic event. The disorder can last a lifetime, as demonstrated in research on combat veterans, prisoners of war, torture victims, and Holocaust survivors (see Basoglu et al., 1994; Sutker et al., 1991).

<u>**INTERIM SUMMARY**</u>   In **anxiety disorders**, people experience frequent, intense, and irrational anxiety. **Generalized anxiety disorder** is characterized by persistent anxiety and excessive worry about life circumstances. A common type of **phobia** (irrational fear) is **social phobia**, which occurs when the person is in a specific social or performance situation. **Panic disorder** is characterized by attacks of intense fear and feelings of doom or terror not justified by the situation. **Agoraphobia** involves a fear of being in places or situations from which escape might be difficult. **Obsessive-compulsive disorder** is marked by recurrent **obsessions** (persistent thoughts or ideas) and **compulsions** (stereotyped acts performed in response to an obsession). **Posttraumatic stress disorder** is marked by flashbacks and recurrent thoughts of a psychologically distressing event outside the range of usual human experience.

Theories of Anxiety Disorders

Like depression, anxiety disorders have many roots.

Genetic and Environmental Factors   As in depression, genetic vulnerability is a contributing, but probably not an essential, factor (Kendler et al., 1992). Twin and family studies show that genetics contributes to many anxiety syndromes, such as panic, simple phobia, and obsessive-compulsive disorder (Fyer et al., 1995; Goldstein et al., 1997; Torgersen, 1983). The mechanism that translates a genetic vulnerability into most anxiety disorders probably involves the neurotransmitter norepinephrine; serotonin may be involved in some anxiety disorders as well (Coplan, 1997; Southwick et al., 1997). Imaging studies find that the amygdala and regions of the frontal cortex to which it projects are particularly active when individuals with anxiety disorders are exposed to threatening stimuli, such as combat-related stimuli in veterans with PTSD (e.g., Shin et al., 1997).

Caution is in order, however, in interpreting research on the biology of anxiety disorders, since both genetic and environmental hypotheses could explain the results of many family history studies. Growing up in a home with a pathologically anxious parent—or parents—poses significant environmental risk even if no genetic risk is present. Even studies showing that medications ameliorate specific symptoms do not necessarily demonstrate the role of biology in *causing* a disorder. Giving a sedative to someone who has just discovered she has cancer and finding that it allays her anxiety does not prove that her anxiety was genetic. Anxiety is mediated by neurotransmitters, which should be overactive in anxious people, but this overactivity could reflect learning, heredity, or both.

In fact, stressful life events have been implicated in the development or exacerbation of many anxiety disorders (Zal, 1987). Roughly 80 percent of patients suffering from panic attacks describe a negative life event that coincided with their first attack (Finaly-Jones & Brown, 1981; Mathews et al., 1981), and panic patients report a higher incidence of stressful life events in the months preceding the onset of their symptoms than comparison subjects (Faravelli & Pallanti, 1989). Stressful events occurring in childhood, such as loss of a parent, also predispose people to anxiety disorders in adulthood (Hafner & Roder, 1987). For example, separation from a parent in childhood makes people more likely to develop PTSD after exposure to a traumatic event in adulthood (Breslau et al., 1997). Interestingly, so does low intelligence: Vietnam veterans with lower IQ prior to service in the military were more likely to develop PTSD when exposed to similar experiences than veterans with higher IQ (Macklin et al., 1998). Although the reasons are not entirely clear, a likely explanation is that greater intelligence allows more flexible coping, and greater verbal ability allows people to put traumatic events into words more easily and hence resolve the experience.

Cognitive-Behavioral Theories Cognitive-behavioral theories focus on how people learn anxiety reactions and on the dysfunctional cognitive patterns that generate and maintain them. From a behaviorist perspective, pathological anxiety, like normal anxiety, typically arises through classical conditioning (Chapter 5). People who are afraid of dogs, for example, may develop the phobia after being frightened by a dog. The emotional response is then elicited each time they see a dog. The anxiety may in turn evoke avoidance behavior, which is negatively reinforced: By avoiding dogs, the person avoids the anxiety associated with them. Unfortunately, avoiding dogs also prevents extinction of the emotional response because extinction in classical conditioning requires exposure to the conditioned stimulus (dogs) without the unconditioned stimulus (the original experience that initially made the individual afraid, such as a dog attacking them).

Cognitive theorists add that negative biases in thinking (such as a tendency to fear the worst) and low self-efficacy expectancies ("I can't do it") contribute to the origin and maintenance of anxiety disorders (Mineka & Sutton, 1992). Anxiety, like depression, makes people see things in a negative light, but unlike depression, it also focuses their attention on threatening stimuli. For example, when presented with pairs of threatening and nonthreatening homophones (words that sound the same but have different spellings), anxious people are likely to select the threatening spelling (e.g., die vs. dye) (Mathews et al., 1989).

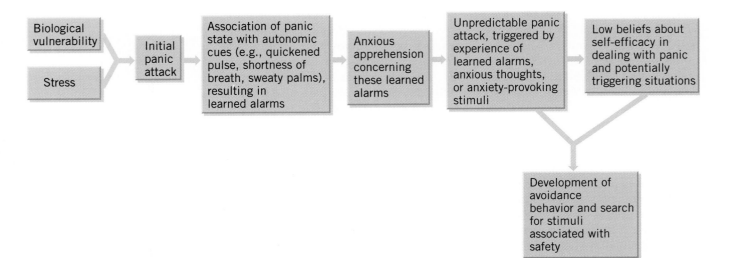

FIGURE 15.10

A cognitive-behavioral view of the development of panic symptoms. Biological vulnerabilities, environmental stresses, or their interaction leads to an initial panic attack. The attack includes autonomic responses that become associated through classical conditioning with the panic state, so whenever the person starts to experience them, she becomes frightened that a panic attack will occur.

David Barlow (1988a,b; Zinbarg et al., 1992) has proposed an integrated cognitive-behavioral model of anxiety disorders (Figure 15.10). In Barlow's view, biological vulnerabilities, environmental stresses, or their interaction lead to an initial panic attack. The attack includes autonomic responses such as quickened pulse, pounding heart, difficulty breathing, dry mouth, and sweaty palms. These responses then become associated with the panic state through classical conditioning, so that whenever the person starts to experience them, she becomes frightened that a panic attack will occur. To put it another way, the individual develops a fear of fear (Goldstein & Chambless, 1978; Kenardy et al., 1992).

People with panic disorders thus become especially aware of their autonomic activity and are constantly on the lookout for signals of arousal. Panic patients show heightened awareness of cardiac changes such as rapid heartbeat and palpitations (Ehlers & Breuer, 1992; Schmidt et al., 1997). They are also more likely to panic when exposed to air that contains slightly more carbon dioxide than normal (Figure 15.11), presumably because they start to feel short of breath (Rapee et al., 1992). In panic-prone individuals, fear of their own autonomic responses magnifies anxiety and may trigger an actual attack.

Repeated experiences of this sort may lead them to avoid situations associated with panic attacks or physiological arousal. People with panic disorders may, for example, give up jogging because it produces autonomic responses such as racing pulse and sweating that they associate with panic attacks. Such avoidance behavior may ultimately lead to agoraphobia.

Psychodynamic Theories   Psychodynamic approaches similarly assert that anxiety disorders stem from mental associations of thoughts and feelings, but they do not assume that actual events, such as being bitten by a dog, necessarily underlie phobias or other recurrent anxieties. Instead, the phobic object is often a source of anxiety because of its unconscious connection to something that is *really* feared, as in the following example. Mr. P sought therapy for a fear of driving. Exploring the thoughts, memories, and fantasies connected with driving uncovered

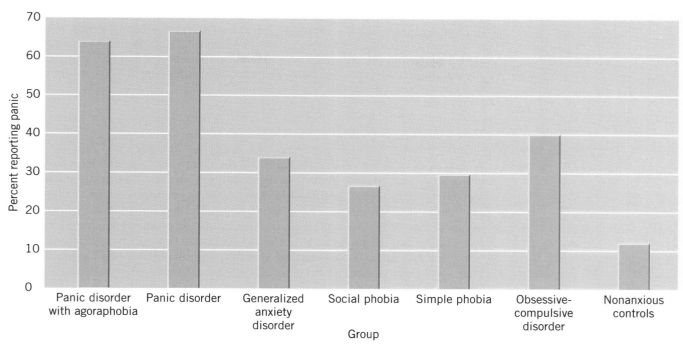

FIGURE 15.11

Precipitation of panic episodes by exposure to carbon dioxide-enriched air. Subjects with various anxiety disorders were exposed to air with a slightly elevated carbon dioxide content (5.5 percent elevation), which makes the air feel harder to breathe. All anxiety-disorder patients were more likely to panic than normal subjects; panic patients were particularly prone to experience panic symptoms. *Source:* Rapee et al., 1992, p. 545.

an occasion when he felt an uncontrollable urge to hit a pedestrian who cavalierly walked across the street in front of his car. He became furious and several other times experienced an urge to hit pedestrians he thought were "being arrogant" in the way they walked across the street or failed to acknowledge his right of way. Mr. P was a chronically angry person who had long-standing concerns about people not taking him seriously, beginning in childhood with his parents. The therapist thus hypothesized that Mr. P's phobia reflected a fear of his own aggressive impulses to hurt pedestrians who do not "take him seriously." What he feared was not really driving but the impulses and fantasies stirred up while driving.

Psychodynamic and cognitive-behavioral views of anxiety may not be entirely incompatible. From both perspectives, anxiety emerges when a contemporary situation (a phobic stimulus, a quickened pulse, or an interpersonal situation) resembles a past situation and activates the associated feeling. This activation may be relatively straightforward, as when the presence of a dog activates a conditioned response and conscious fears ("I can't get away," or "What if it bites me?"). Alternatively, a seemingly innocuous event may activate a network of associations that includes thoughts or memories associated with anxiety, as when Mr. P became frightened behind the wheel because the thought of driving unconsciously activated networks associated with a loss of control and a wish to drive the car *into* someone.

INTERIM SUMMARY   As in other disorders, heredity and environment both contribute to the etiology of anxiety disorders. Both adult and childhood stressors appear to play a role. Behaviorist theories implicate classical conditioning and negative reinforcement of avoidance behavior in the etiology and maintenance of anxiety disorders. Cognitive theorists emphasize negative biases in thinking, such as attention to threatening stimuli. An integrative cognitive-behavioral theory suggests that patients develop classically conditioned fear of their own autonomic responses, which, combined with fearful thoughts, perpetuate anxiety and trigger panic episodes. Psychodynamic theories propose that anxiety disorders reflect unconscious associations.

DISSOCIATIVE DISORDERS

A class of disorders akin to PTSD and usually created by repeated exposure to situations evoking intense anxiety is dissociative disorders. **Dissociative disorders** are characterized by disruptions in consciousness, memory, sense of identity, or perception. The patient may have significant periods of amnesia, may find herself in a new city with no recollection of her old life, or may feel separated from her emotions and experience, as if her mind and body were in two different places. The primary feature is **dissociation**, whereby significant aspects of experience are kept separate and distinct (that is, *dis-associated*) in memory and consciousness. Dissociation is usually a response to overwhelming psychic pain, as when victims of severe physical abuse or rape mentally separate themselves from the situation by experiencing themselves and their feelings outside of their bodies.

The most severe dissociative disorder is **dissociative identity disorder**, otherwise known as *multiple personality disorder*, in which at least two separate and distinct personalities exist within the same person. People with multiple personalities are frequently unaware that they have these alter-selves, as in the following case report (Herzog, 1984):

> Irene, a 29-year-old suicidal woman, told her psychotherapist that she avoided most people because she felt that they were not trustworthy. She was puzzled by the fact that her husband told her that she physically abused their children, since she had no recollection of doing so. Shirley is a young woman who is abusive to other women but sexually provocative with men. She was physically abused by her mother as a young girl and sexually molested by her brother and uncle between the ages of 10 and 17.

Irene and Shirley are part of the same woman; a third personality is "The Man," who surfaces whenever the two women need protection. At the start of her psychotherapy, Shirley was unaware that these were all parts of herself and had no access to memories formed in one state while in another. Another patient with this disorder had two lives, including two addresses, two sets of doctors, and two lovers who did not understand why she was so often unavailable. Some intriguing, but preliminary, data suggest that the different personalities in cases such as these may be both psychologically and physiologically distinct: Not only do they have access to different memories and look strikingly different on personality tests, but they may also differ in physiological qualities such as muscle tension, heart rate, and even allergies (Putnam, 1991).

Individuals with dissociative disorders typically come from chaotic home environments and have suffered physical and sexual abuse in childhood (Bliss, 1984; Chu & Dill, 1990; Gelinas, 1983). In fact, a history of extreme trauma, usually sexual abuse, is found in nearly all cases of dissociative disorder (Lewis et al., 1997; Scroppo et al., 1998). Unlike most psychological disorders, a recent twin study suggests that environmental variables account for the disorder, with little or no genetic influence (Waller & Ross, 1997). The vast majority of cases are female, probably because of the greater incidence of sexual abuse in females. The prevalence of dissociative identity disorder is a matter of controversy. The disorder appears to be quite rare (see Modestin, 1992; Ross et al., 1991), despite the attention it has drawn by gripping accounts such as *Sybil* (Schreiber, 1973) and *The Three Faces of Eve* (Thigpen & Cleckly, 1954).

PERSONALITY DISORDERS

Personality disorders are characterized by enduring maladaptive patterns of thought, feeling, and behavior that lead to chronic disturbances in interpersonal and occupational functioning. For example, a person with **narcissistic personality disorder** has severe trouble in relationships because of a tendency to use people, to devalue or totally dismiss them when they "get in the way," to be hypersensitive to criticism, to feel entitled to special privileges, and to become rageful. Individuals with this disorder show little empathy for other people. One patient who was asked about the feelings of a woman he had just rejected callously remarked, "What do I care? What can she do for me anymore? Hey, that's the breaks of the game—sometimes you dump, sometimes you get dumped. Nobody would be crying if this had happened to me."

Table 15.7 shows the personality disorders delineated in DSM-IV. The prevalence of personality disorders in the general population is unknown, but the best estimates are in the range of 10 percent (Lenzenweger et al., 1997). We examine two of them here, borderline personality disorder, which is more prevalent in women, and antisocial personality disorder, which is more prevalent in men.

Borderline Personality Disorder

The movie *Fatal Attraction* portrayed a disturbed woman who took revenge on a married man with whom she had had an affair. This character, with her dramatic suicidal gestures and extreme mood swings, would likely be diagnosed with a severe borderline personality disorder. **Borderline personality disorder** is marked

TABLE 15.7 DSM-IV PERSONALITY DISORDERS	
PERSONALITY DISORDER	**DESCRIPTION**
Paranoid	Distrust and suspiciousness
Schizoid	Detachment from social relationships and restricted range of emotional expression
Schizotypal	Acute discomfort in close relationships, cognitive or perceptual distortions, and eccentricity
Antisocial	Disregard for, and violation of, the rights of others
Borderline	Impulsivity and instability in interpersonal relationships, self-concept, and emotion
Histrionic	Excessive emotionality and attention seeking
Narcissistic	Grandiosity, need for admiration, and lack of empathy
Avoidant	Social inhibition and avoidance, feelings of inadequacy, and hypersensitivity to negative evaluation
Dependent	Submissive and clinging behavior and excessive need to be taken care of
Obsessive-compulsive	Preoccupation with orderliness, perfectionism, and control
Personality disorder not otherwise specified	Enduring, pervasive, and dysfunctional personality patterns not described by any other personality disorder

Source: Adapted from *Diagnostic and Statistical Manual of Mental Disorders, 4th ed.*, American Psychiatric Association, Washington, DC, 1994, p. 629.

Could a man who would deliberately murder hundreds of people, such as Oklahoma City bomber Timothy McVeigh, be psychologically sound? Where do we draw the line between sickness and badness?

by extremely unstable interpersonal relationships, dramatic mood swings, an unstable sense of identity, intense fears of separation and abandonment, manipulativeness, and impulsive behavior. Also characteristic of this disorder is self-mutilating behavior, such as wrist-slashing, carving words on the arm, or burning the skin with cigarettes.

Although patients with borderline personality disorder may seem superficially normal, the volatility and insecurity of their attachments become clear in intimate relationships. In part, this reflects the ways they form mental representations of people and relationships. Their representations are often simplistic and one-sided, strongly influenced by their moods and needs (Kernberg, 1975; Kernberg et al., 1989; Masterson, 1976; Westen et al., 1990).

Borderline patients are particulary noted for *splitting* their representations into all good or all bad—seeing people as either on their side or bent on hurting or leaving them—and rapidly changing from one view of a person to another (Baker et al., 1992; Kernberg et al., 1989). Splitting makes maintaining relationships extremely difficult. One woman with a borderline personality disorder had been involved with a man for only three weeks before deciding he was "the only man in the world who could love me." She began calling him constantly and suggested they live together. He became concerned about the intensity of her feelings and suggested they see each other only on weekends so they could get to know each other a little more slowly. She was furious and accused him of leading her on and using her. Only hours before he was a knight in shining armor; now he was a demon incarnate. Several studies document that borderline patients are also extremely prone to attribute negative or malevolent intentions to other people and to expect abuse and rejection (Bell et al., 1989; Nigg et al., 1992).

Antisocial Personality Disorder

Antisocial personality disorder is marked by irresponsible and socially disruptive behavior in a variety of areas. Symptoms include stealing and destroying property and a lack of empathy and remorse for misdeeds. These individuals are often unable to maintain jobs because of unexplained absences and harassment of co-workers, lying, stealing, vandalism, impulsive behavior, and recklessness. People with antisocial personality disorders can be exceedingly charming, leading those who have been fooled by them to see them ultimately as con artists.

Typically, an antisocial personality disorder is evident by age 15. The characteristic behaviors are similar to those of childhood conduct disorder. In fact, nearly all adult antisocial personality disorders were conduct-disordered as children, although only 40 to 50 percent of conduct-disordered children become antisocial adults (Lytton, 1990). The syndrome is more prevalent in men (3 percent of adult males) than women (less than 1 percent). It is also more commonly found in poor urban areas (Kaplan & Sadock, 1988).

Antisocial individuals rarely take the initiative to seek treatment; rather, they most commonly wind up in courts, prisons, and welfare departments (Vaillant & Perry, 1985). When they do seek psychiatric treatment, it is usually to avoid some legal repercussion. For example, Mr. C was a tall, muscular man with a scruffy beard and steely blue eyes. He came to a clinic complaining of depression and lack of direction in life. He presented a very moving description of a childhood filled with abuse at the hands of his father and neglect by his severely mentally ill mother, which may well have been accurate. He talked about wanting to come to understand why his life was not going well and wanting to work hard to change. He also described chronic dysphoria and feelings of boredom and worthlessness that are common in antisocial personalities.

By the end of the first session, however, Mr. C disclosed a troubling history of violence, in which he had escalated several bar brawls by hitting people in the face with empty bottles or pool cues. His casual response when asked about whether they were seriously hurt was, "You think I stuck around to pick their face up off the floor?" He also had a history of carrying weapons and spoke of a time in his life during which he had his finger on the trigger "if anybody even looked at me wrong." When asked why he had finally come in for help now, he admitted that he had been "falsely accused" of breaking someone's nose at a bar and that his lawyer thought "seeing a shrink" would help his case—but that this, of course, had nothing to do with his genuine desire to turn his life around.

Theories of Personality Disorders

Once again, both genetic and environmental factors play a role in the genesis of many personality disorders (Nigg & Goldsmith, 1994; Seiver & Davis, 1991). The evidence for biological contributions to borderline personality disorders is not well established, although some recent data are suggestive (Hollander et al., 1994). According to psychodynamic theorists, borderline personality disorder originates in pathological attachment relationships in early childhood, which lead to attachment problems later in life (Adler & Buie, 1979; Kernberg, 1975; Masterson & Rinsley, 1975), and empirical research has begun to support this notion (Ludolph et al., 1990). Several studies also implicate sexual abuse in the etiology of this disorder, which may account for its prevalence in females (Herman et al., 1989; Ogata et al., 1990; Zanarini, 1997). The best available evidence suggests that a chaotic home life (Golomb et al., 1994), a mother with a troubled attachment history, a male relative who is sexually abusive, and a family history of impulsivity and difficulty regulating emotions provide fertile ground for the development of this syndrome.

In many respects, the etiology of antisocial personality disorder resembles that of borderline personality disorder, except that physical abuse is more common than sexual abuse (see Pollock et al., 1990). Both social learning and psychodynamic approaches implicate physical abuse, neglect, and absent or criminal male role models. Young adult experiences can also contribute to the development of the disorder: The extent of combat exposure in Vietnam predicts the extent to which veterans have antisocial symptoms (Barrett et al., 1996); one possible explanation is that men tend to respond to violent traumas with violence.

Adoption studies demonstrate the role of both biological and environmental variables in the etiology of antisocial personality disorder (Cadoret et al., 1995). An adult adoptee whose biological parent had an arrest record for antisocial behavior is four times more likely to have problems with aggressive behavior than a person without a biological vulnerability (Figure 15.12). On the other hand, a person whose *adoptive* parent had antisocial personality disorder is more than three times more likely to develop the disorder, regardless of biological history. Interestingly, twin studies suggest that environmental factors are more important in predicting antisocial behavior in adolescence, whereas genetic factors are more important as individuals get older (Lyons et al., 1997). This finding makes sense in light of other data from behavioral genetics that show that heritability of personality and IQ increase with age—that is, that similarities between biological relatives tend to be stronger as they get older (Chapters 8 and 12).

INTERIM SUMMARY **Dissociative disorders** are characterized by disruptions in consciousness, memory, sense of identity, or perception. In **dissociative identity disorder**, at least two distinct personalities exist within the person. Dissociative disorders generally reflect a history of severe trauma. **Personality disorders** are characterized by enduring maladaptive patterns of thought, feeling, and behavior that lead to chronic disturbances in interpersonal and occupational functioning. **Borderline personality disorder** is marked by extremely unstable interpersonal relationships, dramatic mood swings, an unstable sense

		Aggressivity in adoptee (% of participants)	
		No	Yes
Antisocial personality disorder in biological parent	No	84	16
	Yes	52	48

FIGURE 15.12
Genetic contribution to aggressive behavior problems. Among individuals without an antisocial biological parent, aggressive behavior problems were unusual. In contrast, almost half of the biological offspring of antisocial parents had problems with aggression. *Source:* Adapted from Cadoret et al. (1995). Adoption study demonstrating two genetic pathways to drug abuse. *Archives of General Psychiatry,* 52, p. 48.

of identity, intense fears of separation and abandonment, manipulativeness, impulsive behavior, and self-mutilating behavior. **Antisocial personality disorder** is marked by irresponsible and socially disruptive behavior.

RETHINKING PSYCHOPATHOLOGY

In this chapter, we have examined several psychopathological syndromes. Before concluding, however, we should take a step back and ask three questions about the relation between psychopathology and the categories we use to understand it. First, can disorders really be so neatly classified? Second, to what degree have cultural and political processes shaped the diagnostic categories included in and excluded from DSM-IV? And, finally, can biology and learning be so readily distinguished in the etiology of psychological disorders?

ARE MENTAL DISORDERS REALLY DISTINCT?

Although we have followed DSM-IV in describing discrete disorders, most practicing clinicians question whether psychopathology can be so neatly categorized, and recent research supports their impression. For instance, studies do not clearly support the notion that major depression is a distinct condition; instead, it may simply represent the severe end of a continuum of depression (Kendler & Gardner, 1998).

The most clearly demarcated syndromes are schizophrenia and bipolar disorder. Several studies have shown that bipolar disorder in a first-degree relative (mother, father, brother, or sister) does not elevate a person's risk for schizophrenia, and vice versa, supporting the contention that these are genetically discrete disorders. Yet other studies indicate that over several generations, bipolar disorders do predispose individuals to schizophrenia (Crow, 1986, 1990, 1998). One possibility is that the two disorders may not be entirely discrete; another is that apparent genetic overlap really just reflects diagnostic confusion, because we have not yet identified the categories of psychopathology that actually exist "in nature" (Kendler et al., 1998).

Distinguishing between manic and paranoid schizophrenic episodes can also be difficult. People who are manic often have a delusional belief in their own importance; as a result they may think people are trying to get them because of their elevated position. Conversely, paranoid patients often have grandiose delusions, which can make them difficult to distinguish from patients in a manic episode (Garvey et al., 1980; Zigler & Glick, 1988). Another DSM-IV diagnostic category, **schizoaffective disorder**, is used to describe individuals who seem to have attributes of both schizophrenia and psychotic depression and may not easily fit the criteria for just one or the other. The disorder appears genetically related to both schizophrenia and major depression (Erlenmeyer-Kipling et al., 1997).

To complicate matters further, patients often have symptoms indicative of multiple disorders. Depression tends to occur simultaneously with numerous other syndromes, including anxiety, eating, and substance-related disorders (Coryell et al., 1992; Mineka et al, 1998). Genetic studies show that if one twin has one of these disorders, the other twin is likely to have one or more of the others (Kendler et al., 1995). Cross-cultural evidence suggests that most nonpsychotic disorders involve some mixture of anxiety and depression (Kleinman, 1988), a finding consistent with data on negative affect showing that people who tend to experience one unpleasant emotion tend to experience others (Chapter 11).

Perhaps the most complex questions pertain to the relationship between Axis

I disorders and personality disorders (Axis II). Most patients with severe Axis I disorders of all sorts—anxiety, mood, eating, substance use—have concurrent personality disorders (Green & Curtis, 1988; Shea et al., 1987). Trying to distinguish enduring aspects of personality from specific episodes of illness may be futile when the personality itself is the wellspring of diverse symptoms. For example, a person who cannot maintain relationships and jobs is naturally going to be vulnerable to depression and anxiety, so putting borderline personality disorder on one axis and depression and anxiety on another may be artificial.

▶ ONE STEP FURTHER

The Politics of Diagnosis

Beyond the question of whether psychopathology falls neatly into discrete syndromes is the question of whether DSM-IV identifies the right syndromes in the first place. As we have seen, cultural beliefs and values influence conceptions of mental illness, and this is true of Western scientific conceptions as well. A case in point is homosexuality, which was once considered a mental disorder. As a result of shifting cultural norms, homosexuality was dropped from the DSMs and is no longer considered pathological. Thus, the inclusion and exclusion of syndromes in DSM-IV is a political as well as scientific process.

Even more recently, politics have played a part in a proposed diagnostic category called self-defeating personality disorder (see Caplan, 1991; Frances et al., 1991). A *self-defeating personality disorder* is characterized by a pervasive pattern of self-damaging behavior. The name understates the seriousness of the disorder: People with this disorder are typically involved in physically and emotionally abusive relationships, as in the case of Mary at the beginning of this chapter, and they often do not follow through with treatment recommendations.

The controversy surrounding this disorder stems from its relative prevalence in women. Some feminist critics argue that adding self-defeating personality disorder to the DSM is little more than a medical version of victim blaming, a common psychological mechanism for dealing with injustice or victimization. Advocates of the diagnosis counter that such people clearly exist and typically move from one abusive relationship to another. Thus, staying in an abusive relationship does not solely reflect economic dependence on a particular man, a common explanation offered by opponents. Furthermore, argue proponents, pretending that self-defeating individuals either do not exist or do not suffer from an emotional disturbance is actually harmful because it prevents them from obtaining appropriate treatment and insurance coverage for their treatment, which requires a diagnosable disorder.

Both sides clearly have merit. On the one hand, mental health professionals were quicker to find a label for the women who seek out or remain in abusive relationships than the men who abuse them. On the other hand, few would deny that boys who are physically or sexually abused may develop disturbances that lead them to abuse others. The parallel assertion, however—that women who have been abused may find themselves psychologically compelled to repeat the abuse as victims—seems politically unacceptable. In fact, it has proven so unacceptable that the diagnosis of self-defeating personality disorder was only included in the prior edition of the DSM in an appendix as a diagnosis under consideration; it has been deleted entirely from DSM-IV. Interestingly, neither Mary, who chronically entered into abusive relationships, nor the men who chronically abused her would receive a psychiatric diagnosis. Why males who are disturbed tend to hurt other people, whereas females who are disturbed tend to hurt themselves, is an open question.

FROM MIND TO BRAIN

WHEN NURTURE BECOMES NATURE

Just as the gods of abnormality did not create six discrete disorders and rest on the seventh day, they were not particularly careful to separate nature and nurture. Thus, efforts to reduce the causes of disorders to genetics or environment may be problematic.

Pathogenic experiences—unfortunate life events—can create changes in the brain that become part of an individual's "nature." Monkeys separated from their mothers for prolonged periods show neuropsychological changes—permanent alterations in the number and sensitivity of receptors for neurotransmitters in the postsynaptic membrane (Gabbard, 1992). Similarly, people who undergo traumatic experiences and develop posttraumatic stress disorder also develop abnormalities in hypothalamic and pituitary functioning (Mason et al., 1994; Yehuda et al., 1991). These symptoms may then be amenable to biological treatments such as antidepressant medication, even though the causes were initially environmental. To speak of the causes as completely environmental, however, is not entirely accurate either. Repeated separation from attachment figures only produces biological abnormalities because the brain has evolved to be innately sensitive to attachment-related stimulation. Environmental causes presuppose a nervous system that makes them relevant.

Environmental factors can also activate biological vulnerabilities, so that neither heredity nor environment can alone bear the blame. For example, the amount of sunlight to which people are exposed has an impact on circadian rhythms, mood, eating, and sleep. Most people show mild seasonal mood changes; however, for some, these are extreme (Madden et al., 1996). For some people, lack of sunlight in the winter months can trigger or contribute to seasonal affective disorder (SAD), a depressive syndrome that occurs during a particular season (see Cohen et al., 1992; Teicher et al., 1997). Bingeing increases for some bulimics in winter months as well (Blouin et al., 1992). Although one might therefore consider classifying SAD as a disorder with a clear environmental trigger, a complication is that the tendency to experience SAD is partly heritable (Madden et al., 1996)! Thus, the vulnerability to an environmental event is itself inherited. This is probably true of virtually all environmental circumstances that contribute to psychopathology: Sexual abuse, for example, can probably have the damaging effects it can have only because humans have evolved mechanisms that make incest repugnant and traumatizing—mechanisms that normally prevent inbreeding.

Once a disorder has emerged, biology and experience may weave an even more tangled web. Research suggests that environmentally triggered episodes seem to lay down neural "tracks" that subsequent episodes employ, much as repeated use gradually blazes a trail in the woods. First episodes of mood disorders tend to have a clear precipitant, but later episodes, especially of bipolar disorder, occur after progressively shorter periods of remission and with less input from environmental stressors (Post, 1992). Although schizophrenia may not require an environmental trigger, the longer the interval between development of symptoms and treatment for first-episode schizophrenic patients, the worse the prognosis (Loebel et al., 1992), presumably because the more the disease is able to blaze a trail, the less able the brain is to cover the tracks.

INTERIM SUMMARY   The DSM-IV classification system may overstate the extent to which syndromes are discrete. Distinguishing the roles of nature and nurture in the etiology of psychological disturbances is also not as clear-cut as might first appear, since environmental events can translate into changes in the brain, and inherited characteristics typically determine which environmental events are psychologically toxic.

The longer an episode persists, the more it creates well-worn pathways in the brain that can more easily become reactivated.

SOME CONCLUDING THOUGHTS

We have learned a great deal about psychopathology over the last century. Research has finally dispelled explanations based on demons and spirit possession and replaced them with scientifically grounded theories. Yet it is clear that our categories of thought do not adequately mirror the categories of nature. If the role of science is progressively to narrow the discrepancy between reality and appearance—between the world and our representations of it—we have come a long way, but we have a long way to go. And we probably always will.

SUMMARY

1. **Psychopathology** refers to patterns of thought, feeling, or behavior that disrupt a person's sense of well-being or social or occupational functioning.

THE CULTURAL CONTEXT OF PSYCHOPATHOLOGY

2. The concept of mental illness varies historically and cross-culturally. Cultures differ in the ways they describe and pattern psychopathology, but "mentally ill" is not simply an arbitrary label applied to deviants, as was the claim of **labeling theory**.

CONTEMPORARY APPROACHES TO PSYCHOPATHOLOGY

3. Psychodynamic theorists make a general distinction among **neuroses, personality disorders**, and **psychoses**, which form a continuum of disturbance. A **psychodynamic formulation** involves assessing the person's wishes and fears, cognitive and emotional resources, and experience of the self and others.

4. The **cognitive-behavioral** perspective integrates aspects of classical and operant conditioning with a cognitive-social perspective. Dysfunctional behavior results from environmental contingencies and faulty cognitions.

5. Understanding psychopathology often requires shifting to a biological level of analysis. The biological approach proposes that psychopathology stems

from faulty wiring in the brain, particularly in the abundance, overreactivity, or underreactivity of specific neurotransmitters. **Diathesis–stress models** of psychopathology propose that people with an underlying vulnerability may become symptomatic under stressful circumstances.

6. A **systems approach** attempts to explain an individual's behavior in the context of a social group, such as a couple, a family, or a larger social system. A **family systems model** suggests that the symptoms of any individual are really symptoms of dysfunction in a family.

7. From an evolutionary perspective, psychopathology can reflect random variation, broader population pressures that can produce stable rates of psychopathology if they confer an offsetting advantage, and normally adaptive mechanisms gone awry.

DESCRIPTIVE DIAGNOSIS: DSM-IV AND PSYCHOPATHOLOGICAL SYNDROMES

8. The *Diagnostic and Statistical Manual of Mental Disorders-IV*, or **DSM-IV**, is the official manual of mental illnesses published by the American Psychiatric Association. It is the basis for **descriptive diagnosis**.

9. One disorder usually first diagnosed in childhood or adolescence is **attention-deficit hyperactivity disorder**, characterized by age-inappropriate inattention, impulsiveness, and hyperactivity. Another is **conduct disorder**, a disturbance in which a child persistently violates the rights of others as well as societal norms.

10. **Substance-related disorders** refer to continued use of substances that negatively affect psychological and social functioning. Worldwide, alcoholism is the most common substance use disorder. As with most psychological disorders, the roots of alcoholism lie in genetics, environment, and their interaction.

11. **Schizophrenia** is a disorder or set of disorders in which people lose touch with reality, experiencing both **positive symptoms** (such as **hallucinations**, **delusions**, and **loosening of associations**) and **negative symptoms** (such as **flat affect** and poor social skills). Types of schizophrenia include **paranoid**, **catatonic**, and **disorganized**, as well as **undifferentiated** (mixed) and **residual** (persistent illness but without full-blown psychotic symptoms). Schizophrenia is a highly heritable disease of the brain, although environmental circumstances such as a critical family environment can trigger or worsen it.

12. **Mood disorders** are characterized by disturbances in emotion and mood. In **manic** states, people feel excessively happy and believe they can do anything. The most severe form of depression is **major depressive disorder**. **Dysthymic disorder** refers to a long-standing, less acute depression of more than two years. A **bipolar disorder** is a mood disturbance marked by mania, often alternating with major depressive episodes. Suicide does not occur exclusively in mood disorders, but suicidal thoughts are a common component of depression.

13. Genetics contribute to the etiology of mood disorders, but except for bipolar disorder, which generally requires a biological vulnerability, environmental events alone can precipitate depression. Cognitive theories look for the roots of depression in dysfunctional thoughts. Psychodynamic theories suggest that the nature of and triggers for depression depend on an individual's personality structure.

14. **Anxiety disorders** are characterized by intense, frequent, or continuous anxiety that is not warranted by the situation. **Panic disorders** are distinguished

by attacks of intense fear and feelings of doom or terror not justified by the situation. **Agoraphobia** refers to a fear of being in places or situations from which escape might be difficult. **Obsessive-compulsive disorder** is marked by recurrent **obsessions** (persistent thoughts or ideas) and **compulsions** (intentional behaviors performed in response to an obsession and in a stereotyped fashion). **Posttraumatic stress disorder** is marked by flashbacks and recurrent thoughts of a psychologically distressing event outside the range of usual human experience.

15. Anxiety disorders, like depression, show substantial heritability but do not require a genetic predisposition. Cognitive-behavioral theories link them to conditioned emotional responses and dysfunctional cognitions. Psychodynamic theories link anxiety disorders to unconscious networks of association.

16. **Dissociative disorders** are characterized by disruptions in consciousness, memory, sense of identity, or perception of the environment. The primary feature is **dissociation**, whereby significant aspects of experience are kept separate and distinct in consciousness. The most severe type is **dissociative identity disorder**, also called *multiple personality disorder*.

17. **Personality disorders** are characterized by maladaptive personality patterns that lead to chronic disturbances in interpersonal and occupational functioning. **Borderline personality disorder** is marked by extremely unstable interpersonal relationships, dramatic mood swings, an unstable sense of identity, intense fears of separation and abandonment, manipulativeness, impulsive behavior, and self-mutilating behavior. **Antisocial personality disorder** is marked by a pattern of irresponsible and socially disruptive behavior in a variety of areas. Genetics plays a role in many personality disorders, as do childhood experiences such as abuse and neglect.

RETHINKING PSYCHOPATHOLOGY

18. Diagnostic categories overstate the discreteness of disorders and understate their cultural and political bases. Nature and nurture are so intertwined in the etiology of many syndromes that they cannot be readily distinguished.

George Segal, "Girl on a Chair, Finger to Mouth"/Christies' Images/VAGA.

CHAPTER *16*

Treatment of
Psychological Disorders

*J*enny was a frail, bright, obstinate 19-year-old from a working-class neighborhood in Boston. She came to the hospital under duress: Her parents threatened that if she did not, they would try to have her committed. They had a good case. Jenny was 5′3″ and 72 pounds, suffering from anorexia nervosa. She would likely have been dead two weeks later.

During her 10 weeks in the hospital, Jenny was not the easiest of patients. Like many hospitalized patients with anorexia, she regularly played cat-and-mouse games with her nurses. When weigh-in time came each morning, she had

to wear a hospital gown because otherwise she would fill her pockets with coins to fool the scales. The nurses even had to monitor her first trip to the bathroom each morning before weigh-in so she would not drink huge quantities of water to increase her apparent weight. Jenny also required a watchful eye at mealtime to make certain she did not dispose of her food rather than eat it.

In the hospital, Jenny received several forms of treatment. She met with a psychotherapist three times a week to try to uncover the roots of her need to starve herself. The therapist also set up a behavior plan to reward Jenny for weight gain with increased privileges (beginning with walks on the hospital grounds and eventually trips to the movies) and punish weight loss with increased restrictions. Jenny and her family met twice a week with a family therapist, who explored the role of family dynamics in her disorder. Her mother, a very anxious woman with a severe personality disorder, was dependent on Jenny in many ways. Jenny was completely enmeshed with her mother, taking care of her and sometimes missing school to stay home with her when her mother was anxious. Jenny's mother was especially anxious about Jenny's sexuality and regularly cut out articles from the newspaper about rapes and left them on Jenny's bed. Jenny eliminated any hint of her own sexuality by losing so much weight that she stopped menstruating and lost her feminine shape. Jenny's father was preoccupied with her physically frail, severely mentally retarded sister, whom Jenny always resented for consuming his attention. By becoming so frail herself, Jenny finally caught her father's eye. In addition to individual and family therapy, Jenny participated in a therapy group for patients with eating disorders. In the group her peers confronted her rationalizations about her eating behavior; Jenny could also see in the other group members some of the patterns she could not see in herself.

Once Jenny left the hospital, with her weight stabilized, she spent the next four years in psychotherapy. The therapy focused primarily on the way her anorexic symptoms reflected her discomfort with having any kind of impulses, her need for control over everything (including her body), her fear of her sexuality, her use of starving to regulate feelings of sadness and aloneness, her rage at her sister (which she could not acknowledge to either herself or her parents), and her desperate wish for her father to notice her. At one point during her treatment, when she moved out of her family's home for the first time, she became so anxious at being away from her mother that her therapist also recommended medication for a short time.

By the end of her treatment, Jenny's life-threatening disorder had not returned, and she was no longer preoccupied with food. She was now able to deal more appropriately with her mother, was openly able to acknowledge her mixed feelings toward her sister, had a much more satisfying relationship with her father, and was happily involved in a romantic relationship (something she could not even imagine at the beginning of treatment).

Jenny's case is unusual because people rarely receive so many different forms of treatment. More typically, they find themselves in the office of a clinician who believes their disorder reflects a chemical imbalance and prescribes medication, or that their problem lies in their childhood relationships with their parents and suggests long-term psychotherapy, or that the real problem is their irrational thoughts about themselves and suggests exploring their cognitive distortions, and so forth. In fact, the variety of psychotherapies is astounding—over 400 different types at last count (see Bergin & Garfield, 1994)—and the treatment people receive generally depends less on the nature of the disorder than on the theoretical perspective of the therapist.

In this chapter, we focus on the most widely practiced treatments for psychological disorders: psychodynamic, cognitive-behavioral, humanistic, group, family, and biological (Table 16.1). Each approach has its own theory of etiology and consequently its own prescriptions for treatment. After exploring each of these treatments, we examine the evidence for their effectiveness, the possibility of integrating therapeutic strategies (as in Jenny's treatment), and the role of culture in psychological healing. We conclude with a discussion of who gets—and does not get—treatment and the way treatment is evolving in the context of economic pressures.

PSYCHODYNAMIC THERAPIES

Modern psychotherapy developed in the late 19th century out of the work of Sigmund Freud. Most contemporary psychotherapists report that they rely to some extent on psychodynamic theory and technique (Pope et al., 1987). The psychodynamic approach to therapeutic change rests on two principles: the role of insight and the role of the therapist–patient relationship.

Insight refers to the understanding of one's own psychological processes. According to psychodynamic theory, symptoms reflect unconscious conflicts and compromises among competing wishes and fears and maladaptive ways of coping and defending against unpleasant emotions. Therapeutic change requires that patients come to understand the internal workings of their mind and hence, as one adolescent patient put it, to become "the captain of my own ship." Becoming the captain of one's own ship means acquiring the capacity to make conscious, rational choices as an adult about wishes, fears, and defensive strategies that may have been forged in childhood. Insight is not, however, a cold cognitive act. Psychodynamic clinicians often speak of "emotional insight," stressing that knowing

TABLE 16.1   VARIETIES OF PSYCHOLOGICAL TREATMENT

THERAPY	DESCRIPTION
Psychodynamic	Attempts to change personality patterns through insight (using free association and interpretation) and the therapist–patient relationship (analysis of transference).
Psychoanalysis	Intensive therapy, 3–5 times per week, in which the patient lies on a couch and talks about whatever comes to mind, using free association.
Psychodynamic psychotherapy	Moderately intensive therapy, 1–3 times per week, in which the patient discusses issues that come to mind while sitting face to face with the therapist.
Cognitive-behavioral	Attempts to change problematic behaviors and cognitive processes.
Systematic desensitization	Classical conditioning technique in which the therapist induces relaxation and encourages the patient to approach a phobic stimulus gradually in imagination.
Exposure techniques	Classical conditioning techniques in which the therapist exposes the patient to the feared object in real life, either all at once (flooding) or gradually (graded exposure).
Operant techniques	Therapeutic approach in which the therapist induces change by alternating patterns of reinforcement and punishment.
Participatory modeling	Cognitive-social technique in which the therapist models behavior and encourages the patient to participate in it.
Skills training	Cognitive-social technique in which the therapist teaches behaviors necessary to accomplish goals, as in social skills or assertiveness training.
Cognitive therapy	Therapeutic approach aimed at altering problematic thought patterns that underlie dysfunctional feelings and behavior.
Humanistic	Attempts to restore a sense of genuineness and attunement with inner feelings.
Gestalt	Focuses on the "here and now" and brings out disavowed feelings.
Client-centered	Uses empathy and unconditional positive regard to help patients experience themselves as they really are.
Family and marital	Attempts to change problematic family or marital patterns, such as communication patterns, boundaries, and alliances.
Group	Attempts to use group process and group interaction to help people change problematic patterns, either with the help of a therapist or through self-help.
Biological	Attempts to change problematic brain physiology responsible for psychological symptoms.

intellectually about one's problems is not the same as really confronting intense feelings and fears (such as Jenny's fear that if she did not take care of her mother something terrible might happen).

A second principle of psychodynamic treatment is that the relationship between the patient and therapist is crucial for therapeutic change. A patient has to feel comfortable with the therapist in order to speak about emotionally significant experiences, a phenomenon called the **therapeutic alliance**. Beyond this, many psychodynamic therapists argue, as do some humanistic therapists, that being with someone who listens nonjudgmentally and empathically, rather than critically, is inherently therapeutic. Furthermore, as we explore below, psychodynamic therapists assume that patients often bring enduring and troubling interpersonal patterns into the relationship with the therapist, which can then be more readily explored and changed.

"I UTILIZE THE BEST FROM FREUD, THE BEST FROM JUNG AND THE BEST FROM MY UNCLE MARTY, A VERY SMART FELLOW."

THERAPEUTIC TECHNIQUES

To bring about therapeutic change, psychodynamic psychotherapies rely on three techniques: free association, interpretation, and analysis of transference.

Free Association

If a person becomes anxious without knowing why or starves herself despite knowing the dangers of malnutrition, then an important goal is to understand the unconscious events guiding behavior—or, as Freud put it, "to make the unconscious conscious." The patient and her therapist must find a way to map her unconscious networks of association to see what fears or wishes are linked to her symptoms. **Free association** is a technique for exploring associational networks and unconscious processes involved in symptom formation. The therapist instructs the patient to say whatever comes to mind—thoughts, feelings, images, fantasies, memories, dreams from the night before, or wishes—and to try to censor nothing. The patient and therapist then collaborate to solve the mystery of the symptom, piecing together the connections in what has been said and noting what has *not* been said (that is, what the patient may be defending against). As in any good detective story, the most important clues are often those that are concealed, and only by examining gaps in the suspect's account does one find hidden motives and concealed data. The only difference is that in psychotherapy the patient is both the co-detective and the prime suspect.

Interpretation

Although the patient may work hard to understand her associations, the therapist has two advantages in solving the mystery: The therapist is trained in making psychological inferences and is not personally embroiled in the patient's conflicts and ways of seeing reality. For example, Jenny's aversion to sexuality seemed natural to her until she discovered how she had learned to associate sex and danger

MACBETH: Canst thou not minister to a mind diseas'd, Pluck from the memory a rooted sorrow, Raze out the written troubles of the brain, And with some sweet oblivious antidote Cleanse the stuff'd bosom of that perilous stuff Which weighs upon the heart?
Doctor: Therein the patient must minister to himself.
SHAKESPEARE, *MACBETH*, V.III

from her mother. Thus, a central element of psychodynamic technique is the **interpretation** of conflicts, defenses, and compromise-formations (Chapter 12), whereby the therapist helps the person understand her experiences in a new light.

One patient, for example, repeatedly had affairs with married men. As she talked about sneaking around the wife of one man in order to see him, her associations led to her parents' divorce. At one point, her mother had refused to allow her to see her father, so the patient had arranged secret meetings with him. The therapist interpreted the connection between the patient's pattern of seeking out married men and sneaking around her mother's back to see her father. Apparently, the rage she felt toward her mother for not letting her see her father was now directed toward the wives of the men with whom she had affairs, which allowed her to rationalize sleeping with their husbands.

An important kind of interpretation is the interpretation of **resistance**, barriers to free association, or to the treatment more generally, that the patient creates. As both sleuth and suspect, the patient is consciously on the trail of mental processes that she is unconsciously covering up. Resistance emerges because the patient originally developed her symptoms to reduce anxiety; the closer she comes to its source, the more she is motivated to run from it. Jenny, for example, insisted for two years that her attitudes toward sexuality were totally realistic and refused to discuss the matter further.

Analysis of Transference

The relationship between the patient and the therapist provides a particularly useful source of information in psychotherapy (Freud, 1912; Gill, 1982; Luborsky & Crits-Christoph, 1990). Freud observed that patients tend to play out with their therapists many of the same interpersonal scenarios that give them trouble in their lives. For example, a man who recently came to therapy complaining of problems getting along with people in positions of authority immediately added, "By the way, I don't believe in this psychotherapy crap." In so doing, he had already replicated his symptom with a new authority figure—the therapist—in the first moments of the treatment! The therapy relationship is a very intimate relationship in which the patient communicates personal experiences to someone commonly perceived as an authority. As research documents, this relationship

Freud's office in Vienna.

consequently tends to become a magnet for experiences from prior relationships involving intimacy and authority, particularly parental relationships (Luborsky et al., 1990).

Transference refers to the process whereby people transfer thoughts, feelings, fears, wishes, and conflicts from past relationships, particularly from childhood, onto new relationships, especially with the therapist. For example, one patient had experienced his father as extremely critical and impossible to please. In therapy, the patient tended to interpret even neutral comments from the therapist as severe criticism and would then respond by doing things (like missing appointments without calling) that would elicit criticism and hostility in most relationships. By examining such transferential processes, the patient and therapist can learn about the patient's dynamics directly without relying on self-reports. The intensity of transference can also be a potent force in developing emotional insight. Freud wrote that the relationship between the patient and therapist creates "new editions of the old conflicts" (1917, p. 454). The aim of working with transference is to rewrite the new edition in light of new information.

Experimental research from a cognitive perspective documents transference processes in everyday relationships. In one study the investigators asked participants to describe significant others and then embedded pieces of those descriptions in descriptions of fictional characters (Andersen & Cole, 1991). Thus, if a participant described his mother as intelligent, feminine, gentle, and courageous, the investigators would create a fictional character who was described, among other things, as gentle. The investigators then presented participants with these descriptions and later asked them to remember them. Upon recall, participants attributed qualities of the significant other (such as courage) to these characters, even though these qualities had not been part of the characters' initial description. Essentially, participants transferred aspects of one representation to another.

More recently, these researchers have shown that people similarly transfer *feelings* from significant others onto descriptions of a person who is allegedly in the room next door, and that these feelings lead them either to want to meet or avoid the person (Andersen et al., 1996). Their latest research demonstrates the same effects when descriptions of significant others are embedded in descriptions of hypothetical people and presented *subliminally* (Glassman and Andersen, 1997). Thus, this research documents that transference can influence thought, feeling, and memory, and can occur outside of awareness.

A Case Illustration

The following case study illustrates the principles of psychodynamic psychotherapy. A woman in her early 30s we will call Judy went to a clinic suffering from tremendous anxiety and inexplicable depression. She was developing a relationship with a somewhat older man that was beginning to become physical, and she had never been sexually intimate with anyone as an adult. Although this case occurred in the 1980s, before widespread publicity on repressed memories, the therapist suspected a history of sexual abuse. He noticed a flicker of fear cross her face when he flipped the "Do not disturb" sign on the door. Her response, of which she seemed unaware, could have had many possible meanings; however, the therapist hypothesized that something about being alone with a man who indicated that he did not want to be disturbed might have triggered the fear. The patient was also flirtatious in the sessions and would sit inappropriately in a relatively short skirt. This combination of seductiveness and fear sometimes characterizes sexually abused patients, who may be sexually promiscuous, fearful of men, or both simultaneously.

Ultimately, the patient did recall a history of sexual abuse, in part through dream analysis, another technique used in psychodynamic psychotherapies. In one recurring dream, her mother was selling her as a prostitute. Exploring her associations suggested that this symbolized her belief that her mother had looked the other way when two of her mother's boyfriends sexually molested the patient and her sister, fearing that her boyfriends would leave her if she did not allow it. As the memories began to return, however, the patient was reluctant to disclose them. The therapist wondered aloud whether by discussing something sexual with him the patient felt that something sexual was happening between the two of them and whether that might not be frightening in light of her history. This interpretation made the patient more comfortable in disclosing what she had remembered; it indicated that the therapist was not about to reenact with her a previous trauma. Later in the treatment, she was also able to see how the conflicting signals she sent the therapist in the first session—fear plus flirtatiousness—stemmed from her abuse history and contributed to some confusing and unpleasant experiences with men as an adult.

One important feature of this case was that the therapist had to handle many sensitive issues, particularly around the transference (see Herman, 1992). He needed to help the patient remember what had happened to her so she could begin to control her actions and cope with her emotions. At the same time, he could not move too quickly or she might feel sexually invaded by "demands" for her to disclose, reenacting her experience of helplessness and vulnerability. Working with such intense experiences exerts a pressure on the therapist known as **countertransference**, in which interaction with the patient, and particularly becoming the object of her transference reactions, triggers emotional responses in the therapist. To learn to detect and handle countertransference appropriately, psychodynamic psychotherapists must themselves undergo psychodynamic treatment to explore their own psychological processes.

VARIETIES OF PSYCHODYNAMIC THERAPY

The main contemporary forms of psychodynamic treatment are psychoanalysis and psychodynamic psychotherapy.

Psychoanalysis

The first variety of psychodynamic therapy, developed by Freud, was **psychoanalysis**, in which the patient lies on a couch and the analyst sits behind him. The purpose of the couch is to create an environment in which people can set aside many of their defenses, simply letting associations come to mind. This arrangement can also make disclosing sensitive material easier because the person does not have to look the therapist in the eye. Patients usually undergo psychoanalysis three to five times a week for several years, making it a very intensive, extensive, and expensive form of therapy.

Psychodynamic Psychotherapy

In **psychodynamic psychotherapy**, the patient and therapist sit face-to-face, with the patient in a chair rather than on the couch. The therapy is more conversational than psychoanalysis, although the aim is still exploration of unconscious processes. The techniques are similar to psychoanalysis, but the therapist and patient are usually more goal-directed because time is much more limited.

Psychodynamic psychotherapy is particularly appropriate for addressing repetitive interpersonal patterns or difficulties in relationships, such as consistently choosing the wrong kind of lover or fearing vulnerability in close relationships. This kind of treatment proved crucial for Jenny, who initially had trouble maintaining an appropriate weight after she left the hospital. It allowed her to confront her feelings about herself, her retarded sister, her parents, and her sexuality that contributed to creating a life-threatening symptom. Psychodynamic therapy takes place one to three times a week and, like psychoanalysis, can last several years. (A common misperception about psychodynamic psychotherapy is that the more times a week a person attends, the "sicker" he is. In fact, the purpose of multiple sessions per week is simply to allow more time to explore associational networks, not to "hold the person together.") Versions of psychodynamic therapy are probably the most widely practiced form of therapy (see Svartberg & Stiles, 1991).

In recent years, a number of psychodynamically oriented therapists have developed systems of short-term therapy (Crits-Christoph, 1992; Davanloo, 1985; Mann, 1982; Sifneos, 1987; Binder & Strupp, 1995). Short-term dynamic psychotherapies rely on the same principles as other forms of psychodynamic therapy, but they last only 12 to 50 sessions (Luborsky et al., 1993). Unlike more intensive psychodynamic treatments, short-term therapies tend to have a specific focus, which is formulated in the first few sessions. Formulating the focus usually entails linking the patient's symptom or initial complaint with a hypothesized

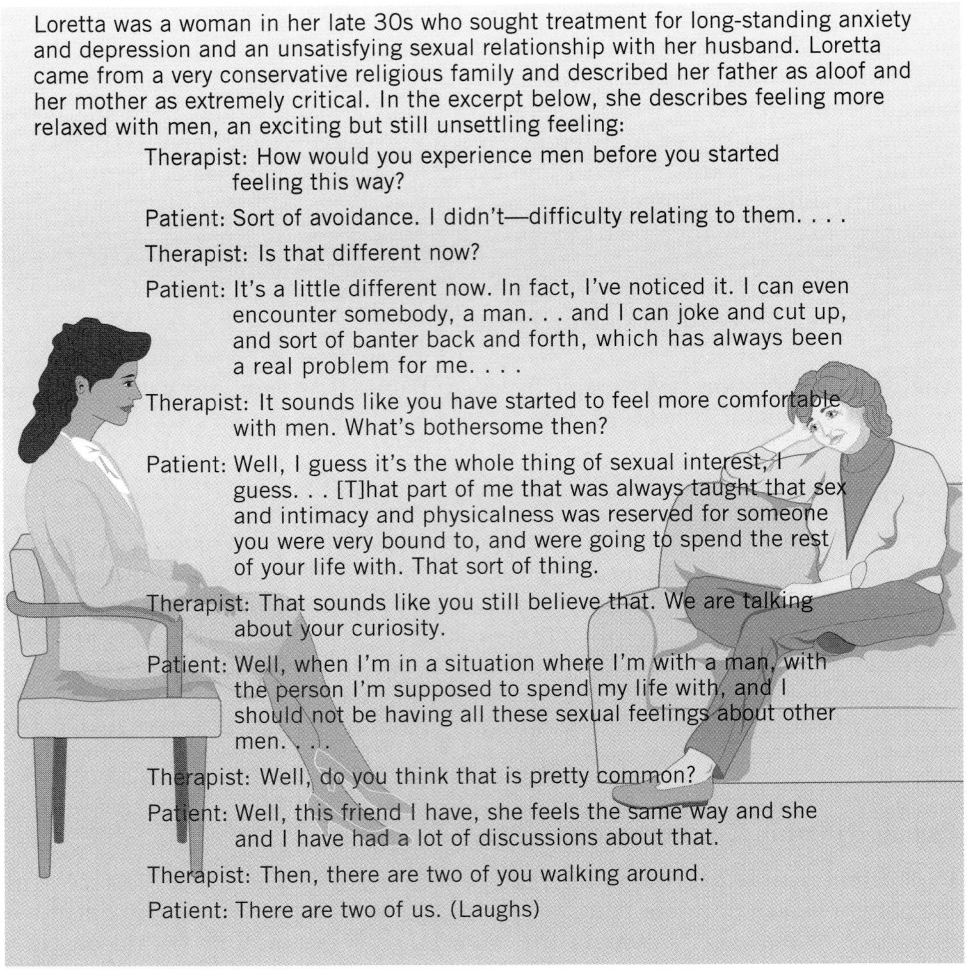

Loretta was a woman in her late 30s who sought treatment for long-standing anxiety and depression and an unsatisfying sexual relationship with her husband. Loretta came from a very conservative religious family and described her father as aloof and her mother as extremely critical. In the excerpt below, she describes feeling more relaxed with men, an exciting but still unsettling feeling:

Therapist: How would you experience men before you started feeling this way?

Patient: Sort of avoidance. I didn't—difficulty relating to them. . . .

Therapist: Is that different now?

Patient: It's a little different now. In fact, I've noticed it. I can even encounter somebody, a man. . . and I can joke and cut up, and sort of banter back and forth, which has always been a real problem for me. . . .

Therapist: It sounds like you have started to feel more comfortable with men. What's bothersome then?

Patient: Well, I guess it's the whole thing of sexual interest, I guess. . . [T]hat part of me that was always taught that sex and intimacy and physicalness was reserved for someone you were very bound to, and were going to spend the rest of your life with. That sort of thing.

Therapist: That sounds like you still believe that. We are talking about your curiosity.

Patient: Well, when I'm in a situation where I'm with a man, with the person I'm supposed to spend my life with, and I should not be having all these sexual feelings about other men. . . .

Therapist: Well, do you think that is pretty common?

Patient: Well, this friend I have, she feels the same way and she and I have had a lot of discussions about that.

Therapist: Then, there are two of you walking around.

Patient: There are two of us. (Laughs)

FIGURE 16.1

Transcript from a short-term psychodynamic psychotherapy. In this excerpt, the therapist helps the patient distinguish between fantasies, for which one need not feel guilty, and actions. The therapist is nonjudgmental and helps Loretta understand that her feelings are normal, through the joke about "two of you walking around." *Source:* Strupp & Binder, 1984.

conflict or dynamic issue, such as unresolved grief, repressed anger, or authority conflicts. A brief transcript from a short-term psychodynamic therapy is reproduced in Figure 16.1.

INTERIM SUMMARY   Psychodynamic therapy rests on two principles: the role of **insight** (coming to an understanding of the way one's mind works, particularly one's conflicts and defenses), and the nature of the relationship between the patient and therapist, such as the extent to which the patient feels comfortable enough to discuss intimate and emotionally significant details (the **therapeutic alliance**). To bring about change, therapists rely on three techniques: **free association** (exploring associational networks by having the patient say whatever comes to mind); **interpretation** (efforts to help the patient come to understand her experiences in a new light); and examination of **transference** (whereby people transfer thoughts, feelings, fears, wishes, and conflicts from past relationships onto the therapist, re-enacting repetitive interpersonal interaction patterns). The main contemporary forms of psychodynamic treatment are **psychoanalysis** (in which the patient lies on the couch and meets with the therapist three or more times a week) and **psychodynamic psychotherapy** (in which the patient and therapist sit face-to-face and usually meet once or twice a week).

COGNITIVE-BEHAVIORAL THERAPIES

In the late 1950s and early 1960s, a number of psychologists, concerned about the lack of scientific data supporting psychoanalysis, sought an approach based in behavioral learning theory (Eysenck, 1952, 1964). They understood psychological symptoms as maladaptive learned behavior patterns that could be changed by applying learning principles (Wolpe, 1964). Today, the majority of clinical psychology faculty members at U.S. universities are **cognitive-behavioral** in their orientation (Sayette & Mayne, 1990), using methods derived from behaviorist and cognitive approaches to learning.

BASIC PRINCIPLES

Cognitive-behavioral therapies are typically short-term. Unlike psychodynamic therapies, they are not concerned with exploring and altering underlying personality patterns or unconscious processes (see Eysenck, 1965, 1987; Goldfried & Davison, 1994; Turner et al., 1992). The focus is on the individual's present behavior, not on childhood experiences or inferred motives. Cognitive-behavioral therapists are far more directive than their psychodynamic counterparts. They suggest specific ways patients should change their thinking and behavior, assign homework, and structure sessions with questions and strategies (Goldfried & Davison, 1994).

Cognitive-behavioral therapists begin with a careful **behavioral analysis**, examining the symptom and the stimuli or thoughts associated with it. They then tailor procedures to address problematic behaviors, cognitions, and emotional responses. The effectiveness of this type of therapy lies in its ability to target specific psychological processes. Panic attacks, for example, include physiological arousal, a subjective experience of terror, anxious thoughts, and a tendency to avoid stimuli associated with anxiety. Panic patients come to associate autonomic

reactions such as a racing heart and a feeling of suffocation with an impending panic attack; they also frequently develop expectancies of helplessness in the face of impending panic and may have catastrophic thoughts such as "I am about to die," or "Everyone will be able to see that I am helpless and incompetent" (Chapter 15). The therapist addresses different components of the problem with different techniques. These may include paced breathing exercises to deal with feelings of breathlessness (Salkovskis et al., 1986), repeated exposure to the experience of a racing heart (for example, through climbing up and down stairs) to extinguish the emotional response, and rational analysis of the accuracy of catastrophic beliefs (Barlow, 1988; Clark, 1994). The success of these treatments in extinguishing fear of autonomic arousal is impressive: Exposing panic patients to air heavy in carbon dioxide (which leads to the feeling of breathlessness) leads roughly 75 percent to experience a panic attack prior to treatment but only 20 percent after treatment (Schmidt et al., 1997).

Cognitive-behavioral therapies focus on altering symptoms rather than exploring their meanings. Although these therapies all take a rational problem-solving approach, their techniques vary considerably. Most therapists who practice **behavior therapy** (treatment based primarily on behaviorist learning principles) also use strategies targeted at cognition, although some behavior therapists rely exclusively on classical and operant conditioning techniques.

CLASSICAL CONDITIONING TECHNIQUES

Some behavioral procedures use classical conditioning to alter emotional responses triggered by particular stimuli. Prominent among these techniques are desensitization and exposure techniques.

Systematic Desensitization

One of the earliest and still most widely used cognitive-behavioral techniques is **systematic desensitization**, in which the patient mentally confronts a phobic stimulus gradually while in a state that inhibits anxiety (Wolpe, 1958). The assumption behind desensitization is that through classical conditioning phobics have learned to fear what should be a neutral stimulus. In classical conditioning of emotional responses (Chapter 5), a previously neutral stimulus comes to elicit an emotion when paired with a stimulus that already elicits the emotion. For example, a person who has an automobile accident feels afraid to drive afterward because being behind the wheel of a car (conditioned stimulus) is associated with a terrifying experience (unconditioned stimulus). Normally, future encounters with the conditioned stimulus (driving) in the absence of the stimulus that elicited the fear (the accident) will extinguish the response (fear). (Whoever penned the proverb about getting right back on the horse after falling off was probably the first behavior therapist.) However, if the person starts walking instead of driving, this short-circuits an adaptive learning process: He avoids the fear by not driving, but this prevents extinction from occurring, so the fear will remain. Thus, phobic responses, like all avoidance responses, become particularly resistant to extinction.

To extinguish irrational fear responses, then, the patient must confront the feared stimulus. This is the aim of systematic desensitization, which takes place in four steps. First, the therapist teaches the patient relaxation techniques, such as tensing and then relaxing muscle groups throughout the body or breathing from the diaphragm. Then the therapist questions the patient about his fears and uses this information to construct a hierarchy of feared imagined stimuli, from scenes that provoke mild anxiety to those that induce intense fear. For the patient who is afraid of driving, the scenes might range from sitting behind the wheel of a non-moving car to driving on a crowded expressway on a rainy night (Figure 16.2). The third step, which usually begins in the third or fourth session, is desensitization proper. The patient relaxes, using the techniques he has learned, and is then instructed to imagine vividly the first, least threatening scene in the hierarchy. When the patient can imagine this scene comfortably, perhaps with additional relaxation instructions, he then imagines the next scene, and so on up the hierarchy. In the fourth step, the therapist encourages the patient to confront his fears in real life and monitors his progress as he does so, desensitizing additional scenes as needed to eliminate anxiety and avoidance.

Desensitization has been used to treat a long list of anxiety-related disorders, including phobias, impotence, nightmares, obsessive-compulsive disorders, social anxiety, and even fears of death (McGlynn et al., 1981; O'Sullivan et al., 1991). In one striking case, desensitization was used to help a 20-year-old woman overcome a fear of babies (Free & Beekhuis, 1985). Initially the patient was unable even to look at photographs of babies long enough to establish a hierarchy. By the end of treatment and at a one-year followup, she could approach babies without discomfort. This form of therapy is markedly different from a psychodynamic therapy, which would have explored what babies meant to her: Was she feeling guilty about an abortion she had had? Was she a victim of incest who unconsciously associated babies with her childhood fear that she was pregnant? In contrast, the cognitive-behavioral therapist aims to extinguish the fear response, not to search for insight into its origins.

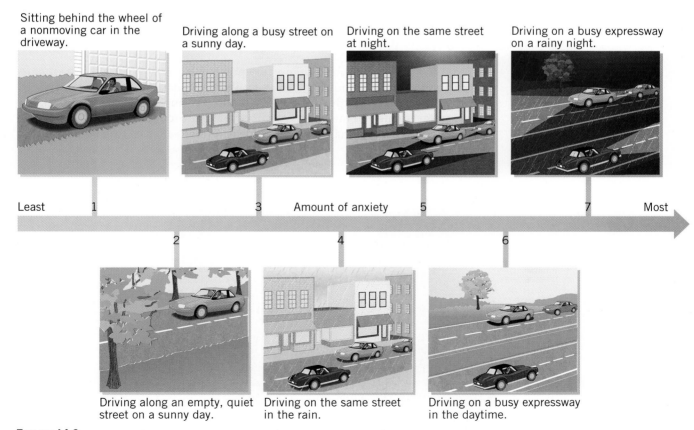

Sitting behind the wheel of a nonmoving car in the driveway.

Driving along a busy street on a sunny day.

Driving on the same street at night.

Driving on a busy expressway on a rainy night.

Least 1   3   Amount of anxiety   5   7   Most

2   4   6

Driving along an empty, quiet street on a sunny day.

Driving on the same street in the rain.

Driving on a busy expressway in the daytime.

FIGURE 16.2
Systemic desensitization. The patient exposes himself to progressively more threatening imagined approximations of the phobic stimulus.

Desensitization works, but the basis for its success is a matter of some dispute (see Levin & Gross, 1985; McGlynn et al., 1981). One theory proposes that desensitization is a **counterconditioning** process; that is, it runs opposite, or counter, to previous conditioning that created the symptom (Wolpe, 1958). Thus, if the person was conditioned to experience anxiety, the therapist tries to create muscular and parasympathetic responses (such as steady breathing) incompatible with anxiety. Another hypothesis is simple extinction: Because the patient's repeated exposure to a stimulus is unaccompanied by a feared outcome, the fear response is extinguished.

Exposure Techniques

Another type of cognitive-behavioral procedure based on classical conditioning is called exposure (or *in vivo* exposure). **Exposure techniques**, unlike desensitization procedures, present the patient with the actual phobic stimulus in real life (*in vivo*), rather than having the patient merely imagine it. In **flooding**, the patient confronts the phobic stimulus all at once. The theory behind flooding is that inescapable exposure to the conditioned stimulus eventually desensitizes the patient through extinction or related mechanisms. Flooding, like desensitization, prevents the person from escaping the onset of the conditioned stimulus (such as sitting in the driver's seat of a running car). From a more cognitive perspective, when faced with inescapable exposure, patients eventually recognize that the situation is not really catastrophic and that they have the self-efficacy to confront it.

One therapist used flooding to treat a young woman with an intense fear of escalators (Nesbitt, 1973). With considerable coaxing from the therapist, the patient rode the escalators in a large department store for hours, first with the therapist and then alone, until the symptom subsided. Exposure techniques such as flooding for simple phobias are some of the most successful treatments devised for any disorder.

From the patient's point of view, flooding can be a frightening procedure. A modification of the technique that is less difficult to endure is graded exposure. Like flooding, **graded exposure** uses real stimuli, but like desensitization, the stimuli are graduated in intensity. One psychologist used graded exposure with a 70-year-old woman who had developed a fear of dogs after having been savagely

Exposure techniques confront the patient with the feared stimulus directly.

THE FAR SIDE   By GARY LARSON

Professor Gallagher and his controversial technique of simultaneously confronting the fear of heights, snakes and the dark.

bitten by one (Thyer, 1980). During the first two sessions, she was exposed to a small dog, first at the other end of the room and then gradually closer until she let it lick her hand. During the third session, she made an hour-long visit to the humane society, where she was exposed to the barking of dozens of dogs. During the fourth and fifth sessions, she repeated the earlier treatments but with large dogs. After five sessions, her symptom disappeared.

OPERANT CONDITIONING TECHNIQUES

In operant conditioning, behavior is controlled by its consequences (Chapter 5). Therapies based on operant conditioning therefore use reinforcement and punishment to modify unwanted behavior, as when Jenny, whose case opened this chapter, was rewarded for gaining weight with increased privileges.

Operant conditioning is the principle behind the **token economy** procedure, in which points or tokens can be cashed in for rewards such as food, privileges, or cigarettes. Token economies were first used with psychotic patients, who received tokens for socially acceptable behaviors and were fined tokens when they were obstreperous, assaultive, or physically destructive (Ayllon & Azrin, 1968). Psychologists have since applied this approach in a number of settings (Hurley and Sovner, 1985; Rimmerman et al., 1992), including institutions for mentally retarded people, who tend to respond well to structured settings and concrete rewards.

Operant techniques can be particularly effective in working with children and their parents because parents often intuitively apply rewards and punishments in ineffective or counterproductive ways (see Kendall, 1993). Skillfully managing the contingencies of reinforcement can bring unwanted behaviors under control, as in the treatment of a 12-year-old girl who repeatedly scratched herself raw and then picked at the scabs (Latimer, 1979). The girl received points for clipping her fingernails and for each half hour that she did not scratch or pick at herself. She could exchange the points for privileges such as reading, watching television, or going on outings.

MODELING

Because people learn not only through their own experiences but also by observing the behavior of others, some cognitive-behavioral therapists rely on modeling procedures. In **participatory modeling**, which tends to be more effective than modeling alone, the therapist models the desired behavior and gradually induces the patient to participate in it. Bandura and his colleagues (1969) demonstrated the effectiveness of participatory modeling in treating patients with snake phobias. In this procedure, the therapist first handles snakes without showing anxiety and without being harmed. (This, of course, presumes fearless therapists and cooperative reptiles.) Then the therapist coaxes the patient to handle the snakes.

By watching the therapist, the patient begins to be desensitized vicariously, enabling him to approach the phobic stimulus. Participatory modeling alters self-efficacy expectancies as well because observing the model safely approach the feared stimulus suggests to the patient that he can, too. Participating with the therapist in snake handling then leads to even more radical revisions of his expectancies.

SKILLS TRAINING

Even if self-efficacy expectancies are high people cannot emit a behavior they lack the competence to perform (Chapter 12). Bandura (cited in Goldfried & Davison, 1994) warns that desensitizing people who are socially phobic but who actually *do* lack the ability to interact in socially competent ways produces little more than "relaxed incompetents." Hence, another cognitive-behavioral technique is **skills training**, which involves teaching the behaviors necessary to accomplish relevant goals. Skills are a form of procedural knowledge and are typically carried out automatically (Chapter 6). Acquiring new skills, however, usually requires that the individual focus conscious awareness on a set of procedures until they gradually become routinized (Meichenbaum, 1977, 1990).

Skills training often draws on theories of problem solving and self-regulation (Chapter 7, 12). For example, skills training with impulsive and hyperactive children teaches them to decide what the problem is, divide it into components, develop ways to solve each part, and use feedback to determine whether each part (and eventually the entire problem) has been successfully handled (Meichenbaum, 1977). In one procedure, the therapist teaches impulsive children to ask themselves a series of questions: "What is my problem?"; "What can I do about it?"; "Am I using my plan?"; "How did I do?" (Figure 16.3).

Clinicians use **social skills training** for people with specific interpersonal deficits, such as shyness or lack of assertiveness. Following assessment, treatment usually begins with direct teaching of skills or modeling of behavior on film, videotape, or in person. The next stage is rehearsal of the new skills—practicing gestures, imagining responses, role-playing various scenarios, and so forth. Patients then receive feedback by observing themselves or others (Ladd & Mize, 1983).

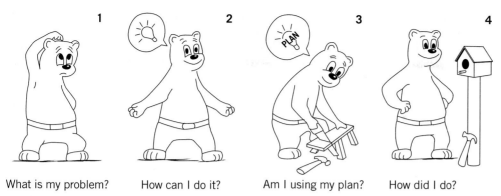

1	2	3	4
What is my problem?	How can I do it?	Am I using my plan?	How did I do?

FIGURE 16.3
Skills training for children. This approach was designed to treat impulsive children. It teaches them how to solve a problem, from framing the problem to self-monitoring and attending to feedback. *Source:* Camp & Bash, 1981.

INTERIM SUMMARY **Cognitive-behavioral** therapists use methods derived from behaviorist and cognitive approaches to learning. Treatment begins with a **behavioral analysis** of the symptom and the stimuli or thoughts associated with it, which define the targets of treatment. Behavioral techniques relying on classical conditioning include **systematic desensitization**, in which the patient mentally confronts a phobic stimulus gradually while in a state that inhibits anxiety; and various **exposure techniques** that present the patient with the actual phobic stimulus. Operant techniques attempt to control maladaptive behavior by altering its consequences. Social learning techniques include **participatory modeling**, in which the therapist models the desired behavior and gradually induces the patient to participate in it; and **skills training**, which involves teaching the behaviors necessary to accomplish relevant goals.

COGNITIVE THERAPY

Whereas most cognitive-behavioral techniques try to alter behavior, **cognitive therapy** focuses on changing dysfunctional cognitions presumed to underlie psychological disorders. Cognitive therapies target the things individuals spontaneously say to themselves and the assumptions they make (Ellis, 1962), or what Aaron Beck calls **automatic thoughts** (Beck, 1976, 1993). By questioning the patient's assumptions and beliefs and asking her to identify the data underlying them, the therapist engages the patient in empirical hypothesis testing (Hollon & Beck, 1985). Cognitive therapies also rely on behavioral techniques but largely to induce patients to implement therapeutic suggestions (see Ellis, 1984). Two approaches to combating cognitive distortions are Ellis's rational-emotive therapy and Beck's cognitive therapy.

Ellis's Rational-Emotive Therapy

Albert Ellis began as a psychoanalyst but came to believe that psychodynamic treatments take too long and are too often ineffective (Ellis, 1962, 1989). According to Ellis, what people think and say to themselves about a situation affects the way they respond to it. He proposed the **ABC theory of psychopathology**, where *A* refers to activating conditions, *B* to belief systems, and *C* to emotional consequences (Ellis, 1977; Yankura & Dryden, 1990). Activating conditions such as loss of a job (*A*) do not lead directly to consequences such as depression (*C*). The process that turns unpleasant events into depressive symptoms involves dysfunctional belief systems, often expressed in a person's self-talk, such as, "I am not a worthy person unless I am very successful" (*B*).

Ellis thus developed **rational-emotive therapy**, which proposes that the patient "can rid himself of most of his emotional or mental unhappiness, ineffectuality, and disturbance if he learns to maximize his rational and minimize his irrational thinking" (Ellis, 1962, p. 36). The therapist continually brings the patient's illogical or self-defeating thoughts to his attention, shows him how they are causing problems, demonstrates their illogic, and teaches alternative ways of thinking (Ellis, 1962, 1977, 1987). If the source of psychological distress is irrational thinking, then the path to eliminating symptoms is increased rationality.

Beck's Cognitive Therapy

Like Ellis, Aaron Beck was a disenchanted psychoanalyst. Also like Ellis, Beck views cognitive therapy as a process of "collaborative empiricism," in which the patient and therapist work together like scientists testing hypotheses (Beck, 1989, 1991). In therapy sessions, which typically number only 12 to 20, the therapist and patient focus on the present, not the past, devising strategies for changing maladaptive patterns of thought and behavior. Often the patient keeps a log, recording thoughts and moods so she can observe the relation between them and track her progress in therapy.

The sessions are highly structured, beginning with setting an agenda. The therapist teaches the patient the theory behind the treatment, often assigning books or articles to read, and trains the patient to fill in the cognitive link between the stimulus that leads to depressed or anxious feelings and the feelings generated in the situation. For example, a patient who felt sad whenever he made a mistake was instructed to focus on his thoughts the next time he made a mistake. At his next session, he reported that he would think, "I'm a dope" or "I never do anything right" (Beck, 1976).

The core of Beck's therapy, like Ellis's, is testing cognitive distortions. The therapist questions the data on which the patient's assumptions are based and identifies errors in thinking. A woman who was suicidal believed she had nothing to look forward to because her husband was unfaithful. Underlying her suicidal feelings were the beliefs that she was nothing without her husband and that she could not save her marriage. The dialogue between the therapist and this patient included the following exchange (Beck, 1976):

> THERAPIST: You say that you can't be happy without Raymond. . . . Have you found yourself happy when you are with Raymond?
> PATIENT: No, we fight all the time and I feel worse.
> THERAPIST: You say you are nothing without Raymond. Before you met Raymond, did you feel you were nothing?
> PATIENT: No, I felt I was somebody.
> THERAPIST: If you were somebody before you knew Raymond, why do you need him to be somebody now?
> PATIENT: [Puzzled] Hmmm. . . .

Eventually, this patient concluded that her happiness did not, in fact, depend on her husband and divorced him, enjoying a more stable life.

Cognitive therapy began as a treatment for depression, but more recently therapists have applied cognitive techniques to other disorders, such as anxiety and eating disorders (Beck, 1991, 1992; Borkovec & Costell, 1993; Chambless & Gillis, 1993; Wilson & Fairburn, 1993). In extending his work to anxiety, Beck has incorporated research on stress, notably Lazarus's (1966, 1991) view that what makes an event stressful is the way the person interprets it (Chapter 11). According to Beck (1985), people with anxiety disorders tend to overestimate the probability and severity of the feared event and underestimate their coping resources.

INTERIM SUMMARY **Cognitive therapy** focuses on changing dysfunctional cognitions presumed to underlie psychological disorders. **Ellis's rational-emotive therapy** attempts to address the belief systems that mediate between activating conditions and maladaptive emotional reactions. Becks' cognitive therapy targets cognitive distortions presumed to underlie psychopathology.

HUMANISTIC, GROUP, AND FAMILY THERAPIES

Psychodynamic and cognitive-behavioral psychotherapies are the most widely practiced, but clinicians have many other alternatives. The most common are humanistic, group, and family therapies.

HUMANISTIC THERAPIES

In the 1950s and 1960s, a number of therapists took issue with what they perceived as mechanistic and dehumanizing aspects of psychoanalysis and behaviorism. **Humanistic therapies**, like humanistic personality theories, focus on the phenomenology of the patient—on the way each person consciously experiences the self, relationships, and the world. The aim is to help people get in touch with their feelings, with their "true selves," and with a sense of meaning in life. The two most widely practiced humanistic therapies are Gestalt therapy and Carl Rogers's client-centered therapy.

Gestalt Therapy

Gestalt therapy developed in response to the belief that people had become too socialized, controlling their thoughts, behaviors, and even their feelings in order to conform to social expectations. According to Gestalt therapists, losing touch with one's emotions and one's authentic inner "voice" leads to psychological problems such as depression and anxiety.

In some respects Gestalt therapy resembles psychodynamic psychotherapy, although Gestalt therapists often try to avoid focusing on childhood antecedents of current difficulties, believing this leads further away from emotions, not toward them (Perls, 1969, 1990). In this view, understanding *why* one feels a certain way is far less important than recognizing *that* one feels that way. Gestalt therapy thus focuses on the "here and now" rather than the "then and there."

A technique commonly used by Gestalt therapists is the **empty chair technique**: The therapist places an empty chair near the client and asks him to imagine that the person to whom he would like to express his feelings (such as a dead parent) is in the chair. The client can then safely express his feelings by "talking" with the person without consequences. A variant of this technique is the **two chair technique**, in which the patient "places" two sides of a dilemma in two different chairs, and expresses each side while sitting in the appropriate chair. For example, one woman was torn between staying with her husband, with whom she felt "dead inside" because of his inability to communicate, and leaving him, which she desperately wanted to do but had trouble admitting to herself because she felt wracked with guilt. In one chair, she described why she wanted to stay with him; in the other, she voiced all her frustrations and disappointments with her husband and their marriage. By the end of the session, what was most striking to her

Les Greenberg using the "two chairs" technique, which encourages clients to resolve business with people "in the other chair" or to express conflicting sides of themselves while taking the perspective of the other chair.

and the therapist was how passionately she voiced her desires to leave and how weakly she really felt toward staying in the marriage.

Client-Centered Therapy

Carl Rogers was among the first to refer to people who seek treatment as *clients* rather than *patients.* He rejected the medical model and suggested that people come to therapy seeking help in solving problems, not cures for disorders. **Client-centered therapy** is based on Rogers's view that people experience psychological difficulties when their concept of self is incongruent with their actual experience (Chapter 12). For example, a man who thought of himself as someone who loved his father came to realize through therapy that he also felt a great deal of rage toward him. He had denied his negative feelings because he learned as a child that he should always be loving and obedient and that feeling otherwise was "bad." The aim of client-centered therapy is to help clients experience themselves as they actually are—in this case, for the man to accept himself as a person who can feel both love and rage toward his father and thus to alleviate tension and anxiety (Rogers, 1961; Rogers & Sanford, 1985).

Rogerian therapy assumes that the basic nature of human beings is to grow and mature. Hence, the goal is to provide a supportive environment in which clients can start again where they left off years ago when they denied their true feelings in order to feel worthy and esteemed by significant others. The therapist creates a supportive environment by demonstrating **unconditional positive regard** for the client—that is, expressing an attitude of fundamental acceptance toward the client, without any requirements or conditions (Rogers, 1961, 1980)—and by listening empathically. Rogers stressed the curative value of *empathy,* the process of becoming emotionally in tune with, and understanding the patient's experience without judging it. Therapeutic change occurs as the client hears his own thoughts and feelings reflected by a caring, empathic, nonjudgmental listener (Rogers, 1961, 1980). The Rogerian therapist, often called a counselor, evaluates clients' thoughts and feelings only for their authenticity, not for their unconscious meanings or their rationality.

INTERIM SUMMARY **Humanistic therapies** focus on the the way each person consciously experiences the self, relationships, and the world; they aim to help people get in touch with their feelings, their "true selves," and a sense of meaning in life. **Gestalt therapy** tries to help people know what they are feeling so they can act in accordance with their true feelings. Rogers's **client-centered therapy** assumes that problems in living result when people's concept of self is incongruent with their actual experience. Therapeutic change occurs as the therapist empathizes with the client's experience, demonstrating **unconditional positive regard** (an attitude of fundamental acceptance).

GROUP THERAPIES

The therapies described thus far all consider the individual as the unit of analysis and treatment. In contrast, group and family therapies treat multiple individuals simultaneously, although they often apply psychodynamic, cognitive-behavioral, or humanistic principles.

In **group therapy**, multiple people meet together to work toward therapeutic goals. Typically eight to ten people meet with a therapist on a regular basis, usually once a week for two hours (Vinogravdov & Yalom, 1989; Yalom, 1995). As in individual therapy, members of the group talk about problems in their own lives, but they also gain from exploring **group process**, or the way members of the group interact with each other. Some cognitive-behavioral therapy also takes place in groups, particularly where the aim is to teach skills that do not require individual instruction, such as stress management.

Group therapy is designed to produce benefits that may not arise from individual therapy (Dies, 1992; Yalom, 1975). For example, for newcomers to a group, the presence of other members who have made demonstrable progress can instill a therapeutic sense of hope. Discovering that others have problems similar to their own may also relieve shame, anxiety, and guilt. In addition, the group provides opportunities for members to repeat, examine, and alter the types of relationships they experienced with their own families, which they may bring with them to many social situations.

Groups assembled for therapy may be more or less heterogeneous. Heterogeneous therapy groups work on the same kinds of problems each person would address in individual therapy, such as anxiety, depression, or trouble finding and maintaining satisfying intimate relationships. Group members typically vary not only in symptoms but also in age, socioeconomic status, and gender. In contrast, homogeneous groups usually focus on a common issue or disorder, such as incest, bulimia, or even borderline personality disorder (Linehan, 1987, 1991). Groups can be quite helpful, in part because members can see and confront in other members what they cannot acknowledge in themselves, as when Jenny observed other obviously emaciated anorexics complain that they were fat. Children and adolescents also benefit from group therapy for issues such as coping with divorce (Kalter, 1987).

A variation on group therapy is the **self-help group**, which is generally not guided by a professional. Self-help groups tend to have a larger membership than other therapy groups. The goal is to help members cope with a specific problem rather than explore individual psychodynamics or make major changes in personality. One of the oldest and best known self-help groups is Alcoholics Anonymous (AA). Research shows that the more committed individuals are to AA, the more likely they are to stay sober (Morgenstern et al., 1997). Other widely attended

An Alcoholics Anonymous meeting.

groups include Adult Children of Alcoholics, Weight Watchers, Gamblers Anonymous, and groups for cancer patients or parents who have lost a child.

Psychotherapists frequently refer patients to self-help groups to supplement individual therapy, particularly if the patient has a problem such as overeating or alcoholism. Although evidence exists that self-help groups can be effective for many people suffering from alcoholism (Baer et al., 1992), eating disorders (Jones, 1992), and smoking addictions (Curry, 1993), their main limitation is a tendency to oversimplify the problem and its causes. Members of some self-help groups may come to believe that all their difficulties can be reduced to being "co-dependent," an "adult child of an alcoholic," and so forth.

FAMILY THERAPIES

Family therapies are predicated on the view that a family is a system of interdependent parts. In this view, the problem lies in the structure of the system itself rather than in the family member who is merely expressing the symptom (Haley, 1971; Simon, 1985; Wynne, 1961) (Chapter 15). The aim of **family therapy** is to change maladaptive family interaction patterns.

As in group and psychodynamic therapy, the focus of family therapy is on *process* rather than simply *content*. In other words, the process that unfolds in the therapy hour—a transference reaction to a therapist, a sibling-like competitive relationship in a group, or a round of accusations and counteraccusations between a husband and wife—is as important as the content of what the patient says. In family therapy the therapist takes a relatively active role and often assigns the family tasks to carry out between sessions.

Approaches to Family Therapy

Family therapy has many schools of thought. Some approaches (called *structural* and *strategic*) focus on the organization (structure) of the family system and use active interventions (strategies) to disrupt dysfunctional patterns. Therapists who operate from this standpoint attend to boundaries between generations, alliances and schisms between family members, the hierarchy of power in the family, and family homeostatic mechanisms (Aponte & VanDeusen, 1981; Elizur & Minuchin, 1989; Minuchin, 1974; Richardson, 1991). In one family with an anorexic daughter, the therapist discovered that the father forbade his children to close the doors to their rooms and felt more intimate with his daughter than his wife. Hypothesizing that the father–daughter relationship might underlie the girl's refusal to eat (particularly since the symptom postponed physical maturation and puberty), the therapist prescribed as a first step that the daughter be allowed to keep her door closed for two hours a day and that the parents spend an hour each evening together in their room with the door closed (Hoffman, 1981).

Another approach to family therapy is the *intergenerational approach* of Murray Bowen (1978; Kerr & Bowen, 1988). Bowen argues that people have difficulty maintaining satisfying relationships when they have not successfully resolved issues from their family of origin. Typically, these issues involve either overdependence or "enmeshment" in the family, or a total break, in which the person is cut off emotionally or physically from important people from the past. Being emotionally caught up with unsettled scores from the past—expressed in either too little or too much emotional distance—can make satisfying involvement with a spouse or child difficult.

Bowen developed an assessment technique used widely by family therapists called a **genogram**, a map of a family over three or four generations (Figure 16.4). The clinician supplements this barebones picture of the family by adding the pa-

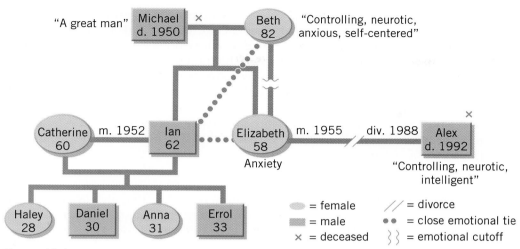

FIGURE 16.4

A genogram. The patient, Elizabeth, sought treatment for anxiety. From the genogram, the therapist could see that she was cut off from her mother, who remained close to her brother, which made Elizabeth feel left out. She also appeared to have married a man somewhat like her mother, and to be anxious like her mother.

tient's comments about each person or relationship depicted in the genogram, looking for possible similarities between current difficulties and the family's past.

Marital Therapy

A variant of family therapy, called **marital** or **couples therapy**, focuses on a smaller system, the marital unit or couple. The therapist may see the members of the couple individually, together, or some combination of the two. Many therapists take a family systems approach to couples work, looking for problematic communication or interaction patterns. For example, one couple was trapped in a cycle in which the husband did something, the wife criticized it, and the husband felt angry and helpless and tried to defend himself (Haley, 1971, pp. 275–276). When the therapist pointed out the pattern, the wife responded, "I have to criticize, because he never does what he should," to which the husband replied, "Well, I try"—which was precisely the pattern repeating itself again.

Marital therapists may also adopt psychodynamic or cognitive-behavioral perspectives. The goal of psychodynamic marital therapy is to help members of the couple recognize and alter patterns of interacting that reflect patterns from the past. A man who complained that his wife was unsupportive repeatedly changed the subject or criticized his wife during therapy sessions every time she was about to do or say something supportive. He appeared to be replaying his experience of his parents' highly critical relationship, which unconsciously guided his expectations of his wife and their interactions.

Behavioral marital therapy addresses the ways spouses often control each other's behavior in ineffective or punishing ways. A phenomenon that has received considerable empirical attention and is related to marital satisfaction and longevity is *negative reciprocity*, the tendency of members of a couple to respond to negative comments or actions by their partner with negative behaviors in return (Gottman, 1998). As a result, arguments spiral out of control without resolution. The aim of the marital therapist is to help couples break these negative spirals. Researchers have recently begin to study, as well, the positive sides of marital interaction: the extent to which behaving in ways that indicate acceptance and validation of the partner predict marital success. As in research on positive and negative affect (Chapter 11) and on parental rejection and acceptance (Chapter 14), the data suggest that negative and positive marital interactions are not simply opposite sides of the same coin; some couples have high rates of both accepting and rejecting behavior toward one another (Arkowitz-Westen, 1998).

Behavioral and cognitive-behavioral therapists use techniques such as building communication skills, assertiveness training, and "good faith" contracts in which each spouse takes responsibility for changing something that is bothering the other (Goldfried & Davidson, 1994). Additionally, cognitively oriented marital therapists focus on irrational beliefs spouses hold about themselves and one another.

INTERIM SUMMARY   In **group therapy**, multiple people meet together to work toward therapeutic goals. A variation on group therapy is the **self-help group**, which is not guided by a professional; the best known self-help group is Alcoholics Anonymous. The aim of **family therapy** is to change maladaptive family interaction patterns. Family therapists often construct a **genogram** (a map of a family over three or four generations) to pinpoint recurring family patterns over generations. **Marital** or **couples therapy** focuses on the relationship between members of a couple, and can rely on psychodynamic, systemic, cognitive, or behavioral principles.

BIOLOGICAL TREATMENTS

The approaches we have examined thus far are all, broadly speaking, psychosocial; that is they use psychological and interpersonal interventions to address psychological problems. A very different type of treatment emerges from the view that psychological disorders reflect pathology of the brain, particularly of the neurotransmitters that carry messages from one neuron to another. Biological treatments use medication to restore the brain to as normal functioning as possible (pharmacotherapy). If medications are ineffective, clinicians may turn to electroconvulsive (shock) therapy or, in extreme cases, psychosurgery. (Unlike psychotherapy, which can be administered by a variety of clinicians, such as psychologists and clinical social workers, biological treatments can only be administered by physicians such as psychiatrists and other authorized medical practitioners.)

FROM MIND TO BRAIN

PSYCHOTROPIC MEDICATIONS

For many years, patients with severe mental illness were sent to state mental hospitals, which provided little more than custodial care in overcrowded wards. But the discovery of **psychotropic medications**—drugs that act on the brain to affect mental processes (Table 16.2)—changed the care of psychiatric patients dramatically. In 1956, chlorpromazine (trade name Thorazine) was introduced to treat schizophrenia. The population of state mental institutions dropped rapidly thereafter (Figure 16.5), and patients who did remain hospitalized were less likely to require physical restraint or isolation. New and better medications have been developed over the ensuing four decades. The recent discovery of new chemical agents, such as clozapine (trade name Clozaril), has led to substantial improvement in an additional 30 to 60 percent of psychotic patients who have not responded to chlorpromazine or other medications (Dufour et al., 1998).

Many of the first drugs for treating mental illness were discovered

TABLE 16.2 PSYCHOTROPIC MEDICATIONS

SYMPTOM	TYPE OF MEDICATION	EXAMPLES
Psychosis	Antipsychotics	Chlorpromazine (Thorazine) Clozapine (Clozaril)
Depression	Tricyclic antidepressants	Trazodone (Desyrel) Amitriptyline (Elavil) Desipramine (Norpamin)
	MAO inhibitors	Phenelzine (Nardil)
	Selective serotonin reuptake inhibitors	Fluoxetine (Prozac)
Mania	Mood stabilizers	Lithium (Lithonate)
Anxiety	Anxiolitics	Benzodiazepines (Valium, Xanax)
	Antidepressants	Fluoxetine (Prozac)

serendipitously, when physicians and researchers using them to treat one medical condition noticed that they altered another. For example, when J. F. Cade, an Australian researcher, gave animals a lithium salt as part of his research into animal metabolism and behavior, he noticed that the animals became calm and quiet. Further investigation showed that lithium was an effective treatment for bipolar disorder.

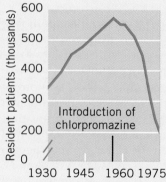

FIGURE 16.5
Impact of chlorpromazine on institutionalization. The populations of state and county psychiatric hospitals declined rapidly after the introduction of the antipsychotic medication, chlorpromazine. *Source:* Adapted from Davis, 1985.

Most psychotropic medications act at neurotransmitter sites (Figure 16.6). Different drugs act in different ways, although their mechanisms of action are still not entirely clear. Some drugs inhibit overactive neurotransmitters or receptors that are overly sensitive and fire too frequently. One way they can do this is by "locking up" the postsynaptic membrane, binding with receptors that would naturally bind with the neurotransmitter (part *a* of Figure 16.6). This renders the postsynaptic receptors unable to fire as frequently or at all.

Other medications have the opposite effect, increasing the action of neurotransmitters that are underactive or in short supply. They may do this in various ways. Some medications prevent the neurotransmitter from being taken back into the presynaptic membrane, causing the neurotransmitter to

(a) Decreases neural transmission by "locking up" receptor sites

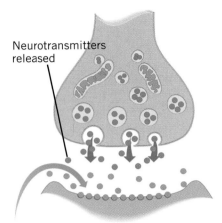

Neurotransmitters released

Drug binds with receptors to prevent them from being activated by the neurotransmitters in the synapse.

(b) Increases neural transmission by blocking reuptake

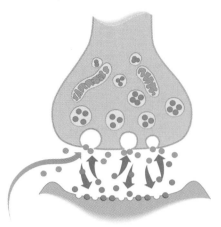

Drug blocks neurotransmitters from being taken back into the presynaptic membrane, leaving the neurotransmitters in the synapse longer.

(c) Increases neural transmission by blocking breakdown of neurotransmitter in synaptic vesicles

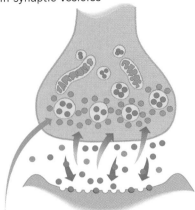

Drug prevents the neurotransmitter returning from the synapse from being broken down for storage, which keeps available at the synapse.

FIGURE 16.6

The therapeutic action of psychotropic medications. This figure depicts three neural mechanisms by which psychotropic medications can reduce symptoms. Psychotropics can decrease neural transmission of overactive neurotransmitters (a), or increase neural transmission where neurotransmitters are depleted (b and c).

remain in the synapse and hence to facilitate further firing (part b of Figure 16.6). Others prevent the neurotransmitter from being broken down once it has returned to the presynaptic neuron, leading to continued availability of the neurotransmitter at the synapse (part c).

Recent theories suggest that some psychotropic medications, particularly for depression, may act at the intracellular level, rather than at the synapse (Duman et al.,1997). Once a neurotransmitter binds with a receptor, a series of events occurs *within* the post-synaptic neuron that affect its rate of firing, as chemicals within the cell carry messages from the receptors to the cell's nucleus and activate the cell's DNA (Chapter 3). Much of thought and memory appears to reflect changes in the way neurons respond to chronic activation from other neurons (Chapter 5). Intracellular mechanisms may help explain why some medications, particularly medications for depression, only begin to have an effect weeks after the person starts to take them. The reason may be that long-term cellular changes, unlike drug-induced changes in neurotransmitter levels, take time to occur.

Not all the beneficial effects of psychotropic medications stem from their molecular structure. Their psychological and cultural "structure" also influence their efficacy. Both Western and non-Western cultures have long known the healing power of the placebo. Because a patient's expectation of cure is influenced by cultural beliefs about the causes of mental illness, even drugs or herbal remedies that have no known physiological action can promote health simply because the person has faith that they will work (Torrey, 1986). In the same way, placebo effects can boost the power of medications that are biologically efficacious. Thus, chemical agents can affect the mind via the brain, or they can affect the brain via the mind.

INTERIM SUMMARY **Psychotropic medications** act on the brain to affect mental processes. Most psychotropic medications act at neurotransmitter sites. Some bind with postsynaptic receptors, hence preventing neural transmission. Others increase the action of underactive or depleted neurotransmitters, often by preventing them from being taken back into the presynaptic membrane or preventing them from being stored once they do return. Others may act at the intracellular level.

ANTIPSYCHOTIC MEDICATIONS

The drugs used to treat schizophrenia and other acute psychotic states are called **antipsychotic medications**. They are also sometimes called *major tranquilizers* because many are highly sedating, but their efficacy is not reducible to their tranquilizing effect.

The most widely accepted biological hypothesis about the positive symptoms of schizophrenia (such as delusions and hallucinations) attributes these symptoms to too much dopamine (Chapter 15). Antipsychotic medications inhibit dopamine and reduce these symptoms. Unfortunately, antipsychotics typically are far less effective for negative symptoms such as flattened affect and interpersonal difficulties (Carpenter, 1992).

Few competent clinicians doubt the enormous utility of antipsychotic medications in treating schizophrenia, which has been documented in thousands of studies (e.g., Volavka et al., 1992). These medications can, however, have significant side effects, some of which can be almost as socially devastating as the disorder itself. Many of these side effects reflect the fact that dopamine is found in multiple regions of the brain and serves many functions. Thus, blocking its overactivity in one region may inhibit its normal functions in another.

The most serious side effect is a movement disorder called **tardive dyskinesia** (*tardive*, meaning late or tardy in onset, and *dyskinesia*, meaning disorder of movement), in which the patient develops involuntary twitching, typically involving the tongue, face, and neck. According to one theory, lowering the amounts of dopamine in the brain leads receptors in motor circuits that require dopamine for normal functioning to become supersensitive. As a result, the neurons in those regions fire readily and unpredictably.

Tardive dyskinesia does not occur in all patients, and it is more likely to arise in people who have taken antispsychotic medications for several years (Sweet et al., 1995), but it is unpredictable, can occur at any point, and is largely irreversible. Between 30 and 40 percent of patients in a long-term ward of a Montreal hospital who had received antipsychotics on the average of 20 years showed symptoms of tardive dyskinesia (Yassa et al., 1990). Because the side effects of prolonged administration can be so severe, and because antipsychotics are often ineffective for treating the more chronic negative symptoms, they are usually prescribed in high doses during acute phases and lower doses between episodes (Gilbert et al., 1995). The discovery of multiple types of dopamine receptors in different parts of the brain, however, is leading to the development of drugs that target specific dopamine receptors and avoid tampering with others (e.g., Gurevich et al., 1997).

ANTIDEPRESSANT AND MOOD-STABILIZING MEDICATIONS

Psychosis is not the only condition amenable to psychotropic drugs. **Antidepressant medications** can also be very effective for some patients, particularly those with severe depressions that include physiological symptoms such as sleep disturbance or loss of appetite (Maj et al., 1992; Montgomery, 1994). Antidepressants increase the amount of norepinephrine, serotonin, or both in synapses; these neurotransmitters are depleted in many cases of depression.

Types of Antidepressants

Several different types of medication have proven effective in treating depression. The **tricyclic antidepressants,** named for their molecular structure, block reuptake of serotonin and norepinephrine into the presynaptic membrane. In other words, they force the neurotransmitter to stay in the synapse longer, compensating for depleted neurotransmitters. Tricyclics can be extremely effective. Double-blind studies, in which neither the patient nor the physician knows whether the patient is taking the drug or a placebo, have found improvement rates of 70 to 80 percent compared to 20 to 40 percent for the placebo (Maj et al., 1992; Prien, 1988). Frequently prescribed tricyclics include trazadone (trade name Desyrel), amitriptyline (Elavil), and desipramine (Norpramin).

Some patients who do not respond well to tricyclics respond to **monoamine oxidase (MAO) inhibitors**. MAO inhibitors keep the chemical MAO from breaking down neurotransmitter substances in the presynaptic neuron, which makes more neurotransmitter available for release into the synapse. MAO inhibitors are more effective than tricyclics in treating many depressed patients with personality disorders, particularly borderline personality disorders (Gardner & Cowdry, 1988; Gunderson, 1986).

A more recently developed class of antidepressants, **selective serotonin reuptake inhibitors (SSRIs),** target serotonin rather than norepinephrine. SSRIs have fewer side effects than other antidepressants and are better tolerated over prolonged periods (Leonard, 1993). The best known SSRI is fluoxetine (Prozac), which has vastly expanded the patient population for whom antidepressants are prescribed. People with severe depression are no longer the only candidates for antidepressants. SSRIs have helped people with chronic mild depression significantly improve their overall mood and social functioning (Kramer, 1993). However, the use of psychotropic medications for people who are not seriously depressed is somewhat controversial. Detractors, who refer to the practice as "cosmetic psychopharmacology," see this as the first step down the road to Aldous Huxley's *Brave New World,* where everyone takes a pill called "soma" to avoid any psychological distress. (Prozac actually has minimal effect on healthy people beyond a placebo response; see Gelfin et al., 1998).

For bipolar disorder, **lithium** is the treatment of choice, although antiseizure medications are often effective for manic patients who are not responsive to it (Goodwin & Ghaemi, 1997). Between 30 and 80 percent of bipolar patients respond to lithium, depending on the sample, although relapse rates range from 50 to 90 percent, in part because bipolar patients frequently stop taking their medication once they feel better (Gershon & Soares, 1997). Lithium acts relatively slowly, often taking three or four weeks before taking effect. In the acute phases of mania patients are therefore usually treated simultaneously with antipsychotics to clear their thinking until the lithium "kicks in." Recent research suggests that lithium may operate less by altering the presence or uptake of neurotransmitters at the synapse than by altering intracellular mechanisms that carry signals from the receptor to the nucleus of the post-synaptic neuron (Manji et al., 1995).

Perhaps the most serious side effect of medications for both unipolar and bipolar depression is that they can be lethal if used for suicide attempts. Prescribing potentially toxic drugs to depressed people obviously carries risks of overdose. Antidepressants can also have minor side effects, including weight gain, dry mouth, sweating, blurred vision, or decreased sexual desire. The side effects of lithium are usually mild compared to the potentially disastrous effects of the disorder or the side effects of antipsychotic medications; patients may experience a fine tremor, weight gain, nausea, and lightheadedness. However, lithium levels in the bloodstream have to be monitored carefully, both because the drug is highly toxic and because if levels drop, the patient may be at risk for relapse.

ANTIANXIETY MEDICATIONS

Antianxiety medications called **benzodiazepines** can be useful for short-term treatment of anxiety symptoms, as with Jenny, who experienced a brief period of intense anxiety. The earliest drug of this class that was widely prescribed was diazepam (Valium); it has since been supplanted by other medications such as alprazolam (Xanax) that are more effective in treating panic symptoms. These medications increase the activity of GABA (Chapter 3), a neurotransmitter that inhibits activation throughout the nervous system. Thus, by increasing the activity of an inhibitory neurotransmitter, they reduce anxiety.

Psychiatrists have more recently been prescribing certain kinds of antidepressants (particularly SSRIs) rather than benzodiazepines for anxiety, particularly for panic disorder (Broocks et al., 1998). While the impact of antidepressants on depression generally takes three to four weeks, anxiety symptoms usually respond within a week. The notion of prescribing antidepressants to treat anxiety seems counterintuitive; however, many neurotransmitters have multiple functions, and neurotransmitter systems are interdependent, so altering one can lead to widespread effects on others. Some neurotransmitters are even used in the synthesis of others; norepinephrine, for example, is synthesized from dopamine.

Antianxiety medications are not without their drawbacks. Patients can become both physiologically and psychologically dependent on them. Many fear that if they get off the medications they will become crippled with panic again. They may in fact be right: The relapse rate after discontinuing antianxiety drugs is very high (see Mavissakalian & Perel, 1992). Nevertheless, some anxiety symptoms such as recurrent panics can be so unpleasant or debilitating that medications are clearly in order, particularly in combination with psychotherapy.

ELECTROCONVULSIVE THERAPY AND PSYCHOSURGERY

Two other biological treatments that were more widely used in previous eras are electroconvulsive therapy and psychosurgery.

Electroconvulsive Therapy

Electroconvulsive therapy (ECT), also known as electroshock therapy, is currently used as a last resort in the treatment of severe depression (see Weiner & Krystal, 1994). Patients lie on an insulated cart or bed and are anesthetized; then electrodes are placed on their heads to administer an electric shock strong enough to induce a seizure. The mechanisms by which ECT works are not known, but its efficacy seems to depend on eliciting a seizure (Frankel, 1984).

The horrifying idea of deliberately shocking a person conjures up images of unscrupulous or overworked mental health professionals using technology to control unruly patients. For many years ECT was clearly used irresponsibly, but today it can be the only hope for some patients with crippling depression and can sometimes be remarkably effective. Studies have found that ECT is more effective than antidepressant drugs in treating many severe depressions, particularly **delusional depressions**, which have psychotic features (Buchan et al., 1992; Goodwin & Roy-Byrne, 1987). As with other therapies for depression, however, relapse rates are high, sometimes requiring readministration a few months later (Weiner

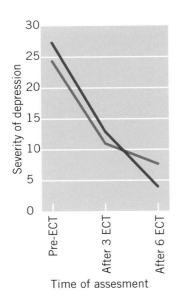

FIGURE 16.7
The effects of unilateral ECT on depressed patients. Applying ECT to either the right or left hemisphere dramatically reduces depressive symptoms. *Source:* Abrams et al., 1989.

& Coffey, 1988). ECT can also sometimes be useful in treating mania (Hanin et al., 1993), but it is ineffective for schizophrenia, for which it was once widely used and abused.

The main side effect of ECT is memory loss. This has been lessened, however, by the discovery that applying electrodes to only one hemisphere is virtually as effective as the bilateral procedures once common. Figure 16.7 demonstrates the dramatic recovery of severely depressed patients treated with ECT applied either to the right or the left hemisphere. After three to six treatments, their depression was eliminated (Abrams et al., 1989).

Those who consider "shock therapy" a brutal invention of technologically developed Western societies are incorrect in another respect. Hieroglyphics on the walls of Egyptian tombs depict the use of electrical fish (such as eels) to numb emotional states, and a number of Greek writers, including Aristotle, refer to the practice. A medieval priest living in Ethiopia observed the use of electrical catfish to drive the devil out of the human body. Today, the San Blas Indians, who live off the coast of Panama and have been relatively untouched by Western culture, use a potion that induces convulsions to quell psychotic states (Torrey, 1986).

Psychosurgery

Another procedure that was once widely practiced is **psychosurgery**, brain surgery to reduce psychological symptoms. Like ECT, psychosurgery is an ancient practice. Fossilized remains from thousands of years ago show holes bored in the skulls, presumably to allow demons to escape from the heads of mentally ill individuals, much the same as in some preliterate cultures studied by anthropologists today.

The most widely practiced Western psychosurgery technique was the **lobotomy**, which involved severing tissue in a cerebral lobe, usually the frontal (Valenstein, 1988). Before the development of psychotropic drugs, some clinicians, frustrated in trying to treat the mentally ill patients who jammed the state institutions, embraced psychosurgery as a way of calming patients who were violent or otherwise difficult to manage. Two leaders in psychosurgery were Egas Moniz, a Portuguese neurologist who introduced the frontal lobotomy in 1935 and received the Nobel Prize for his work, and Walter Freeman, an American neurologist and psychiatrist who popularized the use of lobotomies. Freeman traveled throughout the United States performing his technique, termed a transorbital lobotomy. The procedure involved inserting a cutting tool into the socket of each eye and rotating it to cut the fibers at the base of the frontal lobes.

Lobotomy reached its peak between 1949 and 1952, during which time neurosurgeons performed about 5000 a year in the United States (Valenstein, 1986, 1988). Unfortunately, the procedure rarely cured psychosis (Robin, 1958) and often had devastating side effects. Patients became apathetic and lost self-control and the ability to think abstractly (Freeman, 1959), as portrayed in the popular book and film, *One Flew over the Cuckoo's Nest*. Recently, however, psychiatrists have been experimenting with a much more limited surgical procedure to treat severely debilitating cases of obsessive–compulsive disorder that do not respond to other forms of treatment (Baer et al, 1995; Jenike et al., 1991). Psychosurgery is also the only effective treatment for uncontrollable seizures that do not respond to medication.

INTERIM SUMMARY   **Antipsychotic medications** treat schizophrenia and other acute psychotic states. **Antidepressant medications** can be useful for treating multiple disorders, particularly depression and anxiety disorders. **Lithium** is the treatment of choice for bipolar disorder. Both **benzodiazepines** and antidepressants can be useful for treating anxiety. **Electroconvulsive therapy (ECT)**, also known as electroshock therapy, is currently used as a last resort in the treatment of severe depression. Another treatment of last resort, now primarily used for severe cases of obsessive–compulsive disorder, is **psychosurgery**.

EVALUATING PSYCHOLOGICAL TREATMENTS

One of the most difficult issues facing researchers trying to evaluate the efficacy of various treatments for psychological disorders is that symptoms tend to diminish over time with or without therapeutic intervention. Roughly 30 to 40 percent of patients spontaneously improve without treatment because people seek treatment when they are most distressed and symptomatic and they develop ways of coping with their problems on their own. But what of those individuals who do receive treatment? How effective are the various approaches? And can they be combined to maximize their efficacy?

PHARMACOTHERAPY

The benefits of pharmacotherapy for several disorders are well established. Antipsychotic medication is essential in the treatment of schizophrenia, although full recovery is unusual. Lithium and other mood-stabilizing drugs are similarly indispensable for bipolar disorder (Keller et al., 1992), although some bipolar patients remain chronically unstable. In addition, as we have seen, medication can also be useful in treating many anxiety and mood disorders, particularly major depression, panic, and obsessive–compulsive disorder (Clomipramine Collaborative Study Group, 1991; Thase & Kupfer, 1996).

A major problem associated with biological treatments is the high relapse rate when pharmacotherapy is terminated. One way to minimize this drawback is to continue the medication for a considerable length of time after the treatment has succeeded, usually at a lower dosage (see Montgomery, 1994). As shown in Figure 16.8, most people who experience a major depressive episode will experience another within five years, but continued preventive use of antidepressants can somewhat temper the tendency to relapse (Maj et al., 1992).

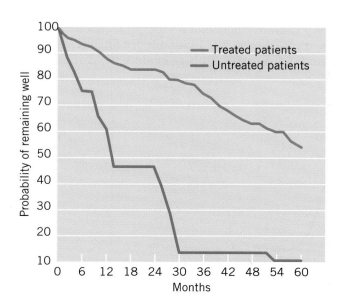

FIGURE 16.8
Relapse rates for major depression with and without medication. The figure shows the effects of the preventive use of antidepressant medication or lithium. Virtually all untreated patients relapsed within three years. Preventative use of medication was clearly helpful, although a substantial minority of patients (46 percent) nevertheless relapsed by five years. *Source:* Maj et al., 1992.

PSYCHOTHERAPY

People who enter into psychotherapy also fare considerably better than those who try to heal themselves (Lambert et al., 1986; Parloff et al., 1986). Researchers have demonstrated this using a statistical technique called **meta-analysis**, which allows them to aggregate, or combine, the findings of diverse studies; the result is a measure of the average effect of psychotherapy.

Is Psychotherapy Useful?

Beginning with a pioneering study in the late 1970s (Smith & Glass, 1977), meta-analyses have shown that the average patient who receives psychotherapy is essentially 25 percent better off than the average control subject, as shown in Figure 16.9 (see Landman & Dawes, 1982). In other words, the bell-shaped curve for subjects who have been treated is shifted in the direction of mental health, so that a person in the 50th percentile of mental health in the group receiving treatment would be in the 75th percentile of subjects if now placed in the control group. This is a substantial shift, equivalent to the difference in reading skill between a third-grader who goes to school and one who stays home and gets no instruction for a year (Lambert et al., 1986).

The Efficacy of Specific Therapies

How useful are the specific psychotherapies we have examined? The answer is more complicated than it seems because many criteria enter into the concept of "successful" treatment. For example, a researcher could measure average improvement, percentage of patients who improve, or relapse rate. One treatment might lead to 90 percent improvement but in only 50 percent of patients, whereas another could reduce symptoms by only 50 percent but do so in 90 percent of patients. Furthermore, one treatment might be very effective but slow and costly; is this, then, a more effective treatment than one that is less ambitious but faster and cheaper? The results of outcome studies also vary depending on who rates improvement: the therapist, the patient, or an outside observer (Lambert et al., 1986). Perhaps most important, estimates of efficacy depend on the time frame: As we will see, many therapies that relieve symptoms in the short run are not efficacious in the long run.

Each of the major approaches has evidence for its efficacy, though to widely varying degrees. The efficacy of cognitive-behavioral therapy is much better established than any other form of psychotherapy, especially for anxiety disorders (Abromowitz, 1997; Chambless & Gillis, 1993; Zinbarg et al., 1992). For example,

FIGURE 16.9
Effectiveness of psychotherapy. Researchers aggregated the findings of 375 studies to assess the effectiveness of psychotherapy. Subjects treated with psychotherapy were, on the average, substantially better off than untreated control subjects. *Source:* Adapted from Smith & Glass, 1977.

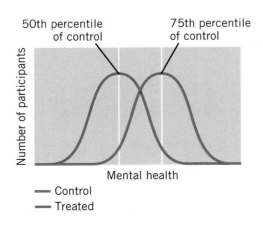

one study compared cognitive-behavioral with Rogerian therapy for panic disorder (Beck et al., 1992). Subjects in the cognitive-behavioral treatment, which addressed patients' fears about panic-related bodily sensations, showed a substantial decrease in panic symptoms; at one-year followup, 87 percent were free of panic attacks, which is as strong a finding as any therapy for any disorder can hope to produce. Cognitive-behavioral therapy is also useful for treating common maladies such as performance anxiety in musicians (Clark & Agras, 1991). Some of the most impressive data have come from cognitive-behavioral treatments of PTSD, which involve exposing the individual to feared thoughts, images, and feelings (Foa & Jaycox, in press).

Considerable research has also demonstrated the efficacy of cognitive therapy in treating depression (Hollon et al., 1993; Scogin & McElreath, 1994; Thase et al., 1991). When efficacy is assessed over longer time frames, however, the data are much less supportive. One recent, well-conducted study of cognitive and behavioral therapies for depression found that roughly half the patients responded to treatment initially, which is an impressive finding. However, at two-year followup only half of *those* patients were still healthy—a success rate of only 25 to 30 percent at two years (Gortner et al., 1998).

Recent research on cognitive-behavioral treatment of panic has produced similar findings (Barlow et al., in press). At one year follow-up, roughly half of patients are panic free; the same is true at two-year follow-up. However, responders at one year are not the same people as responders at two years; that is, roughly half of patients treated for panic are healthy at any given point in a two-year period following treatment, but most patients fluctuate in and out of episodes in which they have relapsed. More sobering, when the researchers imposed stringent criteria for treatment success—the absence of diagnosable disorders or disability—only 20 percent of patients showed what they termed "high end-state functioning" at two years. This suggests that cognitive-behavioral treatment for panic is somewhat efficacious, but that additional treatment is necessary to address other psychiatric problems in panic patients and to maintain therapeutic gains over time.

Psychodynamic, humanistic, group, and marital therapies have not been subjected to as much empirical scrutiny as cognitive-behavioral treatments. Only in recent years have psychodynamic clinicians shown much interest in demonstrating the effectiveness of their techniques (see Blatt et al., 1994; Piper, 1993; Wallerstein, 1989). Empirically sound studies of long-term psychodynamic treatments are very rare, in part because psychoanalysts have long held that the value of their techniques is self-evident, and in part because funding agencies have been reluctant to support studies of treatments lasting longer than six months, which are the most widespread treatments in clinical practice. Thus, we know little about the effectiveness of long-term psychodynamic psychotherapy.

Studies of short-term psychodynamic psychotherapies are much more common and demonstrate a clear advantage over no treatment (Crits-Christoph, 1992; Shefler et al., 1995). Psychodynamic therapy has also proven useful in treating medical conditions that can be affected by psychological factors. For example, psychodynamic treatment stabilized the physical condition of children with life-threatening cases of diabetes who had not responded to medical treatment (Fonagy & Moran, 1990). The only study of marital therapy that has followed patients beyond two years after termination found insight-oriented psychodynamic treatment more beneficial than behavioral marital therapy (Snyder et al., 1991). At four-year followup, only 3 percent of couples treated psychodynamically were divorced, compared with 38 percent of those treated with behavioral techniques.

Humanistic and other treatments are, like psychodynamic psychotherapies, less empirically grounded than cognitive-behavioral therapies. Where evidence exists, however, they are generally as effective as other treatments. For example, in a study of Hispanic children and their families, both psychodynamic and family therapy were superior to a control condition in reducing a range of symptoms, but family therapy was superior in improving family interactions (Szapocznik et al., 1989). Another study found a considerable advantage to adding family therapy to cognitive-behavioral therapy in treating children with anxiety disorders (Barrett et al, 1996). A promising new humanistic therapy (called *experiential therapy*), which integrates Gestalt and Rogerian principles with careful scientific investigation of therapy process and outcome, has also demonstrated considerable efficacy (Greenberg, 1990; Paivio & Greenberg, 1995).

Comparing Psychotherapies

Although advocates of different treatments typically argue for the superiority of their own brand, most research suggests that different therapies yield comparable effects (Smith & Glass, 1977). This is certainly counterintuitive. How could a treatment based on the view that psychopathology stems from unconscious conflicts have the same effect as one that denies their existence or importance?

Common Factors   One possible explanation for the similar outcomes of different treatments is that, despite their specific mechanisms (such as altering defenses or compromise-formations, exposing patients to threatening stimuli, or inhibiting negative automatic thoughts), they share **common factors**—shared elements that produce positive outcomes (Arnkoff et al., 1993; Frank, 1978; Lambert et al., 1986; Weinberger, 1995). Such factors include empathy, a warm relationship between therapist and client, and instilling a sense of hope or efficacy in coping with the problem (Grencavage & Norcross, 1990). Support for this explanation comes from data showing that across a wide variety of studies, the major treatment effect that leads to superiority of the treatment to the control condition occurs by the fifth or sixth session, long before any specific mechanisms (such as astute interpretations of psychodynamic conflicts, or changes in dysfunctional cognitions the patient may have held for years) are likely to have had much effect (Ilardi & Craighead, 1994).

Methodological Challenges in Comparing Treatments   Another possible explanation for the comparable effects of different treatments is methodological. The therapies offered to patients for research purposes frequently bear little resemblance to the way therapy is actually practiced (Persons, 1992). For example, psychodynamic treatments often last three to five years, yet nearly every study ever conducted has assessed treatments averaging six to 20 total *sessions.*

Perhaps the greatest complication in comparing different therapies is experimenter bias: One of the best predictors of the relative efficacy of one treatment over another in any given study is the strength of the investigator's commitment to that treatment (Smith et al., 1980). In fact, a recent study found that experimenter allegiance—that is, the treatment the investigator who performed the study preferred—could account for over 90 percent of the findings in even well-conducted studies of psychotherapy outcome (Berman et al., 1997).

Making matters more complicated, patients differ in their response to different treatments (Beutler, 1991). Even patients who share a diagnosis, such as depression or alcoholism, differ substantially in other respects; thus, comparing mean outcome scores across treatment groups may obscure the fact that different treatments are successful with different patients (see Litt et al., 1992).

The NIMH Collaborative Study   The most definitive evidence yet collected about the relative efficacy of different treatments comes from a nonpartisan study of depression conducted by the National Institutes of Mental Health (NIMH) (Elkin et al., 1989). The NIMH project studied the treatment of 250 patients, a very large sample compared to most prior studies. It compared three treatments for patients with major depression: cognitive therapy, interpersonal therapy (a short-term offshoot of psychodynamic psychotherapy), and imipramine (an antidepressant) combined with supportive clinical management (regular meetings with a concerned physician). A fourth group, control subjects, received a placebo with supportive clinical management. The purpose of giving supportive management to the latter two groups, particularly the placebo group, was to determine whether the effectiveness of psychotherapy is reducible simply to providing regular and kind attention. The study was conducted at several treatment sites, and collaborators from different perspectives administered treatments according to standardized treatment manuals in order to minimize any biases imposed by investigator allegiances.

For all intents and purposes, the three treatments fared equally well. Initial results found both imipramine and interpersonal therapy significantly better than placebo, while the difference between cognitive therapy and placebo fell just short of statistical significance. None of the treatments worked significantly better than the others, although cognitive therapy proved ineffective for more severe depressions. Thus, at short time intervals, short-term treatments tend to have comparable response rates. Once again, however, a more sobering picture emerged when patients were followed up at a two-year interval. Most patients were less depressed than when they began treatment, but relapse was common across all groups, and only a minority met criteria for full recovery (Shea et al., 1992).

Efficacy versus Effectiveness: The Consumer Reports Study Recently researchers have emphasized an important distinction in psychotherapy research, between efficacy and effectiveness (Seligman, 1995). **Efficacy studies** assess treatment outcome under highly controlled conditions: random assignment of patients to different treatment or control groups, careful training of therapists to adhere to a manual, standardized length of treatment, and so forth. **Effectiveness studies** assess treatment outcome under less controlled circumstances, as practiced by therapists in the field rather than in the laboratory. Efficacy studies emphasize internal validity (the validity of the experimental design, maximizing experimenter control), whereas effectiveness studies emphasize external or ecological validity (applicability in the real world).

The overwhelming majority of studies have assessed treatment efficacy under highly controlled conditions. In fact, the NIMH, which is the major source of funding for psychotherapy research, has until recently refused to fund effectiveness studies on the grounds that these studies cannot control relevant variables and hence cannot produce scientifically meaningful results. The American Psychological Association threw its weight behind efficacy studies in 1995 when it published two controversial task force reports distinguishing *empirically validated therapies* from the less structured, longer-term treatments conducted by most practicing clinicians (APA Task Force on Psychological Intervention Guidelines, 1995). Since that time, several advocates of empirically validated treatments (also called *empirically supported treatments*; Kendall, 1998) have argued that clinicians should be trained primarily in these methods and that other forms of treatment are "less essential and outdated" (Calhoun et al., 1998; see also Chambless & Hollon, 1998; Persons & Silberschatz, 1998).

At the same time that the APA came down on the side of efficacy studies, Martin Seligman published a controversial article on the findings of a large *Consumer Reports* survey on the effectiveness of psychotherapy (1995). Seligman described how this survey, involving 2900 respondents who had undergone psychotherapy, led him to reverse his opinion on the superiority of empirically validated treatments. In efficacy studies, patients are seen for a fixed number of sessions, treatments are standardized through the use of manuals that tell thera-

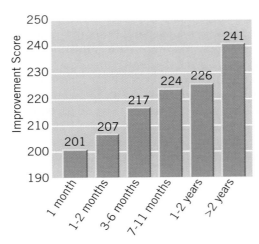

FIGURE 16.10

The *Consumer Reports* study. Like prior research on the relation between length and efficacy of treatment, the *Consumer Reports* study found a direct relation between length and effectiveness. Patients treated for 1–2 months and 3–6 months—the typical length of treatment of many efficacy studies—reported considerably less help from, and satisfaction with, psychotherapy. Satisfaction was measured on a 300-point scale, including reduction of specific problems, general satisfaction with the therapist and the job he or she did, and global life improvement. *Source:* Seligman, 1995, p. 968.

pists what to say and do, and patients meet criteria for a single disorder such as depression. These characteristics may be useful for experimental control, he argued, but they are precisely the characteristics that render a treatment studied difficult to apply or generalize to clinical practice. In everyday clinical practice, the number of sessions depends on the progress of the therapy, treatment is intentionally not standardized because it is self-correcting (that is, the therapist changes course if interventions are not effective), and most patients present with *multiple* concerns rather than just one.

The most striking finding of the *Consumer Reports* study concerned length of treatment: The most successful treatments—that is, those in which respondents reported the greatest decline in symptoms, improvement in overall level of functioning, and general satisfaction—were not empirically supported treatments: They were psychotherapies lasting more than two years. In fact, degree of consumer satisfaction was directly related to length of treatment (Figure 16.10). This is precisely what previous research, using other means of assessing treatment outcome, had shown (Howard et al., 1986, 1994).

Equally striking, and probably a major reason Seligman's article had such an impact, was its source: Seligman, who had an international reputation for his behavioral and cognitive-behavioral research on learned helplessness, had become convinced that long-term therapy, which tends to draw on psychodynamic principles, was more useful than the short-term, largely behavioral and cognitive-behavioral therapies devised by his colleagues.

COMMENTARY
Are All Treatments Created Equal?

Is someone right and someone wrong? As both a researcher and a practicing clinician, I suspect that the current controversy over empirically supported therapies is in some respects a manifestation of the antagonism that has long existed between clinicians and researchers (Chapter 1). Clinicians often find research findings irrelevant and ungeneralizable and hence pay no attention to empirical research. Researchers often find clinical thinking undisciplined and unscientific and hence pay no attention to what their clinical colleagues believe. In retrospect, if clinicians (particularly those who rely on psychodynamic principles, who are the primary practitioners of long-term treatments) had more respect for research, they would have tested the effectiveness of long-term therapy many years ago, rather than simply practicing it without assessing it. They also would have used empirical methods to try to determine which elements of their treatments account for therapeutic change and which can be discarded.

On the other hand, if psychotherapy researchers had more respect for clinicians, they would have asked them years ago how long it typically takes to treat disorders such as depression effectively. This might have made more sense than arbitrarily choosing six to twenty sessions and only beginning to discover, years later, what most clinicians would have told them from the start: Short-term treatments typically yield short-term results. Problems that take years to evolve, and often involve genetic contributions, are not likely to resolve in ten sessions, no matter how good the treatment.

Empirical questions—such as what works, and for whom—require empirical answers (Roth & Fonagy, 1996). We need not abandon scientific methods to assess a complex clinical phenomenon such as response to psychotherapy. The key is to adapt these methods, and use multiple research designs, to try to converge on the most accurate conclusions (see Borkovec & Castonguay, 1998; Goldfried & Wolfe, 1998). When internal and external validity sharply collide, as they have in psychotherapy research, the best strategy is not to err consistently on one side or the other but to conduct studies that err on *each* side, with some aiming to assess causality with the rigor of tightly controlled experimentation and others using quasi-experimental and correlational designs (Chapter 2) that sacrifice an ounce of control for a pound of real-world applicability.

INTERIM SUMMARY Pharmacotherapy is essential for some disorders (such as schizophrenia and bipolar disorder) and can be extremely helpful for others (such as major depression and anxiety disorders), although relapse rates are high when the medication is discontinued, and complete cures are uncommon for most disorders. In general, psychotherapy is effective as well, particularly therapy lasting over two years. An important distinction is between **efficacy studies** that assess treatment outcome under highly controlled conditions and **effectiveness studies** that assess treatment as practiced by clinicians in the field. Both are necessary to establish empirically whether a treatment is useful.

▶ ONE STEP FURTHER

Psychotherapy Integration

All the treatments described in this chapter have their limitations, and each is likely to be more effective with some patients than with others. Thus some mental health professionals argue that the best strategy is **psychotherapy integration**, either choosing techniques selectively to suit the individual case (sometimes called *eclectic* therapy) or relying on theory that cuts across different perspectives (*integrative psychotherapy*) (Beitman et al., 1989; Clarkin et al., 1993; Stricker, 1996).

As noted earlier, Jenny's therapists used many forms of therapy in treating her anorexia. Her individual psychotherapy integrated behavioral and psychodynamic principles. As an outpatient, Jenny's weight was at first precarious, so her therapist required her to weigh in at her doctor's office and bring a slip each week to therapy reporting her weight. Jenny found this acutely embarrassing, so her therapist made a behavioral contract with her: If she maintained her weight for several weeks, he would stop asking to see her weight unless she obviously appeared to be losing again. Aside from reinforcing healthy behavior, this arrangement led to exploration of Jenny's need to be in control, her anger at feeling controlled by her therapist, and ultimately to her longstanding ambivalence about her mother's dependence on her that left her feeling both controlled and controlling. Thus, a behavioral intervention generated a transference reaction that led Jenny to discover her ambivalence toward her mother and a problematic family dynamic of role reversal between mother and daughter.

Although the notion of therapeutic integration is intuitively appealing, it is difficult to practice because the assumptions, methods, and techniques of the various approaches are so different (Arkowitz & Messer, 1984; Messer & Winokur, 1980). How can a clinician integrate principles of therapy based on theories of unconscious conflict and compromise with others that focus on classical and operant conditioning or cognitive distortions?

The best example of an integrative approach is the work of Paul Wachtel (1977, 1993, 1997). Wachtel, who was originally trained psychodynamically, contends that insight into the dynamics of a problem, though often essential to treatment, is not enough: Behavioral techniques can be invaluable in encouraging the patient to confront the problem and developing the necessary skills to master it. For example, a patient who is afraid of his own and other people's anger, and hence avoids confrontations at all costs, may develop a psychodynamic understanding of the ways he runs from anger in many areas of his life and may link this pattern to a fearful relationship with his father as a child. Yet he may remain unable to confront people because the anxiety associated with doing so is a conditioned emotional response that motivates avoidance and needs to be extinguished. The therapist may thus need to take a more active stance, encouraging the patient, applying operant techniques (such as rewarding confrontive behavior with praise), or roleplaying confrontations to desensitize him to real-life confrontations. At the same time, the patient may benefit from examining the way he avoids confrontations with the therapist (examining transference) when he feels the therapist has misunderstood him or made a mistake.

Wachtel has also proposed ways of integrating psychodynamic and family systems therapy, based on the notion that maladaptive interpersonal strategies are maintained through both internal psychodynamic processes and the behavior of significant others, who serve as "accomplices" (Wachtel & Wachtel, 1984). A patient who is depressed and self-hating is often part of a larger family or marital system, and other people in the system may have vested interests in the symptom. The husband of a patient who seeks treatment for low self-esteem may have a need to degrade or dominate his wife, based on a problematic relationship with his own mother; accordingly, he may actively resist his wife's efforts to get better unless he is included in the treatment. Thus, a single mode of treatment—such as treating the wife's self-esteem with cognitive or psychodynamic therapy—may fail because it leaves other important factors that caused or maintain the problem untouched. Helping the husband develop insight into his conflicts with his mother and altering the way the couple communicates may be equally important parts of a treatment plan.   ◄

THE BROADER CONTEXT OF PSYCHOLOGICAL TREATMENT

What clinicians consider therapeutic depends on their perspective, but their views of appropriate treatment also reflect cultural values, beliefs, and economic pressures. In the West, attitudes toward treatment have changed along with attitudes toward psychological distress and disorder. Until recently, the popular assumption was that only "crazy" people sought psychiatric treatment. Although this stigma remains in some quarters, matters have changed dramatically. People today seek treatment for a wide range of problems, from panic attacks to trouble with intimacy or coping with the death of a loved one. The kind of treatment they receive, however, depends as much on economics as on the nature of the problem or the perspective of the practitioner. In this final section, we explore the cultural and economic contexts of treatment.

A GLOBAL VISTA

CULTURE AND PSYCHOTHERAPY

In the industrialized nations of the West, which are highly individualistic by cross-cultural standards, most therapies assume that problems lie in individuals. This is particularly true in the United States (Jansen, 1986), with its historical tradition of rugged individualism. Both psychodynamic and cognitive therapies are predicated on the idea of restoring rational control where unreason has prevailed. The role played by the cognitive-behavioral therapist—who acts in many respects like a mechanic repairing malfunctioning behavioral machinery—is readily understood and embraced by people in a technologically developed society. When, during the 1960s, a segment of the culture rebelled against individualism and rationalism, other treatments emerged, notably group and humanistic therapies that advocated healing through communion with others and experiencing one's emotions (Strupp & Blackwood, 1985).

Cross-culturally, as well as within multicultural societies, methods of treatment similarly depend on cultural value systems and beliefs about personality and psychopathology (Kleinman, 1988, Sue, 1997). Many cultures treat psychological disturbances by bringing the community together in healing rituals (Boesch, 1982; Turner, 1969). These rituals give the ill person a sense of social support and solidarity, similar to the healing properties of empathic relationships in many Western therapies. At the same time, by uniting families or extended kin whose conflicts may be contributing to the individual's symptoms, community healing rituals perform functions similar to family systems therapy.

Among the Ndembu of northwestern Zambia, a ritual doctor thoroughly "researches" the social situation of a person afflicted with illness, mental or physical (Turner, 1967). He listens to gossip and to the patient's dreams and persuades community members to confess any grudges. In one case, the patient held a position of power in the community but was greatly disliked. During the curing ritual, the patient was required to shed some blood, and members of the community were required to confess their hostilities. In this way, the ritual appeased all parties: The patient paid for his character defects with his blood, and the confession repaired social relationships. At the end of the ritual, the mood was jubilant, and people who had been estranged for years joined hands warmly.

To the extent that successful treatment requires faith in the possibility of help, all psychotherapy—if not all medicine—is to some degree "faith healing." The factors that confer faith, however, differ dramatically from culture to culture (Torrey, 1986). Western cultures value academic achievement, and patients tend to respect therapists whose walls are filled with advanced degrees. In non-Western cultures, such as Nigeria, where witch doctors have practiced medicine for generations, family lineage and claims to supernatural powers are more likely to enhance a "therapist's" prestige. Neither academic achievement nor familial descent may have any obvious influence on the degree to which a person can empathize with another, which contributes to therapeutic success and is observed in healers throughout the world (see Triandis, 1994).

THE ECONOMICS OF MENTAL HEALTH CARE

In the West, economic pressures have probably exerted as much impact on treatment as cultural values and beliefs. For example, although research has consistently shown that severely mentally ill patients fare much better if they can rely on the same caregivers over time, hospitals often transfer sicker patients to other hospitals—a phenomenon called "dumping"—in the middle of psychotic episodes because these patients are usually uninsured (Schlesinger et al., 1997). The impact of economics can be seen in the preference for biological treatments, the release of chronically ill patients into the streets, and the failure of many managed care programs to provide even minimal services for mental health.

The Ascent of Biological Treatments

In an environment that sometimes subordinates care to cost, medication is an appealing treatment for mental illness. Medication can be cost-effective and fast-acting and is often the most appropriate treatment. No one should be treated for schizophrenia or bipolar disorder without medication, and a trial of medication is appropriate for most patients with major depression and for many patients with other psychiatric disorders. On the other hand, financial incentives can lead to overuse of medication because a psychiatrist can treat five or six medication patients in an hour, versus the one person per hour seen by a psychotherapist. For example, within a five-year period from the end of the 1980s to the middle of the 1990s, psychiatrists in the United States doubled their rate of prescribing antidepressants, so that antidepressants are now prescribed roughly 50 percent of the time a patient walks into a psychiatrist's office (Olfson et al., 1998). This no doubt reflects in part the increased efficacy of new antidepressants such as Prozac, but it also likely reflects the economics of health care delivery.

Psychiatrists are not the only doctors who rely heavily on mediations. Medical doctors with no training in psychiatry routinely prescribe psychotropic medications, especially for anxiety and depression. Moreover, pharmaceutical companies fund dozens of studies on every new drug, providing vastly more scientific attention than ever devoted to psychological treatments. Thus, biological treatments are better tested and hence preferred by many insurance companies and practitioners. In fact, however, the vast majority of studies that have compared medication alone with medication plus psychotherapy have found that the combination is typically more effective than medication alone, even for severe, biologically based disorders such as bipolar disorder (e.g., Miklowitz, 1996).

The deinstitutionalization movement integrated the severely mentally ill into the community—but certainly not in the way initially intended.

Deinstitutionalization

The development of antipsychotic medications dramatically decreased the warehousing of mental patients but created another problem: deinstitutionalization. Spurred by both the efficacy of medications and outrage at the conditions in many state mental hospitals, the **deinstitutionalization** movement sought to integrate patients whose severe disturbances could be treated with medication into the community. Unfortunately, in the United States, what began as an effort to increase the autonomy of patients gradually evolved into a program of dumping patients onto the street to trim federal and state budgets. The result has been both an abundance of homeless schizophrenic panhandlers (Lamb & Lamb, 1990) and a "criminalization" of mental illness, whereby psychotic patients who cannot care for themselves are incarcerated when their disorders lead to illegal acts, such as disturbing the peace (Abram & Teplin, 1991; Teplin, 1984).

The problems of homelessness, lack of treatment, and criminalization of the mentally ill have been aggravated by laws originally designed to protect people from being locked up without due process. Legal changes in the 1960s often arose from celebrated cases of people who were committed to mental institutions inappropriately. In most states today mentally ill people cannot be hospitalized against their will unless they are both psychotic (grossly out of touch with reality) and demonstrably dangerous to themselves or others.

On the one hand, these changes in the laws have been respectful of the mentally ill and have helped curb abuses of commitment laws. However, an unfortunate result of these changes is that patients who could be treated for their disorders (such as mania, which is usually responsive to medication), who would probably want treatment if they were able to weigh their options rationally, too often wind up on the street because no one has the authority to hospitalize or treat them if they refuse. For paranoid patients, who by definition are distrustful, or manic patients, who may destroy their relationships or spend their life savings while feeling euphoric, these changes in the law have often proven disastrous. Under the guise of civil liberties, municipalities often pass statutes that shield them from the responsibility of caring for deinstitutionalized patients. In one major American city, for example, a person suspected by mental health professionals of being dangerous or suicidal is sent a letter asking him to appear in court for a commitment hearing. If he does not appear, or if he is homeless and has no address, the police do not have the authority to pick him up until he commits a violent crime.

Managed Care

Even for people who seek help for much less disabling conditions, economic pressures are increasingly shaping the kind of treatment they receive. Mental health care, like all health care, costs money. In the United States, people with more money generally receive more and better treatment, although many clinicians and practitioners see some patients on a sliding scale according to ability to pay. To contain spiraling costs, employers and public health programs such as Medicaid are increasingly turning to "managed care" and health maintenance organizations (HMOs). The most effective way for these for-profit health care companies to reduce costs, at least in the short run, is to offer only short-term treatments, such as medication and extremely brief psychotherapies. Thus, HMOs have been criticized for providing the least possible, rather than the best possible, care (Sederer, 1992; Shulman, 1988). At many HMOs, mental health coverage consists of five sessions per year, and case reviewers, some of whom lack training in mental health, frequently decide how long patients stay in the hospital.

Although cost-containment is admittedly a major concern throughout the entire health care system, not just in mental health, HMOs and insurance companies commonly pay tens of thousands of dollars per patient for costly long-term medical treatments for diseases such as cancer, asthma, or emphysema. The policy difference between treatment for mental and physical disorders appears to reflect public attitudes of fear, prejudice, and neglect toward emotional problems (see Melton, 1987). Because unacceptable behaviors, rather than chest pains, may be the symptoms of a severe mental disorder, people have difficulty recognizing that a person suffering from a brain disease like schizophrenia is no more blameworthy or deserving of a life on the street than someone with heart disease. Disparities between coverage for mental and physical disorders are much less prevalent in Canada and other countries where health benefits are nationalized.

INTERIM SUMMARY   Methods of treatment reflect cultural value systems and beliefs about personality and psychopathology. Economic pressures, such as the cost-effectiveness of medication and the rise of managed care, also have a substantial impact on the mental health services people receive.

SOME CONCLUDING THOUGHTS

In this chapter, we have explored a wide variety of techniques used to alleviate psychological distress. Yet all of these approaches treat disorders that have already taken hold. One of the positive outcomes of the interest in cost-effective health care is the increasing recognition that one can often save money—and misery—by preventing illness rather than treating it. Just as exercising, avoiding a high-fat diet, and minimizing stress can promote physical health (Chapter 11), psychologists have long argued that addressing social problems such as poverty, malnutrition, physical and sexual abuse, and some of the factors that influence child and marital abuse (e.g., unemployment) could promote psychological health (Albee, 1986; Masten et al., 1993; Zigler & Berman, 1983).

The basic ideas behind **primary prevention**—efforts to prevent mental health problems rather than simply to treat them after they have arisen—come from the field of public health (Albee & Gullotta, 1997). When experts identify a disease as a public health problem, they take a number of steps, beginning with trying to identify the toxic agents responsible for it. Once they identify the toxin, they attempt to eliminate it, prevent its transmission to the population, or strengthen the resistance of the population to it. Thus, if a large percent of the population is contracting malaria, and malaria is borne by mosquitoes, a sound policy is simultaneously to try to eliminate mosquito breeding grounds, keep people away from areas with high concentrations of mosquitoes that carry the disease, and vaccinate the public. Similarly, if we know that child abuse and marital distress increase at times of high unemployment and that both lead to depression and anxiety in adults and their children, then sound public policy would be to try to reduce the unemployment rate, develop intervention programs for people who lose their jobs, and educate people about child abuse and its effects.

Primary prevention cannot eradicate all forms of mental illness any more than exercising will keep a person from eventually dying. Reducing the unemployment rate will not eliminate genetic causes of mental illness. We cannot control our genes—not yet, anyway—but we can certainly control some of the factors that lead to their maladaptive expression.

SUMMARY

PSYCHODYNAMIC THERAPIES

1. Psychodynamic therapy is predicated on the notion that **insight**—understanding one's own psychological processes—is important for therapeutic change, as are aspects of the **therapeutic relationship**.

2. **Free association** is a technique designed to explore associational networks and unconscious processes involved in symptom formation. Another central element of psychodynamic therapy is the **interpretation** of conflicts, defenses, compromise formations, and transference reactions. **Transference** refers to the displacement of thoughts, feelings, fears, wishes, and conflicts from past relationships, particularly childhood, onto the therapist. Therapists must also carefully watch their own **countertransference**, emotional reactions triggered by interactions with the patient, and particularly by the patient's transference to them.

3. The main contemporary forms of psychodynamic treatment are psychoanalysis (which is very intensive and long-term) and psychodynamic psychotherapy (which relies on the same principles but is more conversational).

COGNITIVE-BEHAVIORAL THERAPIES

4. **Cognitive-behavioral therapies** are relatively short term and directive, and they focus on specific symptoms. They rely on operant and classical conditioning as well as cognitive-social and more strictly cognitive interventions.

5. In **systematic desensitization**, the patient gradually approaches feared stimuli mentally while in a relaxed state. **Exposure techniques**, like desensitization, rely on classical conditioning, but they present the patient with the actual phobic stimulus in real life rather than having the patient merely

imagine it. Therapies based on operant conditioning apply rewards and punishments to modify unwanted behavior, as in **token economies**.

6. In **participatory modeling**, the therapist not only models the desired behavior but also gradually encourages the patient to participate in it. **Skills training** teaches the procedures necessary to accomplish relevant goals; **social skills training** helps people with specific deficits in interpersonal functioning.

7. **Cognitive therapy** attempts to replace dysfunctional cognitions with more useful and accurate ones. Ellis, who developed **rational-emotive therapy**, proposed an **ABC theory** of psychopathology; *A* refers to activating conditions, *B* to belief systems, and *C* to emotional consequences. Beck's cognitive therapy similarly proposes that correcting cognitive distortions is crucial to therapeutic change.

Humanistic, Group, and Family Therapies

8. **Humanistic therapies** focus on the phenomenal (experiential) world of the patient. Rogers's **client-centered therapy** aims at helping individuals experience themselves as they really are, through therapeutic empathy and **unconditional positive regard**.

9. Group, family, and marital therapies treat multiple individuals simultaneously. **Group therapy** focuses on both individual dynamics and group process. A variation on group therapy is the **self-help group**, which is not guided by a professional. **Family therapy** presumes that the roots of symptoms lie in the structure of the family system, so that therapy should target family interaction patterns. A variant of family therapy, **marital** or **couples therapy**, treats the couple as a unit and may employ systems, psychodynamic, behavioral, or cognitive-behavioral techniques.

Biological Treatments

10. The aim of **biological treatments** is to alter the functioning of the brain. **Pharmacotherapy**, the use of medications to treat psychological disorders, is the major type of biological treatment. **Psychotropic medications** affect mental processes by acting at neurotransmitter sites; some also affect intracellular transmission. **Antipsychotic medications** are useful in treating psychotic symptoms, particularly the positive symptoms of schizophrenia. **Tricyclic antidepressants, MAO inhibitors,** and **selective serotonin reuptake inhibitors** can be useful in treating depression, while **lithium** is the treatment of choice for bipolar disorder. Both **benzodiazepines** (antianxiety medications) and certain kinds of antidepressants can be useful in treating anxiety.

11. **Electroconvulsive therapy (ECT)**, or shock therapy, is currently used as a last resort in the treatment of severe depression. Although **psychosurgery** was once widely practiced and abused, today researchers are experimenting with limited forms of psychosurgery as a last resort for obsessive–compulsive disorder.

Evaluating Psychological Treatment

12. Pharmacotherapy is well established as an effective treatment for schizophrenia, bipolar disorder, and many other forms of psychopathology. The two major problems with pharmacotherapy are relapse rates and side effects.

13. Researchers have found that all psychotherapies are relatively effective and none are generally more effective than others, although some treatments are likely superior for some disorders than others. Comparisons among different treatments, however, are methodologically difficult. Cognitive-behavioral treatments have received the most empirical attention and support in **efficacy studies** (carefully controlled experimental studies with relatively homogeneous samples and highly standardized therapeutic procedures), but the long-term **effectiveness** (usefulness in clinical settings with a more heterogeneous population) of short-term treatments is less well established.

THE BROADER CONTEXT OF PSYCHOLOGICAL TREATMENT

14. Cross-culturally, treatment methods depend on cultural value systems and beliefs about personality and psychopathology. In the West, economic conditions often play a part in determining who gets mental health care and what kind.

15. The **deinstitutionalization** movement, designed to maximize the autonomy and community integration of patients whose severe disturbances could be treated with medication, has led to widespread homelessness and lack of care for the severely mentally ill in the United States. Today, economic factors make managed health care more appealing. Policies for treating physical and mental problems differ greatly, however; as a consequence, mental health coverage is becoming progressively less adequate.

16. **Primary prevention** refers to preventative measures aimed at reducing the incidence of mental illness.

Randy Stevens, "They're Here!," 1995.

Attitudes and
Social Cognition

*W*hen most people think of prejudice, they think of apartheid in South Africa, Ku Klux Klan rallies, or the murder of a black man in Texas in 1998 by three white men who tied him to the back of a car and dragged him until his body was completely dismembered. We think of racial and ethnic stereotypes as beliefs people overtly hold or express about other people based on arbitrary qualities such as the color of their skin. But some recent research suggests that negative stereotypes can get *under* the skin in some insidious ways.

In a remarkable series of studies, Claude Steele (1997; Steele & Aronson, 1995) has demonstrated how racial stereotypes can affect even the people who are the targets of them. In one experiment, Steele and his colleagues presented black and white Stanford undergraduates—an elite group selected for their high achievement, who should have few doubts about their intellectual abilities—with difficult verbal items from the Scholastic Assessment Test (SAT) (Steele & Aronson, 1995). Black and white students were matched in SAT scores, so that both groups were of similar intellectual ability. In one condition, students were told that the test did not measure anything significant about them. In the other condition, they were told that it measured their intellect. Black and white students in the first condition performed equally well, as one would expect, since they had similar SAT scores before entering college. In the second condition, however, the performance of black students dropped substantially.

What happened? In the United States, blacks and whites are both exposed to negative stereotypes about the intellectual abilities of blacks. These stereotypes become part of their associative networks—their implicit understanding of race—even if they do not explicitly believe them. So when an African-American student takes a test believed to be diagnostic of his ability, these associations become active. Particularly if scholastic success is important to the student, stereotype activation will generate performance anxiety, which can in turn lead to diminished performance.

Just how much do these processes operate in real life? In a second experiment, Steele and his colleagues once again had black and white Stanford students answer difficult SAT items. The study had two conditions, with a seemingly minor difference between them: In the demographic questionnaire students filled out before taking the test, *race* was included in one condition but not the other. The results are depicted in Figure 17.1: Priming African-American students' racial associations by simply asking them to fill in their race led to a dramatic decline in their performance.

Steele suggests that the impact of processes of this sort are quite profound and likely extend to groups as diverse as the Maori minority in New Zealand and the

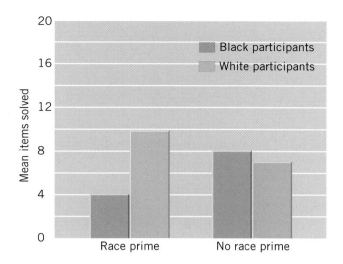

FIGURE 17.1
Performance on a difficult verbal test as a function of whether race was primed. *Source:* From C.M. Steele (1997). A threat in the air: How stereotypes shape intellectual identity and performance. *American Psychologist,* 52, p. 621.

West Indian minority in Britain. (They are also not limited to race: Steele and his colleagues have documented that activation of negative stereotypes about women's mathematical abilities similarly leads to declines in their performance on math tests.) Over time, repeated experiences of anxiety and "choking" on tests caused by stereotype activation lead individuals to stop identifying with scholastic achievement as something self-defining. As a result, they begin to distance themselves from school and stop trying, leading to further declines in performance.

Based on this model, Steele and his colleagues have begun testing an intervention program aimed at breaking this spiral for African-American college students. The standard approach to helping minority students from poor backgrounds is to give them remedial help, often just prior to beginning college, as a way of "catching them up." According to Steele's theory, this approach may actually backfire because it reinforces the associations that lead to decreased performance. An alternative approach is to create a program that gives students from stereotyped groups challenging instead of remedial work, accompanied by the message that they can, in fact, succeed; provide successful role models; and encourage students to continue viewing the academic domain as something relevant and self-defining. Preliminary data suggest that this program leads to substantial increases in grade-point average (GPA) and, perhaps more importantly, decreases in the high drop-out rates of African-American students from largely white colleges.

Steele's research is a classic example of **social psychology**, which examines the influence of social processes on the way people think, feel, and behave (Allport, 1968). Because almost everything people do is social, the subject matter is enormous and varied. In this chapter we focus on interpersonal thinking. We begin with a discussion of attitudes and how they change. This topic is of central concern to advertisers, who try to shape attitudes toward their products, as well as to politicians, who want to shape—and follow—public opinion. Next we examine the processes by which people make sense of each other, from the first impressions they form to enduring beliefs. Among these enduring beliefs are stereotypes, which can lead not only to declines in academic performance but to discrimination and bloodshed. We conclude by considering the way people think about one of the major actors in their social worlds: themselves.

ATTITUDES

Attitudes are probably the most fundamental concept in social psychology because they are involved in all social behavior, from political decisions to stereotyping and prejudice (Allport, 1935).

THE NATURE OF ATTITUDES

An **attitude** is an association between an act or object and an evaluation (Eagly & Chaiken, 1992; Fazio, 1986). To put it another way, an attitude—whether toward Pepsi, Reebok, or Yassir Arafat—is a tendency to evaluate a person, concept, or group positively or negatively (Eagly & Chaiken, 1998). To say that alcohol (the attitude object) leads to major social problems (evaluation) is to express an attitude.

Social psychologists distinguish three components of an attitude: a *cognitive component* or belief (alcohol leads to major social problems); an *emotional* or *evaluative component* (alcohol is bad); and a *behavioral disposition* (alcohol should be avoided). At first glance, attitudes seem relatively straightforward—a person is either for abortion or against it, favorable or unfavorable toward affirmative action, or more positive toward Nike than Reebok or vice versa. Recently, however, researchers have discovered a number of ways in which attitudes vary that make them far more complex than might first appear (see Eagly & Chaiken, 1998).

Attitude Strength

One dimension on which attitudes vary is their strength. Personally, I like the Boston Red Sox, but as someone who is only minimally interested in baseball, my feelings toward the team are relatively weak. If they lose to the Yankees, I do not lose much sleep. Further, my beliefs about the team—the cognitive components of my attitude toward the Red Sox—also tend to sway in the wind. If my barber tells me they are going to be great next year, I am perfectly happy to believe him, and will likely continue believing him until someone else informs me otherwise.

Attitude strength refers to the durability and impact of an attitude (Petty & Krosnick, 1994). An attitude is durable if it tends to persist over time and is resistant to change. An attitude has impact if it affects behavior and influences the way the person thinks and feels. Using this definition, my attitude toward the Red Sox is very weak: It is highly unstable and has minimal impact on what I do on a Saturday afternoon or how I feel if the team loses. It also has little effect on whether I think an umpire made the right call at the plate. Someone with a stronger attitude, in contrast, would be more likely to see the game in person and become outraged at the "injustice" of calls that went against the team.

Attitude Retrieval

Most people are familiar with the concept of attitudes because of the number of opinion polls reported weekly in the media. The idea of polling people about their attitudes suggests that attitudes are stable "things" housed in a mental warehouse and hauled out of storage when someone asks to see them. In reality, like all thoughts and memories, attitudes are constructed "on-line" at any given moment, by combining representations and associations stored in memory with perceptions and feelings at the moment. A person may believe—even strongly—that capital punishment is wrong but construct the momentary attitude that a particular child molester deserves death after hearing the sordid details of the case. In this instance, the emotion of the moment overrides longstanding dispositions or tendencies. At other times, the attitude a person constructs regarding a new object will depend on the extent to which other attitudes are activated. Consider a person who strongly believes in free enterprise but also has strong feelings about protecting children. When asked about his attitudes toward regulating tobacco advertisements to minors, he may report very different attitudes if asked about the issue at a Chamber of Commerce meeting than at a PTA meeting, simply because different values, feelings, and beliefs have been activated by the context.

For an attitude (such as *free enterprise is good*) to have an impact on ongoing thought and behavior, it must be cognitively accessible. **Attitude accessibility** refers to the ease with which an attitude comes to mind (Fazio, 1990, 1995). Highly accessible attitudes come to mind rapidly and automatically when primed by environmental events. For example, a person with negative attitudes toward blacks may have an immediate and negative initial reaction when the doctor at the clinic who comes out to examine him is black. The more accessible an attitude, the more likely it is to affect behavior.

As with emotions, motives, and cognitions, social psychologists are increasingly recognizing the importance of distinguishing between explicit (conscious) attitudes and **implicit attitudes**—associations between attitude objects and feelings about them that regulate thought and behavior unconsciously and automatically (Greenwald & Banaji, 1995). Someone who has just attended a lecture on alcohol-related fatalities is unlikely to stop at the bar on the way home because a conscious attitude is active. He may well, however, overindulge at a happy hour a few days later when his implicit attitudes toward alcohol—which reflect years of associations between drinking and enjoyment—become active. In fact, implicit attitudes of this sort play a more important role in predicting drug and alcohol use than people's conscious attitudes (Stacy, 1997).

Cognitive Components

The cognitive components of an attitude—beliefs—vary on a number of dimensions. These beliefs can be relatively specific (the papparazi who swarmed around Princess Diana were responsible for her death) or general (the media are too intrusive on people's privacy). They can also differ in their complexity (Bieri, 1966; Suedfeld & Granatstein, 1995). Two people with equally positive attitudes toward trade with China can have very different levels of complexity in their beliefs. One person might be positive toward increasing trade with China simply because of the enormous size of the Chinese market: Two billion people translates to a lot of Pepsi. Another person may have carefully weighed the costs and benefits of economic interdependence with China and come to the conclusion that trade is not only economically beneficial but likely to foster the development of a class of entrepreneurs who will ultimately press for more democratic social institutions. On a simple attitude rating from 1 to 7 (where "1" means the person is unfavorable toward increase trade with China, and "7" means the individual is highly favorable), both may rate the question a "5," but the beliefs underlying the attitude are quite different.

Researchers have used some ingenious methods to try to assess the complexity of people's attitudes (Tetlock, 1989). One method is to read political speeches and code them for the extent to which they reflect complex thinking. Using this kind of analysis, researchers have found that people on both political extremes—far right and far left—tend to be less complex in their thinking than people who are politically more moderate. People in the middle may actually know *less* about many political questions than those with more extreme views (Sidanius, 1989), but they may be better able to weigh arguments on both sides than people committed to one extreme or another. Although complex thinking is more likely to produce better judgments, it does not always lead to conclusions that, in retrospect, appear to have been the right ones. Analysis of the speeches and writing of people on both sides of the slavery issue prior to the Civil War in the United States found that the most complex thinkers were in the political center (Tetlock et al., 1994). More generally, people who are moderately liberal in their political beliefs tend to be the most complex in their thinking.

Attitudes also differ in the extent to which they are interconnected with other attitudes (Eagly & Chaiken, 1998). Someone who has strong positive attitudes toward feminism is likely to hold a number of related attitudes: that abortion is a woman's right, that women deserve equal pay for equal or equivalent work, that violence against women should be taken more seriously than it is, and so forth. In contrast, a woman who is relatively conservative politically but has been the victim of rape may strongly believe that violence against women should be taken more seriously but not believe in abortion. Attitudes, like other representations and concepts (Chapter 6 and 7), can be hierarchically ordered; thus, an important dimension on which attitudes vary is the extent to which they are embedded in broader value systems and ideologies (Feather, 1996).

Evaluative Components

The evaluative components of attitudes vary as well. Two important evaluative dimensions are intensity and ambivalence. Some attitudes are associated with strong emotional reactions. Whether the Red Sox win or lose does nothing to my general mood because I am not particularly invested in them. Whether the income disparity between rich and poor increases or decreases, however, is not a matter of indifference to me because I am committed to certain ideals, and these ideals are associated with strong feelings.

Another dimension is the extent to which attitudes involve conflicting feelings. For many years researchers measured attitudes by asking respondents to rate the extent to which they were for or against abortion, liked or disliked President Clinton, and so forth. Periodically, however, attitude researchers have wondered whether this really captures the complexity of people's evaluative judgments. The idea that positive and negative feelings can be placed on a single bipolar continuum from negative to positive makes intuitive sense, but this is a good example in which science has overturned common sense. As we saw in Chapter 11 on emotion, positive and negative affect are somewhat independent and rely on different neural circuits. Thus, a person could associate a single attitude object with both positive and negative feelings.

Researchers studying **attitudinal ambivalence**—the extent to which a given attitude object is associated with conflicting evaluative responses—argue that attitudes include two evaluative dimensions, positive and negative, that are relatively independent (Cacioppo, Gardner, & Berntson, 1997; Priester & Petty, 1996). These components can each be relatively weak or relatively strong. Low positive/low negative attitudes will have minimal impact on behavior because the person does not care much either way about the attitude object. These weakly held attitudes are very different from highly ambivalent attitudes—high positive/high negative—that typically yield precisely the same (moderate) scores on bipolar attitude measures that assume that attitudes run from negative to positive. For example, one study compared people who were low on both positive and negative attitudes toward blood donation with those who were high on both (ambivalent). Those who were essentially indifferent were less willing to donate blood than those who were ambivalent, presumably because the latter were able to harness their social values to overcome their classically conditioned squeamishness (Gardner & Cacioppo, 1996, cited in Cacioppo et al.).

Although researchers have largely focused on positive and negative affect in attitudes, it seems likely that attitudes also differ in the specific feelings associated with them. For a high-achieving African-American student, scholastic success may not just be associated with a mixture of positive and negative feelings but, more specifically, with a combination of pride, happiness, anxiety, and shame (if the student's friends brand achievement as white behavior). Some research on conflict between groups (such as nations) suggests, in fact, a very important difference between attitudes associated with disgust and contempt on the one hand, which tend to lead to avoidance of people from that group or country, and those associated with feelings such as fear, anger, and jealousy, which are associated with escalating conflict and attack (Smith, 1993).

Coherence

A final dimension on which attitudes vary is **attitudinal coherence**—the extent to which an attitude is internally consistent (Eagly & Chaiken, 1998). Logically, the cognitive and emotional aspects of attitudes should be congruent because an emotional evaluation of an object should reflect a cognitive appraisal of its qualities; that is, we should like things we believe have positive consequences. In fact, however, the beliefs and feelings comprising an attitude frequently develop separately and can change independently (see Petty & Cacioppo, 1981, 1986; Edwards, 1991).

A classic example occurred during Ronald Reagan's tenure in the White House. Opinion polls consistently showed that a majority of voters disagreed with many of his policy positions, such as his opposition to abortion, but they maintained a highly favorable attitude toward him anyway. Similarly, during Bill Clinton's first term as President, many Americans disliked his reputation for womanizing but found him approachable and charismatic and associated his Presidency with good economic times. As political consultants well understand, the emotional component of a political attitude—which can be decisive in voting behavior—rests as much on implicit assessments of nonverbal gestures, likability, and apparent sincerity as on the issues (Epstein, 1994). From a cognitive perspective, coherent attitudes, in which beliefs about the object are strongly associated with feelings about it, are likely to be particularly strong and influence the way people act.

INTERIM SUMMARY   An **attitude** is an association between an act or object and an evaluation. **Attitude strength** refers to the durability and impact of an attitude on behavior. **Attitude accessibility** refers to the ease with which an attitude comes to mind. **Implicit attitudes** regulate thought and behavior unconsciously and automatically. The cognitive components of attitudes vary in the extent to which they are general or specific as well as in their complexity. They also vary in the extent to which they are interconnected with other attitudes. The evaluative components of attitudes vary in their intensity and in the extent to which the attitude object is associated with conflicting evaluative responses (**attitudinal ambivalence**). **Attitudinal coherence** refers to the extent to which an attitude (particularly its cognitive and evaluative components) is internally consistent.

ATTITUDES AND BEHAVIOR

Logic would suggest that attitudes should predict behavior. For example, students' attitudes toward cheating should be closely related to how much they

Surprisingly, these people are not much more likely to recycle their glass and plastic at home than the average person.

cheat. Once again, however, the empirical David is mightier than the logical Goliath: Broad attitudes predict behavior, but not very well (Fishbein & Ajzen, 1974). Students' attitudes toward cheating are not very useful predictors of the probability that they will cheat, any more than religious attitudes predict attendance at religious ceremonies (Wicker, 1969).

A striking early demonstration of the incongruence between attitudes and behavior was a study published in 1934 in which a psychologist interested in prejudice wrote to 251 hotels and restaurants to see if they would serve Chinese patrons (LaPiere, 1934). Nearly all said no—yet nearly all of them had actually served the investigator and a young Chinese couple traveling with him several months earlier.

Given that people are often passionate about their attitudes, how could their attitudes have so little effect on the way they behave? Several factors appear to be at work. First, people's attitudes do predict their actions if the attitude and action are at the same level of generality, and particularly if both are relatively specific (Ajzen & Fishbein, 1977; Kraus, 1995). Asking people their attitude toward protecting the environment does not predict whether they will recycle, but asking their attitude toward recycling does (Oskamp, 1991).

Second, and perhaps most importantly, people's attitudes are only one of many influences on what they do (Ajzen & Fishbein, 1977). From a behaviorist perspective, behavior is under the control of environmental consequences. An ecologically minded person who buys one small bag of groceries a week might reuse her own canvas shopping bag each week and thus contribute to the longevity of tropical rain forests. An equally environmentally conscious person who totes groceries for her family up six flights of stairs might find the convenience of plastic bags such overwhelming reinforcement that she contributes instead to the longevity of landfills. From a cognitive perspective, much of behavior is controlled by implicit procedures (Chapter 6), or habits, that people develop through experience, rather than by their explicit (conscious) attitudes (Ouellette & Wood, 1997). As in other areas of research, it seems likely that people's explicit attitudes guide their behavior primarily when they are consciously reflecting on them.

Because attitudes are only one of the factors that influence behavior, they may not be useful in predicting who a person will vote for in a particular election, but over the long run, they will in fact predict the party the individual tends to endorse at the ballot box. As we saw in Chapter 12, human behavior is so complex that a single variable is rarely likely to predict what a person will do in a specific circumstance. By aggregating (averaging) across behaviors, however, researchers get a clearer picture of a person's behavioral tendencies. Attitudes, like personality traits, predict behavior over the long run. And as with both intelligence (Chapter 8) and personality (Chapter 12), some attitudes are relatively general whereas others are specific.

Third, the recognition that attitudes vary along a number of dimensions points to some previously unrecognized complexities in the way attitudes affect behavior. For example, as we will see, people's explicit racial attitudes are often much more liberal than their implicit attitudes. Explicit attitudes predict some behaviors, but much of the time implicit attitudes, which are more automatic, explain the way people act, as when a white person who thinks she is unprejudiced makes less eye contact with black than white strangers.

Finally, the way attitudes are acquired influences their impact on behavior. Attitudes shaped by personal experience are especially likely to influence action (Fazio & Zanna, 1981; Smith & Swinyard, 1983). One study examined students' attitudes toward a campus housing shortage that forced many to sleep on cots in makeshift quarters for weeks (Regan & Fazio, 1977). Both the affected students and their more comfortably housed peers had negative attitudes toward the situation and the way the university handled it; however, those who were personally affected were much more likely to act in accordance with their attitudes by writing letters, signing petitions, and the like.

INTERIM SUMMARY The cognitive, evaluative, and behavioral components of an attitude may vary independently of each other. Although attitudes are generally believed to include a behavioral disposition, they often do not predict specific behaviors, for several reasons: the behavior and the attitude are often at different levels of generality; other variables influence behavior; and attitudes vary in different ways that make prediction complex, such as the extent to which they are implicit or explicit.

PERSUASION

People often have a vested interest in changing others' attitudes, whether they are selling products, running for political office, or trying to convince a lover to reconcile one more time. **Persuasion** refers to deliberate efforts to change an attitude.

Central and Peripheral Routes

People sometimes change their attitudes after considerable conscious reflection. Other times they change their attitudes with little thought. Correspondingly, researchers have identified two routes through which people can be persuaded (Petty & Cacioppo, 1981, 1986; Eagly & Chaiken, 1992; Petty & Wegener, 1998). The first, or **central route,** involves inducing the recipient of a message to think carefully and weigh the arguments. The second, or **peripheral route,** appeals to less rational and thoughtful processes—bypassing the cortex and often heading straight for points south, such as the limbic system, the heart, or the gut. Most beer commercials, for example, have little to offer in terms of rational persuasion. Were weekends really made for Michelob? When you say "Bud," have you *really* said it all?

According to one model, the **elaboration likelihood model** of persuasion, knowing how to appeal to a person requires figuring out the likelihood that they will think much about (or elaborate on) the arguments (Petty & Cacioppo, 1986).

Rational appeals are more likely to change people's attitudes when they are both *motivated* to think about a topic (that is, when they care about the issue) and when they are *able* to think about it (when they have time to consider the arguments). In other words, when elaboration likelihood is high, appeals to logic are most likely to be persuasive. These appeals are not, of course, always successful; the recipient of the message may think about the arguments and find them unpersuasive. Nevertheless, attitudes changed via the central route, which involve high-effort cognitive processing, tend to be stronger.

Much of the time, however, people do not have the time, interest, or ability to weigh every argument about every possible attitude object that crosses their paths. Do I buy Green Giant string beans or Del Monte? Do I get the Guess jeans or the Calvins? If I am a true green bean devotee, I might spend the extra 30 seconds in the aisle at the grocery store pondering the merits of two brands (or walk over to the fresh produce aisle), but as we have seen (Chapter 7), in everyday cognition people have to choose how to allocate their cognitive resources because working memory and time are both limited commodities. People often use simple heuristics (cognitive shortcuts or rules of thumb) to make judgments about attitude objects, such as following the majority opinion (hence laugh tracks on television shows, which tell people that the jokes are funny, in case they did not notice on their own) or passively accepting appeals to unknown experts (e.g., "nine out of ten dermatologists prefer...") (Chaiken, 1980; Chaiken et al., 1997).

The distinction between central and peripheral routes to attitude change parallels the distinction between explicit and implicit judgment and decision making (Chapter 7). Whereas explicit attitude change (the central route) requires conscious deliberation, implicit attitude change (the peripheral route) can occur in several ways. One is through classical conditioning of an object with an emotional response. Advertisers use a catchy slogan and humor so that people will associate their product with a positive feeling, or they populate their commercials with beautiful women and virile men, implying that using their product or drinking their beer will increase consumers' reproductive success (rather than their beer gut). These kinds of conditioning processes can occur outside of awareness. In one study, participants saw slides of a young woman, preceded immediately by subliminal presentation of photographs designed to arouse either positive or negative emotion (Krosnick et al., 1992). When asked their attitudes toward the woman, participants exposed to the positive subliminal pictures were more favorable than those exposed to the negative pictures. Remarkably, simply having people move an object toward or away from themselves while evaluating it can affect their attitudes toward it because pulling objects toward oneself is associated with approach and approach-related emotions, whereas moving the arm away is associated with avoidance (Priester et al., 1996).

Other nonrational appeals can also be persuasive. Simply repeating a message enough times can make people believe it (Arkes et al., 1991). This appears to occur for several reasons. One is simple familiarity: People tend to prefer things that are familiar, which is why advertisers tend to run highly redundant ad campaigns, with familiar faces and jingles (Zajonc, 1968, 1998). It is also why political campaigns often rely heavily on bumper stickers, which convey absolutely no information. A second reason is that repeating a message linking an attitude object with a feeling strengthens the connection between the two through simple mechanisms of association. As Aristotle recognized over 2000 years ago, the repeated association of two events in reality leads to their heightened association in memory (Chapter 5). This works for both positive and negative persuasive appeals. Running a television advertisement that associates a candidate with the nation's flag can be effective, just as repeatedly running an attack ad that associates a candidate with increased taxes can strengthen negative associations. Third, one cue for credibility of a message is the number of times a person hears it. Over time, peo-

ple tend to forget the source and remember the message. This is no revelation to managers of political campaigns, who often repeat false messages about opposing candidates—usually in highly emotional terms—in order to bias public opinion.

Changing someone's attitude, then, requires attention to several variables. If the attitude really matters to the person, if the recipient of the message is knowledgeable about the subject, if the recipient has time to evaluate the arguments, and if the attitude was initially generated rationally by weighing costs and benefits, then the best appeal is to the head (central processing). In this case, the persuader should avoid distractions (glitzy campaigns, jingles, and hoopla) that impede conscious, rational processing and annoy the receiver. If, however, the attitude is not strongly held and is based on minimal knowledge, the best route is usually to the heart or the gut—or at any rate, as far from the frontal lobes as possible (peripheral processing).

Components of Persuasion

Interest in persuasion has a venerable past. Long before modern psychology, Aristotle described *rhetoric*—the art of persuasive speaking—as a combination of *ethos* (characteristics of the speaker), *pathos* (the appeal of the message), and *logos* (the logic of the argument). Psychologists have expanded Aristotle's view to identify several components of persuasion, including the source, message, channel (the medium in which the message is delivered), context, and receiver (Lasswell, 1948; McGuire, 1985; Petty & Wegener, 1998). Attending to each of these aspects is crucial to the success of a persuasive appeal, whether the goal is to sell a car or get someone to agree to a date.

Source Speakers tend to be more persuasive when they appear credible (expert and trustworthy), attractive, likable, powerful, and similar to the recipient of the message (Chaiken, 1980; Simons et al., 1970). For politicians, particularly in countries such as the United States where presidential candidates must appeal directly to voters, winning votes is often a balancing act in which the successful candidate must seem likable but authoritative, powerful yet able to understand the concerns of everyday citizens.

Message The type of appeal (e.g., presenting one side of the argument or both) and the way it is delivered also affect attitude change. As we have seen, the match between the recipient's willingness and ability to think about the message and the way the message is delivered is crucial for persuasion; a jingle about a low-fat margarine will not convince someone who is concerned about her weight and has compared the fat content of multiple brands. Fear appeals—efforts to induce fear to try to change attitudes—can sometimes be effective, but they can backfire if they induce too much fear, leading people to stop attending to the message and instead to focus on managing their anxiety (Insko et al., 1965). For example, messages about AIDS may fall on deaf ears if they are so frightening that people simply deny the realities. Fear can, however, be useful in inducing attitude change if the recipients of the message believe the danger applies to them and that they can do something to avoid it (see Olson & Zanna, 1993).

Channel   The channel of persuasion is the means by which a message is sent—in words or images, verbally or nonverbally, in person or through media such as telephone or television. Choosing the right channel can be as important as selecting the right message. Turning someone down for a date is much more difficult face to face than on the telephone, so suitors of reluctant targets should make their pitch in person. Emotional appeals to contribute to emergency relief funds are similarly more effective when the target of the communication can see starving children with distended stomachs rather than simply hear about their plight.

Context   The context in which a message is presented can also influence attitude change (Petty & Wegener, 1998). Soft music in the background can be useful in leading an ambivalent "target" to agree to a second date, and a roomful of cheering supporters can make a political message seem much more exciting. Distraction (such as washing the dishes while discussing a political issue) can also affect the impact of a persuasive appeal, either increasing its impact by preventing counterarguments or decreasing its impact by reducing attention to it.

Persuasion is often complicated by the fact that someone else has a vested interest in the opposite outcome. Reebok's loss is Nike's gain. Psychologists and advertisers have devised many methods to increase resistance to contrary appeals. One is to get there first: Being the first to make a pitch renders a persuasive appeal more effective (Insko, 1964; Miller & Campbell, 1959). Another method for countering an opposing appeal, called **attitude inoculation,** involves building up the receiver's "resistance" to an appeal, much as a vaccine builds the body's defenses through exposure to small, inert amounts of a virus (McGuire, 1961; McGuire & Papegeorgis, 1962). The speaker presents weak and easily assailable arguments supporting the other point of view or forewarns of a strong attack by the other side, prompting the person to develop counterarguments that serve as attitudinal "antibodies." Salespeople frequently use this technique when they know a customer is about to visit a competitor ("He'll tell you Dell has a better customer service, but don't believe him").

Receiver   Receiver characteristics—qualities of the person the communicator is trying to persuade—also affect the persuasiveness of a communication. People bias their information processing in order to preserve attitudes they do not want to change (MacCoun, 1998). Coffee drinkers, for example, discount messages about the dangers of caffeine (Liberman & Chaiken, 1992). Prior attitude strength also influences the impact of an appeal; people with weaker opinions are obviously easier to persuade. Moreover, some individuals are simply more resistant to attitude change in general (see Haugtvedt & Petty, 1992; Hovland & Janis, 1959).

People also vary in the extent to which they are likely to attend to, elaborate, and reflect on careful arguments—that is, to rely on the central route to attitude formation and change (Jarvis & Petty, 1996). This does not mean, however, that people who focus on the substance of the arguments form "better" attitudes. People can exercise considerable effort in preserving their biases and carefully attacking arguments that do not support their position.

Behavioral Change   One of the most effective strategies for changing attitudes is inducing people first to change their behavior. As we saw in Chapter 16, convincing a person with a snake phobia to get closer and closer to the slithery reptile can change the person's attitudes toward snakes (from intensely fearful to neutral) as well as toward himself (inducing a greater sense of self-efficacy). A persuasive strategy that similarly targets behavioral change is the **foot-in-the-door technique,** based on the principle that once people comply with a small request, they are more likely to comply with a bigger one (Beaman et al., 1983).

In one classic study, experimenters posed as representatives of the Community Committee for Traffic Safety or the Keep California Beautiful Committee (Freedman & Fraser, 1966). They visited over 100 homes in Palo Alto, California and asked residents to comply with one of two requests, either signing a petition or posting a small sign on their lawns reading, "Be a safe driver" or "Keep California Beautiful." About two weeks later, the investigators visited the same homes as well as several others and made a larger request—to install a large "Drive Carefully" sign on their front lawn. Whereas over 55 percent of paricipants who had granted one of the small requests two weeks earlier complied, less than 20 percent of those who received only the second (large) request consented. The same principle may work in dating: If a potential date seems uncertain or ambivalent, suggest lunch (a much smaller investment) before proposing an entire evening out.

INTERIM SUMMARY   **Persuasion** refers to deliberate efforts to change an attitude and can occur through a **central route,** inducing the message recipient to think about the argument, or a **peripheral route,** appealing to less thoughtful processes. According to the **elaboration likelihood model,** the central route to attitude persuasion is more effective when the person is both motivated and able to think about the arguments, whereas the peripheral route is more effective when the likelihood that the person will engage in high-effort cognitive processing is low. Characteristics of the source, message, channel, context, and receiver all affect the effectiveness of persuasive appeals. Getting people to change their behavior can also lead to attitude change.

COGNITIVE DISSONANCE

Although attitude change often involves deliberate efforts at persuasion, another path to attitude change is cognitive dissonance. According to Leon Festinger (1957, 1962), who developed cognitive dissonance theory, attitude change can occur when various objects of thought, which he called "cognitive elements," are logically inconsistent—that is, when they are *dissonant* with one another. These objects of thought can be attitudes, behaviors, new information—virtually anything a person can think about. Thus, if a person holds the belief that smoking is dangerous (element 1) but does not smoke (element 2), she does not experience dissonance; the two cognitive elements are consistent. If, on the other hand, she knows that smoking is dangerous (element 1) but also knows she smokes (element 2), she experiences **cognitive dissonance**—a perceived discrepancy between an attitude and a behavior or between an attitude and a new piece of information.

According to Festinger, this discrepancy leads to a state of psychological tension similar to anxiety. The tension, in turn, motivates the individual to change the attitude, the behavior, or the perception of the inconsistent information to eliminate the discrepancy and the accompanying tension. For example, if the person knows that smoking is bad but she smokes anyway, she may change the belief component of her attitude toward smoking ("it's not really that dangerous—I don't know anyone who has died of lung cancer from smoking"), or she may quit smoking. Alternatively, she may add some additional cognitive element that resolves the dissonance (e.g., "I don't plan to smoke that many years, so it won't hurt me").

Having chosen between two stocks to buy, people are likely to watch closely for even minor gains in the one they chose rather than continue checking the other to see if they should change their investment. Keeping an eye on both stocks might be more useful financially, but it leaves them vulnerable to cognitive dissonance.

Dissonance Reduction

Cognitive dissonance theory is essentially a drive-reduction theory (Chapter 10) in which an attitude change is reinforced by reduction of an uncomfortable emotional state (a drive). Suppose, for example, Linda has been dating Justin for a few weeks. She was really interested in him when they began dating, but he has seemed somewhat indifferent, often preferring to go out with his buddies on weekends. Whether Linda is free to date other people is ambiguous; they are involved enough to suggest otherwise, but Justin's level of commitment hardly seems to imply an exclusive relationship.

The plot thickens when another man, Bob, asks her out for Saturday night. Bob seems like a nice enough guy, and Linda has no intention of spending the evening at home while Justin spends another night out with the boys, so she accepts. Then she begins to worry whether she has made the right choice—a phenomenon called *post-decision regret*. The tension she experiences may lead her to convince herself that Bob is more attractive than he is—essentially justifying a choice she has made that is inconsistent with another choice, dating Justin. She may also talk with her friends about the situation in a way that solicits a particular answer—for example, talking only to friends who dislike the way Justin has treated her, or "talking up" Bob's virtues. These are examples of *post-decision dissonance reduction*—or dissonance reduction after the fact.

Cognitive dissonance can also arise when people carry out an act contrary to their attitudes, which frequently leads to attitude change. In a classic test, Festinger and Carlsmith (1959) had participants perform monotonous tasks for an hour. The experimenters told participants that the aim of this procedure was to test their performance, but the actual purpose was to create a negative attitude toward the tasks. The investigators then instructed some participants to tell the next "participant" (who was really a confederate of the experimenter) that the experiment was enjoyable. They paid the participants either $1 or $20 for their compliance.

One might expect that people who received $20 for hyping a boring task would feel more positive toward the task than those paid only $1. In fact, just the opposite occurred. Those who received only $1 rated the experimental tasks more enjoyable, and they more frequently agreed to participate in a similar experiment again. While these results seem counterintuitive, they exquisitely matched the predictions of dissonance theory: To say that a boring task is interesting for a meager payment creates considerable dissonance. Participants who received only $1 either had to change their attitude toward the task or acknowledge that they had sold their souls rather cheaply. In contrast, those who received $20 reduced their dissonance and thus avoided the need to change their attitude because they could readily explain their behavior in terms of the payment, a considerable amount in the late 1950s. In Festinger's terms, participants in both conditions (1$ and $20 payment) experienced a discrepancy between what they believed (cognitive element 1, "the task is boring") and what they did (cognitive element 2, "I told this poor sucker that the task is interesting"). When participants in the $1 condition tried to explain this to themselves, they had *insufficient justification* for their action, and hence had to change their attitude toward the task. In contrast, participants paid $20 could add a third cognitive element ("I told the guy it was interesting because they paid me a lot to do it"), which relieved the logical inconsistency between what they believed and what they said.

Two variables that influence the extent to which dissonance arises and requires resolution are the perception of choice and the size of rewards and punishments. A person with a gun to his head will not feel much pressure to cling to attitudes he publicly professed at the time. Coerced statements create little dissonance because they are uttered with minimal choice. Similarly, as in Festinger and Carlsmith's study, the smaller the reward or punishment, the greater the attitude change because larger incentives minimize dissonance. This paradoxical finding, that a smaller reward leads to greater attitude change, has obvious implications for teaching children, who must often be induced to perform tasks that do not at first appear intrinsically compelling, such as practicing multiplication tables. Rewarding children too generously for activities they might come to enjoy spontaneously can actually lead them to attribute their enjoyment to the rewards and hence to find the task itself intrinsically unrewarding (Lepper, 1978). This is much more likely to occur with simple, routine tasks, however, than with more complex or creative ones (Eisenberger & Selbst, 1994).

Alternative Explanations

The original formulation of cognitive dissonance theory explained the results of these experiments in terms of the motivation to reduce dissonance. Not all researchers agree, however, that motivation is necessarily involved. An alternative nonmotivational explanation, derived from behaviorism, is self-perception theory. **Self-perception theory** holds that individuals infer their attitudes, emotions, and other internal states by observing their own behavior (Bem, 1967, 1972). Thus, if they see themselves telling someone that they like a task and they have only received $1 for doing so, they conclude that they must have liked it or they would not be saying so. If they slander their country at gunpoint, they conclude that they did so to avoid dying, not because they truly dislike their country. According to self-perception theory, the attitudes people report depend on their behavior; as their behavior changes (because of changes in reinforcement contingencies), so again will their attitude. No motivation, tension, or perceived inconsistency is involved.

Other theories provide alternative motivational explanations other than dissonance reduction to explain the findings of dissonance experiments. A **self-presentation** explanation focuses on the way people try to present themselves to others. According to this view, what appear to be changes in attitudes in dissonance studies are really changes in reported attitudes. Because subjects do not want to look foolish to the experimenter by behaving inconsistently, they report attitudes they do not really hold. Another motivational explanation maintains that people feel guilty, ashamed, or lacking in integrity after doing something that conflicts with their values, such as lying about a task. Thus, they change their attitudes to minimize their discomfort and preserve their self-esteem (see Abelson, 1983; Scher & Cooper, 1989; Steele, 1988).

Most likely, each of these explanations is applicable at various times. When people do things that do not seem "like them" but that do not have unpleasant consequences for other people, simple self-perception processes can sometimes explain why they change their attitudes. On the other hand, experiments measuring physiological responses demonstrate that encountering conflicting information *can* produce emotional arousal that people experience as uncomfortable, and that these feelings can indeed be reduced by changing a belief—or by other emotion-regulation strategies (Chapter 11), such as watching a funny movie, "cleansing their emotional wounds" with alcohol, or misattributing the cause of their discomfort to something irrelevant like a pill they have recently taken (Fried & Aronson, 1995; Steele et al., 1991; Zanna & Cooper, 1974). Unpleasant feeling states are most likely to lead to attitude change when the person has done something that leads to shame, guilt, or anxiety, such as looking foolish to someone else or breaking a moral standard.

The reader may recognize some similarity between these various theories of cognititve dissonance—particularly those that emphasize motivation—and the models of stress and coping and emotion regulation we examined in Chapter 11. In each case, the person makes a primary appraisal of the situation as either problematic or unproblematic—whether the problem is logical inconsistency, immorality, or the appearance of foolishness. If this appraisal leads to a perception of a problem, the person experiences a negative or stressful emotional state that she is motivated to resolve. She then employs coping strategies (such as changing her attitude, changing her behavior, rationalizing her behavior by adding a third cognitive element, or changing the emotion directly by exercising, drinking, etc.) to reduce the unpleasant feeling. Much of this, of course, may occur outside conscious awareness.

Culture and Dissonance

The extent to which cognitive dissonance is universal has recently come into question (Kitayama et al., 1998). One study compared the responses of Japanese and Canadian participants to a procedure that typically elicits dissonance in Western samples (Heine & Lehman, 1997). Prior research had shown that giving people positive feedback prior to a dissonance manipulation decreases dissonance-reduction motivation (because the person is less threatened about his self-worth), whereas negative feedback increases attitude change through dissonance reduction because it essentially heightens the person's sense of incompetence, immorality, lack of integrity, or similar feelings (Steele, 1988). Thus, participants in this study were first given a fake "personality test" and told the results would be available shortly. Next, the investigators asked participants to choose 10 CDs from a list of 40 they would most like to own and to indicate how much they would like each one by making a mark on an unmarked 118-millimeter line labeled "wouldn't like this CD at all" on the left and "would like this CD very much"on the right. Immediately afterward, they were given the "results" of the personality test—some received negative feedback, some positive, and some no feedback at all—and a few minutes to ponder the results. Afterwards, the experimenter came back with the subject's 5th- and 6th-choice CDs and gave them a choice between them. After a few more minutes of filling out some irrelevant information (to give time for dissonance reduction processes to occur), participants again rated each of the ten CDs using the same 118-mm line.

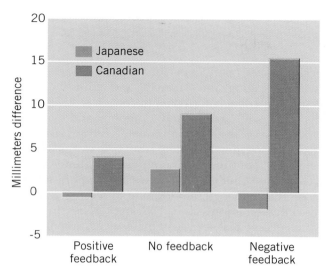

FIGURE 17.2

Dissonance reduction and culture. Canadian participants tended to reduce dissonance by increasing their relative preference for the CD they chose over the one they turned down, as assessed by the difference in the number of millimeters on a line on which they indicated their preference. This was particularly true under conditions of threat to their view of themselves (negative feedback). For Japanese participants, no dissonance reduction occurred under any of the three conditions. *Source:* Heine & Lehman, 1997, p.396.

The results for Canadian participants were just as expected (Figure 17.2). Those who had received no feedback showed a substantial difference between their post-choice ratings of the two CDs; on the average, they preferred the one they had chosen by over 9 mm on a 118-mm line. Those who had been given positive feedback showed a much smaller effect, whereas those who had received negative feedback substantially changed their attitudes in favor of the CD they had chosen, which apparently made them feel better about themselves ("I'm not so stupid after all—I know how to choose a good CD!"). No such effect occurred for the Japanese: They did not show a significant preference for the CD they had chosen under any condition.

Research with other Asian samples has produced similar findings. Why would this be? The authors suggest that the difference lies in the way Asians and North Americans view themselves. North Americans are individualistic and independent. To make a bad choice thus has strong implications for self-esteem, leading to rationalization and attitude change in dissonance experiments. Asians, on the other hand, tend to be much more collectivist and interdependent in their views of themselves (Markus & Kitayama, 1991; Kitayama et al., 1998). Their self-esteem rises and falls more with their ability to meet social expectations and maintain a sense of connection with those around them than with individual choices that indicate how smart or savvy they are. As we will see, this distinction between different ways of representing and experiencing the self may extend well beyond people's behavior in dissonance experiments.

INTERIM SUMMARY **Cognitive dissonance** occurs when a person experiences a discrepancy between an attitude and a behavior or between an attitude and a new piece of information. This leads to a state of tension that can motivate attitude change. According to **self-perception theory,** attitudes change in dissonance experiments as people observe their own behavior. Other explanations emphasize **self-presentation** (trying to look good) or efforts to regulate unpleasant emotions such as guilt and shame. To some extent cognitive dissonance may presume a particular way of thinking about and evaluating the self that is distinctively Western.

Social cognition is all about inference in the face of ambiguity. The most important information— what is going on in another person's mind—is never directly accessible.

SOCIAL COGNITION

A friend has just told you she has the "perfect person" for you. She describes the individual as intelligent, witty, engaging, and articulate, and thinks the two of you would make a great pair. You immediately form an impression of this person, which probably includes traits such as attractive, kind, outgoing, and generous. Now suppose instead your friend describes a potential date with precisely the same words—intelligent, witty, engaging, and articulate—but first warns that this person is a "real con artist." This time your impression probably includes less favorable traits, such as selfish, cold, and ruthless. How does a simple phrase ("perfect for you" versus a "real con artist") change the meaning of a series of adjectives and lead to an entirely different impression? The answer lies in **social cognition,** the processes by which people make sense of themselves, others, social interactions, and relationships.

SOCIAL VERSUS NONSOCIAL COGNITION

The study of social cognition emerged as psychologists began to extend models and metaphors from cognitive psychology into the realm of social information processing. Researchers studying social cognition have closely watched developments in cognitive science, but they have also recognized some important differences between social and nonsocial cognition.

From Cognitive Science to Social Cognition

As we saw in Chapters 6 and 7, psychology is undergoing a second cognitive revolution. A computer metaphor is giving way to a brain metaphor; an exclusive focus on laboratory experimentation is giving way to more eclectic methods, including observation of thought and memory in their everyday contexts; and a focus on conscious, explicit thought and memory is giving way to a recognition that thought and memory include implicit as well as explicit processes. Research in social cognition has in many respects followed developments in cognitive science, and a similar shift is beginning to occur in the understanding of thought and memory in the social realm (Kunda & Thagard, 1996; Read et al., 1997; Smith, 1996, 1998).

Central to this shift are changes in the understanding of representations in social cognition—that is, of how we mentally reconstruct the social world in our minds (Smith, 1998). As we saw in Chapters 6 and 7, cognitive psychologists have relied on a number of different models of how information is represented in long-term memory. Some models emphasize principles of association, arguing that memories are stored as interconnected nodes on networks of association that have become linked through experience. Activation of one node in a network spreads activation to other nodes. Other models emphasize schemas, organized patterns of thought that direct attention, memory, and interpretation. Activation of a schema (such as a theater schema) makes a person more likely to hear the word "play" as referring to a theater production than as something children do in a schoolyard. Still other models focus on concepts, mental representations of categories, such as birds. In these models, categorizing a novel stimulus involves comparing it to an abstract prototype (a generalized image or idea of a class of stimuli), a set of defining features (such as a list of attributes common to all birds), or a salient example or exemplar (such as a robin).

As we saw in Chapter 7, more recently, connectionist models have proposed that representations are not so much "things" that are "stored" in the brain but patterns of activation of networks of neurons. According to these models, when a person sees an object, multiple processing modules are simultaneously activated in parallel. Somehow the system has to weed out less likely hypotheses about what the object is and settle on a solution. It does this by taking into account the multiple constraints imposed by the data. Thus, the presence of wings on an animal in the garden activates multiple possible bird representations (robin, sparrow, etc.). At first, the mind automatically favors the most common birds, which begin with the highest level of activation, because they are the most frequently encountered. However, if the bird's wings are flapping at an extremely rapid pace, this is inconsistent with the representation of garden-variety birds, so these representations are inhibited. The representation that is left "standing" at the end of this battle of competing networks is the one that receives the greatest activation: hummingbird.

These various models or "languages" for speaking about representations all continue to be used in research on social cognition. Researchers are just beginning to sort out the extent to which they are compatible or incompatible and the conditions under which one model may be more accurate than another. However, one of the major new developments in research on social cognition—and in fact in all of social psychology, such as the study of attitudes and cognitive dissonance—is the application of connectionist models to phenomena that have previously been understood using other models of representation. The basic findings to be described below about the way people think about themselves and others remain well documented, but we may be witnessing a mini-revolution in social psychology in the years ahead as concepts such as attitudes, social schemas, and stereotypes begin to come under a broader and more unified conceptual umbrella.

Differences between Social and Nonsocial Cognition

Although social psychologists have followed developments in cognitive science closely, they have also recognized a number of ways in which social cognition differs from nonsocial cognition (see Fiske, 1993, 1995; Markus & Zajonc, 1985). These differences are not black and white, but several of these dimensions are much more salient in social than nonsocial cognition.

First, human action and interaction are ambiguous. A person observing a social interaction is probably missing the most relevant data: the unspoken intentions, thoughts, and feelings of the people involved. Because observers of a social interaction have access only to behaviors, they must infer what those behaviors mean. Ambiguity is thus the rule in social cognition, leaving substantial opportunities for error, bias, and idiosyncratic interpretation.

Second, social cognition is inherently intertwined with emotion. People either like or dislike their roommate; their psychology professor is either interesting or boring; the clerk is either courteous or rude. Thinking about airplane propellers, in contrast, may not engender quite so much feeling (unless we are in the way of them).

Third, although culture influences many cognitive processes such as categorization, it plays a particularly important role in social cognition. An individual who is competitive and driven to accumulate wealth may appear perfectly normal in Western culture, and hence draw little attention, whereas the same person may be classified as antisocial, self-centered, or even dangerous in an agricultural society, where resources are limited. Social cognition is inherently infused with cultural value judgments because categories (such as men, nurses, or students) carry with them implications of how people who fit them *should* behave (Shweder, 1980). Culture also influences the way people interpret interpersonal events by providing intuitive theories of personality and causality. When children and adults in the West explain their successes and failures they rely on concepts such as skill, effort, and luck (Weiner, 1980). In contrast, Buddhist children from Sri Lanka sometimes attribute achievement and failure to good and bad deeds in past lives. Good deeds from another life lead to good karma, a positive moral force that guides one's fate (Little, 1988).

Finally, social cognition is reciprocal. The "object" being perceived in social cognition may respond to the perceiver—and change its actions based on how it believes it is being perceived. Getting annoyed at a textbook for being thick and boring does not change it. Getting annoyed at a professor for the same reasons, however, may well influence the way he lectures.

INTERIM SUMMARY   **Social cognition** refers to the processes by which people make sense of themselves, others, social interactions, and relationships. Changing concepts of representation in cognitive science are beginning to lead to similar changes in the study of social cognition. In particular, connectionist models, which view representations as patterns of activation of networks of neurons operating in parallel, are beginning to shed new light on old phenomena. On the other hand, social psychologists have pointed to a number of ways in which social cognition differs from nonsocial cognition, including its inherent ambiguity, its inseparability from emotion, its heavy cultural foundation, and its reciprocal nature.

PERCEIVING OTHER PEOPLE

Social cognition is pervasive in everyday life, from the first impressions people form of other people to their more enduring knowledge about people, situations, and relationships.

First Impressions

Even before the field of social cognition emerged as a distinct discipline, psychologists interested in interpersonal perception studied **first impressions.** These initial perceptions of another person can have remarkably powerful effects because they create mental representations that influence the processing of subsequent information. For example, participants in one study read the two passages shown in Figure 17.3 (Luchins, 1957). Half read the top paragraph (A) first, whereas the other half read the bottom paragraph (B) first. The order of the material substantially influenced participants' evaluations of the person described: Seventy-eight percent of subjects who read paragraph A first considered Jim friendly, whereas only 18 percent of those who read paragraph B first did so.

One salient piece of information people consider, particularly on first impression, is attractiveness. Individuals who are physically attractive benefit from the tendency to assume that positive qualities cluster together, a phenomenon known as the **halo effect.** Researchers have found halo effects for physical attractiveness across a wide array of situations, such as people's evaluations of the bad behavior of attractive versus unattractive children (Dion, 1972), the sentences recommended by simulated jurors for crimes involving attractive and unattractive criminals and victims (Landy & Aronson, 1969), and the traits ascribed to political and media figures (Lachman & Bass, 1985). A large study of workers in the United States and Canada found that more attractive people tend to earn 5 to 10 percent more than their plainer colleagues (Hamermesh & Biddle, 1994). (Perhaps that explains my meager professor's salary.)

The positive glow of beauty, of course, has its limits (see Eagly et al., 1991; Feingold, 1992). It is most powerful when people have minimal information about each other. It also extends to some traits more than to others. People typically at-

Paragraph A

Jim left the house to get some stationery. He walked out into the sun-filled street with two of his friends, basking in the sun as he walked. Jim entered the stationery store, which was full of people. Jim talked with an acquaintance while he waited for the clerk to catch his eye. On his way out, he stopped to chat with a school friend who was just coming into the store. Leaving the store, he walked toward school. On his way out he met the girl to whom he had been introduced the night before. They talked for a short while, and then Jim left for school.

Paragraph B

After school Jim left the classroom alone. Leaving the school, he started on his long walk home. The street was brilliantly filled with sunshine. Jim walked down the street on the shady side. Coming down the street toward him, he saw the pretty girl whom he had met on the previous evening. Jim crossed the street and entered a candy store. The store was crowded with students, and he noticed a few familiar faces. Jim waited quietly until the counterman caught his eye and then gave his order. Taking his drink, he sat down at a side table. When he had finished his drink he went home.

FIGURE 17.3

First impressions. In this classic study, the order of presentation of two paragraphs had a substantial influence on the impression subjects formed of Jim. *Source:* Luchins, 1957, pp. 34–35.

tribute greater sociability and social competence to attractive people, but they do not expect them to have more integrity, modesty, or concern for others.

Is the perceived correlation between physical and emotional beauty entirely illusory? Actually, some of the beliefs people hold about the relation between physical attractiveness and other qualities have some basis in fact. People rated by panels of judges as more physically attractive tend to report feeling more socially comfortable and less lonely than less attractive subjects. An even more important variable than *actual* physical attractiveness, however, may be how attractive people *perceive* themselves to be. Individuals who perceive themselves as physically attractive report being more extroverted, socially comfortable, and mentally healthy than those less comfortable with their appearance (Feingold, 1992). Although they may simply be deluded in every realm of their lives, it is equally likely that seeing oneself as attractive produces a self-fulfilling prophecy, in which feeling attractive leads to behaviors perceived by others as attractive. In fact, when people feel and act attractive, others are more likely to see them that way.

Schemas and Social Cognition

First impressions are essentially the schemas people form when they encounter someone for the first time. Schemas—the patterns of thought hypothesized to organize human experience (Chapters 4 and 6)—apply in the social realm as in other areas of life (see Fiske, 1993, 1995; Taylor & Crocker, 1980).

Types of Social Schemas **Person schemas** represent information about specific people or types of people. Individuals develop schemas about broad categories (e.g., extroverts, librarians, Hispanics, women) as well as about specific others (e.g., one's father or neighbor). **Situation schemas** represent information about different kinds of social situations, including what to expect and how to act. People know how to behave in a classroom, in a library, or in a restaurant because they have schemas for each of these situations.

Role schemas represent information about what is expected of people in particular social positions or roles, such as student, professor, or parent. Role schemas are generally shared by members of a culture. In contrast, **relationship schemas,** which encode expectations about how the self and others interact in different kinds of relationships, tend to be more idiosyncratic and personal (Baldwin, 1992; Horowitz, 1988). Like other schemas, relationship schemas are typically activated outside awareness. Thus, a student may bristle at a comment by a professor without realizing that the professor's remark triggered a reaction shaped in his relationship with his father—an example that makes sense from both a psychodynamic and a cognitive perspective.

The Impact of Schemas on Social Thought and Memory As in other cognitive domains, social schemas guide information processing. They specify what information is likely to be relevant; direct attention; organize encoding; and influence retrieval. An employer who suspects that a job candidate may be exaggerating his accomplishments is likely to scrutinize his resume with special care and inquire about details that would normally not catch her eye. If later asked about the candidate, the first thing she may remember is that he described a part-time job as a courier at a radio station as a "communications consultant."

People are especially prone to recall *schema-relevant* social information—behaviors or aspects of a situation related to an activated schema (Higgins & Bargh, 1987). For example, participants presented with a vignette about a librarian are likely a week later to remember information congruent with their librarian schema, such as a bun hairstyle and glasses. They are also prone to remember highly discrepant information, such as her tendency to go out dancing every night. If a librarian schema is active during encoding or retrieval, what people are least likely to remember are details irrelevant to the schema, such as her hair color.

INTERIM SUMMARY **First impressions** can have an important influence on subsequent information processing. One of the features that strongly affects the way people perceive others upon first meeting is physical attractiveness. People process information about other people and relationships using several types of schemas, including **person schemas,** which represent information about specific people or types of people; **situation schemas,** which represent information about different kinds of social situations; **role schemas,** which represent information about what is expected of people in particular social positions; and **relationship schemas,** which encode expectations about how the self and others interact in different kinds of relationships. Social schemas guide information processing by directing attention, organizing encoding, and influencing retrieval.

STEREOTYPES AND PREJUDICE

Schemas are essential for social cognition. Without them, people would walk into every new situation without knowing how to behave or how others are likely to act. Schematic processing can go awry, however, when schemas are so rigidly or automatically applied that they preclude the processing of new information. This often occurs with **stereotypes,** characteristics attributed to people based on their membership in specific groups. Stereotypes are often overgeneralized, inaccurate, and resistant to new information. Like other schemas and attitudes, however, they save cognitive "energy"; that is, they simplify experience and allow individuals to categorize others quickly and effortlessly (Allport, 1954; Hamilton & Sherman, 1994; Macrae et al., 1994).

Prejudice, which literally means *pre-judgment,* involves judging people based on (usually negative) stereotypes. In attitude terms, stereotypes are the cognitive component, prejudice is the evaluative component, and **discrimination** is the behavioral component of negative attitudes toward particular groups (Fiske, 1998).

Racial, ethnic, and religious prejudice has contributed to more bloodshed over the past 60 years than perhaps any other force in human history. Its path of destruction can be traced through the violence and institutionalized discrimination against blacks in the United States and South Africa, to the Holocaust, the Arab–Israeli conflict, the tension between Anglophones and Francophones in Quebec, the carnage in Northern Ireland, the tribal warfare and genocide in Rwanda and other African countries, the civil war and atrocities in Bosnia, and the other civil wars that erupted after the breakup of the Soviet Union. The list is, indeed, long and grim.

Since the 1930s, psychologists have proposed a number of explanations for prejudice, based on their answers to two central questions: Do the roots of prejudice lie in individual psychology (such as personality dynamics or cognition) or in social dynamics (the oppression of one group by another)? And are the causes of prejudice found in cognition or motivation—in the way people think or in the way they *want* to think? As we will see, the absence of a single widely accepted theory of prejudice probably reflects the fact that researchers have often tried to choose among these options (see Duckitt, 1992).

The Authoritarian Personality

Around the time of World War II, psychologists turned to psychodynamic theory to explain the racism that was devouring Europe and eating away at the United

"... it required years of labor and billions of dollars to uncover the secret of the atom. It will take still a greater investment to gain the secrets of man's irrational nature. It is easier ... to smash an atom than a prejudice...."

GORDON ALLPORT (1954, P. XI)

(a)

(b)

(c)

Prejudice has a grim history, from the cross-burnings and lynchings of the Klu Klux Klan (a), to the Nazi concentration camps (b), to the more recent camps created by the Bosnian Serbs (c).

States. They noted that acts of racial violence tend to increase in times of economic recession, as people search for scapegoats, or targets for displaced anger (Dollard et al., 1939). For example, the rate of lynchings in the southern United States was inversely correlated with the price of cotton: The harder the economic times, the more lynchings. According to this theory, scapegoats bolster the self-esteem of prejudiced individuals by providing a rationalization for their unemployment or low status; that is, prejudice is a defense mechanism motivated by anger, anxiety, or feelings of low self-worth. More recent data support this hypothesis (Fein & Spencer 1997): Bolstering participants' self-esteem through positive feedback renders them less likely to evaluate a member of a stereotyped group negatively. Conversely, threatening their self-esteem through negative feedback seems to increase their tendency to derogate members of stereotyped groups, which then leads to increases in their own self-esteem.

According to one theory, some people are more likely to be attracted to racist ideology than others. In *The Authoritarian Personality,* Theodore Adorno and his colleagues (1950) isolated a particular personality style, called the **authoritarian personality,** characterized by a tendency to hate people who are different or downtrodden. They found that people who had a dominant, stern, and sometimes sadistic father and a submissive mother—interestingly, like the family of origin of Adolph Hitler—were more authoritarian than those who came from other kinds of families.

According to this explanation, the children in such families fear and hate their fathers, but these feelings are unacceptable to them and would be brutally punished if exposed, so they repress them. As adults, authoritarian individuals displace or project their rage onto groups such as Jews, blacks, homosexuals, or others who do not conform to social norms. Adorno and later researchers found that these personality dynamics were not limited to Nazi Germany but were present in every society studied. Despite criticism of Adorno's methodology, more recent work has supported many of the original findings (Christie, 1978; Snyder & Ickes, 1985), such as the link between this personality style and harsh parenting demanding strict obedience.

Subtle Racism

Psychodynamic concepts of conflict, ambivalence, and unconscious processes (Chapter 12) may be of some relevance to more recent cognitive approaches to prejudice. These approaches emerged from the observation that racism has changed in the last three decades, particularly in the United States. Today, overt racial discrimination against ethnic minorities is generally met with public disapproval. Gone are the days of separate buses, drinking fountains, and bathrooms for whites and blacks.

A Different Kind of Racism?   Several researchers contend, however, that new, more subtle kinds of racism exist in the wake of old-fashioned racism (Devine et al., 1991; Dovidio & Gaertner, 1993; Fiske, 1998). The precise nature of these kinds of racism is a matter of debate; researchers have focused on different types of subtle racism, in part because of changing social climates toward race over the last 25 years, and in part because of changes in theory and methods.

According to one theory developed in the 1970s, many people claim not to be racist but in fact hold one after another attitude that "just happens" to be unfavorable to minorities, such as attitudes toward welfare, immigration, affirmative action, tax breaks for wealthy people, and so forth (McConahay & Hough, 1976). Another kind of subtle racism occurs in people who experience a conflict between two attitudes (Katz & Hass, 1988). On the one hand, they believe in what the sociologist Max Weber called the *Protestant work ethic*, the idea that hard work is the key to "making it," with the implication that people who are not successful have simply not applied themselves. On the other hand, they believe in equality and recognize that all people in their society do not start out at the same place. This ambivalence leads to extreme responses, both positive and negative, depending on the context. This kind of person loved O.J. Simpson when he was a football star because he was smart, articulate, and had overcome the adversity of being black in the United States, and hated him when he appeared to match too closely the stereotype of the dangerous, criminal black male who cannot control his impulses.

Implicit and Explicit Racism   Another form of conflict is between explicit and implicit attitudes toward members of minority groups. Although old-style bigotry is certainly alive and well in some quarters, most people in the West today are explicitly opposed to racism. Nevertheless, like the African-American participants in Steele's studies described at the beginning of the chapter who found themselves prey to their implicit associations, most white people have absorbed negative attitudes toward people of color over the course of their lives (Dovidio & Gaertner, 1993). They (or perhaps, more honestly, we) often express nonbigoted views, but when acting or responding without much conscious attention, unconscious stereotypes slip through the cracks. For example, in ambiguous situations, whites tend to be less helpful to blacks than to other whites, and they are more likely to believe in stiffer penalties for black criminals.

In part, this discrepancy between what people say and what they do reflects a simple cognitive process. When people process information without much conscious thought, they are more likely to rely on stereotypes, to treat people as part of a category rather than as a specific individual (see Olson & Zanna, 1993). Negative stereotypes, like other attitudes, may thus be activated without awareness, as when a white man automatically checks his wallet after standing next to a young black man on the subway. Emotional arousal can also render people more susceptible to stereotypic thinking, in part because it draws limited attentional resources away from conscious reflection (Bodenhausen, 1993). The less people make conscious attributions, the more their unreflective, implicit attitudes prevail (Gilbert, 1995).

A growing body of research has begun to demonstrate just how different people's implicit and explicit racial attitudes can be (Greenwald et al., 1998). These studies have used priming procedures (Chapter 6), activating racial associations and then observing their effects on thought and behavior. In one of the first studies of this kind, the experimenter primed white subjects with words related to stereotypes of blacks, such as aggressive and lazy (Devine, 1989). Subjects then read information about a fictional character. Simply activating stereotypes related to blacks led subjects to rate the character more negatively (e.g., as more hostile) than subjects who were not primed with race-related words.

Another study found that people's implicit and explicit racial attitudes may be completely unrelated to each other—and may control different behavior (Fazio et al., 1995). To measure implicit attitudes, the investigators presented participants with a series of black and white faces followed by either a positive or a negative adjective. The participant's task was simply to press a key indicating whether the adjective was positive or negative. The theory behind the study was that negative attitudes are associatively connected to negative words (because they share the same emotional tone). Thus, the extent to which people have negative associations to blacks should be directly related to how quickly they recognize negative words after exposure to black faces. In other words, the speed with which participants respond to negative adjectives following priming with a black face can serve as a measure of their implicit attitudes toward blacks.

This measure of implicit attitudes was not related to measures of explicit racial attitudes, such as a questionnaire that taps racial attitudes or questions about the Rodney King beating and the riots that followed acquittal of the police officers who beat him. But it did predict something very important: their behavior toward a black confederate of the experimenter who met them at the end of the study. When the confederate simply rated the extent to which they seemed friendly and interested in what she had to say, participants who had responded more quickly to negative adjectives after priming with black faces received lower ratings—regardless of what they believed explicitly. In fact, whether or not participants held consciously racist attitudes bore no relation to the way they interacted with her. Conscious beliefs did, however, predict other conscious beliefs. These findings directly parallel the results of studies distinguishing implicit motives, which predict long-term behavioral trends (such as success in business), from explicit motives, which control behavior only when people are consciously thinking about them (Chapter 10).

A Connectionist Model of the Influence of Stereotypes on Judgments   Recently, researchers have applied connectionist models to social-cognitive and attitudinal phenomena such as stereotyping, demonstrating some of the ways implicit processes can affect ongoing thought and behavior (Kunda & Thagard, 1996). Consider what happens when a white person observes a white or black man shoving someone (Figure 17.4). The person could interpret the shove as an aggressive act (a violent push) or a playful, jovial shove. Because the person associates the category *black* with the trait *aggressive*, activation spreads from *black* to *aggressive* to *violent push,* and simultaneously inhibits interpretation of the action as a jovial shove (because the "weight" connecting the *violent push* and *jovial shove* nodes is strongly negative). In contrast, because *white* is not associated one way or the other with *aggressive* (or may actually be slightly negatively associated with it), less activation spreads to the *violent push* interpretation (represented as a node

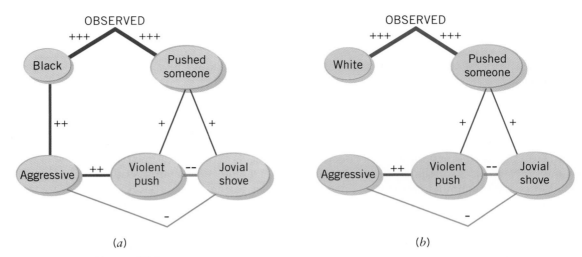

FIGURE 17.4

A connectionist model of the impact of stereotypes on inferences about behavior. The difference between the neural network that leads to interpretation of an ambiguous shove by a black man as a violent push (*a*) and the network that leads to a more benign interpretation of the same action performed by a white man (*b*) lies in the weights that connect the nodes of the networks (the circles). Blue lines indicate positive weights, red lines indicate negative weights (inhibitory connections between nodes), and the thickness of the lines indicates the strength of the connection (either positive or negative). Because *black* is strongly associated with *aggressive,* and *aggressive* activates *violent push* and inhibits *jovial shove* (as indicated by the red line between them), the first network is more likely to settle on the inference that the ambiguous action was a violent shove than the second network, which spreads less activation to that interpretation. *Source:* Adapted from Z. Kunda & P. Thagard (1996). Forming impressions from stereotypes, traits, and behaviors: A parallel-constraint-satisfaction theory. *Psych. Review,* 103, p. 286.

in a network). Thus, in an ambiguous situation, satisfaction of multiple constraints can lead to inferences that are biased by stereotypes.

Suppressing Implicit Racism   Implicit racism (or sexism or homophobia, which show quite similar properties) may interact with motivational factors. No one wants to be a hypocrite. When conscious beliefs and values conflict with deep-seated, automatic negative stereotypes, people may alternate between extreme positions, either laying excessive blame at the feet of members of devalued groups or refusing to hold them accountable for their behavior. Alternatively, they may learn to recognize their unconscious tendencies toward racist thinking and perpetually monitor their reactions to prevent racist attitudes from coloring their actions (Devine & Monteith, 1993).

Researchers have begun examining the conditions under which people will express or suppress their stereotypes. In one series of studies, the investigators used a simple manipulation—the presence of a mirror—to heighten participants' focus on themselves while responding to a questionnaire about the acceptability of stereotypes (Macrae, Bodenhausen, & Milne, 1998). The researchers hypothesized that under conditions of self-focus, people will be more likely to suppress stereotypic attitudes. That is precisely what they found: Participants in the mirror condition considered stereotyping less appropriate than control subjects without the mirror. However, suppressing a stereotype can lead to rebound effects, in which the person later responds even more stereotypically. In another study, participants were asked to evaluate a male hairdresser. After completing the task, the experimenter apologetically told them that some equipment had failed and asked

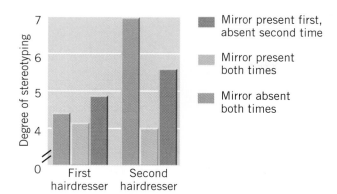

FIGURE 17.5
Stereotype suppression and rebound. Participants who initially suppressed their stereotype because of the presence of a mirror showed a rebound effect if the mirror was not present the second time. *Source:* Adapted from Macrae et al., 1998.

them to do the task again, this time evaluating another male hairdresser. Some participants had the mirror in the room both times, others had the mirror initially but not while evaluating the second hairdresser, and some had no mirror on either occasion. As predicted, those who had the mirror present initially produced less stereotypical descriptions of the first hairdresser. However, participants who had suppressed the stereotype the first time showed a substantial increase in stereotyping the second time if the mirror was removed (Figure 17.5). Thus, fighting a stereotype does not make it go away; in fact, it can intensify its expression when the person least expects it.

INTERIM SUMMARY **Stereotypes** are the characteristics attributed to people based upon their membership in groups. **Prejudice** means judging people based on (usually negative) stereotypes. An early approach to prejudice focused on a personality style called the **authoritarian personality,** characterized by a tendency to project blame and rage onto specific groups. Cognitive researchers have focused on more subtle forms of racism, many of which involve ambivalent attitudes. Of particular importance is implicit racism, which resides in the structure of people's associations toward members of minority groups rather than their explicit attitudes, and often controls everyday behavior unless they monitor and suppress it.

Prejudice and Social Conditions

In the late 1950s and 1960s, the civil rights movement in the United States was at its peak, and social scientists were optimistic about eradicating social evils such as poverty and racism. This optimism in part reflected research suggesting that the roots of prejudice lay less in personality dynamics than in social dynamics, particularly in socialization practices that teach children racist attitudes (Duckitt, 1992; Pettigrew, 1958).

Prejudice is indeed transmitted from one generation to the next, and it takes hold very early. In India, which has seen continued violence between Muslims and Hindus, children show signs of prejudice by age 4 or 5 (Saraswathi & Dutta, 1988). In multiethnic societies such as the United States, children from both minority and majority subcultures tend to express preferences toward the majority culture by the preschool years (see Spencer & Markstrom-Adams, 1990). Learning culturally patterned associations of this sort can make later identity formation difficult for adolescent members of devalued groups, who must somehow integrate a positive view of themselves with negative attitudes and stereotypes others hold of them. As demonstrated by Steele's research on negative stereotype activation in achievement situations, these associations can also lead to self-fulfilling prophecies, as people who fear they will fail begin to do so—and hence confirm the stereotype in their own and others' eyes.

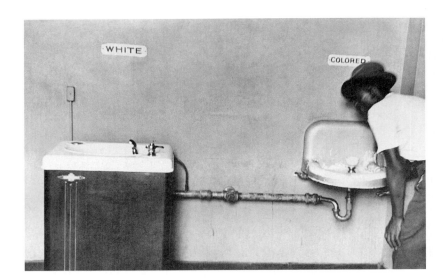

Scenes like this were commonplace in the American South 50 years ago.

The roots of prejudice may lie in social conditions in yet another way. Many theorists, from Karl Marx to contemporary sociologists, have argued that prejudiced social attitudes serve a function: They preserve the interests of the dominant classes. Promulgating the view that blacks are inferior justifies a social order in which whites hold disproportionate power, and teaching black children to devalue themselves discourages them from challenging white authority and persevering in the face of adversity. Disparities in wealth and property ownership often provide the fault lines around which societies crumble with ethnic strife because the haves and have-nots frequently differ in color, religion, or ethnicity.

Ingroups and Outgroups

Prejudice requires a distinction between **ingroups** and **outgroups**—people who belong to the group and those who do not. Human beings make these distinctions with astonishing rapidity, on even the most arbitrary bases (Brewer, 1979; Tajfel, 1981). The impact of ingroups and outgroups was demonstrated by a third-grade teacher named Jane Elliott (1977) in a remarkable classroom experiment in a rural, all-white community. To demonstrate what prejudice and discrimination feel like, Elliott one day announced that the brown-eyed children in her class were superior and the blue-eyed children, inferior. Within minutes, life changed in the classroom; before long, the brown-eyed children refused to play with their blue-eyed classmates and became vicious in their behavior, excluding them from activities. Friendships dissolved as children internalized their labels. The blue-eyed children began to think of themselves as stupid and bad, and their schoolwork deteriorated. When Elliott switched the group labels, placing the blue-eyed children in the superior ingroup and the brown-eyed children in the inferior outgroup, she observed the same type of behavior.

Us and Them   Similar ingroup–outgroup behavior occurs with adults and is particularly powerful in naturally occurring groups such as families, clans, or communities. It is manifestly apparent at sporting events, where taunting and physical violence may erupt between opposing fans whose only commonality lies in their identification with a city, school, or team. People tend to perceive members of outgroups as much more homogeneous than they really are and to emphasize the individuality of ingroup members (Judd & Park, 1988; Moreland, 1985;

Mullen & Hu, 1989). Thus, people of other races "all look alike," and members of other fraternities or sororities are seen to share many core traits—which is highly unlikely, given the tremendous differences in personality that exist within any group of people. In multicultural societies, however, members of minority groups tend to perceive more homogeneity within their own group than outside it, presumably as a way of maximizing identification with other members of their group.

Interpretations of other people's behavior also depend on their ingroup–outgroup status. One set of studies examined the way Hindu and Muslim students in Bangladesh explained the causes of helpful or unhelpful behavior presented in vignettes (Islam & Hewstone, 1993). Participants tended to attribute the helpful behavior of ingroup members to their goodness as a person and unhelpful behaviors to environmental circumstances. The reverse applied to outgroup members: Their positive acts were explained away and their negative behaviors attributed to enduring personality attributes.

Interestingly, these findings were much stronger for the majority Muslims than for the minority Hindus, who are socially disadvantaged and numerically outnumbered in Bangladesh. Weaker findings of this sort are common in minority groups cross-culturally and reflects two opposing mechanisms operating at once. On the one hand, minority groups tend to favor their ingroup because it is their own. On the other, they also show biases toward the majority culture, which is more socially valued in the broader society (see Fletcher & Ward, 1988).

Favoring the ingroup and denigrating the outgroup may at first appear to be polar opposites. However, we have seen in several chapters (11, 14, & 15), research on a number of seemingly unrelated phenomena—positive and negative affect, parental acceptance and rejection, positive and negative interactions in couples, and positive and negative components of attitudes—suggests that what look like opposite ends of a single dimension are often actually separate phenomena. The same is true with positive feelings toward ingroups and negative feelings toward outgroups (Brewer & Brown, 1998). In fact, in most situations, ingroup favoritism is more common than outgroup derogation or devaluation. This suggests that another form of subtle racism or group antagonism may lie less in the presence of hostile feelings than in the absence of the positive feelings that normally bind people together and lead them to help each other (Pettigrew & Meertens, 1995).

The readiness to create and act on ingroup–outgroup distinctions probably rests on both motivational and cognitive processes. From a motivational point of view, casting ingroup members in a positive light gives oneself a positive glow as a member of the group (Tajfel, 1981). In fact, one study showed that after watching their team win, basketball fans showed an increased belief in their abilities at an irrelevant task (Hirt et al., 1992). From a cognitive perspective, ingroup effects reflect the mind's continuous efforts to categorize and schematize information.

Reducing Group Antagonisms Research on ingroups and outgroups inevitably led to interest in techniques for reducing group antagonisms. In a classic experiment, researchers first created friction between two groups of boys, dubbed the Rattlers and the Eagles, at a Boy Scout summer camp (Sherif et al., 1961). The experimenters fostered the formation of strong ingroup sentiments by instructing the children in each group to give their group a name, wear special clothes, and so forth; they encouraged rivalries through competitive activities. Within a short time, the competition became so heated that it degenerated into overt hostility.

Initial attempts to defuse the hostility, such as bringing the groups together for pleasant activities, failed. Another approach was more successful: The experimenters contrived situations that created **superordinate goals**—goals requiring

Based on something as simple as team affiliation, soccer fans can attack each other, demonstrating the power of ingroup-outgroup dynamics.

the groups to cooperate for the benefit of all. In one instance, the experimenters arranged for a truck transporting food for an overnight trip to stall. Eventually, members of both groups cooperated in pulling the truck with a rope. Similar positive interactions occurred when the camp's water supply stopped and the boys from both groups were asked to help solve the problem.

The researchers concluded that contact alone is not enough to reduce conflict; the contact must also involve cooperation (see Sherif & Sherif, 1979). This finding has important implications for social policies such as school desegregation because it suggests that simply placing children from two different races in the same school may not minimize animosities; it may in fact exacerbate them (Stephan, 1987). Other factors that increase the likelihood that contact between groups will lead to reduced conflict rather than increased fear or anger include the potential to get to know one another on an individual basis and relatively equal status (Brewer & Brown, 1998), which is why racial tensions tend to be least noticeable in musical groups and on sports teams. People from different groups also need to have enough shared values, beliefs, interests, culture, and skills that their interactions dissolve stereotypes rather than confirm them. Unfortunately, many of these variables are precisely the ones on which members of various cultures and subcultures differ.

COMMENTARY
Is Prejudice Inevitable?

We are all members of races, ethnic groups, and socioeconomic classes that cherish their values and deliberately display the signs of their social identities. Perhaps to be human in an era of multiculturalism means brushing up against one of the givens of human nature—that what is different, what is "other," what speaks a different language and partakes of different rituals, can evoke fear, distrust, anger, or contempt. Unchecked by knowledge and self-reflection, those emotional reactions may elicit fight or flight.

We are also all members of social groups that enjoy privilege or suffer disadvantages. Thus, we can never address matters of race and prejudice without an underlying agenda of assuaging our guilt, justifying our privilege, or voicing our outrage.

These tensions provide the emotional undercurrent to every public policy debate remotely related to race or ethnicity, whether the issue is welfare, crime, or affirmative action. We are torn between the values we cherish and those we try to accept in others, between an explicit toleration or celebration of diversity and an implicit fear of it. The most dangerous thing we can do is to deny these conflicts within ourselves and remain unaware of the profound ambivalence we all have about people of different colors, ethnicities, and cultures. When we see a disproportionate number of violent crimes committed by people of color, we tend either to lay the blame on these "hoodlums" or on a society that relegates 20 percent of its population to poverty and yet calls itself civilized. Each response alone is a half-truth that resolves conflict and ambiguity at the expense of reality. To deny our ambivalence is to lead us inevitably and unknowingly to continue to judge people, as Martin Luther King, Jr. so eloquently decried, by the color of their skin—or to fail to judge others who deserve our condemnation for the content of their character.

INTERIM SUMMARY Prejudice lies not only in people's minds but in social institutions and socialization practices that foster it. Prejudice requires a distinction between **ingroups** and **outgroups** (people who belong to the group and those who do not). People often attribute more homogeneity to outgroups than ingroups, and make more positive interpretations of the behavior of ingroup members. Ingroup–outgroup distinctions probably reflect both motivational and cognitive factors. Contact between groups can increase rather than decrease prejudice and hostility unless it is accompanied by shared goals, the possibility of personal acquaintance with members of the outgroup, relatively equal status, and enough shared values and culture to dissolve rather than enhance stereotypes.

ATTRIBUTION

Whether trying to understand the causes of inner-city violence or a terse response from a boss, people are constantly thinking about the "whys" of social interaction. The process of inferring the causes of one's own and others' mental states and behaviors is called **attribution.** Attribution plays a central role in virtually every social encounter. For example, the inferences a person makes about her boss's terseness ("Is he trying to tell me something?") can influence her feelings about her boss and ultimately her behavior, such as the decision to look for new employment. The attributions a student makes for a weak performance on a test, as in the example that opened this chapter, can affect her motivation, self-concept, and level of effort in the future.

The extent to which attributions infiltrate virtually every interpersonal decision can be seen in legal decision making. If someone is killed by a handgun, the slayer could be convicted of first-degree murder if the judge or jury determines that his act was both intended and premeditated. Alternatively, the gunman could be convicted of second-degree murder (intention to kill, no planning), manslaughter (no intention), or no crime (accidental mishandling of a gun). In sentencing, the judge may decrease the severity of the sentence if he attributes the murderer's behavior in part to mental illness or a deprived childhood.

Intuitive Science

People attribute causes by observing the covariation of different social stimuli or events, such as situations, people, or behaviors. In other words, they try to assess the extent to which the presence of one variable tends to predict the presence of another (the extent to which they vary together, or co-vary) (Heider, 1958; Kelley, 1973, 1992). The employee who receives a terse reponse to a question may have observed that her boss is always brusque when he is stressed by approaching deadlines. Thus, she attributes his behavior to the situation rather than to his feelings about her.

When people make attributions, they are acting like **intuitive scientists**: They rely on intuitive theories, frame hypotheses, collect data about themselves and others, and draw conclusions as best they can based on the pattern of data they have observed (Heider, 1958; Ross, 1977). In the language of connectionism, they are essentially trying to settle on a solution that takes into account as many of the constraints they have observed as possible.

Making Inferences

Understanding other people's behavior requires trying to figure out when their actions reflect demands of the situation, aspects of their personalities (often called personality *dispositions*), or interactions between the two (the ways specific people behave in particular situations). Thus, people sometimes make **external attribu-**

tions (attributions to the situation), whereas other times they make **internal attributions** (attributions to the person) (Chapter 5). Often they combine the two, as when the employee concludes that her boss tends to become tense and brusque (internal, or dispositional, attribution) when he is stressed by deadlines (external, or situational, attribution).

In making attributions to the person or the situation, people rely on three types of information: consensus, consistency, and distinctiveness (Kelley, 1973, 1979). If everyone in the organization responds tersely to her questions, the employee might attribute her boss's brusque behavior to something situational (such as the organizational culture, or atmosphere of the company) because her boss's behavior is a normative, or **consensus** response. **Consistency** refers to the extent to which the person always responds in the same way to the same stimulus. If her boss is frequently brusque, the employee will likely make an internal attribution. The **distinctiveness** of a person's action refers to the individual's likelihood to respond this way to many different stimuli. Does her boss treat other people this way? If so, she is likely to conclude that brusqueness is an enduring aspect of his personality. Consistency and distinctiveness are the "intuitive scientist's" versions of the concepts of consistency across time and consistency over situations debated by personality psychologists (Chapter 12).

Part of the difficulty in making accurate attributions is that most actions have multiple causes, some situational and some dispositional. In deciding how much to credit or blame a person, people generally adjust for the strength of situational demands through two processes, discounting and augmentation. **Discounting** occurs when people downplay (discount) the role of one variable (such as personality, intelligence, or skill) because they know that others may be contributing to the behavior in question (Heider, 1958; McClure, 1998). A judge may discount the responsibility of a defendant accused of murder because of mental illness, or the employee may discount her boss's bad manners because he is under the strain of an approaching deadline.

The opposite situation occurs with **augmentation,** which means increasing (augmenting) an internal attribution for behavior that has occurred despite situational pressures. The judge may perceive the defendant as particularly morally deficient because he continued to shoot the person repeatedly after he already appeared dead, or the employee may attribute particular coldness to her boss when he continues to respond tersely to her questions when the workload is low.

Making an attribution is typically a three-step process (Gilbert, 1995). First, people categorize the behavior they have observed. They might look at a facial expression and decide that it is angry, or hear a comment and conclude that it is provocative. Next, they categorize the actor's personality based on the way they have interpreted the behavior. An aggressive comment may thus imply a hostile person. Finally, they correct their inference if features of the situation were likely to have elicited the behavior. For instance, they may discount the attribution of hostility when they recognize that the comment was provoked.

Interestingly, once people have identified an action, they are likely to make internal attributions automatically and unconsciously and only correct them with conscious effort. Experimental participants who are distracted while making attributions tend to make internal attributions even when situational variables call for discounting because they have no time to reflect and correct their initial impression (Gilbert, 1995).

INTERIM SUMMARY   **Attribution** is the process of inferring the causes of one's own and others' mental states and behaviors. People attribute causes by observing the covariation of social stimuli or events. People are like **intuitive scientists,** who use intuitive theories, frame hypotheses, and try to draw inferences from the data they have collected. They sometimes make **external attributions** (attributions to the situation), **internal attributions** (attributions to the person), or attributions that reflect the interaction of the two.

▶ **ONE STEP FURTHER**

Self-Attribution

People not only make inferences about the causes of other people's actions; they also attribute causes to their own psychological processes, a process called **self-attribution.** The notion of self-attribution may seem counterintuitive because we tend to assume we have direct access to our own psychological processes. However, people are only conscious of a subset of the events that occur in their minds (Chapter 9) and hence must make educated guesses about their own personalities or the causes of their own actions.

In one study, male participants were asked to rate the attractiveness of photos of nude women while hearing what they believed were their own heartbeats (Valins, 1966). When the "heart" beat faster, participants rated the photos as more attractive. Apparently, they thought that if their heart was beating faster, they must be aroused and assumed the photos were the cause.

In another experiment, male participants crossed either a wobbly suspension bridge high over a canyon, which tended to generate anxiety, or a solid bridge only 10 feet above a brook (Dutton & Aron, 1974). As each participant crossed the bridge, an attractive female research assistant approached and asked him to complete a short questionnaire indicating his interpretaion of some ambiguous pictures of people. Afterward, she gave him her phone number in case he had questions about the study or its results. As predicted, participants on the suspension bridge not only found more sexual themes in the pictures, but they were also much more likely to call the woman. The arousal that occurred on the wobbly suspension bridge was fear, but participants misattributed it to sexual arousal because of the presence of the attractive research assistant. In general, arousal of this sort increases attraction if people do not realize where the feeling is coming from; if they figure out its source, they discount the feeling in making inferences about how attracted they really are (Foster et al., 1998).

Surprisingly, people apply the discounting and augmentation principles to themselves as well as to others. In a study exploring the self-perception of humor, participants listened to two sets of jokes, with a laugh track accompanying one set (Olson, 1992). In one condition, the experimenter told participants that canned laughter increases the perceived humor of jokes. He informed another group that canned laughter actually *decreases* perceived humor, and he told the control group that canned laughter has no effect whatsoever. The logic of the experiment was that people who believe canned laughter enhances the comic appeal should discount the humor of the jokes accompanied by laugh tracks. By contrast, participants who are led to believe that canned laughter diminishes enjoyment should augment for jokes accompanied by the laugh track.

After participants listened to the two sets of jokes, the experimenter left the room, encouraging them to read either of two books from which the jokes had been extracted. The results were as predicted (Table 17.1). Participants who were led to believe that the laugh track inflated their enjoyment

TABLE 17.1	SELF-ATTRIBUTION		
	AVERAGE NUMBER OF SECONDS WITH EACH BOOK		
	TOLD THAT CANNED LAUGHTER INCREASES PERCEIVED HUMOR	TOLD THAT CANNED LAUGHTER DECREASES PERCEIVED HUMOR	TOLD THAT CANNED LAUGHTER HAS NO EFFECT
With laugh track	54.5	117.6	88.3
Without laugh track	107.2	48.1	90.0

Source: Adapted from Olson, 1992, p. 373.

of jokes spent twice as much time reading jokes from the book that had been presented without the laugh track. Participants who believed the laugh track had diminished their mirth spent twice as much time with the joke book that had been "ruined" by the laugh track. Participants in the control condition were as likely to read one book as the other.

BIASES IN SOCIAL INFORMATION PROCESSING

Although individuals often act like intuitive scientists, the "studies" of everyday people often have substantial methodological shortcomings. Indeed, rigorous application of scientific method is so important in social psychology precisely because it prevents researchers from making the same kinds of intuitive errors we all make in everyday life.

Social psychologists have identified several biases in social information processing. Here we examine two of the most widely studied and then explore the cognitive and motivational roots of biases in social cognition.

Correspondence Bias

One of the most pervasive biases in social cognition is the tendency to attribute behaviors to people's personalities and to ignore possible situational causes (Gilbert & Mallone, 1995; Heider, 1958; Ross, 1977). This assumption, that people's behavior corresponds to their internal states rather than external situations, is called the **correspondence bias.** A good example occurs while driving. Whereas in my clinical work I tend to be very careful before drawing conclusions about a patient's personality, I have no such caution on the road, where I seem to be able to make diagnoses of other drivers with extraordinary rapidity. I may, for example, draw highly sophisticated inferences about a person's character (e.g., "what a jerk!") from the fact that he is holding me up on my way to work by driving slowly—only to recognize when I see his license plate that he is from another state and probably has no idea where he is going.

A classic set of studies explored this bias during the height of U.S. tensions with Cuba (Jones & Harris, 1967). Participants read or listened to a discourse in support of or against Fidel Castro's regime. The experimenters led half the participants to believe the attitude was the author's and told the other half that the author had been instructed which position to take.

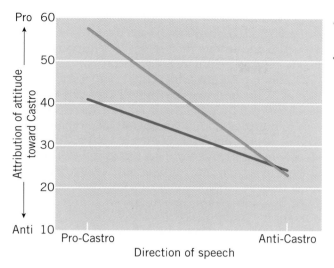

FIGURE 17.6

The correspondence bias. Participants attributed pro-Castro sentiment to speakers who spoke positively of the Castro regime even when informed that the speaker had to take a pro-Castro position. *Source:* Adapted from Jones, 1976, p.301.

Listeners assumed the anti-Castro speech represented the speaker's point of view regardless of whether they were told that it reflected the speaker's own attitude because virtually everyone in the United States at that time was anti-Castro. The more striking finding was that participants who listened to the pro-Castro speech tended to overestimate the pro-Castro position of the speaker even when they had been informed that the author had been assigned a point of view (Figure 17.6). In other words, they attributed the speaker's behavior to internal dispositions even though they knew otherwise.

Although the correspondence bias appears to be common in the West, it may not be universal. Because contemporary Western culture is individualistic, Western subjects tend to emphasize individual responsibility when they make attributions. People outside Western technologically developed societies are more likely to believe that external factors control their lives. For example, one study asked subjects from India and the United States to explain why someone might have carried out various socially acceptable and deviant acts (Miller, 1984). Indian subjects were far less likely to make internal attributions and more likely to explain behavior in terms of social roles and responsibilities. Their responses may reflect not only different cultural explanatory systems but also differences in reality: Indians may well be more heavily influenced or constrained in their behavior by role demands and social obligations (Fletcher & Ward, 1988).

Self-Serving Bias

Another pervasive bias in social cognition is the **self-serving bias:** People tend to see themselves in a more positive light than others see them (Baumeister, 1998; Epstein, 1992; Greenwald, 1980). The self-serving bias takes a number of forms. For example, a majority of people rate themselves above average on most dimensions, which is, of course, statistically impossible (Taylor & Brown, 1988). People are more likely to recall positive than negative information about themselves (Kuiper & Derry, 1982; Kuiper et al., 1985), to see their talents as more striking and unusual than their deficiencies (Campbell, 1986), and to attribute greater respon-

Most of these people believe they are smarter, more personable, and better looking than the person next to them.

sibility to themselves for a group product than other group members attribute to them (Ross & Sicoly, 1979). Similarly, both partners in divorced couples are more likely to see themselves as the victim and to rate themselves less responsible for the breakup and as more willing to reconcile (Gray & Silver, 1990).

Self-serving biases are not without their limits. Most people will not totally ignore reality to perceive themselves in the best possible light. Extroverts who are induced to believe that extroversion is not conducive to academic success start to see themselves as less extroverted, but they do not completely deny their extroversion (see Kunda, 1990).

People also differ tremendously in their tendency to let their needs for self-enhancement interfere with their objectivity. One study observed MBA students interacting over a weekend (John & Robins, 1994). Groups of six students each participated in simulated corporate decision-making meetings. At the end of the weekend, participants ranked themselves and their peers as to who had done the best, second best, and so on, from one to six. Eleven psychologist observers also ranked each participant.

Participants' were fairly objective in ranking their peers' performance; peer and psychologist rankings correlated at about .50. However, they were less objective about themselves. The correlation between self-rankings and psychologist rankings was only about .30. Moreover, 60 percent overestimated their own performance, suggesting a self-serving bias.

Does this mean that people routinely ignore the data to make themselves feel better? Perhaps, but with two substantial qualifications (Table 17.2). First, roughly 50 percent of participants ranked themselves (from 1 to 6) within one rank of the way psychologists and their peers ranked them. Thus, within bounds, half of all subjects were reasonably accurate in their self-perceptions.

Second, the one-third who overestimated themselves by two or more ranks had a distinguishing characteristic: They were more *narcissistic,* that is, self-aggrandizing and self-centered. The tendency to self-enhance in this study correlated around .50 with objective observers' ratings of participants' narcissism. Clinicians suggest that narcissists are prone to distort their accomplishments in order to compensate for underlying feelings of worthlessness or self-doubt (Kernberg, 1975). This study thus suggests that most people wear mildly rose-tinted glasses when they look in the mirror, but people who are narcissistic keep a pair of opaque spectacles on hand in case the spotlight shines too brightly on their flaws.

Like the correspondence bias, the self-serving bias may also depend in part on cultural factors (Kitayama et al., 1998). The bias is pervasive in the West but much less so in Eastern and other collectivist cultures in which people do not define themselves as much in terms of their individual accomplishments. When people in the U.S. describe themselves, they tend to list about five times as many positive as negative traits (Holmberg et al., 1995). This pattern is unheard of in cultures such as Japan and Korea, where people do not toot their horns so loudly, either in private or in public. Recent research suggests that as Asians become assimilated into Western culture, their conscious self-descriptions begin to show the Western bias, but that deeper, implicit processes (assessed, for example, by the speed with which people recognize the words *good* and *bad* after priming with the word *me*) may take a generation to change (Pelham et al., 1998, cited in Kitayama et al., 1998).

Causes of Biases

What causes biases in processing social information? The answers appear to lie in both cognition and motivation.

TABLE 17.2 SELF-SERVING BIASES AND NARCISSISM

(a)

SELF-RANKINGS	COMPARISON	
	PEER RANKINGS	PSYCHOLOGIST RANKINGS
Overestimate > one rank	31%	32%
Within one rank	54%	53%
Underestimate > one rank	15%	15%

(b)

NARCISSISM	SELF-ENHANCEMENT	
	COMPARED WITH PEER RANKINGS	COMPARED WITH PSYCHOLOGIST RANKINGS
Observer rating	.55	.49
Self-report	.34	.38

Source: Adapted from John & Robins, 1994.

Note: Part (*a*) shows the relative accuracy of subjects' self-rankings compared to the way their peers and neutral observers ranked them. Part (*b*) shows the correlations between narcissism scores and the extent to which subjects' self-rankings were inflated when compared to the way they were ranked by peers and psychologists.

Cognitive Biases   Some of the errors people make reflect the same kinds of cognitive biases people display in nonsocial cognition (Chapter 7). For example, people often see what they expect to see and fail to test alternative hypotheses (false confirmation of schemas). This frequently occurs with stereotypes, when the perceiver discounts the implications of meeting a member of a category who does not fit the stereotype by concluding that "she's an exception." A similar process is familiar to many students who have come home from college only to find their parents continuing to see them in an old light, interpreting their behavior through schemas that do not reflect changes they have made, or continuing to impose role schemas more appropriate for a child.

Heuristics (cognitive shortcuts) can lead to biases in social thinking as well, as when people assume that "all politicians are crooks" because of some salient examples that come to mind (the availability heuristic). In fact, one of the main reasons politicians often appear crooked is that their behavior is more closely scrutinized, with the media closely examining their tax returns, business dealings, and so forth. (This example probably just came to mind because I am being audited by the Internal Revenue Service about 6 hours from now—a good example of priming in social cognition.)

People frequently lack the time or information they need to make accurate attributions, so they do the best they can. Often, these rapid, good-enough attributions are just that—good enough. On the other hand, phrases like "I had no idea he would turn out to be that way," or "I can't believe I didn't see that" express the regrets people often feel when they discounted or failed to piece together some initial "clues" about someone with whom they had the misfortune of becoming romantically involved.

Motivational Biases   Other biases reflect motivation (Bruner & Tagiuri, 1954; Fiske, 1992; Kunda, 1990; Westen, 1991, in press). Schemas and attributions are influenced by wishes, needs, and goals. For example, people who are currently involved in romantic relationships tend to perceive opposite-sex peers as

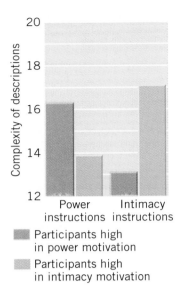

FIGURE 17.7
Motivation and the complexity of social cognition. When the instructions stressed power, participants high in power motivation showed greater cognitive complexity in describing potential research assistants. When the instructions stressed intimacy, participants high in intimacy motivation thought more complexly. *Source:* Woike & Aronoff, 1992, p. 102.

less attractive and sexually desirable than people who are uninvolved (Simpson et al., 1990). This bias is useful because it makes maintaining a monogamous relationship easier.

Motivation can also influence the extent to which people think complexly about themselves and others, as documented in a study comparing people high in need for intimacy with those high in need for power (Woike & Aronoff, 1992). Participants were asked to evaluate potential research assistants by watching them interact with each other on videotape. In one condition, the investigators emphasized the need to be sensitive and empathic toward the applicant. In the other condition, the investigators stressed the importance of taking control of the situation and exercising decision-making power.

After watching the videotapes, the researchers instructed participants to describe the candidates and then coded their responses for the complexity of their social cognition. The investigators reasoned that participants motivated by power would think more deeply and complexly when their power motives were activated, and those high in intimacy motivation would think more complexly when motivated by instructions emphasizing intimacy. These findings were strongly confirmed (Figure 17.7), suggesting that the extent to which people think deeply about others depends on their motivation to do so.

Motivated biases can occur at the societal or national level as well as the personal. Nations on the verge of war systematically distort their attributions about the motives of the other side, often portraying the enemy—but not themselves, of course—as interested in little else but power (Winter, 1987, 1993). Even Abraham Lincoln, not a person known for biased thinking, declared in his Second Inaugural Address, "Both parties depreciated war, but one of them would make war rather than let the nation survive, and the other would accept war rather than let it perish, and the war came."

Lincoln's biased attributions were shared by his countrymen, as demonstrated in a study of motives attributed by Northern and Southern newspapers to Lincoln and his Confederate counterpart, Jefferson Davis, following a series of speeches in 1861 (Winter, 1987). The Northern media exaggerated Davis's power motivation, whereas the Southern media diminished Lincoln's motives for affiliation (Figure 17.8). Similar biases have been documented in British and German newspapers from World War I (Winter, 1993) and have been apparent in more re-

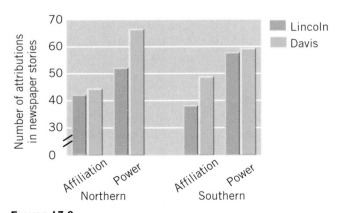

FIGURE 17.8
Motives attributed to Lincoln and Davis by Northern and Southern newspapers. Northern newspapers saw Davis as power hungry, whereas Southern newspapers saw Lincoln as unaffiliative (rather ironically, since he was trying to keep the South from disaffiliating). *Source:* Adapted from Winter, 1987, p. 44.

cent international conflicts, such as Saddam Hussein's repeated conflicts with George Bush and Bill Clinton.

If people are intuitive scientists, then, research suggests that they could use some basic courses in research design. Aside from cognitive errors, social perceivers have many goals besides the scientific objective of seeking truth, and these other agendas often influence their "findings." They are interested in looking good, maintaining positive feelings about themselves, believing good things will happen to them, protecting their idealized views of people they care about, and maintaining negative schemas of people (or groups) they dislike. Because motives play a fundamental role in attention, encoding, retrieval, and problem solving, social cognition is inherently intertwined with social motivation (see Fiske, 1993).

INTERIM SUMMARY The **correspondence bias** is the tendency to attribute behaviors to people's personalities and to ignore possible situational causes. The **self-serving bias** is the tendency to see oneself in a more positive light than one deserves. Biases in social cognition reflect both cognitive factors (such as the use of heuristics) and motivational factors (the impact of wishes, needs, and goals).

THE SELF

Thus far, we have paid little attention to the social stimulus to which people attend more than any other: the self. The concept of self has a long and rather serpentine history in psychology, slithering in and out of vogue. In some eras, such as the present, psychologists have viewed the self as a central aspect of psychological functioning (Epstein, 1994; Markus & Cross, 1990). In others, particularly during the heyday of behaviorism, psychologists viewed the self as a fuzzy, mushy concept, unobservable and hence scientifically unknowable.

One of the greatest challenges in describing the self seems to be defining it. Many behaviorists justifiably complain that psychologists have used the same word to denote dozens of discrete phenomena and hence have failed to provide a coherent, empirically valid view of the self. For years, theorists of nearly every persuasion have defined the self as the self-concept—the way people see themselves. The problem with this definition is that it is logically impossible: If the self-concept is a concept of something, it must be a concept of the self. The self, then, cannot be a self-concept, or the self-concept becomes a person's concept of her self-concept. This is analogous to saying that a person's lamp and her concept of the lamp are the same thing.

The only logically sensible definition, then, is that the **self** is the person, including mental processes, body, and personality characteristics. From this definition several others logically follow. The **self-concept** is the person's concept of herself; it is a concept like any other (Chapter 7), such as squirrel, tree, or hairdresser; **self-esteem** refers to the degree to which the person likes, respects, or esteems the self; and so forth.

APPROACHES TO THE SELF

William James (1890) proposed a fundamental distinction between self as subject and self as object. The self as subject includes the person's experience of self as thinker, feeler, and actor. When I feel an emotion or think a thought, it is "I"—the *self as subject*—who is feeling or thinking. When I take an action, I have a sense that it is I who has made a choice about how to behave. In contrast, the *self as ob-*

ject is the person's view of the self. This is the self-concept on which people reflect when they take the self as an object of thought. The difference between self as subject and as object can be easily remembered grammatically: The self as subject, which James called the "I," is the subject who is capable of thinking about the self as object, the "me." Thus, the statement, "I am thinking about me," contains both elements of self.

Two perspectives have recently given increasing prominence to the self: the psychodynamic and the cognitive (see Baumeister, 1998; Westen, 1992).

Psychodynamic Perspective

Contemporary psychodynamic thinking focuses on **self-representations**—mental models or representations of the self. Object relations theories assert that people's representations of themselves and others play a key role in personality and psychopathology (Chapter 12). Patients with borderline personality disorders, for example, often view themselves as totally unlovable or evil to the core, which can make them vulnerable to suicide (Gunderson, 1984; Kernberg, 1975; Wixom et al., 1993). Most people have multiple emotional states associated with their self-representations, which are activated under various conditions (Horowitz, 1988). For example, a person may have generally positive feelings about herself but be vulnerable to feelings of shame or anxiety about her appearance that get activated by looking in a mirror or having someone look at her.

Self-representations can be conscious or unconscious, explicit or implicit (Sandler & Rosenblatt, 1962). Explicit and implicit representations of self can be at odds or even completely contradictory. One patient with a narcissistic personality disorder was furious and deeply depressed when he was passed over for a supervisory position. At some level he worried that his own failings were the cause, but he convinced himself that the only reason he was passed over was because "mediocrity cannot appreciate true genius." This consciously grandiose representation seemed to mask a very different unconscious or implicit view of himself.

The psychodynamic view of self is thus converging in many respects with contemporary attitude research in emphasizing the likelihood of ambivalence (especially given all the ways we evaluate ourselves) and the distinction between implicit and explicit self-representations. In this sense, the self-concept is essentially an attitude toward the self, which includes beliefs, feelings, and tendencies to behave toward oneself in particular ways.

Cognitive Perspective

Cognitive theorists focus on the way the self-concept shapes thought and memory (see Greenwald & Pratkanis, 1984; Higgins, 1990; Markus & Cross, 1990). Arguing that people are intuitive scientists even when examining themselves, one theorist has proposed that the self-concept is like a theory of oneself (Epstein, 1973, 1994). A good self-theory should have the virtues of a good scientific theory, such as accuracy and internal consistency.

Other cognitive theorists propose that the self-concept is a **self-schema**—a schema about the self—that guides the way we think about and remember information relevant to ourselves (Kuiper & Rogers, 1977; Markus, 1977; Markus & Wurf, 1987). Thus, a person who has a self-schema of herself as incompetent is likely to remember times she failed in exquisite detail, and perhaps to forget occasions in which she was skillful or successful.

Self-schemas may be hierarchically organized (Kihlstrom & Cantor, 1983). At the core of the broader self-schema are fundamental attributes of the self, such as the person's name, sex, physical appearance, relationships to family members,

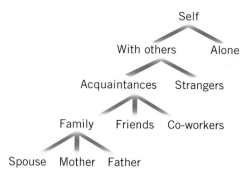

FIGURE 17.9
Hierarchical organization of a self-schema. Self-schemas may be organized hierarchically with multiple components, many defined by relationships, such as the self with family, friends, and co-workers. *Source:* Kihlstrom & Cantor, 1983.

and salient personality traits. Below this general level in the hierarchy are schemas of the self in different situations or relationships (Figure 17.9). Each sub-schema is associated with its own attributes; a person may see herself as annoyed and anxious with her mother but comfortable with friends.

FROM MIND TO BRAIN

PHYSICAL HEALTH AND VIEWS OF THE SELF

People have schemas not only about the way they are but also about the way they wish they were or fear becoming (Markus & Nurius, 1986; Nieden-thal et al., 1992). One theory distinguishes three kinds of self-concepts: actual, ideal, and ought (Higgins, 1987, 1990). The **actual self** refers to people's views of how they actually are. The **ideal self** refers to the hopes, aspirations, and wishes that define the way the person would like to be. The **ought self** includes the duties, obligations, and responsibilities that define the way the person should be.

Thus, a person may see himself as a moderately successful businessman (actual self) but hope to become the chief executive officer of a company (ideal self). At the same time, he may volunteer at a soup kitchen on Thanksgiving to satisfy a nagging sense that he is not contributing enough to his community (ought self). People have actual, ideal, and ought selves from a number of points of view, including their own and those of significant others. A person may feel she is meeting her "ought" standards for herself but that she has failed to meet her mother's expectations.

Discrepancies between these various self-schemas are associated with particular types of emotion (Higgins, 1987; Strauman, 1992). When people perceive discrepancy between their actual self and their ideal self, they tend to feel emotions such as disappointment, dissatisfaction, shame, and embarrassment. These are characteristic feelings of individuals who are depressed, who feel their wishes and hopes are unfulfilled. People who experience a discrepancy between actual self and ought self feel emotions such as anxiety, fear, resentment, guilt, self-contempt, or uneasiness. These feelings are characteristic of anxious individuals, who believe they have failed to meet their obligations and hence may be punished.

Research suggests that these schemas may influence not only mood but physical health. As we have seen (Chapter 11), emotional distress can depress immune-system functioning, making a person vulnerable to ill health. Enduring ways of perceiving the self may thus lead to chronic feelings that increase vulnerability to illness.

One remarkable study demonstrated this by comparing people who were anxious, depressed, or neither (Strauman et al., 1993). The investigators asked participants to describe their actual, ideal, and ought selves, thanked them for their participation, and told them the experiment was over. Six weeks later, their research assistants, allegedly conducting a different experiment, primed discrepancies between actual and ideal self in depressed participants and between actual and ought self in anxious participants; they did this by exposing them to words they had previously mentioned that were related to these discrepancies. For example, the investigators might ask an anxious subject who described his actual self as shy but his ought self as confident to think about the importance of being confident. (They also included words that were irrelevant to the person so that participants would not figure out what was happening.) A week later, the experimenters exposed participants to a set of entirely irrelevant words (actually, taken from other participants), which they compared against the results of the previous session. Control subjects were similarly exposed one day to self-referential words and another day to irrelevant words. After each session, the investigators took blood samples to ascertain levels of natural killer cells, a rough index of immune response.

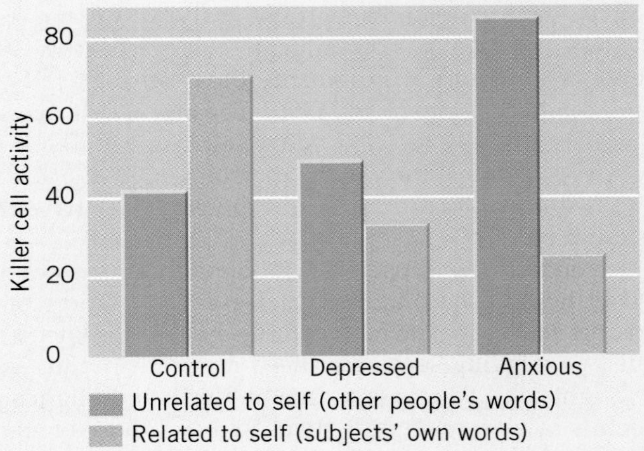

FIGURE 17.10
Self-schemas and immune functioning. Exposing nondepressed, nonanxious control subjects to words related to their ideal and ought selves led to a slight increase in killer cell activity—that is, to heightened immune functioning. For depressed and especially for anxious subjects, in contrast, exposure led to diminished immune functioning. *Source:* Adapted from Strauman et al., 1993, p. 1049.

The main findings are reproduced in Figure 17.10. The killer cell activity of control subjects, who were neither depressed nor anxious, went up slightly when they were exposed to self-referential words. Depressed subjects showed a slight decrease in killer cell activity when exposed to words related to their ideal-self discrepancies, although this was not statistically significant. The most striking finding was for anxious subjects, whose killer cell levels were significantly lower after being exposed to words related to their self-perceived failings (actual/ought discrepancies). Thinking about their unfulfilled obligations or unmet standards made them momentarily more vulnerable to illness. These findings are preliminary, but they strongly suggest that chronic discrepancies between the way one believes one is and the way one ought or ideally should be might have a lasting impact on health.

INTERIM SUMMARY   The **self** refers to the person, including mental processes, body, and personality characteristics. William James distinguished the self as subject, which includes the person's experience of self as thinker, feeler, and actor; and the self as object, or **self-concept** (the person's view or concept of self). Contemporary psychodynamic thinking focuses on **self-representations,** mental models or representations of the self that are typically associated with multiple emotional states and can be implicit or explicit. According to some cognitive theorists, the self-concept is a **self-schema,** or schema about the self, which may be hierarchically organized. People have schemas not only about the way they are but the way they ideally would like to be and ought to be.

SELF-ESTEEM

People have multiple motives that guide the way they think about themselves, such as the motive to see themselves accurately (Baumeister, 1998). As we saw in considering research on self-serving biases, one of the other main motives regarding the self, which often competes with accuracy motivation, is the motivation to maintain self-esteem (Chapter 10). Just as individuals can conjure up a typical or prototypical self-concept, they have a core or global sense of self-esteem (Rosenberg, 1979), a usual way they feel about themselves. They also experience momentary fluctuations in self-esteem, depending on which self-schemas are currently active. An athlete who wins a competition sees herself as a winner and enjoys a momentary boost in self-esteem, regardless of whether being a winner is part of her prototypical self-concept.

Research with Western subjects suggests that self-esteem is hierarchically organized, presumably tied to a hierarchically organized view of the self. Thus, nested below a general level of self-esteem, people have feelings about themselves along specific dimensions, such as their morality, physical appearance, and competence (Coopersmith, 1967; Harter 1998). A person with generally low esteem for his athletic prowess may nevertheless recognize himself to be a decent tennis player. People generally maintain positive self-esteem by giving greater emotional weight to areas in which they are more successful.

Men and women appear to differ in the way they derive self-esteem. Men tend to gain esteem by emphasizing their distinctiveness compared to others—particularly their superiority. Women tend to derive more of their esteem from their capacity to connect with other people (Josephs et al., 1992). To what degree this distinction is changing as gender roles converge is an open question, as women gain more self-esteem from their feelings of competence at work and men increasingly appreciate their ability to nurture and connect with others.

SELF-CONSISTENCY

A less obvious motive toward the self is **self-consistency.** People are motivated to interpret information to fit the way they already see themselves, and they prefer people who verify rather than challenge their views of themselves (Lecky, 1945; Swann, 1990). Most of the time, self-consistency and self-esteem motives produce similar effects. Because most people hold relatively favorable views of themselves, they prefer positive information because it enhances self-esteem and bolsters their existing self-concept.

For people who do not like themselves, however, these two motives can lead them in opposite directions. They want to feel better about themselves, but they also dislike evidence that conflicts with their self-concept. Depressed people actually prefer to interact with others—including marital partners—who have a negative view of them (Chapter 15). Individuals who perceive themselves negatively appear to avoid people who give them feedback to the contrary for several reasons: They consider the feedback untrue, they feel that the relationship will be smoother and more predictable if the other person understands them, and they believe people who view them positively are less perceptive (Swann et al., 1992).

A GLOBAL VISTA

CULTURE AND SELF

The notion that people have a self-concept and some core of selfhood that distinguishes them from others seems intuitively obvious to people living in 20th-century Western societies. This view would not, however, be commonsensical to people in most cultures in most historical epochs (Geertz, 1974; Markus & Kitayama, 1991; Shweder & Bourne, 1982). That the phrase, "the individual" is synonymous with "the person" in contemporary usage demonstrates how the individualism of our culture is reflected in its language. Not coincidentally, the prefix "self-," as in "self-esteem" or "self-representation," did not evolve in the English language until around the time of the Industrial Revolution.

A Relational View of the Self

The contemporary Western view of "the person" is of a bounded individual, distinct from others, who is defined by more or less idiosyncratic attributes. In contrast, most cultures, particularly the nonliterate tribal societies that existed throughout the vast expanse of human history, view the person in her social and familial context, so that the self-concept is far less distinctly bounded. When the Wintu Indians of North America described being with another person who was closely related or intimate with them, they would not use a phrase such as "John and I," but rather, "John we." They reserved "and" to signify distance between people with minimal relation. When anthropologist Dorothy Lee (1950) tried to elicit an autobiography from a

Wintu woman, she received an extensive account of the lives of the woman's ancestors. Only with considerable prompting did the woman eventually discuss "that which was in my mother's womb." Cheyenne autobiographies similarly tend to begin with "My grandfather..." (Straus, 1982).

This relational view of selfhood is not confined to North American tribes. It is common among many African groups, such as the Tshidi of Southern Africa (Comaroff, 1980). It has also been observed among traditional Hindus in India (De Vos et al., 1985), who frequently give their caste and village along with their name when they are asked to identify themselves, and in many Asian cultures.

Why Does the Self Differ Across Cultures?

Two factors seem to explain the differences between contemporary Western and other views of the self. First, some cultures are simply more group-centered, and others, more individualistic (Markus & Kitayama, 1991; Triandis, 1989). Because Japanese culture emphasizes cooperation rather than the Western ideal of autonomy, the Japanese experience the self less in terms of internal states than in terms of social relationships (Cousins, 1989; DeVos et al., 1985). Thus, for the Japanese, sincerity describes behavior that conforms to a person's role expectations (carrying out one's duties), whereas for North Americans it means behaving in accordance with one's inner feelings (DeVos et al., 1985). Sincere behavior in Japan may thus be very insincere to an American. In general, the Western self tends to be conceptualized as more independent, whereas the Asian self tends to be conceptualized as more interdependent (Kitayama et al., 1998).

A second influence on conceptions of selfhood is technological development (Westen, 1985, 1991). Careful examination of historical documents suggests that only a few centuries ago the Western concept of self was much closer to the non-Western, group-centered view (Baumeister, 1986). The values, attitudes, and self-concepts of people in rural Greece, for example, resemble the collectivistic orientation one finds in China more than the individualism of contemporary Athens (see Triandis, 1989).

Ten thousand years ago, before the advent of agriculture, humans lived in bands (small groups) that were not altogether different from the band societies discovered by anthropologists in the 19th and 20th centuries. In these groups, individualism is rarely developed, a concept of self distinct from other people and nature is generally absent, and moral values focus on the interests of the clan or band. With the rise of agriculture, which allowed accumulation of personal resources and stratification into social classes, people became more aware of individuality, but this awareness was countered by cultural proscriptions against it. As one anthropologist observed, in these societies, made up largely of poor peasants, "individual progress is seen as—and in the context of the traditional society in fact is—the supreme threat to community stability" (Foster, 1965, p. 310).

Around the time of the Industrial Revolution, something remarkable happened: The concept of the individual, free of attachments and duties, was born. And the individual has been born again wherever technological development has taken hold.

Technological development seems to facilitate individualism, and with it a more individuated sense of selfhood, for several reasons. The first is geographical mobility. People who remain in a small community with parents,

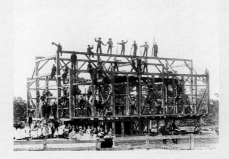

In the 19th century, Americans thought nothing of lending neighbors a hand for days or weeks to build a barn. This seems inconceivable just a century later, with the highly individualized sense of self produced by industrialization.

grandparents, and extended kin throughout their lives are likely to view themselves in a very different context than people who can expect to leave home and relocate hundreds or thousands of miles away. In addition, changing work conditions, such as wage labor and work that is not performed communally with kin or clan, leads to a sense of individual competence. Furthermore, in technologically developed societies people earn much of their status through their actions rather than their family affiliations. They also frequently take up occupations different from those of their parents. When a man is no longer a hunter or farmer like his father, his representations of self and father diverge. Literacy and education also personalize skills and competences, which are no longer experienced as collective knowledge and may be learned through individual study. In addition, increased lifespan and higher standard of living make personal pleasures, desires, and interests more important. Factors such as family size and whether children have their own rooms probably have a subtle influence as well.

Whether cultural differences such as those that divide Japan and the West will remain despite the pressures of industrialization is a profound psychological question that will probably be resolved over the course of the next century.

INTERIM SUMMARY   The self-concept is shaped by at least three motives: accuracy, **self-esteem** (the need to view oneself positively), and **self-consistency** (the motive to interpret information to fit existing self-concepts). The contemporary Western view of self is of an independent, bounded, autonomous individual. This contrasts with other views of self, which are more group-centered, collectivistic, and relational. Some of these differences reflect cultural factors. Others reflect the impact of technological development, which tends to promote individualism for a number of reasons, such as geographical mobility, less communal working conditions, literacy, and increased lifespan.

SOME CONCLUDING THOUGHTS

This chapter has focused on thinking in the social realm, and hence has primarily followed the cognitive perspective. As we saw in Chapters 6 and 7 on memory and thought, however, another perspective has begun to influence our thinking about thinking: the evolutionary perspective. This is likely to be the case in the years ahead with respect to social thought, where evolutionary pressures presumably exerted considerable influence over millions of years of primate evolution.

An evolutionary analysis trains our eyes squarely on the *function* of psychological phenomena (Buss & Kenrick, 1998). Why, for example, do we have attitudes, and why do they take the forms they do? Why, of all the characteristics of people that could catch our eye, do we attend to and remember other people's age, gender, and status?

From an evolutionary perspective, the answers to questions such as these lie in our ancestral past, and in the adaptive pressures that shaped the human brain. Is it an accident that most people have a negative rather than a positive attitude toward death, a strong orientation toward "family values" that maximize the safety and well-being of their children and kin, a negative attitude toward infidelity (at least other people's), or a preference for objects that indicate high status?

Consider the example of status. We take for granted that teenage boys want to wear shoes endorsed by high-status males such as Michael Jordan, or that teenagers of both sexes know precisely where they and everyone else in their social group stands in the status hierarchy. These are characteristics we share with other primates. As we have seen (Chapter 11), in primate societies, low status not only decreases opportunities to mate but also places individuals at greater risk for mortality. It is thus not surprising that people tend to prefer expensive cars if they can afford them, elite schools if they can get into them, and wealthy or physically appealing mates if they can attract them.

The way we think and feel about ourselves and others, and our attitude toward objects of relevance to our well-being, is in part a product of our evolution. This does not mean that our thoughts, feelings, or attitudes are inflexible or genetically determined. The capacity to learn from other people through language and social interaction is itself probably the most important and distinctive aspect of human evolution (Chapter 7). In humans, as in other primates, adaptation is first and foremost adaptation to a community, without which the individual cannot survive or reproduce. As we will see in the final chapter, the most striking aspects of human social behavior—from friendship, love, and altruism to aggression and violence—bear the distinct imprint of our evolutionary past.

SUMMARY

1. **Social psychology** examines the influence of social processes on the way people think, feel, and behave.

ATTITUDES

2. An **attitude** is an association between an object and an evaluation, which usually includes cognitive, evaluative, and behavioral components. These three components can, however, vary independently. Attitudes vary on a number of dimensions, such as their strength and accessibility, as well as whether they are implicit or explicit. Broad attitudes tend not to be good predictors of behavior.

3. **Persuasion** refers to deliberate efforts to change an attitude, and can occur through either careful, explicit thought (the **central route**) or less explicit and rational processes (the **peripheral route**). The effectiveness of a persuasive appeal depends on a number of factors related to the source of the communi-

cation, the message, the channel (the means by which a message is sent), the context, and the receiver. Persuading people to change their behavior can also lead them to change their attitudes.

4. **Cognitive dissonance** occurs when a person experiences a discrepancy between an attitude and a behavior or between an attitude and a new piece of information that does not fit with it. Cognitive dissonance can motivate altitude change.

SOCIAL COGNITION

5. **Social cognition** refers to the processes by which people make sense of others, themselves, social interactions, and relationships. Social cognition differs from nonsocial cognition in its greater ambiguity, links to emotion, cultural basis, and reciprocal nature.

6. **First impressions** are the initial representations people form when they encounter someone for the first time. **Schemas**—the patterns of thought that organize human experience—apply in the social realm as in other areas of life. **Person schemas** represent information about specific people or types of people. **Situation schemas** represent information about different kinds of social situations. **Role schemas** represent culturally patterned information about what is expected of people in particular social positions. **Relationship schemas** encode more idiosyncratic, personal expectations about how the self and others interact.

7. **Stereotypes** are characteristics attributed to people based on their membership in specific groups. **Prejudice** refers to judging an individual based on (usually negative) stereotypes. Racial and ethnic prejudice has roots both in motivation and cognition, and in the person and the broader social system. Stereotypes can be implicit or explicit. Prejudice typically requires the distinction between **ingroups** and **outgroups.**

8. The process of making inferences about the causes of one's own and others' thoughts, feelings, and behavior is called **attribution.** People can make **external attributions** (attributions to the situation), **internal attributions** (attributions to the person), and attributions about interactions between the person and the situation. In making these attributions, they rely on three types of information: **consensus** (how everyone acts in that situation), **consistency** (how this person typically reacts in that situation), and **distinctiveness** (how this person usually reacts in different situations). **Discounting** occurs when people downplay the role of a variable that could acount for a behavior because they know other variables may be contributing to the behavior in question. The opposite situation occurs with **augmentation,** which involves increasing an internal attribution for behavior that has occurred despite situational pressures.

9. Social cognition may be biased in a number of ways, including the tendency to attribute behavior to other people's dispositions even when situational factors could provide an explanation (the **correspondence bias**) and the propensity to see oneself in a more positive light than one deserves (the **self-serving bias**).

THE SELF

10. The **self** refers to the person. The **self as subject** refers to the individual's experience of self as thinker, feeler, and actor. The **self as object,** or self-concept, is the person's concept or view of the self.

11. Contemporary psychodynamic thinking focuses on mental representations of the self, or **self-representations,** which can be conscious or unconscious, and are typically associated with a variety of feelings. From a cognitive perspective, the self-concept is a **self-schema,** which guides thought, attention, and memory. **Self-esteem** refers to a person's feelings toward the self. People's views of themselves are motivated not only by the desire to perceive themselves accurately and by self-esteem motivation but also by the need for **self-consistency,** interpreting information to fit the way they already see themselves.

12. The contemporary Western view of the person is of a bounded individual, distinct from significant others, who is defined by more or less idiosyncratic attributes. In contrast, most cultures have understood the person in social and familial context. Technological development has fostered individualism and taken the self-concept out of its social context.

Elinore Schnurr, "Darkness and Light #18," 1989.

CHAPTER *18*

Interpersonal Processes

*S*amuel Oliner was 12 years old when the Nazis invaded the Jewish ghetto in Poland where he lived. His entire family was killed, but Samuel managed to escape. After two days of hiding, during which he witnessed a child bayoneted and a baby shot with a pistol, he found his way to the home of a Christian woman with whom his father had done business. She fed him and taught him how to pass for a Christian peasant, and he survived the war.

Years later, Oliner wrote a book about the small number of people who risked their lives and the lives of their families to protect Jews during the Holocaust (Oliner & Oliner, 1988). He and his research team interviewed over 400 rescuers and compared them with 72 individuals who neither helped nor hindered the Nazis. They sought to answer a simple question: What made the rescuers perform such extraordinary acts of **altruism**, that is, helping another person with no apparent gain, and even potential cost, to oneself?

The altruism of these individuals seems to defy theories of moral development (Chapter 14). For example, according to cognitive-social theories, reward, punishment, and expectancies control behavior. Everyone in Germany and the occupied countries during the war faced the same contingencies of reinforcement—to be caught rescuing Jews meant certain execution—but several thousand people did so nonetheless. According to cognitive-developmental theories, moral heroism should occur only among people with a high level of moral reasoning. Yet only about half of Oliner's rescuers referred to complex or abstract principles. In fact, several offered strikingly conventional reasons for their actions, such as, "I am an obedient Christian; the Lord wanted us to rescue those people and we did" (Oliner & Oliner, 1988, p. 155).

Rescuers differed from nonrescuers on both *situational* and *dispositional* variables, that is, both in their circumstances and in their personalities and attitudes. Perhaps surprisingly, one of the variables that distinguished the two groups was completely situational: Rescuers had more available rooms in their houses and were more likely to have a cellar. On the dispositional side, rescuers reported having come from closer-knit families and having had parents who sometimes reasoned with them as a mode of discipline, rather than simply punishing them. Overwhelmingly, they reported being taught to treat people fairly regardless of their race, color, or class.

Understanding why some people risked their lives while others did nothing—and why still others have used ultranationalist ideology as an excuse to steal, rape, and murder, much as in Serbian "ethnic cleansing" in our own times—

is the work of social psychologists. The previous chapter focused on the cognitive processes people use to try to understand themselves and others. This chapter addresses motives, emotions, and behaviors that emerge in social interaction.

We begin by examining interpersonal attraction and relationships, from brief encounters through long-term love relationships. We then turn to two very different forms of social interaction, which Oliner encountered in his childhood odyssey: altruism and aggression. Next we investigate the influence of other people on the way individuals behave, as they obey and conform, and consider what happens when individuals participate in groups. We conclude by placing the psychology of our era in its social and historical context and returning to some of the central themes with which we began in the opening chapter.

RELATIONSHIPS

People affiliate, or seek out and spend time with others, for many reasons. Sometimes they interact to accomplish instrumental goals, such as raising money for a charity or meeting over dinner to discuss a business deal. Other interactions reflect family ties, shared interests, desires for companionship, or sexual interest.

When people interact with one another, they may have one or more models of relationships in their minds (Fiske, 1992; Mills & Clark, 1994). For example, they may think about the other person's needs and welfare or be guided by social standards about how the other person should be treated, as typically occurs with friends. At other times, the primary model of relationships that guides people's interactions is more self-interested; among business associates, for example, the expectation is that each will receive a comparable benefit from the relationship. At still other times, the model in people's minds focuses on authority and status—on who is on top. Often, more than one model simultaneously guides the way a person interacts with another, as when colleagues—including those who are at different levels of a status hierarchy—become friends.

Social psychologists have become increasingly interested in the nature of relationships, particularly close relationships (Berscheid & Reis, 1998). Here we focus on two lines of research, one that examines the factors that attract people to each other and another that explores a particular kind of attraction in enduring relationships: love.

FACTORS LEADING TO INTERPERSONAL ATTRACTION

Social psychologists have devoted considerable attention to why people choose to spend time with other people, or **interpersonal attraction**. What draws us to some people but not to others? Researchers have identified several factors.

Proximity

Sometimes the answer is as simple as proximity: Numerous studies have documented that people tend to choose their friends and lovers from individuals nearby. Interviews of 270 residents of a New York City housing project found that nearly 88 percent of their friends in the seven-building project lived in the same building as the respondent; almost half lived on the same floor (Nahemow & Lawton, 1975). Another study surveyed 44 Maryland State Police trainees who had been assigned rooms and classroom seats in alphabetical order of their surnames (Segal, 1974). When the trainees were asked to name their three closest friends on the force, the closer together their surnames, the more likely they were to be friends.

Proximity plays an equally important role in romantic relationships. As one observer wryly commented, "Cherished notions about romantic love notwithstanding, the chances are about 50–50 that the 'one and only' lives within walking distance" (Eckland, cited in Buss & Schmitt, 1993, p. 205). Social-psychological research has repeatedly shown that situational influences such as proximity (or merely having a spare room in Nazi-occupied Germany) have a remarkably strong impact on behavior.

Of course, people neither become friends nor fall in love *simply* because the other person is within walking distance. Rather, proximity allows people to get to know one another. It also sets the stage for familiarity, and familiarity breeds affection. From an evolutionary perspective, the link between familiarity and liking may be part of our genetic endowment because people who are familiar are likely to be safe; they are also likely to be relatives or alliance partners. The preference for the familiar extends to objects as well: We tend to prefer things we have seen before (Zajonc, 1968, 1998). Again, this makes sense from an evolutionary point of view because things we have seen before and not previously associated with ill effects are less likely to pose a threat than novel stimuli.

Interpersonal Rewards

A second factor that influences interpersonal attraction is the degree to which interaction with another person is rewarding. From a behaviorist point of view, the more people associate a relationship with reward, the more likely they are to affiliate (Byrne & Murnen, 1988; Clark & Pataki, 1995; Newcomb, 1956). One ingenious experiment tested a classical conditioning theory of attraction that maintains that children should prefer other children they meet under more enjoyable conditions (Lott & Lott, 1974). The investigators placed first and third graders in groups of three. They gave some participants a chance to succeed on a task, rewarding them for it, and rigged the task so that others would fail. Later, the experimenters asked the children to name someone from the class who they would like to take on a family vacation. One-fourth of the children who succeeded on the task chose one of the children who shared the experience with them. Only one in 20 children who failed made a similar choice.

Social exchange theories, based on behaviorist principles, consider reciprocal reward the foundation of relationships (Homans, 1961). Choosing a relationship is like trying to get the best "bang for the buck"; as in an economic exchange, people try to maximize the value they can obtain with their resources (Kenrick et al., 1993). The resources in social relationships are personal assets: physical attractiveness, wit, charm, intelligence, material goods, and the like. These same assets are the "values" sought in others as well, as a glance at the personal ad in newspapers will attest. In romantic relationships, people tend to choose others of similar value (as culturally defined) because both partners are trying to maximize the value of their mate.

Similarity

A third factor that influences attraction is similarity. People tend to choose casual acquaintances, as well as mates and best friends, on the basis of shared attitudes, values, and interests. One study periodically assessed the attitudes and patterns of affiliation of incoming male college transfer students assigned to the same dormitory (Newcomb, 1961). Over the course of the semester, as the students had a chance to learn one another's attitudes, friendship patterns began to match initial attitude profiles. Surrounding oneself with like-minded others seems to be rewarding, leading to the kind of interpersonal reinforcement described by social exchange theorists.

Folk wisdom that "birds of a feather flock together" thus tends to have more than a grain of truth. So what do we make of the opposite adage, that "opposites attract"? Although people tend to like others who share their values and attitudes, they often prefer being with people whose resources, needs, or behavioral styles *complement* their own (Dryer & Horowitz, 1997; Pilkington et al., 1991). For example, dominant people tend to prefer to interact with others who are more submissive; if both partners in a relationship are dominant, they are likely to butt heads.

Physical Attractiveness

A final factor that influences interpersonal attraction is physical attractiveness (Chapter 17). Even in nonsexual relationships, physically attractive people are magnets. Attractive children tend to be more popular among their peers and are treated more leniently by adults (Clifford & Walster, 1973; Dion & Berscheid, 1974). Attractive adults receive more cooperation and assistance from others (Sigall et al., 1971) and better job recommendations (Cash et al., 1977), and others tend to self-disclose to them more (Brundage et al., 1977).

Not surprisingly, physical attractiveness tends to have a greater impact on romantic than nonromantic relationships. Attractiveness is a major, if not *the* major, criterion college students use in judging initial attraction (e.g., Curran & Lippold, 1975; Walster et al., 1966). One study asked students to indicate whether they were attracted to strangers pictured in photographs. The experimenters gave another group the same photographs but stapled them to surveys showing the strangers' attitudes. Information about the strangers' attitudes had virtually no effect (Byrne et al., 1968). At first meeting, attraction appears to be skin deep.

Given that only a small percentage people can occupy the choice locations on the bell curve of attractiveness, how do the rest of us ever get a date? In reality, people tend to choose partners they perceive to be equally attractive to themselves, not necessarily the most beautiful or handsome (Berscheid et al., 1971). One set of studies clarified how and why this happens. In one condition, male participants were told that a number of different women would gladly date them; in the other condition, they were offered no such assurance. Men in the second condition chose less attractive partners. By doing so, they were apparently trying to maximize the beauty of their partner while minimizing their risk of rejection (see Huston, 1973). Across a number of studies, the average correlation between rated attractiveness of members of a couple is around .50, suggesting that people do indeed tend to find someone of equivalent attractiveness. In economic terms, one of the major "assets" people take on the dating "market" is their appearance, and they tend to exchange "goods" of relatively equal value.

Standards of physical attractiveness vary tremendously from culture to culture (and from individual to individual). Nevertheless, views of beauty are not entirely culture-specific. People across the world tend to rate facial attractiveness in similar ways (Cunningham et al., 1995). Cross-cultural studies have found remarkable consistency in judgments of the attractiveness of faces of different races; correlations between raters across cultures generally exceed .60. Several studies have also found that infants in the West who have not yet been socialized to norms of physical beauty gaze longer at faces rated by adults as attractive than those rated unattractive. This occurs whether the faces are of adults or infants, males or females, or blacks or whites (Langlois et al., 1991).

Just How Shallow Are We?

The research on interpersonal attraction described thus far suggests that we humans are a shallow lot indeed. What we most desire is someone a few doors down, who brings us a beer on a warm afternoon, reminds us of ourselves, and looks like Cameron Diaz or Leonardo di Caprio.

We may be shallow creatures, but probably not quite that shallow. An important caveat about this body of research is that most studies were conducted in brief laboratory encounters between college students who did not know each other. While all the factors identified are probably important, the extent to which each influences interpersonal attraction outside this special circumstance is largely unknown. People tend to emphasize physical attractiveness more during the late teens and early twenties than in any other life stage. Concerns about identity in late adolescence also probably promote a preference for peers who are similar because they reinforce the individual's sense of identity (Sears, 1986).

College students may not be representative for research on relationships for another reason: Few have had long-term relationships, simply by virtue of their age. The importance of various dimensions of attraction waxes and wanes at different points in a relationship, and these fluctuations cannot be observed in first encounters of students brought together in a laboratory or in relationships that typically last only a few months. Studies using broader community samples find that marital satisfaction is typically high initially, lower during child-rearing years (especially when children are toddlers), and higher again once the children leave home, particularly during retirement (Sillars & Zietlow, 1993).

LOVE

Researchers aware of these limitations have turned their attention to long-term adult love relationships in an attempt to convert this enigmatic experience from sonnets to statistics, or from poetry to *p*-values.

Classifying Love

At considerable risk to themselves from Cupid's arrows, some researchers have tried to classify love. A basic distinction is between passionate and companionate love (Walster & Walster, 1978). **Passionate love** is the stuff of Hollywood movies, sleepless nights, and daytime fantasies; it is a wildly emotional condition, marked by intense physiological arousal and absorption in another person. In contrast, **companionate love** involves deep affection, friendship, and emotional intimacy. It grows over time and increasingly takes the place of passionate love—which, alas, does not last forever, despite the fantasies of young lovers who swear their passion will never wane. Companionate love develops over time through shared experiences, emotions, and daily life routines. The two kinds of love often coexist, and people experience resurgences of passionate love at different points in a long relationship (Figure 18.1).

Another taxonomy proposes a *triangular* theory of love (Sternberg, 1988; see also Aron & Westbay, 1996). In an initial study, researchers administered questionnaires to a community sample, inquiring about participants' experiences in love relationships. Using factor analysis, they found that most responses fell into three categories: intimacy, passion, and decision/commitment. The intimacy component includes feelings of closeness, connection, and bonding that provide the warmth of a loving relationship. The passion component describes the physical, sensual, and emotional arousal that attract lovers to one another. The decision/commitment component refers to the decision that one loves the person and

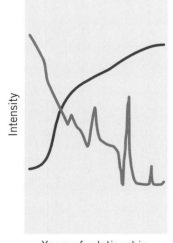

Years of relationship
— Passionate love
— Companionate love

FIGURE 18.1
Passionate and companionate love in a long-term relationship. Passionate love is high at the beginning of a relationship but tends to diminish over time, with periodic resurgences or "spikes." Companionate love usually grows over time.

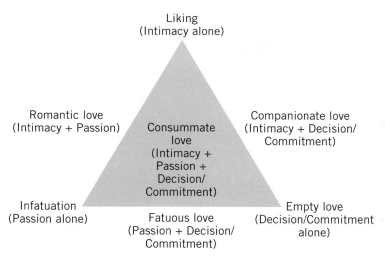

FIGURE 18.2
A triangular theory of love. The triangular theory proposes three components of love: intimacy, passion, and decision/commitment. The combinations of these components produce eight types of relationships: liking (intimacy only), infatuation (passion only), empty love (commitment only, as when a couple stays together for the sake of their children), romantic love (intimacy plus passion), companionate love (intimacy plus commitment), fatuous love (passion plus commitment, as in a whirlwind courtship), and consummate love (in which all three components are present). The eighth type, nonlove, is characteristic of most casual acquaintanceships. *Source:* Adapted from Sternberg, 1988, p. 122.

is committed to the relationship. Together, all the possible combinations of these three components produces a classification of eight basic types of love (Figure 18.2) ranging from infatuation (passion only) to consummate love (all three components combined).

An Evolutionary Perspective

From an evolutionary perspective, the feelings and behaviors we associate with the concept of love are all related to reproductive success (Buss & Kenrick, 1998). Caring for offspring (parental love), courtship, sexual intimacy, and concern for family all maximize the likelihood that we, and those related to us, will reproduce. Romantic love, in this view, is an adaptation that fostered the reproductive success of our ancestors by bonding two people likely to become parents of an infant who would need their reliable care (Hazan & Shaver, 1987, p. 523).

Neither love nor lust, however, inevitably leads to monogamous marriage, and marriage is just one mating strategy among many that occur across species. Even among humans, 80 percent of societies practice polygyny, which permits men multiple wives or mistresses. In Western cultures, premarital sex is virtually ubiquitous, and roughly half of married people at some point have extramarital affairs (Buss & Schmitt, 1993).

Sexual Strategies Evolutionary psychologists have studied the **sexual strategies** (tactics used in selecting mates) people use in different kinds of relationships, from brief romantic liaisons to marriages (Buss & Schmitt, 1993). Unlike most researchers studying interpersonal attraction and relationships, who often generalize across genders, evolutionary theorists argue that males and females face different selection pressures and have thus evolved different sexual strategies. Because a man can have a virtually infinite number of offspring if he can obtain enough willing partners, he can maximize his reproductive success by

Is love unique to humans?

spreading his seed widely, inseminating as many fertile females as possible. In contrast, women can bear only a limited number of children, and they make an enormous initial investment in their offspring during nine months of gestation. As a result, women should be choosier about their mating partners and select only those who can and will commit resources to them and their offspring.

From these basic differences ensues a battle of the sexes. Females maximize their reproductive success by forcing males with resources to commit to them in return for sexual access. Short-term and long-term mating strategies are similar for females; they use short-term liaisons to assess and attract potential long-term mates. For males, by contrast, short-term and long-term sexual strategies are very different. In the short term, the female with the greatest reproductive value is one who is both fertile (young) and readily available for copulation. In the long run, committed relationships provide exclusive sexual access to a female, which allows the male to contribute resources to offspring without uncertainty about paternity. Long-term relationships also bring potential alliances and resources from the woman's family. Thus, ideally, men should prefer less promiscuous long-term partners who are young enough to produce many offspring and attractive enough to elicit arousal over time and increase the man's status. Men should also be choosier in long-term than in short-term encounters because the woman chosen for a long-term relationship will provide half the genes of the offspring in whom they invest.

Aspects of this portrait of male and female sexual strategies probably sound familiar to anyone who has ever dated. Consider the Casanova who professes commitment and then turns out a few months later not to be ready for it; the man who gladly sleeps with a woman on a first date but then does not want to see her again, certainly not for a long-term relationship; or the woman who only dates men of high status and earning potential. From an evolutionary perspective, these are well-known figures because they exemplify common mating strategies. Like other mechanisms for adaptation, sexual strategies were selected in an environment very different from our own, tens or hundreds of thousands of years ago. Their expression should be apparent under particular environmental circum-

"I dreamt I had a Harem, but they all wanted to talk
about the relationship."

stances; they are not rigidly instinctive behaviors like the mating dance of a ring
dove.

The Empirical Evidence How well do the data support evolutionary theory? Although the differences between the sexes are not always enormous, they tend to be consistent. For example, a study of 37 cultures found that in all but one, males tended to value the physical attractiveness of their mates more than females, whereas females were more concerned than males about the resources a spouse could provide (Buss, 1989). Males also consistently prefer females who are younger, and hence have greater reproductive potential; females prefer males who are older and hence are more likely to posses resources, although social and cultural factors obviously influence specific age preferences (Buss & Schmitt, 1993; Kenrick & Keefe, 1992; Kenrick et al., 1993). Figure 18.3 shows the results of some tests of evolutionary hypotheses in several cultures.

Studies of North American undergraduates also corroborate many evolutionary predictions about sexual strategies. For example, when males are asked to identify desired characteristics of potential partners, they prefer good-looking, promiscuous women for the short run but dislike promiscuity and pay somewhat less attention to physical appearance in the long run. In general, compared to women, men report a desire for a greater number of short-term sexual partners, a greater number of sexual partners in a lifetime, and a willingness to engage in intercourse after less time has elapsed (Buss & Schmitt, 1993). In one study, attractive male and female confederates of the experimenter approached opposite-sex students on campus and told them, "I have been noticing you around campus. I find you very attractive." They then asked, among other things, if the student would sleep with them that night (Clark & Hatfield, 1989). Seventy-five percent of the men approached agreed, whereas none of the women accepted the invitation. If the results seem obvious, consider for a moment whether any other theory could have predicted them.

Research examining the content of personal advertisements in newspapers provides intriguing confirmation of the view of "men as success objects and women as sex objects" (Davis, 1990; Mills, 1995). Women tend to advertise their physical beauty and request men who are high in status, prestige, or wealth, and men do the opposite. Men tend to prefer women who are younger, and women are more likely to emphasize that they are seeking a committed long-term relationship. Further, in newspapers read by people of lower socioeconomic status, males tend to be overrepresented among advertisers in the Personals, presumably because low-resource males have more trouble finding mates.

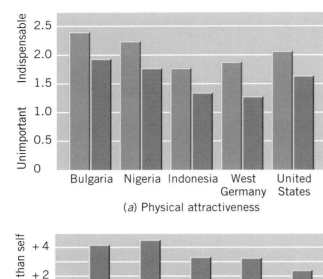

(a) Physical attractiveness

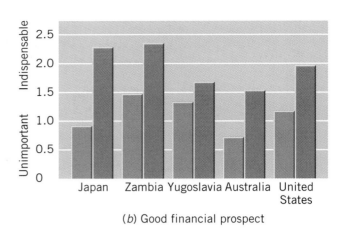

(b) Good financial prospect

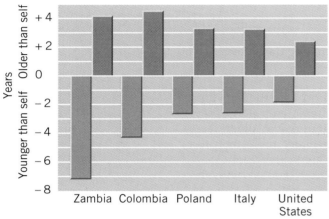

(c) Age difference preferred between self and spouse

FIGURE 18.3

Preferred characteristics of mates across cultures. Across cultures, males show a stronger preference for physically attractive mates than females (a). Financial prospects are more important to females than males in choosing a mate (b). Nearly everywhere, males prefer females who are younger, while females prefer males who are older (c). *Source:* Buss & Schmitt, 1993, pp. 204–232.

These evolutionary hypotheses are, of course, controversial, particularly since they could be used to justify a double standard ("Honey, I couldn't help it, it's in my genes"). They also do not adequately explain the large numbers of extramarital affairs among females, the choice to limit family size or remain childless among couples with plenty of resources in cultures like our own, or homosexuality (although evolutionary theorists have attempted to offer explanations for all these apparently "maladaptive" phenomena). Nevertheless, evolutionary theory does offer some very challenging explanations for phenomena that are not otherwise easily explained.

Romantic Love as Attachment

Another theory of love based on evolutionary principles comes from attachment theory. Romantic love relationships share several features with attachment relationships in infancy and childhood (Hazan & Shaver, 1987, 1994). Adults feel security in their lover's arms, desire physical proximity, and experience distress when their lover is away for a considerable period or cannot be located (Shaver et al., 1988). Adults respond to wartime and job-related marital separations with much the same pattern of depression, anger, and anxiety observed in childhood separations, suggesting that attachment processes continue into adulthood (Vormbrock, 1993). Romantic love also brings security, contentment, and joy, like the satisfaction an infant feels in its mother's arms.

The bond between lovers does, of course, differ from infant attachment in that it involves sexual attraction between people who may have approximately equal power and status, including the power to end the relationship. Furthermore, care for offspring and sexuality are components of adult romantic love absent from infant attachment. Nevertheless, the love between an infant and mother and between two lovers may have more in common than may first appear.

Attachment theorists argue that people pattern their love relationships on the mental models they constructed of earlier attachment relationships. Thus, the way individuals love as adults tends to reflect the way they loved and were loved as children—that is, whether their attachment style was secure or insecure (Chapter 14). Early childhood attachment styles may be especially evident in adults when they are under stress because the attachment system is activated by threats to security.

Striking evidence comes from an experiment on the relation between attachment style and the way members of college-student couples give and receive support (Simpson et al., 1992). After administering attachment style questionnaires to both members of a couple, the investigator told the woman she would shortly be exposed to an experimental procedure that arouses "considerable anxiety and distress in most people" but that he could not explain further (p. 437). Then the experimenter took her to a room that looked like an isolation chamber filled with psychophysiological equipment, told her that the apparatus was not yet ready, and escorted her to a waiting room to sit with her boyfriend for five minutes. While the couple waited for the experiment to begin, their behavior was videotaped and coded for the types of support given and received by each member of the couple. The female's behavior was also rated for level of anxiety.

As predicted, securely attached women sought support from their boyfriends when they were anxious. The opposite was true for avoidantly attached women, who feel uncomfortable being emotionally close to others and tend to shut off attachment needs when stressed; the more anxious they appeared, the less they sought support (Figure 18.4). Also as predicted, securely attached men gave more support, and avoidant men gave less support. No consistent results held for subjects classified as anxiously attached (who crave security but tend to be vulnerable to anxiety and depression).

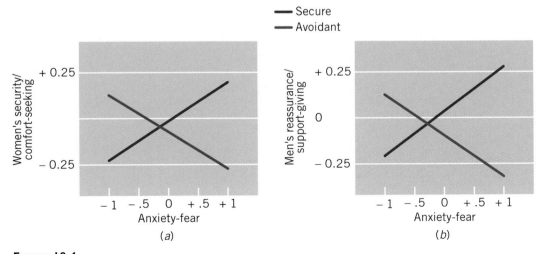

FIGURE 18.4
Relation between attachment style and giving and receiving support. In (*a*), among securely attached women, those who felt more anxious correspondingly sought more comfort from their partners. Precisely the opposite pattern held for avoidantly attached women. In (*b*), the same pattern emerged for support-giving from male partners. Secure men responded with increased support when their girlfriends were more anxious, while avoidant men withdrew as their girlfriends' anxiety increased. *Source:* Simpson et al., 1992, p. 440.

Similar findings emerged in a study of coping mechanisms among Israeli college students during the Gulf War, when Iraq was bombarding civilian areas of Israel (Mikulincer et al., 1993). Subjects who lived in areas directly threatened by missile attacks differed from one another in the ways they coped with the danger. Securely attached subjects tended to seek support from others and generally experienced less distress from the bombings. Avoidantly attached people used distancing strategies (such as, "I tried to forget about the whole thing"). Their distress was manifested primarily in physical symptoms, as might be expected since they tend to be unwilling to feel emotional distress consciously. Ambivalently attached subjects used coping strategies aimed at calming themselves and quelling their emotions, which makes sense given their high level of conscious distress.

A GLOBAL VISTA

LOVE IN CROSS-CULTURAL PERSPECTIVE

Western theorists were not the first to recognize a link between infant and adult love. The Japanese have a concept of love that combines the experience of attachment and dependence, called *amae*, derived from the word for "sweet" (Doi, 1992). *Amae* is both what infants desire with their mothers and what adults feel in the presence of their beloved.

Although adult romantic love may have its origins in the biological proclivity of infants to form attachments, by the time people have participated in relationships for 15 to 20 years, their manner of loving as adults is highly influenced by their culture (Dion & Dion, 1996). Many societies have arranged marriages, which are as much economic bonds linking families or clans as personal and sexual bonds between lovers.

Chinese culture has historically expected couples to consider their obligations to family in choosing a marriage partner: "An American asks, 'How does my heart feel?' A Chinese asks, 'What will other people say?'" (Hsu, 1981, p. 50). Indeed, in Chinese culture, love is so secondary to family obligations that the term *love* does not refer to a legitimate, socially sanctioned relationship between a man and a woman but connotes an illicit, shameful affair (see also Dion & Dion, 1988). In feudal China, passionate love was more

The experience of love differs cross-culturally, but the sentiments of these 18th century Japanese lovers are not difficult to recognize today.

likely to constitute a reason why a couple should *not* marry. The female protagonist in Chinese love stories was more likely to be a concubine than a woman eligible for marriage. The marriage contract was signed by the fathers of the bride and groom; the engaged couple was not required to endorse the contract (Lang, 1946).

Similarly, in many parts of India, where marriages have traditionally been arranged, people may experience passionate love, but they typically hide it (Traiwick, 1990). Public displays of affection are avoided, although they are tolerated more between an unmarried than a married couple. Patterns of marriage and intimacy also vary among castes. In one Untouchable caste, the Chuhras, even private expressions of affection and desire are limited, and spouses do not share sleeping quarters.

A study using data from 42 hunter-gatherer societies from across the globe (gathered by anthropologists over the last century) found evidence of romantic love in 26 of them, or about 60 percent (Harris, 1995). Only 6 cultures allowed pure individual choice of marital partners, however; the other 36 required some degree of parental control, either in the form of veto power over the union of two lovers or arranged marriages.

In the United States, the meaning of marriage has changed substantially over the last three centuries. As in other societies prior to industrialization, marriage was once primarily an arrangement for procreating and managing property and financial unions between families, not a vessel for emotional and sexual intimacy. Based on evidence from diaries and letters written in the 19th century, some historians argue that for women, passion and romance were not absent, but they were often separate from sex and more likely experienced in nonsexual relationships. One mother wrote her daughter, "All the day I muse away, since the sound of your voice no longer rouses me to sympathy. . . . You cannot know how much I miss your affectionate demonstrations" (Smith-Rosenberg, 1975, p. 16).

Contemporary Western culture is unique in its focus on individual satisfaction as a valued end. This orientation extends into relationships, which are viewed as vehicles for personal gratification and are terminated when they are no longer satisfying. The nature and experience of long-term adult love relationships, then, differs not only cross-culturally but even within a single culture over time.

Maintaining Relationships

Maintaining a relationship over time is no easy task. (Oscar Wilde once said something to the effect that the chains of matrimony are so heavy that it often takes three to carry them.) Relationships pass through many phases (Borden & Levinger, 1991), and the majority of marriages in the United States and some other Western countries now end in divorce. This has led many researchers to try to track down the causes of marital satisfaction, dissatisfaction, and dissolution (Gottman, 1998).

According to one line of thinking, people decide whether to stay in a relationship by weighing its relative costs and benefits (Kelley & Thibaut, 1978; Levinger, 1976; Rusbult & Van Lange, 1996). Whether a person remains committed over time depends on the balance of pleasure and discomfort it brings. Commitment to a relationship also depends on how much the person has invested in it and what the alternatives look like. People will tend to stay in a relatively unhappy marriage if they feel they have put so much into it that they cannot leave and if they do not think they can do any better.

Another factor that seems to be associated with satisfying, stable relationships is the extent to which partners overlook each other's faults. Studies of both dating and married couples find that people report greater satisfaction with—and stay longer in—relationships when they have a somewhat idealized or unrealistically positive perception of their partner (Murray & Holmes, 1997). (As a beneficiary of this defensive process, I support it wholeheartedly.) These findings make sense in light of research on "positive illusions" that suggests people often enhance their sense of well-being by holding mildly positive illusions about who they are and what they can accomplish (Chapter 11). In addition, idealizing our mates allows us to believe we have a good deal—and hence resolves the cognitive dissonance that would arise every time we saw an attractive alternative.

Although slightly exaggerating our partners' strengths (and overlooking their warts) can increase satisfaction, having a partner who actually *is* impressive can be a mixed blessing (Beach & Tesser, 1995). Consider a man who is married to a tennis star. If she wins Wimbledon, he is likely to derive considerable satisfaction and even self-esteem from it because he loves her, and his self-concept includes her as his wife. Her wins are his wins. But suppose he, too, is a tennis player—and one who is only ranked in the top 50. In this case, her victories can actually lead to his diminished self-esteem. We tend to bask in the glories of those we love—unless the spotlight on their successes puts our own in the shadows.

INTERIM SUMMARY   Several factors lead to interpersonal attraction, including proximity, interpersonal rewards, similarity, and physical attractiveness. Psychologists have proposed various taxonomies of love. One contrasts **passionate love** (marked by intense physiological arousal and absorption in another person) with **companionate love** (love that involves deep affection, friendship, and emotional intimacy). Some theorists argue that romantic love is a continuation of infant attachment mechanisms. Evolutionary theorists emphasize **sexual strategies**, tactics used in selecting mates, which vary by gender and reflect the different evolutionary selection pressures on males and females. Love appears to be rooted in attachment but is shaped by culture and experience. The decision to stay in a relationship often involves a balancing act, weighing factors such as its costs and benefits, one's prior investment in it, and the attractiveness of alternatives.

ALTRUISM

Thus far, we have focused on the ties that bind. In this section, we examine another interpersonal process that brings people together: altruism. A person who donates blood, volunteers in a soup kitchen, or risks death (like the heroes of Oliner's World War II odyssey that opened this chapter) is displaying altruism. Some altruistic behavior is so common that we take it for granted—holding open a door, giving a stranger directions, or trying to make someone feel comfortable during a conversation. Indeed, charitable contributions in the United States alone exceed $50 billion a year (Batson, 1995). We begin this section by examining theories of altruism. We then consider experimental research on a particular form of altruism, bystander intervention.

THEORIES OF ALTRUISM

For centuries, philosophers have debated whether any prosocial act—no matter how generous or unselfish it may appear on the surface—is truly altruistic. When

Did you never see little dogs caressing and playing with one another, so that you might say there is nothing more friendly? But that you may know what friendship is, throw a bit of flesh among them, and you will learn. Throw between yourself and your son a little estate, then you will know how soon he will wish to bury you and how soon you wish your son to die.... For universally, be not deceived, every animal is attached to nothing so much as to its own interest.... For where the I and Mine are placed, to that place of necessity the animal inclines.

EPICTETUS

people offer money to a homeless person on the subway, is their action motivated by a pure desire to help, or are they primarily alleviating their own discomfort?

Ethical Hedonism

Many philosophers argue for **ethical hedonism**, the doctrine that all behavior, no matter how apparently altruistic, is—and should be—designed to increase one's own pleasure or reduce one's own pain. As one observer put it, "Scratch an 'altruist' and watch a 'hypocrite' bleed (Gheslin, cited in Batson, 1995).

People have many selfish reasons to behave selflessly (Batson, 1991, 1998). People are frequently motivated by their emotions (Chapter 11), and behaving altruistically can produce positive emotions and diminish negative ones. The overwhelming majority of Oliner's subjects who saved Jews from the Nazis reported that their emotions—pity, compassion, concern, or affection—drove them to help (Oliner & Oliner, 1988). Prosocial acts can also lead to material and social rewards (gifts, thanks, and the esteem of others) as well as to positive feelings about oneself that come from meeting one's ideal-self standards.

Behaving prosocially can also reduce negative feelings. Some theorists explain the motivation to act on another's behalf in terms of *empathic distress*: Helping relieves the negative feelings aroused through empathy with a person in distress (Hoffman, 1982). This mechanism does not appear to be unique to humans. In one study, researchers trained rhesus monkeys to pull a chain to receive food (Masserman et al., 1964). Once the monkeys learned the response, the investigators placed another monkey in an adjacent cage, who received an electric shock every time they pulled the chain. Despite the reward, the monkeys stopped pulling the chain, even starving themselves for days to avoid causing suffering in the other monkey.

Empathizing with others apparently does involve actually *feeling* some of the things they feel. In one experiment, participants watched videotaped interactions between spouses and were asked to rate the degree of positive or negative affect one of the spouses was feeling at each instant (Levenson & Ruef, 1992). To assess the accuracy of these ratings, the experimenters correlated participants' ratings with the spouses' own ratings of how they felt at each point. Participants who accurately gauged these feelings showed a pattern of physiology similar to the person with whom they were empathizing, such as a similar level of skin conductance (but this was true only for unpleasant emotions). In other words, when people "feel for" another's pain, they do just that—feel something similar, if less intensely—and use this feeling to gauge the other person's feeling. With positive emotions, people apparently use their head instead of their gut.

Genuine Altruism

An alternative philosophical position is that people can be genuinely altruistic. Jean-Jacques Rousseau, the French Romantic philosopher, proposed that humans have a natural compassion for one another and that the only reason they do not always behave compassionately is that society beats it out of them. Adam Smith, an early capitalist economist, argued that people are generally self-interested but have a natural empathy for one another that leads them to behave altruistically at times.

Some experimental evidence suggests that Rousseau and Smith may have been right. Empathic people who have the opportunity to escape empathic distress by walking away, or who are offered rewards for doing so, still frequently choose to help someone in distress (Batson, 1991). In addition, people at times behave altruistically for the benefit of a group, usually one with which they identify themselves.

Mother Theresa and Princess Diana were both known for their altruistic acts.

How selfish soever man may be supposed, there are evidently some principles in his nature, which interest him in the fortune of others, and render their happiness necessary to him, though he derives nothing from it except the pleasure of seeing it. Of this kind is pity or compassion, the emotion which we feel for the misery of others, when we either see it, or are made to conceive it in a very lively manner.

ADAM SMITH, 1759,
A Theory of Moral Sentiments

An Evolutionary Perspective

Evolutionary psychologists have taken the debate about altruism a step further by redefining self-interest as reproductive success. By this definition, protecting oneself and one's offspring is in an organism's evolutionary "interest."

Evidence of this type of altruistic behavior abounds in the animal kingdom. Some mother birds will feign a broken wing to draw a predator away from their nest, at considerable potential cost to themselves (Wilson, 1975). Chimpanzees "adopt" orphaned chimps, particularly if they are close relatives (Batson, 1995). If reproductive success is expanded to encompass inclusive fitness (Chapter 10), one would expect humans and other animals to care preferentially for themselves, their offspring, and their relatives. Organisms that paid little attention to the survival of related others, or animals that indiscriminately invested in kin and nonkin alike, would be less represented in the gene pool with each successive generation. The importance of these evolutionary mechanisms has been documented in humans, who tend to choose to help related others, particularly those who are young (and hence still capable of reproduction), in life and death situations (Burnstein et al., 1994).

Why, then, do people sometimes behave altruistically toward others unrelated to them? Was Mother Teresa an evolutionary anomaly? And why does a flock of black jackdaws swarm to attack a potential predator carrying a black object that resembles a jackdaw, when it means some may be risking their feathers for a bird to which they are genetically unrelated? To answer such questions, evolutionary theorists invoke the concept of **reciprocal altruism**, which holds that natural selection favors animals that behave altruistically if the likely benefit to each individual over time exceeds the likely cost (Caporael & Barron, 1997; Trivers, 1971). In other words, if the dangers are small but the gains in survival and reproduction are large, altruism is an adaptive strategy.

For example, a jackdaw takes a slight risk of injury or death when it screeches or attacks a predator, but its action may save the lives of many other birds in the flock. If most birds in the flock warn one another, they are *all* more likely to survive than if they wander in solitude through the woods like the Transcendentalist philosopher Henry David Thoreau. Thus, altruism can sometimes be more adaptive than "selfishness" (Simon, 1990).

The same argument applies to humans. Social organization for mutual protection, food gathering, and so forth permits far greater reproductive success for each member on the average than a completely individualistic approach that loses the safety of numbers and the advantages of shared knowledge and culture.

INTERIM SUMMARY Altruism refers to behaviors that help other people, with no apparent gain, or with potential cost, to oneself. Philosophers and psychologists disagree as to whether an act can be purely altruistic or whether all apparent altruism is really intended to make the apparent altruist feel better (**ethical hedonism**). Evolutionary psychologists propose that people act in ways that maximize their inclusive fitness and are more likely to behave altruistically toward relatives than others. Natural selection also favors animals that behave altruistically toward unrelated others if the likely benefit to each individual over time exceeds the likely cost, a phenomenon known as **reciprocal altruism**.

BYSTANDER INTERVENTION

Although philosophers and evolutionists may question the roots of altruism, apparent acts of altruism are so prevalent that their absence can be shocking. A case in point was the brutal 1964 murder of Kitty Genovese in Queens, New York. Arriving home from work at 3:00 A.M., Genovese was attacked over a half-hour period by a knife-wielding assailant. Although her screams and cries brought 38 of her neighbors to their windows, not one came to her assistance or even called the

This quiet street in New York was the scene of a brutal murder—and the impetus for research attempting to understand why Kitty Genovese's neighbors did nothing to help.

police. These bystanders put on their lights, opened their windows, and watched while Genovese was repeatedly stabbed and ultimately murdered.

To understand how a group of law-abiding citizens could fail to help someone who was being murdered, social psychologists John Darley and Bibb Latane (1968) designed several experiments to investigate **bystander intervention**, or helping a stranger in distress. Darley and Latane were particularly interested in whether being part of a group of onlookers affects an individual's sense of responsibility to take action.

In one experiment, male college students arrived for what they thought was an interview (Darley & Latane, 1968). While the students waited to be interviewed, either individually or in groups of three, the investigators pumped smoke into the room through an air vent. Students who were alone reported the smoke 75 percent of the time. In contrast, only 38 percent of the students in groups of three acted, and only 10 percent acted when in the presence of two confederates who behaved as if they were indifferent to the smoke. In another experiment (Latane & Rodin, 1969), college students waited, alone or with one other person, purportedly to participate in a market research study. While waiting, they heard a tape of what sounded like a woman falling and injuring herself in the next room. Seventy percent of the students who were alone or with a friend tried to help, but only 7 percent of those with a nonresponsive confederate did so.

A Model of Bystander Intervention

Based on these experiments, Darley and Latane developed a multi-stage model of the decision-making process that underlies bystander intervention (Figure 18.5). First, bystanders must notice the emergency. Second, they must interpret the incident as an emergency. Finally, they must assume personal responsibility for intervention. After assuming responsibility, bystanders must then decide how, if at all, they can be helpful, and actually try to help. At any point during these stages, a bystander may make a decision that leads to inaction.

The presence of others has a substantial impact on the bystander's decision-making process. If other people are paying little or no attention to the emergency during stage one, the bystander may conclude that nothing significant has happened. Similarly, a bystander is unlikely to interpret an event as an emergency

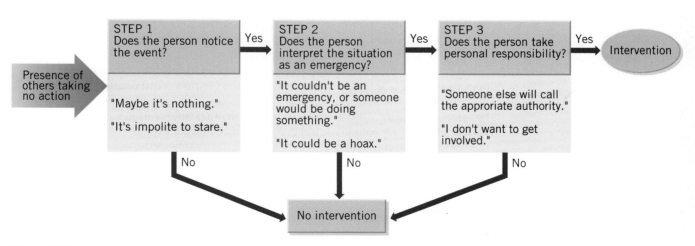

FIGURE 18.5

Bystander intervention. In the first stage of this decision-making model, the bystander must notice the emergency. In stage two, the bystander must interpret the incident as an emergency. In stage three, the bystander must assume responsibility. Once the bystander accepts responsibility, he must then decide what to do and try to do it. *Source:* Adapted from Darley & Latane, 1968, pp. 70–71.

In The Accused, *Jodie Foster plays the part of a woman who was gang-raped in a crowded barroom as bystanders either watched silently or cheered on the attackers. The movie was based on an incident that occurred in New Bedford, Massachusetts.*

during stage two if other people do not seem to take it seriously. This is especially true if the situation is at all ambiguous (see Clark & Ward, 1972, 1974). The presence of others during these two initial stages acts not only as a source of information ("Is there a crisis here or isn't there?") but also as a source of reassurance. Hence, the mere presence of other people decreases the likelihood of intervention, particularly if the others do not appear to be distressed.

During stage three, the presence of others leads to a **diffusion of responsibility**—a diminished sense of personal responsibility to act because others are seen as equally responsible. During this third stage, people also consider the consequences of action. Clearly, people are less willing to intervene if taking action jeopardizes their own safety. Individuals are also less willing to act if they fear they might turn out to be goats instead of heroes; what if the event is really a hoax or they are misinterpreting the situation?

Other factors influence bystander intervention, such as the attractiveness of the victim (Pilliavin et al., 1975). The bystander's perceived similarity to the victim further increases the likelihood of action, apparently because it maximizes empathy (Graf & Riddle, 1972). Bystanders who are anonymous, like Kitty Genovese's neighbors and most German citizens during the reign of Nazism, are less likely to help. Sociologists have long argued that the anonymity of city life reduces individuals' sense of personal responsibility for the welfare of others. Research comparing the responses of urban and rural subjects largely supports this view (see Solomon et al., 1982). Population density—the number of people crammed into a small urban space—is also highly predictive of altruism: The more densely populated a city, the less people help (Levine et al., 1994). This finding supports Darley and Latane's contention that people are less likely to intervene when responsibility is diffused.

How Bleak Is this Picture?

Most of the bystander studies described so far involved simulated emergencies in laboratory settings. Under other experimental conditions, the results are sometimes quite different. One study examined whether bystanders are more likely to respond to an emergency in a natural setting where their compatriots are friends rather than strangers. The investigators staged a rape in a campus parking lot (Harari et al., 1985). When unsuspecting male bystanders observed the female victim struggling with her attacker and heard her cries for help, 85 percent of those walking in groups of two or three responded, versus 65 percent of those walking alone. In this study, the presence of several people increased, rather than decreased, bystander intervention. According to the investigators, the naturalistic setting of the rape, the clarity of the victim's plight, and the ability of group members to see and talk to one another made intervention more likely.

INTERIM SUMMARY   Researchers studying **bystander intervention** have found that individuals often do not help in a crisis in the presence of other people. To intervene, a person must notice the event, define it as an emergency, and assume personal responsibility for intervening. **Diffusion of responsibility**, a diminished sense of personal responsibility to act, is one important reason why people do not intervene.

AGGRESSION

Charitable contributions exceed $50 billion a year in the United States, but that is less than half the military budget. **Aggression**—verbal or physical behavior aimed at harming another person or living being—is at least as characteristic of human interaction as altruism. Aggression is often elicited by anger, as when someone lashes out at a perceived injustice, but it can also be carried out for practical purposes without anger, as when a driver leans on the horn to protest reckless lane-changing that could cause an accident. Calm, pragmatic aggression is called **instrumental aggression** and is often used by institutions such as the judicial system to punish wrongdoers (Geen, 1990, 1998). Aggressive acts are also frequently mixed with other motives. The behavior of kamikaze pilots during World War II, terrorists who carry out suicide bombings, and many soldiers in wartime involve blends of aggression and altruism, depending upon one's point of view.

VIOLENCE AND CULTURE

The prevalence and forms of aggression vary considerably across cultures. Among technologically developed countries, the United States has the highest rates of aggression. Indeed, violence has overtaken communicable diseases as the leading cause of death among the young. Homicide rates are up to 10 times higher in the United States than in Europe (see Lore & Schultz, 1993), and the murder rate in some major U.S. cities dwarfs the number of annual murders in all of Canada. In Canada, roughly 600 people a year die from homicides, compared with 24,000 in the United States. Taking account of the larger population in the United States, the murder rate is still over five times higher in the United States. Cross-cultural data have demonstrated that much of the difference in murder rates is attributable to the ready availability of firearms in the United States (Archer, 1994).

A soccer field in Bosnia converted to a cemetary. How would different perspectives explain such bloodshed among civilized people?

Across and within societies, cultural differences play an important role in violence and aggression. Psychologists have recently begun studying a cultural difference between men (particularly white men) from the Northern and Southern United States that is related to a tendency to behave violently (Nisbett, 1993). Homicide rates are higher in the South, but not for crimes committed during felonies such as burglaries. The difference lies in the tendency of Southern men to resort to violence in the midst of conflicts or arguments.

According to one explanation, the South is characterized by what anthropologists call a *culture of honor,* where small disputes between men can turn violent because they become contests for reputation and status. For reasons rooted in the ancestry, history, and economy of the South, to be dishonored—to show cowardice or a lack of "manliness" in the face of possible insult—is to lose face and status; thus, Southern men are more likely than Northerners to respond with violence to insults or ambiguous situations that *could* suggest an insult.

Researchers demonstrated this in a fascinating study at the University of Michigan. In one condition, an associate of the experimenter bumped into Northern and Southern male students, called them an obscene name, and walked off into another room (Cohen et al., 1996). In a control condition, Northern and Southern participants received no such insult. The researchers measured a number of variables, including observers' ratings of how amused versus angry participants appeared after the bump and how they completed a hypothetical scenario in which a woman complained to her boyfriend that a mutual male friend kept making passes at her. They also assessed participants' physiological stress during the incident by analyzing cortisol levels in their saliva (recall from Chapter 11 that cortisol is, among other things, a hormone secreted during stress) and testosterone levels before and after the incident (testosterone provides, among other things, a physiological index of readiness to fight).

The results were striking. The majority of Northern students responded to the insult with more amusement than anger; in contrast, 85 percent of Southerners displayed more anger then amusement. Roughly half the Northerners who were insulted completed the scenario about the woman complaining to her boyfriend

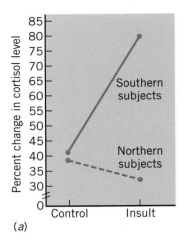

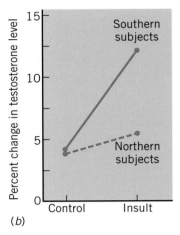

FIGURE 18.6
Changes in cortisol and testosterone levels for insulted and noninsulted Southerners and Northerners. In (*a*), cortisol levels (measured both before and after the experimental manipulation) showed dramatic increases for insulted Southerners. In (*b*), the same was true for testosterone. *Source:* Cohen, D., Nisbett, R., Bowdle, B., & Schwarz, N. (1996). "Insult, aggression, and the Southern culture of honor: An experimental ethnography. *J. of Personality and Social Psych.,* 70, 945–960.

about their friend's inappropriate attention with a violent ending; the percentage who did so was similar in the experimental and control conditions. In contrast, 75 percent of Southerners in the experimental condition (who received the insult) wrote a violent ending, compared with 20 percent of "unbumped" Southerners. Southern men thus appeared to be gentlemen when they were not insulted, but when primed with an insult were ready to act with aggression.

The biological findings led to precisely the same conclusion (Figure 18.6): Whereas Northerners showed virtually no physiological reaction to the insult, both cortisol and testosterone levels jumped dramatically in Southern men who were insulted. Thus, cultural factors can influence not only how people feel, think, and act when confronted with a situation that could potentially lead to violence but also how they respond physiologically.

VIOLENCE AND GENDER

Gender differences in aggression are highly consistent across cultures. In most societies, males commit the majority of criminal and aggressive acts. Male adolescents are particularly likely to be the perpetrators; in fact, fluctuations in crime rates in most countries can be predicted simply from the proportion of adolescent males in the population (see Segall, 1988).

Violence perpetrated by men against men is so universal that it scarcely seems to draw attention. Recently, however, psychologists have come to recognize the extent of male violence perpetrated against women (Goodman et al., 1993). The number of women battered by their male partners is unknown because many women do not report domestic violence, but the U.S. Department of Justice estimates that approximately 2.1 million women are battered each year in the United States (Frieze & Browne, 1989). Other estimates suggest that as many as 10 percent of marriages in the United States are marred by violent assaults, the most severe typically committed by the man (Dutton, 1996). Most batterers do not begin abusing their partners until the woman has made an emotional commitment to them, and attacks are most likely to occur during pregnancy or upon separation or divorce (Russell, 1991).

Sexual aggression against women is as old as the species. Men have traditionally viewed rape as one of the spoils of war. Because most women do not report rape to the police, legal records are not a valid index of its prevalence. Some studies suggest that as many as 14 to 25 percent of women have been forced into sex by strangers, acquaintances, boyfriends, or husbands at some point in their lives (Goodman et al., 1993; Koss, 1993). A substantial percentage of women (27 percent) also report histories of childhood sexual abuse (as do 16 percent of men) (Finkelhor et al., 1990). Many factors influence the tendency of some men to rape, such as the lack of empathy for, and enjoyment of, the victim's pain and fear; hostility toward women; lack of emotional and impulse control; and cognitive processes, such as the tendency to interpret women's actions as seductive or hostile (Geen, 1998; Hall & Hirschman, 1991).

▶ ONE STEP FURTHER

Why Men Rape

Rapists vary in their personalities, motives, and modus operandi. Roy Hazelwood (1993), a counseling psychologist, was a special investigator for many years with the FBI. According to Hazelwood, rapists vary in the extent to which they are motivated by power over their victim or by anger and sadism. The most common and least violent of rapists are usually solitary, socially inadequate men with low self-esteem, whose primary aim is to reassure themselves of their sexual adequacy and masculinity by exercising power over their victim. When interviewed months or years later, they typically report the fantasy that the women they rape will fall in love with them, and their behavior during the rape reflects this fantasy: They tend to kiss and fondle their victims, to compliment them on their beauty, to avoid violence, and to become distressed if the woman becomes too manifestly upset or struggles too much. Prior to being apprehended for a series of rapes, one such man received commendation from his city for heroically subduing an attacker who was brutally raping a woman. When later apprehended himself and asked why he had rescued the woman, he indignantly responded that *he* would never "hurt" a woman (Hazelwood & Harpold, 1986).

The most dangerous type of rapist is the sexual sadist, who is excited by the woman's suffering. These rapists tend to be extremely intelligent and active, often raping dozens of women before being apprehended. They torture their victims and often create their own violent pornography by photographing, videotaping, or audiotaping their crimes. Unlike other rapists, they are typically cool and calm when committing and recounting their crimes, which they carry out with precision and forethought. They often kidnap and torture their victims for days and weeks, work with partners (sometimes their girlfriends or spouses), force their victims to say and do degrading things, and penetrate their victims as violently as possible. Frighteningly, these men generally do not appear odd or peculiar to the people who know them in daily life (Dietz et al., 1990).

Rapists do not all look the part.

One study examined 41 incarcerated serial rapists, who had raped at least 10 women each, accounting as a group for over 800 sexual assaults and another 400 attempted rapes (Hazelwood & Warren, 1989). The men ranged in occupation from professionals to blue-collar workers; most held steady employment. Most had a history of prior sexual offenses, such as voyeurism (being a "peeping tom") or making obscene phone calls, if not prior rapes. Many also had a general history of antisocial behavior; half of those who had been in the military were discharged other than honorably, and over half reported being physically assaultive from the time they were children. Only 33 percent collected pornography. Perhaps the most consistent finding was a history of sexual abuse: 76 percent reported being sexually abused or witnessing sexual abuse in childhood or adolescence. One subject was initiated into rape by his father, who took him out with him while he raped women and initially had to force the boy to participate. ◀

INTERIM SUMMARY   **Aggression** refers to verbal or physical behavior aimed at harming another person or living being. Rates of violence vary cross-culturally, but across cultures, males tend to be more aggressive than females. Researchers are increasingly recognizing the prevalence of male violence perpetrated against women, including battering and rape.

THE ROOTS OF VIOLENCE

The universality of aggression, as well as individual differences in aggressive behavior, have led to considerable controversy about its origins. Some theories maintain that the roots of aggression lie in biology and evolution; others look to the environment and social learning. In this section we explore psychodynamic, evolutionary, and cognitive-social approaches (which integrate cognitive and behavioral perspectives). We also examine the biopsychological processes that underlie aggressive behavior and offer a tentative integration of multiple standpoints.

Psychodynamic Perspective

Freud viewed aggression as a basic instinct in humans, a drive that intensifies over time if not discharged, analogous to hunger and sex (Chapter 10). Most psychodynamic psychologists no longer accept this model; instead, they view aggression as an inborn behavioral potential that is usually activated by frustration and anger. Infants and toddlers bite, scratch, and kick when they are not comfortable or do not get what they want. In every human society ever observed, socialization to control aggressive impulses is one of the most basic tasks of parenting (see Whiting & Child, 1953). This suggests that aggression is a class of behavior that societies inhibit rather than implant through social learning. As children grow older and become increasingly socialized, they do, in fact, tend to use less physical violence against one another (Hartup, 1977).

Psychodynamic theory, unlike other perspectives, argues that aggressive fantasies and behavior can be pleasurable, and that humans are inherently capable of sadism, regardless of their upbringing (Sandler, personal communication, 1993). Although the enjoyment of aggression is perhaps most obvious in sexual sadists, delinquents, and antisocial personalities, psychodynamic psychologists contend that all people enjoy aggression to some degree, if only in very controlled circumstances. Crowds flock to boxing matches and attend hockey games in hopeful anticipation of fistfights. Many people's sexual behavior includes mildly aggressive acts such as squeezing, biting that leaves "passion marks," scratching, pulling skin, light bondage such as holding down a partner's arms, or fantasies of tying up or being tied. Although most men and women would find the actual experience of rape traumatic and repulsive, research documents that both sexes report being sexually aroused by stories of sexual coercion (Malamuth et al., 1980). This fact is obviously known to script writers, who frequently pepper motion pictures with aggressive sex.

From a psychodynamic standpoint, aggression can have many triggers. For example, one psychiatrist, after spending over 20 years working with violent prisoners and conducting extensive interviews, has proposed that a primary trigger for violence is the feeling of *shame* (Gilligan, 1996). In interview after interview, in which he asked prisoners to tell the stories of their violent acts, he heard the same thing: They attacked someone when they felt "dissed," or treated with perceived disrespect. For many of these men, their threshold for feeling worthless and ashamed was so low, and their impulse control so poor, that they were virtually ready to explode with minimal provocation. A wide range of research suggests, more generally, that threats to self-esteem or valued views of the self can trigger

Why are we so captivated by horror films? Here, actress Drew Barrymore, from Scream.

violence (Baumeister et al., 1996). This appears to be most true for people who have an unstable, inflated, or uncertain sense of self-worth, whose ability to maintain *self-respect* in the face of negative events or encounters is low.

Another distinctive feature of the psychodynamic account of aggression regards the ways aggression can be expressed. Despite angry feelings and at times aggressive desires, most people do not wind up in prison, because they learn to control aggressive impulses as they grow up. Over the course of childhood, normal children learn to regulate direct physical aggression just as they learn to regulate other selfish or antisocial impulses (see Hartup, 1998). However, from a psychodynamic point of view, out of sight does not mean out of mind. People still get angry or wish to hurt people who frustrate them, and if they cannot do so directly, they may do so indirectly, often outside of awareness.

For example, a prominent lawyer who was badly abused as a child appeared mild-mannered in all contexts except one—the courtroom—where she "took no prisoners." Hockey players, boxers, and soldiers may find socially acceptable ways to express more overt aggression. Aggression may also be expressed through passive resistance rather than overt action—passive aggression (Chapter 10)—as when a husband "forgets" to pick up the dry cleaning after an argument with his wife. Aggressive impulses may also blend with other motives to produce behavior. Parents who beat their children generally intend to teach the child a lesson, but they are also expressing frustrations and hostilities they cannot safely—or legally—take out on another adult.

An Evolutionary Perspective

Aggression, including killing members of one's own species, occurs in all animals; hence, the capacity for aggression presumably evolved because of its value for survival and reproduction (Lore & Schultz, 1993). Males typically attack other males to obtain access to females and to keep or take over territory. In many animal species, including some lions and monkeys, a male who takes over a "harem" from another male kill all the infants so that the females will breed with him and devote their resources only to *his* offspring, maximizing his reproductive success.

Wolves, unlike humans, know how to stop a confrontation from becoming too dangerous.

Females often try to fight back in these circumstances. Across species, overt female aggression is elicited largely by attacks on their young.

Contemporary evolutionary psychologists, like their psychodynamic colleagues, do not consider aggression a drive that builds up and requires discharge. Rather, many believe that humans, like other animals, have evolved aggressive mechanisms that can be activated when circumstances threaten their survival, reproduction, the reproductive success of their kin, or the survival of alliance partners. To put it another way, aggression is like a pilot light that is always on but can burst into flames if conditions threaten reproductive success (de Waal, 1989).

Although aggression is common to all animal species, the degree of violence toward members of their own species is remarkable in humans, who slaughter each other on a scale unimaginable to even the cruelest of beasts (see Lorenz, 1966). Other animals have evolved inhibitory mechanisms that stop them from ravaging their own. Wolves can call off a potential battle simply by rolling over. In the midst of a vicious fight for territory or status, a wolf whose competitor rolls over and exposes his jugular will immediately halt his attack; a biologically based inhibitory mechanism is activated, and the victor scores a technical knockout. Such mechanisms are particularly prevalent in animals with built-in weaponry, such as powerful jaws.

Primates, including humans, have a variety of appeasement gestures to avoid violence, notably facial expressions, vocalizations, and gestures (deWaals, 1989; Krebs & Miller, 1985). Unfortunately, humans are unique in their capacity to override evolved mechanisms for inhibiting aggression, particularly when divided by nationality, ethnicity, or ideology. Furthermore, as Konrad Lorenz noted, humans have developed the ability to kill one another from a distance. Not seeing our victims suffer prevents activation of natural inhibitions against killing members of the species, such as empathic distress responses, which are probably involved in both inhibiting aggression and promoting altruism. We are not, sadly, as civilized as wolves.

FROM MIND TO BRAIN

THE BIOLOGICAL BASIS OF AGGRESSION

Psychodynamic and evolutionary psychologists presume that aggression is built into the human behavioral repertoire. If a tendency to behave aggressively is innate, it must be rooted in the nervous system and perhaps in the endocrine system as well. Mounting evidence in animals and humans supports this view.

Neural Systems

The neural systems that control aggression, like those involved in other forms of behavior, are hierarchically organized (Figure 18.7). Sensory information (such as the sight of a threatening gesture) transmitted by the thalamus to the amygdala and hypothalamus can instigate aggression because the amygdala and hypothalamus are specialized for emotional reactions and drive states (Chapter 3). Midbrain structures also play a role in aggression. Lesioning parts of the midbrain can eliminate an animal's ability to respond with species-typical aggressive motor movements, such as hissing and bared teeth in cats (Carlson, 1991). More sophisticated processing at the cortical level can

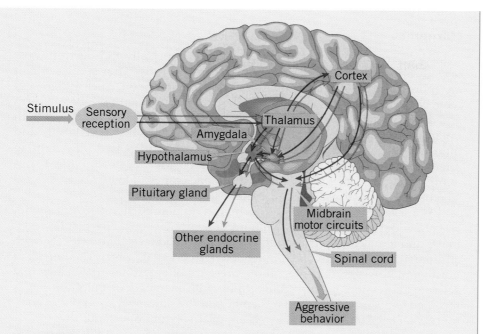

FIGURE 18.7

Areas of the brain involved in aggressive behavior. The neural circuitry for aggression, like other complex psychological functions, is hierarchically organized. Stimulus information (e.g., a threatening gesture) is relayed via the thalamus to the amygdala and hypothalamus for immediate action. The information is also relayed from the thalamus to the cortex for more careful consideration. One or both of these pathways can generate an aggressive response, which requires coordinating motor cortex, midbrain motor mechanisms specialized for species-specific aggressive responses, and other structures involved in control of movement (such as the basal ganglia and cerebellum, not shown here). Information about the emotional significance of the stimulus calculated by the amygdala is transmitted to the hypothalamus, which activates endocrine responses, which in turn affect arousal and readiness for fight or flight.

either inhibit or facilitate aggression instigated at lower levels. A threatening gesture, for example, can be interpreted as either an attack or a joke.

Research documents the role of the hypothalamus and amygdala in aggression. When researchers electrically stimulate regions of the lateral hypothalamus of a normally nonpredatory cat or rhesus monkey, the animal immediately attacks (Egger & Flynn, 1963; Robinson et al., 1969). Similar results occur in humans when electrodes are implanted in the amygdala during surgery. With electrical stimulation, a normally submissive, mild-mannered woman became so hostile and aggressive that she tried to strike the experimenter—who was able to control the outburst by switching off the current (King, 1961). Conversely, numerous animal studies show that destroying the amygdala can make extremely wild, hostile animals so docile they can be picked up and petted (Schreiner & Kling, 1953; Woods, 1956). Neurosurgeons who performed essentially the same operation (a partial or complete amygdalectomy) on extremely violent human patients reported a success rate of 85 to 92 percent in reducing violent behavior (Heimburger et al., 1966; Narabayashi et al., 1963). Unfortunately, this type of surgery also produced unpredictable and permanent damage, such as loss of emotion (see Valenstein, 1988).

Hormones

Outside the central nervous system, hormones, especially androgens (testosterone), appear to be involved in aggression. In species after species, males are more aggressive than females, starting in childhood. Such differences have been linked to the action of androgens on the brain both before birth and during development (Archer & Lloyd, 1985). Recall that hormones both organize and activate neural circuits (Chapter 10). When female rats and monkeys receive testosterone *in utero*, they exhibit increased play fighting after birth (Goy, 1968; Meaney & McEwen, 1986; Meaney et al., 1981). In humans, prenatal exposure to synthetic hormones can lead to increased aggression in childhood and adolescence (Reinisch, 1981).

As for activational effects of hormones on neural circuits, studies with rats show definitively that the amount of aggressive behavior displayed by males and females correlates with circulating blood testosterone levels, with additional hormones involved in females (Albert et al., 1991). The impact of hormones, however, depends on the presence of environmental events that activate aggression, such as competition with members of the same sex or repeated exposure to unfamiliar members of the same species. Without environmental triggers, hormonal levels are relatively unimportant.

The data in humans are less definitive, largely because they rely on correlational designs. Correlational studies show that higher levels of testosterone are associated with aggression, but they cannot distinguish the relative contributions of prenatal and circulating testosterone or the possibility that aggression increases testosterone levels and does not simply reflect them (Archer, 1991). Nevertheless, several studies are suggestive. One examined the relation between physical and verbal aggression and levels of testosterone in adolescent boys (Olweus et al., 1980). Participants with higher levels of testosterone tended to be more impatient and irritable. Men convicted of violent crimes also tend to have higher testosterone levels than nonviolent offenders and nonoffenders (see Archer, 1991). The dramatic increase in male aggression that occurs at sexual maturation (puberty) in many species and cultures is also likely related to a surge in testosterone levels (see Segall, 1988).

Genetics

Genetic factors contribute to individual differences in aggressive behavior. Successful attempts to breed highly aggressive strains of rats, mice, and rabbits demonstrate that among these animals, some individuals inherit a more aggressive temperament than others (see Cologer-Clifford et al., 1992; Moyer, 1983). Questionnaire studies comparing monozygotic and dizygotic twin pairs find aggressive behavior to be heritable in humans, like other personality traits (Caspi, 1998; Rushton, 1986). The evidence seems clear that humans are constructed with a potential for aggression and that innate differences exist both between the two sexes and among individuals.

INTERIM SUMMARY   Although Freud believed aggression is instinctive, most psychodynamic theorists view aggression as an inborn behavioral potential that is usually activated by frustration and anger. Aggression can have many triggers, notably shame and feelings of diminished self-worth. Children learn to regulate their aggression as they grow older, but anger and aggressive feelings do not go away; instead, they are more likely to be expressed indirectly. Evolutionary theorists similarly view aggression as an inborn human potential that gets activated under conditions that affect reproductive success, such as competing for territory or mates and protecting oneself and related others. The neural control of aggression is hierarchically organized, with the amygdala and hypothalamus playing prominent roles. Aggression is also partially controlled by hormones, particularly testosterone.

A Cognitive-Social Perspective

The capacity for aggression appears to be innate, but the activation and inhibition of aggression depends on culture and learning. Harsh parental discipline, for example, produces children who are more aggressive than those whose parents spare the rod (Weiss et al., 1992). According to cognitive-social theories, children and adults learn to behave aggressively through social rewards and punishments and through observational learning such as modeling. As Bandura (1977) demonstrated, when children watch adults abusing Bobo dolls, they are much more likely to do so themselves (Chapter 5).

Such findings have fueled public debates, and a large body of psychological research, on the influence of television violence. To estimate the long-term effects of television violence on behavior is very difficult because people who are aggressive tend to seek out aggressive shows, and they do this from the time they are young. Experimental data show that in the short run, children and adolescents are more likely to behave aggressively immediately after viewing violent television shows, particularly if they are provoked (Singer & Singer, 1981; Wood et al., 1991). This could occur because watching television violence increases arousal, decreases inhibition, provides aggressive models, or desensitizes children to violence by making violent acts seem commonplace (Gunter & McAleer, 1990).

The data are inconclusive for long-term effects (see Gadow & Sprafkin, 1993; McGuire, 1986). Rather than having a global effect on every child or adult, televised violence is likely to have a stronger impact on people who are already highly aggressive. In fact, experimental research suggests that people who are high on the personality trait of aggressiveness not only prefer violent films but become more angry after watching them and are more likely to behave aggressively after doing so (Bushman, 1995). Thus, the impact of televised aggression on violence likely reflects a person-by-situation-interaction (Chapter 12)—that is, a tendency of certain people to behave in certain ways under certain conditions—rather than a general phenomenon.

Similar results emerge from research assessing the effects of pornography on sexual violence. Viewing pornography does not cause sexual violence, but viewing pornographic *aggression* appears to desensitize men to the brutality of rape and other sexual crimes against women (see Malamuth & Donnerstein, 1982). As with television violence, pornographic aggression may affect a person's emotional response to violence or slightly weaken inhibitions in deviant individuals with poor internal controls. Nonetheless, most people will not kill or rape after watching a violent or pornographic movie.

The results of 30 years of research on television violence are not without policy implications. In the United States, politicians periodically browbeat network executives during televised hearings and threaten them with governmental controls if they do not curb violent programming. (Televised aggression apparently begets televised aggression.) Yet the effect of media violence pales as a predictor of aggressive behavior in comparison with violence witnessed at home, in schools, or on the streets (Gunter & McAleer, 1990). The relatively weak and

HERMAN®

12-3   © 1977 Jim Unger/dist. by LaughingStock Licensing Inc.

**"I thought T.V. was supposed
to make you violent."**

sometimes contradictory findings on television violence suggest that lawmakers might better spend their time addressing the abundance of *real* weapons in the nation's cities rather than demonstrating their fierce determination to keep fictional handguns off make-believe streets.

Toward an Integrated View of Aggression

In 1939, John Dollard, Neal Miller, and their colleagues at Yale University presented the **frustration-aggression hypothesis,** which states that when people are frustrated in achieving a goal, they may become aggressive. The child who wants a cookie and is told to wait until after dinner may throw a tantrum, or the college student who had her heart set on a particular graduate school and was rejected may become not only sad but furious.

This model is simple and intuitively appealing. It was initially hailed as a significant advance toward a comprehensive theory because it tied aggression to environmental events rather than solely to instincts. However, researchers soon realized that not all aggression results from frustration and not all frustration leads to aggression. Physical pain may cause aggression, and frustrated goals can lead one person to become aggressive, another to become depressed, and still another to become more determined.

A reformulated frustration-aggression hypothesis suggests that frustration breeds aggression to the extent that a frustrating event elicits unpleasant emotion (Berkowitz, 1989). Blocked goals can be frustrating, as Dollard and his colleagues emphasized, but so can innumerable other unpleasant experiences. Air pollution,

I pray thee, good Mercutio, let's retire:
The day is hot, the Capulets abroad,
And, if we meet, we shall not 'scape a brawl;
For now, these hot days, is the mad blood stirring.

SHAKESPEARE
Romeo and Juliet (III, i)

tobacco smoke, and other noxious odors have all been linked to increases in aggressive behavior (Rotton et al., 1979; Zillman et al., 1981).

The relation between heat and aggression is particularly well documented (Anderson, 1989). As temperature rises, so does temper. One study found a strong correlation between temperature and the incidence of riots in U.S. cities between 1967 and 1971 (Carlsmith & Anderson, 1979). Rape, murder, assault, and prison unrest all vary with the time of the year, peaking in the hot summer months (Figure 18.8). Within countries as diverse as Spain, Italy, France, and the United States, the southern regions typically have the highest rates of violent crime (Anderson, 1989). Even the number of batters hit by pitches in professional baseball varies with the temperature (Reifman et al., 1991).

According to the reformulated frustration-aggression hypothesis, people respond to negative affect with either aggression or withdrawal—fight or flight—depending on their genetic endowment, learning history, and the situation. Unpleasant thoughts, feelings, and behaviors are associatively connected in memory, so that activating one will activate the others. As a result, people can become angry and behave aggressively no matter how the underlying emotional state was elicited—whether through an insult, an uncomfortable temperature, or an unpleasant memory that elicits thoughts of revenge.

The reformulated frustration-aggression hypothesis points the way toward an integrative perspective on aggression that takes seriously both the role of biology and the influence of culture and experience. Although humans are not driven to act aggressively like they are driven to eat, children spontaneously behave aggressively, and humans are endowed with hormonal and neural mechanisms that mediate aggressive responses. Moreover, like other animals, humans, and particularly males, compete for territorial resources and sexual partners, and they are omnivores who hunt prey. That natural selection would have failed to endow them with emotional and behavioral mechanisms that produce aggression under certain circumstances therefore seems inconceivable.

Culture and learning, however, largely define those circumstances. Humans appear biologically constructed to behave aggressively when they feel hurt, deprived, or blocked from reaching their goals, but many goals, as well as strategies

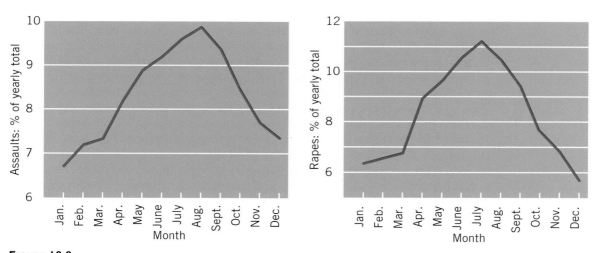

FIGURE 18.8

Aggression and time of year. The number of assaults (*a*) and rapes (*b*) committed varies by the time of year and is highest in the hottest months. Data were averaged across studies from North America and Europe over the last hundred years. *Source:* Anderson, 1989, pp. 85–86.

for dealing with frustration, reflect culture and learning. Prior experiences with aggressive behavior and its consequences, both direct and vicarious, also influence future tendencies to behave aggressively. Wife-beaters who are arrested for their crimes re-victimize their wives at a much lower rate than those who are not arrested, just as children who get a clear message that violence will not be tolerated tend to find other ways of regulating conflicts (Lore & Schultz, 1993). Because the potential for aggression is rooted in our biology, then, does not mean it is uncontrollable. Finally, cognitive processes, especially the attributions people make for the causes of their misfortunes, play a role in eliciting and controlling aggression as well. Individuals are more likely to become aggressive, for example, if they believe someone has willfully and knowingly inflicted harm (see Geen, 1995).

INTERIM SUMMARY   According to cognitive-social theories, people learn to behave aggressively through social rewards and punishments and through observational learning. The **frustration-aggression hypothesis** states that people may become aggressive when they are frustrated in achieving a goal. A reformulated hypothesis suggests that frustrating or unpleasant circumstances are likely to evoke aggression if they elicit unpleasant emotion. The capacity for aggression appears to be innate, but the activation and inhibition of aggression depends on culture and learning.

SOCIAL INFLUENCE

In 1991, the world was shocked by a home video of Los Angeles police officers beating black motorist Rodney King after a high-speed chase. Equally shocking was the acquittal of the officers on April 29 of the following year. After repeatedly viewing the tape in slow motion the jury was convinced that King's continued resistance justified the officers' actions. When news of the acquittal hit the streets, the African-American community erupted in anger. Enraged mobs looted stores, pulled people from their vehicles and beat them senseless, set buildings and cars on fire, and attacked anyone whose race placed him in the wrong neighborhood at the wrong time. The riots left 54 people dead, over 2000 injured, and racial tensions burning like the streets of the city.

By the late 19th century, sociologists and philosophers had recognized that people behave differently in crowds than they do as individuals and that a crowd is more than the mere sum of its parts. In his classic 1895 study, *The Crowd*, Gustave Le Bon argued that people in a crowd may lose their personal identities and ability to judge right and wrong. They become anonymous and no longer consider themselves accountable for their behavior. Le Bon had in mind events of the 18th and 19th centuries, such as the frenzied mobs of the French Revolution, but his reflections could equally apply to the behavior of the police officers who beat Rodney King or the rioters who rampaged through Los Angeles after the officers' acquittal.

Since Le Bon's time, social psychologists have examined a number of forms of **social influence**, or effects of the presence of others on the way people think, feel, and behave. In one of the earliest social-psychological experiments, Norman Triplett (1897) investigated how the mere presence of other people affects performance. When he asked 40 adolescents to wind a fishing reel as quickly as possible, he found that they wound it faster when competing with others than when racing solely against the clock. Psychologists call the performance-enhancing effect of the presence of others **social facilitation** and have observed the phenomenon in a wide variety of species, from humans to cockroaches (Buck et al., 1992;

Zajonc, 1965). In this section we cast aside the cockroaches to explore three forms of social influence in humans: obedience, conformity, and group processes.

OBEDIENCE

In the small South Vietnamese village of My Lai on March 16, 1968, at the height of the Vietnam War, three platoons of American soldiers massacred several hundred unarmed civilians, including children, women, and the elderly. The platoons had arrived in Vietnam only a month before but in that short time had sustained heavy casualties, leaving the survivors scared and vengeful. Any inhibitions the soldiers might have had against killing innocent civilians disappeared when their commander ordered them to shoot the villagers, whom he suspected of being enemy sympathizers. Tremendous controversy ensued: Do soldiers relinquish their duty to judge right and wrong upon receiving an order? And if soldiers remain morally responsible actors who must make their own independent decisions, what happens to the chain of command?

Still saluting after his conviction for mass murder in the town of My Lai, Lt. William Calley began a life prison term in a case that drew controversy about the limits of military obedience.

The Mystery of Obedience

Such tragic consequences of **obedience**, or compliance with authority, are not limited to warfare. In 1978, in the small community of Jonestown, located in a Guyana jungle, over 900 members of the People's Temple cult drank cyanide-laced Kool Aid to commit mass suicide. The cult's leader, Jim Jones, told his people that a "revolutionary suicide" would dramatize their dedication. According to the few survivors, some people resisted, but most took their lives willingly, with mothers giving cyanide to their children and then drinking it themselves. Equally grizzly examples of misplaced obedience include the inferno in Waco, Texas, in which many Branch Davidian cult members lit their own compound ablaze under the leadership of David Koresh, and the mass suicide of California cult members who believed salvation was just around the corner with the arrival of the Hale–Bopp comet.

Psychological research on obedience to authority increased dramatically following World War II, primarily as an attempt to understand the horrors of the Third Reich. Many social psychologists were refugees from the Nazis who presumed that the blind obedience they had witnessed was an aberration or anomaly caused by flaws in the German character or by the political, social, and economic upheaval that left Germany in ruin after the First World War. Subsequent research on authoritarian personality dynamics in their new land (Chapter 17) led instead to a disquieting conclusion: Many people in the United States were also attracted to ideology glorifying blind obedience (Adorno et al., 1950).

The Milgram Experiments

In the 1960s Stanley Milgram (1963, 1974) conducted a series of classic studies on obedience at Yale University that took many people, including psychologists, by surprise. The basic design of the studies was as follows. The experimenter told subjects they were participating in an experiment to examine the effect of punishment on learning. Subjects were instructed to punish a "learner" (actually a confederate of the researcher) in the next room whenever the learner made an error, using an instrument they believed to be a shock generator. Panel switches were labeled from 15 volts (SLIGHT SHOCK) to 450 volts (DANGER: SEVERE SHOCK). The experimenter instructed the subjects to begin by administering a slight shock and increase the voltage each time the learner made an error. The learner actually

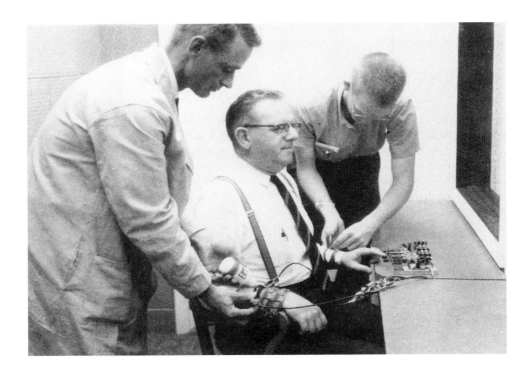

Milgram's research on obedience shocked both psychologists and the lay public who never would have imagined that participants would have been willing to shock a stranger at the command of an authority who told them that he would take responsibility for their action.

received no shocks, but subjects had no reason to disbelieve what they were told—especially since they heard protests and, later, screaming from the next room as they increased the punishment.

Milgram was not actually studying the impact of punishment on learning. Rather, he wanted to determine how far people would go in obeying orders. Before conducting the study, Milgram had asked various social scientists, including psychiatrists, psychologists, sociologists, and social workers to estimate how many subjects would continue with the experiment all the way to 450 volts. Virtually all the experts estimated that less than 5 percent would administer the maximum shock.

They were wrong. Approximately *two-thirds* of subjects administered the full 450 volts, even though the learner had stopped responding (screaming or otherwise) and was apparently either unconscious or dead. The subjects were torn between wanting to obey the experimenter and not wanting to hurt the learner; many were clearly distressed by the experience. Each time they asked if they should continue to administer the shocks, the experimenter told them that the experiment required that they continue. If they inquired about their responsibility for any ill effects the learner might be experiencing, the experimenter told them that he was responsible, and that the procedure might be painful, but it was not dangerous. The experimenter was very scientific and business-like and never overtly tried to coerce subjects to continue; all he did was to remind them of their obligation.

To Milgram, the implications were painfully clear: People will obey, without limitations of conscience, when they believe an order comes from a legitimate authority (Milgram, 1974).

By varying the experimental conditions, Milgram discovered several factors that influence obedience. One is the proximity of the victim to the subject. Obedience declines substantially if the victim is moved from a separate room into the subject's room, if the sound of his voice replaces pounding on the wall, and if the subject has to force the victim's hand onto a shockplate to administer further punishments (see Figure 18.9). Proximity to the experimenter also affects the subject's

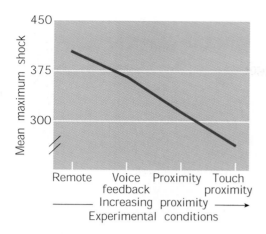

FIGURE 18.9
Effects of proximity on maximum shock delivered. Subjects in the Milgram experiments generally obeyed, but the closer they were to the victim, the less they tended to obey.
Source: Milgram, 1965, p. 63.

decision to obey. The closer the subject is to the experimenter, the more difficult is disobedience; when the experimenter sits in another room, obedience drops sharply. Another factor that influences obedience is an opposing form of social influence. In the presence of dissenters who refuse to proceed, subjects more readily refuse to continue. Personality variables such as authoritarianism and hostility can also influence the likelihood of obedience (Blass, 1991).

Milgram's experiments drew storms of controversy from psychologists concerned that he did not safeguard the rights of his subjects, who were often visibly distressed by the experience. Following the experiment, he did discuss with them any negative feelings they had, and his subjects did not ultimately express regret about their participation. In fact, many claimed that participation was valuable, and that they had learned something important about themselves. Whether the knowledge generated by Milgram's extraordinary results outweighs the possible costs to his subjects remains a matter of debate. With contemporary ethics standards, such studies could not be conducted today. Nevertheless, Milgram's studies suggest that the philosopher Hannah Arendt may have been right when she said that the horrifying thing about the Nazis was not that they were so deviant but that they were "terrifyingly normal."

CONFORMITY

Whereas obedience refers to compliance with the demands of an authority, **conformity** means changing attitudes or behavior to accommodate the standards of peers or groups. The pressure to conform can be immense, even if subtle. Consider how fads and fancies change with the times. Real estate agents can date the interior of a house by the colors and patterns in the kitchen and bathrooms. The loud green and orange wallpaper designs that excited decorators and consumers in the 1960s make contemporary home buyers wince. Wearing a thin tie when wide is in vogue makes many men uncomfortable, as does wearing the wrong brand of tennis shoes for many teenagers.

The Asch Studies

A series of classic studies by Solomon Asch (1955, 1956) documented the power of conformity, much as Milgram's studies established the power of obedience. Asch assembled groups of seven to nine college students and told them they were participating in an experiment on visual judgment. All but one of the students were actually confederates, so their responses were planned in advance. The experi-

Conformity can take many forms.

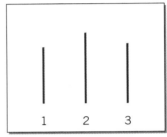

FIGURE 18.10

The Asch conformity experiments. Participants in Asch's experiments on conformity were asked which of the three lines on the right matched the one on the left. Pressure to conform swayed their responses. *Source:* Asch, 1955, p. 193.

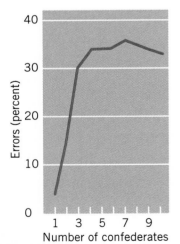

FIGURE 18.11

Effect of number of confederates on performance. Participants in Asch's experiments tended to conform when three or more confederates chose the wrong line. *Source:* Asch, 1955, p. 193.

menter asked the "subjects" to match the lines on two white cards (Figure 18.10). On one card was a line, and on the other were three vertical lines of varying length. One of these three lines was the same length as the line on the other card, while the others were substantially different. The experimenter asked each student to choose which of the three lines matched the line on the other card.

On the first and second trials, everyone—subject and confederates alike—gave the right answer. On subsequent trials, however, the confederates (who went first) unanimously chose a line that was obviously incorrect. Their answers placed the subject in the uncomfortable position of having to choose between publicly opposing the view of the group answering incorrectly.

Without peer pressure to conform, subjects chose the wrong line less than 1 percent of the time. However, when faced with a unanimous (but incorrect) opinion of the confederates, subjects made the same incorrect choice as the confederates 36.8 percent of the time. Up to a point, the more confederates, the greater the tendency to conform (Figure 18.11). Subjects only conformed, however, if the confederates all gave the same answer. If at least one confederate gave a different answer than the others, subjects followed their own judgment most of the time. Apparently, bucking the majority is extremely difficult without at least one other dissenter.

The Asch studies powerfully demonstrate the power of situations to influence behavior and attitudes. Personality factors, however, also influence the tendency to conform. Individuals with low self-esteem and those who are especially motivated by a need for social approval are more likely to conform (Crown & Marlowe, 1964; Dittes, 1959; Moeller & Applezweig, 1957; Strang, 1972). To what extent subjects actually alter their beliefs in the Asch studies rather than simply comply with situational demands to avoid disapproval is a matter of debate. Many of Asch's subjects reported that they believed their (incorrect) answers, perhaps because of cognitive dissonance or a desire not to look foolish. Nevertheless, the main implication of these studies is that many people will change at least the public expression of their beliefs when confronted with a group that disagrees with them.

Conformity and Culture

Conformity varies by culture and appears to be linked to the way people earn their livelihood (Price-Williams, 1985). People in hunter-gatherer societies exercise more independent judgments than people in agricultural societies (Berry, 1979). Agricultural societies depend heavily on communal organization and coordinated action; too much independent judgment can be counterproductive during planting and harvest times, when work needs to be done. Agricultural societies also have much higher population density, whereas hunter-gatherer societies are often highly dispersed across a territory and may thus require less compliance with social norms (see Barry et al., 1957). In general, conformity is higher in collectivist than in more individualistic cultures (Bond & Smith, 1996). To what extent this reflects the tendency of collectivist cultures to be agricultural cultures with dense populations is unclear.

Conformity also varies within cultures. In both North America and Australia, low-income and rural parents tend to emphasize obedience and conformity in their child-rearing practices compared with urban and middle-class parents (Cashmore & Goodnow, 1986; Peterson & Peters, 1985). This finding, too, makes adaptive sense because parents typically prepare their children for work similar to their own (LeVine, 1982), and laborers have less autonomy than professionals.

INTERIM SUMMARY   **Social influence** refers to the effects of the presence of others on the way people think, feel, and behave. **Obedience** refers to compliance with authority. The **Milgram experiments** demonstrated that most people will obey, without limitations of conscience, when they believe an order comes from a legitimate authority. **Conformity** means changing attitudes or behavior to accommodate the standards of peers or groups. The **Asch experiments** demonstrated that people tend to conform rather than be the lone dissenting voice. Conformity varies across and within cultures and tends to reflect economic and ecological demands.

GROUP PROCESSES

The Asch conformity experiments illustrate just how powerful group processes can be. A **group** is a collection of people whose actions affect the other group members. When a collection of people congregate for even relatively short periods of time, their interactions tend to become patterned in various ways. In fact, many similar patterns emerge in informal groups that come together on the spur of the moment and in enduring institutions such as families and corporations. Features common to many groups include norms, status, roles, and leadership.

Norms

All groups develop **norms**, or standards for behavior. Norms guide thought, feeling, and behavior, from the way people dress to their attitudes about sex, Republicans, and lawyers. Sometimes norms are explicit (e.g., a written dress code), but much of the time they are implicit (men do not wear dresses). Different groups have different norms, and particularly in complex societies, people must pick and choose the norms to obey because they belong to many groups, which may have conflicting norms. Adolescents, for example, frequently find themselves choosing between the norms of adults and peers.

The way people respond to norms depends on their attitude toward the groups with which the norms are associated. Groups whose norms matter to an individual, and hence have an impact on the individual's behavior, are known as **reference groups**, because these are the groups to which a person *refers* when taking action. A reference group can be positive or negative. A reference group is considered *positive* if the person tries to emulate its members and meet their standards. When a teenage boy gets drunk on weekends because his friends do, his friends are a positive reference group (but not necessarily a positive influence). A reference group is *negative* if a person rejects its members and disavows their standards. If a teenager gets drunk every weekend to establish his independence from his teetotaling parents, his parents are a negative reference group. In both cases, the reference group is influencing the teenager's behavior (which he might be loath to admit), but the direction of influence is different.

Status

Members' **status** in a group reflects the amount of power they hold. Status distinctions emerge rapidly in many groups, and they become solidified over time in groups of longer duration such as families and organizations. Status distinctions emerge quickly in other primate groups as well, where power often reflects physical stature (de Waal, 1989). In many species, status distinctions arise through physical confrontations or threats of confrontation, which result in a pecking order that each partner in a potential conflict recognizes (or learns the hard way).

Humans, like other animals, usually have little difficulty reading signs of status and recognizing who defers to whom. People high in status in a group tend to talk more and are freer to interrupt. They also display their status nonverbally, by standing erect, maintaining eye contact longer, and generally displaying signs of confidence (Levine & Moreland, 1998).

Roles

Not only do members of a group vary in status, but they differ in the roles they play in the group. A **role** is a position in a group that has norms specifying appropriate behavior for its occupants (see Merton, 1957; Parsons, 1951). Roles are essentially norms that are specific to particular people or subgroups. Roles reflect shared expectations about how particular members of a group are supposed to behave. They tend to be flexible, allowing the individual to make decisions about specific actions, much like roles in improvisational theater. A mother can decide how she will care for her child in a given circumstance, but her culture provides general guidelines for acceptable maternal behavior, such as whether she should stay home with her child or what forms of discipline she should employ.

Role theorists often use a theatrical metaphor: Roles are the parts individuals play in life's drama; society directs them until their time on the stage has passed and another actor takes their place. Individuals internalize roles as role schemas (Chapter 17), which direct their behavior when they are in a particular role and lead them to expect certain responses from people with complementary roles (such as husband and wife, teacher and student).

The Influence of Roles on Behavior   Several roles routinely emerge in groups, even in brief, unstructured ones (see Bales, 1953). When strangers enter into groups in the laboratory and are asked to solve problems, some group members usually take responsibility for seeing that the group completes its tasks; these

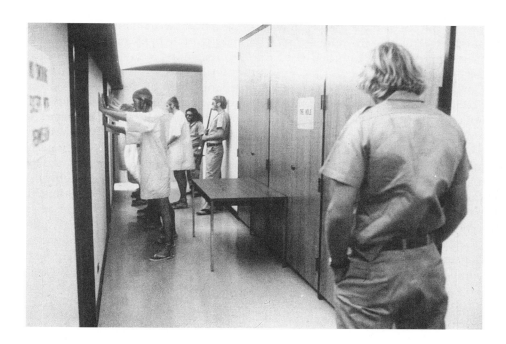

Zimbardo's prison study showed how powerful the demands of roles and situations can be on individual behavior.

are called **task leaders**, or instrumental leaders. Others, called **social-emotional leaders**, try to keep the group working cohesively and with minimal animosity. Sometimes a group member takes on a **tension-release role**, making jokes to relieve the pressure that builds as the group tries to accomplish its tasks. Although people in this role may appear at times to interfere with the group's progress, their presence in a jury room or corporate meeting can actually help the group function.

Because people often define themselves by their roles, roles can have a profound impact on attitudes. One classic study examined the way workers' attitudes change as a result of job promotions (Lieberman, 1956). The researcher measured the attitudes of plant workers and then reassessed them after some were promoted to foreman (a management position) or shop steward (a union position). Not surprisingly, after their promotions, the foremen were more pro-company than they had been as workers, whereas the shop stewards had become more pro-union. More interestingly, however, when the company later experienced financial problems and had to demote some of the foremen to their previous rank-and-file positions, they returned to their original attitudes.

Zimbardo's Prison Study   One of the most dramatic illustrations of the influence of roles on social behavior occurred in a study by Philip Zimbardo (1972, 1975). Twenty-two male college student volunteers played the roles of prisoners and guards in a simulated prison. To make the experiment as realistic as possible, students designated as prisoners were arrested at their homes and searched, handcuffed, fingerprinted, and booked at a police station. They were then blindfolded and driven to the simulated prison where they were stripped, sprayed with a delousing preparation (actually a deodorant spray), and told to stand alone naked in the cell yard. After a short time, they were given a uniform and placed in a cell with two other "prisoners." The guards received minimal instructions and were free to devise their own rules. The only prohibition was against physical punishment.

Soon after the experiment began, Zimbardo noted marked differences between the behavior of the guards and the prisoners. The guards became increasingly aggressive, treating the prisoners as less than human, seldom using their names (instead calling them by number, if referring to them as individuals at all), and subjecting them to roll calls that could last for hours. Many acted with clear sadistic pleasure.

The prisoners, for their part, initiated progressively fewer actions and appeared increasingly depressed. Half the prisoners (five participants) suffered such extreme depression, anxiety, or psychosomatic illness that they had to leave the experiment. The prisoners talked almost exclusively about prison life, maintaining the illusion of their roles. By the fifth day, those who remained were brought before a mock parole board, which would determine whether or not they would be released. Most were willing to forfeit all the money they had earned in the experiment if they could be released. When their requests for parole were denied, they obediently returned to their cells.

The study was originally designed to last two weeks, but the shocking results led Zimbardo to abort it after only six days. The study provides a powerful demonstration of the way roles structure people's behavior and ultimately their emotions, attitudes, and even their identities. Although participants were, in reality, college students randomly assigned to be prisoners or guards, within days they had *become* their roles—in action, thought, and feeling.

INTERIM SUMMARY   A **group** is a collection of people whose actions affect the other group members. All groups develop **norms**, or standards for behavior. Members' **status** in a group reflects the amount of power they hold. People also frequently play particular **roles** in groups (positions in the group that have norms specifying appropriate behavior for their occupants). **Task leaders** take responsibility for seeing that the group completes its tasks; **social-emotional leaders** try to keep the group working cohesively and with minimal conflict. Roles can have a dramatic influence on attitudes and behaviors, as demonstrated in Zimbardo's prison experiment, which had to be aborted because people became immersed too deeply in their assigned roles.

Leadership

As we have seen, groups tend to have formal or informal **leaders**, people who exercise greater influence than the average member. A major initial impetus to research on leadership was Adolf Hitler. Social scientists were astonished that an individual so manifestly disturbed and filled with rage could arouse such popular sentiment and create such a well-oiled war machine. Could democratic forms of leadership be as efficent?

Leadership Styles   In a classic study, Kurt Lewin and his colleagues (1939) randomly assigned 10-year-old boys to one of three groups for craft activities after school. Each group was led by an adult who took one of three leadership styles: He made all the decisions (an *autocratic* leadership style); involved himself in the group and encouraged members to come to decisions themselves (a *democratic* style); or simply let things happen, intervening as little as possible (a *laissez-faire* style).

Boys with an autocratic leader produced more crafts, but they were more likely to stray from the task when the leader left the room, and their products were judged inferior to those produced in the democratic condition. Boys in the democratic group expressed greater satisfaction and displayed less aggression than the others. Laissez-faire leadership led to neither satisfaction nor efficiency. Lewin and his colleagues concluded that autocratic leadership breeds discontent among group members but can be efficient. In contrast, democratic leadership seems to be both efficient and motivating. Lewin's leadership categories largely parallel Baumrind's findings on parenting styles (Chapter 14), which showed that authoritative parenting (equivalent to democratic leadership) is more effective than either authoritarian (autocratic) or permissive (laissez faire).

In recent years, industrial/organizational (I/O) psychologists have conducted much of the research on leadership, trying to translate theory and research on effective leadership into interventions to make organizations more efficient. Contemporary organizational psychologists emphasize two factors implicit in Lewin's typology: *task orientation* and *relationship orientation* (see Blake & Mouton, 1964; Hersey & Blanchard, 1982; Misumi & Peterson, 1985; Stogdill & Coons, 1957). In other words, leaders differ in the extent to which they focus on efficiency and on the feelings of their employees. The distinction is similar to the two major clusters of psychosocial motives found cross-culturally—agency and communion (Chapter 10). Leaders can be high or low on one or both dimensions, although the extent to which the two correlate is a matter of debate (see Dipboye et al., 1994). Some research suggests, for example, that people who are highly attentive to tasks tend to be less attentive to the feelings of their subordinates.

Intuitively, one would assume that the best leader is one who is interested in both the product and the producer and who therefore takes a strong but democratic leadership style. This is not always the case, however. A physician cannot effectively perform delicate surgery by seeking consensus every step of the way, any more than a company in a rapidly changing field such as computer software can encourage innovative thinking with an autocratic leadership style. Many situational factors influence the effectiveness of a particular management style, such as the motivation and ability of employees, the extent to which tasks require autonomy and creativity, the leader's position in the organizational hierarchy, the degree of pressure to produce, the type of organization, and the extent to which the environment is competitive (Dipboye et al., 1994).

Cultural values and norms also guide leadership styles (see Gerstner & Day, 1994). Managers in traditional societies like Greece and India tend to prefer autocratic leadership styles with passive subordinates; by contrast, leaders in technologically developed societies like Japan, the United States, Canada, and England prefer subordinates who are active and participatory (Barrett & Franke, 1969; Negandhi, 1973). A study of managers in the United States, Hong Kong, and China found American managers more concerned with worker productivity and Chinese managers more concerned with maintaining a harmonious work environment (Ralston et al., 1992). Hong Kong managers expressed moderate concerns about both productivity and harmony, presumably reflecting Hong Kong's economic similarity to the United States and cultural similarity to China.

North American executives are now trying to adapt some of the more participatory, less hierarchical forms of management that have made Japanese organizations so productive (Deming, 1986; Sahney et al., 1991). Some companies, for example, have tried variants of the Japanese *ringi* procedure, in which work groups at lower levels draft a plan, which is then circulated up the organizational ladder (Berry et al., 1992). The result is that employees, from the lowest levels up, can see their influence on company decisions and feel responsible for them.

Leadership style and effectiveness also depend on the leader's personality (Hogan et al., 1994). Research on the Five Factor model and similar dimensions of personality (Chapter 12) finds that successful leaders tend to be high on extroversion (including dominance, energy, and orientation toward status), agreeableness, and conscientiousness. Thus, effective leaders tend to be outgoing, energetic, powerful, kind, hard-working, and attentive to the task at hand. Ineffective leaders tend to be perceived as arrogant, untrustworthy, selfish, insensitive, and overambitious—in a word, narcissistic. These generalizations, however, require the same caveat as all generalizations about personality traits: They are more likely to apply in some situations than in others (Chapter 12).

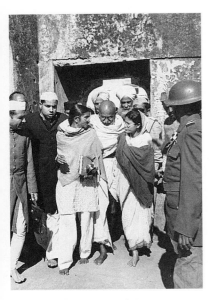

Gandhi was one of the most powerful charismatic leaders of the 20th century.

Charismatic Leaders   A type of leader prevalent today, as in most periods of rapid social change, is the charismatic leader. A **charismatic leader** is one who inspires obedience by the force of his personality (House, 1977; Weber, 1924). This century has witnessed charismatic leaders from Martin Luther King, Jr., Mahatma Gandhi, and John Kennedy to Adolf Hitler and David Koresh. As this list suggests, leaders can harness charisma for good or for ill.

Charismatic leadership generally reflects the interaction of a singular personality and a singular time. According to Erik Erikson, charismatic leaders are often motivated to greatness or infamy by their own inner turmoil, yet their actions simultaneously answer the needs of their followers. In Erikson's artful words, "Now and again. . . an individual is called upon (called by whom, only the theologians claim to know, and by what, only bad psychologists) to lift his individual patienthood to the level of a universal one and to try to solve for all what he could not solve for himself alone" (1958, p. 67). For example, Hitler felt controlled and persecuted by an autocratic father (Erikson, 1963). His resulting fantasies of rebellion and domination touched a sympathetic chord in many Germans, who had suffered as children at the hands of autocratic parents and who as a nation had suffered humiliating defeat in World War I.

Charismatic leaders offer their followers a vision of a better life and redemption from suffering (House & Singh, 1987), which are particularly appealing to people who feel oppressed, humiliated, confused by rapid cultural change, or conflicted about their identity. Charismatic leaders capture the hearts of their followers because their political message is not merely pragmatic but infused with cultural or spiritual meaning. This infusion was especially evident in Gandhi's leadership of the Indian independence movement (Erikson, 1969). Gandhi's success as a leader lay in developing a strategy for political action—passive resistance—that was compatible with traditional Indian collectivistic and nonviolent values while fostering independence from British colonialism.

INTERIM SUMMARY   **Leaders** are people who exercise greater influence than the average member of a group. Leaders tend to vary in the extent to which they are *task oriented* or *relationship oriented*. Leadership styles that are optimal or considered appropriate in one culture or setting may not be optimal in others. Leadership style and effectiveness differs across cultures as well as across individuals. At least in the West, effective leaders tend to be extroverted, agreeable, and conscientious. A **charismatic leader** is one who inspires obedience by the force of his personality.

SOME CONCLUDING THOUGHTS

Our psychological odyssey is rapidly coming to an end. We have traveled through the hills and valleys of the brain and traversed the seemingly impenetrable jungles of culture. In the process, we have encountered four soothsayers, each offering a different perspective on the psychological terrain that lies between brain and culture. One implores us to remember that humans are fundamentally animals, whose reason is always at the service of their motivation, and whose motivation is only partially available for conscious inspection. A second exhorts us to remember that human behavior, like that of other animals, is first and foremost a response to environmental events, and that what may look like freely chosen behavior is always controlled by its consequences. A third perspective reminds us of the power of human thought—of the capacity to transform simple sensations into complex ideas and to call them up moments or even years later to solve problems. The fourth reminds us that people think, feel, and behave for a reason, and that the method behind the mind's madness is the handiwork of millions of adaptations to an environment that is always one step ahead of us.

So is the mind a battleground on which internal forces compete and conflict, a machine, a computer or set of neural circuits, or a repository of adaptive "wisdom" shaped by millenia of evolution? The human mind is no doubt all of these and none of these. We will surely someday encounter other soothsayers bearing new metaphors, but they will have to save their sooth for another book and another time.

As psychologists, we view human nature from a scientific standpoint but cannot escape our own historical and cultural vista. Our knowledge of mental life and behavior is the knowledge of a particular people at a particular time. The only way to catch a glimpse of what lies beyond this limited vista is to train our eyes on the observer—ourselves—as we study the observed. This means examining our idiosyncratic reactions as we try to comprehend our nature as well as recognizing our own cultural and historical context.

These are very special times to study psychology. In the 20th century, we witnessed the most momentous period of social change in human history, as the vast majority of the world's people shifted from agricultural, nomadic, or hunter-gatherer societies to industrial nation-states. Not since the rise of agriculture thousands of years ago has the structure of human society changed so dramatically, and never as rapidly as in the present epoch. A century ago, most people lived with their extended families and believed in the values of their parents and ancestors. Within a few brief generations, traditional values and beliefs have broken down, and technology has advanced beyond anyone's wildest predictions.

People cope with social change in many ways. Some embrace new ideologies, technologies, and values. Others, coping with spiritual unease or feelings of envy, inferiority, and hatred of the dominant cultures that swept away their traditions, search for the future in the past, embracing fundamentalist ideologies that rigidly define good and evil, eliminate ambiguity, and offer a blueprint for how to live (Lifton, 1963). Another route to personal meaning lies in transferring loyalties from family and clan to large nation-states (see Geertz, 1963). Unfortunately, this process can produce the kind of fervent nationalism that has left so many dead in the 20th century, from Nazi Germany to Bosnia. Still another strategy for coping with social change is to synthesize the old and the new, to preserve a continuity with the past while somehow mooring one's identity in the future, as was Gandhi's path.

These psychological responses to the social and political realities of our age lie at the intersection of mind, brain, and culture. The aggression that fuels conflicts between nations, like the powerful feelings of kinship and solidarity that unite people and give their lives meaning, springs from a brain constructed to make possible the passions that divide and unite. We all share a core of human nature rooted in biology. But the way that nature develops and expresses itself is as diverse as the cultures and individuals who populate the globe.

The twentieth century brought more dramatic social change than any other century in human history, presenting people everywhere with profound psychological challenges.

SUMMARY

RELATIONSHIPS

1. Several factors lead to **interpersonal attraction**, including proximity, similarity, rewards, and physical attractiveness. **Social exchange theory** holds that the foundation of relationships is reciprocal rewards.

2. Psychologists have proposed various taxonomies of love. One contrasts **passionate love** (marked by intense physiological arousal and absorption in an-

other person) with **companionate love** (love that involves deep affection, friendship, and emotional intimacy). Another divides love into three components—intimacy, passion, and decision/commitment.

3. Evolutionary theorists understand love in terms of its functions for maximizing reproductive success. From this point of view, romantic love is a continuation of infant attachment mechanisms. Evolutionary theorists emphasize **sexual strategies,** tactics used in selecting mates, which vary by gender and reflect the different evolutionary selection pressures on males and females. The capacity for love is rooted in biology, but its specific nature is shaped by culture.

ALTRUISM

4. **Altruism** means behaving in a way that helps another person, with no apparent gain, or with potential cost, to oneself. Philosophers and psychologists disagree as to whether any act can be genuinely altruistic or whether all apparent altruism is really aimed at making the apparent altruist feel better (**ethical hedonism**). Altruistic behavior probably reflects a blend of selfish and unselfish motives. Evolutionary psychologists propose that people act in ways that maximize their inclusive fitness and hence are most likely to behave altruistically toward their relatives. Natural selection favors animals that behave altruistically toward unrelated members of the species if the likely benefit to each individual over time exceeds the likely cost, a phenomenon known as **reciprocal altruism**.

5. Researchers studying **bystander intervention** have found that in the presence of other people who do not take action, people often do not help in a crisis. In part this reflects a **diffusion of responsibility** (a diminished sense of personal responsibility to act).

AGGRESSION

6. **Aggression** refers to verbal or physical behavior aimed at harming another person or living being. Across cultures, males tend to be more aggressive than females. Researchers are increasingly recognizing the prevalence of male violence perpetrated against females, including battering and rape.

7. Psychodynamic and evolutionary psychologists view aggression as rooted in biology. The neural control of aggression is hierarchically organized, with the amygdala and hypothalamus playing prominent roles. Aggression is also partially controlled by hormones, particularly testosterone. The cognitive-behavioral perspective explains aggressive behavior as a result of social learning (such as modeling) and rewards and punishments.

8. The **frustration-aggression hypothesis** asserts that aggressive behavior arises from frustrated desires or needs. A reformulated hypothesis suggests that frustrating or unpleasant circumstances are likely to evoke aggression if they elicit unpleasant emotion.

SOCIAL INFLUENCE

9. **Social influence** refers to the ways in which the presence of other people influences thought, feeling, and behavior. **Obedience** is a social influence process whereby individuals follow the dictates of an authority. The Milgram

studies demonstrated that most people will obey without limitations of conscience if they believe the authority is legitimate.

10. **Conformity** is the process by which people change their attitudes or behavior to accommodate the standards of peers or groups. Asch's studies demonstrated that a substantial number of people will conform when confronted by a group with a consensus opinion, even if the opinion is manifestly wrong. Conformity is highest in agricultural societies with dense populations, where independence can be maladaptive.

11. A **group** is a collection of people whose actions affect the other group members. Naturally occurring groups routinely have **norms** (standards for the behavior of group members), **status** systems (distributions of power within the group), **roles** (socially patterned positions within a group that define appropriate behavior for the people occupying them), and **leaders** (people who exercise greater influence than the average member).

12. The massive social changes in the last century, such as rapid technological development and the breakdown of traditional family structures and values, have created profound psychological changes and dilemmas for coping.

A

ABC theory Albert Ellis's theory of psychopathology, in which A refers to activating conditions, B to belief systems, and C to emotional consequences.

absolute threshold The minimum amount of physical energy (stimulation) needed for an observer to notice a stimulus.

absorptive phase Phase of metabolism during which the person is ingesting food.

accommodation In vision, the changes in the shape of the lens that focus light rays; in Piaget's theory, the modification of schemas to fit reality.

acculturative stress The stress people experience while trying to adapt to a new culture.

acetylcholine (ACh) A neurotransmitter involved in muscle contractions, learning, and memory.

achievement test A test of knowledge in a specific area.

acquisition Initial learning of a conditioned response.

action potential A temporary shift in the polarity of the cell membrane, which leads to the firing of a neuron.

activational effects Effects of hormones activating brain circuitry to produce psychobiological changes.

actualizing tendency The primary motivation in humans, according to Carl Rogers, which includes a range of needs that humans experience, from the basic needs for food and drink to the needs to be open to experience and express one's true self.

adaptive A term applied to traits that help organisms adjust to their environment.

additive color mixture The color that results when light of differing wavelengths simultaneously strike the retina; the perception is the result of adding or combining the wavelengths.

adrenal glands Endocrine glands located above the kidneys that secrete epinephrine and other hormones during emergency situations.

adrenalin A hormone that leads to arousal.

adrenogenital syndrome A condition in which the adrenal glands secrete too much androgen, leading to the masculinization of the genitals in females.

adult attachment Patterns of mental representation, emotion, and proximity-seeking in adults related to childhood attachment patterns.

aerial perspective A monocular cue for depth perception, in which objects farther away appear fuzzier and more bluish than those nearby because of reduction and filtering of light by the atmosphere.

affect A positive or negative feeling state that typically includes arousal, subjective experience, and behavioral expression.

afferent neuron Neuron that carries sensory information to the brain or spinal cord, also called sensory neuron.

affiliation motive A need for some kind of satisfying interaction with others.

affordance Personal implication of objects or events.

afterimage Visual image that persists after a stimulus has been removed.

age changes Changes in functioning associated with age.

age differences Differences among people of different ages.

age regression Reliving an experience from a prior age under hypnosis.

ageism A form of prejudice against old people comparable to racism and sexism.

agency motives Motives for achievement, mastery, power, autonomy, and other self-oriented goals.

aggression Verbal or physical behavior aimed at harming another person or living being.

agoraphobia Fear of being in places or situations from which escape might be difficult.

alarm stage The first stage of the general adaptation syndrome that involves the release of epinephrine and other hormones such as cortisol.

alcoholism Tendency to use or abuse alcohol to a degree that leads to social or occupational dysfunction.

alexithymia Psychological disorder in which individuals are unable to describe their emotional experience.

algorithm Systematic problem-solving procedure that inevitably produces a solution.

all-or-none The quality characteristic of the depolarization of an axon membrane; an action potential either occurs, or it does not.

altered states of consciousness Deviations in subjective experience from a normal waking state.

altruism Behaving in a way that helps another person with no apparent gain, or with potential cost, to oneself.

Alzheimer's disease A progressive and incurable illness that destroys neurons in the brain, causing severe impairment of memory, reasoning, perception, language, and behavior.

ambivalence Conflicting feelings or intentions.

amnesia Memory loss.

amphetamine Drug that leads to hyperarousal and a feeling of "speeding."

amplitude The difference between the minimum and maximum pressure levels in a sound wave, measured in decibels; amplitude corresponds to the psychological property of loudness.

amygdala Brain structure associated with the expression of rage, fear, and calculation of the emotional significance of a stimulus.

anal stage   Psychosexual phase occurring roughly around ages 2 to 3, which is characterized by conflicts with parents over compliance and defiance.

analysis of variance (ANOVA)   Statistic that assesses the likelihood that mean differences between groups occurred by chance.

androgen insensitivity syndrome   A condition in which androgens are secreted in utero, but a genetic defect leads to an absence of androgen receptors, so that a genetic male develops female genitalia.

anhedonia   Lack of any pleasure in life.

anima   In Jungian theory, an unconscious feminine archetype that exists in all men.

animus   In Jungian theory, an unconscious masculine archetype that exists in all women.

anorexia nervosa   Eating disorder in which a person refuses to eat, starving herself to the point that physical complications and sometimes death may occur.

anterograde amnesia   A loss of memory for events since the damage to the brain.

antibodies   Protein molecules that attach themselves to foreign agents in the body, marking them for destruction.

antidepressant medication   Biological treatment of depression that increases the amount of norepinephrine and/or serotonin available in synapses.

antipsychotic medication   Medication used to treat schizophrenia and other psychotic states, which has sedating effects and reduces positive symptoms such as hallucinations and delusions.

antisocial personality disorder   A personality disorder marked by irresponsible and socially disruptive behavior in a variety of areas.

anxiety disorder   A disorder characterized by intense, frequent, or continuous anxiety, which may lead to disruptive avoidance behavior.

aphasia   Language disorders.

aplysia   A marine snail with very large cells that are easy to study.

aptitude   Potential for performing well.

aqueous humor   Clear fluid filling the space between the cornea and lens of the eye.

archetypes   According to Jung, mythological motifs that emerge in dreams and cultural practices, express basic human needs, and are represented by symbols in the collective unconscious.

artificial intelligence   The use of computers to perform tasks that require intelligence when performed by humans.

assimilation   The interpretation of actions or events in terms of one's present schemas.

association areas   Areas of cortex involved in putting together perceptions, ideas, and plans.

associationism   The school of philosophy that focused on the way thoughts and ideas become associated with each other in the mind.

attachment   Enduring affectional ties that children form with their primary caregivers and become the basis for later love relationships.

attachment motivation   The desire for physical and psychological proximity to an attachment figure.

attention   The process of focusing consciousness on a limited range of experience.

attention-deficit/hyperactivity disorder (ADHD)   A disorder characterized by age-inappropriate inattention, impulsiveness, and hyperactivity.

attitude   An association between an action or object and an evaluation.

attitude accessibility   The ease with which an attitude comes to mind or is activated.

attitude inoculation   Building up a receiver's resistance to an opposing attitude by presenting weak arguments for it or forewarning of a strong opposing persuasive appeal.

attitude strength   The durability of an attitude (its persistence and resistance to change) and its impact on behavior.

attitudinal ambivalence   A condition in which an attitude object is associated with conflicting evaluative responses.

attribution   The process of making inferences about the causes of one's own and others' thoughts, feelings, and behavior.

audition   Hearing.

auditory canal   Part of the outer ear, an inch-long passageway just inside the skull in which sound waves resonate and are amplified.

auditory nerve   The bundle of sensory neurons that transmit auditory information from the ear to the brain.

augmentation   Attributional phenomenon in which people emphasize an internal explanation for a behavior because it occurred despite situational pressures.

authoritarian parenting style   A way of parenting that places high value on obedience and respect for authority.

authoritarian personality   Personality type that is prone to hate people who are different or downtrodden.

authoritative parenting style   A way of parenting that sets standards for children and firmly enforces them but also provides explanations for the parents' actions and encourages verbal give-and-take.

autocratic   A leadership style identified in which the leader makes all the decisions.

automatic thoughts   The things people say spontaneously to themselves, which can lead to irrational feelings and behaviors.

automatization   The process of executing mental processes with increasing efficiency, so that they require less and less attention.

autonomic nervous system (ANS)   The part of the peripheral nervous system that serves visceral or internal bodily structures connected with basic life processes, such as the beating of the heart and breathing. It consists of two parts: the sympathetic nervous system and the parasympathetic nervous system.

autonomy versus shame and doubt   In Erikson's theory, the stage in which children begin to walk, talk, and get a sense of themselves as independent sources of will and power.

availability heuristic   A strategy that leads people to judge the frequency of a class of events or the likelihood of something happening on the basis of how easy it is to retrieve from explicit memory.

avoidance learning   Negative reinforcement procedure in which the behavior of an organism is reinforced by the prevention of an expected aversive event.

awareness   A continuum of experience that ranges from consciousness to peripheral awareness.

axon   The extension from the cell body of a neuron through which electrical impulses pass.

axon hillock   The juncture of the axon and the cell body, the site of the action potential that adds up the total voltage change from all the graded potentials sent along the dendrites and cell body.

B

B cells   Cells in the immune system that produce antibodies.

babbling   A child's earliest language utterances that are spontaneous and incomprehensible.

backward conditioning   Classical conditioning procedure in which the conditioned stimulus is presented after the unconditioned stimulus has occurred.

barbiturate   Drug that depresses the action of the nervous system.

basal ganglia   A set of structures involved in the control of movement.

basic emotions   Feeling states common to the human species from which other feeling states are derived.

basic level The level of categorization to which people naturally go; the level at which objects share distinctive common attributes.

basic trust versus mistrust In Erikson's theory, the stage in which infants come to trust others or to perceive the social world as unfriendly or unreliable.

basilar membrane Membrane that separates two of the cochlea's chambers and is flexed by pressure waves in the cochlear fluid, leading to transduction of sound.

behavior therapy Treatment based on behaviorist learning principles of classical and operant conditioning.

behavior-outcome expectancy Belief that a certain behavior will lead to a particular outcome.

behavioral analysis In cognitive-behavior therapy, the process of assessing the symptom and the stimuli or thoughts associated with it.

behavioral approach system (BAS) The anatomical system that is associated with pleasurable emotional states and is responsible for approach-oriented operant behavior.

behavioral environment The environment as mentally represented within the individual that orients the person to time, space, and people.

behavioral inhibition system (BIS) The anatomical system that is associated with anxiety and avoidance behavior.

behavioral neuroscience Field of investigation that examines the physical basis of psychological phenomena such as motivation, emotion, and stress (also called *biopsychology*).

behaviorism Perspective pioneered by John Watson and B. F. Skinner that focuses on the relation between observable behaviors and environmental events or stimuli.

benzodiazepines Antianxiety medications that indirectly affect the action of norepinephrine.

Big Five factors Five superordinate personality traits: extroversion, agreeableness, conscientiousness, neuroticism, and openness to experience.

binocular cells Neurons that receive information from both eyes.

binocular cues Visual input integrated from two eyes that provides perception of depth.

biofeedback A procedure for monitoring autonomic physiological processes and learning to alter them at will.

biopolar cells Neurons in the retina that combine information from many receptors and excite ganglion cells.

biopsychology The field that examines the physical basis of psychological phenomena such as motivation, emotion, and stress.

bipolar disorder A psychological disorder marked by extreme mood swings; also called manic-depression.

bleaching Process by which photoreceptors lose their characteristic color when exposed to light.

blind spot The point on the retina where the optic nerve leaves the eye and which contain no receptor cells; also called optic disk.

blind studies Studies in which subjects are kept unaware of or "blind" to important aspects of the research.

blindsight A phenomenon in which individuals with cortical lesions have no conscious visual awareness but can make discriminations about objects placed in front of them.

blocking When a stimulus fails to elicit a conditioned response because it is combined with another stimulus that already elicits the response.

borderline personality disorder A personality disorder characterized by extremely unstable interpersonal relationships, dramatic mood swings, an unstable sense of identity, intense fears of abandonment, manipulativeness, and impulsive behavior.

bottom-up processing Perceptual processing that starts with raw sensory data that feed "up" to the brain; what is perceived is determined largely by the features of the stimuli reaching the sense organs.

boundaries In family systems theory, the physical and psychological limits of a family or system.

bounded rationality The notion that people are rational within constraints imposed by their environment, goals, and abilities.

brain grafting Neural tissue transplants.

brightness Sensory counterpart of visual stimulus intensity.

Broca's aphasia Language disorder caused by damage to Broca's area of the left frontal cortex, in which a person has difficulty speaking, putting together grammatical sentences, understanding complex sentences, and articulating words.

Broca's area Brain structure located in the left frontal lobe at the base of the motor strip, involved in the ability to talk and use grammar.

buffering hypothesis The view that social support acts as a protective factor against the harmful effects of stress.

bulimia A disorder characterized by a binge-and-purge syndrome in which the person binges on food and then either induces vomiting or uses laxatives to purge.

bystander intervention A form of altruism involving helping a person in need.

C

Cannon-Bard theory A theory of emotion that asserts that emotion-inducing stimuli elicit both emotional experience and bodily response.

case study In-depth observation of one subject or a small group of subjects.

castration complex In Freud's theory, the fear the boy has in the phallic stage that his father will castrate him for his wishes toward his mother.

catastrophes Rare, unexpected disasters such as earthquakes, floods, and other traumatic events that affect a group of people.

catatonic schizophrenia Type of schizophrenia marked by peculiar motor behavior, such as an extended period of frozen movement and stupor.

categorical variable A variable comprised of groupings, classifications, or categories.

categorization The process of identifying an object as an instance of a category, recognizing its similarity to some objects and dissimilarity to others.

cell body (soma) Part of the neuron which includes a nucleus containing the genetic material of the cell (the chromosomes) as well as other microstructures vital to cell functioning.

central fissure The deep divide in cortical tissue that separates the primary motor and somatosensory cortex.

central nervous system The brain and spinal cord.

centration The tendency to focus or center on one perceptually striking feature of an object without considering other features that might be relevant.

cerebellum A large bulge in the dorsal or back area of the brain, responsible for the coordination of smooth, well-sequenced movements as well as maintaining equilibrium and regulating postural reflexes.

cerebrum The "thinking" center of the brain, which includes the cortex and subcortical structures such as the basal ganglia and limbic system.

chaining Process of learning in which a sequence of already established behaviors is reinforced step by step.

charismatic leader A leader who inspires obedience by the force of his or her personality.

chi-square (X^2) test Inferential statistic that compares the observed data with the results one would expect by chance and tests the likelihood the differences between observed and expected are accidental.

childhood amnesia The inability to recall early childhood memories.

chromosomes Strands of DNA arranged in pairs.

chunking The process of organizing information into small, meaningful bits to aid memory.

cilia Dendrite-like protections from olfactory receptor cells that extend through the mucous layer into the nasal cavity.

circadian rhythms Biological rhythms that evolved around the daily cycles of light and dark.

classical conditioning A procedure by which a previously neutral stimulus comes to elicit a response after it is paired with a stimulus that automatically elicits that response.

client-centered therapy Therapeutic approach developed by Carl Rogers, based on the assumption that psychological difficulties result from incongruence between one's concept of self and one's actual experience, and that empathy is curative.

clinical psychology The field that studies the nature and treatment of psychopathology.

clinical syndrome A constellation of symptoms that tend to occur together.

closure A Gestalt rule of perception which states that people tend to perceive incomplete figures as complete.

cocaine A stimulant that increases the activity of norepinephrine and dopamine.

cochlea Three-chambered tube in the inner ear in which sound is transduced.

cognition Thought and memory.

cognitive dissonance Phenomenon in which a person experiences a discrepancy between an attitude and a behavior or between an attitude and a new piece of information incongruent with it, which leads to a state of tension and a subsequent change in attitude, behavior, or perception.

cognitive distortions Cognitive mechanisms by which a depressed person transforms neutral or positive information in a depressive direction.

cognitive maps Mental representations of visual space.

cognitive social theory A theory of learning that emphasizes the role of thought and social learning in behavior.

cognitive therapy A psychological treatment that focuses on the thought processes that underlie psychological symptoms.

cognitive unconscious Information processing mechanisms that operate outside of awareness, such procedural memory and implicit associative processes, as opposed to the psychodynamic unconscious, which includes information the person is *motivated* to keep from awareness.

cognitive-behavioral therapy Psychotherapy that uses methods derived from behaviorist and cognitive learning theories.

cohort Age group born around the same time.

cohort effects Differences among age groups associated with differences in the culture.

collective unconscious A repository of ideas, feelings, and symbols that are shared by all humans and passed genetically from one generation to another, according to Jung.

color constancy The tendency to perceive the color of objects as stable despite changing illumination.

color-opponent cells Neurons excited by wavelengths that produce one color but inhibited by those that produce another.

companionate love Love that involves deep affection, friendship, and emotional intimacy.

competence An ability to perform a behavior even if never performed in the past.

competencies Skills and abilities used for solving problems.

complex cells Feature detectors in the visual cortex that respond when a stimulus of the right orientation falls anywhere within their receptive field; the cells respond most vigorously to lines of a specific orientation moving in a particular direction.

complexity The extent to which a sound wave is composed of multiple frequencies.

compromise formations A single behavior, or a complex pattern of thought and action, which typically reflects compromises among multiple (and often conflicting) forces.

compulsion An intentional behavior or mental act performed in a stereotyped fashion.

computerized axial tomography (CT scan) Brain scanning technique used to detect lesions.

concept A mental representation of a category of objects, ideas, or events that share common properties.

concrete operational stage Piaget's third stage of cognitive development, in which children are capable of mentally manipulating internal representations of concrete objects in ways that are reversible.

conditioned emotional response An emotional response that is learned by pairing an unconditioned stimulus or previously conditioned stimulus with a formerly neutral stimulus.

conditioned response In classical conditioning, a response that has been learned.

conditioned stimulus A stimulus that the organism has learned to associate with the unconditioned stimulus.

conditioning trial Each pairing of the conditioned stimulus and the unconditioned stimulus during the acquisition of the conditioned response.

conditions Values or versions of the independent variable that vary across experimental groups.

conditions of worth In Carl Rogers' theory, standards children internalize that they must meet in order to esteem themselves.

conduct disorder A childhood disorder in which a child persistently violates the rights of others as well as societal norms.

conduction loss Type of hearing defect in which the outer or middle ear fails to conduct sound to the hair cells.

cones One of two types of photoreceptors, which are specialized for color vision and allow perception of fine detail.

confederates Individuals posing as subjects, who assist an experimenter, in a deception experiment.

confirmation bias The tendency for people to search for information that confirms their expectations.

conflict A battle between opposing motives.

conflict model Theoretical model of adolescence that holds that conflict and crisis are normal in adolescence.

conformity The process of changing attitudes or behavior to accommodate the standards of a group.

confounding variable A variable that produces effects of independent variables.

conscious mental processes In psychoanalytic theory, mental processes of which people are aware.

consciousness The subjective awareness of mental events.

consensus In attribution theory, a normative response in a social group.

conservation Recognition that basic properties of an object remain stable even though superficial properties may change.

consistency In attribution theory, the extent to which a person always responds in the same way to the same stimulus.

consolidation The processes by which knowledge becomes stored in long-term memory systems.

context of discovery Part of scientific process in which phenomena are observed, hypotheses are framed, and theories are built.

context of justification Part of scientific process in which hypotheses are tested.

continuity model Theoretical model that holds that adolescence for most individuals is essentially continuous with childhood and adulthood and not distinguished by turbulence.

continuous development   Steady and gradual change, as opposed to major qualitative transformations; see also **stages.**

continuous schedule of reinforcement   When the environmental consequences are the same each time an organism emits a behavior.

continuous variable   A variable that can be placed on a continuum, from none or little to much.

control group   Subjects in an experiment who receive a relatively neutral condition to serve as a comparison group.

conventional morality   Level of morality in which individuals define what is right by the standards they have learned from other people, particularly respected authorities.

convergence   The turning inward of the eyes as an object gets closer; a binocular cue for depth perception.

coping   Ways people deal with stressful situations.

core feature   Aspect of a concept not shared by other concepts that clearly distinguishes the concept from others.

cornea   Tough, transparent tissue covering the front of the eyeball.

corpus callosum   A band of fibers that connect the two hemispheres of the brain.

correlation coefficient   An index of the extent to which two variables are related.

correlation matrix   A table presenting the correlations among several variables.

correlational research   Research that assesses the degree to which two variables are related, so that knowing the value of one can lead to prediction of the other.

cortex   The many-layered surface of the cerebrum that allows complex movement and information processing.

counterconditioning   A technique by which the patient learns physiological and muscular processes that are the opposite of a previously conditioned anxiety response.

countertransference   The phenomenon in which transference reactions of the patient trigger emotional responses in the therapist.

couples therapy   Psychotherapy that treats a couple.

covariation   The extent to which the presence of one variable implies the presence of another.

creativity   The ability to produce valued outcomes in a novel way.

critical period   A period of special sensitivity to specific types of learning that shapes the capacity for future development.

cross-cultural psychology   The field that attempts to test psychological hypotheses in different cultures.

cross-sectional studies   Type of research that compares groups of different-aged subjects at a single time to see whether differences exist among them.

crystallized intelligence   People's store of knowledge.

culture pattern approach   Approach to personality and culture that views culture as an organized set of beliefs, rituals, and institutions that shape individuals to fit its patterns.

culture-free   Not dependent on a particular cultural experience.

cycle   A single round of expansion and contraction of the distance between molecules of air in a sound wave.

D

daily hassles   The small, but irritating demands that characterize daily life.

dark adaptation   The eyes' adjustment to dim light.

daydreaming   Part of the flow of consciousness in which attention turns from external stimuli to internal thoughts.

decay theory of forgetting   The notion that memories are lost as a result of a fading of the memory trace.

decibels (dB)   Unit of measure of amplitude (loudness) of a sound wave.

decision criterion   In signal detection theory, the subject's readiness to report detecting a signal when uncertain; also called response bias.

decision making   The process by which people weigh the pros and cons of different alternatives in order to make a choice among two or more options.

declarative memory   Knowledge that can be consciously retrieved and "declared."

deductive reasoning   The process of reasoning that draws logical conclusions from premises.

deep structure   The underlying meaning conveyed by a sentence.

default value   Standard information that fills in for missing data in schematic processing.

defense mechanisms   Unconscious mental processes aimed at protecting a person from experiencing unpleasant emotions, especially anxiety.

deficiency needs   In Maslow's hierarchy of needs, motives generated by a lack of something.

degree of relatedness   The probability that two people share any particular gene.

deinstitutionalization   A movement to increase the autonomy of severely psychiatrically impaired people and to integrate them in community life.

delta sleep   A deep characterized by relaxation of muscles and a reduction in biological processes such as rate of respiration and body temperature.

delusion   A false belief firmly held despite evidence to the contrary.

delusional depression   Severe depression with psychotic features.

demand characteristics   The influence of subjects' perception of the researchers' goals on subjects' behavior.

dementia   A disorder marked by global disturbance of higher mental functions.

demographic characteristics   Subject characteristics such as age, sex, and race.

dendrites   Branch-like extensions of the cell body, which receive information from other cells.

denial   A defense mechanism in which the person refuses to acknowledge external realities or emotions.

dependent variables   Subjects' responses in a study, hypothesized to depend on the influence of the independent variables.

depolarization   Process by which the inside of the cell membrane of a neuron becomes less negative (a decrease in polarization) resulting from the stimulation of a neuron's dendrites or cell body by impulses from other neurons.

depressant   Drug that slows down the nervous system.

depth of processing   The degree to which information is processed in a meaningful way.

depth perception   The organization of perception in three dimensions.

descriptive diagnosis   Classification of mental disorders in terms of clinical syndromes.

descriptive research   Research methods that cannot unambiguously demonstrate cause and effect, including case studies, naturalistic observation, survey research, and correlational methods.

descriptive statistics   Numbers that describe the data from a study in a way that summarizes their essential features.

developmental model   In Freud's theory, the model of psychosexual stages.

developmental psychology   The field that studies the way thought, feeling, and behavior develop through the lifespan.

developmental task   Challenge that is normative for a particular period of life.

Diagnostic and Statistical Manual of Mental Disorders-IV (DSM-IV)   Manual of clinical syndromes published by the American Psychiatric Association and used for descriptive diagnosis.

diathesis-stress model   Model of psychopathology which proposes that people with an underlying vulnerability (also called a diathesis) may develop a disorder under stressful circumstances.

dichotic listening   A procedure in which different information is presented to the left and right ears simultaneously.

difference threshold   The smallest difference in intensity between two stimuli that a person can detect.

diffusion of responsibility   The phenomenon in which the presence of other people leads to a diminished sense of personal responsibility to act.

direct perception   A theory which states that sensory information intrinsically carries meaning.

discounting   Attributional phenomenon in which people downplay the role of one variable that might explain a behavior because they know another may be contributing.

discrimination   The behavioral component of prejudiced attitudes.

discriminative stimulus   A stimulus that signals that particular contingencies of reinforcement are in effect.

disorganized schizophrenia   Type of schizophrenia marked by extremely poor contact with reality and bizarre behavior.

display rules   Patterns of emotional expression that are considered acceptable in a given culture.

dissociation   A disturbance in memory and consciousness in which significant aspects of experience are kept separate and distinct (or dis-associated).

dissociative disorders   Disorders characterized by disruptions in consciousness, memory, sense of identity, or perception of the environment.

dissociative identity disorder   The most severe dissociative disorder, also known as multiple personality disorder.

distinctiveness   In attribution theory, the extent to which an individual responds in a particular way to many different stimuli.

divergent thinking   Generating multiple possibilities from a given situation.

divided attention   The process by which attention is split between two or more sets of stimuli.

dizygotic (DZ) twins   Fraternal twins who, like other siblings, share only about half of their genes.

doctrine of specific nerve energies   Formulated by Johannes Müller in 1826; states that whether a neural message is experienced as light, sound, or some other sensation results less from differences in stimuli than from the particular neural pathways excited by them.

dominant   Cortical hemisphere more involved in certain functions than the other.

dopamine   A neurotransmitter with wide-ranging effects, involved in movement, thought, and emotion.

double-blind study   Study in which both subjects and researchers are blind to the status of subjects.

Down syndrome   Disorder caused by an extra 21st chromosome, resulting in severe mental retardation.

drive   According to Freud, an internal tension state that builds up until satisfied; according to behaviorist theory, an unpleasant tention state that motivates behavior, classified as either primary or secondary (acquired).

drive model   Freud's theory of motivation, which held that people are motivated by sexual and aggressive instincts or drives.

drive-reduction theories   Mid-twentieth century behaviorist theories which proposed that motivation stems from a combination of drive and reinforcement, in which stimuli become reinforcing because they are associated with reduction of a state of biological deficit.

dysthmymia   Chronic low-level depression of more than two years' duration, with intervals of normal moods that never last more than a few weeks or months.

E

eardrum   Thin, flexible membrane that marks the outer boundary of the middle ear; the eardrum is set in motion by sound waves and in turn sets in motion the ossicles; also called the tympanic membrane.

early memories   Memories of events that took place early in one's life.

echoic storage   An auditory sensory registration process by which people retain an echo or brief auditory representation of a sound to which they have been exposed.

echolocation   Process used by bats and other animals to sense objects by emitting waves of sounds and sensing the echoes as these waves bounce off the objects.

ecological approach   Approach to the development of perception which attempts to understand perception in its environmental, adaptive context.

educational psychology   Field that studies psychological processes in learning and applies psychological knowledge to practical problems in educational settings.

effectiveness studies   Studies that assess the outcome of psychotherapy as it is practiced in the field rather than in the laboratory.

efferent neuron (motor neuron)   Neuron that transmits commands from the brain to the glands or musculature of the body, typically through the spinal cord.

efficacy studies   Studies that assess psychotherapy outcome under highly controlled conditions, such as random assignment of patients to different treatment or control groups, careful training of therapists to adhere to a manual, and standardized length of treatment.

ego   The structure in Freud's model of the mind that must somehow balance desire, reality, and morality.

ego functioning   The person's ability to function autonomously, make sound decisions, think clearly, and regulate impulses and emotions.

egocentrism   Being thoroughly embedded in one's own point of view.

eidetic imagery   A kind of visual representation that is of photographic accuracy.

elaborative rehearsal   An aid to long-term memory storage that involves thinking about the meaning of information in order to process it with more depth; see also **depth of processing.**

electroconvulsive therapy (ECT)   A last-resort treatment for severe depression, in which an electric shock to the brain is used to induce a seizure.

electroencephalograph (EEG)   Instrument that assesses electrical activity in the brain, used especially in sleep research and diagnosis of epilepsy.

elevation   Monocular depth cue in which distant objects are higher on the person's plane of view.

embryonic period   Second phase of prenatal development that extends from the beginning of the third week to about the eighth week of gestation.

emotional expression   The variety of models (e.g., facial expression, posture, hand gestures, voice tone) through which people express feelings.

empathic distress   Feeling upset for another person.

empathy   Feeling for another person who is hurting, which includes a cognitive component (understanding what the person is experiencing) and an emotional component (experiencing a feeling of empathic discomfort; in Rogers's theory of personality, the capacity to understand another person's experience cognitively and emotionally.

empty chair technique   A technique associated with Gestalt therapy, in which clients practice emotional expression by imagining that the person to whom they would like to speak is seated in the chair.

encoding   The process by which information is put into a representational form that can be stored and accessed from memory.

encoding specificity principle   The notion that the match between the way information is encoded and the way it is retrieved is important to remembering.

endocrine system   Collection of ductless glands that secrete hormones into the bloodstream and control various bodily and psychological functions.

endogenous   Produced within the body.

endorphins   Chemicals in the brain similar to morphine that act as analgesics.

environmental psychology   Area of psychology that applies psychological knowledge to the design of buildings and landscapes.

epinephrine   Hormone secreted by the adrenal glands.

episodic memory   Memories of particular episodes or events from personal experience.

equilibration   According to Piaget, a balancing of assimilation and accommodation in trying to adapt to the world.

ERG theory   A theory of worker motivation distinguishing existence, relatedness, and growth needs.

error   That part of a subject's score on a test that is unrelated to the true score.

escape learning   Negative reinforcement procedure in which the behavior of an organism is reinforced by the cessation of an aversive event that already exists.

estrogens   Hormones produced by the female gonads, the ovaries, which control sex drive as well as the development of secondary sex characteristics.

ethical hedonism   School of philosophical thought that asserts that all behavior, no matter how apparently altruistic, is and should be designed to increase one's own pleasure or reduce one's own pain.

ethology   Field that studies animal behavior from a biological and evolutionary perspective.

etiology   Causes of a disorder.

Eustachian tube   Passage that connects the middle ear to the throat and allows release of pressure.

evolutionary perspective   Viewpoint built on Darwin's principle of natural selection; argues that human behavioral proclivities must be understood in the context of their evolutionary and adaptive significance.

excitatory neurotransmitters   Chemicals that depolarize the postsynaptic cell membrane, making an action potential more likely.

excitement phase   First phase of the sexual response cycle, characterized by increased muscle tension, engorgement of blood vessels in the genitals, and often a skin flush.

exhaustion stage   The third stage of the general adaptation syndrome in which the body's physiological defenses break down.

existential dread   The recognition that life has no absolute value or meaning, that any meaning that does exist we create for ourselves, and that ultimately, we all face death.

existentialism   A school of modern philosophy that focuses on each individual's subjective existence or phenomenology and on the way the individual comes to terms with basic issues such as meaning in life and mortality.

expectancies   Expectations relevant to desired outcomes.

expectancy-value theories   Theories which assert that motivation is a joint function of the value people place on an outcome and the extent to which they believe they can attain it.

expected utility   A combined assessment of the value and probability of different options.

experience sampling   Technique designed to study the flow of consciousness in which subjects may talk through a task or report their thoughts when beeped on a pager.

experimental research   Research design in which investigators manipulate some aspect of a situation and examine the impact of this manipulation on the way subjects respond.

explanatory style   The way people make sense of events or outcomes, particularly aversive ones.

explicit cognition   Thinking that involves conscious manipulation of representations.

explicit memory   Conscious recollection of facts and events.

exposure techniques   Behavior therapy techniques based on classical conditioning in which the patient is confronted with the actual phobic stimulus.

expressed emotion   A family climate that includes criticism, hostile interchanges, and emotional overinvolvement or intrusiveness on the part of family members, which predicts relapse in schizophrenia and other forms of psychopathology.

external attribution   Explanation of behavior that attributes it to the situation rather than the person.

external validity   The extent to which the findings of a study can be generalized to situations outside the laboratory.

extinction   In classical conditioning, the process by which a conditioned response is weakened by presentation of the conditioned stimulus without the unconditioned stimulus; in operant conditioning, the process by which the connection between an operant and a reinforcer or punishment is similarly broken.

extroversion   Tendency to be sociable, active, and willing to take risks.

F

factor analysis   A statistical technique for identifying common factors that underlie performance on a wide variety of measures.

false confirmation   The tendency to look for information that confirms beliefs and to ignore information that does not.

false self   Condition in which people mold themselves to other people's expectations and to the demands of the roles they play.

familiar size   A monocular cue for depth perception in which familiar objects are assumed to be their usual size, so that if they appear small they are perceived as farther away.

family alliances   Patterns of taking sides in family conflicts.

family homeostatic mechanisms   Methods members use to preserve equilibrium in a family.

family roles   Parts individuals play in repetitive family interaction patterns.

family systems model   Model of psychopathology which suggests that an individual's symptoms are really symptoms of dysfunction in a family.

family therapy   A psychological treatment that attempts to change maladaptive interaction patterns among members of a family.

farsightedness   Condition in which the eye focuses light on a point beyond the retina, leading to decreased acuity at close range; also called hyperopia.

fasting phase   The second stage of metabolism, when the body converts glucose and fat into energy.

feature detector   Neuron that fires only when stimulation in its receptive field matches a particular pattern or orientation.

Fechner's law   Law of psychophysics proposed by Gustav Fechner, that the subjective magnitude of a sensation grows as a proportion of the logarithm of the stimulus.

feedback   Information about the extent to which a system is meeting a goal.

fetal alcohol syndrome   A condition affecting up to half of babies born to alcoholic mothers, which leads to birth defects.

fetal period The third phase of prenatal development, from about 9 weeks to birth.

fight/flight system Anatomical system associated with unconditioned escape and defensive aggression and the emotions of terror and rage.

figure-ground perception A fundamental rule of perception described by Gestalt psychology which states that people inherently differentiate between figure (the object they are viewing, sound to which they are listening, etc.) and ground (background).

firing When a neuron is activated enough to send information to other neurons.

first impressions Initial perceptions of another person that can be powerful in shaping future beliefs about the person.

fixations In psychoanalytic theory, prominent conflicts and concerns focused on wishes from a particular period.

fixed interval schedules When the organism receives rewards for its responses only after a fixed amount of time.

fixed ratio schedules When the organism receives reinforcement at a fixed rate, according to the number of responses emitted.

flashbulb memories Especially vivid memories of exciting or highly consequential events.

flat affect Blunted emotional response, which is often found in schizophrenic patients.

flooding Cognitive-behavioral technique designed to eliminate phobias, in which the patient confronts the real phobic stimulus all at once.

fluid intelligence Intellectual capacities that have no specific content but are used in processing information.

foot-in-the-door technique Persuasive technique often used by salespeople, which involves getting people to comply with a small request in order to induce their compliance with a larger request.

forebrain In humans, the most evolutionary recent part of the brain, which allows complex emotional reactions, thought processes, and movement patterns.

forgetting Inability to retrieve memories.

form perception The organization of sensations into meaningful shapes and patterns.

formal operational stage Piaget's fourth stage of cognitive development, which begins at about age 12 to 15, and is characterized by the ability to manipulate abstract as well as concrete objects, events, and ideas mentally.

forward conditioning When the conditioned stimulus precedes the unconditioned stimulus.

fovea The central region of the retina, where light is most directly focused by the lens.

free association Therapeutic technique for exploring associational networks and unconscious process involved in symptom formation.

free nerve endings Receptors in the skin that appear sensitive to pain.

free will versus determinism The philosophical question of whether people act on the basis of their freely chosen intentions, or whether their actions are caused or determined by physical processes in their bodies or in the environment in which they live.

frequency In a sound wave, the number of cycles per second, expressed in hertz and responsible for subjective experience of pitch.

frequency distribution A way of organizing data to show how frequently subjects received each of the many possible scores.

frequency theory Theory of pitch which asserts that perceived pitch reflects the rate of vibration of the basilar membrane.

frontal lobes Brain structures involved in coordination of movement, attention, planning, social skills, conscience, abstract thinking, and aspects of personality.

frustration-aggression hypothesis Hypothesis that when people are frustrated in achieving a goal, they may become aggressive.

functional fixedness The tendency to ignore other possible functions of an object when one already has a function in mind.

functionalism An early school of thought in psychology influenced by Darwinian theory that looked for explanations of psychological processes in terms of their role, or function, in helping the individual adapt to the environment.

fuzzy concept Concept that is not reliably understood but rather has different meanings in different contexts.

G

g-factor The general intelligence factor that emerges through factor analysis of IQ tests.

GABA Acronym for gamma-aminobutyric acid, one of the most widespread neurotransmitters in the nervous system, which largely plays an inhibitory role in the brain.

galvanic skin response An electrical measure of the amount of sweat on the skin that is produced during states of anxiety or arousal; also called skin conductance or electrodermal activity (EDA).

ganglion cells Nerve cells in the retina that integrate information from multiple bipolar cells, the axons of which bundle together to form the optic nerve.

gate control theory Theory of pain perception which proposes that cells in the spinal cord act as neurological "gates," allowing some pain signals through while blocking others.

gender The psychological meaning of being male or female.

gender constancy The recognition that people's gender cannot be altered by changes in appearance or activities.

gender identity Categorization of oneself as either male or female.

gender roles The range of behaviors considered appropriate by society for males and females.

gender schemas Representations that associate psychological characteristics with one sex or the other.

gender stability The understanding that one's gender remains constant over time.

gene The unit of hereditary transmission.

general adaptation syndrome The three-stage process (alarm, resistance, exhaustion) by which a person responds to stressful conditions.

general intelligence The general quickness and efficiency of solving problems that differs among individuals.

generalizability Applicability of a study's finding to the entire population of interest.

generalized anxiety disorder Persistent anxiety at a moderate but disturbing level.

generativity Concern for the next generation as well as an interest producing something of lasting value to society.

generativity versus stagnation In Erikson's theory, the stage in which people in mid-adulthood experience concern for the next generation as well as an interest in producing something of lasting value to society.

genital stage In Freudian theory, psychosexual stage that occurs at approximately age 12 and beyond, when conscious sexuality resurfaces after years of repression.

genogram A map of a family over three or four generations, drawn by a therapist to explore possible similarities between current difficulties and the family's past.

genotype Genetic blueprints underlying phenotypic variance.

germinal period   First two weeks of pre-natal development, when the fertilized egg becomes implanted in the uterus.

gerontologist   Scientist who studies the elderly.

Gestalt therapy   A psychological treatment based on the assumption that psychological distress results from losing touch with one's emotions and one's authentic inner voice, and that focusing on the "here and now" is curative.

gestation   Period of prenatal development.

giftedness   The high extreme of the intellectual spectrum.

glucoreceptors   Neurons that monitor glucose levels.

glucose   A simple carbohydrate or sugar that is a source of energy for humans and other animals.

glucostatic theory   A theory of hunger which proposes that hunger arises when glucose "thermostats" in the nervous system–or "glucostats"–detect low levels of glucose in the bloodstream.

glutamate   One of the most widespread neurotransmitters in the nervous system, which largely plays an excitatory role; also called glutamic acid.

goal state   The final stage of problem solving in which the problem is solved.

goal-setting theory   Theory of motivation which suggests that conscious goals regulate much human action, particularly performance tasks.

gonads   Endocrine glands that control much of sexual development and behavior.

good continuation   A Gestalt rule of perception which states that, if possible, the brain organizes stimuli into continuous lines or patterns rather than discontinuous elements.

graded exposure   A modified version of the behaviorist flooding technique for treating anxiety, in which stimuli are real but are presented to the patient in a gradual manner.

graded potential   Spreading voltage change that occurs when the neural membrane receives a signal from another cell.

grammar   A system of rules for generating understandable and acceptable language utterances.

group   A collection of people whose actions affect the other group members.

group process   The interactions among members of a group.

group test   A pencil-and-paper measure of intelligence or similar qualities that can be administered simultaneously to a roomful of people.

group therapy   Treatment method in which multiple people meet together to work toward therapeutic goals.

growth needs   Motives to expand and develop one's skills and potential.

gustation   Taste.

gyrus   Cortical "hill."

H

hair cells   Receptors for sound attached to the basilar membrane.

hallucination   Sensation and perception that occurs in the absence of any external stimulation.

hallucinogen   Drug that produces hallucinations.

halo effect   A tendency to attribute additional positive characteristics to someone who has one salient quality, such as physical attractiveness.

health psychology   Field that lies at the intersection of psychology and medicine, looking at psychological factors involved in health and disease.

heritability   The extent to which individual differences in phenotype are determined by genetic factors or genotype.

heritability coefficient   Statistic that quantifies the degree to which a trait is heritable.

hermeneutic   Interpretive approach to methodology which proposes that a science of human action should aim to understand personal meaning, not predict behavior.

hertz (Hz)   Unit of measurement of frequency of sound waves.

heuristics   In problem solving, cognitive shortcuts or rules of thumb.

hierarchical organization of memory   When information is organized first by broad, general categories which are in turn comprised of narrower subcategories, and ultimately of representations of specific information.

hierarchy of needs.   Maslow's theory that needs are arranged hierarchically, from physiological needs, safety needs, belongingness needs, and esteem needs, through self-actualization needs.

hindbrain   Part of the brain above the spinal cord that includes the medulla cerebellum, and parts of the reticular formation.

hippocampus   A structure in the limbic system involved in the acquisition and consolidation of new information in memory.

histogram   A graph that plots ranges of scores along the x axis and the frequency of scores in each range on the y axis.

homeostasis   The body's tendency to maintain a relatively constant state that permits cells to live and function.

hormone   Chemical secreted directly into the bloodstream by the endocrine glands.

hue   the sensory quality people normally consider color.

humanistic psychology   Branch of psychology that asserts the importance of free will, abandons the view that environmental and genetic variables determine all behavior, and thus questions the applicability of scientific methods to human psychology.

humanistic therapies   Psychological treatments that focus on the patient's conscious or lived experience and on the way each person uniquely experiences relationships and the world.

hyper-complex cells   A type of feature detector in the visual cortex that responds to moving lines of a specific length and to moving angles of a specific size.

hypermnesia   Recalling forgotten memories during hypnosis.

hyperopia   Condition in which the eye focuses light on a point beyond the retina, leading to decreased acuity at close range. Also called farsightedness.

hyperpolarization   Process by which the inside of the cell membrane of a neuron becomes more negative (increasing the polarization), decreasing the likelihood that the neuron will fire.

hypersomnia   Sleep disorder in which the individual sleeps too much.

hypnosis   Altered state of consciousness characterized by deep relaxation and suggestibility which a person voluntarily enters through the efforts of a hypnotist.

hypnotic analgesia   Under hypnosis, an apparent lack of pain despite pain-inducing stimulation.

hypnotic susceptibility   The capacity to enter into a deep hypnotic state.

hypothalamus   Brain structure situated directly below the thalamus, involved in the regulation of eating, sleeping, sexual activity, movement, and emotion.

hypothesis   A tentative belief or educated guess that purports to predict or explain the relationship between two or more variables.

hypothesis testing   In problem solving, a strategy that involves pursuing an educated guess.

hypothyroidism   Disorder in which the thyroid gland is underactive.

I

iconic storage   A visual sensory registration process by which people retain an afterimage of a visual stimulus.

id   In Freudian theory, the reservoir of sexual and aggressive energy, which is driven by impulses and is characterized by primary process thinking.

ideal self   A person's view of what she/he should be like.

identification   Making another person part of oneself by imitating the person's behavior, changing the self-concept to see oneself as more like that person, and attempting to become more like the person by accepting his or her values and attitudes.

identified patient   In a family system model of psychopathology, the person identified as needing help, or the symptom bearer.

identity   A stable sense of knowing who one is and what one's values and ideals are.

identity confusion   Condition in which the individual fails to develop a coherent and enduring sense of self, and has difficulty committing to roles, values, people, and occupational choices in his or her life.

identity versus identity confusion   In Erikson's theory, stage in which adolescents develop a stable sense of who they are and a stable set of values and ideals.

ill-defined problem   A situation in which both the information needed to solve a problem and the criteria that determine whether the goals are attained are vague.

imaging techniques   Methods for studying the brain that use computer programs to convert the data taken from brain scanning devices into visual images; this is sometimes also called *neuroimaging.*

immune system   A system of cells throughout the body that fights disease.

implicit attitudes   Attitudes that regulate thought and behavior unconsciously and automatically.

implicit cognition   Thinking that occurs outside awareness.

implicit memory   Memory that cannot be brought to mind consciously but can be expressed in behavior.

impoverished thought   Negative symptom of schizophrenia, characterized by lack of complex thought in response to environmental stimuli.

incentive   An external motivating stimulus (as opposed to an internal need state).

inclusive fitness   The notion that natural selection favors organisms that survive, reproduce, and foster the survival and reproduction of their kin.

independent variable   The variable an experimenter manipulates, or whose effects the experimenter assesses.

individual differences   The way people resemble and differ from one another in personality or intelligence.

inductive reasoning   The process of reasoning from specific observations to generate propositions.

industry versus inferiority   In Erikson's theory, the stage in which children develop a sense of competence as they begin to practice skills they will use in productive work.

inferential statistics   Procedures for assessing whether the results obtained with a sample are likely to reflect characteristics of the population as a whole.

information processing   The transformation, storage, and retrieval of environmental inputs through thought and memory.

informed consent   Subject's ability to agree to participate in a study in an informed manner.

ingroup   People perceived as belonging to a valued group.

inhibition to the unfamiliar   A temperamental variable involving shyness and fear of novel stimuli.

inhibitory neurotransmitter   Neurotransmitter that hyperpolarizes the membrane, reducing the likelihood that the postsynaptic neuron will fire.

initial state   The first stage of problem solving that involves the recognition that a problem exists.

initiation rites   Ceremonies such as the rites found in many cultures in adolescence, which initiate a person into a new social role, such as adulthood.

initiative versus guilt   In Erikson's theory, the stage in which children develop a sense of planfulness and responsibility.

insight   In learning theory, the ability to perceive a connection between a problem and its solution; in psychodynamic treatments, the understanding of one's own psychological processes.

insomnia   The inability to sleep.

instinct   Relatively fixed pattern of behavior that animals produce without learning.

instinct model   Freud's theory of motivation, which held that people are motivated by sexual and aggressive instincts or drives.

instrumental aggression   Calm, pragmatic aggression that may or may not be accompanied by anger.

instrumental conditioning   Learning that results when an organism associates a response that occurs spontaneously with a particular effect; also called operant conditioning.

instrumental leader   See task leader.

integrity versus despair   In Erikson's theory, stage in which older people look back on their lives with a sense of satisfaction that they have lived it well, or with despair, regret, and loss for loved ones who have died.

intelligence   The application of cognitive skills and knowledge to learn, solve problems, and obtain ends that are valued by an individual or culture.

intelligence quotient (IQ)   A score originally derived by dividing mental age and chronological age and multiplying by 100, but now generally established by comparing the individual's performance to norms of people his or her own age.

intelligence test   Measure designed to assess an individual's level of cognitive capabilities compared to other people in a population.

intensity   In sensation, the strength of a stimulus.

inter-rater reliability   A measure of the similarity with which different raters apply a measure.

intergenerational approach   Approach to family therapy that examines the ways in which problems are repeated across generations of a family.

intermittent schedule of reinforcement   Operant procedure in which an organism is reinforced only some of the time it emits a behavior.

intermodal processing   The capacity to associate sensations of an object from different senses, or to match one's own actions to behaviors that are observed visually; also called cross-modal processing.

internal attribution   Explanation of behavior that attributes it to the person rather than the situation.

internal consistency   A type of reliability that assesses whether the items in a test measure the same construct.

internal validity   The extent to which a study is methodologically adequate.

internal working model   Mental representation of the attachment relationship, which forms the basis for expectations in close relationships.

interneuron   Neuron that connects other neurons to each other, found only in the brain and spinal cord.

interpersonal attention   The factors that lead people to choose to spend time with other people.

interposition   Monocular depth cue in which one object blocks part of another leading to perception of the occluded (blocked) object as more distant.

interpretation   A therapeutic technique whereby the therapist helps the patient understand his or her experiences in a new light.

interstimulus interval   The duration of time between presentation of the conditioned stimulus and the unconditioned stimulus.

interval schedules of reinforcement   Operant conditioning procedures in which rewards are delivered according to intervals of time.

interview Research tool in which the investigator ask the subject questions.

intimacy A kind of closeness characterized by self-disclosure, warmth, and mutual caring.

intimacy versus isolation In Erikson's theory, the stage in which young adults establish enduring, committed friendships and romantic relationships.

intrinsic motivation Motivation to perform a behavior for its own sake, rather than for some kind of external (or extrinsic) reward.

introspection Method used by Wundt and other structuralists in which trained subjects verbally reported everything that went through their minds when presented with a stimulus or task; more generally, refers to the process of looking inward at one's own mental contents or process.

intuitive scientist Conception of people as lay scientists who use intuitive theories, frame hypotheses, collect data about themselves and others, and examine the impact of various experimental manipulations when trying to understand themselves and others; also called intuitive psychologist.

iris The ring of pigmented tissue that gives the eye its blue, green, or brown color; its muscle fibers cause the pupil to constrict or dilate.

J

James-Lange theory A theory of emotion that asserts that emotion originates with peripheral arousal, which people then label as an emotional state.

just noticeable difference (jnd) The smallest difference in intensity between two stimuli that a person can detect.

K

kinesthesia Sense that provides information about the movement and position of the limbs and other parts of the body; receptors in joints transduce information about the position of the bones, and receptors in the tendons and muscles transmit messages about muscular tension.

knowledge base Accumulated information stored in long-term memory.

Korsakoff's syndrome Disorder related to chronic alcoholism that impairs the ability to acquire and consolidate new information in memory.

L

labeling theory Theory that psychiatric diagnosis is a way of labeling individuals a society considers deviant.

laissez-faire A leadership style in which the leader intervenes as little as possible.

language The system of symbols, sounds, meanings, and rules for their combination that constitutes the primary mode of communication among humans.

Language Acquisition Device (LAD) The prewired, innate mechanism that allows for the acquisition of language hypothesized by Noam Chomsky.

latency stage Psychosexual phase that occurs roughly around ages 6 to 11, when children repress their sexual impulses.

latent content According to Freud's dream theory, the meaning that underlies the symbolism in a dream.

latent learning Learning that has occurred but is not currently manifest in behavior.

lateral geniculate nucleus Group of neurons in the thalamus that transmit information from the eye to the visual cortex.

lateralized Localized on one or the other side of the brain

law of effect Law proposed by Thorndike which states that the tendency of an organism to produce a behavior depends on the effect the behavior has on the environment.

laws of association First proposed by Aristotle, basic principles used to account for learning and memory, which describe the conditions under which one thought becomes connected, or associated, with another.

laws of learning Invariant causal connections between environmental events and the way individuals behave.

leader A person who exercises greater influence than the average member of a group.

learned helplessness The expectancy that one cannot escape from aversive events.

learning Any relatively permanent change in the way an organism responds based on its experience.

learning goals Motives to increase one's competence, mastery, or skill.

left hemisphere Left half of the cerebrum.

lens Disc-shaped, elastic structure of the eye that focuses light.

level of processing The degree to which information is elaborated, reflected upon, or processed in a meaningful way during encoding of memory.

libido In Freudian theory, the human sexual drive, which refers as much to pleasure-seeking and love as to sexual intercourse.

life events Stressful experiences that require change and adaptation.

life history method Method of personality assessment whose aim is to understand the whole person in the context of his or her life experience and environment.

life tasks The conscious, self-defined problems people attempt to solve.

light The form of electromagnetic radiation to which the eye is sensitive.

light adaptation The eyes' adjustment to bright light after exposure to darkness.

limbic system Subcortical structures responsible for emotional reactions, many motivational processes, and aspects of memory.

linear perspective A monocular cue for depth perception in which parallel lines appear to converge as they recede into the distance.

lithium The drug treatment of choice for bipolar disorder.

lobe Section of the cortex.

lobotomy A surgical treatment no longer practiced involving removal of part of the brain (usually the frontal lobes) to try to treat schizophrenia.

localization of functioning The extent to which different parts of the brain control different aspects of functioning.

locus of control Generalized expectancies people hold about whether or not their own behavior will bring about the outcomes they seek.

long-term memory (LTM) Memory for facts, images, thoughts, feelings, skills, and experiences that may last as long as a lifetime.

longitudinal fissure Deep sulcus or valley in the brain that divides the cortex down the middle from front to back.

longitudinal study Type of research that follows the same individuals over time.

loosening of associations A tendency common in individuals with schizophrenia, in which conscious thought is directed along associative lines rather than by controlled, logical, purposeful processes.

loudness The psychological property corresponding to a sound wave's amplitude.

low-effort syndrome Phenomenon in which members of a racial or ethnic group experience an upper limit, or ceiling, on their ability to succeed as a result of repeated exposure to situations in which effort and academic success are thwarted, producing frustration, anger and decreased effort.

lysergic acid diethylamide (LSD) Synthetic hallucinogenic drug.

M

magnetic resonance imaging (MRI) Brain scanning technique.

maintenance rehearsal The process of repeating information over and over to maintain it momentarily in STM.

major depressive disorder Form of psychopathology characterized by depressed mood, loss of interest in pleasurable activities, and disturbances in appetite, sleep, energy level, and concentration.

major tranquilizers Another name for antipsychotic medications.

mania An excessively euphoric, elevated, or expansive mood.

manifest content The obvious story line of a dream.

marijuana Drug that leads to a state of feeling high (euphoric, giddy, unselfconscious, or contemplative).

marital therapy A psychological treatment that focuses on maladaptive interaction patterns between a couple.

mastery goals Motives to increase one's competence, mastery, or skill.

maturation Biologically based development.

mean The statistical average of the scores of all subjects on a measure.

measure A concrete way of assessing a variable.

measures of central tendency Statistical concepts that provide an index of the way a "typical" subject responded on a measure.

mechanoreceptors Pressure receptors that transduce mechanical energy in the skin.

median The score that falls in the middle of the distribution of scores, with half of subjects scoring below it and half above it.

medical model A model of psychopathology that assumes that mental disorders fall into discrete categories like other medical illnesses.

meditation A relaxation practice, often associated with religion, characterized by a state of tranquility.

medulla oblongata An extension of the spinal cord, essential to life, controlling such vital physiological functions as heartbeat, circulation, and respiration.

memory scanning Combing or scanning long-term memory to find information.

memory systems Discrete but interdependent processing units responsible for different kinds of remembering.

menopause The cessation of the menstrual cycle.

mental age (MA) The average age at which children can be expected to achieve a particular score on an intelligence test.

mental image A visual representation of a stimulus.

mental models Representations that describe, explain, or predict the way things work.

mental representation A mental model of a stimulus or category of stimuli.

mental retardation Significantly subaverage general intellectual functioning, existing concurrently with deficits in adaptive behavior and manifested during childhood.

mental simulation Problem-solving strategy in which people imagine the steps to problem solving mentally before actually undertaking them.

mental status The intactness of memory, orientation to reality, state of consciousness, reasoning ability, and ability to think abstractly.

mere exposure effect The phenomenon in which people feel more positively toward stimuli as their exposure to the stimuli increases.

meta-analysis Statistical technique that allows researchers to combine findings from various studies and make comparisons between the effects of treatment and no treatment.

metabolism The processes by which the body transforms food into energy.

metacognition People's understanding of the way they perform cognitive tasks such as remembering, learning, or solving problems.

metamemory People's recognition about their own memory.

method of loci A memory aid or mnemonic device in which images are remembered by fitting them into an orderly arrangement of locations.

midbrain Section of the brain above the hindbrain that is involved in some auditory and visual functions, movement, and conscious arousal and activation.

mind-body dualism The view that the mind and body are two distinct realms, with different principles explaining each realm.

mind-body problem The question of how mental and physical events interact.

mnemonic devices Systematic strategies for remembering information.

mode The most common or most frequent score or value of a variable observed in a sample.

modeling Social learning procedure in which a person learns to reproduce behavior exhibited by a model.

modules Independently functioning systems of neurons.

monamine oxidase inhibitor (MAOI) A class of medications for depression that prevents monoamine oxidase from breaking down neurotransmitters, thus increasing neurotransmitter availability in the synapse.

monocular cues Visual input from a single eye alone that contributes to depth perception.

monozygotic (MZ) twins Twins identical in their genetic makeup.

mood Relatively extended emotional states that do not shift attention or disrupt ongoing activities.

mood disorder Disorder characterized by disturbances in emotion and mood.

moral development Development of the values and rules a person uses for balancing or adjudicating the conflicting interests of the self and others.

morepheme In language, basic unit of meaning.

motion parallax A monocular depth cue involving the relative movements of retinal images of objects; nearby objects appear to speed across the field of vision, whereas distant objects barely seem to move.

motivated forgetting Forgetting for a reason, which leads to inhibition of retrieval.

motivation The moving force that energizes behavior.

motor cortex The primary zone of the frontal lobes responsible for control of motor behavior.

motor neuron Neuron that transmits commands from the brain to the glands or musculature of the body, typically through the spinal cord; also called efferent neuron.

Müller-Lyer illusion Perceptual illusion in which two lines of equal length appear different in size.

multiaxial system of diagnosis System used in DSM-IV that places mental disorders in their social and biological context, assessing the patient on five axes.

multiple measures The use of several ways of assessing a variable to minimize the impact of measurement error.

myelin sheath A coat of cells composed primarily of lipids, which serves to insulate the axon from chemical or physical stimuli that might interfere with the transmission of nerve impulses and speeds neural transmission.

myopia Condition in which light waves from distant objects converge in front of the retina rather than on it, leading to decreased acuity for distant objects; also called nearsightedness.

N

nanometer (nm) One-billionth of a meter, used to measure wavelengths.

narcissism Tendency to be self-centered and focused on gratifying one's own needs.

narcissistic personality disorder A personality disorder characterized by feelings of entitlement, tendencies to use or devalue others, and a lack of empathy.

narcolepsy   A disorder in which people are prone to sudden sleep attacks and fall into rapid eye movement sleep during daytime activities.

nasal cavity   Region hollowed out of bone in the skull that contains smell receptors.

natural killer cells   Cells that fight viruses and tumors.

natural selection   Theory proposed by Darwin, which states that natural forces select traits in organisms that help them adapt to their environment.

naturalistic observation   The in-depth observation of a phenomenon in its natural setting.

nature-nurture controversy   The question of degree to which inborn biological processes or environmental events determine human behavior.

nearsightedness   Condition in which light waves from distant objects converge in front of the retina rather than on it, leading to decreased acuity for distant objects; also called myopia.

need for achievement   A motive to do well, to succeed, and to avoid failure.

negative affect   A general category of emotions related to feeling bad.

negative correlation   Relation between two variables in which the higher one is, the lower the other tends to be.

negative identity   Taking on a role that society defines as bad but that nevertheless provides one with a sense of being something.

negative reinforcement   The process whereby a behavior is made more likely because it is followed by the removal of an aversive stimulus.

negative reinforcer   Aversive or unpleasant stimulus that strengthens a behavior by its removal.

negative symptoms   Symptoms of schizophrenia such as flat affect, socially inappropriate behavior, and intellectual impairments that reflect a deficit or a loss of something that was once present or should be present.

negative triad   In Beck's cognitive theory of depression, negative outlook on the world, the self, and the future.

neo-Freudians   Theorists who accepted the influence of unconscious processes and conflicts among psychological forces but rejected Freud's instinct theory, particularly his insistence on the centrality of sexuality in psychological functioning.

neo-Piagetian theories   Theories that attempt to wed a stage model of cognitive development with research on information processing and domain-specific knowledge.

nerves   Bundles of neurons.

nervous system   The interacting network of nerve cells that underlies all psychological activity.

network of association   A cluster of interconnected information stored in long-term memory.

neurons   Cells in the nervous system.

neuroses   Problems in living, such as phobias, chronic self-doubts, and repetitive interpersonal problems.

neuroticism   A continuum from emotional stability to emotional instability.

neurotransmitter   Chemical substance that transmits information from one neuron to another.

New Look   An approach to perception that integrated perceptual research with personality theory and focused on the influence of motives on perception.

niche   The particular environmental circumstance to which an organism adapts.

night terrors   Dramatic experiences during sleep of intense terror or panic, in which the sufferer can rarely recall the dream content associated with the panic.

nightmare   A vivid bad dream, often associated with fears of falling, calamity, or death.

node   A cluster or piece of information along a network of association.

nodes of Ranvier   Small spaces between the cells that form the myelin sheath.

noise   Irrelevant, distracting information in any sensory modality.

non-REM (NREM) sleep   States of sleep in which rapid eye movements (REM sleep) are not present.

nonverbal communication   Mode of communication that relies on gestures, expressions, intonation, body language, and other unspoken signals.

normal distribution   A frequency distribution in which most subjects' scores fall in the middle of the bell-shaped distribution, and progressively fewer subjects have scores at either extreme.

normalization   The movement to take mentally retarded individuals out of institutions and place them, as much as possible, within the community.

norms   Standards for the behavior of group members.

O

obedience   Overt compliance with authority.

obesity   Condition characterized by a body weight over 15 percent above the ideal for one's height and age.

object permanence   In Piaget's theory, the recognition that objects exist in time and space independent of one's actions on, or observation of, them.

object relations   Behavioral patterns in intimate relationships and the motivational, cognitive, and affective processes that produce them.

object relations theories   Theories that attempt to account for the capacity for intimacy or the lack thereof in individuals with severe personality disorders.

observational learning   Learning that occurs by observing the behavior of others.

obsession   Persistent unwanted thought or idea.

obsessive-compulsive disorder   Disorder characterized by recurrent obsessions and compulsions that cause distress and significantly interfere with an individual's life.

occipital lobes   Brain structures located in the rear portion of the cortex involved in vision.

Oedipus complex   In Freudian theory, process that occurs during the phallic stage of development when the child desires an exclusive, sensual/sexual relationship with the opposite sex parent.

olfaction   Smell.

olfactory bulb   Multilayer structure that combines information from the olfactory nerve.

olfactory epithelium   Thin pair of structures in which transduction of smell occurs.

olfactory nerve   The bundle of axons from sensory receptor cells that transmits information from the nose to the brain.

operant   A behavior that is emitted by the organism rather than elicited by the environment.

operant conditioning   Learning that results when an organism associates a response that occurs spontaneously with a particular environment effect.

operation   In Piagetian theory, a mental action that the individual can use to manipulate, transform, and return an object of thought to its original state.

operationalizing   Turning an abstract concept or variable into a concrete form that can be defined by some set of operations or actions.

operator   In problem solving, mental and behavioral process aimed at transforming the initial state into the goal state.

opponent-process theory   A theory of color vision that proposes the existence of three antagonistic color systems: a blue-yellow system, a red-green system, and a black-white system; according to this theory, the blue-yellow and red-green systems are responsible for hue, while the black-white system contributes to perception of brightness and saturation.

optic chiasm   The point at which the optic nerve splits.

optic disk The point on the retina where the optic nerve leaves the eye and which contain no receptor cells; also called blind spot.

optic nerve The bundle of axons of ganglion cells that carries information from the retina to the brain.

optic tract The bundle of neurons that carries combined information from the two eyes to higher centers in the brain.

oral stage In Freudian theory, the psychosexual phase occurring roughly in the first year of life, when children explore the world through their mouths.

organizational effects Effects of hormones that influence the structure of the brain.

orgasm The third phase of the sexual response cycle characterized by a release of built-up tension.

orienting reflex The tendency of humans, even from birth, to pay more attention to novel stimuli than to stimuli to which they have grown accustomed.

ossicles Three tiny bones in the middle ear (the malleus, incus, and stapes) that amplify sound through mechanical leverage when set in motion by the vibration of the eardrum.

outcome expectancy An expectation about the type of consequence that will be produced by a given behavior.

outgroup People perceived as not belonging to a valued group.

oval window Membrane covering the cochlea that vibrates when struck by the stirrup, causing pressure waves in the fluid filling the cochlea.

ovaries The female gonads.

P

***p*-value** The probability that obtained findings were accidental or just a matter of chance.

painful neuropathy Neurological disorder in which normal touch sensations are experienced as excruciating pain.

pancreas Endocrine gland located near the stomach, which produces various hormones that control blood-sugar level.

panic disorder Disorder characterized by attacks of intense fear and feelings of doom or terror not justified by the situation.

papillae Small bumps on the surface of the tongue in which taste buds are located.

paradigm A broad system of theoretical assumptions employed by a scientific community to make sense out of a domain of experience.

paradoxical conditioning Classical conditioning process in which the conditioned response represents an effort by the organism to counteract the effects of a stimulus that is about to occur.

parallel distributed processing (PDP) Model of human cognitive processes in which many cognitive processes occur simultaneously (i.e., in parallel), so that a representation is spread out (i.e., distributed) throughout a network of interacting processing units.

paranoid schizophrenia Type of schizophrenia marked by preoccupation with delusions of persecution.

parasympathetic nervous system The part of the autonomic nervous system involved in conserving and maintaining the body's energy resources.

parietal lobes Brain structures located in front of the occipital lobes and involved in a number of functions, including sense of touch and the experience of one's own body in space and in movement.

Parkinson's disease Disorder characterized by uncontrollable tremors, repetitive movements, and difficulty initiating movements.

participants The individuals who participate in a study (also called *subjects*).

participatory modeling A cognitive-behavioral technique in which the therapist models desired behavior and gradually induces the patient to participate in it.

passionate love A highly emotional form of love marked by intense physiological arousal and absorption in another person.

passive aggression The indirect expression of anger toward others.

pathogens Agents that cause physical illness.

peg method A memory aid or mnemonic device in which information to be remembered is imagined or visualized to hang on mental pegs.

penis envy In Freudian theory, feeling of envy that emerges in girls, who feel that because they lack a penis they are inferior to boys.

perceived stress The extent to which a person himself regards an experience as stressful.

percentile scores A method of representing subjects' scores on a variable that shows the percentage of scores that fall below a score.

perception The process by which the brain selects, organizes, and interprets sensations.

percepts Meaningful perceptual units, such as images of particular objects.

perceptual constancy The organization of changing sensations into percepts that are relatively stable in size, shape, and color.

perceptual defense The unconscious tendency of people to resist perceiving anxiety-provoking stimuli.

perceptual illusions Perceptual misinterpretations produced in the course of normal perceptual processes.

perceptual interpretation The process of generating meaning from sensory experience.

perceptual organization The process of integrating sensations into meaningful perceptual units.

perceptual set The expectations an observer brings to a situation which influence what is perceived, notably context and schemas.

performance goals Motives to achieve at a particular level, usually one that meets a socially defined standard.

performance-approach goals Goals that center on approaching or attaining a standard.

performance-avoidance goals Goals that center on avoiding failure, particularly publicly observable failure.

peripheral nervous system (PNS) Component of the nervous system that includes neurons that travel to and from the central nervous system; includes the somatic nervous system and the autonomic nervous system.

permissive parenting style A way of parenting that imposes few controls on children, allowing the children to make their own decisions whenever possible.

person schemas Knowledge structures that represent information about specific people or types of people.

person-by-situation interaction Process by which some personality dispositions are activated only under certain circumstances.

person-centered approach Carl Rogers' theory of personality, which focuses on understanding the individual's phenomenal world.

personal constructs Mental representations of the people, places, things, and events that are significant in a person's life.

personal value The importance individuals attach to various stimuli and to the outcomes they expect as a result of their behavior.

personality The enduring patterns of thought, feeling, and behavior that are expressed by individuals in different circumstances.

personality disorder Chronic and severe disorder that substantially inhibits the capacity to love and to work.

perspective taking The ability to understand other people's viewpoints or perspectives.

persuasion Deliberate efforts to induce attitude change.

pessimistic explanatory style A tendency to explain bad events that happen in a self-blaming manner, viewing their causes as global and stable.

phallic stage   In Freudian theory, the psychosexual phase occurring roughly around ages 4 to 6, when children discover that they can get pleasure from touching their genitals.

phantom limb pain   Pain felt in an amputated limb.

pharmacotherapy   Drug therapy for mental illness.

phenomenal experience   The way individuals conceive of reality and experience themselves and their world.

phenomenological   Having to do with subjective experience.

phenotype   Observable psychological attributes that reflect genetic variation.

phenylketonuria (PKU)   Disorder produced by a single recessive gene which causes a deficiency in the enzyme responsible for converting the amino acid phenylalanine into another amino acid, resulting in severe mental retardation.

pheromone   Chemical secreted by organisms in some species that allow communication between organisms.

phobia   Irrational fear of a specific object or situation.

phoneme   The smallest unit of speech that distinguishes one linguistic utterance from another.

phonemic restoration   Process by which listeners replace a sound that has been obliterated by background noise.

photoreceptors   Light receptors located at the back of the retina.

phrase   Group of words that act as a unit and convey a meaning.

pinna   The projecting external portion of the ear.

pitch   The psychological property corresponding to the frequency of a sound wave; the quality of a tone from low to high.

pituitary gland   Often referred to as the "master gland" of the endocrine system because some of the hormones it releases stimulate and thus regulate the hormonal action of other endocrine glands.

place theory   A theory of pitch which proposes that different areas of the basilar membrane are maximally sensitive to different frequencies.

placebo effect   Phenomenon in which an experimental intervention produces an effect because subjects believe it will produce an effect.

plasticity   Flexibility of the brain to adapt to changing circumstances or damage.

plateau phase   Second phase of the sexual response cycle during which maximum arousal occurs.

polysensory association area   Cortical region that receives information from more than one sensory system.

population   Group of people or animals of interest to a research from which a sample is drawn.

position correlation   Relation between two variables in which the higher one is, the higher the other tends to be.

positive affect   A general category of emotions related to feeling good.

positive reinforcement   The process by which a behavior is made more likely because of the presentation of a rewarding stimulus.

positive reinforcer   A rewarding stimulus that strengthens a behavior when it is presented.

positive symptoms   Symptoms of schizophrenia such as delusions and hallucinations that reflect the presence of something that was not there previously and is not normally present.

positron emission tomography (PET) Computerized brain scanning technique that allows observation of the brain in action.

possession trance   A type of religiously patterned altered state that involves the alleged possession of the soul by a spirit.

post-traumatic stress disorder (PTSD) An anxiety disorder characterized by symptoms such as flashbacks and recurrent thoughts of a psychologically distressing event outside the normal range of experience.

postconventional morality   In Kohlberg's theory, the level of morality in which individuals follow abstract, self-defined principles which may or may not accord with the dominant mores or morals of the times.

posthypnotic suggestion   A suggestion to perform a behavior on demand once out of the hypnotic trance.

postsynaptic neuron   The cell receiving a neural impulse as neurotransmitters are released across the synapse.

preconscious mental processes Thoughts that are not conscious but could become conscious at any point, much like information stored in long-term semantic memory.

preconventional morality   In Kohlberg's theory, the level of morality in which children follow moral rules either to avoid punishment or to obtain reward.

prefrontal cortex   Anterior (front) section of frontal lobes, implicated, among other functions, in attention and working memory.

prejudice   Judging people based on negative stereotypes.

prenatal   Before birth.

preoperational stage   Piaget's second stage of cognitive development, beginning roughly around age 2 and lasting until age 5 to 7, characterized by the emergence of symbolic thought.

prepared learning   Responses to which an organism is predisposed because they were selected through natural selection.

presbycusis   The inability to hear high-frequency sounds, which usually occurs with aging.

presynaptic neuron   The cell that is sending an impulse and releasing neurotransmitters.

primacy effect   The superiority of memory for words presented at the beginning of a list than for words presented later.

primary appraisal   The first stage in the process of stress and coping in which the person decides whether the situation is benign, stressful, or irrelevant.

primary area   Area of the cortex involved in sensory functions and in the direct control of motor movements.

primary drive   Innate drive such as hunger, thirst, and sex.

primary prevention   Preventative mental health measures.

primary process thought   Associative thinking described by Freud, in which ideas connected in people's minds through experience come to mind automatically when they think about related ideas; primary process thought is also wishful and unrealistic.

primary reinforcer   Stimulus that is innately rewarding to an organism.

priming   The process by which a person's performance is influenced by recent exposure to associatively connected stimuli.

priming effects   The processing of specific information is facilitated by prior exposure to the same or similar information.

proactive interference   Phenomenon in which old memories that have already been stored interfere with the retrieval of new information.

probability value   The probability that obtained findings were accidental or just a mater of chance; also called *p*-value.

problem solving   The process of transforming one situation into another that meets a goal.

problem solving strategy   Technique used to solve problems.

procedural memory   Knowledge of procedures or skills that emerges when people engage in activities that require them.

prodigy   An individual with early-developing genius in one area and normal abilities otherwise.

programmed learning   Learning that proceeds at the learner's own rate, with reinforcement received upon mastery of each task.

projection Defense mechanism in which a person attributes his own unacknowledged feelings or impulses to others.

projective test Personality assessment method in which subjects are confronted with an ambiguous stimulus and asked to define it in some way; the assumption underlying these tests is that when people are faced with an unstructured, undefined stimulus, they will project their own thoughts, feelings, and wishes into their responses.

proposition The smallest unit of meaning that can stand alone as an assertion and can be judged to be true or false.

proprioceptive senses Senses that provide information about body position and movement; the two proprioceptive senses are kinesthesia and vestibular sense.

prosocial behavior Behavior that benefits either specific individuals or society as a whole.

prosopagnosia Neurological disorder involving an inability to recognize different people's faces.

prospective memory Memory for things that need to be done in the future.

prototype Particularly good example of a category.

proximity A Gestalt rule of perception which states that, other things being equal, the brain groups objects together that are close to each other.

psychoactive substance Any drug that operates on the nervous system to alter patterns of mental activity.

psychoanalysis An intensive therapeutic process in which the patient meets with the therapist three to five times in week, lies on a couch, and uses free association, interpretation, and transference.

psychodynamic formulation A set of hypotheses about the patient's personality structure and the meaning of a symptom.

psychodynamic perspective The perspective initiated by Sigmund Freud that focuses on the dynamic interplay of mental forces.

psychodynamic psychotherapy A form of psychotherapy based on psychodynamic principles, in which the patient meets the therapist somewhat less frequently than in psychoanalysis and sits face to face with the therapist.

psychodynamics A view analogous to dynamics among physical forces in which psychological forces such as wishes, fears, and intentions have a direction and an intensity.

psychological anthropology Field that studies psychological phenomena in other cultures by observing the way the natives behave in their daily lives.

psychological perspectives Broad ways of understanding psychological phenomena, including theoretical propositions, shared metaphors, and accepted methods of observation.

psychology The scientific investigation of mental processes and behavior.

psychometric approach Approach to the study of intelligence, personality, and psychopathology which tries to derive some kind of theoretical meaning empirically from statistical analysis of psychometric test findings.

psychometric instruments Psychological "yardsticks" that compare individuals.

psychomotor slowing A slowing in the time between sensory input and cognitive and motor output that occurs with aging.

psychopathology Problematic patterns of thought, feeling, or behavior that disrupt an individual's sense of well-being or social or occupational functioning.

psychophysics Branch of psychology that studies the relationship between attributes of the physical world and the psychological experience of them.

psychosexual stages In Freudian theory, the developmental phases that represent the child's evolving quest for pleasure and growing realization of the social limitations of this quest.

psychosis Gross disturbance involving a loss of touch with reality.

psychosocial motives Personal and interpersonal motives that lead people to strive for such ends as mastery, achievement, power, self-esteem, affiliation, and intimacy with other people.

psychosocial stages In Erikson's theory, the stages in the development of the person as a social being.

psychosurgery Brain surgery to reduce psychological symptoms.

psychotherapy integration Choosing therapeutic techniques from different treatment approaches selectively or integrating across perspectives.

psychoticism A dimension whose low end is defined by people who display empathy and impulse control and the high end is defined by people who are aggressive, egocentric, impulsive, and antisocial.

psychotropic medications Drugs that act on the brain to affect mental processes.

puberty The stage at which individuals become capable of reproduction.

punishment Conditioning process that decreases the probability that a behavior will occur.

pupil The opening in the center of the iris that constricts or dilates to regulate the amount of light entering the eye.

Q

Q-sort A procedure for assessing personality (or other domains) in which a rater sorts items into piles, depending on how much the items describe a person.

quality In sensation, the nature of the stimulus sensed (e.g., color, pitch, taste, etc.).

quasi-experimental design A research design that employs the logic of experimental methods but lacks absolute control over variables.

questionnaire Research tool in which the investigator asks subjects to respond to a written list of questions or items.

R

random sample Sample of subjects selected from the population in a relatively arbitrary manner.

range A measure of variability that represents the difference between the highest and the lowest value on a variable obtained in a sample.

rapid eye movement (REM) sleep Period of sleep during which darting eye movements occur, autonomic activity increases, and patterns of brain activity resemble those observed in waking states.

ratio schedules of reinforcement Operant conditioning procedures in which an organism is reinforced for some proportion of responses.

rational-emotive psychotherapy A psychological treatment in which the therapist helps uncover and alter the illogical thoughts that provoke psychological distress.

rationalist philosophy School of philosophical thought that emphasizes the role of reason in creating knowledge.

rationalization Defense mechanism that involves explaining away actions in a seemingly logical way to avoid uncomfortable feelings.

reaction formation Defense mechanism in which the person turns unacceptable feelings or impulses into their opposites.

reasoning The process by which people generate and evaluate arguments and beliefs.

recall Explicit (conscious) recollection of material from long-term memory.

recency effect The superiority of memory for items presented at the end of a list.

receptive field A region within which a neuron responds to appropriate stimulation.

receptors In neurons, protein molecules in the postsynaptic membrane that pick up neurotransmitters; in sensation, specialized cells of the sensory systems that respond to the environmental stimuli and typically activate sensory neurons.

reciprocal altruism Theory that natural selection favors animals that behave altruistically if the likely benefit to each individual over time exceeds the likely cost to each individual's reproductive success.

recognition Explicit (conscious) knowledge of whether something currently perceived has been previously encountered.

reference group Group to which a person refers when taking a particular action.

regression Reverting to conflicts or modes of managing emotion characteristic of an earlier particular stage.

rehearsal Repeating or studying information to retain it in memory.

reinforcer An environmental consequence that increases the probability that a behavior will occur.

relatedness motives Interpersonal motives for connectedness with other people; these motives also called *communion motives.*

relationship schemas Knowledge structures that encode expectations about how the self and others interact in different kinds of relationships.

relative size A monocular cue for depth perception in which looking at two objects known to be of similar size leads to the perception of the smaller object as farther away.

reliability A measure's ability to produce consistent results.

religious experience Altered state of consciousness in which the individual feels at one with nature or the supernatural.

religious experiences Subjective experiences of being in contact with the divine, which can range from relatively ordinary experiences, such as listening passively to a sermon, to altered states of consciousness in which a person feels at one with nature or the supernatural.

repertory grid technique A technique for assessing personal constructs indirectly.

replicate To repeat a study to see if the same findings are obtained.

representative A sample that reflects characteristics of the population as a whole.

representativeness heuristic A cognitive shortcut used to assess whether an object or incident belongs in a particular class.

repression Defense mechanism in which thoughts that are too anxiety-provoking to acknowledge are kept from conscious awareness.

reproductive success The capacity to survive and reproduce offspring.

resistance Barriers to psychotherapy created by the patient in an effort to reduce anxiety.

resistance stage The second stage of the general adaption syndrome, in which blood glucose levels are elevated and the body uses its resources at an accelerated rate.

resolution The fourth phase of the sexual response cycle when the body gradually returns to normal physiological functioning, and psychological arousal is also reduced.

response bias In signal detection theory, the readiness of an observer to report detecting a stimulus when uncertain; also called decision criterion.

resting potential Condition in which the neuron is not firing.

reticular formation A network of neural nuclei and axons in the brainstem that maintains consciousness and regulates activity states throughout the central nervous system.

retina The light-sensitive layer of tissue at the back of the eye that transduces light into neural impulses.

retinal disparity The slight difference between the retinal images of the right and left eyes; the degree of disparity is greater for close objects and diminishes as objects move away.

retrieval Bringing information from long-term memory into short-term, or working, memory.

retrieval cues Stimuli or thoughts that can be used to stimulate retrieval.

retroactive interference Interference of new information with the retrieval of old information.

retrograde amnesia Loss of memory for events prior to brain damage.

retrospective memory Memory for events that have already occurred.

right hemisphere Right half of the cerebrum.

rites of passage Ceremonies that initiate the child into adulthood or other major life transitions and impose a socially bestowed identity.

rods One of two types of photoreceptors; allow vision in dim light.

role A position within a group that defines appropriate behavior for the person occupying it.

role reversal Situations in which a child and parent switch roles and the child's role is to take care of the parent.

role schemas Knowledge structures that represent information about what is expected of people in particular social positions or roles.

rooting reflex Reflex that helps ensure infants will get the nourishment they need; when touched on the cheek, the infant turns its head and opens its mouth to suck.

Rorschach inkblot test A projective personality test in which a subject views a set of inkblots and tells the tester what each inkblot resembles.

S

s-factors Specific cognitive abilities.

sample A subgroup of a population likely to be representative of the population as a whole.

saturation Purity of sensed color.

savant Individual with extraordinary ability in one area who has comparatively low functioning in other areas.

scapegoat A role that may emerge in a group in which a person is blamed for the group's problems.

scatterplot graph A graph that charts subjects' scores on two variables showing correlations.

Schacter-Singer theory Theory which assets that emotion involves cognitive interpretation of general physiological arousal.

schema Integrated pattern of knowledge stored in memory that organizes information and guides the acquisition of new information.

schema-relevant information Information about behaviors or aspects of a situation related to an activated schema.

schizoaffective disorder A disorder characterized by both schizophrenia symptoms and psychotic depression.

schizophrenia Psychotic disorders characterized by disturbances in thought, perception, behavior, language, communication, and emotion.

scripts Schemas that specify how to do something socially.

secondary appraisal The second stage in the process of stress and coping during which the person evaluates the options and decides how to respond.

secondary drive Motive learned through classical conditioning and other leaning mechanisms such as modeling; also called acquired drive.

secondary process thought Rational, logical, goal-directed thinking.

secondary reinforcer A stimulus that acquires reinforcement value after an organism learns to associate it with stimuli that are innately reinforcing.

selective inattention The process by which important information is ignored.

selective serotonin reuptake inhibitor (SSRI) A class of antidepressant medications, including Prozac, that blocks the presynaptic membrane from taking back serotonin, and hence leaves it acting longer in the synapse.

self The person, including mental processes, body, and attributes.

self as object The person's view of the self.

self as subject The person's experience of self as a thinker, feeler, and actor.

self-actualization needs In Maslow's theory, the needs to express oneself, grow, and actualize or attain one's potential.

self-attribution Phenomenon in which people attribute causes to their own psychological processes.

self-conflict A person's view of him/herself.

self-consistency The motivation to interpret information to fit the self-concept and to prefer people who verify rather than challenge it.

self-efficacy expectancy A person's conviction that he can perform the actions necessary to produce an intended behavior.

self-esteem The degree to which a person likes, respects, or esteems the self.

self-esteem motivation The desire to feel good about oneself.

self-fulfilling prophecy A false definition of a situation that evokes a new behavior, which makes the originally false concept come true.

self-help groups Groups that are leaderless or guided by a nonprofessional, in which members assist each other in coping with a specific problem, as in Alcoholics Anonymous.

self-perception theory Alternative explanation of cognitive dissonance phenomena which holds that individuals become aware of their attitudes, emotions, and other internal states by observing their own behavior.

self-preservation Ways individuals try to make themselves appear to others; an alternative explanation for cognitive dissonance phenomenon.

self-regulation Setting goals, evaluating one's own performance, and adjusting one's behaviors flexibly to achieve these goals in the context of ongoing feedback.

self-representations Mental models of the self.

self-schema A schema or pattern of thought about the self.

self-serving bias Phenomenon in which people tend to see themselves in a more positive light than they deserve.

semantic memory General world knowledge or facts.

semicircular canals Vestibular organs that sense acceleration and deceleration.

sensation The process by which the sense organs gather information about the environment.

sensitive period Developmental period during which environmental input is especially important, but not absolutely required, for future development in a domain.

sensorimotor stage Piaget's first stage of cognitive development, from birth to about 18 months of age, with thinking primarily characterized by action.

sensorineural loss Form of deafness involving failure of receptors in the inner ear or of neurons in any auditory pathway in the brain.

sensory adaptation The tendency of sensory systems to respond less to stimuli that continue without change.

sensory modalities Senses that provide ways of knowing about stimuli.

sensory neuron Neuron that carries sensory information to the brain or spinal cord; also called afferent neuron.

sensory process According to signal detection theory, the first of two processes occurring when an observer detects a stimulus; the sensory process involves sensation and reflects the observer's sensitivity to the stimulus.

sensory registers Memory systems that hold information for a very brief period of time.

sensory representation Information that is represented in one of the sense modalities.

sentence A unit of language that combines a subject and predicate and expresses a thought or meaning.

separation anxiety Distress at separation from attachment figures.

septal area Limbic structure of unknown function, possibly involved in the sensation of pleasure.

sequential study Type of research in which multiple cohorts are studied over time.

serial position effect The phenomenon that people are more likely to remember information that appears first and last in a list than information in the middle of the list.

serotonin Neurotransmitter involved in the regulation of mood, sleep, eating, arousal, and pain.

set point The value of some variable that the body is trying to maintain, such as temperature.

sex typing The process by which children come to acquire personality traits, emotional responses, skills, behaviors, and preferences that are culturally considered to be appropriate to their sex.

sex-role ideology Beliefs about appropriate behaviors of the sexes.

sexual dysfunction Problem that impairs sexual functioning.

sexual orientation The direction of a person's enduring sexual attraction—to members of the same sex, the opposite sex, or both.

sexual response cycle Pattern of physiological changes during sexual stimulation consisting of four phases: excitement, plateau, orgasm, and resolution.

sexual strategies Tactics used in selecting mates.

shading Monocular depth cue that uses shadows to indicate depth or distance.

shape constancy The perception that an object's shape remains constant despite the changing shape of the retinal image as the object is viewed from varying perspectives.

shaping The process of teaching a new behavior by reinforcing closer and closer approximations of the desired response.

short-term memory (STM) Memory for information that is available to consciousness for roughly 20 to 30 seconds.

signal detection theory A theory which asserts that the ability to detect a stimulus depends on both sensitivity to the stimulus (a sensory process) and response bias (a decision process).

similarity A Gestalt rule of perception which states that the brain tends to group similar elements within a perceptual field.

simple cells Feature detectors in the visual cortext that respond most vigorously to lines of a specific orientation.

simplicity A Gestalt rule of perception which states that people tend to perceive the simplest pattern possible.

simultaneous conditioning Conditioning procedure in which the conditioned stimulus and the unconditioned stimulus are presented simultaneously.

single-blind study Study in which subjects are kept blind to crucial information, notably about the experimental condition in which they have been placed.

single-cell recording Procedure in which researchers insert a tiny electrode into an animal's brain and map the response of specific cells in response to stimulation.

situation schemas Knowledge structures that represent information about different kinds of social situations, including what to expect and how to act.

situational variables Aspects of the situation that interact with aspects of the person to produce behavior.

size constancy The perception that an object's size of the retinal image as the subject is seen from different distances.

skills training A technique that involves teaching behaviors or procedures for accomplishing specific goals.

skin conductance An electrical measure of the amount of sweat on the skin that is provided during states of anxiety or arousal, also called galvanic skin response (GSR) or electrical activity (EDA).

sleep apnea A disorder in which a person's breathing is interrupted during sleep and the person is awakened gasping for air.

sleep disorder Chronic syndrome of disrupted sleep.

social cognition The processes by which people make sense of others, themselves, social interactions, and relationships.

social comparison Process that becomes prominent in children's thinking in middle childhood, in which children size themselves and others up on various dimensions such as intelligence, athletic ability, and popularity.

social development Predictable changes in interpersonal thought, feeling, and behavior.

social exchange theories Theories based on behaviorist principles that suggest the foundation of relationships is reciprocal reward.

social facilitation The phenomenon in which the presence of other people facilitates performance.

social influence The ways in which the presence of other people influences a person's thought, feeling, or behavior.

social intelligence The ability to store, retrieve, and understand social information.

social psychology Field of psychology that examines the way thought, feeling, and behavior are influenced by the actual, imagined, or implied presence of other.

social psychology Subdiscipline that examines the influence of social processes on the way people think, feel, and behave.

social skills training Cognitive-behavioral technique that involves instruction and modeling, and was designed to help people develop interpersonal competence.

social support Relationships with others that provide resources for coping with stress.

social-emotional leader A role that may emerge in a group in which that member seeks to maximize group cohesion and minimize hostility.

socialization Process by which children and adults learn the rules, beliefs, values, skills, attitudes, and patterns of behavior of their society.

socialization agents Individuals, groups, and organizations that transmit social values.

sociology Field that explores evolutionary and biological bases of human social behavior.

soma (cell body) Part of the neuron which includes a nucleus containing the genetic material of the cell (the chromosomes) as well as other microstructures vital to cell functioning.

somatic nervous system Division of the peripheral nervous system that consists of sensory and motor neurons that transmit sensory information and control intentional actions.

somatosensory cortex Primary area of the parietal lobes, located behind the central tissue, which receives sensory information from different sections of the body.

sound wave Pulsation of acoustic energy.

spacing effect The superior long-term retention of information rehearsed in sessions spread out over longer intervals of time.

spacing of rehearsal The interval between rehearsal sessions, which influences memory retention.

spinal cord Part of the central nervous system that transmits information from sensory neurons to the brain, and from the brain to motor neurons that initiate movement; it is also capable of reflex actions.

spinal nerves Bundles of axons to and from the spinal cord to the periphery that carry sensory and motor information.

split-brain Condition that results when the corpus callosum has been surgically cut, blocking communication between the two cerebral hemispheres.

spontaneous recovery The spontaneous re-emergence of a response or an operant that has been extinguished.

spreading activation The theory that the presentation of a stimulus triggers activation of closely related nodes.

stages Relatively discrete steps through which everyone progresses in the same sequence.

standard deviation (SD) The amount that the average subject deviates from the mean of the sample on a measure.

standardized procedures Procedures applied uniformly to subjects to minimize unintended variation.

Stanford-Binet Scale IQ test initially devised in the early part of the twentieth century, which introduced the intelligence quotient, or IQ.

state-dependent memory The phenomenon in which information encoded in a particular state can better be recalled when the person is again in that state.

states of consciousness Different ways of orienting to internal and external events, such as awake states and sleep states.

statistical significance The degree to which the results of a study are likely to have occurred simply by chance.

stereotypes Schemas about characteristics ascribed to a group of people based on qualities such as race, ethnicity, or gender rather than achievements or actions.

Stevens's power law Law of sensation proposed by S. S. Stevens, which states that the subjective intensity of a stimulus grows as a proportion of the actual intensity raised to some power.

stimulant Drug that increases alertness, energy, and autonomic reactivity.

stimulus An object or event in the environment that elicits a response in an organism.

stimulus control When behavior emitted by an organism is under the control of the stimulus.

stimulus discrimination The tendency for an organism to respond to a very restricted range of stimuli.

stimulus generalization The tendency for learned behavior to occur in response to stimuli that were not present during conditioning but that are similar to the conditioned stimulus.

stimulus substitution The explanation of classical conditioning that focuses on the way in which the conditioned stimulus acts as substitute for the unconditioned stimulus.

Strange Situation Research design for studying attachment, in which the mother leaves her child alone in a room of toys; the child is joined for a brief time by a friendly stranger, after which the mother returns and greets the child, and coders observe the child's response to the mother.

strategic therapy Family therapy that tries to change the basic organization of the family.

stratified random sample Sample selected to represent subpopulations proportionately, randomizing only within groups (such as age or race).

stress A challenge to a person's capacity to adapt to inner and outer demands, which may be physiologically arousing, emotionally taxing, and cognitively and behaviorally activating.

stressors Situations that often lead to stress, including life events, catastrophes, and daily hassles.

stroke Condition that occurs when blood flow to parts of the brain is cut off by disease of the blood vessels, leading to brain damage.

structural model Freud's model of conflict between desires and the dictates of conscience or the constraints of reality, which posits three sets of mental forces or structures: id, ego, and superego.

structural therapy Family therapy that tries to change the organization of the family.

structuralism An early school of thought in psychology developed by Edward Titchener, which attempted to use introspection as a method for uncovering the basic elements of consciousness and the way they combine with each other into ideas.

structure of personality The way enduring patterns of thought, feeling, and behavior are organized within an individual.

structure of thought In Piaget's theory, a distinct underlying logic used by a child at a given stage.

subcortical   Below the cortex.

subjects   The individuals whom a researcher observes in a study.

sublimation   Defense mechanism that involves converting sexual or aggressive impulses into socially acceptable activities.

subliminal perception   The perception of stimuli below the threshold of consciousness.

subordinate level   A level of categorization below the basic level in which more specific attributes are shared by members of a category.

substance P   A chemical believed to be released by damaged cells that activates pain receptors.

substance-related disorders   Disorders involving continued use of a substance (such as alcohol or cocaine) that negatively affects psychological and social functioning.

subtractive color mixing   The process by which pigments are combined before reaching the eye, so that each pigment absorbs, or subtracts, a portion of the visual spectrum, leaving only the remaining wavelengths to perceive.

sucking reflex   Infant reflex of rhythmic sucking in response to stimulation three or four centimeters inside the mouth.

sulcus   Cortical "valley."

superego   In Freudian theory, the structure that acts as conscience and source of ideals, or the parental voice within the person, established through identification.

superior colliculus   A clump of neurons in the midbrain involved in controlling eye movements, detecting the position of objects in space, and integrating sensory input from the eyes and ears.

superordinate goals   Goals requiring groups to cooperate for the benefit of all.

superordinate level   The most abstract level of categorization in which members of a category share few common features.

surface structure   The particular way that words are combined in a sentence to express meaning.

survey research   Research asking a large sample of subjects questions, often about attitudes or behaviors, using questionnaires or interviews.

survivors' guilt   A feeling of intense guilt at the seeming unfairness of having survived when others have been harmed or killed in traumatic circumstances.

syllogism   A formal statement of deductive reasoning, which consists of two premises that lead to a logical conclusion.

symbolic interactionists   Sociological theorists who argue that the way people see themselves depends heavily on the way others see them.

sympathetic nervous system   Branch of the autonomic nervous system typically activated in response to threats to the organism, which readies the body for "fight-or-flight" reactions.

symptom bearer   In a family systems model of psychopathology, the person identified as needing help, or the symptom bearer; also called identified patient.

synapse   Placed at which transmission of information between neurons occurs.

synaptic cleft   Space between two neurons.

synaptic vesicles   Small sacs in the terminal buttons of a neuron that contain neurotransmitters.

syntax   Rules that govern the placement of specific words or phrases within a sentence.

systematic desensitization   A cognitive-behavioral procedure in which the patient is induced to approach feared stimuli gradually, in a state that inhibits anxiety.

T

T cells   Cells in the immune system that directly attack foreign agents in the body or that stimulate other immunologic activity.

t-test   Inferential statistic that compares the mean scores of two groups.

tardive dyskinesia   A serious, unpredictable, irreversible side effect of prolonged use of antipsychotic medications, in which a patient develops involuntary or semivoluntary twitching, usually of the tongue, face, and neck.

task leader   Group member who takes responsibility for seeing that the group completes its tasks.

taste buds   Structures that line the walls of the papillae of the tongue (and elsewhere in the mouth) that contain taste receptors.

tectorial membrane   Membrane in the inner ear that flexes when sound waves pass through the cochlear fluid, contributing to movement of hair cells, which trigger action potentials in the sensory neurons forming the auditory nerve.

tectum   Midbrain structure involved in vision and hearing.

tegmentum   Midbrain structure that includes a variety of neural structures, related mostly to movement and conscious arousal and activation.

telegraphic speech   Speech used by young children that leaves out all but the essential words in a sentence.

temperament   Basic personality dispositions heavily influenced by genes.

temporal lobes   Brain structures located in the lower side portion of the cortex that are important in audition (hearing) and language.

tension-release role   Group member who makes jokes to relieve the pressure that builds as the group tries to accomplish its tasks.

teratogen   Harmful environmental agent, such as drugs, irradiation, and viruses that cause maternal illness, which can produce fetal abnormalities or death.

terminal buttons   Structures at the end of the neuron that receive nerve impulses from the axon and transmit signals to adjacent cells.

test-retest reliability   A measure of the tendency of a psychometric instrument to yield relatively similar scores for the same individual over time.

testes   The male gonads.

testosterone   Hormone produced by the testes.

texture gradient   A monocular cue for depth perception, in which the pattern of textured surfaces appears coarser at closer range and finer and more densely packed at greater distances.

thalamus   Structure located deep in the center of the brain which acts as a relay station for sensory information.

Thematic Apperception Test (TAT)   A projective test consisting of a series of ambiguous pictures about which subjects are asked to make up a story.

theory   A systematic way of organizing and explaining observations.

theory of mind   An implicit set of ideas about the existence of mental states, such as beliefs and feelings, in oneself and others that children begin to develop in the toddler years.

theory of multiple intelligences   Howard Gardner's theory of seven intelligences used to solve problems or produce culturally significant products.

therapeutic alliance   The patient's degree of comfort with the therapist, which allows him or her to speak about emotionally significant experiences.

thinking   Manipulating mental representations for a purpose.

three-mountain task   Piagetian procedure for assessing egocentrism, in which a child must describe the view of three mountains from a perspective other than her own.

thyroid gland   Endocrine structure located next to the trachea and larynx in the neck, which releases hormones that control growth and metabolism.

timbre   The psychological property corresponding to a sound wave's complexity; the texture of a sound.

token economy   An operant conditioning technique used to modify undesirable behavior, in which points or tokens that can be exchanged for rewards (e.g., candy) are given or taken away.

top-down processing   Perceptual processing that starts with the observer's expectations and knowledge.

topographic model   Freud's model of conscious, preconscious, and unconscious processes.

traits   Emotional, cognitive, and behavioral tendencies that constitute underlying dimensions of personality on which individuals vary.

transduction   The process of converting physical energy into neural impulses.

transference   The phenomenon in which the patient displaces thoughts, feelings, fears, wishes, and conflicts from past relationships, especially childhood relationships, onto the therapist.

transformational grammar   A field of study that attempts to describe and define the conversion from surface to deep structure and vice versa.

trichromatic theory of color   A theory of color vision initially proposed by Thomas Young and modified by Herman Von Helmholtz that proposes that the eye contains three types of receptors, each sensitive to wavelengths of light that produce sensations of blue, green, and red; by this theory, the colors that humans see reflect blends of the three colors to which the retina is sensitive; also called the Young-Helmholtz theory.

tricyclic antidepressant   A class of medications for depression that compensates for depleted neurotransmitters.

true self   A core aspect of being, untainted by the demands of others.

tumor   Abnormal tissue growth.

tutelage   The teaching of concepts or procedures primarily through verbal explanation or instruction.

two-factor theory   Theory derived by Charles Spearman which holds that two types of factors or abilities underlie intelligence.

tympanic membrane   Eardrum.

Type A behavior pattern   A pattern of behavior and emotions that includes ambition, competitiveness, impatience, and hostility.

U

unconditioned positive regard   An attitude of total acceptance expressed by the therapist toward the client in client-centered therapy.

unconditioned reflex   A reflex that occurs naturally, without any prior learning.

unconditioned response   An organism's unlearned, automatic response to a stimulus.

unconditioned stimulus   A stimulus that produces a reflexive response without any prior learning.

unconscious   Mental processes that are not conscious; in Freud's topographic model, mental processes that are inaccessible to consciousness because they are too anxiety-provoking to acknowledge.

unconscious mental processes   In Freud's theory, mental processes that are inaccessible to consciousness, many of which are repressed.

unipolar depression   Mood disorder involving only depression; see also bipolar disorder.

utility   In expectancy value theories, the value of alternatives that are considered in decision making.

V

validation   Demonstrating the validity of a measure by showing that it consistently relates to other phenomena in theoretically expected ways.

validity   The extent to which a test measures the construct it attempts to assess, or a study adequately addresses the hypothesis it attempts to assess.

variability   The extent to which subjects tend to vary from each other in their scores on a measure.

variable   Phenomenon that changes across circumstances or varies among individuals.

variable interval schedule of reinforcement   Operant conditioning procedure in which an organism receives a reward for its responses after an amount of time that is not constant.

variable ratio schedule of reinforcement   An organism receives a reward for a certain percentage of behaviors that are emitted, but this percentage is not fixed.

ventricles   Fluid-filled cavities of the brain that are enlarged in schizophrenics suggesting neuronal atrophy.

verbal representations   Information represented in words.

vertebrate   Animal with a spinal cord.

vestibular sacs   Organs located in the inner ear at the base of the semicircular canals that sense gravity and the position of the head in space.

vestibular sense   Sense that provides information about the position of the body in space by sensing gravity and movement.

vicarious conditioning   The process by which an individual learns the consequences of an action by observing its consequences for someone else.

visual acuity   Sharpness of vision.

vitreous humor   The clear, gelatinous liquid that fills the space between the lens and the retina.

W

wavelength   The distance over which a wave of energy completes a full oscillation.

Weber fraction   The proportion by which two stimuli must differ for a person to detect a just noticeable difference.

Weber's law   Perceptual law described by Ernst Weber which states that for two stimuli to be perceived as differing in intensity, the second must differ from the first by a constant proportion.

Wechsler Adult Intelligence Scale-Revised (WAIS-R)   Intelligence test for adults that yields scores for both verbal and nonverbal (performance) IQ scores.

Wechsler Intelligence Scale for Children-Revised (WISC-R)   Intelligence test for children up to age 16 that yields verbal and nonverbal (performance) IQ scores.

weighted utility   In expectancy value theory, a combined measure of the importance of an attribute and how well a given option satisfies it.

well-defined concept   Concept that has properties clearly setting it apart from other concepts.

well-defined problem   Problems in which there is adequate information to solve the problem and clear criteria by which to determine whether the problem has been solved.

Wernicke's aphasia   Language disorder caused by damage to Wernicke's area, in which the individual has difficulty understanding language.

Wernicke's area   Brain structure located in the left temporal lobe, involved in language comprehension.

Whorfian hypothesis of linguistic relativity   The notion that language shapes thought.

working memory   Conscious "workspace" used for retrieving and manipulating information, maintained through maintenance rehearsal; also called short-term memory.

Y

Young-Helmholtz theory   A theory of color vision initially proposed by Young and modified by Helmholtz which proposes that the eye contains three types of receptors, each sensitive to wavelengths of light that produce sensations of blue, green, and red; by this theory, the colors that humans see reflect blends of the three colors to which the retina is sensitive; also called trichromatic theory.

References

AARP News Bulletin. (January 1989). New study finds older drivers "capable, safe." *30*, 14.

Abelson, R. B. (1995). *Statistics as principled argument.* Hillsdale, NJ: Lawrence Erlbaum Associates, Inc.

Abelson, R. P. (1983). Whatever became of consistency theory? *Personality and Social Psychology Bulletin, 9*, 37–54.

Abelson, R. P. (1997). On the surprising longevity of flogged horses: Why there is a case for the significance test. *Psychological Science, 8*, 12–15.

Abraham, H. D., & Duffy, F. H. (1996). Stable quantitative EEG difference in post-LSD visual disorder by split-half analysis: Evidence for disinhibition. *Psychiatry Research: Neuroimaging, 67,* 173–187.

Abram, K. M., & Teplin, L. (1991). Co-occurring disorders among mentally ill jail detainees: Implications for public policy. *American Psychologist, 46,* 1036–1045.

Abramov, I., & Gordon, J. (1994). Color appearance: On seeing red—or yellow, or green, or blue. *Annual Review of Psychology, 45,* 451–485.

Abramowitz, J. S. (1997). Effectiveness of psychological and pharmacological treatments for obsessive-compulsive disorder: A quantitative review. *Journal of Consulting & Clinical Psychology, 65,* 44–52.

Abrams, D. B., & Wilson, G. T. (1983). Alcohol, sexual arousal, and self control. *Journal of Personality and Social Psychology, 45,* 188–198.

Abrams, R., Swartz, C. M., & Vedak, C. (1989). Antidepressant effects of right versus left unilateral ECT and the lateralization theory of ECT action. *American Journal of Psychiatry, 146,* 1190–1192.

Abramson, L. Y., Seligman, M.E.P., & Teasdale, J. D. (1978). Learned helplessness in humans: Critique and refor-mulation. *Journal of Abnormal Psychology, 87,* 49–74.

Adams, B. D. (1985). Age, structure, and sexuality. *Journal of Homosexuality, 11,* 19–33.

Adams, C. (1991). Qualitative age differences in memory for text: A life-span development perspective. *Psychology and Aging, 6,* 323–336.

Adams, H. E., Wright, L. W., & Lohr, B. A. (1996). Is homophobia associated with homosexual arousal? *Journal of Abnormal Psychology 105,* 440–445.

Adams, P. R., & Adam, G. R. (1984). Mount Saint Helens' Ashfall: Evidence for a disaster stress reaction. *American Psychologist, 39,* 252–260.

Adams, R., Courage, M., & Mercer, M. (1994). Systematic measurement of human neonatal color vision. *Vision Research, 34,* 1691–1701.

Adams, R. J. (1989). Newborns' discrimination among mid- and long-wavelength stimuli. *Journal of Experimental Child Psychology, 47,* 130–141.

Adelson, E., & Fraiberg, S. (1974). Gross motor development in infants blind from birth. *Child Development, 45,* 114–126.

Ader, R., & Cohen, N. (1985). CNS immune system interactions: Conditioning phenomena. *Behavioral and Brain Sciences, 8,* 379–426.

Ader, R., & Cohen, N. (1993). Psychoneuroimmunology: Conditioning and stress. *Annual Review of Psychology, 44,* 53–85.

Adler, A. (1929). *The practice and theory of individual psychology.* (2nd ed.). London: Routledge & Kegan Paul.

Adler, N., & Matthews, K. (1994). Health psychology: Why do some people get sick and some stay well? *Annual Review of Psychology, 45,* 229–259.

Adorno, T. W., Frenkel–Brunswik, E., Levinson, D., & Sanford, R. N. (1950). *The authoritarian personality.* New York: W.W. Norton.

Affleck, G., Tennen, H., Urrows, S., & Higgins, P. (1994). Person and contextual features of daily stress reactivity: Individual differences in relations of undesirable daily events with mood disturbance and chronic pain intensity. *Journal of Personality and Social Psychology, 66,* 329–340.

Aggleton, J. P. (Ed). (1992). *The amygdala: Neurobiological aspects of emotion, memory, and mental dysfunction.* New York: Wiley-Liss.

Ainsworth, M. D. (1991). Salter. Attachments and other affectional bonds across the life cycle. In C. M. Parkes, J. Stevenson-Hinde, et al. (eds.), *Attachment across the life cycle.* (pp. 33–51). London, UK: Tavistock/Routledge.

Ainsworth, M.D.S. (1967). *Infancy in Uganda.* Baltimore, Md.: Johns Hopkins University.

Ainsworth, M.D.S. (1973). The development of infant–mother attachment. In B. Caldwell & H. Ricciuti (Eds.) *Review of Child Development Research,* Vol. 3. Chicago: University of Chicago Press.

Ainsworth, M.D.S. (1979). Infant–mother attachment. *American Psychologist, 34,* 932–937.

Ainsworth, M.D.S., & Bell, S. M. (1970). Attachment, exploration, and separation: Illustrated by the behavior of one-year-olds in a strange situation. *Child Development, 41,* 49–67.

Ainsworth, M. S., & Bowlby, J. (1991). An ethological approach to personality development. *American Psychologist, 46,* 333–341.

Ajzen, I., & Fishbein, M. (1977). Attitude-behavior relations: A theoretical analysis and review of empirical research. *Psychological Bulletin, 84,* 888–918.

al-Absi, M., & Rokke, P. D. (1991). Can anxiety help us tolerate pain? *Pain, 46,* 43–51.

Alba, J. W. & Hasher, L. (1983). Is memory schematic? *Psychological Bulletin, 93,* 203–231.

Albee, G. W. (1986). Toward a just society: Lessons from observations on the primary prevention of psychopathology. *American Psychology, 41,* 891–898.

Albee, G. W., & Gullotta, T. P. (Eds.). (1997). *Primary prevention works.* Thousand Oaks: Sage Publications, Inc.

Albert, D. J., Jonik, R. H., & Walsh, M. (1991). Hormone-dependent aggression in the female rat: Testosterone plus estradiol implants prevent the decline in aggression following ovariectomy. *Physiology & Behavior, 49,* 673–677.

Albert, M. K. (1993). Parallelism and the perception of illusory contours. *Perception, 22,* 589–595.

Alberts, A. C. (1989). Ultraviolet visual sensitivity in desert iguanas: Implications for pheromone detection. *Animal Behaviour, 38,* 129–137.

Albrecht, J. E., & Myers, J. L. (1995). Role of context in accessing distant information during reading. *Journal of Experimental Psychology: Learning, Memory, & Cognition, 21,* 1459–1468.

Alderfer, C. (1972). Existence, relatedness, and growth: *Human needs in organizational settings.* New York: Free Press.

Alderfer, C. P. (1989). Theories reflecting my personal experience and life development. *Journal of Applied Behavioral Science, 25,* 351–365.

Aldrich, M. S. (1990). Narcolepsy. *New England Journal of Medicine, 323,* 389–394.

Alexander, G. M., Swerdloff, R. S., Wang, C. W., & Davidson, T. (1997). Androgen-behavior correlations in hypogonadal men and eugonadal men: I. Mood and response to auditory sexual stimuli. *Hormones & Behavior, 31,* 110–119.

Alexander, I. (1990). *Personology: Method and content in personality assessment and psychobiography.* Durham, NC: Duke University Press.

Alexander, J. M., & Schwanenflugel, P. J. (1994). Strategy regulation: The role of intelligence, metacognitive attributions, and knowledge base. *Developmental Psychology, 30,* 709–723.

Alexander, P. C. (1992). Application of attachment theory to the study of sexual abuse. *Journal of Consulting and Clinical Psychology, 60,* 185–195.

Alivisatos, B., & Petrides, M. (1997). Functional activation of the human brain during mental rotation. *Neuropsychologia, 35,* 111–118.

Allgulander, C., & Lavori, P. (1991). Excess mortality among 3302 patients with "pure" anxiety neurosis. *Archives of General Psychiatry, 48,* 599–602.

Allison, D. B., Heshka S., Neale, M. C., & Lykken, D. T. (1994). A genetic analysis of relative weight among 4,020 twin pairs, with an emphasis on sex effects. *Health Psychology, 13,* 362–365.

Alloy, L. B., Acocella, J. R., & Bootzin, R. R. (1996). *Abnormal psychology: Current perspectives* (7th ed.). New York: McGraw-Hill Book Company.

Allport, G. (1937). *Personality: A psychological interpretation.* New York: Henry Holt & Co.

Allport, G. (1954). *The nature of prejudice.* Cambridge, MA: Addison-Wesley.

Allport, G. (1968). The historical background of modern social psychology. In G. Lindzey & E. Aronson (Eds.), *Handbook of social psychology,* Vol. I. Reading, MA: Addison-Wesley.

Allport, G., & Odbert, H. (1936). *Trait-names: A Psycho-lexical study.* Psychological Monographs, Vol. 47, No. 1. Princeton, NJ: Psychological Review Co.

Allport, G. W. (1935). Attitudes. In C. Murchison (Ed.), *Handbook of social psychology* (pp. 798–844). Worcester, MA: Clark University Press.

Alonso, L., & Jeffrey, W. D. (1988). Mental illness complicated by the santeria belief in spirit possession. *Hospital and Community Psychiatry, 39,* 1188–1191.

Alvarez–Borda, B., Ramirez–Amaya, V., Perez–Montfort, R., & Bermudez–Rattoni, F. (1995). Enhancement of antibody production by a learning paradigm. *Neurobiology of Learning & Memory, 64,* 103–105.

Amabile, T. M. (1996). Creativity in context. *Update to "The Social Psychology of Creativity."* Boulder, CO: Westview Press.

Ambady, N., & Rosenthal, R. (1993). Half a minute: Predicting teacher evaluations from thin slices of nonverbal behavior and physical attractiveness. *Journal of Personality and Social Psychology, 64,* 431–441.

American Psychiatric Association (1994). *Diagnostic and statistical manual of mental disorders* (4th ed.). Washington, DC: Author.

American Psychological Association, Committee for the Protection of Human Participants in Research. (1973). *Ethical principles in the conduct of research with human subjects.* Washington, DC.

American Psychological Association. (1997). Report of the ethics committee, 1996. *American Psychologist, 52,* 897–905.

Amsterdam, B. (1972). Mirror self–image reactions before age two. *Developmental Psychology, 5,* 297–305.

Anand, B., & Brobeck, J. (1951). Hypothalamic control of food intake in rats and cats. *Yale Journal of Biological Medicine, 24,* 123–140.

Anastasi, A. (1958). Heredity, environment, and the question "How?" *Psychological Review, 65,* 197–208.

Anastasi, A., & Urbina, S. (1997). *Psychological testing* (7th ed.). Upper Saddle River, NJ: Prentice Hall.

Andersen, S., & Cole, S. (1991). Do I know you? The role of significant others in general social perception. *Journal of Personality and Social Psychology, 59,* 384–399.

Andersen, S. M., Reznik, L., & Manzella, L. M. (1996). Eliciting facial affect, motivation, and expectancies in transference: Significant-other representations in social relations. *Journal of Personality and Social Psychology, 71,* 1108–1129.

Anderson, C. (1989). Temperature and aggression: Ubiquitous effects of heat on occurrence of human violence. *Psychological Bulletin, 106,* 74–96.

Anderson, D. J., & Ricklefs, R. E. (1995). Evidence of kin-selected tolerance by nestlings in a siblicida bird. *Behavioral Ecology & Sociobiology, 37,* 163–168.

Anderson, J. (1983). *The architecture of cognition.* Cambridge, MA: Harvard University Press.

Anderson, J. R. (1985). *Cognitive psychology and its implications.* (2nd ed.). New York: Freeman.

Anderson, J. R. (1993). Problem solving and learning. *American Psychologist, 48,* 35–44.

Anderson, J. R. (1995). *Learning and memory: An integrated approach.* New York: John Wiley.

Anderson, J. R. (1996). ACT: A simple theory of complex cognition. *American Psychologist, 51,* 355–365.

Anderson, N. C., Arndt, S., Alliger, R., Miller, D., & Flaum, M. (1995). Symptoms of schizophrenia: Methods, meanings, and mechanisms. *Archives of General Psychiatry, 52,* 341–351.

Anderson, R. C., & Pitchert, J. (1978). Recall of previously unrecalled information following a shift in perspective. *Journal of Verbal Learning and Verbal Behavior, 17,* 1–12.

Andersson, B. (1992). Effects of day-care on cognitive and socioeconomic competence of thirteen-year-old Swedish schoolchildren. *Child Development, 63,* 20–36.

Andreasen, N., & Glick, I. (1988). Bipolar affective disorder and creativity: Implications and clinical management. *Comprehensive Psychiatry, 29,* 207–217.

Andreasen, N. C., Rice, J., Endicott, J., Coryell, W., Grove, W. M., & Reich, T. (1987). Familial rates of affective disorder: A report from the National Institute of Mental Health collaborative study. *Archives of General Psychiatry, 44,* 461–469.

Andreason, N., Swayze, V., Flaum, M., Alliger, R., & Cohen, G. (1990). Ventricular abnormalities in affective disorder: Clinical and demographic correlates. *American Journal of Psychiatry, 147,* 893–900.

Andreasen, N. C., Arndt, S., Miller, D., Flaum, M., et al. (1995). Correlational studies of the Scale for the Assessment of Negative Symptoms and the Scale for the Assessment of Positive Symptoms: An overview and update. *Psychopathology, 28,* 7–17.

Andreasson, S., & Brandt, L. (1997). Mortality and morbidity related to alcohol. *Alcohol & Alcoholism, 32,* 173–178.

Andrzejewski, S. J., Moore, C. M., Corvette, M., & Hermann, D. (1991). Prospective memory skill. *Bulletin of the Psychonomic Society, 29,* 304–306.

Angel, I., Hauger, R., Giblin, B., & Paul, S. (1992). Regulation of the anorectic drug recognition site during glucoprovic feeding. *Brain Research Bulletin, 28,* 201–207.

Angrist, B., Sathananthan, G., Wilk, S., & Gershon, S. (1974). Amphetamine psychosis: Behavioral and biochemical aspects. *Journal of Psychiatric Research, 11,* 13–23.

Annett, J. M. (1996). Olfactory memory: A case study in cognitive psychology. *The Journal of Psychology, 130,* 309–319.

Anthony, E., & Cohler, B. (Eds.) (1987). *The invulnerable child.* New York: Guilford Press.

Antoch M. P., Song E. J., Chang A. M., Vitaterna M. H., Zhao Y. L., Wilsbacher L. D., et al. (1997). Functional identification of the mouse circadian clock gene by transgenic bac rescue. *Cell, 89,* 655–667.

Antrobus, J. (1991). Dreaming: Cognitive processes during cortical activation and high afferent thresholds. *Psychological Review, 98,* 96–121.

Aparicio, C. F., & Baum, W. M. (1997). Comparing locomotion with lever-press travel in an operant simulation of foraging. *Journal of the Experimental Analysis of Behavior, 68,* 177–192.

Aponte, H. J., & VanDeusen, J. M. (1981). Structural family therapy. In A. S. Gurman and D. P. Kniskern (Eds.), *Handbook of family therapy.* New York: Brunner/Mazel.

Applebaum, P. S., Uyehara, L. A., & Elin, M. R., Eds. (1996). *Trauma and memory: Clinical and legal controversies.* New York: Oxford University Press.

Archer D. (1994). American violence: How high and why? *Law Studies, 19,* 12–20.

Archer, J. (1991). The influence of testosterone on human aggression. *British Journal of Psychology, 82,* 1–28.

Archer, J., & Lloyd, B. (1985). *Sex and gen-*

der. (2nd ed.). New York: Cambridge University Press.

Ardila, A., Monanes, P., & Gempeler, J. (1986). Echoic memory and language perception. *Brain and Language, 29,* 134–140.

Arena, J. G., & Blanchard, E. B. (1996). Biofeedback and relaxation therapy for chronic disorders. In R. J. Gatchel, and D. C. Turk et al. (Eds.). *Psychological approaches to pain management: A practitioner's handbook.* (pp. 179–230). New York, NY: Guilford Press.

Arendt, R. E., Minnes, S., Singer, L. T. (1996). Fetal cocaine exposure: Neurologic effects and sensory-motor delays. In L. S. Chandler, and S. J. Lane (Eds.), *Children with prenatal drug exposure* (pp. 129–144). New York: Haworth Press, Inc.

Arkes, H., Boehm, L., & Xu, G. (1991). Determinants of judged validity. *Journal of Experimental Social Psychology, 27,* 576–605.

Arkowitz, H. (1997). Integrative theories of therapy. In P. L. Wachtel, S. B. Messer et al. (Eds.). *Theories of psychotherapy: Origins and evolution.* (pp. 227–288). Washington, DC: American Psychological Association.

Arkowitz, H., & Messer, S. B., (Eds.) (1984). *Psychodynamic therapy and behavior therapy: Is integration possible?* New York: Plenum Press.

Arndt, J., Greenberg, J., Solomon, S., Pyszczynski, T., & Simon, L. (1997). Suppression, accessibility of death-related thoughts, and cultural worldview defense: Exploring the psychodynamics of terror management. *Journal of Personality and Social Psychology, 73,* 5–18.

Arnkoff, D., Victor, B., & Glass, C. (1993). Empirical research on factors in psychotherapeutic change. In G. Stricker & J. Gold (Eds.), *Comprehensive handbook of psychotherapy integration* (pp. 27–42). New York: Plenum Press.

Aron, A., & Westhay, L. (1996). Dimensions of the prototype of love. *Journal of Personality and Psychology, 70,* 535–555.

Aron, L. (1996). *A meeting of minds: Mutuality in psychoanalysis.* Hillside, NJ: Analytic Press.

Aronson, E. (1978). *The jigsaw classroom.* Beverly Hills, CA: Sage.

Arrigo, J. A., & Pezdek, K. (1997). Lessons from the study of psychogenic amnesia. *Current Directions in Psychological Science, 5,* 148–152.

Arvey, R. D., Bouchard, T. J., Segal, N. L., & Abraham, L. M. (1989). Job satisfaction: Environmental and genetic components. *Journal of Applied Psychology, 74,* 187–192.

Asch, S. E. (1955). Opinions and social pressure. *Scientific American, 193,* 31–35.

Asch, S. E. (1956). Studies of independence and conformity: A minority of one against unanimous majority. *Psychological Monographs: General and Applied, 70,* 1–69.

Asendorph, J., & Baudonniere, P. (1993). Self-awareness and other-awareness: Mirror self-recognition and synchronic imitation among unfamiliar peers. *Developmental Psychology, 29,* 88–95.

Asendorph, J., & Scherer, K. (1983). The discrepant repressor: Differentiation between low anxiety, high anxiety, and repression of anxiety by autonomic-facial-verbal patterns of behavior. *Journal of Personality and Social Psychology, 45,* 1334–1346.

Ashford, J. W., Schmitt, F. A., & Kumar, V. (1996). Diagnosis of Alzheimer's disease. *Psychiatric Annals, 26,* 262–268.

Atkinson, J. W. (1977). Motivation for achievement. In Blass, T. (Ed.), *Personality Variables in Social Behavior.* Hillsdale, NJ: Erlbaum.

Atkinson, J. W., & Litwin, G. H. (1960). Achievement motive land test anxiety conceived as motive to approach success and motive to avoid failure. *Journal of Abnormal and Social Psychology, 60,* 52–63.

Atkinson, R. C., & Shiffrin, R. N. (1968). Human memory: A proposed system and its control processes. In K. W. Spence and J. T. Spense (Eds.), *The psychology of learning and motivation,* Vol. 2. New York: Academic Press.

Atwater, L. E. (1992). Beyond cognitive ability: Improving the prediction of performance. *Journal of Business and Psychology, 7,* 27–44.

Ayllon, T., & Azrin, N. H. (1968). *The token economy: A motivational system for therapy and rehabilitation.* New York: Appleton-Century-Crofts.

Baars, B. (1995). Tutorial commentary: Surprisingly small subcortical structures are needed for the stage of waking consciousness, while cortical projection areas seem to provide perceptual contents of consciousness. *Consciousness and Cognition, 4,* 159–162.

Baars, B. J. (1988). Momentary forgetting as a "resetting" of a conscious global workspace due to competition between incompatible contexts. In M. J. Horowitz (Ed.), *Psychodynamics and cognition* (pp. 269–293). University of California.

Baars, B. J. (1997). *In the theater of consciousness: The workspace of the mind.* New York: Oxford University Press.

Baars B. J., & McGovern, K. (1996). Cognitive views of consciousness: What are the facts? How can we explain them? In M. Velmans (Ed.), *The science of con-*

sciouness: Psychological, neuropsychological and clinical reviews (pp. 63–95). London.

Babor, T., Hoffman, M., DelBoca, F., Hesselbrock, V., Meyer, R. E., Dolinsky, Z., & Rounsaville, B. (1992). Types of alcoholics, I: Evidence for an empirically derived typology based on indicators of vulnerability and severity. *Archives of General Psychiatry, 49,* 599–608.

Baddeley, A., Gathercole, S., & Papagno, C. (1998). The phonological loop as a language learning device. *Psychological Review, 105,* 158–173.

Baddeley, A. D. (1992). Working memory. *Science, 255,* 556–559.

Baddeley, A. D. (1995). Working memory. In M. Gazzaniga (Ed.), *The cognitive neurosciences* (pp. 754–764). Cambridge, MA: Bradford/MIT Press.

Baddeley, A. D., & Patterson, K. (1971). The relation between long-term and short-term memory. *British Medical Bulletin, 27,* 237–242.

Baer, J. S., Marlatt, G., Kivlahan, D., & Fromme, K. (1992). An experimental test of three methods of alcohol risk reduction with young adults. *Journal of Consulting and Clinical Psychology, 60,* 974–979.

Baer, L., Rauch, S. L., Ballantine, H. T., Martuza, R., Cosgrove, R., Cassem, E., et al. (1995). Cingulotomy for intractable obsessive-compulsive disorder: Prospective long-term follow-up of 18 patients. *Archives of General Psychiatry, 52,* 384–392.

Bahrick, H. P. (1985). Associationism and the Ebbinghaus legacy. Journal of Experimental Psychology: *Learning, Memory, & Cognition, 11,* 439–443.

Bahrick, H. P., Bahrick, L. E., Bahrick, A. S., & Bahrick, P. E. (1993). Maintenance of foreign language vocabulary and the spacing effect. *Psychological Science, 4,* 316–321.

Bahrick, H. P., & Hall, L. K. (1991). Lifetime maintenance of high school mathematics content. *Journal of Experimental Psychology: General, 120,* 20–33.

Bahrick, H. P., Hall, L. K., & Berger, S. A. (1996). Accuracy and distortion in memory for high school grades. *Psychological Science, 7,* 265–271.

Bailey, C. H., & Kandel, E. R. (1995). Molecular and structural mechanisms underlying long-term memory. In M. S. Gazzaniga et al. (Eds.), *The cognitive neurosciences.* (pp. 19–36). Cambridge, MA: MIT Press.

Bailey, J. M., & Pillard, R. (1991). A genetic study of male sexual orientation. *Archives of General Psychiatry, 48,* 1089–1096.

Bailey, J. M., & Zucker, K. (1995). Childhood sex-typed behavior and sexual

orientation: A conceptual analysis and quantitative review. Special Issue: Sexual orientation and human development. *Developmental Psychology, 31,* 43–55.

Bailey, J. M., Pillard, R. C., Neale, M. C., & Agyei, Y. (1993). Heritable factors influence sexual orientation in women. *Archives of General Psychiatry, 50,* 217–223.

Bailey, J. M., Willerman, L., & Parks, C. (1991). A test of the maternal stress theory of human homosexuality. *Archives of Sexual Behavior, 20,* 277–293.

Baker, L., Silk, K. R., Westen, D., Nigg, J. T., & Lohr, N. E. (1992). Malevolence, splitting, and parental ratings by borderlines. *Journal of Nervous and Mental Disease, 180,* 258–264.

Baldessarini, R. J., & Tarazi, F. I. (1996). Brain dopamine receptors: A primer on their current status, basic and clinical. *Harvard Review of Psychiatry, 3,* 301–325.

Baldwin, M. (1992). Relational schemas and the processing of social information. *Psychological Bulletin, 112,* 461–484.

Bales, R. F. (1953). The equilibrium problem in small groups. In T. Parsons, R. F. Bales, & E. A. Shils (Eds.), *Working papers in the theory of action.* Glencoe, Ill: Free Press.

Baltes, P. (1987). Theoretical propositions of life-span developmental psychology: On the dynamics between growth and decline. *Developmental Psychology, 23,* 611–626.

Baltes, P. B. (1997). On the incomplete architecture of human ontogeny: Selection, optimization, and compensation as foundation of developmental theory. *American Psychologist, 52,* 366–380.

Banaji, M. R., & Crowder, R. G. (1989). The bankruptcy of everyday memory. *American Psychologist, 44,* 1485–1193.

Bandler, R. (1982). Identification of neuronal cell bodies mediating components of biting attack behavior in the cat: Induction of jaw opening following microinjections of glutamate into hypothalamus. *Brain Research, 245,* 192–197.

Bandura, A. (1967). The role of modeling personality development. In C. Lavatelli & F. Stendler (Eds.). *Readings in childhood and development* (pp. 334–343). New York: Harcourt Brace Jovanovich.

Bandura, A. (1977). Self-efficacy: Toward a unifying theory of behavioral change. *Psychological Review, 84,* 191–215.

Bandura, A. (1977). *Social learning theory.* Englewood Cliffs, NJ: Prentice-Hall.

Bandura, A. (1982). Self-efficacy mechanisms in human agency. *American Psychologist, 37,* 122–147.

Bandura, A. (1986). *Social foundations of thought and action: A social cognitive the-*

ory, Englewood Cliffs, NJ: Prentice-Hall.

Bandura, A. (1989). Human agency in social cognitive theory. *American Psychologist, 44,* 1175–1184.

Bandura, A. (1991). Social cognitive theory of self-regulation. *Organizational Behavior and Human Decision Processes 50,* 248–287.

Bandura, A. (1995). *Self-efficacy in changing societies.* New York: Cambridge University Press.

Bandura, A., Blanchard, E. B., & Ritter, B. (1969). Relative efficacy of desensitization and modeling approaches for inducing behavioral, affective, and attitudinal changes. *Journal of Personality and Social Psychology, 13,* 173–199.

Bandura, A., Ross, D., & Ross, S. (1961). Transmission of aggression through imitation of aggressive models. *Journal of Abnormal and Social Psychology, 66,* 3–11.

Bandura, A., Ross, D., & Ross, S. (1963). Vicarious reinforcement and imitative learning. *Journal of Abnormal and Social Psychology, 67,* 601–607.

Banerjee, M. (1997). Hidden emotions: Preschoolers' knowledge of appearance-reality and emotion display rules. *Social Cognition 15(2),* 107–132.

Banks, M. S., & Salapatek, P. (1983). Infant visual perception. In M. M. Haith & J. J. Campos (Eds.), *Handbook of child psychology: Vol. 2, Infancy and developmental psychobiology.* New York: John Wiley.

Bard, P. (1934). On emotional expression after desortation with some remarks on certain theoretical views. *Psychological Review, 41,* 309–328.

Bardwick, J. (1971). *Psychology of women.* New York: Harper & Row.

Bargh, J. (in press). The automaticity of everyday life. In J. S. Wyer, Jr. (Ed.), *Advances in social cognition, Vol. 10.* Hillsdale, NJ: Lawrence Erlbaum.

Bargh, J., & Barndollar, K. (1996). Automaticity in action: The unconscious as repository of chronic goals and motives. In P. M. Gollwitzer, & J. Bargh (Eds.), *The psychology of action: Linking cognition and motivation to behavior* (pp. 457–481). New York: Guilford.

Bargh, J. A., & Tota, M. E. (1988). Context-dependent automatic depression: Accessibility of negative constructs with regard to self but not others. *Journal of Personality and Social Psychology, 54,* 925–939.

Barinag, M. (1997). New imaging methods provide a better view into the brain. *Science, 276,* 1974–1976.

Barling, J., Kelloway, E. K., & Cheung, D. (1996). Time management and achievement striving interact to predict car sales performance. *Journal of Applied Psychology, 81,* 821–826.

Barlow, D. H. (1988). *Anxiety and its disorders.* New York: Guilford Press.

Barlow, D. H. (1988). Current models of panic disorder and a view from emotion theory. In A. J. Frances & R. E. Hales (Eds.), *Review of psychiatry,* Vol. 7. Washington, DC: American Psychiatric Press.

Barlow, D. H., Chorpita, B. F., & Turovsky, J. (1996). Fear, panic, anxiety, and disorders of emotion. In D. A. Hope, et al. (Eds.), *Nebraska Symposium on Motivation, 1995: Perspectives on anxiety, panic, and fear. Current theory and research in motivation,* Vol. 43. (pp. 251–328). Lincoln, NE: University of Nebraska Press.

Barlow, D. H., Esler, J. L., & Vitali, A. E. (1998). Psychosocial treatments for panic disorders, phobias, and generalized anxiety disorder. In P. E. Nathan, J. M. Gorman, et al. (Eds.), *A guide to treatments that work.* (pp. 288–318). New York: NY: Oxford University Press.

Barnes, D. M. (1990). Silver Spring monkeys yield unexpected data on brain reorganization. *Journal of NIH, 2,* 19–20.

Baron, A., & Mattila, W. (1989). Response slowing of older adults: Effects of time-limit contingencies on single- and dual-task performances. *Psychology and Aging, 4.*

Baron, R. S., Cutrona, C. E., Hicklin, D., Russel, D. W., & Lubaroff, D. M. (1990). Social support and immune function among spouses of cancer patients. *Journal of Personality and Social Psychology, 59,* 344–352.

Baron-Cohen, S., Baldwin, D. A., & Crowson, M. (1997). Do children with autism use the speaker's direction of gaze strategy to crack the code of language? *Child Development, 68,* 48–57.

Barr, H., Pytkowicz, Streissguth, Darby, B., & Sampson, P. (1990). Prenatal exposure to alcohol, caffeine, tobacco, and aspirin: Effects on fine and gross motor performance in 4-year-old children. *Developmental Psychology, 26,* 339–348.

Barrett, D. H., Resnick, H. S., Foy, D. W., Dansky, B. S., Flanders, W. D., & Stroup, N. E. (1996). Combat exposure and adult psychosocial adjustment among U.S. Army veterans serving in Vietnam, 1965–1971. *Journal of Abnormal Psychology, 105,* 575–581.

Barrett, G. V., & Depinet, R. L. (1991). A reconsideration of testing for competence rather than for intelligence. *American Psychologist, 46,* 1012–1024.

Barrett, G. V., & Franke, R. H. (1969). Communication preference and performance: A cross-cultural comparison. *Proceedings of the 77th Annual American Psychological Association Convention,* 597–598.

Barrett, P. M., Dadds, M. R., & Rapee, R. M. (1996). Family treatment of childhood anxiety: A controlled trial. *Journal of Consulting and Clinical Psychology, 64,* 333–339.

Barron, F., & Harrington, D. M. (1981). Creativity, intelligence, and personality. *Annual Review of Psychology, 32,* 439–476.

Barry, H. M., et al. (1957). A cross-cultural survey of some sex differences in socialization. *Journal of Abnormal Social Psychology, 55,* 327–332.

Barta, P., Pearlson, G., Powers, R. E., Richards, S. S., & Tune, L. (1990). Auditory hallucinations and smaller superior temporal gyral volume in schizophrenia. *American Journal of Psychiatry, 147,* 1457–1462.

Bartlett, F. C. (1932). *Remembering: A study in experimental and social psychology.* Cambridge: Cambridge University Press.

Bartoshuk, L. M., & Beauchamp, G. K. (1994). Chemical senses. *Annual Review of Psychology, 45,* 419–449.

Basoglu, M. (1997). Torture as a stressful life event: A review of the current status of knowledge. In T. W. Miller (Ed.), *Clinical disorders and stressful life events* (pp. 45–70). Madison, CT: International Universities Press, Inc.

Basoglu, M., Paker, M., Paker, O., Ozmen, E., Marks, I., Sahin, D., & Sarimurat, N. (1994). Psychological effects of torture: A comparison of tortured with nontortured political activists in Turkey. *American Journal of Psychiatry, 151,* 6–81.

Basso, M. R., Schefft, B., & Hoffmann, R. G. (1994). Mood-moderating effects of affect intensity on cognition: Sometimes euphoria is not beneficial and dysphyoria is not detrimental. *Journal of Personality and Social Psychology, 66,* 363–368.

Bates, J. E., Marvinney, D., Kelley, T., Dodge, K. E., Bennett, D. S., & Pettit, G. S. (1994). Child-care history and kindergarten adjustment. *Developmental Psychology, 39,* 690–700.

Bates, M. S. (1987). Ethnicity and pain: A biocultural model. *Social Science and Medicine, 24,* 47–50.

Batson, C. D. (1991). Evidence for altruism: Toward a pluralism of prosocial motives. *Psychological Inquiry, 2,* 107–122.

Batson, C. D. (1995). Altruism. In A. Tesser (Ed.), *Advanced social psychology.* New York: McGraw-Hill.

Batson, C. D. (1998). Altruism and prosocial behavior. In D. T. Gilbert, S. T. Fiske, and G. Lindzey (Eds.), *The Handbook of Social Psychology Vol. 2* (4th ed.). (pp. 282–316). Boston, MA: McGraw-Hill.

Battacchi, M. W., Pelamatti, G., Umilta, C., & Michelotti, E. (1981). On the acoustic information stored in echoic memory. *International Journal of Psycholonguistics, 8,* 17–29.

Batteau, D. W. (1967). The role of the pinna in human localization. Proceedings of the *Royal Society of London, Series, B, 168,* 158–180.

Batuev, A. S., & Gafurov, B. G. (1993). The chemical natrue of the hypothalamo-cortical activation underlying drinking behavior. *Neuroscience of Behavioral Psychology, 23,* 35–41.

Bauer, P. J. (1995). Recalling past events: From infancy to early childhood. In R. Vasta (Ed.), *Annals of child development: A research annual* (Vol. 11, pp. 25–71). England: Jessica Kingsley Publishers.

Baumeister, R. (1991). *Meanings of life.* New York: Guilford Press.

Baumeister, R., & Leary, M. R. (1995). The need to belong: Desire for interpersonal attachments as a fundamental human motive. *Psychological Bulletin, 117,* 497–529.

Baumeister, R. F., Smart, L., & Boden, J. M. (1996). Relation of threatened egotism to violence and aggression: The dark side of high self-esteem. *Psychological Review, 103,* 5–33.

Baumeister, R. F., Stillwell, A. M., & Heatherton, T. F. (1994). Guilt: An interpersonal approach. *Psychological Bulletin, 115,* 243–267.

Baumeister, R. J. (1998). The self. In D. T. Gilbert, S. T. Fiske, and G. Lindzey (Eds.), *The Handbook of Social Psychology Vol. 2* (4th ed.). (pp. 680–740). Boston, MA: McGraw-Hill.

Baumrind, D. (1967). Child care practices anteceding three patterns of preschool behavior. *Genetic Psychology Monographs, 75,* 43–88.

Baumrind, D. (1971). Current patterns of parental authority. *Developmental Psychology Monograph, 4,* 1–103.

Baumrind, D. (1985). Research using intentional deception: Ethical issues revisited. *American Psychologist, 40,* 165–174.

Baumrind, D. (1987). A developmental perspective on adolescent risk taking in contemporary America. *New Directions for Child Development, 37,* 93–125.

Baumrind, D. (1991). The influence of parenting style on adolescent competence and substance use. *Journal of Early Adolescence, 11,* 56–95.

Baxter, D. W., & Olszewski, J. (1960). Congenital universal insensitivity to pain. *Brain, 83,* 381–393.

Baydar, N., & Brooks-Gunn, J. (1991). Effects of maternal employment and child-care arrangements on preschoolers' cognitive and behavioral outcomes: Evidence from the children of the National Longitudinal Survey of Youth. *Developmental Psychology, 27,* 932–945.

Bazler, J., & Simonis, D. (1991). Are high school chemistry textbooks gender fair? *Journal of Research in Science Teaching, 28,* 353–362.

Beaman, A. L., Barnes, P. J., Klentz, B., & McQuirk, B. (1978). Increasing helping rates through information dissemination: Teaching pays. *Personality and Social Psychology Bulletin, 4,* 406–411.

Beaman, A. L., Cole, C. M., Preston, M., Klentz, B., & Steblay, N. M. (1983). Fifteen years of foot-in-the-door research: A meta-analysis. *Personality and Social Psychology Bulletin, 9,* 181–196.

Bearden, C. (1994). The nightmare: Biological and psychological origins. *Dream, 4,* 139–152.

Bechara, A., Tranel, D., Damasio, H., Adolphs, R., Rockland, C., & Damasio, A. (1995). Double dissociation of conditioning and declarative knowledge relative to the amygdala and hippocampus in humans. *Science, 29,* 1115–1118.

Beck, A. (1985). *Anxiety disorders and phobias: A cognitive perspective.* New York: Basic Books.

Beck, A. (1989). *Cognitive therapy in clinical practice: An illustrative casebook.* New York: Routledge.

Beck, A. (1991). Cognitive therapy: A 30-year retrospective. *American Psychologist, 46,* 368–375.

Beck, A. (1992). Cognitive therapy: A 30 year retrospective. In J. Cottraux, P. Legeron, et al. (Eds.), Which psychotherapies in year 2000? *Annual series of European research in behavior therapy, 6.* (pp. 13–28). Amsterdam, The Netherlands: Swets & Zeitlinger.

Beck, A., & Freeman, A. (1990). *Cognitive therapy of personality disorders.* New York: Guilford Press.

Beck, A. T. (1976). *Cognitive therapy and the emotional disorders.* New York: International Universities Press.

Beck, A. T. (1993). Cognitive therapy: Past, present, and future. *Journal of Consulting and Clinical Psychology, 61,* 194–198.

Beck, A. T., & Emery, G. (1985). *Anxiety disorders and phobias: A cognitive perspective.* New York: Basic Books.

Beck, A. T., Sokol, L., Clark, D. A., Berchick, R., & Wright, R. (1992). A crossover study of focused cognitive therapy for panic disorder. *American Journal of Psychiatry, 149,* 778–783.

Beck, J. G., & Barlow, D. H. (1984). Current conceptualizations of sexual dysfunction: A review and an alternative perspective. *Clinical Psychology Review, 4,* 363–378.

Becker, E. (1973). *The denial of death.* New York: Free Press.

Becker, G. (1978). *The mad genius controversy.* Beverly Hills, CA: Sage.

Beckwith, J., Geller, L., & Sarkar, S. (1991). Sources of human psychological differences: The Minnesota Study of Twins Reared Apart: Comment. *Science, 252,* 191.

Beckwith, L., Rodning, C., & Cohen, S. (1992). Preterm children at early adolescence and continuity and discontinuity in maternal responsiveness from infancy. *Child Development, 63,* 1198–1208.

Bee, H. (1982). Prediction of IQ and language skill from perinatal status, child performance, family characteristics, and mother-infant interaction. *Child Development, 53,* 1134–1156.

Beets, J. G. T. (1978). Odor and stimulant structure. In E. C. Carterette & M. P. Friedman (Eds.), *Handbook of perception.* New York: Academic Press.

Beitman, B. D., Goldfried, M. R., & Norcross, J. C. (1989). The movment toward integrating the psychotherapies: An overview. *American Journal of Psychiatry, 146,* 138–147.

Bekesy, G. von. (1959). Synchronism of neural discharges and their demultiplication in pitch perception on the skin and in learning. *Journal of the Acoustical Society of America, 31,* 338–349.

Bekesy, G. von. (1960). *Experiments in hearing.* New York: McGraw-Hill.

Bekesy, G. von, & Rosenblith, W. A. (1951). The mechanical properties of the ear. In S. S. Stevens (Ed.), *Handbook of experimental psychology.* New York: John Wiley & Sons.

Bell, A. P., Weinberg, M. S., & Hammersmith, S. (1981). *Sexual preference: Its development in men and women.* Bloomington: University of Indiana Press.

Bell, R. M. (1985). *Holy anorexia.* Chicago: University of Chicago Press.

Bell, R. Q. (1968). A reinterpretation of the direction of effects in studies of socialization. *Psychological Review, 75,* 71–85.

Bellack, A., & Mueser, K. (1992). Social skills training for schizophrenia? *Archives of General Psychiatry, 49.*

Bellack, L., Hurvich, M., & Geldman, H. (1973). *Ego functions in schizophrenics, neurotics, and normals.* New York: John Wiley.

Bellah, R. N., et al. (1985). *Habits of the heart: Individualism and commitment in American life.* Berkeley: University of California Press.

Bellivier, F., Leboyer, M., Courtet, P., Buresi, C., Beufils, B., Samolyk, D., et al. (1998). Association between the tryptophan hydroxylase gene and

manic-depressive illness. *Archives of General Psychiatry, 55,* 33–37.

Belo, J. (1955). Balinese children's drawing. In M. Mead & M. Wolfenstein (Eds.), *Childhood in Contemporary Cultures* (pp. 52–69). Chicago: University of Chicago Press.

Belsky, J., Hsieh, K.-H., & Crnic, K. (1996). Infant positive and negative emotionality: One dimension or two? *Developmental Psychology, 32,* 289–298.

Belsky, J., Hsieh, K.-H., & Crnic, K. (1996). Infant positive and negative emotionality: One dimension or two? *Developmental Psychology, 32,* 289–298.

Belsky, J., & Isabella, R. (1988). Maternal, infant, and social-contextual determinants of attachment security. In J. Belsky & T. Nezworsky (Eds.), *Clinical implications of attachment* (pp. 41–94). Hillsdale, NJ: Erlbaum.

Belsky, J., & Nezworski, T. (Eds.). (1987). *Clinical implications of attachment theory.* Hillsdale, NJ: Erlbaum.

Belsky, J., & Pensky, E. (1988). Marital change across the transition to parenthood. *Marriage and Family Review, 12,* 133–156.

Belsky, J., & Rovine, M. J. (1988). Nonmaternal care in the first year of life and the security of infant-parent attachment. *Child Development, 59,* 157–167.

Bem, D. J. (1967). Self perception: An alternative interpretation of cognitive dissonance phenomena. *Psychological Review, 74,* 183–200.

Bem, D. J. (1972). Self-perception theory. In L. Berkowitz (Ed.), *Advances in experimental social psychology* (Vol. 6). New York: Academic Press.

Bem, D. J., & Allen, A. (1974). On predicting some of the people some of the time: The search for cross-situational consistencies in behavior. *Psychological Review, 81,* 506–520.

Bem, S. L. (1983). Gender schema theory and its implications for child development: Raising gender-aschematic children in a gender-schematic society. *Signs, Journal of Women in Culture and Society, 8,* 354–364.

Bem, S. L. (1985). Androgyny and gender schema theory: A conceptual and empirical integration. In T. B. Sonderegger (Ed.), *Nebraska symposium on motivation: Psychology and gender,* Vol. 32. Lincoln: University of Nebraska Press.

Bemporad, J. R. (1996). Self-starvation through the ages: Reflections on the pre-history of anorexia nervosa. *International Journal of Eating Disorders, 19,* 217–237.

Benasich, A. A., & Brooks-Gunn, J. (1996). Maternal attitudes and knowledge of child-rearing: Associations with family and child outcomes. *Child Development, 67*, 1186–1205.

Benbow, C., & Stanley, J. (1983). Sex differences in mathematical reasoning ability: More facts. *Science, 222*, 1029–1030.

Bendersky, M., & Lewis, M. (1998). Arousal modulation in cocaine-exposed infants. *Developmental Psychology, 34*, 555–564.

Benedict, R. (1934). *Patterns of culture.* New York: Mentor/New American Library.

Benes, F. (1989). Myelination of cortical-hippocampal relays during late adolescence. *Schizophrenia Bulletin, 15*, 585–593.

Benes, F., Turtle, M., Khan, Y., & Farol, P. (1994). Myelination of a key relay zone in the hippocampal formation occurs in the human brain during childhood, adolescence, and adulthood. *Archives of General Psychiatry, 51*, 477–484.

Benet-Martinez, V., & Waller, J. G. (1997). Further evidence for the cross-cultural generality of the Big Seven factor model: Indigenous and imported Spanish personality constructs. *Journal of Personality, 65*, 567–598.

Benton, M. K., & Schroeder, H. E. (1990). Social skills training with schizophrenics: A meta-analytic evaluation. *Journal of Consulting and Clinical Psychology, 58*, 741–747.

Berg, C. (1992). Perspectives for viewing intellectual development throughout the life course. In R. J. Sternberg & C. A. Berg (Eds.), *Intellectual development* (pp. 1–15). New York: Cambridge University Press.

Berger, R. J., & Phillips, N. H. (1995). Energy conservation and sleep. *Behavioural Brain Research, 69*, 65–73.

Berkowitz, L. (1989). Frustration-aggression hypothesis: Examination and reformulation. *Psychological Bulletin, 106*, 59–73.

Berkowitz, L. (1993). *Aggression: Its causes, consequences, and control.* New York: McGraw-Hill Book Company.

Berkowitz, L. B. (1994). *Aggression: Its causes, consequences, and control.* New York: McGraw-Hill.

Berman, E. (1973). *Scapegoat.* Ann Arbor, Michigan: University of Michigan Press.

Berman, P. W., & Pedersen, F. A. (1987). Research on men's transitions to parenthood: An integrative discussion. In P. W. Berman and F. A. Pederson (Eds.), *Men's transitions to parenthood: Longitudinal studies of early family experience.* Hillsdale, NJ: Erlbaum.

Berman, B., Fasotti, L., Nieuwenhuyse, B., & Schuerman, J. (1991). Spinal cord lesions, peripheral feedback and intensi-

ties of emotional feelings. *Cognition and Emotion, 5*, 201–220.

Bernstein, I. L. (1991). Aversion conditioning in response to cancer and cancer treatment. *Clinical Psychology Review, 11*, 185–191.

Berquier, A., & Ashton, R. (1992). Characteristics of the frequent nightmare sufferer. *Journal of Abnormal Psychology, 101*, 246–250.

Berridge, K., & Valenstein, E. (1991). What psychological process mediates feeding evoked by electrical stimulation of the lateral hypothalamus? *Behavioral Neuroscience, 105*, 3–14.

Berridge, K., & Zajonc, R. (1991). Hypothalamic cooling effects elicit eating: Differential effects on motivation and pleasure. *Psychological Science, 2*, 184–189.

Berridge, K. C. (1996). Food reward: Brain substrates of wanting and liking. Special Issue: Society for the Study of Ingestive Behavior, Second Independent Meeting. *Neuroscience & Biobehavioral Reviews, 20*, 1–25.

Berry, J. W. (1979). A cultural ecology of social behavior. In L. Berkowitz (Ed.), *Advances in experimental social psychology,* Vol. 12. New York: Academic Press.

Berry, J. W. (1989). Psychology of acculturation. In J. Berman (Ed.), *Nebraska Symposium on Motivation,* Vol. 37 (pp. 201–234). Lincoln: University of Nebraska Press.

Berry, J. W., & Bennet, J. A. (1992). Cree conceptions of cognitive competence. *International Journal of Psychology, 27*, 73–88.

Berry, J. W., Dasen, P. R., Saraswathi, T. S. (Eds., 1997). *Handbook of cross-cultural psychology, Vol. 2: Basic processes and human development* (2nd ed.). Boston: Allyn & Bacon, Inc.

Berry, J. W., & Irvine, S. H. (1986). Bricolage: Savages do it daily. In R. J. Sternberg, & R. K. Wagner (Eds.), *Practical Intelligence: Nature and Origins of Competence in the Everyday World* (pp. 271–303). New York: Cambridge University Press.

Berry, J. W., Poortinga, Y. H., Segall, M. H., & Dasen, P. R. (1992). *Cross-cultural psychology: Research and applications.* New York: Cambridge University Press.

Berscheid, E., Dion, K., Walster, E., & Walster, G. (1971). Physical attractiveness and dating choice: A test of the matching hypothesis. *Journal of Experimental Social Psychology, 7*, 173–189.

Berscheid, E., & Reis, H. T. (1998). Attraction and close relationships. In D. T. Gilbert, S. T. Fiske, et al. (Eds.), *The handbook of social psychology, Vol. 2* (4th ed.). (pp. 193–281). Boston, MA: McGraw-Hill.

Best, D. L. (1993). Inducing children to generate mneumonic organizational strategies: An examination of long-term retention and materials. *Developmental Psychology, 29*, 324–336.

Best, D. L., & Williams, J. E. (in press). Cross-cultural viewpoint. In A. E. Beall & R. J. Steinberg (Eds.), *Perspectives on the psychology of gender.* New York: Guilford Press.

Best, D. L., Williams, J. E., Cloud, J. M., Davis, S. W. Robertson, L. S., Edwards, J. R., Giles, H., & Fowles, J. (1977). Development of sex-trait stereotypes among young children in the United States, England, and Ireland. *Child Development, 48*, 1375–1384.

Beutler, L. E. (1991). Have all won and must all have prizes? Revisiting Luborsky et al's verdict. *Journal of Consulting and Clinical Psychology, 59*, 226–232.

Beyene, Y. (1986). Cultural significance and physiological manifestations of menopause. A biocultural analysis. *Culture, Medicine, & Psychiatry, 10*, 47–71.

Beyer, C., Caba, M., Banas, C., & Komisaruk, B. R. (1991). Vasoactive intestinal polypeptide (VIP) potentiates the behavior effect of substance P intrathecal administration. *Pharmacology, Biochemistry, and Behavior, 39*, 695–698.

Bickel, W. K., Green, L., & Vuchinich, R. E. (1995). Behavioral economics. Special Issue: Behavioral economics. *Journal of the Experimental Analysis of Behavior, 64*, 257–262.

Bidell, T. R., & Fischer, K. W. (1992). Beyond the stage debate: Action, structure, and variability in Piagetian theory and research. In R. Sternberg & C. Berg (Eds.), *Intellectual development* (pp. 100–140). Cambridge: Cambridge University Press.

Biederman, I. (1987). Recognition by components: A theory of human image understanding. *Psychological Review, 94*, 115–147.

Biederman, I. (1990). Higher-level vision. In D. N. Osherson, S. M. Kosslyn, et al. (Eds.), *Visual cognition and action: An invitation to cognitive science, Vol. 2.* (pp. 41–72). Cambridge, MA, USA: MIT Press.

Biederman, I., Glass, A. L., & Stacy, E. W., Jr. (1973). Searching for objects in real-world scenes. *Journal of Exerimental Psychology, 97*, 22–27.

Biederman, I., Mezzanotte, R. J., & Rabinowitz, J. C. (1982). Scene perception: Detecting and judging objects undergoing relational violations. *Cognitive Psychology, 14*, 143–177.

Biederman, I., Mezzanotte, R. J., Rabinowitz, J. C., Francolini, C. M., & Plude, D. (1981). Detecting the unexpected in photointerpretation. *Human Factors, 23,* 153–164.

Biederman, J., Faraone, S., Milberger, S., Guite, J., Mick, E., Chen, L., et al. (1996). A Prospective 4-Year Follow-up Study of Attention-Deficit Hyperactivity and Related Disorders. *Archives of General Psychiatry, 53,* 437–446.

Biederman, J., Milberger, S., Faraone, S. V., Kiely, K., Guite, J., Mick, E., et al. (1995). Family-environment risk factors for attention-deficit hyperativity disorder: A test of Rutter's indicators of adversity. *Archives of General Psychiatry, 52,* 464–470.

Bierer, L. M., Hof, P. R., Purohit, D. P., Carlin, L., et al. (1995). Neocortical neurofibrillary tangles correlate with dementia severity in Alzheimer's disease. *Archives of Neurology, 52,* 81–88.

Bieri, J. (1966). Cognitive complexity and personality development. In O. J. Jarvey (Ed.), *Experience, Structure and adaptability.*

Bierman, K. L., Miller, C. L., & Stabbo, S. D. (1987). Improving the social behavior and peer acceptance of rejected boys: Effects of social skill training with instructions and prohibitions. *Journal of Consulting and Clinical Psychology, 55,* 194–200.

Binet, A., & Simon, T. (1908). Le developpement de l'intelligence chez les enfants. *L'Annee Psychologique, 14,* 1–94.

Birenbaum, A., & Cohen, H. J. (1993). On the importance of helping families: Policy implications from a national study. *Mental Retardation, 31,* 67–74.

Birnbaum, D. W. (1983). Preschooler's stereotypes about sex differences in emotionality: A reaffirmation. *Journal of Genetic Psychology, 143,* 139–140.

Bishop, J. A., & Cook, L. M. (1975). Moths, melanism and clean air. *Scientific American, 232,* 90–99.

Bixler, E., Kales, A., Soldatos, C., Kales, J., & Healey, S. (1979). Prevalence of sleep disorders in the Los Angeles metropolitan area. *American Journal of Psychiatry, 136,* 1257–1262.

Bjork, E. L., & Bjork, R. A. (1996). Continuing influences of to-be-forgotten information. *Consequences & Cognition: An International Journal, 5,* 176–196.

Bjork, E., Bjork, R., & Anderson, M. C. (1998). Varieties of goal-directed forgetting. In J. M. Golding & C. M. MacLeod (Eds.), *Intentional forgetting: Interdisciplinary approaches* (pp. 103–137). Mahway, NJ: Lawrence Erlbaum.

Bjorklund, A., & Gage, F. (1985). Neural grafting of neutrodegenerative diseases in animal models. *Annals of the New York Academy of Sciences, 457,* 53–81.

Bjorklund, D., & Harnishfeger, K. (1990). The resources construct in cognitive development: Diverse sources of evidence and a theory of efficient inhibition. *Developmental Review, 10,* 48–71.

Black, B., & Hazen, N. (1990). Social status and patterns of communication in acquainted and unacquainted children. *Developmental Psychology, 27,* 379–387.

Black, D. W., Goldstein, R. B., & Mason, E. E. (1992). Prevalence of mental disorder in 88 morbidly obese bariatric clinic patients. *American Journal of Psychiatry, 149,* 227–234.

Blair, S. N., Kohl, H. W., Paffenbarger, R., Clark, D. G., Cooper, K. H., & Gibbons, L. W. (1989). Physical fitness and all-cause mortality: A prospective study of healthy men and women. *Journal of the American Medical Association, 262,* 2395–2401.

Blake, R., & Hirsch, H. V. B. (1975). Deficits in binocular depth perception in cats after alternating monocular deprivation. *Science, 190,* 1114–1116.

Blake, R., & Mouton, J. (1964). *The managerial grid.* Houston, TX.: Gulf.

Blakemore, C., & Cooper, G. F. (1970). Development of the brain depends on the visual environment. *Nature, 228,* 477–478.

Blanchard, R., & Bogaert, A. F. (1997). Additive effects of older brothers and homosexual brothers in the prediction of marriage and cohabitation. *Behavior Genetics, 27,* 45–54.

Blanchard, R., & Zucker, K. J. (1994). Reanalysis of Bell, Weinberg, and Hammersmith's data on birth order, sibling sex ratio, and parental age in homosexual men. *American Journal of Psychiatry, 151,* 1375–1376.

Blanchard-Fields, F., & Chen, Y. (1996). Adaptive cognition and aging. *American Behavioral Scientist, 39,* 231–248.

Blass, T. (1991). Understanding behavior in the Milgram obedience experiment: The role of personality, situations, and their interactions. *Journal of Personality and Social Psychology, 60,* 398–413.

Blatt, S. (1992). The differential effect of psychotherapy and psychoanalysis with anaclitic and introjective patients: The Menninger Psychotherapy Research Project revisited. *Journal of the American Psychoanalytic Association, 40,* 691–724.

Blatt, S., Ford, R., Berman, W., Cook, B., Cramer, P., & Robins, C. E. (1994). *Therapeutic change: An object relations perspective.* New York: Plenum Press.

Blatt, S., & Zuroff, D. (1992). Interpersonal relatedness and self-definition: Two prototypes for depression. *Clinical Psychology Review, 12,* 527–562.

Blatt, S. J., & Homann, E. (1992). Parent child interaction in the etiology of de-pendent and self-critical depression. *Clinical Psychology Review, 12,* 47–91.

Blatt, S. J., & Lerner, H. (1983). Investigations in the psychoanalytic theory of object relations and object representations. In J. Mashling (Ed.), *Empirical studies of psychoanalytic theories,* Vol. 1, pp. 189–249. Hillsdale, NJ: Erlbaum.

Blatt, S. J., Sanislow, C. A., Pilkonis, P. A., Zuroff, D. A. (1996). Characteristics of effective therapists: Further analyses of data from the national institute of mental health treatment of depression collaborative research program. *Journal of Consulting and Clinical Psychology, 64,* 1275–1284.

Blaustein, A. R., & Waldman, B. (1992). Kin recognition in anuran amphibians. *Animal Behavior, 44,* 207–221.

Blaxton, T., Zeffiro, T., Gabrieli, J. D. E., Bookheimer, S., Carillo, et al. (1996). Functional mapping of human learning: A positron emission tomography activation study of eyeblink conditioning. The *Journal of Neuroscience, 16,* 4032–4040.

Bliss, E. L. (1984). A symptom profile of patients with multiple personalities, including MMPI results. *Journal of Nervous & Mental Disease, 172,* 197–202.

Block, J. (1977). Advancing the psychology of personality: Paradigmatic shift or improving the quality of research? In D. Magnusson & N. Endler (Eds.), *Psychology at the crossroads: Current issues in interactional psychology* (pp. 37–63). Hillsdale, NJ: Erlbaum.

Block, J. (1995). A contrarian view of the five-factor approach to personality description. *Psychological Bulletin, 117,* 187–215.

Block, J., Block, J. H., & Keyes, S. (1988). Longitudinally foretelling drug usage in adolescence: Early childhood personality and environmental precursors. *Child Development, 59,* 336–355.

Block, J., & Kremen, A. (1996). IQ and ego-resiliency: Conceptual and empirical connections and separateness. *Journal of Personality and Social Psychology, 70,* 349–361.

Block, J. H. (1978). Another look at sex differentiation in the socialization behaviors of mothers and fathers. In J. Sherman & F. L. Denmark (Eds.), *The psychology of women: Future directions of research.* New York: Psychological Dimensions.

Block, J. H., Gjerde, P., & Block, J. H. (1991). Personality antecedents of depressive tendencies in 18-year-olds: A prospective study. *Journal of Personality and Social Psychology, 60,* 726–738.

Block, R., Farinpour, R., & Schlechte, J. (1991). Effects of chronic marijuana use of testosterone. *Drug and Alcohol Dependence, 28,* 121–128.

Block, R. I., Farinpour, R., & Schlechte, J. A. (1991). Effects of chronic marijuana use on testosterone, luteinizing hormone, follicle stimulating hormone, prolactin and cortisol in men and women. *Drug & Alcohol Dependence, 28,* 121–128.

Blokland, A. (1997). Acetylcholine: A neurotransmitter for learning and memory? *Brain Research Reviews, 21,* 285–300.

Bloom, L. (1993). *The transition from infancy to language: Acquiring the power of expression.* New York: Cambridge University Press.

Blos, P. (1962). *On adolescence: A psychoanalytic interpretation.* New York: Free Press.

Blos, P. (1967). The second individuation process of adolescence. *Psychoanalytic study of the Child, 22,* 162–186.

Blouin, A., Blouin, J., Aubin, P., Carter, J., Goldstein, C., Boyer, H., & Perez, E. (1992). Seasonal patterns of bulimia nervosa. *American Journal of Psychiatry, 149,* 73–81.

Blum, G. S. (1954). An experimental reunion of psychoanalytic theory with perceptual vigilance and defense. *Journal of Abnormal and Social Psychology, 49,* 94–98.

Blumer, D., & Benson, D. (1984). Personality changes with frontal and temporal lesions. In D. F. Benson & F. Blumer (Eds.), *Psychiatric aspects of neurologic disease.* New York: Grune & Stratton.

Blurton-Jones, N., & Konner, M. (1976). !Kung knowledge of animal behavior. In R. B. Lee & I. De Vore (Eds.), *Kalahari hunter-gatherers* (pp. 326–348). Cambridge, MA: Harvard University Press.

Bock, P. (1988). *Rethinking psychological anthropology: Continuity and change in the study of human action.* San Francisco: Freeman.

Boden, J. M., & Baumeister, R. F. (1997). Repressive coping: Distraction using pleasant thoughts and memories. *Journal of Personality and Social Psychology, 73,* 45–62.

Bodenhausen, G. (1993). Emotions, arousal, and stereotypic judgments: A heuristic model of affect and stereotyping. In D. Mackie & D. Hamilton (Eds.), *Affect, cognition, and stereotyping: Interactive processes in group perception.* New York: Academic.

Boehm, C. (1996). Emergency decisions, cultural-selection mechanics, and group selecton. *Current Anthropology, 37,* 763–793.

Boehm, C. (1996). Emergency decisions, cultural-selection mechanics, and group selection. *Current Anthropology, 37,* 763–793.

Boersch, E. E. (1982). Ritual und Psy-chotherapie. *Zeitschrift fur Klinische Psychologie und Psychotherapie, 30,* 214–234.

Bogen, J. E. (1995). On the neurophysiology of consciousness: I. An overview. *Consciousness & Cognition: An International Journal, 4,* 52–62.

Bohannon, J. N., & Bonvillian, J. D. (1997). Theoretical approaches to language acquisition. In J. B. Gleason (Ed.), *The development of language,* 4th ed. (pp. 259–316). Boston: Allyn and Bacon.

Boiten, F. (1996). Autonomic response patterns during voluntary facial action. *Psychophysiology, 33,* 123–131.

Bolger, N., Foster, M., Vinokur, A. D., & Ng, R. (1996). Close relationships and adjustment to a life crisis: The case of breast cancer. *Journal of Personality and Social Psychology, 70,* 283–294.

Bolles, R. C. (1975). *Learning theory.* New York: Holt, Rinehart & Winston.

Bondareff, W. (1985). The neural basis of aging. In J. Birren & K. W. Schaie (Eds.). *Handbook of the psychology of aging.* (2nd ed.). New York: Van Nostrand.

Bondolfi, G., Dufour, H., Patris, M., Billeter, U., Eap, C. B., & Baumann, P. (1998). Risperidone Study Group. Risperidone versus clozapine in treatment-resistant chronic schizophrenia: A randomized double-blind study. *American Journal of Psychiatry, 155,* 499–504.

Bonebakker, A. E., Bonke, B., Klein, J., & Wolters, G. (1996). Information processing during general anesthesia: Evidence for unconscious memory. *Memory & Cognition, 24,* 766–776.

Bonvillian, J. D. (in press). Sign language development. In M. Barrett (Ed.), *The development of language.* London: UCL Press.

Borbely, A. (1986). *Secrets of sleep.* New York: Basic.

Borden, V. M. H., & Levinger, G. (1991). Interpersonal transformations in intimate relationships. In W. H. Jones, D. Perlman, et al. (Eds.), *Advances in personal relationships: A research annual, Vol. 2. Advances in personal relationships.* (pp. 35–56). London: Jessica Kingsley Publishers.

Boring, E. G. (1930). A new ambiguous figure. *American Journal of Psychology, 42,* 444–445.

Borjeson, M. (1976). The aetiology of obesity in children. *Acta Paediatrica Scandinavica, 65,* 279–287.

Borkovec, T. D., & Costello, E. (1993). Efficacy of applied relaxation and cognitive-behavioral therapy in the treatment of generalized anxiety disorder. *Journal of Consulting and Clinical Psychology, 61,* 611–619.

Bornstein, M. H. (1989). Sensitive periods in development: Structural characteristics and causal interpretations. *Psychological Bulletin, 105,* 179–197.

Borod, J. (1992). Interhemispheric and intrahemispheric control of emotion: A focus on unilateral brain damage. *Journal of Consulting and Clinical Psychology, 60,* 339–348.

Bors, D. A., & Forrin, B. (1998). The effects of post-weaning environment, biological dam, and nursing dam on feeding neophobia, open field activity, and learning. *Canadian Journal of Experimental Psychology, 50,* 197–204.

Boszormenyi-Nagy, I., & Sparks, G. (1973). *Invisible loyalties.* New York: Harper & Row.

Bouchard, C. (1989). Genetic factors in obesity. *Medical Clinics of North America, 73,* 67–81.

Bouchard, T. J., Lykken, D. T., McGue, M., & Segal, N. L. (1990). Sources of human psychological differences: The Minnesota study of twins reared apart. *Science, 250,* 223–228.

Bouchard, T. J., Lykken, D. T., McGue, M., & Segal, N. L. (1991). Sources of human psychological differences: The Minnesota study of twins reared apart: Response. *Science, 252,* 191–192.

Bourgignon, E. (1979). *Psychological anthropology: An introduction to human nature and cultural differences.* New York: Holt, Rinehart & Winston.

Bovbjerg, D., Redd, W. H., Maier, L. A., Holland, J. C., Leske, L. M., Niedzwiecki, D., Rubin, S. C., & Herkes, T. B. (1990). Anticipatory immune suppression and nausea in women receiving cyclic chemotherapy for ovarian cancer. *Journal of Consulting and Clinical Psychology, 58,* 153–157.

Bowd, A. D. (1990). A decade of animal research in psychology: Room for consensus? *Canadian Psychology, 31,* 74–82.

Bowd, A. D., & Shapiro, K. J. (1993). The case against laboratory animal research in psychology. *Journal of Social Issues, 49,* 133–142.

Bowden, S. C. (1990). Separating cognitive impairment in neurologically asymptomatic alcoholism from Wernicke-Korsakoff syndrome: Is the neuropsychological distinction justified? *Psychological Bulletin, 107,* 355–366.

Bowen, M. (1978). *Family therapy in clinical practice.* New York: Jason Aronson.

Bowen, M. (1991). Alcoholism as viewed through family systems theory and family psychotherapy. *Family Dynamics of Addiction Quarterly, 1,* 94–102.

Bower, G. (1975). Cognitive psychology: an introduction. In W. K. Estes, (Ed.), *Handbook of Learning and Cognitive Processes,* Vol. 1, Introduction to concepts and Issues (pp. 25–80). Hillsdale, NJ: Erlbaum.

Bower, G. H. (1970). Analysis of a mnemonic device. *American Scientist, 58,* 496–510.

Bower, G. H. (1981). Mood and memory. *American Psychologist, 36,* 129–148.

Bower, G. H. (1989). In search of mood-dependent retrieval. *Journal of Social Behavior & Personality, 4,* 121–156.

Bower, T. G. R. (1971). The object in the world of the infant. *Scientific American, 225,* 30–38.

Bower, T. G. R. (1982). *Development in infancy.* (2nd ed.). San Francisco: W. H. Freeman.

Bowers, J. S., & Schacter, D. L. (1990). Implicit memory and test awareness. *Journal of Experimental Psychology: Learning, Memory, and Cognition, 16,* 404–416.

Bowers, K. (1976). *Hypnosis for the seriously curious.* Monterey, CA: Brooks/Cole Publishing Co.

Bowers, K. S. (1984). On being unconsciously informed and uninformed. In K. S. Bowers & D. Meichenbaum (Eds.), *The unconscious reconsidered.* New York: John Wiley.

Bowers, K., Regenr, G., Balthazard, C., & Parker, K. (1990). Intuition in the context of discovery. *Cognitive Psychology, 22,* 72–110.

Bowlby, J. (1969). *Attachment and loss.* Vol. I. *Attachment.* New York: Basic Books.

Bowlby, J. (1973). *Separation, attachment, and loss: Vol. 2.* New York: Basic Books.

Bowlby, J. (1988). *A secure base: Parent-child attachment and healthy human development.* New York: Basic Books.

Boysen, Sarah T., & Berntson, G. G. (1995). "Responses to quantity: Perceptual versus cognitive mechanisms in chimpanzees (Pan troglodytes). *Journal of Experimental Psychology: Animal Behavior Processes, 21,* 82–86, ch 7. 3e

Bradberry, J. S. (1989). Gender differences in mathematical attainment at 16+. *Educational Studies, 15,* 301–314.

Bradley, C. L., & Marcia, J. E. (1998). Generativity-stagnation: A five-category model. *Journal of Personality, 66,* 39–64.

Brainerd, C. J. (1996). Piaget: A centennial celebration. *Psychological Science, 7,* 191–195.

Braitenberg, V. (1977). *On the texture of brains.* New York: Springer-Verlag.

Brandao, M., Cardoso, S. H., Melo, L. L., Motta, V., and Coimbra, N. C. (1994). Neural substrate of defensive behavior in the midbrain tectum. *Neuroscience and Biobehavioral Reviews, 18,* 339–346.

Brandimonte, M., Einstein, G. O., & McDaniel, M. A. (Eds.). (1996). *Prospective memory: theory and applications.* Mahwah: L. Erlbaum.

Braun, A. R., Balkin, T. J., Wesensten, N. J., Gwadry, F., Carson, R. E., Varga, M., et al. (1998). Dissociated pattern of activity in visual cortices and their projections during human rapid movement sleep. *Science, 279,* 91–95.

Braun, S. (1996). New experiments underscore warnings on maternal drinking. *Science, 273,* 738–739.

Braungart, J., Plomin, R., DeFries, J., & Fulker, D. (1992). Genetic influence on tester-rated infant temperament as assessed by Bayley's infant behavior record: Nonadoptive and adoptive siblings and twins. *Developmental Psychology, 28,* 40–47.

Brazelton, T. B. (1972). Implications of infant development among the Mayan Indians of Mexico. *Human Development, 15,* 90–111.

Breer, H., Wanner, I., & Strogmann, J. (1996). Molecular genetics of mammalian olfaction. *Behavior Genetics, 26,* 209–219.

Bregman, J. D., & Hodapp, R. M. (1991). Current developments in the understanding of mental retardation. *Journal of the American Academy of Child and Adolescent Psychiatry, 30,* 707–719.

Breier, A., Schreiber, J. L., Dyer, J., & Pickar, D. (1991). National Institute of Mental Health Longitudinal Study of chronic schizophrenia: Prognosis and predictors of outcome. *Archives of General Psychiatry, 48,* 239–246.

Breier, A., Wolkowitz, O., Roy, A., Potter, W. Z., & Pickar, D. (1990). Plasma norepinephrine in chronic schizophrenia. *American Journal of Psychiatry, 147,* 1467–1470.

Breiter, H. C., Rauch, S. L., Kwong, K. K., Baker, J. R., Weisskoff, R. M., Kennedy, D.N, et al. (1996). Functional magnetic resonance imaging of symptom provocation in obsessive-compulsive disorder. *Archives of General Psychiatry, 53,* 595–606.

Breland, K., & Breland, M. (1961). The misbehavior of organisms. *American Psychologist, 16,* 681–684.

Brennan, K. A., Clark, C. L., & Shaver, P. (in press). Self-report measurement of adult romantic attachment: an overview. In J. A. Simpson & W. S. Rholes (Eds.), *Attachment theory and close relationships.* New York: Guilford.

Brennan, W., Ames, E., & Moore, R. (1966). Age differences in infants' attention to patterns of different complexity. *Science, 151,* 354–356.

Brennen, T., Baguley, T., Bright, J., & Bruce, V. (1990). Resolving semantically induced tip-of-the-tongue states for proper nouns. *Memory & Cognition, 18,* 339–347.

Brenner, C. (1982). *The mind in conflict.*

New York: International Universities Press.

Breslau, N., Davis, G. C., Andreski, P., & Peterson, E. (1991). Traumatic events and posttraumatic stress disorder in an urban population of young adults. *Archives of General Psychiatry, 48,* 216–222.

Breslau, N., Davis, G. C., Andreski, P., Peterson, E. L., Schultz, L. R. (1997). Sex Differences in Posttraumatic Stress Disorder. *Archives of General Psychiatry, 54,* 1044–1048.

Bretherton, I. (1985). Attachment theory: Retrospect and prospect. In I. Bretherton & E. Waters (Eds.), Growing points of attachment theory and research. *Monographs of the Society for Research in Children Development, 50* (1–2, serial No. 209), 3–35.

Bretherton, I. (1990). Communication patterns, internal working models, and the intergenerational transmission of attachment relationships. *Infant Mental Health Journal, 11,* 237–257.

Brett, E. A., Spitzer, R. L., & Williams, J. B. W. (1988). DSM-III-R criteria for posttraumatic stress disorder. *American Journal of Psychiatry, 145,* 1232–1236.

Breuer, K. (1985). Intentionality and perception in early infancy. *Human Development, 28,* 71–83.

Brewer, M. (1979). Ingroup bias in the minimal intergroup situation: A cognitive motivational analysis. *Psychological Bulletin, 86,* 307–324.

Brewer, M., & Kramer, R. M. (1985). The psychology of intergroup attitudes and behavior. *Annual Review of Psychology, 36,* 219–243.

Brewer, M. B., & Brown, R. J. (1998). Intergroup relations. In D. T. Gilbert, S. T. Fiske, et al. (Eds.), *The handbook of social psychology, Vol. 2* (4th ed.). (pp. 554–594). Boston: McGraw-Hill.

Brewer, N., and Smith, J. M. (1989). Social acceptance of mentally retarded children in regular schools in relation to years mainstreamed. *Psychological Reports, 64,* 375–380.

Brewer, W. F., & Treyens, J. C. (1981). Role of schemata in memory for places. *Cognitive Psychology, 13,* 207–230.

Brewerton, T. D. (1995). Toward a unified theory of serotonin dysregulation in eating and related disorders. *Psychoneuroendocrinology, 20,* 561–590.

Briere, J., & Conte, J. R. (1993). Self-reported amnesia for abuse in adults molested as children. *Journal of Traumatic Stress, 6,* 21–31.

Brim, O. G. (1976). Theories of the male mid-life crisis. *Counseling Psychologist, 6,* 2–9.

Brislin, R. M. (1986). The culture general assimilator: Preparation for various types of sojourns. Special issue: Theories and methods in cross-cultural orientation. *International Journal of Intercultural Relations, 10,* 215–234.

Brislin, R. W., & Keating, C. F. (1976). Cultural differences in the perception of a three-dimensional Ponzo illusion. *Journal of Cross-Cultural Psychology, 7,* 397–412.

Broadbent, D. E. (1958). The hidden preattentive processes. *American Psychologist, 32,* 109–118.

Broberg, A., Wessels, H., Lamb, M. E., & Hwang, C. P. (1997). Effects of day care on the development of cognitive abilities in 8-year-olds: A longitudinal study. *Developmental Psychology, 33,* 62–69.

Brody, L., & Hall, J. A. (1993). Gender and emotion. In M. Lewis & J. Haviland (Eds.), *Handbook of emotions* (pp. 447–460). New York: Guilford Press.

Brody, N. (1992). *Intelligence* (2nd ed.). San Diego, CA: Academic Press, Inc.

Broocks, A., Bandelow, A., Pekrun, G., George, A., Meyer, T., Bartmann, U., et al. (1998). Comparison of aerobic exercise, clomipramine, and placebo in the treatment of panic disorder. *American Journal of Psychiatry, 155,* 603–609.

Brookoff, D., O'Brien, K., Cook, C. S., & Thompson, T. D. (1997). Characteristics of participants in domestic violence. *JAMA: Journal of the American Medical Association, 277,* 1369–1373.

Broughton, J. (1978). Development of concepts of self, mind, reality, and knowledge. *New Directions for Child Development, 1,* 75–100.

Brown, A., Bransford, J., Ferrara, R., Campione, J. (1983). Learning, remembering, and understanding. In E. M. Markman, & J. H. Flavell, (Eds.), *Carmichael's Manual of Child Psychology,* Vol. III. New York: John Wiley.

Brown, G., Bhrolchain, M., & Harris, T. (1975). Social class and psychiatric disturbance among women in an urban poulation. *Sociology, 9,* 225–254.

Brown, G. W., & Harris, T. O. (1978). *Social origins of depression: A study of psychiatric disorder in women.* New York: Free Press.

Brown, G. W., Andrews, B., Harris, T. O., Adler, Z., et al. (1986). Social support, self esteem and depression. *Psychological Medicine, 16,* 813–831.

Brown, G. W., & Harris, T. O. (1989). Depression. In G. W. Brown & T. O. Harris (Eds.), *Life events and illnesses.* New York: Guilford Press.

Brown, G. W., Harris, T. O., & Hepworth, C. (1994). Life events and endogenous depression: A puzzle reexamined. *Archives of General Psychiatry, 51,* 525–534.

Brown, J., & Smart, S. A. (1991). The self and social conduct: Linking self-representations to prosocial behavior. *Journal of Personality and Social Psychology, 60,* 368–375.

Brown, J. B. (1991). Staying fit and staying well: Physical fitness as a moderator of life stress. *Journal of Personality and Social Psychology, 61,* 555–561.

Brown, L. L., Tomarken, A. J., Orth, D. N., Loosen, P. T., Kalin, N. H., & Davidson, R. J. (1996). Individual differences in repressive-defensiveness predict basal salivary cortisol levels. *Journal of Personality and Social Psychology, 70,* 362–371.

Brown, N. O. (1959). *Life against death: The psychoanalytic meaning of history.* Middleton, CT: Wesleyan University Press.

Brown, P. K., & Wald, G. (1964). Visual pigments in single rods and cones in the human retina. *Science, 144,* 45–52.

Brown, R. (1973). *A first language: The early stages.* Cambridge, MA: Harvard University Press.

Brown, R., & Chiesa, M. (1990). An introduction to repertory grid theory and technique. *British Journal of Psychotherapy, 6,* 411–419.

Brown, R., & Fraser, C. (1963). The acquisition of syntax. In C. N. Cofer & B. Musgrave (Eds.), *Verbal behavior and learning: Problems and processes* (pp. 158–201). New York: McGraw-Hill.

Brown, R., & Hanlon, C. (1970). Derivational complexity and order of acquisition in child speech. In J. R. Hayes (Ed.), *Cognition and the development of language.* New York: John Wiley.

Brown, R., & Kulik, J. (1977). Flashbulb memories. *Cognition, 5,* 73–99.

Brown, R. W., Galanter, E., Hess, D., & Mandler, G. (1962). *New directions in psychology.* New York: Holt.

Brown, R. W., & McNeill, D. (1966). The tip-of-the-tongue phenomenon. *Journal of Verbal Learning and Verbal Behavior, 5,* 325–337.

Brown, S. L. (1985). "Two adolescents at risk for schizophrenia: A family case study": Discussion. *International Journal of Family Therapy, 7,* 149–154.

Brownell, H. H., Potter, H. H., Bihrle, A. M., & Gardner, H. (1986). Inference deficits in right brain-damaged patients. *Brain & Language, 27,* 310–321.

Brownell, K., & Rodin, J. (1994). The dieting maelstrom: Is it pssible and advisable to lose weight? *American Psychologist, 49,* 781–791.

Brownell, K. D., & Rodin, J. (1994). The dieting maelstrom: Is it possible and advisable to lose weight? *American Psychologist, 49,* 781–791.

Brownell, K. D., & Wadden, T. A. (1992). Etiology and treatment of obesity: Understanding a serious, prevalent, and refractory disorder. *Journal of Consulting and Clinical Psychology, 60,* 505–517.

Bruce, D., & Bahrick, H. P. (1992). Perceptions of past research. *American Psychologist, 47,* 319–328.

Bruch, H. (1970). Eating disorders in adolescence. *Proceedings of the American Psychopathology Association, 59,* 181–202.

Bruch, H. (1973). *Eating disorders: Obesity, anorexia nervosa, and the person within.* New York: Basic Books.

Brundage, L. E., Derlega, V. J., & Cash, T. F. (1977). The effects of physical attractiveness and need for approval on self-disclosure. *Personality and Social Psychology Bulletin, 3,* 63–66.

Bruner, J. S. (1992). Another look at New Look 1. *American Psychologist, 47,* 780–783.

Brunstetter, R. W., & Silver, L. B. (1985). Attention deficit disorder. In H. I. Kaplan & B. J. Sadock (Eds.), *Comprehensive textbook of psychiatry.* (4th ed.). Baltimore, MD: Williams & Wilkins.

Bruyer, R. (1991). Covert face recognition in prosopagnosia: A review. *Brain and Cognition, 15,* 223–235.

Bryson, G., Bell, M., & Lysaker, P. (1997). Affect recognition in schizophrenia: A function of global impairment or a specific cognitive deficit. *Psychiatry Research, 71,* 105–113.

Bucci, W. (1997). *Psychoanalysis and cognitive science: A multiple code theory.* New York: The Guilford Press.

Buchan, H., Johnstone, E., McPherson, K., & Palmer, R. L. (1992). Who benefits from electroconvulsive therapy? Combined results of the Leicester and Northwick Park trials. *British Journal of Psychiatry, 160,* 355–359.

Buchsbaum, M. S., Someya, T., Teng, C. Y., Abel, L., Chin, S., Najafi, A., et al. (1996). PET and MRI of the thalamus in never-medicated patients with schizophrenia. *American Journal of Psychiatry, 153,* 191–199.

Buck, R. (1986). The psychology of emotion. In J. E. LeDoux and W. Hirst (Eds.), *Mind and brain: Dialogues in cognitive neuroscience.* New York: Cambridge University Press.

Buck, R., Losow, J., & Murphy, M. (1992). Social facilitation and inhibition of emotional expression and communication. *Journal of Personality and Social Psychology, 63,* 962–968.

Buglass, D. (1977). A study of agoraphobic housewives. *Psychological Medicine, 7,* 73–86.

Buhrich, N., Bailey, J. M., Martin, N. G. (1991). Sexual orientation, sexual identity, and sex-dimorphic behaviors in male twins. *Behavior Genetics, 21,* 75–96.

Buhrmester, D. (1990). Intimany of friendship, interpersonal competence, and adjustment during preadolescence and adolescence. *Child Development, 61,* 1101–1111.

Bukowski, W., Gauze, C., Hoza, B., & Newcomb, A. (1994). Differences and consistency beween same-sex and other-sex peer relationships during early adolescence. *Developmental Psychology, 29,* 255–263.

Bulik, C. M., Sullivan, P. F., Carter, F. A., & Joyce, P. R. (1996). Lifetime anxiety disorders in women with bulimia nervosa. *Comprehensive Psychiatry, 37,* 368–374.

Bunney, W. E., Jr. (1981). Current biological strategies for anxiety. *Psychiatric Annals, 11,* 21–29.

Buri, J., Louiselle, P., Misukanis, T., & Mueller, R. (1988). Effects of parental authoritarianism on self-esteem. *Personality and Social Psychology Bulletin, 14,* 271–282.

Burke, A., Heuer, F., Reisberg, D. (1992). Remembering emotional events. *Memory & Cognition, 20,* 277–290.

Burke, W., & Cole, A. M. (1978). Extraretinal influences on the lateral geniculate nucleus. *Review of Physiology, Biochemistry, and Pharmacology, 80,* 105–166.

Burkett, L. (1991). Parenting behaviors of women who were sexually abused as children in their families of origin. *Family Process, 30,* 421–434.

Burks, B. (1938). On the relative contributions of nature and nurture to average group differences in intelligence. *Proceedings of the National Academy of Sciences, 24,* 276–282.

Burks, B. S. (1928). The relative influence of nature and nurture upon mental development: A comparative study of foster parent-foster child resemblance and true parent-true child resemblance. *27th Yearbook of the National Society for the Study of Education, 27,* 219–316.

Burnstein, E., Crandall, C., & Kitayama, S. (1994). Some neo-Darwinian decision rules for altruism: Weighing cues for inclusive fitness as a function of the biological importance of the decision. *Journal of Personality & Social Psychology, 67,* 773–789.

Bushman, B. J. (1997). Effects of alcohol on human aggression: Validity of proposed explanations. In M. Galanter (Ed.). *Recent developments in alcoholism, Vol. 13: Alcohol and violence: Epidemiology, neurobiology, psychology, family issues* (pp. 227–243). New York: Plenum Press.

Bushman, B. J., & Cooper, H. M. (1990). Effects of alcohol on human aggression: An integrative research review. *Psychological Bulletin, 107,* 341–354.

Buss, D. (1989). Sex differences in human mate preferences: Evolutionary hypotheses tested in 37 cultures. *Behavioral and Brain Sciences, 12,* 1–49.

Buss, D. M. (1988). Love act: The evolutionary biology of love. In R. J. Sternberg & M. L. Barnes (Eds.), *The anatomy of love.* New Haven, CT: Yale University Press.

Buss, D. M. (1991). Evolutionary personality psychology. *Annual Review of Psychology, 42,* 459–492.

Buss, D. M. (1993). Strategic individual differences: The evolutionary psychology of selection, evocation, and manipulation. In T. Bouchard Jr., P. Propping, et al. (Eds.). *Twins as a tool of behavioral genetics. Life sciences researches report, 53.* (pp. 121–137). Chichester, England: John Wiley & Sons.

Buss, D. M. (1995). Evolutionary psychology: A new paradigm for psychological science. *Psychological Inquiry, 6,* 1–30.

Buss, D. M., & Schmitt, D. P. (1993). Sexual strategies theory: An evolutionary perspective on human mating. *Psychological Review, 100,* 1–29.

Buss, D. M., Kenrick, D. T. (1998). Evolutionary social psychology. In D. T. Gilbert, S. T. Fiske, et al. (Eds.), *The handbook of social psychology, Vol. 2* (4th ed.). (pp. 982–1026). Boston: McGraw-Hill.

Buss, D. M., Larsen, R. J., Westen, D., & Semmelroth, J. (1992). Sex differences in jealousy: Evolution, physiology, and psychology. *Psychological Science, 3,* 251–255.

Butler, A. B., & Hodos, W. (1996). *Comparative vertebrate neuroanatomy: Evolution and adaptation.* New York: Wiley-Liss.

Butler, C. A. (1976). New data about female sexual response. *Journal of Sex and Marital Therapy, 2,* 40–46.

Butler, R. N. (1969). Age-ism: Another form of bigotry. *The Gerontologist, 9,* 243–246.

Butler, R. N. (1975). *Why survive? Being old in America.* New York: Harper & Row.

Butler, R. N. (1984). Senile dementia: Reversible and irreversible. *Counseling Psychology, 12,* 75–79.

Butt, A., Testylier, G., & Dykes, R. (1997). Acetylcholine release in rat frontal and somatosensory cortex is enhanced during lactile discrimination learning. *Psychobiology, 25,* 18–33.

Butterfield, E. C. (1964). The interruption of tasks: Methodological, factual, and theoretical issues. *Psychologial Bulletin, 62,* 309–322.

Butters, N., Heindel, W. C., & Salmon, D. (1990). Dissociation of implicit memory in dementia: Neurological implications. *Bulletin of the Psychonomic Society, 28,* 359–366.

Butterworth, A. (1978). A review of a primer of infant development. *Perception, 17,* 363–364.

Butzlaff, R. L., & Hooley, J. M. (1998). Expression emotion and psychiatric relapse: A meta-analysis. *Archives of General Psychiatry, 55,* 547–552.

Buunk, B. P., Angleitner, A., Oubaid, V., & Buss, D. M. (1996). Sex differences in jealousy in evolutionary and cultural perspective: Tests from the Netherlands, Germany, and the United States. *Psychological Science, 7,* 359–363.

Buysse, D. J., Morin, C. M., & Reynolds, C. F. III (1995). Sleep disorders. In G. O. Gabbard (Ed.), *Treatment of psychiatric disorders* (2nd ed.) (Vol. 2) (pp. 2395–2453). Washington, DC: American Psychiatric Press.

Bye, L., & Jussim, L. (1993). A proposed model for the acquisition of social knowledge and social competence. *Psychology in the Schools, 30,* 143–161.

Bynum, C. W. (1987). *Holy feast and holy fast.* Berkeley: University of California Press.

Byrd, K. R. (1994). The narrative reconstructions of incest survivors. *American Psychologist, 49,* 439.

Byrne, D. (1971). *The attraction paradigm.* New York: Academic Press.

Byrne, D., et al. (1968). The effects of physical attractiveness, sex, and attitude similarity on interpersonal attraction. *Journal of Personality, 36,* 259–271.

Byrne, D., & Murnen, S. (1988). Maintaining loving relationships. In R. Sternberg & M. L. Barnes (Eds.), *The psychology of love* (pp. 293–310). New Haven, CT: Yale University Press.

Cabeza, R., Kapur, S., Craik, F. I. M., & McIntosh, A. R. (1997). Functional neuroanatomy of recall and recognition: A PET study of episodic memory. *Journal of Cognitive Neuroscience, 9,* 254–265.

Cacioppo, J. T., Gardner, W. L., & Berntson, G. G. (1997). Beyond bipolar conceptualizations and measures: The case of attitudes and evaluative space. *Personality and Social Psychology Review, 1,* 3–25.

Cadoret, R. J., O'Gorman, T. W., Troughton, E., & Heywood, E. (1985). Alcoholism and antisocial personality. *Archives of General Psychiatry, 42,* 161–167.

Cadoret, R. J., Yates, W. R., Troughton, E., Woodworth, G., & Stewart, M. A. (1995). Genetic-environmental interaction in the genesis of aggressivity and conduct disorders. *Archives of General Psychiatry, 52,* 916–924.

Caggiula, A. R., Epstein, L. H., Antelman, S., Seymour, M., & Taylor, S. S. (1991). Conditioned tolerance to the anorectic and corticosterone-elevating effects of nicotine. *Pharmacology, Biochemistry, and Behavior, 40,* 53–59.

Cahill, L., Prins, B., Weber, M., & McGaugh, J. L. (1994). β-Adrenergic activation and memory for emotional events. *Nature, 371,* 702–704.

Calhoun, K. S., Moras, K., Pilkonis, P. A., & Rehm, L. P. (1998). Empirically supported treatments: Implications for training. *Journal of Consulting & Clinical Pshcology, 66,* 151–162.

Campbell, D. T., & Stanley, J. C. (1963). *Experimental and quasiexperimental designs for research.* Chicago: Rand McNally.

Campbell, J. D. (1986). Similarity and uniqueness: The effects of attribute type, relevance, and individual differences in self-esteem and depression. *Journal of Personality and Social Psychology, 50,* 281–294.

Campbell, S. B. (1985). Hyperactivity in preschoolers: Correlates and prognostic implications. *Clinical Psychology Review, 5,* 405–428.

Campbell, S. S., & Tobler, I. (1984). Animal sleep: A review of sleep duration across phylogeny. *Neuroscience & Biobehavioral Reviews, 8,* 269–300.

Campfield, L., Arthur, S., Francoise, J., Rosenbaum, M., & Hirsch, J. (1996). Human eating: Evidence for a physiological basis using a modified paradigm. Special Issue: Society for the Study of Ingestive Behavior, Second Independent Meeting. *Neuroscience & Biobehavioral Reviews, 20,* 133–1137.

Campfield, L., Brandon, P., & Smith, F. J. (1985). On-line continuous measurement of blood glucose and meal pattern in free-feeding rats: The role of glucose in meal initiation. *Brain Research Bulletin, 14,* 605–617.

Campione, J. C., Brown, A. L., & Ferrara, R. A. (1982). Mental retardation and intelligence. In R. J. Sternberg (Ed.), *Handbook of human intelligence* (pp. 393–490). New York: Cambridge University Press.

Campos, J. J., Barrett, K. C., Lamb, M. E., Goldsmith, H. H., & Stenberg, C. (1983). Socioemotional development. In P. H. Mussen (Ed.), *Handbook of Child Psychology: Vol. II. Infancy and Developmental Psychobiology.* New York: John Wiley.

Canfield, R. L., & Ceci, S. J. (1992). Integrating learning into a theory of intellectual development. In R. J. Sternberg & C. A. Berg (Eds.), *Intellectual Development.* New York: Cambridge University Press.

Cannon, T. D., Kaprio, J., Lönnqvist, J., Huttunen, M., & Koskenvuo, M. (1998). The genetic epidemiology of schizophrenia in a Finnish twin cohort: A population-based modeling study characterization of psychotic conditions. *Archives of General Psychiatry, 55,* 67–74.

Cannon, W., & Washburn, A. (1912). An explanation of hunger. *American Journal of Physiology, 29,* 441–454.

Cannon, W. B. (1927). The James-Lange theory of emotions: A critical examination and an alternative theory. *American Journal of Psychiatry, 39,* 106–124.

Cannon, W. B. (1932). *The wisdom of the body.* New York: W. W. Norton.

Cantor, N. (1990). From thought to behavior: Having and doing in the study of personality and cognition. *American Psychologists, 45,* 735–750.

Cantor, N., & Blanton, H. (1996). Effortful pursuit of personal goals in daily life. In P. M. Gollwitzer, J. A. Bargh, et al. (Eds.), *The psychology of action: Linking cognition and motivation to behavior.* (pp. 338–359). New York: Guilford Press.

Cantor, N., & Harlow, R. (1994). Personality, strategic behavior, and daily-life problem solving. Current Directions in *Psychologial Science 3,* 169–172.

Cantor, N., & Kihlstrom, J. F. (1987). Personality and social intelligence. Englewood Cliffs, NJ: Prentice-Hall.

Cantwell, D. P. (1976). Genetic factors in the hyperkinetic syndrome. *Journal of the American Academy of Child Psychiatry, 15,* 214–223.

Capaldi, E., & VandenBos, G. (1991). Taste, food exposure, and eating behavior. *Hospital and Community Psychiatry, 42,* 787–789.

Caplan, D., & Waters, G. S. (1990). Short-term memory and language comprehension: A critical review of the neuropsychological literature. In G. Vallar and T. Shallice (Eds.), *Neuropsychological impairments of short-term memory* (pp. 337–389). Cambridge, England: Cambridge University Press.

Caplan, P. J. (1991). How do they decide who is normal? The bizarre, but true, tale of the DSM process. *Canadian Psychology, 32,* 162–170.

Caplan, P. J., Crawford, M., Hyde, J. S., & Richardson, J. T. E. (1997). *Gender differences in human cognition.* New York: Oxford University Press.

Cardon, L. R., Fulker, D. W., DeFries, J. C., & Plomin, R. (1992). Multivariate genetic analysis of specific cognitive abilities in the Colorado Adoption Program at age 7. *Intelligence, 16,* 383–400.

Carlsmith, J. M., & Anderson, C. A. (1979). Ambient temperature and the occurrence of collective violence: A new analysis. *Journal of Personality and Social Psychology, 37,* 337–344.

Carlson, E. B., & Rosser-Hogan, R. (1991). Trauma experiences, posttraumatic stress, dissociation, and depression in Cambodian refugees. *American Journal of Psychiatry, 148,* 1548–1551.

Carlson, N. R. (1994). *Physiology of behavior* (5th ed.). Boston: Allyn & Bacon, Inc.

Carlson, S. (1990). Visually guided behavior of monkeys after early binocular visual deprivation. *International Journal of Neuroscience, 50,* 185–194.

Carolsfeld, J., Tester, M., Kreiberg, H., & Sherwood, N. M. (1997). Pheromone-induced spawning of Pacific herring: I. Behavioral characterization. *Hormones & Behavior, 31,* 256–268.

Carone, B. J., Harrow, M., & Westermeyer, J. F. (1991). Posthospital course and outcome in schizophrenia. *Archives of General Psychiatry, 48,* 247–253.

Carpenter, P. A., Miyaka, A., & Just, M. A. (1995). Language comprehension: Sentence and discourse processing. *Annual Review, 46,* 91–120.

Carpenter, W. T. (1992). The negative symptom challenge. *Archives of General Psychiatry, 49,* 236–237.

Carroll, J. B. (1993). Human cognitive abilities: *A survey of factor-analytic studies.* New York: Cambridge University Press.

Cartwright, R. D. (1996). Dreams and adaptation to divorce. In D. Barrett (Ed.), *Trauma and dreams* (pp. 179–185). Cambridge, MA: Harvard University Press.

Carver, C. S., Scheier, M. F., & Weintraub, J. K. (1989). Assessing coping strategies: A theoretically based approach. *Journal of Personality and Social Psychology, 56,* 267–283.

Carver, M., & Scheier, H. (1981). *Attention and self-regulation: A control-theory approach to human behavior.* New York: Springer-Verlag.

Case, R. (1984). The process of stage transitions: A neo-Piagetian view. In R. J. Sternberg (Ed.), *Mechanisms of cognitive development.* New York: Freeman.

Case, R. (1985). *Intellectual development: Birth to adulthood.* New York: Academic Press.

Case, R. (1992). Neo-Piagetian theories of child development. In R. J. Sternberg & C. A. Berg, *Intellectual development* (pp. 161–196). New York: Cambridge University Press.

Casey, M. B., Nuttall, R. L., & Pezaris, E. (1997). Mediators of gender differences in mathematics college entrance test scores: A comparison of spatial skills with internalized beliefs and anxieties. *Development Psychology, 33,* 669–680.

Cash, T. F., Gillen, B., & Burns, D. S. (1977). Sexism and "beautyism" in personnel consultant decision making. *Journal of Applied Psychology, 62,* 301–310.

Cashmore, J. A., & Goodnow, J. J. (1986). Influences on Australian parents' values: Ethnicity versus socioeconomic status. *Journal of Cross-Cultural Psychology, 17,* 441–454.

Casper, R. C., Hedeker, D., & McClough, J. F. (1992). Personality dimensions in eating disorders and their relevance for subtyping. *Journal of the American Academy of Child and Adolescent Psychiatry, 31,* 830–840.

Caspi, A. (1998). Personality development across the lifespan. In W. Damon (Ed.), *Handbook of child psychology. Vol. 3, Social, emotional, and personality development* (N. Eisenberg, Vol. Ed.) (pp. 311–388). New York: Wiley.

Caspi, A., Elder, G. E., & Herbener, E. (1990). Childhood personality and the prediction of life-course patterns. In L. N. Robins & M. Rutter (Eds.), *Straight and devious pathways from childhood to adulthood* (pp. 13–35). New York: Cambridge University Press.

Caspi, A., Lynam, D., Moffitt, T., & Silva, P. (1993). Unraveling girls' delinquency: Biological, dispositional, and contextual contributions to adolescent misbehavior. *Developmental Psychology, 29,* 19–30.

Cassidy, J., Kirsh, S. J., Scolton, K., & Parke, R. D. (1996). Attachment and representations of peer relationships. *Developmental Psychology, 32,* 892–904.

Castle, D. J., & Ames, F. R. (1996). Cannabis and the brain. *Australian & New Zealand Journal of Psychiatry, 30,* 179–183.

Catania, J. A., Coates, T. J., Stall, R., Turner, H., Peterson, J., Hearst, N., Dolcini, M. M., Hudes, E., Gagnon, J., Wiley, J., & Groves, R. (1992). Prevalence of AIDS-related risk factors and condom use in the United States. *Science, 258,* 1101–1106.

Cattell, R. B. (1941). Some theoretical issues in adult intelligence testing. *Psychological Bulletin, 38,* 592.

Cattell, R. B. (1957). *Personality and motivation: Structure and measurement.* Yonkers-on-Hudson, NY: World Book Co.

Cattell, R. B. (1990). Advances in Cattellian personality theory. In L. Pervin (Ed.), *Handbook of personality: Theory and research* (pp. 101–110). New York: Guilford Press.

Cave, C. B. (1997). Very long-lasting priming in picture naming. *Psychological Science, 8,* 322–325.

Ceci, S. J. (1990). Framing intellectual assessment in terms of a person-process-context model. *Educational Psychologist, 25,* 269–291.

Ceci, S. J., & Bronfenbrenner, U. (1991). On the demise of everyday memory: "The rumors of my death are much exaggerated" (Mark Twain). *American Psychologist, 46,* 27–31.

Cerella, J. (1990). Aging and information-processing rate. In J. E. Birren & K. W. Schaie (Eds.), *Handbook of the psychology of aging.* (3rd ed.). New York: Van Nostrand Reinhold.

Cervantes, C. A., & Callahan, M. (1998). Labels and explanations in mother-child emotion talk: Age and gender differentiation. *Developmental Psychology, 34,* 88–98.

Chaiken, S. (1980). Heuristic versus systematic information processing and the use of source versus message cues in persuasion. *Journal of Personality and Social Psychology, 39,* 752–766.

Chambless, D. C., & Gillis, M. M. (1993). Cognitive therapy of anxiety disorders. *Journal of Consulting and Clinical Psychology, 61,* 248–260.

Chambless, D. L., Hollon, S. D. (1998). Defining empirically supported therapies. *Journal of Consulting & Clinical Psychology, 66,* 7–18.

Champoux, M., & Suomi, S. J. (1994). Behavioral and adrenocortical responses of rhesus macaque mothers to infant separation in an unfamiliar environment. *Primates, 35,* 191–202.

Chance, P. (1988). *Learning and behavior.* (2nd ed.). Belmont, CA: Wadsworth.

Chandler, L. S., Richardson, G. A., Gallagher, J. D., & Day, N. L. (1996). Prenatal exposure to alcohol and marijuana: Effects on motor development of preschool children. Alcoholism: *Clinical & Experimental Research, 20,* 455–461.

Chapman, L., & Chapman, J. (1980). Scales for rating psychotic and psychotic-like experiences as continua. *Schizophrenia Bulletin, 6,* 476–489.

Chapman, L., Chapman, J., & Fowles, D. (1993). *Progress in experimental personality and psychopathology research,* Vol. 16. New York: Springer.

Chen, J., & Gardner, H. (1997). Alternative assessment from a multiple intelligences theoretical perspective. In D. P. Flanagen, J. L. Genshaft, and P. L. Harrison, Eds. *Contemporary intellectual assessment: Theories, tests, and issues* (pp. 105–121). New York: Guilford Press.

Chen, S., Shechter, D., & Chaiken, S. (1996). Getting at the truth or getting along: Accuracy-versus impression-motivated heuristic and systematic processing. *Journal of Personality and Social Psychology, 71,* 262–275.

Chess, S., & Thomas, A. (1986). *Temperament in clinical practice.* New York: Guilford Press.

Chess, S., & Thomas, A. (1987). *Origins and evolution of behavior disorders: From infancy to early adult life.* Cambridge, MA: Harvard University Press.

Cheyette, S. R., & Cummings, J. L. (1995). Encephalitis lethargica: Lessons for contemporary neuropsychiatry. Journal of *Neuropsychiatry & Clinical Neurosciences, 7,* 125–134.

Chi, M. T. H. (1976). Short-term memory limitations in children: Capacity or processing deficits? *Memory and Cognition, 4,* 559–572.

Chi, M. T. H. (1978). Knowledge structures and memory development. In R. Siegler (Ed.), *Children's thinking: What deficits?* Hillsdale, NJ: Erlbaum.

Chi, M. T. H., Glaser, R., & Rees, E. (1982). Expertise in problem solving. In R. J. Sternberg (Ed.), *Advances in the psychology of human intelligence,* Vol. 1 (pp. 7–76). Hillsdale, NJ: Erlbaum.

Chiu, L-H. (1990). A comparison of moral reasoning in American and Chinese school children. *International Journal of Adolescence and Youth, 2,* 185–198.

Chomsky, N. (1957). *Syntactic structures.* The Hague: Mouton.

Chomsky, N. (1959). Review of Skinner's Verbal Behavior. *Language, 35,* 26–58.

Chomsky, N. (1986). *Knowledge of language: Its nature, origins, and use.* New York: Praeger.

Christenfeld, N. (1997). Memory for pain and the delayed effects of distraction. *Health Psychology, 16,* 327–330.

Christensen, A. (1988). Deception in psychological reseach: When is it justified? *Personality & Social Psychology Bulletin, 14,* 663–675.

Christianson, S. A. (1992). Emotional stress and eyewitness memory: A critical review. *Psychological Bulletin, 112(2)Z,* 284–309.

Chu, J. A., & Dill, D. (1990). Dissociative symptoms in relation to childhood physical and sexual abuse. *American Journal of Psychiatry, 147,* 887–892.

Church, A. T., & Burke, P. J. (1994). Exploratory and confirmatory tests of the Big Five and Tellegen's three- and four-dimensional models. *Journal of Personality and Social Psychology, 66,* 93–114.

Church, A. T., & Lonner, W. J. (1998). The cross-cultural perspective in the study of personality: Rationale and current research. *Journal of Cross-Cultural Psychology, 29,* 32–62.

Cicirelli, V. (1991). Sibling relationships in adulthood. *Marriage and Family Review, 16,* 291–310.

Cillessen, A., van IJzendoorn, H. W. [sic], & van Lieshout, C. (1992). Heterogeneity among peer-rejected boys: Subtypes and stabilities. *Child Development, 63,* 893–905.

Clark, A. S., & Goldman-Rakic, P. (1989). Gonadal hormones influence the emergence of cortical function in nonhuman primates. *Behavioral Neuroscience, 103,* 1287–1295.

Clark, D. B., & Agras, W. S. (1991). The assessment and treatment of performance anxiety in musicians. *American Journal of Psychiatry, 148,* 598–605.

Clark, D. M. (1994). Cognitive therapy for panic disorder. In B. E. Wolfe, J. D. Maser, et al. (Eds.), *Treatment of panic disorder: A consensus development conference.* (pp. 121–132). Washington: American Psychiatric Press, Inc.

Clark, M. S., & Pataki, S. (1995). Interpersonal processes influencing attraction and relationships. In A. Tesser (Ed.), *Advanced social psychology.* New York: McGraw-Hill.

Clark, R., & Hatfield, E. (1989). Gender differences in receptivity to sexual offers. *Journal of Psychology & Human Sexuality, 2,* 39–55.

Clark, R., Hyde, J. S., Essex, M., & Klein, M. H. (1997). Length of maternity leave and quality of mother-infant interaction. *Child Development, 68,* 364–383.

Clark, R. D., III, & Word, L. E. (1972). Why don't bystanders help? Because of ambiguity? *Journal of Personality and Social Psychology, 24,* 392–400.

Clark, R. D., III, and Word, L. E. (1974). Where is the apathetic bystander? Situational characteristics of the emergency. *Journal of Personality and Social Psychology, 29,* 279–287.

Clayton, P. J., Desmarais, L., & Winokur, G. (1968). A study of bereavement. *American Journal of Psychiatry, 125,* 168–178.

Clayton, P. J., Halikas, J. A., & Maurice, W. L. (1972). The depression of widowhood. *British Journal of Psychiatry, 120,* 71–78.

Cleare, A., & Bond, A. (1997). Does central cooserotonergic function correlate inversely with aggression? A study using d-fenfluramine in healthy subjects. *Psychiatry Research, 69,* 89–95.

Cleghorn, J. M., Peterfy, G., Pinter, E. J., & Pattee, C. J. (1970). Verbal anxiety and the beta adrenergic receptors: A facilitating mechanism? *Journal of Nervous and Mental Disease, 151,* 266–272.

Clifford, M. M., & Walster, E. (1973). The effect of physical attractiveness on teacher expectations. *Sociological Education, 46,* 248–258.

Clomipramine Collaborative Study Group. (1991). Comipramine in the treatment of patients with obsessive-compulsive disorder. *Archives of General Psychiatry, 48,* 730–738.

Cloninger, C. R., Bohman, M., & Sigvardsson, S. (1981). Inheritance of alcohol abuse. *Archives of General Psychiatry, 38,* 861–868.

Cloninger, C. R., Svrakic, D. M., & Przybeck, T. R. (1993). A psychobiological model of temperament and character. *Archives of General Psychiatry, 50,* 975–990.

Coccarro, E. F., Siever, L. J., Klar, H. M., Maurer, G., Cochrane, K., Cooper, T. B., Mohs, R. C., & Davis, K. L. (1989). Serotonergic studies on patients with affective and personality disorders: Correlates with suicidal and impulsive aggressive behavior. *Archives of General Psychiatry, 46,* 587–599.

Cohen, D. (1983). *Piaget: Critique and reassessment.* New York: St. Martin's Press.

Cohen, J. (1994). The earth is round (p. <.05). *American Psychologist, 49,* 997–1003.

Cohen, L. B., Diehl, R. L., Oakes, L. M., & Loehlin, J. L. (1992). Infant perception of /aba/ versus /apa/: Building a quantitative model of infant categorical discrimination. *Developmental Psychology, 28,* 261–272.

Cohen, L. J., Test, M. A., & Brown, R. L. (1990). Suicide and schizophrenia: Data from a prospective community treatment study, *American Journal of Psychiatry, 147,* 602–607.

Cohen, R. M., Gross, M., Nordahl, T., Semple, W., Oren, D., & Rosenthal, N. (1992). Preliminary data on the metabolic brain pattern of patients with Winter seasonal affective disorder. *Archives of General Psychiatry, 49,* 545–552.

Cohen, S., & Herbert, T. B. (1996). Health psychology: Psychological factors and physical disease from the perspective of human psychoneuroimmunology. *Annual Review, 47,* 113–142.

Cohen, S., Tyrrell, D. A. J., & Smith, A. P. (1991). Psychological stress and susceptibility to the common cold. *New England Journal of Medicine, 325,* 606–612.

Cohen, S., & Williamson, G. M. (1991). Stress and infectious disease in humans. *Psychological Bulletin, 109,* 5–24.

Cohen, S., & Wills, T. A. (1985). Stress, social support, and the buffering hypothesis. *Psychological Bulletin, 98,* 310–357.

Coie, J., & Dodge, K. (1983). Continuities and changes in children's social status: A five year longitudinal study. *Merrill-Palmer Quarterly, 29,* 261–282.

Colby, A., & Kohlberg, L. (1984). Invariant squence and internal consistency in moral judgment stages. In W. M. Kurtines & J. L. Gewirtz (Eds.), *Morality, moral behavior and moral development.* New York: John Wiley.

Cole, D. (1991). Underground potlatch: How the Kwakiutl kept the faith. *Natural History, 100,* 50–53.

Cole, M. (1975). An ethnographic psychology of cognition. In R. Brislin et al. (Eds.), *Cross-cultural Perspectives on Learning.* New York: Sage Publications.

Cole, M. (1997). Cultural mechanisms of cognitive development. In E. Amsel, K. A. Renninger, et al. (Eds.), *Change and development: Issues of theory, method, and application. The Jean Piaget symposium series.* (pp. 245–263). Mahwah, NJ: Lawrence Erlbaum Associates, Inc., Publishers.

Cole, M., Gay, J., Glick, J. A., & Sharp, D. W. (1971). *The cultural context of learning and thinking.* New York: Basic Books.

Cole, P. M., Zahn-Waxler, C., Fox, N. A., & Usher, B. A. (1996). Individual differences in emotion regulation and behavior problems in preschool children. *Journal of Abnormal Psychology, 105,* 518–529.

Collett, T. S., & Baron, J. (1994). Biological compasses and the coordinate frame of landmark memories in honeybees. *Nature, 368,* 137–140.

Collier, G., Johnson, D. F., & Berman, J. (1998). Patch choice as a function of procurement cost and encounter rate. *Journal of the Experimental Analysis of Behavior, 69,* 5–16.

Collings, G. (1989). Stress containment through meditation. *Prevention in Human Services, 6,* 141–150.

Collins, A., & Loftus, E. F. (1975). A spreading-activation theory of semantic processing. *Psychological Review, 82,* 407–428.

Collins, R. L., Lapp, W. M., Emmons, K. M., & Isaac, L. M. (1990). Endorsement and strength of alcohol expectancies. *Journal of Studies on Alcohol, 51,* 336–342.

Collins, W. A., & Gunnar, M. R. (1990). Social and personality development. *Annual Review of Psychology, 41,* 387–416.

Cologer-Clifford, A., Simon, N., & Jubilan, B. (1992). Genotype, uterine position, and testosterone sensitivity in older female mice. *Physiology and Behavior, 51,* 1047–1050.

Colvin, C. R. (1993). Judgable people: Personality, behavior, and competing explanations. *Journal of Personality and Social Psychology, 64,* 861–873.

Colvin, C. R., Block, J., & Funder, D. C. (1995). Overly positive self-evaluations and personality: Negative implications for mental health. *Journal of Personality & Social Psychology, 68,* 1152–1162.

Comaroff, J. (1980). Healing and the cultural order: The case of the Barolong boo Ratshidi of Southern Africa. *American Ethnologist, 7,* 637–657.

Compas, B., Hinden, B. R., & Gerhardt, C. (1995). Adolescent development: Pathways and processes of risk and resilience. *Annual Review of Psychology, 46,* 265–293.

Compton, W. M., Helzer, J., Hai-Gwo, H., Eng-Kung, Y., McEvoy, L., Tipp, J., & Spitznagel, E. (1991). New methods in cross-cultural psychiatry: Psychiatric illness in Taiwan and the United States. *American Journal of Psychiatry, 148,* 1697–1704.

Conger, R., Conger, K., Elder, G., Lorenz, F., Simons, R., & Whitbeck, L. (1993). Family economic stress and adjustment of early adolescent girls. *Developmental Psychology, 29,* 206–219.

Conley, J. J. (1985). Longitudinal stability of personality traits: A multitrait-multimethod-multioccasion analysis. *Journal of Personality and Social Psychology, 49,* 1266–1282.

Contrada, R., Leventhal, H., & O'Leary, A. (1990). Personality and health. In L. Pervin (Ed.), *Handbook of personality: Theory and research* (pp. 638–669). New York: Guilford Press.

Conway, M. A. (1995). *Flashbulb memories.* Mahwah, New Jersey: Lawrence Erlbaum.

Conway, M. A., Collins, A. F., Gathercole, S. E., & Anderson, S. J. (1996). Recollections of true and false autobiographical memories. *Journal of Experimental Psychology: General, 125,* 69–95.

Cook, S. P., Vulchanova, L., Hargreaves, K. M., Elde, R., et al. (1997). Distinct ATP receptors on pain-sensing and stretch-sensing neurons. *Nature, 387,* 505–508.

Cooley, C. H. (1902). *Human nature and the social order.* New York: Scribner's.

Coombs, C., & Lehner, P. E. (1984). Conjoint design and analysis of the bilinear model: An application to judgments of risk. *Journal of Mathematical Psychology, 28,* 1–42.

Coombs, G. (1980). Decision theory and subsistence strategies: Some theoretical considerations. In T. Earle & A. Christenson (Eds.), *Modeling change in prehistorical subsistence econmies.* New York: Academic Press.

Coon, H., Fulker, D. W., DeFries, J. C., & Plomin, R. (1990). Home environment and environmental etiologies. *Developmental Psychology, 26,* 459–468.

Cooper, J., Bloom, F., & Roth, R. (1991). *The biochemical basis of neuropharmcology.* (6th ed.). New York: Oxford University Press.

Cooper, L. A. (1975). Mental rotation of random two-dimensional shapes. *Cognitive Psychology, 7,* 20–43.

Cooper, L. A. (1976). Demonstration of a mental analog of an external rotation. *Perception and Psychophysics, 19,* 296–302.

Cooper, L. A., & Shepard, R. N. (1973). Chronometric studies of the rotation of mental images. In W. G. Chase (Ed.), *Visual information processing.* New York: Academic.

Cooper, L. A., & Shepard, R. N. (1973). The time required to prepare for a rotated stimulus. *Memory and Cognition, 1,* 246–250.

Coopersmith, S. (1967). *The antecedents of self-esteem.* San Francisco: Freeman.

Coplan, J. D., Papp, L. A., Pine, D., Martinez, J., Cooper, T., Rosenblum, L. A. et al. (1997). Clinical Improvement With Fluoxetine Therapy and Noradrenergic Function in Patients With Panic Disorder. *Archives of General Psychiatry, 54,* 643–648.

Cork, R. C. (1996). Implicit memory during anesthesia. In S. R. Hameroff, A. W. Kaszniak, & A. C. Scott (Eds.), *Toward a science of consciousness: The first Tucson discussions and debates. Complex adaptive systems* (pp. 295–302). Cambridge: MIT Press.

Cornblatt, B. A., & Kelip, J. G. (1994). Impaired attention, genetics, and the pathophysiology of schizophrenia. *Schizophrenia Bulletin, 20,* 31–46.

Corr, P. J., Pickering, A. D., & Gray, J. A. (1995). Personality and reinforcement in associative and instrumental learning. *Personality & Individual Differences, 19,* 47–71.

Coryell, W., Endicott, J., Keller, M., Andreason, N., Grove, W., Hirschfeld, R., & Scheftner, W. (1989). Bipolar affective disorder and high achievement: A familial association. *American Journal of Psychiatry, 146,* 983–988.

Coryell, W., Endicott, J., & Winokur, G. (1992). Anxiety syndromes as epiphenomena of primary major depression: Outcome and familial psychopathology. *American Journal of Psychiatry, 149,* 100–107.

Cosmides, L. (1989). The logic of social exchange: Has natural selection shaped how humans reason? Studies with the Wason selection task. *Cognition, 31,* 187–276.

Cosmides, L., & Tooby, J. (1995). From evolution to adaptations to behavior. Toward an integrated evolutionary psychology. In R. Wong, et al. (Eds.), *Biological perspectives on motivated activities.* (pp. 11–74). Norwood: Ablex Publishing Corp.

Costa, P. T. Jr., & McCrae, R. R. (1988). Personality in adulthood: A six-year longitudinal study of self-reports and spouse ratings on the NEO Personality Inventory. *Journal of Personality and Social Psychology, 54,* 853–863.

Costa, P. T. Jr., & McCrae, R. R. (1990). Personality: Another "hidden factor" in stress research. *Psychological Inquiry, 1,* 22–24.

Costa, P. T. Jr., McCrae, R. R. (1997). Stability and change in personality assessment: The Revised NEO Personality Inventory in the Year 2000. *Journal of Personality Assessment, 68,* 86–94.

Cotman, C. W. (1990). Synaptic plasticity, neurotropic factors, and transplantation in the aged brain. In E. L. Schneider & J. W. Rowe (Eds.), *Handbook of the biology of aging* (3rd ed.). San Diego: Academic Press.

Courtney, S. M., et al. (1998). An area specialized for spatial working memory in human frontal cortex. *Science, 279,* 1347–1351.

Courtney, S. M., Ungerleider, L. G., Keil, K., & Haxby, J. V. (1997). Transient and sustained activity in a distributed neural system for human working memory. *Nature, 386,* 608–611.

Cousins, S. (1989). Culture and self-perception in Japan and the United States. *Journal of Personality and Social Psychology, 56,* 124–131.

Cowan, N. (1994). Mechanisms of verbal short-term memory. *Current Directions in Psychological Science, 3,* 185–189.

Cowan, W. M. (1979). The development of the brain. *Science American, 241,* 112–133.

Cowdry, R. W., & Gardner, D. L. (1988). Pharmacotherapy of borderline personality disorder: Alprazolam, carbamazepine, trifluoperazine, and tranylcypromine. *Archives of General Psychiatry, 45,* 111–119.

Cowey, A. (1991). Grasping the essentials. *Nature, 349,* 102–103.

Cox, M. J., Owen, M. T., Henderson, V., & Margand, N. (1992). Prediction of infant-father and infant-mother attachment. *Development Psychology, 28,* 474–483.

Coyle, J. (1991). Molecular biological and neurobiological contributions to our understanding of Alzheimer's disease. In A. Tasman & S. Goldfinger, (Eds.), *American Psychiatric Press Review of Psychiatry,* Vol. 10 (pp. 515–527). Washington, DC: American Psychiatric Press.

Coyle, J. Y., Price, D. L., & DeLong, M. R. (1983). Alzheimer's disease: A disorder of cortical cholinergic innervation. *Science, 219,* 1184–1190.

Craik, F., & Lockhart, R. (1972). Levels of processing: A framework for memory research. *Journal of Verbal Learning and Verbal Behavior, 11,* 671–684.

Craik, F. I. M., Govoni, R., Naveh-Benjamin, M., & Anderson, N. D. (1996). The effects of divided attention on encoding and retrieval processes in human memory. *Journal of Experimental Psychology: General, 125,* 159–180.

Cramer, P. (in press). Identity, narcissism, and defense mechanisms in late adolescence. *Journal of Research in Personality.*

Cramer, P., & Block, J. (1998). Preschool antecedents of defense mechanism use in young adults: A longitudinal study. *Journal of Personality and Social Psychology, 74,* 159–169.

Crandall, C. (1994). Prejudice against fat people: Ideology and self-interest. *Journal of Personality and Social Psychology, 66,* 882–894.

Crandall, C. S., & Martinez, R. (1996). Culture, ideology, and antifat attitudes. *Personality & Social Psychlogy Bulletin, 22,* 1165–1176.

Crano, W. D. (1997). Vested interest, symbolic politics, and attitude-behavior consistency. *Journal of Personality and Social Psychology, 72,* 485–491.

Crick, F., & Mitchison, G. (1983). The function of dream sleep. *Nature, 304,* 111–114.

Crits-Christoph, P. (1992). The efficacy of brief dynamic psychotherapy: A meta-analysis. *American Journal of Psychiatry, 149,* 151–158.

Crook, T. H., Youngjohn, J., Larrabee, G., & Salama, M. (1992). Aging and everyday memory. *Neuropsychology, 6,* 123–136.

Cross-national Collaborative Group (1992). The changing rate of major depression: Cross-national comparisons. *Journal of the American Medical Association, 268,* 3098–3105.

Crow, T. J. (1980). Molecular pathology of schizophrenia: More than one disease process? *British Medical Journal, 280,* 66–68.

Crow, T. J. (1986). The continuum of psychosis and its implication for the structure of the gene. *British Journal of Psychiatry, 149,* 419–429.

Crow, T. J. (1990). The continuum of psychosis and its genetic origins. *British Journal of Psychiatry, 156,* 788–797.

Crow, T. J. (1998). From Kraepelin to Kretschmer leavened by Schneider: The transition from categories of psychosis to dimensions of variation intrinsic to Homo sapiens. *Archives of General Psychiatry, 55,* 502–504.

Crowder, R. (1993). Systems and principles in memory theory: Another critique of pure memory. In A. F. Collins, S. Gathercole, M. A. Conway, and P. E. Morris (Eds.), *Theories of memory* (pp. 139–161). Hillsdale: Lawrence Erlbaum Associates, Ltd.

Crowell, J. A., & Feldman, S. S. (1991). Mothers' working models of attachment relationships and mother and child behavior during separation and reunion. *Developmental Psychology, 27,* 597–605.

Crowne, D. P., & Marlow, D. (1964). *The approval motive: Studies in evaluative dependence.* New York: John Wiley.

Croyle, R., & Cooper, J. (1983). Dissonance arousal: Physiological evidence. *Journal of Personality and Social Psychology, 45,* 782–791.

Csikszentmihalyi, M. (1992). *Validity and reliability of the experience sampling method.* Cambridge: Cambridge University Press.

Csikszentmihalyi, M., & Larson, R. (1984). *Being adolescent: Conflict and growth in the teenage years.* New York: Basic Books.

Culp, R. E., Watkins, R. V., Lawrence, H., & Letts, D. (1991). Maltreated children's language and speech development: Abused, neglected, and abused and neglected. *First language, 11,* 377–389.

Cummings, J. L. (1992). Depression and Parkinson's disease: A review. *American Journal of Psychiatry, 149,* 443–454.

Cummins, R. A., Livesey, P. J., & Evans, J. G. M. (1977). A developmental theory of environmental enrichment. *Science, 197,* 692–694.

Cunningham, M., & Cunningham, J. D. (1997). Patterns of symptomatology and patterns of torture. *Australian & New Zealand Journal of Psychiatry, 31,* 555–565.

Cunningham, M. R. (1979). Weather, mood, and helping behavior: The sunshine Samaritan. *Journal of Personality and Social Psychology, 37,* 1947–1956.

Cunningham, M. R., Roberts, A. R., Barbee, A. P., Druen, P. B., et al. (1995). "Their ideas of beauty are, on the whole, the same as ours": Consistency and variability in the cross-cultural perception of female physical attractiveness. *Journal of Personality & Social Psychology, 68,* 261–279.

Curcio, C. A., & Drucker, D. N. (1993). Retinal ganglion cells in Alzheimer's disease and aging. *Annals of Neurology, 33,* 248–257.

Curran, J. P., & Lippold, S. (1975). The effects of physical attraction and attitude similarity on attraction in dating dyads. *Journal of Personality and Social Psychology, 43,* 528–539.

Curry, S. J. (1993). Self-help interventions for smoking cessation. *Journal of Consulting and Clinical Psychology, 61,* 790–803.

Curtiss, S. (1977). *Genie: A psycholinguistic study of a modern-day wild child.* New York: Academic Press.

Curtiss, S. (1989). The independence and task-specificity of language. In A. Bornstein & J. Bruner (Eds.), *Interaction in human development.* Mahwah, NJ: Erlbaum.

Cutler, S. E., Larsen, R. J., & Bunce, S. C. (1996). Repressive coping style and the experience and recall of emotion: A naturalistic study of daily affect. *Journal of Personality, 64,* 379–405.

D'Amico, E. J., & Fromme, K. (1997). Health risk behaviors of adolescent and young adult siblings. *Health Psychology, 16,* 426–432.

D'Andrade, R. G. (1992). Cognitive anthropology. In T. Schwartz, G. M. White, et al. (Eds.), New directions in psychological anthropology. *Publications of the Society for Psychological Anthropology, 3.* (pp. 47–58). Cambridge, UK: Cambridge University Press.

D'Esposito, M., Detre, J., Aquirre, G., Stallcup, M., Alsop, D., Tippet, L., & Farah, M. (1997). A functional MRI study of mental image generation. *Neuropsychologia, 35,* 725–730.

D'Esposito, M., Detre, J. A., Alsop, D. C., Shin, R. K., Atlas, S., & Grossman, M. (1995). The neural basis of the central executive system of working memory. *Nature, 378,* 279–281.

D'Zurilla, T., & Sheedy, C. (1991). Relation between social problem-solving and subsequent level of psychological stress in college students. *Journal of Personality and Social Psychology, 61,* 841–846.

Daly, M., & Wilson, M. (1988). Evolutionary social psychology and family homicide. *Science, 242,* 519–524.

Damasio, A. R. (1994). *Descartes' error: Emotion, reason, and the human brain.* New York: Grosset/Putnam.

Damon, W. (1977). *The social world of the child.* San Francisco: Jossey-Bass.

Damon, W., & Hart, D. (1988). Self-understanding in childhood and adolescence.

New York: Cambridge University Press.

Daneman, M., & Merikle, P. (1996). Working memory and language comprehension: A meta-analysis. *Psychonomic Bulletin and Review, 3,* 422–433.

Darley, J., & Schultz, T. R. (1988). Moral rules: Their content and acquisition. *Annual Review of Psychology, 41,* 525–556.

Darling, C. A., Davidson, J. K., & Jennings, D. A. (1991). The female sexual response revisited: Understanding the multiorgasmic experience in women. *Archives of Sexual Behavior, 20,* 527–540.

Darou, W. G. (1992). Native Canadians and intelligence testing. *Canadian Journal of Counseling, 26,* 96–99.

Darwin, C. (1872). *The expression of the emotions in man and animals.* London: John Murray/Julian Friedmann, 1979.

Dasen, P. (1975). Concrete operational development in three cultures. *Journal of Cross-Cultural Psychology, 6,* 156–172.

Dasen, P., & Heron, A. (1981). Cross-cultural tests of Piaget's theory. In H. C. Triandis & A. Heron (Eds.), *Handbook of cross-cultural psychology:* Vol. 4, *Developmental psychology.* Boston: Allyn & Bacon.

Davanloo, H. (1985). Short-term dynamic psychotherapy. In H. I. Kaplan & B. J. Sadock (Eds.), *Comprehensive Textbook of Psychiatry.* (4th ed.). Baltimore, MD: Williams & Wilkins.

Davidson, R. (1992). Emotion and affective style: Hemispheric substrates. *Psychological Science, 3,* 39–43.

Davidson, R. (1995). Cerebral asymmetry, emotion and affective style. In R. J. Davidson & K. Hugdahl (Eds.), *Brain asymmetry* (pp. 361–387). Cambridge, MA: MIT Press.

Davidson, R. J. (1992). Emotion and affective style: Hemispheric substrates. *Psychological Science, 3,* 39–43.

Davis, D. L., & Whitten, R. G. (1987). The cross-cultural study of human sexuality. *Annual Review of Anthropology, 16,* 69–98.

Davis, H. (1996). Underestimating the rat's intelligence. *Cognitive Brain Research, 3,* 291–298.

Davis, H., & Perusse, R. (1988). Numerical competence in animals: Definitional issues, current evidence, and a new research agenda. *Behavioral and Brain Sciences, 11,* 561–615.

Davis, J. M. (1985). Minor tranquilizers, sedatives, and hypnotics. In H. I. Kaplan, & B. J. Sadock (Eds.), *Comprehensive textbook of psychiatry.* (4th ed.). Baltimore, MD: Williams & Wilkins.

Davis, K. L., Kahn, R. S., Ko, G., & Davidson, M. (1991). Dopamine in schizophrenia: A review and reconceptualiza-tion. *American Journal of Psychiatry, 148,* 1474–1486.

Davis, S. (1990). Men as success objects and women as sex objects: A study of personals advertisements. *Sex Roles, 23,* 43–50.

Dawes, R. (1997). Judgment, decision making, and interference. In D. Gilbert, S. Fiske, & G. Lindzey (Eds.), *Handbook of social psychology* (pp. 497–549). Boston: McGraw-Hill.

Deacon, T. W. (1996). *The making of language.* Edinburgh: Edinburgh University Press.

Deary, I. J., & Stough, C. (1996). Intelligence and inspection time: Achievements, prospects, and problems. *American Psychologist, 51,* 599–608.

Deater-Deckard, K., Dodge, K. A., Bates, J. E., & Pettit, G. S. (1996). Physical discipline among African American and European American mothers: Links to children's externalizing behaviors. *Developmental Psychology, 32,* 1065–1072.

de Castro, J., & Brewer, M. (1992). The amount eaten in meals by humans is a power function of the number of people present. *Physiology and Behavior, 51,* 121–125.

de Castro, J. M. (1993). Genetic influences on daily intake and meal patterns of humans. *Physiology & Behavior, 53,* 777–782.

Deci, E. L., & Ryan, R. M. (1985). *Intrinsic motivation and self-determination in human behavior.* New York: Plenum Press.

Decker, A., Connor, D., & Thal, I. (1991). The role of choinergic projections from the nucleus basalis in memory. *Neuroscience & Behavioral Reviews, 15,* 299–317.

Deglin, V. L., & Kinsbourne, M. (1996). Divergent thinking styles of the hemispheres: How syllogisms are solved during transitory hemisphere suppression. *Brain & Cognition, 31,* 285–307.

Dehaene, S., Tzourio, N., Frak, V., Raynaud, L., et al. (1996). Cerebral activations during number multiplication and comparison: A PET study. *Neuropsychologia, 34,* 1097–1106.

Delgado, P., Charney, D., Price, L., Aghajanian, G., Landis, H., & Heninger, R. (1990). Serotonin function and the mechanism of antidepressant action. *Archives of General Psychiatry, 47,* 411–418.

DeLoache, J. S., Miller, K. F., & Rosengren, K. S. (1997). The credible shrinking room: Very young children's performance with symbolic and nonsymbolic relations. *Psychological Science, 8,* 308–313.

DeLongis, A., Folkman, S., & Lazarus, R. S. (1988). The impact of daily stress on health and mood: Psychological and social resouces as mediators. *Journal of Personality and Social Psychology, 54(3),* 486–495.

Dembroski, T. M., & Costa, P. T. (1987). Coronary prone behavior: Components of the Type A pattern and hostility. *Journal of Personality, 55,* 211–235.

Dement, W. C., & Kleitman, N. (1957). The relation of eye movements during sleep to dream activity: An objective method for the study of dreaming. *Journal of Experimental Psychology, 55,* 543–553.

Dement, W. C., & Wolpert, E. A. (1958). The relation of eye movements, body motility, and external stimuli to dream content. *Journal of Experimental Psychology, 55,* 543–553.

Deming, W. (1986). *Out of crisis.* Cambridge, MA: MIT Press.

Demorest, A. P., & Siegel, P. F. (1996). Personal influences on professional work: An empirical case study of B. F. Skinner. *Journal of Personality, 64,* 243–261.

Demorest, M. E. (1986). Problem solving: Stages, strategies, and stumbling blocks. *Journal of Academic Rehabilitation Audiology, 19,* 13–26.

Dempster, F. N. (1996). Distributing and managing the conditions of encoding and practice. In E. L. Bjork, R. A. Bjork, (Eds.), *Memory. Handbook of perception and cognition* (2nd ed. pp. 317–344). San Diego: Academic Press Inc.

Denham, S., & Holt, R. W. (1993). Preschoolers' likability as cause or consequence of their social behavior. *Developmental Psychology, 29,* 271–275.

Denney, N. R., & Denney, N. W. (1973). The use of classification for problem solving: A comparison of middle and old age. *Developmental Psychology, 9,* 275–278.

Denney, N. W., & Palmer, A. M. (1981). Adult age differences on traditional and practical problem-solving measures. *Journal of Gerontology, 36,* 323–328.

De Pascalis, V., & Perrone, M. (1996). EEG asymmetry and heart rate during experience of hypnotic analgesia in high and low hypnotizables. International *Journal of Psychophysiology, 21,* 163–175.

Deregowski, J. B. (1970). Effect of cultural value of time upon recall. *British Journal of Social and Clinical Psychology, 9(11),* 37–41.

De Renzi, E., & Nichelli, P. (1975). Verbal and non-verbal short-term memory impairment following hemispheric damage. *Cortex, 11,* 341–354.

DeRosier, M., & Kupersmidt, J. (1991). Costa Rican children's perceptions of their social networks. *Developmental Psychology, 27,* 656–662.

Derryberry, D., & Tucker, D. M. (1992). Neural mechanisms of emotion. *Journal of Consulting and Clinical Psychology, 60,* 329–338.

DeSteno, D. A., & Salovey, P. (1996). Genes, jealousy, and the replication of misspecified models. *Psychological Science, 7,* 376–377.

Deutsch, H. (1945). *Psychology of women: A psychoanalytic interpretation.* New York: Grune & Stratton.

Deutsch, J. A., & Gonzalez, M. E. (1980). Gastric nutrient content signals satiety. *Behavioral and Neural Biology, 30,* 113–116.

DeValois, R. L., & DeValois, K. (1975). Neural coding of color. In E. C. Carterette & M. P. Friedman (Eds.), *Handbook of perception.* New York: Acaemic Press.

Devine, P. (1989). Stereotypes and prejudice: Their automatic and controlled components. Journal of Personality and *Social Psychology, 56,* 5–18.

Devine, P. (1995). Prejudice and outgroup perception. In A. Tesser (Ed.), *Constructing social psychology.* New York: McGraw-Hill.

Devine, P., Monteith, M., Zuwerink, J., & Elliot, A. (1991). Prejudice with and without compunction. *Journal of Personality and Social Psychology, 60,* 817–830.

Devine, P. G., & Monteith, M. J. (1993). The role of discrepancy-associated affect in prejudice reduction. In D. M. Mackie, D. L. Hamilton, et al. (Eds.), *Affect, cognition and stereotyping: Interactive processes in group perception.* (pp. 317–344). San Diego: Academic Press, Inc.

Devolder, P., & Pressley, M. (1989). Metamemory across the adult lifespan. *Canadian Psychology, 30,* 578–587.

DeVries, R. (1975). Constancy of generic identity in the years three to six. *Monographs of the Society for Research on Child Development, 34* (Whole No. 127).

de Waal, F. (1989). *Peacemaking among primates.* Cambridge: Harvard University Press.

de Wijk, R. A., Schab, F. R., & Cain, W. S. (1995). Odor identification. In F. R. Schab, R. G. Crowder, et al. (Eds.), *Memory for odors.* (pp. 21–37). Mahwah, NJ: Lawrence Erlbaum Associates, Inc.

De Witte, P. (1996). The role of neurotransmitters in alcohol dependence: Animal research. *Alcohol and Alcoholism, 31,* 13–16.

De Wolffe, M. S., & van Ijzendoorn, M. (1997). Sensitivity and attachment: A meta-analysis on parental antecedents of infant attachment. *Child Development, 68,* 571–591.

Dews, P. B. (1959). Some observations on an operant in the octopus. *Journal of the Experimental Analysis of Behavior, 2,* 57–63.

Diamond, I. T., & Hall, W. C. (1969). Evolution of the neocortex. *Science, 164,* 551–562.

Diamond, M. C. (1978). The aging brain: Some enlightening and optimistic results. *American Psychologist, 66,* 66–71.

Diaz-Guerrero, R. (1979). The development of coping style. *Human Development, 2,* 320–331.

DiBartolo, P. M., & Barlow, D. H. (1996). Perfectionism, marital satisfaction, and contributing factors to sexual dysfunction in men with erectile disorder and their spouses. *Archives of Sexual Behavior, 25,* 581–588.

Di Chiara, G., Acquas, E., & Tanda, G. (1996). Ethanol as a neurochemical surrogate of conventional reinforcers: The dopamine-opioid link. *Alcohol, 13,* 13–17.

Diener, E., Smith, H., & Fujita, F. (1995). The personality structure of affect. *Journal of Personality and Social Psychology, 69,* 130–141.

Dies, R. (1992). The future of group therapy. *Psychotherapy, 29,* 58–64.

Dietz, D., Hazelwood, R., & Warren, J. (1990). The sexually sadistic criminal and his offenses. *Bulletin of the American Academy of Psychiatry and Law, 18,* 27–32.

Dil, N. (1984). Noverbal communication in young children. *Topics in Early Childhood Special Education, 4,* 82–99.

Dimberg, U. (1990). Facial electromyography and emotional reactions. *Psychophysiology, 27,* 481–494.

Dion, K. K. (1972). Physical attractiveness and evaluations of children's transgressions. *Journal of Personality and Social Psychology, 24,* 207–213.

Dion, K. K., & Berscheid, E. (1974). Physical attractiveness and peer perception among children. *Sociometry, 37,* 1–12.

Dion, K. K., & Dion, K. L. (1996). Cultural perspectives on romantic love. *Personal Relationships, 3,* 5–17.

Dion, K. L., & Dion, K. K. (1988). Romantic love: Individual and cultural perspectives. In R. Sternberg, and M. Barnes (Eds.), *The psychology of love.* New York Conn.: Yale University Press.

Dipboye, R., Smith, C. S., & Howell, W. C. (1994). *Understanding industrial and organizational psychology: An integrated approach.* Fort Worth, Tex.: Harcourt Brace.

DiPietro, J. A., Hodgson, D. M., Costigan, K. A., & Johnson, T. R. B. (1996). Fetal antecedents of infant temperament. *Child Development, 67,* 2568–2583.

DiPietro, J. A., Hodgson, D. M., Costigan, K. A., Hilton, S. C., & Johnson, T. R. B. (1996). Fetal neurobehavioral development. *Child Development, 67,* 2553–2567.

Dishion, T. (1990). The family ecology of boys' peer relations in middle childhood. *Child Development, 61,* 874–892.

Dittes, J. E. (1959). Effect of changes in self-esteem upon impulsiveness and deliberation in making judgments. *Journal of Abnormal Social Psychology, 53,* 100–107.

Dixon, N. F. (1971). *Subliminal perception: The nature of a controversy.* New York: McGraw-Hill.

Dixon, N. F. (1981). *Preconscious processing.* New York: John Wiley.

Doane, J. A., et al. (1981). Parental communication deviance and affective style: Predictors of subsequent schizophrenia spectrum disorders in vulnerable adolescents. *Archives of General Psychiatry, 38,* 679–685.

Dobson & Teller (1978). Visual acuity in human infants: A review and comparison of behavioral and electrophysiological studies. *Visual Research, 18,* 1469–1483.

Dodd, B. (1979). Lip reading in infants: Attention to speech presented in-and out-of-synchrony. *Cognitive Psychology, 11,* 478–484.

Dodge, K., Lochman, J., Harnish, J., Bates, J. E., & Pettit, G. (1997). Reactive and proactive aggression in school chidlren and psychiatrically impaired chronically assaultive youth. *Journal of Abnormal Psychology, 106,* 37–51.

Dodge, K., Pettit, G., Bates, J. E., & Valente, E. (1995). Social information-processing patterns partially mediate the effect of early physical abuse on later conduct problems. *Journal of Abnormal Psychology, 104,* 632–643.

Dodge, K., Price, J. M., Bachorowski, J., & Newman, J. P. (1990). Hostile attributional biases in severely aggressive adolescents. *Journal of Abnormal Psychology, 99,* 385–392.

Doi, T. (1992). On the concept of amae. *Infant Mental Health Journal, 13,* 7–11.

Dollard, J., Doob, L., Miller, N. E., Mowrer, O., & Sears, R. (1939). *Frustration and aggression.* New Haven Conn.: Yale University Press.

Dollard, J., & Miller, N. (1950). *Personality and psychotherapy: An analysis in terms of learning, thinking, and culture.* New York: McGraw-Hill.

Domhoff, G. W. (1996). *Finding meaning in dreams: A quantitative approach.* New York: Plenum Press.

Dorfman, J., Shames, V. A., & Kihlstrom, J. F. (1996). Intuition, incubation, and insight: Implicit cognition in problem solving. In G. Underwood (Ed.), *Implicit cognition.* (pp. 257–296). New York: Oxford University Press.

Dornbusch, S. M., Ritter, P. L., Leiderman, P. H. (1987). The relation of parenting styles to adolescent school performance. *Child Development, 58,* 1244–1257.

Dorner, G., Geier, T., Ahrens, L., Krell, L., Munx, G., Sieler, H., Kittner, E., & Muller, H. (1980). Prenatal stress and possible aetiogenic factor homosexuality in human males. *Endokrinologie, 75,* 365–368.

Dorner, G., Schenk, B., Schmiedel, B., & Ahrens, L. (1983). Stressful events in prenatal life of bi- and homosexual men. *Experimental and Clinical Endocrinology, 81,* 83–87.

Doty, R. L., Green, P. A., Ram, C., & Tandeil, S. L. (1982). Communication of gender from human breath odors: Relationship to perceived intensity and pleasantness. *Hormones and Behavior, 16,* 13–22.

Douglas, M. (1966). *Purity and danger: An analysis of concepts of pollution and taboo.* Middlesex: Penguin.

Douvan, E., & Adelson, J. (1966). *The adolescent experience.* New York: John Wiley.

Dovidio, J., & Gaertner, S. (1993). Stereotypes and evaluative intergroup bias. In D. Mackie & D. Hamilton (Eds.), *Affect, cognition, and stereotyping: Interactive processes in group perception.* San Diego: Academic Press.

Dozier, M., & Kobak, R. (1992). Psychophysiology in attachment interviews: Converging evidence for deactivating strategies. *Child Development, 63,* 1473–1480.

Draguns, J. G. (1986). Culture and psychopathology: What is known about their relationship? *American Journal of Psychology, 38,* 329–338.

Draguns, J. G. (1990). Normal and abnormal behavior in cross-cultural perspective: Specifying the nature of their relationship. In J. J. Beeman (Ed.), *Cross-Cultural perspectives. Current theory and research in motivation.*

Drasdo, N. (1977). The neural representation of visual space. *Nature, 266,* 554–556.

Drewnowski, A. (1991). Obesity and eating disorders. Cognitive aspects of food preference and food aversion. *Bulletin of the Psychonomic Society, 29,* 261–264.

Dreyfus, H., & Dreyfus, S. (1986). Why computers may never think like people. *Technology Review, 89,* 42–61.

DuBois, C. (1944). *The people of Alor: A social psychological study of an East Indian.* Minneapolis: University of Minnesota Press.

Duckitt, J. (1992). Psychology and prejudice: A historical analysis and integrative framework. *American Psychologist, 47,* 1882–1197.

Dudley, R. (1991). IQ and heritability. *Science, 252,* 191–192.

Duman, R. S., Heninger, G. R., & Nestler, E. J. (1997). A molecular and cellular theory of depression. *Archives of General Psychiatry, 54,* 597–606.

Dumaret, A. (1985). I.Q., scholastic performance and behavior of sibs raised in contrasting environments. *Journal of Child Psychology and Psychiatry and Allied Disciplines, 26,* 553–580.

Duncker, K. (1946). On problem solving. *Psychological Monographs, 158, 5,* #270.

Dunn, J., Bretherton, I., & Munn, P. (1987). Conversations about feeling states between mothers and their young children. *Developmental Psychology, 23,* 132–139.

Dunn, J., & McGuire, S. (1992). Sibling and peer relationships in childhood. *Journal of Child Psychology and Psychiatry, 33,* 67–105.

Durand, R. P., Fincher, R. E., Reigart, J. R., & Lancaster, C. J. (1991). Association between third year medical students' abilities to organize hypotheses about patients' problems and to order appropriate diagnostic tests. *Academic Medicine, 66,* 702–704.

Durkheim, E. (1915). *The elementary forms of the religious life.* New York: Free Press.

Dutton, D. G. (1996). *The domestic assault of women.* Vancouver: University of British Columbia Press.

Dutton, D. G., & Aron, A. P. (1974). Some evidence for heightened sexual arousal under conditions of high anxiety. *Journal of Personality and Social Psychology, 30,* 510–517.

Dweck, C. (1975). The role of expectations and attributions in the alleviation of learned helplessness. *Journal of Personality and Social Psychology, 31,* 674–685.

Dweck, C. (1986). Motivational processes affecting learning. *American Psychologist, 41,* 1040–1048.

Dworkin, R. H., Hartsetin, G., Rosner, H., Walther, R., Sweeney, E. W., & Brand, L. (1992). A high-risk method for studying psychosocial antecedents of chronic pain: The prospective investigation of herpes zoster. *Journal of Abnormal Psychology, 101,* 200–205.

Eagle, M. (1959). The effects of subliminal stimuli of aggressive content upon conscious cognition. *Journal of Personality, 27,* 678–688.

Eagly, A., Ashmore, R., Makhijani, M., & Longo, L. (1991). What is beautiful is good, but . . . : A meta-analytic review of research on the physical attractiveness stereotype. *Psychological Bulletin, 110,* 109–128.

Eagly, A., & Chaiken, S. (1992). *The psy-chology of attitudes.* San Diego: Harcourt, Brace.

Eagly, A. H. (1983). Gender and Social Influence: A social psychological analysis. *American Psychologist, 38,* 971–981.

Eagly, A. H. (1995). The science and politics of comparing men and women. *American Psychologist, 50,* 145–158.

Eagly, A. H., & Chaiken, S. (1998). Attitude structure and function. In D. T. Gilbert, S. T. Fiske, et al. (Eds.), *The handbook of social psychology, Vol. 2* (4th ed.). (pp. 269–322). Boston: McGraw-Hill.

Earls, F., Escobar, J. I., & Manson, S. M. (1990). Suicide in minority groups: Epidemiologic and cultural perspectives. In S. J. Blumenthal and D. J. Kupfer (Eds.), *Suicide over the life cycle: Risk factors, assessment, and treatment of suicidal patients.* Washington, DC: American Psychiatric Press.

Easterbrooks, M. A., & Goldberg, W. A. (1985). Effects of early maternal employment on toddlers, mothers, and fathers. *Developmental Psychology, 21,* 774–783.

Ebbinghaus, H. (1885). *Memory.* New York: Columbia University/Dover, 1964.

Eberhardt, J. L., & Randall, J. L. (1997). The essential notion of race. *Psychological Science, 8,* 198–203.

Eckert, E. D., Bouchard, T. J., Bohlen, J., & Heston, L. (1986). Homosexuality in monozygotic twins reared apart. *British Journal of Psychiatry, 148,* 421–425.

Eder, R. (1990). Uncovering young children's psychological selves: Individual and developmental differences. *Child Development, 61,* 849–863.

Edwards, C. P., & Whiting, B. B. (1983). Differential socialization of girls and boys in light of cross-cultural research. In W. Damon (Ed.), *Social and personality development: Essays on the growth of the child.* New York: W. W. Norton.

Edwards, D. A., & Einhorn, L. C. (1986). Preoptic and midbrain control of sexual motivation. *Physiology and Behavior, 37,* 329–335.

Edwards, W. (1977). How to use multiattribute utility measurement for social decision making. *IEEE Transactions in Systems Man and Cybernetics, 17,* 326–340.

Egeland, B., & Hiester, M. (1995). The long-term consequences of infant daycare and mother-infant attachment. *Child Development, 66,* 474–485.

Egger, M. D., & Flynn, J. P. (1963). Effect of electrical stimulation of the amygdala on hypothalamically elicited attack behavior in cats. *Journal of Neurophysiology, 26,* 705–720.

Ehlers, A., & Breuer, P. (1992). Increased cardiac awareness in panic disorder.

Journal of Abnormal Psychology, 101, 371–382.

Ehrman, R., Ternes, J., O'Brien, C. P., & McLellan, A. T. (1992). Conditioned tolerance in human opiate addicts. *Psychopharmacology, 108,* 218–224.

Eichenbaum, H. (1996). Learning from LTP: A comment on recent attempts to identify cellular & molecular mechanisms of memory. *Learning & Memory, 3,* 61–73.

Eichenbaum, H. (1997). Declarative memory: Insights from cognitive neurobiology. *Annual Review, 48,* 547–572.

Eimas, P. (1985). The perception of speech in early infancy. *Scientific American, 252,* 46–52.

Eimas, P. D. (1985). The perception of speech in early infancy. *Scientific American, 252,* 120.

Eimas, P. D., Siqueland, E. R., Jusczyk, P., & Vigorito, J. (1971). Speech perception in infants. *Science, 171,* 303–306.

Einstein, G. O., & McDaniel, M. A. (1990). Normal aging and prospective memory. *Journal of Experimental Psychology: Learning, Memory, & Cognition, 16,* 717–726.

Einstein, G. O., Smith, R. E., McDaniel, M. A., & Shaw, P. (1997). Aging and prospective memory: The influence of increased task demands at encoding and retrieval. *Psychology & Aging, 12,* 479–488.

Eisenberg, N., Fabes, R. A., & Murphy, B. C. (1996). Parent's reactions to children's negative emotions: Relations to children's social competence and comforting behavior. *Child Development, 67,* 2227–2247.

Eisenberg, N., Fabes, R. A., Shepard, S. A., & Murphy, B. C. (1997). Contemporaneous and longitudinal prediction of children's social functioning from regulation and emotionality. *Child Development, 68,* 642–664.

Eisenberg, N., Miller, P. A., Shell, R., McNalley, S., & Shea, C. (1991). Prosocial development in adolescence: A longitudinal study. *Developmental Psychology 27,* 849–857.

Eisenberger, R., & Selbst, M. (1994). Does reward increase or decrease creativity? *Journal of Personality and Social Psychology, 66,* 1116–1127.

Ekman, P. (1971). Universals and cultural differences in facial expression. In J. K. Cole (Ed.), Nebraska Symposium on Motivation. Lincoln: University of Nebraska Press.

Ekman, P. (1977). Biological and cultural contributions to body and facial movement. In J. Blacking (Ed.), *The anthropology of the body.* A.S.A. Monograph 15. London: Academic Press.

Ekman, P. (1992). Facial expressions of emotion: New findings, new questions. *Psychological Science, 3,* 34–38.

Ekman, P., & Davidson, R. (1993). Voluntary smiling changes regional brain activity. *Psychological Science, 4,* 342–345.

Ekman, P., & Davidson, R. J. (1993). Voluntary smiling changes regional brain activity. *Psychological Science, 4,* 342–345.

Ekman, P., & Friesen, W. V. (1975). *Unmasking the face: A guide to recognizing emotions from facial cues.* Englewood Cliffs, NJ: Prentice-Hall.

Ekman, P., Friesen, W. V., & Ellsworth, P. (1982). What are the similarities and differences in facial behavior across cultures? In P. Ekman (Ed.), *Emotion in the human face* (2nd ed.). New York: Cambridge University Press.

Ekman, P., & Keltner, D. (1997). Universal facial expressions of emotion: An old controversy and new findings. In U. C. Segerstrale, P. Molnar, et al. (Eds.), *Nonverbal communication: Where nature meets culture.* (pp. 27–46). Mahwah, NJ: Lawrence Erlbaum Associates, Inc.

Ekman, P., Levenson, R., & Friesen, W. (1983). Autonomic nervous system activity distinguishes between emotions. *Science, 221,* 1208–1210.

Ekman, P., & Oster, H. (1979). Facial expressions of emotion. *Annual Review of Psychology, 30,* 527–554.

El Hassan Al Awad, A., & Sonuga-Barke, E. (1992). Childhood problems in a Sudanese city: A comparison of extended and nuclear families. *Child Development, 63,* 906–914.

Elder, G. (1998). The life course as developmental theory. *Current Directions in Psychological Science, 69,* 1–12.

Elder, G. H., Jr. (1998). The life course as developmental theory. *Child Development, 69,* 1–12.

Elias, M., Elias, J., & Elias, P. (1990). Biological and health influences on behavior. In J. Birren & K. W. Schaie (Eds.), *Handbook of the psychology of aging,* (pp. 80–102). (3rd ed.). New York: Academic Press.

Elizur, J., & Minuchin, S. (1989). *Institutionalizing madness: Families, therapy, and society.* New York: Basic Books.

Elkin, I. (1994). The NIMH Treatment of Depression Collaborative Research Program: Where we began and where we are. In A. Bergin & S. Garfield (Eds.), *Handbook of psychotherapy and behavior change* (pp. 114–139). (4th ed.) New York: John Wiley.

Elkin, I., Shea, M. T., Watkins, J., & Imber, S. (1989). National Institute of Mental Health Treatment of Depression Collaborative Research Program: General effectiveness of treatments. *American Journal of Psychiatry, 46,* 971–982.

Elkind, D. (1981). Children's discovery of the conservation of mass, weight, and volume: Piaget replications studies II. *Journal of Genetic Psychology, 98,* 37–46.

Elkins, H., Friedman, L., Wise, A., & Meltzer, H. Y. (1995). Meta-analyses of studies of ventricular enlargement and cortical sulcal prominence in mood disorders. *Archives of General Psychiatry, 52,* 735–746.

Elkins, I. J., Cromwell, R. L., & Asarnow, R. (1992). Span of apprehension in schizophrenic patients as a function of distractor masking and laterality. *Journal of Abnormal Psychology, 101,* 53–60.

Elkins, I. J., Mcgue, M., & Iacono, W. G. (1997). Genetic and environmental influences on parent-son relationships: Evidence for increasing genetic influence during adolescence. *Developmental Psychology, 33,* 351–363.

Ellicott, A., Hammen, C., Gitlin, M., Brown, G., & Jamison, K. (1990). Life events and the course of bipolar disorder. *American Journal of Psychiatry, 147,* 1194–1198.

Elliot, A. J., & Church, M. A. (1997). A hierarchical model of approach and avoidance achievement motivation. *Journal of Personality & Social Psychology, 72,* 218–232.

Elliot, A. J., & Harackiewicz, J. M. (1996). Approach and avoidance achievement goals and intrinsic motivation: A mediational analysis. *Journal of Personality and Social Psychology, 70,* 461–475.

Elliot, A., & Devine, P. (1994). On the motivational nature of cognitive dissonance: Dissonance as psychological discomfort. *Journal of Personality and Social Psychology, 67,* 382–394.

Elliot, R. (1988). Tests, abilities, race, and conflict. *Intelligence, 12,* 333–350.

Elliott, E. S., & Elliot, C. S. (1988). Goals: An approach to motivation and achievement. *Journal of Personality and Social Psychology, 54,* 5–12.

Elliott, J. (1977). The power and pathology of prejudice. In P. G. Zimbardo and F. L. Ruch (Eds.), *Psychology and Life.* (9th ed.). Glenview, Ill: Scott, Foresman.

Ellis, A. (1962). *Reason and emotion in psychotherapy.* New York: Lyle Stuart.

Ellis, A. (1977). The basic clinical theory of rational-emotive therapy. In A. Ellis and R. Grieger (Eds.), *Handbook of rational-emotive therapy.* New York: Springer.

Ellis, A. (1984). Rational-emotive therapy. In R. J. Corsini (Ed.), *Current psychotherapies.* (2nd ed.). Itasca, Ill: Peacock Publishers.

Ellis, A. (1987). Cognitive therapy and rational-emotive therapy: A dialogue.

Journal of Cognitive Psychotherapy, 1, 205–255.

Ellis, A. (1989). *Inside rational-emotive therapy: A critical appraisal of the theory and therapy of Albert Ellis.* New York: Academic.

Ellis, L., & Ames, M. A. (1987). Neurohormonal functioning and sexual orientation: A theory of homosexuality-heterosexuality. *Psychological Bulletin, 101,* 233–258.

Ember, M. (1997). Evolution of the human relations area files. *Cross-Cultural Research: The Journal of Comparative Social Science, 31,* 3–15.

Eme, R., Maisiak, R., & Goodale, W. (1979). Seriousness of adolescent problems. *Adolescence, 14,* 93–99.

Emmons, R., & King, L. A. (1988). Conflict among personal strivings: Immediate and long-term implications for psychological and physical well-being. *Journal of Personality and Social Psychology, 54,* 1040–1048.

Engel, S., Zhang, X., & Wandell, B. (1997). Colour tuning in human visual cortex measured with functional magnetic resonance imaging. *Nature, 388,* 68–71.

Engen, T. (1982). *The perception of odors.* New York: Academic.

Epstein, S. (1973). The self-concept revisited, or a theory of a theory. *American Psychologist, 28,* 404–416.

Epstein, S. (1979). The stability of behavior: On predicting most of the people much of the time. *Journal of Personality and Social Psychology, 37,* 1097–1126.

Epstein, S. (1986). Does aggregation produce spuriously high estimates of behavior stability? *Journal of Personality and Social Psychology, 50,* 1199–1210.

Epstein, S. (1990). Cognitive-experiential self theory. In L. Pervin (Ed.), *Handbook of personality: Theory and research* (pp. 165–192). New York: Guilford.

Epstein, S. (1992). Coping ability, negative self-evaluation, and overgeneralization: Experiment and theory. *Journal of Personality and Social Psychology, 62,* 826–836.

Epstein, S. (1994). Integration of the cognitive and the psychodynamic unconscious. *American Psychologist, 49,* 709–724.

Epstein, S. (1997). This I have learned from over 40 years of personality research. *Journal of Personality, 65,* 3–32.

Epstein, S., & Katz, L. (1992). Coping ability, stress, productive load, and symptoms. *Journal of Personality and Social Psychology, 62,* 813–825.

Era, P., Jokela, J., & Heikkinen, E. (1986). Reaction and movement times in men of different ages: A population study. *Perceptual and Motor Skills, 63,* 111–130.

Erdelyi, M. H. (1985). *Psychoanalysis:*

Freud's cognitive psychology. New York: W. H. Freeman.

Erhardt, A. A., & Baker, S. W. (1974). Fetal androgens, human central nervous system differentiation, and behavior sex differences. In R. C. Friedman, R. M. Richart & R. L. Vande Wiele (Eds.), *Sex differences in behavior.* New York: John Wiley.

Ericcson, K., & Chase, W. G. (1982). Exceptional memory. *American Scientist, 70,* 607–614.

Ericsson, K. A. (1985). Memory skill. *Canadian Journal of Psychology, 39,* 188–231.

Erikson, E. (1963). *Childhood and society.* New York: W. W. Norton.

Erikson, E. (1968). *Identity: Youth and crisis.* New York: W. W. Norton.

Erikson, E. (1969). *Gandhi's truth: On the origin of militant nonviolence.* New York: W. W. Norton.

Erikson, E. H. (1958). *Young Man Luther.* New York: W. W. Norton.

Erlenmeyer-Kimling, L., Adamo, U. H., Rock, D., Roberts, S. A., Bassett, A. S., Squires-Wheeler, E., et al. (1997). The New York High-Risk Project Prevalence and Comorbidity of Axis I Disorders in Offspring of Schizophrenic Parents at 25-Year Follow-up. *Archives of General Psychiatry, 54,* 1096–1102.

Ernst, B. (1976). *The magic mirror of M. C. Escher.* New York: Random House.

Estes, W. K. (1994). *Classification and cognition.* New York: Oxford University Press.

Euler, H. A., & Weitzel, B. (1996). Discriminative grandparental solicitude as reproductive strategy. *Human Nature, 7,* 39–59.

Evans, D. L., Folds, J., Petitto, J., Golden, R. N., Pedersen, C., & Corrigan, M. (1992). Cirulating natural killer cell phenotypes in men and women with major depression: Relation to cytotoxic activity and severity of depression. *Archives of General Psychiatry, 49,* 388–395.

Evans, G. W., Palsane, M. N., & Carrere, S. (1987). Type A behavior and occupational stress: A cross-cultural study of blue-collar workers. *Journal of Personality and Social Psychology, 52,* 1002–1007.

Evans, K. K., & Singer, J. A. (1994). Studying intimacy through dream narratives: The relationship of dreams to self-report and projective measures of personality. *Imagination, Cognition & Personality, 14,* 211–226.

Evans-Pritchard, E. E. (1956). *Nuer religion.* Oxford: Clarendon Press.

Everitt, B. J., & Robbins, T. W. (1997). Central cholinergic systems and cognition. *Annual Review, 48,* 649–684.

Everson, C. A. (1997). Sleep deprivation

and the immune system. In M. R. Pressman, and W. C. Orr (Eds.), *Understanding sleep: The evaluation and treatment of sleep disorders. Application and practice in health psychology* (pp. 401–424). Washington, DC: American Psychological Association.

Eysenck, H. (1987). The growth of a unified scientific psychology: Ordeal by quakery. In A. Staats & L. Mos (Eds.), *Annals of theoretical psychology,* Vol. 5 (pp. 91–113). New York: Plenum Press.

Eysenck, H. (1987). *Theoretical foundations of behavior therapy.* New York: Plenum Press.

Eysenck, H. J. (1953). *The structure of human personality.* New York: John Wiley.

Eysenck, H. J. (1967). *The biological basis of personality.* Springfield, Ill.: Charles C. Thomas.

Eysenck, H. J. (1983). Human learning and individual differences: The genetic dimension. *Educational Psychology, 3,* 169–188.

Eysenck, H. J. (1983). The roots of creativity: Cognitive ability or personality trait? *Roeper Review, 5,* 10–12.

Eysenck, H. J. (1990). Biological dimensions of personality. In L. A. Pervin (Ed.), *Handbook of personality: Theory and research* (pp. 244–276). New York: Guilford Press.

Eysenck, H. J. (1993). Creativity and personality: Suggestions for a theory. *Psychological Inquiry, 4,* 147–178.

Fabrega, H. (1989). On the significance of an anthropological approach to schizophrenia. *Psychiatry, 52,* 45–65.

Fagot, B. I. (1985). Changes in thinking about early sex role development. *Developmental Review, 5,* 83–98.

Fagot, B. I., & Patterson, G. R. (1969). An in vivo analysis of reinforcing contingencies for sex-role behaviors in the preschool child. *Developmental Psychology.*

Fairbairn, W. (1954). *An object-relations theory of personality.* New York: Basic Books.

Fantz, R. L. (1966). Pattern discrimination and selective attention as determinants of perceptual developmental from birth. In A. H. Kidd & L. J. Rivoire (Eds.), *Perceptual development in children.* New York: International Universities Press.

Fantz, R. L., Fagan, J. F., III, & Miranda, S. B. (1975). Early visual selectivity. In L. B. Cohen & P. Salapatek (Eds.), *Infant perception: From sensation to cognition: Vol. I. Basic visual processes.* New York: Academic Press.

Faravelli, C., & Pallanti, S. (1989). Recent

life events and panic disorder. *American Journal of Psychiatry, 146,* 622–626.

Farel, A. (1980). Effects of preferred maternal roles, maternal employment, and sociodemographic status on school adjustment and competence. *Child Development, 51,* 1179–1196.

Farmer, I. P., Meyer, P. S., Ramsey, D. J., & Goff, D. C. (1996). Higher levels of social support predict greater survival following acute myocardial infarction: *The Corpus Christi Heart Project. Behavioral Medicine, 22,* 59–66.

Fass, P. S. (1980). The I.Q.: A cultural and historical framework. *American Journal of Education,* 431–458.

Fazio, R. (1990). Multiple processes by which attitudes guide behavior: The MODE model as an integrative framework. In L. Berkowitz (Ed.), *Advances in Experimental Social Psychology, 23,* 75–109.

Fazio, R., Jackson, J. R., Dunton, B., & Williams, C. J. (1995). Variability in automatic activation as an unobtrusive measure of racial attitudes: A bona fide pipeline? *Journal of Personality and Social Psychology, 69,* 1013–1027.

Fazio, R., & Zanna, M. (1981). Direct experience and attitude-behavior consistency. In L. Berkowitz (Ed.), *Advances in experimental social psychology,* Vol. 14. New York: Academic.

Fazio, R. H. (1986). How do attitudes guide behavior? In R. M. Sorrentino and E. T. Higgins (Eds.), *The handbook of motivation and cognition: Foundations of social behavior.* New York: Guilford Press.

Fazio, R. H. (1995). Attitudes as object-evaluation associations: Determinants, consequences, and correlates of attitude accessibility. In R. E. Petty, J. A. Krosnick, et al. (Eds.), *Attitude strength: Antecedents and consequences.* Ohio State University series on attitudes and persuasion, Vol. 4. (pp. 247–282). Mahwah, NJ: Lawrence Erlbaum Associates Inc.

Feather, N. T. (1996). Values, deservingness, and attitudes toward high achievers: Research on tall poppies. In C. Seligman, J. M. Olson, et al. (Eds.), The psychology of values: The Ontario symposium, Vol. 8. *The Ontario symposium on personality and social psychology,* Vol. 8. (pp. 215–251). Mahwah, NJ: Lawrence Erlbaum Associates, Inc.

Federoff, J. P., et al. (1992). Depression in patients with acute traumatic brain injury. *American Journal of Psychiatry, 149,* 918–923.

Fehm-Wolfsdorf, G., Soherr, U., Arndt, R., Kern, W., et al. (1993). Auditory reflex thresholds elevated by stress-induced cortisol secretion. *Psychoneuroendocrinology, 18,* 579–589.

Feingold, A. (1992). Good-looking people are not what we think. *Psychological Bulletin, 111,* 304–341.

Feingold, A. (1994). Gender differences in personality: A meta-analysis. *Psychological Bulletin, 116,* 429–456.

Feldman, D. E., Brainard, M. S., & Knudsen, E. I. (1996). Newly learned auditory responses mediated by NMDA receptors in the owl inferior colliculus. *Science, 271,* 525–528.

Feldman, D. H. (1980). *Beyond universals in cognitive development.* Norwood, NJ: Ablex.

Feldman, R. S., & Rime, B., Eds. (1991). *Fundamentals of nonverbal behavior.* New York: Cambridge University Press.

Fenton, W., & McGlashan, T. (1991). Natural history of schizophrenia subtypes, I: Longitudinal study of paranoid, hebephrenic, and undifferentiated schizophrenia. *Archives of General Psychiatry, 48,* 969–977.

Fernald, A., & Kuhl, P. (1987). Acoustic determinants of infant preference for motherese speech. *Infant Behavior and Development, 10,* 279–293.

Fernald, R. D. (1996). Recognition of visual signals; Eyes specialize. In C. F. Moss, S. J. Shettleworth, et al. (Eds.), *Neuroethological studies of cognitive and perceptual processes.* (pp. 229–249). Boulder: Westview Press.

Ferster, C. B., & Skinner, B. F. (1957). *Schedules of reinforcement.* New York: Appleton-Century-Crofts.

Festinger, L. (1957). *A theory of cognitive dissonance.* New York: Harper & Row.

Festinger, L. (1962). Cognitive dissonance. *Scientific American, 107,* 409–415.

Festinger, L., & Carlsmith, J. M. (1959). Cognitive consequences of forced compliance. *Journal of Abnormal and Social Psychology, 58,* 203–210.

Field, T. (1991). Quality infant day care and grade school behavior and performance. *Child Development, 62,* 863–870.

Finkelhor, D. (1994). The international epidemiology of child sexual abuse. *Child Abuse & Neglect, 18,* 409–417.

Finkelhor, D., et al. (1990). Sexual abuse in a national survey of adult men and women: Prevalence, characteristics, and risk factors. *Child Abuse and Neglect, 14,* 19–28.

Finkelhor, D., Hotaling, G., Lewis, I. A., & Smith, C. (1990). Sexual abuse in a national survey of adult men and women: Prevalence, characteristics, and risk factors. *Child Abuse & Neglect, 14,* 19–28.

Finlay, B. L., & Darlington, R. (1995). Linked regularities in the development and evolution of mammalian brains. *Science, 268,* 1578–1583.

Fischer, K. W. (1980). A theory of cognitive development: The control and construction of hierarchies of skills. *Psychological Review, 87,* 477–531.

Fischer, K. W., Shaver, P. R., & Carnochan, P. (1990). How emotions develop and how they organize development. *Cognition and Emotion, 4,* 81–127.

Fischhoff, B., & Downs, J. (1997). Accentuate the relevant. *Psychological Science, 8,* 154–158.

Fishbein, M., & Ajzen, I. (1974). Attitudes towads objects as predictors of single and multiple behavioral criteria. *Psychologial Review, 81,* 59–74.

Fisher, S., & Greenberg, R. (1985). *The scientific credibility of Freud's theories and therapy.* New York: Columbia University Press.

Fiske, S. (1992). Thinking is for doing: Portraits of social cognition from daguerreotype to laserphoto. *Journal of Personality and Social Psychology, 63,* 877–889.

Fiske, S. (1995). Social cognition. In A. Tesser (Ed.), *Constructing social psychology.* New York: McGraw-Hill.

Fiske, S., & Taylor, S. (1991). *Social cognition.* (2nd ed). Reading, MA: Addison-Wesley.

Fiske, S. T. (1993). Social cognition and social perception. *Annual Review of Psychology, 44,* 155–194.

Fiske, S. T. (1998). Stereotyping, prejudice, and discrimination. In D. T. Gilbert, S. T. Fiske, et al. (Eds.), *The handbook of social psychology, Vol. 2* (4th ed.). (pp. 357–411). Boston: McGraw-Hill.

Fitzpatrick, K. M. (1993). Exposure to violence and presence of depression among low-income African-American youth. *Journal of Consulting and Clinical Psychology,* 528–531.

Flavell, J. (1992). Cognitive development: past, present, and future. *Developmental Psychology, 28,* 998–1005.

Flavell, J., Green, F. L., Flavell, E., & Grossman, J. B. (1997). The development of children's knowledge about inner speech. *Child Development, 68,* 39–47.

Flavell, J. H. (1982). Structures, stages, and sequences in cognitive development. In W. A. Collins (Ed.), *The concept of development:* Vol. 15. Hillsdale, NJ: Erlbaum.

Flavell, J. H. (1996). Piaget's legacy. *Psychological Science, 7,* 200–203.

Flavell, J. H., Beach, D. R., & Chinsky, J. M. (1966). Spontaneous verbal rehearsal in a memory task as a function of age. *Child Development, 37,* 283–299.

Flavell, J. H., Botkin, P. T., Fry, C. L. Jr., Wright, J. W., & Jarvis, P. E. (1968). *The development of role-taking and communications skills in children.* New York: John Wiley.

Flavell, J. H., Friedrichs, A. G., & Hoyt, J. D. (1970). Developmental changes in memorization processes. *Cognitive Psychology, 1,* 324–340.

Flavell, J. H., & Wellman, H. M. (1977). Metamemory. In R. V. Kail & J. W. Hagen (Eds.), *Memory in cognitive development.* Hillsdale, NJ: Erlbaum.

Fletcher, G. (1986). Attributional complexity: An individual differences measure. *Journal of Personality and Social Psychology, 51,* 875–884.

Fletcher, G., & Ward, C. (1988). Attribution theory and processes: A cross-cultural perspective. In M. Bond (Ed.), *The cross-cultural challenge to social psychology.* Beverly Hills, CA: Sage.

Flor, H., Haag, G., & Turl, D. C. (1986). Long term efficacy of EMG biofeedback for chronic rheumatic back pain. *Pain, 27,* 195–202.

Flynn, J. R. (1987). Massive IQ gains in 14 nations: What IQ tests really measure? *Psychological Bulletin, 101,* 171–191.

Foa, E., & Meadows, E. A. (1997). Psychosocial treatments for posttraumatic stress disorder. A critical review. *Annual Review of Psychology, 48,* 449–480.

Foa, E. B., & Meadows, E. A. (1997). Psychosocial treatments for posttraumatic stress disorder: A critical review. *Annual Review, 48,* 449–480.

Fodor, J. (1983). *The modularity of mind.* Cambridge, MA: MIT.

Fogel, A., Melson, G. F., & Mistry, J. (1986). Conceptualizing the determinants of nurturance: A reassessment of sex differences in nurturance. In A. Fogal & G. F. Melson (Eds.), *Origins of nurtuance.* Hillsdale, NJ: Erlbaum.

Fonagy, P., & Moran, G. S. (1990). Studies on the efficacy of child psychoanalysis. *Journal of Consulting and Clinical Psychology, 58,* 684–695.

Fonagy, P., Steele, H., & Steele, M. (1991). Maternal representations of attachment during pregnancy predict the organization of infant-mother attachment at one year of age. *Child Development, 62,* 891–905.

Fong, G. T., & Nisbett, R. E. (1991). Immediate and delayed transfer of training effects in statistical reasoning. *Journal of Experimental Psychology: General, 120,* 34–45.

Ford, M. (1979). The construct validity of egocentrism. *Psychological Bulletin, 86,* 1169–1188.

Foreyt, J. P. (1987). Issues in the assessment and treatment of obesity. *Journal of Consulting and Clinical Psychology, 55,* 677–684.

Forgas, J. P. (1995). Mood and judgment: The affect infusion model (AIM). *Psychological Bulletin, 117,* 39–66.

Foster, G. (1965). Peasant society and the image of limited good. *American Anthropologist, 67,* 293–315.

Fouts, R. S., Hirsch, A. D., & Fouts, D. H. (1982). Cultural transmission of a human language in a chimpanzee mother-infant relationship. In H. E. Fitzgerald, J. A. Mullins, & P. Gage (Eds.), *Child Nurturance,* Vol. 3. New York: Plenum Press.

Fowles, D. C. (1992). Schizophrenia: Diathesis-stress revisited. *Annual Review of Psychology, 43,* 303–336.

Fox, N. (1991). Hemispheric specialization and attachment behaviors: Developmental processes and individual differences in separation protest. In J. Gewirtz & W. Kurtines (Eds.), *Intersections with attachment* (pp. 147–164). Hillsdale, NJ: Erlbaum.

Fox, N. (1991). If it's not left, it's right: Electroencephalograph asymmetry and the development of emotion. *American Psychologist, 46,* 863–872.

Fox, N. A., Rubin, K. H., Calkins, S. D., Marshall, T. R., Coplan, R. J., Porges, S. W., et al. (1995). Frontal activation asymmetry and social competence at four years of age. *Child Development, 66,* 1770–1784.

Foxx, R. M., & Faw, G. (1992). An eight-year followup of three social skills training studies. *Mental Retardation, 30,* 63–66.

Fozard, J. (1990). Vision and hearing in aging. In J. Birren & K. W. Schaie (Eds.), *Handbook of the psychology of aging.* (3rd ed.). New York: Academic Press.

Fraiberg, S. (1975). The development of human attachments in infants blind from birth. *Merrill-Palmer Quarterly, 21,* 315–334.

Frances, A., Widiger, T., First, M. B., & Pincus, H. (1991). DSM-IV: Toward a more empirical diagnostic system. *Canadian Psychology, 32,* 171–173.

Frank, E., Anderson, B., Reynolds, C. F., Ritenour, A., & Kupfer, D. J. (1994). Life events and the research diagnostic criteria endogenous subtype: A confirmation of the distinction using the Bedford College methods. *Archives of General Psychiatry, 51,* 519–524.

Frank, R. (1997). Nonverbal communication and the emergence of moral sentiments. In U. C. Segerstrale, & P. Molnar (Eds.), *Nonverbal communication: Where nature meets culture* (pp. 275–292). New Jersey: Lawrence Erlbaum Associates, Inc.

Frankel, F. H. (1984). Electroconvulsive therapy. In American Psychiatric Commission on Psychiatric Therapies, *The psychiatric therapies.* Washington, DC: American Psychiatric Association.

Frankl, V. (1959). *Man's search for meaning: An introduction to logotherapy.* New York: Pocket Books.

Franklin, J., Donohew, L., Dhoundiyal, V., & Cook, P. L. (1988). Attention and our

recent past: The scaly thumb of the reptile. *American Behavioral Scientist, 31,* 312–326.

Franz, C., McClelland, D., & Weinberger, J. (1991). Childhood antecedents of conventional social accomplishment in midlife adults: A 36-year prospective study. *Journal of Personality and Social Psychology, 60,* 586–595.

Frederiksen, N., Glaser, R., & Lesgold, A. (Eds.). *Diagnostic monitoring of skill and knowledge acquisition.* Hillsdale, NJ: Erlbaum.

Freedman, J. L., & Fraser, S. C. (1966). Compliance without pressure: The foot-in-the-door technique. *Journal of Personality and Social Psychology, 4,* 195–202.

Freeman, W. (1959). Psychosurgery. In S. Aneti (Ed.), *American handbook of psychiatry II.* New York: Basic Books.

Freud, A. (1936). *The ego and the mechanisms of defense.* New York: International Universities Press.

Freud, A. (1958). Adolescence, *Psychoanalytic study of the child, 13,* 255–278.

Freud, S. (1895). Project for a scientific psychology. *In the standard edition of the complete psychological works of Sigmund Freud.* J. Strachey (Ed.), Vol. 1. London: Hogarth Press, 1966.

Freud, S. (1900). *The interpretation of dreams.* New York: Avon, 1965.

Freud, S. (1905). *Three contributions to the theory of sexuality.* New York: E. P. Dutton, 1962.

Freud, S. (1912). The dynamics of transference. In J. Strachey (Ed. & Trans.), *The standard edition of the complete psychological works of Sigmund Freud,* Vol. 12 (pp. 97–108). London: Hogarth, 1958.

Freud, S. (1915). The unconscious. In P. Rieff (Ed.), *Freud: General psychological theory.* New York: Collier, 1963.

Freud, S. (1917). Mourning and melancholia. In P. Reiff (Ed.), *Freud: General psychological theory.* New York: Collier, 1963.

Freud, S. (1922). Certain neurotic mechanisms in jealousy, paranoia, and homosexuality. In J. Strachey (Ed. & Trans.), *The standard edition of the complete psychological works of Sigmund Freud,* Vol. 1, London: Hogarth Press, 1966.

Freud, S. (1923). *The ego and the id.* New York: W. W. Norton.

Freud, S. (1925). An autobiographical study. J. Strachey (Ed. & Trans.), *The standard edition of the complete psychological works of Sigmund Freud,* Vol. 20. London: Hogarth Press, 1952.

Freud, S. (1933). *New introductory lectures on psychoanalysis.* New York: W. W. Norton, 1965.

Freyd, J. J. (1994). Circling creativity. *Psychological Science, 5,* 122–126.

Frick, R. W. (1985). Communicating emotion: The role of prosodic features. *Psychological Bulletin, 97,* 412–429.

Fried, C. B., & Aronson, E. (1995). Hypocrisy, misattribution, and dissonance reduction. *Personality & Social Psychology Bulletin, 21,* 925–933.

Fried, P. A. (1995). The Ottawa Prenatal Prospective Study (OPPS): Methodological issues and findings: It's easy to throw the baby out with the bath water. Special Issue: 1994 International Symposium on Cannabis and the Cannabinoids: Developmental effects. *Life Sciences, 56,* 2159–2168.

Friedman, H. R., & Goldman-Rakic, P. (1994). Coactivation of prefrontal cortex and inferior parietal cortex in working memory tasks revealed by 2DG functional mapping in the rhesus monkey. *Journal of Neuroscience, 14,* 2775–2788.

Friedman, M., & Rosenman, R. H. (1959). Association of specific overt behavior pattern with blood and cardiovascular findings—blood cholesterol level, blood clotting time, incidence of arcus senilis, and clinical coronary heart disease. *Journal of the American Medical Association, 162,* 1286–1296.

Friedman, M. A., & Brownell, K. D. (1995). Psychological correlates of obesity: Moving to the next research generation. *Psychological Bulletin, 117,* 3–20.

Friedman, R. C., & Stern, L. O. (1980). Juvenile aggressivity and sissiness in homosexual and heterosexual males. *Journal of American Academy of Psychoanalysis, 8,* 427–440.

Frieze, I. H., & Browne, A. (1989). Violence in marriage. In L. Ohlin & M. Tonry (Eds.), *Family violence.* Chicago: University of Chicago Press.

Frisch, R. E., Wyshak, G., & Vincent, L. (1980). Delayed menarch and amenorrhea of ballet dancers. *New England Journal of Medicine, 303,* 17–19.

Frith, C., & Dolan, R. (1996). The role of the prefrontal cortex in higher cognitive functions. *Cognitive Brain Research, 5,* 175–181.

Frock, J., & Money, J. (1992). Sexuality and the menopause. *Psychotherapy and Psychosomatics, 57,* 29–33.

Fromkin, V., Krashen, S., Curtiss, S., Rigler, D., & Rigler, M. (1974). The development of language in Genie: A case of language acquisition beyond the critical period. *Brain and Language, 1,* 81–107.

Fromm, E. (1947). *Man for himself: An inquiry into the psychology of ethics.* New York: Holt, Rinehart & Winston.

Fromm, E. (1955). *The sane society.* Greenwich, CT: Fawcett Books.

Frustaci, J. (1988). A survey of agoraphobics in self-help groups. *Smith College Studies in Social Work, 58,* 193–211.

Fry, A. F., & Hale, S. (1996). Processing speed, working memory, and fluid intelligence: Evidence for a developmental cascade. *Psychologial Science, 7,* 237–241.

Fukuda, T., Kanada, K., & Saito, S. (1990). An ergonomic evaluation of lens accommodation related to visual circumstances. *Ergonomics, 33,* 811–831.

Fukunishi, I., Maeda, K., Kubota, M., & Tomino, Y. (1997). Association of alexithymia with low utilization and perception on a measure of social support in patients on peritoneal dialysis. *Psychological Reports, 80,* 127–130.

Fuller, J. L., & Thompson, W. R. (1978). *Foundations of behavior genetics.* New York: John Wiley.

Funder, D., & Colvin, C. R. (1991). Explorations in behavioral consistency: Properties of persons, situations, and behaviors. *Journal of Personality and Social Psychology, 60,* 773–794.

Furman, W., & Buhrmester, D. (1992). Age and sex differences in perceptions of networks of personal relationships. *Child Development, 63,* 103–115.

Fussell, S. R., & Krauss, R. M. (1992). Coordination of knowledge in communication: Effects of speakers' assumptions about what others know. *Journal of Personality and Social Psychology, 62,* 378–391.

Fuster, J. (1989). *The prefrontal cortex.* (2nd ed.) New York: Raven.

Fyer, A. J., Mannuzza, S., Chapman, T. F., Martin, L. Y., & Klein, D. F. (1995). Specificity in familial aggregation of phobic disorders. *Archives of General Psychiatry, 52,* 564–573.

Gabbard, G. (1992). Psychodynamic psychiatry in the "decade of the brain." *American Journal of Psychiatry, 149,* 991–998.

Gabbay, F. (1992). Behavior-genetic strategies in the study of emotion. *Psychological Science, 3,* 50–55.

Gabrieli, J. D. E. (1998). Cognitive neuroscience of human memory. *Annual Review of Psychology, 49,* 87–115.

Gabrieli, J. D., Desmond, J. E., Demb, J. B., Wagner, A. D., Stone, M. V., Vaidya, C. J., & Glover, G. H. (1996). Functional magnetic resonance imaging of semantic memory processes in the frontal lobes. *Psychological Science, 7,* 278–283.

Gackenbach, J., & Bosveld, J. (1989). Take control of your dreams. *Psychology Today,* 27–32.

Gadow, K., & Sprafkin, J. (1993). Television violence and children with emotional and behavioral disorders. *Journal of Emotional and Behavioral Disorders, 1,* 54–63.

Gaertner, S., Mann, J., Dovidio, J., Murrell, A., & Pomare, M. (1990). How does cooperation reduce intergroup bias? *Journal of Personality and Social Psychology, 59,* 692–704.

Gagnon, J., & Simon, W. (1973). *Sexual conduct.* Chicago: Aldine.

Gamsa, A. (1990). Is emotional disturbance a precipitator or a consequence of chronic pain? *Pain, 42,* 183–195.

Ganley, R. (1989). Emotion and eating in obesity: A view of the literature. *International Journal of Eating Disorders, 8,* 343–361.

Gannon, P. J., Holloway, R. L., Broadfield, D. C., & Braun, A. R. (1998). Asymmetry of chimpanzee planum temporale: Humanlike pattern of Wernicke's brain language, area homolog. *Science, 279,* 220–222.

Gao, J-H, Parsons, L. M., Bower, J. M., Xiong, J., & Fox, P. (1996). Cerebellum implicated in sensory acquisition and discrimination rather than motor control. *Science, 272,* 545–547.

Garb, H. N. (1984). The incremental validity of information used in personality assessment. *Clinical Psychological Review, 40,* 641–655.

Garbarino, J., & Kostelny, K. (1996). The effects of political violence on Palestinian children's behavior problems: A risk accumulation model. *Child Development, 67,* 33–43.

Garcia, J. (1979). I.Q.: The conspiracy. In J. B. Maas (Ed.), *Readings in psychology today* (pp. 198–202) (4th ed.). New York: Random House.

Garcia, J., & Garcia y Robertson, R. (1985). Evolution of learning mechanisms. In B. L. Hammonds (Ed.), *The Master Lecture Series,* Vol. 4. Washington, DC: American Psychological Association.

Garcia, J., & Koelling, R. (1966). Relation of cue to consequence in avoidance learning. *Psychonomic Science, 4,* 123–124.

Garcia, J., Lasiter, P., Bermudez-Rattoni, & Deems, D. (1985). A general theory of aversion learning. *Annals of the New York Academy of Sciences, 443,* 8–21.

Gardner, B. T., & Gardner, R. A. (1975). Evidence for sentence constituents in the early utterances of child and chimpanzee. *Journal of Experimental Psychology: General, 104,* 244–267.

Gardner, H. (1975). *The shattered mind.* New York: Alfred A. Knopf.

Gardner, H. (1983). *Frames of mind: The theory of multiple intelligences.* New York: Basic Books.

Gardner, H. (1985). *The mind's new science: A history of the cognitive revolution.* New York: Basicbooks, Inc.

Garn, S. M. (1980). Human growth. *Annual Review of Anthropology, 9,* 275–292.

Garner, D. M., & Wooley, S. (1991). Confronting the failure of behavioral and dietary treatments for obesity. *Clinical Psychology Review, 11,* 729–780.

Garrison, R. J., & Castelli, W. P. (1985). Weight and thirty-year mortality of men in the Framingham study. *Annals of Internal Medicine, 103,* 1006–1009.

Garrow, J. S., & Warwick, P. M. (1978). Diet and obesity. In J. Yudkin, (Ed.), *The Diet of Man: Needs and Wants.* Barking: Applied Science Pub., 127–144.

Garver, D. L. (1997). The etiologic heterogeneity of schizophrenia. *Harvard Review of Psychiatry, 4,* 317–327.

Gauthier, J. G., Ivers, H., & Carrier, S. (1996). Nonpharmacological approaches in the management of recurrent headache disorders and their comparison and combination with pharmacotherapy. *Clinical Psychology Review, 16,* 543–571.

Gazzaniga, M. (1967). The split brain in man. *Scientific American, 217,* 24–29.

Gazzaniga M. (Ed.), (1996). *The cognitive neurosciences* (pp. 855–870). Cambridge: MIT Press.

Ge, X., Conger, R. D., & Elder, G. (1996). Coming of age too early: Pubertal influences on girls' vulnerability to psychological distress. *Child Development, 67,* 3386–3400.

Geary, D. C., Rumsey, M., Bow-Thomas, C. C., & Hoard, M. K. (1995). Sexual jealousy as a facultative trait: Evidence from the pattern of sex differences in adults from China and the United States. *Ethology & Sociobiology, 16,* 355–383.

Gebhard, P. H. (1971). Human sexual behavior: A summary statement. In D. S. Marshall, & R. C. Suggs, (Eds.) *Human Sexual Behavior: Variations in the Ethnographic Spectrum.* New York: Basic Books.

Geen, R. (1990). *Human aggression.* Pacific Grove, CA: Brooks–Cole.

Geen, R. G. (1985). Human motivation: New perspectives on old problems. In V. P. Makosky, (Ed.), *G. Stanley Hall Lecture Series, 6.* Washington, DC: American Psychological Association.

Geen, R. G. (1995). Human aggression. In A. Tesser (Ed.), *Advanced social psychology.* New York: McGraw-Hill.

Geen, R. G. (1998). Aggression and antisocial behavior. In D. T. Gilbert & S. T. Fiske, et al. (Eds.), *The handbook of social psychology, Vol. 2* (4th ed.). (pp. 317–356). Boston: McGraw-Hill.

Geertz, C. (1963). The integrative revolution: Primordial sentiments and civil politics in the new states. In C. Geertz (Ed.), *Old societies and new states.* New York: Free Press.

Geertz, C. (1973). *The interpretation of cultures.* New York: Basic Books.

Geertz, C. (1974). From the natives' point of view. *American Academy of Arts and Sciences Bulletin, 28,* 26–43.

Geis, F. (1978). Machiavellianism. In H. London and J. E. Exner (Eds.), *Dimensions of personality.* New York: Wiley.

Geiselman, R. E., Fisher, R. P., MacKinnon, D. P., & Holland, H. L. (1985). Eyewitness memory enhancement in the police interview: Cognitive retrieval mnemonics versus hypnosis. *Journal of Applied Psychology, 70,* 401–412.

Geldard, G. A. (1972). *The human senses.* (2nd ed.). New York: Wiley.

Gelfin, Y., Gorfine, M., & Lerer, B. (1998). Effect of clinical dose of Fluoxetine on psychological variables in healthy volunteers. *American Journal of Psychiatry, 155,* 290–292.

Gelinas, D. J. (1983). The persisting negative effects of incest. *Psychiatry, 46,* 312–332.

Gelman, R., & Baillargeon, R. (1983). A review of Piagetian concepts. In J. H. Flavell & E. M. Markman (Eds.), *Handbook of child psychology: Cognitive development* (Vol. 3). New York: John Wiley.

Gentner, D., & Holyoak, K. J. (1997). Reasoning and learning by analogy: Introduction. *American Psychologist, 52,* 32–34.

Gentner, D., & Markman, A. B. (1997). Structure mapping in analogy and similarity. *American Psychologist, 52,* 45–46.

Geoghehan, W. H. (1976). Polytypy in folk biological taxonomies. *American Ethnologist, 3,* 469–480.

Gerald, C., Walker, M. W., Criscione, L., Gustafson, E. L., et al. (1991). A receptor subtype involved in neuropeptide-Y-induced food intake. *Nature, 382,* 168–171.

Gerken, L., & McIntosh, B. J. (1993). Interplay of function morphemes and prosody in early language. *Developmental Psychology, 29,* 448–457.

Gershkoff-Stowe, L. Thal, D., Smith, L. J., & Namy, L. (1997). Categorization and its developmental relation to early language. *Child Development, 68,* 843–859.

Gershon, S., & Soares, J. C. (1997). Current Therapeutic Profile of Lithium. *Archives of General Psychiatry, 54,* 16–20.

Gerstner, C., & Day, D. V. (1994). Cross-cultural comparison of leadership prototypes. *Leadership Quarterly, 5,* 121–134.

Gest, S. D. (1997). Behavioral inhibition: Stability and associations with adaptation from childhood to early adulthood. *Journal of Personality and Social Psychology, 72,* 467–475.

Gibbs, R. W., Jr. (1981). Your wish is my command: Convention and context in interpreting indirect requests. *Journal of Verbal Learning and Verbal Behavior, 20,* 431–444.

Gibson, E. J. (1984). Perceptual development from the ecological approach. In M. E. Lamb, A. L. Brown, & B. Rogoff, *Advances in developmental psychology, Vol. 3.*

Gibson, E. J., & Walk, R. D. (1960). The "visual cliff." *Scientific American, 202,* 64–71.

Gibson, H. B. (1996). Sexual functioning in later life. In R. T. Woods, et al. (Eds.), *Handbook of the clinical psychology of ageing.* (pp. 183–193). Chichester, UK: John Wiley & Sons.

Gibson, J. J. (1966). *The senses considered as perceptual systems.* Boston: Houghton Mifflin.

Gibson, J. J. (1979). *The ecological approach to visual perception.* Boston: Houghton Mifflin.

Gigerenzer, G., & Goldstein, D. G. (1996). Reasoning the fast and frugal way: Models of bounded rationality. *Psychological Review, 103,* 650–669.

Gilbert, D. (1989). Thinking lightly about others: Automatic components of the social inference process. In J. S. Uleman & J. A. Bargh (1989), *Unintended thought* (pp. 189–211). New York: Guilford Press.

Gilbert, D., Pelham, B., & Krull, D. (1988). On cognitive busyness: When person perceivers meet persons perceived. *Journal of Personality and Social Psychology, 54,* 733–740.

Gilbert, P. L., Harris, M. J., McAdams, L. A., & Jeste, D. V. (1995). Neuroleptic withdrawal in schizophrenic patients: A review of the literature. *Archives of General Psychiatry, 52,* 173–188.

Gilert, D. T., & Malone, P. S. (1995). The correspondence bias. *Psychological Bulletin, 117,* 21–38.

Gilhooly, K. J. (1989). Human and machine problem solving: Toward a comparative cognitive science. In K. J. Gilhooly (Ed.), *Human and machine problem solving.* New York: Plenum Press.

Gill, M. (1982). *The analysis of transference.* Vol. 1. *Theory and technique. Psychological Issues, Monograph,* No. 53.

Gilligan, C. (1982). *In a different voice.* Cambridge, MA: Harvard University Press.

Gilligan, J. (1996). Exploring shame in special settings: A psychotherapeutic study. In C. Cordess, M. Cox, et al. (Eds.), *Forensic psychotherapy: Crime, psychodynamics and the offender patient,*

Vol. 2: Mainly practice. Forensic focus series, No. 1. (pp. 475–489). London, England UK: Jessica Kingsley Publishers, Ltd.

Gilligan, S., & Bower, G. (1984). Cognitive consequences of emotional arousal. In C. E. Izard, J. Kagan, & R. B. Zajonc (Eds.), *Emotion, cognition, and behavior* (pp. 547–588). Cambridge: Cambridge University Press.

Gitlin, M. J., & Altshuler, L. L. (1997). Unanswered Questions, Unknown Future for One of Our Oldest Medications. *Archives of General Psychiatry, 54,* 21–23.

Gladue, B. A., Green, R., & Hellman, R. E. (1984). Neuroendocrine response to estrogen and sexual orientation. *Science, 225,* 1496–1499.

Gladwin, T. (1970). *East is a big bird.* Cambridge, MA: Belknap Press.

Glassman, J. B., Burkhart, B. R., Grant, R. D., & Vallery, G. G. (1978). Density, expectation, and extended task performance: An experiment in the natural environment. *Environment and Behavior, 10,* 299–316.

Glassman, N., & Andersen, S. (1997). Activating transference without consciousness: Using significant-other representations to go beyond the subliminally given information. Unpublished manuscript, Department of Psychology, New York University.

Gleitman, L. R., Gleitman, H., Landau, B., & Warner, E. (1988). Where learning begins: Initial representations for language learning. In F. Newmeyer (Ed.), *Linguistics: The Cambridge survey.* Vol. III. *Language: Psychological and biological aspects.* Cambridge: Cambridge University Press.

Gluck, M. A., & Myers, C. E. (1997). Psychobiological models of hippocampal function in learning and memory. *Annual Review, 48,* 481–514.

Godden, D. R., & Baddeley, A. D. (1975). Context-dependent memory in two natural environments: On land and underwater. *British Journal of Psychology, 66,* 325–331.

Gold, J. M., Carpenter, C., Randolph, C., Goldberg, T. E., Weinberger, D. E. (1997). Auditory Working Memory and Wisconsin Card Sorting Test Performance in Schizophrenia. *Archives of General Psychiatry, 54,* 159–165.

Gold, M. S., & Pearsall, H. R. (1983). Hypothyroidism—or is it depression? *Psychosomatics, 24,* 646–656.

Gold, S. N., Hughes, D., & Hohnecker, L. (1994). Degree of repression of sexual abuse memories. *American Psychologist, 49,* 441.

Goldberg, L. R. (1981). Language and individual differences: The search for universals in personality lexicons. In L. Wheeler (Ed.), *Review of Personality and Social Psychology,* Beverly Hills, CA: Sage Publications.

Goldberg, L. R. (1993). The structure of phenotypic personality traits. *American Psychologist, 48,* 26–34.

Goldberg, W. A., Greenberger, E., & Nagel, S. K. (1996). Employment and achievement: Mothers' work involvement in relation to children's achievement behaviors and mothers' parenting behaviors. *Child Development, 67,* 1512–1527.

Golden, R. M., & Rumelhart, D. E. (1993). A parallel distributed processing model of story comprehension and recall. *Discourse Processes, 16,* 203–237.

Goldfield, B. A., & Snow, C. E. (1989). Individual differences in language acquisition. In J. Berko Gleason (Ed.), *The development of language.* (2nd ed.). Columbus, OH: Merrill.

Goldfried, M., & Davison, G. (1994). *Clinical behavior therapy.* (2nd ed.). New York: Holt, Rinehart & Winston.

Goldfried, M. R., Castonguay, L. G., Hayes, A. M., Drozd, J. F., & Shapiro, D. A. (1997). A comparative analysis of the therapeutic focus in cognitive-behavioral and psychodynamic-interpersonal sessions. *Journal of Consulting and Clinical Psychology, 65,* 740–748.

Goldfried, M. R., & Wolfe, B. E. (1998). Toward a more clinically valid approach to therapy research. *Journal of Consulting & Clinical Psychology, 66,* 143–150.

Goldin-Meadow, S., & Mylander, C. (1984). Gestural communication in deaf children: The effects and noneffects of parental input on early language development. *Monographs of the Society for Research in Child Development, 49,* 1–121.

Goldin-Meadow, S., & Mylander, C. (1998). Spontaneous sign systems created by deaf children in two cultures. *Nature, 391,* 279–281.

Goldman-Rakic, P. (1995). Cellular basis of working memory. *Neuron, 14,* 477–485.

Goldman-Rakic, P. (1996). Regional and cellular fractionation of working memory. *Proceedings of the National Academy of Sciences, 93,* 13473–13476.

Goldsmith, H. H., & Alansky, J. A. (1987). Maternal and infant temperamental predictors of attachment: A meta-analytic review. *Journal of Consulting and Clinical Psychology, 55,* 805–816.

Goldsmith, H. H., & Harman, C. (1994). Temperament and attachment: Individuals and relationships. *Current Directions in Psychological Science, 3,* 53–57.

Goldsmith, S. K., Shapiro, R. M., & Joyce, J. N. (1997). Disrupted Pattern of D2 Dopamine Receptors in the Temporal Lobe in Schizophrenia: A Postmortem Study. *Archives of General Psychiatry, 54,* 649–658.

Goldstein, A. J., & Chambless, D. J. (1978). A reanalysis of agoraphobia. *Behavior Therapy, 9,* 47–59.

Goldstein, M. J. (1988). The family and psychopathology. *Annual Review of Psychology, 39,* 283–299.

Goldstein, R. B., Wickramaratne, P. J., Horwath, E., & Weissman, M. M. (1997). Familial Aggregation and Phenomenology of 'Early'-Onset (at or Before Age 20 Years) Panic Disorder. *Archives of General Psychiatry, 54,* 271–278.

Goleman, D. (1995). *Emotional intelligence.* New York: Bantam Books, Inc.

Golomb, A., Ludolph, P., Westen, D., Block, M. J., et al. (1994). Maternal empathy, family chaos, and the etiology of borderline personality disorder. *Journal of the American Psychoanalytic Association, 42,* 525–548.

Gong-Guy, E. Cravens, R., & Patterson, T. E. (1991). Clinical issues in mental health service delivery to refugees. *American Psychologist, 46,* 642–648.

Good, B. J., & Kleinman, A. M. (1985). Culture and anxiety: Cross-cultural evidence for the patterning of anxiety disorders. In A. Tuma, J. D. Maser, et al. (Eds.), *Anxiety and the anxiety disorders.* (pp. 297–323). Hillsdale, NJ: Lawrence Erlbaum Associates, Inc.

Goodman, L., Koss, M., Fitzgerald, L., Russo, N., & Keita, G. (1993). Male violence against women: Current research and future directions. *American Psychologist, 48,* 1054–1058.

Goodman, L., Saxe, L., & Harvey, M. (1991). Homelessness as psychological trauma: Broadening perspectives. *American Psychologist, 46,* 1219–1225.

Goodman, W. K., Price, L., Delgado, P., Palumbo, J., Krystal, J., Nagy, L., Rasmussen, S., Heninger, G., & Charney, D. (1990). Specificity of serotonin reuptake inhibitors in the treatment of obsessive-compulsive disorder. *Archives of General Psychiatry, 47,* 577–585.

Goodnow, J. J. (1976). The nature of intelligent behavior: Questions raised by cross-cultural studies. In L. B. Resnick (Ed.), *The nature of intelligence* (pp. 169–188). Hillsdale, NJ: Erlbaum.

Goodwin, F. K., & Ghaemi, S. N. (1998). Understanding manic-depressive illness. *Archives of General Psychiatry, 55,* 23–25.

Goodwin, F. K., & Roy-Byrne, P. (1987). Treatment of bipolar disorders. In A. J. Frances and R. E. Hales (Eds.), *Psychiatric Update Annual Review,* Vol. 6.

Goody, J. (1977). *The domestication of the savage mind.* Cambridge University Press.

Gopnik, A. (1993). How we know our minds: The illusion of first-person intentionality. *Behavioral and Brain Sciences, 16,* 1–14.

Gordis, E. (1996). Alcohol research: At the cutting edge. *Archives of General Psychiatry, 53,* 199–201.

Gordon, M., & Shankweiler, P. J. (1971). Different equals less: Female sexuality in recent marriage manuals. *Journal of Marriage and the Family, 33,* 459–466.

Gordon, P. (1990). Learnability and feedback. *Developmental Psychology, 26,* 217–220.

Gorski, R. A., & Barraclough, C. A. (1963). Effects of low dosages of androgen on the differentiation of hypothalamic regulatory control of ovulation in the rat. *Endocrinology, 73,* 210–216.

Gortner, E. T., Gollan, J. K., Dobson, K. S., & Jacobson, N. S. (1998). Cognitive-behavioral treatment for depression: Relapse prevention. *Journal of Consulting & Clinical Psychology, 66,* 377–384.

Goschke, T., & Kuhl, J. (1993). Representations of intentions: Persisting activation in memory. *Journal of Experimental Psychology: Learning, Memory, and Cognition, 19,* 1211–1226.

Gotlib, I. H. (1993). Depressive disorders. In A. S. Bellack, M. Hersen, et al. (Eds.), *Psychopathology in adulthood.* (pp. 179–194). Boston: Allyn & Bacon, Inc.

Goto, H. (1971). Auditory perception by normal Japanese adults of the sounds "I" and "r." *Neuropsychologia, 9,* 317–323.

Gottesman, I. I. (1991). *Schizophrenia genesis: The origins of madness.* New York: W. H. Freeman & Co.

Gottesman, I. I., & Bertelsen, A. (1989). Confirming unexpressed genotypes for schizophrenia: Risks in the offspring of Fischer's Danish identical and fraternal discordant twins. *Archives of General Psychiatry, 50,* 527–540.

Gottlieb, G. (1991). Experiential canalization of behavioral development: Theory. *Developmental Psychology, 27,* 4–13.

Gottlieb, G. (1991). Experimental canalization of behavioral development: Theory. *Developmental Pshchology, 27,* 4–13.

Gottlieb, J. (1990). Mainstreaming and quality education. *American Journal on Mental Retardation, 95,* 16–17.

Gottman, J. (1998). Psychology and the study of marital processes. *Annual Review of Psychology, 49,* 169–197.

Gottman, J. M. (1998). Psychology and the study of the marital processes. *Annual Review of Psychology, 49,* 169–197.

Gould, E., Tanapat, P., McEwen, B. S., Flugge, G., & Fuchs, E. (1998). Proliferation of granule cell precursors in the dentate gyrus of adult monkeys is diminished by stress. *Proceedings of the National Academy of Sciences, 95,* 3168–3171.

Gould, S. J. (1981). *The mismeasure of man.* New York: W. W. Norton.

Gove, W. (1982). Labeling theory's explanation of mental illness: An update of recent evidence. *Deviant Behavior, 3,* 307–327.

Grabowski, J., & VandenBos, G. (1992). *Psychopharmacology: Basic mechanisms and applied interventions.* Washington, DC: American Psychological Association.

Gracely, R., Lynch, S., & Bennett, G. J. (1992). Painful neuropathy: Altered central processing maintained dynamically by peripheral input. *Pain, 51,* 175–194.

Graesser, A. C., Millis, K. K., & Zwaan, R. (1997). Discourse comprehension. *Annual Review of Psychology, 48,* 163–189.

Graf, P., & Schacter, D. L. (1987). Selective effects of interference on implicit and explicit memory for new associations. *Journal of Experimental Psychology: Learning, Memory, & Cognition, 13,* 45–53.

Graf, R. G., & Riddell, J. C. (1972). Helping behavior as a function of interpersonal perception, *Journal of Social Psychology, 86,* 227–231.

Granholm, E., Morris, S. K., Sarkin, A. J., Asarnow, R. F., & Jeste, D. V. (1997). Pupillary responses index overload of working memory resources in schizophrenia. *Journal of Abnormal Psychology, 106,* 458–467.

Grattan, L., & Eslinger, P. (1991). Frontal lobe damage in children and adults: A comparative review. *Developmental Neuropsychology, 7,* 283–326.

Gray, J. A. (1987). *The psychology of fear and stress.* (2nd ed.). New York: Cambridge Univesity Press.

Gray, J. A. (1990). Brain systems that mediate both emotion and cognition. *Cognition and Emotion, 4,* 269–288.

Graziadei, P. P. C. (1969). The ultra-structure of vertebrate taste buds. In C. Pfaffman (Ed.), *Olfaction and taste,* Vol. 3. New York: Rockefeller University Press.

Green, L., & Freed, D. E. (1993). The substitutability of reinforcers. *Journal of the Experimental Analysis of Behavior, 60,* 141–158.

Green, M. A., & Curtis, G. C. (1988). Personality disorders in panic patients: Response to termination of antipanic medication. *Journal of Personality Disorders, 2,* 303–314.

Green, M. F., Nuechterlein, K. H., Breitmeyer, B, (1997). Backward masking performance in unaffected siblings of schizophrenic patients: Evidence for a vulnerability indicator. *Archives of General Psychiatry, 54,* 465–472.

Green, R. (1987). *The 'sissy boy' syndrome and the development of homosexuality.* New Haven, CT: Yale University Press.

Greenberg, C., & Powers, S. M. (1987). Memory improvement among adult learners. *Educational Gerontology, 13,* 263–280.

Greenberg, J. (1977). The brain and emotions: Crossing a new frontier. *Science News, 112,* 74–75.

Greenberg, J., Pyszczynski, T., Solomon, S., Rosenblatt, A., Veeder, M., Kirkland, S., & Lyon, D. (1990). Evidence for terror management theory II: The effects of mortality salience on reactions to those who threaten or bolster the cultural worldview. *Journal of Personality and Social Psychology, 58,* 308–318.

Greenberg, J., Pyszczynski, T., Solomon, S., Simon, L., et al. (1994). Role of consciousness and accessibility of death-related thoughts in mortality salience effects. *Journal of Personality & Social Psychology, 67,* 627–637.

Greenberg, R. P., Bornstein, R. F., Greenberg, M. D., & Fisher, S. (1992). A meta-analysis of antidepressant outcome under "blinder" conditions. *Journal of Consulting & Clinical Psychology, 60,* 664–669.

Greeno, C. G., & Wing, R. R. (1994). Stress-induced eating. *Psychological Bulletin, 115,* 444–464.

Greeno, J. G. (1978). Natures of problem-solving abilities. In W. K. Estes (Ed.), *Handbook of Learning and Cognitive Processes,* Vol. 5. Hillsdale, NJ: Erlbaum.

Greenough, W., Black, J., & Wallace, C. (1987). Experience and brain development. *Child Development, 58,* 539–559.

Greenough, W. T. (1991). Experience as a component of normal development: Evolutionary considerations. *Developmental Psychology, 27,* 14–17.

Greenspan, S., and Granfield, M. (1992). Reconsidering the construct of mental retardation: Implications of a model of social competence. *American Journal on Mental Retardation, 96,* 442–453.

Greenwald, A., Pratkanis, A. R., Leippe, M. R., & Baumgardner, M. H. (1986). Under what conditions does theory obstruct research progress? *Psychological Review, 93,* 216–229.

Greenwald, A. G. (1980). The totalitarian ego: Fabrication and revision of personal history. *American Psychologist, 35,* 603–618.

Greenwald, A. G., & Banaji, M. (1995). Implicit social cognition: Attitudes, self-esteem, and stereotypes. *Psychological Review, 102,* 4–27.

Gregory, R. (1970). *The intelligent eye.* New York: McGraw-Hill.

Gregory, R. (1978). *Eye and brain: The psychology of seeing.* (3rd ed.). New York: McGraw-Hill.

Gregory, R. L. (1971). *Eye and brain.* (3rd ed.). New York: McGraw-Hill.

Greist, J. H., Jefferson, J. W., Kobak, K. A., Katzelnick, D. J., & Ierlin, R. C. (1995). Efficacy and tolerability of seratonin transport inhibitors in obsessive compulsive disorder. *Archives of General Psychiatry, 52,* 53–60.

Grencavage, L. M., & Norcross, J. C. (1990). Where are the commonalities among the therapeutic common factors? *Professional Psychology: Research and Practice, 21,* 372–378.

Grice, H. P. (1975). Logic and conversation. In P. Cole & J. L. Morgan (Eds.), *Syntax and semantics: Speech acts* (pp. 41–58). San Diego: Academic Press.

Griffin, D. R. (1959). *Echoes of bats and man.* New York: Anchor Books/Doubleday.

Griffith, D. R., Azuma, S. D., & Chasnoff, I. J. (1994). Three-year outcome of children exposed prenatally to drugs. Special Section: Cocaine babies. *Journal of the American Academy of Child and Adolescent Psychiatry, 33,* 20–27.

Griffith, E. E., Young J. L., & Smith. (1984). An analysis of the therapeutic elements in a Black church service. *Hospital and Community Psychiatry, 35,* 464–469.

Griffitt, W. (1987). Females, males, and sexual responses. In K. Kelley, (Ed.), *Females, males, and sexuality: Theories and research,* Albany: State University of New York Press.

Griggs, R. A., & Cox, J. R. (1982). The elusive thematic-materials effect in Wason's selection task. *British Journal of Psychology, 73,* 407–420.

Grob, C., & Dobkin de Rios, M. (1992). Adolescent drug use in cross-cultural perspective. *Journal of Drug Issues, 22,* 121–138.

Gross, J. J. (1998). Antecedent- and response-focused emotion regulation: Divergent consequences for experience, expression, and physiology. *Journal of Personality & Social Psychology, 74,* 224–237.

Gross, J. J., & Levenson, R. W. (1997). Hiding feelings: The acute effects of inhibiting negative and positive emotion. *Journal of Abnormal Psychology, 106,* 95–103.

Gross, R. T., & Duke, P. M. (1980). The effect of early versus late physical maturation on adolescent behavior. *Pediatric Clinic of North America, 27.*

Group for the Advancement of Psychiatry (GAP) Committee on Alcoholism and the Addictions (1991). Substance abuse disorders: A paychiatric priority. *American Journal of Psychiatry, 148,* 1291–1300.

Grunbaum, A. (1984). *The foundations of psychoanalysis: A philosophical critique.* Berkeley: University of California Press.

Grunewald, K. (1979). Mentally retarded children and young people in Sweden. *Acta Paediatrica Scandinavica,* suppl. 275, no. 75, 75–84.

Grusec, J. E., Goodnow, J. J. (1994). Summing up and looking to the future. *Developmental Psychology, 30,* 29–31.

Guilford, J. P. (1956). The structure of intellect. *Psychological Bulletin, 53,* 267–293.

Gumperz, J. J., & Levinson, S. C. (Eds., 1996). *Rethinking linguistic relativity.* Cambridge, UK: Cambridge University Press.

Gunderson, John G. (1986). Pharmacotherapy for patients with borderline personality disorder. *Archives of General Psychiatry, 43,* 698–700.

Gunnar, M., Larson, M. C., Hertsgaard, L., Harris, M. L., & Brodersen, L. (1992). The stressfulness of separation among nine-month-old infants: Effects of social context variables and infant temperament. *Child Development, 63,* 290–303.

Gunter, B., & McAleer, J. (1990). *Children and television: The one eyed monster?* London: Routledge.

Gur, R. E., Cowell, P., Turetsky, B. I., Gallacher, F., Cannon, T., Bilker, W., & Gur, R. C. (1998). A follow-up magnetic resonance imaging study of schizophrenia relationship of neuroanatomical changes to clinical and neurobehavioral measures. *Archives of General Psychiatry, 55,* 145–152.

Gurevich, E. V., Bordelon, Y., Shapiro, R. M., Arnold, S. E., Gur, R. E., & Joyce, J. N. (1997). Mesolimbic dopamine D3 receptors and use of antipsychotics in patients with schizophrenia: A postmortem study. *Archives of General Psychiatry, 54,* 225–232.

Gust, D., Gordon, T., Brodie, A., & McClure, H. (1994). Effect of a preferred companion in modulating stress in adult female rhesus monkeys. *Physiology and Behavior, 4,* 681–684.

Gustavson, C. R., Kelly, D. J., Sweeny, M., & Garcia, J. (1976). Prey-lithium aversions: I: Coyotes and wolves. *Behavioral Biology, 17,* 61–72.

Guttman, D. (1974). The country of old men: Cross cultural studies in the psychology of later life. In R. LeVine (Ed.), *Culture and personality: Contemproary readings.* Chicago: Aldine.

Hadley, J. A., Holloway, E. L., & Mallinckrodt, B. (1993). Common aspects of object relations and self-representations in offspring from disparate dysfunctional families. *Journal of Counseling Psychology, 40,* 348–356.

Hafner, R. J., & Roder, M. J. (1987). Agoraphobia and parental bereavement. *Australian and New Zealand Journal of Psychiatry, 21,* 340–344.

Haggerty, J. J., Stern, R., Mason, G., & Beckwith, J. (1993). Subclinical hypothyroidism: A modifiable risk factor for depression? *American Journal of Psychiatry, 150,* 508–510.

Hagman, G. (1995). Mourning: A review and reconsideration. International *Journal of Psycho-Analysis, 76,* 909–925.

Halasz, P. (1993). Arousals without awakening: Dynamic aspect of sleep. *Physiology & Behavior, 54,* 795–802.

Hale, S., Bronik, M., & Fry, A. (1997). Verbal and spatial working memory in school-age children: Differences in susceptibility to interference. *Developmental Psychology, 33,* 364–371.

Haley, J. (1971). Family therapy: A radical change. In J. Haley (Ed.), *Changing families: A family therapy reader.* New York: Grune & Stratton.

Haley, J. (1976). *Problem-solving therapy.* San Francisco: Jossey-Bass.

Halford, G. (1989). Reflections on 25 years of Piagetian cognitive developmental psychology, 1963–1988. *Human Development, 32,* 325–357.

Halford, W., & Hayes, R. (1991). Psychological rehabilitation of chronic schizoprephrenic patients: Recent findings on social skills training and family psychoeducation. *Clinical Psychology Review, 11,* 23–44.

Hall, G. C. N., & Hirschman, R. (1991). Toward a theory of sexual aggression: A quadripartite model, *Journal of Consulting & Clinical Psychology,* 662–669.

Hall, G. S. (1904). *Adolescence: Its psychology and its relations to physiology, anthropology, sociology, sex, crime, religion, and education.* Vols. 1–2: New York: Appleton-Century-Crofts.

Hallowell, A. I. (1955). *Culture and experience.* Philadelphia: University of Pennsylvania Press.

Hallstrom, T. (1973). *Mental disorder and sexuality in the climacteric.* Gotenborg: Scandinavian University Books.

Halmi, K. A., Goldberg, S., & Cunningham, S. (1977). Perceptual distribution of body image in adolescent girls: Distortion of body image in adolescence. *Psychological Medicine, 7,* 253–257.

Hamermesh, D. S., & Biddle, J. E. (1994). Beauty and the labor market. American *Economic Review, 94,* 1174–1195.

Hamilton, D., & Sherman, J. (1994). Stereotypes. In R. S. Wyer, Jr., & T. K. Srull, (Eds.), *Handbook of social cognition,* Vol. 1, *Basic processes,* (pp. 1–68) (2nd ed.). Hillsdale, NJ: Erlbaum.

Hamilton, W. D. (1964). The genetical theory of social behavior. *Journal of Theoretical Biology, 6*, 1–52.

Hammen, C., Burge, D., & Adrian, C. (1991). Timing of mother and child depression in a longitudinal study of children at risk. *Journal of Consulting and Clinical Psychology, 59*, 341–345.

Hammen, C., Ellicott, A., Gitlin, M., & Jamison, K. R. (1989). Sociotropy/autonomy and vulnerability to specific life events in patients with unipolar depression and bipolar disorders. *Journal of Abnormal Psychology, 98*, 154–160.

Hanin, B., Sprour, N., Margolin, J., & Braun, P. (1993). Electroconvulsive therapy in mania: Successful outcome despite short duration of convulsions. *Convulsive Therapy, 9*, 50–53.

Hansen, W. B., & O'Malley, P. M. (1996). Drug use. In R. J. DiClemente, W. B. Hansen, et al. (Eds.), *Handbook of adolescent health risk behavior. Issues in clinical child psychology.* (pp. 161–192). New York: Plenum Press.

Harari, H., Harari, O., & White, R. V. (1985). The reaction to rape by American male bystanders. *Journal of Social Psychology, 125*, 653–658.

Hardin, C. L., & Maffi, L. (eds.). (1997). *Color categories in thought and language.* New York: Cambridge University Press.

Harlow, H. F., & Zimmerman, R. R. (1959). Affectional responses in the infant monkey. *Science, 130*, 421–432.

Harlow, R., & Cantor, N. (1994). Personality as problem solving: A framework for the analysis of change in daily-life behavior. *Journal of Personality Integration, 4*, 355–386.

Harlow, R. E., & Cantor, N. (1996). Still participating after all these years: A study of life task participation in later life. *Journal of Personality and Social Psychology, 71*, 1235–1249.

Harmon-Jones, E., & Allen, J. J. B. (1998). Anger and frontal brain activity: EEG asymmetry consistent with approach motivation despite negative affective valence. *Journal of Personality & Social Psychology, 74*, 1310–1316.

Harris, B. (1979). Whatever happened to little Albert? *American Psychologist, 34*, 151–160.

Harris, C. R., & Christenfeld, N. (1996). Gender, jealousy, and reason. *Psychological Science, 7*, 364–366.

Harris, J. E. (1980). Memory aids people use: Two interview studies. *Memory and Cognition, 8*, 31–38.

Harris, M. B., Walters, L. C., & Waschull, S. (1991). Gender and ethnic differences in obesity-related behaviors and attitudes in a college sample. *Journal of Applied Social Psychology, 21*, 1545–1566.

Harris, Y. H. (1995). *The opportunity for romantic love among hunter-gatherers.* Paper presented at the annual convention of the Human Behavior and Evolution Society, June, Santa Barbara, California.

Hart, B., & Risley, T. (1992). American parenting of language-learning children: Persisting differences in family-child interactions observed in natural home environments. *Developmental Psychology, 28*, 1096–1105.

Harter, S., & Monsour, A. (1992). Development analysis of conflict caused by opposing attributes in the adolescent self-portrait. *Developmental Psychology, 28*, 251–260.

Hartline, H. K. (1938). The response of single optic nerve fibers of the vertebrate eye to illuminate of the retina. *American Journal of Physiology, 121*, 400–415.

Hartman, D. S., & Civelli, O. (1996). Molecular attributes of dopamine receptors: New potential for antipsychotic drug development. *Annals of Medicine, 28*, 211–219.

Hartmann, H. (1939). *Ego psychology and the problem of adaptation.* New York: International Universities Press.

Hartstein, N. B. (1996). Suicide risk in lesbian, gay, and bisexual youth. In R. P. Cabaj, T. S. Stein et al. (Eds.), *Textbook of homosexuality and mental health.* (pp. 819–837). Washington: American Psychiatric Press, Inc.

Hartup, W. (1989). Social relationships and their developmental significance. *American Psychologist, 44*, 120–126.

Hartup, W., & van Lieshout, C. F. M. (1995). Personality development in social context. *Annual Review of Psychology, 46*, 655–687.

Hartup, W. W. (1977). Aggression in childhood: Developmental perspectives. In M. Hertherington and D. Ross (Eds.), *Contemporary readings in child psychology.* New York: McGraw-Hill.

Hartup, W. W. (1996). The company they keep: Friendships and their developmental significance. *Child Development, 67*, 1–13.

Hartup, W. W. (1998). Cooperation, close relationships, and cognitive development. In W. M. Bukowski, A. F. Newcomb, et al. (Eds.), *The company they keep: Friendship in childhood and adolescence. Cambridge studies in social and emotional development.* (pp. 213–237). New York: Cambridge University Press.

Hartup, W. W., & Stevens, N. (1997). Friendships and adaptation in the life course. *Psychological Bulletin, 121*, 355–370.

Harvey J. H., & Weary, G. (1981). *Perspec-* tives on attributional processes. Dubuque, Iowa: William C. Brown.

Harwood, R. L., Schoelmerich, A., Ventura-Cook, E., Schulze, P. A., & Wilson, S. P. (1996). Culture and class influence on Anglo and Puerto Rican mothers' beliefs regarding long-term socialization goals and child behavior. *Child Development, 67*, 2446–2461.

Hasselhorn, M. (1990). The emergence of strategic knowledge activation in categorical clustering during retrieval. *Journal of Experimental Child Psychology, 50*, 59–80.

Hasselquist, D., & Bensch, S. (1991). Trade-off between mate guarding and mate attraction in the polygynous great reed warbler. *Behavioral Ecology and Sociobiology, 28*, 187–193.

Haugtvedt, C., & Petty, R. (1992). Personality and persuasion: Need for cognition moderates the persistence and resistance of attitude changes. *Journal of Personality and Social Psychology, 63*, 308–319.

Hay, D. F., Caplan, M., Castle, J., & Stimson, C. A. (1991). Does sharing become increasinngly 'rational' in the second year of life? *Developmental Psychology, 27*, 987–993.

Hayes, S. C., & Wilson, K. (1994). Acceptance and commitment therapy: Altering the verbal support for experiential avoidance. Special Section: Clinical behavior analysis. *Behavior Analysis, 17*, 289–303.

Hazan, C., & Shaver, P. (1987). Romantic love conceptualized as an attachment process. *Journal of Personality and Social Psychology, 57*, 731–739.

Hazan, C., Shaver, P. (1994). Attachment as an organizational framework for research on close relationships. *Psychological Inquiry, 5*, 1–22.

Hazelwood, R. (1993). Analyzing the rape and profiling the offenders. In R. Hazelwood & A. Burgess (Eds.), *Practical aspects of rape investigation: A multidisciplinary approach.* Boca Raton, FL: CRC Press.

Hazelwood, R., & Harpold, J. (1986). Rape: The dangers of providing confrontational advice. *FBI Law Enforcement Bulletin.*

Hazelwood, R., & Warren, J. (1989). The serial rapist: His characteristics and victims. *FBI Law Enforcement Bulletin, 58*, 10–17.

Healy, A. F., & McNamara, D. S. (1996). Verbal learning and memory: Does the modal model still work? *Annual Review, 47*, 143–172.

Healy, S. D. (1996). Ecological specialization in the avian brain. In C. F. Moss, S. J. Shettleworth, et al. (Eds.), *Neu-*

roethological studies of cognitive and perceptual processes. (pp. 84–110). Boulder, CO: Westview Press.

Heather-Greener, G. Q., Comstock, D., & Joyce, R. (1996). An investigation of the manifest dream content associated with migraine headaches: A study of the dreams that precede nocturnal migraines. *Psychotherapy & Psychosomatics, 65,* 216–221.

Hebl, M. R., & Heatherton, T. F. (1998). The stigma of obesity in women: The difference is black and white. *Personality & Social Psychology Bulletin, 24,* 417–426.

Hedricks, C. A. (1994). Female sexual activity across the human menstrual cycle. *Annual Review of Sex Research, V,* 122–172.

Hegarty, J. Baldessarini, R., Tohen, M., Waternaux, C., & Oepen, G. (1994). One hundred years of schizophrenia: A meta-analysis of the outcome literature. *American Journal of Psychiatry, 151,* 1409–1416.

Heider, F. (1958). *The psychology of interpersonal relations.* New York: John Wiley.

Heimburger, R. F., et al. (1966). Stereotaxic amygdalotomy for epilepsy with aggressive behavior. *Journal of American Medical Association, 198,* 165–169.

Heine, S. J., & Lehman, D. R. (1997). Culture, dissonance, and self-affirmation. *Personality & Social Psychology Bulletin, 23,* 389–400.

Held, R., & Hein, A. (1963). Movement-produced stimulation in the development of visually deprived behavior. *Journal of Comparative and Physiological Psychology, 56,* 872–876

Heller, D. (1986). *The children's God.* Chicago: University of Chicago Press.

Helmholtz, H. von. (1863). *Die Lehre von den tonempfindungen als physiolgisdne grundlage fur die theorie der musik.* Brunswick: Vierweg-Verlag.

Helms, J. E. (1997). The triple quandary of race, culture, and social class in standardized cognitive ability testing. In D. P. Flanagan, J. L., Genshaft and P. L. Harrison. (Eds.), *Contemporary intellectual assessment: Theories, tests, and issues* (pp. 517–532). New York: Guilford Press.

Helson, R., & Klohnen, E. C. (1998). Affective coloring of personality from young adulthood to midlife. *Personality & Social Psychology Bulletin, 24,* 241–252.

Helson, R., & Moane, G. (1987). Personality change in women from college to midlife. *Journal of Personality and Social Psychology, 53,* 176–186.

Hemphill, S. A. (1996). Characterisics of conduct-disordered children and their families: A review. *Australian Psychologist, 31,* 108–118.

Henley, K., & Morrison, A. R. (1974). A re-evaluation of the effects of lesions of the positive tegmentum and locus coeruleus on phenomena of paradoxical sleep in the cat. *Act Neurobiologica Experimental, 34,* 215–232.

Henry, W. P., Schacht, T. E., & Strupp, H. (1990). Patient and therapist introject, interpersonal process, and differential psychotherapy outcome. *Journal of Consulting and Clinical Psychology, 58,* 768–774.

Herbert, T. B., & Cohen, S. (1993). Depression and immunity: A meta-analytic review. *Psychological Bulletin, 113,* 472–486.

Herdt, G. (1997). *Same sex, different cultures: Gays and lesbians across cultures.* Boulder, CO: Westview Press.

Herdt, G. H. (Ed.). (1984). *Ritualized Homosexuality in Melanesia.* Berkeley, CA: University of California Press.

Hering, E. (1878). *Zur lehre vom lichtsinne.* Vienna: Gerold.

Hering, E. (1920). *Grundzuge, der Lehr vs. Lichtsinn.* Berlin: Springer-Verlag.

Heritch, A., Henderson, K., & Westfall, T. (1990). Effects of social isolation on brain catecholamines and forced swimming in rats. *Journal of Psychiatric Research, 24,* 251–258.

Herman, J., Perry, J. C., & Van der Kolk, B. A. (1989). Childhood trauma in borderline personality disorder. *American Journal of Psychiatry, 146,* 490–495.

Herman, J. L. (1992). *Trauma and recovery: The aftermath of violence—from domestic violence to political terror.* New York: Basic Books.

Hernandez, L., & Hoevel, B. (1989). Food intake and lateral hypothalamic self-stimulation covary after medial hypothalamic lesions or ventral midbrain 6-hydroxydopamine injections that cause obesity. *Behavioral Neuroscience, 103,* 412–422.

Herrmann, D., McEvoy, C., Hertzod, C., Hertel, P., & Johnson, M. K. (eds.). (1996). *Basic and applied memory research* (Vols. 1–2). Mahwah, NJ: Lawrence Erlbaum Associates.

Herrmann, D. J., Crawford, M., & Holdsworthy, M. (1992). Gender-linked differences in everyday memory performance. *British Journal of Psychology, 83,* 221–231.

Herrnstein, R. J. (1970). On the law of effect. *Journal of the Experimental Analysis of Behavior, 13,* 243–266.

Herrnstein, R. J., & Murray, C. A. (1994). *The bell curve: Intelligence and class structure in American life.* New York: Free Press.

Hersen, M. (Ed.). (1988). *Behavioral assessment: A practical handbook.* New York: Pergamon.

Hersey, P., & Blanchard, K. (1982). *Management of organizational behavior: Utilizing human resources.* (2nd ed.). Englewood Cliffs, NJ: Prentice-Hall.

Hertzog, C., Dixon, R., & Hultsch, D. (1990). Relationships between metamemory, memory predictions, and memory task performance in adults. *Psychology and Aging,* 215–227.

Herzog, A. (1984). On multiple personality: Comments on diagnosis, etiology, and treatment. *International Journal of Clinical & Experimental Hypnosis, 32,* 210–221.

Hetherington, A. W., & Ranson, S. W. (1940). Hypothalamic lesions and adiposity in the rat. *The Anatomical Record, 78,* 149–172.

Heyser, C. T., Hampson, R. E., & Deadwyler, S. A. (1993). Effcts of delta-9-tetrahydrocannabinol on delayed match to sample performance in rats: Alterations in short-term memory associated with changes in task specific firing of hippocampal cells. *Journal of Pharmacology and Experimental Therapeutics, 264,* 294–307.

Hicks, R. A., & Pellegrini, R. (1991). The changing sleep habits of college students. *Perceptual & Motor Skills, 72,* 631–636.

Higgins, E. T. (1987). Self-discrepancy: A theory relating self and affect. *Psychological Review, 94,* 319–340.

Higgins, E. T. (1990). Lay epistemic theory and the relation between motivation and cognition. *Psychological Inquiry, 1,* 209–210.

Higgins, E. T. (1990). Personality, social psychology, and person-situation relations: Standards and knowledge activation as a common language. In L. Pervin (Ed.), *Handbook of personality: Theory and research* (pp. 301–338). New York: Guilford Press.

Higgins, E. T., & Bargh, J. A. (1987). Social cognition and social perception. *Annual Review of Psychology, 38,* 369–425.

Higley, J., Mehlman, P., Taub, D., Higley, S., Suomi, S., Linnoila, M., & Vickers, J. H. (1992). Cerebrospinal fluid momoamine and adrenal correlates of aggression in free-ranging rhesus monkeys. *Archives of General Psychiatry, 49,* 436–441.

Hilgard, E. R. (1965). *Hypnotic susceptibility.* New York: Harcourt Brace Jovanovich.

Hilgard, E. R. (1986). *Divided consciousness: Multiple controls in human thought and action.* New York: John Wiley.

Hilgard, E. R., & Hilgard, J. R. (1975). *Hypnosis in the relief of pain.* Los Altos, CA: William Kaufman.

Hilliard, R. B. (1993). Single-case methodology in psychotherapy process and outcome research. *Journal of Consulting and Clinical Psychology, 61,* 373–380.

Hilsenroth, M. J., & Fowler, J. C., Padawer, J. R., & Handler, L. (1997). Narcissism in the Rorschach revisted: Some reflections on empirical data. *Psychologial Assessment, 9,* 113–121.

Hilts, P. (1980). Bulldozers, bassoons, and silicone chips. *Science, 80,* 77–79.

Hinde, R. (1982). *Ethology: Its nature and relations with other sciences.* New York: Oxford University Press.

Hindmarch, I. (1991). Residual effects of hypnotics: An update. *Journal of Clinical Psychiatry, 52*(s), 14–15.

Hinkle, L. E. Jr., & Plummer, N. (1952). Life stress and industrial absenteeism. *Industrial Medicine and Surgery, 21,* 363–375.

Hinz, L. D., & Williamson, D. A. (1987). Bulimia and depression: A review of the affective variant hypothesis. *Psychological Bulletin, 102,* 150–158.

Hirsch, J. (1997). Some history of heredity-vs-environment, genetic inferiority at Harvard (?), and The (incredible) Bell Curve. *Genetica, 99,* 207–224.

Hirsch, J., & Knittle, J. L. (1970). Cellularity of obese and nonobese human adipose tissue. *Federation Proceedings, 29,* 1516–1521.

Hirshberg, L., & Svejda, M. (1990). When infants look to their parents: II. Twelve-month-olds' response to conflicting parental emotional signals. *Child Development, 61,* 1187–1191.

Hirshman, E., & Henzler, A. (1998). The role of decision processes in conscious recollection. *Psychological Science, 9,* 61–65.

Hirst, W. (1986). The psychology of attention. In J. Ledoux & W. Hirst (Eds.), *Mind and brain: Dialogues in cognitive neuroscience* (pp. 105–142). Cambridge: Cambridge University Press.

Hirt, E. R., Zillmann, D., Erickson, G. A., Kennedy, C. (1992). Costs and benefits of allegiance: Changes in fans' self-ascribed competencies after team victory versus defeat. *Journal of Personality & Social Psychology, 63,* 724–738.

Hittner, J. B. (1997). Alcohol-related outcome expectancies: Construct overview and implications for primary and secondary prevention. *Journal of Primary Prevention, 17,* 297–314.

Hobson, J. A. (1988). *The dreaming brain.* New York: Basic Books.

Hobson, P. R. (1985). Self-representing dreams. *Psychoanalytic Psychotherapy, 1,* 43–53.

Hock, E., & DeMeis, D. (1990). Depression in mothers of infants: The role of maternal employment. *Developmental Psychology, 26,* 285–291.

Hoebel, B. G., & Teitelbaum, P. (1966). Weight regulation in normal and hyperphagic rats. *Journal of Comparative and Physiological Psychology, 61,* 189–193.

Hoek, H. W. (1993). Review of the epidemiological studies of eating disorders. *International Review of Psychiatry, 5,* 61–74.

Hoff-Ginsberg, E. (1990). Maternal speech and the child's development of syntax: A further look. *Journal of Child Language., 17,* 85–99.

Hoff-Ginsberg, E., & Shatz, M. (1982). Linguistic input and the child's acquisition of language. *Psychological Review, 92,* 3–26.

Hoffman, L. (1981). *Foundations of family therapy.* New York: Basic Books.

Hoffman, L. (1991). A reflexive stance for family therapy. *Journal of Strategic and Systemic Therapies., 10,* 4–17.

Hoffman, M. (1990). Empathy and justice motivation. *Motivation and Emotion, 14,* 151–172.

Hoffman, M. L. (1978). Psychological and biological perspectives on altruism. *International Journal of Behavioral Development, 1,* 323–339.

Hoffman, M. L. (1982). Development of prosocial motivation: Empathy and guilt. In N. Eisenberg (Ed.), *The development of prosocial behavior.* New York: Academic Press.

Hoffman, M. L., & Saltzstein, H. D. (1967). Parent discipline and the child's moral development. *Journal of Personality and Social Psychology, 5,* 45–47.

Hoffman, P. (1997). The endorphin hypothesis. In W. P. Morgan, et al. (Eds.), *Physical activity and mental health. Series in health psychology and behavioral medicine.* (pp. 163–177). Washington: Taylor & Francis.

Hoffman, W. S., Carpentier-Alting, P., Thomas, D., & Hamilton, V. L. (1991). Initial impact of plant closings on automobile workers and their families. *Families in Society, 72,* 103–107.

Hogan, R. (1983). What every student should know about personality psychology. In A. M. Rogers and J. Scheirer (Eds.), *G. Stanley Hall Lecture Series,* vol. 6, Washington, DC: American Psychological Association.

Hogan, R. (1987). Personality psychology: Back to basics. In J. Aronoff et al. (Eds.), *The emergence of personality.* New York: Springer.

Hogan, R., Curphy, G., & Hogan, J. (1994). What we know about leadership: Effectiveness and personality. *American Psychologist, 49,* 493–304.

Hohmann, G. W. (1966). Some effects of spinal cord lesions on experienced emotional feelings. *Psychophysiology, 3,* 143–156.

Holcomb, H. H., Cascella, N. G., Thaker, G. K., Medoff, D. R., Dannals, R. F., & Tamminga, C. A. (1996). Functional sites of neuroleptic drug action in the human brain: PET/FDG studies with and without halperidol. *American Journal of Psychiatry, 153,* 41–49.

Holden, C. (1980). Identical twins reared apart. *Science, 207,* 1323–1325.

Holden, C. (1987). Creativity and the troubled mind. *Psychology Today, 21,* 9–10.

Holland, A. J., & Oliver, C. (1995). Down's syndrome and the links with Alzheimer's disease. *Journal of Neurology, Neurosurgery & Psychiatry, 59,* 111–114.

Holland, J., Holyoak, K., Nisbett, R., & Thagard, P. (1986). *Induction: Processes of inference, learning, and discovery.* Cambridge, MA: MIT Press.

Hollander, E., Stein, D. J., DeCaria, C. M., Cohen, L., Saoud, J. B., Skodol, A. E., Kellman, D., Rosnick, L., & Oldham, J. M. (1994). Serotonergic sensitivity in borderline personality disorder: Preliminary findings. *American Journal of Psychiatry, 151,* 277–280.

Hollingworth, L. S. (1926). *Gifted children: Their nature and nurture.* New York: Macmillan.

Hollingworth, L. W. (1942). *Children above 180 IQ Stanford-Binet: Origin and development.* Yonkers, NY: World Book.

Hollis, K. L. (1997). Contemporary research on Pavlovian conditioning: A "new" functional analysis. *American Psychologist, 52,* 956–965.

Hollon, S. (1988). Cognitive therapy. In Lyn Y. Abramson (Ed.), *Social cognition and clinical psychology: A synthesis* (pp. 204–253). New York: Guilford Press.

Holmes, D. (1990). The evidence for repression: An examination of sixty years of research. In J. L. Singer, (Ed.), *Repression and dissociation: Implications for personality theory, psychopathology, and health* (pp. 85–102). Chicago, IL: University of Chicago Press.

Holmes, T. H., & Rahe, R. H. (1967). The social readjustment rating scale. *Journal of Psychosomatic Research, 11,* 213–218.

Holroyd, K. A., & Penzien, D. B. (1990). Pharmacological versus non-pharmacological prophylaxis of recurrent migraine headache: A meta-analytic review of clinical trials. *Pain, 42,* 1–13.

Holt, R. (1976). Drive or wish? A reconsideration of the psychoanalytic theory of motivation. In M. Gill & P. Holzman (Eds.), *Psychology vs. metapsychology: Psychoanalytic essays in memory of George Klein. Psychological Issues,* Monograph 36, Vol. 9, No. 4.

Holt, R. R. (1985). The current status of psychoanalytic theory. *Psychoanalytic Psychology, 2,* 289–315.

Holtzworth-Monroe, A., & Stuart, G. L. (1994). Typologies of male batterers: Three subtypes and the differences among them. *Psychological Bulletin, 116,* 476–497.

Holyoak, K. J., & Spellman, B. A. (1993). Thinking. *Annual Review of Psychology, 44,* 265–315.

Holyoak, K. J., & Thagard, P. (1989). Analogical mapping by constraint satisfaction. *Cognitive Science, 13,* 295–355.

Holyoak, K. J., & Thagard, P. (1995). *Mental leaps: Analogy in creative thought.* Cambridge: MIT Press.

Holyoak, K. J., & Thagard, P. (1997). The analogical mind. *American Psychologist, 52,* 35–41.

Homans, G. (1961). *Social behavior: Its elementary forms.* London: Routledge & Kegan Paul.

Honeybourne, C., Matchett, G., & Davey, G. (1993). Expectancy models of laboratory preparedness effects: A UCS-expectancy bias in phylogenetic and ontogenetic fear-relevant stimuli. *Behavior Therapy, 24,* 253–264.

Hooks, M. S., Jones, G. H., Juncos, J. L., Neill, D. B., et al. (1994). Individual differences in schedule-induced and conditioned behaviors. *Behavioural Brain Research, 60,* 199–209.

Hooley, J., & Teasdale, J. D. (1989). Predictors of relapse in unipolar depressives: Expressed emotion, marital distress and perceived criticism. *Journal of Abnormal Psychology, 98,* 229–235.

Horn, J. C., & Meer, J. (1987). The vintage years. *Psychology Today, 21,* 76–90.

Horn, J. L., & Cattell, R. B. (1967). Age differences in fluid and crystallized intelligence. *Acta Psychologica, 26,* 107–129.

Horn, J. L., & Hofer, S. M. (Eds.). Major abilities and development in the adult period. In R. J. Sternberg & C. A. Berg (1992), *Intellectual development* (pp. 44–99). New York: Cambridge University Press.

Horn, J. L., & Noll, J. (1997). Human cognitive capabilities: gf-gc theory. In: D. P. Flanagen, J. L. Genshaft, and P. L. Harrison, Eds. *Contemporary intellectual assessment: Theories, tests and issues* (pp. 53–91). New York: Guilford Press.

Horn, J. M., Loehlin, J. C., & Willerman, L. (1979). Intellectual resemblance among adoptive and biological relatives: The Texas Adoption Project. *Behavior Genetics, 9,* 177–207.

Horner, T. M., & Chethik, L. (1986). Conversation attentiveness and following in 12- and 18-week-old infants. *Infant Behavior and Development, 9,* 203–213.

Horowitz, M. (1988). *Introduction to psychodynamics: A synthesis.* New York: Basic Books.

House, J. S., Landis, K. R., & Umberson, D. (1988). Social relationships and health. *Science, 241,* 540–545.

House, J. S., Umberson, D., & Landis, K. R. (1988). Structures and processes of social support. *American Review of Sociology, 14,* 293–318.

House, R. J. (1977). A 1976 theory of charismatic leadership. In J. G. Hunt & L. L. Larson (Eds.), *Leadership: The cutting edge* (pp. 189–207). Carbondale, IL: Southern Illinois University Press.

House, R. J., & Singh, J. V. (1987). Organizational behavior: Some new directions for I/O psychology. *Annual Review of Psychology, 38,* 669–718.

Hovland, C. (1937). The generalization of conditioned responses: IV. The effects of varying amounts of reinforcement upon the degree of generalization of conditioned responses. *Journal of General Psychology, 21,* 261–276.

Hovland, C. I., Irving, L. J., & Harold, H. K. (1953). *Communication and persuasion: Psychological studies of opinion changes.* New Haven, CT: Yale University Press.

Hovland, C. I., & Janis, I. (1959). *Personality and persuasibility.* New Haven, CT: Yale University Press.

Howard, K. I., Kopta, S. M., Krause, M. S., & Orlinsky, D. E. (1986). The dose-effect relationship in psychotherapy. *American Psychologist, 41,* 159–164.

Howes, C. (1990). Can the age of entry into child care and the quality of child are predict adjustment in kindergarten? *Developmental Psychology, 26,* 292–303.

Howes, C., & Hamilton, C. E. (1992). Children's relationships with child care teachers: Stability and concordance with parental attachments. *Child Development, 63,* 867–878.

Howes, C, Hamilton, C. E., & Philiopsen, L. C. (1998). Stability and comorbidity of child-caregiver and child-peer relationships. *Child Development, 69,* 418–426.

Howes, C., Phillips, D. A., & Whitebook, M. (1992). Thresholds of quality: Implications for the social development of children in center-based child care. *Child Development, 63,* 449–460.

Hsu, F. L. K. (1981). *Americans and Chinese: Passage to difference.* (3rd ed.). Honolulu: University Press of Hawaii.

Hsu, L. K. G. (1989). The gender gap in eating disorders: Why are the eating disorders more common among women. *Clinical Psychology Review, 9,* 393–407.

Hubel, D. H., & Wiesel, T. N. (1959). Receptive fields of single neurons in the cat's striate cortex. *Journal of Physiology, 148,* 574–591.

Hubel, D. H., & Wiesel, T. N. (1963). Single-cell responses in striate cortex of kittens deprived of vision in one eye. *Journal of Neuropsychology, 26,* 1003–1009.

Hubel, D. H., & Wiesel, T. N. (1979). Brain mechanisms of vision. *Scientific American, 241,* 150–162.

Hugdahl, K., Berardi, A., Thompson, W. L., Kosslyn, S., Macy, R., Baker, D. P., et al. (1995). Brain mechanisms in human classical conditioning: A PET blood flow study. *NeuroReport, 6,* 1712–1718.

Hughes, J. N., & Hasbrouck, J. E. (1996). Television violence: Implications for violence prevention. *School Psychology Review, 25,* 134–151.

Hulka, B. S., & Meirik, O. (1996). Research on the menopause. *Maturitas, 23,* 109–112.

Hull, C. L. (1943). *Principles of behavior: An introduction to behavior theory.* New York: Oxford University Press.

Hull, C. L. (1952). *A behavior system: An introduction to behavior theory concerning the individual organism.* New Haven, CT: Yale University Press.

Hull, J. G., & Bond, C. F. (1986). Social and behavioral consequences of alcohol consumption and expectancy: A meta-analysis. *Psychological Bulletin, 99,* 347–360.

Hulme, C., Maughan, S., & Brown, G. D. A. (1991). Memory for familiar and unfamiliar words: Evidence for a long-term memory contribution to short-term memory span. *Journal of Memory and Language, 30,* 685–701.

Hultsch, D., & Dixon, R. (1990). Learning and memory in aging. In J. Birren & K. W. Schaie (Eds.), *Handbook of the psychology of aging.* (3rd ed.). New York: Academic Press.

Hunter, J. E. (1997). Needed: A ban on the significance test. *Psychological Science, 8,* 3–7.

Hupka, R. B., Zaleski, Z., Otto, J., Reidl, L., et al. (1997). The colors of anger, envy, fear, and jealousy: A cross-cultural study. *Journal of Cross-Cultural Psychology, 28,* 156–171.

Hurley, A. D., & Sovner, R. (1985). Behavior modification: III. The token economy. *Psychiatric Aspects of Mental Retardation Reviews, 4,* 1–4.

Hurvich, L. M., & Jameson, D. (1957). An opponent-process of color vision. *Psychological Review, 64,* 384–404.

Huston, A. C. (1983). Sex-typing. In M. Hetherington (Ed.), *Handbook of child psychology: Vol. 4. Social and personality development.* New York: John Wiley.

Huston, T. L. (1973). Ambiguity of acceptance, social desirability, and dating choice. *Journal of Experimental Social Psychology, 9,* 32–42.

Huttenlocher, J., & Hedges, L. V. (1994). Combining graded categories: Membership and typicality. *Psychological Review, 101,* 157–165.

Hyde, J. S. (1984). How large are gender differences in aggression? A developmental meta-analysis. *Developmental Psychology, 20,* 722–736.

Hyde, J. S. (1990). Meta-analysis and the psychology of gender differences. *Signs, 16,* 55–73.

Hyde, J. S., Krajnik, M., & Skuldt-Niederberger, K. (1991). Androgyny across the life span: A replication and longitudinal follow-up. *Developmental Psychology, 27,* 516–519.

Hyman, I. E., & Billings, F. J. (1998). Individual differences and the creation of false childhood memories. *Memory, 6,* 1–20.

Ickes, W. J. (1997). *Empathic accuracy.* New York: Guilford Press.

Inciardi, J. A., Surratt, H. L., & Saum, C. A. (1997). *Cocaine-exposed infants: Social, legal, and public health issues.* Thousand Oaks, CA: Sage Publications, Inc.

Inhelder, B., & Piaget, J. (1958). *The growth of logical thinking from childhood to adolescence.* New York: Basic Books.

Inkeles, A., & Smith, D. H. (1974). *Becoming modern: Individual change in six developing countries.* Cambridge, MA: Harvard University Press.

Innis, N. K. (1992). Early research on the inheritance of the ability to learn. *American Psycologist, 47,* 190–197.

Insko, C. A. (1964). Primacy versus recency in persuasion as a function of the timing of arguments and measures. *Journal of Abnormal and Social Psychology, 69,* 381–391.

Insko, C. A., Arkoff, A., & Insko, V. M. (1965). Effects of high and low fear-arousing communications upon opinions toward smoking. *Journal of Experimental Social Psychology, 1,* 156–266.

Intons-Peterson, M. J., & Fournier, J. (1986). External and internal memory aids: When and how often do we use them? *Journal of Experimental Psychology, General, 115,* 267–280.

Intons-Peterson, M. J., & Fournier, J. (1986). External and internal memory aids: When and how often do we use them? *Journal of Experimental Psychology: General, 115,* 267–280.

Irwin, M., Schafer, G., & Fieden, C. (1974). Emic and unfamiliar category sorting of Mano farmers and U.S. undergradutes. *Journal of Cross-Cultural Psychology, 5,* 407–423.

Irwin, M. H., & McLaughlin, D. H. (1970). Ability and preference in category sorting by Mano school children and adults. *Journal of Social Psychology, 82,* 15–24.

Isen, A. (1984). Toward understanding the role of affect in cognition. In R. S. Wyer, Jr. & T. K. Srull (Eds.), *Handbook of social cognition,* Vol. 3. Hillsdale, NJ: Erlbaum.

Isen, A. (1993). Positive affect and decision making. In M. Lewis, & J. M. Haviland (Eds.), *Handbook of emotions* (pp. 261–277). New York: Guilford.

Islam, M. R., & Hewstone, M. (1993). Intergroup attributions and affective consequences in majority and minority groups. *Journal of Personality and Social Psychology, 64,* 936–950.

Ito, T. A., Miller, N., & Pollock, V. E. (1996). Alcohol and aggression: A meta-analysis on the moderating effects of inhibitory cues, triggering events, and self-focused attention. *Psychological Bulletin, 120,* 60–82.

Ittenbach, R. F., Bruininks, R. H., Thurlow, M. L., & McGrew, K. S. (1993). Community integration of young adults with mental retardation: A multivariate analysis of adjustment. *Research in Developmental Disabilities, 14,* 275–290.

Iwashita, Y., Kawaguchi, S., & Murata, M. (1994). Restoration of function by replacement of spinal cord segments in the rat. *Nature, 367,* 167–169.

Izard, C. (1990). Facial expressions and the regulation of emotions. *Journal of Personality and Social Psychology, 58,* 487–498.

Izard, C. E. (1971). *The face of emotion.* New York: Appleton.

Izard. C. E. (1977). *Human emotions.* New York: Plenum Press.

Izard, C. E. (1997). *Emotions and facial expressions: A perspective from Differential Emotions Theory.* New York: Cambridge University Press.

Izard, C. E., & Buechler, S. (1980). Aspects of consciousness and personality in terms of differential emotions theory. In R. Plutchik & H. Kellerman (Eds.), *Emotion: Theory, Research, and experience, Vol. I: Theories of emotion.* New York: Academic Press.

Izard, C. E., Libero, C., Putnam, P., & Haynes, O. M. (1993). Stability of emotional experiences and their relations to traits of personality. *Journal of Personality and Social Psychology, 64,* 847–860.

Izquierdo, I., & Medina, J. H. (1997). The biochemistry of memory formation and its regulation by hormones and neuromodulators. *Psychobiology, 25,* 1–9.

Jablenski, A. (1989). Epidemiology and cross-cultural aspects of schizophrenia. *Psychiatric Annals, 19,* 516–524.

Jackendoff, R. (1996). The architecture of the linguistic-spatial interface. In P. Bloom, M. A. Peterson, et al. (Eds.), *Language and space. Language, speech, and communication.* (pp. 1–30). Cambridge: MIT Press.

Jacklin, C. (1989). Female and male: Issues of gender. *American Psychologist, 44,* 127–133.

Jacob, T., Krahn, G. L., & Leonard, K. (1991). Parent-child interactions in families with alcoholic fathers. *Journal of Consulting and Clinical Psychology, 59,* 176–181.

Jacob, T., & Leonard, K. (1991). Experimental drinking procedures in the study of alcoholics and their families: A consideration of ethnical issues. *Journal of Consulting and Clinical Paychology, 59,* 249–255.

Jacobs, T. J., & Charles, E. (1980). Life events and the occurrence of cancer in children. *Psychosomatic Medicine, 42,* 11–24.

Jacobsen, T., & Hofmann, V. (1997). Children's attachment representations: Longitudinal relations to school behavior and academic competency in middle childhood and adolescence. *Developmental Psychology, 33,* 703–710.

Jacobson, E. (1964). The self and the object world. *Psychoanalytic Study of the Child, 9,* 75–127.

Jacobson, J., Jacobson, S., Padgett, R., Brumitt, G., & Billings, R. (1992). Effects of prenatal PCB exposure on cognitive processing efficiency and sustained attention. *Developmental Psychology, 28,* 297–307.

Jacobson, J. L., Jacobsen, S. W., Sokol, R. J., Martier, S. S. (1993). Teratogenic effects of alcohol on infant development. *Alcoholism: Clinical and Experimental Research, 17,* 174–183.

Jacobson, J. L., & Wille, D. E. (1986). The influence of attachment pattern on developmental changes in peer interaction from the toddler to the preschool period. *Child Development, 57,* 338–347.

Jacoby, L. L., & Kelley, C. M. (1987). Unconscious influences of memory for a prior event. *Personality and Social Psychology Bulletin, 13,* 314–336.

Jacques, E. (1965). Death and the mid-life crisis. *International Journal of Psychoanalysis, 46,* 502–514.

Jaeger, J. J. (1992). 'Not by the chair of my hinny hin hin': Some general properties of slips of the tongue in young children. *Journal of Child Language, 19,* 335–366.

Jaeger, T., & van der Kooy, D. (1996). Separate neural substrates mediate the motivating and discriminative properties of morphine. *Behavioral Neuroscience, 110,* 181–201.

Jahoda, A., Markova, I., & Cattermole, M. (1988). Stigma and the self concept of people with a mild mental handicap. *Journal of Mental Deficiency Research, 32,* 103–115.

Jahoda, G. Psychology and social change in developing countries. In *Proceedings of the XVIth International Congress of Applied Psychology.* Amsterdam: Swets and Zeitlinger.

James, W. (1884). What is emotion? *Mind, 19,* 188–205.

James, W. (1890). *Principles of psychology,* Vol. 1. New York: Henry Holt.

James, W. (1902). *Varieties of Religious Experience.* New York: American Library, 1958.

James, W. (1910). The Self. *In Psychology: The briefer course.* New York: Henry Holt and Co. Reprinted in C. Gordon & K. J. Gergen, *The self in social interaction,* 1968. New York: John Wiley.

Jamison, K. R. (1989). Mood disorders and patterns of creativity in British writers and artists. *Psychiatry, 52,* 125–134.

Jamison, K. R. (1993). *Touched with fire.* New York: Free Press.

Jangid, R. K., Vyas, J. N., & Shukla, T. R. (1988). The effects of the transcendental meditation programme on the normal individuals. *Journal of Personality and Clinical Studies, 4,* 145–149.

Janis, I. (1972). *Victims of groupthink: A psychological study of foreign-policy decisions and fiascos.* Boston: Houghton Mifflin.

Janoff-Bulman, R. (1992). *Shattered assumptions: Towards a new psychology of trauma.* New York: Free Press.

Janos, P. M., & Robinson, N. M. (1985). Psychosocial development in intellectually gifted children. In Horowitz, F. D., & O'Brien, M. (Eds.) The gifted and talented: *Developmental perspectives* (pp. 149–195). Washington, DC: American Psychological Association.

Janowitz, H. D., & Grossman, M. I. (1949). Some factors affecting the food intake of normal dogs and dogs esophagostomy and gastric fistula. *American Journal of Physiology, 159,* 143–148.

Jansen, M. A. (1986). Mental health policy: Observations from Europe. *American Psychologist, 41,* 1273–1278.

Jarvis, W. B. G., & Petty, R. E. (1996). The need to evaluate. *Journal of Personality and Social Psychology, 70,* 172–194.

Jasmos, T. M., & Hakmiller, K. I. (1975). Some effects of lesion level, and emotional cues of affective expression in spinal cord patients. *Psychological Reports, 37,* 859–870.

Jeffery, K. J. (1997). LTP and spatial learn-ing—Where to next? *Hippocampus, 7,* 95–110.

Jemmott, J. B., III, Boryseko, J. Z., Borysenko, M., McClelland, D. C., Chapman, R., Meyer, D., & Benson, H. (1983). Academic stress, power motivation, and decrease in salivary secretory immunoglobin A secretion rate. *Lancet, 1,* 1400–1402.

Jemmott, J. B. III, & Locke, S. E. (1984). Psychosocial factors, immunologic mediation, and human susceptibility to infectious diseases: How much do we know? *Psychological Bulletin, 95,* 78–108.

Jenike, M., Baer, L., Ballantine, T., & Martuza, R. (1991). Cingulotomy for refractory obsessive-compulsive disorder: A long-term follow-up of 33 patients. *Archives of General Psychiatry, 48,* 548–555.

Jenike, M. A. (1983). Obsessive compulsive disorder. *Comprehensive Psychiatry, 24,* 99–111.

Jenkins, J. H., & Karno, M. (1992). The meaning of expressed emotion: Theoretial issues raised by cross-cultural research. *American Journal of Psychiatry, 149,* 9–21.

Jensen, A. R. (1969). How much can we boost IQ and scholastic achievement? *Harvard Educational Review, 39,* 1–123.

Jensen, A. R. (1973). *Educability and group differences.* New York: Harper & Row.

Jensen, A. R. (1980). *Bias in mental testing.* New York: Free Press.

Jensen, A. R., & Reynolds, C. R. (1982). Race, social class and ability patterns on the WISC-R. *Personality and Individual Differences, 3,* 423–438.

Jewesbury, E. C. O. (1951). Insensitivity to pain. *Brain, 74,* 336–353.

Jimerson, D. C., Wolfe, B. E., Brotman, A. W., Metzger, Eran D., & Jimerson, D. C. (1996). Medications in the treatment of eating disorders. *Psychiatric Clinics of North Ameica, 19,* 739–754.

Jockin, V., McGue, M., & Lykken, D. (1996). Personality and divorce: A genetic analysis. *Journal of Personality and Social Psychology, 71,* 288–299.

John, O., & Robins, R. (1994). Accuracy and bias in self-pereption: Individual differences in self-enhancement and the role of narcissism. *Journal of Personality and Social Psychology, 66,* 206–219.

John, O. P. (1990). The big five factor taxonomy: Dimensions of personality in the natural language and in questionnaires. In L. Pervin (Ed.), *Handbook of personality: Theory and research* (pp. 66–100). New York: Guilford Press.

Johnson, J. V., Stewart, W., Hall, E. M., Fredlund, P., et al. (1996). Long-term psychosocial work environment and cardiovascular mortality among Swedish men. *American Journal of Public Health, 86,* 324–331.

Johnson, K., Churchill, L., Klitenick, M. A., Hooks, M. S. (1996). Involvement of the ventral tegmental area in locomotion elicited from the nucleus accumbens or ventral pallidum. *Journal of Pharmacology & Experimental Therapeutics, 277,* 1122–1131.

Johnson, K. O., & Lamb, G. H. (1981). Neural mechanisms of spatial tactile discrimination: Neural patterns evoked by Braille-like dot patterns in the monkey. *Journal of Physiology, 310,* 117–144.

Johnson, K. O., Hsiao, S. S., & Twombly, I. A. (1995). Neural mechanisms of tactile form recognition. In M. S. Gazzaniga, et al. (Eds.), *The cognitive neurosciences.* (pp. 253–267). Cambridge: MIT Press.

Johnson, M. K., Kim, J. K., & Risse, G. (1985). Do alcoholic Korsakoff's syndrome patients acquire affective reactions? *Journal of Experimental Psychology: Learning, Memory, & Cognition, 11,* 22–36.

Johnson, R., & Murray, F. (1992). Reduced sensitivity of penile mechanoreceptors in aging rats with sexual dysfunction. *Brain Research Bulletin, 28,* 61–64.

Johnson-Laird, P. N. (1995). Mental models, deductive reasoning, and the brain. In M. S. Gazzaniga, et al. (Eds.), *The cognitive neurosciences.* (pp. 999–1008). Cambridge: MIT Press.

Johnson-Laird, P. N. (1996). The process of deduction. In D. Steier, & T. M. Mitchell (Eds.), *Mind matters: A tribute to Allen Newell. Carnegie Mellon Symposia on cognition.* (pp. 363–399). New Jersey: Lawrence Erlbaum Associates, Inc.

Johnson-Laird, P. N., Legrenzi, P., & Legrenzi, M. S. (1972). Reasoning and a sense of reality. *British Journal of Psychology, 63,* 395–400.

Jones, A. (1992). Community self-help groups for women with bulimic and complsive eating problems. *British Review of Bulimia and Anorexia Nervosa, 6,* 63–71.

Jones, E. E. (1976). How do people perceive the causes of behavior? *American Scientist, 64,* 300–305.

Jones, E. E., & Harris, V. A. (1967). The attribution of attitudes. *Journal of Experimental Social Psychology, 3,* 1–24.

Jones, K. L., Smith, D. W., Ulleland, C. N., & Streissguth, A. (1973). Pattern of malformation in offspring of chronic alcoholic mothers. *Lancet, 1,* 1267–1271.

Jones, L. (1990). Unemployment and child abuse. *Families in Society, 71,* 579–588.

Jones, P. B., Rantakallio, P., Hartikainen, A., Isohanni, M., & Sipila, P. (1998). Schizophrenia as a long-term outcome of pregnancy, delivery, and perinatal complications: A 28-year follow-up of the 1966 North Finland General Population Birth Cohort. *American Journal of Psychiatry, 155,* 355–364.

Jordaan, G. P., Roberts, M. C., & Emsley, R. A. (1996). Serotonergic agents in the treatment of hypothalamic obesity syndrome: A case report. *International Journal of Eating Disorders, 20,* 111–113.

Josephs, R, Markus, H., & Tafarodi, R. (1992). *Journal of Personality and Social Psychology, 63,* 391–402.

Judd, C. M., & Park, B. (1988). Out-group homogeneity: Judgments of variability at the individual and group levels. *Journal of Personality and Social Psychology, 54,* 778–788.

Judd, T. (1988). The varieties of musical talent. In L. K. Obler, & D. Fein (Eds.), *The exceptional brain: Neuropsychology of talent and special abilities* (pp. 127–155). New York: Guilford Press.

Jung, C. G. (1923). *Psychological types.* New York: Pantheon Books.

Jung, C. G. (1961). *Memories, dreams, reflections.* New York: Random House.

Jung, C. G. (1968). *Analytical psychology: Its theory and practice.* New York: Vintage Books, 40–45.

Just, M. A., & Carpenter, P. A. (1992). A capacity theory of comprehension: Individual differences in working memory. *Psychological Review, 99,* 122–149.

Kaas, J. H. (1987). Somatosensory cortex. In G. Adelman (Ed.), *Encyclopedia of neuroscience.* Vol. 2. Boston: Birkhauser.

Kagan, J. (1976). Emergent themes in human development. *American Scientist, 64,* 186–196.

Kagan, J. (1983). Stress and coping in early development. In N. Garmezy & M. Rutter (Eds.), *Stress, coping, and development in children.* New York: McGraw-Hill.

Kagan, J. (1984). *The nature of the child.* New York: Basic Books.

Kagan, J. (1989). Temperamental contributions to social behavior. *American Psychologist, 44,* 668–674.

Kagan, J., Kearsley, R. B., & Zelazo, P. R. (1978). *Infancy: Its place in human development.* Cambridge, MA: Harvard University Press.

Kagan, J., & Snidman, N. (1991). Temperamental factors in human development. *American Psychologist, 46,* 856–862.

Kahn, R. S., Davidson, M., & Davis, K. L. (1996). Dopamine and schizophrenia revisted. In S. J. Watson, et al. (Eds.), *Biology of schizophrenia and affective disease.* (pp. 369–391). Washington: American Psychiatric Press, Inc.

Kahn, S., Zimmerman, G., Csikszentmihalyi, M., & Getzels, J. (1985). Relations between identity in young adulthood and intimacy at midlife. *Journal of Personality and Social Psychology, 49,* 1316–1322.

Kahneman, D., & Tversky, A. (1979). Prospect theory: An analysis of decision under risk. *Econometrica, 47,* 263–291.

Kail, R. (1991). Developmental change in speed of processing during childhood and adolescence. *Psychological Bulletin, 109,* 490–501.

Kail, R. (1991). Processing time declines exponentially during childhood and adolescence. *Developmental Psychology, 27,* 259–266.

Kail, R., & Pelligrino, J. W. (1985). *Human intelligence: Perspectives and prospects.* New York: Freeman.

Kalat, J. W. (1988). *Biological psychology.* (3rd ed.). Belmont, CA: Wadsworth.

Kalivas, P. W., Bush, L., & Hanson, G. (1996). High and low behavioral response to novelty is associated with differences in neurotensin and substance P content. In J. N. Crawley, S. McLean, et al. (Eds.), *Neuropeptides: Basic and clinical advances. Annals of the New York Academy of Sciences, Vol. 780.* (pp. 164–167). New York: New York Academy of Sciences.

Kalter, N. (1987). Long-term effects of divorce on children: A developmental vulnerability model. *American Journal of Orthopsychiatry, 57,* 587–600.

Kalter, N. (1990). *Growing up with divorce: Helping your child avoid immediate and later emotional problems.* New York: Free Press; London: Collier Macmillan, Ltd.

Kamas, E. N., & Reder, L. M. (1995). The role of familiarity in cognitive processing. In R. F. Lorch, E. J. O'Brien, et al. (Eds.), *Sources of coherence in reading.* (pp. 177–202). Hillsdale, NJ: Lawrence Erlbaum Associates, Inc.

Kamen, L. P., & Seligman, M. E. P. (1987). Explanatory style and health. *Current Psychological Research & Reviews, 6,* 207–218.

Kamil, A. C., & Jones, J. E. (1997). The seed-storing corvid Clark's nutcracker learns geometric relationships among landmarks. *Nature, 390,* 276–279.

Kamin, L. J. (1969). Predictability, surprise, attention, and conditioning. In B. A. Campbell & R. M. Church (Eds.), *Punishment and aversive behavior.* New York: Appleton-Century-Crofts.

Kamin, L. J. (1974). *The science and politics of I.Q.* Hillsdale, NJ: Erlbaum.

Kaminer, Y., & Hrecznyj, B. (1991). Lysergic acid diethylamide-induced chronic visual disturbances in an adolescent. *Journal of Nervous and Mental Disease, 179,* 173–174.

Kan, S. (1986). The 19th century Tlinglit potlatch: A new perspective. *American Ethnoloist, 13,* 191–212.

Kandel, E. R. (1989). Genes, nerve cells, and the remembrance of things past. *Journal of Neuropsychiatry and Clinical Neurosciences, 1,* 103–125.

Kandel, E. R., & Schwartz, J. H. (1982). Molecular biology of learning: Modulation of transmitter release. *Science, 218,* 433–434.

Kanizsa, G. (1976). Subjective contours. *Scientific American, 234,* 48–52.

Kanner, A. D., Coyne, J. C., Schaefer, C., & Lazarus, R. S. (1981). Comparison of two modes of stress measurement: Daily hassles and uplifts versus major life events. *Journal of Behavioral Medicine, 491,* 1–39.

Kaplan, H. I., & Sadock, B. J. (1988). *Synopsis of psychiatry: Behavioral sciences clinical psychiatry* (5th Ed.). Baltimore: Williams & Wilkins Co.

Kaplan, H. S. (1981). *The new sex therapy: Active treatment of sexual dysfunctions.* New York: Brunner/Mazel.

Kaplan, J. P. (1996). Psychologists' attitudes towards corporal punishment. *Dissertation Abstracts International: Section B: the Sciences & Engineering, 56,* 5151.

Kapur, S., Tulving, E., Cabeza, R., & McIntosh, A. R. (1996). The neural correlates of intentional learning of verbal materials: A PET study in humans. *Cognitive Brain Research, 4,* 243–249.

Karadi, Z., Oomura, Y., Nishino, H., & Scott, T. R. (1990). Complex attributes of lateral hypothalamic neurons in the regulation of feeding of alert rhesus monkeys. *Brain Research Bulletin, 25,* 933–939.

Kardiner, A. (1945). *The psychological frontiers of society.* New York: Columbia University Press.

Karlson, J. L. (1978). *Inheritance of creative intelligence.* Chicago: Nelson-Hall.

Karni, A., Tanne, D., Rubenstien, B. S., Askenasy, J. J. M. (1994). Dependence on REM sleep of overnight improvement of a perceptual skill. *Science, 265,* 679–682.

Kasl, S. V., Evans, A. S., & Neiderman, J. C. (1979). Psychosocial risk factors in the development of infectious mononucleosis. *Psychosomatic Medicine, 41,* 445–466.

Kassin, S., & Kiechel, K. (1996). The social psychology of false confessions: Compliance, internationalization, and confabulation. *Psychologial Science, 7,* 125–128.

Katafuchi, T., Oomura, Y., & Yoshimatsu, H. (1985). Single neuron activity in the rat lateral hypothalamus during 2-deoxy-d-glucose induced and natural feeding behavior. *Brain Research, 359,* 1–9.

Katahn, M., & McMinn, M. (1990). Obesity: A biobehavioral point of view. *Annals of the New York Academy of Arts and Sciences, 602,* 189–204.

Katigbak, M., Church, A. T., & Akamine, T. (1996). Cross-cultural generalizability of personality dimensions: Relating indigenous and imported dimensions in two cultures. *Journal of Personality and Social Psychology, 70,* 99–114.

Katz, H., & Beilin, H. (1976). A test of Bryant's claims concerning the young children's understanding of quantitative invariance. *Child Development, 47,* 877–880.

Katz, I., & Hass, R. (1988). Racial ambivalence and American value conflict: Correlational and priming studies of dual cognitive structures. *Journal of Personality and Social Psychology, 55,* 893–905.

Katz, J., & Melzack, R. (1990). Pain "memories" in phantom limbs: Review and clinical observations. *Pain, 43,* 319–336.

Kausler, D. (1990). Motivation, human aging, and cognitive performance. In J. Birren & K. W. Schaie (Eds.), *Handbook of the psychology of aging* (3rd ed.). New York: Academic Press.

Kazdin, A. E., & Tuma, A. H. (1982). *Single-case research designs.* San Francisco: Jossey-Bass.

Keating, D. P. (1983). The creative potential of mathematically precocious boys. In R. S. Albert (Ed.), *Genius and eminence: The social psychology of creativity and exceptional achievement* (pp. 128–138). Elmsford, NY: Pergamon Press.

Keesey, R. E., & Corbett, S. W. (1984). Metabolic defense of the body weight set-point. In A. J. Stunkard & E. Stellar (Eds.), *Eating and its disorders.* New York: Raven Press.

Keesey, R. E., & Powley, T. L. (1986). The regulation of body weight. *Annual Review of Psychology, 37,* 109–134.

Keller, M., Lavori, P., Kane, J., Gelenbert, A., Rosenbaum, J. F., Waltzer, E., & Baker, L. A. (1992). Subsyndromal symptoms in bipolar disorder: A comparison of standard and low serum levels of lithium. *Archives of General Psychiatry, 49,* 371–376.

Kelley, H. H. (1973). The process of causal attribution. *American Psychologist, 28,* 107–128.

Kelley, H. H. (1979). *Personality relationships.* Hillsdale, NJ: Erlbaum.

Kelley, H. H. (1992). Common-sense psychology and scientific psychology. *Annual Review of Psychology, 43,* 1–23.

Kelley, H. H., & Thibaut, J. W. (1978). *Interpersonal relations: A theory of interdependence.* New York: Wiley.

Kelley, J. E., & Lumley, M. A., & Leisen, J. C. C. (1997). Health effects of emotional disclosure in rheumatoid arthritis patients. *Health Psychology, 16,* 331–340.

Kelley, M. L., Power, T. G., & Wimbush, D. (1992). Determinants of disciplinary practices in low-income Black mothers. *Child Development, 63,* 573–582.

Kelly, G. A., (1955). *Psychology of personal constructs.* New York: W. W. Norton.

Kelly, M. D., Grant, I., Heaton, R. K., Marcotte, T. D. et al. (1996). Neuropsychological findings in HIV infection and AIDS. In I. Grant, K. M. Adams, et al. (Eds.), *Neuropsychological assessment of neuropsychiatric disorders.* (2nd ed.). (pp. 403–422). New York: Oxford University Press.

Kenardy, J., Evans, L., & Tian, P. (1992). The latent structure of anxiety symptoms in anxiety disorders. *American Journal of Psychiatry, 149,* 1058–1061.

Kendall, P. C. (1993). Treating anxiety disorders in children: Results of a randomized clinical trial. *Journal of Consulting and Clinical Psychology, 62,* 100–110.

Kendall, P. C. (1998). Empirically supported psychological therapies. *Journal of Consulting & Clinical Psychology, 66,* 3–6.

Kendler, K., MacLean, C., Neale, M., Kessler, R., Heath, A., & Eaves, L. (1991). The genetic epidemiology of bulimia nervosa. *American Journal of Psychiatry, 148,* 1627–1637.

Kendler, K., Neale, M., Kessler, R., Heath, A., & Eaves, L. (1992). Generalized anxiety disorder in women: A population-based twin study. *Archives of General Psychiatry, 49,* 267–272.

Kendler, K., Neale, M., Kessler, R., Heath, A., & Eaves, L. (1992). The genetic epidemiology of phobias in women: The interrelationship of agoraphoia, social phobia, situational phobia, and simple phobia. *Archives of General Psychiatry, 49,* 273–281.

Kendler, K., Neale, M., Kessler, R., Heath, A., & Eaves, L. (1992). A population-based twin study of major depression in women. *Archives of General Psychiatry, 49,* 257–266.

Kendler, K. S., & Diehl, S. R. (1993). The genetics of schizophrenia: A current, genetic-epidemiologic perspective. *Schizophrenia Bulletin, 19,* 261–285.

Kendler, K. S., & Gardner, C. O., Jr. (1998). Boundaries of major depression: An evaluation of DSM-IV criteria. *American Journal of Psychiatry, 155,* 172–177.

Kendler, K. S., Neale, M. C., Heath, A. C., Kessler, R. C., & Eaves, L. J. (1994). A twin-family study of alcoholism in women. *American Journal of Psychiatry, 151,* 707–715.

Kendler, K. S., Neale, M. C., Kessler, R.C., & Heath, A. C. (1993). A test of the equal-environment assumption in twin studies of psychiatric illness. *Behavior Genetics, 23,* 21–27.

Kendler, K. S., Prescott, C. A., Neale, M. C., & Pedersen, N. L. (1997). Temperance Board Registration for Alcohol Abuse in a National Sample of Swedish Male Twins, Born 1902 to 1949. *Archives of General Psychiatry, 54,* 178–184.

Kendler, K. S., Walters, E. E., Neale, M. C., Kessler, R. C., Heath, A. C., & Eaves, L. J. (1995). The structure of the genetic and environmental risk factors for six major psychiatric disorders in women: Phobia, generalized anxiety disorder, panic disorder, bulimia, major depression, and alcoholism. *Archives of General Psychiatry, 52,* 374–383.

Kenealy, P. M. (1997). Mood-state-dependent retrieval: The effects of induced mood on memory reconsidered. *Quarterly Journal of Experimental Psychology: Human Experimental Psychology, 50,* 290–317.

Kenrick, D., & Keefe, R. (1992). Age preferences in mates reflect sex differences in human reproductive strategies. *Behavioral and Brain Sciences, 15,* 75–113.

Kenrick, D., Groth, G., Trost, M., & Sadalla, E. (1993). Integrating evolutionary and social exchange perspectives on relationships: Effects of gender, self-appraisal, and involvement level on mate selection criteria. *Journal of Personality and Social Psychology, 64,* 951–969.

Kenrick, D. T., & Stringfield, D. O. (1980). Personality traits and the eye of the beholder: Crossing some traditional philosophical boundaries in the search for consistency in all of the people. *Psychological Review, 87,* 88–104.

Kernberg, O. (1975). *Borderline conditions and pathological narcissism.* New York: Aronson.

Kernberg, O. (1984). *Severe personality disorders: Psychotherapeutic strategies.* New Haven, CT: Yale University Press.

Kernberg, O. F., Selzer, M. A., Koenigsberg, H. W., Carr, A. C., & Appelbaum, A. H. (1989). *Psychodynamic psychotherapy of borderline patients.* New York: Basic Books, Inc.

Kerr, M., & Bowen, M. (1988). *Family evaluation: An approach based on Bowen theory.* New York: Norton.

Kessler, R. C., House, J. S., & Turner, J. B. (1987). Unemployment and health in a community sample. *Journal of Health and Social Behavior, 28,* 51–59.

Kessler, R. C., Kendler, K., Heath, A., Neale, M. C., & Eaves, L. J. (1992). Social support, depressed mood, and adjustment to stress: A genetic epidemiologic investigation. *Journal of Personality and Social Psychology, 62,* 257–272.

Kessler, R. C., McGonagle, K. A., Zhao, S., Nelson, C. B., Hughes, M., Eshleman, S., Wittchen, H., & Kendler, K. S. (1994). Lifetime and 12-month prevalence of DSM-III-R psychiatric disorders in the United States. *Archives of General Psychiatry, 51,* 8–19.

Kessler, R. C., Price, R. H., & Wortman, C. B. (1985). Social factors in psychopathology: Stress, social support, and coping processes. *Annual Review of Psychology, 36,* 531–572.

Kessler, R. C., Sonnega, A., Bromet, E., Hughes, M., & Nelson, C. B. (1995). Posttraumatic stress disorder in the national comorbidity survey. *Archives of General Psychiatry, 52,* 1048–1060.

Kessler, R. C., Stein, M. B., & Berglund, P. (1998). Social phobia subtypes in the National Comorbidity Survey. *American Journal of Psychiatry, 155,* 613–619.

Kessler, R. C., Turner, J. B., & House, J. S. (1987). Intervening processes in the relationship between unemployment and health. *Psychological Medicine, 17,* 949–961.

Kessler, R. C., Turner, J. B., & House, J. S. (1989). Unemployment, reemployment, and emotional functioning in a community sample. *American Sociological Review, 54,* 648–657.

Kety, S. S., Rosenthal, D., Wender, P. H., Schulsinger, F., & Jacobsen, B. (1975). Mental illness in the biological and adoptive families of adopted individuals who have ecome schizophrenic: A preliminary report based on psychiatric interviews. In Fieve, Rosenthal, & Brill (Eds.), *Genetic research in psychiatry.* Baltimore, MD: Johns Hopkins University Press.

Khatena, J. (1982). Myth: Creativity is too difficult to measure. *Gifted Child Quarterly, 26,* 21–23.

Kihlstrom, J. F. (1987). The cognitive unconscious. *Science, 237,* 1445–1452.

Kihlstrom, J. F. (1996). Unconscious processes in social interaction. In S. R. Hameroff, A. W. Kasniak, & A. C. Scott (Eds.), *Toward a science of consciousness: The first Tucson discussions and debates. Complex adaptive systems* (pp. 93–104). Cambridge: MIT Press.

Kihlstrom, J. F., & Cantor, N. (1983). Mental representations of the self. In L. Berkowitz (Ed.), *Advances in experimental social psychology,* Vol. 15. New York: Academic Press.

Kimble, D. P. (1992). *Biological psychology* (2nd ed.). Ft. Worth: Harcourt Brace Jovanovich, Inc.

Kimura, D. (1987). Are men's and women's brains really different? *Canadian Psychology, 28,* 133–148.

Kinder, D. R. (1998). Opinion and action in the realm of politics. In D. T. Gilbert, S. T. Fiske, et al. (Eds.), *The handbook of social psychology,* Vol. 2 (4th ed.). (pp. 778–867). Boston: McGraw-Hill.

King, A. J., & Carlile, S. (1995). Neural coding for auditory space. In M. S. Gazzaniga et al. (Eds.). *The cognitive neurosciences* (pp. 279–293). Cambridge: MIT Press.

King, H. E. (1961). Psychological effects of excitation in the limbic system. In D. E. Sheer (Ed.). *Electrical stimulation of the brain.* Austin: University of Texas Press.

King, M., & McDonald, E., (1992). Homosexuals who are twins: A study of 46 probands. *British Journal of Psychiatry, 160,* 407–409.

King, W., & Ellison, G. (1989). Long-lasting alterations in behavior and brain neurochemistry following continuous low-level LSD administration. *Pharmacology, Biochemistry & Behavior, 33,* 69–73.

Kinney, D. K., Holzman, P. S., Jacobsen, B., Jansson, L., Faber, B., Hildebrand, W., et al. (1997). Thought disorder in schizophrenic and control adoptees and their relatives. *Archives of General Psychiatry, 54,* 475–479.

Kinomura, S., Larsson, J., Gulyas, B., & Roland, P. E. (1996). Activation of attention by the human reticular formation and thalamic intralaminar nuclei. *Science, 271,* 512–515.

Kinsbourne, M., & Smith, W. L. (1974). *Hemispheric disconnection and cerebral function.* Springfield, IL: Charles C. Thomas.

Kinsey, A. C., Pomeroy, W. B., & Martin, C. E. (1948). *Sexual behavior in the human male.* Philadelphia: W. B. Saunders.

Kinsey, A. C., Pomeroy, W. B., Martin, C. E., & Gebhard, P. (1953). *Sexual behavior in the human female.* Philadelphia: W. B. Saunders.

Kintsch, W., & Greeno, J. G. (1985). Understanding and solving word arithmetic problems. *Psychological Review, 92,* 109–129.

Kirasic, K. C., Allen, G. A., Dodson, S. H., & Binder, K. S. (1996). Aging, cognitive resources, and declarative learning. *Psychology & Aging, 11,* 658–670.

Kirsch, I., & Lynn, S. J. (1995). The altered state of hypnosis: Changes in the theoretical landscape. *American Psychologist, 50,* 846–858.

Kirsch, I., Montgomery, G., & Sapirstein, G. (1995). Hypnosis as an adjunct to cognitive behavioral psychotherapy: A meta-analysis. *Journal of Consulting & Clinical Psychology, 63,* 214–220.

Kitayama, S., & Markus, H. R. (Eds., 1994). *Emotion and culture: Empirical studies of mutual influence.* Washing-

ton: American Psychological Association.

Klaczynski, P. (1997). Bias in adolescents' everyday reasoning and its relationship with intellectual ability, personal theories, and self-serving motivation. *Developmental Psychology, 33,* 273–283.

Klayman, J., & Ha, Y. (1989). Hypothesis testing in rule discovery: Strategy, structure, and content. *Journal of Experimental Psychology: Learning, Memory, and Cognition, 15,* 596–604.

Kleinman, A. (1988). *Rethinking psychiatry: From cultural category to personal experience.* New York: Macmillan.

Kleven, M., & Seiden, L. (1991). Repeated injection of cocaine potentiates methamphetamine-induced toxicity to dopamine-containing neurons in rat striatum. *Brain Research, 557,* 340–343.

Kline, D. W., & Schieber, F. (1985). Vision and aging. In J. E. Birren, K. W. Schaie, et al. (Eds.), Handbook of the psychology of aging (2nd ed.). *The handbooks of aging.* (pp. 296–331). New York: Van Nostrand Reinhold Co., Inc.

Klinger, E. (1992). What will they think of next? Understanding daydreaming. In G. Brannigan & M. Merrens (Eds.), *The undaunted psychologist: Adventures in research.* New York: McGraw-Hill.

Klinnert, M. D., Campos, J. J., Sorce, J. F., Emde, R. R., & Svejda, M. (1983). Emotions as behavior regulators: Social reference in infancy. In R. Plutchik & H. Kellerman (Eds.), *Emotion: Theory, research, and experience:* Vol. 2, *Emotions in early development.* San Diego: Academic Press.

Kluckhohn, F., & Strodtbeck, F. (1961). *Variations in value orientations.* Evanston, IL: Row, Peterson.

Kluger, A., & DeNisi, A. (1996). The effects of feedback interventions on performance: A historical review, a meta-analysis, and a preliminary feedback intervention theory. *Psychological Bulletin, 119,* 254–284.

Kluver, H., & Bucy, P. (1939). Preliminary analysis of functions of the temporal lobe in monkeys. *Archives of Neurology & Psychiatry, 42,* 979–1000.

Knupfer, G. (1991). Abstaining for foetal health: The fiction that even light drinking is dangerous. *British Journal of Addiction, 86,* 1063–1073.

Kobak, R. R., & Sceery, A. (1988). Attachment in late adolescence: Working models, affect regulation, and presentations of self and others. *Child Development, 59,* 135–146.

Kochanska, G. (1997). Multiple pathways to conscience for children with different temperaments: From toddlerhood to age 5. *Developmental Psychology, 33,* 228–240.

Kochanska, G. (1997). Mutually responsive orientation between mothers and their young children: Implications for early socialization. *Child Development, 68,* 94–112.

Koestner, R., Weinberger, J., & McClelland, D. C. (1991). Task-intrinsic and social-extrinsic sources of arousal for motives assessed in fantasy and self-report. *Journal of Personality, 59,* 57–82.

Koestner, R., Zuroff, D., & Powers, T. (1991). Family origins of adolescent self-criticism and its continuity into adulthood. *Journal of Abnormal Psychology, 100,* 191–197.

Kohlberg, L. (1963). The development of children's orientations toward a moral order. I. Sequence in the development of moral thought. *Vita Humana, 6,* 11–33.

Kohlberg, L. (1969). Stage and sequence: The cognitive-developmental approach to socialization. In D. Goslin (Ed.), *Handbook of socialization and research* (pp. 347–480). Chicago: Rand-McNally.

Kohlberg, L. (1976). Moral stages and moralization: The cognitive-developmental perspective. In T. Lickona (Ed.), *Moral development and behavior: Theory, research, and social issues.* New York: Holt, Rinehart, & Winston.

Kohlberg, L., & Kramer, R. (1969). Continuities and discontinuities in childhood and adult moral development. *Human Development, 12,* 93–120.

Kohlberg, L. A. (1966). A cognitive-developmental analysis of children's sex-role concepts and attitudes. In E. E. Maccoby (Ed.), *The development of sex differences.* Stanford, CA: Stanford University Press.

Kohlenberg, R. J., & Tsai, M. (1994). Improving cognitive therapy for depression with functional analytic psychotherapy: Theory and case study. *Behavior Analyst, 17,* 305–319.

Kohnken, G., & Maass, A. (1988). Eyewitness testimony: False alarms on biased instructions? *Journal of Applied Psychology, 73,* 363–370.

Kohut, H. (1971). *The analysis of the self: A systematic approach to the treatment of narcissistic personality disorders.* New York: International Universities Press.

Kohut, H. (1977). *The restoration of the self.* New York: International Universities Press.

Kolb, B., & Gibb, R. (1991). Environmental enrichment and cortical injury: Behavioral and anatomical consequences of frontal cortex lesions. *Cerebral Cortex, 1,* 189–198.

Kolb, F., & Whishaw, I. (1990). *Fundamentals of human neuropsychology* (3rd ed.). New York: Freeman.

Konishi, M. (1995). Neural mechanisms of auditory image formation. In M. S. Gazzaniga et al. (Eds.), *The cognitive neurosciences.* (pp. 269–277). Cambridge: MIT Press.

Konner, M. (1991). Universals of behavioral development in relation to brain myelination. In K. R. Gibson & A. C. Petersen (Eds.), *Brain maturation and cognitive development: Comparative and cross-cultural perspectives.* New York: Aldine de Gruyter.

Koocher, G. P. (1991). Questionable methods in alcoholism research. *Journal of Consulting and Clinical Psychology, 59,* 246–248.

Kopp, C. B. (1989). Regulation of distress and negative emotions: A developmental view. *Developmental Psychology, 25,* 343–354.

Koriat, A., & Goldsmith, M. (1996). Memory metaphors and the real-life/laboratory controversy: Correspondence versus storehouse conceptions of memory. *Behavioral & Brain Sciences, 19,* 167–228.

Korn, J. H., Davis, R., Davis, S. F. (1991). Historians' and chairpersons' judgments of eminence among psychologists. *American Psychologist, 46,* 789–792.

Korten, A. E., Henderson, A. S., Christensen, H., Jorm, A. F., et al. (1997). A prospective study of cognitive function in the elderly. *Psychological Medicine, 27,* 919–930.

Kosmitzki, C., & John, O. (1993). The implicit use of explicit conceptions of social intelligence. *Personality and Individual Differences, 15,* 11–23.

Koss, M. (1993). Rape: Scope, impact, interventions, and public policy responses. *American Psychologist, 48,* 1062–1069.

Kosslyn, S. M. (1983). *Ghosts in the mind's machine.* New York: Norton.

Kosslyn, S. M., Alpert, N. M., Thompson, W. L., Maljokovic, V., et al. (1993). Visual imagery activates topographically organized visual cortex: PET investigations. *Journal of Cognitive Neuroscience, 5*(3), 263–287.

Kosslyn, S. M., Digirolamo, G. J., Thompson, W. L., & Alpert, N. M. (1998). Mental rotation of objects versus hands: Neural mechanisms revealed by positron emission tomography, *Psychophysiology, 35,* 151–161.

Kosslyn, S. M., Thompson, W. L., Kim, I. J., & Alpert, N. M. (1995). Topographical representations of mental images in primary visual cortex. *Nature, 378,* 496–498.

Kouri, E., Pope, H. G., Yurgelun-Todd, D., Gruber, S. (1995). Attributes of heavy vs. occasional marijuana smokers in a college population. *Biological Psychiatry, 38,* 475–481.

Kovacs, D. M., Parker, J. G., & Hoffman, L. W. (1996). Behavioral, affective, and social correlates of involvement in cross-sex friendship in elementary school. *Child Development, 67,* 2269–2286.

Kraemer, G. (1992). A psychobiological theory of attachment. *Behavioral and Brain Sciences, 15,* 493–541.

Kramer, L., & Gottman, J. (1992). Becoming a sibling: "With a little help from my friends." *Developmental Psychology, 28,* 685–699.

Kramer, P. (1993). *Listening to Prozac.* New York: Viking Press.

Kraus, N., Malmfors, T., & Slovic, P. (1992). Intuitive toxicology: Expert and lay judgments of chemical risks. *Risk Analysis, 12,* 215–232.

Kraus, S. J. (1995). Attitudes and the prediction of behavior: A meta-analysis of the empirical literature. *Personality & Social Psychology Bulletin, 21,* 58–75.

Kring, A. M., & Gordon, A. H. (1998). Sex differences in emotion: Expression, experience, and physiology. *Journal of Personality & Social Psychology, 74,* 686–703.

Kripke, D., Simons, R. N., Garfinkel, L., & Hammond, E. C. (1979). Short and long sleep and sleeping pills. *Archives of General Psychiatry, 36,* 103–116.

Krishnan, K. R. (1993). Neuroanatomic substrates of depression in the elderly. *Journal of Geriatric Psychiatry and Neurology, 6,* 39–58.

Krosnick, J., Betz, A., Jussim, L., Lynn, A., & Stephens, L. (1992). Subliminal conditioning of attitudes. *Personality and Social Psychology Bulletin, 18,* 152–162.

Kruesi, M., Hibbs, E., Zahn, T., & Keysor, C. (1992). A 2-year prospective follow-up study of children and adolescents with disruptive behavior disorders: Prediction by cerebrospinal fluid 5-hydroxyindoleacetic acid, homovanillic acid, and autonomic measures? *Archives of General Psychiatry, 49,* 429–435.

Kuebli, J., Butler, S., & Fivush, R. (1995). Mother-child talk about past emotions: Relations of maternal language and child gender over time. *Cognition and Emotion, 9,* 265–283.

Kuhl, P. K., & Meltzoff, A. N. (1988). Speech and an intermodal object of perception. In A. Tonas (Ed.), *Minnesota symposium on child psychology: Vol. 20. Perceptual development in infancy.* Hillsdale, NJ: Erlbaum.

Kuhl, P. K., Williams, K. A., Lacerda, F., & Stevens, K. N. (1992). Linguistic experience alters phonetic perception in infants by 6 months of age. *Science, 255*(5044), 606–608.

Kuhn, D. (1976). Short-term longitudinal evidence for the sequentiality of Kohlberg's early stages of moral judgment. *Developmental Psychology, 12,* 162–166.

Kuhn, T. S. (1970). *The structure of scientific revolutions.* (2nd ed.). Chicago: University of Chicago Press.

Kuiken, D., (Ed.) (1991). *Mood and memory: Theory, research, and applications.* Newbury Park, CA: Sage.

Kuiper, N. A., & Derry, P. A. (1982). Depressed and nondepressed content self-reference in mild depression. *Journal of Personality, 50,* 67–79.

Kuiper, N. A., Olinger, L. J., MacDonald, M. R., & Shaw, B. F. (1985). Self-schema processing of depressed and nondepressed content: The effects of vulnerability on depression. *Social Cognition, 3,* 77–93.

Kunda, Z. (1990). The case for motivated reasoning. *Psychological Bulletin, 108,* 480–498.

Kunda, Z., & Thagard, P. (1996). Forming impressions from stereotypes, traits, and behaviors: A parallel-constraint-satisfaction theory. *Psychological Review, 103,* 284–308.

Kunzendorf, R. G., Spanos, N. P., & Wallace, B. (Eds.) (1996). *Hypnosis and imagination. Imagery and human development series.* New York: Baywood Publishing Co., Inc.

Kuo-shu, Y., & Bond, M. H. (1990). Exploring implicit personality theories with indigenous or imported constructs: The Chinese case. *Journal of Personality and Social Psychology, 58,* 1087–1095.

Kvavilashvili, L. (1987). Remembering intention as a distinct form of memory. *British Journal of Psychology, 78,* 507–518.

LaBar, K. S., & LeDoux, J. E. (1996). Partial disruption of fear conditioning in rats with unilateral amygdala damage: Correspondence with unilateral temporal lobectomy in humans. *Behavioral Neuroscience, 110,* 991–997.

Labouvie-Vief, G. (1985). Intelligence and cognition. In J. E. Birren & K. W. Schaie (Eds.), *Handbook of the psychology of aging.* (2nd ed.). New York: Van Nostrand.

Labouvie-Vief, G., & Gonda, J. N. (1976). Cognitive strategy training and intellectual performance in the elderly. *Journal of Gerontology, 31,* 327–332.

Labouvie-Vief, G., & Schell, D. A. (1982). Learning and memory in late life. In B. B. Wolman (Ed.), *Handbook of developmental psychology.* Englewood Cliffs, NJ: Prentice-Hall.

Lachman, S. J., & Bass, A. R. (1985). A direct study of halo effect. *Journal of Psychology, 119,* 535–540.

Ladd, G. W., & Mize, J. (1983). A cognitive-social learning model of social skill training. *Psychologial Review, 90,* 127–157.

LaFreniere, P. J., & Sroufe, L. A. (1985). Profiles of peer competence in the preschool: Interrelations between measures, influences of social ecology, and relation to attachment history. *Developmental Psychology, 21,* 56–69.

Laing, D. G., Prescott, J., Bell, G. A., & Gilmore, R. (1993). A cross-cultural study of taste discrimination with Australians and Japanese. *Chemical Senses, 18,* 161–168.

Lakoff, G. (1985). *Women, fire, and dangerous things.* Chicago: University of Chicago Press.

Lakoff, G. (1989). A suggestion for a linguistics with connectionist foundations. In D. Touretzky, G. E. Hinton, et al. (Eds.), *Proceedings of the 1988 Connectionist Models Summer School.* (pp. 301–314). San Mateo, CA: Morgan Kaufmann, Inc.

Lakoff, G. (1997). How unconscious metaphorical thought shapes dreams. In D. J. Stein (Ed.), *Cognitive science and the unconscious. Progress in psychiatry* (No. 52) (pp. 89–120). Washington, DC: American Psychiatric Press.

Lamb, H. R., & Lamb, D. M. (1990). Factors contributing to homelessness among the chronically and severely mentally ill. *Hospital and Community Psychiatry, 41,* 301–305.

Lamb, M. E. (1987). Introduction: The emergent American father. In M. E. Lamb (Ed.), *The father's role: Cross-cultural perspective.* Hillsdale, NJ: Erlbaum.

Lamb, M. E., & Roopnarine, J. L. (1979). Peer influences on sex-role development in preschoolers. *Child Development, 50,* 1219–1222.

Lambert, M. J., Shapiro, D. A., & Bergin, A. E. (1986). The effectiveness of psychotherapy. In S. L. Garfield and A. E. Bergin, (Eds.), *Handbook of psychotherapy and behavior change.* New York: John Wiley.

Lamberts, K. (1996). Exemplar models and prototype effects in similarity-based categorization. *Journal of Experimental Psychology: Learning, Memory, & Cognition, 22,* 1503–1507.

Lame Deer, J., & Erdoes, R. (1972). *Lame Deer, seeker of visions.* New York: Simon & Schuster.

Landau, E., & Weissler, K. (1993). Parental environment in families with gifted and nongifted children. *Journal of Psychology, 127,* 129–142.

Landesman, S., & Butterfield, E. C. (1987). Normalization and deinstitutionalization of mentally retarded individuals: Controversy and facts. *American Psychologist, 42,* 809–816.

Landesman-Dwyer, S., & Butterfield, E. C. (1983). Mental retardation: Developmental issues in cognitive and social adaptation. In M. Lewis (Ed.), *Origins of intelligence: Infancy and early childhood* (2nd ed.). New York: Plenum Press.

Landman, J. T., & Dawes, R. M. (1982). Psychotherapy outcome: Smith and Glass' conclusions stand up under scrutiny. *American Psychologist, 37,* 504–516.

Lane, C., & Hobfoll, S. E. (1992). How loss affects anger and alienates potential supporters. *Journal of Consulting and Clinical Psychology, 6,* 935–942.

Lang, P. (1995). The emotion probe: Studies of motivation and attention. *American Psychologist, 50,* 372–385.

Lang, P. J. (1994). The varieties of emotional experience: A meditation on James-Lange theory. *Psychological Review, 101,* 212–221.

Lange, C. G. (1885). The amotions: A psychophysiological study, trans. I. A. Haupt. In C. G. Lange & W. James (Eds.), *Psychology classics,* Vol. I. Baltimore, MD: Williams & Wilkins, 1922.

Langlois, J., Ritter, J. M., Roggman, L., & Vaughn, L. S. (1991). Facial diversity and infant preferences for attractive faces. *Developmental Psychology, 27,* 79–84.

Langlois, J. H., & Downs, A. C. (1980). Mothers, fathers, and peers as socialization agents of sex-typed play behaviors in young children. *Child Development, 51,* 1217–1247.

Langs, O. (1946). Chinese family and society. New Haven, CT: Yale University Press.

Lanzetta, J. T., Cartwright-Smith, J., & Kleck, R. E. (1976). Effects of nonverbal dissimulation on emotional experience and autonomic arousal. *Journal of Personality and Social Psychology, 33,* 354–370.

Laroche, S., Doyere, V., Redini-Del Negro, C., & Burette, F. (1995). Neural mechanisms of associative memory: Role of long-term potentiation. In J. L. McGaugh, N. M. Weinberger, et al. (Eds.), *Brain and memory: Modulation and mediation of neuroplasticity.* (pp. 277–302). New York: Oxford University Press.

Larsen, K. S. (1990). The Asch conformity experiment: Replication and trans-historical comparisons. *Journal of Social Behavior and Personality, 5,* 163–168.

Larsen, R. J., & Diener, E. (1987). Affect intensity as an individual differences characteristic: A review. *Journal of Research in Personality, 21,* 1–39.

Larsen, R. J., Billings, D. W., & Cutler, S. E. (1996). Affect intensity and individual differences in informational style. *Journal of Personality, 64,* 185–207.

Larson, R. W. (1997). The emergence of solitude as a constructive domain of experience in early adolescence. *Child Development, 68,* 80–93.

Larson, R. W., Richards, M. H., Moneta, G., Holmbeck, G., & Duckett, E. (1996). Changes in adolescents' daily interactions with their families from ages 10 to 18: Disengagement and transformation. *Developmental Psychology, 32,* 744–754.

Larson, R., Csikszentmihalyi, M., & Graef, R. (1980). Mood variability and the psychosocial adjustment of adolescents. *Journal of Youth and Adolescence, 9,* 469–490.

Larsson, G., Bohlon, A., & Turnell, R. (1985). Prospective study of children exposed to various amounts of alcohol in utero. *Archives of Disease in Childhood, 60,* 306–321.

Larzelere, R. (1986). Moderate spanking: Model or deterrent of children's aggression in the family? *Journal of Family Violence, 1,* 27–36.

Larzelere, R. E., Schneider, W. N., Larson, D. B., & Pike, P. L. (1996). The effects of discipline responses in delaying toddler misbehavior recurrences. *Child & Family Behavior Therapy, 18,* 35–57.

Lasswell, H. D. (1948). The structure and function of communication in society. In L. Bryson (Ed.), *Communication of ideas.* New York: HarperCollins.

Latane, B., & Rodin, J. (1969). A lady in distress: Inhibiting effects of friends and strangers on bystander intervention. *Journal of Experimental Social Psychology, 5,* 189–202.

Latimer, P. R. (1979). The behavior treatment of self-excoriation in a twelve-year-old girl. *Journal of Behavioral Therapy and Experimental Psychiatry, 10,* 349–352.

Laub, J. B., & Sampson, R. J. (1995). The long-term effect of punitive discipline. In J. McCord (Ed.), *Coercion and punishment in long-term perspectives* (pp. 247–258). New York: Cambridge University Press.

Laudenslager, M. L., & Boccia, M. L. (1996). Some observations on psychosocial stressors, immunity, and individual differences in nonhuman primates. *American Journal of Primatology, 39,* 205–221.

Lavie, P. (1996). *The enchanted world of sleep* (A. Berris, Trans.). New Haven: Yale University Press.

Lavigne, V., & Finley, G. E. (1990). Memory in middle-aged adults. *Educational Gerontology, 16,* 447–461.

Lavond, D. G., Kim, J. J., & Thompson, R. F. (1993). Mammalian brain substrates

of aversive classical conditioning. *Annual Review of Psychology, 44,* 317–342.

Lazarus, R. (1981). The stress and coping paradigm. In C. Eisdorfer, D., Cohen, A. Kleinman & P. Maxim (Eds.), *Models for clinical psychopathology.* New York: Spectrum.

Lazarus, R. S. (1966). *Psychological stress and the coping process.* New York: McGraw-Hill.

Lazarus, R. S. (1991). Cognition and motivation in emotion. *American Psychologist, 46,* 352–367.

Lazarus, R. S. (1993). From psychological stress to the emotions: A history of changing outlooks. *Annual Review of Psychology, 44,* 1–21.

Lazarus, R. S., & McCleary, R. A. (1951). Autonomic discrimination without awareness: A study of subception. *Psychological Review, 58,* 113–122.

Leahy, A. M. (1935). Nature-nurture and intelligence. *Genetic Psychological Monographs,* 237–308.

Leaper, C., Anderson, K. J., & Sanders, P. (1998). Moderators of gender effects on parents' talk to their children: A meta-analysis. *Developmental Psychology, 34,* 3–27.

Lecky, P. (1945). *Self-consistency: A theory of personality.* New York: Island Press.

LeDoux, J. (1995). Emotion: Clues from the brain. *Annual Review of Psychology, 46,* 209–235.

LeDoux, J. E. (1986). The neurobiology of emotion. In J. E. LeDoux & W. Hirst (Eds.), *Mind and brain: Dialogues in cognitive neuropsychology.* New York: Cambridge University Press.

LeDoux, J. E. (1989). Cognitive-emotional interactions in the brain. *Cognition and Emotion, 3,* 267–289.

LeDoux, J. E. (1992). Emotional memory systems in the brain. *Behavioural Brain Research, 58,* 69–79.

LeDoux, J. E., Wilson, D. H., & Gazzinaga, M. S. (1977). Manipulo-spatial aspects of central lateralization. *Neuropsychologia, 15,* 743–750.

Lee, D. (1950). The conception of the self among the Wintu Indians. In D. Lee (Ed.), *Freedom and culture.* Englewood Cliffs, NJ: Prentice-Hall, 1959.

Lee, E. (1951). Negro intelligence and selective migration: A Philadelphia test of Klineberg's hypothesis. *American Sociological Review, 61,* 227–233.

Lee, H. J. (1991). Relationship of hardiness and current life events to perceived health in rural adults. *Research in Nursing and Health, 14,* 351–359.

Lee, Y., & Seligman, M. E. P. (1997). Are Americans more optimistic than the Chinese? *Personality & Social Psychology Bulletin, 23,* 32–40.

Leff, J. (1988). *Psychiatry around the globe: A transcultural view.* (2nd ed.) London: Gaskell.

Legerstee, M., Anderson, D., & Schaffer, A. (1998). Five- and eight-month-old infants recognize their faces and voices as familiar and social stimuli. *Child Development, 69,* 37–50.

Lehman, D. R., Lempert, R. O., & Nisbett, R. E. (1988). The effects of graduate training on reasoning: Formal discipline and thinking about everyday-life events. *American Psychologist, 43,* 431–442.

Lehman, D. R., & Nisbett, R. E. (1990). A longitudinal study of the effects of undergraduate training on reasoning. *Developmental Psychology, 26,* 952–960.

Lehman, D. R., Wortman, C. B., & Williams, A. F. (1987). Long-term effects of losing a spouse or child in a motor vehicle crash. *Journal of Personality and Social Psychology, 52,* 218–231.

Lehmann, H. E. (1985). Affective disorders: Clinical features. In H. I. Kaplan & B. J. Sadock (Eds.), *Comprehensive textbook of psychiatry.* (4th ed.), Baltimore, MD: Williams & Wilkins.

Lehmann, H. E., & Cancro, R. (1985). Schizophrenia: Clinical features. In H. Kaplan & B. J. Sadock (Eds.), *Comprehensive textbook of psychiatry* (4th ed.). Baltimore, MD: Williams & Wilkins.

Lehrman, D. S. (1956). On the organization of maternal behavior and the problem of instinct. In *L'instinct dans le Comportement des Animaux et de l'homme.* Paris: Masson et Cie.

Lempers, J. D., Flavell, E. R., & Flavell, J. H. (1977). The development in very young children of tacit knowledge concerning visual perception. *Genetic Psychology Monographs, 95,* 3–53.

Lenneberg, E. (1967). *The biological foundations of language.* New York: John Wiley.

Leonard, B. (1993). The comparative pharmacology of new antidepressants. *Journal of Clinical Psychiatry, 54,* 3–15.

Lepper, M. R., & Greene, D. (1978). *The hidden costs of reward: New perspectives on the psychology of motivation.* New York: Halstead.

Lerner, R. (1991). Changing organism-context relations as the basic process of development: A developmental contextual perspective. *Developmental Psychology, 27,* 27–32.

LeVay, S. (1991). A difference in hypothalamic structure between heterosexual and homosexual men. *Science, 253,* 1034–1037.

Levenson, J. L., & Bemis, C. (1991). The role of psychological factors in cancer onset and progression. *Psychosomatics, 32,* 124–132.

Levenson, R., & Ruef, A. (1992). Empathy: A physiological substrate. *Journal of Personality and Social Psychology, 63,* 234–246.

Levenson, R. W. (1992). Autonomic nervous system differences among emotions. *Psychological Science, 3, 23–27.*

Levenson, R. W., Ekman, P., & Friesen, W. (1990). Voluntary facial action generates emotion-specific autonomic nervous system activity. *Psychophysiology, 27, 363–385.*

Levenson, R. W., Ekman, P., Heider, K., & Friesen, W. V. (1992). Emotion and autonomic nervous system activity in the Minangkabau of West Sumatra. *Journal of Personality and Social Psychology, 62,* 972–988.

Leventhal, E. A., Leventhal, H., Shacham, S., & Easterling, D. V. (1989). Active coping reduces reprots of pain from childbirth. *Journal of Consulting and Clinical Psychology, 57,* 365–371.

Leventhal, H., & Tomarken, A. J. (1986). Emotion: Today's problems. *Annual Review of Psychology, 37,* 565–610.

Levin, R. B., & Gross, A. M. (1985). The role of relaxation in systematic desensitization. *Behavior Research and Therapy, 23,* 187–196.

Levine, J. M., & Moreland, R. L. (1998). Small groups. In D. T. Gilbert, S. T. Fiske, et al. (Eds.), *The handbook of social psychology, Vol. 2* (4th ed). (pp. 415–469). Boston: McGraw-Hill.

Levine, L. J., & Burgess, S. L. (1997). Beyond general arousal: Effects of specific emotions on memory. *Social Cognition, 15,* 157–181.

LeVine, R. (1982). *Culture, behavior, and personality.* (2nd ed.). Chicago: Aldine.

LeVine, R. A., & LeVine, B. B. (1963). Nyasongo: A Gusii Community in Kenya. In B. Whiting (Ed.), *Six cultures: Studies in child rearing* (pp. 19–202). New York: John Wiley.

Levine, R. V., Martinez, T., Brase, G., & Sorenson, K. (1994). Helping in 36 U.S. cities. *Journal of Personality and Social Psychology, 67,* 69–82.

Levinger, G. (1976). Social psychological perspectives on marital dissolution. *Journal of Social Issues, 32,* 21–47.

Levinson, D. (1978). *The seasons of a man's life.* New York: Ballantine Books.

Levinson, D. J., Darrow, C. N., Klein, E. B., Levinson, M. H., McKee, B. (1978). *The seasons of a man's life.* New York: Alfred A. Knopf.

Levy, B., & Langer, E. (1994). Aging free from negative stereotypes: Successful memory in China and among the American deaf. *Journal of Personality & Social Psychology, 66,* 989–997.

Lewes, K. (1988). *The psychoanalytic theory of male homosexuality.* New York: Simon & Schuster.

Lewicki, P. (1985). Nonconscious biasing effects of single instances on subsequent judgments. *Journal of Personality and Social Psychology, 48,* 563–574.

Lewicki, P. (1986). *Nonconscious social information processing.* New York: Academic Press.

Lewin, K. (1939). Field theory and experiment in social psychology: Concepts and methods. *American Journal of Sociology, 44,* 868–897.

Lewinsohn, P. M., Gotlibm, I. H., Lewinsohn, M., Seeley, J. R., & Allen, N. B. (1998). Gender differences in anxiety disorders and anxiety symptoms in adolescents. *Journal of Abnormal Psychology, 107,*109–117.

Lewis, D. O., Yeager, C. A., Swica, Y., Pincus, J. H., & Lewis, M. (1997). Objective documentation of child abuse and dissociation in 12 murderers with dissociative identity disorder. *American Journal of Psychiatry, 154,* 1703–1710.

Lewis, J. E., Malow, R. M., & Ireland, S. J. (1997). HIV/AIDS in heterosexual college students: A review of a decade of literature. *Journal of American College Health, 45,* 147–158.

Lewis, M. B. G. J. (1979). *Social cognition and the acquisition of self.* New York: Plenum Press.

Lewis, M., & Bendersky, M. (1995). *Mothers, babies, and cocaine: The role of toxins in development.* New Jersey: Lawrence Erlbaum Associates, Inc.

Liben, L., & Signorella, M. (1993). Gender-schematic processing in children: The role of initial interpretations of stimuli. *Developmental Psychology, 29,* 141–149.

Liberman, A., & Chaiken, S. (1992). Defensive processing of personally relevant health messages. *Journal of Experimental Social Psychology.*

Lieberman, J., Bogerts, B., Degreef, G., Ashtari, M., Lantos, G., & Alvir, J. (1992). Qualitative assessment of brain morphology in acute and chronic schizophrenia. *American Journal of Psychiatry, 149,* 784–794.

Lieberman, S. (1956). The effects of changes in roles on the attitudes of role occupants. *Human Relations, 9,* 385–402.

Lifton, R. J. (1963). *Thought reform and the psychology of totalism: A study of brainwashing in China.* New York: W. W. Norton.

Lifton, R. J. (1980). Nuclearism. *Journal of Clinical Child Psychology, 9,* 119–124.

Light, L. (1990). Interactions between memory and language in old age. In J. E. Birren & K. W. Schaie (Eds.), *Handbook of the Psychology of Aging.* (3rd ed.). NewYork: Van Nostrand Reinhold.

Lin, E., & Peterson, C. (199). Pessimistic explanatory style and response to illness. *Behaviour Therapy & Research, 28,* 243–248.

Lindberg, M. (1980). Is knowledge base development a necessary and sufficient condition for memory development? *Journal of Experimental Child Psychology, 30,* 401–410.

Lindley, R. H., & Smith, W. R. (1992). Coding tests as measures of IQ: Cognitive or motivation? *Personality and Individual Differences, 13,* 25–29.

Linehan, M. (1987). Dialectical behavior therapy for borderline personality disorder: Theory and method. *Bulletin of the Menninger Clinic, 51,* 261–276.

Linehan, M. M. (1987). Dialectical behavioral therapy: A cognitive behavioral approach to parasuicide. *Journal of Personality Disorders, 1,* 328–333.

Lisspers, J., & Ost, L. (1990). Long-term follow-up of migraine treatment: Do the effects remain up to six years? *Behaviour Therapy and Research, 28,* 313–322.

Litt, M., Babor, T., DelBoca, F., Kadden, R., & Cooney, N. (1992). Types of alcoholics, II: Application of an empirically derived typology to treatment matching. *Archives of General Psychiatry, 49,* 609–614.

Liu, H., Mantyh, P. W., & Basbaum, A. I. (1997). NMDA-receptor regulation of substance P release from primary afferent nociceptors. *Nature, 386,* 721–724.

Livesley, W. J., & Bromley, D. B. (1973). *Person perception in childhood and adolescence.* London: John Wiley.

Livingstone, M., & Hubel, D. H. (1988). Segregation of form, color, movement, and depth: Anatomy, physiology, and perception. *Science, 240,* 740–749.

Livson, F. B. (1976). Patterns of personality development in middle-aged women: A longitudinal study. *International Journal of Aging and Human Development, 7,* 107–115.

Livson, F. B. (1981). Paths to psychological health in the middle years: Sex differences. In D. Eichorn, J. Clausen, N. Haan, M. Honzik & P. Mussen (Eds.), *Present and past in middle life.* New York: Academic Press.

Lochman, J., Coie, J., Underwood, M., & Terry, R. (1993). Effectiveness of a social relations intervention program for aggressive and nonaggressive, rejected children. *Journal of Consulting and Clinical Psychology, 61,* 1053–1058.

Locke, E. A. (1991). Goal theory vs. control theory: Contrasting approaches to understanding work motivation. *Motivation and Emotion, 15,* 9–27.

Locke, E. A. (1996). Motivation through conscious goal setting. *Applied and Preventive Psychology, 5,* 117–124.

Locke, E., & Latham, G. (1990). *A theory of goal-setting and task performance.* Englewood Cliffs, NJ: Prentice-Hall.

Locke, J. (1950). *An essay concerning human understanding.* New York: Dover.

Lockhart, R. S., & Craik, F. (1990). Levels of processing: A retrospective commentary on a framework for memory research. *Canadian Journal of Psychology, 44,* 87–112.

Loeb, R. C., Horst, L., & Horton, P. J. (1980). Family interaction patterns associated with self-esteem in preadolescent girls and boys. *Merill-Palmer Quarterly, 26,* 203–217.

Loebel, A., Lieberman, J. A., Alvir, J., Mayerhoff, D., Geisler, S., & Syzmanski, S. (1992). Duration of psychosis and outcome in first-episode schizophrenia. *American Journal of Psychiatry, 149,* 1183–1188.

Loehlin, J. (1992). *Genes and environment in personality development.* New York: Guilford Press.

Loehlin, J. C. (1988). Human behavior genetics. *Annual Review of Psychology, 39,* 101–133.

Loehlin, J. C. (1989). Partitioning environmental and genetic contributions to behavioral development. *American Psychologist, 44,* 1285–1292.

Loehlin, J. C., Horn, J. M., & Willerman, L. (1989). Modeling IQ change: Evidence from the Texas Adoption Project. *Child Development, 60,* 993–1004.

Loehlin, J. C., Horn, J. M., & Willerman, L. (1997). Heredity, environment and IQ in the Texas Adoption Project. In R. J. Sternberg, E. L. Grigorenko, et al. (Eds.), *Intelligence, heredity, and environment.* (pp. 105–125). New York: Cambridge University Press.

Loehlin, J. C., Lindzeg, G., & Spuhler, J. N. (1975). *Race differences in intelligence.* San Francisco, CA: Freeman.

Loehlin, J. C., Willerman, L., & Horn, J. M. (1987). Personality resemblance in adoptive families: A 10-year follow-up. *Journal of Personality and Social Psychology, 53,* 961–969.

Loehlin, J. C., Willerman, L., & Horn, J. M. (1988). Human behavior genetics. *Annual Review of Psychology, 39,* 101–133.

Loehlin, J., Horn, J., & Willerman, L. (1990). Modeling IQ change: Evidence from the Texas Adoption Project. *Child Development, 60,* 993–1004.

Loevinger, J. (1976). *Ego development.* San Francisco: Jossey-Bass.

Loevinger, J. (1985). Revision of the sentence completion test for ego development. *Journal of Personality and Social Psychology, 48,* 420–427.

Loewenstein, W. R. (1960). Biological transducers. *Scientific American,* 98–108.

Loftus, E. (1997a). Creating false memories. *Scientific American, 277,* 70–75.

Loftus, E. (1997b). Memory for a past that never was. *Current Directions in Psychological Science, 6,* 60–65.

Loftus, E. F. (1993). The reality of repressed memories. *American Psychologist, 48*(5), 518–537.

Loftus, E. F., Levidow, B., & Duensing, S. (1992). Who remembers best? Individual differences in memory for events that occurred in a science museum. *Applied Cognitive Psychology, 6,* 93–107.

Loftus, E. F., & Palmer, J. C. (1974). Reconstruction and automobile destruction. An example of the interaction between language and memory. *Journal of Verbal Learning and Verbal Behavior, 13,* 585–589.

Loftus, E. F., Polonsky, S., & Fullilove, M. T. (1994). Memories of childhood sexual abuse: Remembering and repressing. *Psychology of Women Quarterly, 18,* 67–84.

Loftus, E. F., & Zanni, G. (1975). Eyewitness testimony: the influence of the wording of a question. *Bulletin of the Psychonomic Society, 5,* 86–88.

Logie, R. (1996). The seven ages of working memory. In J. T. E. Richardson, R. W. Engle, L. Hasher, R. Logie, E. Stoltzfus, and R. Zacks (Eds.), *Working memory and human cognition* (pp. 31–65). New York: Oxford University Press.

Lonner, W. J., & Malpass, R. (1994). *Psychology and Culture.* Needham Heights, MA: Allyn and Bacon.

Lonner, W., & Malpass R. (Eds.) (1994). *Readings in psychology and culture.* Boston: Allyn & Bacon.

Lopez, A., Atran, S., Coley, J. D., Medin, D. L., & Smith, E. E. (1997). The tree of life: Universal and cultural features of folkbiological taxonomies and inductions. *Cognitive Psychology, 32,* 251–295.

Lopez-Villegas, D., Kulisevsky, J., Deus, J., & Junque, C. (1996). Neuropsychological alterations in patients with computed tomography—Detected basal ganglia calcification. *Archives of Neurology, 53,* 251–256.

Lore, R., & Schultz, L. A. (1993). Control of human aggression: A comparative perspective. *American Psychologist, 48,* 16–25.

Lorenz, K. (1966). *On aggression.* New York: Harcourt, Brace & World.

Lorenz, K. (1979). *King Solomon's ring.* New York: HarperCollins.

Lott, A., & Lott, B. (1974). The role of reward in the formation of positive interpersonal attitudes. In T. Huston (Ed.), *Foundations of interpersonal attraction.* New York: Academic.

Low, B. S. (1989). Cross-cultural patterns in the training of children: An evolutionary perspective. *Journal of Comparative Psychology, 103,* 311–319.

Lozoff, B., Klein, N. K., Nelson, E. C., McClish, D., Manuel, M., & Chacon, M. (1998). Behavior of infants with iron-deficiency anemia. *Child Development, 69,* 24–36.

Lu, C., Shaikh, M. B., & Siegel, A. (1992). Role of NMDA receptors in hypothalamic facilitation of feline defensive rage elicited from the midbrain pariaqueductal gray. *Brain Research, 581,* 123–132.

Luborsky, L., Barber, J. P., & Crits-Christoph, P. (1990). Theory-based research for understanding the process of dynamic psychotherapy. *Journal of Consulting and Clinical Psychology, 58,* 281–287.

Luborsky, L., & Crits-Christoph, P. (1990). *Understanding transference: The core conflictual relationship theme method.* New York: Basic Books.

Luborsky, L., Docherty, J. P., Miller, N. E., & Barber, J. P. (1993). What's here and what's ahead in dynamic therapy research and practice? In N. E. Miller, L. Luborsky, et al. (Ed.), *Psychodynamic treatment research: A handbook for clinical practice.* (pp. 536–553). New York: Basicbooks, Inc.

Lubow, R. E., & Gewirtz, J. C. (1995). Latent inhibition in humans: Data, theory, and implications for schizophrenia. *Psychological Bulletin, 117,* 87–103.

Luchins, A. (1957). Primacy-recency in impression formation. In C. Hovland (Ed.), *The order of presentation in persuasion* (pp. 33–61). New Haven, CT: Yale University Press.

Ludolph, P. S., Westen, D., Misle, B., Jackson, A., et al. (1990). The borderline diagnosis in adolescents: Symptoms and developmental history. *American Journal of Psychiatry, 147,* 470–476.

Luria, A. R. (1973). *The working brain.* Harmondsworth: Penguin.

Lutz, C. (1988). Ethnographic perspectives on the emotion lexicon. In V. Hamilton, G. H. Bower, & N. Frijda (Eds.), *Cognitive perspectives on emotion and motivation* (pp. 399–419). Kluwer: Dordrecht.

Lutz, C. (1992). Culture and consciousness: A problem in the anthropology of knowledge. In F. S. Kessel, P. M. Cole, & D. L. Johnson (Eds.), *Self and consciousness: Multiple perspectives* (pp. 64–87). Hillsdale, NJ: Lawrence Erlbaum.

Lykken, D. T., Bouchard, T. J., McGue, M., & Tellegen, A. (1993). Heritability of interests: A twin study. *Journal of Applied Psychology, 78,* 649–661.

Lykken, D. T., McGue, M., Tellegen, A., & Bouchard, T. J. (1992). Emergenesis: Genetic traits that may not run in families. *American Psychologist, 47,* 1565–1577.

Lynch, O. M. (1990). The social construction of emotion in India. In O. M. Lynch (Ed.), *Divine passions: The social construction of emotion in India* (pp. 3–34). Berkeley: University of California Press.

Lynn, B., & Perl, E. R. (1996). Afferent mechanisms of pain. In L. Kruger, et al. (Eds.) *Pain and touch. Handbook of perception and cognition* (2nd ed.). (pp. 213–241). San Diego: Academic Press, Inc.

Lynn, S. J., Lock, T., Myers, B., & Payne, D. G. (1997). Recalling the unrecallable: Should hypnosis be used to recover memories in psychotherapy? *Current Directions in Psychological Science, 6,* 79–83.

Lyons, M. J., Eisen, S. A., Goldberg, J., True, W., Lin, N., Meyer, J. M., et al. (1998). A registry-based twin study of depression in men. *Archives of General Psychiatry, 55,* 468–472.

Lyons-Ruth, K., Connell, D., Grunebaum, H., & Botein, S. (1990). Infants at social risk: Maternal depression and familiy support services as mediators of infant development and security of attachment. *Child Development, 61,* 85–98.

Lyons-Ruth, K., Easterbrooks, M. A., & Cibelli, C. D. (1997). Infant attachment strategies, infant mental lag, and maternal depressive symptoms. Predictors of internalizing and externalizing problems at age 7. *Developmental Psychology, 33,* 681–692.

Lytton, H. (1990). Child and parent effects in boys' conduct disorder: A reinterpretation. *Developmental Psychology, 26,* 683–697.

Maccoby, E. (1992). The role of parents in the socialization of children: An historical overview. *Developmental Psychology, 28,* 1006–1017.

Maccoby, E. E., & Jacklin, C. N. (1974). *The psychology of sex differences.* Stanford, CA: Stanford University Press.

Maccoby, E. E., & Jacklin, C. N. (1980). Sex differences in aggression: A rejoinder and reprise. *Child Development, 51,* 964–980.

MacCorquodale, K. (1970). On Chomsky's review of Skinner's verbal behavior. *Journal of the Experimental Analysis of Behavior, 13,* 83–89.

MacCoun, R. J. (1998). Biases in the interpretation and the use of research results. *Annual Review of Psychology, 49,* 259–287.

Mace, R. (1996). Biased parental investment and reproductive success in Gabbra pastoralists. *Behavioral Ecology & Sociobiology, 38,* 75–81.

MacKinnon, D. F., Jamison, K. R., & DePaulo, J. R. (1997). Genetics of manic depressive illness. *Annual Review of Neuroscience, 10,* 355–373.

MacKinnon-Lewis, C., Starnes, R., Volling, B., & Johnson, S. (1997). Perceptions of parenting as predictors of boys' sibling and peer relations. *Developmental Psychology, 33,* 1024–1031.

Macklin, M. L., Metzger, L. J., Litz, B. T., McNally, R. J., Lasko, N. B., Orr, S. P., & Pitman, R. K. (1998). Lower precombat intelligence is a risk factor for posttraumatic stress disorder. *Journal of Consulting & Clinical Psychology, 66,* 323–326.

MacLean, P. D. (1982). On the origin and progressive evolution of the triune brain. In E. Armstrong & D. Falk, (Eds.), *Primate brain evolution.* New York: Plenum Press.

MacLean, P. D. (1990). A reinterpretation of memorative functions of the limbic system. In E. Goldberg, et al. (Eds.), *Contemporary neuropsychology and the legacy of Luria. Institute for research in behavioral neuroscience.* (pp. 127–154). Hillsdale, NJ: Lawrence Erlbaum Associates, Inc.

Macrae, C. N., Bodenhausen, G. V., & Milne, A. B. (1998). Saying no to unwanted thoughts: Self-focus and the regulation of mental life. *Journal of Personality & Social Psychology, 74,* 578–589.

Macrae, C. N., Milne, A. B., & Bodenhausen, G. (1994). Stereotypes as energy-saving devices: A peek inside the cognitive toolbox. *Journal of Personality and Social Psychology, 66,* 37–47.

MacWhinney, B. (1998). Models of the emergence of language. *Annual Review of Psychology, 49,* 199–227.

Madden, P. A. F., Heath, A. C., Rosenthal, N. E., & Martin, N. G. (1996). Seasonal changes in mood and behavior: The role of genetic factors. *Archives of General Psychiatry, 53,* 47–55.

Madigan, S., & O'Hara, R. (1992). Short-term memory at the turn of the century: Mary Whiton Calkin's memory research. Special Issue: The history of American psychology. *American Psychologist, 47,* 170–174.

Madrid, A., & Schwartz, M. (1991). Maternal-infant bonding and pediatric asthma: An initial investigation. *Pre- and Peri-natal Psychology Journal, 5,* 347–358.

Magee, W. J., Eaton, W. W., Wittchen, H., McGonagle, K. A., & Kessler, R. C. (1996). Agoraphobia, simple phobia, and social phobia in the National Comorbidity Survey. *Archives of General Psychiatry, 53,* 159–168.

Magnusson, D. (1996). The patterning of antisocial behavior and autonomic re-

activity. In D. M. Stoff, R. B. Cairns, et al. (Eds.), *Aggression and Violence: Genetic, Neurobiological, and Biosocial Perspectives.* (pp. 291–308). Mahwah, NJ: Lawrence Erlbaum Associates, Inc., Publishers.

Mahler, M., Pine, F., & Bergman, A. (1975). *The psychological birth of the human infant: Symbiosis and individualization.* New York: Basic Books.

Mahowald, M. W., & Schenck, C. H. (1989). In M. H. Kryger, T. Roth, & W. C. Dement (Eds.), *Principles and practice of sleep medicine.* Philadelphia: Saunders (pp. 389–401).

Main, M. (1990). Cross-cultural studies of attachment organization: Recent studies, changing methodologies, and the concept of conditional strategies. *Human Development, 33,* 48–61.

Main, M. (1995). Recent studies in attachment: Overview, with selected implications for clinical work. In S. Goldberg, R. Muir, et al. (Eds.). *Attachment Theory: Social, Developmental, and Clinical Perspectives.* (pp. 407–474). Hillsdale, NJ: Analytic Press, Inc.

Main, M., Kaplan, N., & Cassidy, J. (1985). Security in infancy, childhood, and adulthood: A move to the level of representation. In I. Bretherton & E. Waters (Eds.), Growing points of attachment theory and research. *Monographs of the Society for Research in Child Development, 50* (No. 1–2), 67–104.

Main, M., & Solomon, J. (1986). Discovery of a new, insecure-disorganized/disoriented attachment pattern. In T. Brazelton & M. Yogman, (Eds.), *Affective development in infancy* (pp. 95–124). Norwood, NJ: Ablex.

Maj, M., Veltro, F., Pirozzi, R., Lobrace, S., & Magliano, L. (1992). Pattern of recurrence of illness after recovery from an episode of major depression: A prospective study. *American Journal of Psychiatry, 149,* 795–800.

Major, B., Zubek, J. M., Cooper, M. L., Cozzarelli, C., et al. (1997). Mixed messages: Implications of social conflict and social support within close relationships for adjustment to a stressful life event. *Journal of Personality & Social Psychology, 72,* 1349–1363.

Malamuth, N. M., & Donnerstein, E. (1982). The effects of aggressive-pornographic mass media stimuli. In L. Berkowitz (Ed.) *Advances in Experimental Social Psychology,* Vol. 15. New York: Academic Press.

Malamuth, N. M., Heim, M., & Feshbach, S. (1980). Sexual responsiveness of college students to rape depictions: Inhibitory and disinhibitory effects. *Journal of Personality and Social Psychology, 38,* 399–408.

Maletsky, B., McFarland, B., & Burt, A. (1994). Refractory obsessive compulsive disorder and ECT. *Convulsive Therapy, 10,* 34–42.

Malt, B., & Smith, E. E. (1984). Correlated properties in natural categories. *Journal of Verbal Learning and Verbal Behavior, 23,* 250–269.

Malt, B. C. (1993). Concept structure and category boundaries. In G. V. Nakamura, D. L. Medin, and R. Taraban (Eds.), Categorization by humans and machines. *The psychology of learning and motivation: Advances in research and theory* (Vol. 29) (pp. 363–390). San Diego: Academic Press, Inc.

Mandler, G. (1980). Recognizing: The judgment of previous occurrence. *Psychological Review, 87,* 252–271.

Mandler, G. (1997). *Human nature explored.* New York: Oxford University Press.

Mandler, G., & Nakamura, Y. (1987). Aspects of consciousness. *Personality and Social Psychology Bulletin, 13,* 299–313.

Mangelsdorf, S., Gunnar, M., Kestenbaum, R., Lang, S., & Andreas, D. (1990). Infant proneness-to-distress temperament, maternal personality, and mother-infant attachment: Associations and goodness of fit. *Child Development, 61,* 820–831.

Manis, M., Nelson, T. E., & Shedler, J. (1988). Stereotypes and social judgment: Extremity, assimilation, and contrast. *Journal of Personality and Social Psychology, 55,* 28–36.

Manis, M., Paskewitz, J., & Cotler, S. (1986). Stereotypes and social judgment. *Journal of Personality and Social Psychology, 50,* 461–473.

Manji, H. K., Chen, G., Shimon, H., Hsiao, J. K., Potter, W. Z., & Belmaker, R. H. (1995) Guanine nucleotide-binding proteins in bipolar affective disorder: Effects of long-term lithium treatment. *Archives of General Psychiatry, 52,* 135–144.

Mann, J. (1982). *A casebook in time-limited psychotherapy.* New York: McGraw-Hill.

Mann, J. J., McBridge, P. A., Brown, R. P., Linnoila, M., Leon, A. C., et al. (1992). Relationship between central and peripheral serotonin indexes in depressed and suicidal psychiatric inpatients. *Archives of General Psychiatry, 49,* 442–446.

Mannuzza, S., Klein, R. G., Bessler, A., Malloy, P., & Lpadula, M. (1998). Adult psychiatric status of hyperative boys grown up. *American Journal of Psychiatry, 155,* 493–498.

Mannuzza, S., Klein, R. G., Bonagura, N., Malloy, P., Giampino, T., & Addali, K. (1991). Hyperactive boys almost grown up, V: A replication of psychiatric status. *Archives of General Psychiatry, 48,* 77–83.

Manson, J. E., Colditz, G. A., Stampfer, M. J., Willett, W. C., Rosner, B., Monson, R. R., Speizer, F., & Hennekens, C. (1990). A prospective study of obesity and risk of coronary heart disease in women. *New England Journal of Medicine, 322,* 882–889.

Maquet, P., Peters, J., Aerts, J., Delfiore, G., et al. (1996). Functional neuroanatomy of human rapid-eye-movement sleep and dreaming. *Nature, 383,* 163–166.

Marcel, A. J. (1983). Conscious and unconscious perception: Experiments on visual masking and word recognition. *Cognitive Psychology, 15,* 197–237.

Marcia, J. (1987). The identity status approach to the study of ego identity development. In T. Honess & K. Yardley (Eds.), *Self and identity: Perspectives across the lifespan* (pp. 161–171). Boston: Routledge & Kegan Paul.

Marcotte, A., & Morere, D. (1990). Speech lateralization in deaf populations: Evidence for a developmental critical period. *Brain & Language, 39,* 134–152.

Marcus, D. E., & Overton, W. E. (1978). The development of cognitive gender constancy and sex role preferences. *Child Development, 49,* 434–444.

Marcus, G. F. (1993). Negative evidence in language acquisition. *Cognition, 46,* 53–85.

Margolskee, R. (1995). Receptor mechanisms in gustation. In R. L. Doty (Ed.), *Handbook of olfaction and gustation.* New York: Marcel Dekker.

Marks, G. (1984). Thinking one's abilities are unique and one's opinions are common. *Personality and Social Psychological Bulletin, 10,* 203–208.

Marks, I. M. (1969). *Fears and phobias.* New York: Academic Press.

Markus, H. (1977). Self-schemata and processing information about the self. *Journal of Personality and Social Psychology, 35,* 63–78.

Markus, H., & Cross, S. (1990). The interpersonal self. In L. Pervin (Ed.), *Handbook of personality: Theory and research* (pp. 576–608). New York: Guilford Press.

Markus, H., & Kitayama, S. (1991). Culture and the self: implications for cognition, emotion, and motivation. *Psychological Review, 98,* 224–253.

Markus, H., & Nurius, P. (1986). Possible selves. *American Psychologist, 41,* 954–969.

Markus, H., & Wurf, E. (1987). The dynamic self-concept: A social psychological perspective. *Annual Review of Psychology, 38,* 299–337.

Markus, H., & Zajonc, R. B. (1985). The cognitive perspective in social psychology. In G. Lindzey and E. Aronson (Eds.), *Handbook of social psychology.* Reading, MA: Addison-Wesley.

Marlatt, G. A., & Baer, J. S. (1988). Addictive behaviors: Etiology and treatment. *Annual Review of Pychology, 39,* 223–252.

Marsh, R. L., Hiscks, J. L., & Bink, M. L. (1998). Activation of completed, uncompleted, and partially completed intentions. *Journal of Experimental Psychology: Learning, Memory and Cognition, 24,* 350–361.

Marshall, D. A., & Moulton, D. G. (1981). Olfactory sensitivity to a-ionone in humans and dogs. *Chemical Senses, 6,* 53–61.

Marshall, D. S. (1971). Sexual behavior on Mangaia. In D. S. Marshall, & R. C. Suggs (Eds.) *Human sexual behavior: Variations in the ethnographic spectrum.* New York: Basic Books.

Marshall, G., & Zimbardo, P. G. (1979). Affective consequences of inadequately explained physiological arousal. *Journal of Personality and Social Psychology, 37,* 970–988.

Martikainen, P., & Valkonen, T. (1996). Mortality after the death of a spouse: Rates and causes of death in a large Finnish cohort. *American Journal of Public Health, 86,* 1087–1093.

Martin, C. L., Wood, C. H., & Little, J. K. (1990). The development of gender stereotype components. *Child Development, 61,* 1891–1904.

Martin, M. (1986). Ageing patterns of change in everyday memory and cognition. *Human Learning Journal of Practical Research and Application, 5,* 63–74.

Martin, M. A. (1985). Students' applications of self-questioning study techniques: An investigation of their efficacy. *Reading Psychology, 6,* 69–83.

Martinez, J. L., & Derrick, B. E. (1996). Long-term potentiation and learning. *Annual Review, 47,* 173–203.

Marx, K. (1972). *The Marx-Engels Reader,* R. Tucker, Ed. New York: Norton.

Maslach, C. (1979). Negative emotional biasing of unexplained arousal. *Journal of Personality and Social Psychology, 37,* 953–969.

Masling, J. M., Bornstein, R. F. (Eds., 1994). *Empirical perspectives on object relations theory.* Washington: American Psychological Association.

Maslow, A. H. (1962). *Toward a psychology of being.* Princeton, NJ: Van Nostrand.

Maslow, A. H. (1970). *Motivaiton and personality* (2nd Ed.). New York: Harper & Row.

Mason, J., Southwick, S., Yehuda, R., & Wang, S. (1994). Elevation of serum free triiodothyronine, total triiodothyronine, thyroxine-binding globulin, and total thyroxine levels in combat-related posttraumatic stress disorder. *Archives of General Psychiatry, 51,* 629–641.

Masten, A. S., Price, A., Charney, D., & Heninger, G. (1993). Children in homeless families: Risks to mental health and development. *Journal of Consulting and Clinical Psychology, 61,* 335–343.

Masters, W., & Johnson, V. (1966). *Human sexual response.* Boston: Little, Brown.

Masters, W. H., & Johnson, V. E. (1970). *Human sexual inadequacy.* Boston: Little, Brown.

Mathews, A., & Macleod, C. (1994). Cognitive approaches to emotion. *Annual Review of Psychology, 45,* 25–50.

Mathews, A., Richards, A., & Eysenck, M. (1989). Interpretation of homophones related to treatment in anxiety states. *Journal of Abnormal Psychology, 98,* 31–34.

Mathews, H., & Moore, C., (Eds.) (1998). *The psychology of cultural experience.* Cambridge: Cambridge University Press.

Matjucha, I. C. A., & Katz, B. (1994). Neuro-ophthalmology of aging. In M. L. Albert, J. E. Knoefel et al. (Eds.), *Clinical neurology of aging* (2nd ed.). (pp. 421–447). New York: Oxford University Press.

Matlin, M. M. (1983). *Perception.* Boston: Allyn & Bacon.

Matsuoka, S. (1990). Theta rhythms: State of consciousness. *Brain Topography, 3,* 203–208.

Matthies, H. (1989). Neurobiological aspects of learning and memory. *Annual Review of Psychology, 40,* 381–404.

Mauro, R., Sato, K., & Tucker, J. (1992). The role of appraisal in human emotions: A cross-cultural study. *Journal of Personality and Social Psychology, 62,* 301–317.

Mavissakalian, M., & Perel, J. (1992). Protective effects of imipramine maintenance treatment in panic disorder with agoraphobia. *American Journal of Psychiatry, 149,* 1053–1057.

May, R. (1953). *Man's search for himself.* New York: Signet Books.

May, R., Angel, E., & Ellenberger, H. F. (1958). *Existence: A new dimension in psychiatry and psychology.* New York: Basic Books.

Mayberry, R., & Eichen, E. B. (1991). The long-lasting advantage of learning sign language in childhood: Another look at the critical period for language acquisition. *Journal of Memory and Language, 30,* 486–512.

Mayer, J. (1955). Regulation of energy intake and body weight. The glucostatic and the lipostatic hypothesis. *Annals of the New York Academy of Science, 63,* 15–43.

Mayer, J. D., & Geher, G. (1996). Emotional intelligence and the identification of emotion. *Intelligence, 22,* 89–114.

Mayer, J. D., & Salovey, P. (1997). What is emotional intelligence? In P. Salovey & D. Sluyter (Eds.), *Emotional development and emotional intelligence: Implications for educators.* New York: Basic Books.

Mayer, J., Gasche, Y., Braverman, D., & Evans, T. (1992). Mood-congruent judgment is a general effect. *Journal of Personality and Social Psychology, 63,* 119–132.

Mayer, R. E. (1983). *Thinking, problem solving, cognition.* New York: Freeman.

Mayman, M. (1968). Early memories and character structure. *Journal of Projective Techniques and Personality Assessment, 32,* 303–316.

McAdams, D. (1992). The five-factor model in personality: A critical appraisal. *Journal of Personality, 60,* 329–361.

McAdams, D. (1992). The intimacy motive. In C. P. Smith, J. W. Atkinson, D. McClelland, & J. Veroff (Eds.), Motivation and personality: *Handbook of thematic content analysis* (pp. 224–228). Cambridge: Cambridge University Press.

McAdams, D., & de St. Aubin, E. (1992). A theory of generativity and its assessment through self-report, behavioral acts, and narrative themes in autobiography. *Journal of Personality and Social Psychology, 62,* 1003–1015.

McAdams, D., & Vaillant, G. (1982). Intimacy motivation and psychosocial adjustment: A longitudinal study. *Journal of Personality Assessment, 46,* 586–593.

McAdams, D., & West, S. G. (1997). Introduction: Personality psychology and the case study. *Journal of Personality, 65,* 757–783.

McAdams, D. P., de St. Aubin, E., & Logan, R. L. (1993). Generativity among young, midlife, and older adults. *Psychology and Aging, 8,* 221–230.

McAdams, D. P., Hoffman, B. J., Mansfield, E. D., & Day, R. (1996). Themes of agency and communion in significant autobiographical scenes. *Journal of Personality, 64,* 339–377.

McAdams, J. (1986). Status polarization of social welfare attitudes. *Political Behavior, 8,* 313–334.

McCartney, K., Scarr, S., Phillips, D., Grajek, S., & Schwartz, J. C. (1982). Environmental differences among day care centers and their effect on children's development. In E. F. Zigler & E. W. Gordon (Eds.), *Day care: scientific and social policy issues.* Boston: Auburn House.

McCaul, K. D., & Malott, J. M. (1984). Distraction and coping with pain. *Psychological Bulletin, 95,* 516–533.

McCauley, C., & Jacques, S. (1979). The popularity of conspiracy theories of presidential assassination: A Bayesian

analysis. *Journal of Personality and Social Psychology, 37,* 637–644.

McClelland, D. C. (1961). *The achieving society.* Princeton, NJ: D. Van Nostrand.

McClelland, D. C. (1978). Managing motivation to expand human freedom. *American Psychologist, 33,* 201–210.

McClelland, D. C. (1985). *Human motivation.* Glenview, Ill.: Scott, Foresman.

McClelland, D. C., Atkinson, J. W., Clark, R. A., & Lowell, E. L. (1953). *The achievement motive.* New York: Appleton-Century-Crofts.

McClelland, D. C., Koestner, R., & Weinberger, J. (1989). How do self-attributed and implicit motives differ? *Psychological Review, 96,* 690–792.

McClelland, D. C., & Pilon, D. A. (1983). Sources of adult motives in patterns of parent behavior in early childhood. *Journal of Personality and Social Psychology, 44,* 564–554.

McClelland, D. C., & Winter, D. G. (1969). *Motivating economic achievement.* New York: Free Press.

McClelland, J. L. (1995). Constructive memory and memory distortions: A parallel-distributed processing approach. In D. L. Schacter (Ed.), *Memory distortions: How minds, brains, and societies reconstruct the past.* (pp. 69–90). Cambridge: Harvard University Press.

McClintock, M. K. (1971). Menstrual synchrony and suppression. *Nature, 229,* 244–245.

McCloskey, M., & Egeth, H. E. (1983). Eyewitness identification: What can a psychologist tell a jury? *American Psychologist, 38,* 550–563.

McCloskey, M., & Macaruso, P. (1995). Representing and using numerical information. *American Psychologist, 50,* 351–363.

McComb, K., Packer, C., & Pusey, A. (1994). Roaring and numerical assessment in contests between groups of female lions, Panthera leo. *Animal Behaviour, 47,* 379–387.

McConaghy, N. (1979). Maternal deprivation: Can its ghost be laid? *Australian and New Zealand Journal of Psychiatry, 13,* 209–217.

McConahay, J., & Hough, J. (1976). Symbolic racism. *Journal of Social Issues, 32,* 23–45.

McConkey, K. M. (1995). *Hypnosis, memory, and behavior in criminal investigation.* New York: Guilford Press.

McCrae, C. N., Bodenhausen, G., & Milne, A. B. (1998). Saying no to unwanted thoughts: Self-focus and the regulation of mental life. *Journal of Personality and Social Psychology, 74,* 578–589.

McCrae, R. (1993). Agreement of personality profiles across observers. *Mulivariate Behavioral Research, 28,* 25–40.

McCrae, R. R. (1996). Social consequences of experiential openness. *Psychological Bulletin, 120,* 323–337.

McCrae, R. R., & Costa, P. (1997). Personality trait structure as a human universal. *American Psychologist, 52,* 509–516.

McCrae, R. R., & Costa, P. T. (1990). *Personality in adulthood.* New York: Guilford Press.

McCrae, R. R., Costa, P., del Pilar, G., Rolland, J-P., & Parker, W. D. (1998). Cross-cultural assessment of the five-factor model: The revised NEO Personality Inventory. *Journal of Cross-Cultural Psychology, 29,* 171–188.

McDaniel, M. A., Robinson-Riegler, B., & Einstein, G. O. (1998). Prospective remembering: Perceptually driven or conceptually driven processes? *Memory and Cognition, 26,* 121–134.

McDonald, J. L. (1997). Language acquisition: The acquisition of linguistic structure in normal and special populations. *Annual Review, 48,* 215–241.

McDonough, L. (1994). Very long-term recall in infants: Infantile amnesia reconsidered. In R. Fivush (Ed.). *Long-term retention of infant memories. Memory* (Vol. 2, No. 4, pp. 339–352). Englewood, NJ: Lawrence Erlbaum Associates, Inc.

McEvoy, G. M., & Cascio, W. F. (1989). Cumulative evidence of the relationship between employee age and job performance. *Journal of Applied Psychology, 74,* 11–17.

McFadden, D., & Pasanen, E. G. (1998). Comparison of the auditory systems of heterosexuals and homosexuals: Click-evoked otoacoustic emissions. *Proceedings of the National Academy of Sciences, 95,* 2705–2713.

McGaugh, J., Weinberger, N., & Lynch, G. Eds. (1995). *Brain and memory: Modulation and Mediation of Neuroplasticity.* New York: Oxford University Press.

McGeorge, P., Crawford, J. R., Kelley, S. W. (1996). The relationship between WAIS—R abilities and speed of processing in a word identification task. *Intelligence, 23,* 175–190.

McGlashan, T., & Fenton, W. (1992). The positive-negative distinction in schizophrenia: Review of natural history validators. *Archives of General Psychiatry, 49,* 63–72.

McGlynn, F. D., Mealies, W. L. Jr., & Landau, D. L. (1981). The current status of systematic desensitization. *Clinical Psychology Review, 1,* 149–179.

McGue, M., Bacon, S., & Lykken, D. (1993). Personality stability and change in early adulthood: A behavior genetic analysis. *Developmental Psychology, 29,* 96–109.

McGue, M., Pickens, R. W., & Svikis, D. (1992). Sex and age effects on the inheritance of alcohol problems: A twin study. *Journal of Abnormal Psychology, 101,* 3–17.

McGuffin, P., Katz, R., Watkins, S., & Rutherford, J. (1996). A Hospital-Based Twin Register of the Heritability of DSM-IV Unipolar Depression. *Archives of General Psychiatry, 53,* 129–136.

McGuire, W. (1986). The myth of massive media impact: Savagings and salvagings. In G. Comstock (Ed.), *Public communication and behavior* (Vol. 1). New York: Academic Press.

McGuire, W. J. (1961). The effectiveness of supportive and refutational defenses in immunizing and restoring beliefs against persuasion. *Sociometry, 24,* 184–197.

McGuire, W. J. (1985). Attitudes and attitude change. In G. Lindzey and E. Aronson (Eds.), *Handbook of Social Psychology.* Reading, MA: Addison-Wesley.

McGuire, W. J., & Papageorgis, D. (1962). Effectiveness of forewarning in developing resistance to persuasion. *Public Opinion Quarterly, 26,* 24–34.

McKenna, R. J. (1972). Some effects of anxiety level and food cues on the eating behavior of obese and normal subjects. *Journal of Personality and Social Psychology, 23,* 311–319.

McKinnon, W., Weisse, C. S., Reynolds, C. P., Bowles, C. A., & Baum, A. (1989). Chronic stress, leukocyte subpopulations, and humoral response to latent viruses. *Health Psychology, 8,* 389–402.

McKoon, G., & Ratcliff, R. (1998). Memory-based language processing: Psycholinguistic research in the 1990s. *Annual Review of Psychology, 49,* 25–42.

McLoyd, V. (1989). Socialization and development in a changing economy: The effects of paternal job and income loss on children. *American Psychologist, 44,* 293–302.

McNally, R. (1987). Preparedness and phobias: A review. *Psychologial Bulletin, 101,* 283–303.

Mead, M. (1928). *Coming of age in Samoa: A psychological study of primitive youth for Western civilization.* New York: Morrow & Co.

Meaney, M., & McEwen, B. (1986). Testosterone implants into the amygdala during the neonatal period masculinize the social play of juvenile female rats. *Brain Research, 398,* 324–328.

Medin, D. L., & Smith, E. E. (1981). Strategies and classification learning. *Journal of Experimental Psychology: Human Learning and Memory, 7,* 241–253.

Medin, D. L., Lynch, E. B., Coley, J. D., & Atran, S. (1997). Categorization and reasoning among tree experts: Do all roads lead to Rome? *Cognitive Psychology, 32,* 49–96.

Medin, D. L., & Smith, E. E. (1985). Concepts and concept formation. *Annual Review of Psychology, 35,* 113–138.

Mednick, S. A., Gabrielli, W. F., & Hutchings, B. (1984). Genetic influences in criminal convictions: Evidence from an adoption cohort. *Science, 224,* 891–894.

Meece, J. L., Wigfield, A., & Eccles, J. S. (1990). Predictors of math anxiety and its influence on young adolescents' course enrollment intentions and performance in mathematics. *Journal of Educational Psychology, 82,* 60–70.

Meehl, P. (1962). Schizotaxia, schizotypy, schizophrenia. *American Psychologist, 17,* 827–838.

Meehl, P. (1989). Schizotaxia revisted. *Archives of General Psychiatry, 46,* 935–944.

Meichenbaum, D. (1977). *Cognitive-behavior modification: An integrative approach.* New York: Plenum Press.

Meichenbaum, D. (1990). Cognitive perspective on teaching self-regulation. *American Journal of Mental Retardation, 94,* 367–369.

Melcher, J. M., & Schooler, J. W. (1996). The misremembrance of wines past: Verbal and perceptual expertise differentially mediate verbal overshadowing of taste memory. *Journal of Memory and Language, 35,* 231–245.

Mellers, B., Schwartz, A., & Cooke, A. D. J. (1998). Judgment and decision making. *Annual Review of Psychology, 49,* 447–477.

Mellers, B., Schwartz, A., Ho, K., & Ritov, I. (1997). Decision affect theory: Emotional reactions to the outcomes of risky options. *Psychological Science, 8,* 423–429.

Melton, G. B. (1987). Fear, prejudice, and neglect: Discrimination against mentally disabled persons. *American Psychologist, 42,* 1007–1026.

Meltzoff, A. (1990). Towards a developmental cognitive science: The implications of cross-modal matching and imitation for the development of representation and memory in infancy. *Annals of the New York Academy of Sciences, 608,* 1–7.

Meltzoff, A. N. (1995). What infant memory tells us about infantile amnesia: Long-term recall and deferred imitation. Special Issue: Early memory. *Journal of Experimental Child Psychology, 59,* 497–515.

Meltzoff, A. N., & Moore, M. K. (1977). Imitation of facial and manual gestures by human neonates. *Science, 198,* 75–78.

Melzack, R. (1970). Phantom limbs. *Psychology Today,* 63–68.

Melzack, R. (1973). *The puzzle of pain.* New York: Basic Books.

Melzack, R. (1980). Psychological aspects

of pain. In J. Bonica (Ed.), *Pain*. New York: Raven.

Melzack, R. (1993). Pain: Past, present and future. *Canadian Journal of Experimental Psychology, 47*, 615–629.

Melzack, R. (1995). Phantom-limb pain and the brain. In B. Bromm, J. E. Desmedt (Eds.), *Pain and the Brain: From Nociception to Cognition. Advances in Pain Research and Therapy* (Vol. 22, pp. 73–82). New York: Raven Press.

Melzack, R., & Wall, P. D. (1965). Pain mechanisms: A new theory. *Science, 150*, 971–979.

Melzack, R., & Wall, P. D. (1983). *The challenge of pain*. New York: Basic Books.

Menard, M. T., Kosslyn, S., Thompson, W. L., Alpert, N. M., et al. (1996). Encoding words and pictures: A positron emission tomography study. *Neuropsychologia, 34*, 185–194.

Menninger, K., Mayman, M., & Pruyser, P. (1963). *The vital balance*. New York: Viking.

Merckelbach, H., Arntz, A., & de Jong, P. (1991). Conditioning experiences in spider phobics. *Behaviour Research & Therapy, 29*, 333–335.

Merckelbach, H., Arntz, A., & deJong, P. (1991). Conditioning experiences in spider phobics. *Behavior Research and Therapy, 29*, 333–335.

Merluzzi, T., Taylor, C. B., Boltwood, M., & Gotestam, K. G. (1991). Opioid antagonist impedes exposure. *Journal of Consulting and Clinical Psychology, 59*, 425–430.

Merriam, A. P. (1971). Aspects of sexual behavior among the Bala (Basongye). In D. S. Marshall, & R. C. Suggs (Eds.) *Human sexual behavior: Variations in the ethnographic spectrum*. New York: Basic Books.

Merton, R. K. (1957). *Social theory and social structure*. Glencoe, IL: Free Press.

Mervis, C. B., & Rosch, E. (1981). Categorization of natural objects. *Annual Review of Psychology, 32*, 89–115.

Mesquita, B., Frijda, N. H., & Scherer, K. R. (1997). Culture and emotion. In J. W. Berry, P. R. Dasen, et al. (Eds.), *Handbook of cross-cultural psychology, Vol. 2: Basic processes and human development (2nd ed.). Handbook of cross-cultural psychology.* (pp. 255–297). Boston: Allyn & Bacon, Inc.

Messer, S., & Winokur, M. (1980). Some limits to the integration of psychodynamic and behavior therapy. *American Psychologist, 35*, 818–827.

Messer, S., Sass, L. H., & Woolfolk, R. L., (Eds.). (1988). *Hermeneutics and psychologial theory*. New Brunswick, NJ: Rutgers University Press.

Metz, M. E., Pryor, J. L., Nesvacil, L. J., & Abuzzahab, F. Sr. (1997). Premature ejaculation: A psychophysiological review. *Journal of Sex & Marital Therapy, 23*, 3–23.

Michelson, L., & Marchione, K. (1991). Behavioral, cognitive, and pharmacological treatments of panic disorder with agoraphobia: Critique and synthesis. *Journal of Consulting and Clinical Psychology, 59*, 100–114.

Mickelson, K. D., Kessler, R. C., & Shaver, P. R. (1997). Adult attachment in a nationally representative sample. *Journal of Personality & Social Psychology, 73*, 1092–1106.

Middlebrooks, J. C., & Green, D. M. (1991). Sound localization by human listeners. *Annual Review of Psychology, 42*, 135–159.

Middleton, D., & Edwards, D. (1990). Introduction. In D. Middleton & D. Edwards (Eds.), *Collective remembering*. London: Sage.

Miklowitz, D. J. (1996). Psychotherapy in combination with drug treatment for bipolar disorder. *Journal of Clinical Psychopharmacology, 16*, 56S–66S.

Mikulincer, M., & Florian, V. (in press). Maternal-fetal bonding, coping strategies, and mental health during pregnancy: The contribution of attachment style. *Journal of Social and Clinical Psychology*.

Mikulincer, M., Florian, V., & Weller, A. (1993). Attachment styles, coping strategies, and posttraumatic psychological distress: The impact of the Gulf War in Israel. *Journal of Personality and Social Psychology, 64*, 817–826.

Milgram, S. (1963). Behavioral study of obedience. *Journal of Abnormal and Social Psychology, 67*, 371–378.

Milgram, S. (1965). Some conditions of obedience and disobedience to authority. *Human Relations, 18*, 57–76.

Milgram, S. (1974). *Obedience to authority: An experimental view*. New York: Harper & Row.

Miller, C. B., Rothblum, E., Barbour, L., Brand, P. A., & Felicio, D. (1991). Social interactions of obese and nonobese women. *Journal of Personality, 58*, 365–380.

Miller, G. A. (1956). The magical number seven, plus or minus two: Some limits in our capacity for processing information. *Psychological Review, 63*, 81–97.

Miller, G. A., Galanter, E., & Pribram, K. H. (1960). *Plans and the structure of behavior*. NewYork: Holt, Rinehart & Winston.

Miller, I. J., Jr. (1995). Anatomy of the peripheral taste system. In R. L. Doty (Ed.), *Handbook of olfaction and gustation*. New York: Marcel Dekker.

Miller, J. G. (1984). Culture and the development of everyday social explanation. *Journal of Personality and Social Psychology, 46*, 961–978.

Miller, J. G. (1994). Cultural diversity in the morality of caring: Individually oriented versus duty-based interpersonal moral codes. *Cross-cultural Research, 28*, 3–39.

Miller, J. G. (1997). A cultural-psychology perspective on intelligence. In R. J. Sternberg and E. L. Grigorenko (Eds.), *Intelligence, heredity, and environment.* (pp. 269–302). New York: Cambridge University Press.

Miller, J. L., & Eimas, P. (1995). Speech perception: From signal to word. *Annual Review of Psychology, 46*, 467–492.

Miller, L. C., Bettencourt, B. A., DeBro, S., & Hoffman, V. (1993). Negotiating safer sex: Interpersonal dynamics. In J. Pryor and G. Reeder (Eds.), *The social psychology of HIV infection*. Hillsdale, NJ: Erlbaum.

Miller, L. K. (1997). *Principles of everyday behavior analysis*. Pacific Grove, CA: Brooks/Cole Publishing Company.

Miller, L. T., & Vernon, P. A. (1997). Developmental changes in speed of information processing in young children. *Developmental Psychology, 33*, 549–554.

Miller, M. W. (1992). Circadian rhythm of cell proliferation in the telencephalic ventricular zone: Effect of in utero exposure to ethanol. *Brain Research, 595*, 17–24.

Miller, N. (1951). Learnable drives and rewards. In S. S. Stevens (Ed.), *Handbook of experimental psychology* (pp. 435–472). New York: John Wiley.

Miller, N., & Campbell, D. T. (1959). Recency and primacy in persuasion as a function of the timing of speeches and measurement. *Journal of Abnormal and Social Psychology, 59*, 1–9.

Miller, N. E. (1983). Behavioral medicine: Symbiosis between laboratory and clinic. *Annual Review of Psychology, 34*, 1–31.

Miller, N. E. (1985). The value of behavioral research on animals. *American Psychologist, 40*, 423–440.

Miller, N. E. (1992). Some examples of psychophysiology and the unconscious. *Biofeedback and Self-Regulation, 17*, 3–16.

Miller, P. A., Eisenberg, N., Fabes, R., & Shell, R. (1996). Relations of moral reasoning and vicarious emotion to young children's prosocial behavior toward peers and adults. *Developmental Psychology, 32*, 210–219.

Miller, P. J., Wiley, A. R., Fung, H., & Liang, C.-H. (1997). Personal story-telling as a medium of socialization in Chinese and American families. *Child Development, 68*, 557–568.

Miller, T. Q., Smith, T. W., Turner, C. W.,

Guijarro, M. L., & Hallet, A. J. (1996). A meta-analytic review of research on hostility and physical health. *Psychological Bulletin, 119,* 322–348.

Miller, T. W., & Kraus, R. F. (1990). An overview of chronic pain. *Hospital and Community Psychiatry, 41,* 433–440.

Miller, W. A., Ratliff, F., & Hartline, H. K. (1961). How cells receive stimuli. *Scientific American, 222–238.*

Mills, J., & Clark, M. S. (1994). Communal and exchange relationships: Controversies and research. In R. Erber, R. Gilmour, et al. (Eds.), *Theoretical frameworks for personal relationships.* (pp. 29–42). Hillsdale, NJ: Lawrence Erlbaum Associates Inc.

Mills, M. (1995). *Characteristics of personals ads differ as a function of publication readership SES.* Paper presented at the annual convention of the Human Behavior and Evolution Society, June, Santa Barbara, California.

Milner, B., Corkin, S., & Teuber, H. L. (1968). Further analysis of the hippocampal amnesic syndrome: Fourteen year follow-up study of H.M. *Neuropsychologia, 6,* 215–234.

Milner, P. (1991). Brain-stimulation reward: A review. *Canadian Journal of Psychology, 45,* 1–36.

Mineka, S., & Sutton, S. K. (1992). Cognitive biases and the emotional disorders. *Psychological Science, 3,* 65–69.

Mineka, S., Watson, D., & Clark, L. A. (1998). Comorbidity of anxiety and unipolar mood disorders. *Annual Review of Psychology, 49,* 377–412.

Minsky, M. (1975). A framework for representing knowledge. In P. H. Winston (Ed.), *The psychology of computer vision.* New York: McGraw-Hill.

Minuchin, S. (1974). *Families and family therapy.* Cambridge, MA: Harvard University Press.

Mirsky, A. F., & Duncan, C. C. (1986). Etiology and expression of schizophrenia: Neurobiological and psychosocial factors. *Annual Review of Psychology, 37,* 291–319.

Mischel, W. (1968). *Personality and assessment.* New York: John Wiley.

Mischel, W. (1973). Toward a cognitive social learning reconceptualization of personality. *Psychological Review, 39,* 351–364.

Mischel, W. (1979). On the interface of cognitive and personality: Beyond the person-situation debate. *American Psychologist, 34,* 740–754.

Mischel, W. (1990). Personality dispositions revisited and revised: A view after three decades. In L. Pervin (Ed.), *Handbook of personality: Theory and research* (pp. 111–134). New York: Guilford Press.

Mischel, W., Cantor, N., & Feldman, S. (1996). Principles of self-regulation: The nature of willpower and self-control. In E. T. Higgins, A. W. Kruglanski, et al. (Eds.), *Social psychology: Handbook of basic principles.* (pp. 329–360). New York: Guilford Press.

Mischel, W., & Mischel, H. N. (1976). A cognitive social-learning approach to morality and self-regulation. In T. Lickona (Ed.), *Moral development and behavior: Theory, research, and social issues.* New York: Holt, Rinehart, & Winston.

Mischel, W., & Shoda, Y. (1995). A cognitive-affective system theory of personality: Reconceptualizing situations, dispositions, dynamics, and invariance in personality structure. *Psychological Review, 102,* 246–268.

Mishra, R. C. (1997). Cognition and cognitive development. In J. W. Berry, P. R. Dasen, and T. S. Swanaswathi (Eds.), *Handbook of cross-cultural psychology, Vol. 2: Basic processes and human development (2nd ed.). Handbook of cross-cultural psychology* (pp. 143–175). Boston: Allyn & Bacon, Inc.

Mistlin, A., & Perrett, D. (1990). Visual and somatosensory processing in the macaque temporal cortex: The role of "expectation." *Experimental Brain Research, 82,* 437–450.

Mistry, J., & Rogoff, B. (1985). A cultural perspective on the development of talent. In F. D. Horowitz, & M. O'Brien (Eds.), *The gifted and talented: Developmental perspectives* (pp. 125–144). Washington, DC: American Psychological Association.

Mitchell, S. A. (1988). *Relational concepts in psychoanalysis: An integration.* Cambridge, MA: Harvard University Press.

Moatti, J., Hausser, D., & Agrafiotis, D. (1997). Understanding HIV risk-related behaviour: A critical overview of current models. In L. V. Campenhoudt, M. Cohen, G. Guizzardi, & D. Hausser (Eds.), *Sexual interactions and HIV risk: New conceptual perspective in European research. Social aspects of AIDS.* (pp. 100–126). Washington, DC: Taylor & Francis.

Mobilization for Animals. (1984). *Direct action program 1984.* Columbus, Ohio.

Modestin, J. (1992). Multiple personality disorder in Switzerland. *American Journal of Psychiatry, 149,* 88–92.

Moeller, G., & Applezweig, M. M. (1957). A motivational factor in conformity. *Journal of Abnormal Social Psychology, 55,* 114–120.

Moen, I. (1993). Functional lateralization of the perception of Norwegian word tones: Evidence from a dichotic listening experiment. *Brain & Language, 44,* 400–413.

Moerk, E. L. (1992). *A first language taught and learned.* Baltimore, MD: Brookes.

Moloney, D. P., Bouchard, T., & Segal, N. (1991). A genetic and environmental analysis of the vocational interests of monozygotic and dizygotic twins reared apart. *Journal of Vocational Behavior, 39,* 76–109.

Money, J. (1987). Sin, sickness, or status? Homosexual gender identity and psychoneuroendocrinology. *American Psychologist, 42,* 384–399.

Money, J., & Ehrhardt, A. A. (1972). *Man & woman. Boy & girl.* Baltimore, MD: Johns Hopkins University Press.

Money, J., Schwartz, M., & Lewis, V. G. (1984). Adult heterosexual status and fetal hormonal masculinization and demasculinization. *Psychoneuroendocrinology, 9,* 405–414.

Monk, T. H. (1997). Shift work. In M. R. Pressman and W. C. Orr (Eds.), *Understanding sleep: The evaluation and treatment of sleep disorders. Application and practice in health psychology* (pp. 249–266). Washington, DC: American Psychological Association.

Monroe, S. M., & Simons, A. D. (1991). Diathesis-stress theories in the context of life stress research: Implications for the depressive disorders. *Psychological Bulletin, 110,* 406–425.

Montemayor, R., & Eisen, M. (1977). A developmental sequence of self-conceptions from childhood to adolescence. *Developmental Psychology, 13,* 314–319.

Montgomery, S. (1994). Long-term treatment of depression. *British Journal of Psychiatry, 165,* 31–36.

Montgomery, S. A. (1994). Antidepressants in long-term treatment. *Annual Review of Medicine, 45,* 447–457.

Monti, P., Rohsenow, D., Rubonis, A., & Niaura, R. (1993). Cue exposure with coping skills treatment for male alcoholics: A preliminary investigation. *Journal of Consulting and Clinical Psychology, 61,* 1011–1019.

Moos, R. H., & Billings, A. G. (1982). Conceptualizing and measuring coping resources and processes. In L. Goldberger and S. Breznitz (Eds.), *Handbook of stress.* New York: Macmillan.

Moos, R. H., & Schaefer, J. A. (1986). Life Transitions and Crises. In R. H. Moos and J. A. Schaefer (Eds.), *Coping with life crises: An integrated approach.* New York: Plenum Press.

Moray, N. (1969). *Attention: Selective processes in vision and hearing.* London: Hutchinson.

Moreland, R. L. (1985). Social categorization and the assimilation of new group members. *Journal of Personality and Social Psychology, 48,* 1173–1190.

Morelli, G., Rogoff, B., Oppenheim, D., &

Goldsmith, D. (1992). Cultural variation in infants' sleeping arrangements: Questions of independence. *Developmental Psychology, 28,* 604–613.

Morgan, J. (1986). *From simple input to complex grammar.* Cambridge, MA: MIT Press.

Morgan, J., & Travis, L. (1989). Limits on negative information in language input. *Journal of Child Language, 16,* 531–552.

Morgenstern, J., Labouvie, E., McCrady, S., Kahler, C. W., & Frey, R. M. (1997). Affiliation with Alcoholics Anonymous after treatment: A study of the therapeutic effects and mechanisms of action. *Journal of Consulting and Clinical Psychology, 65,* 768–777.

Morris, J. S., Frith, C. D., Perrett, D. I., Rowland, D., Young, A. W., Calder, A. J., & Dolan, R. J. (1996). A differential neural response in the human amygdala to fearful and happy facial expressions. *Nature, 383,* 812–815.

Morris, R. G., & Baddeley, A. D. (1988). Primary and working memory functioning in Alzheimer-type dementia. *Journal of Clinical and Experimental Neuropsychology, 10,* 279–296.

Morse, J. M., & Park, C. (1988). Differences in cultural expectations of the perceived painfulness of childbirth. In K. Michaelson (Ed.), *Childbirth in America: Anthropological Perspectives.* South Hadley, MA: Bergin & Garvey.

Mould, D. E. (1990). A reply to Page: Fraud, pornography, and the Meese commission. *American Psychologist, 45,* 777–778.

Mowrer, O. H. (1947). On the dual nature of learning: A reinterpretation of conditioning and problem-solving. *Harvard Educational Review, 17,* 102–148.

Mowrer, O. H. (1960). *Learning theory and behavior.* New York: John Wiley.

Moyer, K. E. (1983). The physiology of motivation: Aggression as a model. In C. James Scheirer & Anne M. Rogers (Eds.), *G. Stanley Hall Lecture Series* (Vol. 3.) Washington, DC: American Psychological Association.

Mullen, B., & Hu, L. (1989). Perceptions of ingroup and outgroup variability: A meta-analytic integration. *Basic and Applied Social Psychology, 10,* 233–252.

Mulligan, R. (1966). Dental pain. In J. Barber (Ed.), *Hypnosis and suggestion in the treatment of pain: A clinical guide* (pp. 185–208). New York: W. W. Norton & Co., Inc.

Mumaw, R., & Pellegrino, J. (1984). Individual differences in complex spatial processing. *Journal of Educational Psychology, 76,* 920–939.

Mumford, D. B. (1993). Eating disorders in different cultures. *International Review of Psychiatry, 5,* 109–113.

Munk, M., Roelfsema, P., Konig, P., Engel, A. K., & Singer, W. (1996). Role of reticular activation in the modulation of intracortical synchronization. *Science, 272,* 271–274.

Murphy, G. L., & Medin, D. L. (1985). The role of theories in conceptual coherence. *Psychological Review, 92,* 289–316.

Murphy, J., & Slorach, N. (1983). The language development of preschool hearing children of deaf parents. *British Journal of Disorders of Communications, 18,* 118–126.

Murphy, J. M. (1976). Psychiatric labeling in cross-cultural perspective. *Science, 191,* 1019–1028.

Murphy, L. R. (1996). Stress management in work settings: A critical review of the health effects. *American Journal of Health Promotion, 11,* 112–135.

Murphy, S. T., & Zajonc, R. (1993). Affect, cognition, and awareness: Affective priming with optimal and suboptimal stimulus exposures. *Journal of Personality and Social Psychology, 64,* 723–739.

Murray, H. A. (1938). *Explorations in personality.* New York: Oxford University Press.

Murray, H. A. (1943). *Thematic Apperception Test.* Cambridge, MA: Harvard University Press.

Murray, S. L., & Holmes, J. G. (1997). A leap of faith? Positive illusions in romantic relationships. *Personality and Social Psychology Bulletin, 23,* 586–604.

Murrey, G. J., Cross, H. J., & Whipple, J. (1992). Hypnotically created pseudomemories: Further investigation into the "memory distortion or response bias" question. *Journal of Abnormal Psychology, 101,* 75–77.

Myers, D. G. (1993). *Social psychology.* (4th ed.). New York: McGraw-Hill.

Myers, D. G., & Diener, E. (1995). Who is happy? *Psychological Science, 6,* 10–19.

Myerson, J., Ferraro, F. R., Hale, S., & Lima, S. (1992). General slowing in semantic priming and word recognition. *Psychology and Aging, 7,* 257–270.

Nadeau, S. E., & Crosson, B. (1995). A guide to the functional imaging of cognitive processes. *Neuropsychiatry, Neuropsychology & Behavioral Neurology, 8,* 143–162.

Nader, K., Bechara, A., Van der Kooy, D. (1997). Neurobiological constraints on behavioral models of motivation. *Annual Review, 48,* 85–114.

Nader, K., & van der Kooy, D. (1997). Deprivation state switches the neurobiological substrates mediating opiate reward in the ventral tegmental area. *Journal of Neuroscience, 17,* 383–390.

Nahemow, L., & Lawton, M. P. (1975).

Similarity and propinquity in friendship formation. *Journal of Personality and Social Psychology, 32,* 205–213.

Nakao, M., Nomura, S., Shimosawa, T., Yoshiuchi, K., Kumano, H., Kuboki, T., et al. (1997). Clinical effects of blood pressure biofeedback treatment on hypertension by auto-shaping. *Psychosomatic Medicine, 59,* 331–338.

Narabayashi, H., et al. (1963). Stereotaxic amygdalotomy for behavior disorders. *Archives of Neurology, 9,* 1016.

Naroll, R., Michik, G. L., & Naroll, F. (1976). *Worldwide theory testing.* New Haven: Human Relations Area Files.

Nash, M. R. (1988). Hypnosis as a window on regression. *Bulletin of the Menninger Clinic, 52,* 383–403.

Nathan, S. G. (1986). The epidemiology of the DSM-III psychosexual dysfunctions. *Journal of Sex & Marital Therapy, 12,* 267–281.

Nathans, J. (1987). Molecular biology of visual pigments. *Annual Review of Physiology, 10,* 163–194.

National Research Council. (1989). Obesity and eating disorders. In *Diet and health: Implications for reducing chronic disease risk* (pp. 563–592.). Washington, DC: National Academy Press.

Negandhi, A. R. (1973). *Management and economic development: The case of Taiwan.* The Hague: Martinus Nijhoff.

Neher, A. (1991). Maslow's theory of motivation: A critique. *Journal of Humanistic Psychology, 31,* 89–112.

Neisser, U. (1967). *Cognitive psychology.* New York: Appleton-Century-Crofts.

Neisser, U. (1976). *Cognition and reality.* San Francisco: Freeman.

Neisser, U. (1976). General, academic, and artificial intelligence. In L. Resnick (Ed.), *Human intelligence: Perspectives on its theory and measurement* (pp. 179–189). Norwood, NJ: Ablex.

Neisser, U. (1978). Anticipations, images, and introspection. *Cognition, 6,* 169–174.

Neisser, U. (1991). A case of misplaced nostalgia. *American Psychologist, 46,* 34–36.

Neisser, U., Boodoo, G., Bouchard, T. J., Jr., Boykin, A. W., Brody, N., Ceci, S. J. et al. (1996). Intelligence: Knowns and unknowns. *American Psychologist, 51,* 77–101.

Nelson, C. A. (1995). The ontogeny of human memory: A cognitive neuroscience perspective. *Developmental Psychology, 31,* 723–738.

Nelson, K. (1987). What's in a name? Reply to Seidenberg and Petitto. *Journal of Experimental Psychology: General, 116,* 293–296.

Nelson, K. (1997). Cognitive change as collaborative construction. In E. Amsel, K. A. Renninger, et al. (1997). *Change and* development: Issues of theory, method, and application. The Jean Piaget symposium series. (pp. 99–115). Mahwah, NJ: Lawrence Erlbaum Associates, Inc., Publishers.

Nelson, M. D., Saykin, A. J., Flashman, L. A., & Riordan, H. J. (1998). Hippocampal Volume Reduction in Schizophrenia as Assessed by Magnetic Resonance Imaging: A Meta-analytic Study. *Archives of General Psychiatry, 55,* 433–440.

Nesbitt, E. B. (1973). An escalator phobia overcome in one session of flooding in vivo. *Journal of Behavior Therapy and Experimental Psychiatry, 4,* 405–406.

Nesse, R. M. (1988). An evolutionary view. *Psychiatric Annals, 18,* 478–483.

Nesse, R. M., & Berridge, K. C. (1997). Psychoactive drug use in evolutionary perspective. *Science, 278,* 63–66.

Nettelbeck, T., & Wilson, C. (1997). Speed of information processing and cognition. In W. E. MacLean Jr. (Ed.), *Ellis' handbook of mental deficiency, psychological theory and research* (3rd ed.) (pp. 245–274). New Jersey: Lawrence Erlbaum Associates, Inc., Publishers.

Neugarten, B. L. (1977). Personality and aging. In J. E. Birren & K. W. Schaie (Eds.), *Handbook of the psychology of aging.* New York: Academic.

Neutra, M., & Leblond, C. P. (1969). The golgi apparatus. *Scientific American,* 100–107.

Newcomb, T. M. (1956). The predictions of interpersonal attraction. *American Psychologist, II,* 575–586.

Newcomb, T. M. (1961). *The acquaintance process.* New York: Holt, Rinehart, & Winston.

Newcombe, N., Drummey, A. B., & Lie, E. (1995). Children's memory for early experience. Special Issue: Early memory. *Journal of Experimental Child Psychology, 59,* 337–342.

Newcombe, N., & Dubas, J. S. (1992). A longitudinal study of predictors of spatial ability in adolescent females. *Child Development, 63,* 37–46.

Newell, A. (1969). Heuristic programming: Ill-structured problems. In J. Aronofsky (Ed.), *Progress in Operations Research,* Vol. 3. New York: John Wiley.

Newell, A., & Simon, H. A. (1972). *Human problem solving.* Englewood Cliffs, NJ; Prentice-Hall.

Newman, E. A., & Hartline, P. H. (1982). The infrared "vision" of snakes. *Scientific American,* 116–127.

Newman, H. G., Freeman, F. N., & Holzinger, K. J. (1937). *Twins: A study of heredity and environment.* Chicago: University of Chicago Press.

Newman, J. (1995). Thalamic contributions to attention and consciousness. *Consciousness and Cognition, 4,* 172–193.

Newman, L. S., Duff, K., and Baumeister, R. (1997). A new look at defensive projection: Thought suppression, accessibility, and biased person perception. *Journal of Personality and Social Psychology, 72,* 980–1001.

Newport, E. L. (1990). Maturational constraints on language learning. *Cognitive Science, 14,* 11–28.

Newport, E. L., Gleitman, H., & Gleitman, L. R. (1977). Mother, I'd rather do it myself: Some effects and noneffects of maternal speech style. In C. Snow & C. A. Ferguson (Eds.), *Talking to children: Language input and acquisition.* Cambridge, England: Cambridge University Press.

Newsom, C., Flavall, J., & Rincover, A. (1983). Side effects of punishment. In S. Axelrod & J. Apsche (Eds.), *The effects of punishment on human behavior.* New York: Academic.

Newsome, W. T., Britten, K. H., & Moushon, J. A. (1989). Neuronal correlates of a perceptual decision. *Nature, 341,* 52–54.

Newton, T. L., & Contrada, R. J. (1992). Repressive coping and verbal autonomic response dissociation: the influence of social context. *Journal of Personality and Social Psychology, 62,* 159–167.

NICHD Early Child Care Research Network (1997). The effects of infant child care on infant-mother attachment security: Results of the NICHD study of early child care. *Child Development, 68,* 860–879.

Niedenthal, P. M., & Cantor, N. (1986). Affective responses as guides to category-based inferences. *Motivation & Emotion, 10,* 217–232.

Niedenthal, P., Setterlund, M., & Wherry, M. B. (1992). Possible self-complexity and affective reactions to goal-relevant evaluation. *Journal of Personality and Social Psychology, 63,* 5–16.

Nigg, J. T., & Gold, H. H. (1994). Genetics of personality disorders: Perspectives from personality and psychopathology research. *Psychological Bulletin, 115,* 346–380.

Nigg, J. T., & Goldsmith, H. H. (1994). Genetics of personality disorders: Perspectives from personality and psychopathology research. *Psychological Bulletin, 115,* 346–380.

Nigg, J. T., Lohr, N. E., Westen, D. Gold, L. J., & Silk, K. (1992). Malevolent object representations in borderline personality disorder and major depression. *Journal of Abnormal Psychology, 101,* 61–67.

Nisbett, R. (1993). Violence and U.S. regional culture. *American Psychologist, 48,* 441–449.

Nisbett, R. E., & Ross, L. (1980). *Human inference: Strategies and shortcomings of social judgment.* Englewood Cliffs, NJ: Prentice-Hall.

Nisbett, R. E., & Wilson, T. D. (1977). Telling more than we can know: verbal reports on mental processes. *Psychological Review, 84,* 231–259.

Noll, R. (1994). Hypnotherapy for warts in children and adolescents. *Journal of Developmental and Behavioral Pediatrics, 15,* 170–173.

Norman, W. T. (1963). Toward an adequate taxonomy of personality attributes: Replicated factor structure in peer nomination personality ratings. *Journal of Abnormal and Social Psychology, 66,* 574–583.

Novak, M. A., & Harlow, H. F. (1975). Social recovery of monkeys isolated for the first year of life: rehabilitation and therapy. *Developmental Psychology, 11,* 453–465.

Nwadiora, E., & McAdoo, H. (1996). Acculturative stress among Amerasian refugees: Gender and racial differences. *Adolescence, 31,* 477–487.

Nyber, L. (1998). Mapping episodic memory. *Behavioral Brain Research, 90,* 107–114.

Oakhill, J., & Garnham A. (1993). On theories of belief bias in syllogistic reasoning. *Cognition, 46,* 87–92.

Oakhill, J., Johnson-Laird, P. N., & Garnham, A. (1989). Believability and syllogistic reasoning. *Cognition, 31,* 117–140.

Oatley, K., & Jenkins, J. M. (1992). Human emotion: Function and dysfunction. *Annual Review of Psychology, 43,* 55–85.

Oberle, K., Paul, P., Wry, J., & Grace, M. (1990). Pain, anxiety and analgesics: A comparative study of elderly and younger surgical patients. *Canadian Journal on Aging, 9,* 13–22.

O'Brien, T. B., & DeLongis, A. (1996). The interactional context of problem-, emotion-, and relationship-focused coping: The role of the Big Five personality factors. *Journal of Personality, 64,* 775–813.

O'Connor, T. G., McGuire, S., Reiss, D., Hetherington, E. M., & Plomin, R. (1998). Co-occurrence of depressive symptoms and antisocial behavior in adolescence: A common genetic liability. *Journal of Abnormal Psychology, 107,* 27–37.

Oettingen, G., & Seligman, M. (1990). Pessimism and behavioral signs of depression in East versus West Berlin. *European Journal of Social Psychology, 20,* 207–220.

Oettingen, G., Little, T. D., Lindenberger, U., & Baltes, P. B. (1994). Causality, agency, and control beliefs in East versus West Berlin children: A natural experiment on the role of context. *Journal of Personality and Social Psychology, 66,* 579–595.

Offer, D., & Offer, J. (1975). *From teenage to young manhood: A psychological study.* New York: Basic Books.

Offer, D., Ostrov, E., Howard, K., & Atkinson, R. (1990). Normality and adolescence. *Psychiatric Clinics of North America, 13,* 377–388.

Ogata, N., Voshii, M., & Narahashi, T. (1989). Psychotropic drugs block voltage-gated ion channels in neuroblastoma cells. *Brain Research, 476,* 140–144.

Ogata, S. N., Silk, K. R., Goodrich, S., Lohr, N. E., et al. (1990). Childhood sexual and physical abuse in adult patients with borderline personality disorder. *American Journal of Psychiatry, 147,* 1008–1013.

Ogbu, J. (1991). Minority coping responses and school experience. *Journal of Psychohistory, 18,* 434–456.

Ohman , A. (1994). "Unconscious anxiety": Phobic responses to masked stimuli. *Journal of Abnormal Psychology, 103,* 231–240.

Ohman, A., Fredrikson, M., Hugdahl, K., & Rimmon, P. (1976). The premise of equipotentiality in human classical conditioning. *Journal of Experimental Psychological General, 105,* 313–337.

Okagaki, L., & Sternberg, R. J. (1993). Arental beliefs and children's school performance. *Child Development, 64,* 36–56.

Okasha, A., El Akabaw, A. S., Snyder, K. S., Wilson, A. K., Youssef, I. & El Dawla, A. S. (1994). Expressed emotion, perceived criticism, and relapse in depression: A replication. *American Journal of Psychiatry, 151,* 1001–1005.

Olds, J., & Milner, P. (1954). Positive reinforcement produced by electrical stimulation of septal areas and other regions of rat brains. *Journal of Comparative and Physiological Psychology, 47,* 419–427.

O'Leary, A. (1990). Stress, emotion, and human immune function. *Psychological Bulletin, 108,* 363–382.

O'Leary, A., Brown, S., & Suarez-Al-Adam, M. (1997). Stress and immune function. In T. W. Miller (Ed.), *Clinical disorders and stressful life events* (pp. 181–215). Madison, CT: International Universities Press, Inc.

Olfson, M., Marcus, S. C., Pincus, H. A., Zito, J. M., Thompson, J. W., & Zarin, D. A. (1998). Antidepressant prescribing practices of outpatient psychiatrists. *Archives of General Psychiatry, 55,* 310–316.

Oliner, S., & Oliner, P. (1988). *The altruistic personality: Rescuers of Jews in Nazi Europe.* New York: Free Press.

Olivier, B., Mos, J., VanderHeyden, J., & VanderPoel, G. (1992). Preclinical evidence for the anxiolytic activity of 5 ht sub 3 receptor antagonists: A review. *Stress Medicine, 8,* 117–136.

Olson, D. (1985). Circumplex model VII: Validation and FACES III. *Family Process, 25,* 337–351.

Olson, G. B. (1981). Perception of melodic contour through intrasensory matching and intersensory transfer by elementary school students. *Journal of Educational Research, 74,* 358–362.

Olson, J. M. (1992). Self-perception of humor: Evidence for discounting and augmentation effects. *Journal of Personality and Social Psychology, 62,* 369–377.

Olson, J. M., & Zanna, M. (1993). Attitudes and attitude change. *Annual Review of Psychology, 44,* 117–154.

Olson, S. L., Bates, J. E., & Bayles, K. (1989). Predicting long-term developmental outcomes from maternal perceptions of infant and toddler behavior. *Infant Behavior & Development, 12,* 77–92.

Olweus, D. (1980). Familial and temperamental determinants of aggressive behavior in adolescent boys: A causal analysis. *Developmental Psychology, 16,* 644–666.

Omark, D. R., Omark, M., & Edelman, M. (1975). Formation of dominance hierarchies in young children. In T. R. Williams (Ed.), *Psychological anthropology.* The Hague: Mouton.

O'Neill, R. M., Greenberg, R. P., & Fisher, S. (1992). Humor and anality. *Humor: International Journal of Humor Research, 5,* 283–291.

Oppenheim, D., Emde, R., & Warren, S. (1997). Children's narrative representations of mothers: Their development and associations with child and mother adaptation. *Child Development, 68,* 127–138.

Orne, M. T., Sheehan, P. W., & Evans, F. J. (1968). *Journal of Personality and Social Psychology, 9,* 189–196.

Ornstein, R. E. (1986). *The psychology of consciousness.* (2nd ed.). NewYork: Penguin Books.

Ortony, A., Clore, G. L., & Collins, A. (1988). *The cognitive structure of emotions.* New York: Cambridge University Press.

Ortony, A., & Turner, T. J. (1990). What's basic about basic emotions? *Psychological Review, 97,* 315–331.

Oskamp, S. (1991). Factors influencing household recycling behavior. *Environment & Behavior, 23,* 494–519.

Ost, L. (1991). Acquisition of blood and injection phobia and anxiety response patterns in clinical patients. *Behavior Research and Therapy, 29,* 323–332.

O'Sullivan, G., Noshirvani, H., Marks, I., & Monteira, W. (1991). Six-year follow-up after exposure and clomipramine therapy for obsessive compulsive disorder. *Journal of Clinical Psychiatry, 52,* 150–155.

O'Sullivan, J. T., Howe, M. L., & Marche, T. (1996). Children's beliefs about long-term retention. *Child Development, 67,* 2989–3009.

Ouellette, J. A., & Wood, W. (1997). Habit: Predicting frequently-occurring behaviors in constant contexts. Manuscript submitted.

Packard, J. (1986). Tone production in nonfluent aphasic Chinese speech. *Brain & Language, 29,* 212–223.

Packwood, J., & Gordon, B. (1975). Steropsis in normal domestic cat, Siamese cat, and cat raised with alternating monocular occlusion. *Journal of Neurophysiology, 38,* 1485–1499.

Paivio, A. (1991). Dual coding theory: Retrospect and current status. *Canadian Journal of Psychology, 45,* 255–287.

Paivio, S. C., & Greenbery, L. S. (1995). Resolving "unfinished business"; efficacy of experimental therapy using empty-chair dialogue. *Journal of Consulting and Clinical Psychology, 63,* 419–425.

Palumbo, R., & Gillman, I. (1984). Effects of subliminal activation of Oedipal fantasies on competitive performance. *Journal of Nervous and Mental Disease, 172,* 737–741.

Papez, J. W. (1937). A proposed mechanism of emotion. *Archives of Neurology and Psychiatry, 38,* 725–743.

Paran, E., Amir, M., & Yaniv, N. (1996). Evaluating the response of mild hypertensives to biofeedback-assisted relaxation using a mental stress test. *Journal of Behavior Therapy & Experimental Psychiatry, 27,* 157–167.

Pargament, K. I., & Park, C. L. (1995). Merely a defense? The variety of religious means and ends. *Journal of Social Issues, 51,* 13–32.

Park, D. C., Smith, A. D., Lautenschlager, G., & Earles, J. L. (1996). Mediators of long-term memory performance across the life span. *Psychology & Aging, 11,* 621–637.

Park, S. (1995). Spatial working memory deficits in the relatives of schizophrenia patients. *Archives of General Psychiatry, 52,* 821–828.

Park, S., & Holzman, P. S. (1993). Association of working memory deficit and eye tracking dysfunction in schizophrenia. *Schizophrenia Research, 11,* 55–61.

Parke, R. D., & Slaby, R. G. (1983). The development of aggression. In P. H. Mussen (Ed.), *Carmichael's Manual of Child Psychology*, Vol. 4: *Socialization, personality, and social development.* New York: John Wiley.

Parker, J. G., & Herrera C. (1996). Interpersonal processes in friendship: A comparison of abused and nonabused children's experiences. *Developmental Psychology, 32,* 1025–1038.

Parkin, A. J., Walter, B. M., & Hunkin, N. M. (1995). Relationships between normal aging, frontal lobe function, and memory for temporal and spatial information. *Neuropsychology, 9,* 304–312.

Parloff, M. B., London, P., & Wolfe, B. (1986). Individual psychotherapy and behavior change. *Annual Review of Psychology, 37,* 321–349.

Parsons, T. (1951). *The social system.* Glencoe, IL: Free Press.

Pascual-Leone, A., Cammarota, A., Wassermann, E., & Brasil-Neto, J. (1994). Modulation of cortical motor output maps during development of implicit and explicit knowledge. *Science, 263,* 1287–1289.

Pascual-Leone, A., & Torres, F. (1993). Plasticity of the sensorimotor cortex representations of the reading finger in Braille. *Brain.*

Passaro, K. T., & Little, R. E. (1997). Childbearing and alcohol use. In R. W. Wilsnack, and S. C. Wilsnack (Eds.), *Gender and alcohol: Individual and social perspectives* (pp. 90–113). New Jersey: Rutgers Center of Alcohol Studies.

Patterson, D. G., & O'Gorman, E. C. (1989). Sexual anxiety in sexual dysfunction. *British Journal of Psychiatry, 155,* 374–378.

Patterson, D. R., & Ptacek, J. T. (1997). Baseline pain as a moderator of hypnotic analgesia for burn injury treatment. *Journal of Consulting & Clinical Psychology, 65,* 60–67.

Patterson, D. R., Everett, J. J., Burns, G. L., & Marvin, J. A. (1992). Hypnosis for the treatment of burn pain. *Journal of Consulting & Clinical Psychology, 60,* 713–717.

Patterson, G. R., & Bank, L. (1986). Bootstrapping your way in the nomological thicket. *Behavioral Assessment, 8,* 49–73.

Paulesu, E., Frith, U., Snowling, M., Gallagher, A., Morton, J., Frackowiak, R. S. J., & Frith, C. D. (1996). Is developmental dyslexia a disconnection syndrome? Evidence from PET scanning. *Brain, 119,* 143–157.

Paulhus, D., Fridhandler, B., & Hayes, S. (1997). Psychological defense: Contemporary theory and research. In R. Hogan, J. Johnson, & S. R. Briggs (Eds.), *Handbook of personality psychology*

(pp. 543–579). San Diego: Academic Press.

Paulus, P. B. et al. (1988). *Prison crowding: A psychological perspective.* New York: Springer-Verlag.

Paunonen, S. V., Jackson, D. N., Trzebinski, J., & Forsterling, F. (1992). Personality structure across cultures: A multimethod evaluation. *Journal of Personality and Social Psychology, 62,* 447–456.

Pause, B. M., Bernfried, S., Krauel, K., Fehm-Wolfsdorf, Gabriele, & Ferstl, R. (1996). Olfactory information processing during the course of the menstrual cycle. *Biological Psychology, 44,* 31–54.

Pavlov, I. P. (1927). *Conditioned reflexes.* New York: Oxford University Press.

Pavone, L., Meli, C., Nigro, F., Lisi, R. et al. (1993). Late diagnosed phenylketonuria patients: Clinical presentation and results of treatment. *Developmental Brain Dysfunction, 6,* 184–187.

Payne, D. G., Neuschatz, Lampien, J., & Lynn, S. J. (1997). Compelling memory illusions: The qualitative characteristics of false memories. *Current Directions in Psychological Science, 6,* 56–60.

Pearce, J. M. (1987). A model for stimulus generalization in Pavlonian conditioning. *Psychologial Review, 94,* 61–73.

Pedersen, D. M., & Wheeler, J. (1983). The Muller-Lyer illusion among Navajos. *Journal of Social Psychology, 121,* 3–6.

Pedersen, N., McClearn, G., Plomin, R., & Nesselroade, J. R. (1991). The Swedish adoption/twin study of aging: An update. *Acta Geneticae Medicae et Gemellogiae: Twin Research, 40,* 7–20.

Pederson, D. R., Moran, G., Sitko, C., Campbell, K., Ghesquire, K., & Acton, H. (1990). Maternal sensitivity and the security of infant-mother attachment: A q-sort study. *Child Devleopment, 61,* 1974–1983.

Peele, S. (1986). Implications and limitations of genetic models of alcoholism and other addictions. *Journal of Studies on Alcohol, 47,* 63–73.

Pennebaker, J. (1992). Putting stress into words: Health, linguistic and therapeutic implications. *Behavior Research & Therapy, 31,* 539–548.

Pennebaker, J. (1997). *Opening up: The healing power of expressing emotions* (rev. ed.). New York: Guilford Press.

Pennebaker, J. (1997). Writing about emotional experiences as a therapeutic process. *Psychological Science, 8,* 162–166.

Pennebaker, J. W., Barger, S. D., & Tiebout, J. (1989). Disclosure of traumas and health among Holocaust survivors. *Psychosomatic Medicine, 51,* 577–589.

Pennebaker, J. W., Mayne, T. J., & Francis,

M. E. (1997). Linguistic predictors of adaptive bereavement. *Journal of Personality & Social Psychology, 72,* 863–871.

Pennebaker, J., Colder, M., & Sharp, L. K. (1990). Accelerating the coping process. *Journal of Personality and Social Psychology, 58,* 528–537.

Penner, L., & Rioux, S. (1995). *The prosocial personality and memories of parents.* Nags Head Invitation Conference on the Social Sciences, Highland Beach, June.

Perdue, C., Dovidio, J., Gurtman, M., & Tyler, R. (1990). Us and them: Social categorization and the process of intergroup bias. *Journal of Personality and Social Psychology, 59,* 475–486.

Perdue, C., & Gurtman, M. (1990). Evidence for the automaticity of ageism. *Journal of Experimental Social Psychology, 26,* 199–216.

Perlmutter, M. (1978). What is memory aging the aging of? *Developmental Psychology, 14,* 330–345.

Perlmutter, M. (1983). Learning and memory through adulthood. In M. W. Riley, B. B. Hess, & K. Bond (Eds.), *Aging in society: Selected reviews of recent research.* Hillsdale, NJ: Erlbaum.

Perlmutter, M., Dams, C., Berry, J., Kaplan, M., Pearson, D., & Verdonik, J. (1990). Aging and memory. *Annual Review of Gerontology and Geriatrics, 7,* 57–92.

Perlmutter, M., & Nyquist, L. (1990). Relationship between self-reported physical and mental health and intelligence performance across adulthood. *Journal of Gerontology, 45,* 145–155.

Perris, E. E., Myers, N. A., & Clifton, R. K. (1990). Long-term memory for a single infancy experience. *Child Development, 61,* 1796–1807.

Perry, G. D., & Bussey, K. (1979). The social learning theory of sex differences: Imitation is alive and well. *Journal of Personality and Social Psychology, 37,* 1699–1712.

Perry, J. C., & Cooper, S. H. (1987). Empirical studies of psychological defense mechanisms. In R. Michels & J. O. Cavenar, Jr. (Eds.), *Psychiatry.* Philadelphia: J. B. Lippincott.

Persons, J. B., & Silberschatz, G. (1998). Are results or randomized controlled trials useful to psychotherapists? *Journal of Consulting & Clinical Psychology, 66,* 126–135.

Pervin, L. (1996). Personality: A view of the future based on a look at the past. *Journal of Research in Personality, 30,* 309–318.

Peselow, E., Robins, C. J., Sanfilipo, M. P., Block, P., & Fieve, R. (1992). Sociotropy and autonomy: Relationship to antidepressant drug treatment response and endogenous-nonendogenous dichotomy. *Journal of Abnormal Psychology, 101,* 479–486.

Peskin, J. (1992). Ruse and representations: On children's ability to conceal information. *Developmental Psychology, 28,* 84–89.

Peterson, C. (1988). Explanatory style as a risk factor for illness. *Cognitive Therapy and Research, 12,* 119–132.

Peterson, C. (1995). Explanatory style and health. In G. M. Buchanan, M. E. P. Seligman, et al. (Eds.), *Explanatory style.* (pp. 233–246). Hillsdale, NJ: Lawrence Erlbaum Associates, Inc.

Peterson, C., & Seligman, M. E. P. (1984). Causal explanations as a risk factor for depression: Theory and evidence. *Psychological Review 91,* 347–374.

Peterson, C., Seligman, M., & Vaillant, G. (1988). Pessimistic explanatory style is a risk factor for physical illness: A thirty-five-year longitudinal study. *Journal of Personality & Social Psychology, 55,* 23–27.

Peterson, G., & Peters, D. (1985). The socialization values of low-income Appalachian White and rural Black mothers: A comparative study. *Journal of Comparative Family Studies, 16,* 75–91.

Peterson, J. (1925). *Early conceptions and tests of intelligence.* Yonkers-on-Hudson, NY: World Book Co.

Peterson, L. R., and Peterson, M. J. (1959). Short-term retention of individual items, *Journal of Experimental Psychology, 61,* 12–21.

Pettigrew, T. (1958). Personality and socio-cultural factors in intergroup attitudes: A cross-national comparison. *Journal of Conflict Resolution, 2,* 29–42.

Petty, R., & Cacioppo, J. (1981). *Attitudes and persuasion: Classic and contemporary approaches.* Dubuque, Iowa: W. C. Brown.

Petty, R., & Cacioppo, J. (1986). *Communication and persuasion: Central and peripheral routes to attitude change.* New York: Springer-Verlag.

Petty, R., & Cacioppo, J. T. (1986). The elaboration likelihood model of persuasion. In L. Berkowitz (Ed.), *Advances in Experimental Social Psychology, 19,* 123–205.

Petty, R., & Krosnick, J. (1994). *Attitude strength: Antecedents and consequences.* Hillsdale, NJ: Erlbaum.

Petty, R. E., & Wegener, D. T. (1998). Matching versus mismatching attitude functions: Implications for scrutiny of persuasive messages. *Personality & Social Psychology Bulletin, 24,* 227–240.

Pfaffman, C. (1955). Gustatory nerve impulses in rat, cat and rabbit. *Journal of Neurophysiology, 18,* 429–440.

Phillips, C. D., & Dinitz, S. (1982). Labeling and juvenile court dispositions: Official responses to a cohort of violent juveniles. *Sociological Quarterly, 23,* 267–278.

Phillips, M. L., Young, A. W., Senior, C., Brammer, M., Andrews, C., Calder, A. J., et al. (1997). A specific neural substrate for perceiving facial expressions of disgust. *Nature, 389,* 495–498.

Piaget, J. (1926). *The language and thought of the child.* New York: Humanities Press, 1951.

Piaget, J. (1932). *The moral judgment of the child* (M. Gabrain, Trans.). New York: Free Press.

Piaget, J. (1954). *The construction of reality in the child* (M. Cook, Trans.). New York: Basic Books.

Piaget, J. (1970). Piaget's theory. In P. Mussen, (Ed.), *Carmichael's manual of child psychology.* New York: John Wiley.

Piaget, J. (1972). Development and learning. In C. S. Lavatelli & F. Stendler (Eds.), *Readings in child behavior and development.* (3rd ed.). New York: Harcourt Brace Jovanovich.

Piaget, J., & Inhelder, B. (1956). *The child's conception of space* (F. J. Langdon & J. L. Lunzer, Trans.). London: Routledge & T. K. Paul.

Piaget, J., & Inhelder, B. (1969). *The psychology of the child.* New York: Basic Books.

Pickar, D. (1988). Perspectives on a time-dependent model of neuroleptic action. *Schizophrenia Bulletin, 14,* 255–268.

Pickens, R., Svikis, D., McGue, M., Lykken, D., Heston, L., & Clayton, P. (1991). Heterogeneity in the inheritance of alcoholism: A study of male and female twins. *Archives of General Psychiatry, 48,* 19–28.

Piers, G., & Singer, M. (1953). *Shame and guilt: A psychoanalytic and a cultural study.* Springfield, Ill.: C. Thomas.

Pihl, R., Peterson, J., & Finn, P. (1990). Inherited predisposition to alcoholism: Characteristics of sons of male alcoholics. *Journal of Abnormal Psychology, 99,* 291–301.

Pillard, R. C., Poumadere, J., & Carretta, R. A. (1981). Is homosexuality familial? A review, some data, and a suggestion. *Archives of Sexual Behavior, 10,* 465–73.

Pillard, R. C., Poumadere, J., & Carretta, R. A. (1982). A family study of sexual orientation. *Archives of Sexual Behavior, 11,* 511–520.

Pillemer, D. B. (1984). Flashbulb memories of the assassination attempt on President Reagan. *Cognition, 16,* 63–80.

Pinker, S. (1994). *The language instinct: How the mind creates language.* New York: HarperCollins.

Pinker, S. (1995). Language acquisition. In L. R. Gleitman, & M. Liberman, et al. (Eds.), *Language: An invitation to cognitive science, Vol. 1 (2nd ed.). An invitation to cognitive science.* (pp. 135–182). Cambridge: MIT Press.

Piper, W. E., Joyce, A., McCallum, M., & Azim, H. (1993). Concentration and correspondence of transference interpretations in short-term psychotherapy. *Journal of Consulting and Clinical Psychotherapy, 61,* 586–595.

Plomin, R. (1990). *Nature and nurture.* Pacific Grove, CA: Brooks-Cole.

Plomin, R., Chipuer, H., & Loehlin, J. C. (1990). Behavioral genetics and personality. In L. Pervin (Ed.), *Handbook of personality: Theory and research* (pp. 225–243). New York: Guilford Press.

Plomin, R., & DeFries, J. (1980). Genetics and intelligence: Recent data. *Intelligence, 4,* 15–24.

Plomin, R., DeFries, J. C., McClearn, G. E., & Rutter, R. (1997). *Behavioral genetics,* (3rd ed.). New York: W. H. Freeman.

Plomin, R., Reiss, D., Hetherington, E. M., & Howe, G. W. (1994). Nature and nurture: Genetic contributions to measures of the family environment. *Developmental Psychology, 30,* 32–43.

Plomin, R., & Rende, R. (1991). Human behavioral genetics. *Annual Review of Psychology, 42,* 161–190.

Plomin, R., Willerman, L., & Loehlin, J. C. (1976). Resemblance in appearance and the equal environments assumption in twin studies of personality. *Behavior Genetics, 6,* 43–52.

Plous, S. (1991). An attitude survey of animal rights activists. *Psychological Science, 2,* 194–196.

Plutchik, R. (1980). *Emotions: A psychoevolutionary synthesis.* New York: Harper & Row.

Plutchik, R. (1997). The circumplex as a general model of the structure of emotions and personality. In R. Plutchik, H. R. Conte, et al. (Eds., 1997). *Circumplex models of personality and emotions* (pp. 17–45). Washington: American Psychological Association.

Poldrack, R. A., Desmond, J. E., Glover, G. H., & Gabrieli, J. D. E. (1998). The neural basis of visual skill learning: An fMRI study of mirror reading. *Cerebral Cortex, 8,* 1–10.

Pollock, V. E., Briere, J., Schneider, L., Knop, J., Mednick, S., & Goodwin, D. W. (1990). Childhood antecedents of antisocial behavior: Parental alcoholism and physical abusiveness. *American Journal of Psychiatry, 147,* 1290–1293.

Ponds, R., Brouwer, W., & Van Wolffelaar, P. (1988). Age differences in divided attention in a simulated driving task. *Journal of Gerontology, 43,* 151–156.

Poon, L., Clayton, P. M., Martin, P., Johnson, M. A., Courtenay, B., Sweaney, A., Merriam, S., Pless, B. S., & Thielman, S. (1992). The Georgia Centenarian study. *International Journal of Aging and Human Development, 34,* 1–17.

Pope, H., McElroy, S., Keck, P., & Hudson, J. (1991). Valproate in the treatment of acute mania. *Archives of General Psychiatry, 48,* 62–68.

Pope, H. G., Gruber, A. J., & Yurgelun-Todd, D. (1995). The residual neuropsychological effects of cannabis: The current status of research. *Drug & Alcohol Dependence, 38,* 25–34.

Pope, K., Tabachnick, B., & Keith-Spiegel, P. (1987). Ethics of practice: The beliefs and behaviors of psychologists as therapists. *American Psychologist, 42,* 993–1006.

Popper, K. (1963). *Conjectures and refutations: The growth of scientific knowledge.* New York: Basic Books.

Porcerelli, J., Hill, K., & Dauphin, V. B. (1995). Need-gratifying object relations and psychopathology. *Bulletin of the Menninger Clinic, 59,* 99–106.

Porkka-Heiskanen, T., Strecker, R. E., Thakkar, M., & Bjorkum, A. A. (1997). Adenosine: A mediator of the sleep-induced effects of prolonged wakefulness. *Science, 276,* 1265–1268.

Posner, M. I. (1995). Attention in cognitive neuroscience: An overview. In M. S. Gazzaniga, et al. (Eds.), *The cognitive neurosciences.* (pp. 615–624). Cambridge: MIT Press.

Posner, N. I., & Raichle, M. E. (1996). Precis of image and mind. *Behavioral and Brain Sciences, 18,* 327–383.

Posner, R. M., Boies, S., Eichelman, W. H., & Taylor, R. L. (1969). Retention of visual and name codes of single letters. *Journal of Experimental Psychology, 79.*

Pospisil, L. (1963). *Kapauka Papuan political economy.* New Haven, Conn.: Yale University Publications in Anthropology, No. 67.

Post, R. M. (1992). Transduction of psychosocial stress into the neurobiology of recurrent affective disorder. *American Journal of Psychiatry, 149,* 999–1010.

Post, R. M. (1997). Molecular Biology of Behavior: Targets for Therapeutics. *Archives of General Psychiatry, 54,* 607–608.

Povinelli, D., & Simon, B. B. (1998). Young children's understanding of briefly versus extremely delayed images of the self: Emergence of the autobiographical stance. *Developmental Psychology, 34,* 188–194.

Powers, W. T. (1973). *Behavior: The control of perception.* Chicago: Aldine.

Prakash, P. (1984). Second language acquisition and critical period hypothesis. *Psycho-Lingua, 14,* 13–17.

Premack, A. J., & Premack, D. (1972). Teaching language to an ape. *Scientific American, 227,* 92–99.

Premack, D. (1962). Reversibility of the reinforcement relation. *Science, 136,* 235–237.

Premack, D. (1965). *Reinforcement theory.* In D. Levine (Ed.), Nebraska Symposium on motivation (Vol. 3, pp. 123–180). Lincoln: University of Nebraska Press.

Prentky, R. A. (1980). *Creativity and psychopathology.* New York: Praeger.

Preti, G., Cutler, W. B., Garcia, G. R., Huggins, M., & Lawley, J. J. (1986). Human axillary secretions influence women's menstrual cycles: The role of donor extract from females. *Hormones and Behavior, 20,* 474–482.

Pribram, K. H. (1980). The biology of emotions and other feelings. In R. Plutchik and H. Kellerman (Eds.), *Emotion: theory, research, and experience,* Vol. I: Theories of emotion. New York: Academic Press.

Pribram, K. H., & Gill, M. M. (1976). *Freud's project reassessed.* New York: Basic Books.

Price, D. L., Cork, L. C., Struble, R. G., Whitehouse, P. J., Kitt, C. A., & Walker, L. C. (1985). The functional organization of the basal forebrain cholinergic system in primates and the role of this system in Alzheimer's disease. In D. S. Olton, E. Gamzu, & S. Corkin (Eds.), *Memory dysfunctions: An integration of animal and human research from preclinical and clinical perspectives.* New York: New York Academy of Sciences.

Price, L. H., Charney, D. S., Delgado, P., & Heninger, G. (1991). Serotonin function and depression: Neuroendocrine and mood responses to intravenous L-tryptophan in depressed patients and healthy comparison subjections. *American Journal of Psychiatry, 148,* 1518–1525.

Price-Williams, D. (1975). *Explorations in cross-cultural psychology.* San Francisco: Chandler & Sharp.

Price-Williams, D. (1981). Concrete and formal operations. In R. H. Munroe, R. L. Munroe, & B. D. Whiting (Eds.), *Handbook of cross-cultural human development.* New York: Garland Press.

Price-Williams, D., Gordon, W., & Ramirez, M. (1969). Skill and conservation: A study of pottery-making children. *Developmental Psychology, 1,* 769.

Price-Williams, D. R. (1985). In G. Lindzey and E. Aronson (Eds.), *Handbook of social psychology.* Reading, MA: Addison-Wesley.

Prien, R. F. (1988). Somatic treatment of unipolar depressive disorder. In A. J. Frances and R. E. Hales (Eds.), *Review of Psychiatry,* Vol. 7. Washington, DC: American Psychiatric Press.

Priester, J. R., Cacioppo, J. T., & Petty, R. E. (1996). The influence of motor processes on attitudes toward novel versus familiar semantic stimuli. *Personality & Social Psychology Bulletin. Vol. 22,* 442–447.

Prince, A., & Smolensky, P. (1997). Optimality: From Neural Networks to Universal Grammar. *Science, 275,* 1604–1610.

Prochaska, J. D. (1984). *The transtheoretical approach: Crossing traditional boundaries of therapy.* Homewood, Ill.: Dow Jones-Irwin.

Puce, A., Allison, T., Asgari, M., Gore, J. C., & McCarthy, G. (1996). Differential sensitivity of human visual cortex to faces, letterstrings, and textures: A functional magnetic resonance imaging study. *Journal of Neuroscience, 16,* 5205–5215.

Putnam, F. W. (1991). Dissociative disorders in children and adolescents: A developmental perspective. *Psychiatric Clinics of North America, 14,* 519–531.

Putnam, H. (1973). Reductionism and the nature of psychology. *Cognition, 2,* 131–146.

Quinn, N. (1975). Decision models of social structure. *American Ethnologist, 2,* 19–45.

Quitkin, F., Harrison, W., Stewart, J., & McGrath, P. (1990). Response to phenelzine and imipramine in placebo nonresponders with atypical depression: A new application of the crossover design. *Archives of General Psychiatry, 48,* 319–323.

Quitkin, F. M., Harrison, W., Stewart, J. W., McGrath, P. J., et al. (1991). Response to phenelzine and imipramine in placebo nonresponders with atypical depression: A new application of the crossover design. *Archives of General Psychiatry, 48,* 319–323.

Rabbitt, P. (1996). Speed of processing and ageing. In R. T. Woods (Ed.), *Handbook of the clinical psychology of ageing* (pp. 59–72). New York: Wiley.

Rachlin, H., Green, L., Kagel, J. H., & Battalio, R. C. (1976). Economic demand theory and psychological studies of choice. In G. H. Bower (Ed.), *The psychology of learning and motivation* (Vol. 10, pp. 129–154). New York: Academic.

Rachman, S. J. (1978). *Fear and courage.* San Francisco: Freeman.

Rafal, R., & Robertson, L. (1995). The neurology of visual attention. In M. S. Gazzaniga, et al. (Eds.), *The cognitive neurosciences.* (pp. 625–648). Cambridge: MIT Press.

Rain, A., & Venables, P. H. (1984). Electrodermal nonresponding, antisocial behavior, and schizoid tendencies in adolescents. *Psychophysiology, 21,* 424–433.

Rajaram, S. (1993). Remembering and knowing: Two means of access to the personal past. *Memory and Cognition, 21,* 89–102.

Rallison, M. (1986). *Growth disorders in infants, children, and adolescents.* New York: John Wiley.

Ralston, D., Gustafson, D., Elsass, P., & Cheung, F. (1992). Eastern values: A comparison of managers in the United States, Hong Kong, and the People's Republic of China. *Journal of Applied Psychology, 77,* 664–671.

Ramos, A., Berton, O., Mormede, P., & Chaouloff, F. (1997). A multiple-test study of anxiety-related behaviours in six inbred rat strains. *Behavioural Brain Research, 85,* 57–69.

Rand, C. S., & Kuldau, J. M. (1990). The epidemiology of obesity and self-defined weight problem in the general population: Gender, race, age, and social class. *International Journal of Eating Disorders, 9,* 329-343.

Randhawa, B. (1991). Gender differences in academic achievement: A closer look at mathematics. *Alberta Journal of Educational Research, 37,* 241–257.

Rao, S. C., Rainier, G., & Miller, E. K. (1997). Integration of what and where in the primate prefrontal cortex. *Science, 276,* 821–824.

Rao, S. M., Huber, S. J., & Bornstein, R. A. (1992). Emotional changes with multiple sclerosis and Parkinson's disease. *Journal of Consulting and Clinical Psychology, 60,* 369–378.

Rapee, R. (1991). Generalized anxiety disorder: A review of clinical features and theoretical concepts. *Clinical Psychology Review, 11,* 419–440.

Rapee, R. M., Brown, T. A., Antony, M., & Barlow, D. (1992). Response to hyperventilation and inhalation of 5.5% carbon dioxide-enriched air across the DSM-III-R anxiety disorders. *Journal of Abnormal Psychology, 101,* 538–552.

Rapoport, J. L., Ryland, D., & Kriete, M. (1992). Drug treatment of canine acral lick. *Archives of General Psychiatry, 49,* 517–521.

Rashidy-Pour, A., Motaghed-Larijani, Z., & Bures, J. (1995). Reversible inactivation of the medial septal area impairs consolidation but not retrieval of passive avoidance learning in rats. *Behavioural Brain Research, 72,* 185–188.

Ray, O. S., Ksir, C. (1993). *Drugs, society & human behavior.* (6th ed.). St. Louis: Mosby-Year Book.

Rea, C. P., & Modigliani, V. (1988). Educational implications of the spacing effect. In M. M. Gruneberg, P. E. Morris, et al. (Eds.), *Practical aspects of memory: Current research and issues, Vol. 1: Memory in everyday life.* (pp. 402–406). New York: John Wiley & Sons.

Read, P. B. (1982). Foreword. In D. H. Feldman (Ed.), *New directions for child development:* No. 17 (1–4), *Developmental approaches to giftedness and creativity.* San Francisco: Jossey-Bass.

Read, S. J., Vanman, E. J., & Miller, L. C. (1997). Connectionism, parallel constraint satisfaction processes, and Gestalt principles: (Re)introducing cognitive dynamics to social psychology. *Personality and Social Psychology Review 1,* 26–53.

Reber, A. S. (1989). Implicit learning and tacit knowledge. *Journal of Experimental Psychology: General, 118,* 219–235.

Reber, A. S. (1992). The cognitive unconscious: An evolutionary perspective. *Consciousness and Cognition, 1,* 93–133.

Recanzone, G. H., Schreiner, C. E., & Merzenich, M. M. (1993). Plasticity in the frequency representation in the primary auditory cortex following discontinuous training in adult owl monkeys. *Journal of Neuroscience.*

Reder, L. M., & Schunn, C. D. (1996). Metacognition does not imply awareness: Strategy choice is governed by implicit learning and memory. In L. M. Reder (Ed.), *Implicit memory and metacognition* (pp. 45–77). Mahwah, NJ: Erlbaum.

Rees, G., Frackowiak, R., & Firth, C. (1997). Two modulatory effects of attention that mediate object categorization in human cortex. *Science, 275,* 835–838.

Reeve, R. A., & Brown, A. L. (1985). Metacognition reconsidered: Implications for intervention research. *Journal of Abnormal Child Psychology, 13,* 343–56.

Regan, D., & Fazio, R. (1977). On the consistency between attitudes and behavior: Look to the method of attitude formation. *Journal of Experimental Social Psychology, 13,* 28–45.

Regan, J. W. (1971). Guilt, perceived injustice, and altruistic behavior. *Journal of Personality and Social Psychology, 18,* 124–132.

Regan, P. C. (1996). Rhythms of desire: The association between menstrual cycle phases and female sexual desire. *Canadian Journal of Human Sexuality, 5,* 145–215.

Reifman, A., Larrick, R., & Fein, S. (1991). Temper and temperature on the dia-

mond: The heat-aggression relationship in major league baseball. *Personality & Social Psychology Bulletin, 17,* 580–585.

Reiman, P., Chi, M. T. H. (1989). Human expertise. In K. J. Gilhooly (Ed.), *Human and machine problem solving.* New York: Plenum Press.

Reinisch, J. M. (1981). Prenatal exposure to synthetic progestins increases potential for aggression in humans. *Science, 211,* 1171–1173.

Reis, H. J., & Shaver, P. (1988). Intimacy as an interpersonal process. In S. Duck (Ed.), *Handbook of personal relationships: Theory, relationships and interventions.* New York: John Wiley.

Reisberg, D. (1997). *Cognition: Exploring the science of the mind.* New York: Norton.

Reisberg, D., & Heuer, F. (1995). Emotion's multiple effects on memory. In J. L. McGaugh, N. Weinberger, & G. Lynch (Eds.), *Brain and memory: Modulation and mediation of neuroplasticity* (pp. 84–92). New York: Oxford University Press.

Reisenzein, R. (1983). The Schachter theory of emotion: Two decades later. *Psychological Bulletin, 94,* 239–264.

Repacholi, B., & Gopnik, A. (1997). Early reasoning about desires: Evidence from 14- and 18-month-olds. *Developmental Psychology, 33,* 12–21.

Rescorla, R. A. (1988). Pavlovian conditioning: It's not what you think it is. *American Psychologist, 43,* 151–160.

Rescorla, R. A., & Holland, P. C. (1982). Behavioral studies of associative learning in animals. *Annual Review of Psychology, 33,* 265–308.

Rescorla, R. A., & Wagner, A. R. (1972). A theory of Pavlovian conditioning: Variations in the effectiveness of reinforcement and non-reinforcement. In A. H. Black & W. F. Prokasy (Eds.), *Classical conditioning: II. Current research and theory.* New York: Appleton.

Rest, J. R. (1983). Morality. In J. H. Flavell & E. M. Markman (Eds.), *Handbook of child psychology: Vol. 3. Cognitive development.* New York: John Wiley.

Revelle, W. (1992). Personality processes. *Annual Review of Psychology, 46,* 295–328.

Reynolds, A. J., Mehana, M., & Temple, J. A. (1995). Does preschool intervention affect children's perceived competence? *Journal of Applied Development Psychology, 16,* 211–230.

Reynolds, C. F. III, Kupfer, D. J., Buysee, D. J., et al. (1991). Subtyping DSM-III-R primary insomnia: A literature review by the DSM-IV work group on sleep disorders. *American Journal of Psychiatry, 148,* 432–438.

Rholes, W. S., Simpson, J. A., Blakely, B.

S., Lanigan, L., & Allen, E. A. (1997). Adult attachment styles, the desire to have children, and working models of parenthood. *Journal of Personality, 65,* 357–385.

Richards, B. J. (1990). Language development and individual differences: A study of auxiliary verb learning. Cambridge: Cambridge University Press.

Richards, J. B., Sabol, K. E., & Freed, C. R. (1990). Conditioned rotation: A behavioral analysis. *Physiology and Behavior, 47,* 1083–1087.

Richards, M. H., Crowe, P. A., Larson, R., & Swarr, A. (1998). Developmental patterns and gender differences in the experience of peer companionship during adolescence. *Child Development, 69,* 154–163.

Richards, R. (1994). Creativity and bipolar mood swings: Why the association? In M. P. Shaw and M. A. Runco (Eds.), *Creativity and affect* (pp. 44–72). Norwood: Ablex.

Richards, R., & Kinney, D. K. (1990). Mood swings and creativity. *Creativity Research Journal, 3,* 202–217.

Richards, R., Kinney, D. K., Daniels, H., & Linkins, K. (1992). Everyday creativity and bipolar and unipolar affective disorder: Preliminary study of personal and family history. *European Psychiatry, 7,* 49–52.

Richards, R., Kinney, D., Lunde, I., Benet, M., & Merzel, A. (1988). Creativity in manic-depressives, cyclothymes, and their normal relatives, and control subjects. *Journal of Abnormal Psychology, 97,* 281–288.

Richardson, D. (1991). Structural and strategic family therapy techniques: Application to chemically dependent families. *Journal of Chemical Dependency Treatment, 4,* 29–39.

Richardson, J. T. E. (1996). Evolving concepts of working memory. In J. T. E. Richardson, R. W. Engle, L. Hasher, R. Logie, E. Stoltzfus, and R. Zacks (Eds.), *Working memory and human cognition* (pp. 3–29). New York: Oxford University Press.

Richardson, J. T. E. (1996). Evolving issues in working memory. In J. T. E. Richardson, R. W. Engle, L. Hasher, R. Logie, E. S. Stoltzfus, and R. Zacks (Eds.), *Working memory and human cognition* (pp. 121–152). New York: Oxford University Press.

Richardson, J. T. E., Engle, R., Hasher, & Logie, R. (1996). *Working memory and human cognition.* New York: Oxford University Press.

Richardson, S. A., & Koller, H. (1996). *Twenty-two years: Causes and consequences of mental retardation.* Cambridge: Harvard University Press.

Richman, A. L., Miller, P. M., & LeVine, R. (1992). Cultural and educational variations in maternal responsiveness. *Developmental Psychology, 28,* 614–621.

Rickels, K., Schweizer, E., Clary, C., Fox, I., et al. (1994). Nefazodone and imipramine in major depression: A placebo-controlled trial. *British Journal of Psychiatry, 164,* 802–805.

Ricks, M. H. (1985). The social transmission of parental behavior: Attachment across generations. In I. Bretherton & E. Waters (Eds.), Growing points of attachment theory and research. *Monographs of the Society for Research in Child Development, 50,* (1–2, Serial No. 209), 211–227.

Riesen, A. H. (1960). The effects of stimulus deprivation on the development and atrophy of the visual sensory system. *American Journal of Orthopsychiatry, 30,* 23–36.

Riesen, A. H. (1965). Effects of early deprivation of photic stimulation. In S. Osler & R. Cooke (Eds.), *The biosocial bases of mental retardation.* Baltimore, MD: John Hopkins University Press.

Riley, A. J. (1991). Sexuality and the menopause. *Sexual and Marital Therapy, 6,* 135–145.

Rimmerman, A., Finn, H., Schnee, J., & Klein, I. (1992). The rehabilitation of persons with severe mental illness in adult homes: The NYPCC study. *Psychosocial Rehabilitation Journal, 15,* 55–66.

Rinn, W. E. (1984). The neuropsychology of facial expression: A review of the neurological and psychological mechanisms for producing facial expressions. *Psychological Bulletin, 95,* 52–77.

Riordan, R. J., & Beggs, M. S. (1988). Some critical differences between self-help and therapy groups. *Journal for Specialists in Group Work, 13,* 24–29.

Rips, L. (1990). Reasoning. *Annual Review of Psychology, 41,* 321–353.

Rips, L. J. (1995). Deduction and cognition. In E. E. Smith, D. N. Osherson, et al. (Eds.), *Thinking: An invitation to cognitive science, Vol. 3 (2nd ed.). An invitation to cognitive science* (2nd ed.) (pp. 297–343). Cambridge: MIT Press.

Robben, H. S., Webley, P., Weigel, R., & Warneryd, K-E. (1990). Decision frame and opportunity as determinants of tax cheating: An international experimental study. *Journal of Economic Psychology, 11,* 341–364.

Robbins, T. W. (1997). Arousal systems and attentional processes. *Biological Psychology, 45,* 57–71.

Roberson, E. D., English, J. D., & Seweatt, J. D. (1996). A biochemist's view of long-term potentiation. *Learning & Memory, 3,* 1–24.

Roberts, W. A. (1995). Simultaneous numerical and temporal processing in the pigeon. Current Directions in *Psychological Science, 4,* 47–51.

Robertson, J., & Robertson, J. (1971). Young children in brief separation: A fresh look. *Psychoanalytic study of the child, 26,* 264–315.

Robin, A. A. (1958). A controlled study of the effects of leucotomy. *Journal of Neurology, Neurosurgery and Psychiatry, 21,* 262–269.

Robin, N., & Holyoak, K. (1995). Relational complexity and the functions of the prefrontal cortex. In M. Gazzaniga (Ed.), *The cognitive neurosciences* (pp. 987–997). Cambridge: MIT Press.

Robins, L. H., & Kulbok, P. A. (1988). Epidemiologic studies in suicide. In A. J. Frances and R. E. Hales (Eds.), *Review of psychiatry,* Vol. 7. Washington, DC: American Psychiatric Press.

Robins, R. W., John, O. P., Caspi, A., Moffitt, T.E., & Stouthamer-Loeber, M. (1996). Resilient, overcontrolled, and undercontrolled boys: Three replicated personality types. *Journal of Personality and Social Psychology, 70,* 157–71.

Robinson, B. W., et al. (1969). Dominance reversal resulting from aggressive responses evoked by brain telestimulation. *Physiology and Behavior, 4,* 749–752.

Robinson, F. P. (1961). *Effective study.* New York: Harper & Row.

Robinson, G. (1996). Cross cultural perspectives on menopause. *The Journal of Nervous and Mental Disease, 184,* 453–458.

Robinson, K. J., & Roediger, H. L., III. (1997). Associative processes in false recall and false recognition. *Psychological Science, 8,* 231–237.

Robinson, N. M. (1978). Mild mental retardation: Does it exist in the People's Republic of China? *Mental Retardation, 16,* 295–299.

Rodin, J. Schank, D., & Striegel-Moore, R. (1989). Psychological features of obesity. *Medical Clinics of North America, 73,* 47–66.

Rodman, H. R. (1997). Temporal cortex. In G. Adelman & B. Smith (Eds.), *Encyclopedia of Neuroscience.* Amsterdam: Elsevier.

Roediger, H. L. (1990). Implicit memory: Retention without remembering. *American Psychologist, 45*(9), 1043–1056.

Roediger, H. L., & McDermott, K. B. (1995). Creating false memories: Remembering words not presented in lists. *Journal of Experimental Psychology: Learning, Memory, and Cognition, 21,* 803–814.

Rogers, C. (1959). A theory of therapy, personality, and interpersonal relationships, as developed in the client-centered framework. S. Koch (Ed.),

Psychology: A study of a science, Vol. 3. New York: McGraw-Hill.

Rogers, C. R. (1951). *Client-centered therapy: Its current practice, implications, and theory.* Boston: Houghton Mifflin.

Rogers, C. R. (1961). *On becoming a person: A therapist's view of psychotherapy.* Boston: Houghton Mifflin.

Rogers, C. R. (1980). *A way of being.* Boston: Houghton Mifflin.

Rogers, C. R., & Sanford, M. A. (1985). Client-centered psychotherapy. In H. I. Kaplan, H., & B. J. Sadock (Eds.), *Comprehensive textbook of psychiatry.* (4th ed.). Baltimore, MD: Williams & Wilkins.

Rogler, L. H., Cortes, D. E., & Malgady, R. G. (1991). Acculturation and mental health status among hispanics: Convergence and new directions for research. *American Psychologist, 46,* 585–592.

Rogoff, B., & Lave, J. (Eds.) (1984). *Everyday cognition: Its development in social context.* Cambridge, MA: Harvard University Press.

Rohner, R. (1975). Parental acceptance-rejection and personality development: A universalist approach to behavioral science. In R. W. Brislin et al. (Eds.), *Cross-cultural perspectives on learning* (pp. 251–269). New York: Sage.

Rohner, R. (1975). *They love me, they love me not.* New Haven, CT.: HRAF Press.

Rohner, R. P. (1986). *The warmth dimension: Foundations of parental acceptance-rejection theory.* Beverly Hills, CA: Sage Publications, Inc.

Rollin, B. E. (1985). The moral status of research animals in psychology. *American Psychologist, 40,* 920–926.

Romney, K., & Romney, R. (1963). The Mixtecans of Juxtlahuaca, Mexico. In B. Whiting (Ed.), *Six cultures: Studies in child rearing* (pp. 541–691). New York: John Wiley.

Ron, M. (1989). Psychiatric manifestations of frontal lobe tumours. *British Journal of Psychiatry, 155,* 735–738.

Rosch, E. (1973). On the internal structure of perceptual and semantic categories. In T. E. Moore (Ed.), *Cognitive development and the acquisition of language.* New York: Academic Press.

Rosch, E. (1978). Principles of categorization. In E. Rosch & B. Lloyd (Eds.), *Cognition and categorization.* New York: John Wiley.

Rosch, P. J. (1996). Stress and sleep: Some startling and sobering statistics. *Stress Medicine, 12,* 207–210.

Roscoe, A. K., & Myers, R. D. (1991). Hypothermia and feeding induced simultaneously in rats by perfusion of neuropeptide Y in preoptic area. *Pharmacology, Biochemistry & Behavior, 39,* 1003–1009.

Roseman, I. J., Antoniou, A. A., & Jose, P. E. (1996). Appraisal determinants of emotions: Constructing a more accurate and comprehensive theory. *Cognitive & Emotion, 10,* 241–277.

Roseman, I. J., Dhawan, N., Rettek, S. I., Naidu, R. K., et al. (1995). Cultural differences and cross-cultural similarities in appraisals and emotional responses. *Journal of Cross-Cultural Psychology, 26,* 23–48.

Roseman, I., Spindel, M., & Jose, P. (1990). Appraisals of emotion-eliciting events: Testing a theory of discrete emotions. *Journal of Personality and Social Psychology, 59,* 899–915.

Rosen, A. B., & Rozin, P. (1993). Now you see it, now you don't: The preschool child's conception of invisible particles in the context of dissolving. *Developmental Psychology, 29,* 300–311.

Rosen, J., Reynolds, C. F. III, Yeager, A. L., Houck, P. R., & Hurwitz, L. F. (1991). Sleep disturbances in survivors of the nazi holocaust. *American Journal of Psychiatry, 148,* 62–66.

Rosen, J. C., & Gross, J. (1987). The prevalence of weight reducing and weight gaining in adolescent girls and boys. *Health Psychology, 6,* 131–147.

Rosen, K. S., & Rothbaum, F. (1993). Quality of parental caregiving and security of attachment. *Developmental Psychology, 29,* 358–367.

Rosen, R. C. (1996). Erectile dysfunction: The medicalization of male sexuality. *Clinical Psychology Review, 16,* 497–519.

Rosen, R. C., Taylor, J. F., Leiblum, S. R., & Bachmann, G. A. (1993). Prevalence of sexual dysfunction in women: Results of a survey study of 329 women in an outpatient gynecological clinic. *Journal of Sex & Marital Therapy, 19,* 171–188.

Rosenberg, M. (1979). *Conceiving the self.* New York: Basic Books.

Rosenblatt, A., Greenberg, J., Solomon, S., Pyszczynski, T., & Lyon, D. (1989). Evidence for terror management theory: I. The effects of mortality salience on reactions to those who violate or uphold cultural values. *Journal of Personality and Social Psychology, 57,* 681–690.

Rosenhan, D. L. (1973). On being sane in insane places. *Science, 179,* 252–258.

Rosenwald, G. (1988). The multiple case study method. *Journal of Personality, 56,* 239–264.

Rosenzweig, M. R. (1984). Experience, memory, and the brain. *American Psychologist, 39,* 365–376.

Rosenzweig, M. R., Bennett, E. L., & Diamond, M. C. (1972). Brain changes in response to experience. *Scientific American, 226,* 22–29.

Rosenzweig, M. R., & Leiman, A. L.

(1989). *Physiological psychology.* (2nd ed.). New York: McGraw-Hill.

Ross, C. A., Anderson, G., Fleisher, W., & Norton, G. R. (1991). The frequency of multiple personality disorder among psychiatric inpatients. *American Journal of Psychiatry, 148,* 1717–1720.

Ross, L. (1977). The intuitive psychologist and his shortcomings: Distortions in the attribution process. *Advances in Experimental Social Psychology, 10,* 173–220.

Ross, M., & Sicoly, F. (1979). Egocentric biases in availability and attribution. *Journal of Personality and Social Psychology, 37,* 322–336.

Ross, R. J., Ball, W. A., Sullivan, K. A., et al. (1989). Sleep disturbance as the hallmark of posttraumatic stress disorder. *American Journal of Psychiatry, 146,* 697–707.

Ross, S. M., & Ross, L. E. (1971). Comparison of trace and delay classical eyelid conditioning as a function of interstimulus interval. *Journal of Experimental Psychology, 91,* 165–167.

Roth, A., Fonagy, P., Parry, G., Target, M., et al. (1996). *What works for whom? A critical review of psychotherapy research.* New York: Guilford Press.

Roth, M. (1978). Epidemiological studies. In R. Katzman, R. D. Terry, & K. L. Bick (Eds.), *Alzheimer's disease: Senile dementia and related disorders.* New York: Raven.

Rothblum, E. (1992). The stigma of women's weight: Social and economic realities. *Feminism and Psychology, 2,* 61–73.

Rothenberg, S. A. (1997). Introduction to sleep disorders. In M. R. Pressman and W. C. Orr (Eds.), *Understanding sleep: The evaluation and treatment of sleep disorders. Application and practice in health psychology* (pp. 57–72). Washington, DC: American Psychological Association.

Rotter, J. (1971). External control and internal control. *Psychology Today,* June, 40–45.

Rotter, J. B. (1954). *Social learning and clinical psychology.* New York: Englewood Cliffs, NJ: Prentice-Hall.

Rotter, J. B. (1966). Generalized expectancies for internal versus external control of reinforcement. *Psychological Monographs* (Whole No. 609).

Rotter, J. B. (1990). Internal versus external control of reinforcement: A case history of a variable. *American Psychologist, 45,* 489–493.

Rotton, J. et al. (1979). The air pollution experience and physical aggression. *Journal of Applied Social Psychology, 9,* 397–442.

Rovee-Collier, C. (1990). The "memory system" of prelinguistic infants. In A. Diamond (Ed.), *Development and neural bases of higher cognitive functions* (pp. 517–542). New York: New York Academy of Sciences Press.

Roy, A., Karoum, F., & Pollock, S. (1992). Marked reduction in indexes of dopamine metabolism among patients with depression who attempt suicide. *Archives of General Psychiatry, 49,* 447–450.

Rubenstein, C. (1982). Psychology's fruit flies. *Psychology Today, 16,* 83–84.

Rubin, D. C. (1995). *Memory in oral traditions: The cognitive psychology of epic, ballads, and counting-out rhymes.* New York: Oxford University Press.

Rubin, D. C., & Kozin, M. (1984). Vivid memories. *Cognition, 16,* 81–95.

Rubin, D. C., Rahhal, T. A., & Poon, L. W. (1998). Things learned in early childhood are remembered best. *Memory and Cognition, 26,* 3–19.

Rumbaugh, D. M. (1992). Learning about primates' learning, language, and cognition. In G. G. Brannigan & M. R. Merrens (Eds.), *The undaunted psychologist: Adventures in research.* New York: McGraw-Hill.

Rumbaugh, D. M., & Gill, T. V. (1977). Lana's acquisition of language skills. In D. M. Rumbaugh (Ed.), *Language learning by a chimpanzee: The Lana project* (pp. 165–192). New York: Academic Press.

Rumelhart, D. (1984). Schemata and the cognitive system. In R. S. Wyer & T. K. Srull (Eds.), *Handbook of social cognition.* Vol. 1. Hillsdale, NJ: Erlbaum.

Rumelhart, D. E., McClelland, J. L., & the PDP Research Group (1986). *Parallel distributed processing: Explorations in the microstructure of cognition.* Cambridge, MA: MIT Press.

Rundus, D. (1971). Analysis of rehearsal process in free recall. *Journal of Experimental Psychology, 89,* 63–77.

Runyan, W. M. (1984). *Life histories and psychobiography: Explanations in theory and method.* New York: Oxford University Press.

Rusbult, C. E., & Van Lange, P. A. M. (1996). Interdependence processes. In E. T. Higgins, A. W. Kruglanski, et al. (Eds.), *Social psychology: Handbook of basic principles.* (pp. 564–596). New York: Guilford Press.

Rushton, J. P. (1986). Altruism and aggression: The heritability of individual differences. *Journal of Personality and Social Psychology, 50,* 1192–1198.

Rushton, W. A. H. (1962). Visual pigments in man. *Scientific American,* 120–132.

Russell, D. (1991). Wife rape. In A. Parot & L. Bechhofer (Eds.), *Acquaintance rape: The hidden crime* (pp. 129–139). New York: John Wiley.

Russell, J. A. (1991). Culture and the categorization of emotions. *Psychological Bulletin, 110,* 426–450.

Russell, J. A. (1994). Is there universal recognition of emotion from facial expression? A review of the cross-cultural studies. *Psychological Bulletin, 115,* 102–141.

Russell, J. D., & Roxanas, M. (1990). Psychiatry and the frontal lobes. *Australian & New Zealand Journal of Psychiatry, 24,* 113–132.

Russell, M. J. (1976). Human olfactory communication. *Nature, 260,* 520–522.

Russo, R., & Parkin, A. J. (1993). Age differences in implicit memory: More apparent than real. *Memory and Cognition, 21,* 73–80.

Rutter, M., Quinton, D., & Liddle, C. (1983). Parenting in two generations: Looking backwards and looking forwards. In N. Madge (Ed.), *Families at risk* (pp. 60–98). London: Heineman.

Ryan, E. B. (1992). Beliefs about memory changes across the adult life span. *Journal of Gerontology, 47,* 41–46.

Ryder, R., & Bartle, S. (1991). Boundaries as distance regulators in personal relationships. *Family Process, 30,* 393–406.

Rymer, R. (1993). *Genie: An abused child's flight from silence.* New York: HarperCollins.

Sacks, O. (1973). *Awakenings.* London: Duckworth.

Sacks, O. (1993). A neurologist's notebook: To see and not see. *New Yorker,* May 10, 59–73.

Sadock, B. J. (1985). Group psychotherapy, combined individual and group psychotherapy, and psychodrama. In H. I. Kaplan & B. J. Sadock (Eds.), *Comprehensive textbook of psychiatry.* (4th ed.). Baltimore, MD: Williams & Wilkins.

Saegert, S., & Winkel, G. H. (1990). Environmental psychology. *Annual Review of Psychology, 41,* 441–477.

Saffran, J., Aslin, R., & Newport, E. (1996). Statistical learning by 8-month-old infants. *Science, 274,* 1926–1928.

Sagi, A. (1990). Attachment theory and research from a cross-cultural perspective. *Human Development, 33,* 10–22.

Sagi, A., van IJzendoorn, M. H., Aviezer, O., Donnell, F., & Mayseless, O. (1994). Sleeping out of the home in a kibbutz communal arrangement: It makes a difference for infant-mother attachment. *Child Development, 65,* 971–991.

Sakurai, T., et al. (1998). Orexins and orexin receptors: A family of hypothalamic neuropeptides and g protein-coupled receptors that regulate feeding behavior. *Cell, 92,* 573–585.

Salisbury, D. F., Shenton, M. E., Sherwood, A. R., Fischer, I. A., Yurgelun-Todd, D. A., Tohen, M., & McCarley, R. W. (1998). First-Episode Schizophrenic Psychosis Differs From First-Episode Affective Psychosis and Controls in P300 Amplitude Over Left Temporal Lobe. *Archives of General Psychiatry, 55,* 173–180.

Salkovskis, P. M., Jones, D. R., & Clark, D. M. (1986). Respiratory control in the treatment of panic attacks: Replication and extension with concurrent measurement of behavior and PCPs. *British Journal of Psychiatry, 148,* 526–532.

Salovey, P., & Sluyter, D. (Eds.) (1997). *Emotional development and emotional intelligence: Educational implications.* New York: Basic Books, Inc.

Salovey, P., Rothman, A. J., & Rodin, J. (1998). Health behavior. In D. T. Gilbert, S. T. Fiske, et al. (Eds.), *The handbook of social psychology, Vol. 2* (4th ed.). (pp. 633–683). Boston: McGraw-Hill.

Salthouse, T. (1985). Speed of behavior and its implications for cognition. In J. E. Birren & K. W. Schaie (Eds.), *Handbook of the psychology of aging* (2nd ed.). New York: Van Nostrand Reinhold.

Salthouse, T. (1992). The information-processing perspective on cognitive aging. In R. Sternberg & C. Berg (Eds.), *Intellectual development.* Cambridge: Cambridge University Press.

Salthouse, T. A. (1996). General and specific speed mediation of adult age differences in memory. *Journals of Gerontology Series B- Psychological Sciences & Social Sciences, 51B,* P30–P42.

Sameroff, A., Seifer, R., Baldwin, A., & Baldwin, C. (1993). Stability of intelligence from preschool to adolescence: The influence of social and family risk factors. *Child Development, 64,* 80–97.

Sandler, J., & Rosenblatt, B. (1962). The concept of the representational world. *Psychoanalytic Study of the Child, 17,* 128–145.

Sapir, E. (1949). *Culture, language and personality.* Berkeley: University of California Press.

Sarason, B. R., Sarason, I. G., & Gurung, R. A. R. (1997). Close personal relationships and health outcomes: A key to the role of social support. In S. Duck, et al. (Eds.), *Handbook of personal relationships: Theory, research and interventions* (2nd ed.). (pp. 547–573). Chichester, UK: John Wiley & Sons, Inc.

Saraswathi, T., & Dutta, R. (1988). Current trends in developmental psychology: A life span perspective. In J. Pandey (Ed.), *Psychology in India: The state-of-the-art,* Vol. 1, *Personality and mental processes* (pp. 93–152). London: Sage.

Sarnat, H. B., & Netsky, M. G. (1974). *Evolution of the nervous system.* New York: Oxford University Press.

Sarter, M., & Markowitsch, H. J. (1985). Involvement of the amygdala in learning and memory: A critical review, with emphasis on anatomical relation. *Behavioral Neuroscience, 99,* 342–380.

Sartre, J. P. (1971). Being and nothingness: An essay in phenomenological ontology, H. E. Barnes (Trans.). New York: Citadel Press.

Satel, S. L., Southwick, S. M., & Gawin, F. H. (1991). Clinical features of cocaine-induced paranoia. *American Journal of Psychiatry, 148,* 495–498.

Saundino, K. (1997). Moving beyond the heritability question: New directions in behavioral genetic studies of personality. *Current Directions in Psychological Science, 6,* 86–89.

Savage-Rumbaugh, E. S. (1990). Language acquisition in a nonhuman species: Implications for the innateness debate. *Developmental Psychobiology, 23,* 599–620.

Savage-Rumbaugh, E. S., Pate, J. L., Lawson, J., Smith, S. T., & Rosenbaum, S. (1983). Can a chimpanzee make a statement? *Journal of Experimental Psychology: General, 112,* 457–492.

Savage-Rumbaugh, E. S., Rumbaugh, D. M., & Boysen, S. (1978). Symbolic communication between two chimpanzees. *Science, 201,* 641–644.

Savage-Rumbaugh, S., McDonald, K., Sevcik, R., Hopkins, W., & Rupert, E. (1986). Spontaneous symbol acquisition and communicative use by pygmy chimpanzees (pan paniscus). *Journal of Experimental Psychology: General, 115,* 211–235.

Savin-Williams, R. C., & Small, S. A. (1986). The timing of puberty and its relationship to adolescent and parent perceptions of family interactions. *Developmental Psychology, 22,* 342–47.

Sayette, M., & Mayne, T. (1990). Survey of current clinical and research trends in clinical psychology. *American Psychologist, 45,* 1263–1266.

Scarr, S. (1997). Why child care has little impact on most children's development. *Current Directions in Psychological Science, 6,* 143–148.

Scarr, S. (1998). American child care today. American Psychologist, 53, 95–108.

Scarr, S., & Carter-Saltzman, L. (1982). Genetics and intelligence. In R. J. Sternberg (Ed.), *Handbook of human intelligence* (pp. 792–896). New York: Cambridge University Press.

Scarr, S., & Eisenberg, M. (1993). Child care research: Issues, perspectives, and results. *Annual Review of Psychology, 44,* 613–644.

Scarr, S., Pakstis, A. J., Katz, S. H., & Barker, W. B. (1977). The absence of a relationship between degree of white ancestry and intellectual skills within a black population. *Human Genetics, 39,* 69–86.

Scarr, S., & Weinberg, R. A. (1976). IQ test performance of black children adopted by white families. *American Psychologist, 31,* 726–739.

Scarr, S., & Weinberg, R. A. (1983). The Minnesota adoption studies: Genetic differences and malleability. *Child Development, 54,* 260–267.

Scarr, S., & Yee, D. (1980). Heritability and educational policy: Genetic and environmental effects on I.Q., aptitude, and achievement. *Educational Psychologist, 15,* 1–22.

Schab, F. R., & Crowder, R. G. (1995). Odor recognition memory. In F. R. Schab, Frank R. G. Crowder, et al. (Eds.), *Memory for odors.* (pp. 9–20). Mahwah, NJ: Lawrence Erlbaum Associates, Inc.

Schachter, F. F., Shore, E., Hodapp, R., Chalfin, S., & Bundy, C. (1978). Do girls talk earlier? Mean length of utterance in toddlers. *Developmental Psychology, 14,* 388–392.

Schachter, S., & Singer, J. (1962). Cognitive, social, and physiological determinants of emotional state. *Psychological Review, 69,* 379–399.

Schacter, D. (1995). Implicit memory: A new frontier for cognitive neuroscience. In M. Gazzaniga (Ed.), *The cognitive neurosciences* (pp. 815–824). Cambridge: MIT Press.

Schacter, D. (1995). *Memory and distortion: How minds, brains, and societies recollect the past.* Cambridge: Harvard University Press.

Schacter, D. (1997). False recognition and the brain. *Current Directions in Psychological Science, 6,* 65–70.

Schacter, D., Cooper, L. A., & Valdiserri, M. (1992). Implicit and explicit memory for novel visual objects in older and younger adults. *Psychology and Aging, 7,* 299–308.

Schacter, D. L. (1966). *Searching for memory: The brain, the mind, and the past.* New York: Basic Books, Inc.

Schacter, D. L. (1992). Understanding implicit memory: A cognitive neuroscience approach. *American Psychologist, 47,* 559–569.

Schacter, D. L., & Buckner, R. L. (1998). Priming and the brain. *Neuron, 20,* 185–195.

Schacter, D. L., Cooper, L. A., & Valdiserri, M. (1992). Implicit and explicit memory for novel visual objects in older and younger adults. *Psychology & Aging, 7,* 299–308.

Schacter, D. L., Verfaellie, M., Anes, M., & Racine, C. (in press). When true recognition suppresses false recognition: Evidence from amnesic patients. *Journal of Cognitive Neuroscience.*

Schafe, G. E., & Bernstein, I. L. (1996). Taste aversion learning. In E. D. Capaldi (Ed.), Why we eat what we eat: *The psychology of eating* (pp. 31–51). Washington, DC: American Psychological Association.

Schaie, K. W. (1988). Ageism in psychological research. *American Psychologist, 43,* 179–183.

Schaie, K. W. (1990). Intellectual development in adulthood. In J. E. Birren & K. W. Schaie (Eds.), *Handbook of the psychology of aging.* (3rd ed.). New York: Van Nostrand Reinhold.

Schaie, K. W. (1994). The course of adult intellectual development. *American Psychologist, 49,* 304–313.

Schaie, K. W., & Willis, S. L. (1986). *Adult development and aging.* (2nd ed.). Boston: Little, Brown.

Scheff, T. J. (1970). Schizophrenia as ideology. *Schizophrenia Bulletin, 1,* 15–20.

Scheier, M., & Carver, C. (1993). On the power of positive thinking: The benefits of being optimistic. *Current Directions in Psychological Science, 2,* 26–30.

Scheier, M. F., & Bridges, M. W. (1995). Person variables and health: Personality predispositions and acute psychological states as shared determinants for disease. *Psychosomatic Medicine, 57,* 255–268.

Scheier, M. F., Matthews, K. A., Owens, J., Magovern, G. J., Lefebvre, R. C., Abbott, R., & Carver, C. S. (1989). Dispositional optimism and recovery from coronary artery bypass surgery: The beneficial effects on physical and psychological well-being. *Journal of Personality and Social Psychology, 57,* 1024–1040.

Scheper-Hughes, N. (1979). *Saints, scholars, and schizophrenics: Mental illness in rural Ireland.* Berkeley: University of California Press.

Scher, S., & Cooper, J. (1989). Motivational basis of the dissonance: The singular role of behavioral consequences. *Journal of Personality and Social Psychology, 56,* 899–906.

Scherer, K., & Wallbott, H. (1994). Evidence for universality and cultural variation of differential emotion response patterning. *Journal of Personality & Social Psychology, 66,* 310–328.

Scherer, K. R. (1997). Profiles of emotion-antecedent appraisal: Testing theoretical predictions across cultures. *Cognition & Emotion, 11,* 113–150.

Schiavi, R. C., Schreiner-Engel, P., White,

D., & Mandeli, J. (1991). The relationship between pituitary-gonadal function and sexual behavior in healthy aging men. *Psychosomatic Medicine, 53,* 363–374.

Schiavi, R. C., Schreiner-Engle, P., Mandeli, J., Schanzer, H., et al. (1990). Healthy aging and male sexual function. *American Journal of Psychiatry, 147,* 766–771.

Schiele, J. H. (1991). An epistemological perspective on intelligence assessment among African American children. *Journal of Black Psychology, 17,* 23–26.

Schiff, M., Duyme, M., Dumaret, A., & Tomkiewicz, S. (1982). How much could we boost scholastic achievement and IQ scores? A direct answer from a French adoption study. *Cognition, 12,* 165–196.

Schiffman, H. R. (in press). *Sensation and perception.* (4th ed.) New York: John Wiley.

Schiller, P. H. (1965). Monoptic and dicroptic visual masking by patterns and flashes. *Journal of Experimental Psychology, 69,* 193–199.

Schlesinger, M., Dorwart, R., Hoover, C., & Epstein, S. (1997). Competition, ownership, and access to hospital services: Evidence from psychiatric hospitals. *Medical Care, 35,* 974–992.

Schlesser, M. A., & Altshuler, K. Z. (1983). The genetics of affective disorder: Date, theory, and clinical applications. *Hospital and Community Psychiatry, 34,* 415–422.

Schmajuk, N. A., Lamoureux, J. A., & Holland, P. C. (1998). Occasion setting: A neural network approach. *Psychological Review, 105,* 3–32.

Schmidt, N. B., Lerew, D. R., & Trakowski, J. H. (1997). Body vigilance in panic disorder: Evaluating attention to bodily perturbations. *Journal of Consulting and Clinical Psychology, 65,* 214–220.

Schmidt, N. B., Trakowski, J. H., & Staab, J. P. (1997). Extinction of a panicogenic effects of a 3% CO2 challenge in patients with panic disorder. *Journal of Abnormal Psychology, 106,* 630–640.

Schmitt, R. C. (1966). Density, health, and social disorganization. *American Institute of Planners Journal, 32,* 38–40.

Schnapf, J., Kraft, T., Nunn, B., & Baylor, D. (1989). Transduction in primate cones. *Neuroscience Research, Suppl 10,* 9–14.

Schneider, M. L., Roughton, E. C., & Lubach, G. R. (1997). Moderate alcohol consumption and psychological stress during pregnancy induce attention and neuromotor impairments in primate infants. *Child Development, 68,* 747–759.

Schneider, W., & Pressley, M. (1989). *Memory development between 2 and 20.* New York: Springer-Verlag.

Schraw, G. Dunkle, M. E., & Bendixen, L. D. (1995). Cognitive processes in well-defined and ill-defined problem solving. *Applied Cognitive Psychology, 9,* 523–538.

Schreiner, L., & Kling, A.(1953). Behavioral changes in following rhinencephalic injury in cats. *Journal of Neurophysiology, 16,* 643–658.

Schrieber, F. (1974). *Sybil.* New York: Warner Books.

Schroeder, S. R., Schroeder, C. S., & Landesman, S. (1987). Psychological services in educational settings to persons with mental retardation. *American Psychologist, 42,* 805–808.

Schuckit, M. (1984). Relationship between the course of primary alcoholism in men and family history. *Journal of Studies on Alcohol, 45,* 334–338.

Schuckit, M. (1987). Biological vulnerability to alcoholism. *Journal of Consulting and Clinical Psychology, 55,* 301–309.

Schuckit, M. A. (1994). Low level of response to alcohol as a predictor of future alcoholism. *American Journal of Psychiatry, 151,* 184–189.

Schultz, T., & Schliefer, M. (1983). Towards a refinement of attribution concepts. In J. Jaspars, F. Fincham, & M. Hewstone (Eds.), *Attribution theory and research: Conceptual, developmental, and social dimensions* (pp. 37–62). New York: Academic Press.

Schultz, W., Dayan, P., & Montague, P. R. (1997). A neural substrate of prediction and reward. *Science, 275,* 1593–1599.

Schuster, D. T. (1990). Fulfillment of potential, life satisfaction, and competence: Comparing four cohorts of gifted women at midlife. *Journal of Educational Psychology, 82,* 471–478.

Schwartz, C. E., Snidman, N., & Kagan, J. (1996). Early childhood temperament as a determinant of externalizing behavior in adolescence. *Development & Psychopathology, 8,* 527–537.

Schwartz, G. E. (1987). Personality and health: An integrative health science approach. In V. P. Makosky, (Ed.), *The G. Stanley Hall Lecture Series,* Vol. 7. Washington, DC: American Psychological Association.

Scialfa, C., Garvey, P. M., Tyrell, R., & Leibowitz, H. (1992). Age differences in dynamic contrast thresholds. *Journal of Gerontology, 47,* 172–175.

Scogin, F., & McElreath, L. (1994). Efficacy of psychosocial treatments for geriatric depression: A quantitative review. *Journal of Consulting and Clinical Psychology, 62,* 69–74.

Scott, J. P. (1980). The function of emotions in behavioral systems: A systems theory analysis. In R. Plutchik and H. Kellerman (Eds.), *Emotion vol. 1: Theories of emotion.* New York: Academic Press.

Scott, K. G., & Carran, D. T. (1987). The epidemiology and prevention of mental retardation. *American Psychologist, 42,* 801–804.

Scott, S. K., Young, A. W., Calder, A. J., & Hellawell, D. J. (1997). Impaired auditory recognition of fear and anger following bilateral amygdala lesions. *Nature, 385,* 254–257.

Scoville, W. B., & Milner, B. (1957). Loss of recent memory after bilateral hippocampal lesions. *Journal of Nerology, Neurosurgery, and Psychiatry, 20,* 11–21.

Scribner, S. (1986). Thinking in action: some characteristics of practical thought. In R. J. Sternberg & R. K. Wagner (Eds.), *Practical intelligence: Nature and origins of competence in the everyday world* (pp. 13–40). New York: Cambridge University Press.

Scroppo, J. C., Drob, S. L., Weinberger, J. L., & Eagle, P. (1998). Identifying dissociative identity disorder: A Self-report and projective study. *Journal of Psychology, 107,* 272–284.

Scully, D., & Bart, P. (1973). A funny thing happened on the way to the orifice: Women in gynecology textbooks. In J. Huber (Ed.), *Changing women in a changing society.* Chicago: University of Chicago Press.

Seagall, M., Campbell, D., & Herskovits, M. (1966). *The influence of culture on visual perception.* New York: Bobbs Merrill.

Searle, J. (1987). Minds, brains and programs. In Rainer Born (Ed.), *Artificial intelligence: The case against.* London: Croom Helm.

Sears, D. O. (1986). College sophomores in the laboratory: Influences of a narrow data base on social psychological view of human nature. *Journal of Personality and Social Psychology, 51,* 515–530.

Sederer, L. (1992). Judicial and legislative responses to cost containment. *American Journal of Psychiatry, 149,* 1157–1161.

Seelinger, G., & Schuderer, B. (1985). Release of male courtship display in Periplaneta americana: Evidence for female contact sex pheromone. *Animal Behaviour, 33,* 599–607.

Seeman, P., & Lee, T. (1975). Antipsychotic drugs: Direct correlation between clinical potency and presynaptic action on dopamine neurons. *Science, 188,* 1217–1219.

Segal, M. W. (1974). Alphabet and attraction: An unobtrusive measure of the effect of propinquity in a field setting. *Journal of Personality and Social Psychology, 30,* 654–657.

Segal, N. L. (1997). Same-age unrelated

siblings: A unique test of within-family environmental influences on IQ similarity. *Journal of Educational Psychology, 89,* 381–390.

Segall, M. H. (1988). Cultural roots of aggressive behavior. In M. H. Bond (Ed.), *The cross-cultural challenge to social psychology.* Newbury Park, CA: Sage.

Segall, M. H., Dasen, P. R., Berry, J. W., & Poortinga, Y. H. (1990). *Human behavior in global perspective: An introduction to cross-cultural psychology.* New York: Pergamon Press, Inc.

Seger, C. A. (1994). Implicit learning. *Psychological Bulletin, 115,* 163–196.

Seidenberg, M. S. (1997). Language acquisition and use: Learning and applying probabilistic constraints. *Science, 275,* 1599–1603.

Seidenberg, M. S., & Petitto, L. A. (1987). Communication, symbolic communication, and language: Comment on Savage-Rumbaugh, McDonald, Sevcik, Hopkins, & Rupert (1986). *Journal of Experimental Psychology: General, 116,* 279–287.

Seidman, S., & Reider, R. (1994). A review of sexual behavior in the United States. *American Journal of Psychiatry, 151,* 330–341.

Sekular, R., & Blake, R. (1994). *Perception.* (3rd ed.). New York: McGraw-Hill.

Selemon, L. D., Rajkowska, G., & Goldman-Rakic, P. S. (1995). Abnormally high neuronal density in the Schizophrenic cortex: A morphometric analysis of prefrontal area 9 and occipital area 17. *Archives of General Psychiatry, 52,* 805–818.

Seligman, L. (1975). Skin potential as an indicator of emotion. *Journal of Counseling Psychology, 22,* 489–493.

Seligman, M. E. P. (1970). On the generality of the laws of learning. *Psychological Review, 77,* 406–418.

Seligman, M. E. P. (1971). Phobias and preparedness. *Behavior Therapy, 193,* 323–325.

Seligman, M. E. P. (1995). The effectiveness of psychotherapy: The Consumer reports study. *American Psychologist, 50,* 965–974.

Selman, R. L. (1980). *The growth of interpersonal understnading.* New York: Academic Press.

Selye, H. (1936). A syndrome produced by diverse nocuous agents. *Nature, 138,* 32.

Selye, H. (1976). *The stress of life.* New York: McGraw-Hill.

Serpell, R. (1989). Dimensions endogenes de l'intelligence chez les A-chewa et autres peuples africans. In J. Retschitzky, M. Bossel-Lagos, & P. Dasen (Eds.), *La recherche interculturelle.* Paris: L'Harmattan.

Sethi, S., & Seligman, M. (1993). Opti-

mism and fundamentalism. *Psychological Science, 4,* 256–259.

Sewall, L., & Wooten, B. R. (1991). Stimulus determinants of achromatic constancy. *Journal of the Optical Society of America, 8,* 1794–1809.

Sewell, K. W., Adams-Webber, J., Mitterer, J., & Cromwell, R. L. (1992). Computerized repertory grids: Review of the literture. *International Journal of Personal Construct Psychology, 5,* 1–23.

Shantz, C. U. (1983). Social cognition. In J. H. Flavell & E. M. Markman (Eds.), *Handbook of child psychology: Vol. 3. Cognitive Development.* New York: John Wiley.

Shapira, Z. (1995). *Risk taking: A managerial perspective.* New York: Russell Sage Foundation.

Shapiro, S., & Vukovich, K. R. (1970). Early experience effects upon cortical dendrites: A proposed model for development. *Science, 167,* 292–294.

Shapley, R. (1995). *Parallel neural pathways and visual function. In M. S. Gazzaniga, et al. (1995). The cognitive neurosciences.* (pp. 315–324). Cambridge: MIT Press.

Sharps, M. J., & Price-Sharps, J. L. (1996). Visual memory support: An effective mnemonic device for older adults. *Gerontologist, 36,* 706–708.

Shaver, P., Hazan, C., & Bradshaw, D. (1988). Love as attachment. In R. J. Sterberg, & M. L. Barnes, *The psychology of love.* New Haven, Conn.: Yale University Press.

Shaver, P., Schwartz, J., Kirson, D., & O'-Connor, G. (1987). Emotion knowledge: Further exploration of a prototype approach. *Journal of Personality and Social Psychology, 52,* 1061–1086.

Shaywitz, B. A., Shaywitz, S. E., Pugh, K. R., Constable, R. T., et al. (1995). Sex differences in the functional organization of the brain for language. *Nature, 373,* 607–609.

Shaywitz, S., Shaywitz, B., Pugh, K. R., Fulbright, R. K., Constable, R. T., Mencl, W. E., et al. (1998). Functional disruption in the organization of the brain for reading in dyslexia. *Proceedings of the National Academy of Science, 95,* 2636–2641.

Shea, M., Glass, D., Pilkonis, P., Watkins, J., & Docherty, J. (1987). Frequency and implications of personality disorders in a sample of depressed outpatients. *Journal of Personality Disorders, 1,* 27–42.

Shea, M. T., Elkin, I., Imber, S., & Sotsky, S. (1992). Course of depressive symptoms over follow-up: Findings from the National Institute of Mental Health Treatment of Depression Collaborative Research Program. *Archives of General Psychiatry, 49,* 782–787.

Shedler, J., & Block, J. (1990). Adolescent

drug use and psychological health: A longitudinal inquiry. *American Psychologist, 45,* 612–630.

Shedler, J., Mayman, M., & Manis, M. (1993). The illusion of mental health. *American Psychologist, 48,* 1117–1131.

Sheehy, G. (1976). *Passages.* New York: E. P. Dutton.

Shefler, G., Dasberg, H., & Ben-Shakhar, G. (1995). A randomized controlled outcome and follow-up study of Mann's time-limited psychotherapy. *Journal of Consulting and Clinical Psychology, 63,* 585–593.

Sherif, M. et al. (1961). *Intergroup conflict and cooperation: The Robber's Cave experiment.* Norman: University of Oklahoma Press.

Sherif, M., & Sherif, C. W. (1979). Research on intergroup relations. In W. G. Austin and S. Worchel (Eds.), *The social psychology of intergroup relations.* Monterey, CA: Brooks/Cole.

Sherman, R. L. (1994). The rock ceiling: A study of African-American women managers' experiences and perceptions of barriers restricting advancement in the corporation. Dissertation Abstracts International Section A: *Humanities & Social Sciences, 54,* 3226.

Sherwin, B. (1993). *Menopause myths and realities.* Washington, DC: American Psychiatric Press.

Shettleworth, S. J. (1988). Foraging as operant behavior and operant behavior as foraging: What have we learned? In G. H. Bower, et al. (Ed.), *The psychology of learning and motivation: Advances in research and theory,* Vol. 22. (pp. 1–49). San Diego: Academic Press, Inc.

Shevrin, H., Bond, J. Brakel, L., Hertel, R., & Williams, W. J. (1996). *Conscious and unconscious processes: Psychodynamic, cognitive, and neurophysiological convergences.* New York: Guilford.

Shields, J. (1962). *Monozygotic twins brought up apart and brought together.* London: Oxford University Press.

Shimamura, A. P. (1995). *Memory and frontal lobe function. In M. S. Gazzaniga, et al. (Eds.), The cognitive neurosciences.* (pp. 803–813). Cambridge: MIT Press.

Shimizu, N., Oomura, Y., Novin, D., Grijalva, C., & Cooper, P. H. (1983). Functional correlations between lateral hypothalamic glucose-sensitive neurons and hepatic portal glucose-sensitive units in rats. *Brain Research, 265,* 49–54.

Shin, L. M., Kosslyn, S. M., McNally, R. J., Alpert, N. M., Thompson, W. L., Rauch, S. L., et al. (1997). Visual Imagery and Perception in Posttraumatic Stress Disorder: A Positron Emission Tomographic Investigation. *Archives of General Psychiatry, 54,* 233–241.

Shoda, Y., & Mischel, W. (1996). Toward a

unified, intra-individual dynamic conception of personality. *Journal of Research in Personality, 30,* 414–428.

Shrom, S. H., Lief, H. I., & Wein, A. J. (1979). Clinical profile of experience with 130 consecutive cases of impotent men. *Urology, 13,* 511–15.

Shulman, M. E. (1988). Cost containment in clinical psychology: Critique of biodyne and the HMOs. *Professional Psychology Research and Practice, 19,* 298–307.

Shweder, R. (1991). *Thinking through cultures: Expeditions in cultural psychology.* Cambridge, MA: Harvard University Press.

Shweder, R. A. (1980). Scientific thought and social cognition. In W. A. Collins (Ed.), Development of cognition, affect, and social relations: Minnesota *Symposium on Child Development,* Vol. 13, Hillsdale, NJ: Erlbaum.

Shweder, R. A. & Bourne, E. J. (1982). Does the concept of the person vary cross-culturally? In A. J. Marsella and G. M. White (Eds.), *Cultural conceptions of mental health and therapy.* Boston: D. Reidel.

Siegel, R. K. (1990). *Intoxication.* New York: Pocket Books.

Siegel, S. (1984). Pavlonian conditioning and heroin overdose: Reports by overdose victims. *Bulletin of the Psychonomic Society, 22,* 428–430.

Siegler, R. S. (1991). *Children's thinking.* (2nd ed.). Englewood Cliffs, NJ: Prentice-Hall Press.

Siegler, R. S., & Ellis, S. (1996). Piaget on childhood. *Psychological Science, 7,* 211–215.

Siegman, A. W. (1994). From Type A to hostility to anger: Reflections on the history of coronary-prone behavior. In A. W. Siegman, T. W. Smith, et al. (Eds.). *Anger, hostility, and the yeart.* (pp. 1–21). Hillsdale, NJ: Lawrence Erlbaum Associates, Inc.

Sifneos, P. (1973). The prevalence of alexithymic characteristics in psychosomatic patients. *Psychotherapy and Psychosomatics, 22,* 255–262.

Sifneos, P. (1987). *Short-term dynamic psychotherapy: Evaluation and technique,* (2nd ed.) New York: Plenum.

Sigall, H., Page, R., & Brown, A. C. (1971). Effort expenditure as a function of evaluation and evaluator attractiveness. *Representative Research in Social Psychology, 2,* 19–25.

Sillars, A. L., & Zietlow, P. (1993). Investigations of marital communication and lifespan development. In N. Coupland & J. Nussbaum (Eds.), *Discourse and lifespan identity: Language and language behaviors,* Vol. 4 (pp. 237–261). Newbury Park, CA: Sage Publications.

Silverstein, B., Perdue, L., Peterson, B., Vogel, L., & Fantini, D. A. (1986). Possible causes of the thin standard of bodily attractiveness for women. *International Journal of Eating Disorders, 5,* 907–916.

Silverstein, L. B. (1991). Transforming the debate about child care and maternal employment. *American Psychologist, 46,* 1025–1032.

Simmons, L. W. (1990). Pheromonal cues for the recognition of kin by female field crickets, Gryllus bimaculatus. *Animal Behaviour, 40,* 192–195.

Simmons, R. G., & Blythe, D. A. (1987). *Moving into adolescence.* Hawthorne, NY: Aldine.

Simon, H. (1990). Invariants of human behavior. *Annual Review of Psychology, 41,* 1–19.

Simon, H. A. (1978). Information-processing theory of human problem solving. In W. K. Estes (Ed.), *Handbook of learning and cognitive processes.* Hillsdale, NJ: Erlbaum.

Simon, H. A. (1990). A mechanism for social selection and successful altruism. *Science, 150,* 1665–1668.

Simon, R. (1985). Family therapy. In H. I. Kaplan & B. J. Sadock (Eds.), *Comprehensive textbook of psychiatry.* (4th ed.). Baltimore, MD: Williams & Wilkins.

Simons, H. W., Berkowitz, N. N., & Moyer, R. J. (1970). Similarity, credibility, and attitude change: A review and a theory. *Psychological Bulletin, 73,* 1–16.

Simonton, D. K. (1994). *Greatness: Who makes history and why?* New York: Guilford.

Simonton, D. K. (1997). Creative productivity: A predictive and explanatory model of career trajectories and landmarks. *Psychological Review, 104,* 66–89.

Simpson, J., Gangestad, S., & Lerma, M. (1990). Perception of physical attractiveness: Mechanisms involved in the maintenance of romantic relationships. *Journal of Personality and Social Psychology, 59,* 1192–1201.

Simpson, J., Rholes, W., & Nelligan, J. (1992). Support seeking and support giving within couples in an anxiety-provoking situation: The role of attachment styles. *Journal of Personality and Social Psychology, 62,* 434–446.

Simpson, J. A., Rholes, W. S., & Phillips, D. (1996). Conflict in close relationships: An attachment perspective. *Journal of Personality and Social Psychology, 71,* 899–914.

Singer, J. L. (1975). *The inner world of daydreaming.* New York: Harper & Row.

Singer, J. L. (1986). Is television bad for children? *Social Science, 71,* 178–182.

Singer, J. L. (1990). *Repression and dissociation: Implications for personality theory, psychopathology, and health.* Chicago: University of Chicago Press.

Singer, J. L., & Kolligian, J., Jr. (1987). Personality: Developments in the study of private experience. *Annual Review of Psychology, 38,* 533–574.

Singer, J. L., & Singer, D. G. (1981). Television, imagination, and aggression: A study of preschoolers, Hillsdale, NJ: Erlbaum.

Skeels, H. M. (1966). Adult states of children with contrasting early life experiences: A follow-up study. *Monographs of the Society for Research in Child Development, 31,* (serial No. 105), 70.

Skinner, B. F. (1938). *The behavior of organisms.* New York: Appleton-Century-Crofts.

Skinner, B. F. (1948). *Walden Two.* New York: Macmillan.

Skinner, B. F. (1951). How to teach animals. *Scientific American, 185,* 26–29.

Skinner, B. F. (1953). *Science and human behavior.* New York: Macmillan.

Skinner, B. F. (1957). *Verbal behavior.* New York: Appleton-Century-Crofts.

Skinner, B. F. (1974). *About behaviorism.* New York: Vintage Books.

Skinner, B. F. (1977). Hernstein and the evolution of behaviorism. *American Psychologist, 32,* 1006–1012.

Skinner, B. F. (1990). Can psychology be a science of mind? *American Psychologist, 45,* 1206–1210.

Skodak, M., & Skeel, H. M. (1949). A final follow-up study of one hundred adopted children. *Journal of Genetic Psychology, 75,* 85–125.

Slade, L. A., & Rush, M. C. (1991). Achievement motivation and the dynamics of task difficulty choices. *Journal of Personality and Social Psychology, 60,* 165–172.

Slob, A., Bax, C. M., Hop, W. C. J., & Rowland, D. L. (1996). Sexual arousability and the menstrual cycle. *Psychoneuroendocrinology, 21,* 545–558.

Sloboda, J. A., Hermelin, B., & O'Connor, N. (1985). An exceptional music memory. *Music Perception, 3,* 155–169.

Slochower, J. (1987). The psychodynamics of obesity: A review. *Psychoanalytic Psychology, 4,* 145–159.

Slutske, W. S., Heath, A. C., Kinwiddie, S. H., Madden, P. A. F., Buholz, K. K., Dunne, M. P. et al. (1997). Modeling genetic and environmental influences in the etiology of conduct disorder: A study of 2682 adult twin pairs. *Journal of Abnormal Psychology, 106,* 266–279.

Smith, C., & Lloyd, B. (1978). Maternal behavior and perceived sex of infant: Revisited. *Child Development, 49,* 1263–1265.

Smith, C. A., & Ellsworth, P. (1985). Patterns of cognitive appraisal in emotion.

Journal of Personality and Social Psychology, 48, 813–838.

Smith, D. E., & Seumour, R. B. (1994). LSD: History and toxicity. *Psychiatric Annals, 24,* 145–147.

Smith, E. E. (1995). Concepts and categorization. In E. E. Smith, D. N. Osherson, et al. (Eds.), Thinking: An invitation to cognitive science, Vol. 3 (2nd ed.). *An invitation to cognitive science* (2nd ed.). (pp. 3–33). Cambridge: MIT Press.

Smith, E. R. (1993). Social identity and social emotions: Toward new conceptualizations of prejudice. In D. M. Mackie, D. L. Hamilton, et al. (Eds.), *Affect, cognition, and stereotyping: Interactive processes in group perception* (pp. 297–315). San Diego, CA: Academic Press.

Smith, E. R. (1996). What do connectionism and social psychology offer each other? *Journal of Personality and Social Psychology, 70,* 893–912.

Smith, E. R. (1998). Mental representation and memory. In D. T. Gilbert, S. T. Fiske, et al. (Eds.), *The handbook of social psychology,* Vol. 2 (4th ed.). (pp. 391–445). Boston: McGraw-Hill.

Smith, J. A., Hauenstein, N. M. A., & Buchanan, Laurie B. (1996). Goal setting and exercise performance. *Human Performance, 9,* 141–154.

Smith, K. (1984). Drive: In defence of a concept. *Behaviorism, 12,* 71–114.

Smith, M. B. (1978). Perspectives on selfhood. *American Psychologist, 33,* 1053–1063.

Smith, M. B. (1988). Can there be a human science? *Symposium of the American Psychological Association,* Atlanta, GA.

Smith, M. B. (1994). Selfhood at risk: Postmodern perils and the perils of postmodernism. *American Psychologist, 49,* 405–411.

Smith, M. L., & Glass, G. V. (1977). Meta-analysis of psychotherapy outcome studies. *American Psychologist, 32,* 752–760.

Smith, M. L., Glass, G. V., & Miller, T. I. (1980). *The benefits of psychotherapy.* Baltimore: Johns Hopkins University Press.

Smith, P. F., & Darlington, C. L. (1996). The development of psychosis in epilepsy: A re-examination of kindling hypothesis. *Behavioural Brain Reseach, 75,* 59–66.

Smith, P. K., & Daglish, L. (1977). Sex differences in parent and infant behavior. *Child Development, 48,* 1250–1254.

Smith, R. E., & Swinyard, W. R. (1983). Attitude-behavior consistency: The impact of product trial versus advertising. *Journal of Marketing Research, 20,* 257–267.

Smith, S. (1988). Calculating Prodigies. In L. K. Obler & D. Fein (Eds.), *The exceptional brain: Neuropsychology of talent and special abilities* (pp. 19–47). New York: Guilford Press.

Smith, V. L., & Ellsworth, P. C. (1987). The social psychology of eyewitness accuracy: Misleading questions and communicator expertise. *Journal of Applied Psychology, 72,* 294–300.

Smith-Rosenberg, C. (1975). The female world of love and ritual: Relations between women in 19th century America. *Signs,* Autumn, 1–29.

Smolensky, P. (1997). Connectionist modeling: Neural computation/mental connections. In J. Haugeland, et al. (Eds.), *Mind design 2: Philosophy, psychology, artificial intelligence* (2nd ed., pp. 233–250). Cambridge: The MIT Press.

Smotherman, W. P., & Robinson, S. R. (1996). The development of behavior before birth. *Developmental Psychology, 32,* 425–434.

Snyder, D. K., Wills, R. M., & Grady-Fletcher, A. (1991). Long-term effectiveness of behavioral versus insight-oriented marital therapy: A 4-year follow-up study. *Journal of Consulting and Clinical Psychology, 59,* 138–141.

Snyder, M., & Ickes, W. (1985). In G. Lindzey and E. Aronson (Eds.), *Handbook of social psychology,* Reading, MA: Addison-Wesley.

Sobal, J., & Stunkard, A. (1989). Socioeconomic status and obesity: A review of the literature. *Psychological Bulletin, 105,* 260–275.

Solomon, D. A., Keller, M. B., Leon, A. C., Mueller, T. I., Shea, M. T., Warshaw, M., et al. (1997). Recovery from major depression: A 10-year prospective follow-up across multiple episodes. *Archives of General Psychiatry, 54,* 1001–1006.

Solomon, S., Greenberg, J., & Pyszczynski, T. (1991). A terror management theory of social behavior: The psychological functions of self-esteem and cultural worldviews. In L. Berkowitz (Ed.), *Advances in Experimental Social Psychology, 24,* 93–159.

Sommer, R., & Sommer, B. A. (1983). Mystery in Milwaukee: Early intervention, I.Q., and psychology textbooks. *American Psychologist, 38,* 982–985.

Sorensen, P. W. (1996). Biological responsiveness to pheromones provides fundamental and unique insight into olfactory function. *Chemical Senses, 21,* 245–256.

Sorenson, P. W., Hara, T. J., & Stacey, N. E. (1991). Sex pheromones selectively stimulate the medial olfactory tracts of male goldfish. *Brain Research, 558,* 343–347.

Sorrentino, R. M., & Higgins, E. T. (Eds., 1996). *Handbook of motivation and cognition,* Vol. 3: The interpersonal context. New York: Guilford Press.

Southwick, S. M., Krystal, J. H., Bremer, J. D., Morgan, C. A., Nicolaou, A. L., Nagy, L. M., et al. (1997). Noradrenergic and Serotonergic Function in Posttraumatic Stress Disorder. *Archives of General Psychiatry, 54,* 749–758.

Spain, D., Ed. (1992). Psychoanalytic anthropology after Freud. New York: Psyche Press.

Spangler, W. D., & House, R. J. (1991). Presidential effectiveness and the leadership motive profile. *Journal of Personality and Social Psychology, 60,* 439–455.

Spanos, N. P., Burgess, C. A., Cross, P. A., & MacLeod, G. (1992). Hypnosis, response bias, and suggested negative hallucinations. *Journal of Abnormal Psychology, 101,* 192–199.

Spanos, N. P., Burgess, C. A., Wallace-Capretta, S., & Ouaida, N. (1996). Simulation, surreptitious observation and the modification of hypnotizability: Two tests of the compliance hypothesis. *Contemporary Hyponosis, 13,* 161–176.

Spanos, N. P., Stenstrom, R. J., & Johnston, J. C. (1988). Hypnosis, placebo, and suggestion in the treatment of warts. *Psychosomatic Medicine, 50,* 245–260.

Spearman, C. (1904). General intelligence, objectively determined and measured. *American Journal of Psychology, 15,* 201–293.

Spearman, C. (1927). *The abilities of man: Their nature and measurement.* New York: Macmillan.

Spector, I., & Carey, M. P. (1990). Incidence and prevalence of the sexual dysfunctions: A critical review of the empirical literature. *Archives of Sexual Behavior, 19,* 389–408.

Speicher, B. (1994). Family patterns of moral judgement during adolescence and early adulthood. *Developmental Psychology, 30,* 624–632.

Spelke, E., Hirst, W., & Neisser, U. (1979). Skills of divided attention. *Cognition, 4,* 215–230.

Spellman, B. A., & Holyoak, K. (1992). If Saddam is Hitler then who is George Bush? Analogical mapping between systems of social roles. *Journal of Personality and Social Psychology, 62,* 913–933.

Spence, A. P. (1989). *Biology of human aging.* Englewood Cliffs, NJ: Prentice-Hall.

Spence, S. H. (1997). Sex and relationships. In W. K. Halford, and H. J. Markman (Eds.), *Clinical handbook of marriage and couples interventions.* (pp. 73). England: John Wiley & Sons, Inc.

Spencer, M. B., & Markstrom-Adams, C. (1990). Identity processes among racial and ethnic minority children in America. *Child Development, 61,* 290–310.

Sperling, G. (1960). The information available in brief visual presentations. *Psychological Monographs, 74,* 1–29.

Sperry, R. (1984). Consciousness, personal identity and the divided brain. *Neuropsychologia, 22,* 661–673.

Spiegel, D., & Kato, P. M. (1996). Psychological influences on cancer incidence and progression. *Harvard Review of Psychiatry, 4,* 10–26.

Spillman, L. (1994). The Mermann grid illusion: A tool for studying human perceptive field organization. *Perception, 23,* 691–708.

Spirduso, W., & MacRae, P. (1990). Motor performance and aging. In J. E. Birren & K. W. Schaie (Eds.), *Handbook of the psychology of aging.* (3rd ed.). New York: Van Nostrand Reinhold.

Spiro, M. (1965). *Context and meaning in cultural anthropology.* New York: Free Press.

Spitz, R. A. (1945). Hospitalism: An inquiry into the genesis of psychiatry conditions in early childhood. *The Psychoanalytic Study of the Child, 1,* 53–74.

Spitzer, R., Williams, J. B. W., Gibbon, M., & First, M. (1992). The structured clinical interview for DSM-III-R (SCID) I: History, rationale, and description. *Archives of General Psychiatry, 49,* 624–629.

Spitzer, R. L. (1985). DSM-III and the politics-science dichotomy syndrome: A response to Thomas E. Schacht's "DSM-III and the politics of truth." *American Psychologist, 40,* 522–526.

Sporer, S., Malpass, R., & Koehnken, G., Eds. (1996). *Psychological issues in eyewitness identification.* Mahwah, NJ: Lawrence Erlbaum.

Spray, D. (1986). Cutaneous temperature receptors. *Annual Review of Physiology, 48,* 625–638.

Spreen, O., Tupper, D., Risser, A., Tuokko, H., & Edgell, D. (1984). *Human developmental neuropsychology.* New York: Oxford University Press.

Squire, L. R. (1986). Mechanisms of memory. *Science, 232,* 1612–1619.

Squire, L. R. (1987). *Memory and brain.* New York: Oxford University Press.

Squire, L. R. (1989). On the course of forgetting in very long-term memory. *Journal of Experimental Psychology: Learning, Memory, and Cognition, 15,* 241–245.

Squire, L. R. (1992). Declarative and nondeclarative memory: Multiple brain systems supporting learning and memory. *Journal of Cognitive Neuroscience, 4,* 232–243.

Squire, L. R. (1995). Memory and brain systems. In R. D. Broadwell, et al. (ed.), *Neuroscience, memory, and language. Decade of the brain,* Vol. 1. (pp. 59–75).

Washington: US Government Printing Office.

Squire, L. R., & Zola-Morgan, S. (1991). The medial temporal lobe memory system. *Science, 253,* 1380–1386.

Srivastava, A., Borries, C., & Sommer, Volker. (1991). Homosexual mounting in free-ranging female langurs (*Presbytis entellus-R*). *Archives of Sexual Behavior, 20,* 487–512.

Sroufe, L. A. (1983). Individual patterns of adaptation from infancy to preschool. In M. Perlmutter (Ed.), *Minnesota symposium on child psychology:* Vol. 16. Hillsdale, NJ: Erlbaum.

Sroufe, L. A. & Fleeson, J. (1986). Attachment and the construction of relationships. In W. W. Hartup & Z. Rubin (Eds.), *Relationships and development* (pp. 51–72). Hillsdale, NJ: Erlbaum.

Sroufe, L. A. & Waters, E. (1977). Attachment as an organizational construct. *Child Development, 48,* 1184–1199.

Stacy, A. W. (1997). Memory activation and expectancy as prospective predictors of alcohol and marijuana use. *Journal of Abnormal Psychology, 106,* 61–73.

Stallings, M., Hewitt, J., Cloninger, C. R., Heath, A. C., & Eaves, L. J. (1996). Genetic and environmental structure of the Tridimensional Personality Questionnaire: Three or four temperament dimensions? *Journal of Personality and Social Psychology, 70,* 127–140.

Stattin, H., & Magnusson, D. (1989). The role of early aggressive behavior in the frequency, seriousness, and types of later crime. *Journal of Consulting and Clinical Psychology, 57,* 710–718.

Stearns, P. (1994). *American cool: Constructing a twentieth-century emotional style.* New York: New York University Press.

Steele, C., & Aronson, J. (1995). Stereotype threat and the intellectual test performance of African Americans. *Journal of Personality and Social Psychology, 69,* 797–811.

Steele, H., Steele, M., & Fonagy, P. (1996). Associations among attachment classifications of mothers, fathers, and their infants. *Child Development 67,* 541–555.

Stein, B. E., & Meredith, M. A. (1990). Multisensory integration: Neural and behavioral solutions for dealing with stimuli from different sensory modalities. *Annals of the New York Academy of Sciences, 608,* 51–70.

Stein, J., Newcomb, M., & Bendler, P. (1994). Psychosocial correlates and predictors of AIDS risk behaviors, abortion, and drug use among a community sample of young adult women. *Health Psychology, 13,* 308–318.

Stein, Z., & Susser, M. (1975). Public health and mental retardation: New power and new problems. In M. Begab & S. Richardson (Eds.), *The Mentally re-*

tarded and society: A social science perspective. Baltimore, MD: University Park Press.

Steinberg, L. (1988). Reciprocal relation between parent-child distance and pubertal maturation. *Developmental Psychology, 24,* 122–128.

Steinberg, L., Lamborn, S. D., Darling, N., & Mounts, N. S. (1994). Over-time changes in adjustment and competence among adolescents from authoritative, authoritarian, indulgent, and neglectful families. *Child Development, 65,* 754–770.

Steinhausen, H. C., Willms J., & Spohr, H. L. (1993). Long-term psychopathological and cognitive outcome of children with fetal alcohol syndrome. *Journal of the American Academy of Child and Adolescent Psychiatry, 32,* 990–994.

Stephens, D. W., & Krebs, J. R. (1986). *Foraging theory.* Princeton: Princeton University Press.

Stern, K., & McClintock, M. K. (1998). Regulation of ovulation by human pheromones. *Nature, 392,* 177–179.

Sternberg, R. J. (Ed.). (1984). *Mechanisms of cognitive development.* New York: Freeman.

Sternberg, R. J. (1985). *Beyond IQ: A triarchic theory of human intelligence.* New York: Cambridge University Press.

Sternberg, R. J. (1988). Triangulating love. In R. Sternberg & M. L. Barnes (Eds.), *The psychology of love.* New Haven, Conn.: Yale University Press.

Sternberg, R. J. (1996). Costs of expertise. In K. A. Ericsson (ed.), *The road to excellence: The acquisition of expert performance in the arts and sciences, sports, and games.* (pp. 347–354). New Jersey: Lawrence Erlbaum Associates, Inc.

Sternberg, R. J. (1997). *Satisfaction in close relationships.* New York: The Guilford Press.

Sternberg, R. J. (1997). The triarchic theory of intelligence. In D. P. Flanagan, J. L. Genshaft, & P. L. Harrison (Eds.), *Contemporary intellectual assessment: Theories, tests, and issues* (pp. 92–104). New York: Guilford Press.

Sternberg, R. J., & Davidson, J. E. (1985). Cognitive development in the gifted and talented. In F. D. Horowitz & M. O'Brien (Eds.), *The gifted and talented: Developmental perspectives* (pp. 37–73). Washington, DC: American Psychological Association.

Sternberg, R. J., & Lubart, T. I. (1996). Investing in creativity. *American Psychologist, 51,* 677–688.

Sternberg, R. J., & Salter, W. (1982). Conceptions of intelligence. In R. J. Sternberg (Ed.), *Handbook of human intelligence* (pp. 3–28). New York: Cambridge University Press.

Sternberg, R. J., & Wagner, R. K. (1993). The geocentric view of intelligence and job performance is wrong. Current *Directions in Psychological Science, 2,* 1–5.

Sternberg, R. J., Wagner, R. K., Williams, W. M., & Horvath, J. A. (1995). Testing common sense. *American Psychologist, 50,* 912–927.

Sternberg, R. J., & Williams, W. M. (1997). Does the Graduate Record Examination predict meaningful success in the graduate training of psychology? A case study. *American Psychologist, 52,* 630–641.

Stevens, A., & Coupe, P. (1978). Distortions in judged spacial relations. *Cognitive Psychology, 10,* 422–437.

Stevens, C. F. (1979). The neuron. *Scientific American, 241,* 54–65.

Stevens, S. S. (1961). Psychophysics of sensory function. In W. Rosenblith (Ed.), *Sensory communication* (pp. 1–33). Cambridge, MA: MIT Press.

Stevens, S. S. (1975). *Psychophysics: Introduction to its perceptual, neural, and social prospects.* New York: John Wiley.

Stevens, S. S., & Newman, E. B. (1934). The localization of pure tone. *Proceedings of the National Academy of Sciences, 20,* 593–596.

Stewart, D. E., & Robinson, G. E. (1997). *A clinician's guide to menopause.* Washington: Health Press International.

Stewart, W. A. (1969). On the use of Negro dialect in the teaching of reading. In J. C. Baratz & R. W. Schuy (Eds.), *Teaching black children to read* (pp. 156–219). Washington, DC: Center for Applied Linguistics.

Stice, E., & Barrera, M. (1995). A longitudinal examination of the reciprocal relations between perceived parenting and adolescents' substance use and externalizing behaviors. *Developmental Psychology, 31,* 322–334.

Stogdill, R., & Coons, A. (1957). *Leader behavior: Its description and measurement.* Columbus, Ohio: Ohio State University Bureau of Business Research.

Stokes, J. P. (1985). The relation of social network and individual differences variables to loneliness. *Journal of Personality and Social Psychology, 48,* 981–990.

Stokes, P. E., Maas, J. W., Davis, J. M., Koslow, S. H., Casper, R. C., & Stoll, P. M. (1987). Biogenic amine and metabolic levels in depressed patients with high versus normal hypothalamic-pituitary-adrenocortical activity. *American Journal of Psychiatry, 144,* 868–872.

Strang, D. J. (1972). Conformity, ability, and self-esteem. *Representative Research in Social Psychology, 3,* 97–103.

Strauman, T. (1992). Self-guides, autobiographical memory, and anxiety and dysphoria: Toward a cognitive model of vulnerability to emotional distress. *Journal of Abnormal Psychology, 101,* 87–95.

Strauman, T., Lemieux, A., & Coe, C. (1993). Self-discrepancy and natural killer cell activity: Immunological consequences of negative self-evaluation. *Journal of Personality and Social Psychology, 64,* 1042–1052.

Straus, A. S. (1977). Northern Cheyenne ethnopsychology. *Ethos, 5,* 326–357.

Straus, A. S. (1982). The structure of the self in Northern Cheyenne culture. In B. Lee (Ed.), *Psychosocial theories of the self.* New York: Plenum Press.

Straus, M. A., & Kantor, G. K. (1994). Corporal punishment of adolescents by parents: A risk factor in the epidemiology of depression, suicide, alcohol abuse, child abuse, and wife beating. *Adolescence, 29,* 543–561.

Strauss, C., & Quinn, N. (1997). *A cognitive theory of cultural meaning.* New York: Cambridge University Press.

Strauss, D. H., Spitzer, R. L., & Muskin, P. R. (1990). Maladaptive denial of physical illness: A proposal for DSM-IV. *American Journal of Psychiatry, 147,* 1168–1172.

Strauss, J., Carpenter, W. T., & Bartko, J. (1974). The diagnosis and understanding of schizophrenia, III: Speculations on the processes that underlie schizophrenic symptoms and signs. *Schizophrenia Bulletin, 1,* 61–69.

Strauss, J., & Ryan, R. M. (1987). Autonomy disturbances in subtypes of anorexia nervosa. *Journal of Abnormal Psychology, 96,* 254–258.

Strayer, J. (1993). Children's concordant emotions and cognitions in response to observed emotions. *Child Development, 64,* 188–201.

Strayer, J., & Roberts, W. (1997). Facial and verbal measures of children's emotions and empathy. *International Journal of Behavioral Development, 20,* 627–649.

Streissguth, A., Barr, H., Johnson, Martin, D., & Kirchner, G. (1985). Attention and distraction at age 7 years related to maternal drinking during pregnancy. *Alcoholism: Clinical and experimental research, 9,* 195.

Streissguth, A., Sampson, P., & Barr, H. (1989). Neurobehavioral dose-response effects of prenatal alcohol exposure in humans from infancy to adulthood. *Annals of the New York Academy of Sciences, 562,* 145–158.

Stricker, G. (1991). Ethical concerns for alcohol research. *Journal of Consulting and Clinical Psychology, 59,* 256–257.

Stricker, G., & Gold, J. R. (1996). Psychotherapy integration: An assimilative, psychodynamic approach. *Clinical Psychology-Science & Practice, 3,* 47–58.

Stricker, G., & Healey, B. J. (1990). Projective assessment of object relations: A review of the empirical literature. *Psychological Assessment, 2,* 219–230.

Striegel-Moore, R. H., Silberstein, L. R., & Rodin, J. (1986). Toward an understanding of risk factors for bulimia. *American Psychologist, 41,* 246–263.

Stroebel, C. F. (1985). Biofeedback and behavioral medicine. In H. I. Kaplan & B. J. Sadock (Eds.), *Comprehensive textbook of psychiatry.* Baltimore, MD: Williams & Wilkins.

Stroebe, M., Gergen, M., Gergen, K., & Stroebe, W. (1996). Broken hearts or broken bonds? In D. Klass, P. R. Silverman, et al. (Eds.), *Continuing bonds: New understandings of grief. Series in death education, aging, and health care.* (pp. 31–44). Washington: Taylor & Francis.

Stromswold, K. (1995). The cognitive and neural bases of language acquisition. In M. S. Gazzaniga (Ed.), *The cognitive neurosciences.* (pp. 855–870). Cambridge: MIT Press.

Stroufe, L. A., & Fleeson, J. (1986). Attachment and the construction of relationships. In W. W. Hartup & Z. Rubin (Eds.), *Relationships and development* (pp. 51–72). Hillsdale, NJ: Erlbaum.

Stroufe, L. A., & Waters, E. (1977). Attachment as an organizational construct. *Child Development, 48,* 1184–1199.

Struckman-Johnson, C. (1990). Male victims of acquaintance rape. In A. Parrot & L. Bechhofer (Eds.), *Acquaintance rape: The hidden crime.*

Strupp, H., & Binder, J. L. (1984). *Psychotherapy in a new key: A guide to time-limited dynamic psychotherapy.* New York: Basic Books.

Strupp, H. H., & Blackwood, G. L., Jr. (1985). Recent methods of psychotherapy. In H. I. Kaplan, & B. J. Sadock (Eds.), *Comprehensive textbook of psychiatry.* (4th ed.). Baltimore, MD: Williams & Wilkins.

Stumpf, H. (1993). The factor structure of the Personality Research Form: A cross-national evaluation. *Journal of Personality, 61,* 1–26.

Stunkard, A., Sorensen, T. I. A., Harris, C., Teasdale, T. W., Chakraborty, R., Schull, W., & Schulsinger, F. (1986). An adoption study of human obesity. *New England Journal of Medicine, 314,* 193–198.

Stuss, D. T., & Benson, D. F. (1984). Neuropsychological studies of the frontal lobes. *Psychological Bulletin, 95,* 3–28.

Stuss, D. T., Gw, C. A., & Hetherington, C. R. (1992). "No longer Gage": Frontal lobe dysfunction and emotional changes. *Journal of Consulting and Clinical Psychology, 60,* 349–359.

Suarez-Orozco, M., Spindler, G., & Spindler, L. (1994). *The making of psychological anthropology II.* Fort Worth, Tex.: Harcourt Brace Jovanovich.

Suedfeld, P., & Pennebaker, J. W. (1997). Health outcomes and cognitive aspects of recalled negative life events. *Psychosomatic Medicine, 59,* 172–177.

Sullivan, H. S. (1953). *The interpersonal theory of psychiatry.* New York: W. W. Norton.

Suls, J., David, J. P., & Harvey, J. H. (1996). Personality and coping: Three generations of research. *Journal of Personality, 64,* 711–735.

Suls, J., Green, P., & Hillis, S. (1998). Emotional reactivity to everyday problems, affective inertia, and neuroticism. *Personality & Social Psychology Bulletin, 24,* 127–136.

Sundstrom, L., Chapuisat, M., & Keller, L. (1996). Conditional manipulation of sex ratios by ant workers: A test of kin selection theory. *Science, 274,* 993–995.

Super, C. M. (1981). Cross-cultural research on infancy. In H. C. Triandis & A. Heron (Ed.), *Handbook of cross-cultural psychology: Vol. 4. Developmental psychology.* Boston: Allyn & Bacon.

Super, C. M., & Harkness, S. (1980). *Anthropological perspectives on child development.* San Francisco: Jossey-Bass.

Surman, O. S., Gottlieb, S. K., Hackett, T. P., & Silverberg, E. L. (1983). Hypnosis in the treatment of warts. *Advances, 1,* 19–24.

Susser, E., Neugebauer, R., Hoek, H. W., Brown, A. S., Lin, S., Labovitz, D., & Gorman, J. M. (1996). Schizophrenia After Prenatal Famine Further Evidence. *Archives of General Psychiatry, 53,* 25–31.

Sutker, P., Winstead, D., Galina, Z., & Allai, A. (1991). Cognitive deficits and psychopathology among former prisoners of war and combat veterans of the Korean conflict. *American Journal of Psychiatry, 148,* 67–72.

Sutton, S. K., & Davidson, R. J. (1997). Prefrontal brain asymmetry: A biological substrate of the behavioral approach and inhibition systems. *Psychological Science, 8,* 204–210.

Svartberg, M., & Stiles, T. C. (1991). Comparative effects of short-term psychodynamic psychotherapy: A meta-analysis. *Journal of Consulting and Clinical Psychology, 59,* 704–714.

Swain, I., Zelano, P., & Clifton, R. K. (1993). Newborn infants' memory for speech sounds retained over 24 hours. *Developmental Psychology, 29,* 312–323.

Swain, S. A., Polkey, C. E., Bullock, P., & Morris, R. G. (1998). Recognition memory and memory for order in script-based stories following frontal lobe excisions. *Cortex, 34,* 25–45.

Swann, W. (1990). To be adored or to be known: The interplay of self-enhancement and self-verification. In R. M. Sorrentino & E. T. Higgins (Eds.), *Handbook of motivation and cognition.* Vol. 2, (pp. 408–448). New York: Guilford Press.

Swann, W., Stein-Seroussi, A., & Giesler, R. B. (1992). Why people self-verify. *Journal of Personality and Social Psychology, 62,* 392–401.

Swann, W., Wenzlaff, R., Krull, D. S., & Pelham, B. (1992). Allure of negative feedback: Self-verification strivings among depressed persons. *Journal of Abnormal Psychology, 101,* 293–306.

Swarr, A. E., & Richards, M. H. (1996). Longitudinal effects of adolescent girls' pubertal development, perceptions of pubertal timing, and parental relations on eating problems. *Developmental Psychology, 32,* 636–646.

Sweet, R. A., Mulsant, B. H., Gupta, B., Rifai, A. H., Pasternak, R. E., McEachran, A., & Zubenko, (1995). Duration of neuroleptic treatment and prevelence of tardive dyskinesia in late life. *Archives of General Psychiatry, 52,* 478–486.

Swets, J. A. (1992). The science of choosing the right decision threshold in high-stakes diagnostics. *American Psychologist, 47,* 522–532.

Szapocznik, J., Rio, A., Murray, E., Cohen, R., Scopetta, M., et al. (1989). Structural family versus psychodynamic child therapy for problematic Hispanic boys. *Journal of Consulting and Clinical Psychology, 57,* 571–578.

Szasz, T. (1974). *The myth of mental illness: Foundations of a theory of personal conduct,* (Rev. ed.). New York: Harper & Row.

Szasz, T. (1989). *Laws, liberty, and psychiatry: An inquiry into the social uses of mental health practices.* Syracuse, NY: Syracuse University Press.

Szeto, H. H., Wu, D. L., Decena, J. A., & Cheng, Y. (1991). Effects of single and repeated marijuana smoke exposure on fetal EEG. *Pharmacology, Biochemistry, and Behavior, 40,* 97–101.

Szymusiak, R., Iriye, T., & McGinty, D. (1989). Sleep-walking discharge of neurons in the posterior lateral hypothalamic area of cats. *Brain Research Bulletin, 23,* 111–120.

Tajfel, H. (1981). *Human groups and social categories: Studies in social psychology.* Cambridge: Cambridge University Press.

Tamminga, C., Thaker, G., Buchanon, R., Kirkpatrick, B., Alpha, L., Chase, T., & Carpenter, W. T. (1992). Limbic system abnormalities identified in schizophrenia using positron emission tomography with fluorodeoxyglucose and neocortical alterations with deficit syndrome. *Archives of General Psychiatry, 49,* 522–530.

Tamura, T., Nakatani, K., & Yau, K.-W. (1989). Light adaptation in cat retinal rods. *Science, 245,* 755–758.

Tan, C. C. (1991). Occupational health problems among nurses. *Scandinavian Journal of Work, Environment, and Health. 17,* 221–230.

Tanabe, T., Lino, M., & Tagaki, S. F. (1975). Discrimination of odors in olfactory bulb, pyriform-amygadaloid areas and orbito-frontal cortex of the monkey. *Journey of Neurophysiology, 38,* 1284–1296.

Tanaka, J. W., & Taylor, M. (1991). Object categories and expertise: Is the basic level in the eye of the beholder? *Cognitive Psychology, 23,* 457–482.

Tandberg, E., Larsen, J. P., Aarsland, D., & Cummings, J. L. (1996). The occurrence of depression in Parkinson's disease: A community-based study. *Archives of Neurology, 53,* 175–179.

Tanner, J. E., & Byrne, R. W. (1996). Representation of action through iconic gesture in a captive lowland gorilla. *Current Anthropology, 37,* 162–173.

Tanner, J. M. (1978). *Fetus into man: Physical growth from conception to maturity.* Cambridge, MA: Harvard University Press.

Tarr, M. J., Buelthoff, H. H., Zabinski, M., & Blanz, V. (1997). To what extent do unique parts influence recognition across changes in viewpoint? *Psychological Science, 8,* 282–289.

Tassinary, L. G., & Cacioppo, J. (1992). Unobservable facial actions and emotion. *Psychological Science, 3,* 28–33.

Taylor, S. (1991). *Health psychology.* (2nd ed.). New York: McGraw-Hill.

Taylor, S., & Crocker, J. (1980). Schematic bases of social information processing. In E. T. Higgins, P. Herman, & M. Zanna (Eds.), *Social cognition: The Ontario Symposium.* Hillsdale, NJ: Erlbaum.

Taylor, S. E., & Armor, D. A. (1996). Positive illusions and coping with adversity. *Journal of Personality, 64,* 873–898.

Taylor, S. E., & Brown, J. D. (1988). Illusion and well-being: A social psychological perspective on mental *health. Psychological Bulletin, 103,* 193–210.

Taylor, S. E., & Koivumaki, J. H. (1976). The perception of self and others: Acquaintanceship, affect, and actor-observer differences. *Journal of Personality and Social Psychology, 33,* 403–408.

Taylor, S. E., Pham, L., Rivkin, I., & Armor, D. (1998). Harnessing the imagination: Mental stimulation, self-regulation, and coping. *American Psychologist, 53,* 429–439.

Teicher, M. H., Glod, C. A., Magnus, E., Harper, D., Benson, G., Krueger, K., McGreenery, C. E. (1997). Circadian Rest-Activity Disturbances in Seasonal Affective Disorder. *Archives of General Psychiatry, 54,* 124–130.

Teitelbaum, P. (1961). Disturbances in feeding and drinking behavior after hypothalamic lesions. *Nebraska Symposium on Motivation, 39*–68.

Tellegen, A., Lykken, D. T., Bouchard, T. J. Jr., Wilcox, K. J., & Rich, S. (1988). Personality similarity in twins reared apart and together. *Journal of Personality and Social Psychology, 54*, 1031–1039.

Teplin, L. A. (1984). Criminalizing mental disorder: The comparative arrest rate of the mentally ill. *American Psychologist, 39*, 794–803.

Terman, L. M. (1925). *Genetic studies of genius: Vol. 1, Mental and physical traits of a thousand gifted children.* Stanford, CA: Stanford University Press.

Terman, L. M., & Oden, M. H. (1947). *Genetic studies of genius: Vol. 4. The gifted child grows up: Twenty-five years' follow-up of a superior group.* Stanford, CA: Stanford University Press.

Terman, L. M., & Oden, M. H. (1959). *Genetic studies of genius: Vol. 5. The gifted group at mid-life.* Stanford, CA: Stanford University Press.

Terrace, H. S. (1979). How Nim Chimsky changed my mind. *Psychology Today, 3,* 65–76.

Tesser, A. (1991). Social versus clinical approaches to self psychology: The self-evaluation maintenance model and Kohutian object relations theory. In R. C. Curtis (Ed.), *The relational self: theoretical convergences in psychoanalysis and social psychology* (pp. 257–281). New York: Guilford Press.

Tetlock P., Armor, D., & Peterson, R. S. (1994). The slavery debate in antebellum America: Cognitive style, value conflict, and the limits of compromise. *Journal of Personality and Social Psychology, 66,* 115–126.

Tetlock, P., Peterson, R., McGuire, C., Change, S., & Feld, P. (1992). Assessing political group dynamics: A test of the groupthink model. *Journal of Personality and Social Psychology, 63,* 403–425.

Tetlock, P. E. (1989). Structure and function in political belief systems. In A. R. Pratkanis, S. J. Breckler, et al. (Eds.), *Attitude structure and function. The third Ohio State University volume on attitudes and persuasion.* (pp. 129–151). Hillsdale, NJ: Lawrence Erlbaum Associates, Inc.

Thase, M., Simons, A. D., Cahalane, J., McGeary, J., & Harden, T. (1991). Severity of depression and response to cognitive behavior therapy. *American Journal of Psychiatry, 148,* 784–789.

Thayer, R. E., Newman, J. R., McClain, T. M. (1994). Self-regulation of mood: Strategies for changing a bad mood, raising energy, and reducing tension. *Journal of Personality & Social Psychology, 67,* 910–925.

Thelen, E. (1995). Motor development: A new synthesis. *American Psychologist, 50,* 79–95.

Thelen, E., & Smith, L. B. (1994). *A dynamic systems approach to the development of cognition and action.* Cambridge: MIT Press.

Thigpen, C. H., & Cleckley, H. (1954). *The thress faces of Eve.* Kingsport, TN: Kingsport Press.

Thomas, D. G., & Lykins, M. S. (1995). Event-related potential measures of 24-hour retention in 5-month-old infants. *Developmental Psychology, 31,* 946–957.

Thomas, W., & Znaniecki, F. (1927). *The Polish peasant in Europe and America.* New York: Alfred A. Knopf.

Thompson, D. A., & Campbell, R. G. (1977). Hunger in humans induced by 2-deoxy-D-glucose: Clucoprivic control of taste preference and food intake. *Science, 198,* 1065–1068.

Thompson, V. A., & Paivio, A. (1994). Memory for pictures and sounds: Independence of auditory and visual codes. *Canadian Journal of Experimental Psychology, 48,* 380–398.

Thurstone, L. L. (1938). Primary mental abilities. *Psychometric Monographs,* Vol. 1. Chicago: Chicago University Press.

Thurstone, L. L., & Thurstone, T. G. (1962). *Primary mental abilities.* Chicago: Science Research Associates.

Thyer, B. A. (1980). Prolonged in vivo exposure therapy with a 70-year-old woman. *Journal of Behavior Therapy and Experimental Psychiatry, 11.*

Tienari, P. (1991). Interaction between genetic vulnerability and family environment: The Finnish adoptive family study of schizophrenia. *Act Psychiatrica Scandinavica, 84,* 460–465.

Tinbergen, N. (1951). *The study of instinct.* Oxford: Clarendon Press.

Tizard, B., & Hodges, J. (1978). The effects of early institutional rearing on the development of eight-year old children. *The Journal of Child Psychology and Psychiatry, 19,* 99–108.

Tolliver, L. M. (1983). Social and mental health needs of the aged. *American Psychologist, 38,* 316–318.

Tolman, E. C. (1948). Cognitive maps in rats and men. *The Psychological Review, 55,* 189–208.

Tolman, E. C., & Honzik, C. H. (1930). Insight in rats. *University of California Publications in Psychology, 4,* 215–232.

Tomarken, A. J., Davidson, R. J., Wheeler, R. E., & Doss, R. C. (1992). Individual differences in anterior brain asymmetry and fundamental dimensions of emotion. *Journal of Personality & Social Psychology, 62,* 676–687.

Tomkins, S. S. (1962). *Affect, imagery, consciousness,* Vol. 1: *The positive affects.* New York: Springer-Verlag.

Tomkins, S. S. (1980). Affect as amplification: Some modifications in theory. In R. Plutchik & H. Kellerman (Eds.), *Emotion: Theory, research, and experience,* Vol. I: *Theories of emotion.* New York: Academic Press.

Tomkins, S. S. (1986). Script theory. In J. Aronoff, A. I. Radin, and R. Zucker (Eds.), *The emergence of personality* (pp. 147–216). New York: Springer.

Tomlinson-Keasey, C., and Little, T. D. (1990). Predicting educational attainment, occupational achievement, intellectual skill, and personal adjustment among gifted men and women. *Journal of Educational Psychology, 82,* 442–455.

Tooby, J., & Cosmides, L. (1990). On the universality of human nature and the uniqueness of the individual: The role of genetics and adaptation. *Journal of Personality, 58,* 17–68.

Tooby, J., & Cosmides, L. (1992). The psychological foundations of culture. In J. H. Barkow, L. Cosmides, & J. Tooby (Eds.), *The adapted mind: Evolutionary psychology and the generation of culture* (pp. 19–136). New York: Oxford University Press.

Toorey, E. F. (1986). *Witchdoctors and psychiatrists: The common roots of psychotherapy and its future.* New York: Aronson.

Tootell, R. B. H., Reppas, J. B., Dale, A. M., & Look, R. B. (1995). Visual motion aftereffect in human cortical area MT revealed by functional magnetic resonance imaging. *Nature, 375,* 139–141.

Tootell, R. B. H., Reppas, J. B., Kwong, K. K., & Malach, R. (1995). Functional analysis of human MT and related visual cortical area using magnetic resonance imaging. *Journal of Neuroscience, 15,* 3215–3230.

Torgersen, S. (1988). Genetic factors in anxiety disorders. *Archives of General Psychiatry, 40,* 1085–1089.

Traiwick, M. (1990). The ideology of love in a Tamil family. In O. M. Lynch (Ed.), *Divine passions: The social construction of emotion in India.* Berkeley: University of California Press.

Trandis, H. (1990). Cross-cultural studies of individualism and collectivism. In J. Berman (Ed.), *Nebraska symposium on motivation, 1989* (pp. 42–133). Lincoln: University of Nebraska Press.

Trappey, C. (1996). A meta-analysis of consumer choice and subliminal advertising. *Psychology & Marketing, 13,* 517–530.

Treisman, A. (1986). Properties, parts, and objects. In Boff, K., Kaufman, L., & Thomas, J. (Eds.), *Handbook of perception and human performance* (Vol. 2) (pp. 3501–3570). New York: Wiley.

Triandis, H. (Ed.) (1980). *Handbook of cross-cultural psychology*, 6 vols. Boston: Allyn & Bacon.

Triandis, H. (1989). The self and social behavior in differing cultural contexts. *Psychological Bulletin, 96*, 506–520.

Triandis, H. (1994). *Culture and social behavior*. New York: McGraw-Hill.

Triandis, H. C., Valsiner, J., Berry, J. W., Hui, C. H., & Keats, D. M. (1989). Culture and socialisation. In J. P. Forgas, J. M. Innes, et al. (Eds.), *Recent advances in social psychology: An international perspective*. (pp. 491–534). Amsterdam, The Netherlands: North-Holland.

Triplett, N. (1897). The dynamogenic factors in pacemaking and competition. *American Journal of Psychology, 9*, 507–533.

Trivers, R. (1972). Parental investment and sexual selection. In B. Campbell (Ed.), *Sexual selection and the descent of man: 1871–1971* (pp. 136–179). Chicago: Aldine.

Trivers, R. L. (1971). The evolution of reciprocal altruism. *Quarterly Review of Biology, 46*, 35–57.

Tronick, E., Morelli, G., & Ivey, P. (1992). The Efe forager infant and toddler's pattern of social relationships: Multiple and simultaneous. *Developmental Psychologist, 28*, 568–577.

Tsai, G., Passani, L. A., Slusher, B. S., Carter, R., Baer, L., Kleinman, J. E., & Coyle, J. T. (1995). Abnormal excitatory neurotransmitter metabolism in schizophrenic brains. *Archives of General Psychiatry, 52*, 829–836.

Tucker, D. M., Novelly, R. A., & Walker, P. J. (1987). Hyperreligiosity in temporal lobe epilepsy: Redifining the relationship. *Journal of Nervous and Mental Disease, 175*, 181–184.

Tuddenham, R. D. (1962). The nature & measurement of intelligence. In L. Postman (Ed.), *Psychology in the making: Histories of selected research problems* (pp. 469–525). New York: Alfred A. Knopf.

Tulving, E. (1972). Episodic and semantic memory. In E. Tulving and W. Donaldson (Eds.), *Organization of memory* (pp. 381–403). New York: Academic Press.

Tulving, E. (1987). Multiple memory systems and consciousness. *Human Neurobiology, 6*(2), 67–80.

Tulving, E., & Thomson, D. M. (1973). Encoding specificity and retrieval processes in episodic memory. *Psychological Review, 80*, 359–380.

Turiel, E. (1998). The development of morality. In W. Damon (Ed.), *Handbook of child psychology, Vol. 3, Social, emotional, and personality development* (N. Eisenberg, Vol. Ed.) (pp. 863–932). New York: Wiley.

Turkheimer, E. (1991). Individual and group differences in adoption studies of IQ. *Psychological Bulletin, 110*, 392–405.

Turner, J. R., Sherwood, A., & Light, K. (Eds.). (1992). *Individual differences in cardiovascular response to stress*. New York: Guilford Press.

Turner, S. M., Beidel, D. C., Long, P. J., & Greenhouse, J. (1992). Reduction of fear in social phobics: An examination of extinction patterns. *Behavior Therapy, 23*, 389–403.

Turner, V. (1969). *The ritual process*. Chicago: Aldine.

Turner, V. W. (1967). *A forest of symbols: Aspects of Ndembu ritual*. Ithaca, New York: Cornell University Press.

Turvey, M. T. (1996). Dynamic touch. *American Psychologist, 51*, 1134–1154.

Tversky, A. (1977). Features of similarity. *Psychological Review, 84*, 327–352.

Tversky, A., & Kahneman, D. (1973). Availability: A heuristic for judging frequency and probability. *Cognitive Psychology, 5*, 207–232.

Tversky, A., & Kahneman, D. (1974). Judgment under uncertainty: Heuristics and biases. *Science, 185*, 1124–1131.

Tversky, A., & Kahneman, D. (1981). Extensional vs. intuitive reasoning: The conjunction fallacy in probability judgment. *Psychological Review, 90*, 293–315.

Tyler, L. E. (1965). *The psychology of human differences*. New York: Appleton-Century-Crofts.

Udry, J. R., Billy, J. O. G., Morris, N. M., Groff, T. R., & Raj, J. H. (1985). Serum androgenic hormones motivate sexual behavior in adolescent boys. *Fertility and Sterility, 43*, 90–94.

Uleman, J. S., & Bargh, J. A. (Eds.). (1989). *Unintended thought*. New York: Guilford Press.

Ullman, S. (1989). Aligning pictorial descriptions: An approach to object recognition. *Cognition, 32*, 193–254.

Ullman, S. (1995). The visual analysis of shape and form. In M. S. Gazzaniga et al. (Eds.), *The cognitive neurosciences*. (pp. 339–350). Cambridge: MIT Press.

Ulrich, R. E. (1991). Animal rights, animal wrongs, and the question of balance. *Psychological Science, 2*, 197–201.

Ulrich, R. S. (1984). View through a window may influence recovery from surgery. *Science, 224*, 420–421.

Urban, J., Carlson, E., Egeland, B., & Sroufe, L. A. (1991). Patterns of individual adaptation across childhood. *Development and Psychopathology, 3*, 445–460.

Vaillant, G. (1977). *Adaptation to life*. Boston: Little, Brown.

Vaillant, G. (Ed.) (1992). *Ego mechanisms of defense: A guide for clinicians and researchers*. Washington: American Psychiatric Association Press.

Vaillant, G., & Perry, J. C. (1985). Personality disorders. In H. I. Kaplan & B. J. Sadock (Eds.), *Comprehensive textbook of psychiatry*. (4th ed.) Baltimore, MD: Williams & Wilkins.

Vaillant, G., & Vaillant, C. (1990). Natural history of male psychology health: XII. A 45-year study of predictors of successful aging at age 65. *American Journal of Psychiatry, 147*, 31–37.

Vaillant, G. E. (1992). The historical origins and future potential of Sigmund Freud's concept of the mechanisms of defence. *International Review of Psycho-Analysis, 19*, 35–50.

Vaillant, G. E. (1996). A Long-term Follow-up of Male Alcohol Abuse. *Archives of General Psychiatry, 53*, 243–249.

Valenstein, E. S. (1986). *Great and desperate cures*. New York: Basic Books.

Valenstein, E. S. (1988). The history of lobotomy: A cautionary tale. *Michigan Quarterly, 27*, 417–437.

Valins, S. (1966). Cognitive effects of false heart-rate feedback. *Journal of Personality and Social Psychology, 4*, 400–408.

Vallerand, R. J., Pelletier, L. G., Blais, M. R., Briere, N. M., Senecal, C., & Vallieres, E. F. (1993). On the assessment of intrinsic, extrinsic, and a motivation in education: Evidence on the concurrent and construct validity of the Academic Motivation Scale. *Educational and Psychological Measurement, 53*, 159–172.

van der Staay, F. J., & Blockland, A. (1996). Behavioral differences between outbred Wistar, inbred Fischer 344, Brown Norway, and hybrid Fischer 344 Brown Norway rats. *Physiology & Behavior, 60*, 97–109.

van Duijn, C. M. (1996). Epidemiology of the dementias: Recent developments and new approaches. *Journal of Neurology, Neurosurgery & Psychiatry, 60*, 478–488.

Van Essen, D. C., Anderson, C. H., Felleman, D. J. (1992). Information processing in the primate visual system: An integrated systems perspective. *Science, 255*, 419–423.

van IJzendoorn, M. (1995). Adult attachment representations, parental responsiveness, and infant attachment: A meta-analysis on the predictive validity of the Adult Attachment Interview. *Psychological Bulletin, 117*, 387–403.

Van IJzendoorn, M. (in press). Attachment representations in mothers, fathers, adolescents, and clinical groups: A meta-analytic search for normative data. *Journal of Consulting and Clinical Psychology*.

van IJzendoorn, M., & Kroonenberg, P. (1988). Cross-cultural patterns of attachment: A meta-analysis of the strange situation. *Child Development, 59,* 147–156.

van IJzendoorn, M.H., & De Wolf, M. S. (1997). In search of the absent father—Meta-analyses of infant-father attachment: A rejoinder to our discussants. *Child Development, 68,* 604–609.

Vance, E. B., & Wagner, N. D. (1976). Written descriptions of orgasm: A study of sex differences. In R. Green (Ed.), *Archives of Sexual Behavior,* Vol. 5.

Varley, C. K. (1984). Attention deficit disorder (the hyperactivity syndrome): A review of selected issues. *Developmental and Behavioral Pediatrics, 5,* 254–258.

Vaughn, B. E., Stevenson-Hinde, J., Waters, E., & Kotsaftis, A. (1992). Attachment security and temperament in infancy and early childhood: Some conceptual clarifications. *Developmental Psychology, 28,* 463–473.

Velez-Blasini, C. J. (1997). A cross-cultural comparison of alcohol expectancies in Puerto Rico and the United States. *Psychology of Addictive Behaviors, 11,* 124–141.

Venables, P. H. (1996). Schizotypy and maternal exposure to influenza and to cold temperature: The Mauritius Study. *Journal of Abnormal Psychology, 105,* 53–60.

Vernon, P. A., & Weese, S. E. (1993). Predicting intelligence with multiple speed of information-processing tests. *Personality and Individual Differences, 14,* 413–419.

Veroff, J., Kulka, R., & Douvan, E. (1981). *Mental health in America: Patterns of help-seeking from 1957–1976.* New York: Basic Books.

Vigliocco, G., Antonini, T., & Garrett, M. F. (1997). Grammatical gender is on the tip of Italian tongues. *Psychological Science, 8,* 314–317.

Viinamaeki, H., Koskela, K., & Niskanen, L. (1996). Rapidly declining mental well being during unemployment. *European Journal of Psychiatry, 10,* 215–221.

Viken, R. J., Rose, R. J., Kaprio, J., & Koskenvuo, M. (1994). A developmental genetic analysis of adult personality: Extraversion and neuroticism from 18 to 59 years of age. *Journal of Personality and Social Psychology, 66,* 722–730.

Vinogravdov, S., & Yalom, I. (1989). *Concise guide to group psychotherapy.* Washington, DC: American Psychiatric Press.

Vitaro, F., Tremblay, R. E., Kerr, M., Pagani, L., & Bukowski, W. M. (1997). Disruptiveness, friends' characteristics, and delinquency in early adolescence: A test of two competing models of development. *Child Development, 68,* 676–689.

Vitousek, K., & Manke, F. (1994). Personality variables and disorders in anorexia nervosa and bulimia nervosa. *Journal of Abnormal Psychology, 103,* 137–147.

Vokey, J. R., & Read, D. (1985). Subliminal messages: Between the devil and the media. *American Psychologist, 11,* 1231–1239.

Volavka, J., Cooper, T., Crobor, P., Bitter, I., Meisner, M., et al. (1992). Haloperidol blood levels and clinical effects, agpaloperidol blood levels and clinical effects. *Archives of General Psychiatry, 49,* 354–361.

Von Dras, D., & Blumenthal, H. T. (1992). Dementia of the aged: Disease or atypical accelerated aging? Biopathological and psychological perspectives. *Journal of the American Geriatrics Society, 40,* 285–294.

Von Senden, M. (1960). *Space and sight.* (Public Health transcript). New York: Free Press.

Vormbrock, J. (1993). Attachment theory as applied to wartime and job-related marital separation. *Psychological Bulletin, 114,* 122–144.

Vygotsky, L. (1978). *Mind in society: The development of higher psychological processes.* M. Cole, V. John-Steiner, S. Scribner, & E. Souberman (Eds.). Cambridge, Cambridge University Press.

Wachtel, P. (1977). *Psychoanalysis and behavior therapy: toward an integration.* New York: Basic Books.

Wachtel, P. (1993). *Therapeutic communication.* New York: Guilford.

Wachtel, P. (1997). *Psychoanalysis, behavior therapy, and the relational world.* Washington: American Psychological Association Press.

Wachtel, P. L. (1987). *Action and insight.* New York: Guilford Press.

Wagner, R. K. (1987). Tacit knowledge in everyday intelligent behavior. *Journal of Personality & Social Psychology, 52,* 1236–1247.

Wagstaff, G. F. (1984). The enhancement of witness memory by "hypnosis": A review and methodological critique of the experimental literature. British *Journal of Experimental and Clinical Hypnosis, 2,* 3–12.

Wakeling, A. (1996). Epidemiology of anorexia nervosa. *Psychiatry Research, 62,* 3–9.

Wald, G. (1968). Molecular basis of visual excitation. *Science, 162,* 230–239.

Waldrop, M. M. (1988). Toward a unified theory of cognition. *Science, 241,* 27–29.

Walker, B. M. (1996). A psychology for adventurers: An introduction to personal construct psychology from a social perspective. In D. Kalekin-Fishman, B. M. Walker, et al. (Eds.), *The construction of group realities: Culture, society, and personal construct theory* (pp. 7–26). Malabar, FL: Robert E. Krieger Publishing Co., Inc.

Walker, E. F., & Diforio, D. (1997). Schizophrenia: A neural diathesis-stress model. *Psychological Review, 104,* 667–685.

Walker, J. R., El-Guebaly, N., Ross, C., & Currie, R. F. (1992). Where do you turn for help? A community survey of the use of professinals, reading materials, and group programs for three problems in living. *Journal of Community Psychology, 20,* 84–89.

Wallace, A. F. C. (1956). Revitalization movements. *American Anthropologist, 58,* 264–281.

Wallace, A. F. C. (1959). Cultural determinants of response to hallucinatory experiences. *Archives of General Psychiatry, 1,* 58–69.

Wallace, B. (1993). Day persons, night persons, and variability in hypnotic susceptibility. *Journal of Personality and Social Psychology, 64,* 827–833.

Wallace, P. (1977). Individual discrimination of humans by odor. *Physiology and Behavior, 19,* 577–579.

Wallach, M. A. (1970). Creativity. In P. H. Mussen (Ed.), *Carmichael's Manual of Child Psychology,* Vol. 1. (pp. 1211–1272). (3rd ed.). New York: John Wiley.

Wallach, M. A. (1985). Creativity testing and giftedness. In F. D. Horowitz & M. O'Brien (Eds.), *The gifted and talented: Developmental perspectives* (pp. 99–123). Washington, DC: American Psychological Association.

Waller, N., Kojetin, B., Bouchard, T., & Lykken, D. (1990). Generic and environmental influences on religious interests, attitudes, and values: A study of twins reared apart and together. *Psychological Science, 1,* 138–142.

Waller, N. G., & Ross, C. A. (1997). The prevalence and biometric structure of pathological dissociation in the general population: Taxometric and behavior genetic findings. *Journal of Abnormal Psychology, 106,* 499–510.

Wallerstein, J. S. (1988). Children after divorce: Wounds that don't heal. *Perspectives in Psychiatric Care, 24,* 107–113.

Wallerstein, R. S. (1988). One psychoanalysis or many? *International Journal of Psycho-Analysis, 69,* 5–22.

Wallerstein, R. S. (1989). The psychotherapy research project of the Menninger Foundations: An overview. *Journal of Consulting and Clinical Psychology, 57,* 195–205.

Walsh, B. T., Hadigan, C. M., Devlin, M. J., Gladis, M., & Roose, S. (1991).

Long-term outcome of antidepressant treatment for bulimia nervosa. *American Journal of Psychiatry, 148,* 1206–1212.

Walsh, James K., & Lindblom, Scott S. (1997). Psychophysiology of sleep deprivation and disruption. In M. R. Pressman, W. C. Orr, et al. (Eds.), *Understanding sleep: The evaluation and treatment of sleep disorders. Application and practice in health psychology.* (pp. 73–110).Washington: American Psychological Association.

Walster, E., Aronson, V., Abrahams, D., & Rottman, L. (1966). The importance of physical attractiveness in dating behavior. *Journal of Personality and Social Psychology, 4,* 508–516.

Walster, E., & Walster, G. W. (1978). *A new look at love.* Reading, MA: Addison-Wesley Publishing Company.

Walters, J. M., & Gardner, H. (1986). The theory of multiple intelligences: Some issues and answers. In R. J. Sternberg & R. K. Walters, (Eds.), *Practical Intelligence: Nature and origins of competence in the everyday world.* New York: Cambridge University Press.

Wanke, M., Schwartz, N., & Bless, H. (1995). The availability heuristic revisted: Experienced case of retrieval in mundane frequency estimates. *Acta Psychologica, 89,* 83–90.

Warburton, E., Wise, R. J. S., Price, C. J., Weiller, C., Hadar, U., Ramsay, S., & Frackowiak, R. S. J. (1996). Noun and verb retrieval by normal subjects: Studies with PET. *Brain, 119,* 159–179.

Ward, I. L. (1984). The prenatal stress syndrome: Current status. *Psychoneuroendocrinology, 9,* 3–11.

Ward, T. B., Smith, S. M., and Vaid, J. (Eds.) (1997). *Creative thought: An investigation of conceptual structures and processes.* Washington: American Psychological Association.

Ware, J. Catesby, & Morin, Charles. M. (1997). Sleep in depression and anxiety. In M. Pressman, & W. Orr (Eds.), *Understanding Sleep: The evaluation and treatment of sleep disorders* (pp. 483–503). Washington: American Psychological Association.

Warner, L. A., Kessler, R. C., Hughes, M., Anthony, J. C., & Nelson, C. B. (1995). Prevalence and correlates of drug use and dependence in the United States: Results from the national comorbidity survey. *Archives of General Psychiatry, 52,* 219–229.

Warwick, Z. S., Hall, W. G., Pappas, T. N., & Schiffman, S. S. (1993). Taste and smell sensations enhance the satiating effect of both a high-carbohydrate and a high-fat meal in humans. *Physiology and Behavior, 53,* 553–563.

Wason, P., & Johnson-Laird, P. (1972). *The psychology of reasoning: Structure and content.* Cambridge, MA: Harvard University Press.

Wason, P. C. (1960). On the failure to eliminate hypotheses in a conceptual task. *Quarterly Journal of Experimental Psychology, 12,* 129–140.

Wason, P. C. (1968). Reasoning about a rule. *Quarterly Journal of Experimental Psychology, 20,* 273–281.

Wasserman, E. A., & Miller, R. R. (1997). What's elementary about associative learning? *Annual Review, 48,* 573–607.

Watanabe, S., Sakamoto, J., & Wakita, M. (1995). Pigeons' discrimination of painting by Monet and Picasso. *Journal of the Experimental Analysis of Behavior, 63,* 165–174.

Waters, E. Wippman, J., & Sroufe, J. A. (1979). Attachment, positive affect, and competence in the peer group: Two studies of construct validation. *Child Development, 50,* 821–829.

Watkin, L. R., & Mayer, D. J. (1982). Organization of endogenous opiate and nonopiate pain control systems. *Science, 216,* 1185–1193.

Watson, D., & Clark, L. A. (1992). Affects separable and inseparable: On the hierarchical arrangement of the negative affects. *Journal of Personality and Social Psychology, 62,* 489–505.

Watson, D., & Tellegen, A. (1985). Toward a consensual structure of mood. *Psychological Bulletin, 98,* 219–225.

Watson, J. (1925). *Behaviorism.* New York: W. W. Norton, 1970.

Watson, J., & Rayner, R. (1920). Conditioned emotional reactions. *Journal of Experimental Psychology, 3,* 1–14.

Watson, M. W., & Getz, K. (1990). The relationship between Oedipal behaviors and children's family role concepts. *Merrill-Palmer Quarterly, 36,* 487–505.

Waugh, N. C., & Norman, D. A. (1975). Primary memory. *Psychological Review, 72,* 89–104.

Weale, R. (1982). *Focus on vision.* Cambridge, MA: Harvard University Press.

Weber, M. (1924). Bureaucracy. In H. Gerth & C. W. Mills (Eds.), *From Max Weber: Essays in sociology.* New York: Oxford University Press, 1946.

Wegesin, D. J. (1998). A neuropsychologic profile of homosexual and heterosexual men and women. *Archives of Sexual Behavior, 27,* 91–108.

Wegner, D. (1992). You can't always think what you want: Problems in the suppression of unwanted thoughts. *Advances in Experimental Social Psychologyt, 25,* 193–225.

Wegner, D., Shortt, J., Blake, A. W., & Page, M. S. (1990). The suppression of

exciting thoughts. *Journal of Personality and Social Psychology, 58,* 409–418.

Weinberg, R. A. (1989). Intelligence and IQ: Landmark issues and great debates. *American Psychologist, 44,* 98–104.

Weinberg, R. A., Scarr, S., & Waldman, I. D. (1992). The Minnesota Transracial Adoption Study: A follow-up of IQ test performance at adolescence. *Intelligence, 16,* 117–135.

Weinberger, D. A. (1990). The construct validity of the repressive coping style. In J. L. Singer (Ed.), *Repression and dissociation: Implications for personality, psychopathology and health.* Chicago: University of Chicago Press.

Weinberger, D. R., Berman, K. F., Suddath, R., & Torrey, E. F. (1992). Evidence of dysfunction of a prefrontal-limbic network in schizophrenia: A magnetic resonance imaging and regional cerebral blood flow study of discordant monozygotic twins. *American Journal of Psychiatry, 149,* 890–897.

Weinberger, J. (1995). Common factors aren't so common: The common factors dilemma. *Clinical Psychology-Science & Practice, 2,* 45–69.

Weinberger, J. (in press). Heart and head: Are they one? In H. Kurtzman (Ed.), *Cognition and psychodynamics.* New York: Oxford University Press.

Weinberger, J., & Hardaway, R. (1990). Subliminal separating science from myth in subliminal psychodynamic activation. *Clinical Psychological Review, 10,* 727–756.

Weinberger, J., & Silverman, L. (1988). Testability and empirical verification of psychoanalytic dynamic propositions through subliminal psychodynamic activation. *Unpublished manuscrupt,* H. A. Murray Center, Harvard University.

Weiner, B. (1974). *Achievement motivation and attribution theory.* Morristown, NJ: General Learning Press.

Weiner, B. (1985). An attributional theory of achievement motivation and emotion. *Psychological Review, 92,* 548–573.

Weiner, B. (1985). 'Spontaneous' causal thinking. *Psychological Bulletin, 97,* 74–84.

Weiner, H. (1985). Schizophrenia: Etiology. In H. I. Kaplan & B. J. Sadock (Eds.), *Comprehensive textbook of psychiatry.* (4th ed.). Baltimore, MD: Williams & Wilkins.

Weiner, R. D., & Coffee, C. E. (1988). Indications for use of electroconvulsive therapy. In A. J. Frances & R. E. Hales (Eds.), *Review of Psychiatry,* Vol. 7. Washington, DC: American Psychiatric Press.

Weiner, R. D., & Krystal, A. D. (1994). The present use of electroconvulsive therapy. *Annual Review of Medicine, 45,* 273–281.

Weinstein, S. (1960). *Intensive and extensive aspects of tactile sensitivity as a function of body part, sex, and laterality.* In D. Kenshalo (Ed.), The Skin Senses. Springfield, IK: Thomas.

Weisberg, P., & Waldrop, P. B. (1972). Fixed-interval work habits of congress. *Journal of Applied Behavior Analysis, 5,* 93–97.

Weisberg, R. W. (1994). Genius and madness? A quasi experimental test of the hypothesis that manic-depression increases creativity. *Psychological Science, 5,* 361–367.

Weisenberg, M., Tepper, I., & Schwarzwald, J. (1995). Humor as a cognitive technique for increasing pain tolerance. *Pain 63,* 207–212.

Weiskrantz, L. (1997). *Consciousness lost and found: A neuropsychological exploration.* England: Oxford University Press.

Weiskrantz, L., Warrington, E., Sanders, M. D., & Marshall, J. (1974). Visual capacity in the hemianopic field following a restricted occipital ablation. *Brain, 97,* 709–728.

Weiss, B., Dodge, K., Bates, J., & Pettit, G. (1992). Some consequences of early harsh discipline: Child aggression and a maladaptive social information processing style. *Child Development, 63,* 1321–1335.

Weiss, G., Hechtman, L., Milroy, T., & Perlman, T. (1985). Psychiatric status of hyperactives as adults: A controlled prospective 15-year follow-up of 63 hyperactive children. *Journal of the American Academy of Child Psychiatry, 24,* 211–220.

Weiss, L. H., & Schwarz, J. C. (1996). The relationship between parenting types and older adolescents' personality, academic achievements, adjustment, and substance use. *Child Development, 67,* 2101–2114.

Weiss, R. S. (1986). Continuities and transformations in social relationships from childhood to adulthood. In W. W. Hartup & Z. Rubin (Eds.), *Relationships and development,* pp. 95–110. Hillsdale, NJ: Erlbaum.

Weiss, V. (1992). Major genes of general intelligence. *Personality and Individual Differences, 13,* 1115–1134.

Weisse, C. S. (1992). Depression and immunocompetence: A review of the literature. *Psychological Bulletin, 111,* 475–489.

Weissman, M. M., Bland, R. C., Canino, G. J., Faravelli, C., Greenwald, S., Hwu, H., et al. (1997). The Cross-national Epidemiology of Panic Disorder. *Archives of General Psychiatry, 54,* 305–309.

Weissman, M. M., & Boyd, J. H. (1985). Affective disorders: Epidemiology. In H. I. Kaplan & B. J. Sadock (Eds.), *Comprehensive textbook of psychiatry.* (4th ed.). Baltimore, MD: Williams & Wilkins.

Wells, G. L., & Loftus, E. F. (Eds.) (1984). *Eyewitness testimony: Psychological perspectives.* Cambridge: Cambridge University Press.

Wells, G. L., & Turtle, J. W. (1987). Eyewitness testimony: Current knowledge and emerging controversies. *Canadian Journal of Behavioural Science, 19*(4), 363–388.

Wentzel, K. R., & Asher, S. R. (1995). The academic lives of neglected, rejected, popular, and controversial children. *Child Development, 66,* 754–763.

Werker, J. F., & Tees, R. C. (1984). Cross-language speech perception: Evidence for perceptual reorganization during the first year of life. *Infant Behavior and Development, 7,* 49–63.

Werner, E. (1979). *Cross-cultural child development: A review from the planet earth.* Monterey, CA: Brooks/Cole.

Werner, H. (1948). *Comparative psychology of mental development.* (rev. ed.). Chicago: Follett.

Wertenbaker, L. (1981). *The eye: Window to the world.* Washington, DC: U.S. News books.

Wertsch, J., & Kanner, B. (1992). A sociocultural approach to intellectual development. In R. Sternberg & C. A. Berg (Eds.), *Intellectual development* (pp. 328–349). New York: Cambridge University Press.

Wesley, F., & Sullivan, E. (Eds.). (1986). *Human Growth and Development.* New York: Human Services Press.

Wessinger, C. M., Fendrich, R., & Gazzaniga, M. S. (1997). Islands of residual vision in hemianopic patients. *Journal of Cognitive Neuroscience, 9,* 203–221.

West, R. L. (1996). An application of prefrontal cortex function theory to cognitive aging. *Psychological Bulletin, 120,* 272–292.

Westen, D. (1985). *Self and society: Narcissism, collectivism, and the development of morals.* New York: Cambridge University Press.

Westen, D., (1990). Psychoanalytic approaches to personality. In L. Pervin (Ed.), *Handbook of personality: Theory and research* (pp. 21–65). New York: Guilford Press.

Westen, D. (1991). Social cognition and object relations. *Psychological Bulletin, 109,* 429–455.

Westen, D. (1992). The cognitive self and the psychoanalytic self: Can we put our selves together? *Psychological Inquiry, 3,* 1–13.

Westen, D. (1994). Toward an integrative model of affect regulation: Applications to social-psychological research. *Journal of Personality, 62,* 641–647.

Westen, D. (1995). A clinical-empirical model of personality: Life after the Mischelian ice age and the NEOlithic era. *Journal of Personality, 63,* 495–524.

Westen, D. (1997a). Toward an empirically and clinically sound theory of motivation. *International Journal of Psycho-Analysis, 78,* 521–548.

Westen, D. (1997b). Divergences between clinical and research methods for assessing personality disorders: Implications for research and the evolution of Axis II. *American Journal of Psychiatry, 154,* 895–903.

Westen, D. (in press). The scientific legacy of Sigmund Freud: Toward a psychodynamically informed psychological science. *Psychological Bulletin.*

Westen, D., Klepser, J., Ruffins, S., Silverman, M., Lifton, N., & Boekamp, J. (1991). Object relations in childhood and adolescence: The development of working representations. *Journal of Consulting and Clinical Psychology, 59,* 400–409.

Westen, D., Lohr, N., Silk, K., Gold, L., & Kerber, K. (1990). Object relations and social cognition in borderlines, major depressives, and normals: A TAT analysis. *Psychological Assessment: A Journal of Consulting and Clinical Psychology, 2,* 355–364.

Westen, D., Muderrisoglu, S., Fowler, C., Shedler, J., & Koren, D. (1997). Affect regulation and affective experience: Individual differences, group differences, and measurement using a Q-sort procedure. *Journal of Consulting and Clinical Psychology, 65,* 429–439.

Wetherick, N. (1975). The role of semantic information in short-term memory. *Journal of Verbal Learning and Verbal Behavior, 14,* 471–480.

Whalen, C., & Henker, B. (1991). Therapies for hyperactive children: Comparisons, combinations, and compromises. *Journal of Consulting and Clinical Psychology, 59,* 126–137.

Wheeler, M. A., Stuss, D. T., & Tulving, E. (1995). Frontal lobe damage produces episodic memory impairment. *Journal of the International Neuropsychological Society, 1,* 525–533.

Wheeler, M. A., Stuss, D. T., & Tulving, D. (1997). Toward a theory of episodic memory: The frontal lobes and autonoetic consciousness. *Psychological Bulletin, 121,* 331–354.

Whipple, B., Josimovich, J. B., and Komisaruk, B. R. (1990). Sensory thresholds during the antepartum, intrapartum and postpartum periods. *International Journal of Nursing Studies, 27,* 213–221.

Whitam, F., & Mathy, R. (1991). Childhood cross-gender behavior of homosexual females in Brazil, Peru, the Philippines, and the United States. *Archives of Sexual Behavior, 20,* 151–170.

Whitbourne, S. K. (1996). Psychological perspectives on the normal aging process. In L. L. Cartensen, B. A. Edelstein, & L. Dornbrand (Eds.), *The practical handbook of clinical gerontology* (pp. 3–35). Thousand Oaks, CA: Sage Publications, Inc.

Whitbourne, S. K., & Hulicka, I. (1990). Ageism in undergraduate psychology texts. *American Psychologist, 45,* 1127–1136.

Whitbourne, S. K., Zuschlag, M. K., Elliot, L. B., & Waterman, A. S. (1992). Psychosocial development in adulthood: A 22-year sequential study. *Journal of Personality & Social Psychology, 63,* 260–271.

White, C. B. (1978). Moral development in Bahamian school children: A 3-year examination of Kohlberg's stages of moral development. *Developmental Psychology, 14,* 58–65.

White, R. W. (1959). Motivation reconsidered: The concept of competence. *Psychological Review, 66,* 297–333.

Whiting, B., & Edwards, C. P. (1973). A cross-cultural analysis of the behavior of children aged 3–11. *Journal of Social Psychology, 91,* 171–188.

Whiting, B. B., & Whiting, J. W. M. (1975). *Children of six cultures: A psychocultural analysis.* Cambridge, MA: Harvard University Press.

Whiting, J. (1964). The effects of climate on certain cultural practices. In W. Goodenough (Ed.), *Explorations in cultural anthropology: Essays in honor of George Peter Murdock* (pp. 511–544). New York: McGraw-Hill.

Whiting, J. W. M., & Child, I. L. (1953). *Child training and personality: A cross-cultural study.* New Haven, Conn.: Yale University Press.

Whiting, J. W. M., & Whiting, B. B. (1973). Altruistic and egoistic behavior is six cultures. In L. Nader & T. W. Marekzki (Eds.), *Cultural illness and helath: Essays in human adaptation.* Washington, DC: American Anthropological Association.

Whorf, B. L. (1956). *Language, thought, and reality.* Cambridge, MA: MIT Press.

Wicker, A. W. (1969). Attitudes versus action: The relationship of verbal and overt behavioral responses to attitude objects. *Journal of Soc. Issues, 25,* 41–78.

Wicklegren, I. (1996). Marijuana: Harder than thought? *Science, 276,* 1967–1968.

Wiesel, T. N. (1982). Postnatal development of the visual cortex and the influence of environment. *Nature, 299,* 583–591.

Wiesel, T. N., & Hubel, D. H. (1960). Receptive fields of ganglion cells in the cat's retina. *Journal of Physiology, 153,* 583–594.

Wilfley, D. E., Agras, W. S., Telch, C., & Rossiter, E. (1993). Group cognitive-behavioral therapy and group interpersonal psychotherapy for the non-purging bulimic individual: A controlled comparison. *Journal of Consulting and Clinical Psychology, 61,* 296–305.

Wilkins, M. C. (1982). The effect of changed material on ability to do formal syllogistic reasoning. *Archives of Psychology, 16,* 1–83.

Wilkinson, R., & Allison, S. (1989). Age and simple reaction time: Decade differences for 5,325 subjects. *Journal of Gerontology, 44,* 29–36.

Wilkinson, S. C. (1993). WISC-R profiles of children with superior intellectual ability. *Gifted Child Quarterly, 37,* 84–91.

Williams, C., & Bybee, J. (1994). What do children feel guilty about? Developmental and gender differences. *Developmental Psychology, 30,* 617–623.

Williams, C. D. (1959). The elimination of tantrum behavior by extinction procedures. *Journal of Abnormal and Social Psychology, 59,* 269.

Williams, D. E., & Thompson, J. K. (1993). Biology and behavior: A set-point hypothesis of psychological functioning. *Behavior Modification, 17,* 43–57.

Williams, G.-J., Power, K. G., Millar, H. R., & Freeman, C. P. (1993). Comparison of eating disorders and other dietary/weight groups on measures of perceived control, assertiveness, self-esteem, and self-directed hostility. *International Journal of Eating Disorders, 14,* 27–32.

Williams, J. E., & Best, D. L. (1982). *Measuring sex stereotypes: A thirty-nation study.* Beverly Hills, CA: Sage.

Williams, J. E., & Best, D. L. (1990). *Sex and psyche: Gender and self viewed cross-culturally.* Newbury Park, CA: Sage.

Williams, J. H. (1983). The emergence of gender differences. In W. Damon (Ed.), *Social and personality development.* New York: W. W. Norton.

Williams, L. M. (1994). Recall of childhood trauma: A prospective study of women's memories of child sexual abuse. *Journal of Consulting and Clinical Psychology, 62,* 1167–1176.

Williams, W. M., & Ceci, S. J. (1997). Are Americans becoming more or less alike? Trends in race, class, and ability differences in intelligence. *American Psychologist, 52,* 1226–1235.

Wilpert, B. (1995). Organizational behavior. *Annual Review of Psychology, 46,* 59–90.

Wilson, E. D. (1963). Phermones. *Scientific American,* 2–11.

Wilson, E. O. (1975). *Sociobiology: A new synthesis.* Cambridge, MA: Harvard University Press.

Wilson, E. O., & Bossert, W. H. (1996). Chemical communication among animals. In L. D. Houck & L. C. Drickamer (Eds.), *Foundations of animal behavior: Classic papers with commentaries* (pp. 602–645). Chicago: University of Chicago Press.

Wilson, G., & Fairburn, C. (1993). Cognitive treatments for eating disorders. *Journal of Consulting and Clinical Psychology, 61,* 261–269.

Wilson, T., Lisle, D., Schooler, J., & Hodges, S. (1993). Introspecting about reasons can reduce post-choice satisfaction. *Personality & Social Psychology Bulletin, 19,* 331–339.

Wilson, T. D., Lisle, D. J., & Schooler, J. W. (1990). Some undesirable effects of self-reflection. Unpublished manuscript, University of Virginia, Department of Psychology, Charlottesville.

Winblad, B., Hardy, J., Backman, L., & Nilsson, L-G. (1985). Memory function and brain biochemistry in normal aging and in senile dementia. In D. S. Olton, E. Gamzu, & S. Corkin (Eds.), *Memory dysfunctions: An integration of animal and human research from preclinical and clinical perspectives.* New York: New York Academy of Sciences.

Winchel, R., & Stanley, M. (1991). Self-injurious behavior: A review of the behavior and biology of self-mutilation. *American Journal of Psychiatry, 148,* 306–317.

Windholz, G. (1997). Ivan P. Pavlov: An overview of his life and psychological work. *American Psychologist, 52,* 941–946.

Winn, P. (1995). The lateral hypothalamus and motivated behavior: An old syndrome reassessed and a new perspective gained. *Current Directions in Psychological Science, 4,* 182–187.

Winograd, E., & Neissier, U. (Eds.). (1993). *Affect and accuracy in recall: Studies of "flashbulb" memories.* New York: Cambridge University Press.

Winokur, G. C. W., Keller, M., Endicott, J., & Leon, A. (1995). A family study of manic-depressive (bipolar I) disease: Is it a distinct illness separate from primary unipolar depression? *Archives of General Psychiatry, 52,* 367–373.

Winslow, R. W., Franzini, L., & Hwang, J. (1992). Perceived peer norms, casual sex, and AIDS prevention. *Journal of Applied Psychology, 22,* 1809–1827.

Winson, J. (1985). *Brain and psyche: The biology of the unconscious.* New York: Anchor.

Winter, D. (1993). Power, affiliation, and war: Three tests of a motivational model. *Journal of Personality and Social Psychology, 65,* 532–545.

Winter, D. G. (1987). Enhancement of an enemy's power motivation as a dynamic of conflict escalation. *Journal of Personality and Social Psychology, 42,* 41–46.

Winterbottom, M. R. (1953). The relation of childhood training in independence to achievement motivation. *Unpublished doctoral dissertation,* Univeristy of Michigan, Ann Arbor.

Witkin, H. A., Dyk, R. B., Faterson, H. F., Goodenough, D. R., & Karp, S. A. (1962). *Psychological differentiation.* London: John Wiley.

Wixom, J., Ludolph, P., & Westen, D. (1993). Quality of depression in borderline adolescents. *Journal of the American Academy of Child & Adolescent Psychiatry, 32,* 1172–1177.

Wixted, J., & Ebbesen, E. (1991). On the form of forgetting. *Psychological Science, 2,* 409–415.

Wober, M. (1987). Perceived risk of disease from alcohol, asbestos, and AIDS: Links with television viewing? *Health Educational Research 2,* 175–184.

Woike, B., & Aronoff, J. (1992). Antecedents of complex social cognitions. *Journal of Personality and Social Psychology, 63,* 97–104.

Wolpe, J. (1958). *Psychotherapy by reciprocal inhibition.* Stanford, CA: Stanford University Press.

Wolpe, J. (Ed.). (1964). *The conditioning therapies: The challenge in psychotherapy.* New York: Holt, Rinehart, & Winston.

Wong, M. M., & Csikszentmihalyi, M. (1991). Motivation and academic achievement: The effects of personality traits and the quality of experience. *Journal of Personality, 59,* 539–574.

Wong, P., Shevrin, H., & Williams, W. J. (1994). Conscious and nonconscious processes: An ERP index of an anticipatory response in a conditioning paradigm using visually masked stimuli. *Psychophysiology, 31,* 87–101.

Wood, J. M., Bootzin, R., Rosenhan, D., Nolen-Hocksema, S., & Jourden, F. (1992). Effects of the 1989 San Francisco earthquake on frequency and content of nightmares. *Journal of Abnormal Psychology, 101,* 219–224.

Wood, R., & Bandura, A. (1989). Social cognitive theory of organizational management. Special issue: Theory development forum. *Academy of Management Review, 14,* 361–384.

Wood, W., Wong, F., & Chachere, J. G. (1991). Effects of media violence on viewers' aggression in unconstrained social interaction. *Psychologial Bulletin, 109,* 371–383.

Woodall, K., & Matthews, K. (1993). Changes in and stability of hostile characteristics: Results from a 4-year longitudinal study of children. *Journal of Personality and Social Psychology, 64,* 491–499.

Woods, J. W. (1956). Taming of the wild Norway rat by rhinencephalic lesions. *Nature, 178,* 869.

Worthington, E. L., Jr., Martin, G. A., Shumate, M., & Carpenter, J. (1983). The effect of brief Lamaze training and social encouragement on pain endurance ina cold pressor tank. *Journal of Applied Social Psychology, 13,* 223–233.

Wright, L. B., Treiber, F. A., Davis, H., & Strong, W. B. (1996). Relationship of John Henryism to cardiovascular functioning at rest and during stress in youth. *Annals of Behavioral Medicine, 18,* 146–150.

Wright, M. R. (1989). Body image satisfaction in adolescent girls and boys. *Journal of Youth and Adolescence, 18,* 71–84.

Wyatt, G. E. (1988). The relationship between child sexual abuse and adolescent sexual functioning in Afro-American and White American women. In R. A. Prentky, V. L. Quinsey, et al. (Eds.), *Human sexual aggression: Current perspectives.* Annals of the New York Academy of Sciences, Vol. 528. (pp. 111–122). New York: New York Academy of Sciences.

Wyatt, G. E., Peters, S. D., & Guthrie, D. (1988a). Kinsey revisited: I. Comparisons of the sexual socialization and sexual behavior of White women over 33 years. *Archives of Sexual Behavior, 17,* 201–239.

Wyatt, G. E., Peters, S. D., & Guthrie, D. (1988b). Kinsey revisted: II. Comparisons of the sexual socialization and sexual behavior of Black women over 33 years. *Archives of Sexual Behavior, 17,* 289–332.

Wyatt, R. J. (1996). Neurodevelopmental Abnormalities and Schizophrenia: A Family Affair. *Archives of General Psychiatry, 53,* 11–18.

Wyatt, R. J., Freed, W. J., & Hoffer, B. (1985). Functional brain grafts: A distant hope for patients with irreversible brain lesions. *Integrative Psychiatry, 3,* 27–31.

Wyer, R. S., Jr., & Srull, T. K. (1986). Human cognition in its social context. *Psychological Review, 93,* 322–359.

Wylie, R. (1979). *The self-concept, Vol. 2.* Lincoln: University of Nebraska Press.

Wynne, L. C. (1961). The study of intrafamilial alignments and splits in exploratory family therapy. In N. Ackerman et al. (Eds.), *Exploring the base for family therapy.* New York: Family Service Association of America.

Wynne, L. C., & Singer, M. T. (1963). Thought disorder and family relations of schizophrenics. *Archives of General Psychiatry, 9,* 191–198.

Wyrwicka, W. (1976). The problem of motivation in feeding behavior. In D. Novin, W. Wyrwicka, and G. Bray, *Hunger: Basic Mechanisms and Clinical Implications.* New York: Raven.

Yadin, E., & Thomas, E. (1996). Stimulation of the lateral septum attenuates immobilization-induced stress ulcers. *Physiology & Behavior, 59,* 883–886.

Yamamoto, D., Ito, H., Fujitani, K. (1996). Genetic dissection of sexual orientation: Behavioral, cellular, and molecular approaches in Drosophila melanogaster. *Neuroscience Research, 26,* 95–107.

Yaniv, I., Meyer, D. (1987). Activation and metacognition of inaccessible stored information: Potential bases for incubation effects in problem solving. *Journal of Experimental Psychology: Learning, Memory, and Cognition, 13,* 187–205.

Yankura, J., & Dryden, W. (1990). *Doing RET: Albert Ellis in action.* New York: Springer.

Yarrow, M. R., Waxler, C. Z., & Scott, P. M. (1971). Child effects on adult behavior. *Developmental Psychology, 5,* 300–311.

Yassa, R., Nair, N., Iskandar, H., & Schwartz, G. (1990). Factors in the development of severe forms of tardive dyskinesia. *American Journal of Psychiatry, 147,* 1156–1163.

Yehuda, R., Lowy, M., Southwick, S. M., Shaffer, D., & Giller, E. (1991). Pymphocyte glucocoricoid receptor number in posttraumatic stress disorder. *American Journal of Psychiatry, 148,* 499–504.

Yehuda, R., McFarlane, A. C., Eds. (1997). *Psychobiology of posttraumatic stress disorder.* New York: New York Academy of Sciences.

Yeomans, F. E., Hull, J. W., & Clarkin, J. C. (1994). Risk factors for self-damaging acts in a borderline population. *Journal of Personality Disorders, 8,* 10–16.

Young, A. W. (1994). Face recognition. In G. d'Ydewalle, P. Eelen, et al. (Eds.), *International perspectives on psychological science,* Vol. 2: The state of the art. (pp. 1–27). Hove, UK: Lawrence Erlbaum Associates, Inc.

Youniss, J., & Haynie, D. (1992). Friendship in adolescence. *Developmental and Behavioral Pediatrics, 13,* 59–66.

Yu, B., Zhang, W., Jing, Q., Peng, R., Zhang, G., & Simon, H. A. (1985). STM capacity for Chinese and English language materials. *Memory and Cognition, 13,* 202–207.

Yuille, J. C. (1980). A critical examination of the psychological and practical implications of eyewitness research. *Law and Human Behavior, 4,* 335–345.

Yussen, S. R., & Levy, V. M., Jr. (1975). Developmental changes in predicting one's own span of short-term memory. *Journal of Experimental Child Psychology, 19,* 502–508.

Zahn-Waxler, C., Radke-Yarrow, M., Wagner, E., & Chapman, M. (1992). Development of concern for others. *Developmental Psychology, 28,* 126–136.

Zahn-Waxler, C., Robinson, J., & Emde, R. (1992). The development of empathy in twins. *Developmental Psychology, 28,* 1038–1047.

Zajonc, R. (1980). Feeling and thinking: Preferences need no inferences. *American Psychologist, 35,* 151–175.

Zajonc, R. B. (1965). *Social facilitation. Science, 149,* 269–274.

Zajonc, R. B. (1968). The attitudinal effects of mere exposure. *Journal of Personality and Social Psychology, 9,* 1–27.

Zajonc, R. B. (1998). Emotions. In D. T. Gilbert, S. T. Fiske, et al. (Eds.), *The handbook of social psychology,* Vol. 2 (4th ed.). (pp. 591–632). Boston: McGraw-Hill.

Zal, H. M. (1987). Panic disorder: Is it emotional or physical? *Psychiatric Annals, 17,* 497–505.

Zanarini, M. C. (Ed., 1997). *Role of sexual abuse in the etiology of borderline personality disorder.* Washington: American Psychiatric Press, Inc.

Zanarini, M., Gunderson, J., Marino, M., Schwartz, E., & Frankenburg, F. (1990). Psychiatric disorders in the families of

borderline outpatients. In P. Links (Ed.), *Family environment and borderline personality disorder* (pp. 69–84). Washington, DC: American Psychiatric Press.

Zanarini, M. C., Gunderson, J. G., Marino, M. F., Schwartz, E. D., & Frankenberg, F. R. (1989). Childhood experience of borderline patients. *Comprehensive Psychiatry, 30,* 18–25.

Zanna, M. P., & Cooper, J. (1974). Dissonance and the pill: An attribution approach to studying the arousal properties of dissonance. *Journal of Personality and Social Psychology, 9,* 703–709.

Zaragosta, M., & Mitchell, K. J. (1996). Repeated exposure to suggestion and the creation of false memories. *Psychological Science, 7,* 294–300.

Zatzick, D. F., & Dimsdale, J. E. (1990). Cultural variations in response to painful stimuli. *Psychosomatic Medicine, 52,* 544–557.

Zborowski, M., & Herzog, E. (1952). *Life is with people.* New York: International Universities Press.

Zeanah, C. H., & Zeanah, P. D. (1989). Intergenerational transmission of maltreatment: Insights from attachment theory and research. *Psychiatry, 52,* 177–196.

Zelazo, P. D., Helwig, C. C., & Lau, A. (1996). Intention, act, and outcome in behavioral prediction and moral judgment. *Child Development, 67,* 2478–2492.

Zervas, I. M., Augustine, A., & Fricchione, G. L. (1993). Patient delay in cancer: A view from the crisis model. *General Hospital Psychiatry, 15,* 9–13.

Zigler, E., & Berman, W. (1983). Discerning the future of early childhood intervention. *American Psychologist,* 894–906.

Zigler, E., & Glick, M. (1988). Is paranoid

schizophrenia really camouflaged depression? *American Psychologist, 43,* 294–290.

Zigler, E., Hodapp, R. M., & Edison, M. R. (1990). From theory to practice in the care and education of mentally retarded individuals. *American Journal of Mental Retardation, 95,* 1–12.

Zillman, D., Baron, R. A., & Tamborini, R. (1981). Special costs on smoking: Effects of tobacco smoke on hostile behavior. *Journal of Applied Social Psychology, 11,* 548–561.

Zimbardo, P. G. (1972). Pathology of imprisonment. *Society,* 4–8.

Zimbardo, P. G. (1975). Transforming experimental research into advocacy for social change. In M. Deutsch and H. A. Hornstein (Eds.), *Applying social psychology: Implications for research, practice, and training.* Hillsdale, NJ: Erlbaum.

Zinbarg, R., Barlow, D., Brown, T., & Hertz, R. (1992). Cognitive-behavioral approaches to the nature and treatment of anxiety disorders. *Annual Review of Psychology, 43,* 235–267.

Zipursky, R. B., Lambe, E. K., Kapur, S., & Mikulis, D. J. (1998). Cerebral Gray Matter Volume Deficits in First Episode Psychosis. *Archives of General Psychiatry, 55,* 540–546.

Zuckerman, M. (1994). *Behavioral expression and biosocial bases of sensation seeking.* New York: Cambridge University Press.

Zuckerman, M., Koestner, R., DeBoy, T., Garcia, T., Maresca, B., & Sartois, J. (1988). To predict some of the people some of the time. A reexamination of the moderator variable approach in personality theory. *Journal of Personality and Social Psychology, 54,* 1006–1019.

Gamma Liaison. Page 373 (right): Randi Anglin/The Image Works. Page 376: F. Paolini/Sygma. Page 378 (top): Marks Product/The Image Bank. Page 378 (bottom): Renee Lynn/Tony Stone Images/New York, Inc. Page 381: R. Schneider/The Image Bank. Page 387 (center): Culver Pictures, Inc. Page 383: Cindy Karp/Black Star. Page 387 (left): UPI/Bettmann. Page 387 (right): Malmberg/Black Star.

Chapter 9 Page 392: Josh Gosfield, "Girl and a Clock," 1990. Private collection. Page 394: Jerzy Kolacz/The Image Bank. Page 397: David Yound Wolff/Tony Stone Images/New York, Inc. Page 402: ©SIGNET Penguin Books USA, Inc. Page 410: Malcolm Piers/The Image Bank. Page 412: Weinberg/Clark/The Image Bank. Page 421: Françoise Suaze/Science Photo Library/Photo Researchers. Page 427: Jose Azel/Woodfin Camp & Associates. Page 429 (left): Michael K. Nichols/Magnum Photos, Inc. Page 429 (right): Greenlar/The Image Works.

Chapter 10 Page 434: Peter Malone, "Dreams." Copyright 1994 Duncan Baird Publishers. Reproduced with permission. Page 436: Rhoda Sidney/Stock, Boston. Page 438: Carolina Biological Supply Company/Phototake. Page 442: Acme/UPI/Bettmann. Page 443: © Leo Cullum/The Cartoon Bank, Inc. Page 444: Lew Merrin/Monkmeyer Press Photo. Page 447: Hans Neleman/The Image Bank. Page 448: John Blaustein/Gamma Liaison. Page 450: ©Sidney Harris. Page 451: Courtesy American Museum of Natural History. Page 453: ©1990 Jim Unger/LaughingStock Licensing, Inc. Page 454: Courtesy Neal E. Miller. Page 457: CLOSE TO HOME, ©John McPherson. Reprinted with permission of UNIVERSAL PRESS SYNDICATE. All rights reserved. Page 458 (top): Giraudon/Art Resource. Page 458 (center): Topham/The Image Works. Page 458 (bottom): Maria C. Valentino/Sygma. Page 463 (left): Steven Weinberg/Tony Stone Images/New York, Inc. Page 463 (right): Shattil/Rozinski S.I./Stock Imagery. Page 464: Fabricius & Taylor/Gamma Liaison. Page 469: Rick Maiman/Sygma. Page 471: Camille Tokerud/Photo Researchers. Page 472 (top): ©1997 Timothy Greenfield-Sanders. Page 472 (center): Lisa Quinones/Black Star. Page 472 (bottom): Allen/Gamma Liaison. Page 473: Bruno Barbey/Magnum Photos, Inc.

Chapter 11 Page 480: Robert Birmelin, "The Telephone Rings," 1994/Hackett-Freedman Gallery. Acrylic on canvas, 78"x60". Page 482: Agence France Presse/Corbis-Bettmann. Pages 488 and 490: Courtesy P. Ekman, Human Interaction Lab, University of California San Francisco. Page 491: Photofest. Page 503 (top): Art Wolfe/Tony Stone Images/New York, Inc. Page 503 (center): Joe McDonald/Bruce Coleman, Inc. Page 503 (bottom): Tom Hussey/The Image Bank. Page 508 (top): Dirck Halstead/Gamma Liaison. Page 508 (center): Mike Keza/Gamma Liaison. Page 511: Vanessa Vick/Photo Researchers. Page 513: Roger Lemoyne/Gamma Liaison. Page 514: W. Karel/Sygma Photo News. Page 517: Manfred Kage/Peter Arnold, Inc. Page 520 (top left): Steve Powell/Allsport/PNI. Page 520 (top right): Mike Powell/Allsport/PNI. Page 520 (center): Manfred Kaoe/Peter Arnold, Inc. Page 520 (bottom): Science Photo Library/Photo Researchers. Page 523: James D. Wilson/Gamma Liaison. Page 524: Daniel J. Cox/Tony Stone Images/New York, Inc.

Chapter 12 Page 528: Diana Ong, "Parts Equal the Whole IV,"1940/SuperStock. Page 530: Francis Picabia, 1878-1953, "Aello," 1930/ Collection Jean-Jacques Lebel, Paris. Oil on canvas, 169x169 cm. Reproduced with permission of Artists' Rights Society, NY. Page 534: Courtesy Jerry Ohlinger's Movie Material Store. Page 535: Sandra Lousada/Woodfin Camp & Associates. Page 536 (top): John Running/Tony Stone Images/New York, Inc. Page 536 (bottom): Andy Sacks/Tony Stone Images/New York, Inc. Page 537: Sestini/Barchielli/Gamma Liaison. Page 540: UPI/Bettmann. Page 544 (top): ©1921 Roschach, Psychodiagnostics, Hans Huber- Medical Publisher, Bern. Page 545: ©Sidney Harris. Page 549: ©Jim Unger, Laughingstock Licensing, Inc. Page 560: Courtesy Jerome Kagan, Harvard University. Page 565: ©Sygma. Page 568: Lippo di Dalmasio, "The Madonna of Humility," The National Gallery, London. Page 569: Courtesy New York Public Library Picture Collection.

Chapter 13 Page 574: Suzy Kitman, "Flying Baby: Ellie: #3," 1997. Oil on paper, 38"x50". Page 576: Lisa Quinones/Black Star. Page 579: From

S. Carlson, *International Journal of Neuroscience*, 1980, p. 189; courtesy The Gordon and Breach Publishers, Switzerland. Reproduced with permission. Page 583 (top): Tony Stone Images/New York, Inc. Page 583 (center): Neil Harding/Tony Stone Images/New York, Inc. Page 583 (bottom left): CLOSE TO HOME, ©John McPherson. Reprinted with permission of UNIVERSAL PRESS SYNDICATE. All rights reserved. Page 583 (bottom right): Petit Format/Nestle/ScienceSource/Photo Researchers. Page 584: Courtesy James W. Hanson, University of Iowa Hospital and Clinics. Page 588: Tom Raymond/Tony Stone Images/New York, Inc. Page 591: Keren Su/Tony Stone Images/New York, Inc. Page 594: From A.N. Meltzoff & M.K. Moore, *Science* 198:75-78, 1977. Reproduced with permission. Page 597: Courtesy Wayne Behling, Ypsilanti Press, Mich. Page 599: Jeffrey W. Myers/Stock, Boston. Page 602: Elizabeth Crews. Page 605: David M. Grossman/Photo Researchers. Page 608 (left): UPI/Corbis-Bettmann. Page 608 (right): Jeffrey Markowitz/Sygma. Page 610: Roz Chast, ©1993 The New Yorker Collection/The Cartoon Bank. All rights reserved. Page 612: ©Mugshots/Gabe Palmer/The Stock Market. Page 617 (left and center): Science Source/Photo Researchers. Page 617 (right): Cecil Fox/Science Source/Photo Researchers.

Chapter 14 Page 620: Diana Ong, "Faces I"/SuperStock. Page 622: David Sams/Stock, Boston. Page 624: Nina Leen/Life Magazine, copyright Time, Inc. Page 626 (left): Tom McHugh/Photo Researchers. Page 626 (right): ©Stephanie Maze/Woodfin Camp & Associates. Page 632: Ira Wyman/Sygma. Page 635: François Charton/Black Star. Page 637: Photo courtesy Cora du Bois, "The People of Alor: A Social-Psychological Study of an East Indian Island," University of Minnesota Press, 1944. Reproduced with permission. Page 643 (left): Jeff Greenberg/The Image Works. Page 643 (right): Tom, Dee Ann McCarthy/The Stock Market. Page 647: ©W. Steis/The Cartoon Bank, Inc. Page 651: Joan Clifford/The Picture Cube. Page 652: ©Sidney Harris. Page 654 (top): Lisa Quinones/Black Star. Page 654 (center): Andrew Holbrooke/The Stock Market. Page 654 (bottom): Dave Kennerly/UPI/Corbis-Bettmann. Page 657: Greg Smith/SABA. Page 659: UPI/Corbis-Bettmann. Page 662 (left): Andy Berhaut/Photo Researchers. Page 662 (center): Bill Strode/Woodfin Camp & Associates. Page 662 (right): Don Smetzer/Tony Stone Images/New York, Inc. Page 667: Ron Dahlquist/Tony Stone Images/New York, Inc.

Chapter 15 Page 670: Freshman Brown, "Loss," 1996/SuperStock. Page 672: Rosanne Percivalle/The Image Bank. Page 674: Eric Roth/The Picture Cube. Page 683: Callahan/Levin Represents. Page 689 (left): Giannia Tobtoli/Photo Researchers. Page 689 (right): Michael Weisbrot/Stock, Boston. Page 692: Courtesy Monte Buchsbaum, M.D., Mt. Sinai Medical Center. Reproduced with permission. Page 694 (top): ©1992 Ziggy and Friends, Inc. Distributed by Universal Press Syndicate. Page 694 (bottom): From Sander L. Gilman, *Seeing The Insane*. Page 696: Courtesy Monte Buschbaum, Mt. Sinai Medical Center, NY. Reproduced with permission. Page 697: From Lieberman et al, *The American Journal of Psychiatry*, 1992. Copyright 1998, The American Psychiatric Association. Reprinted by permission. Page 705: David Butow/Black Star. Page 707: ©1993 Jennifer Berman, Humerus Cartoons. Page 708: Peter Marlow/Magnum Photos, Inc. Page 714: Bob Daemmrich/Sygma. Page 719: Ken M. Johns/Photo Researchers.

Chapter 16 Page 722: George Segal, "Girl on a Chair, Finger to Mouth," Christie's Images/Licensed by VAGA, New York, NY. Page 724: Arlene Colins/Monkmeyer Press Photo. Page 727: ©Sidney Harris. Page 728: Photograph ©Edwin Engelman. Pages 729 and 733: ©Sidney Harris. Page 736: Dr. R. Nesse/©Andrew Sacks. Page 737: THE FAR SIDE, ©1986 FARWORKS, Inc. Distributed by Universal Press Syndicate. Reprinted with permission. All rights reserved. Page 742: Courtesy Les Greenberg. Page 744: Hank Morgan/Science Source/Photo Researchers. Page 763: Vivianne Moos/SABA.

Chapter 17 Page 768: Randy Stevens, "They're Here!," 1995/Newbury Fine Arts. Page 770: Kevin Horan/Tony Stone Images/New York, Inc. Page 776: G. Brad Lewis/Tony Stone Images/New York, Inc. Page 779: ©Tribune Media Services. Reprinted with permission. Page 782: J. P. Williams/Tony Stone Images/New York, Inc. Page 786: Stefan May/Tony

Stone Images/New York, Inc. Page 791 (top left): Anna Flynn/Stock, Boston. Page 791 (top right): US Signal Corp./AP Wide World Photos. Page 791 (center): ITN/ F.S.P./Gamma Liaison. Page 796: Elliott Erwitt/ Magnum Photos, Inc. Page 797: Topham/The Image Works. Page 803: Bob Thomas/Tony Stone Images/New York, Inc. Page 812: ©Sidney Harris. Page 814: Courtesy Selz/Seabolt Communications, Inc.

Chapter 18 Page 818: Elinore Schnurr, "Darkness and Light #18, "1989, 23"x23 1/2". Page 820: Keystone Paris/Sygma. Page 827: Callahan/Levin Represents. Page 828: David C. Tomlinson/Tony Stone Images/New York,

Inc. Page 830: Kitagawa Utamaro, Japanese British Library/SuperStock. Page 833: Gamma Liaison. Page 834: Edward Hausner/New York Times Pictures. Page 836: Photofest. Page 837: Wesley Bocxe/Photo Researchers. Page 839: Chris Maynard/Gamma Liaison. Page 840: Photofest. Page 841: Carl S. Sams, II/Peter Arnold, Inc. Page 846: ©Jim Unger/Laughingstock Licensing, Inc. Page 849: UPI/Corbis-Bettmann. Page 850: Courtesy Yale Interaction Library, Yale University. Page 851: Bill Horsman/Stock, Boston. Page 852: William Vandivert. Page 855: Courtesy Philip G. Zimbardo, Dept. of Psychology, Stanford University. Page 858: Henri Cartier-Bresson/Magnum Photos, Inc. Page 859: Paul Griffin/Stock, Boston.

Text and Illustration Credits

Chapter 1 Figure 1.4: From Cave, C.B. (1997). Long-lasting priming in picture naming. *Psychological Science, 8*, 322–325. Copyright © 1997. Reprinted with the permission of Blackwell Science, Inc. and the author.

Chapter 2 Figure 2.1: From Pennebaker, J., Colder, M., & Sharp, L.K. (1990). Accelerating the coping process. *Journal of Personality and Social Psychology, 58*, 528–537. Copyright © 1990 by the American Psychological Association. Reprinted and adapted with the permission of the APA and the authors. Figure 2.5: From Bower, G.H. (1981). Mood and memory. *American Psychologist, 36*, 129–148. Copyright © 1981 by the American Psychological Association. Reprinted with the permission of the APA and the author. Figure 2.7: From D'Esposito, M., Detre, J.A., Aguirre, G.K., Stallcup, M., Alsop, D.C., Tippet, L.J., & Farah, M.J. (1997). A functional MRI study of mental image generation. *Neuropsychologia, 35*, (5) 725-730. Copyright © 1997 by Elsevier Science Ltd. Reprinted with the permission of Elsevier Science Limited. Table 2.3: From Izard, C.E., Libero, C., Putnam, P., & Haynes, O.M. (1993). Stability of emotion experiences and their relationship to traits of personality. *Journal of Personality and Social Psychology, 64*, 847–860. Copyright © 1993 by the American Psychological Association. Reprinted with the permission of the APA and the authors. Table 2S.4: From Zahn-Waxler, C., Radke-Yarrow, M.J., Wagner, E., & Chapman, M. (1992). Development and concern for others. *Developmental Psychology, 28*, 126–136. Copyright © 1992 by the American Psychological Association. Reprinted with the permission of the APA and the authors.

Chapter 3 Figure 3.4: From Björklund, A. & Gage, F. (1985). Neural grafting of neurodegenerative diseases in animal models. *Annals of the New York Academy of Sciences, 437*, 53-81. Copyright © 1985 by the Annals of the New York Academy of Sciences. Reprinted and adapted with the permission of the Annals of the New York Academy of Sciences and the authors. Figure 3.9: From Kolb & Whishaw (1990). *Fundamentals of Human Neuropsychology*, 3rd Edition. Copyright © 1980, 1985, 1990, 1996 by W.H. Freeman and Company. Reprinted with the permission of the publishers. Figure 3.12: From Gad et al. Cerebellum implicated in sensory acquisition. *Science, 272, April 1996*, 545–547. Copyright © 1996 by American Academy for the Advancement of Science. Reprinted with the permission of *Science*. Figure 3.16: From Penfield, W. & Rasmussen, T. (1950). *The Cerebral Cortex of Man*. Copyright 1950 by the Macmillan Publishing Company, copyright renewed © 1978 by Theodore Rasmussen. Reprinted with the permission of Simon & Schuster. Figure 3.17: From Gazzaniga, M.S. (August 1967). The split brain in man. *Scientific American*. Copyright © 1967 by Scientific American. Reprinted with the permission of the publishers. All rights reserved.

Chapter 4 Figure 4.2: From Sekuler, R. & Blake, R. (1994). *Perception, 3rd Edition*. New York: McGraw-Hill, Inc. Copyright © 1994, 1990, 1985 by McGraw-Hill, Inc. Reprinted and adapted with the permission of the pub-

lishers. Figure 4.3: From Griffin, D.R. (1959). *Echoes of Bats and Men*. New York: Bantam Doubleday Dell Publishing Group. Copyright © 1959 by Donald R. Griffin. Reprinted with the permission of the author. Figure 4.11, 4.15 and 4.23: From Sekuler, R. & Blake, R. (1994). *Perception, 3rd Edition*. New York: McGraw-Hill, Inc. Copyright © 1994, 1990, 1985 by McGraw-Hill, Inc. Reprinted and adapted with the permission of the publishers. Figure 4.30: From Boring, E.G. (1930). A new ambiguous figure. *American Journal of Psychology, 42*, 444–445. Copyright 1930 by the University of Illinois Press. Adapted with the permission of the publishers. Figure 4.31: From Kanisza, G. (April 1976). Subjective contours. *Scientific American, 234*, 48. Copyright © 1976 by Scientific American, Inc. Reprinted with the permission of the publishers. Figure 4.32: From Biederman, I. (1990). Higher level vision. In D.N. Osherson et al. (Eds.), *An Invitation to Cognitive Science, Volume 2*. Copyright © 1990 by the Massachusetts Institute of Technology. Reprinted with the permission of The MIT Press. Figure 4.33: From Biederman, I. (1987). Recognition by components. *Computer Visions, Graphics, and Image Processing, 32*, 29–73. Copyright © 1985 by Academic Press, Inc. Reprinted with the permission of Academic Press and the author. Figure 4.40: From De Lucia, P.R. & Hochberg, J. (1991). Geometrical illusions in solid objects under ordinary viewing conditions. *Perception and Psychophysics, 50 (6)*, 547-555. Copyright © 1991 by the Psychonomic Society, Inc. Reprinted with the permission of the authors. Figure 4.44: From Mistlin, A. & Perrett, D. (1990). Expectations and neural firing. *Experimental Brain Research, 82*, 442. Copyright © 1990 by Springer-Verlag. Reprinted with the permission of the publishers. Figure 4.45: From Kosslyn, S.M. et al. (Unpublished study). Visual mental imagery activates primary visual cortex: A PET study. Reprinted with the permission of Dr. S. M. Kosslyn, Harvard University. Table 4.1: From Brown, R., Galanter, E., & Hess, E.H. (1962). *New Directions in Psychology*. New York: Harcourt Brace & Co. Reprinted with the permission of Roger W. Brown, Harvard University.

Chapter 5 Figure 5.2: From Pavlov, I. P. (1927). *Conditioned Reflexes*. New York: Oxford University Press. Copyright 1927. Reprinted with the permission of Oxford University Press, Ltd. Figure 5.4: From Alvarez-Burda, B., Ramirez-Amaya, V., Perez-Montfort, R., & Bermudez-Rattoni, F. (1995). Enhancement of antibody production by a learning paradigm. *Neurobiology of Learning and Memory, 64*, 103–105. Copyright © 1995 by Academic Press, Inc. Reprinted with the permission of Academic Press and the authors. Figure 5.5: From Hovland, C.I. (1937). The generalization of conditioned responses: the sensory generalization of conditioned responses with varying frequencies of time. *The Journal of General Psychology, 17*, 125–148, 1937. Copyright 1937. Reprinted with the permission of the Helen Dwight Reid Educational Foundation. Figure 5.7: From Garcia, J. & Koelling, R. (1966). Relation of cue to consequence in avoidance learning. *Psychonomic Science, 4*, 123–124. Copyright © 1966. Reprinted with the permission of Psychonomic Society, Inc. Figure 5.12: From Weisberg, P. & Waldrop, P.B. (1972). Fixed-interval work habits of Congress. *Journal of Applied Behavior Analysis.* Copyright © 1972 by Journal of Applied Behavior Analysis. Reprinted by permission. Figure 5.13: From Gray, J.A. (1988). "Gray's Three Behavioral Systems" from *The Psychology of Fear and Stress, 2nd Edition.* New York: Cambridge University Press. Copyright © 1988. Reprinted with the permission of Cambridge University Press and the author. Figure 5.15: From Rotter, J. (1971, June). External control and internal control: Locus of control. *Psychology Today, 42.* Copyright © 1971 by Sussex Publishers, Inc. Reprinted with the permission of Psychology Today Magazine. Figure 5.16: From Bandura, A. (1967). In *The Young Child: Reviews of Research,* W. Hartup & N. Smothergill (Eds.). Washington, DC: National Association for the Education of Young Children. Copyright © 1967 by NAEYC. Reprinted by permission. Table 5.1: From Flor, H., Haag, G., & Turk, D. (1986). Longterm efficacy of emg biofeedback for chronic rheumatic back pain. *Pain,* 198–199. Copyright © 1986 by Elsevier Science. Reprinted with the permission of Elsevier Science and the authors.

Chapter 6   Figure 6.4: From Atkinson & Schifflin (1968). Human memory: A proposed system and its control processes. In K.W. Spence & J.T Spense (Eds.), *The psychology of learning and motivation,* Vol. 2. Copyright © 1968 by Academic Press, Inc. Adapted with the permission of Academic Press and the authors. Figure 6.5: From Rundus, D. (1971). Analysis of rehearsal process in free recall. *Journal of Experimental Psychology, 89,* 63–77. Copyright © 1971 by the American Psychological Association. Reprinted with the permission of the APA and the author. Figure 6.7: From Logie, R. (1996). The seven ages of working memory. In J.T.E. Richardson et al., *Working Memory and Cognition.* Copyright © 1996. Reprinted with the permission of Oxford University Press, Inc. Figure 6.8: From Courtney et al. (1997). Transient and sustained activity in a distributed neural system for human working memory. *Nature, 386,* (6625), p. 610. Copyright © 1997 by Macmillan Magazines Ltd. Reprinted with the permission of *Nature* and the authors. Figure 6.9: From Rao et al. (1997). Integrating the what and where in the primate prefrontal cortex. *Science, 276,* (May 2), p. 822. Copyright © 1997 by American Academy for the Advancement of Science. Reprinted with the permission of *Science.* Figure 6.10: From Ericsson & Chase (1982). Exceptional memory. *American Scientist, 70,* pp. 607–614. Copyright © 1982 by American Scientist. Adapted with the permission of the publishers. Figure 6.12: From Hermann, D.J., Crawford, M., & Holdsworth, M. (1992). Gender-linked differences in everyday memory performance. *British Journal of Psychology, 83,* 221–231. Copyright © 1992. Reprinted with the permission of the British Psychological Society and the authors. Figure 6.13: From Gabrieli, et al. (1996). Functional magnetic resonance imaging of semantic memory processes in the frontal lobes. *Psychological Science, 7,* p. 281. Copyright © 1996. Reprinted with the permission of the publishers. Figure 6.14: From Bahrick, H., et al. (1993). Maintenance of foreign language vocabulary and the spacing effect. *Psychological Science, 4,* p. 319. Copyright © 1993. Reprinted with the permission of the publishers. Figure 6.18: From Brewer & Treyens (1981). The psychology of intergroup attitudes and behavior. *Annual Review of Psychology, 36,* 219–243. Copyright © 1981 by Annual Reviews, Inc. Reprinted with the permission of the publishers. Figure 6.20: Adapted from Bahrick, et al. (1996). Accuracy and distortion in memory for high school grades. *Psychological Science, 7,* p. 266. Copyright © 1996. Reprinted with the permission of the publishers.

Chapter 7   Figure 7.1: Adapted from Cooper, L.A. & Shepard, R.N. (1973). *Memory and Cognition, 1,* (3), 246–250. Copyright © 1973. Reprinted with the permission of the Psychonomic Society, Inc. Figure 7.4: From Lehman, D.R. & Nisbett, R.E. (1990). A longitudinal study of the effects of undergraduate training on reasoning. *Developmental Psychology, 26,* 952-960. Copyright © 1990 by the American Psychological Association. Reprinted with the permission of the APA and the authors. Figure 7.5: From Wason, P.C. (1968). Reasoning about a rule. *Quarterly Journal of Experimental Psychology, 20,* 273–281. Copyright © 1968. Reprinted with the permission of Lawrence Erlbaum Associates, Ltd., Hove, UK and the author. Figure 7.6: Adapted from Griggs, R.A. & Cox, J.R. (1982). The elusive thematic-materials effect in Watson's selection task. *British Journal of Psychology, 73,* 407–420, extract. Reprinted and adapted with the permission of the British Psychological Society and the authors. Figure 7.8: From Taylor et al.

(1998). Harnessing the imagination: Mental stimulation, self-regulation and coping. *American Psychologist, 53,* no. 4, 434. Copyright © 1998 by the American Psychological Association. Reprinted with the permission of the APA and the author. Figure 7.10: Adapted from Rumelhart, D. (1984). Schemata and the cognitive system. In R.S. Wyler and T.K. Strull (Eds.), *Handbook of social cognition,* Vol. 1. Hillsdale, New Jersey: Erlbaum. Copyright © 1984. Reprinted and adapted with the permission of Lawrence Erlbaum Associates and the author. Figure 7.13: From Frith & Dolan (1996). The role of the prefrontal cortex in higher cognitive functions. *Cognitive Brain Research, 5,* 178. Copyright © 1996. Reprinted with the permission of Elsevier Science Limited. Figure 7.14: From Damasio, A. (1994). *Descartes' error: Emotion, reason and the human brain,* p. 210. Copyright © 1994 by Antonio R. Damasio. Reprinted with the permission of Penguin Putnam, Inc. Figure 7.17: From Eimas, P. (January 1985). The perception of speech in early infancy. *Scientific American, 252,* 46–52. Copyright © 1985 by Scientific American, Inc. All rights reserved. Reprinted with permission. All rights reserved. Figure 7.18: From Premack, A.J. & Premack, D. (October 1972). Teaching language to an ape. *Scientific American, 227,* 92–99. Copyright © 1972 by Scientific American, Inc. All rights reserved. Reprinted with permission. All rights reserved. Figure 7.20: Adapted from Pinker, S. (1994). *The language instinct: How the mind creates language.* Copyright © 1994 by Stephen Pinker. Reprinted with the permission of HarperCollins Publishers, Inc. Table 7.2: Adapted from Irwin, M., Schafer, G., & Feiden, C. (1974). Emic and unfamiliar category sorting of Mano farmers and U.S. undergraduates. *Journal of Cross-Cultural Psychology, 5,* 407–423. Copyright © 1974 by Sage Publications, Inc. Reprinted and adapted with the permission of the publishers. Tables 7.3 and 7.4: Adapted from Edwards, W. (1977). How to use multiattribute utility measurement for social decision making. *IEEE Transactions in Systems, Man and Cybernetics, 17,* 326–340. Copyright © 1977 by IEEE. Reprinted with the permission of the publishers. Table 7.6: From Brown, R. & Fraser, C. (1963). The acquisition of syntax. In C.N. Cofer & B. Musgrave (Eds.), *Verbal behavior and learning: Problems and processes.* Copyright © 1963 by McGraw-Hill, Inc. Reprinted with the permission of the publishers.

Chapter 8   Figure 8.3: From Horn, J. & Noll, J. (1997). Human cognitive capacity: Gf - Gc theory. In D.P. Flanagan, J.L. Gershaft & P.L. Harrison (Eds.), *Contemporary Intellectual Assessment.* Copyright © 1997. Reprinted with the permission of The Guilford Press. Figure 8.5: From Posner, R.M., et al. (1969). Retention of visual and name codes of single letters. *Journal of Experimental Psychology, 79.* Copyright © 1969 by the American Psychological Association. Reprinted with the permission of the APA and the authors. Figure 8.6: From Mumaw, R. & Pellegrino, J. (1984). Individual differences in complex spatial processing. *Journal of Educational Psychology, 76,* 920–939. Copyright © 1984 by the American Psychological Association. Reprinted with the permission of the APA and the authors. Figure 8.7: From Sameroff, A., Baldwin, A., & Baldwin, C. (1993). Stability of intelligence from preschool to adolescence: The influence of social and family risk factors. *Child Development, 64,* 89. Copyright © 1993 by the Society for Research in Child Development. Reprinted and adapted with permission. Table 8.1: From the Wechsler Adult Intelligence Scale, Third Edition. Copyright © 1997, 1981 and 1955 by The Psychological Corporation. Reprinted with permission. All rights reserved. Table 8.4: Adapted from Henderson, N.D. (1982). Correlations in IQ for pairs of people with varying degrees of genetic relatedness and shared environment. *Annual Review of Psychology, 33,* 219–243. Copyright © 1982 by Annual Reviews, Inc. Reprinted and adapted with the permission of the author and the publishers. Table 8.5: Adapted from Loehlin, J., Horn, J., & Willerman, L. (1990). Modeling IQ change: Evidence from the Texas Adoption Project. Child Development, 60, 993–1004. Copyright © 1990 by the Society for Research in Child Development. Reprinted and adapted with permission.

Chapter 9   Figure 9.2: From Csikszentmihalyi, M. & Larson, R. (1984). *Being adolescent: Conflict and growth in the teenage years.* Copyright © 1984 by Basic Books, Inc. Reprinted with the permission of Basic Books, a member of Perseus Books, L.L.C. Figure 9.4: From Eagle, M. (1959). The effects of subliminal stimuli of aggressive content upon conscious cognition. *Journal of Personality, 27,* 678–688. Copyright © 1959 by Duke University Press. Reprinted with the permission of the publishers. Figure 9.5:

From Marcel, J. (1983). Conscious and unconscious perception: Experiments in visual masking and word recognition. *Cognitive Psychology, 15,* 197–237. Copyright © 1983 by Academic Press, Inc. Reprinted with the permission of the publishers. Figure 9.7: Adapted from Squire, L.R. (1986). Priming effects in amnesia. *Science, 232,* 1612–1619. Copyright © 1986 by American Association for the Advancement of Science. Reprinted and adapted with the permission of the publisher and author. Figure 9.10: Adapted from Kripke, D.F, Simons, R.N., Garfinkel, L., & Hammond, E.C. (1979). Short and long sleep and sleeping pills: Is increased mortality associated? *Archives of General Psychiatry, 36,* 103–116. Copyright © 1979 by the American Medical Association. Reprinted and adapted with permission. Figure 9.12: From Cartwright, R.D. (1978). *A Primer on Sleep and Dreaming.* Reading: Addison-Wesley, Inc. Copyright © 1978 by R. D. Cartwright. Reprinted with the permission of the author. Figure 9.13: From Hilgard, E.R. (1986). *Divided Consciousness,* p. 190. New York: John Wiley. Copyright © 1986. Reprinted with the permission of the author. Table 9.1: Adapted from Lavie, P. (1996). In *The Enchanted World of Sleep* (pp. 176–177), translated by A. Berris. New Haven, CT: Yale University Press. Copyright © 1996 by Yale University. Reprinted with the permission of Yale University Press.

Chapter 10   Figure 10.2: Adapted from Simmons, L.W. (1990). Pheromonal cues for the recognition of kin by female field crickets, Gryllus bimaculutus. *Animal Behavior, 40,* 194. Copyright © 1990 by Academic Press Inc. Reprinted and adapted with the permission of the publishers. Figure 10.8: From Thompson, D.A. & Campbell, R.G. (1977). Hunger in humans induced by 2 deoxy-d glucose: Glucoprivic control of taste preference and food intake. *Science, 198,* 1065-1068. Copyright © 1977 by the American Association for the Advancement of Science. Reprinted with the permission of *Science.* Figure 10.9: From Masters, W.H. & Johnson, V.E. (1966). *Human Sexual Response,* p. 5. Boston: Little, Brown and Company. Copyright © 1966 by the Masters and Johnson Institute. Reprinted with permission. Figure 10.10: From Gladue, B.A., Green, R. & Hellman, R.E. (1984). Neuroendocrine response to estrogen and sexual orientation. *Science, 225,* 1496. Copyright © 1984 by American Association for the Advancement of Science. Reprinted with the permission of *Science.* Figure 10.12: Adapted from Elliott, A. J. & Church, M. A. (1997). *Journal of Personality and Social Psychology, 72,* 227. Copyright © 1997 by the American Psychological Association. Reprinted with the permission of the publishers. Table 10.1: From Rand, C.S. & Kuldau, J.M. (1990). The epidemiology of obesity and self-defined weight problems in the general population. *International Journal of Eating Disorders, 9,* 333-334. Copyright © 1990 by John Wiley & Sons, Inc. Reprinted with the permission of the publishers. Table 10.2: From Butler, C.A. (1976). New data about female sexual response. *Journal of Sex and Marital Therapy, 10,* 42. Copyright © 1976 by Brunner/Mazel, Inc. Reprinted with the permission of Brunner/Mazel, Inc. and the author. Table 10.3: Adapted from Whitam, F. & Mathy, R. (1991). Childhood cross-gender behavior of homosexual females in Brazil, Peru, the Philippines and the U.S. *Archives of Sexual Behavior, 20,* 151-170. Copyright © 1991 by Plenum Publishing Corporation. Reprinted and adapted with the permission of Plenum Publishing Corporation and the authors. Table 10.4: Adapted from Nathan, S.G. (1986). The epidemiology of the DSM-III psychosexual dysfunctions. *Journal of Sex and Marital Therapy, 12,* 267-281. Copyright © 1986 by Brunner/Mazel, Inc. Reprinted and adapted with the permission of Brunner/Mazel, Inc. and the author. Table 10.5: Adapted from McClelland, D.C., Atkinson, J.W., Clark, R.A., & Lowell, E.L. (1953). *The Achievement Motive,* p. 294. New York: Irvington Publishers. Copyright 1953 by Appleton Century Crofts. Reprinted and adapted with the permission of Irvington Publishers, Inc.

Chapter 11   Figure 11.2: From Myers, D. & Diener, E. (1995). Who is happy? *Psychological Science, 6,* no. 1, 13. Copyright © 1995. Reprinted with the permission of the publishers. Figure 11.4: From Ekman, P. et al. (1983). Autonomic nervous system activity distinguishes among emotions. *Science, 221,* 1209. Copyright © 1984 by the American Association for the Advancement of Science. Reprinted with the permission of *Science.* Figure 11.6: From Fischer K. et al. (1990). How emotions develop and how they organize development. *Cognition and Development, 4,* no. 2: 90. Copyright © 1990. Reprinted with the permission of Lawrence Erlbaum Associ-

ates, Ltd., Hove, UK and Kurt Fischer, Harvard University. Figure 11.7a and 11.7b: Adapted from LeDoux, J.E. (1986). The neurobiology of emotion. In J.E. LeDoux & W. Hirst (Eds.), *Mind and brain: Dialogues in cognitive neuropsychology,* p. 329. New York: Cambridge University Press. Copyright © 1986. Reprinted and adapted with the permission of Cambridge University Press and the author. Figure 11.8: Adapted from Tomarken, A., Davidson, R.J., Wheeler, R.E., & Doss, R.C. (1992). Individual difference in interior brain asymmetry and fundamental dimensions of emotion. *Journal of Personality and Social Psychology, 62,* 681. Copyright © 1992 by the American Psychological Association. Reprinted and adapted with the permission of the APA and the authors. Figure 11.9: From Shedler, J., Mayman, M., & Maris, M. (1993). The illusion of mental health. *American Psychologist, 11,* 1117-1131. Copyright © 1993 by the American Psychological Association. Reprinted and adapted with the permission of the APA and the authors. Table 11.1: Adapted from Plutchik, R. (1980). A general psychoevolutionary theory of emotion. In R. Plutchik & H. Kellerman (Eds.), *Emotion: Theory, Research and Experience, Volume I: Theory of Emotion,* p. 16. Orlando, Florida: Academic Press. Copyright © 1980 by Academic Press, Inc. Reprinted and adapted with the permission of Academic Press and the authors. Figure 11.11: From Buss, D.M., Larsen, R., Westen, D., & Semmelroth, J. (1992). Sex differences in jealousy: Evolution, Physiology and Psychology. *Psychological Science, 3,* 251-255. Copyright © 1992. Reprinted with the permission of the publishers and Dr. David M. Buss, Department of Psychology, The University of Michigan. Figure 11.12: Adapted from Miller, N.E. (1992). Some examples of psychophysiology and the unconscious. *Biofeedback and Self-Regulation, 17,* 3-16. Copyright © 1992. Reprinted and adapted with the permission of Plenum Publishing Corporation and the author. Figure 11.13: Adapted from Westen, D. (1991). Social cognition and object relations. *Psychological Bulletin, 109,* 429-455. Copyright © 1991 by the American Psychological Association. Reprinted with the permission of the APA and author. Table 11.2: From Holmes, T.H. & Rahe, R.E. (1967). The social readjustment rating scale. *Journal of Psychosomatic Research, 11,* 213-218. Copyright © 1967 by Elsevier Science, Inc. Reprinted with the permission of the publishers. Figure 11.14: From Martikainen P. & Valkonen, T. (1996). Mortality after the death of a spouse: Rates and causes of death in a large Finnish cohort. *American Journal of Public Health, 86,* 1090. Copyright © 1996. Reprinted with the permission of American Public Health Association. Figure 11.15: From Adams, P.R. & Adams, G.R. (1984). Mount Saint Helens's ashfall: Evidence for a disaster stress reaction. *American Psychologist, 39 (3),* 257. Copyright © 1984 by the American Psychological Association. Reprinted with the permission of the APA and the authors. Figure 11.16: Adapted from Cohen, S. & Williamson, G.M. (1991). Stress and infectious diseases in humans. *Psychological Bulletin, 109,* 5. Copyright © 1991 by the American Psychological Association. Reprinted and adapted with the permission of the APA and the authors. Figure 11.17: From Brown, J.B. (1991). Staying fit and staying well: Physical fitness as a moderator of life stress. *Journal of Personality and Social Psychology, 61,* 559. Copyright © 1991 by American Psychological Association. Reprinted and adapted with the permission of the APA and the author. Table 11.3: From Kanner, A.D., Coyne, J.C., Schaefer, C., & Lazarus, R.S. (1981). Comparison of two modes of stress measurements: Daily hassles and uplifts versus major life events. *Journal of Behavioral Medicine, 4,* 14. Reprinted with the permission of Plenum Publishing Corporation and Allen D. Kanner, Ph.D. Figure 11.18: From Cohen, S., Ytrrell, P.A.J., & Smith, A.P. (1991). Psychological stress and susceptibility to the common cold. *New England Journal of Medicine, 325,* 609-610. Copyright © 1991 by Massachusetts Medical Society. Reprinted with the permission of *The New England Journal of Medicine* and the authors. Text: C. Bukowski (1980). From "the shoelace." *Mockingbird Wish Me Luck,* p. 114. Santa Rosa: Black Sparrow Press. Copyright © 1972 by Charles Bukowski. Reprinted with the permission of Black Sparrow Press.

Chapter 12   Figure 12.6: From Wood, R. & Bandura, A. (1989). Impact of conceptions of ability on self-regulatory mechanisms and complex decision making. *Journal of Personality and Social Psychology, 56,* 411-413. Copyright © 1988 by the American Psychological Association. Reprinted with the permission of the APA and the authors. Figure 12.7: Adapted from Eysenck, H.J. (1953). *The Structure of Human Personality,* p. 13. London: Methuen & Co. Copyright 1953. Reprinted with the permission of the publishers. Figure 12.8: From Kagan, J. & Snidman, N. (1991). Temperamental factors in human development. *American Psychologist, 46,* 859. Copyright © 1991 by the American Psychological Association. Reprinted with the permission of the APA and the authors. Table 12.1: Adapted from Emmons, R. & King, L.A. (1988). Conflict among siblings: Immediate and long-term implications for psychological and physical well-being. *Journal of Personality and Social Psychology, 54,* 1044. Copyright © 1988 by the American Psychological Association. Reprinted and adapted with the permission of the APA and the authors. Table 12.3: Adapted from McCrae, R.R. & Costa, P.T., Jr. (1997). Personality trait structure as a human universal. *American Psychologist 52,* 513. Copyright © 1997 by the American Psychological Association. Reprinted and adapted with the permission of the APA and the authors. Table 12.4: From Tellegen, A., Lykken, D.T., Bouchard, T.J., Jr., Wilcox, K.J., & Rich, S. (1988). Personality similarity in twins reared apart and together. *Journal of Personality and Social Psychology, 54,* 1033. Copyright © 1988 by the American Psychological Association. Reprinted with the permission of the APA and the authors. Table 12.5: Adapted from Plomin, R., Chiperer, H., & Loehlin, J.C. (1990). *Handbook of Personality: Theory and Research,* p. 231. New York: Guilford Press. Copyright © 1990. Reprinted and adapted with the permission of The Guilford Press and the authors. Table 12.6: Adapted from Zuckerman, M., DeRoy, T., Garcia, T., Maresa, B., & Sartoris, J. (1988). To predict some of the people some of the time: A reexamination of the moderator variable approach in personality theory. *Journal of Personality and Social Psychology, 54,* 1013-1014. Copyright © 1988 by the American Psychological Association. Reprinted and adapted with the permission of the APA and the authors. Table 12.7: Adapted from Block, J.M., Gjerde, P., & Block, J.H. (1991). Personality antecedents of depressive tendencies in 18-year-olds: A prospective study. *Journal of Personality and Social Psychology, 60,* 726-738. Copyright © 1991 by the American Psychological Association. Reprinted and adapted with the permission of the APA and the authors.

Chapter 13   Figure 13.5: Adapted from Frankenburg, W.K. & Dodds, J.B (1967). The Denver Developmental Screening Test. *Journal of Pediatrics, 91,* 181-191. Copyright © 1991 by Mosby-Year Book, Inc. Reprinted and adapted with permission. Figure 13.6: From Perdue, C. & Gurtman, M. (1990). Evidence for the automaticity of ageism. *Journal of Experimental and Social Psychology, 26,* 12. Copyright © 1990 by Academic Press, Inc. Reprinted with the permission of Academic Press and the authors. Figure 13.8: From Meltzoff, A.N. & Borton, R.W. (1979). Intermodal matching by human neonates. *Nature, 282,* 403-404. Copyright © 1979 by Macmillan Magazines Ltd. Reprinted with the permission of *Nature* and the authors. Figure 13.9: Adapted from Bower, T.G.R. (1971). The object in the world of the infant. *Scientific American, 225,* 30-38. Copyright © 1971 by Scientific American, Inc. Reprinted and adapted with permission. All rights reserved Figure 13.12: Adapted from Fry, A. & Hale, S. (1996). Processing speed, working memory and fluid intelligence: Evidence for a developmental cascade. *Psychological Science, 7,* 238. Copyright © 1996. Reprinted with the permission of the publishers. Figure 13.14: From Crook, T.H., Youngjohn, J., Larrabee, G., & Salama, M. (1992). Aging and everyday memory. *Neuropsychology, 6,* 133. Copyright © 1992 by the American Psychological Association. Reprinted with the permission of the APA and the authors. Figure 13.15: Adapted from Cerella, J. (1990). Aging and information processing rate. In J. Birren & K.W. Schaie (Eds.), *Handbook of the Psychology of Aging* (3rd edition), p. 203. Orlando, Florida: Academic Press. Copyright © 1990 by Academic Press, Inc. Reprinted and adapted with the permission of Academic Press and the author. Figure 13.16: From Horn, J. & Hofer, S. (1992). Major abilities and development in the adult period. In R. Sternberg & C. Berg (Eds.), *Intellectual Development,* p. 79. New York: Cambridge University Press. Copyright © 1992. Reprinted with the permission of the publishers. Figure 13.17: Adapted from Schaie, K.W. (1990). Intellectual development in adulthood. In J. Birren & K.W. Schaie (Eds.), *Handbook of the Psychology of Aging* (3rd edition), p. 297. Orlando, Florida: Academic Press. Copyright © 1990 by Academic Press, Inc. Reprinted and adapted with the permission of Academic Press and the author.

Chapter 14   Figure 14.2: From Kagan, J. (1983). Stress and coping in early development. In N. Garmezy & M. Rutter (Eds.), *Stress, Coping and Development in Children,* p. 198. New York: McGraw-Hill, Inc. Copyright © 1983 by Center for Advanced Study in the Behavioral Science. Reprinted with the permission of McGraw-Hill, Inc. Table 14.1: Adapted from Dozier, M. & Kosback, R. (1992). Psychophysiology in attachment interviews: Converging evidence for deactivating strategies. *Child Development, 64,* 1473-1480. Copyright © 1992 by The Society for Research in Child Development. Reprinted and adapted with permission. Table 14.2: Adapted from Rohner, R. (1975). Parental acceptance-rejection and personality development: A universalist approach to behavioral science. In R.W. Brislin (ed.), *Cross-Cultural Perspectives on Learning,* p. 260. Thousand Oaks, CA.: Sage Publications, Inc. Copyright © 1975 by Sage Publications, Inc. Reprinted and adapted with the permission of the author and publishers. Figure 14.3: From Montemayor, R. & Eisen, M. (1977). A developmental sequence of self-conceptions from childhood to adolescence. *Developmental Psychology, 13,* 317-318. Copyright © 1977 by the American Psychological Association. Reprinted with the permission of the APA and Raymond Montemayor. Figure 14.4: From Westen, D., Lohr, N., Silk, K., Gold, L., & Kerber, K. (1991). Object relations and social cognition in borderlines, major depressives and normals: A TAT analysis. *Psychological Assessment: A Journal of Consulting and Clinical Psychology, 2,* 355-364. Copyright © 1991 by the American Psychological Association. Reprinted with the permission of the APA and the authors. Table 14.3: From Williams, J.E. & Best, D.L. (1982). *Measuring Sex Stereotypes: A Thirty Nation Study,* p. 77. Thousand Oaks, CA.: Sage Publications, Inc. Copyright © 1982 by Sage Publications, Inc. Reprinted and adapted with the permission of the publishers. Table 14.4: Adapted from Kohlberg, L. (1969). Stage and sequence: The cognitive-developmental approach to socialization. In D.A. Goslin (ed.), *Handbook of Socialization and Research,* 347-380. New York: Houghton-Mifflin. Copyright © 1969 by David A. Goslin. Reprinted and adapted with permission. Figure 14.6: Adapted from Darley, J. & Schultz, T.R. (1990). Moral rules: Their content and acquisition. *Annual Review of Psychology, 41,* 532. Copyright © 1990 by Annual Reviews, Inc. Reprinted and adapted with the permission of the publishers. Table 14.5: Adapted, in part, from Erikson, E.H. (1963). *Childhood and society, second edition.* Copyright 1950, © 1963 by W. W. Norton & Company, Inc., renewed © 1978, 1991 by Erik H. Erikson. Reprinted with the permission of W. W. Norton & Company, Inc.

Chapter 15   Table 15.1: Adapted from Compton, W.M., Helzer, J., Hai-Gwo, H., Eng-Kung, Y., McEvoy, L., Tipp, J., & Spitznagel, E.(1991). New methods in cross-cultural psychiatry: Psychiatric illness in Taiwan and the U.S. *American Journal of Psychiatry, 148,* 1700-1701. Copyright © 1991 by the American Psychiatric Association. Reprinted and adapted with the permission of the publishers and the authors. Table 15.2, 15.3, 15.5, and 15.7: Adapted from American Psychiatric Association (1994). *Diagnostic and Statistical Manual of Mental Disorders* (4th edition). Washington, DC: American Psychiatric Association. Copyright © 1994 by American Psychiatric Association. Reprinted and adapted with the permission of the publishers. Figure 15.3: From Shedler, J. & Block, J. (1990). Adolescent drug use and emotional health: A longitudinal perspective. *American Psychologist, 45,* 624. Copyright © 1990 by the American Psychological Association. Reprinted with the permission of the APA and the authors. Table 15.6: Adapted from Gottesman, I. (1991). *Schizophrenia Genesis,* p. 96. New York: W.H. Freeman and Company. Copyright © 1991 by Irving I. Gottesman. Reprinted and adapted with the permission of W.H Freeman and Company. Figure 15.7: Based on MacKinnon, D.F., Jamison , K.R., & De-Davlo, J.R. (1997). Genetics of manic depressive illness. *Annual Review of Neuroscience, 20,* 335-373. Copyright © 1997 by Annual Reviews, Inc. Reprinted and adapted with the permission of the publishers. Figure 15.8: From Swann, W.B., Wenzlaff, R., Krull, D.S., & Pelham, B. (1992). Allure of negative feedback: Self-evaluation striving among depressed persons. *Journal of Abnormal Psychology, 101,* 296. Copyright © 1992 by the American Psychological Association. Reprinted with the permission of the APA and the authors. Figure 15.9: From Beck, A.T. (1976). *Cognitive Therapy and the Emotional Disorders,* p. 256. Madison, CT.: International Universities Press, Inc. Copyright © 1976. Reprinted with permission. Figure 15.10: Adapted from Barlow, D.H. (1988). Current models of panic disorder and a view from emotion theory. In A.J. Frances & R.E. Hales (Eds.), *Review of Psychiatry, 7.* Copyright © 1988 by American Psychiatric Association. Reprinted and adapted with the permission of the publishers and the au-

Name Index

Subject Index